PUBLIC POLICIES
TOWARD BUSINESS

THE IRWIN SERIES IN ECONOMICS

Consulting Editor
LLOYD G. REYNOLDS
Yale University

PUBLIC POLICIES
TOWARD BUSINESS

CLAIR WILCOX

Late Professor of Political
Economy, Swarthmore College

Fourth Edition

1971

 Richard D. Irwin, Inc. Homewood, Illinois
IRWIN-DORSEY LIMITED, GEORGETOWN, ONTARIO

Fourth Edition

First Printing, March, 1971

Library of Congress Catalog Card No. 73-124163

Printed in the United States of America

TO THOSE OF MY STUDENTS WHO

HAVE WARMED MY HEART BY

BECOMING ECONOMISTS

PREFACE

This is the fourth edition of a text designed for college and university courses dealing with public policy toward business enterprise. In its approach, the book seeks to give equal emphasis to the economic and political aspects of the policies that it examines. In balance, it seeks to give equal attention to the major types of public policy toward business activity: controlling monopoly by maintaining competition, by regulation, and through public enterprise; controlling competition to protect consumers, investors, and future generations, and to serve the interests of organized producer groups. Its general theme is an appraisal of the comparative merits and demerits of these policies in the light of past experience, from the standpoint of their consequences for the general welfare.

In the process of revision, the organization employed in the third edition has been retained, introducing, first, the various means of controlling monopoly; and second, the various policies directed toward the moderation of competition. Placed at the end are two chapters presenting conclusions concerning monopolistic controls and anticompetitive policies. Each part, however, is self-contained, and the several parts can be taught in whatever sequence the instructor may desire. A new chapter has been added dealing with the rapidly growing field of communications and their regulation, and new sections have been inserted in a number of other chapters to cover recent developments. Some of the material has been rewritten, and all of it has been brought up to date, incorporating legislation, court decisions, and new literature in the field up to late 1970.

The analysis presented in these pages is an outgrowth of some 40 years, off and on, of reading, writing, and teaching in this field in courses and seminars at Swarthmore College. It is also a product of several years of service, while on leave of absence, as an adviser or administrator with various agencies of the federal government, including the National Recovery Administration, the Temporary National Economic Committee, the Office of Price Administration, and the Office of International Trade Policy of the Department of State. This experience, in particular, convinced me that business cannot always be expected so to govern itself as to serve the public interest, but must be subjected to external discipline; that competition affords a more effective discipline than public regulation; that the officers of regulatory agencies are often skillful, industrious, and conscientious; but that regulatory controls are bound to be cumbersome and costly; that such controls, in solving one problem, inevitably raise a host of others; that conflicts arising, in their application, between considerations of economics and those of politics are usually resolved by subordinating economics to politics; that the price system is one of the greatest achievements of civilization and that governmental action, however necessary, is at best a poor substitute.

I have made no attempt, in this text, to conceal my own judgments. The student will not have to be acutely perceptive to discover, for instance, that I am a believer in the antitrust laws and a critic of legislation encouraging cartels; that I am not impressed by the performance of most public utility commissions but am an admirer of the Tennessee Valley Authority; that I favor laws to protect consumers and investors against misrepresentation and am sceptical concerning laws designed to subsidize the members of political pressure groups. I have felt that it would be at once more honest and more entertaining if I were to let my bias show. The reader, accordingly, is forewarned. But it may be well for me to make my point of view explicit, lest I be accused of seeking subtly to subvert the youth.

In my hierarchy of values, I put freedom first, and plenty and progress above equality, stability, and security. I believe that these values are better served by the dispersion than by the concentration of power. I therefore prefer competition to monopoly, private enterprise to public enterprise, and free markets to administrative controls. In judging economic policies, my standard is that of consumer welfare, as measured by the quantity, quality, and variety of goods and services that are made available. But I recognize the need for compromise. I would not leave the worker or the farmer entirely at the mercy of the market. I see the wisdom of employing a rule of reason in the enforcement of the antitrust laws. I believe that government should take the initiative in controlling the flow of water in river valleys and in assuring the quality of the environment. If this be subversion, make the most of it.

I shall not attempt to repeat the acknowledgment of my indebtedness to the many people named in the prefaces to the earlier editions, though the indebtedness remains. Marcia Lincoln Wilcox, still to be emancipated by the Women's Liberation Front, not only permitted me to devote a year of my presumed retirement to this project, but also assisted, as usual, in preparing the indexes and reading the proof.

Swarthmore, Pa.   Clair Wilcox
February, 1971

CONTENTS

PART III. Controlling Monopoly by Regulation

nings of Regulation. Regulation of Telephone Industry: *Quality of Service. Rate Regulation by State Commissions. Holding Company Policies. Regulation by the FCC.* Current Issues in Regulation: *The Rate Level. The Problem of Western Electric. The Rate Structure. The Problem of Western Union.* Changing Technology and Emerging Competition: *Communications Satellites. Telephone Attachments. Microwave Communications. Computers and Communications.* Future Communications Policy.

Background of Regulation: *Beginnings of Control. Broadcasting under the Communications Act. Interests in Broadcasting.* Allocation of Airspace: *The AM Allocation. The FM Allocation. The TV Allocation.* Control of Technology: *Introduction of FM and TV. Introduction of Color.* Competition and Monopoly: *Competition between Media. Competition among Stations. The Networks in Radio. The Networks in TV.* Policy and Practice in Licensing: *Criteria for Licensing. Practice in Licensing. Reform of Licensing.* Program Content: *Freedom of the Air. Quality of Programs. Control of Programs. Revocation of Licenses.* Diversity in Broadcasting: *Subscription TV. Cable TV. Educational Broadcasting. Public TV.*

The Regulatory Commission: *Is Expertness Desirable? Are Several Heads Better Than One? Is Independence Attainable? Is Independence Desirable?* Weaknesses of Regulation: *The Results of Regulation. External Limitations. Internal Shortcomings. The Life Cycle of Regulation. Reform of Regulation.* Inherent Defects of Regulation: *Regulation as a Substitute for Competition. Regulation-Mindedness. Power without Responsibility.*

PART IV.   Controlling Monopoly by Public Enterprise

The Meaning of Public Enterprise. Public Enterprise in Other Countries: *Traditional Fields of Public Enterprise. The Nationalization Movement. The Scope of Public Enterprise. Denationalization.* Public Enterprise in the United States: *Character and Extent of Public Enterprise. Causes of Public Enterprise. Obstacles to Public Enterprise. Public Competition with Private Enterprise.* Local Government Enterprises: *Urban Transit. Municipal Electric Systems. Public Housing.* State Government Enterprises: *State Insurance Programs. State Liquor Stores. Transport and Terminal Facilities. State Power Systems.* Federal Government Enterprises: *Administration of Public Lands.*

Federal Lending Agencies. Federal Insuring Agencies. Federal Trading Agencies. Federal Transport Enterprises. Federal Manufacturing Enterprises.

River Valley Development: *Single-Purpose Development. Flood Control. Multipurpose Development. Criteria for Investment in Valley Development. Practice in Determining Investment. Organization for Valley Development. Politics in Valley Development.* Issues in Power Development: *Disposition of Power. Price Policy. Allocation of Joint Costs. Yardstick Regulation. Expansion of Power Operations.* The Tennessee Valley Authority: *The TVA Power Program. Are TVA Consumers Subsidized? Nonpower Activities. The TVA since 1953.* Other Valley Developments: *The Colorado River. The Columbia River. The Missouri River. The St. Lawrence River.* Public Power Policy.

The Postal Service: *Organization and Administration. Post Office Personnel. Quality of Service. Technical Progress. Postal Rates and Deficits. Postal Reform.* The Atomic Energy Industry: *Atomic Energy Act of 1946. Atomic Energy Act of 1954. The Atomic Energy Commission. The Contract System. Technical Progress. Secrecy. Congress and the AEC.* Atom-Fired Electric Power: *Economic Feasibility of Atomic Power. Promotion of Atomic Power. Subsidization. Regulation of Atomic Power.* Future Administration of the Atomic Program.

Efficiency and Progress: *Comparisons of Efficiency. Factors Affecting Costs. Forms of Organization. Administrative Boards. Overcentralization. Labor Relations. Advancement of Technology.* Public Enterprise and the Consumer: *The Price Level. The Price Structure. Consumer Protection.* Efficiency versus Accountability: *The Government Department. The Costs of Bureaucracy. The Public Corporation. The Problem of Accountability.* Change of Ownership: *Nationalization. Denationalization.*

PART V.   Setting the Plane of Competition

The Consumer and the Law: *The Consumer at Common Law. Establishment of Legal Standards. Requirement of Truthful Disclosure. Truth in Packaging. Truth in Lending. Protection of Public Health and Safety. Protection against Swindlers.* Foods, Drugs, and Cosmetics:

PART VI.   Moderating Competition

Control of Terms of Sale. Control of Prices. Allocation of Markets. Control of Production. Control of Capacity. Control of the Channels of Distribution. Penalties. The End of NRA. An Appraisal of NRA. The Philosophy of Cost Protection. Exceptions to Antitrust: *Labor and Agriculture in the Clayton Act. Agricultural and Fisheries Cooperatives. Agreements and Combinations in Transport and Communications. Export Trade Associations. Insurance. Bank Mergers. Newspapers. Professional Sports. Exceptions to State Antitrust Laws. The Scope of Exceptions.*

The Competitive Struggle: *Changing Patterns of Distribution. The Attack on the Mass Distributor.* The A&P Case: *Practices in Selling. Advantages in Buying. Vertical Integration. The Central Issue. The Consent Decree.* Resale Price Maintenance: *State Fair Trade Laws. Fair Trade in Operation. The Miller-Tydings Act. The McGuire-Keogh Act. Erosion of Fair Trade. The Case Pro. The Case Con. Consequences of Fair Trade. Scope and Enforceability.* Promotional Devices: *Trading Stamps. Lotteries.* Regulation of Liquor Dealers.

Minimum Labor Standards: *Protection for Women and Children. Protection against Industrial Hazards. Maximum Hours and Minimum Wages. Fair Employment Practices. Social Insurance.* Policy toward Unionization: *Discouragement of Unionization. Neutrality toward Unionization. Promotion of Unionization. Regulation of Union-Management Relations. The National Labor Relations Board.* Unions and the Worker: *Exclusion from Membership. Compulsion of Membership. Relations within Unions.* Unions and the Innocent Bystander: *Limitation of Strikes and Boycotts. Mediation, Investigation, and Publicity. Compulsory Arbitration and Seizure.* Unions and the Consumer: *Monopolization of Product Markets. Unions under the Antitrust Laws. The Productivity of Labor. Monopolization of Labor Markets. The Level of Wages. Cost-Push Inflation.*

The Farm Problem: *The Structure of Agriculture. The Level of Farm Income. The Unreliability of Farm Prices. The Instability of Farm Income. The Agricultural Revolution.* Evolution of Parity and Price Supports: *Forerunners of Parity. The First AAA, 1933. The Soil Conservation Stopgap. The Second AAA, 1938. Wartime Goals and Controls.* Price Supports in Operation: *Parity Price. Issues in Price Supports. Loans, Purchases, and Storage. Surplus Disposal. Control of Production. Land Retirement.* Parity and Price Supports Appraised:

The Ethics of Parity. Consequences for the Farmer. Cost to Taxpayers and Consumers. Malallocation of Resources. Direct Payments: *The Wool Program. Farm Programs in the Sixties. Direct Payments: Pro and Con.*

The Background of Cartelization: *Types of Cartels. Enforcement of Restraints. Cartels Abroad. Cartels in the United States.* Petroleum Prorationing: *Development of State Prorationing. Development of Federal Regulation. The Present Pattern of Control. Methods of Quota Allocation. Stabilization and Conservation.* The Sugar Quota System: *The Pattern of Control. Determination of National Quotas. Effects of the Quota System.* Marketing Agreements and Orders: *Agreement and Order Procedures. Control for Special Crops.* Milk Market Controls: *Urban Milk Markets. Milk Price Structures. Public Intervention in Milk Markets. Federal Milk Market Orders. State Milk Controls. Effects of Milk Controls.*

Forms of Subsidization: *Free Services. Sales at Low Prices. Purchases at High Prices. Reduction of Taxes. Exclusion of Competitors.* Subsidies to Transport: *Subsidies to Railroads. Subsidies to Highway Transport. Subsidies to Shipping. Subsidies to Aviation.* Subsidies to Business: *Subsidies to Shipbuilders. Promotion of Housing. Promotion of Atomic Power. Subsidies to the Oil Industry.* Subsidies to Agriculture: *Free Land and Services. Irrigation. Agricultural Credit. Rural Electrification. Crop Insurance. Aid to Low-Income Farmers.* Appraisal of Subsidies: *The Politics of Subsidies. The Economics of Subsidies.*

PART VII.   Which Controls?

Comprehensive Noncompetitive Controls: *The Greater Difficulty of the Task. Market Economy or Planned Economy? Experience with Wartime Controls.* Selective Noncompetitive Controls: *Shortcomings of Noncompetitive Controls. Where Regulation? Where Public Enterprise? Strengthening Noncompetitive Controls.* Reinforcing the Maintenance of Competition: *Attacking Anticompetitive Behavior. Attacking Unreasonable Market Power. Strengthening Antitrust. Consistency of Policy. Promoting Competition.*

Goals of Policy: *Consumer Welfare. Other Goals of Policy. Choice and Compromise.* Political Pressure Groups: *Organized Business.*

Organized Labor. Organized Agriculture. Response to Group Pressures: *Conferring Special Favors. Reducing Uncertainty. Preserving Small Producers. Easing Adjustment to Change. Equalizing Bargaining Power. Settling Disputes.* Significance of Curbs to Competition: *The Cost to the Consumer. From Market to Legislature. The Threat of Inflation.* Policies in Perspective.

INDEXES

PART I

Government and Business

Chapter **PUBLIC CONTROL OF**
1 **BUSINESS**

Business, in the United States, is affected in many ways by the activities of government. Indeed, it is government that provides the institutional foundation upon which business rests, the legal framework within which it functions, and many of the instruments through which its activities are carried on. Government establishes the status of the business unit, grants the privilege of incorporation, and makes the laws that control bankruptcy and reorganization. It defines and maintains the rights of ownership, enforces private contracts, and provides for the adjudication of disputes. It coins money, issues currency, controls credit, and regulates banking, thus freeing business from barter and providing it with a medium of exchange. It establishes standards of weight and measurement, sets up systems for grading commodities, inspects shipments, and regulates central markets, thus facilitating the processes of trade. It directs traffic on streets and highways, maintains police forces and fire departments, builds dams and dikes, inspects ships and aircraft, issues warnings of coming storms, operates lighthouses, and patrols the coasts, thus affording protection against the loss of life and property.

Government also renders valuable services to business, extends to it various forms of public assistance, and promotes its activities in many ways. It collects and disseminates data that provide businessmen with information on the availability of productive resources, credit, and investment funds, on methods and costs of production and distribution, on trends of business activity, on present market conditions and future market prospects. It engages in fundamental research relating to the problems of agriculture, industry, and public health, tests the properties of materials and the effectiveness of productive processes, contributes to the advancement of technology, and makes its discoveries available for general use. Through its system of public education, government trains the labor force and cultivates consumer demand. Through its consular service, it assists business in finding markets abroad. Through its diplomatic service, it seeks to protect investments made in other lands. Government offers technical advice to small business and makes loans to finance productive activities. It supports transport, agriculture, and mining, in some measure, by providing public subsidies. In all of these matters, business leans heavily on government.

3

The economic system within which business functions is shaped by government; the character of its performance depends upon decisions that are made by government. The demand for the products of business and the nature of its costs are influenced by public regulations, by the character of public expenditures, and by the types of taxes that are used in raising public revenues. Its expectations—of stability or instability, of prosperity or depression, of profit or loss—depend upon the policies adopted by central banking authorities in controlling the volume of credit and on those pursued by government in balancing its budget, accumulating a surplus, or running a deficit. Its daily operations must be carried on within the limits that are fixed by a variety of public controls.

It is the purpose of this book, not to examine all of the activities of government that have significance for business, but rather to analyze, in some detail, the nature and consequences of particular controls. In this introductory chapter, however, it is desirable to consider, in more general terms, the nature of public controls, the attitude of business toward them, the need for them, and the forms that they may take.

THE NATURE OF CONTROLS

We begin by defining the phrase "public control of business" and then go on to indicate the character of such control: its pervasiveness, its long history, and its continued growth.

The Meaning of "Public Control of Business"

By "business," of course, is meant that part of economic activity that has to do with the production, distribution, and sale of goods and services. By "public," in this connection, is meant some agency of government. The general public influences business, to be sure, through channels other than those of government: through buying or failing to buy its products, for instance, or through the force of public opinion. But it is only with control through government that we shall be concerned.

What, then, is "control"? Business is influenced, inevitably, by all of the activities of government. But many of them are not to be included in the concept of control. This is true, for instance, of such services as police and fire protection, public health and education, and national defense. It is true, too, of those activities that create the general environment within which business may be carried on, such as the provision of legal status for the business unit, the establishment of a monetary system, and the enforcement of contracts. The meaning of "control," as the word is used here, is confined to the deliberate adoption, by government, of measures designed to cause the policies of business managements to differ, in material respects, from those that they would voluntarily pursue. Control thus comprehends a great variety of measures that differ in purpose, method, and effect. Their common feature is modification of the behavior of business in response to pressures applied through government.

The Pervasiveness of Control

Government, in the United States, has gone a long way toward telling the businessman just what he can and cannot do. It tells him that he can neither misrepresent the securities that he sells to raise capital nor manipulate the markets in which they are subsequently bought and sold. It puts an upper limit on the hours that he can require of labor and a lower limit on the wages that he can pay. It compels him to bargain collectively with his workers and to insure them against accident, unemployment, and dependent old age. It forbids him either to take unfair advantage of his competitors or to agree with them upon the quantities that he will produce or the prices at which he will sell. It requires him to give full weight and measure and establishes standards to govern the quality of many of his products. It restrains him from misrepresenting the goods that he offers for sale and limits his freedom to discriminate among his customers. In some cases, it keeps him from producing goods by curtailing the quantity that he may sell, by taxing his output, or by imposing outright prohibitions. In others, it requires him to obtain permission before he may engage in production, specifies the character of the services that he must render, and fixes the rates that he may charge. In time of depression, it has forbidden him to sell below a minimum price and imposed widespread restrictions on his freedom to produce. In time of threatened inflation, it has forbidden him to sell above a maximum price and allocated his output among his customers. Business has more freedom in the United States than in almost any other country in the world. But, even here, its freedom has been sharply limited.

The Long History of Control

The control of business is not a new departure in public policy. Government has always regulated business in the United States. Even before specific statutes were enacted, the practices of business were subject to decisions of the courts under the rules of common law: agreements to restrain trade were held to be unenforceable, unfair methods of competition were enjoined, enterprises affected with a public interest were required to serve all comers—adequately, speedily, continuously, and without discrimination—and persons who sustained injury at the hands of business were awarded damages. The enactment of state laws requiring safe and sanitary conditions of employment dates back to 1877; laws forbidding the misrepresentation of securities to 1911; laws insuring workers against industrial accidents and laws establishing maximum hours and minimum wages for women to 1911 and 1912. Commissions set up by the states have regulated banking since 1838, railroads since 1844, insurance companies since 1854, and public utilities since 1907. Intervention by the federal government, in the form of the restrictive tariff and the patent system, is as old as our national history. Federal regulation of the railroads goes back to the first administration of Grover Cleveland in 1887, and the Sherman Antitrust Act to the administration of Benjamin Harrison in 1890. The Pure Food and Drug Law was enacted under Theodore Roosevelt in 1906; the Clayton and Federal Trade Commission Acts under Woodrow Wilson in 1914. The first conservation laws date from the seventies; the first law controlling the methods used in producing oil and gas was passed in Texas in 1919. A number of regulatory agencies, set up under Franklin D. Roosevelt in the early years of the New Deal, have now seen more than three decades of service. Regulation of business in the public interest is by no means alien to American tradition. It is an outgrowth of generations of experience.

The Growth of Control

The scope of public regulation has grown steadily with the passage of time. A century ago controls were few and simple. In the economy of that day they were all that seemed to be required. In relation to its great resources the population of the country was small. There were still free lands to be occupied, virgin forests to be cut, and deposits of minerals waiting to be tapped. Productive activity centered in agriculture, in the extractive industries, in handicrafts and small manufactures, and in petty trade. Enterprises were organized, in the main, as individual proprietorships or partnerships. They were managed by their owners; employers dealt directly with employees. The scale of industrial operations was small; the production of goods and services was scattered among many firms. Economic independence was the general rule.

Now all of these conditions have changed. The population has grown; the land has been settled, and its natural wealth exploited. Agriculture has declined in relative importance; manufacturing, transport, and the public utilities have grown. The individual proprietorship and the partnership have given way, in many fields, to the modern corporation. Ownership has been divorced from management, and labor has been organized. Technology has advanced: new products, new materials, new machines, and new methods have been introduced. The scale of industrial operations has grown; production, in many industries, has come to be concentrated in the hands of a few large firms. Economic relationships have steadily grown in complexity. Interdependence, rather than independence, has come to be the rule.

These changes have brought with them a host of new problems, and as these problems have arisen solutions have been sought through the extension of public controls. New laws have been enacted, new agencies established, and new methods of regulation devised. But the process of adapting political institutions to economic change has not been a steady one. Public sentiment has swung from radicalism to conservatism and back again, and legislation has come in spurts as abuses have become so evident as to call for reform. But even during the conservative administration of President Eisenhower, control was extended to the labeling of furs, textiles, and hazardous substances, to the sale of flammable fabrics, and to the pricing of natural gas at the wellhead; the minimum wage was raised, insurance benefits were provided to the totally disabled, old-age benefits were extended to millions of additional workers, and the level of these benefits was raised. Controls have been extended most rapidly when deep depression has emphasized the need for individual security and in periods when preparation for the nation's defense has placed a heavy burden on the whole economy. These controls have generally been abandoned when the emergency has passed. But other controls, once adopted, have usually been retained. Regulation often advances; it seldom retreats.

OPPOSITION TO CONTROLS

Businessmen tend to view government with suspicion and distaste. Government, they say, is sterile; its spending is unproductive. It is inefficient, extravagant, wasteful; its deficits are harmful to business; its taxes are harmful, too. It is inherently evil, driving the nation to socialism and worse. In the eyes of business, the politician, the routine bureaucrat, and the academic bureaucrat are all to be distrusted; the first is probably dishonest, the second incompetent, and the third impractical. None of them is clear-, level-, or hard-headed. All are engaged in activities disturbing to business confidence.[1]

New controls that circumscribe the freedom of business have always been denounced by businessmen. "The Sherman Antitrust Law of 1890," said Henry Lee Higginson, the banker, "is probably the most vicious and unreasonable law that was ever passed by any legislative body, and there is nothing in any state that I know of any worse than the Interstate Commerce Law and its various amendments, giving more power to a half a dozen lawyers than is possessed by the Czar of Russia. . . ."[2] The policies of Theodore Roosevelt were denounced as vigorously in their time as were those of Franklin D. Roosevelt thirty years later.

The usual complaint of businessmen is that government is interfering with business and meddling in private affairs. Implied in this complaint is the view that the behavior of business is a private matter with which the public has no legitimate concern, that government is an entity that exists apart from the rest of the community, that is imposes controls of its own volition in pursuance of its own purposes, and that its activities as a regulator are neither invited nor desired by business itself. Each of these propositions merits some examination.

Private Enterprise and the Public Interest

The behavior of business is not a matter that affects business alone. A single enterprise may use the savings of thousands of investors, employ other thousands of workers, and serve still other thousands of customers. The opportunity that it affords and the security that it provides for investment and employment, the income that it distributes in the form of wages, salaries, interest, and dividends, the quantity and quality of the goods and services that it produces, and the prices at which it sells may influence the well-being of

1 / See Francis X. Sutton, Seymour E. Harris, Carl Kaysen, and James Tobin, *The American Business Creed* (Cambridge, Mass.: Harvard University Press, 1956), chap. ix.
2 / Quoted in *ibid.*, p. 206.

thousands on thousands of citizens. If it possesses a monopoly, suppliers may have no alternative but to sell to it and consumers no alternative but to buy from it. If it competes with other concerns, the methods it employs may affect everyone who invests in, works for, or buys from, its competitors. If it engages in the exploitation of exhaustible resources, the methods it uses may threaten the nation's security and do damage to generations yet to come. If the products that it supplies are not pure, if the working conditions that it provides are not safe, if its wastes go down the stream and up the flue, polluting the water and the air, it may impair the health of the whole community. The behavior of business inescapably affects the general welfare; it is properly a matter of public concern.

It is not always safe to leave business to its own devices; experience has shown that its freedom will sometimes be abused. Investors have been defrauded by promoters, corporate insiders, and market manipulators. Men, women, and children have been put to work under needless hazards, amid unhealthful surroundings, for long hours, at low pay, and without assurance of future security. Competitors have been harassed by malicious and predatory tactics, handicapped by discrimination, excluded from markets and sources of supply, and subjected to intimidation, coercion, and physical violence. Consumers have been victimized by short weights and measures, by adulteration, and by misrepresentation of quality and price; they have been forced to contribute to the profits of monopoly. Water and air have been polluted with the wastes of industry; the nation's resources have been dissipated through extravagant methods of exploitation. These abuses have not characterized all business at all times, but they have occurred with sufficient frequency to justify the imposition of controls. Regulation is clearly required, not only to protect the investor, the worker, the consumer, and the community at large against the unscrupulous businessman, but also to protect the honest businessman against his dishonest competitor.

The Origin of Controls

When government moves to extend its controls, it does not act of its own volition. Government, in the United States, is not an independent entity; it does not possess a will of its own; it is not animated by purposes that are alien to the desires of its citizens. The American government is a creature of the American people; it responds to the pressures that they bring to bear upon it; its policies and its programs, wise or unwise, find their origin in organized demand and depend for their survival upon popular sufferance. If government regulates the securities markets and the stock exchanges, it is because investors demand protection. If it establishes maximum hours and minimum wages, requires collective bargaining, and sets up a system of social insurance, it is because labor demands protection. If it outlaws unfair methods of competition and curbs discrimination in the prices that are quoted to competing firms, it is because competitors demand protection. If it prohibits the sale of impure foods and drugs, if it forbids falsehood in advertising, if it enforces competition in one industry and regulates monopoly in another, it is because consumers demand protection. If it seeks to conserve the nation's resources, it is because a substantial body of public opinion insists that it do so. Government does not willfully interfere with business. It intervenes only when it is forced to intervene. It acts reluctantly, deliberately, and tardily, in response to overwhelming pressures. Criticism of public intervention is criticism, not of dictatorship, but of the results of the democratic process.

It must be noted, moreover, that many of the laws that now regulate business have been enacted, not in the face of business opposition, but at the urgent solicitation of business itself. There are tariffs that prevent businessmen from buying goods abroad, statutes that prevent them from doing business across state lines, and ordinances that exclude them from local markets. There are patents that keep businessmen from competing with the patentees, and licensing requirements that deny them entry into sheltered trades. There are regulations that prevent businessmen from reducing the costs of production, from introducing new methods, and from employing new materials. There are laws that handicap the efficient businessman and laws that subsidize the inefficient one. There are laws that prevent the businessman from increasing his output and laws that prevent him from reducing his price. None of these are measures which an aggressive government has forced upon a reluctant business community. All of them are measures which government has adopted at the behest of business itself. If government is interfering with business, it is largely because business has invited it to interfere.

The Attitudes of Business

Business has prospered despite regulation—or even because of it. But businessmen, nonetheless, have tended to view their regulators with hostility. The reason for this attitude is to be found not so much in the economic costs of regulation as in its psychic costs. In a study of manufacturers in Connecticut, Robert E. Lane offers this explanation of their antagonism toward new controls: "First, the regulation challenged the businessman's belief system, profaned his idols, and depreciated his myths. . . . Second, it denigrated the businessman himself, lowered his status in the community, and allocated to him a role subordinate to the one he had enjoyed. . . ."[3] This resulted in frustration and gave rise to anxiety. In such a state of mind the businessman reacted aggressively. His hostility was directed, in the main, toward the bureaucrats who enforced the hated regulations. They were strangers to him. Their value systems, their group loyalties, their occupational traits, even their vocabularies differed from his.

The first consequence of the new controls was violation of the law, litigation to hamper its enforcement, lobbying to change its terms, and pressure to

3 / Robert E. Lane, *The Regulation of Businessmen* (New Haven: Yale University Press, 1954), p. 19.

influence its administration. In time, however, hostility was tempered by adaptation and adjustment. The regulations came to be accepted as a matter of course. As controls have been extended, this process has been repeated again and again. In certain industries, in fact, managements have become so habituated to regulation that they could not conceive of doing business in any other way. As new problems have arisen, moreover, the response of management has often been to seek their solution through an expansion of controls. Businessmen confronted by threatening competitors have displayed strong regulation-mindedness.

THE NEED FOR CONTROL

The case for private enterprise, as it was developed by economists and expounded by teachers of economics for a century and a half, was based upon the assumption that competition would prevail. Businessmen were selfish; they would seek to maximize their profit by paying too little and charging too much. But their competitors, though equally selfish, would prevent them from doing so by paying more and charging less. Competition would thus harness selfishness and make it serve the common weal.

With the growth of big business, in later years, it has appeared to many observers that competition has declined. If this were true, the selfishness of the businessman was no longer held in check. A new defense of private enterprise was thus required. One was found in the doctrine of social responsibility. This is the view that recent changes in the structure of the corporation, the character of management, and the environment of enterprise have so transformed the motivation of businessmen that they seek, now, to serve the general interest.

In this view, social responsibility is assumed voluntarily; it is not compelled. Another theory rests upon a new form of compulsion—countervailing power. According to this theory, protection against the selfishness of big business is afforded, not by the competition of other enterprises on the same side of the market, but by the emergence of equally large units on the other side of the market. Big sellers thus find themselves confronted by big buyers, and vice versa, so that neither one can take advantage of the other.

Each of these theories argues that business will serve the general interest, whether tnrough the discipline of competition, the assumption of social responsibility, or the force of countervailing power. What need is there, then, for the imposition of public controls?

The Rationale of Competition

Private enterprise is justified, in the defense long offered by economists, by the service it renders to people in their capacity as consumers. Private enterprise seeks profit. But, to obtain profit, it must serve consumers, for this is the only way to profit that competition will allow. It is thus on the foundation of competition that the case for private enterprise is built.

Human wants are many and growing; the productive resources through which they can be satisfied—land, labor, capital, materials, and power—are scarce. The central problem of economics is to determine how these resources shall be allocated; to decide what goods shall be produced. The goods produced by private enterprise, in a market economy, will be those that the consumer demands. In such an economy, the consumer exercises sovereign power. Each time he spends a dollar he casts a vote for the production of the thing he buys. His dollar votes, recorded in his purchases, express the character of his demands. Where his demand for a commodity declines, its price will fall. Where demand increases, price will rise. When producers, in their turn, compete against each other to obtain resources, those with products where demand is weak will find themselves outbid by those with products where demand is strong. Resources will be diverted from the one field to the other, away from producing goods that are wanted less and toward producing goods that are wanted more. Competition is thus the regulator that compels producers to follow the guidance of consumer choice.

Competition serves the consumer in other ways. It operates negatively to protect him against extortion. If the quality of the product offered by one producer is low, the quality of that offered by another may be high. If the price charged by one producer is high, that asked by another may be low. The consumer is not at the mercy of the one as long as he has the alternative of buying from the other. More than this, competition operates affirmatively to enhance quality and reduce price. The producer who wishes to enlarge his profits must increase his sales. To do so, he must offer the consumer more goods for less money. As he adds to quality and subtracts from price, his rivals are compelled to do the same. The changes which he initiates soon spread throughout the trade. Every consumer of its products gets more and pays less. Competition also makes for efficiency. It leads some producers to eliminate wastes and cut costs so that they may undersell others. It compels others to adopt similar measures in order that they may survive. It weeds out those whose costs remain high and thus operates to put production in the hands of those whose costs are low. As the former are superseded by the latter, the general level of industrial efficiency is accordingly enhanced. Competition is congenial to material progress. It keeps the door open to new blood and new ideas. It communicates to all producers the improvements made by any one of them. Competition is cumulative in its effects. When competitors cut their prices, consumers buy more goods, output increases, and unit costs may decline. The lower prices compel producers to seek still further means of cutting costs. The resulting gains in efficiency open the way to still lower prices. Goods are turned out in increasing volume, and the general plane of living is raised.

Competition is thus held to be a stern disciplinarian. It has long been recognized, however, that there still is need, in a competitive economy, for public controls. The existence of competition is not always assured. Many firms may agree among themselves that they will not compete. Two or more firms may combine to make a single unit. One or a few firms may come to dominate an industry, through the employment of unfair methods or through the enjoyment of special advantages. If the consumer is to reap the benefits of competition, government must make sure that competition is maintained.

Opposite to the benefits of competition are the evils of monopoly. Monopoly prevents the allocation of resources in accordance with the pattern of consumer choice. The monopolist is likely to increase his profit by raising his price. He will then limit his output to the quantity that the market will take at the price that he has fixed. Consumers who would be willing to purchase larger quantities of his product at a lower price are left, instead, to buy goods that are wanted less. Resources are thus diverted from those things which the community prefers to those which are, at best, a second choice. The resources that are excluded from the superior occupation compete with others for employment in inferior ones and their productivity declines. Monopoly, moreover, affords the consumer no protection against extortion. The monopolist may persist in offering inferior quality at a high price, since the purchasers of his product lack the alternative of turning to other sources of supply. He may obtain his profit, not by serving the community, but by refusing to serve it. Monopoly inflicts no penalty on inefficiency. The monopolist may eliminate wastes and cut costs, but he is under no compulsion to do so. Through inertia, he may cling to accustomed techniques. His hold upon the market is assured. Monopoly, as such, is not conducive to progress. The large firm may engage in research and invent new products, materials, methods, and machines. But when it possesses a monopoly, it will be reluctant to make use of these inventions if they would compel it to scrap existing equipment or if it believes that their ultimate profitability is in doubt. The monopolist may introduce innovations and cut costs, but instead of moving goods by reducing prices he is prone to spend large sums on alternative methods of promoting sales. His refusal to cut prices deprives the community of any gain. Monopoly impedes the improvement of levels of living. Because it does not compel the enhancement of quality or the reduction of price, because it fails to penalize inefficiency, because it is not conducive to progress, it makes the total output of goods and services smaller than it otherwise would be.

The maintenance of competition protects the community against the evils of monopoly. But this is not enough, for harm may also be done by the behavior of competitors. Competing sellers and competing buyers may not be equally well informed, and those who possess information may take advantage of those who lack it. Sellers and buyers may not be equally able to bargain, and those who are strong may impose upon those who are weak. Sellers seeking present profits and buyers seeking present satisfactions may waste scarce natural resources, thus impairing the well-being of future generations. Government must therefore be concerned, not only with the preservation of competition, but also with the ways in which men compete. It must act to equip traders with accurate information, to protect the weak against the strong, and to safeguard future needs against present wastes. Public control is thus required to facilitate the operation of competitive markets and to protect them against abuse.

The Doctrine of Social Responsibility

Business is driven to serve the common interest, according to a view now popular with businessmen,[4] not by the force of competition, but by a sense of social responsibility. Such service is not compelled; it is rendered voluntarily.

The notion that business conduct may be influenced by moral considerations is not entirely new. Business has long had its unwritten code of ethics—pay thy debts, fulfill thy contracts, satisfy thy customers, deal fairly with thy competitors—honored sometimes in the breach but often in the observance. Associations of businessmen have also had their written codes of ethics for many years. These codes, modeled on those of the professions, give formal expression to even higher standards of social obligation. But this is often little more than window dressing. The high standards may not be observed; they cannot be enforced. And behind their facade, the codes go on to ban competitive behavior as unethical. Even in the professions, codes of ethics are designed to give protection to the members of the group. One doctor, for instance, is not to ctiticize the diagnosis or treatment given by another. But the professions do assume responsibility for the service rendered by their members. Doctors may be excluded from hospitals, and lawyers may be disbarred. Business, however, has none of the characteristics of a profession. It requires no common training. It does not stand in a confidential personal relationship with those it serves. Its associations assume no responsibility for the quality of the products sold by their members. They have no means of imposing professional discipline. Business codes have never been regarded, therefore, as a substitute for public law.[5]

The doctrine of social responsibility, in its present form, has to do only with big business. In the modern corporation, ownership has come to be separated from control. Ownership is scattered among thousands of shareholders whose contact with the enterprise is limited to filling out proxy statements and cashing dividend checks. Control is in the hands of a self-perpetuating management. Participation in management has come increasingly to require formal training. The decisions of management are made in the full light of publicity. In such a situation, the manager holds himself responsible not only—or even primarily—to the stockholders but also to suppliers, workers, consumers, and the community at large. He serves as a mediator among these groups, balancing their interests, one against another. His motivation differs sharply from that of the primitive entrepreneur. He takes little interest in immediate profit, looking rather toward the security of the corporation as an institution and its growth in the longer future. He seeks his satisfaction in the prestige that is accorded to success and

4 / See Howard R. Bowen, *Social Responsibilities of the Businessman* (New York: Harper & Bros., 1953).

5 / See J. M. Clark, *Social Control of Business* (2d ed.; New York: McGraw-Hill Book Co., 1939), chap. xii.

progress. He wields his power benevolently, making each decision in the light of its social effects.[6]

There have been changes, says the doctrine, not only within the corporation but also in its environment. The manager, today, comes into frequent contact with labor leaders and with agencies of government. He must reckon with public opinion and with the possibility of further regulation. But these checks on his discretion are remote. The picture that is painted is that of an oligarch, held responsible by nothing but his own conscience, who is free to collect the profits of monopoly, but chooses instead to serve his fellow man.

The doctrine of social responsibility cannot be taken in disproof of the need for public control. Most men do not kill or steal, but laws against murder and theft are needed because some men do. Socially-minded men are undoubtedly to be found, in large and growing numbers, within the ranks of corporate management, but it would not be wise to assume that all managers of all corporations are of this type. Even though most managers were socially responsible, laws would still be needed to regulate the few who were not. The doctrine assumes, moreover, that the public interest is properly to be defined, and the social responsibility of business determined, by businessmen themselves. But such a view is not to be accepted; it is by society as a whole, acting through its political instruments, that these determinations should be made. Performance in the public interest should not be bestowed upon the community as a gift; it should be rendered because it is required.

The Theory of Countervailing Power

The theory of countervailing power, like the doctrine just examined, has to do with big business. As advanced by J. K. Galbraith,[7] this theory asserts that the presence of concentrated power on one side of the market will evoke the development of offsetting power on the other. Where a buyer is powerful, sellers will organize. Where a seller is powerful, strong buyers will appear. Big business, therefore, cannot abuse its power, because it must deal with those possessing equal power.

This theory does describe the situation that exists in many markets. The big employer bargains with the big union; the big milk distributor with the cooperative association of milk producers. The big meat-packer sells to the big chain stores. But there are many other markets in which strong buyers have long dealt with weak sellers; strong sellers with weak buyers. Countervailing power may emerge. But there is no reason to believe that it must necessarily do so, or that, when it does, it will be equal to the power that it was designed to offset.

Even where the power of sellers and buyers is equal, moreover, it does not follow that the public interest will be served. Instead of fighting one another, the

6 / See A. A. Berle, *The Twentieth Century Capitalist Revolution* (New York: Harcourt, Brace & Co., 1954) and J. K. Galbraith, *The New Industrial State* (Boston, Mass.: Houghton Mifflin Co., 1967), ch. 6 and 11-13.

7 / J. K. Galbraith, *American Capitalism* (Boston: Houghton Mifflin Co., 1952).

two may join hands to exploit somebody else. The steel workers and the steel companies may agree to raise both wages and the price of steel. The producers association and the milk distributors may agree to raise the farm price and the retail price of milk. Indeed, Galbraith himself admits that in a period of inflation this is exactly what they will do. The meat-packers and the chain stores, however, are unlikely to agree to raise the retail price of meat. But this is not because sellers and buyers in the wholesale market have equal power. It is because the business of food retailing is highly competitive. If the buying power of the mass distributor is to be of service to the consumer, competition in distribution must be maintained.

The theory of countervailing power thus leaves wide scope for the exercise of public control. There is need for control where countervailing power does not exist and where power on the two sides of the market is unequal. There is also need for control to prevent powerful adversaries from resolving their differences at the expense of the ultimate consumer.

FORMS OF CONTROL

The purposes for which government applies controls to business are many: maintenance of internal order, defense against external aggression, preservation of individual freedom, reduction of inequality of income, assurance of economic stability and social security, and improvement of consumer welfare. It is only with measures adopted for the last of these purposes, and with those related to them and affecting them, that the present volume is concerned.

To promote the welfare of consumers, levels of living must be raised; men must be given more leisure in which to enjoy more goods and services. To this end, waste must be reduced, efficiency increased, and costs cut; innovation must be encouraged, new methods developed, and new products introduced; quality must be improved and prices cut. The oldest and most comprehensive form of control applied to business for this purpose is that of maintaining competition. In particular industries, however, policy has substituted administrative control of enterprise as a regulator, or substituted public for private enterprise. In important fields, moreover, controls have modified competition in a variety of other ways.

Controlling Monopoly

Government has sought, in general, to maintain competition. It has preserved freedom of entry into markets, forbidden agreements to curtail production or fix prices, broken up existing combinations and prevented the formation of new ones, and outlawed competitive methods that would destroy competition and make for monopoly. This form of control is to be discussed in Part II of this book.

In a few industries, notably those providing transport and public utility services, government has accepted monopoly as unavoidable, and has substituted administrative regulation for competition as a method of control. This has involved control of entry and abandonment, of securities and accounts, of the quality of service and the level and the structure of rates. In transport, this type of control has been retained even though the field has grown increasingly competitive. In the case of radio and television, regulation is necessitated by the shortage of desirable channels; it has to do with problems of organization, technology, and service that are incidental to the allocation of airspace. These controls form the subject matter of Part III.

In industries where monopoly is inevitable, public enterprise affords an alternative to administrative regulation. Its present scope, in the United States, is small. In a few fields, such as the postal service, public enterprise is traditional. In others, it is largely an outgrowth of depression and war. The case in which it is at issue today is electric power. Public enterprise is to be examined in Part IV.

Controlling Competition

Honesty in business dealings must be assured. Consumers must not be cheated, investors swindled, or tradesmen deprived of sales by the crookedness of their competitors. Government has therefore sought to raise the plane of competition by preventing fraud. To this end, it has established standards, forbidden adulteration and misrepresentation, required publicity, inspected business operations, and regulated organized exchanges. It is also necessary, in the interest of future generations, to prevent competitive enterprises from employing wasteful methods in the exploitation of natural resources. For this reason, government requires observance of conservation practices. These matters are to be considered in Part V.

Competition has been moderated, finally, as a means of promoting the development of new industries, relieving the distress of declining industries, preserving small enterprises, and increasing the profits of organized producing groups. To these ends, government has limited entry to the market, controlled output, fixed prices, and provided other sorts of subsidies. Such measures are to be discussed in Part VI.

Chapter

2

METHODS AND LIMITS OF CONTROL

The behavior of business is influenced by society in many ways: through custom and tradition, through codes of personal morality and business ethics, through the recognition of status and the award of prestige, through the force of public opinion, the action of consumers in buying or failing to buy, and the exercise of control by government. All of these influences are important, but it is only with control by government that we are here concerned. In the present chapter, we shall examine the techniques employed in such control and the limits imposed upon their use, in the United States, by the structure and powers of government and by the requirements of constitutional law.

THE METHODS OF CONTROL

The word "control" seems to imply coercion through the imposition of penalties. And, indeed, this is a major method of control. But the means employed by government are frequently more subtle and less harsh. Compliance may be obtained by mere persuasion, by offering inducements, or by threatening business with unfavorable publicity. And even where formal procedures are employed, they may lead to nothing more than an order directing an enterprise to obey the law. Business policy is influenced, in the vast majority of cases, without imposing fines on businessmen or putting them in jail.

The Common Law

Most of the regulations affecting business, at the present time, are based on statutes or ordinances enacted by the legislative bodies of federal, state, or local governments. But statutory law was long preceded by the common law, a body of decisions handed down by courts in cases brought by private litigants. The common law had its origin in England in the days before America was colonized. It embodied the customs and the concepts that grew out of an economy of agriculture, handicrafts, and petty trade. As conditions changed, however, new problems arose, and cases presenting novel issues were brought before the courts. And as decision followed decision, each of them built on old precedents, each of them creating a new precedent, the law developed, adapting its requirements to the changing circumstances of the times. It was through the English common law, transplanted and growing in America, that business in this country was first controlled.

Control by this method was incidental to protection of the rights of parties to private suits. When such suits were brought, the courts might refuse to enforce contracts on the ground that they were contrary to public policy. They might award damages in case of injury. They might enjoin defendants from doing certain things and punish for contempt those who disobeyed them. In this way, at common law, the courts refused to enforce contracts in restraint of trade and afforded redress to persons injured by unfair methods of competition and by the creation of monopolies. And, at the same time, the courts recognized certain occupations as common callings and required those who engaged in them to give adequate service to all comers, at reasonable rates, and without discrimination. They thus anticipated the antitrust laws and the regulation, by statute, of railways and public utilities.

This method of control, however, has its limitations. A person who has suffered injury may not know it. And if he does, he many lack the funds to sue. The prosecution of offenders is bound to be sporadic; offenses that harm the public may not give rise to suits. The procedures of litigation are cumbersome and   time consuming. The courts are wanting in special competence to deal with issues of business policy. They decide the cases that are brought before them; whatever the urgency for action, they are granted no initiative. They can award damages to those who are injured; unless asked to do so, they cannot move to prevent infliction of an injury.

Statutes and Ordinances

A legislature may enact a statute—or a city council pass an ordinance—that does no more than reaffirm the rulings of the common law. More often, however, these rulings will be modified and acts will be prohibited that formerly were allowed. The legislature, however, may still leave enforcement to the initiative of private litigants, the government merely providing courts to adjudicate disputes and sheriffs to help carry their decisions into effect. It may encourage the entry of suits by providing, as a punitive measure, for the assessment of multiple damages. But if it goes no farther than this, it advances little beyond the method of the common law.

Provision is usually made, however, for the enforcement of statutes and ordinances by public agencies. Businesses subject to such enactments may be required to register and make reports. Their activities may be subjected to periodic inspection. Compliance with the law may thus be obtained through persuasion without the application of sanctions. More than this, the law may authorize public prosecutors to bring civil suits to enjoin illegal behavior, to collect damages, and to apply remedies. It may direct the police to apprehend lawbreakers and the prosecutors to bring criminal suits, empowering the courts to impose the penalties of fine and imprisonment. And here, the method of the statute is more effective than the method of the common law.

The prohibitions of a statute may be set forth in general terms, their administration entrusted to an executive agency, and their ultimate interpretation to the courts. Or they may be spelled out at length and in considerable detail. In the former case, the law will be uncertain in content but flexible in its adjustment to changing needs. In the latter, it will be definite but rigid, and may soon go out of date. In 1907 West Virginia passed a law that fixed passenger fares on railroads at 2 cents per mile, and North Dakota a law that required the daily operation of at least one passenger train and one freight train on every line within the state. As conditions change, requirements of this sort must be adjusted, and this necessitates amendment of the law. But legislatures are not continually in session, and their attention, when they meet, may well be claimed by many other things. Their action is certain to be tardy and likely to be clumsy and ill informed. If precise detail is modified by more precise detail, it, too, will soon go out of date. The statute is a good method for laying down general principles. It is a poor method of administering detailed controls.

Franchises, Certificates, and Licenses

A device that is frequently employed as a means of enabling government to establish and maintain control over a business is that of requiring enterprises to obtain permission from a public agency in order to enter the field. Entry into the business of providing utility services is limited by the necessity of obtaining from the local government a franchise which gives the right (usually an exclusive right) to construct and operate facilities along a city's streets. Entry into the utilities business, along with the transport and communications industries, is also restricted by laws requiring entrants to obtain certificates of public convenience and necessity from state or federal authorities. Admission to many other occupations is controlled by laws requiring licenses.

A franchise is contractual in character; its terms can be enforced by suits brought in the courts. Its duration may be perpetual, for a long term or a short one, or indeterminate. Franchises have been used, in the past, as means both of preventing and of exercising control over municipal utilities. Sweeping grants of monopoly power, obtained in perpetuity by bribing venal politicians, have stood, in certain cases, as contractual barriers to regulation in the public interest. But control of monopoly has been sought, on the other hand, by writing detailed requirements into franchises. Here, as in the case of statutes, rigid provisions obstructed adjustment to change. But here, adjustment was made more difficult by the contractual character of the instrument in which they were contained. The franchise has proved to be a clumsy means of regulating in detail. Today, this task is left to administrative agencies; the franchise does little more than govern the use of city streets.

The requirement of certificates of public convenience and necessity is deliberately designed to exclude competitors from the transport, communications, and utilities industries, where it is thought that better service is to be afforded by monopolies. It is usually accompanied by public regulation of services and rates. Certificates do not confer contractual rights; they are issued as a privilege.

Licenses are required as a condition of entry into many other fields. State and local governments make this requirement of doctors, dentists, pharmacists, barbers, brokers, plumbers, and those in other callings; of distributors of liquor, tobacco, milk, and other goods; and of operators of restaurants, hotels, theaters, pool rooms, dance halls, taxicabs, and those in other service trades. The federal government, in its regulations of trucking and shipping, requires certificates of common carriers, permits of contract carriers, and licenses of private carriers. It uses the licensing technique in controlling equipment and personnel in transport and in allocating broadcasting channels among radio and television companies.

A licensing system may be used primarily as a source of revenue, as a method of obtaining registration for policing purposes, or as a means of protecting the public against unqualified practitioners of a profession or unsafe conditions in a trade. Licenses may be granted freely to all who make an application, or the system may be so designed or administered as to exclude competitors from a preempted field. Like the certificate, the license confers a privilege to which its holder has no legal right. It is usually temporary, renewable, and revocable. The government's power to refuse an application enables it—if it chooses—to impose conditions on its licensees. And its power to refuse renewal or to revoke a license affords a sanction whereby these conditions may be enforced. This penalty, however, is so harsh that it may seldom be applied.

Administrative Regulation

Where the policies of an industry are to be supervised in some detail, this task is now assigned, almost invariably, to a specialized administrative agency. The legislature typically enacts a statute, expressing its purposes in general terms, and empowers the agency to put them into effect. It may assign this responsibility to an existing officer or to a new office set up within one of the established departments of government. Or it may set up a new agency for the purpose. Characteristically, this will take the form of a board or commission with three or more members. This body will have its own identity, its own appropriation, and its own staff. Its members may be elected or appointed. They may be made subservient to the executive or given a measure of independence by requiring bipartisan representation, by fixing overlapping terms, and by forbidding removal until these terms expire.

An administrative agency may exercise wide discretion under a grant of legislative authority. The law may authorize the establishment of standards for agricultural commodities. But the actual grades will be fixed by the Secretary of Agriculture. The law may say that public utility service must be adequate, rates just and reasonable, and discrimination not unreasonable or undue. The regulatory commission will go on to specify standards of service, to fix the general level of rates, and to pass upon complaints concerning differences in the charges paid by different customers. Its determinations will then be subject, on appeal, to confirmation or reversal by the courts.

Administrative regulation is widespread in both state and federal governments. Banks and insurance companies are regulated, for instance, by state superintendents of banking and insurance. The food and drug industry is regulated by a federal food and drug administrator, and price ceilings have been fixed for all industries, in wartime, by a federal price administrator. The first commission in the United States was established by Massachusetts in 1838 to regulate the banking business. Railroad commissions with limited powers were set up by five New England states before the Civil War. Commissions were given mandatory powers over grain elevators and warehouses by Illinois in 1871 and over railroads by Illinois, Wisconsin, and Minnesota in 1874. The first such federal agency—the Interstate Commerce Commission—was established by Congress in 1887. State commissions, some of them formerly railroad commissions, were given authority over municipal utilities by Wisconsin, New York, and Georgia in 1907, by 25 other states by 1913, and by all the states but Delaware by 1927. Other federal commissions were established or reestablished during the thirties, among them the Securities and Exchange Commission, the Federal Communications Commission, the Federal Power Commission, and the Civil Aeronautics Board.

The advantages of administrative regulation lie in its possible combination of expert knowledge, continuous oversight, informal procedure, and prompt action, and its emphasis on prevention rather than punishment. Its disadvantages are those inherent in democratic politics and bureaucratic administration. They will be discussed in greater detail later on.

Taxes, Expenditures, and Subsidies

Taxation, though its primary function it that of obtaining revenue, may also be used as a method of control. Taxes have been imposed on liquor, tobacco, and various luxury goods for the purpose of discouraging consumption; on stock and commodity transfers to lessen speculation; and on narcotic drugs, white phosphorus matches, and the products of child labor at rates designed to prevent their production and sale. They have been levied on imported goods, on oleomargarine, and on chain stores to handicap them in their competition with domestic producers, dairymen, and independent retailers. Tax exemption, also, has been employed to induce the sorts of conduct that governments have desired. By granting exemptions from property taxes, local governments have encouraged the construction of new dwellings and the establishment of new industries. By taxing those who did not cooperate and exempting those who did, the federal government has forced the producers of bituminous coal and various agricultural commodities to adhere to programs fixing prices and restricting output and sales. Taxation of corporate income has been manipulated, too, in ways designed to stimulate the discovery and development of minerals and to promote investment in productive facilities.

Government also influences business through its purchases and sales. The federal government has promoted transport by spending money on highways, waterways, and airways, fostered aviation by paying excessive sums for carrying the mails, and supported silver mining by buying the product to bury it again. It has instructed its procurement officers to "buy American," and attached to appropriations for foreign aid the instruction that the goods supplied be carried in American ships. By releasing metals from its strategic stockpiles and by increasing the cut of timber permitted in public forests, government has checked inflation, holding down the prices of such materials when they threatened to rise.

Government affects business by lending as well as by spending. In this way, it has promoted the ownership of homes and farms, the construction of low-rent housing in urban centers, and the extension of electrical power to rural areas. By making loans to one industry rather than another, it has determined where expansion should occur. By denying loans to farmers who do not cooperate in limiting production, it has induced adherence to its agricultural policies.

Subsidies may be concealed in purchases made at more than market prices or in loans made at rates of interest that fail to cover their costs. They may be hidden in sales made at less than market prices or in services rendered at a loss. This is the case when the government pays high prices for facilities and equipment in wartime and sells them at low prices as soon as the war is won. It is the case, too, when the Post Office delivers periodicals at a fraction of what the service costs. But subsidies may also be visible. Thus, in the 19th century, public lands were given to the railroads to open the country and to homesteaders to insure its settlement. And thus, at the present time, cash payments are made to builders and operators of merchant ships in order to keep the shipyards busy and the flag afloat upon the seas. In any of these cases, the payment of a subsidy may be accompanied by conditions laid down by the government. But here, compliance is voluntary. It is not commanded; it is bought.

Contracts

Government has sometimes effected control of an industry by writing regulatory provisions into public contracts. Under laws passed in the thirties, the federal government has required firms accepting such contracts to maintain, at a specified level, the wages paid to laborers. Since 1951, it has forbidden its contractors to discriminate, on grounds of race or color, in offering opportunities for employment. This method of control has been most important, however, in the case of atomic energy. Here, a major industry has been created, developed, and regulated through the terms written into contracts between the Atomic Energy Commission and private companies. The method has advantages: the control is flexible; it is accepted voluntarily. But control by contract is limited in scope: it can be effected only in those cases where government has something to buy or sell.

Industry Self-Government

Another method of control, employed extensively during the depression of the thirties, is called self-government in industry. Under this method, rules are adopted by agreement among the members of a trade, submitted for approval to a public agency, modified if rejected, given legal status when accepted, and then enforced, not only by industry itself, but also by the government. This was the method used in regulating business from 1933 to 1935, under the codes adopted and approved in accordance with the National Industrial Recovery Act. It is the method still employed in regulating the securities markets, export trade associations, transport rate-fixing bureaus, and marketing agreements set up by the producers, processors, and distributors of certain agricultural commodities. The main advantage of the method is that it eases enforcement by enlisting the voluntary cooperation of industry. Its principal disadvantage is that it may give official endorsement to rules adopted in the interest of organized producers with little or no regard for the interests of consumers or the well-being of the whole community.

Investigations and Publicity

Government has sometimes called upon public opinion, employing no further sanctions, to influence the behavior of business. Congress set up a Bureau of Corporations in the Department of Commerce and Labor in 1903 and empowered it to investigate and report on business practices. This function was transferred to the Federal Trade Commission in 1914, the new agency being expected to keep business under control, in President Wilson's words, by "pitiless publicity." This method has been employed repeatedly in an effort to prevent or settle strikes. Boards established by Congress or set up by the President have conducted investigations, issued factual reports, and presented recommendations which employers and workers were under no compulsion to accept. But it was hoped that the pressure of informed opinion would make for peaceful settlements. Congressional investigations, in recent years, have focused the spotlight of publicity on such matters as the diversion of union funds by labor leaders and the prices of coffee, gasoline, and drugs.

Publicity, unaided by compulsion, has sometimes worked. Committee hearings, reported in the press, have served, without legislation, to bring about changes in business policy. An investigation of the relationship between the large automobile manufacturers and their dealers, made by a committee of the Senate in 1955, led to a radical alteration in the terms of dealer contracts. The example set by the Tennessee Valley Authority in establishing promotional rates for electricity, and publication by the Federal Power Commission of rate comparisons for public and private companies in different cities, may have done more than commission regulation to modify the rate structures of privately owned utilities.

But publicity, like other methods, has its limitations. It is violently resented by those against whom it is directed, and steps may be taken to limit the powers and to cut the appropriations of any agency employing it. Counterpropaganda may be issued, and the public, instead of being informed, will merely be confused. It is not always possible to bring public opinion to bear. Its ultimate sanction is the boycott. But consumers may be unable to go without a product, even though convinced that its producers are at fault. And if they do refuse to buy, they may be unable to punish the guilty without injuring the innocent.

Wage-Price Guide Posts

Presidents have repeatedly admonished labor and business leaders to forestall inflation by moderating their wage demands and foregoing price increases. During the depression of the thirties, President Roosevelt appealed to businessmen to raise wages without raising prices. And during the prosperity of the fifties, President Eisenhower cautioned labor and business to restrain their proclivities to boost both wages and prices. In both cases, their appeals fell on deaf ears. In January 1962, the President's Council of Economic Advisers published guide posts for noninflationary wage and price action, suggesting that increases in an industry's wages be kept within the rate of overall increases in productivity, and that its prices be kept stable if its own increase in productivity equalled the overall average, cut if it exceeded the average, and increased only if it fell below the average. In April 1962, the union and the companies in the steel industry concluded a wage agreement that fell within the guideposts. Shortly thereafter, the United States Steel Corporation announced price increases that exceeded the guideposts. President Kennedy, in a nation-wide broadcast, denounced this action as a "wholly unjustifiable and irresponsible defiance of the public interest." The increases were rescinded when the administration succeeded in persuading some of the smaller companies not to follow the Corporation's lead. For the next four years, the level of prices was fairly stable. During this period, it is possible that the guideposts played a minor role in checking discretionary increases in wages and prices. But after 1965, inflation got out of hand. During this period, the effect of the guideposts was small. Whenever government greatly increases its expenditures without increasing taxes in the same proportion, as was the case during the war in Vietnam, the level of wages and prices will be bound to rise. Labor will reject the guideposts; business will ignore them.[1]

1 / See Grant McConnell, *Steel and the Presidency, 1962* (New York: W. W. Norton & Co., 1963) and John Sheahan, *The Wage-Price Guide Posts* (Washington, D.C.: Brookings Institution, 1967).

Emergency Controls

In time of war, or threat of war, the market has been largely superseded, as the governor of the economy, by authoritarian controls. Production has been diverted from civilian to military purposes. Prices and wages have been fixed, consumers' goods rationed, and materials and manpower allocated among competing demands. Laws have been piled upon laws, orders on orders. Administrative agencies have multiplied. All of the available methods of control have been put to use; all of the usual sanctions employed. And there have been two others: the conscription of labor, which has been little used; and the seizure of productive facilities, which has been used repeatedly.

Laws authorizing seizure have been enacted by Congress at least 18 times, the first of them during the Civil War, and others during the two world wars and the war in Korea. These laws have authorized the President to take possession of factories, power plants, mines, and transport and communications facilities, in the event of war or other national emergency, in order to insure production of essential goods and services and continued operation during wage disputes. The powers thus provided were exercised by the President three times during the Civil War, eleven times druing World War I, and 58 times during World War II. Seizure was used by President Truman in a dozen labor cases in the years that followed the war, the industries taken over including petroleum, meat-packing, bituminous coal, the railroads, and iron and steel. The President's action, in all but the last of these cases, was based upon wartime statutes that had not expired. His seizure of the steel industry, on April 8, 1952, was without Congressional authority.

Seizure has come to find its principal significance in the attempted settlement of industrial disputes. It does not involve the public ownership or operation of the properties that are seized. Public officials are placed in positions of nominal authority. But private managements are appointed to run their own concerns, and private owners continue to receive their dividends. The purpose of seizure is to maintain continued operation of essential services by preventing or ending a strike. The properties involved are returned to their owners as soon as this purpose has been served.

Government Ownership and Operation

Ownership and operation gives government the power directly to determine the policies of an industry. It thus affords a possible alternative to indirect controls. If extended to many fields, it makes for comprehensive economic planning. If limited to a few, it is consistent with the preservation of a free economy. This is the case, of course, in the United States. Water systems are owned and operated by most cities, liquor stores by many states, the postal service and the production of atomic energy by the federal government. Other activities are carried on by semiautonomous corporations, such as the Port of

New York Authority and the TVA, whose directors are publicly appointed but whose managements are removed, to a degree, from the pressures of politics and the hampering rules of state and federal bureaucracies. The principal questions raised concerning public ownership, in such cases, are those of character of service and comparative efficiency.

THE STRUCTURE AND POWERS OF GOVERNMENT

In the government of the United States, four fundamental principles affect the application of controls: (1) Under the federal system, powers are distributed between the nation and the several states. The national government possesses the express powers that are delegated to it by the Constitution, the implied powers that may be inferred therefrom, the resulting powers—such as the power to issue paper money and make it legal tender—that are consequent upon a combination of express powers, and the inherent powers—relating primarily to international affairs—that are an attribute of national sovereignty. Under the Tenth Amendment, all other powers were reserved to the states. (2) Within both state and federal governments there is a separation of legislative, executive, and judicial powers. Protection against arbitrary action is thus afforded by a system of checks and balances. (3) These governments rest on written constitutions, containing guarantees of individual rights through which their powers are limited. (4) The acts of legislators and executives are subject to judicial review. The constitutions and the laws are interpreted, laws found to be unconstitutional are voided, and the acts of administrators are approved, modified, or reversed by the courts. This structure of government, and these limitations to its powers, determine whether a particular method of control may be employed and, if so, by whom, and how.

The Distribution of Powers

The economic powers delegated to the federal government by the states, as enumerated in Article I, Section 8 of the Constitution are these:

To lay and collect Taxes, Duties, Imposts and Excises, to pay the Debts
and provide for the common Defence and the general Welfare. . . .
To borrow Money. . . .
To regulate Commerce with foreign Nations and among the several States
. . . and with the Indian tribes;
To establish . . . uniform laws on the subject of Bankruptcies. . . .
To coin Money, regulate the value thereof . . . and fix the Standard of
Weights and Measures. . . .
To establish Post Offices and post Roads;
To promote the progress of Science and useful Arts, by securing for
limited Times to Authors and Inventors the exclusive Right to their
respective Writings and Discoveries. . . .

The most important of these clauses, for public control of business in time of peace, is the one—generally referred to as the interstate commerce clause—that gives the Congress power "To regulate Commerce . . . among the several States. . . ." Of even greater importance, however, are the extensive powers, conferred by subsequent clauses, to declare and wage war. And also significant, in some cases, is the fact that the states are forbidden to enter into treaties by Article I, Section 10 of the Constitution, while the President and the Senate are authorized to do so by Article II, Section 2.

The enumerated powers of the federal government are those expressly set forth in the Constitution. The implied powers are those inferred from the final clause of Article I, Section 8 of that document which authorized the Congress "To make all laws which shall be necessary and proper for carrying into Execution the foregoing Powers, and all other Powers vested by this Constitution in the Government of the United States. . . ." This may not have been intended as a grant of further powers, but it was so interpreted by the Supreme Court in the famous case of *McCulloch* v. *Maryland* in 1819.[2] The state of Maryland had imposed a tax on notes issued by a bank established by the federal government. When sued, it advanced the defense that nothing in the Constitution had empowered the Congress to set up a bank. The Court admitted that this power was not explicit, but held that it could reasonably be deduced from those that were. Said Chief Justice John Marshall, "Let the end be legitimate, let it be within the scope of the Constitution, and all means which are appropriate . . . which are not prohibited, but consist with the letter and spirit of the Constitution, are constitutional. . . ." This decision, as must be obvious, was of paramount importance in extending the scope of federal powers. From this time on, the national government was permitted, not only to do things that the Constitution said, but also to do things that the Court was willing to infer.

All governmental powers, save those denied them by the Constitution, are retained by the several states. Laws affecting business have thus been enacted, in the interest of public safety, health, and morals, and the general welfare, under what has been known as the police power of the states. This power, though not mentioned in the Constitution, has long been recognized by the courts.[3] Without definite limits, it has afforded a basis for such activities as the licensing of automobile drivers to insure public safety, the inspection of dairies to protect public health, the censorship of motion pictures to safeguard public morals, and the payment of mothers' pensions to promote the general welfare.

When state and federal powers come into conflict, the latter must prevail. "This Constitution," says Article VI, "and the Laws of the United States which shall be made in Pursuance thereof . . . shall be the supreme Law of the Land." And this phrase was repeated by Justice Marshall in *McCulloch* v. *Maryland*, when he denied the states the right to tax a federal agency. "The government of the United States," he said, "though limited in its powers, is supreme; and its

2 / 4 Wheaton 316.

3 / *Brown* v. *Maryland*, 12 Wheaton 419 (1827); *Charles River Bridge* v. *Warren Bridge*, 11 Peters 420 (1837); *Cooley* v. *Board of Wardens of Port of Philadelphia*, 12 Howard 299 (1852).

laws, when made in pursuance of the Constitution, form the supreme law of the land."

There has been a steady trend, over the years, toward increasing centralization of functions in the federal government. The reasons for this development are not hard to find. (1) Some regulatory activities require the establishment of uniform standards throughout the country if they are adequately to be performed. This is true, for instance, of the grading of commodities. (2) In other cases, the industries controlled extend beyond state borders, and controls must be given equal scope if they are to work at all. It was the failure of state regulation that led to the federal regulation of railway transport and interstate sales of gas and electricity. (3) Elsewhere, a state may fail to act because its producers, if compelled to incur higher costs, would be placed at a disadvantage in competing with producers in surrounding states. Here, if competitors are to be put upon an equal footing, federal action is required. The establishment of a system of unemployment insurance is a case in point. (4) Sometimes, responsibility for a service is assumed by the federal government because it has not been met by the states. This is why Washington went into the business of conserving natural resources and providing social security. (5) The federal government can raise more money than the states. There is no constitutional limit on its power to borrow. And it can reach the larger incomes with progressive taxes, wherever their possessors may reside. As a result, it has been in a stronger position than the states to finance additional activities. (6) Each of these factors makes for centralization. But the great centralizers are war and depression. And war, depression, and war, since 1917, have contributed heavily to the growth of federal activities.

In some cases, common programs have been undertaken in regions larger than the separate states without concentrating their management in Washington. Three means of doing this have been devised. (1) The federal government has made grants, when matched by state appropriations, laying down certain conditions, but leaving detailed administration to the states. This method has been used in building roads, in providing low-rent housing, and in giving assistance to dependent children and the aged. (2) The federal government has imposed a tax, but granted exemptions where states have levied a comparable tax to finance a specified activity. It was through the tax offset device that unemployment insurance systems were set up in the several states. (3) The Constitution, in Article I, Section 10, forbids the states to enter into compacts with one another without the consent of Congress. In certain cases, this consent has been obtained. Interstate compacts have governed the sharing of water rights on lakes and rivers and provided for curtailment of the production of petroleum. They might well have been used with greater frequency had not interpretation allowed so broad a scope to federal powers.

The Separation of Powers

Within the state and federal governments, distinct responsibilities are traditionally assigned to three separate branches: the enactment of laws to the legislature, their enforcement to the executive, and their interpretation to the judiciary. Under the constitutions, these branches are equal. None has authority over the others, but each of them can check the others. The executive can veto a bill passed by the legislature. The legislature can pass it over his veto. The courts can change its meaning by interpretation. The legislature can revise the law, restating its former purpose, and pass it again. The executive may change the complexion of the courts when he appoints new judges. But these appointments must be confirmed by the upper house of the legislature. Through such checks and balances, protection is afforded against precipitate and ill-considered action and against the arbitrary exercise of power.

Though the three branches of government are equal, the courts have succeeded in establishing their own supremacy in one respect. The state courts can find a local ordinance or a state law to be in violation of the state or federal constitutions; in interpreting a state constitution, the highest court in the state is the final authority. The federal courts can find state or federal laws to be in violation of the federal Constitution, and here the Supreme Court of the United States is the final authority. The power of the Supreme Court to invalidate state laws is clearly indicated in the provision of Article VI that the Constitution itself, and the enactments of the Congress, shall be the supreme law of the land. Its power to invalidate federal legislation was not mentioned in the Constitution but asserted by the Court in the historic case of *Marbury* v. *Madison* in 1803.[4] In the words of Justice Marshall, "an act of the legislature, repugnant to the Constitution, is void. . . ." The doctrine of judicial supremacy, thus established, now has behind it the prestige of tradition and the force of popular support.

The practice of government departs in another respect from the nominal pattern of three coequal branches, each with a distinctive duty to perform The legislature has been forced, by the increasing complexity of the problems with which it must deal, to delegate authority to the executive. It may assert the broad outlines of a policy, but must leave it to administration to fill in the details. In doing so, it confers the power to legislate. Executive agencies—departments and commissions—may issue rules and regulations that come to have the force of law. They may perform judicial functions, too, hearing complaints and rendering decisions, subject to appeal, in much the manner of a lower court. They thus combine, in varying degrees, the work of the administrator, the legislator, and the judge.

The blueprint of governmental organization is further complicated by the independent status usually accorded the regulatory commission. It is located within the executive branch. Its members are appointed by the governor or the President. But usually they may not be removed except for serious misconduct. And their terms of office may be so arranged as to make it difficult for him readily to obtain a majority committed to his policies. The independent commission is dependent on the executive to initiate its appointments, on the legislature to provide its powers and appropriations, on the judiciary to interpret its statute and enforce its rules. Sometimes described as a fourth branch of government, it is still a creature of the other three.

4 / 1 Cranch 137.

Constitutional Safeguards for Individual Rights

In both state and federal constitutions, the rights of citizens are protected against invasion by the acts of governments. State constitutions limit state action, some of them setting forth restrictions in elaborate detail, all of them safeguarding the rights of person and property in general terms. The federal Constitution imposes limitations on both state and federal governments. The limitations on control of business by the federal government are found in the due process clause of the Fifth Amendment and in its protection against abuse of the right of eminent domain: "No person shall . . . be deprived of life, liberty, or property without due process of law; nor shall private property be taken for public use, without just compensation." This Amendment was adopted when the Constitution was ratified, as a part of the Bill of Rights. The limitations on the power of the states to exercise controls over business are contained in the contracts clause in Article I, Section 10 of the Constitution itself, "No State shall . . . pass any . . . Law impairing the Obligation of Contracts . . . ," and in the clauses contained in the Fourteenth Amendment—adopted in connection with the abolition of slavery at the time of the Civil War—which relate (1) to the privileges and immunities of citizens, (2) to due process of law, and (3) to equal protection of the laws: "No State shall make or enforce any law which shall abridge the privileges or immunities of citizens of the United States; nor shall any State deprive any person of life, liberty, or property, without due process of law; nor deny to any person within its jurisdiction the equal protection of the laws." These provisions should be memorized, together with the enumeration of Congressional powers set forth above, for it is upon them that the system of law that governs the public control of business in the United States is based.

Judicial Review

The courts are at once powerful and impotent. They can invalidate or modify an act if it is brought before them. They cannot question it if it is not. They can veto legislation or, in effect, rewrite it. But they cannot initiate a law. They must wait for someone—a public prosecutor or a private plaintiff—to sue or to appeal a suit. It is only then they can speak.

The courts interpret the Constitution and the laws, determining whether laws shall stand, by giving the Constitution one meaning or another, and giving meanings to the laws themselves. In the process of interpretation, they follow precedents. But the precedents on both sides of an issue may be so numerous that judges are free to pick and choose. The Supreme Court of the United States, moreover, does not consider itself to be bound by earlier decisions. It may overrule them explicitly; it may do so silently; it may reverse them, in actuality, while arguing persuasively that it has made no change. The last word spoken by the last court, at any moment, is the law.

Interpretation has seemed to be narrow, ambiguous and inconsistent, shifting and even reversing its direction from time to time. This may be true, in part, because judges are influenced by their background, training, and social outlook, because the Supreme Court, as Mr. Dooley once remarked, "follows th' illiction returns," and because the composition of the Court has changed. With the replacement (or conversion) of a single judge, the minority in a 5 to 4 division may form a majority in the next 5 to 4 vote. It is true, too, because decisions are handed down in specific cases, where issues may differ in detail, because differences in skill of presentation may lead to different judgments on similar facts, and because the courts confine themselves to narrow issues, leaving the way open to arrive at different decisions on the basis of somewhat different facts. It is true, finally, because the problems brought to judgment are complex and confusing, because lawyers and judges—and economists—fail to understand them, and because the answers, at best, are far from clear. It is easy to berate the judiciary, more difficult to fulfill the duties of a judge.

JUDICIAL LIMITATIONS ON CONTROL

When the validity of a law or an order regulating business is questioned, the courts may decide against it on any one of several grounds. They may find that the government enacting it has exceeded its powers: that a state has attempted to control an industry that is in interstate commerce, that the federal government has attempted to control one that is not, that it has made improper use of its taxing power, or gone beyond its power to make treaties or its power to wage war. They may hold that the separation of governmental functions has been disregarded: that the executive branch has acted without legislative authority, or that the legislature has made an undue delegation of powers. They may conclude that the safeguards of individual rights have been violated: that property has been taken without just compensation, that contracts have been impaired, that persons have been denied equality of treatment, or deprived of liberty or property without due process, whether by the procedures employed in a law's administration or by the substance of the law itself. The courts thus have wide latitude in passing judgment on controls established and administered by other branches of the government, and they have used it, from time to time, with varying effects.

Interstate Commerce

The Supreme Court first defined the word "commerce" in the case of *Gibbons* v. *Ogden*[5] in 1824. The scope it gave the term was broad. Commerce, said Justice Marshall, "is traffic, but it is something more. . . . It describes the commercial intercourse between nations and parts of nations, in all its branches. . . ." The concept was thus extended beyond the act of buying and selling across state lines to comprehend all of the processes through which trade is carried on.

5 / 9 Wheaton 1.

The Court applied it specifically to navigation in the Gibbons case, and to other forms of transport and communications in cases decided in 1872 and 1877.[6] But it has gone much farther. In 1871 it upheld federal regulation of a steamer carrying goods between two ports in Michigan on the ground that the out-of-state origin and destination of these goods made the vessel "an instrument" of interstate commerce.[7] In 1914 it permitted the federal government to fix railway rates between points within the borders of a state because this traffic bore "such a close and substantial relation to interstate traffic that the control is essential or appropriate."[8] And in 1922 it approved the regulation of grain elevators and stockyards, saying that such enterprises, though tied to one location, were situated in the "stream" or "flow" of commerce.[9]

The trend of opinion, in these decisions, favored the federal government. But federal controls, in other cases, were limited in scope or completely outlawed, for many years, through narrow interpretations of the commerce clause. Thus, in 1887 and 1895, the Court ruled that manufacturing was not commerce, excluding the entire area from the scope of federal power.[10] In 1918 it invalidated a law prohibiting interstate shipment of the products of child labor, on the ground that their production was not interstate.[11] In 1935 it found the National Industrial Recovery Act to be unconstitutional, for one reason, because the relation between industries covered by NRA codes, on the one hand, and interstate commerce, on the other, was remote.[12] And in 1936, invalidating a law providing for wage and price fixing in the coal industry, the Court asserted that the federal government could not control an intrastate activity unless its effect on interstate commerce was not merely "close and substantial," but "direct."[13]

The restrictive effect of these decisions was sharply reversed in 1937, when the Court upheld the constitutionality of the National Labor Relations Act. This law, requiring collective bargaining and giving a federal board the power to deal with unfair labor practices, was challenged by companies manufacturing steel, trailers, and men's clothing. In each case the Court held that the law applied.[14] Congress cannot be held powerless to regulate, said Chief Justice Hughes, "when

---

6 / *Railway* v. *Van Husen*, 95 U.S. 465 (1872); *Pensacola Tel. Co.* v. *Western Union*, 96 U.S. 1 (1877).

7 / *Steamer Daniel Bell* v. *U.S.*, 10 Wallace 557.

8 / *The Shreveport Rate Cases*, 234 U.S. 342.

9 / *Lemke* v. *Farmers Grain Co.*, 258 U.S. 50 (1922); *Stafford* v. *Wallace*, 258 U.S. 495 (1922).

10 / *Kidd* v. *Pearson*, 128 U.S. 1 (1887); *U.S.* v. *E. C. Knight Co.*, 156 U.S. 1 (1895).

11 / *Hammer* v. *Dagenhart*, 247 U.S. 251.

12 / *Schechter* v. *U.S.*, 295 U.S. 495.

13 / *Carter* v. *Carter Coal Co.*, 298 U.S. 238.

14 / *NLRB* v. *Jones & Laughlin Steel Corp.*, 301 U.S. 1; *NLRB* v. *Fruehauf Trailer Co.*, 301 U.S. 49; *NLRB* v. *Friedman-Harry Marks Clothing Co.*, 301 U.S. 58.

industries organize themselves on a national scale, making their relation to interstate commerce the dominant factor in their activities. . . ." In later decisions the law was also held to cover a cannery that shipped only a third of its output to other states [15] and a power company that sold an insignificant fraction of its current across state lines. [16] In 1941 the Court went on to approve the Fair Labor Standards Act, a law forbidding interstate shipment of goods made by persons paid less than legally determined wages or required to work for more than legally determined hours, thus reversing the position it had taken in 1918, when the same method was used to eliminate child labor.[17] And in 1942, it upheld the Agricultural Adjustment Act of 1938, which enabled the federal government to control the quantity of a crop that a farmer could offer for sale.[18] In this decision, the Court explicitly rejected the rule it had laid down in the case of the coal industry in 1936: "Even if the appellee's activity be local and though it may not be regarded as commerce, it may still, whatever its nature, be reached by Congress if it exerts a substantial economic effect on interstate commerce, and this irrespective of whether such effect is what might at some earlier time have been defined as 'direct' or 'indirect.' "[19] In 1944 the Court upheld the application of a federal statute to the insurance business,[20] and in 1945 to retail trade.[21] It thus appears that the interpretation of the commerce clause is no longer likely to impose significant limits on federal power.

The clause may still be used, however, to reject regulation by the states. Laws that incidentally affect interstate commerce are usually allowed to stand. But those that unduly burden or obstruct it may be found to trespass on federal authority. And where state and federal regulations overlap, those of the federal government are given precedence and those of the states must be made to conform.[22]

The General Welfare

The Supreme Court has shown no desire to restrict the activities of the federal government under its war or treaty powers. It has, however, rejected efforts by Congress, made under cover of its power to tax, to impose controls for which it had no other authority. The Constitution gives Congress the power "To lay and collect Taxes . . . and provide for the common Defence and general Welfare. . . ." But the Court long held that this reference to the general welfare

15 / *Santa Cruz Packing Co.* v. *NLRB*, 303 U.S. 453 (1938).

16 / *Consolidated Edison Co.* v. *NLRB*, 305 U.S. 197 (1938).

17 / *U.S.* v. *Darby Lumber Co.*, 312 U.S. 100.

18 / *Wickard* v. *Filburn*, 317 U.S. 111.

19 / *Ibid.*, p. 125.

20 / *U.S.* v. *South-Eastern Underwriters*, 322 U.S. 533.

21 / *U.S.* v. *Frankfort Distilleries*, 324 U.S. 293.

22 / *The Shreveport Rate Cases*, 234 U.S. 342.

conferred no power in itself, but merely described the purposes for which tax money would be used. It did not object to the imposition of taxes to check the sale of oleomargarine,[23] narcotics,[24] or firearms,[25] accepting the fiction that the levies were intended as a source of revenue. But in 1922 it branded as unconstitutional a second Congressional attempt to outlaw child labor, this time by taxing the profits of the children's employers.[26] In 1936 it nullified the Agricultural Adjustment Act of 1933 on the ground that collection of taxes from processors and payment of benefits to producers of agricultural commodities, in order to curtail their output, involved the use of taxation not for revenue but in the interest of a special group, in order to exercise control where power had not been delegated to Congress but reserved to the states.[27] And in the same year, in rejecting regulation of the coal industry, the Court denounced the effort to compel adherence to minimum wages and prices by taxing producers who did not cooperate in the program and exempting those who did.[28]

With the tax power, as with the commerce power, interpretation was reversed in 1937. In that year the Court was called upon to consider two programs of social insurance adopted under the Social Security Act of 1935. In the first, the federal government induced the states to enact unemployment insurance laws by taxing payrolls and allowing an offset where the states imposed such taxes to finance insurance benefits. In the second, it levied further taxes on wages and payrolls but obligated itself to pay annuities to wage earners upon their retirement from work. Each of these programs was held to be constitutional. Under the first, said Justice Cardozo, the tax was legitimate as a source of revenue, and the offset did not involve coercion of the states, in contravention of the Constitution, but merely afforded a temptation to cooperate.[29] Under the second, the taxes were again legitimate, and the decision of Congress to provide benefits for the aged lay within its power to spend for the general welfare. The concept of welfare, said Justice Cardozo, is not a static one; it changes with the times. Its content is for Congress to decide. The courts will not interfere "unless the choice is clearly wrong, a display of arbitrary power, not an exercise of judgment."[30] The power to control by taxing and spending, in consequence, is virtually unlimited.

The police power, as we have seen, was retained by the several states. Nowhere in the Constitution or in the decisions of the courts is this power given to the federal government. But Congress has none the less acted, under the authority of its other powers, to protect public safety, health, and morals, and

23 / *McCray* v. *U.S.*, 195 U.S. 27 (1904).

24 / *U.S.* v. *Doremus*, 249 U.S. 87 (1919).

25 / *Sonzinsky* v. *U.S.*, 300 U.S. 506.

26 / *Bailey* v. *Drexel Furniture Co.*, 259 U.S. 20.

27 / *U.S.* v. *Butler* (the Hoosac Mills case), 297 U.S. 1.

28 / *Carter* v. *Carter Coal Co.*, 298 U.S. 238.

29 / *Steward Machine Co.* v. *Davis*, 301 U.S. 548.

30 / *Helvering* v. *Davis*, 301 U.S. 619.

to promote the general welfare. In addition to taxing oleo, narcotics, and firearms and providing insurance benefits, it has also excluded fraudulent and obscene materials from the mails and prohibited the interstate movement of lottery tickets, stolen automobiles, and women for immoral purposes. It has used its powers, too, to insure the purity of foods and drugs, to enforce grain standards and plant quarantines, to improve conditions of labor, and to prevent misrepresentation in the distribution of securities. As a result, reference is sometimes made to the police powers of the federal government. Strictly speaking, no such powers exist. But their absence, today, presents no handicap.

Powers of the Executive

Action may be reversed not only because it exceeds the powers conferred upon the government but also because it violates the separation of powers. It may be found that the executive branch has gone beyond its own authority, or that the legislative branch has gone too far in delegating authority to the executive.

On April 8, 1952, in order to prevent a strike, President Truman seized the steel mills. When a district court injunction staying this action was carried to the Supreme Court, the government did not contend that it was authorized by any legislation then in force, but argued that it fell within the inherent powers of the President. This argument was rejected by the Court. Said Justice Black:

> In the framework of our Constitution, the President's power to see that the laws are faithfully executed refutes the idea that he is to be a lawmaker. The Constitution limits his functions in the lawmaking process to the recommending of laws he thinks wise and the vetoing of laws he thinks bad. And the Constitution is neither silent nor equivocal about who shall make laws which the President is to execute. The first section of the first article says that "All legislative powers herein granted shall be vested in a Congress. . . ."
>
> The President's order does not direct that a Congressional policy be executed in a manner prescribed by Congress—it directs that a Presidential policy be executed in a manner prescribed by the President . . . The founders of this nation entrusted the lawmaking power to the Congress alone in both good times and bad . . . [T]his seizure order cannot stand.[31]

It does not appear, from the positions taken by the several justices, that executive action said to be justified by inherent powers will never be upheld. But it is clear that seizure is not permitted in time of peace unless authorized by Congress.

In 1935 the National Industrial Recovery Act was twice found to be unconstitutional, not only because it went beyond the authority conferred by

31 / *Youngstown Sheet and Tube Co.* v. *Sawyer,* 343 U.S. 579 (1952).

the interstate commerce clause, but also because it involved an excessive delegation of legislative powers. In the first case, Section 9-c of the Act, permitting the President to prevent interstate shipment of oil produced in excess of state quotas, was rejected because Congress had neither set forth a statement of policy nor prescribed standards of behavior but had left unfettered discretion to the executive.[32] The second case was broader in scope, involving the NRA program as a whole. This program permitted the President to approve codes, prepared by trade associations, for the government of their respective industries. It was found to involve a virtual abdication of Congressional authority. The Act, said Justice Hughes, "does not undertake to prescribe rules of conduct to be applied to particular states of fact determined by appropriate administrative procedure. Instead of prescribing rules of conduct, it authorizes the making of codes to prescribe them." Under this procedure, said Justice Cardozo, "anything that Congress may do within the limits of the commerce clause for the betterment of business may be done by the President upon the recommendation of a trade association by calling it a code. This is delegation running riot." The program was rejected by a unanimous court.[33]

In most cases where the delegation of power has been questioned, it has been upheld. Congress, in general, is permitted to delegate where it states its purposes and lays down rules to limit the exercise of delegated powers.[34]

The Obligation of Contracts

State laws impairing contracts may be invalidated under Article I, Section 10 of the Constitution. Federal laws having the same effect may be held to be in violation of the due process clause of the Fifth Amendment. The safeguards against impairment apply both to private contracts and to those to which a government is a party, such as charters and franchises. They do not apply to commitments that are lacking in consideration or to contracts involving commitments that are contrary to public policy. The safeguards are not absolute. Impairment is permitted when incidental to legislation enacted under the police powers of a state. The only condition laid down by the courts is that the end sought by a law must be legitimate and the means employed appropriate. This interpretation is inescapable, since, in its absence, a multitude of contracts would bar the enactment of legislation in the public interest.

One of the most serious issues that has arisen here relates to the constitutionality of laws giving relief to debtors in periods of business depression. Such laws do impair the obligation of contracts. But they may also

---

32 / *Panama Refining Co.* v. *Ryan,* 293 U.S. 388.

33 / *Schechter* v. *U.S.,* 295 U.S. 495.

34 / See *U.S.* v. *Shreveport Grain & Elevator Co.,* 287 U.S. 77 (1932), upholding the Food and Drug Act; *U.S.* v. *Rock Royal Cooperative,* 307 U.S. 533 (1939), upholding the Agricultural Marketing Agreements Act; *Yakus* v. *U.S.,* 321 U.S. 414 (1944), upholding the Emergency Price Control Act; *American Power & Light Co.* v. *SEC,* 329 U.S. 90 (1946), upholding the Public Utility Holding Company Act; and *Lichter* v. *U.S.,* 332 U.S. 742 (1948), upholding the renegotiation of war contracts.

preserve human values and social stability in times of stress and strain. Here the Supreme Court has applied the test of reasonableness, upholding laws that postponed payments for a limited period but compensated the creditor for his loss, and invalidating those that seemed to go too far in depriving the creditor of his rights.[35]

Any Person

The Fifth Amendment forbade the federal government to deprive any *person* of life, liberty, or property without due process of law; and the Fourteenth Amendment forbade the states (1) to abridge the privileges or immunities of *citizens*, (2) to deprive any *person* of life, liberty, or property without due process of law, and (3) to deny to any *person* the equal protection of the laws. The clause relating to privileges and immunities has never been employed to limit regulation of business, since business units have not been held to qualify as *citizens*. But the other clauses have been so employed, ever since the Supreme Court decreed, in 1886, that a corporation is a *person*. In 1873, when a corporation challenged a Louisiana law zoning slaughterhouse locations, the Court had rejected this interpretation, and Justice Miller had expressed the view that the Fourteenth Amendment would never be used for any purpose other than its obvious one of protecting the Negro against discrimination.[36] But 13 years later, in the case of *Santa Clara County* v. *Southern Pacific Railway*,[37] the Court extended the scope of the two amendments to cover corporate enterprise. This position was challenged, in 1938, by Justice Black, who stated flatly, in a dissenting opinion, "I do not believe that the word 'person' in the Fourteenth Amendment includes corporations."[38] But this was not the view of the majority; the rule of 1886 still stands.

When applied to corporations, the clause assuring equal protection has been used to invalidate laws that discriminate against one business in favor of another. But this clause has not been so interpreted as to prevent distinctions based on principles of classification that are not arbitrary or capricious. The Supreme Court has thus upheld a minimum wage law for women, in Arizona, that exempted railway restaurants;[39] a tax on retail stores, in Indiana, that was graduated in accordance with the number of stores in a chain;[40] and a federal tax on payrolls that did not apply to employers with fewer than eight employees.[41] The equal protection clause, moreover, adds little to the

---

35 / *Home Building & Loan Assn.* v. *Blaisdell,* 290 U.S. 398 (1933), upholding the Minnesota moratorium law; and *Louisville Joint Stock Land Bank* v. *Radford,* 295 U.S. 955 (1935), invalidating the Frazier-Lemke Act.

36 / *The Slaughter House Cases,* 16 Wallace 36.

37 / 118 U.S. 394.

38 / *Connecticut General Life Insurance Co.* v. *Johnson,* 303 U.S. 77, 85.

39 / *Dominion Hotel* v. *Arizona,* 249 U.S. 265 (1919).

40 / *Indiana* v. *Jackson,* 283 U.S. 527 (1937).

41 / *Steward Machine Co.* v. *Davis,* 301 U.S. 548 (1937).

safeguards of the law. For where a measure is rejected as discriminatory, it can also be found to violate due process. It is under the heading of due process that the most serious restrictions on public control have been imposed.

Liberty or Property

The liberty that is guaranteed by the due process clause has been held by the Supreme Court to include the freedom to enter into contracts. And the preservation of this freedom has been advanced by the Court, from time to time in the past, as its reason for rejecting laws that provided for the establishment of maximum hours and minimum wages. In 1905 the provisions of a New York law limiting the hours of bakers to 10 per day or 60 per week were denounced as "mere meddlesome interferences with the rights of the individual." [42] But in 1908 an Oregon law limiting the hours of women was upheld on the ground that the state, under its police powers, might safeguard the health of mothers in order to preserve the health of the community. [43] And in 1917 an Oregon law establishing a 10 hour daily limit for men as well as women, in factories, was also upheld as falling within the police powers of the state. [44] In 1923, however, the Court invalidated a law fixing minimum wages for women in the District of Columbia. The differences between the sexes, said Justice Sutherland, "have now come almost if not quite to the vanishing point." Consequently, "we cannot accept the doctrine that women of mature age *sui juris* require or may be subjected to restrictions upon their liberty of contract. . . ." [45] And again in 1936, in the Tipaldo case, [46] a New York law fixing minimum wages for women was overthrown, by a 5 to 4 decision, on the same ground.

On this point, as on others, the Court reversed itself in 1937, its decision in the Parrish case [47] upholding a Washington law providing minimum wages for women. Said Justice Hughes: "The Constitution does not speak of freedom of contract. It speaks of liberty and prohibits the deprivation of liberty without due process of law. In prohibiting that deprivation, the Constitution does not recognize an absolute and uncontrollable liberty. . . . The liberty safeguarded is liberty in a social organization which requires the protection of law against the evils which menace the health, safety, morals and welfare of the people." The Parrish decision, also rendered by a 5 to 4 vote, came but a few months after the decision in the Tipaldo case. There had been no change in the composition of the Court. There had been a change, however, in the mind of Mr. Justice Roberts.

To prevent persons (i.e., human beings) from being deprived of *liberty*

42 / *Lochner* v. *New York*, 198 U.S. 45.

43 / *Muller* v. *Oregon*, 208 U.S. 412.

44 / *Bunting* v. *Oregon*, 243 U.S. 426.

45 / *Adkins* v. *Children's Hospital*, 261 U.S. 525.

46 / *Morehead* v. *New York ex rel. Tipaldo*, 298 U.S. 587.

47 / *West Coast Hotel Co.* v. *Parrish*, 300 U.S. 379.

without due process, it is no longer held that men and women must work for long hours at low pay. But to prevent persons (i.e., corporations) from being deprived of *property* without due process, it is still held that measures affecting the size of corporate incomes or the value of corporate assets, if questioned, must have the approval of the courts. And it is here that the due process clause has found its major use.

Affected with a Public Interest

Recognizing the necessity of approving regulation of the services rendered and the prices charged by natural monopolies, but unwilling to permit extension of such controls, under the due process clause, to industry in general, the Supreme Court, in 1877, hit upon the device of establishing a separate category of businesses affected with a public interest, and confining regulation to those that it might so define. In the famous case of *Munn* v. *Illinois*,[48] decided in that year, the Court approved a law, enacted by the state of Illinois, controlling the charges made by grain elevators and warehouses. In the words of its opinion: "Property does become clothed with a public interest when used in a manner to make it of public consequence, and affect the community at large. When, therefore, one devotes his property to a use in which the public has an interest, he, in effect, grants to the public an interest in that use, and must submit to be controlled by the public for the common good. . . ." The elevators along the Chicago waterfront were found to stand "in the very gateway of commerce, and take toll from all who pass." It was permissible, therefore, that they be regulated, so that they might "take but reasonable toll."

This concept was subsequently employed in approving public regulation of such industries as the railroads, and water, gas, electric, and telephone companies. It was called upon in 1914 in upholding a Kansas law providing for the regulation of fire insurance rates.[49] But it was used for a decade to invalidate laws extending public controls to other fields. In 1923 the Court rejected a Kansas law providing for compulsory arbitration of labor disputes in basic industries;[50] in 1927, a New York law fixing the markup of theater ticket agencies;[51] in 1928, a New Jersey law regulating the fees of employment agencies;[52] in the same year, a Tennessee law controlling the price of gasoline;[53] and in 1932, an Oklahoma law retricting entry into the ice business.[54] In each of these cases, the Court, usually speaking through Justice Sutherland, held that the business concerned was not affected with a public interest. But no standards of judgment were consistently applied. Whether an industry could be regulated

48 / 94 U.S. 113.

49 / *German Alliance Insurance Co.* v. *Kansas*, 233 U.S. 389.

50 / *Wolff Packing Co.* v. *Court of Industrial Relations*, 262 U.S. 522.

51 / *Tyson* v. *Banton*, 273 U.S. 418.

52 / *Ribnik* v. *McBride*, 277 U.S. 350.

53 / *Williams* v. *Standard Oil Co.*, 278 U.S. 235.

54 / *New State Ice Co.* v. *Liebmann*, 282 U.S. 262.

depended on no objective criteria, but upon the undisclosed predispositions of the members of the Court.

The concept of a peculiar category of industries affected with a public interest was abandoned in 1934 when the Court handed down its decision in the Nebbia case.[55] The state of New York had set up a milk control board and empowered it to fix the retail price of milk. The board had fixed the price at 9 cents per quart. Nebbia, a grocer in Rochester, had sold two quarts for 18 cents and thrown in a loaf of bread. When sued for violating the law, he argued that the milk business was competitive rather than monopolistic, having none of the characteristics of a public utility, and that the state was therefore powerless to regulate the prices that it charged. The Court, in a 5 to 4 decision, rejected this defense. Said Justice Roberts,

> It is clear that there is no closed class or category of businesses affected with a public interest. . . . The phrase "affected with a public interest" can, in the nature of things, mean no more than that an industry, for adequate reason, is subject to control for the public good. . . . So far as the requirement of due process is concerned . . . a state is free to adopt whatever economic policy may reasonably be deemed to promote public welfare. . . . If the laws passed are seen to have a reasonable relation to a proper legislative purpose, and are neither arbitrary nor discriminatory, the requirements of due process are satisfied. . . .

Having thus broken with the past, the Court went on, in the next few years, to uphold a state law fixing the charges of tobacco warehouses,[56] federal laws requiring inspection of tobacco,[57] restricting the quantities of tobacco that could be marketed,[58] providing for the establishment of minimum prices for milk,[59] and providing—a second time—for minimum prices for bituminuous coal,[60] and a state law curtailing the output of petroleum.[61] This legislation, arising largely from conditions of business depression, carried state and federal governments into new regions of control. Its approval by the Court removed a major barrier to the further extension of regulatory activity.

Due Process: Procedural and Substantive

The concept of due process originally had to do with the criminal law. Its extension to administration was a later development. In recent times, however, the courts have evolved a set of rules to govern the procedures of administrative agencies. Such agencies must have jurisdiction over the matters with which they

55 / *Nebbia* v. *New York,* 291 U.S. 502.

56 / *Townsend* v. *Yeomans,* 301 U.S. 441 (1937).

57 / *Currin* v. *Wallace,* 306 U.S. 1 (1939).

58 / *Mulford* v. *Smith,* 307 U.S. 38 (1939).

59 / *U.S.* v. *Rock Royal Cooperative,* 307 U.S. 533 (1939).

60 / *Sunshine Anthracite Coal Co.* v. *Adkins,* 310 U.S. 381 (1940).

61 / *R. R. Commission* v. *Rowan & Nichols Oil Co.,* 310 U.S. 573 (1940).

deal. They must give fair hearings to all persons affected by their rulings. They must give adequate notice of such hearings well in advance of the dates when they are held. Their officers must be impartial, with no personal interest in the questions upon which they are called to pass. Their decisions must be based upon substantial evidence. In the orders they issue, specific findings of law and fact must be set forth. The persons affected by such orders must be given an opportunity to appeal. This is due process, in the procedural sense of the term.

Such safeguards against arbitrary administrative action are clearly in the public interest. There is danger, however, that administrative agencies might come to be so bound by procedural requirements that it would be impossible for them to operate efficiently. This danger is illustrated by two decisions handed down by the Supreme Court. In the first,[62] where the Secretary of Agriculture had issued an order on the advice of a trial examiner, following extensive hearings, the Court complained that the Secretary had not himself read each of the 13,000 pages of testimony and 1,000 pages of exhibits in the transcript. In the second,[63] it invalidated one of the Secretary's orders on the grounds that the respondents had not received a copy of the trial examiner's intermediate report in time to use it in preparing their final brief. Whatever the merits of these two cases, it is clear that administration might well be put in a strait jacket if the courts were too meticulous in their insistence on form.

In the name of due process, the courts have gone on to interest themselves not only in form but also in substance. Instead of confining themselves to determining whether administrative orders were based upon sufficient evidence, they have arrived at independent judgments by going into the evidence themselves. From a review of questions of law they have slipped over into a review of questions of fact. When the Supreme Court upheld state regulation of public utility rates, in *Munn* v. *Illinois* in 1877, it did not attempt to pass upon the rates themselves. But in 1886 the Court issued a warning that the "power to regulate is not a power to destroy."[64] In 1890 it asserted that "the reasonableness of a rate . . . is eminently a question for judicial investigation."[65] And in 1898, in the historic case of *Smyth* v. *Ames*[66] (to be considered at length in Chapter 13), it enumerated the matters of substance that commissions would be required to take into consideration in fixing rates in order to give assurance that due process had been observed. From then on for nearly half a century the Court undertook to pass judgment, not only on the procedures employed in rate making, but also on the legitimacy of the rates themselves.

This position was substantially modified by the decisions handed down in the Natural Gas Pipeline and Hope Natural Gas cases[67] in 1942 and 1944. Said the

---

62 / *Morgan* v. *U.S.*, 298 U.S. 468 (1936).

63 / *Morgan* v. *U.S.*, 304 U.S. 1 (1948).

64 / *Stone* v. *Farmers' Loan & Trust Co.*, 166 U.S. 307.

65 / *Chicago, Milwaukee & St. Paul Rwy.* v. *Minnesota*, 134 U.S. 418.

66 / 169 U.S. 466.

67 / *FPC* v. *Natural Gas Pipeline Co.*, 315 U.S. 575; *FPC* v. *Hope Natural Gas Co.*, 320 U.S. 591.

Court, in the first of these cases: "The Constitution does not bind rate-making bodies to the service of any single formula or combination of formulas. . . . Once a fair hearing has been given, proper findings made, and other statutory requirements satisfied, the courts cannot intervene in the absence of a clear showing that the limits of due process have been overstepped. If the Commission's order, as applied to the facts before it and viewed in its entirety, produces no arbitrary result, our inquiry is at an end." [68] The boundaries of court review were thus narrowed by judicial self-restraint. Concern with the end result was not abandoned, but the presumption was made to run in favor of the substantive determinations of administrative agencies.

Ownership and Operation

Although the courts have handicapped the federal, state, and local governments in their efforts to preserve the system of private enterprise through the maintenance of competition and the regulation of monopoly, they have interposed no obstacles to public ownership. If a government seeks to socialize an existing private business whose owners do not wish to sell, it may do so by exercising the sovereign right of eminent domain. Under federal and state constitutions, the usual limitations are that the property must be taken for public use, and that just compensation must be paid. The courts have shown little disposition to question legislative judgment as to public use, or to check acquisition of property by supporting an unconscionable price. If a government goes into business by obtaining the assets of a private company through voluntary sale, or by itself constructing new facilities, the constitutional limits are those upon its power to spend. And these require only that expenditures be made for a public purpose or to promote the general welfare. The projects challenged on this basis have invariably been upheld.[69] The courts for many years strained at the gnat of public regulation and swallowed the camel of public ownership.

The Changing Constitution

For the better part of a century the Supreme Court raised no serious barriers to the expansion of public authority. From the founding of the republic to the end of the Civil War it declared only two acts of the Congress to be unconstitutional. It approved the granger legislation of the seventies, including the regulation of services and rates. But from the middle eighties until the middle thirties, a period of 50 years, the Court made of the Constitution an instrument with which to impose upon the country the philosophy of laissez

68 / 315 U.S. 586.

69 / See *Jones* v. *City of Portland*, 246 U.S. 217 (1917); *Green* v. *Frazier*, 253 U.S. 233 (1920); *Standard Oil Co.* v. *City of Lincoln*, 275 U.S. 504 (1927); *Puget Sound Power & Light Co.* v. *Seattle*, 291 U.S. 619 (1934); *Ashwander* v. *TVA*, 297 U.S. 288 (1936); *Tennessee Electric Power Co.* v. *TVA*, 306 U.S. 118 (1939); *Oklahoma* v. *Atkinson Co.*, 313 U.S. 508 (1941).

faire. It restricted the regulatory powers of government, extended to corporate enterprise the guarantees of personal freedom, and transformed procedural safeguards into substantive restraints. The convervatism of the courts, during this period, led to repeated demands for judicial reform. It was Theodore Roosevelt who proposed, in 1912, that decisions declaring laws unconstitutional should be subject to reversal by popular vote.

In the middle thirties, as has been noted again and again in the preceding pages, interpretation of the Constitution was sharply changed. Between 1933 and 1937 a dozen federal laws and more than fifty state laws were invalidated by the Supreme Court, including some of the major legislation of the New Deal—the Railroad Retirement Act, providing the first federal program of social insurance, the National Industrial Recovery Act, the Agricultural Adjustment Act of 1933, and the Bituminous Coal Conservation Act, and also the New York minimum wage law for women. In February, 1937, following his reelection, Franklin D. Roosevelt asked the Congress, in effect, to empower him to add as many as six new judges to the bench, thus turning its hostile majority into a powerless minority. This proposal evoked a violent storm of protest, and the power he asked was not obtained. Within the next two years, however, five vacancies occurred through death or retirement, and Mr. Roosevelt had appointed a majority of the justices. But the course of interpretation had been reversed before the first of these appointments was made. In March, 1937, the minimum wage law of the state of Washington was upheld, two weeks later the National Labor Relations Act, and two months later the Social Security Act. The President had lost—and won—his fight.

Since 1937 the courts have shown but little resistance to the application of controls. The institution of judicial review has been preserved by the exercise of moderation in its use.

PART II

Controlling Monopoly by Maintaining Competition

Chapter 3   THE ANTITRUST ·LAWS

Government, confronted by the problem of monopoly, may follow one of four courses. First, it may take no action, trusting the public interest to be served by the voluntary choice of the monopolist. Second, it may seek to break up existing monopolies and to prevent the formation of new monopolies, protecting the public interest by restoring and preserving the force of competition. Third, it may acquiesce in the existence of monopoly and seek to safeguard the public interest by regulating the services rendered and the prices charged by the monopolist. Fourth, it may take monopoly into public ownership.

There are dangers, for a society that values freedom, progress, and plenty, in a policy of laissez faire. Freedom demands ready access to markets; monopoly excludes newcomers from preempted fields. Progress requires hospitality to innovation—to new products and processes, new materials and methods, new blood and new ideas. Monopoly emphasizes the security of fixed investments; it protects existing ways of doing things; it resists change. Plenty depends upon continuous expansion of output; monopoly may augment its profits by restricting the production of goods and services. If freedom is to be preserved, progress encouraged, and plenty achieved, monopoly must be prevented or subjected to control. Government must make its choice between the maintenance of competition and the extension of public regulation or public ownership.

It is the stated policy of the government of the United States to prevent monopoly and to maintain a competitive economy. This policy, it must be admitted, has not been pursued consistently, continuously, or comprehensively. It has been accompanied by measures, such as the tariff and the patent system that have operated to check competition and to promote monopoly. It has been abandoned temporarily in time of business depression and in time of war. In the case of public utilities it has given way to the administrative regulation of monopoly. In other cases it has been modified by excepting certain practices and by granting exemptions to particular industries. But despite these qualifications, the maintenance of competition has been and still remains a dominant goal of public policy.

America has stood almost alone in its official opposition to monopoly. It is only in Canada, among industrial nations, that a similar policy has been pursued. In Germany, France, Belgium, Holland, Italy, and elsewhere in Europe, before the second World War, public policy supported the organization of major industries into giant combines and the regulation of production and trade by powerful cartels. In Japan, where industrialism had been imposed upon a feudal society, control of business remained in the hands of a few great families. In Great Britain, where the growth of monopoly had long been impeded by competition from abroad, free trade was abandoned in 1932, and government subsequently acquiesced in the rapid cartelization of the domestic economy. International trade, among these nations and between them and the rest of the world, was controlled by supranational cartels.

In many of these countries, both industrial structure and public policy have undergone some modification since the war. In Germany and Japan the occupying powers undertook, with indifferent success, to break up the prewar cartels. In Great Britain and in some of the countries of Western Europe, tentative steps have been taken toward the suppression of monopoly. Regulatory provisions have been written into the treaties that govern the European Coal and Steel Community and the European Economic Community. Consideration has also been given, through agencies of the United Nations, to means of controlling the restrictive practices of international cartels. Whether these developments will prove to have permanent significance remains to be seen. The policy of maintaining competition still finds its fullest expression in the antitrust laws of the United States.

HISTORICAL BACKGROUND OF THE ANTITRUST LAWS

Long before statutes condemning monopoly were enacted by state and federal legislatures, its legality was questioned in cases brought before the courts. In some of these cases the plaintiff sought to compel the defendant to adhere to the terms of a contract that limited his freedom to compete. In others, the plaintiff sued for damages, charging that he had been injured by the defendant's monopolistic practices. Judges, confronted by these issues, looked for precedents. They found them in decisions handed down by the courts of the several states, built on earlier decisions rendered by courts in the American colonies, and reaching back to still earlier decisions made by courts in England. It is through this chain of precedents, constituting the body of the common law, that rules defining the legality of monopolistic behavior first emerged.

The Common Law

In England, during the 17th century, the courts denounced as illegal grants of monopoly by the Crown. Their disapproval did not extend to grants conferred by Parliament, to monopolies acquired through individual effort, or to those resulting from private agreement. In the 18th century, however, monopolistic agreements were also condemned. Up to this time, the concept of conspiracy had been confined to cases in which the conspirators had attempted to obstruct the course of justice. But now the two concepts—monopoly and conspiracy—were brought together in the doctrine of conspiracy to monopolize. Under this doctrine a monopoly held by a single owner still remained undisturbed. But agreements to limit competition were disapproved, persons injured by them were awarded damages, and the courts refused to enforce their terms.

The courts, since the 15th century, had also refused to enforce contracts in restraint of trade. This concept, however, had been given a narrow meaning: trade was held to be restrained when a person selling a business, a partner withdrawing from it, or an employee leaving it, agreed to refrain from competition with its purchaser, a remaining partner, or a former employer. In the eyes of the courts, such agreements were opposed to public policy because they deprived the community of the contracting party's services and restricted his freedom to follow his trade. In the 18th century, this rule was modified: the courts came to enforce such restrictions where they were needed to preserve the value of a business that had been sold and where they were so limited in extent and in duration as not to be unreasonable; but general restraints on former owners, partners, and employees were still held to be unenforceable.

These precedents in the common law were drawn upon, during the 19th century, as cases involving monopolistic agreements were brought before the courts. The doctrine of restraint of trade took on new meaning as it was extended to cover any arrangement whereby competitors sought to exclude outsiders from the market or otherwise to limit freedom to compete. From state to state decisions differed in detail. But in most jurisdictions the courts came to reject all contracts that involved such practices as curtailment of output, division of territories, fixing of prices, and pooling of profits. And here no rule of reason was applied: these practices were held, by their very nature, to be prejudicial to the public interest, and contracts that required them were not enforced.

The maintenance of competition was thus supported by the common law. But as an instrument of public policy the common law was limited in its effectiveness. Initiative in taking action was left to plaintiffs in private suits. Where contracts were brought before the courts, refusal of enforcement weakened the position of monopoly. Where injury was proven, assessment of damages penalized monopoly. But where all of the participants in an agreement voluntarily adhered to its terms, and where no one had the courage or the means to sue for damages, no case was brought and here monopoly continued undisturbed. If competition were to be restored, in such cases, it was necessary to make provision, through legislative enactment, for public prosecution and the imposition of public penalties.

The Antitrust Movement

In the United States, during the years that followed the Civil War, the pattern of industrial organization was rapidly transformed. With the construction of a network of railways, local and regional markets gave way to markets that were national in scope. With the boundaries of markets thus extended, the scale of industrial operations was increased, production was mechanized, and small shops were displaced by large factories. As factories increased in size, larger accumulations of capital were required, and the independent proprietor was supplanted by the corporation. The corporate form of organization, in turn, facilitated industrial consolidation and made for increasing concentration of control. In this situation the growth of monopoly was stimulated by a steady decline in the general level of prices, accompanied by recurring periods of business depression. Concerns with large investments, entailing heavy fixed charges, were impelled successively to slash their prices in an effort to cover some portion of their costs. Competition, on this basis, threatened to become mutually destructive, and business sought refuge in monopolistic agreements and in the combination of competing firms. This movement was stimulated, too, by the prospect of profits that were to be obtained in the process of promoting corporate reorganizations and those that were to be realized through the exercise of monopoly power. In consequence, during the 1880's, many of the country's major industries were brought under some form of concentrated control. In petroleum, cottonseed oil, linseed oil, meat packing, cordage, sugar, lead, coal, whisky, tobacco, matches, gunpowder, and elsewhere, power over markets was attained through the devices of monopoly.

As this process continued, many groups in the community—farmers, producers of raw materials, small businessmen, and laborers—suffered injury. The farmers, in particular, experiencing a persistent decline in farm prices, complained of high freight rates charged by the railroads, high interest rates charged by the banks, and high prices charged by the makers of agricultural implements and other manufactured goods. Producers of raw materials, where manufacturing was monopolized, found themselves selling to a single buyer who manipulated the market to depress the prices they received. Independent businessmen, if they refused to be absorbed, were ruthlessly driven from the field. Workers were crowded into growing cities, made dependent on industrial employment, and faced with increasing competition for uncertain jobs.

All of these developments gave rise to widespread discontent. With the growth of corporate concentration, it appeared that the welfare and the independence of the common man were threatened. With the disappearance of the frontier, it seemed that the door to opportunity was being closed. Out of these fears, there developed a strong political movement against monopoly. Findings its roots in farmers' organizations in the West and South, this movement drew support, as well, from labor unions and from independent businessmen. During the eighties, it brought about the formation of farmer-labor parties, ran an antimonopoly candidate for the presidency, elected a number of members to Congress, and came to control the legislatures of several states. As it grew in strength, the older parties sought to win the votes of its adherents by themselves professing opposition to monopoly. In this way, the movement soon achieved its purpose: antitrust laws were enacted, toward the end of the decade, by state and federal governments.

The antitrust laws owe their name to a method of business combination that has long been obsolete. In pursuit of this method, the owners of controlling shares of stock in competing corporations transferred legal title to these shares to a group of trustees, receiving trust certificates in return. The trustees then voted the stocks in all of the participating companies, electing their directors, controlling their policies, and running them, in effect, as a single enterprise. The holders of the trust certificates were entitled merely to participate in the profits of the combined concerns. This form of organization was first devised by the promoters of the Standard Oil combination in 1879; it was adopted by a number of other industries in the following decade. These combinations were properly designated as trusts. But the term was shortly generalized to cover all monopolistic combinations, whatever the devices through which they were achieved. The antimonopoly statutes were thus christened the antitrust laws. And when the trust, as a legal device, was abandoned, the word survived.

The State Antitrust Laws

Starting with Kansas in 1889, 18 states had enacted antitrust laws by 1891. Such laws are now found on the statute books of most of the states. These laws differ in detail: some of them forbid specific monopolistic practices, such as curtailment of output, division of markets, price fixing, and price discrimination; others condemn monopolization and agreement in restraint of trade in more general terms. In most cases the laws are enforced through suits brought by county or district attorneys under the direction of state attorneys general. They carry criminal penalties, with fines running up to $5,000 and imprisonment, typically, to one year. Provision is also made for private suits leading to the issuance of injunctions or to punitive awards of triple damages.

These laws, however, have proved to be a feeble instrument for the prevention of monopoly. Although in a dozen states there has been some effort to enforce them; in most of the states, there has not. Furthermore, appropriations for enforcement have been meager. Officials have been deterred from bringing suits by the fear that such action might discourage the entry of new industries or drive existing industries to other states. State laws, at best, are limited in application; they are powerless to control agreements or combinations in major industries whose operations, extending beyond state borders, are not within their reach. There are some trades, to be sure, in which local markets may be confined within the boundaries of a single state: building construction, real estate operations, and the sale of sand and gravel, stone, and common brick; job printing, newspaper publishing, and the production of cut flowers, baked goods, beer, and ice; retailing, personal and professional services, and the operation of laundries, cleaning and dyeing establishments, garages, repair shops, theaters, restaurants, and hotels. But, even here, the laws are spasmodically enforced. The task of maintaining competition has been left, almost entirely, to the federal government.

SUBSTANTIVE PROVISIONS OF THE ANTITRUST LAWS

In the national campaign of 1888, the two major parties competed for the votes of farmers by professing opposition to monopoly. The Democrats, then in office, denounced the tariff as the mother of the trusts. The Republicans, proposing higher duties, replied that they could compel competition at home while preventing competition from abroad. Both party platforms promised enactment of legislation against monopoly. Following the Republican victory, President Harrison sent a message to Congress, in 1889, asking that this pledge be redeemed. A number of antimonopoly bills were introduced, one of them by Senator Sherman of Ohio. There was little popular interest in the legislation at the time. Attention was centered, rather, on the effort to grant business and labor further protection against competition by raising the tariff and on the effort to assure farmers higher prices by passing the Silver Purchase Act. The antitrust law was included in the legislative package to quiet the critics of these measures. No hearings were held; the bill that finally emerged from the Congressional committees was enacted, following a brief debate that raised no fundamental issues, with only one dissenting vote in the Senate and without a record vote in the House. It was signed by the President on July 2, 1890. Bearing little or no resemblance to the bill originally introduced by Senator Sherman, it was given his name.

The Sherman Act

The Sherman Act, unlike most Acts of Congress, is short and simple. Its major provisions could easily be memorized:

Sec. 1. Every contract, combination in the form of a trust or otherwise, or conspiracy, in restraint of trade or commerce among the several states, or with foreign nations, is hereby declared to be illegal. Every person who shall make any such contract or engage in any such combination or conspiracy, shall be deemed guilty of a misdemeanor. . . .

Sec. 2. Every person who shall monopolize, or attempt to monopolize, or combine or conspire with any other person or persons, to monopolize any part of the trade or commerce among the several states, or with foreign nations, shall be deemed guilty of a misdemeanor. . . .

The Act thus took over the concepts of restraint of trade and monopolization from the common law, without attempting further to define their meaning. Its first section applies only to agreements in which two or more persons are involved. Its second section is broader, applying also to individual efforts to monopolize.

In substance, the legislation contained nothing that was new. Its real contribution was to turn restraint of trade and monopolization into offenses against the federal government, to require enforcement by federal officials, and to provide for the imposition of penalties. United States district attorneys, acting under the direction of the Attorney General, were instructed to institute proceedings in equity to compel observance of the law. It was also their duty to bring criminal suits against those who violated its terms. Such violations were made punishable by fines up to $5,000, imprisonment up to one year, or both.

Persons injured by illegal restraints or monopolies were entitled to sue for triple damages.

The Sherman Act, with the continued support of both major parties, remained the only important antitrust law to be enacted for nearly a quarter of a century. In the Wilson Tariff Act of 1894, similar provisions were applied to persons importing goods into the United States. In legislation granting rights to certain lands, in 1908 and 1910, violation of the Sherman Act was made a basis for cancellation of these rights. In the Panama Canal Act of 1912, violators operating boats were denied the privilege of passing through the canal. But it was not until 1914 that major additions to the law were made.

The Clayton and Federal Trade Commission Acts

There was increasing dissatisfaction, in the years before 1914, with the operation of the Sherman Act. During the administrations of Cleveland and McKinley, the laws had scarcely been enforced. Powerful new combinations had been formed in steel, tin cans, corn products, farm machinery, and many other industries. During the administrations of Roosevelt and Taft, monopolistic abuses had been disclosed in hearings before committees of Congress, in the reports of public agencies, and in the evidence presented in cases brought before the courts. Though it was shown that competition had been eliminated by particular business practices, these practices had not been held to be in violation of the law. And in 1911 the Supreme Court had declared that combinations that were not unreasonable would be allowed to stand. Following these developments, the trusts again became an issue in the national campaign of 1912. Monopoly was denounced and further legislation promised by the Democrats, the Roosevelt Progressives, and the Republicans.

In 1913 the new Democratic Congress reduced the tariff, set up the Federal Reserve System, and inaugurated the income tax; in 1914 it turned to the problem of monopoly. Consideration of the problem was now more thorough than that accorded it a quarter-century before: the issues raised were subjected to exhaustive hearings and extended debate. President Wilson had recommended that uncertainty concerning the meaning of the Sherman Act be removed by prohibiting, item by item, each of the devices by which competition might be eliminated and monopoly obtained. He had also proposed that a specialized administrative agency be established to strengthen the observance and enforcement of the law. An Act setting up such a body—the Federal Trade Commission—was eventually forthcoming. But agreement on a comprehensive list of monopolistic practices was not to be obtained: opinions differed with respect to particular practices; it was difficult to define existing practices and impossible to frame definitions that would cover future practices; there was fear that such definitions would be so narrowly interpreted as to limit the scope of the law and seriously to impair its effectiveness. The attempt was finally abandoned; the list of devices to be specifically outlawed was reduced to four and provisions forbidding them were written into the Clayton Act; the other devices that had been debated were covered by a general prohibition of unfair methods of competition which was incorporated in the Federal Trade Commission Act. The two Acts were passed by substantial majorities in both houses of Congress and signed by the President in the fall of 1914.

The particular devices that were outlawed by the Clayton Act were discrimination in prices, exclusive and tying contracts, intercorporate stockholdings, and interlocking directorates.

> Section 2 of the Act forbade sellers "to discriminate in price between different purchasers of commodities," but permitted such discrimination where there were "differences in the grade, quality, or quantity of the commodity sold," where the lower prices made "only due allowance for differences in the cost of selling or transportation," and where they were offered "in good faith to meet competition."
>
> Section 3 forbade sellers to "lease or make a sale or contract for sale of . . . commodities . . . on the condition that the lessee or purchaser thereof shall not use or deal in the . . . commodity . . . of a competitor. . . ."
>
> Section 7 forbade any corporation engaged in commerce to acquire the shares of a competing corporation or to purchase the stocks of two or more corporations that were competitors.

It should be noted that none of these prohibitions was absolute; the three practices were forbidden only where their effect, in the words of the law, "may be to substantially lessen competition or tend to create a monopoly. . . ."

> Section 8 prohibited interlocking directorates between corporations engaged in commerce where one of them had a capital and surplus of more than $1 million and where "the elimination of competition . . . between them would constitute a violation of any of the provisions of the antitrust laws."

The broader prohibition contained in Section 5 of the accompanying Federal Trade Commission Act provided, simply, "that unfair methods of competition in commerce are hereby declared unlawful."

In substance, these statutes added little to the content of the law. The specific practices that were prohibited might well have been attacked, as conspiracies in restraint of trade or as attempts to monopolize, under the provisions of the Sherman Act. Unfair methods of competition were already condemned, moreover, by the common law. There were, however, important differences. The Sherman Act was general in its terms; the Clayton Act was explicit. The older law dealt with monopoly as an accomplished fact; the new laws were concerned with the methods through which monopoly was attained. The one placed emphasis on punishment; the others were directed toward prevention. Practices that had not been held to violate the law unless pursued as part of a proved conspiracy were now forbidden in and of themselves. Even more important was the fact that enforcement was strengthened, as we shall see, by other provisions of the Clayton and Trade Commission Acts. Under the latter

Act, moreover, attacks on unfair methods of competition, instead of being left to suits brought by private litigants on their own initiative and at their own expense, were to be made by public officials and financed by appropriations from the federal treasury. It is in these respects that the new legislation made its most significant contribution to the force of the law.

The Robinson-Patman Act

Section 2 of the Clayton Act, relating to price discrimination, was completely revised with the passage, in 1936, of the Robinson-Patman Act. The original section had been designed primarily to prevent large manufacturers from eliminating their smaller rivals by temporarily cutting prices on particular products and in particular markets while prices elsewhere were maintained, a notorious practice of certain of the early trusts. The new law was an outgrowth of a different situation. Independent wholesalers and retailers, in the years following World War I, found themselves faced with increasing competition from chain stores and other mass distributors. The lower prices that these organizations charged were to be attributed, in part at least, to the lower prices that they paid. Their bargaining power enabled them to obtain concessions from suppliers in many forms: brokers' commissions where no broker was employed, services provided by suppliers in addition to the delivery of goods, allowances for advertising the suppliers' products and rendering them other services, and discounts for purchasing in large quantities. The independents, contending that these concessions were larger than could be justified, demanded that the freedom of suppliers to discriminate be more strictly limited. The Robinson-Patman Act was passed in response to their demands.

Section 2 of the Act, amending Section 2 of the Clayton Act, flatly forbids the payment of a broker's commission in cases where an independent broker is not employed. It forbids sellers to provide supplementary services to buyers or to make allowances for services rendered them by buyers unless such concessions are available to all buyers "on proportionally equal terms." Other forms of discrimination, such as quantity discounts, are prohibited in cases where the effect (in the words of the Clayton Act, with the split infinitive corrected) "may be substantially to lessen competition or tend to create a monopoly in any line of commerce," either among sellers or among buyers. Persons accused of such discrimination may defend themselves by proving that their lower prices made only "due allowance" for differences in cost or were offered "in good faith to meet an equally low price of a competitor. . . ." But even where larger discounts can be justified by lower costs, the Federal Trade Commission is authorized to establish quantity limits beyond which discounts cannot be given, if such action is required to prevent large buyers from obtaining a monopoly. The section makes it unlawful, finally, for any person "knowingly to induce or receive" a prohibited discrimination in price.

Section 3 of the Act provides criminal penalties for three offenses. It flatly forbids giving or receiving a larger discount than that made available to competitors buying the same goods in the same quantity. It also forbids the establishment, in one locality, of prices lower than those charged elsewhere, and prohibits the sale of goods "at unreasonably low prices" where either of these practices is adopted "for the purpose of destroying competition or eliminating a competitor." Violation of any of these provisions is punishable by fines up to $5,000, or imprisonment up to one year, or both.

The Wheeler-Lea Act

The ability of the Federal Trade Commission to prevent the use of unfair methods in competition was seriously restricted by a decision handed down by the Supreme Court in 1931. In this case,[1] the Commission had ordered the Raladam Company, manufacturers of Marmola, to cease and desist from representing their product as a remedy for obesity. The court recognized that consumers had been deceived by Raladam's advertisements, but it vacated the order, finding that misrepresentation was common among the vendors of such nostrums and concluding, on this basis, that no injury had been done to Raladam's competitors. The Commission was thus denied authority to protect consumers in cases where injury to competitors could not be shown.

This loophole was closed when Section 5 of the Federal Trade Commission Act was amended by the passage of the Wheeler-Lea Act in 1938. The section, as thus amended, now outlaws not only "unfair methods of competition" but also "unfair or deceptive acts or practices."

The Celler-Kefauver Antimerger Act

The effectiveness of Section 7 of the Clayton Act—forbidding one corporation to acquire the shares of a competing corporation or to buy the stocks of two or more corporations that were competitors, where such action might substantially lessen competition or tend toward monopoly—was similarly impaired by subsequent decisions of the Supreme Court. In 1926 the court decided, in the Swift and Thatcher cases,[2] that the Federal Trade Commission could not order a company to divest itself of the assets of a competitor if it had effected a merger, while the proceeding was pending, by voting stock which it had unlawfully acquired. And again in 1934 the court decided, in the Arrow-Hart & Hegeman case,[3] that the Commission was powerless to act when a holding company, after acquiring the shares of two competing corporations, had distributed them to its stockholders who had thereupon voted to merge the two concerns. In the years that followed there was heavy traffic over the detour that the court had built around the law.

This situation was finally corrected, after repeated efforts, by the enactment of an amendment extending the prohibitions of Section 7 to cover not only the

1 / *FTC* v. *Raladam Co.*, 283 U.S. 643.
2 / *Thatcher Manufacturing Co.* v. *FTC, Swift & Co.* v. *FTC*, 272 U.S. 554.
3 / *Arrow-Hart & Hegeman Electric Co.* v. *FTC*, 291 U.S. 587.

acquisition of stock but also "the use of such stock by the voting or granting of proxies or otherwise" and the acquisition of "the whole or any part of the assets" of a competing corporation or those of two or more corporations in competition with one another. Such acquisitions were made illegal where the effect, as before, "may be substantially to lessen competition or to tend to create a monopoly." But the test was now applied, more clearly than before, "in any line of commerce in any section of the country." The amendment was signed by President Truman on December 29, 1950.[4]

Summary

The prohibitions contained in the antitrust laws may now be summarized. It is illegal:

1. To enter into a contract, combination, or conspiracy in restraint of trade (Sherman Act, Section 1);
2. To monopolize, attempt to monopolize, or combine or conspire to monopolize trade (Sherman Act, Section 2).

In cases where the effect may be substantially to lessen competition or tend to create a monopoly, it is illegal:

3. To acquire the stock or the assets of competing corporations (Clayton Act, Section 7 as amended by Celler-Kefauver Act);
4. To enter into exclusive and tying contracts (Clayton Act, Section 3);
5. To discriminate among purchasers to an extent that cannot be justified by a difference in cost or as an attempt made, in good faith, to meet the price of a competitor (Clayton Act, Section 2 as amended by Robinson-Patman Act, Section 2-a).

And, in general, it is also illegal:

6. To pay a broker's commission if an independent broker is not employed (Robinson-Patman Act, Section 2-c);
7. To provide supplementary services to a buyer or to make allowance for services rendered by a buyer unless such concessions are equally available to all buyers (Robinson-Patman Act, Sections 2-d and 2-e);
8. To give larger discounts than those given others buying the same goods in the same quantity, or to charge lower prices in one locality than in another (Robinson-Patman Act, Section 3);
9. Knowingly to induce or receive an illegal discrimination in price (Robinson-Patman Act, Section 2-a);
10. To serve as a director of competing corporations (Clayton Act, Section 8);
11. To use unfair methods of competition (Federal Trade Commission Act, Section 5);
12. To employ unfair or deceptive acts or practices (Federal Trade Commission Act, Section 5 as amended by Wheeler-Lea Act, Section 3).

4 / 81st Cong., 2d Sess., Public Law No. 889.

In the main these provisions are designed to prevent monopoly and to maintain a competitive economy. But some of them have other purposes. It is the purpose of the Robinson-Patman Act, for instance, less to maintain competition than to preserve the small competitor. In some cases the law may check the growth of monopoly by controlling discrimination; in others, it may merely moderate the force of competition by reducing the competitive advantage of the larger firm. It is the purpose of Section 5 of the Federal Trade Commission Act, not only to preclude the attainment of monopoly through unfair methods of competition, but also to prevent the employment of such methods where no danger of monopoly exists. And it is the purpose of the Wheeler-Lea amendment, not to maintain competition, but to protect the consumer against deceptive practices. It should be noted, too, that Congress has acted, from time to time, to except certain practices and to exempt particular industries from the provisions of these laws, subjecting some of them to other methods of control. These matters are to be considered, in some detail, in Part VI. It is with the enforcement of the policy of maintaining competition that the present section is concerned.

Chapter 4   THE TASK OF ANTITRUST

The problems that confront the administration of the antitrust laws are many and diverse. They are raised both by the elimination of competition among independent enterprises and by the attainment of monopoly by a single concern. They relate not only to forms of business organization, but also to the character of business practices. In some cases, violation is obvious and flagrant; in others, it is hidden and discreet. In the former evidence is readily available; in the latter it is difficult to obtain. There are activities, moreover, that may be either innocent or dangerous and others whose legality or illegality is still unclear. The line between competition and monopoly is sometimes hard to draw. The task of antitrust, in consequence, is one of great complexity. It is well, therefore, to examine the various types of cases to which the law must be applied.

Competition among independent enterprises may be eliminated in a variety of ways: (1) by simple conspiracy, (2) by formal organization, (3) by intercorporate relations, and (4) by habitual identity of behavior. Problems of quite a different nature are presented by concerns that stand alone or overtop their rivals in their respective fields. (1) Such a firm may have sought or may be seeking to obtain or to retain monopolistic powers by employing unfair methods to handicap or to eliminate its competitors. (2) It may have accomplished the same purpose by absorbing or merging with its competitors. (3) It may have achieved monopoly without employing unfair methods of competition or combining with other firms. (4) It may not even possess monopolistic powers but may so overshadow its rivals as to enjoy pronounced competitive advantages. More than one of these problems may be presented by a single case. But, for the purpose of analysis, they are logically separable. Each of them will be examined in turn.

SIMPLE CONSPIRACIES

Where several independent firms are present in a market, some or all of them may participate in overt arrangements that are designed to eliminate competition among themselves and to prevent competition by others. They may establish the prices at which they will sell and fix the other terms and conditions that govern their sales. They may curtail their output as a means of raising the prices that may be charged. They may divide up territories or customers so that each of them will enjoy a monopoly within his allotted field. They may seek to coerce other firms, already in the market, and to exclude outsiders from entry. They may enforce these restrictions by methods that range from peaceful persuasion to the extremes of violence. Such arrangements have repeatedly been found in local, regional, and national markets in the United States.

Rackets

The most spectacular and the most obviously objectionable of these arrangements are those whose provisions have been enforced by a resort to violence. At various times, in several local trades, thugs and gunmen, employed by racketeers, have damaged goods, destroyed them, and interfered with their movement, broken windows, thrown bombs, demolished equipment, set fires to places of business, and assaulted, kidnapped, and even murdered tradesmen and their employees. Among the most notorious of these rackets was one which formerly controlled the market for live poultry in metropolitan New York:

> For many years a ring of 27 to 30 commission men fixed the price of chickens bought from producers in 40 states and the price of those sold to some 200 slaughter houses and several hundred retailers in New York City. In alliance with four trade unions, the ring was able to exclude other commission men from the market by denying them access to the supply of labor. It augmented its profits by granting one company a monopoly of the business of providing coops, another a monopoly of the business of selling chicken feed, and a third a monopoly of the trucking service. It compelled slaughter houses and distributors to deal with these concerns by calling strikes against those who turned elsewhere for supplies or services. It prevented poultry from reaching the market through other channels by having trucks overturned, chickens fed sand and gravel and plaster of paris or sprinkled with poison or kerosene. Ex-convicts and plug-uglies policed the trade; ten murders were committed within a period of five years. In this way, prices were maintained and profits realized by members of the ring.[1]

This sort of terrorism has sometimes characterized the various branches of the construction industry. It has been employed in the coercion of cleaners and dyers, laundrymen, barbers, undertakers, window washers, junkmen, truckers, operators of garages and filling stations, operators of juke boxes, distributors of ice, milk, candy, and soft drinks, and dealers in fish, fresh fruits, and vegetables. In method, such arrangements are universally condemned; in purpose and effect, they differ little from restraints enforced by measures that are more polite.

1 / Clair Wilcox, *Competition and Monopoly in American Industry,* Temporary National Economic Committee, Monograph 21 (Washington, D.C.: Government Printing Office, 1940), pp. 294-95.

Bidding Rings

In buying supplies for public agencies and in purchasing construction services, it is customary to publish specifications, to invite sellers to submit bids, and to award the contract to the seller who submits the lowest bid. Where sellers act independently, their bids will reflect their varying estimates of cost. Where they are in collusion, however, all bids may be identical or differing bids may merely reflect agreement that one bidder is to get the job. The formalities of bidding may be preserved, though competition itself has been suppressed. Such collusion has been frequent among subcontractors in various branches of the building trades:

> In some cases, a group of subcontractors operates a central estimating bureau which either maintains a uniform costing system and circulates specifications for the material and labor to be included in each job, thus enabling all of its members to arrive at the same bid, or itself calculates the cost of jobs and tells its members what to charge. Since identical bids result, contract-letting authorities are forced to award contracts by lot and every member of the bidding group is ultimately afforded an equal share in the market, each of them accepting the particular jobs that come to him by chance. In other cases, the group determines in advance which of its members is to get a job and so arranges the bids that his is lower than the rest. In still others, it maintains a depository where copies of estimates and bids are filed. Here members may open, read, and revise their bids before submitting them to architects or general contractors. They may raise the level of these bids by making certain that they conform to prescribed prices for materials, labor, and overhead, or by requiring that an arbitrary sum be added to each. They may allocate contracts according to some general rule, making the lowest bidder withdraw his bid and submit a new one higher than the highest, averaging the bids and throwing out those that fall more than 10 percent below the average, or assigning each job to the bidder whose bid comes closest to the average and requiring those whose bids fall below this figure to submit new bids to exceed it. Or they may merely decide which of their number is to receive each contract and rig the bids accordingly.[2]

Such activities have been found to exist among excavating, masonry, roofing, flooring, plumbing, heating, plastering, painting, glazing, tile, electrical, and other contractors in various cities. They have also been encountered among suppliers submitting bids on government contracts.

A nationwide bidding ring in the electrical manufacturing industry was disclosed in 1960 when 29 manufacturers of heavy electrical equipment and 45 of their officials, including General Electric and Westinghouse and 16 of their officials, pleaded guilty or offered no defense in 20 criminal suits charging them

2 / *Ibid.,* p. 289.

with conspiring to fix the prices of such equipment, constituting a substantial share of the industry's sales. The defendants had allocated contracts, selecting the low bidder by drawing names out of a hat, by rotating them in alphabetical order, and by making allotments according to a formula based upon the phases of the moon. The low bidder had then informed the others regarding his bid, and they had adjusted their bids accordingly. The conspirators had met under assumed names in luxury hotels in various cities, in motels, in mountain-top retreats, in cabins in the Canadian woods, and at a Milwaukee bar known as "Dirty Helen's." To maintain secrecy, they had used codes in referring to the companies and their executives, called one another from public telephones, sent letters to their homes rather than their offices, in plain envelopes without return addresses, and destroyed these communications when received. The conspiracy was disclosed when examination of bids revealed a pattern that indicated collusion, when examination of expense accounts showed that company officials had regularly congregated in the same places at the same times, and when some of the participants were thereupon persuaded to testify.[3]

Other Restrictive Agreements

In local markets, where sellers have got together, competition has been eliminated in many other ways. Bakers have entered into agreements limiting the sizes, regulating the weights, and fixing the prices of loaves of bread. Automobile dealers have sought, through various devices, to control the allowances made on trade-ins. Druggists have informed one another concerning their charges by marking copies of prescriptions in accordance with a code in which the successive letters of the word "pharmocist" or "pharmecist" stand for the numerals 1 to 0. Operators of filling stations have disciplined price cutters by sending several trucks to blockade their driveways at the busiest time of day, each driver buying one gallon of gasoline, utilizing all of the free services of the station, proffering a $50 bill in payment, and waiting for his change. Similar restraints have been experienced in other local trades.

In national markets, too, agreements among nominal competitors have frequently obtained. One complicated case involved the rigging of the price of gasoline. Here, eight major companies and four smaller ones, producing about 85 percent of the gasoline sold in ten midwestern states, raised and maintained prices during 1935 and 1936 by purchasing from independent refiners, producing the other 15 percent, any portion of their output that would depress the market if it were freely sold:

> Most of the output was distributed through filling stations owned by the major firms or sold under long-term contracts to independent jobbers who sold in turn to independent retailers. Daily exchanges at the independent refineries constituted no more than 5 to 7½ percent of total

3 / See John G. Fuller, *The Gentlemen Conspirators* (New York: Grove Press, 1962), and Myron W. Watkins, "Electrical Equipment Antitrust Cases," *University of Chicago Law Review,* Vol. XXIX (1961), pp. 97-110.

sales. The price established in these transactions, however, was quoted as the spot market price and the contracts under which the jobbers obtained their supplies required them to pay this price. Retailers who bought from jobbers added their margins to this price. As a consequence, the major companies, by controlling the price at which the small volume of spot market gasoline changed hands, were in a position to fix the retail price. The firms participating in the program accordingly agreed to subject the spot quotation to control. Each of them selected an independent refiner as a "dancing partner" and assumed responsibility for his "surplus" output. Buying in the spot market, in small quantities, at progressively higher figures, they contrived to raise the price and to maintain it at an artificial level for the better part of two years. Independent refinery output no longer depressed the spot quotation. Independent jobbers, compelled to buy at this figure, advanced their own charges. Independent retailers were forced to follow suit. The integrated majors, protected thus from competition, augmented their profits by exacting higher prices from the consumers of gasoline.[4]

In 1969, 15 of the country's largest manufacturers of plumbing fixtures were found to have met in a hotel room in Chicago to set the prices of bathtubs, toilets, and sinks, and three of the leading pharmaceutical houses were found to have agreed upon the prices to be charged for antibiotic "wonder drugs." Agreements restricting competition in national markets have occurred in scores of other cases, ranging from eyeglasses to explosives and including such important products as soap, cheese, watches, electric lamps, typewriters, ball bearings, newsprint paper, stainless steel, fertilizers, and various chemicals.

Vulnerability of Simple Conspiracy

Since understandings of the type described are clearly in violation of the law, their existence is usually shrouded in secrecy. But this fact presents no serious obstacle to enforcement. For, in the words of Corwin D. Edwards:

> There is scarcely a collusive agreement of any size or duration which does not leave unmistakable traces. If there are many persons in the conspiracy, one of them is almost sure to develop a grievance and turn state's evidence. If the plan is complicated, it is almost certain to leave written records. If no letters or memoranda are written, there is evidence that meetings were held and evidence of the identity of action which followed the meetings. If files have been stripped, stray carbons and references to missing documents in other documents make it possible to trace what happened. Once proved, a collusive agreement is relatively easy to terminate by law, since it operates through a system of joint action which may be stopped.[5]

4 / Wilcox, *op. cit.*, pp. 135-36.

5 / Corwin D. Edwards, "Can the Antitrust Laws Preserve Competition?" *American Economic Review,* suppl. (March, 1940), pp. 164-80, esp. p. 175.

If these were the only ways in which firms might conspire to restrain trade, the task of antitrust would be a fairly simple one. Unfortunately, they are not.

TRADE ASSOCIATIONS

Where traders are few in number, competition may be eliminated by simple agreement. Where they are numerous, it is more difficult to bring them together and to keep them in line. Some sort of contractual arrangement or formal organization is usually required. In Western Europe this need has long been satisfied by the activities of cartels. In the United States, it has frequently been met through the efforts of trade associations.

A trade association is an agency through which the sellers of a like commodity unite to promote their common interests. It exists solely to serve its members; it does not itself engage in the production or sale of goods. It is usually governed by a board of directors elected by its members and financed by dues which they contribute in proportion to their output, payrolls, capital, or sales. Its activities are typically administered by a salaried secretary and carried on by a paid staff. In some cases, however, administration may be delegated to one among the hundred or more firms of management engineers that specialize in this work. Association membership may number as few as a dozen or as many as several thousands; it may comprise a majority or minority of the firms in an industry and cover a large or a small part of its sales. The members of such an association retain their legal independence; they are free to enter or withdraw from it at will; they cannot even be compelled to pay their dues. An association, therefore, may be strong or weak, according to the force of circumstances making for voluntary cooperation within the trade. The number of these organizations runs into the thousands; they are found in every market and in every industry in the United States.

Restrictive Activities

In more than 200 cases brought before the Federal Trade Commission and the courts, trade associations have been found to have eliminated competition in a variety of ways. They have established uniform prices. They have allocated markets and customers among their members. They have required their members to hold production to some fraction of past output or capacity. They have assigned to each of their members a quota in a permitted volume of sales. These activities are illustrated in the program developed by the firm of Stevenson, Jordan & Harrison when it was employed, in 1932, to manage the affairs of one national association and 12 regional associations comprising 165 manufacturers of fiberboard shipping containers:

> The firm developed a "Basic Unit Plan" under which the numerous varieties of the industry's products were reduced to comparable elements. It prepared and circulated "Industry Estimating Manuals" containing

"formulas, factors, and differentials" which were to be used by members in computing their prices. It urged members to ignore their actual costs and to employ the arbitrary estimates set forth in these manuals. It enforced compliance through a plan of "Invoice or Order Analysis" which required each member to submit copies of invoices or orders giving complete details on every sale. Association officials followed up members who failed to submit this information, checked the figures reported, and applied the "formulas, factors, and differentials" to members' sales in order to determine whether they were adhering to them in fixing their charges. They also prepared and circulated reports and charts which compared each member's basic unit price with the average for the industry. These materials were discussed at frequent meetings and members with prices below the average were urged to raise them. The program also involved the allocation of production under a plan which was variously designated as "Prorationing of Business," "Equitable Sharing of Available Business," and "Live and Let Live." The Stevenson firm divided the country into zones and made surveys of the volume of business transacted by each member in each zone during a "normal" or "base" period of three years. On the basis of these surveys, it assigned to members definite percentages of the business in their zones. Members agreed that they would adhere to their quotas and supplied copies of invoices in order to enable officials to determine whether they were doing so. Association employees prepared bi-weekly reports and charts showing each member's share in the sales made and comparing it with his quota. These materials were discussed at association meetings and members who had exceeded their quotas were urged to curtail production.[6]

Arrangements such as these have been enforced by campaigns of education and exhortation, by personal remonstrance and persuasion, by requiring members to make deposits against which the association may levy fines, and by the organization of boycotts. Associations have sought to confine the business of a trade to members, to force nonmember competitors to join the association or to withdraw from the field, and to compel members and nonmembers alike to adhere to association rules. To these ends, loyal association members have applied concerted pressure, directly by refusing to deal with recalcitrant members and nonmember competitors, and indirectly by refusing to buy from suppliers who have sold to them or to sell to purchasers who have bought from them.

Such arrangements, when they involve large numbers of participants, are readily attacked by antitrust. The detailed instructions and elaborate procedures required for their effectuation make them conspicuous and therefore highly vulnerable. Illegal activities, however, are by no means characteristic of all associations; nine out of ten have never been charged with violation of the law. But there are other practices, more widely followed and not illegal in themselves,

6 / Wilcox, *op. cit.,* pp. 254-55.

that may pass by almost imperceptible degrees from innocent cooperation to dangerous conspiracy. And it is here that trade associations present a problem of peculiar difficulty to the law.

Cooperative Activities

Many of the functions performed by trade associations do not appear to be inconsistent with the preservation of competition; many others may involve the imposition of restraints. Typical association activities include industrial research, market surveys, the development of new uses for products, the operation of employment bureaus, collective bargaining with organized labor, mutual insurance, commercial arbitration, the publication of trade journals, joint advertising and publicity, and joint representation before legislative and administration agencies—all of them undertakings that may serve a trade without disservice to its customers. But they also include the establishment of common cost accounting procedures, the operation of price reporting plans, the collection and dissemination of statistics, the standardization of products and terms of sale, the provision of credit information, the interchange of patent rights, the joint purchasing of supplies, and the promulgation of codes of business ethics—each of them a practice which may operate to restrain competition in quality, service, price, or terms of sale.

Cost Accounting

Conspicuous among association activities is the promotion of cost accounting or, in association parlance, cost education. As described by Arthur R. Burns,[7] this educational work is carried on through six grades:

In the first, the association provides its members with standard forms for use in cost determination. This is expected to eliminate any price cutting that might arise from ignorance of costs. It may also carry the suggestion that no seller's price should fall below his costs as set forth on the standard forms. In the second grade, the association prescribes detailed procedures for computing costs, showing its members the proper way to figure charges for materials, the proper way to compute depreciation, and the proper way to distribute overhead. This is designed to reduce the price disparities that might result from the employment of diverse methods of calculation. In the third grade, the association suggests a uniform mark-up. Each of its members is encouraged to add the same per cent of profit to his costs to get his price. But one member may undersell another if he has lower costs. In the fourth grade, however, the association publishes some sort of an average of the costs of all the firms in the trade. Where this figure is adopted by members in place of their individual actual costs, it

---

7 / For a more complete description in his own words, see *The Decline of Competition* (New York: McGraw-Hill Book Co., 1936), pp. 47-55.

affords a basis for the establishment of a common price. But prices may still vary if members do not add a uniform markup to the uniform cost. In the fifth grade, therefore, some associations have taken the final step and included an allowance for profit in the so-called average costs. Average costs then become merely a suggested selling price, uniform for all, and provide a means by which to define and detect price cutting and a stimulus to attempts to eliminate it. In the sixth and final grade, the association undertakes to enfore adherence to the average "costs." Through editorials published in trade journals, through resolutions passed at association meetings, and through conferences, and correspondence between association officials and members of the trade, it endeavors to persuade all sellers that they should adopt the common estimate of "cost" and therefore charge a common price.[8]

It would scarcely be wise to prohibit the promotion of cost accounting as such; it certainly would not be safe to give this activity a free rein.

Price Reporting

Price reporting systems are operated by some associations; they were found in 15 percent of those covered in a survey made by Charles A. Pearce in 1939.[9] Through these systems, association members make available to one another, and sometimes to outsiders, information concerning the prices at which products have been, are being, or are to be sold. It is argued that such systems, by increasing the amount of knowledge available to traders, must lessen the imperfection of markets and make for more effective competition. Whether they do so, in fact, depends upon the characteristics of the industries which use them and upon the characteristics of the plans themselves:

For a price reporting system to increase the effectiveness of competition in a trade, many conditions must be fulfilled. As for the characteristics of the trade: Sellers must be numerous, each of them relatively small, and no one of them dominant. Entrance to the field must not be obstructed by legal barriers or by large capital requirements. Otherwise a reporting system may implement a price agreement, or promote price leadership, and facilitate the application of pressure against price cutters. Moreover, the market for the trade must not be a declining one. Supply, demand, and price must not be subject to violent fluctuation. The product must consist of small units turned out in large volume and sales must be frequent. Otherwise sellers will have a stronger incentive than usual to restrict competition and, even though numerous, they may agree upon a common course of action. Under such circumstances, a price reporting plan may serve as a convenient instrument for the administration of a

8 / Wilcox, *op. cit.,* pp. 226-27.

9 / Charles A. Pearce, *Trade Association Survey,* T.N.E.C. Monograph 18 (Washington, D.C.: Government Printing Office, 1940), p. 374.

scheme of price control. And finally, the demand for the product of the trade must be elastic, falling as prices rise and rising as prices fall. Otherwise it is not to be expected that the provision of fuller information would force a seller to reduce his price.

So, too, with the characteristics of the reporting plan itself: The price reports must not be falsified. If members do not return their lowest prices, if the association excludes such prices from the figures it reports, competitive reductions to meet the lowest figure actually charged will not occur. The reports must be available to all sellers on equal terms. If they are not, the sellers who fail to see them will not be informed of lower prices that they otherwise might meet. The reports must also be available to buyers. If information is withheld from them, they cannot seek out the seller who has filed the lowest price or compel another seller to meet this price to make a sale. The reports must not identify individual traders. The reporting agency must be neutral, keeping each seller's returns in confidence and transmitting the collective information to all concerned. If price cutters are openly or secretly identified, those who desire to sell at higher prices may employ persuasion or even sterner methods to bring them into line. The prices reported must be limited to past transactions. If current or future prices are exchanged, sellers will hesitate to cut their charges to make a sale, since they will know that lower figures will instantly be met. Each seller must be free to change his price at any time. If a seller cannot cut a price until sometime after he has filed the lower figure, thus affording his rivals an opportunity to meet it instantly, the chances that he will do so are accordingly reduced. The plan must carry no recommendation as to price policy. If the publication of average "costs" suggests the figures to be filed, if uniform charges are voted at trade meetings, then the reporting system becomes a method of policing the observance of a common price. The system, finally, must make no provision for the supervision of prices charged or for the imposition of penalties on those who sell below the figures they have filed. If association officials supervise the filing and persuade sellers whose quotations are low to raise them, if penalties are imposed on those who quote figures below those recommended or sell at figures below those quoted, then the reporting plan becomes but an incident in the whole price-fixing scheme. When every one of these conditions is fulfilled, a price reporting system may promote effective competition. But where any one of them is unsatisfied, price reporting is likely to implement the noncompetitive arrangements within the trade.[10]

Other Ambiguous Activities

Other association activities, not necessarily inconsistent with the maintenance of competition, may be carried to a point where they restrain the freedom of

10 / Wilcox, *op. cit.,* pp. 229-30.

members to compete. Circulation of statistics on production, inventories, unfilled orders, idle capacity, sales, and shipments may serve merely to inform traders concerning the state of the market; it may also be used to facilitate a scheme for curtailment of output and sharing of sales. Standardization of products may contribute to convenience and lessen waste; it may also lessen competition in quality and restrict the consumer's range of choice. Standardization of terms of sale may benefit purchasers by saving time, preventing misunderstandings, and affording a common basis for price comparisons; it may also promote collusion by preventing indirect departures from an established price. Provision of information on credit risks may increase the safety with which credit may be granted; reporting on customers may also be employed as a means of boycotting those who deal with outsiders or fail to observe a recommended price. The pooling of patents may afford a readier access to technology; it may be so administered that technology is monopolized. Joint purchasing may increase efficiency in buying; it may be used to establish prices that are unfair to suppliers and to exact concessions that are unfair to competitors. The promulgation of a code of ethics is avowedly designed to raise standards of conduct among the members of a trade, but such codes frequently contain provisions denouncing practices that are found to be offensive merely because they are competitive. Where an association lacks the power of enforcement, these prohibitions are merely persuasive. But where some measure of coercion is at hand, they may take on the force of law.

Cooperation or Conspiracy?

As Adam Smith remarked in 1776: "People of the same trade seldom meet together, even for merriment and diversion, but the conversation ends in a conspiracy against the public or in some contrivance to raise prices." [11] Does this observation apply to the modern trade association? How far do the members of these organizations engage in activities which enable them, without sacrificing their essential independence of action, to cooperate in increasing efficiency, reducing costs, and improving their service to the public? How far do they engage in activities which secure their adherence to common policies governing production and price? No one knows. There are thousands of trade association offices in the United States. In each of them a staff is working, presumably five days in every week and 52 weeks in every year, to administer activities in which competitors do not compete. Upon occasion the Federal Trade Commission or the Department of Justice makes an investigation and certain practices of an association are proscribed by the Commission or the courts. But no such sporadic action can be expected to disclose each of the cases in which competition is restrained. Nor can there ever be assurance that the merriment, diversion, and conversation of which Adam Smith spoke do not lead to the conspiracies or contrivances which he feared, unless an agent of the government is placed in every trade association office to read all correspondence,

11 / *Wealth of Nations,* Book I, chap. x, Part II.

memoranda, and reports, attend all meetings, listen to all conversations, participate in all the merriment and diversion, and issue periodic reports on what transpires. No such systematic oversight is authorized by law.

INTERCORPORATE RELATIONS

Competition may also be impaired by bringing nominally independent corporations under some form of common control. This may be done through common ownership of voting stock, through interlocking directors and officers, through joint undertakings, and through various ties of a less tangible sort. Where a common front is thus effected, firms are less likely to compete.

Common Stockholdings

A corporation can obtain control of a competing corporation by purchasing its shares, or a holding company can obtain control of two or more competitors in this way. Such behavior is highly visible and can be prevented under the provisions of the law. But a similar effect is achieved when the shares of competing companies are owned by the same indivudals. Thus, 27 years after the dissolution of the Standard Oil trust, each of 58 of the largest stockholders in 17 major oil companies owned shares in 2 to 5 of them; 48 owned shares in 6 to 10; and 14 owned shares in 11 to 15. Members of several families indentified with the trust continued to hold stock in two or more successor companies.[12] In view of the extent to which these concerns were owned by the same people, it seems unlikely that any one of them would pursue a course which was prejudicial to the interests of the others. Such a situation, however, is less readily brought within the purview of the law.

Interlocking Directorates

Unity of action may also be achieved through interlocking directorates. It is illegal, under Section 8 of the Clayton Act, for one person to serve on the boards of two companies that produce the same goods or services. In 1968, the Department of Justice broke up a number of interlocks between automobile manufacturers and major oil companies both of whom were selling batteries, spark plugs, and lubricants to owners of automobiles. Such interlocks are rare. But an officer of one company may serve as a director of another, and directors of two competing companies may sit together on the board of a third. There are interlocks, moreover, between potential competitors, and interlocks between companies and their bankers, suppliers, or customers that may assure them preferred access to capital, materials, or markets. The staff of the Antitrust Subcommittee of the House of Representatives reported, in 1965, that 1,206

---

12 / *Hearings before the Temporary National Economic Committee,* Part 14-A, pp. 7776-78; National Resources Committee, *The Structure of the American Economy* (Washington, D.C.: Government Printing Office, 1939), Part I, p. 311.

board members of 74 of the largest banks, insurance companies, and industrial firms had a total of 4,608 links with other concerns. The prohibition contained in the Clayton Act applies to only one among many means whereby competition may be impaired through interlocks.

Joint Ventures

Two companies that compete in the sale of one product may set up a jointly owned subsidiary to produce another. Thus, Pennsalt Chemicals and Olin Mathieson, manufacturers of a variety of chemical products, set up the Penn-Olin Chemical Company to produce and sell sodium chlorate. When such a subsidiary is established, potential competition in the sale of its product will probably be foreclosed, since neither of the parent companies is likely to compete with their progeny. Nor are the parents apt to compete, in this field, with one another. Their joint interest in the one product may operate, moreover, to moderate their competition in others. In the Penn-Olin case, the joint venture was permitted to stand by an equally divided court.[13] But other arrangements of the sort may run afoul of antitrust.

Interest Groupings

It has sometimes been noted that the security issues of competing corporations have been underwritten by the same investment banking houses, that their bonds have been held by the same banks and insurance companies, that their books have been audited by the same accountants, and that they have been served by the same law firms, engineering firms, advertising agencies, and public relations counselors. Many writers have perceived, in these facts, influences that may discourage competition and make for uniformity of policy. They doubt that companies can be completely independent of one another when their financing is carried on through the same channels and their policies formulated and reviewed within a common climate of opinion. Important as these influences may be, they are too tenuous to fall within the strictures of the law. The climate of opinion is beyond the reach of antitrust.

CONSCIOUS PARALLELISM OF ACTION

In markets characterized by oligopoly, where the entire output of a product is controlled by a few firms, or where the bulk of it is in the hands of firms that are much larger than any of the rest, the decisions made by each large seller will have an appreciable effect upon supply and price. If any one of them increases his output or reduces his price, the others are likely to retaliate, and the profits of the trade may be impaired. The threat of this development has sometimes led to arrangements, of the sort described above, whereby independent action is

13 / *Penn-Olin Chemicals Co.* v. *U.S.*, 378 U.S. 158 (1964); *U.S.* v. *Penn-Olin Chemicals Co.*, 389 U.S. 308 (1967).

forestalled. It may also lead, by force of circumstances or through long experience, to an identity of behavior that is achieved, without overt agreement or formal organization, through mutual forbearance by common consent. "Men may move in lockstep," as Walton Hamilton and Irene Till have put it, "not by agreement among themselves, but in automatic response to identical stimuli." [14] Such behavior has been described by the Federal Trade Commission as "conscious parallelism of action." It has manifested itself in the conventional sharing of markets, in price leadership and followership, and in the computation of delivered prices in accordance with a common formula.

Conventional Market Sharing

In certain industries competition is avoided by behavior which maintains a settled distribution of the business in the field. Here the dominant concerns amicably share supplies and markets, no one of them attempting to trespass on another's ground, each of them habitually abstaining from bidding against the others in making purchases and sales. In some cases they have acted in conformity with the terms of an explicit agreement; in others, they merely follow the conventions of the trade. Market sharing, either by agreement or by convention, has long existed in the meat-packing industry:

In 1918, the Federal Trade Commission reported that the distribution of livestock purchases, slaughtering, and sales among the Swift, Armour, Morris, Wilson, and Cudahy companies, during the five years previous, had remained the same from week to week and month to month, regardless of the total quantity of sales. Again in 1925, the Commission reported that the percentage distribution of the slaughter in the five preceding years had shown little change. In 1940, William H. Nicholls published an analysis of the proportionate weekly purchases of hogs, cattle, and calves made by the "Big Four" companies in each of five terminal markets during the years from 1931 through 1937. Each packer's share of the "Big Four" purchases of each type of livestock in each of these markets was found to remain strikingly constant from week to week and from year to year. When the distribution of purchases in this period was compared with that which the Federal Trade Commission had published for 1913–1917, it was found that the situation had remained virtually unchanged for a quarter of a century.[15]

"As it weaves its way into the structure of an industry," say Hamilton and Till, "restraint shifts its home from collusion to the folkways." [16] And this, according to a Complaint issued by the Department of Justice in 1948, is what happened

---

14 / Walton Hamilton and Irene Till, *Antitrust in Action*, T.N.E.C., Monograph 16 (Washington, D.C.: Government Printing Office, 1940), p. 14.

15 / Wilcox, *op. cit.,* pp. 183-85.

16 / Hamilton and Till, *op. cit.,* p. 15.

in the meat industry. "During the first quarter of a century of the conspiracy, defendants engaged in joint enterprises and held numerous meetings to control their buying and selling activities. . . . During this period, each company adopted substantially identical policies and methods of doing business. . . .By about 1920, the executives of each concern had become so habituated to the use of these identical methods and policies that they were expert in conducting the operations of their respective companies along parallel noncompetitive lines." [17] In such an arrangement, as in cases where market sharing is formally organized, no participant can increase his share of the market by paying higher prices or by charging lower ones. As a consequence, there is no incentive to do so. Nor is there pressure to improve the quality of products, to offer better service, to increase efficiency, or to reduce costs. As far as the consumer is concerned, the situation is much the same as if a single firm possessed a complete monopoly.

Price Leadership

Where a single firm overtops its rivals, it may invariably take the initiative in announcing changes in price. The smaller firms in such a field will follow the changes that are announced. They may sell at the prices that are set, or at a constant discount that is necessitated by inferior quality, service, or acceptibility. But they will follow the leader. Not only will they follow him down, as competition would dictate; they will also follow him up, as it would not. They may do so because they fear annihilation in the warfare that might be provoked by an attempt to undercut the leader, because they hope to obtain larger profits by taking refuge under the price umbrella which he holds over the trade, or merely because they find it convenient to follow his lead. In any case, they abandon independence of judgment and adopt his decisions as their own.

In the steel industry, United States Steel has been the leader. As a former president of the Corporation told a committee of the Senate in 1936: "We generally make the prices." [18] And the president of Bethlehem Steel subsequently testified that his company welcomed "the opportunity to follow the Corporation's lead in the publishing of new base prices," [19] recalling no instance in which it had failed to follow these prices either up or down. [20] In the glass container industry, according to officials of the leading companies: "Thatcher sets a price on milk bottles. . . .Hazel-Atlas . . . initiates the prices covering wide-mouthed container ware . . . tumblers and table ware. As to prices on proprietary and prescription ware, we adopt the schedules of . . . Owens-Illinois

17 / *U.S.* v. *Armour & Co. et al., Complaint,* September 15, 1948. The government dropped its suit against the industry in 1953.

18 / *Hearings before the Committee on Interstate Commerce, U.S. Senate, 74th Cong., 2d Sess. on S. 4055,* p. 595.

19 / *Hearings before the T.N.E.C.,* Part XIX, p. 10592.

20 / *Ibid.,* p. 10603.

. . . and make their prices ours. . . . .We adopt the prices as published by . . . Ball Brothers . . . as our prices for fruit jars, jelly glasses, and fruit jar tops." [21] There has also been evidence of the leader-follower relationship among producers of agricultural implements, anthracite coal, bananas, biscuits and crackers, canned salmon, cement, cigarettes, copper, corn products, fertilizers, gasoline, industrial alcohol, lead, newsprint paper, sulfur, and tin cans. [22]

In markets that are occupied by a number of large concerns, initiative in changing prices may shift from one to another from time to time. Here, each firm will exercise its own judgment, following the leader only when it finds its interest served by doing so. Such a leader serves, in effect, as a barometer, holding his position while his action expresses the industry's consensus as to market prospects. In this position, he cannot ignore the forces of potential competition.

Where a dominant firm invariably assumes the role of leadership, however, the prices that it sets are not effectively competitive. The leader, controlling a substantial portion of the output of the trade, estimates the sales revenues and the production costs incident to the quantities salable at various prices and produces the amount, and sells at the figure, that is calculated to yield him the largest net return. In short, he behaves as a monopolist. When other sellers adopt the same figure, they offer buyers no real alternative. Leader and followers alike exact a monopoly price.

Delivered Pricing

In many industries where the cost of transporting the product is high, sellers located at different places have contrived to charge identical prices at any location where goods are delivered. This identity was once accomplished through the use of common basing points. Under such a system, each seller refuses to quote a price for the sale of goods at the door of his own mill and insists on making quotations that include a charge for their delivery to his customers. In computing this charge, all sellers employ the same city or cities as basing points, and each of them figures the freight on a particular sale from the same point. Goods may be shipped by water or by truck at rates that are lower than by rail, but every price is calculated on the basis of an all-rail haul. One railroad may quote a lower rate than another, but the freight included in the price is that recorded in a common rate book. As a result, all sellers, wherever located, charge the same amount at any destination. [23]

The character and the consequences of various delivered pricing systems will be analyzed in some detail in Chapter 10. It is sufficient, at this stage, to point out that such a system may enable sellers to eliminate competition without

21 / *Ibid.*, Part II, pp. 530, 547-48.

22 / Burns, *op. cit.*, pp. 77-140; Wilcox, *op. cit.*, pp. 121-32; George W. Stocking and Myron W. Watkins, *Monopoly and Free Enterprise* (New York: Twentieth Century Fund, 1951), pp. 132-84.

23 / On basing point pricing in the steel industry, see Wilcox, *op. cit.*, pp. 149-50.

affording evidence of overt agreement or formal organization in restraint of trade. Faithful adherence to a common formula for computing prices is all that is required.

Constructive Conspiracy

Such patterns of behavior, once learned, continue of their own momentum. Compared with obvious conspiracy, they may be difficult to prosecute. The contrast is described by Hamilton and Till:

> Where units are many, heat has marked the struggle for markets, feelings have grown tense, suspicions have been quickened. As a result, the getting together has hard going. The meetings must be frequent, the talk frank, the understandings clean-cut, explicit, above board. The procedure generates evidence as it goes forward; the industry virtually invites a suit through the very ease of getting proof. But where very few units are involved, where co-operation is a practice of long standing, where a large body of understandings is a matter of course, the situation is otherwise. The necessity for conference is infrequent, minutes of meetings are prepared in advance by skilled attorneys, the question direct is never put. Action is taken without fanfare of trumpets; conduct is clothed in accepted practice; records are barren of evidence to the overt act.[24]

In such a situation, the evidence available may be purely circumstantial. Statistics of purchases, sales, and prices may have to bear the burden of proof. Agreement may have to be inferred from identity of behavior. A case of conspiracy may have to be constructed on the basis of a probability that each of several firms adopting some common course of conduct has done so in the light of knowledge that all the others would do the same. Conscious parallelism of action thus presents a problem of particular difficulty to antitrust.

MONOPOLISTIC ABUSES

The unfair methods that may be used by a single firm are much the same as those employed by several independent enterprises in accordance with the terms of a restrictive agreement or in conformity with the provisions of a trade association plan. They include such practices as maliciously interfering with the production and sale of competitive goods, excluding competitors from access to supplies, obtaining unduly discriminatory prices in purchasing supplies, excluding competitors from access to markets, obtaining preferential markets for themselves, squeezing the margins of nonintegrated independents, and engaging in discriminatory and predatory pricing in an effort to drive competitors to the wall.

24 / Hamilton and Till, *op. cit.,* p. 20.

Malicious Interference

Large firms have sometimes undertaken to eliminate their smaller rivals by maliciously interfering with the production and sale of their goods. The classic case of such behavior, dating back to the end of the last century, is that of the National Cash Register Company:

> The company set out deliberately to destroy its competitors. It hired their employees away from them. It bribed their employees and the employees of railroads and telephone and telegraph companies to spy on them and disclose their business secrets. It spread false rumors concerning their solvency. It instructed its agent to misrepresent the quality of their goods, interfere with their sales, and damage the mechanism of their machines in establishments where they were in use. It publicly displayed their cash registers under labels which read, "Junk." It made, and sold at less than cost, inferior machines called "knockers," which it represented to be just as good as theirs. It threatened to bring suit against them and their customers for alleged infringements of patent rights. It induced their customers to cancel their orders and repudiate their contracts. It intimidated prospective investors in competing plants by publishing lists of defunct competitors and by exhibiting in a "grave yard" at its factory samples of the machines which they had formerly made. Such practices, carried on over a period of twenty years, gave the company control of 95 per cent of the nation's production of cash registers.[25]

Behavior of this sort clearly violates the law. Being conspicuous, it is easy to attack. While not unknown today, it has largely disappeared. The methods of monopolization that are currently employed are usually more circumspect.

Exclusive and Discriminatory Buying

Firms dominant in a field have sometimes prevented the emergence or survival of competitors by excluding them from access to productive facilities, credit, equipment, and materials. They have made preemptive purchases, buying in quantities greater than those required to satisfy their needs. They have forced suppliers to sign exclusive contracts, refusing to buy from those who sold to their competitors. They have also handicapped their rivals by demanding and obtaining from suppliers discriminatory concessions that could not be justified by differences in cost. Such practices were characteristic of the early trusts. The American Can Company prevented its competitors from obtaining up-to-date equipment by entering into exclusive contracts with the manufacturers of automatic can-making machinery; its connection with the American Tin Plate Company not only enabled it to obtain secret rebates on its raw material but

25 / Wilcox, *op. cit.,* p. 68.

also threatened to interfere with the delivery of plate to other producers and even to cut them off completely from their source of supply.[26] Several of the trusts persuaded the railroads to grant them substantial rebates; Standard Oil not only recovered 40–50 percent of the sums which it paid the roads for carrying its own products but also collected a similar share of the rates paid by its rivals.[27] The Aluminum Company of America, enjoying a patent monopoly in its early years, made preemptive purchases of deposits of bauxite and sites for the generation of hydroelectric power, and bought power elsewhere under contracts which forbade suppliers to sell to other producers of aluminum; it eliminated one prospective competitor by purchasing the site he was arranging to develop and acquired the property of another when he could find no bankers to finance his enterprise.[28] To the same end, more recently, producers of the leading brands of cigarettes bought up the stocks of tobacco required for the production of 10-cent brands;[29] and exhibitors of motion pictures prevented other houses from obtaining films by renting more features than they had time to display in their own theaters.[30]

Exclusive Selling

Large concerns have frequently attempted to exclude their smaller rivals from the market by imposing upon distributors contracts forbidding them to handle goods produced by other firms. Contracts of this sort have been employed, in the past, in the sale of biscuits and crackers, cameras, dress patterns, canned sirups, petroleum products, and many other goods. Their use is now limited by Section 3 of the Clayton Act. Where products are small, simple, and relatively inexpensive, they are usually distributed by independent retailers who may be compelled by heavy advertising to carry the large firm's brand and may therefore find it necessary to accept exclusive contracts. When this occurs, smaller producers are seriously handicapped in reaching the market by exclusion from normal contacts with potential customers. Where goods are bulky, complicated, and expensive, they are usually distributed through exclusive agencies, and any firm that seeks to enter the market must establish an agency system of its own. The difficulties involved in doing so may operate to bar newcomers from the field.

Firms facing little or no competition in the sale of one product and substantial competition in the sale of another have employed restrictive

26 / *U.S.* v. *American Can Co.,* 230 Fed. 859 (1916).

27 / Eliot Jones, *The Trust Problem in the United States* (New York: Macmillan Co., 1921), pp. 49-52.

28 / *U.S.* v. *Aluminum Co. of America,* 148 F. 2d 416 (1945); Donald H. Wallace, *Market Control in the Aluminum Industry* (Cambridge, Mass.: Harvard University Press, 1937), pp. 115-17; 132-37.

29 / *American Tobacco Co.* v. *U.S.,* 328 U.S. 781 (1946).

30 / Walter Adams, *The Structure of American Industry* (New York: Macmillan Co., 1950), p. 286.

contracts of another type, refusing to supply a purchaser with the first product unless he would agree to rely upon the same supplier for the second, thus closing the market to competitors in the latter field. Such a practice was followed, for many years, by the United Shoe Machinery Corporation:

> Instead of selling its patented machines, the company adopted the policy of leasing them, charging shoe manufacturers a royalty for each pair of shoes on which they were used. It inserted in its leases a clause which forbade the manufacturer to use any other maker's machine for any process in which one of its own machines was employed. It denied him the right to use its own machines on shoes which were processed at any stage of their production on machines made by its rivals. By means of the latter device, the company extended its control from its exclusive fields to those in which it had formerly been faced by competition. The shoe manufacturer, who could obtain a lasting machine only by leasing it from the United Shoe Machinery Corporation was compelled to turn to it also for his welter, stitcher, and metallic fastener, and the independent producers of these machines were robbed of their customers.[31]

In the same way, competitors were once excluded from the market for radio tubes by a provision in licenses granted by the Radio Corporation of America, under its patents, to manufacturers of radio sets, requiring them to buy their tubes from RCA.[32] Tying contracts of this sort have also been used in the sale of stencils and ink to purchasers of mimeograph machines, jute bagging to purchasers of steel ties for baling cotton, installment financing services to dealers in automobiles, motion picture films to lessees of projectors, tabulating cards to lessees of tabulating machines, and various materials to lessees of many other types of machinery, in each case giving the producer of the second good or service a marked advantage over his competitors in the production of the first.

Firms selling a large number of products have sometimes followed a similar practice, refusing to supply any of them to purchasers who would not agree to take several or all of them. Companies manufacturing a full line of agricultural implements once forced their distributors to carry every product in the line, forbidding them to handle equipment produced by other firms. This full-line forcing excluded the specialized manufacturer from thousands of retail outlets; in rural markets which were too small to support more than two or three dealers he may not have been represented at all.[33] The major producers of motion pictures have likewise imposed upon independent exhibitors, who must turn to them for the great majority of their feature attractions, contracts including a block-booking clause which compels these houses to take many pictures they do not want in order to obtain the ones they do. Independent producers have

---

31 / Wilcox, *op. cit.,* pp. 72-73.

32 / *Lord et al.* v. *Radio Corporation of America,* 24 F. 2d 565 (1928).

33 / Federal Trade Commission, *The Agricultural Implements and Machinery Industry* (Washington, D.C.: Government Printing Office, 1938), pp. 276-83.

consequently been unable to rent their films to exhibitors whose programs were thus crowded with the products of the major firms.[34] Through such devices, firms producing several different goods have contrived to handicap competitors whose operations were narrower in scope.

Reciprocal Dealing

A favored market is also obtained, at the expense of competitors, when Company A refuses to buy product x from Company B unless Company B will buy product y from Company A. Thus, General Motors was charged, in 1963, with telling railroads that if they did not buy GM locomotives, GM would ship freight on other lines. Consolidated Foods was found, in 1965, to have forced its suppliers to buy dried onions and garlic from one of its subsidiaries and U.S. Steel agreed, in 1969, to discontinue the practice of providing its purchasing agents with records of its sales so that they would buy from its customers. This "you-scratch-my-back-and-I'll-scratch-yours" practice, according to *Business Week,* is followed by thousands of companies in doing business with one another.[35] When the firm involved controls a small share of the market for the goods it buys and when it invites reciprocal purchases rather than requiring them, the harm done its competitors will be small. But when it is a major buyer and when it uses coercion to force reciprocal purchases, its competitors may find their market opportunities substantially curtailed.

Abuses of Vertical Integration

Another means of foreclosing the opportunities of competitors is presented when one company controls a second at an earlier or a later stage of the processes of production and distribution. Clearly, vertical integration is not to be condemned as such. The baker who has his display cases in the front room and his ovens in the back is vertically integrated, as is the manufacturer of hats or shoes who operates his own retail stores. The purposes of a concern that gets control of another company, up or down the line, may be entirely legitimate. Control of a producer of raw materials may assure a more dependable quality and a steadier supply. Control of retail outlets may afford a surer access to markets and promote sales by combining selling and servicing. Such developments are not properly to be attacked.

But vertical integration may also be employed to lessen competition by handicapping competitors or even by excluding them from access to sources of supply and to channels of distribution. The common ownership of anthracite mines and railroads once made it possible for the companies concerned to withhold cars and to collect high transport rates from other mines. Ownership of pipelines has afforded the major oil companies a similar advantage over

34 / *U.S.* v. *Paramount Pictures,* 334 U.S. 131 (1948).
35 / *Business Week,* February 9, 1963, pp. 45-46.

independent refineries. Ownership of theater chains by major producers of motion pictures has made it difficult both for independent producers to obtain desirable outlets and for independent exhibitors to obtain desirable films. Ownership of one subsidiary that operated sleeping cars and of another that manufactured them enabled the Pullman Company to exclude other manufacturers from the market for such equipment until recent years. Ownership of telephone operating companies and of the Western Electric Company by American Telephone and Telegraph has long excluded other manufacturers from markets for telephonic apparatus and materials. Such arrangements, however, are open and aboveboard. Their correction, therefore, has not been handicapped by lack of proof.

The most celebrated of these cases, in recent years, has been that of du Pont and General Motors. At the end of World War I, du Pont, which was to become the world's largest chemical company, began buying the common stock of General Motors, which was to become the world's largest manufacturing company. From 1918 on, it always held 23 percent or more of these shares. This concentrated minority, together with proxies obtained from smaller holders, gave du Pont working control of GM. In addition, du Pont officials sat on the General Motors board of directors and dominated the principal committees of the board. In this way, they were enabled to control the appointment, promotion, and compensation of the GM executives. Its purpose in all of this, according to du Pont, was merely to diversify its risks and protect its investment. But it should be noted that du Pont was a manufacturer of finishes and fabrics for automobiles, and that General Motors had almost half of the market for such goods. The purchasing agents of the GM subsidiaries may have continued to deal at arm's length, as du Pont has protested, buying only on the basis of quality and price. Or they may have been influenced, as the government charged in an antitrust suit brought against the companies in 1949, by the fact that du Pont was in control. In either case, the fact remains that GM was buying two thirds of its supplies of finishes and around half of its supplies of fabrics from du Pont in 1946 and 1947. And to the extent that du Pont was thus thus afforded a preferred market, other producers of finishes and fabrics were excluded from the field. In the same way, du Pont control of U.S. Rubber, through stockholdings, may have operated to give du Pont a preferred market for tire fabrics and U.S. Rubber a preferred market—among the GM companies— for tires. [36]

The Squeeze

A large concern that is vertically integrated, controlling operations at each of the successive stages of production, may turn out at each stage the exact amounts that it requires for use at the next, entering the market only as a seller of finished goods. But integration may also be disproportionate; an integrated

36 / *U.S. v. du Pont,* 353 U.S. 586.

company may enter the market at earlier stages as a seller of materials; its nonintegrated competitors at later stages may depend upon it for supplies. To the integrated firm, the prices charged and the margins allowed at successive stages are a matter of convenience; to its nonintegrated competitors, they are a matter of life and death. Such a concern is thus in a position to squeeze its rivals by raising prices in the markets where they buy and reducing prices in the markets where they sell. Thus, the Aluminum Company of America, competing with independent companies in the fabrication of aluminum products, was for many years the only source from which these independents could obtain their supply of aluminum ingots and sheets; by raising the price of raw materials and lowering the price of finished products, the company has been said to have made it unprofitable for its rivals to remain in business.[37] A similar squeeze has been experienced by independent refiners of petroleum.[38] The squeeze is difficult for antitrust authorities to attack, since price changes may be adjudged competitive or monopolistic according to their motivation, and motives are difficult to prove.

Discriminatory and Predatory Pricing

It is not unusual for sellers to fix different prices for different buyers. Nor is such differentiation necessarily unfair. For differences in price may reflect real differences in the cost at which particular sales are made. But there are cases in which differentiation cannot be so justified. Discriminatory reductions may carry particular prices far below real costs, and losses may be deliberately incurred for the purpose of driving weaker rivals from the field.

Discrimination of this sort is most likely to be practiced by a firm that operates in many different markets or produces many different goods. Such a seller enjoys a marked advantage over those whose operations are confined to a single market or a single line. He can cut a particular price to a point where he loses money and still preserve his solvency by maintaining prices elsewhere. But his smaller rivals, incurring losses on their entire output, may shortly be driven into bankruptcy. The diversified seller is thus in a position to select particular firms for destruction, picking them off at his pleasure, one at a time. He may discriminate among localities, temporarily cutting his price in one area and raising it again when he has eliminated his local competitors. He may discriminate among products, setting up bogus independents or producing fighting brands to sell at ruinous prices, and cutting them off when their purpose has been served. Such practices were employed by the early trusts to build up positions of monopoly in oil, sugar, tobacco, meat-packing, and tin cans. They are now forbidden by the Clayton and Robinson-Patman Acts.

A firm possessing large financial resources, instead of engaging in discrimination, may reduce its prices uniformly, setting them below its costs at levels that

37 / Burns, *op. cit.,* p. 441; Corwin D. Edwards, *Maintaining Competition* (New York: McGraw-Hill Book Co., 1949), p. 172.

38 / Wilcox, *op. cit.,* pp. 167-68.

make it impossible for its weaker rivals to survive, and accepting the resulting losses as an investment to be recovered in the later profits of monopoly. This was a common practice in the heyday of the trusts. Firms were combined, prices were raised, new competition was attracted, prices were slashed, the new-comers were bought up or driven out of business, and prices were raised again. Reduction of prices, under these circumstances, was monopolistic in purpose and effect.

Predatory price cutting may now be held to violate the law. But the practice is by no means easy to identify. The test of predation is intent, but the price cutter's purpose is known only to himself, is only to be inferred by others. In cases of flagrant discrimination, the inference may be plain; in cases of general price reduction, it is less so. The competitor who finds it difficult to meet another's price may well believe that his rival intends to eliminate him, but this conviction cannot be taken as sufficient proof of such intent. Every act of competition is designed to attract business to one competitor rather than another and, to that extent, to eliminate the latter from the field. The line beyond which such activity is properly to be attacked as predatory is not an easy one to draw.

COMBINATION WITHOUT ABUSE

A firm may acquire possession of the property of its competitors by employ-ing methods of competition that are so oppressive as to leave them no choice but to sell out. And this, indeed, has frequently occurred. But business com-binations may also be effected, without coercive pressure, through the volun-tary choice of the participants. And where the firms combined produce the bulk of a product, monopoly may be painlessly achieved. In any case, combina-tion is a process that should be examined apart from the unfair methods by which it has often been induced.

Forms of Combination

Two or more enterprises may be brought under common direction in a variety of ways: by the purchase of assets, by merger, by amalgamation, by intercorporate stockholding, and by the formation of a holding company. In the first case, Company A offers to purchase the assets of Company B, the stockholders of B consent to the sale, A pays cash to B and takes possession of its assets, B distributes the cash to its stockholders and goes out of business. In the case of a merger, A proposes to absorb B, the stockholders of B agree, they receive the stock in A in return for stock in B, and B disappears. In both cases, A retains its identity. In the case of amalgamation, it is proposed to establish a new Company C for the purpose of absorbing both A and B, the stockholders of A and B agree to the proposal, they surrender their stock and get stock in C, thereafter C survives and A and B both disappear. In all three cases, two com-panies are fused and one or both of them loses its identity. In the case of intercorporate stockholding, A goes into the market and purchases a majority or a controlling minority of the voting stock of B, the stockholders of B do not vote on the deal, B retains its corporate identity, but A now selects its directors and officers and determines its policies. In the holding company case, a new corporation H is established, H goes into the market and purchases controlling stock in A and B, the stockholders of A and B do not vote on the deal, A and B both retain their identity, but H now selects their directors and officers and determines their policies. The latter devices have two advantages: they do not necessitate the payment of cash or the issuance of securities to cover the full value of the companies brought under control, and they do not require the assent of their stockholders.

The types of activity that are brought under common direction by any of the methods described may differ fundamentally in character. Combinations may be classified as horizontal, chain, vertical, lateral, and conglomerate. The horizontal combination brings together firms at the same stage of production, turning out the same product, and selling it in the same market. This was the pattern adopted by the early trusts. The chain combination unites companies at the same stage of production that sell the same product in different local markets. It is typified by public utility and branch banking systems and by chains of restaurants, hotels, and retail stores. Vertical integration reaches forward or backward or both to combine firms at successive stages of production. It is seen in the ownership of iron mines by steel mills and movie theaters by producing companies. Lateral combination brings together companies engaged in the production of goods that are related but not competitive. General Foods and Standard Brands are examples of this type. Here a common trademark or a common selling organization may be used for the various products in a corporate family. Conglomerate combination unites enterprises whose products may not be related in any way. There are a dozen such concerns among the 125 American corporations with sales exceeding $1 billion a year. Conspicuous among them have been Textron, with subsidiaries producing helicopters, poultry feed, eye glasses, and watch bands; Ling-Temco-Vought, with units manufacturing aircraft, ships, mobile homes, electronic products, chemicals, and drugs, processing meats and other food products, and operating airlines, insurance companies, and banks; and Litton Industries, with units producing ships, submarines, office machinery, furniture, movie cameras, X-Ray equipment, and surgical instruments, publishing books, and operating paper mills and food services.

The Merger Movement

The historical development of corporate combination, usually referred to as the merger movement, has been characterized by three widely separated periods of heightened activity, the first around the turn of the century, the second following World War I, and the last dating from the middle fifties. The first of these periods opened with prosperity in 1897, reached a peak with the formation of 1,200 mergers in 1899, and ended with the depression of 1903. It was marked primarily by the use of the holding company device to effect horizontal combinations in mining and manufacturing. During this period a number of gigantic combines were formed and many of the country's basic industries were monopolized. The second period began with prosperity in the twenties, peaked with the creation of more than 1,200 mergers in 1929, and ended with the stock market crash in that year. It was marked by extension of the movement to the public utilities, banking, and the distributive and service trades, by combinations among firms of moderate size, and by the emergence of many different patterns of combination: chain, vertical, lateral, and conglomerate as well as horizontal. In both of these periods, the movement was facilitated by the existence of a ready market for corporate securities and stimulated by the prospect of realizing quick profits through promotional and speculative activities.

The third period, dating from the fifties, has been longer in duration and larger in scale than the other two. The number of mergers effected from 1960 through 1968 exceeded 18,000, reaching a high of more than 4,000 in the latter year. The movement was marked by vertical integration and diversification as well as by the merger of firms engaged in like activities. There was extensive public discussion of the growth of conglomerates, but a minor fraction of the combinations (around a twentieth in 1967) took this form. In most cases, the mergers united firms of moderate size, with larger enterprises acquiring the shares or the assets of smaller ones. A small fraction (around a thirtieth) involved really large concerns. But there were a number of mergers, many of them conglomerates, where the acquiring company and the acquired company were of substantial size. In 74 cases, in 1968, the acquiring company was among the country's 200 largest corporations, and in 192 cases the acquired companies had assets of more than $10,000,000. [39]

Purposes and Effects of Mergers

The significance of such figures is by no means clear since the effects of combination on competition will vary from case to case. Horizontal combination, where the companies involved control the whole supply of a product, will result in a complete monopoly. But where one small firm absorbs another, it may increase the vigor of competition by strengthening their ability to compete. In other forms of combination, where the units brought together do not sell the same product in the same market, the purpose may be something other than the attainment of monopoly: chain combination may be directed toward economies that are to be realized through mass buying, standardized operations, and unified management; vertical integration toward the assurance of raw material supplies and market outlets; lateral combination toward the employment of a common sales organization and the exploitation of a common brand. One company may acquire another as a ready means of expanding its capacity, entering new lines or new markets, or obtaining access to managerial talent or to research

39 / *Business Week*, April 19, 1969, p. 36.

capacity. It may seek to reduce the cost of credit, of advertising, and the like by enhancing its market power. It may seek competitive advantage by engaging in reciprocal dealing and by using the profits of a successful line temporarily to support an unsuccessful one. A prosperous company may acquire a declining company because its assets can be bought at a bargain, or because its losses will offset the buyer's profits, thus reducing his liability under the corporate income tax. In the case of conglomerate combinations, the motivation appears to be less to realize economies in production or to suppress competition than to obtain the gains in security values and in executive compensation that come as a result of corporate growth. In some cases, a combination may contribute indirectly to the impairment of competition by giving a large concern an unfair advantage over its small competitors. In others, it may have no such effect. And in still others, its results may be indeterminate. Combination must therefore be judged by its consequences, case by case. Over the years, it appears to have contributed less to business size than has expansion through internal growth.[40]

The Control of Combination

Since combination is an overt act, its prosecution is not handicapped by lack of proof. It is a simple matter, moreover, to issue an order forbidding new acquisitions of stock or assets. But it is not so easy to break up a combination that has existed for many years. Where there is evidence of serious abuse, the courts are likely to find a combination to be in violation of the law. But where the position of a monopolistic combination is so secure that unfair methods are no longer needed, they may be reluctant to act. It is not easy to unscramble eggs that were scrambled many years ago. Where combination has been effected through intercorporate stockholdings or through the holding company device, divorcement can be accomplished by requiring the holders to sell their stock. But where firms have been merged or amalgamated, a complete reorganization is required. In either case, the task of reshuffling property interests, while not impossible, is difficult. The courts may also fear that dismemberment of a corporate giant would reduce efficiency and impede progress. They may doubt that competition would be restored or the public interest really served. In the face of difficulty, and in the light of uncertainty, it is easier to leave ill enough alone.

MONOPOLY WITHOUT COMBINATION

Combination is the principal method by which a single firm is likely to attain a position of monopoly but is not the only one. Monopolistic powers are granted, in many cases, by local, state, and federal governments. There are

---

40 / See J. Fred Weston, *The Role of Mergers in the Growth of Large Firms* (Berkeley: University of California Press, 1953). See also John Lintner and J. Keith Butters, "Effect of Mergers on Industrial Concentration," in *Review of Economics and Statistics* for February, 1950.

franchises, certificates of public convenience and necessity, permits, and licenses which confer upon their holders exclusive privileges in the employment of limited facilities and the provision of important services. Such monopolies, being subject to other forms of regulation, are beyond the reach of antitrust. There are also patents, trademarks, and copyrights which give their owners the exclusive right to control the use of certain machines and processes and the manufacture and sale of certain goods, to employ certain names or symbols, or to publish certain materials. Trademark protection may be permanent; patents and copyrights are limited in time.

There are also fields in which the characteristics of the product, the scope of the market, or the location of resources are such that competition cannot be expected to obtain. A novelty is likely to be produced exclusively, for a time, by the company that was first in the field. The market for another product may be so small that a single firm can satisfy the whole demand. The supply of a mineral may be so concentrated as to give the owner of one deposit a monopoly. This was true, at one time, in the case of nickel, magnesium, and molybdenum. But such advantages will usually be temporary. Unless it is permanently protected by law, a monopoly is likely to be lost as markets expand, as substitutes are developed, as new resources are discovered, and as new competitors enter the field. In some cases, however, it is possible that a position of monopoly, once established, may be maintained, not through legal privilege, resort to unfair tactics, or combination with others, but simply by growing as the market grows. An outstanding example of such growth is that of the Aluminum Company of America. Another is International Business Machines.

In 1969, IBM was the nation's seventh largest corporation. Its stock was worth $42 billion. Its annual sales amounted to $6.88 billion; its profits to $871 million. The company had a number of products, in some of which it faced substantial competition. But it dominated the new computer industry in a way in which no other company dominated a major market. IBM shipped more than three quarters, in value, of all the general-purpose computers supplied in the United States in 1967; its two closest rivals, taken together, accounted for less than a tenth of the sales. The company supplied two thirds of the computers used in the world as a whole. In 1968 and 1969, it was made a defendant in antitrust suits brought by two of its small competitors and by the Department of Justice. The company was charged with monopolizing the computer industry, not by absorbing its competitors, not by engaging in illegal practices, but through its exploitation of the dominant position accorded it by its early occupancy of the field and by its subsequent rapid growth.

Monopolies based on legal grants are excluded from the operation of antitrust laws. But other monopolies are covered by Section 2 of the Sherman Act, which forbids any person to "monopolize or attempt to monopolize," and these words are separate from the ones which prohibit combination or conspiracy. Here again, however, enforcement is handicapped by the difficulties of dissolution and by uncertainty as to its consequences.

SIZE WITHOUT MONOPOLY

It would be a mistake to identify little business with competition, big business with monopoly. It is not the absolute size of a business unit that is significant, but its size in relation to the size of the market in which it operates. In a limited market a tiny firm may possess a complete monopoly. In a larger market a corporate giant may face severe competition. In many small towns there are only one or two bankers, butchers, plumbers, pharmacists, undertakers, hotels, garages, coal dealers, and lumberyards. The largest corporations in the country, on the other hand, include such firms as Sears Roebuck, Macy's, and the A&P, all of them facing active competition in the markets where they buy and sell.

The large concern, however, possesses marked competitive advantages. Its vast resources and the scale of its operations give it a preferred position in buying and selling, in obtaining capital and credit, in conducting litigation, and in dealing with the government. It can obtain low prices from suppliers, not only by buying in quantity, but also by threatening to divert its purchases or to produce for itself. It can influence demand by spending huge sums on advertising and, in some cases, by providing assurance of trade-in values, continued supplies of parts, and servicing. It can obtain easy access to credit and find a ready market for its securities. It can afford to sue and be sued and can withstand the cost of repeated appeals. It can contribute heavily to campaign funds and make substantial investments in contacts with legislators and administrative agencies. Such a firm obtains still further advantages when its activities are diversified. As Edwards has observed:

> Its operations are spread across so many customers, so many geographical markets, and, in the case of the conglomerate enterprise, so many different types of commodities and services that its fortunes do not depend upon profit or loss in a particular transaction, a particular location, or a particular activity. This diversity of interests not only immunizes it from the effects of business fluctuations which would mean disaster to an enterprise operating more narrowly, but also gives it the power to lose money deliberately at any one point for the sake of disciplining or destroying its more specialized rivals.[41]

Even though the large concern lacks a monopoly in any of the fields in which it operates, the many advantages which it enjoys may thus threaten the survival of its smaller competitors.

If the corporate giant resorts to unfair methods of competition, it may be found to violate the law. But if it employs its powers with due restraint, it probably cannot be held to do so. It is sometimes asserted that the preservation, for its own sake, of an economy of numerous small units was the motivating

41 / Edwards, op. cit., p. 101.

purpose of the framers of the Sherman Act. But this is not what the law says. It is monopoly that is condemned, not size as such. And though antitrust has often been accused of attacking size alone, its proceedings against large firms have invariably been based on allegations of illegal behavior.

But the line between legality and illegality, in such a case, is not an easy one to draw. An integrated firm, in the words of Dirlam and Kahn,

> ... must, if it is to compete vigorously, charge little more than incremental costs in some of its markets, relying on others to make up the larger portion of the joint costs of integrated operations. Yet in so doing it cannot avoid "squeezing" non-integrated competitors in the more competitive markets, in the sense that it is accepting prices there which it could not long continue to accept but for the returns it obtains elsewhere. It is practically impossible, therefore, for a large integrated firm to exploit its socially acceptable advantages, or even to meet competition, without at the same time exploiting those advantages which are purely strategic.[42]

The problem of size thus presents a serious dilemma to public policy. If differential advantages are not to be disturbed, the competitive struggle will go forward on unequal terms. But if they were, the law would be directed, not toward the maintenance of competition, but toward the preservation of small competitors. And this is quite a different thing. For it is often the large concern that sets the pace for competition in a trade. To break it up, in such a case, would be to sacrifice the force that makes for progress in efficiency. Protection of small business may be defended, however, on other than economic grounds. Personal independence and self-reliance may have their social and political advantages. Their preservation might be taken, in itself, as an objective of public policy. But this is not the stated purpose of the law.

42 / Joel B. Dirlam and Alfred E. Kahn, *Fair Competition: The Law and Economics of Antitrust Policy* (Ithaca, N.Y.: Cornell University Press, 1954), p. 151.

Chapter 5 | ENFORCEMENT OF ANTITRUST

The provisions of the antitrust laws are made effective through actions brought against violators, case by case. A decision or an order resulting from such an action does not apply to industry in general but only to those who are named as respondents or defendants in a particular case. The Sherman Act is enforced through criminal or civil suits brought in the federal courts by the Department of Justice and through suits initiated by private litigants. Section 5 of the Federal Trade Commission Act is enforced by orders issued by the Commission and, when these orders become final, through suits brought by the Department of Justice. The two agencies have been given concurrent jurisdiction in the enforcement of the Clayton Act. The procedures that they follow have been specified, in part, by statute and developed, in part, through administrative experience.

MAINTAINING COMPETITION THROUGH LITIGATION

When the Sherman Act is violated, it is expected that a public prosecutor or a private plaintiff will bring suit, asking that penalties be imposed, remedies provided, or payment of damages required. The role played by the private suit, however, is a supporting one. Enforcement must be sought, in the main, through cases brought by the government. The success or failure of enforcement will depend, therefore, upon the character of the organization established to detect and prosecute violations, the adequacy with which it is staffed and financed, the policies it adopts, and the procedures it employs. The outcome of enforcement will depend, too, upon the nature of the processes of litigation and the effectiveness of the penalties and remedies to which they lead.

The Antitrust Division

Until 1903 no separate staff was set up in the Department of Justice to enforce the Sherman Act. In that year an Antitrust Division was established and an Assistant Attorney General was placed in charge. The Division is now required by Congress to enforce some 40 laws and also to enforce the orders issued by a number of administrative agencies. Its principal function, however, is the enforcement of the Sherman Act.

The sums appropriated by Congress for this purpose have always been small. For the first 13 years, no separate appropriation was made, the work being undertaken by the Department of Justice as a part of its general activities. After the Antitrust Division was established, its annual appropriation ran around $100,000 until 1908, below $300,000 until 1935, and under $800,000 through 1939. The figure did not reach $1,000,000 for 50 years. Then it rose, to $1,300,000 in 1940, to $2,300,000 in 1942, and to $3,400,000 in 1949. It stood at $8,350,000 in 1969. But it is still small when compared with the character of the Division's responsibility, with the sums spent by defendants in antitrust suits, and with those spent by the government on less important activities. Since a single suit may cost anywhere from $100,000 to $500,000, the modest size of the Division's appropriation has seriously limited the number that could be brought. In some years, curiously enough, these appropriations have been surpassed by fines collected from violators.

The size of the Division's appropriation has been reflected in the size of its staff. Under Theodore Roosevelt, it had seven lawyers. Under Woodrow Wilson, it had 18. Under Harding, Coolidge, and Hoover, it had 25. It was not until 1939 that the number reached 200, not until 1949 that it approached 300. The Division had a staff of about 275 lawyers and 25 economists in 1969. This was still a microscopic figure in the federal bureaucracy. Counsel for the government in antitrust cases have usually found themselves outnumbered by counsel for the defense. In the Hartford-Empire case the Antitrust Division had 5 lawyers and the defendants 30. In the Madison oil case, the respective numbers were 5 and 103. In 1969, the salary range for antitrust lawyers was between $10,000 and $30,000. Counsel for the defense might well get 10 times more than this. As a result, perhaps, the rate of turnover in the Division has been high. From 1903 to 1969, moreover, there were 33 assistant attorneys general in charge of antitrust, an average of one for each two years. Even when a national administration has undertaken vigorously to enforce the law, it has been handicapped by paltry appropriations, scanty staffs, low pay, rapid turnover, and shifting leadership.

Enforcement Policy

Vigorous enforcement has not always been administration policy. Harrison, Cleveland, and McKinley showed little interest in the law. In nearly three years remaining in Harrison's term only seven cases were brought. In Cleveland's second term there were only eight. Under McKinley there were only three. Initiative and leadership in enforcement were taken for the first time by Theodore Roosevelt, who came to be pictured by cartoonists as wielding the Big Stick of antitrust. Roosevelt started 44 suits in his two terms. Taft started 90 in one. Wilson also started 90; his good beginning was interrupted by World War I. Under three years of Harding there were 50 cases, under five years of Coolidge 83, under four years of Hoover only 38; during these administrations, according to Charles Stevenson, head of an industrial engineering firm in New York, "industry enjoyed, to all intents and purposes, a moratorium from the Sherman Act, and, through the more or less effective trade associations which were developed in most of our industries, competition was, to a very considerable extent, controlled. The Department of Justice acted with great restraint and intelligence and only enforced the Sherman Act against those industries who violated the laws in a flagrant and unreasonable manner."[1] Up to the late thirties, says Corwin D. Edwards, "prosecutions were merely symbolic in character. In any one year, from half a dozen to a dozen instances of law violation were arbitrarily selected for investigation and trial. . . . With all available resources committed . . . the prosecution of a few lawbreakers became in effect a guarantee of immunity to the rest."[2] This has been described by Paul T. Homan as " 'token' or 'ritual' enforcement, a system of 'selective justice' in which it is hoped a few 'examples' will have a sufficiently deterring effect."[3]

As a part of the New Deal, inaugurated under Franklin D. Roosevelt at the depth of the Great Depression in 1933, the antitrust laws were suspended and agreements to restrain trade were given enthusiastic approval as a means of promoting industrial recovery.[4] In 1935, however, the National Industrial Recovery Act was found to be unconstitutional and, in 1937, the administration reversed its policy, proceeding with equal enthusiasm to the vigorous enforcement of antitrust. This campaign was carried forward by Thurman Arnold, who served as Assistant Attorney General from 1938 to 1943. The new lease on life which Arnold gave to the Antitrust Division was carried over into later years. By 1969, more than 2,000 suits had been brought by the Department of Justice under the Sherman and Clayton Acts. But of these, less than 500 had been instituted during the first 50 years, and more than 1,500 during the last 30. Enforcement, on a major scale, is a phenomenon of recent times.

With the advent of the Eisenhower administration, there was some speculation that enforcement might be cut back to the level of earlier days, but this did not prove to be the case. A committee of lawyers and economists appointed to advise the Attorney General on antitrust policy brought in a report in which the existing trend of enforcement and interpretation was generally approved. The number of cases initiated by the Antitrust Division rose from 29 in 1953 to 90 in 1960. Approval was denied for the proposed merger of Bethlehem Steel and Youngstown Sheet and Tube. The large electrical manufacturing companies were convicted of criminal conspiracy. The du Pont company was ordered to relinquish its control of General Motors.

At the beginning of the Kennedy administration, after the President had publicly chided the steel industry for raising its prices, it was said that the Department of Justice would let up on antitrust prosecutions in order to mollify big business. But 92 cases, a record high, were brought in 1962. Real progress

---

1 / Quoted by Corwin D. Edwards in *American Economic Review,* Vol. XXX suppl. (1940), p. 167.

2 / Corwin D. Edwards, *Maintaining Competition* (New York: McGraw-Hill Book Co., 1949), p. 293.

3 / Paul T. Homan, "Notes on the Antitrust Law Policy," in *Readings in the Social Control of Industry,* ed. Edgar M. Hoover, Jr., and Joel Dean (Homewood, Ill.: Richard D. Irwin, Inc., 1942), pp. 226-62, esp. p. 247.

4 / This experience will be discussed in Chapter 28.

was made on the enforcement of the antimerger law. Early in the Johnson administration, too, it was rumored that antitrust officials had been instructed to take a friendlier attitude toward business. In 1965, the President put Donald F. Turner, Professor of Law at Harvard University, in charge of the Antitrust Division. During Professor Turner's tenure, the number of cases instituted ran around 50 per year. Suits were brought, as before, against anticompetitive agreements. But increasing emphasis was placed, in prosecuting restrictive practices and in attacking mergers, on analyses of their economic effects. The Division concerned itself with such novel problems as reciprocal dealing and the significance of large expenditures on advertising as barriers to market entry. It developed a set of guidelines to govern its enforcement of the antimerger law. It favored civil rather than criminal action and sought, where possible, to effect settlements without resorting to litigation. In the view of enthusiastic trustbusters, Professor Turner's administration was too soft. In the view of legal scholars, he deserved high credit for introducing economic rationality into the body of the law.

With the advent of the Nixon Administration in 1969, Richard W. McLaren, a lawyer long experienced in defending large corporations in antitrust suits, was made Assistant Attorney General for antitrust. It might have been supposed that this appointment signalled relaxation in enforcement of the law. But Mr. McLaren moved immediately to make it clear that this was not the case. With regard to mergers, in particular, he took a tougher line than had his predecessor, instituting a number of suits against combinations of large concerns and announcing that his Division would henceforth oppose the combination of any two companies among the largest 200 in manufacturing or the acquisition by any one of the top 200 of any firm that is a leader in its field. It thus appeared that antitrust enforcement, bipartisan since 1936, was to continue so.

Initiating Action

In most cases, the Antitrust Division takes action, not on its own initiative, but on the basis of complaints brought to it by a company's competitors or its customers. This procedure, obviously, has its limitations, since complaints are not received in cases where these groups have been intimidated or where all of those participating in an illegal arrangement are contented with the way it works. Nor does every complaint lead to the initiation of a suit. Some cases are dropped and others picked for prosecution. This choice is made by the lawyers on the staff of the Division; the economists do not participate. It may well turn on considerations other than the comparative economic significance of the cases at hand. In any case, enforcement is haphazard and sporadic rather than systematic and sustained.

Thurman Arnold's major contribution to antitrust procedure was the inauguration of industry-wide investigations leading to a series of related suits. One such program, covering restraints in urban housing, involved the simultaneous presentation of evidence to grand juries in eleven cities and the subsequent initiation of around a hundred suits against manufacturers and distributors of building materials, and general contractors, subcontractors, and labor unions in the building trades. Similar campaigns were directed against restraints among processors of foodstuffs, holders of patents, and participants in international cartels. This procedure made for comprehensive and systematic enforcement. But it did not become the general rule.

Proposed mergers are sometimes brought to the attention of the Antitrust Division when the companies concerned ask whether the mergers would be legal under the Celler-Kefauver Act. They are discovered more frequently through stockholder inquiries, investment brochures, and stories in trade journals and in the financial press. But a third of the mergers examined by the Division had been consummated before they were discovered or before its investigation was complete. A succession of bills introduced in Congress would have required concerns proposing a merger, where the combined assets would exceed $10,000,000, to notify the Division and the Federal Trade Commission and then wait 60 days before putting their plans into effect. None of them was passed. In 1969, however, the Commission, acting under its general powers of investigation, issued an order requiring any two companies planning to merge, where their combined assets exceeded $250,000,000, and any company with such assets planning to acquire a company with assets of $10,000,000 or more, to report to the Commission and to wait for 60 days before proceeding with its plans. By facilitating preventive action, this requirement should make for better enforcement of the law.

Preparing a Case

The Division must accumulate a convincing body of evidence if it is to win a case. But it has no investigators of its own. For this purpose it is dependent on the Federal Bureau of Investigation. When a case is pending, it submits a written memorandum to the FBI, outlining the information that is sought. The Bureau, following its usual routine, gathers the data through its local agents, none of whom is trained to meet the particular requirements of antitrust. The resulting materials are then assembled and forwarded to the Division in a written report. As a method of industrial research, and even as mere detective work, the procedure leaves something to be desired. As Wallace and Douglas have put it: "The clean-cut lads of the F.B.I. deserve the respect and admiration of the country. But when they are sent out . . . to find evidence of a price-fixing conspiracy, they are likely to return empty handed. The reason is that their innocent routine is to search business files for evidence which is usually not there. Even if the evidence had once been there, counsel would almost surely have made management aware of its risky significance."[5] Files may have been stripped, witnesses silenced, and evidence destroyed. To piece a case together

5 / Robert A. Wallace and Paul H. Douglas, "Antitrust Policies and the New Attack on the Federal Trade Commission," *University of Chicago Law Review,* Summer, 1952, p. 18. See also, Committee on Small Business, *Antitrust Law Enforcement,* pp. 56-59.

from the fragments that remain may well require a specialization of training and coordination of effort that the FBI does not provide.

If a case appears to have some substance, litigation may be started and further evidence obtained once it is under way. When a criminal suit has been taken to a grand jury, books and records can be subpoenaed and witnesses compelled to testify. In a civil suit, however, until recently, evidence could not be demanded until a complaint had been filed in court. Criminal indictments were therefore sought as a means of obtaining information in cases where civil actions would otherwise have sufficed. To correct this situation, Congress enacted a law in 1962 empowering the Attorney General to issue civil investigative demands, enforceable by the courts, requiring companies under investigation to make documentary material available. It is no longer necessary for the Antitrust Division to sue first and investigate afterward.

The Case at Law

The prosecutor, in a criminal case, must first go before a grand jury and convince it that evidence pointing toward the guilt of the defendants is sufficient to justify a trial. If he succeeds in doing so, an indictment will be returned and the case will be set for trial before a jury in a district court. At this stage, if the defendants decide that they will not contest the suit, they may enter a plea of *nolo contendere,* involving no admission of their guilt. If the court accepts the plea, however, criminal penalties may be imposed. The government may drop a case, at any stage of the proceedings, by entering a *nolle prosequi.* In the absence of such actions, the case will go on trial.

It is by no means easy to win an antitrust suit. In a civil action guilt must be established by a preponderance of evidence. In a criminal suit it must be proven beyond a reasonable doubt. The evidence, however, may be largely circumstantial; documentary proof may be wanting and witnesses reluctant to testify. The complexities of business organization and practice may be difficult for the prosecution to explain and for the jury and the judge to understand. The defendants may be eminently respectable, members of the best clubs, active in charitable enterprises, and pillars of the church. The course of conduct of which they are accused may appear to be quite normal. The jury may hesitate to convict, the judge to provide appropriate remedies. A trial, moreover, may drag on for many months. The trial of the Aluminum Company in the District Court ran from June 1, 1938, to August 14, 1940. The judge, when asked on a second occasion by the same attorney to grant a day's adjournment at the birth of a child, warned that such favors were not to be expected when grandchildren began to come along.

Litigation has its shortcomings as an instrument of public policy. The matter at stake in a trial is the behavior of an industry in the future. The matter discussed is the evidence of its wrongdoing in the past. The economic staff of the Antitrust Division is not invited to participate in defining the issues in a case, but only in preparing the evidence that may help to win a decision. Whatever the issues, the prosecution must seek a conviction, the defense an acquittal. And the outcome will be influenced by the technicalities of the law. The procedure has been best described by Hamilton and Till:

It brings to the settlement of questions of economic order the processes, hazards, confusions, evasions, circumlocutions, delays, of the legal folkways. . . . Persons competent in the habits of industry must give way to those skilled in the techniques of legal combat. . . . The opposing champions are well versed in demurrer, interlocutory motion, the tactics of seeking or avoiding a general engagement. They are less at home with overhead cost, Pittsburgh-plus, the fiction of the quoted price. . . . The staging of the question as an adversary proceeding sets lawyer against lawyer. . . . Every move, every witness, every fact, every document becomes a counter in a legal game. "The record" has come to do vicarious duty for an analysis of the industry in operation; and every item, favorable to one side, can win admission only against the heavy cross-fire of the other. Every procedural device which may arrest or speed action, flank or snipe the verbal minions of the enemy, color the conduct on parade with innocence or guilt is called into play. . . . Again and again the attorney and the witness raise their antiphonal voices; the counsel for the adverse party chants the approved formula "incompetent, irrelevant, and immaterial"; the judge from the loft above interjects a responsive "sustained" or "overruled"; and the loser, who intends to fight another day, comes in dramatically with "exception". . . . It takes the final summing up of the lawyers to bring the jury back to the dominant legal issue. And somehow antitrust as an instrument of public policy has gotten lost in the scuffle.[6]

The case presents peculiar difficulties to the judge:

He is expected to have a critical mastery of corporate finance, marketing practice, industrial structure; to have a sound grasp of physics, chemistry, electrodynamics, in fact the fundamentals of all the mechanical arts. . . . In a word, he must be alike omnicompetent in law and industry—an expert in the multiplex of affairs and disciplines which converge upon the case. . . . In the face of his own ordeal, his tendency is to retire somewhat from the domain of industrial reality and to fortify his judicial performance with a meticulous observance of the technicalities. . . . Even the judge himself becomes an obstacle to bringing into sharp relief the pattern of the industry and its points of restraint.[7]

In preparing his opinion, the judge makes no investigation of his own, but chooses among the alternatives presented to him by counsel for the prosecution and counsel for the defense. The record that he must study may be voluminous. In the A&P case, the judge was confronted with 45,000 pages of testimony and

6 / Walton Hamilton and Irene Till, *Antitrust in Action,* T.N.E.C. Monograph No. 16 (Washington, D.C.: Government Printing Office, 1940), pp. 59-62.
7 / *Ibid.,* pp. 71-72.

7,000 exhibits; in the Aluminum case with 58,000 pages of testimony and 15,000 pages of documents. From such a mass of materials, the judge must make his findings of fact and his application of the law to these facts. To work his way through the complexities of the arrangements involved, he must take time. In the Sugar Institute case, the judge spent 14 months writing a 50-page finding of facts and a 178-page opinion.[8]

Judges have long been supplied with law clerks to assist them in working through the legal issues presented by a case. But it was not until 1945 that they were authorized, by a modification in the rules of judicial procedure, to employ economists as expert witnesses to aid in analyzing the facts. The practice was first adopted when Judge Charles E. Wyzanski, Jr., of the District Court in Boston engaged Carl Kaysen to work on the United Shoe Machinery case. But it has not commended itself, in general, to the bench, since it affords neither adversary an opportunity to present arguments to counter the advice which is given to the judge in private, and this runs counter to legal tradition.

An appeal from the decision of a lower court is taken on the basis of error, and error is concerned exclusively with points of law. In the words of Hamilton and Till, "The jurists who must correct error—and are presumed not to err themselves—live in a rarified atmosphere where they never see a litigant, observe a witness, or smell the sweat and blood of battle. In their forum quarreling persons are the abstract 'appellant' and 'appellee'; industrial problems, legal contentions; actuality, verbal currency."[9] Here, again, the highly developed skills that are brought to bear on questions of economic policy are those, not of economic analysis, but of the law.

Between the date when an offense occurs and the date when the last court has spoken its final word there may be a span of many years. There is delay until a suit is brought, delay until a decision is rendered by a District Court, delay until it has been reviewed by a Court of Appeals, further delay until the case has been rejected or reviewed by the Supreme Court, and still further delay until the District Court has prepared a remedy. On the average, it has taken 5½ years to complete a litigated antitrust case.[10] The U.S. Steel Corporation was formed in 1901, sued in 1912, and finally acquitted in 1920. The proceeding against the Aluminum Company was extended for 20 years. While its legality is discussed at leisure, monopoly may persist. And when, at long last, it is found unlawful, it may have assumed another guise.

The Private Suit

The laws are also enforced through private suits. Under the Sherman Act, persons injured by violations may sue for threefold damages. Under Section 16 of the Clayton Act, injunctive relief may also be granted to plaintiffs in private

8 / Mark S. Massel, *Competition and Monopoly* (Washington, D.C.: Brookings Institution, 1962), p. 145.

9 / Hamilton and Till, *op. cit.,* p. 73.

10 / Massel, *op. cit.,* p. 123.

suits. In Section 5 of the Clayton Act, moreover, the position of such plaintiffs was greatly strengthened by permitting them to introduce, as prima facie evidence, decisions handed down by the courts in criminal and civil cases brought against the same defendants by the government. Defeat in public cases may thus lead to further penalties by inviting the initiation of private suits for triple damages.

The possible award of threefold damages in private suits was designed, not only to punish violators of the law, but also to encourage those who were injured to sue. This encouragement was needed to overcome the obstacles to starting such a suit. Litigation is costly; the resources of the plaintiff may be small and those of the defendant large; to start a suit involves assumption of a serious risk. The burden of proof, moreover, is heavy. The plaintiff must establish (1) that the antitrust laws have been violated, (2) that the violation has caused him injury, and (3) that the injury has amounted to a certain sum. As prima facie evidence on the first point, he may present the decision of a court in a case brought by the government. But the government moves slowly. And where, as in the usual case, it accepts a consent decree or a plea of *nolo contendere*, there is no admission or finding of guilt.

During the first 50 years of the Sherman Act, there were only three or four private suits per year. The plaintiffs succeeded, moreover, in less than a tenth of these. In later years, however, such suits came to be more important. In 1947, a Chicago movie exhibitor collected $360,000 in damages from a movie distributor who refused to lease him first-run films. Profiting by this example, a number of other exhibitors sued to collect similar damages. Attorneys for plaintiffs found such litigation to be lucrative. Business concerns and agencies of state and local governments brought increasing numbers of suits. From 1957 through 1961, there were 1,200; in 1962 and 1963, there were nearly 2,400. Plaintiffs, moreover, have been successful, winning two fifths of their cases, with damages running into millions of dollars in a single case. Such suits, however, can supplement, but not supplant, the efforts of enforcement agencies. They are brought on the initiative of private litigants. They cannot be expected to assure the comprehensiveness and the continuity that are required in the administration of the law.[11]

Criminal Penalties

If the defendants in a criminal case are acquitted, the case is closed. If they are convicted, they may appeal. Again, if the Court of Appeals acquits them, the case is closed. If it upholds the lower court, they may petition the Supreme Court for review. This petition may be granted or denied. It is only when the

11 / Until 1957, the federal government was not permitted to sue for damages when injured, as a purchaser, by conspiracies or combinations in restraint of trade, the Supreme Court holding that the government was not a "person" within the meaning of the section of law that authorizes "any person" to bring suit for damages. In 1955, however, Congress amended the Clayton Act to permit the government to sue for simple (rather than threefold) damages.

final court to hear the case has spoken that criminal penalties may be imposed.

The penalties originally provided in the Sherman Act applied to individuals and to corporations found guilty of violating the law. But the directors and officers of guilty corporations could not be punished unless their personal guilt was proved. In Section 14 of the Clayton Act, however, Congress fixed responsibility for the conduct of a corporation on its directors and officers and extended to them the penalties of fine or imprisonment or both. The fine that might be imposed under the Sherman Act was originally limited to $5,000, but this figure was raised to $50,000 by Congress in 1955. Fines running into the hundreds of thousands have been collected, however, in a single case. Even before 1955, the legal penalty could be exacted under each of the counts in an indictment (monopolizing, attempting to monopolize, conspiring, and restraining trade) and imposed on each of the defendants in a suit, i.e. on a trade association, on every company that belongs to the association, and on each of their directors and officers.[12]

Businessmen who wish to avoid the imposition of these penalties may enter into consultation with the Department of Justice, presenting their plans for proposed combinations or for the adoption of particular practices. If it appears, upon full disclosure, that nothing illegal is involved, the Department may commit itself not to bring criminal proceedings against such parties, at a later date, for participation in the activities described. But it will reserve the right to take civil action if competition should subsequently be restrained.

When the government won a criminal suit, the penalties that were applied, until recently, could not, in themselves, have much force as a deterrent. Imprisonment was rare; the fines imposed were usually insignificant. From 1890 until 1958, defendants sentenced to prison numbered 206. But, of the first 198 of them, 108 were members of the labor unions, 75 were petty racketeers, 8 were wartime spies, and only 7 were businessmen. In the latter cases, moreover, the sentences were suspended. No important industrialist had ever spent a day in jail for violation of the Sherman Act. The typical outcome of a criminal suit had been a plea of *nolo contendere* followed by a small fine. The average fine levied on corporations from 1955 to 1965 was only $12,778; the average fine on individuals was only $3,226.[13] The total of all the fines imposed on the defendants in a particular case might be much higher, the figure having reached $105,000 in the case of the Aluminum Company, $175,000 in the case of the A&P, and $312,000 in that involving the three largest manufacturers of cigarettes. But such penalties became insignificant when compared with earnings of

12 / The Sherman Act also provided for seizure, in the course of transport, of the goods involved in an illegal conspiracy and their forfeiture to the United States. Further penalties have been provided in other acts: denial of passage through the Panama Canal, forfeiture of certain land and mineral rights, and revocation of broadcasting licenses. Violation of the antitrust laws by patentees and trademark owners has also been made a defense available to persons against whom the violators might bring infringement suits.

13 / James M. Clabault and John F. Burton, Jr., *Sherman Act Indictments*, 1955-65 (New York: Federal Legal Publications, Inc., 1966) p. 104.

the companies concerned. Antitrust fines from 1936 to 1948, taken as a percentage of net profits in 1948, amounted to .001 percent for General Motors, .017 percent for du Pont, .037 percent for Alcoa, and .113 percent for A&P.[14]

The real punishment in a criminal case was to be found less in the sentence imposed by the court than in the cost of the defense and in the unfavorable publicity attending an indictment and a trial. An antitrust suit may have been derided by a powerful defendant. But it could not be shrugged off as unimportant, since it might impair the good will of an enterprise and be damaging to its prestige. And this, in itself, may have deterred some of those who otherwise would have broken the law.

In 1959 a district judge in Ohio sentenced four officers of companies convicted of restraining trade in hand tools to 90 days in jail.[15] Following this precedent in 1960, a judge in Pennsylvania imposed 30-day sentences on 31 of the defendants in the electrical manufacturing conspiracy described in Chapter 4. Twenty-four of the sentences were suspended, but seven officials, including two vice presidents and a division general manager of General Electric and a vice president and a division sales manager of Westinghouse, served time in jail. The fines imposed on the corporate and individual defendants in this case amounted to $1,924,500. But, more than this, the conviction gave rise to 1,900 treble damage suits, among them one by Consolidated Edison of New York for $100 million and one by Commonwealth Edison of Chicago for $75 million. In the first suit to go to trial, Philadelphia Electric proved damages of $9,600,000 and was awarded $28,800,000. The manufacturers then undertook to settle the remaining cases out of court. The ultimate cost of the antitrust violation was estimated at $600 million.[16] The impact of this penalty was softened by the fact that the Treasury permitted the companies (but not the individuals) to deduct their payments from gross income in determining net income for the purpose of the income tax, with the effect that roughly half of the payments could be met with money that would otherwise have gone to the government. But the remaining cost would still be around $300 million. It could no longer be said that the penalty for violating the antitrust laws was negligible.

But a criminal penalty, whatever its severity, does not provide a remedy. Defendants may be fined but an industry's structure and its practices left unchanged. In its case against the major cigarette companies, decided by the Supreme Court in 1946, the government won a sweeping victory, and heavy fines were imposed. But the companies were left in predominant possession of the market, and their methods of buying tobacco and selling cigarettes were not perceptibly disturbed. The suit, in the opinion of William H. Nicholls, who has analyzed its outcome, may have brought somewhat lower cigarette prices in the short run. But market sharing and price leadership still appeared to be the

14 / *Hearings before the Committee on the Judiciary, House of Representatives, on H.R. 6679* (81st Cong., 2d Sess.), pp. 13, 38.

15 / *U.S.* v. *McDonough Co.,* 1959 Trade Cases 69482 at 75887.

16 / *Business Week,* October 14, 1967, p. 130.

rule.[17] If behavior that violates the law is to be corrected, civil remedies must be sought.

Injunctions and Decrees

The government may normally proceed against offenders by bringing a criminal suit or a civil suit or both. In the latter case, the two actions may be brought either simultaneously or successively. It is the purpose of a civil suit, not to deter violation by inflicting punishment, but to restore competitive conditions by providing remedies. Such a suit is not initiated through an indictment or tried before a jury. Whatever the decision in a lower court, the government as well as the defendants may appeal. The provision of remedies, however, is the duty of the lower courts. When the government's contentions are sustained, upon appeal, the case will be remanded to a district court. Here, after hearings in which the remedies proposed by the government are debated by both parties, the court will issue a decree.

Under the wording of the Sherman Act, violations of the law may be "enjoined or otherwise prohibited." The latitude afforded by the phrase "or otherwise prohibited" is wide. The Supreme Court has held, however, that the provisions of decrees must be limited to parties brought before the courts, must be related to their past offenses, must not be punitive in character, must not impose new duties on defendants, and must be reasonably specific in their terms. But it has also held that the effects of illegal behavior may be corrected, that the pattern of industrial organization may be changed, and that doubts concerning the proper content of decrees may be resolved in favor of the government. The discretion accorded to the courts is, therefore, broad.

The provisions contained in decrees are of two main types. Of these, the first is negative in character, enjoining offenders from taking certain actions that they had planned or admonishing them no longer to do things that they had previously done. An injunction may prevent a proposed merger. It may forbid the repetition of illegal acts, such as discriminating in prices or entering into exclusive or tying contracts. In this case, the guilty are not punished for their past misdeeds but are merely told to go and sin no more. Since the practices enjoined are already outlawed, it may be asked whether anything is gained through the issuance of a decree. The answer is that here, as elsewhere, the violators of an injunction may be adjudged guilty of contempt of court and punished by fine or imprisonment or both.

Injunctions are limited in scope and in effect. They apply only to the parties that are named and to the particular matters that are described. An injunction can forbid only those practices that have been found to violate the law. Although one firm has been ordered to abandon a practice, another may continue to use it until this firm, too, has been prosecuted and enjoined. Although one practice has been prohibited, another practice may be used to achieve the same result

17 / William H. Nicholls, *Price Policies in the Cigarette Industry* (Nashville: Vanderbilt University Press, 1951), chap. xxviii.

until another suit is brought and another injunction obtained. The rules that are issued by the courts cannot be taken as a general code to govern business conduct. They cannot anticipate wrongdoing and forbid it in advance.

Injunctions, however, have been effective in their application, case by case. They have been successful in breaking up restraints where markets have been controlled through artificial devices and contractual relationships. They have put an end, in many instances, to exclusive dealing, tying contracts, and discriminatory pricing, and have outlawed procedures through which identity of delivered prices has been obtained. They have gone far toward preventing the restrictive use of patent rights.

Injunctions can be effective, too, in preventing mergers, pending decisions as to their legality. The courts, however, have been sparing in their use of such orders. From 1953 through 1964, they granted the Antitrust Division only 13; in 1965, only one of the four it sought. The FTC was granted no antimerger injunctions until it won a case on appeal to the Supreme Court in 1966.[18]

Provisions of a second type in court decrees are positive in character, requiring that certain things be done. They may break the grip of a monopoly by compelling it to take such action as selling rather than leasing patented machines or granting patent licenses to competitors. They may order the abolition of a trade association, the liquidation of a holding company, the reorganization of a corporate combination, or the sale of controlling shares of stock.

Dissolution, Divorcement, and Divestiture

In markets that are shared by a few large firms, the restoration of effective competition may call for a rigorous application of the three D's of antitrust: dissolution, divorcement, and divestiture. These three measures are closely allied. Dissolution breaks up a business unit into several parts. Divorcement separates the units in a combination. Divestiture requires defendants to dispose of particular assets: either physical properties or stockholdings in other concerns. Whatever the legal form of action, each of them involves disintegration of a common enterprise.

Disintegration has been sought in a minority of suits. It had been ordered up to 1960 in less than a hundred cases. In most of these, moreover, the unit dissolved was not an industrial undertaking but a trade association or a common selling agency. The number of productive enterprises broken up was less than 30. The list includes, in the earlier years, a number of railroads, the oil, tobacco, and gunpowder trusts, the meat packing and stockyard companies, and concerns making corn products and photographic equipment and supplies. In 1932 General Electric and Westinghouse were ordered to relinquish their control of RCA. In 1943 the National Broadcasting Company was required to sell its Blue Network which became the foundation for the American Broadcasting Company. In 1944 the Pullman subsidiary that operated sleeping cars was separated

18 / *FTC* v. *Dean Foods Co.,* 384 U.S. 597.

from the one that manufactured them. In 1948, after several years of unsuccessful experimentation with milder methods of restoring competition to the motion picture industry, the large producers were divorced from the large exhibitors. In 1958, United Fruit accepted a consent decree requiring it to create, out of its assets, before 1970, a competitor capable of handling 35 percent of the bananas imported into the United States. In 1962, the Supreme Court ordered the largest divestiture in history when it ruled that the du Pont company, the family, and its corporations must dispose of their controlling shares in General Motors. Divestiture was also ordered, during the sixties, in a number of cases brought under the Celler-Kefauver Act. And in 1969, United Shoe Machinery agreed to dispose of half of its shoe-making equipment business, thus reducing its share of the market (formerly nine tenths) to a third.

The difficulties presented by dissolution, though great, are not insuperable. It is relatively easy to abolish a trade association or a common sales agency, difficult for one corporation to dispose of its stock in another, more difficult to liquidate a holding company, and even more difficult to divide a single corporation into several parts. In all but the first of these cases important property interests are involved. And in the latter ones, painstaking corporate reorganizations are required. But the problems involved are capable of solution, as has been shown by the experience of the Securities and Exchange Commission under the Public Utility Holding Company Act.[19]

In antitrust, however, what man hath joined together the courts may hesitate to put asunder. In the absence of flagrant abuse, they are loath to modify established rights of property. Unable to foresee the consequences of disintegration, they are reluctant to risk a possible impairment of efficiency. Where other remedies are available, therefore, they are usually preferred. The courts will turn to dissolution only as a last resort.

Consent Decrees

A civil suit may be concluded, before a court has rendered a decision, by the negotiation of an agreement between the defendants and the government. This agreement, with the approval of the court, will be embodied in a consent decree. Such decrees had been employed in other fields before 1890, but no provision was made in the Sherman Act for their use in settling antitrust suits. They were recognized by implication, however, when they were mentioned in the Clayton Act. The first consent decree in an antitrust case was accepted in 1906. At the present time, nine tenths of the civil suits started by the government are settled in this way.

Settlement by consent is initially proposed by counsel for the defense. The terms first offered are usually rejected by the Antitrust Division as inadequate. There follows a series of informal negotiations between the lawyers for the two

19 / See Chap. 15.

sides. In these negotiations, as in any case of bilateral bargaining, differences are gradually narrowed as proposals lead to counterproposals and these to counter-counterproposals until agreement is finally attained. The terms agreed upon will depend upon the bargaining power and skill of the antagonists. If the government's case is strong, it will get more in the decree; if weak, it will get less. It is given leverage, however, by the fact that a *nolle prosequi* in a pending criminal suit or a consent decree in the civil suit is desired by the defendants, since it involves no conviction of antitrust violation, thus depriving plaintiffs in possible private suits of prima facie evidence of guilt. The settlement resulting from the bargaining process is taken by each side as the best it can get. It is then accepted by a district court—usually without examination or questioning—and is issued in the same manner and with the same effect as any other court decree.

The method has much to commend it. It saves time and money. It takes less than half as long to negotiate a consent decree as it does to fight a case through the courts. Since 1954, moreover, the terms of many settlements have been negotiated before bringing suit and the costs of litigation have been spared. The method is more flexible than litigation. It permits decrees to be drafted in conformity with the peculiar characteristics of particular industries. It may go beyond the negative provisions of the law to shape affirmative remedies. It sometimes obtains acceptance for reforms more sweeping than those that would have been demanded by the courts.

But the method also has its dangers. The negotiations are conducted in private. No record of the proceedings is disclosed. If representatives of the government were to become corrupt or incompetent, offenders might be let off lightly without the facts becoming known. Approval by a court, in the absence of any basis for appraisal, affords no guarantee against abuse. Until recently, the terms of consent decrees were not revealed until they had been made effective. Then, if interested parties found them to be objectionable, it was too late to protest. Since 1961, however, proposed decrees are made public 30 days before they are taken to court and such parties are thus afforded an opportunity to present objections before they are put into effect.

The consent decree, depending on the manner of its use, may either strengthen or relax enforcement of the law. In 1959, the Antitrust Subcommittee of the House of Representatives issued a lengthy report on such decrees in which a majority of its members criticized as inadequate the terms of certain decrees accepted in the previous years. The majority recommended more sparing use of the procedure, complaining that it had weakened antitrust enforcement by depriving private plaintiffs of ammunition that they might have used in treble damage suits.

The formulation of antitrust decrees is the work of men trained in the law. The economists on the staff of the Antitrust Division do not participate. The contribution that they might make, from their special knowledge, to the reformation of business organization and practice is foregone. The remedies provided may therefore be less realistic than might otherwise have been the case. Here, as elsewhere, antitrust enforcement is a lawyer's show.

Policing the Courts' Decrees

Antitrust decrees are permanent. Their provisions may grow obsolete with the passage of time. But they remain in force unless a court terminates or modifies them at a defendant's request. In some cases, such as those necessitating the determination of royalties where patent licensing has been required, administration of a decree imposes on a court responsibility for continued regulation of an industry. In others, where dissolution or divestiture has been ordered, the government maintains its contact with the defendants until the decree is carried out. Usually, however, cases have been regarded as closed when the last court has spoken.

Antitrust decrees, throughout the years, have not been systematically enforced. The Antitrust Division has lacked the money and the staff to follow them up and check on the observance of their terms. Decrees may have been ignored, but no action has been taken until someone who was injured has complained. Up to 1970, only 34 defendants had been sued for contempt of court in cases involving violation of an antitrust decree. The Federal Trade Commission Act requires the Commission, upon request by the Attorney General, to report upon observance of such decrees. Until 1961, a report had been requested in only one case. In that year, the Attorney General asked the Commission to investigate the observance of 56 decrees, including all of those handed down in major cases since 1940. This was done. But no such request has been made since that time.

MAINTAINING COMPETITION THROUGH ADMINISTRATIVE PROCESSES

The judicial process as a method of maintaining competition has obvious weaknesses. It is cumbersome, inexpert, confusing, and frequently ineffective. It was not designed to serve as an instrument of industrial control. The proposal is therefore made, from time to time, that antitrust be removed from the arena of litigation and placed in the hands of an administrative agency, composed of men possessing an intimate knowledge of business, serving as impartial experts, and empowered to issue regulations, industry by industry, forbidding industrial combinations and business practices that would tend to restrain trade or promote monopoly. Such an agency could act speedily, skillfully, and flexibly. It would seek not to punish but to prevent. As a safeguard to business, its regulations would be subject to judicial review. But administrative rather than judicial processes would be adopted initially as being more appropriate to the nature of the task at hand.

The proposal is not a new one. Something of the sort is involved, of course, in the practice of giving advisory opinions and in the negotiation of consent decrees. But it is in the Federal Trade Commission that the closest approach to administrative enforcement of competition has been made.

Most of the cases that come before the FTC relate to the use of unfair methods or deceptive practices in competitive industries. The Commission, however, was given concurrent jurisdiction with the Department of Justice in enforcing the prohibitions against monopolistic devices contained in the Clayton Act. It has also proceeded against agreements to curtail output, divide markets, and fix prices, condemning them as unfair methods of competition within the meaning of Section 5 of the Trade Commission Act. Such agreements, of course, instead of being methods of competition, give evidence of failure to compete. But the Commission's authority to move against them has long been upheld, by implication, by the courts; [20] it was recognized explicitly in the decision handed down by the Supreme Court in the Cement case in 1948. [21] "The Commission," said the Court, "has jurisdiction to declare that conduct tending to restrain trade is an unfair method of competition even though the selfsame conduct may also violate the Sherman Act." The Commission has thus come to play an important part, not only in preventing the use of unfair methods, but also in maintaining competition itself.

The Federal Trade Commission

The Federal Trade Commission is an independent administrative agency composed of five commissioners who are appointed by the President, with the advice and consent of the Senate, for terms of seven years. No more than three of its members may belong to the same political party, and continuity is afforded by provision for overlapping terms. Until 1950 the Commission's chairmanship rotated among its members, each of them serving, in turn, for a single year. Since that time, the Chairman has been designated by the President and has been made responsible for administration of the Commission's activities.

The Commission's functions include research and the publication of reports, promotion of compliance, investigation of unfair methods of competition, deceptive practices, monopolistic devices, and agreements in restraint of trade, and prosecution of those who violate the law. In addition to its duties under the Clayton and Trade Commission Acts, the Commission administers the antitrust exemption granted to export trade associations under the Webb-Pomerene Act of 1918; polices the advertising of foods, drugs, and cosmetics under the Wheeler-Lea Act of 1938; and enforces the Wool Products Labeling Act of 1939, the Fur Products Labeling Act of 1951, the Flammable Fabrics Act of 1953, the Textile Fiber Products Identification Act of 1958, and the Fair Packaging and Labeling Act of 1966.

As first envisaged, the Commission was to have been a vigorous agency, composed of experts, equipped with economic and legal staffs, given broad powers to investigate and report on business organization and practices, and authorized to issue orders that would have the force of law. It was to bring the skill of the

20 / *FTC* v. *Pacific States Paper Trade Assn.*, 273 U.S. 52 (1927).
21 / *FTC* v. *Cement Institute*, 333 U.S. 683.

specialist and the flexibility of the administrative process to the solution of the problems of monopoly. It was to explore the frontiers of legality and to break new ground in the development of policy.

After more than 50 years, these hopes are far from being realized. It is true that the Commission has embarked, from time to time, upon campaigns against powerful antagonists. It conducted a crusade against basing point pricing in the cement and steel industries. It has attacked mergers in a number of cases involving large concerns. It has sought to force the manufacturers of cigarettes to warn smokers that the habit endangers their health. But apart from such sporadic undertakings, the agency has occupied itself with trivia, devoting its energies, in the main, to inconsequential cases of misbranding and deceptive advertising in petty trade where no problem of monopoly has been involved. Instead of taking vigorous action, the Commission has functioned passively, as if it were a court, waiting for outsiders to bring complaints. Its procedures have been clumsy and time consuming. Cases have lingered on its docket for years. The initiative, informality, and dispatch supposedly inherent in the administrative process have not as yet been seen.

Much of the responsibility for these shortcomings can be laid at the doors of Congress. The appropriations made for the work of the Commission ran around $500,000 a year until 1918, around $1 million until 1930, reaching $2 million in 1935 and $3 million in 1949. At the end of fiscal 1950, the agency had only 650 employees, with fewer than 300 lawyers, less than 100 of them engaged in antimonopoly work. In one case, where the respondents were represented by 102 law firms, the Commission itself was represented by one principal attorney and two part-time assistants. Congress thus expected the FTC to keep watch on American business with the aid of a corporal's guard.

The White House was equally indifferent. No sooner had the Commission been established, under Woodrow Wilson, than the attention of the administration was diverted by World War I. The Harding, Coolidge, and Hoover administrations were unsympathetic. William E. Humphrey, appointed by President Coolidge in 1925, dominated the Commission until 1933. The function of the agency, in his view, was less to police the activities of business than to promote its interest. Shortly after Franklin D. Roosevelt was inaugurated, he asked Commissioner Humphrey to resign. When the Commissioner refused to do so, the President removed him. Humphrey appealed to the courts and, after his death, the Supreme Court held that the President lacked the power of removal, save for the causes specified in the Trade Commission Act: "inefficiency, neglect of duty, or malfeasance in office." [22] Thereafter, the Roosevelt and Truman administrations showed little interest in the FTC. A succession of lame duck appointments set a pattern of mediocrity from which a full recovery was never made.

During the fifties and the sixties, the Commission was given more adequate

22 / *Humphrey's Executor* v. *U.S.*, 295 U.S. 602 (1935).

support by Congress, its budget standing at $15,000,000 in 1968 and its staff numbering more than 1,200. There were improvements, too, in its personnel. But independent appraisals published in 1969, like those appearing in earlier years, found the quality of its performance to be low. [23]

Investigations and Publicity

Quite apart from the inquiries made into the specific practices of particular concerns, in preparing cases for legal action, the Commission makes studies and publishes reports of a more general character. Section 6 of its basic statute gave the agency power (1) on its own initiative "to gather and compile information concerning, and to investigate from time to time the organization, business, conduct, practices, and management of any corporation engaged in commerce," to require such corporations to file annual and special reports, and to publish such information, "except trade secrets and names of customers, as it shall deem expedient in the public interest," and (2) "upon the direction of the President or either House of Congress to investigate and report the facts relating to any alleged violations of the antitrust Acts. . . ." The Commission, in the opinion of its sponsors, was to possess "full inquisitorial powers." Its investigatory function was held to be an integral part of the regulatory process. Business conduct was to be controlled, not only by legal action, but also, in Woodrow Wilson's phrase, by "pitiless publicity."

In its discharge of this responsibility, however, the Commission was handicapped for many years by adverse decisions of the courts. In 1924, when the FTC had asked the American Tobacco Company to provide it with information, in pursuance of a Senate resolution, and the company had declined to do so, the Commission asked that disclosure be enforced. But the Supreme Court refused, noting that the Senate had not alleged a violation of the law and holding that the guarantee against unreasonable searches and seizures contained in the Fourth Amendment to the Constitution would be abrogated if the government were to conduct "fishing expeditions into private papers on the possibility that they may disclose evidence of crime. [24] This limitation was removed, however, by a sweeping decision handed down by the Court in 1950. In this instance, the Commission had brought suit against the Morton Salt Company for refusing to heed its request for a report on the company's compliance with an order against illegal discrimination in price. The Commission's authority to demand information for any purpose within its duties was upheld by a unanimous court: "An administrative agency charged with seeing that the laws are enforced . . . does not depend upon a case or controversy for power to get evidence but can investi-

23 / See Edward F. Cox, Robert C. Fellmeth, and John E. Schultz, *The Nader Report on the Federal Trade Commission* (New York: Richard W. Baron, 1969) and the report to President Nixon by a panel of the American Bar Association, *New York Times,* September 16, 1969.

24 / *FTC* v. *American Tobacco Co.,* 264 U.S. 298, p. 306.

gate merely on suspicion that the law is being violated, or even just because it wants assurance that it is not." [25]

The studies made by the FTC, throughout the years, have been uneven in quality. Some of them have been superficial and apologetic; others have been searching and significant. Studies of general economic interest have dealt with national wealth and income, industrial concentration, the merger movement, interlocking directorates, and international cartels. Studies of business practices have covered open price reporting, delivered pricing, resale price maintenance, and the marketing of gasoline. Studies of particular industries have included among others: copper, motor vehicles, petroleum, pipelines, and electrical utilities. They have also included, in response to agricultural interests, industries from whom the farmers buy or to whom they sell: farm machinery, fertilizer, flour milling, meat packing, and the distribution of milk and dairy products, and fruits and vegetables. The information provided by such investigations has led to the enactment of a number of important statutes, the outstanding example being that of the 78-volume report on the electrical utility industry which laid the foundation for the Public Utility Holding Company Act of 1935.

Promotion of Voluntary Compliance

The FTC undertakes, in a variety of ways, to promote observance of the provisions of the Trade Commission Act. It approves codes of trade practice rules, promulgates trade regulation rules, issues industry guides, gives advisory opinions, and settles some cases by accepting assurances that objectionable practices will not be followed.

Formulation of trade practice rules was begun in 1919. Under this program, the FTC, in conference with the members of an industry, agrees upon a code enumerating practices that are held to be unfair. These codes add nothing to the content of the law. But they make its application explicit, call its provisions to attention, and thus, it is hoped, promote compliance. The rules are only advisory; compliance is not policed; violators are prosecuted only as complaints happen to come in.

Industry guides, which have been issued since 1958, deal with widespread deceptive practices. They set forth the views of the FTC on such matters as "bait advertising" (where the goods advertised are not really available for sale), "preticketing" (where fictitious prices are shown to give the appearance of a markdown), "free" deals, and other forms of deceptive pricing.

The trade practice codes have been supplemented, since 1962, by the promulgation of trade regulation rules. These rules identify practices which the FTC holds to be unlawful. They may apply to an industry as a whole or to a particular product or market. In preparing such a rule, the Commission first publishes a tentative draft and invites written comments, then may revise the draft and hold a public hearing, finally adopting the rule to become effective within 30

25 / *U.S.* v. *Morton Salt Co.,* 338 U.S. 632.

days. Thereafter, the rule serves notice that the Commission intends to act if it is violated.

Members of the FTC staff have long given advisory opinions on request. The Commission itself has done so since 1961. When a firm inquires about the legality of a practice it plans to adopt, the Commission tells whether it is likely to object. In doing so, it reserves its right to prosecute if the practice is later found to be objectionable. In this event, however, it promises not to make use of information obtained in this way without first giving the firm an opportunity to discontinue the practice in question.

In another procedure, adopted in 1963, the FTC gives a firm charged with infraction of the law an opportunity to dispose of the matter without formal action. If the Commission, in such an instance, has confidence in the firm's good faith, it accepts written assurance that a questioned practice has been discontinued and will not be resumed. Here, in the view of the Commission, informal settlement is quicker and cheaper than the issuance of formal orders and may be equal in effectiveness. Originally, this procedure was confined to minor offenses, such as deceptive advertising and the use of unfair methods in petty trade, but increasingly it has come to be employed in handling more serious matters, such as restrictive agreements and monopolistic practices. In neither case is violation of an assurance subject to any penalty. It may be questioned, therefore, whether the public interest is adequately protected by the mere existence of a written promise to behave.

Formal Procedures

A case may be brought to the attention of the FTC by a company's competitors, its suppliers, or its customers, or initiated by the Commission itself. Thousands of applications for complaints are filed each year. Each of them is investigated by members of the Commission's staff. Many cases will be dropped at this point. If, however, the Commission decides to proceed, it will prepare a formal document known as a complaint, naming as respondents the parties accused of violation and presenting the charges against them. It will then notify the offenders of its intention to file the complaint, sending them, without publicity, a copy of the proposed draft and giving them 10 days in which to say whether they want the action to be settled by consent. If they reply in the affirmative, an agreement must be negotiated and a consent order filed with the Commission within 30 days. Such an order does not imply an admission of guilt. It is thus analogous to an antitrust consent decree. The great majority of the cases brought before the FTC are now settled by a written assurance or a consent order.

If the offenders do not reply, or if negotiations for a consent order do not succeed, the Commission will make public its complaint and formal proceedings will ensue. The case will be heard, in the first instance, by a member of the Commission's staff known as a trial examiner. Action may be terminated at this stage by dismissal of the complaint or, if the respondents are found guilty, by the issuance of a cease and desist order directing them to abstain from their illegal acts. Such an order will be supported by findings of fact and conclusions as to points of law. It will become effective unless reviewed by the Commission on its own motion or upon appeal. In this case, a final hearing will be held before the Commission sitting as a court. After considering the briefs and the arguments presented, the Commission may dismiss the complaint, or it may issue a cease and desist order. This is the only mandatory action the Commission is empowered to take. Among the thousands of cases brought to the Commission's attention and the hundreds of cases investigated in any year, only a score will eventuate in an order to cease and desist.

A cease and desist order has serious weaknesses. It is purely negative in character. It can forbid a practice that is in itself illegal; it cannot forbid one that would otherwise be lawful on the ground that it is an integral part of an unlawful plan. It can tell respondents what they are not to do; it cannot require them to take affirmative action to rectify past wrongs or to afford assurance against future ones. The order is strictly limited in scope. It is confined to a particular offense by a particular offender in a particular case. It leaves the respondent free to offend in a different way, and leaves his neighbor free to offend in the same way, until an order has been issued in another case. No matter how often a practice has been condemned, further offenses cannot be punished until each procedural step has been taken again and again.

Enforcement of Commission Orders

The parties named in an order may carry it for review to a Circuit Court of Appeals. When an order is reviewed, the Commission's findings of fact, if supported by evidence, are conclusive. But the Commission may be reversed on points of law. The court may enter a decree affirming an order, requiring its modification, or setting it aside. Unless the Supreme Court grants a further review, an order becomes final when it has been affirmed by a Circuit Court. Violators of final orders can be prosecuted by the Department of Justice for contempt. But the law, as it was written in 1914, specified no penalty.

Until 1938, if an order were violated, the FTC had to ask a Court of Appeals for an injunction directing the violators to obey. It was thus necessary to prove a first violation before the Commission could issue an order, a second before it could obtain an injunction, and a third before the violator could be punished for contempt. In 1938, however, the Wheeler-Lea Act gave final effect to orders issued under the Federal Trade Commission Act if not appealed by respondents within 60 days. In 1959, Congress extended this provision to orders issued under the Clayton Act. In 1938, the law further provided that a fine, up to $5,000, might be imposed for each violation of a final order. In 1950, almost by inadvertance, this penalty was increased. In that year Congress repealed a federal tax on oleomargarine but sought to protect the dairy interests by requiring that margarine be plainly labeled, by compelling eating places that served the product to call this fact to the attention of their customers, and by making advertisement of margarine as a dairy product a deceptive practice within the meaning of the

Trade Commission Act. To enforce these provisions, it further provided that each day of continuing violation of any Commission order, when final, should constitute a separate offense for which a fine of $5,000 might be imposed. Nominally, the Commission's authority was greatly strengthened. It appeared that the parties named in an order must appeal it, obey it, or face the imposition of substantial penalties. In practice, this has not been the case.

The Commission has made little effort, over the years, to determine whether its orders have actually been observed. When issuing them, it has directed respondents to submit reports on their compliance within 60 or 90 days. Its power to require a second such report was upheld by the Supreme Court in the Morton Salt case in 1950, the defendants in this case subsequently being fined a total of $80,000 for refusing to make it. So reports have been received, examined, and filed. And when this has been done, it has been assumed that compliance has been obtained. The Commission has seldom moved to punish violations of its orders unless outsiders have brought renewed complaints. Criminal cases have rarely been brought. Fines have been the exception rather than the rule.

Political Vulnerability

Litigation, with all its faults, has one outstanding advantage: it is familiar, it is understood, it is clothed with prestige; as a consequence, it is accepted, if not with enthusiasm, at least with tolerance. The prosecutors and the courts are likely to be permitted to do their work. An administrative agency, by contrast, is peculiarly vulnerable to political attack. If inert, lenient, and ineffective, its placid existence may be undisturbed. But if vigorous in the performance of its duties, it will be headed for trouble. Its powers may be curtailed, its appropriation slashed, its administrators refused confirmation, its personnel subjected to persecution, its very existence jeopardized.

When the Supreme Court upheld its orders against basing point pricing, in 1948, the hue and cry was raised against the FTC. It was said that the Commission had exceeded its authority, that it had usurped the prerogatives of Congress, that it was embracing alien ideologies. The basing point lawyer who served as counsel for an investigating committee of the Senate demanded that the Commission be dismembered, its research functions being transferred to the Department of Commerce and its antitrust function to the Department of Justice.[26] The clock was thus to be turned back to the days before World War I. If it values survival, an agency thus attacked is likely to draw in its horns.

THE PROBLEM OF DUAL ENFORCEMENT

The authors of the Federal Trade Commission Act intended that the Commission should play a major role in the enforcement of antitrust. At the request of

---

26 / William Simon, "The Case against the Federal Trade Commission," *University of Chicago Law Review,* Vol. XIX, p. 297. See also Wallace and Douglas, *op. cit.*

the court, in an antitrust suit, the Commission was to serve as a master in chancery to prepare a tentative decree. At the request of the Attorney General, it was to draw up plans for the reorganization of illegal combinations. Neither of these functions has been performed, since the requests that were contemplated have not been forthcoming, and the Commission has been unwilling to enter where its presence has not been desired. The integration of the two agencies of enforcement, clearly contemplated by Congress, has not occurred. As a result, in the words of the House Committee on Small Business, "The antitrust program today is being conducted in a series of isolated skirmishes under two separate forces and two separate commands."[27]

Formal liaison was established between the Commission and the Antitrust Division in 1948, and one agency or the other now obtains priority in particular actions through a system of clearances. Overlapping is thus avoided, but omissions are not. Some offenders may escape entirely. Whether others are made the objects of cease and desist orders or criminal suits will depend upon the chance that FTC or Justice was the first to take a case. Each agency formulates its own program. If the two coincide, it is by accident rather than design. In the absence of central direction, it is not surprising if antitrust is characterized by inadequacy of coverage, errors in timing, and inconsistency of policy.

To correct this situation, three different solutions have been proposed. The first would combine the Antitrust Division and the FTC in a single agency under common direction. This was rejected by the Hoover Commission on governmental reorganization in 1949 on the ground that the two bodies complement one another: "As one went into temporary eclipse, the other kept alive the government's antitrust policy."[28] The second proposal would separate the jurisdiction of the two agencies, giving all conspiracy and combination cases to the Antitrust Division and all trade practice cases to the FTC. This proposal was rejected in 1955 by the Attorney General's National Committee on Antitrust Policy, who found the purposes of antitrust well served by the simultaneous use of the different types of proceedings available to the two agencies.[29] The third proposal calls for coordination of the work of the two bodies through closer cooperation at every level and continuous consultation at the top. This solution is obviously to be desired. But, given the folkways of bureaucracy, it is difficult to achieve.

---

27 / Committee on Small Business, *Antitrust Law Enforcement*, p. 70.

28 / Commission on Organization of the Executive Branch of the Government, *Task Force Report on Regulatory Commissions* (Washington, D.C.: Government Printing Office, 1949), p. 132.

29 / *Report of the Attorney General's National Committee to Study the Antitrust Laws*, pp. 372-73.

Chapter 6

COLLUSION AND OLIGOPOLY IN THE COURTS

The Sherman Act forbade restraint of trade, monopolization, and attempts to monopolize. The Clayton Act outlawed certain practices when their effect might be substantially to lessen competition or to tend toward monopoly. The Trade Commission Act condemned unfair methods of competition. But Congress did not attempt, in any of these laws, to define the terms it used. What is restraint of trade, monopoly, and competition? When is the lessening of competition substantial? When are methods of competition unfair? The answers to these questions were left to the courts. The problems that Congress faced were so diverse, complex, and ever changing that precision of language was not to be obtained. As a result the laws have meant whatever the judges in particular cases have decided they should mean. Judicial interpretation has thus been crucial in determining their application and effect.

The number of cases brought before the courts, involving monopoly and restraint of trade, runs well beyond two thousand; the number carried to the Supreme Court reaches several score. In reviewing the history of interpretation, it will be possible only to consider the leading decisions and to indicate the major trends. The cases will be presented, not chronologically, but according to the issues which they raise.

THE SCOPE OF THE LAW

The first case to come before the Supreme Court under the Sherman Act, the E. C. Knight case,[1] decided in 1895, involved the sugar trust. The American Sugar Refining Company, already controlling 65 percent of the sugar refined in the United States, had purchased the stock of the E. C. Knight Company and three other independent refiners, thus increasing its control to 98 percent. The government sought, not to break up the American company, but merely to compel it to dispose of its stock in the Knight company and the three other concerns. The Court admitted that American had a monopoly, but it decided against the government on the ground that the Act applied only to commerce, that sugar refining was manufacturing, and that manufacturing was not com-

---

1 / *U.S.* v. *E.C. Knight Co.,* 156 U.S. 1.

merce. This interpretation, had it stood, would have confined the law to firms engaged in moving goods from state to state. In decisions that shortly followed, however, though not overruled, it was consistently ignored. And in upholding the constitutionality of the National Labor Relations Act in 1937, the Court found explicitly that manufacturing involved commerce and thus fell within the scope of federal power.[2]

Groups Covered

Aside from its temporary aberration in the Knight case, the Court has given antitrust wide scope. In 1897, rejecting the contention that since common carriers were covered by the Interstate Commerce Act they were not included in the Sherman Act, it applied the law to railroads;[3] in 1917, extended it to ocean shipping companies.[4] In 1939, though association of farmers in agricultural cooperatives had been exempted by Congress in the Clayton Act and other measures, the Court held that an organization of milk producers was subject to the law when it joined with milk distributors, a milk wagon drivers union, and local health authorities to control the supply and fix the price of milk in Chicago.[5] In 1943, when a medical society in Washington, D.C., was charged with attempting to prevent the operation of a group health plan by expelling doctors from membership, denying them consultation privileges, and excluding them from hospitals, and the defendants argued that physicians, not being engaged in trade or commerce, were exempt, the Court ruled that restraint on the practice of medicine was restraint of trade.[6] In 1944, when fire insurance companies contended that insurance contracts were intrastate in character, that their business was regulated by state governments, and that decisions upholding such regulation exempted them from federal law, the Court found that documents, communications, and money were transmitted in interstate commerce and held that the Sherman Act applied.[7] In 1945, despite the exemption granted to export trade associations in the Webb-Pomerene Act of 1918, the Court held that it was illegal for such associations to participate in the restrictive activities of international cartels.[8] In the same year, rejecting the defense that transmission of news is not commerce, the Court applied the law to the Associated Press.[9] In 1950, it held the real estate brokerage business to be a trade within the meaning of the Sherman Act.[10] In 1951, it held that application of the law to a news-

2 / *NLRB* v. *Jones & Laughlin Steel Corp.*, 301 U.S. 1.
3 / *U.S.* v. *Trans-Missouri Freight Assn.*, 166 U.S. 290.
4 / *Thomsen* v. *Cayser*, 243 U.S. 66.
5 / *U.S.* v. *Borden Co.*, 308 U.S. 188.
6 / *U.S.* v. *American Medical Assn.*, 317 U.S. 519.
7 / *U.S.* v. *South-Eastern Underwriters Assn.*, 322 U.S. 533.
8 / *U.S. Alkali Export Assn.* v. *U.S.*, 325 U.S. 196.
9 / *U.S.* v. *Associated Press*, 326 U.S. 1.
10 / *U.S.* v. *National Assn. of Real Estate Boards*, 339 U.S. 485.

paper publisher did not violate the constitutional guarantee of freedom of the press.[11] And in 1954, it applied the law to building construction.[12]

In 1953, in a suit brought by a baseball player against a club in one of the major leagues, the Court was asked to rule on the applicability of the Sherman Act to organized baseball. In view of the commercial nature of the business, and in light of the precedents just cited, it might well have held the law to apply. But it refused to do so, reaffirming a decision made in 1922 in which it was held that baseball was not a trade.[13] This precedent, however, was not followed in subsequent decisions. In 1955, the law was applied to the legitimate theater[14] and to professional boxing;[15] in 1956 to professional basketball[16] and wrestling;[17] and in 1957 to professional football.[18] Justice Clark, speaking for the Court in the latter case, admitted that the distinction it had made between baseball and other sports might be regarded as "unrealistic, inconsistent, or illogical" and suggested that it be rectified by Congress. Bills for this have been introduced and hearings held, but no action has been taken.

It is principally in the case of labor that interpretation now limits the boundaries of antitrust. The legality of union activities in restraint of trade is to be considered in Chapter 30.

In many cases where judicial interpretation has brought particular groups within the scope of the law, Congress has subsequently exempted them. Rate agreements among shipping companies were legalized and brought under the authority of the United States Maritime Commission by the Shipping Act of 1916. Agreements among agricultural cooperatives, the processors, and the distributors of agricultural products, if approved by the Secretary of Agriculture, were authorized by the Agricultural Adjustment Act of 1933 and the Agricultural Marketing Agreements Act of 1937. Suits against insurance companies were suspended, under a Congressional moratorium, from 1945 to 1948, to give the states an opportunity to strengthen their regulation of insurance rates; following the enactment of more effective statutes, antitrust is now confined to the prosecution of boycotts and agreements preventing the filing of lower rates. Rate agreements among railroads were removed from the jurisdiction of the Antitrust Division and brought under the authority of the Interstate Commerce Commission by the Reed-Bulwinkle Act, passed over the veto of President

11 / *Lorain Journal Co.* v. *U.S.*, 342 U.S. 143.

12 / *U.S.* v. *Employing Plasterers' Assn.*, 347 U.S. 186.

13 / *Federal Baseball Club of Baltimore* v. *National League*, 259 U.S. 200 (1922); *Toolson* v. *New York Yankees*, 346 U.S. 356 (1953). On the economic and legal issues involved here, see "Monopsony in Manpower: Organized Baseball Meets the Antitrust Laws," *Yale Law Journal*, Vol. LXII (1953), pp. 576-639.

14 / *U.S.* v. *Shubert*, 348 U.S. 222.

15 / *U.S.* v. *International Boxing Club*, 348 U.S. 236.

16 / *Washington Professional Basketball Corp.* v. *National Basketballers' Assn.*, 147 F. Supp. 154.

17 / *U.S.* v. *National Wrestling Alliance*, 1956 Trade Cases Par. 68,507.

18 / *Radovich* v. *National Football League*, 352 U.S. 445.

Truman in 1948. The significance of such exemptions, legislative and judicial, will be considered in Chapter 28.

Activities Covered

Enforcement of the Sherman Act has not been handicapped by decisions preventing its application to particular forms of restrictive activity. In the second and third cases to come before the Supreme Court, the Act was applied to rate agreements,[19] and in the fourth to market sharing through collusive bidding.[20] In the fifth, the Northern Securities Company, created in 1901 to control the Northern Pacific and Great Northern Railways, challenged its application to the holding company device, contending that the company had been authorized by its New Jersey charter to hold the stock of other concerns, and that denial of such authority, by federal action, would interfere with the internal commerce of a state. In a 5 to 4 decision, handed down in 1904, the Court rejected this defense, declaring that the power of a state to grant a corporate charter does not override the power of the federal government to eliminate combinations that restrain trade.[21] In subsequent decisions, the Court applied the Act to outright consolidation,[22] to control through minority stockholdings,[23] and to trade association activities,[24] saying, in the American Tobacco case, that the policy of the law could not be frustrated "by resorting to any disguise or subterfuge of form." With respect to the Sherman Act, this position has been consistently maintained. But under the Clayton Act, as previously noted, the Court refused to break up combinations, in the Thatcher, Swift, and Arrow-Hart & Hegeman cases, holding the acquisition of assets to be legal, even though effected through the illegal acquisition of stock.[25] This loophole has now been closed by law.

Regions Covered

The Sherman Act applies only to trade "among the several states, or with foreign nations." But here, too, interpretation has been liberal. Restraints by local traders in intrastate markets have been held subject to the law where it could be shown that such restraints affected interstate trade.[26] Restraints initi-

---

19 / *U.S.* v. *Trans-Missouri Freight Assn.*, 166 U.S. 290 (1897); *U.S.* v. *Joint Traffic Assn.*, 171 U.S. 505 (1898).

20 / *U.S.* v. *Addyston Pipe & Steel Co.*, 175 U.S. 211 (1899).

21 / *Northern Securities Co.* v. *U.S.*, 193 U.S. 197.

22 / *U.S.* v. *American Tobacco Co.*, 221 U.S. 106 (1911).

23 / *U.S.* v. *Union Pacific Railway Co.*, 226 U.S. 61 (1912).

24 / *U.S.* v. *Eastern States Retail Lumber Assn.*, 234 U.S. 600 (1914).

25 / *Thatcher Mfg. Co.* v. *FTC* and *Swift & Co.* v. *FTC*, 272 U.S. 554 (1926); *Arrow-Hart & Hegeman Electric Co.* v. *FTC*, 291 U.S. 587 (1934). See above, p. 56.

26 / *Mandeville Island Farms* v. *American Crystal Sugar Co.*, 334 U.S. 219 (1948); *U.S.* v. *Employing Lathers Assn. of Chicago*, 347 U.S. 198 (1954).

ated or carried out in other countries have also been held liable where they have affected the nation's foreign trade. Thus, when a number of American companies undertook, through a purchasing agent in Mexico, to monopolize the shipment of sisal into this country, they affected the import trade of the United States.[27] When a number of American concerns combined to set up joint subsidiaries abroad, they curtailed American exports.[28] And when, on various occasions, American companies entered into cartel agreements with foreign companies, sharing world markets, they cut both imports from the other countries involved and exports to the markets assigned to them.[29] In some cases, moreover, the law has been applied not only to the American participants but also to their foreign partners in international cartels. Where foreign companies carry on activities outside the boundaries of the United States, they are beyond its jurisdiction. But where they do business and own property in this country, they can be held subject to its laws.

THE RULE OF REASON

The first word in the Sherman Act applies the law to *every* contract, combination, and conspiracy in restraint of trade. If interpreted strictly, the Act might thus be held to prohibit an agreement between firms controlling an insignificant share of a market, to prevent one small competitor from merging with another, and even to forbid normal contractual relationships. It is obvious that the Act cannot be so interpreted. The rule against restraint of trade was not so interpreted at common law.

The common law distinguished between ancillary and nonancillary restraints. An ancillary restraint is incidental to a legal purpose; it may occur, for instance, when a person selling a business, a partner withdrawing from it, or an employee leaving it undertakes to preserve its value by refraining from competition with its purchaser, a remaining partner, or a former employer. Here the courts came to apply a rule of reason, enforcing such restrictions when they were limited in duration and extent, and refusing to do so when they were not. Nonancillary restraints, on the other hand, are those suppressing competition in a market as a whole. And here, though some American courts followed English precedents in applying a rule of reason, more of them did not.

In the earliest cases brought before the Supreme Court under the Sherman Act, it was argued that the rule of reason should apply. For many years, however, this contention was rejected by the Court. In a decision handed down in the Trans-Missouri case in 1897, Justice Peckham held that Congress had not intended merely to give statutory effect to common-law precedents and found,

27 / *U.S.* v. *Sisal Sales Corp.,* 274 U.S. 268 (1927).

28 / *U.S.* v. *Minnesota Mining and Manufacturing Co.,* 92 F. Supp. 947 (1950).

29 / *U.S.* v. *American Tobacco Co.,* 221 U.S. 106 (1911); *U.S.* v. *National Lead Co.,* 332 U.S. 319 (1947); *U.S.* v. *General Electric Co.,* 82 F. Supp. 753 (1949); *U.S.* v. *Alkali Export Assn.,* 86 F. Supp. 59 (1949); *U.S.* v. *Timken Roller Bearing Co.,* 341 U.S. 593 (1951); *Holophane Co.* v. *U.S.,* 352 U.S. 903 (1956).

accordingly, that the Act was not confined to unreasonable agreements but applied, as it said, to every agreement in restraint of trade, even though it may have been valid at common law. [30] In his decision in the Addyston Pipe case in 1898, Judge Taft took a different line. It was the intention of Congress, he said, to adopt the principles of the common law. But the rule of reason, at common law, was confined to restrictions that were ancillary to lawful contracts and did not apply to nonancillary restraints on competition, since these restraints were made unlawful by their purposes. [31] Under either interpretation, the rule of reason was not to be employed.

So the law stood for twenty years, until Chief Justice White handed down the decisions of the Supreme Court in the Standard Oil and American Tobacco cases in 1911. [32] In each of these cases the Court upheld the government. But it went on, in an obiter dictum, to write the rule of reason into the law. Justice White agreed with Judge Taft that Congress had intended to follow the common law. But he found, by going back to English precedents, emphasizing consistent American decisions, and ignoring many inconsistent ones, that the rule of reason had applied to nonancillary as well as to ancillary restraints. The purpose of the Sherman Act, he said, "was not to restrain the right to make and enforce contracts . . . which did not unduly restrain interstate or foreign commerce, but to protect that commerce from being restrained by methods . . . which would constitute an interference, that is, an undue restraint." [33] The Act applied, he admitted, to every agreement in restraint of trade, but this meant every unreasonable agreement, since reasonable agreements did not involve restraint. And, arguing further that Section 2 of the Act was complementary to and therefore must be harmonized with Section 1, he went on to apply the rule of reason, not only to restraint of trade, but also to monopolization and attempts to monopolize.

To both of these decisions, Justice Harlan appended vigorous dissents, saying, in the Tobacco case, that

> . . . the Court, in accordance with what it denominates the "rule of reason," in effect inserts in the Act the word "undue" which means the same as "unreasonable," and thereby makes Congress say what it did not say, what, I think, it plainly did not intend to say, and what, since the passage of the Act, it has explicitly refused to say. . . . In short, the Court, now, by judicial legislation, in effect amends an Act of Congress relating to a subject over which that department of the Government has exclusive cognizance. [34]

But Congress, instead of reversing the Court, limited the application of the

30 / *U.S.* v. *Trans-Missouri Freight Assn.,* 166 U.S. 290.

31 / *U.S.* v. *Addyston Pipe & Steel Co.,* 85 Fed. 271.

32 / *Standard Oil Co. of N.J.* v. *U.S.,* 221 U.S. 1; *U.S.* v. *American Tobacco Co.,* 221 U.S. 106.

33 / *Standard Oil Co. of N.J.* v. *U.S.,* 221 U.S. 1, 59.

34 / *U.S.* v. *American Tobacco Co.,* 221 U.S. 106, 192.

Clayton Act, passed three years later, to cases in which the lessening of competition might be substantial, and the rule of reason came to be accepted and employed, thereafter, in interpreting the law.

Is this development to be commended or condemned? It is evident that the word "every" could not be taken literally. Even Justice Peckham had not found all agreements among competitors to be illegal, holding that those which failed to affect the competitive character of a market did not involve restraint of trade. But the door was opened wider by Justice White. Under the terms of his decision, the Court may find that agreements and combinations suppressing competition in a market, being reasonable, are immune. And no criteria for separating the reasonable from the unreasonable are supplied. The meaning of the law is thus uncertain; its application may be lax or stringent, depending on the judgment of the Court. But some uncertainty is inescapable, given the nature of the problems with which the law must deal. Its very vagueness, moreover, endows the Act with greater flexibility, permitting its adaptation to changing needs. Where judges look with favor on monopoly, the rule of reason may be open to abuse; where they believe in competition, it may have its use.

THE LAW ON RESTRICTIVE AGREEMENTS

From the beginning the Court has upheld the government, with only minor exceptions, in cases brought against overt agreements involving price fixing—whether direct or indirect—control of output, market sharing, and the exclusion of competitors by boycotts or other coercive practices. Here the rule of reason has rarely been applied. Behavior that was held, before 1911, to restrain trade is still held to do so. In cases involving the price reporting and statistical activities of trade associations, however, interpretation has been less consistent and the legal status of such activities is less clear. In another group of cases, the Court has come to find illegal conspiracy in dealings between parent corporations and their subsidiaries. The leading decisions in each of these areas will now be reviewed.

Simple Conspiracies

The earliest cases involving restrictive agreements among competitors were those of the Trans-Missouri Freight Association in 1897,[35] the Joint Traffic Association in 1898,[36] and the Addyston Pipe & Steel Company in 1899.[37] In the Trans-Missouri and Joint Traffic cases, groups of railroads had fixed and enforced freight rates. In the Addyston case, six producers of cast iron pipe had assigned certain markets to each of their number and determined the allocation of contracts elsewhere by operating a bidding ring. In all three cases the de-

35 / *U.S.* v. *Trans-Missouri Freight Assn.*, 166 U.S. 290.
36 / *U.S.* v. *Joint Traffic Assn.*, 171 U.S. 505.
37 / *Addyston Pipe & Steel Co.* v. *U.S.*, 175 U.S. 211.

fendants argued that their restrictions were required to prevent ruinous competition and that the resulting rates and prices were reasonable. And, in each case, the Court rejected this defense, holding the arrangements to be illegal in themselves.

These precedents were followed faithfully for 20 years, decisions being rendered against collusive bidding by purchasers of livestock,[38] exclusion of competing railways from a terminal,[39] the use of patent licenses to fix the price of bathtubs,[40] and the operation of a boycott by retail lumber dealers.[41] In 1918, in a decision of limited significance, the Court refused to condemn a rule adopted by the Chicago Board of Trade requiring those buying and selling grain outside of trading hours to do so at the price at which the market closed.[42] In 1923, it decided against the government in a case involving control of the output of hand-blown window glass.[43] Under the terms of an agreement between the National Association of Window Glass Manufacturers, representing 50 firms, and the National Window Glass Workers, a union of skilled glass blowers, operation of the plants in this industry was limited to 4½ months in the year, half of them being open during one period and half during another, the workers moving from plant to plant. The Court's acquiescence in this arrangement is explained by the fact that it was devised to meet the peculiar problems of a declining trade in a dying industry. The plan reduced costs by enabling plants to operate, for short periods, at full capacity, assured employment to labor, and eased the transfer of resources from the field. The case does not appear to have involved a serious departure from precedent.

The leading decision on restrictive agreements came in 1927 in the Trenton Potteries case.[44] Firms producing four fifths of the domestic output of vitreous enamel bathroom fixtures had agreed to fix prices and to sell exclusively through jobbers. The Court was emphatic in its refusal to accept the reasonableness of the prices fixed as a defense:

> The aim and result of every price-fixing agreement, if effective, is the elimination of one form of competition. The power to fix prices, whether reasonably exercised or not, involves power to control the market and to fix arbitrary and unreasonable prices. The reasonable price fixed today may, due to economic and business changes, become the unreasonable price of tomorrow. Once established it may be maintained unchanged because of the absence of competition. . . . Agreements which create such potential power may well be held to be in themselves unreasonable or

38 / U.S. v. *Swift & Co.,* 196 U.S. 375 (1906).
39 / U.S. v. *Terminal R.R. Assn.,* 224 U.S. 383 (1912).
40 / U.S. v. *Standard Sanitary Mfg. Co.,* 226 U.S. 20 (1912).
41 / U.S. v. *Eastern States Retail Lumber Assn.,* 234 U.S. 600 (1914).
42 / *Chicago Board of Trade* v. *U.S.,* 246 U.S. 231.
43 / *National Assn. of Window Glass Mfrs.* v. *U.S.,* 263 U.S. 403.
44 / U.S. v. *Trenton Potteries Co.,* 273 U.S. 392.

unlawful restraint, without the necessity of minute inquiry, whether a particular price is reasonable or unreasonable as fixed, and without placing on the government in enforcing the Sherman law the burden of ascertaining from day to day whether it has become unreasonable. . . .[45]

The purpose of the law, said the Court, is to protect the public by maintaining competition. Every agreement to fix prices, however reasonable, is therefore to be condemned.

Doubts concerning this position were raised, however, by the Court's decision in the Appalachian Coals case in 1933.[46] In this case 137 companies, producing a tenth of the bituminous coal mined east of the Mississippi River and around two thirds of that mined in the Appalachian territory, had set up a joint agency to handle all their sales. The Court recognized that this arrangement established common prices for the firms involved, but it went on to find that the industry was seriously depressed, that competition in the sale of coal had been subject to various abuses, and that the selling agency did not control enough of the supply to enable it to fix the market price. It therefore concluded that: "A cooperative enterprise, otherwise free from objection, which carries with it no monopolistic menace, is not to be condemned as an undue restraint merely because it may affect a change in market conditions, where the change would be in mitigation of recognized evils and would not impair, but rather foster, fair competitive opportunities.[47] On this basis, the arrangement was allowed to stand.

This precedent, had it been followed in later cases, would substantially have modified the meaning of the law. In its decision in the Socony-Vacuum case[48] in 1940, however, the Court reaffirmed the rule of Trenton Potteries. This case involved an agreement, described in Chapter 4, under which the major oil companies in ten midwestern states raised and maintained the price of gasoline by purchasing marginal supplies from independent refineries. The Court again rejected the defense that the price established was no more than fair. Said Justice Douglas:

Any combination which tampers with price structures is engaged in an unlawful activity. Even though the members of the price-fixing group were in no position to control the market, to the extent that they raised, lowered, or stabilized prices they would be directly interfering with the free play of market forces. The Act places all such schemes beyond the pale. . . . Under the Sherman Act, a combination formed for the purpose and with the effect of raising, depressing, fixing, pegging, or stabilizing the price of a commodity in interstate or foreign commerce is illegal per se. . . . Whatever economic justification particular price-fixing agree-

45 / Ibid., pp. 397-98.
46 / Appalachian Coals, Inc. v. U.S., 288 U.S. 344.
47 / Ibid., pp. 373-74.
48 / U.S. v. Socony-Vacuum Oil Co., 310 U.S. 150.

ments may be thought to have, the law does not permit an inquiry into their reasonableness. They are banned because of their actual or potential threat to the central nervous system of the economy. [49]

The ruling of the Court could not have been more sweeping; any such agreement, even though affecting a minor portion of the market, was forbidden; any manipulation of prices, whatever its purpose, was against the law.

The Court was not troubled by its inconsistency. The oil agreement, it said, had the purpose and effect of controlling market prices; the coal agreement did not. But the two cases are not so easily to be reconciled; In coal the decision permitted a minority to fix prices; in the words of the oil decision, price fixing—even by a minority—was condemned. The contrast is to be explained, in part, perhaps, by the fact that there had been changes between 1933 and 1940 in the composition of the Court, in the prosperity of the country, and in the attitude of the public toward monopoly; in part, by the fact that bituminous coal had been produced by many small firms engaged in active competition, while oil had been refined by large concerns whose pattern of behavior was that of oligopoly. The Appalachian case must be regarded as an exception, and the Socony-Vacuum case as a restatement of the general rule.

The government has been highly successful in cases brought against restrictive agreements under the Sherman Act. A tabulation of decrees down to 1951 reveals 437 instances (69 in litigated decrees and 368 in consent decrees) in which price fixing, market sharing, control of output, collusive bidding, and the use of a common buying or selling agent were enjoined. [50] It should be noted, moreover, that the Court has long upheld the authority of the Federal Trade Commission to proceed against such agreements under Section 5 of the Trade Commission Act. It is in this area that interpretation has been most consistent in supporting the enforcement of the law.

Trade Association Activities

During the twenties, four cases came before the Court involving the price and other statistical reporting activities of trade associations in the hardwood lumber, linseed oil, maple flooring, and cement industries. In all four cases the associations concerned were engaged in collecting and disseminating data on production, stocks, orders, sales and shipments, in preparing and circulating reports on prices and terms of sale, in operating delivered pricing systems, and in holding meetings where prices and production were discussed. In none of the cases was there explicit evidence of agreement as to price and production policy. In the Hardwood and Linseed cases [51] decided in 1921 and 1923, the

49 / *U.S.* v. *Socony-Vacuum Oil Co.,* 310 U.S. 150, 221-26.

50 / Arthur T. Dietz, *An Analysis of Decrees under the Sherman Act,* unpublished doctoral dissertation, Princeton University, 1953, pp. 336-53, 365.

51 / *American Column and Lumber Co.* v. *U.S.,* 257 U.S. 377; *U.S.* v. *American Linseed Oil Co.,* 262 U.S. 371.

plans were held to be illegal; in the Maple Flooring and Cement cases [52] decided in 1925, they were not. Said the Court, in the Hardwood case: "Genuine competitors do not make daily, weekly, and monthly reports of the minutest details of their business to their rivals. . . . This is not the conduct of competitors but . . . clearly that of men united in an agreement, express or implied, to act together and pursue a common purpose under a common guide. . . ." [53] And in the Linseed case: "With intimate knowledge of the affairs of other producers . . . the subscribers went forth to deal with widely separated and unorganized customers. . . . Obviously, they were not *bona fide* competitors; their claim in that regard is at war with common experience." [54] But in the Maple Flooring case the Court decided: "that trade associations . . . which openly and fairly gather and disseminate information . . . without, however, reaching or attempting to reach any agreement or any concerted action with respect to prices or production or restraining competition, do not thereby engage in unlawful restraint of commerce." [55] Such activities, said the Court, are not to be condemned "merely because the ultimate result . . . may be to stabilize prices or limit production through a better understanding of economic laws and a more general ability to conform to them." [56]

How is the shift in the Court's position to be explained? The plans that were followed in the two sets of cases differed in detail. The prices that were reported in the Hardwood and Linseed cases were those to be charged in future transactions, firms making quotations were identified, and reports were withheld from customers. In the Hardwood case, moreover, the information provided was accompanied by interpretive comments and strong suggestions as to policy. And in the Linseed case adherence to quoted prices was required. In the Maple Flooring case, on the other hand, prices were reported for past transactions, sellers were not identified, and the reports were given wide publicity. Here, as in the Cement case, it was noted that members retained their freedom to take such action as they chose.

The plans adopted by the Maple Flooring and Cement associations, however, were not as innocent as they seemed. The former group prepared and distributed estimates showing the average cost of producing each of the grades and dimensions of flooring, and both groups compiled and circulated common freight-rate books. The activities of both associations were designed to implement delivered pricing systems. And under these systems, with the base price built on the reported costs or established through price leadership, overt agreement as to prices was not required. This fact, however, was not made known to the Court.

52 / *Maple Flooring Mfrs. Assn.* v. *U.S.*, 268 U.S. 563; *Cement Mfrs. Protective Assn.* v. *U.S.*, 268 U.S. 588.

53 / 257 U.S. 377, 410.

54 / 262 U.S. 371, 389-90.

55 / 268 U.S. 563, 586.

56 / *Ibid.*, p. 584.

The government's case was poorly prepared: the prosecution confined itself to showing that the practices followed in the later cases resembled those found in the earlier ones. The defense presented evidence to show that the effects of these practices, however restrictive elsewhere, were not restrictive here. And this evidence was not refuted by the government. No agreement to control output or to fix prices was charged or proved. The Court rendered its decision accordingly: "We realize that such information, gathered and disseminated among the members of a trade or business, may be the basis of agreement or concerted action to lessen production arbitrarily or to raise prices. . . . But in the absence of proof of such agreement or concerted action . . . we can find no basis in the gathering and dissemination of such information . . . for the inference that such concerted action will necessarily result. . . ."[57] None of these decisions was generalized; each of them was limited to the facts of a particular case.

The next trade association program to come before the Court was that of the Sugar Institute. The program was an elaborate one, having as its purpose the elimination of all indirect methods of competition and the requirement of adherence to the seller's reported price. The association standardized terms of sale, limited cash discounts, classified purchasers and forbade long-term contracts, sales on consignment, quantity discounts, and allowances for returned bags, storage, and advertising, together with many other practices. It imposed a boycott on distributors performing both brokerage and wholesaling functions. It eliminated certain consignment points and ports of entry for sugar, operated a delivered pricing system, and published a common freight-rate book. It reported to its members on the production, sales, and stocks of individual refiners, and to its customers only on total production, sales, and stocks. It reported filed prices to buyers and sellers alike, but forbade departure from these prices without filing prior notice of the change. There was no evidence of agreement as to prices themselves, but such agreement was clearly facilitated when every other aspect of each transaction had been standardized.

In 1934 the District Court found this program to be in restraint of trade and, while refusing to dissolve the Institute, issued an injunction prohibiting further adherence to 45 specific practices, including those relating to the operation of the delivered pricing system and the standardization of other aspects of a sale. It required that buyers be given access to statistics on production, sales, deliveries, and stocks, and to "any other statistical information of a similar character," enjoined the practice of reporting and disseminating future prices, and forbade agreement to adhere to the prices that were filed. Two years later the Supreme Court affirmed the decision of the lower court, with two exceptions. It permitted "any other statistical information of a similar character" to be kept in confidence. And, finding that prior announcement of prices conformed to the established practice of the industry, it ruled that future prices might be filed. "The unreasonable restraint which defendants imposed," said the Court, "lay

57 / *Ibid.*, p. 586.

not in advance announcements, but in the steps taken to secure adherence without deviation to prices and terms thus announced."[58] Agreement to observe filed prices was enjoined.

About 10 cases involving restrictive trade association activities are brought by the Antitrust Division each year. These are usually settled by consent decrees. In serious cases, they are likely to end in dissolution of the associations concerned. The Federal Trade Commission regularly gives advisory opinions on association activities. It may warn an association, for instance, not to agree on wages that are to be reflected in setting prices, not to recommend certain profit margins as being fair, or not to use a common rate book in pricing services. The Commission, however, now rarely makes a formal complaint against an association or issues an order to cease and desist.

The courts, in general, have refrained from passing on particular elements of a trade association program, directing attention rather toward the consequences of the program as a whole. They have refused to generalize their rulings, confining each decision to the case in hand. As a result the legality of particular practices and programs may be unclear. It would appear, however, that such programs are lawful when they limit price reports to past transactions, preserve the anonymity of individual traders, make data available to buyers as well as sellers, and permit departure from the prices that are filed. Practices and programs may be viewed with disfavor where future prices are reported, traders are identified, information is withheld from buyers, and discussions are held, statements issued, and recommendations made on price and production policies. Such programs are certain to be condemned when they involve elaborate standardization of the conditions surrounding a sale and require adherence to a filed price.

Intra-Enterprise Conspiracy

Conspiracies in restraint of trade have been found to exist not only between independent enterprises but also between the corporations in an integrated structure that is under common ownership, each of them being regarded as a separate person within the meaning of the law. In 1941 General Motors and its subsidiary, the General Motors Acceptance Corporation, were held to have violated the Sherman Act when GM required its dealers to finance installment sales of automobiles through GMAC, thus excluding competitors from the financing business.[59] In 1947 in the Yellow Cab case, a manufacturer of taxicabs had acquired control of companies operating cabs in several cities and required them to purchase their cabs from him, excluding other manufacturers from the market and preventing the operating companies from buying where they chose. The Court rejected the defense that sales within a corporate family cannot involve conspiracy. An unreasonable restraint, it said, "may result as readily from a

58 / *U.S.* v. *Sugar Institute,* 15 F. Supp. 817 (1934); *Sugar Institute* v. *U.S.,* 297 U.S. 553 (1936) 601.

59 / *General Motors Corp.* v. *U.S.,* 121 F. 2d 376, certiorari denied, 314 U.S. 618.

conspiracy among those who are affiliated or integrated under common owner-ship as from a conspiracy among those who are otherwise independent." [60]

These precedents were followed in later cases. In 1948 in the Griffith case, a company operating a chain of movie houses was found to have conspired with its subsidiaries when it pooled their buying power to bargain for choice pictures, first runs, and long clearances in regions where it had competitors. [61] In 1951 the Seagram Company, which owned the controlling shares of its nominal com-petitor Calvert, was found to be conspiring with Calvert when it required Calvert to adopt Seagram's prices for whisky. [62] And in the same year, the Timken Roller Bearing Company was held to have conspired with the subsidiaries that it owned jointly with its British and French competitors to divide the roller-bearing markets of the world. [63]

Of itself, elimination of competition between a parent corporation and its subsidiary, or between two subsidiaries, is not illegal. As the Court remarked in the Columbia Steel case, "A subsidiary will in all probability deal only with its parent for goods the parent can furnish. That fact, however, does not make the acquisition invalid." [64] Where such relationships are held to be conspiratorial, it is because the trade of strangers to the corporate family has been restrained.

The State of the Law

The state of the law on restrictive agreements among competitors is set forth by Corwin D. Edwards in the following classification of types of agreements that are presumed to be illegal: [65]

I. Exclusion of competitors from the market.
 A. Agreement to preempt or deprive others of access to facilities for doing business . . . or to afford such access to others only upon discriminatory terms. . . .
 B. Agreement upon exclusive or preferential dealing arrangements de-signed to impair access by competitors to markets.
 C. Agreement not to use specified channels of distribution, or to make exclusive use of certain designated channels.
 D. Agreement to undertake discriminatory price cutting designed to destroy competition.

60 / *U.S.* v. *Yellow Cab Co.,* 332 U.S. 218, 227. The Supreme Court reversed the lower court on the point of law and remanded the case for trial on the facts. The lower court acquitted Yellow Cab, finding no intent to monopolize. The Supreme Court allowed this decision to stand (*U.S.* v. *Yellow Cab Co.,* 338 U.S. 338, 1949).

61 / *U.S.* v. *Griffith,* 334 U.S. 100.

62 / *Kiefer-Stewart Co.* v. *Joseph E. Seagram & Sons,* 340 U.S. 211.

63 / *Timken Roller Bearing Co.* v. *U.S.,* 341 U.S. 593.

64 / *U.S.* v. *Columbia Steel Co.,* 334 U.S. 495, p. 523.

65 / Corwin D. Edwards, *Maintaining Competition* (New York: McGraw-Hill Book Co., 1949), pp. 41-42. Reproduced with permission.

    E. Agreement to exact discriminatory prices or terms that prevent or destroy competition.

    F. Agreement to require the purchase of certain goods or services as a condition of supplying others.

    G. Discriminatory patent pools designed to destroy nonparticipants.

II. Restriction of output or of purchases.

    A. Agreement to restrict production, sales, or inventory accumulations.

    B. Agreements to restrict purchases or imports.

    C. Agreement not to construct or acquire additional equipment.

    D. Agreement not to use new processes or not to produce, sell, purchase or use new types of materials or equipment.

    E. Agreement to limit research.

    F. Agreement to shut down or destroy existing equipment, or to acquire equipment from competitors for such purposes.

    G. Agreement not to produce low-cost products.

    H. Agreement to limit the quality or durability of goods sold or the extent of services rendered.

III. Division of markets.

    A. Allocation of territories in which to sell or purchase.

    B. Allocation of customers.

    C. Rotation of bids or orders.

    D. Agreement on proportion of total sales or purchases to be made by each concern.

    E. Allocation of products to be made or sold or processes to be used.

IV. Price Fixing.

    A. Agreement upon selling bids or prices.

    B. Agreement upon and enforcement of resale prices (except as specifically exempted by law).

    C. Agreement upon purchase prices to be paid.

    D. Agreement to fix price differentials, discounts, or important terms of sale or to designate groups of customers who shall be eligible for discounts.

    E. Agreement to add arbitrary charges to sale prices or to make arbitrary deductions from purchase prices.

V. Elimination of opportunity or incentive to compete.

    A. Agreement to sell through the same agents.

    B. Agreement to pool profits.

VI. Coercion. Agreement to use boycotts and other coercive devices to further any of the foregoing restraints.

THE LAW ON OLIGOPOLY

Where markets are shared by a few large firms confronted with similar conditions, each of them is likely to react in the same way, fully expecting that the others will follow suit. The identity of behavior that thus results from tacit agreement among the few may restrain trade as seriously as that resulting from overt agreement among the many. But there may be, in this behavior, no evidence of agreement, no witnesses or documents to prove the existence of conspiracy. Oligopoly thus presents to antitrust the most serious of the problems it has to face. An approach to a solution has been provided by the doctrine of conscious parallelism, a phrase originated by the Federal Trade Commission and first used in describing the behavior of firms adhering to basing point systems of delivered pricing.

The Doctrine of Conscious Parallelism

It has long been recognized that unlawful agreement may be proven, in the absence of witnesses or documents, by circumstantial evidence. "It is elementary," said the Supreme Court in the Eastern States Lumber case in 1914, "that conspiracies are seldom capable of proof by direct testimony, and may be inferred from the things actually done. [66] In several cases in recent years the Court has gone even further, holding that knowing participation in a common course of action, without proof of agreement, may constitute conspiracy. In the Interstate Circuit case in 1939 the operator of a chain of movie houses in Texas had entered into separate contracts with eight distributors of films, agreeing to show their pictures for an admission charge of 40 cents, on condition they not be rented later to be shown for less than 25 cents or run on a double bill. There was no evidence that the distributors had consulted one another or agreed among themselves. But such evidence said the Court, "was not a prerequisite to an unlawful conspiracy. It was enough that, knowing that concerted action was contemplated and invited, the distributors gave their adherence to the scheme and participated in it. . . . Acceptance by competitors, without previous agreement, is sufficient to establish an unlawful conspiracy under the Sherman Act." [67] A similar position was taken in the Masonite case in 1942. Here, a manufacturer of hardboard had signed an agency agreement with each of his competitors, authorizing them to distribute his product and fixing the prices at which they could sell. And here, again, there was no evidence of agreement among the other companies. But the Court found the plan to be illegal, holding that each of them must have been "aware of the fact that its contract was not an isolated transaction but a part of a larger arrangement." [68]

In these cases there was evidence that plans had been proposed by Interstate and Masonite; the inference of conspiracy among the other companies was drawn from their adherence to these plans. In the second American Tobacco case, a criminal suit against the three leading producers of cigarettes, decided in 1946, no such proposal was in evidence. Statistics of purchases, sales, and prices were relied upon for proof. In buying tobacco, it was shown, these companies had purchased fixed shares of the supply, each of them paying the same price on the same day. In selling cigarettes, they had adopted identical price lists,

66 / *Eastern States Retail Lumber Assn.* v. *U.S.*, 234 U.S. 600, 612.
67 / *Interstate Circuit Co.* v. *U.S.*, 306 U.S. 208, 226-27.
68 / *U.S.* v. *Masonite Corp.*, 316 U.S. 265, 275.

changing their prices simultaneously. In other practices, too, there was striking uniformity. But the case, says William Nicholls, "was probably unique in that there was not a whit of evidence that a common plan had even been contemplated or proposed. The government's evidence was admittedly wholly circumstantial. The fact of identity of behavior was offered as the basis for inferring both the existence and the elements of the alleged common plan and the defendants' knowledge of that plan. Each was alleged to have acted similarly with the knowledge that the others would so act, to their mutual self-interest." [69] But the character of the evidence did not deter the Court. Conspiracy, it said, "may be found in a course of dealings or other circumstances as well as in an exchange of words." [70] The companies were found, accordingly, to be in violation of the law. The decision, says Nicholls, "brought wholly tacit, nonaggressive oligopoly wholly within the reach of the conspiracy provisions of the Sherman Act." [71]

Conspiracy was also found by the Supreme Court in cases where firms had agreed to identical provisions in the licenses granted them by the owner of a patent [72] and in cases brought under the Trade Commission Act where each of the members of an industry had adhered to a delivered pricing system in the knowledge that all the others would do the same. "It is enough to warrant a finding of 'combination' within the meaning of the Sherman Act," said the Court in the Cement Institute case in 1948, "if there is evidence that persons, with knowledge that concerted action was contemplated and invited, give adherence and then participate in a scheme." [73] In a case decided by a lower court in the same year, the manufacturers of rigid steel conduit had been prosecuted under two counts: the first charged overt agreement to adhere to a system of delivered pricing; the second made no mention of such agreement, merely charging that each defendant had adhered to the system in the knowledge that the others were doing so. The court found the manufacturers guilty on both counts. [74] When the case was appealed in 1949, the Supreme Court divided 4 to 4. The conviction on the second count, charging conscious parallelism, was thus allowed to stand.

The doctrine was carried furthest in the case of *Milgram* v. *Loew's* in 1950. Here, eight distributors of motion pictures had been sued by a drive-in movie for refusing to supply it with first-run films. A district court found the distributors guilty of conspiracy, holding that their common refusal to supply first runs could not have been due to independent business judgment but was sufficient, in itself, to establish violation of the law. A meeting of minds need not be proven; identity of behavior was all that was required. [75]

69 / William H. Nicholls, "The Tobacco Case of 1946," *American Economic Review*, Vol. XXXIX, No. 3 (1949), pp. 284-96, esp. p. 285.

70 / *American Tobacco Co.* v. *U.S.*, 328 U.S. 781, 810.

71 / Nicholls, *op. cit.*, p. 285.

72 / *U.S.* v. *Line Material Co.*, 333 U.S. 282 (1948); *U.S.* v. *U.S. Gypsum Co.*, 333 U.S. 364 (1948).

73 / *FTC* v. *Cement Institute*, 333 U.S. 683 at p. 716.

74 / *Triangle Conduit & Cable Co.* v. *FTC*, 168 F. 2d 157.

75 / *Milgram* v. *Loews's, Inc.*, 94 F. Supp. 416.

The Limits of Conscious Parallelism

When this decision was handed down, the Federal Trade Commission made known its intention, in future cases, to infer conspiracy from evidence of identical behavior. Within five years, however, the Commission and the courts began to retreat from the doctrine of conscious parallelism. Early in 1953 the Commission ordered manufacturers of lead pigments to discontinue matching prices through adherence to a system of zone-delivered pricing, inferring conspiracy from the existence of price identity. Commissioner Mason dissented, saying, "No one claims the evidence has to show one secret meeting in a smoke-filled room, or any number of meetings, nor do all the conspirators have to be present at any one time and sign their names in blood. But a charge of conspiracy must mean something besides a handle on which to hang an order. . . . In my opinion, some kind of overt act which implements a meeting of the minds is a 'must' in a conspiracy. . . ." [76] With a shift occurring shortly in the Commission's membership, this came to be the view of the majority. In 1953, too, a case against the investment banking companies was dismissed by a district judge, who brushed aside the charge that markets were shared through conventional adherence to historical relationships between bankers and borrowers, finding no evidence of conspiracy. [77] In 1954, in a suit against the major meat-packing companies, another district judge ruled that the government could not present evidence relating to the period before 1930 in support of its charge that the packers were now habitually sharing markets in accordance with a pattern that had been created through overt agreement some 50 years ago. At the government's request, the case was then dismissed "without prejudice." [78]

In 1953, another case involving the distribution of movies came to the Supreme Court. In this instance, the distributors had restricted first runs to downtown theaters and provided features to suburban houses only for later runs after lengthy clearances. But this time, the District Court had found their action to be legal, attributing it to the independent exercise of business judgment. The Supreme Court refused to review. [79] In the following year, the issue was presented again in the Theater Enterprises case. This time, the Court handed down a decision flatly rejecting an exhibitor's contention that the distributors' refusals to supply first runs constituted an illegal conspiracy. Said Justice Clark: "This court has never held that proof of parallel business behavior conclusively establishes agreement or, phrased differently, that such behavior itself constitutes a Sherman Act offense. Circumstantial evidence of consciously parallel behavior

76 / New York Times, January 16, 1953.

77 / U.S. v. Morgan, Civil No. 43-757, District Court of the U.S., Southern District of New York, October 14, 1953.

78 / U.S. v. Armour & Co., Civil 48-C-1351, discontinued March, 1954.

79 / Fanchon & Marco v. Paramount Pictures, 100 F. Supp. 84, certiorari denied, 345 U.S. 964.

may have made heavy inroads into the traditional judicial attitude toward conspiracy, but 'conscious parallelism' has not yet read conspiracy out of the Sherman Act entirely."[80]

Since this decision, the courts have been less ready to infer conspiracy. To explain identical behavior, they have first looked for other factors, external to the members of a group. But in the absence of such factors, they have still been willing to convict. In the Esco case, in 1965, the government had shown that distributors of stainless steel pipe on the Pacific coast had discussed their prices and had subsequently practiced parallelism in pricing. It was unable, however, to prove that they had agreed to do so. But the Court of Appeals held that no such proof was required.[81] The doctrine of conscious parallelism, though less potent than once supposed, still has some force.

The State of the Law

Evidence of identical behavior by a few large firms is not enough, in itself, to prove conspiracy. If it were, oligopoly would be illegal per se. Such behavior may result, in fact, from the independent discovery of identical solutions to a common business problem. Beyond this, some proof of agreement is required. Proof of overt agreement is likely to be present where substantial markets are brought under effective control. But even where such proof is lacking, identity of behavior may be so complex, so pervasive, and so persistent that agreement can safely be inferred. Collusive oligopoly is thus with the reach of antitrust.

80 / *Theater Enterprises, Inc.* v. *Paramount Film Distributing Corp.*, 346 U.S. 537, 540.
81 / *Business Week*, February 13, 1965, p. 42.

Chapter 7 : MONOPOLIZATION AND MERGERS IN THE COURTS

Trade may be restrained by agreements—overt or tacit—among competitors. It may be restrained more effectively by a combination of competitors and by monopolization of a market by a single firm. Collusive agreements are constantly tending to break down; they are unenforceable at law. Combinations, on the other hand, are permanent; their constituent parts are brought under common control. Monopoly power attained through combination or through internal growth persists unless attacked by outer force.

Combination to restrain trade violates Section 1 of the Sherman Act. Combination to monopolize violates Section 2. Mergers violate Section 7 of the Clayton Act where the effect may be substantially to lessen competition or tend to create a monopoly. In each of these provisions, more than one defendant is involved: it takes at least two firms to combine. But Section 2 of the Sherman Act also applies to two other offenses: monopolizing and attempting to monopolize. And these offenses may be committed by a single firm.

In the earlier history of antitrust, suits against agreements were many; those against combinations were comparatively few; those against monopolization were virtually nonexistent. From 1895 to 1927, The Supreme Court handed down only 14 decisions on combinations; from 1927 to 1948 there were none. It was not until 1945 that a case was decided on monopolization, as such. In these cases, moreover, the rule of the law was less clear and less consistent than in those involving agreements among competitors. Since the middle fifties, however, the courts have been called upon to pass on many cases brought under the Celler-Kefauver Antimerger Act. And here, the interpretation of the law, while incomplete, has rapidly been taking form.

COMBINATION UNDER THE SHERMAN ACT

During the first half century of the Sherman Act, the Supreme Court was quick to condemn combinations involving railroads, hesitant to condemn those involving manufacturers. The Court found every railroad combination brought before it to be in violation of the law. At first, it held that the law did not apply to manufacturers. Then, abandoning this position, it struck down manufacturing combinations that had engaged in predatory practices. But those not guilty of such practices were allowed to stand.

132

The Bad Trusts

In 1904, the Court ordered the dissolution of the Northern Securities Company, a holding company that controlled the Great Northern and Northern Pacific railroads, parallel competing roads that were in competition with other transcontinental lines.[1] In 1912, it found that joint ownership of the Terminal Railroad Association of St. Louis by a number of railroads entering that city was an illegal combination and ordered the Association to admit, on reasonable terms, any other road that might apply.[2] In the same year, the Union Pacific Railroad came before the Court. The Union Pacific's line had stopped at Ogden, Utah. The Company had sought to extend it to the coast by buying stock in the Southern Pacific which controlled the Central Pacific which ran from Ogden to San Francisco. The Court held that this acquisition violated the law even though the two lines served different cities and operated between different termini.[3] In 1922, moreover, the Court held Southern's ownership of stock in Central to be illegal, though they were not competing lines.[4] Two other cases involved joint ownership of railroads and anthracite coal mines. In 1920, the Court ordered dissolution of the Reading Company, a holding company which controlled the Reading Railroad and mines producing a third of the country's supply of anthracite.[5] And it ordered the Lehigh Valley Railroad to divest itself of shares in mines producing another fifth of the supply.[6] In all of these cases, the Court held that the attainment of market power through combination was illegal even though that power was not abused.

The first case of a manufacturing combination to come before the Court was the E. C. Knight case, involving the sugar trust. Here, the Court held, in 1895, that the law did not apply because its scope was limited to business engaged in interstate commerce and thus did not cover manufacturing.[7] If this interpretation had stood, the application of the law would have been strictly limited. In fact, it was ignored.

In 1911, in cases involving the Standard Oil trust[8] and the American Tobacco trust,[9] the Court applied the law to manufacturing. It was in these cases that it enunciated the rule of reason. But it ordered each of the combinations to be dissolved. Standard Oil controlled all of the important pipelines and nearly 90 percent of the country's refining capacity. It had attained its position by exacting rebates from the railroads on its own shipments and on those of its com-

1 / *Northern Securities Co.* v. *U.S.*, 193 U.S. 197.
2 / *U.S.* v. *Terminal Railroad Assn.*, 224 U.S. 383.
3 / *U.S.* v. *Union Pacific Railroad Co.*, 226 U.S. 61.
4 / *U.S.* v. *Southern Pacific Co.*, 259 U.S. 214.
5 / *U.S.* v. *Reading Co.*, 253 U.S. 26.
6 / *U.S.* v. *Lehigh Valley Railroad Co.*, 254 U.S. 255.
7 / *U.S.* v. *E. C. Knight Co.*, 156 U.S. 1.
8 / *Standard Oil Co. of N.J.* v. *U.S.*, 221 U.S. 1.
9 / *U.S.* v. *American Tobacco Co.*, 221 U.S. 106.

petitors, by cutting prices in one region at a time to drive its local rivals out of business, and by resorting to other predatory practices, the mere listing of which filled some 57 pages of the record. American Tobacco controlled three quarters of the country's output of smoking tobacco and around nine tenths of its output of chewing tobacco, cigarettes, and little cigars. This company, too, had attained its position by unfair methods of competition: by excluding its rivals from sources of supply, by buying plants to shut them down, by local price cutting, and by the production of fighting brands which were sold at a loss to destroy competitors and abandoned when their purpose had been served. In its decisions in these cases, the Court placed its emphasis, not on the fact of combination or even on the attainment of monopoly, but on the monopolistic intent of the defendants and on their use of unfair tactics in eliminating competition and excluding new competitors. It dissolved the trusts, not because they possessed monopoly power, but because they had so flagrantly abused it.

The Good Trusts

In 1916, five years after these decisions, a lower court refused to break up the American Can Company, controlling nine tenths of the output of tin cans, because the defendant "had done nothing of which any competitor or consumer of cans complains or anything which strikes a disinterested outsider as unfair or unethical." [10] In its decision in the U.S. Steel case in 1920 the Supreme Court revealed a similar complacency. It was the doctrine contained in this decision that, for the next 25 years, granted virtual immunity to monopolistic combinations in manufacturing.

The United States Steel Corporation, created in 1901, was a combination of 12 concerns, themselves resulting from earlier combinations of 180 separate companies. It was the largest merger in the nation's history, extending vertically from mining to fabrication and horizontally to all the types of steel mill products, and controlling, at its inception, around two thirds of the output of the industry. When this colossus came before the Court, it still controlled one half of the supply of steel. But in a 4 to 3 decision, with two of its members abstaining, the Court found that the combination did not violate the law. [11]

The majority reasoned as follows: (1) The organizers of the Corporation had intended to monopolize the industry, but they had not succeeded in doing so and, recognizing their failure, had abandoned the attempt. The law was directed, said Justice McKenna, not against an expectation of monopoly but against its realization. Its specific prohibition of attempts to monopolize was thus ignored. (2) Admittedly, the Corporation had conspired with other companies, in earlier years, to fix the price of steel. But this only served to prove its lack of monopoly. The practice, moreover, had been abandoned; the evidence showed that the industry was now competitive. The monopolistic character of the Pittsburgh-plus

10 / *U.S.* v. *American Can Co.*, 230 F. 859, 861 (1916).
11 / *U.S.* v. *U.S. Steel Corp.*, 251 U.S. 417 (1920).

delivered pricing system was not explained or understood. (3) The decision was thus confined to a narrower issue: the legal status of a combination controlling half of an industry. Certainly the Corporation was big and powerful. But, said the Court, "the law does not make mere size an offense. It . . . requires overt acts and trusts to its prohibition of them and its power to repress and punish them." [12] (4) The question, then, was whether the Corporation had abused its power. Had it acted, by itself, to fix monopolistic prices? Had it excluded others from the market? On the contrary, said the Court, its behavior was exemplary: "It resorted to none of the brutalities or tyrannies that the cases illustrate of other combinations. It did not secure freight rebates; it did not increase its profits by reducing the wages of its employees . . . , by lowering the quality of its products, nor by creating an artificial scarcity of them; . . . it did not undersell its competitors in some localities by reducing its prices there below those maintained elsewhere . . . ; there was no evidence that it attempted to crush its competitors or drive them from the market." [13] In short, though the Corporation was big, it was not bad. And, accordingly, it was not dissolved. The law was thus held by the majority of the Court, as Justice Day remarked in his dissent, to be "intended merely to suppress unfair practices." [14]

When this decision was announced, the government withdrew its appeals in several pending cases, including the one against American Can. The issue of size was presented to the Court again in 1927, however, when the government sought to break up the International Harvester Company. This concern, a combination of five producers of agricultural implements and machinery, controlled 85 percent of the output of such equipment when it was established in 1902, and 64 percent when it was brought before the Court. Its leadership in setting prices was followed by the other members of the industry. These facts, however, did not impress the justices. Six of them, with three abstaining, adhered to the precedent set in the case of U.S. Steel. The law, they said, "does not make the mere size of a corporation, however impressive, or the existence of unexerted power on its part, an offense, when unaccompanied by unlawful conduct in the exercise of its power." [15] Price leadership was rejected as offering evidence of monopoly. In the words of the opinion: "The fact that competitors may see proper, in the exercise of their own judgment to follow the prices of another manufacturer, does not establish any suppression of competition or show any sinister domination." [16] International Harvester, like U.S. Steel, was a good trust.

The State of the Law

It would be difficult to reconcile the positions taken by the Court in this group of cases. In Steel and Harvester, combinations controlling half and two thirds of the market, respectively, were allowed to stand; in Reading and Lehigh,

12 / *Ibid.*, p. 451.   13 / *Ibid.*, p. 441.   14 / *Ibid.*, p. 464.
15 / *U.S.* v. *International Harvester Co.*, 274 U.S. 693, 708.
16 / *Ibid.*, pp. 708-9.

combinations controlling a third and a fifth were dissolved. In Steel, where there was clear intent to monopolize, the combination was permitted; in Northern Securities, Union Pacific, and Southern Pacific, where there was no such intent, the combinations were condemned. In the railroad cases, it was the attainment of market power that was held to be unlawful; in Steel and Harvester, such power was held to be innocent if it were not abused. Under the circumstances, the legality of a prospective combination was unpredictable. The law, after half a century, still was shrouded in uncertainty.

In the interpretation of the law as it applied, on the one hand, to agreement among competitors and, on the other, to combination, there was also inconsistency. Where market power had been attained through agreement, the courts had been strict. But where it had been attained through combination, they had faltered and enforcement frequently had failed. This judicial schizophrenia had a curious result. Firms once convicted of conspiracy for entering agreements were allowed to go untouched when they proceeded to combine. A statute that had been designed to prevent and break up combinations was so distorted, through interpretation, as to offer them encouragement.

Vertical Integration

In a number of cases coming before the courts over the years, the combination in question has been vertical rather than—or as well as—horizontal. In the Yellow Cab and other cases described above, bringing transactions between holding companies and their subsidiaries within the purview of the law, it appeared that the Supreme Court might be prepared to question vertical integration as such. But this has not been the rule. In the Paramount case in 1948, the Court said that vertical integration might become illegal if it were undertaken "to gain control over an appreciable segment of the market and to restrain or suppress competition,"[17] or if the integrated company possessed the power and the intent to restrict the access of competitors to materials or markets. But it was careful to state that it did not hold such integration to be illegal per se. In the Columbia Steel case in the same year, Columbia, a subsidiary of U.S. Steel, was allowed to acquire control of Consolidated Steel, a fabricator on the Pacific coast. The government had charged that the acquisition excluded Columbia's competitors from the market for rolled steel products on the coast. The Court found, however, that Consolidated's purchases of such products were only 3 percent of the total. "It seems clear to us," it said, "that vertical integration, without more, cannot be held violative of the Sherman Act."[18]

In several cases, however, disintegration has been required. In each of these cases it appeared that the dominant position occupied by a company at one stage of production gave it an unfair advantage over its competitors at another.

---

17 / *U.S.* v. *Paramount Pictures,* 334 U.S. 131, 174.
18 / *U.S.* v. *Columbia Steel Co.,* 334 U.S. 495, 525.

In the Reading and Lehigh cases, discussed above, where it appeared that common ownership of railroads and coal mines enabled the companies to discriminate against other coal producers in providing railway service, the combinations were dissolved. In the Swift case, where a meat-packing house had extended its operations backward into the stockyards and forward into the distribution of foodstuffs to the detriment of its suppliers and competitors, a consent decree entered in 1920 required it to withdraw from both these fields. In 1932, when the company asked that the decree be modified to permit it to engage in distribution, the Supreme Court refused. [19] In the Pullman case in 1943, where a company that manufactured sleeping cars and also operated all such cars in use on American railroads employed its control of the market to exclude competitors from the manufacturing business, divorcement of the two functions was required. [20] And in the A&P case, where the company was found in 1946 to be employing its wholesale produce subsidiary, the Atlantic Commission Company, to obtain discriminatory advantages over its competitors, a consent decree accepted in 1954 provided that ACCO be dissolved. [21]

One of the most important of the disintegration decrees is that in the Paramount case. This case involved five of the major producers of motion pictures who also operated first-run theaters in the larger cities and chains of smaller theaters throughout the country. The government charged that these concerns had favored their own houses in supplying films, and had required block booking, minimum admission charges, and protracted intervals between successive showings in leasing films to others, thus making it difficult for independent producers and distributors to compete. It sought the separation of production and exhibition, the elimination of block booking, and the prohibition of other coercive practices. The lower court enjoined the practices complained of and required that films, instead of being booked in blocks, be leased through competitive bidding. The Supreme Court found this remedy to be inadequate, insisting also that production and exhibition be divorced. [22] The reorganizations were completed by 1952, the five companies being broken into ten: five of them producers and five operating chains of theaters. As a result, markets were opened to independent producers and films made more readily available to independent exhibitors.

The issue of vertical integration was raised again by a suit against A.T.&T. and its manufacturing subsidiary, the Western Electric Company. The government charged that the combination excluded other manufacturers from the market for telephonic equipment and asked that it be dissolved. In the end, however, it accepted a consent decree that required A.T.&T. to license these

19 / *U.S.* v. *Swift & Co.,* 286 U.S. 106.

20 / *U.S.* v. *Pullman Co.,* 50 F. Supp. 123.

21 / *U.S.* v. *N.Y. Great A.&P. Tea Co.,* 67 F. Supp. 626 (1946); affirmed 173 F. 2d 79 (1949); Civil Action 52-139, District Court of the U.S. Southern District of N.Y., Consent Decree, January 19, 1954.

22 / *U.S.* v. *Paramount Pictures,* 334 U.S. 131 (1948).

manufacturers under its patents but permitted it to retain control of Western Electric. [23]

MONOPOLIZATION UNDER THE SHERMAN ACT

The position taken by the Supreme Court in the case of U.S. Steel prevailed for a quarter of a century. Then decisions were issued by lower courts in two cases of equal importance: the first, in 1945, involved the Aluminum Company of America; the second, in 1953, involved the United Shoe Machinery Corporation. Each of these concerns had attained a virtually complete monopoly. Each of them had done so, in the main, through patent protection and internal growth. Each of the cases thus presented to the Court the issue of monopolization as such. The decisions entered in these cases brought a sharp change in the interpretation of the law.

Acquisition of Monopoly Power

The government brought suit against the Aluminum Company of America in 1937, charging that it had monopolized the manufacture of virgin aluminum and the sale of various aluminum products, in violation of Section 2 of the Sherman Act, and asking that it be broken into several parts. The monopoly, originating in a basic patent now expired, had been extended and preserved, according to the government's complaint, by resorting to oppressive tactics, including the elimination of competing fabricators by squeezing the spread between the price charged them for crude aluminum and the prices offered customers for finished goods. After a trial that ran for more than two years the District Court found Alcoa not guilty and the government appealed. [24] When the justices who had previously been connected with the prosecution disqualified themselves, however, the Supreme Court could not muster a quorum of six to hear the case. The judicial code was then amended by Congress to enable a Court of Appeals to serve, in such circumstances, as a court of last resort. The case was certified to the Court in the second circuit, and the decision of this Court, having the effect of a Supreme Court ruling, was rendered by Judge Learned Hand in 1945. [25]

The Court found that Alcoa manufactured more than nine tenths of the virgin aluminum ingot used in the United States, the rest coming in from abroad, and concluded that this was "enough to constitute a monopoly." [26] It then considered the argument that the power conferred by this monopoly, though it existed, had not been exercised. This distinction, said the Court, "is . . . purely formal; it would be valid only so long as the monopoly remained wholly inert;

23 / *U.S.* v. *Western Electric Co.,* D.C. of U.S. for D. of N.J., Civil No. 17-49, Consent Decree, 1956.
24 / *U.S.* v. *Aluminum Co. of America,* 44 F. Supp. 97 (1942).
25 / *U.S.* v. *Aluminum Co. of America,* 148 F. 2d 416.
26 / *Ibid.,* p. 424.

it would disappear as soon as the monopoly began to operate; for, when it did— that is, as soon as it began to sell at all—it must sell at some price and the only price at which it could sell is a price which it itself fixed. Thereafter the power and its exercise must needs coalesce." [27] The doctrine of the Steel and Harvester cases, that the mere existence of unexerted power is no offense, was thus explicitly reversed. Price fixing was found to be inherent in monopoly. The acquisition of market power became the test of illegality. The double standard of interpretation, which condoned the single-firm monopoly while holding agreements among competitors to be unlawful, was rejected as "absurd."

Alcoa had attained its position, however, not by combining with others, but by reinvesting its earnings and expanding its capacity as the market grew. Was this against the law? The Sherman Act does not forbid monopoly as such; it prohibits the act of monopolization and attempts to monopolize. It did not follow from the company's position, said the Court, "that it 'monopolized' the ingot markets; it may not have achieved monopoly; monopoly may have been thrust upon it." [28] But Alcoa might have avoided this development:

> It was not inevitable that it should always anticipate increases in the demand for ingots and be prepared to supply them. Nothing compelled it to keep doubling and redoubling its capacity before others entered the field. It insists that it has never excluded competitors; but we can think of no more effective exclusion than progressively to embrace each new opportunity as it opened, and to face every newcomer with new capacity already geared into a great organization, having the advantage of experience, trade connections, and the elite of personnel. [29]

To retain monopolistic power merely by growing with the market was thus to violate the law. Nor could the fact of monopolization be excused by the absence of intent to monopolize. To read Section 2 of the Sherman Act "as demanding any 'specific' intent makes nonsense of it, for no monopolist monopolizes unconscious of what he is doing. So here, 'Alcoa' meant to keep, and did keep, that complete and exclusive hold upon the ingot market with which it started. That was to 'monopolize' that market, however innocently it otherwise proceeded." [30] The defense of good behavior was likewise unavailing. The Court condemned the use of squeeze tactics in the past and enjoined their repetition in the future but made clear that it was holding Alcoa guilty of monopolization "regardless of such practices." The firm was not found to be abusing its position at the time of the trial, but a verdict for the government was held not to require the proof of such abuse. Congress, said the Court, "did not condone 'good trusts' and condemn 'bad' ones; it forbade all." [31] The antitrust laws were not intended merely to regulate business practices. It was one of their purposes "to perpetuate and preserve for its own sake and in spite

27 / *Ibid.*, pp. 427-28.   30 / *Ibid.*, p. 432.
28 / *Ibid.*, p. 429.   31 / *Ibid.*, p. 427.
29 / *Ibid.*, p. 431.

of possible costs, an organization of industry into small units which can effectively compete with each other."[32]

Judge Hand's decision is a landmark in the interpretation of the law. It made a clean break with the Steel and Harvester precedents. It resurrected Section 2 of the Sherman Act. It opened the way to enforcement of the law against monopolization as well as against conspiracy. But the decision was not without its own peculiarities. In holding expansion with the market through reinvestment of earnings to constitute monopolization, the Court created a precedent under which ordinary business foresight might be questioned and desirable improvements held in check. And in finding the preservation of smallness for its own sake to be a purpose of the law, it gave hostage to those who would use it, not to preserve competition, but to preserve the weak competitor.

In principle, the government won a sweeping victory in the Aluminum case. In fact, it obtained much less than it had sought. In 1950, in the district court to which Judge Hand had returned the Aluminum case for the preparation of a remedy, Judge Knox announced his decree. He first laid down a general rule:

> In determining the extent of permissible power that is consistent with the antitrust laws in a particular industry, the following factors are relevant: the number and strength of the firms in the market; their effective size from the standpoint of technological development, and from the standpoint of competition with substitute materials and with foreign trade; national security interest in the maintenance of strong productive facilities, and maximum scientific research and development; together with public interest in lowered costs and uninterrupted production.[33]

Aluminum, said the Court, must compete with other materials made by large concerns. Dismemberment of Alcoa's research staff and its managerial personnel would lessen its ability to do so. Success in interproduct competition "can be achieved only by companies that are rich in resources, and which are capable of undertaking extensive scientific and market experimentations. At the present juncture, the weakening of any aluminum producer would lessen the buoyancy of the industry as a whole."[34] The Court therefore denied the government's request that Alcoa be broken in two, finding its remedy in provisions requiring the company to license other domestic producers under its patents and to sever its ties with Aluminum, Ltd. of Canada, thus opening the way to competition from other firms.

The doctrine enunciated by Judge Hand in the Aluminum case was explicitly endorsed by the Supreme Court, in 1946, in the second American Tobacco case, discussed above. In this case three sellers, rather than a single seller, were involved. But the Court held that they could be convicted of monopolization,

---

32 / *Ibid.*, p. 429.
33 / *U.S.* v. *Aluminum Co. of America*, 91 F. Supp. 333, 347.
34 / *Ibid.*, p. 416.

under Section 2 of the Sherman Act, without proof that they had abused their power. Possession of power and the intention to use it were all that was required. Intent, however, could be inferred from identity of behavior. The existence of power was all that needed to be proved. In the words of the decision, "the material consideration in determining whether a monopoly exists is not that prices are raised and that competition actually is excluded, but that power exists to raise prices or to exclude competition when it is desired to do so." [35] The ghost of the steel decision was thus laid by the Supreme Court itself.

The Court returned to the issue of monopolization in the Griffith case, involving a chain of movie houses, in 1948. Said Justice Douglas: "It is not always necessary to find a specific intent to restrain trade or build a monopoly. . . . It is sufficient that a restraint of trade or monopoly results as the consequence of a defendant's conduct or business arrangements. . . . Monopoly power, whether lawfully or unlawfully acquired, may itself constitute an evil and stand condemned under Section 2 even though it remains unexercised." [36]

Sources of Monopoly Power

The United Shoe Machinery Corporation, a combination of three concerns, controlling 95 percent of the output of shoe machinery, was brought before the Supreme Court in 1913 charged with violation of the Sherman Act. At that time, the Court found the combination to be innocent, holding that each of the companies had been given a legal monopoly by its patent rights, and that the machines they made were not competitive but complementary. [37] Forty years later, the company, still maintaining its dominant position, was again tried on the same charge. But this time it was found to have violated Section 2 of the Sherman Act by monopolizing the industry. The decision in the case was handed down by Judge Charles Wyzanski in 1953. [38] It followed the precedent established in the Aluminum case. But Judge Wyzanski's reasoning went beyond that of Judge Hand. Monopoly, he agreed, is lawful if it is "thrust upon" the monopolist. A concern's monopoly power is unlawful, however,

if that power is to any substantial extent the result of barriers erected by its own business methods (even though not predatory, immoral, or restraining trade in violation of Section 1 of the Sherman Act), unless the enterprise shows that the barriers are *exclusively* the result of superior skill, superior products, natural advantages, technological or economic efficiency, scientific research, low margins of profit maintained permanently and without discrimination, legal licenses, or the like. [39]

35 / *American Tobacco Co.* v. *U.S.*, 328 U.S. 781, 811.
36 / *U.S.* v. *Griffith*, 334 U.S. 100, 105-7.
37 / *U.S.* v. *Winslow*, 227 U.S. 202.
38 / *U.S.* v. *United Shoe Machinery Corp.*, 110 F. Supp. 295.
39 / *Ibid.*, pp. 296-97. Italics supplied.

The offense of attempting to monopolize requires evidence of intent; the offense of monopolizing does not. The means employed, in themselves, may be lawful; the result may be monopolization, which is not lawful. United's business practices—such as leasing rather than selling its machines and making long-term contracts on exclusive terms—were not per se immoral or illegal. But the company had not achieved and maintained its overwhelming strength solely by virtue of its "ability, economies of scale, research, and adaptation to inevitable economic laws." Instead, given its dominant position, its business practices, however legal in themselves, had operated to exclude competitors from the field. Judge Wyzanski, thus, did not find monopolization to be illegal as such. But he imposed on the monopolist a stricter standard of conduct than that applying to competitive concerns. The former, he said, must be denied the right to follow practices in which the latter may safely be permitted to engage. The decision was appealed by the company and was upheld in 1954 by the Supreme Court.[40]

The government asked the court to split United into three competing firms. Judge Wyzanski refused to do so, ordering the company, instead, to sell as well as lease its machines, shorten its leases, modify their terms, and grant licenses under its patents to its competitors. During the next decade, United diversified its business, reducing shoe machinery to 10 percent of its sales and reducing its share of the shoe machinery market to 60 percent. The Antitrust Division asked that the case be reopened, holding that 60 percent was still too large a share. The judge refused, the government appealed, and his decision was overruled by a unanimous Supreme Court.[41] In 1969, accordingly, the company was required to dispose of enough of its shoe machinery business to reduce its share of that market to a third.

The issue of monopolization was raised again in the suits brought against International Business Machines in 1968 and 1969. Here, it was charged that the company's methods of selling or leasing computers and related materials and services operated to give it a virtual monopoly of the computer industry. It remained to be seen whether IBM.s dominance of this industry would be held to constitute illegal monopolization and, if so, whether the law would be satisfied by a change in the company's business practices or whether a more drastic remedy would be required.

The State of the Law

The meaning of the law on combination and monopolization is clearer since the Aluminum and Shoe Machinery decisions than it was before. Size, in itself, as the Supreme Court said in 1920, is no offense. Monopoly as such is legal where it has been "thrust upon" the monopolist. This may be the case where a firm owns the sole deposit of a mineral, where it has been given a patent or an

40 / 347 U.S. 521.
41 / *U.S.* v. *United Shoe Machinery Corp.,* 391 U.S. 244 (1968).

exclusive license, where it is the first to produce a new product, to introduce a new process or a new technique of marketing, where it has bested its rivals by reducing prices, raising quality, or improving service, or where demand is so small and the optimum scale of production so large that there is no room for a second plant. Attempts to monopolize will be held illegal where intent to monopolize can be shown. Monopolization itself may be held illegal, and here no proof of intent is required. Possession of monopoly power may be held unlawful even though the power was lawfully acquired. Abuse of monopoly power will be condemned. But such power may also be condemned, even though it has never been abused. If it has the effect of barring the entry of others to a market, it may be held to violate the law.

The force of the law depends upon the effectiveness of the remedies which it applies. Where competitors have agreed, the courts have long been vigorous in striking down restraints. Where a single firm has possessed a monopoly, they have increasingly shown themselves willing so to limit its powers and reform its practices as to open the way to the entry and growth of possible competitors. But they are still reluctant to break up closely knit combinations and will do so only where it appears that there is no other solution to be found. Whatever the judges may have said, the hand of the law has fallen more heavily on those who have conspired, more lightly on those who have monopolized.

MERGERS UNDER THE CLAYTON ACT

The Sherman Act, in its application to combinations, was punitive and corrective. Section 7 of the Clayton Act was designed to be preventive. The test of illegality in the Sherman Act was strict: it required proof of accomplished monopolization or of intent to monopolize. The test in the Clayton Act was easier to meet: it required only a reasonable probability that competition would be substantially lessened at some future time. Convictions should thus have been easier to obtain under the Clayton than under the Sherman Act. But here, again, judicial interpretation robbed the law of force.

The Impotence of Section 7

The Clayton Act sought to prevent monopolistic combinations by forbidding a company to hold the shares of a competitor or a third company to hold the shares of two competing firms. It was soon discovered that this method of control left open an escape. The shares that one concern held in another could be voted to effect an acquisition of the latter's assets before the case was brought to court. In 1926, the Supreme Court held, in the Swift and Thatcher cases, that the FTC could not order a meat-packing company to divest itself of assets acquired in this way.[42] And again, in 1934, the Court decided, in the Arrow-Hart & Hegeman case, that the Commission was powerless to act when a

42 / *Thatcher Mfg. Co.* v. *FTC, Swift & Co.* v. *FTC,* 272 U.S. 554.

holding company, after acquiring the shares of two competing corporations, had distributed them to its stockholders who had thereupon voted to merge the two concerns. [43]

Section 7 established a broad and a narrow test of legality, making it illegal (1) for a corporation to acquire stock in another corporation where the effect might be to restrain commerce or tend to create a monopoly, and (2) for a corporation to acquire stock in a competing corporation where the effect might be "to substantially lessen competition between the corporation whose stock is acquired and the corporation making the acquisition." The latter test proved to be so narrow that the next combination brought before the Court was also allowed to stand. In this case, the International Shoe Company, the largest manufacturer of shoes in the United States had acquired McElwain Shoe Company, the fourth or fifth in size. The two concerns produced shoes of different types and sold them through different channels to different customers. The Court held, in 1930, that there had been no competition between them and that the law, therefore, did not apply.[44]

Section 7 was thus rendered ineffective by its failure to cover the acquisition of assets as well as the acquisition of stock and by its limitation to cases in which the competition lessened was not competition in the market as a whole but competition between the concerns that were combined. It was believed, moreover, that the law applied only to horizontal combinations, since firms at different stages of production were not competitors. In the 36 years between the enactment of the Clayton Act and its amendment by the Celler-Kefauver Act, only 29 cases were brought by the government under Section 7 and none were brought in cases where vertical integration was involved.

The Sleeping Giant

The government won its only important victory under the original Section 7 in 1957. Here the issue was vertical integration and the defendants were du Pont and General Motors. The government brought suit against these companies in 1949, under the Sherman Act and incidentally under Section 7 of the Clayton Act, charging that du Pont's acquisition of GM stock had had the purpose and effect of controlling GM and using this control to obtain a preferred market for du Pont's automobile finishes and fabrics. The district court held, in 1954, that the government had failed to prove its case. The evidence, it said, did not show that du Pont had sought or exercised control of GM or received any preference in GM purchases. The government appealed, and the Supreme Court, in a 4 to 2 decision handed down in 1957, took the opposite view of the facts, holding that du Pont had sought and obtained a preferred position in the GM market.[45]

The significance of the decision lay in the force which it gave to the old

43 / *Arrow-Hart & Hegeman Electric Co.* v. *FTC*, 291 U.S. 587.
44 / *International Shoe Co.* v. *FTC*, 280 U.S. 291.
45 / *U.S.* v. *du Pont*, 353 U.S. 586.

Section 7 of the Clayton Act. The Court might have found that du Pont violated the Sherman Act by having obtained and used control of GM to further its own interest. Instead, it found the company in violation of the Clayton Act on the ground that its acquisition of GM stock—effected 40 years before—now had the potentiality of substantially lessening competition. In doing so, it explicitly applied Section 7 (using the broader test of legality) to vertical integration, thus enabling the government to prosecute such combinations, even though effected before 1950, at any time in the future when the threat of lessening competition may appear. Said the minority, in commenting on the "newly discovered teeth" of the Clayton Act, "it now becomes apparent for the first time that Section 7 has been a sleeping giant all along." [46]

MERGERS UNDER THE CELLER-KEFAUVER ACT

The defects of Section 7 were rectified in 1950 when Congress passed the Celler-Kefauver Act. The law was made to apply to the acquisition of assets as well as stock. And such acquisitions were made illegal where the effect "may be substantially to lessen competition or tend to create a monopoly" in the market as a whole. The force of the law that was designed to prevent monopolistic combinations was thus restored.

The Department of Justice and the Federal Trade Commission have concurrent jurisdiction in enforcement of the law. Here, as elsewhere, the division of labor between the two is largely a matter of chance. With mergers running between 1,000 and 4,000 a year in the fifties and the sixties, these agencies have been able to do no more than select for prosecution in any year a score of cases which they believe to be important because large firms are involved or because they present significant points of law for interpretation by the courts. By 1970, as many as 300 actions had been instituted by the government under the Celler-Kefauver Act, around three fifths of them by the Department of Justice and two fifths by the FTC. These had involved three types of combinations: horizontal, vertical, and conglomerate. In each of these areas, the government has scored impressive victories in the courts.

Horizontal Combinations

The first case to be brought before the courts by the government under the new law involved a proposed merger between Bethlehem Steel and Youngstown Sheet and Tube. Bethlehem, the nation's second largest steel producer, had notified the Department of Justice in 1956 that it planned to acquire Youngstown, the sixth largest, thus raising its own share of the nation's output from 15 percent to 20 percent, and the share of U.S. Steel and Bethlehem together from 45 percent to 50 percent. The Department sued to enjoin the merger, and the case went to trial in 1958 under Judge Edward Weinfeld in a federal district

46 / *Ibid.*, p. 611.

court. The defense argued that the merger would make the industry more competitive, since it would enable Bethlehem to compete more effectively with U.S. Steel. It directed the court's attention, in particular, to the market near Chicago. Here, Bethlehem had no plant and shipped in less than 1 percent of its output. By acquiring and expanding Youngstown's Chicago facilities, it would provide more vigorous competition for U.S. Steel in this area. These contentions were rejected by Judge Weinfeld. The merger, he said,

> offers an incipient threat of setting into motion a chain reaction of further mergers by the other but less powerful companies in the steel industry. If there is logic to the defendants' contention that their joinder is justified to enable them . . . to offer "challenging competition to United States Steel . . ." then the remaining large producers in the "Big Twelve" could with equal logic urge that they, too, be permitted to join forces . . . in order to give more effective competition to the enhanced "Big Two"; and so we reach a point of more intense concentration in an industry already highly concentrated—indeed we head in the direction of triopoly.

The judge was not persuaded that the merger afforded the only means by which the supply of steel in the Chicago area could be increased. In any case, he said, the argument was irrelevant, since Congress "made no distinction between good mergers and bad mergers. It condemned all which came within the reach of the prohibition of Section 7." The merger was enjoined.[47] Bethlehem did not appeal.

The first decision in which the Supreme Court undertook to interpret the Celler-Kefauver Act was handed down by a unanimous court in the Brown Shoe case in 1962.[48] The Brown Shoe Company, which manufactured 4.0 percent of the nation's output of shoes, had acquired the Kinney Company, which manufactured 0.5 percent. Brown was the third largest distributor of shoes with 1,230 retail stores; Kinney the eighth with 350 stores. In certain local markets for particular types of shoes, the combined share of the two concerns amounted to 20 percent or more. The Court put less emphasis on the existing structure of the market than on the historical trend toward increasing concentration in the shoe industry. "We cannot avoid the mandate of Congress," it said, "that tendencies toward concentration in industry are to be curbed in their incipiency, particularly when these tendencies are being accelerated through giant steps striding across a hundred cities at a time. In the light of the trends in this industry, we agree . . . that this is an appropriate place at which to call a halt."[49] The Court observed that Congress did not intend to prevent a merger between two small companies that would enable them to compete better with larger ones or a merger between a corporation which is financially healthy and one that is failing and is thus unable effectively to compete. But elsewhere, according

47 / *U.S.* v. *Bethlehem Steel Corp.,* 168 F. Supp. 576.
48 / *Brown Shoe Co.* v. *U.S.,* 370 U.S. 294.
49 / *Ibid.,* p. 345.

to the Court's interpretation, any merger in an important market may be challenged if a trend toward concentration exists. And it may be held illegal unless the merging companies can show that it is likely to increase competition and thus to serve the public interest.

The Court went on, in 1964, to uphold the application of the law in cases where an acquired firm produced a tiny portion of total output and where the competition of such a firm was only potential. The Aluminum Company of America, producing 27.8 percent of aluminum conductor output, had purchased the Rome Cable Corporation, producing only 1.3 percent. But the Court found that Rome was "an aggressive competitor . . . a pioneer" with "special aptitude and skill . . . and an effective research and sales organization." It was "the prototype of the small independent that Congress aimed to preserve by Section 7." [50] The El Paso Natural Gas Company, the only firm bringing gas into California, had acquired the Pacific Coast Pipeline Company, which operated outside the state. Pacific had attempted to enter the California market without success. But its efforts, said the Court, "had a powerful influence on El Paso's business attitudes." [51] Its potential competition should be preserved. In both cases, the Court ordered divestiture.

The Court also upheld the government, in 1966, in a case involving the merger of two retail food chains in Los Angeles. Here, Von's Grocery, the third largest food chain in the area, had acquired the Shopping Bag, the sixth largest, thus moving into second place. But Von's share of the market, after the merger, was only 7.5 percent. The share of all the market leaders was declining, and there was no barrier to the entry of new concerns. But the Court noted that the number of stores operated by individual owners had fallen. And it found the merger to be unlawful on the ground that it was the purpose of the law "to prevent concentration in the American economy by keeping a large number of small competitors in business." [52]

The government has been victorious in many other cases of horizontal combination, challenging projected mergers which were thereupon abandoned, negotiating consent decrees, winning decisions in the lower courts which were not appealed, and being upheld in the Supreme Court. It has also been upheld in cases involving vertical combinations and conglomerates.

Vertical Combinations

Congress, when it passed the Celler-Kefauver Act, eliminated the wording in the old Section 7 that made mergers illegal where the effect "may be to substantially lessen competition between the corporation whose stock is acquired and the corporation making the acquisition." It thus made clear that the new law was not to be limited to horizontal combinations but was to apply to

50 / *U.S.* v. *Aluminum Co. of America*, 377 U.S. 271, 280.
51 / *U.S.* v. *El Paso Natural Gas Co.*, 376 U.S. 651, 659.
52 / *U.S.* v. *Von's Grocery Co.*, 384 U.S. 280 (1966).

vertical and conglomerate combinations as well. The application of the law to vertical combinations was considered by the Supreme Court in the Brown Shoe case.

Brown manufactured shoes. Kinney, the company acquired by Brown, sold shoes in 350 retail stores. It accounted for less than 2 percent of the sales of shoes in the United States, for a higher percentage of sales of particular types of shoes in particular markets. The Court held the data as to market shares to be relevant but not determinative. It was concerned, rather, with the likelihood that Brown would require Kinney to carry Brown's shoes, closing the Kinney market to Brown's competitors. Such a development, said the Court, would be inherently anticompetitive. In an industry moving toward increasing concentration, it would exclude competition from a substantial share of the relevant markets. In its vertical as well as in its horizontal aspect, the combination was therefore in violation of Section 7.[53]

The Court did not hold vertical integration to be illegal per se. The standard it applied was similar to that employed in judging the legality of exclusive dealing under Section 3 of the Act. In both cases, it is the foreclosure of substantial markets to competitors that makes exclusive arrangements unlawful.

Conglomerate Combinations

A conglomerate combination brings together businesses that are unlike in character, being neither competitive nor vertically related. But such a combination may nonetheless have an adverse effect on competition. It may increase the market power of a leading firm in a concentrated industry. It may forestall potential competition by eliminating a possible entrant to the market. It may put the conglomerate, as a large purchaser of goods from other companies, in a position to insist that they reciprocate by purchasing its own goods or those of its affiliates. Its exercise of this power may give it an unfair advantage over its competitors.

Three cases against conglomerates were brought before the Supreme Court in the sixties. Each of them involved reciprocal dealing. In the first, decided in 1965, the Consolidated Foods Corporation, operating a nationwide chain of groceries and buying large quantities of processed food, had acquired Gentry, Inc., a small wholesaler making a third of the nation's sales of dehydrated onions and garlic. Consolidated was thus enabled to require the food processors who sold to it to buy their onions and garlic from Gentry, thereby excluding Gentry's competitors from its market for these commodities. The Court held that the reciprocity made possible by the merger was anticompetitive. "We do not say," it went on, "that any acquisition, no matter how small, violates Section 7 if there is a probability of reciprocal buying. . . . But where, as here, the acquisition is of a company that commands a substantial share of the market, a finding of probability of reciprocal buying by the Commission should be honored."[54]

53 / *Brown Shoe Co.* v. *U.S.* 370 U.S. 294, 322-23.
54 / *FTC* v. *Consolidated Foods Corporation,* 380 U.S. 592.

In a second case, decided in 1967, Procter & Gamble, a leading manufacturer of detergents, had acquired control of Clorox, the producer of half of the nation's output of liquid bleaches. Procter & Gamble was the nation's largest advertiser, its annual expenditures for this purpose running to more than $175 million. As a major customer of the television networks, it received quantity discounts when it purchased time. Used in promoting Clorox, the company's economic power could give it a marked advantage over other producers of liquid bleaches. The Supreme Court held the acquisition to be illegal and ordered divestiture.[55]

In the third case, decided in 1968, General Foods had acquired S.O.S., the leading manufacturer of steel wool scouring pads. The FTC charged that the market power of General Foods might be employed to enable S.O.S. to obtain an even larger share of the scouring pad business. Its order for divestiture was upheld by the courts.[56]

The State of the Law

The Celler-Kefauver Act does not bar all mergers. Two small concerns may combine. A healthy concern may acquire a failing one. But the fact that a merger would enable a firm to reduce its costs does not justify its approval. Nor does the fact that it would enable a firm to compete more successfully with the leaders in its industry. The law forbids the elimination of potential as well as actual competitors. It not only outlaws a combination of firms that sell the same product in the same market; it also outlaws combinations of firms that sell unlike products where the effect may be to lessen competition by enhancing market power.

It is the policy of the antimerger law, as now interpreted, to check increasing concentration in its incipiency. The law permits the attainment of oligopolistic status through internal growth. But it seeks to prevent its attainment through combination. Though the competition of giants might well be more effective than that of pygmies, the law seeks not only to maintain competition but also to preserve small concerns. Said the Court in the Brown Shoe case,

> It is competition, not competitors, which the Act protects. But we cannot fail to recognize Congress' desire to promote competition through the protection of viable, small, locally owned businesses. Congress appreciated that occasional higher costs and prices might result from the maintenance of fragmented industries and markets. It resolved these competing considerations in favor of decentralization.[57]

The two purposes—maintaining competition and preserving small concerns—are not the same. Mergers that increase efficiency may rob the independent com-

55 / FTC v. Procter & Gamble, 386 U.S. 568.
56 / FTC v. General Foods Corp., 386 F. 2d 836; 391 U.S. 919, Cert. den.
57 / Brown Shoe Co. v. U.S., 370 U.S. 294, 343.

petitor of sales. Integration that cuts costs may make life more difficult for the nonintegrated firm. The growth of the larger enterprise may drive its smaller rival out of business. But this is the way of competition. And hard as it may be on the small producer, it operates to serve the interest of the consumer.

Antimerger Guidelines

In their enforcement of the Celler-Kefauver Act, in the fifties and the sixties, the Antitrust Division and the Federal Trade Commission were upheld by the courts in every major action they brought and on every issue involving the interpretation of the law. With mergers running up to 4,000 a year, they found themselves embarrassed by their success. Possessing legal authority to stem the tide, they lacked the time and the staff to do so. Nor did they always wish to make the attempt. In three instances where large automobile manufacturers merged—Kaiser with Willys, Nash with Hudson, and Packard with Studebaker—the enforcement agencies entered no complaint, doubtless hoping that the combinations would increase the ability of these concerns to compete with General Motors, Ford, and Chrysler. When Ford acquired Philco, too, they took no action, possibly influenced by the fact that General Motors had been left in possession of Frigidaire. Indeed, there was some disposition in Washington to take the view that the government should pause to digest its legal victories and to base its future program of enforcement on more careful economic analyses.

The Division and the Commission both made such analyses. But they proceeded in quite different ways. The Division issued guidelines of general applicability, indicating the circumstances under which it was and was not prepared to prosecute for violation of the law. The Commission confined its pronouncements to particular industries, basing them on the facts revealed in case by case studies of these industries.

In cases of horizontal combinations among distributors of dairy products and retail food chains, the FTC found anticompetitive effects where the combinations had reached a certain absolute size or captured a certain share of the market; it therefore promised to investigate all cases where such a size or share was attained. In the cement industry, the Commission found that vertical combinations between the manufacturers of cement and local producers of ready-mixed concrete operated to exclude other manufacturers from these markets and it promised to attack such combinations whenever they occurred. In the case of automotive tires, the Commission's staff found the industry to be so highly concentrated that all future acquisitions by the major companies, whether horizontal or vertical, should be banned. These pronouncements took all of the economic circumstances in the industries into account. Their meaning was plain, but their applicability was limited.

The Antitrust Division's guidelines, in preparation for three years, were published in 1968. In accordance with their provisions, the Division announced that it was prepared to challenge a merger under any of the following circumstances:

Horizontal mergers
  A. On the basis of market structure:
      1. If the four largest firms have 75% of the market and
            the acquiring firm has   4% and the acquired firm 4% or
            the acquiring firm has 10% and the acquired firm 2% or
            the acquiring firm has 15% and the acquired firm 1%.
      2. If the four largest have less than 75% of the market and
            the acquiring firm has   5% and the acquired firm 5% or
            the acquiring firm has 10% and the acquired firm 4% or
            the acquiring firm has 15% and the acquired firm 3% or
            the acquiring firm has 20% and the acquired firm 2% or
            the acquiring firm has 25% and the acquired firm 1%.
  B. On the basis of increasing concentration:
        If the acquired firm has 2% of the market and the share of the
        largest two to eight firms has risen 7% or more in the last five to
        ten years.
  C. Without regard to market shares:
        If the acquired firm is unusually competitive, actually or poten-
        tially, or has assets conferring an unusual competitive advantage.
Vertical mergers
  A. If a firm that is a customer for a product makes 6% of the purchases
      and a firm supplying the product makes 10% of the sales, unless
      their merger raises no significant barrier to entry.
  B. If a firm that is a customer for a product has 10% of its own market,
      if the product is essential to its business, and if a firm supplying the
      product makes 20% of the sales.
  C. If a customer or a supplier is acquired by a major firm in an industry
      with a significant trend toward vertical integration, if such a com-
      bination would raise barriers to entry, and if it does not promise to
      cut the costs of production.
  D. If a customer or a supplier is acquired for the purpose of barring
      competitors from the market or otherwise putting them at a disad-
      vantage.
Conglomerate mergers
  A. If a firm that has a large share of a market seeks to acquire a firm
      that is the only potential entrant to the market or one of the only
      two potential entrants.
  B. If a merger creates the danger of substantial reciprocal buying.
  C. In other circumstances where further investigation suggests the pres-
      ence of anticompetitive effects.

It will be noted that these guidelines are set forth, in the main, in terms of
market structure, with the boundaries of relevant markets defined and the
shares of individual firms measured. They are concerned with concentration of
control. They are based on the assumption that an industry's performance in

the public interest will be worse when the degree of concentration is high; better when it is low. As a general rule, this is true. But there are cases where increased concentration would make for improved service and lowered costs. If undesirable combinations are to be prevented and desirable combinations permitted, criteria involving something more than market structure may be required.

THE RELEVANT MARKET

In order to determine whether a defendant is guilty of monopolizing or attempting to monopolize, under the Sherman Act, a court must decide not only whether he has engaged in the illegal activities known as monopolization or attempted monopolization but also whether—as a matter of economic fact— he has obtained or sought a monopoly. It must therefore define the market that is relevant to its decision and determine what share of that market is to be regarded as conferring monopoly power. In order to find whether a merger, under the Celler-Kefauver Act, may substantially lessen competition or tend to create a monopoly "in any line of commerce in any section of the country," the court, again, must define the market and denominate the illegal share. These decisions may be crucial. If markets are narrowly defined, monopolization and the substantial lessening of competition will be frequent; if markets are broadly defined, they will be rare. If the market share conferring monopoly power or substantially lessening competition is set low, convictions will be many; if it is set high, they will be few. Definition of relevant markets and determination of market shares have therefore commanded the attention of the courts.

The Line of Commerce

To determine a relevant market, a court may find it necessary to define the commodity with which it is concerned. This problem does not arise with products such as cigarettes and shoe machinery. But where a product has close substitutes, the court must decide whether to exclude or include them when it measures market power. If substitution were to be ignored, every brand would have a monopoly. If all possible substitutes were to be taken into account, monopoly would be rare indeed. The question is where to draw the line.

Like products may have different physical characteristics; they may have different end uses; they may sell in different price lines; their markets, therefore, may be distinct. Like products, on the other hand, may be readily interchangeable; their market, therefore, will be the same. The degree of interchangeability is to be measured by cross-elasticity of demand. Cross-elasticity defines the extent to which a change in the price of one product affects the sales of another. If a slight change in the price of product A results in a large change in the sales of product B, cross-elasticity is high. Conversely, if a sharp change in the price of A has little effect on sales of B, cross-elasticity is low. In the first case, substitution occurs so readily that the two products can be held to occupy a single market. In the second, the possibility of substitution is so remote that the markets for the two must be regarded as separate.

The concept of cross-elasticity is potentially a useful one. But it is only recently that it has begun to find its way into the decisions of the courts. In most of the earlier cases, products were narrowly defined. Thus, sea-green slate, linen rugs, red-cedar shingles produced in the state of Washington, parchment paper, and hydraulic oil well pumps were held to occupy distinct markets, though in each case substitutes were readily available. [58]

In the Aluminum case, too, a finding of monopoly turned upon a faulty definition of the product and the market with which the court was concerned. By excluding aluminum scrap in measuring the supply of raw materials and including not only the ingots Alcoa sold to others but also the ingots it consumed itself, Alcoa's share of the market was found to stand at 90 percent. But scrap competes with ingots and was excluded on the ground that it had been derived from products made from ingots that Alcoa had once produced, though evidence was lacking that Alcoa controlled the scrap supply. Had scrap been included in measuring the market, Alcoa's share would have stood at 60-64 percent. And if Alcoa's consumption of its own ingots had been excluded, its share of the open market would have stood at 33 percent. By adopting the first of these definitions of the market, the Court was enabled to make a finding of monopoly. For it went on to hold that 90 percent "is enough to constitute a monopoly; it is doubtful whether 60 or 64 percent would be enough; and certainly 33 percent is not." [59]

The definition of markets cuts both ways. It convicted the Aluminum Company. It freed the *Times-Picayune*. This newspaper had a monopoly of the morning field in New Orleans. It also published an evening edition, and here it had a competitor. The paper refused to sell advertising space in its morning edition alone but required advertisers to purchase space in its evening edition as well. The government sued to break the tie. In its decision, in 1953, the Supreme Court laid down the rule that a tying contract is illegal per se when a seller has a monopoly in the tying product and when a substantial volume of commerce in the tied product is thus restrained. But it went on to find that the *Times-Picayune* had no monopoly, having reached this conclusion by defining the market to include all three dailies instead of separating the morning and evening markets and recognizing the *Times-Picayune* monopoly in the morning field. Under the former definition, the contract was held to be legal. [60] Under the latter, following the Court's own rule, it would have been enjoined.

The problems involved in defining the relevant market were more thoroughly explored by the courts in the case of cellophane. Du Pont, the producer of

58 / *O'Halloran* v. *American Sea Green Slate Co.*, 207 Fed. 187 (1913); *U.S.* v. *Klearflax Linen Looms*, 63 F. Supp. 32 (1945); *Gibbs* v. *McNeeley*, 118 Fed. 120 (1902); *Story Parchment Co.* v. *Paterson Paper Parchment Co.*, 282 U.S. 555 (1931); *Kobe, Inc.* v. *Dempsey Pump Co.*, 198 F. 2d 416 (1952).

59 / *U.S.* v. *Aluminum Co. of America*, 148 F. 2d 416, 424.

60 / *Times-Picayune Publishing Co.* v. *U.S.*, 345 U.S. 594.

cellophane, was charged (1) with attempting and conspiring to monopolize and (2) with monopolizing the market for this product. There was evidence to support the first of these charges, but it was not pressed by the government. Guilt or innocence under the second charge depended upon the definition of the market. If the market in question were that for cellophane alone, it was clear that the company had a monopoly, since it accounted for 75 percent of the output of the product and, together with its licensee Sylvania, for all of it. But if the market were that for flexible packaging materials, including glassine, parchment papers, waxed papers, pliofilm, and aluminum foil, du Pont's share was only 18 percent. The first definition was urged by the government; the second by du Pont. Judge Leahy, in the district court, found for the defense. The company, he said, had pioneered in developing the product. It had increased its sales by reducing its price. There was evidence of frequent and continuing shifts, in many uses, between cellophane and competing materials; the cross-elasticity of demand was high. "The record," said the judge, "reflects not the dead hand of monopoly but rapidly declining prices, expanding production, intense competition stimulated by creative research, the development of new products and uses and other benefits of a free economy." This verdict was sustained by a 4 to 3 vote of the Supreme Court in 1956. In defining a relevant market, said the Court, "commodities reasonably interchangeable by consumers for the same purposes" establish the boundaries. In this case, as Judge Leahy had found, cross-elasticity of demand was high and competition intense. The relevant market, therefore, was that for flexible packaging materials. [61]

This decision was open to criticism. The price of cellophane had, indeed, been sharply cut. But the reduction could have been the act of an intelligent monopolist. The fact that prices of other packaging materials held steady or even rose made it clear that their producers did not regard them as competitive. From 1924 to 1950, moreover, the price of cellophane was from seven times to two times that of the other materials. This fact appeared significant to the Court's minority:

> We cannot believe that . . . practical businessmen would have bought cellophane in increasing amounts over a quarter of a century if close substitutes were available at from one seventh to one half cellophane's price. That they did so is testimony to cellophane's distinctiveness. [62]

There seemed to be danger in the Court's formula of reasonable interchangeability that markets would thereafter be defined so broadly that monopoly would rarely be found. Thus, aluminum, copper, and steel might be held to compete in the market for metals, and rugs, carpets, and linoleum in the market for floor coverings. In the next year, however, the Court's decision in the case of du Pont and General Motors put such fears to rest.

The Court was strict in defining the product market. The defense had argued

---

61 / *U.S.* v. *du Pont,* 118 F. Supp. 41 (1953).
62 / *U.S.* v. *du Pont,* 351 U.S. 377.

that du Pont's sales of automobile finishes to GM were only 3.5 percent of all its sales of industrial finishes, and its sales of fabrics to GM only 1.6 percent of all its sales of fabrics. But the Court held that the characteristics of automotive finishes and fabrics were sufficiently peculiar to make them distinct, and that GM in itself constituted a substantial market for these products.[63] It thus retreated from the broadening of markets toward which it had moved in the cellophane case the year before. It is probably significant that the composition of the Court was changed between the two decisions, the minority in cellophane becoming the majority in GM. In any case, the product was defined in terms, not of interchangeability, but of its peculiar characteristics.

In the Bethlehem Steel case in 1958, the defendants sought to have their product so defined as to include nonferrous and plastic substitutes, following the precedent established in cellophane. Judge Weinfeld refused, holding that the line of commerce involved was a series of products having characteristics sufficiently peculiar to make them distinct, thus following the precedent established in du Pont—GM.

The judge went on to list the product markets in the case as iron and steel products as a whole and ten specific products, including track spikes. This reasoning is hard to follow. One can agree that each of the specific products listed is a separate line of commerce and that Section 7 is violated if competition may be substantially lessened in one or more of them. But it can scarcely be said that all iron and steel products, on the one hand, and track spikes, on the other, constitute separate lines. The market is either for iron and steel in general or for track spikes; it cannot be for both.

The Supreme Court returned to the problem of product-market definition in the Brown Shoe case in 1962. It recognized three markets: those for men's, women's, and children's shoes. The defense sought recognition for infants' and babies' shoes, misses' and children's shoes, and youths' and boys' shoes and, within the sex and age groups, for medium-priced and low-priced shoes. The Court refused, presenting its reasoning as follows:

> The outer boundaries of a product market are determined by the reasonable interchangeability of use or the cross-elasticity of demand between the product itself and substitutes for it. However, within this broad market, well-defined submarkets may exist which, in themselves, constitute product markets for antitrust purposes. The boundaries of such a submarket may be determined by examining such practical indicia as industry or public recognition of the submarket as a separate economic entity, the product's peculiar characteristics and uses, unique production facilities, distinct customers, distinct prices, sensitivity to price changes, and specialized vendors.[64]

In short, cross-elasticity of demand between shoes and hats, let us say, or gloves,

63 / *U.S. v. du Pont,* 353 U.S. 586.
64 / *Brown Shoe Co.* v. *U.S.,* 370 U.S. 294, 324.

can be used in defining the market for all shoes. But cross-elasticity cannot be used in distinguishing the markets for misses' dancing pumps and men's hob-nailed boots, those for dress shoes and work shoes, or those for Brown's shoes and Kinney's shoes. If the Court had agreed to define the markets in a different way, the outcome of the case might well have been the same. But here, again, judicial logic leaves something to be desired.

In the Rome Cable case in 1964, the District Court had defined the product as including both aluminum and copper conductors. The Supreme Court found that the two types of conductors had different uses, aluminum being used overhead and insulated copper underground. It found, too, that aluminum cable sold at half to two thirds of the price of copper cable and that elasticity of demand between them was low. It therefore reversed the District Court, defining the product as aluminum conductor alone.

The government won the Rome Cable case on a narrow definition of the product market. It won the Continental case, decided in the same month, on a broad definition. The metal containers made by Continental and the glass containers made by Hazel-Atlas were found to constitute a single product. "In our view," said the Court, "there is and has been a rather general confrontation between metal and glass containers and competition between them for the same end uses which is insistent, continuous, effective, and quantitywise very sub-stantial. [65] The prices of the two containers differed and cross-elasticity of demand between them was low. But these facts, while recognized as relevant, were held to be inconclusive. For price is only one factor in the canner's choice. Consumer preference (the housewife's preference, for instance, for glass rather than metal in the packaging of baby foods) may lead him to use a container that costs him more. "This may not be price competition," concluded the Court, "but it is nevertheless meaningful competition between interchangeable containers." [66] And here the Court was on solid ground.

The Section of the Country

In geographic extent, the relevant market may be local, regional, national, or international. The incidence of monopolization or of a probability of sub-stantially lessened competition will vary accordingly. Definition of spatial boundaries was crucial in two cases arising under the Sherman Act. In a case involving two publishers of farm papers, decided in 1934, where a Court of Appeals had found for the defendant on the ground that it did not have a monopoly of the national market for farm advertising, the Supreme Court reversed the decision, holding that the relevant market was confined to the eight states in which the papers of the plaintiff and the defendant had their major circulation. [67] In the Paramount case in 1948, where the lower court had

---

65 / *Continental Can Co.* v. *U.S.,* 378 U.S. 441, 489.

66 / *Ibid.,* p. 492.

67 / *Indiana Farmer's Guide* v. *Prairie Farmer,* 293 U.S. 268.

found that the five major producers of motion pictures did not have a monopoly of the business of exhibiting pictures, the Supreme Court held that they did have a monopoly of exhibition at the first-run theaters in the 92 largest cities of the country.[68]

Determination of the relevant geographic markets is equally important under the Celler-Kefauver Act. In defining these markets in the Bethlehem Steel case, Judge Weinfeld listed them as (a) the United States as a whole, (b) the northeast quadrant of the United States, (c) Michigan, Ohio, Pennsylvania, and New York, (d) Michigan and Ohio, (e) Michigan, and (f) Ohio. Such a definition makes little sense. If the market within which supply and demand operate to affect the price of steel-mill products is the United States, or its northeast quadrant, or a four-state or two-state area, it cannot be confined to Michigan or to Ohio alone. It is true, however, that the projected merger would have lessened competition in Michigan and along the border of Ohio and Pennsylvania, where Bethlehem and Youngstown had both made sales. On this basis, the merger was properly held to be in violation of the law.

In the Brown Shoe case, the Supreme Court found different markets to be relevant in considering the probable effects of horizontal combination and vertical integration. The combination of retail outlets, it held, would affect competition in "every city with a population exceeding 10,000 and its immediate contiguous surrounding territory in which both Brown and Kinney sold shoes at retail through stores they either owned or controlled.[69] The integration of manufacturing and distribution would affect competition in the United States as a whole.

In the Philadelphia-Girard case, the defendants argued that the combined bank would be in a stronger position to compete for business with banks in New York City and asked that the market be defined to include New York. The Court refused:

> The proper question to be asked . . . is not where the parties to the merger do business or even where they compete, but where, within the area of competitive overlap, the effect of the merger on competition will be direct and immediate. . . . In banking . . . convenience of location is essential to effective competition. Individuals and corporations typically confer the bulk of their patronage on banks in their local community; they find it impractical to conduct their banking business at a distance. [70]

On this basis, the Court found the relevant market to consist of the four-county area of metropolitan Philadelphia.

Interpretation of the law regarding geographic market boundaries was given a curious twist by the Court in the Pabst Brewing Co. case [71] in 1966. Pabst had

---

68 / *U.S.* v. *Paramount Pictures,* 334 U.S. 141.
69 / *Brown Shoe Co.* v. *U.S.,* 370 U.S. 294, 336.
70 / *U.S.* v. *Philadelphia National Bank,* 374 U.S. 321, 409-10.
71 / *U.S.* v. *Pabst Brewing Co.,* 384 U.S. 546.

acquired the Blatz Brewing Co., giving it 24 percent of the market for beer in Wisconsin, 11.3 percent of the market in the three states of Wisconsin, Illinois, and Michigan, and 4.5 percent of the market in the United States as a whole. The government contended that Wisconsin and the three-state area were the markets involved. The district court dismissed the case, finding the relevant market to be the country as a whole. The Supreme Court reversed this action, ordering the combination dissolved. But Mr. Justice Black, in its decision, brushed aside the issue of market boundaries, holding that the law did not require these boundaries to be delimited but demanded only a showing that competition had been substantially impaired "anywhere in the United States." Mr. Justice Harlan disagreed, insisting that all of the statistics presented in a case relate, of necessity, to a particular geographic market, and that this market must therefore be defined. Justice Harlan would appear to have the better of the argument.

The Market Share

Having defined the relevant market, the Court must go on to determine the share of that market that is to betoken monopolization or threaten substantial lessening of competition. In neither case is there a clear rule. The Supreme Court, over the years, has outlawed combinations controlling a fifth to a third of a market and absolved others controlling half to nine tenths. Fortunately, the Court has not embraced the dictum of Judge Hand that 90 percent constitutes a monopoly but 64 percent may not and 33 percent certainly does not. For if this rule were followed, the firms that could be convicted under Section 2 of the Sherman Act would be few and far between. The Court flatly refused, in the Columbia Steel case, to specify a percentage to be used in the future as a test of monopoly power. Such a figure, said the Court, would mean nothing in itself. Its significance would depend upon the whole complex of market factors in which it occurred. But in the Philadelphia-Girard case, the Court did set a figure beyond which it is prepared to find defendants guilty of violating the Celler-Kefauver Act. The merger, it said, "will result in a single bank's controlling at least 30 percent of the commercial banking business in the four-county Philadelphia metropolitan area. Without attempting to specify the smallest share which would still be considered to threaten undue concentration, we are clear that 30 percent presents that threat." [72]

The State of the Law

The boundaries of the market and the size of the market share that constitute monopolization or threaten substantially to lessen competition are not to be determined by resorting to a simple formula. Judgment must be exercised in deciding where to draw the line along a range of possible substitutes; where to set the limits of a trading area. Factors other than market shares are relevant. Account must be taken of potential as well as actual competition, conditions of entry, aggressiveness of market rivals, their financial strength and ability to grow. The statistics needed properly to delimit market boundaries and to measure market shares may not be readily available. Even if they are, decisions cannot be based on these data alone. More in the way of economic analysis is required. In the face of such difficulties, the courts have been feeling their way. They have yet to arrive at a position that gives real clarity to the law. And until they do, the legality of monopolization and merger, in particular cases, will still be unpredictable.

| *Chapter* | PATENTS, TRADEMARKS, |
| 8 | AND COPYRIGHTS |

To encourage the advancement of technology, government grants patents to inventors. To prevent sellers from misrepresenting the origin of their goods, it registers trademarks. To promote the creative arts, it records the copyrights of authors, artists, and composers. In each of these cases, it establishes a monopoly—a monopoly that could not exist unless protected by law. As a result, competitors are prevented from employing the patented process, using the registered mark, or reproducing the copyrighted material. The policies that find expression in the patent, trademark, and copyright laws are thus in conflict with the policy embodied in the antitrust laws. In some cases this conflict may not be serious: a copyright applies to but one among the many expressions given to ideas; a patent may cover a process for which there are alternatives; a trademark may be attached to goods that are in competition with others of their kind. But elsewhere the conflict may be serious indeed: a collection of patents may enable their owner to monopolize an entire industry; a name belonging to a single seller may be the only one by which the product of an industry is known. It is in such cases that the exclusive rights conferred by government create a problem of peculiar difficulty for antitrust.

THE PATENT GRANT

A patent is an exclusive right conferred on an inventor, for a limited period, by a government. It authorizes him to make, use, transfer, or withhold whatever may be patented. This he might do in any case; what the patent adds is the right to exclude others or to admit them on his own terms. Without a patent, he might attempt to preserve a monopoly by keeping his invention secret; to get a patent, it must be disclosed.

The policy of promoting invention by granting temporary monopolies to inventors, a policy that had been followed in England for nearly two centuries, was written into the Constitution of the United States. The framers of the Constitution did not mention patents, but they did empower the Congress, in Article I, Section 8, Paragraph 8, "To promote the progress of Science and useful Arts, by securing for limited Times to Authors and Inventors the exclusive Right to their respective Writings and Discoveries. . . ." It is upon this authority that the American patent system is based.

160

The Patent System

Congress passed the first patent law in 1790, offering protection to all inventors of novel and useful processes and devices who would disclose their nature in sufficient detail to "enable a workman or other person skilled in the art of manufacture . . . to make, construct . . . or use the same." Under this law a committee composed of the Secretary of State (Thomas Jefferson, himself an inventor of some note), the Secretary of War, and the Attorney General granted 57 patents during the next three years. In 1793 a second law relieved the cabinet officers of this burden, authorizing the Department of State to issue patents to everyone who might register inventions, without questioning their novelty or usefulness, leaving their validity to be determined by the courts. This act resulted in a flood of worthless patents and clogged the courts with litigation. It was superseded in 1836, by a third law which set up a Patent Office under a Commissioner of Patents, required that applications be examined to determine whether the inventions claimed were really new, and provided that patents should be issued only when such inventions were deemed by the Commissioner to be "sufficiently useful and important." The American patent system still rests upon the foundations established by the Act of 1836.

Patents have been obtainable in the United States since 1790 on any useful "art, manufacture, engine, machine," since 1793 on a "composition of matter," since 1842 on "ornamental designs," and since 1930 on botanical plants, and on improvements to any of them. The law thus covers processes of production (art, manufacture), the implements employed in such processes (engine, machine), and the products resulting from them (manufacture, composition of matter, and botanical plants). It covers, as a "composition of matter," not only such chemical products as dyestuffs, plastics, and synthetic fibers, but also foods and medicines—products to which the patent privilege is not generally extended under the laws of other countries. Patents on "ornamental designs" may relate to the design of the article itself or to designs that are incorporated in it or affixed to it. Designs, however, may be protected more cheaply and for longer periods by obtaining copyrights. Design protection is afforded to products that are durable, such as jewelry and furniture. But fashions, in which the element of design is important, are neither patented nor copyrighted, not because the law excludes them, but because they change too rapidly to be protected by the usual legal processes. Patents are not granted on methods of doing business, or on fundamental scientific discoveries. But otherwise the law is generous in its coverage.

Patents are issued to individuals, not to corporations. Under the law, a patent is granted only to a person called "the sole and true inventor." But patent rights can be transferred to others through assignment. An inventor may sell his rights in an invention he has already made. Or he may accept employment under a contract which binds him to transfer his rights in any invention that he may come to make. In the usual case, he will file his assignment along with his application for a patent, and the corporation that employs him will be the assignee. In legal theory, patents are issued to individual inventors; in practice, 70 percent of them are assigned to corporations.

The territorial scope of a patent is limited to the jurisdiction of the country that grants it. An American who wishes to protect his invention in other countries must take out patents under their laws. Foreigners may likewise take out patents in the United States. A patent may be exploited in one country, in another, or in both, and rights in different countries may be assigned to different firms. Products that are patented may not be imported in violation of domestic patent rights.

In England in 1643 the duration of a patent was fixed at 14 years, a period sufficient to enable a craftsman to train two successive groups of apprentices. This term was adopted in the first patent law in the United States. In 1861, however, an effort to extend the term to 20 years resulted in a compromise that fixed it at 17, and 17 years is still the nominal duration of the monopoly conferred by the patent grant.

In most other countries the patent holder is required to put his invention to work. In some countries this requirement is absolute. In others, it may be waived if the holder can show good cause or prove that a reasonable effort has been made. Failure to work an invention may be penalized by revocation or by the requirement that it be licensed to others. Licensing may also be required where enforcement of one patent would prevent the development of an invention covered by another, where refusal to license would prejudice the trade of other groups, and where the output of patented goods falls short of meeting public needs. No such obligations attach to patents issued by the United States. Within the limits laid down by the courts, the owner of a patent may refuse to work it, work it himself and refuse to license it to others, or license it on such terms as he may choose. In the lightness of its requirements, as in the breadth of its grants, the American patent law is noted for its liberality.

How Patents Are Issued and Validated

It is the function of the Patent Office merely to accept or to reject the applications that are brought before it. Each application must describe, with some precision, the nature of the invention that is claimed. This description takes the form of drawings or formulae accompanied by exposition couched in technical phraseology; no working models have been required since 1890. The monopoly awarded to an applicant will be confined within the boundaries of his claims. These claims are usually formulated by a patent lawyer employed by the inventor or, more often, by the corporate assignee. Their preparation is an art in itself. The broader they can be made, without appearing to be limitless, the wider will be the area of the monopoly. The less informative they can be made, without appearing to withhold essential facts, the less is the likelihood that the technology involved will be disclosed to possible competitors. When the application, thus carefully prepared, is submitted to the Patent Office, it must be accompanied by a $65 fee. when the patent is obtained, another $100 must be paid. The fee or salary of the patent lawyer is the major cost of patenting.

Applications are not made public by the Patent Office. Persons who may hold patents on similar inventions are not informed of the proceedings. Persons who might be injured by a grant of monopoly are not notified. Agencies of government charged with the maintenance of competition are not represented. Interests adverse to the grant are given no opportunity to protest. Whether a patent shall be issued is determined as a matter not of public interest but of private privilege.

An invention is not supposed to be patented unless it is new and useful and actually works. But the number of applications presented to the Patent Office is so large, and the resources available for handling them are, by comparison, so small, that rigorous standards of appraisal cannot, in practice, be maintained. The Office does not undertake to determine whether an invention is workable; it has no laboratories or testing bureaus of its own; it lacks the funds and the time required to seek the technical advice of private agencies. With respect to usefulness, it adheres to the standard established by Justice Story in 1817. The word "useful," he said, "is incorporated in the Act in contradistinction to mischievous or immoral."[1] An invention is thus presumed to be useful unless there is evidence that it would do positive harm. Nor is there real assurance that the invention covered by a patent is new. The burden imposed on the Patent Office is so heavy and its resources, in comparison, so limited, that a thorough search of prior technology cannot be made.

Applications for patents run around 100,000 per year, with more than 200,000 pending at any one time, each of them being taken up in its turn. The Patent Office has a staff of 70 examiners and 1,000 assistant examiners. The typical assistant examiner is an engineering graduate who is studying law at night, preparing to become a patent attorney. The turnover in this group, amounting to 20 percent per year, is one of the highest in the government. Each assistant examiner handles 70 to 80 patent applications per year. In each case, he must analyze the application and search the prior art as revealed in Patent Office files and in scientific publications in the United States and abroad. In the case of certain chemicals, this process has been speeded by computerizing some of the relevant data; in other fields, however, mechanization is more difficult and has not yet been undertaken. An examiner typically rejects one or more claims in an initial application, giving the applicant six months in which to file an amended application, which he then considers in its turn. He has, on the average, three working days in which to take all the steps that may be required from his first receipt of an application until a final determination can be made. Two out of five applications are finally abandoned or rejected; three are allowed. The typical patent, when granted, has been pending more than three years.[2]

If the examiner rejects an application, it may be carried to the Board of Appeals in the Patent Office where, in a third to a half of the cases, he is likely

1 / *Lowell* v. *Lewis,* 15 Fed. Cases, 1018, 1019.

2 / U.S. Senate, Committee on the Judiciary, Subcommittee on Patents, Trademarks, and Copyrights, Study No. 29, *The Examination System in the U.S. Patent Office* (Washington, D.C.: Government Printing Office, 1961).

to be reversed. If the examiner is sustained, the applicant may go on to the Court of Customs and Patent Appeals where his chance of obtaining a patent may be one in five. Out of this process, there emerged an average annual crop of 22,000 patents during the eighties and the nineties, more than 35,000 from 1900 to 1920, more than 46,000 in the twenties and thirties, around 35,000—with somewhat more rigorous standards prevailing—in the forties, and around 50,000 in the fifties and sixties. In this flood of claims to monopolistic rights, granted as carelessly as must be the case, there will be many that will overlap.

The Patent Office does not guarantee its product. It does not warrant that the patentee is the true inventor or insure that his claim will be upheld. If he is sued for infringing another patent, he can argue that his own is different or superior. But the Patent Office will not come to his assistance. It leaves to him the burden and the cost of his defense. All that it gives him is a claim upon which he himself can enter suit. If another uses his invention without permission, he can seek an injunction and ask for damages. But the defendant may counter with a patent of his own, or may argue that the plaintiff's patent covers a process or a product that has long been common property. The resolution of such conflicts is the duty of the courts.

Judges have had their training, not in physics, chemistry, and engineering, but in the law. They are seldom expert in industrial technology. But they must decide whether a patent covers a real invention, whether it was issued to the true inventor, and whether it has been infringed. And it is their judgment that determines the existence, the ownership, and the scope of the patent monopoly. Invention of the telephone was claimed by Daniel Drawbaugh, Elisha Gray, and Alexander Graham Bell. Gray's patents were acquired by the Bell interests when their suit against Western Union was settled out of court, and the telegraph company withdrew from the telephone industry. Drawbaugh's telephone was invented in 1869 and put to work in 1871; Bell's was patented in 1876. When Bell's suit against Drawbaugh reached the Supreme Court, two judges did not sit, three voted for Drawbaugh and four for Bell. It was on this foundation that the telephone monopoly was built.[3] More often, however, the courts have found that the plaintiff's patent was not infringed or that it was lacking in validity. Among 124 infringement suits brought before the Supreme Court from 1900 to 1960, 28 were found to be based on valid patents that had been infringed, 27 on patents that were valid but not infringed, and 69 on patents that were void.[4] It is a rare patent, however, that is taken to court, and an even rarer one that is appealed to the higher courts. The currency that is issued by the Patent Office thus passes at face value, save in those cases where the courts have found it to be counterfeit.

Monopoly and the Advancement of Technology

Inventive activity is not to be attributed exclusively, or even largely, to

---

3 / *The Telephone Cases,* 126 U.S. 1 (1887).

4 / E. Burke Inlow, *The Patent Grant* (Baltimore: Johns Hopkins Press, 1950), pp. 142-43; and 85th Cong., 2d Sess., Senate Report 1430, p. 19.

desire for monetary gain. No one can say what actuated the inventors of the wheel, the wedge, the lever, the pulley, the mill, the screw, the drill, the lathe, the keel, the oar, the sail. Certain it is, however, that these contrivances emerged from cultures where the patent was unknown. Many men in later times have been driven to construct devices which could bring them no possible profit. Leonardo da Vinci, Benjamin Franklin, Thomas Jefferson never left off inventing things, never attempted to turn their inventions to practical account. Taussig, who studied the lives of the great utilitarian inventors found that they, too, "were constantly experimenting on all sorts of schemes, promising and unpromising. . . ." With these men, "schemes and experiments begin in child-hood, and persist so long as life and strength hold. It matters not whether a fortune is made or pecuniary distress is chronic."[5] And when the Patent, Trademark, and Copyright Foundation asked a long list of inventors if the availability of patent protection had stimulated their inventive activity, one fifth of those who replied said yes; four fifths said that it was not essential or made little difference.[6] The nature and the motivation of invention have been something other than the law assumes.

The patent system was established in an agricultural and handicraft economy. The first patents were awarded for a plow of cast iron, a cradle to be used in cutting grain, and improvements on the tools employed by artisans. Inventions were put to work by the inventors who developed them. Following the industrial revolution, with machine production, the factory system, and the growth of corporate enterprise, the process of invention underwent a striking change. Technology grew in scale and in complexity. Scientific knowledge came increasingly to be specialized. Invention came to require elaborate and costly equipment and to depend for its success on organized research. Corporations began to build their own laboratories and to hire their own technicians, putting them to work inventing for a salary. As an improvement emerged from a corporate laboratory, one of its employees was designated to play the part of the sole and true inventor when a patent was obtained. But the profits of the patent monopoly did not accrue to him. They belonged to his employer to whom the patent was assigned. And this is the basis on which the great majority of new inventions are made and patented today.

This change has given to the patent system a new and entirely different rationale. Research is costly, and the commercial development of innovations may demand substantial sums. The ideas that succeed must provide the revenues to pay for those that fail. If competitors were straightway free to imitate the successes and avoid the failures, sharing in the profits of innovation without contributing to its costs, it would be less worth while to make the investments that are required to finance invention and to assume the risks that are involved. It is the temporary monopoly afforded by the patent that encourages the investments and justifies the risks. The patent system thus finds its function less in the

5 / F. W. Taussig, *Inventors and Moneymakers* (New York: Macmillan Co., 1915), pp. 21-23.

6 / U.S. Congress, Joint Economic Committee, *Invention and the Patent System* (Washington, D.C.: Government Printing Office, 1964), p. 47.

stimulation of invention than in the promotion of corporate research and development.

Even here, the essentiality of patent protection is open to question. When the Harvard Business School asked a number of corporations how important patents were to investment in research, a tenth replied that patents were very important, nine tenths that they were not.[7] Melman concludes his study of *The Impact of the Patent System on Research* by saying that

> business expenditure for research . . . would not be appreciably diminished by the elimination of opportunities for claiming patent rights. . . . Competitive pressures along product and production cost lines that now impel the expansion of industrial research outlays would . . . continue to be operative.[8]

And Machlup, in his *Economic Review of the Patent System,* finding patents numerous in the chemical and electrical industries, says that "even without any patents, past, present, or future, firms in these industries would carry on research, development, and innovation because the opportunities for the search for new processes and new products are so excellent in these fields that no firm could hope to maintain its position in the industry if it did not constantly strive to keep ahead of its competitors. . . ."[9]

PATENTS AND COMPETITION

The maintenance of competition necessarily has to do, not with the usefulness of the patent system, which is generally acknowledged, but with the possibility that it may be abused. Patent monopolies have been sought and granted on supposed inventions that have contributed little or nothing to the advancement of technology. In some cases, ownership of patents that cover the whole of an industry's technology has been concentrated in the hands of one or a few large firms. Patent litigation has been deliberately employed as a means of eliminating and excluding competitors. Common control of patents has been established by cross-licensing or through the operation of patent pools. Patent procedures have been so manipulated as to extend the duration of exclusive rights beyond the legal term of 17 years. The scope of patent protection has been extended horizontally to monopolize unpatented goods and vertically to control successive stages of production and distribution. Patent owners have refused to license their patents or have granted licenses on restrictive terms. Patent licensing has been employed as a means of controlling the output, divid-

7 / Otto J. Bachmann, *Patents and the Corporation* (Boston, Mass.: processed, 1958), p. 106.

8 / U.S. Senate, Committee on the Judiciary, Subcommittee on Patents, Trademarks, and Copyrights, Study No. 11 (Washington, D.C.: Government Printing Office, 1958), p. 56.

9 / U.S. Senate, Committee on the Judiciary, Subcommittee on Patents, Trademarks, and Copyrights, Study No. 15 (Washington, D.C.: Government Printing Office, 1958), p. 78.

ing the markets, and fixing the prices of entire industries. In the present section consideration will be given to each of these perversions of the patent law.

Patents without Inventions

The volume of patents has clearly been greater than the quantity of significant invention. Patents have been granted on mere gadgets, on contrivances expressing the lowest order of mechanical ability, and on ideas involving little in the way of novelty. Patents have covered an indentation on the head of a screw, an eraser on the end of a pencil, rubber hand grips on bicycle handlebars, a bosom or dickie sewn onto the front of a shirt, the use of flat cord instead of round cord in the loop at the ends of suspenders, and the use of an oval rather than a cylindrical shape in a roll of toilet paper. The patent that gave the Johns-Manville Corporation a monopoly of the business of insulating previously constructed buildings by blowing mineral wool into the space between the outer and the inner walls was one that applied, not to the manufacture of the wool itself, nor to the machinery used in blowing it, but to the process of "providing openings to afford access to the air spaces" in existing structures, "inserting the outlet end of a conduit through said openings, and forcing through the said conduit comminuted heat insulating material. . . ." In short, it was a patent on the idea of blowing through a hole.[10] When such patents reach the courts, they will rarely be allowed to stand. But until they do, they continue to afford a basis for industrial monopoly.

Suppression of Technology

Under American law the patentee is not required to work his patent. As a consequence, the law may be employed not to promote but to retard the introduction of advances in technology. It has frequently been charged—and as frequently denied—that new inventions are deliberately suppressed. While proof is not sufficient to support this charge, it is certain that patents outnumber the inventions that are put to work. In 1959, there were nearly 600,000 patents outstanding. Of these, 150,000 to 300,000 were in use; half to three quarters were not.[11] But failure to work a patent need not involve suppression of technology. A patent may cover a product for which demand appears to be inadequate or a process that appears to be inferior to the one already employed. But a patentee's judgment as to these matters may well be influenced by the fact that he has substantial sums invested in a competing product or in a process that embodies an earlier technology. A vested interest may lead him to postpone

10 / Clair Wilcox, *Competition and Monopoly in American Industry,* T.N.E.C. Monograph No. 21 (Washington, D.C.: Government Printing Office, 1940), pp. 164-65.

11 / U.S. Senate, Committee on the Judiciary, Subcommittee on Patents, Trademarks, and Copyrights, Study No. 29, *The Examination System in the Patent Office,* pp. 36-37.

an innovation that would otherwise be made. Under active competition, the rate of change is determined by the market. Under the patent monopoly, it is determined by the patentee. Insofar as suppression of patented inventions does occur, it clearly defeats the fundamental purpose of the patent law.

The Monopolization of Patent Monopolies

Not only does a single patent confer a monopoly, but many related patents may be accumulated by one or a few large firms or brought together by agreement among them. There is no limit to the number of patents that may be held by a single company. The large corporation will usually obtain a steady flow of patents through assignment from members of its own research staff and will supplement them by purchases from outsiders. Among the companies receiving patents from 1939 to 1956, there were 39 with more than 1,000 and 15 with more than 2,000 each; du Pont received 6,338; Westinghouse, 7,567; RCA, 7,894; A.T.&T. 8,539; and GE 10,757.[12] The existence of competing patents, where their ownership is diffused, may be conducive to active competition. But concentration of patent ownership, on so great a scale, may place in the hands of a single firm control over each of the possible methods by which a good may be produced, enabling it to monopolize the technology of an entire industry.

Where a few large corporations hold patents that overlap, each is likely to share its rights with the others through cross-licensing. Such agreements may call for exclusive or nonexclusive licensing, and may cover future as well as present patent rights. The companies participating will usually agree to refrain from attacking the validity of patents held by other members of the group. Where the participants are engaged in different industries, each of them may be given an exclusive right, in his own field, to all of the patents that are involved. The agreement that settled the contest between Bell and Western Union in 1879 divided the communications industry, leaving the telegraph to Western Union and giving the telephone to Bell. Some years later, A.T.&T. entered into a series of agreements with RCA giving each interest an exclusive field within which to exploit the patents owned by both, RCA getting broadcasting, radio telegraphy, and other wireless services; A.T.&T. getting wireless telephony and all the wire services, including wire facilities used in broadcasting. Where the participants in a cross-licensing arrangement are engaged in the same industry, all of the technology in the field may thus be brought under unified control. It was a series of treaties between Hartford-Empire, a company holding patents on machinery for making glass containers, and each of the major producers of such containers that enabled Hartford to establish its dominance over the container field.

Patent Warfare

Large firms have sometimes undertaken to fortify a position of monopoly by

12 / U.S. Senate, Committee on the Judiciary, Subcommittee on Patents, Trademarks, and Copyrights, Study No. 3, *Distribution of Patents Issued to Corporations* (Washington, D.C.: Government Printing Office, 1957).

accumulating an arsenal of patents to be used in attacking possible competitors. Their lawyers have flooded the Patent Office with a constant stream of applications to cover every process, every machine, and every product that their technicians have invented or might conceivably invent. Hartford-Empire, according to a policy memorandum taken from its files, applied for patents designed "to block the development of machines which might be constructed by others for the same purpose as our machines, using alternative means" and for other patents "on possible improvements of competing machines so as to 'fence in' those and prevent their reaching an improved stage." [13] In addition to "blocking" and "fencing" patents, there are "umbrella," "accordion," and "drag-net" patents, drawn up with claims so broad, so expansible, and so effective as to cover and seize upon extensive areas of industrial technology. According to Alfred E. Kahn: "The great research laboratories are only incidentally technological centers. From the business standpoint they are patent factories; they manufacture the raw material of monopoly. Their product is often nothing but a 'shot-gun,' a basis for threatening infringement suit and scaring off competitors; or a 'scare-crow,' a patent which itself represents little or no contribution but seems . . . to cover an important part of a developing art and hence permits threat of suit." [14]

Litigation has been deliberately employed as a weapon of monopoly. Between 1877 and 1893, when the first Bell patent expired, the telephone company initiated more than 600 infringement suits. [15] Patent warfare was similarly employed to build the power of National Cash Register, Eastman Kodak, and United Shoe Machinery. [16] Hartford-Empire, in later years, repeatedly brought suit against competing manufacturers of container machinery, against the purchasers of such machinery, and against concerns that undertook to produce containers with their own machines.

In patent warfare there is no assurance that the adversary with the better claim will be victorious. Litigation is costly, and the outcome is likely to favor the party with the longer purse. Suits may be brought in different jurisdictions and under many different claims. A firm may see its markets vanish as suits are brought against its customers. Such litigation, moreover, may drag on for years. Its victim may well conclude that capitulation is preferable to bankruptcy. When Eastman Kodak sued the Boston Camera Co. in 1894, obtaining a temporary injunction against the sale of Boston's wares, Eastman was finally adjudged the real infringer, but Boston had by then been broken and was thereupon absorbed. [17] When the predecessor of the Aluminum Company of America sued the Cowles Brothers, it was found, after 10 years, to have infringed their

13 / Wilcox, *op. cit.*, p. 74.

14 / Alfred E. Kahn, "Fundamental Deficiencies of the American Patent Law," *American Economic Review*, Vol. XXX (1940), pp. 475-91.

15 / Walton H. Hamilton, *Patents and Free Enterprise*, T.N.E.C. Monograph No. 31 (Washington, D.C.: Government Printing Office, 1941), p. 89.

16 / Floyd L. Vaughan, *Economics of Our Patent System* (New York: Macmillan Co., 1925), pp. 149-52.

17 / Hamilton, *op. cit.*, p. 47.

patents, but they agreed to accept a cash settlement and retired from the field. [18] In many other cases, suits have been settled before the courts have passed upon the rival patent claims. A weaker firm with a valid patent may thus sell out to a stronger firm with a patent of dubious validity. Or it may recognize the latter's patent as valid, take out a license, and agree to abide by its terms. Exclusive rights thus tend to gravitate to large concerns, regardless of the legal status of their claims.

Extending the Boundaries of Monopoly

The normal duration of the monopoly conferred under the patent system is not 17 years but around 20. An invention may be worked for a year before a patent is applied for, and the usual application remains pending in the Patent Office for three years more. The period of pendency has been further extended by the withdrawal and amendment of applications and through the initiation of interference proceedings by the Patent Office when two applications appear to cover the same ground. The duration of monopoly has also been prolonged by dividing a complicated invention into several parts—the steps in a process, the elements in a compound, or the sections of a machine—and applying for separate patents at judicious intervals. During the life of a basic patent, its owner will seek to develop and patent improvements. He will also be the only buyer to whom patents on improvements made by others can be sold. When one grant of monopoly has expired, another will be ready to take its place. During its period of patent protection, moreover, a firm may have developed a productive organization, market outlets, control over materials, and a monopoly of skilled personnel that will make it difficult, if not impossible, for others to enter the field when its patents have expired. The patent system, in its operation, thus involves a longer tenure of power than that envisaged by the framers of the law.

The monopoly power afforded by patents has been extended in space as well as in time. Monopoly has been extended horizontally from one patented product to another and from patented to unpatented goods. Whether by contract or by persuasion, the shoe manufacturer who has leased one of his machines from the United Shoe Machinery Corporation has also obtained the rest of his machinery and supplies from United Shoe, the canner who has leased his canning machinery from American Can or Continental has also bought his cans from the same concern, and the office that has leased an International Business Machine has ordered its tabulating cards from IBM. Monopoly has also been extended vertically from one stage of production and distribution to the next. The Hartford-Empire patents covered a machine used in making glass containers, but they were used not only to monopolize the container machinery business but also to cartelize the container industry itself. Machines were leased to manufacturers of jars and bottles, and each of them was licensed to turn out

18 / George W. Stocking and Myron W. Watkins, *Cartels in Action* (New York: Twentieth Century Fund, 1946), p. 221.

a certain quantity of a certain product and sell it in a certain market at a certain price. The jars and bottles were not patented, but their production and sale was effectively controlled. In these and other cases, extension of the boundaries of patent monopoly has been found to be illegal. But, in the meantime, the profits of wider monopoly have been obtained.

Restrictive Licensing

The patent holder may fail to work his patent himself; he may refuse to license others to do so. The Hartford-Empire Co. consistently refused to grant licenses to firms which undertook to enter into competition with its established licensees. According to its policy memorandum, the company "licensed the machines only to manufacturers of the better type, refusing many licensees who we thought would be price cutters. . . ." This policy was quite acceptable to manufacturers of the better type. "With the plans we now have," wrote one of them, "there is certain to be a curtailment of the promiscuous manufacture of milk bottles. . . ."[19]

The patentee who grants a license gives someone else the right to share in his monopoly. He promises, in effect, that he will not bring suit against the licensee. Licenses may be granted to one firm or to many. They may permit the licensee to produce and sell in any quantity, in any market, and at any price, or they may sharply restrict his liberty. Output may be limited by imposing quotas or by charging graduated royalties. Hartford-Empire's contract with the Florida Glass Co. provided "that the licensee shall not produce in any calendar year . . . more than 21,000 gross of such bottles."[20] Under its contract with General Electric, Westinghouse formerly paid a royalty of 1 percent on lamp sales which did not exceed 25.4 percent of the combined sales of the two concerns and 30 percent on sales made in excess of this share.[21] License contracts may authorize each licensee to sell in a different market, thus giving each of them a regional monopoly. Hartford's contract with the Northwestern Glass Co. permitted the latter to sell its wares only in Oregon, Idaho, Montana, and Alaska; the contract with the Laurens Glass works directed that concern to sell its bottles to two buyers in Spartanburg, South Carolina.[22] A patent holder may also undertake to fix the prices that are charged by subsequent distributors. Thus, U.S. Gypsum required its licensees to sell on a delivered basis under a multiple basing point system and to observe the minimum prices which it prescribed and Masonite licensed competing manufacturers of hardboard and fixed the prices they could charge.[23] In each of these ways, the patentee imposes restraints on competition. In some cases he may overstep the bounds of

19 / Wilcox, *op. cit.*, pp. 76-77.
20 / *Ibid.*, p. 75.
21 / *Ibid.*, p. 104.
22 / *Ibid.*, p. 76.
23 / *Ibid.*, pp. 161-64.

legality. In others, he may be within his rights. The alternative to restrictive licensing, it should be remembered, may be no licensing at all.

Patent Pools

In industries where essential patents are controlled by many firms, they may be brought together in a common pool. Under such an arrangement, patents may be assigned to a trade association or to a corporation set up for the purpose, and licenses granted to each of the participants under all of the patents in the pool. Licenses may be restricted or unrestricted; royalties may be collected and distributed, or patents may be licensed royalty free. A pool may be confined to patents relating to a single product or may include all those important to an industry. It may be limited to older patents, sharing the earlier inventions, but leaving to innovators, for a time, the advantage of exclusive use. But whatever its characteristics, the patent pool in every case will centralize control over a substantial segment of industrial technology.

Patent pooling may be employed either to liberate competition or to intensify monopoly. Under such arrangements, improvements resulting from invention are made available to all of the participants and costs are reduced by eliminating litigation within the group. If unrestricted licenses are granted to all applicants on reasonable terms, outsiders are afforded access to the industry's technology. In the automobile industry, since 1915, patents have been pooled and licenses freely given without restriction and without charge. Patents covering all but the more recent inventions are thus thrown open to the entire industry, and smaller and newer firms may use them without contributing inventions of their own. Since the pool was first established, no manufacturers of automobiles have appeared as plaintiff and defendant in an infringement suit. But agreements combining patents may also be administered with less liberality. A pool controlling all of the inventions in an industry will be the only purchaser of future patents and the only source of patent licenses. By refusing to license, by charging exorbitant royalties, and by drawing upon the combined resources of its members in prosecuting and defending patent suits, it may eliminate outsiders from the field. By including in its contracts provisions which restrict the quantity a licensee may produce, the area in which he may sell, and the prices he may charge, it may regiment an entire industry. Whether cross-licensing and patent pooling make for competition or for monopoly depends therefore upon the purposes for which they are established and the way in which they are administered.

PATENTS AND THE COURTS

Most of the problems outlined in the preceding section have been presented in cases brought before the courts. Decisions in such cases have dealt with the standard of patentability; with concentration of patent ownership; with the right of the patentee to deny licenses to others, and to grant licenses on restrictive terms; with his efforts to extend his monopoly to other products and to later stages of production, to control output, to divide markets, and to fix prices; with cross-licensing; and with the operation of patent pools. In general, the earlier decisions were favorable to the patent holder. But the courts have come increasingly, in recent years, to limit the scope and check the abuses of patent monopoly.

The Standard of Patentability

Until 1835 no patent was found invalid for want of novelty. Thereafter a succession of cases involving patents on gadgets led to the development of a judicial standard of patentability. In 1850, the Supreme Court held that a door-knob made of clay or porcelain rather than metal or wood was "the work of the skilled mechanic, not that of the inventor."[24] This distinction continued to govern the decisions handed down for the better part of a century, and patents were upheld if they were deemed to embody a degree of skill that was greater than that of the artisan. But as invention came increasingly to be the product of corporate research, the standard of patentability was raised. And finally, in the Cuno case[25] in 1941, the Court held that usefulness and novelty in a wireless lighter "does not necessarily make the device patentable." Said Justice Douglas: "Under the statute, the device must not only be 'new and useful,' it must also be an 'invention' or 'discovery' . . . That is to say, the new device, however useful it may be, must reveal the flash of creative genius, not merely the skill of the calling. If it fails, it has not established its right to a private grant on the public domain."[26] The standard thus became one that distinguished, not between the skill of the mechanic and that of the inventor, but between mere skill and the flash of genius.

This standard rested upon nothing more than subjective judgment. It was rejected by Congress when it passed the Patent Act of 1952. Inventions still are not patentable if "the subject matter as a whole would have been obvious at the time the invention was made to a person having ordinary skill in the art." But "patentability shall not be negatived by the manner in which the invention was made." A flash of genius is no longer required; dogged research will suffice. A patent is to be issued if the differences between an invention and the prior art are substantial.[27] But the obviousness of inventions and the substantiality of their differences from the prior art is still a matter of judgment. Whether an invention is patentable depends, as it has always depended, on the opinion of the courts. In three cases decided in 1966, the Supreme Court found patents on

24 / *Hotchkiss* v. *Greenwood,* 11 How. 248.
25 / *Cuno Corp.* v. *Automatic Devices Corp.,* 314 U.S. 84.
26 / *Ibid.,* p. 91.
27 / Patent Codification Act of 1952, Sec. 103.

two inventions (one that placed the shank on a vibrating shank plow above the hinge plate, and one that provided a leak-proof cap for a finger-operated spray dispenser) to be invalid, and a third patent (on a water-activated battery of a radically new design) to be valid, on the ground that the first two would have been obvious to an artisan having ordinary skill in the prior art, while the third would not.[28] The Court took note of the laxity of the standards employed by the Patent Office and cautioned the office to adhere more closely to the standards enunciated by the courts.

Concentration of Patent Ownership

Where a single company has clearly sought to monopolize an industry's patents as a means of monopolizing the industry itself, its action has been condemned. Thus, the Kobe company undertook to monopolize the rodless pump industry by buying up all the patents in the field and getting the sellers to agree not to compete. It then sued the Dempsey Pump Co. for infringement and organized a boycott among Dempsey's customers in order to eliminate it as a competitor. Here, a circuit court refused to find infringement, holding that Kobe's suit was an integral part of a scheme to monopolize the industry.[29] In itself, however, the ownership of many patents by a single company has not been found to violate the law.

The issue was raised in the United Shoe Machinery case. The company held nearly 4,000 patents, about 95 percent of them the product of its own research, only 5 percent of them purchased from others. The government charged that the company "has been for many years, and is now, engaged in a program of engrossing all patents and inventions of importance relating to shoe machinery for the purpose of blanketing the shoe machinery industry with patents under the control of United and thereby suppressing competition in the industry."[30] This was one among the factors that led to a finding of illegality. Here, the court found no evidence that the patent right had been abused. United had put a third of its patents to work; it had not suppressed the others or used them to threaten possible competitors. It had not offered or been asked to grant licenses, but it had not refused to do so. It had not resorted to litigation as a means of harassing competitors but had acted in good faith in bringing infringement suits. It had adopted certain policies, however, that operated to handicap competitors. It had refused to sell its machines, making them available only on long-term leases. It had included in its leases provisions that discriminated against customers who might install competing machines. It had required them to use its own machines at full capacity on all the shoes they made. It had entered into blanket contracts covering not only the lease of machines but also

28 / *Graham* v. *John Deere Co.* and *Calmar, Inc.* v. *Cook Chemical Co.*, 383 U.S. 1; *U.S.* v. *Adams*, 383 U.S. 39.

29 / *Kobe, Inc.* v. *Dempsey Pump Co.*, 198 F. 2d 416 (1952).

30 / *U.S.* v. *United Shoe Machinery Corp.*, Civil Action No. 7198, District Court of the U.S., District of Mass., Complaint, December 15, 1947.

the provision of supplies and services. None of these policies was held to be illegal per se. But their combined effect, given United's dominant position in the field, was found to prove monopolization, in violation of Section 2 of the Sherman Act.[31]

The issue of concentration of patent ownership was also raised in cases involving Western Electric, the manufacturing subsidiary of A.T.& T., and International Business Machines, but here the legality of such concentration was not determined, each of the cases being settled in 1956 by a consent decree. Apart from coercive tactics like those employed by Kobe or a complex of practices such as those followed by United, a monopoly of patents is yet to be condemned.

Tying Contracts

Many decisions of the courts have dealt with the efforts of a patentee to extend the scope of his monopoly beyond the boundaries of the patent grant. In some cases the patentee has sought to prevent a competitor from selling an unpatented product for use in a patented combination. In 1909, the Supreme Court held an unpatented record to be an integral part of a patented phonograph, licensed to users by the Victor company, and found that Victor's patent was infringed by the sale of Leeds & Catlin's records.[32] This position was emphatically reversed by the Court's decision in the Mercoid Case[33] in 1944. Mercoid had been sued by Minneapolis-Honeywell when it sold an unpatented switch to be used in connection with a patented combination of thermostats in controlling furnace heat. The Court found no infringement, holding Honeywell's effort to extend the scope of its patent to be illegal per se. "An unpatented part of a combination patent," said Justice Douglas, "is no more entitled to monopolistic protection than any other unpatented device."

In other cases the patent holder has included in his license contracts provisions requiring his licensees to purchase some other product that he has for sale. Before the passage of the Clayton Act such tying contracts were upheld. Since that Act was passed, however, they have consistently been condemned. The courts have struck down contracts, among others, requiring radio manufacturers licensed under RCA patents to buy their tubes from RCA;[34] requiring lessees of International Business Machines to buy their tabulating cards from IBM;[35] and requiring the purchase of rivets by lessees of patented riveting machines.[36] In these cases, the contracts were found substantially to lessen competition, within the meaning of the Clayton Act, because the patentee

31 / *U.S.* v. *United Shoe Machinery Corp.*, 110 F. Supp. 295.

32 / *Leeds & Catlin* v. *Victor Talking Machine Co.*, 213 U.S. 325.

33 / *Mercoid Corp.* v. *Minneapolis-Honeywell Regulator Co.*, 320 U.S. 680.

34 / *Lord* v. *Radio Corp. of America*, 24 F. 2d 505 (1928).

35 / *International Business Machines Corp.* v. *U.S.*, 298 U.S. 131 (1936).

36 / *Judson Thompson* v. *FTC*, 150 F. 2d 952 (1945).

dominated the market for the process or product to which the unpatented commodity was tied. But tying contracts have also been invalidated in cases where the patentee was far from having a monopoly. Thus, in the International Salt case, [37] the Supreme Court held that a contract requiring the users of a patented salt dispenser to purchase salt from its producer was unreasonable per se. It is evident that the courts will not now tolerate the use of tying clauses, under any circumstances, to extend the boundaries of a patent monopoly.

Restrictive Licenses

Where a patent owner grants a license to use a patented machine or process or to make and sell a patented product, the courts have generally upheld his right to limit the licensee to a certain geographic area [38] or a certain field of industry, [39] to restrict his output, [40] and to fix the price that he may charge when he sells the patented goods. The leading decision on the latter point was handed down by the Supreme Court in the General Electric case [41] in 1926. One of the issues raised in this case related to the right of General Electric, under its basic patents on the electric lamp, to fix the prices charged by Westinghouse. This right was upheld by the Court, and license contracts fixing a licensee's prices on patented products are still permitted by the law.

Surrender of title to a patented good, however, has long been held to terminate the patentee's authority over its subsequent use and sale. His right to control the price at which patented products, once sold by him, are resold by others has therefore been denied. In the case of *Bauer* v. *O'Donnell* [42] in 1913, it was held that O'Donnell had not infringed Bauer's patent on Sanatogen when he resold it for less than the price that Bauer had printed on the package. And this precedent has generally been followed since that time. General Electric, however, has circumvented this rule by treating its distributors as agents, shipping its bulbs on consignment, and retaining title until they are sold. The Court, in its 1926 decision, found this arrangement to be legitimate and permitted the company to fix the prices that its thousands of "agents" could charge.

Restrictive licensing of another manufacturer was permitted in the General Electric case, where it applied to a single licensee. But it has been held to be illegal when employed for the purpose of eliminating competition among many licensees. In the Gypsum case [43] in 1948, the Supreme Court condemned the establishment of common prices for manufacturers of gypsum board through

---

37 / *International Salt Co.* v. *U.S.*, 332 U.S. 392 (1947).

38 / *Providence Rubber Co.* v. *Goodyear*, 9 Wall. 788 (1869).

39 / *General Talking Pictures Corp.* v. *Western Electric Corp.*, 304 U.S. 175 (1938).

40 / *Rubber Tire Wheel Co.* v. *Milwaukee Rubber Works Co.*, 154 F. 328 (1907), 210 U.S. 439 (1908).

41 / *U.S.* v. *General Electric Co.*, 272 U.S. 476.

42 / 229 U.S. 1.

43 / *U.S.* v. *U.S. Gypsum Co.*, 333 U.S. 364.

provisions contained in separate contracts for patent licensing. The General Electric precedent, said the Court, "gives no support for a patentee, acting in concert with all members of an industry, to issue substantially identical licenses . . . under which industry is completely regimented." When each of several licensees accepts restrictive terms on the condition or with the knowledge that others will do so, they are guilty, in the eyes of the Court, of conspiracy in restraint of trade.

On a number of occasions, the government has asked the Court to reverse the rule of the G.E. decision permitting a patentee to fix the prices that may be charged by a single licensee. In the Gypsum case, in 1948, four of the judges were willing to do so, but this fell short of a majority. In the Huck case [44] in 1965, the Court split 4 to 4 on a similar request. Sooner or later, it is likely that the rule will be reversed.

Cross-Licensing and Patent Pools

Cross-licensing and patent pooling have never been held to be illegal per se. But their employment as a means of eliminating competition among patent owners and licensees has usually been condemned. In the leading case on patent pooling, the Standard Sanitary case [45] decided in 1912, where patents covering the production of enameled iron bathtubs and other sanitary wares had been pooled with a trade association, the inclusion in licenses issued to firms producing 85 percent of the output of such wares of provisions restricting output, fixing prices and discounts, and controlling channels of trade was held to violate the Sherman Act. In the Standard Oil of Indiana case [46] in 1931, however, a pool controlling patents covering methods of cracking gasoline was allowed to stand. But here the Court was impressed by the fact that many other cracking processes remained outside the pool, that licensees under the pooling arrangement did little more than half of the cracking of gasoline, and that cracking provided only a fourth of the total supply. The pool, thus faced with competition, was found to be powerless to fix prices and was therefore held to be within the law. In the Hartford-Empire case [47] decided in 1945, Hartford had employed the patents in its pool to dominate completely the glass container industry, curtailing output, dividing markets, and fixing prices through restrictive licenses; the Court found in Hartford's behavior, as a whole, convincing evidence of unlawful conspiracy.

So, too, with cross-licensing. In the Line Material case [48] in 1948, the court was emphatic in its condemnation of a plan that eliminated competition through cross-licensing. Here, each of two small companies producing patented fuse cutouts had licensed the other and fixed the prices it might charge. Their agree-

44 / *Huck Manufacturing Co.* v. *U.S.*, 382 U.S. 197.
45 / *Standard Sanitary Mfg. Co.* v. *U.S.*, 226 U.S. 20.
46 / *Standard Oil Co.* (*Indiana*) v. *U.S.*, 283 U.S. 163.
47 / *Hartford-Empire Co.* v. *U.S.*, 323 U.S. 386.
48 / *U.S.* v. *Line Material Co.*, 333 U.S. 287.

ment to do so was held to be illegal per se. "This price fixing scheme," said the Court, "does far more than secure to inventors 'the exclusive right' to their discoveries. . . . It gives them a leverage on the market which only a combination, not a patent by itself can create." In the Besser case [49] in 1952, the Court held an agreement between two patent holders to refuse licenses to others to be a boycott and, as such, to be illegal per se. And in the Singer case [50] in 1963, where Singer had exchanged licenses with Swiss and Italian manufacturers of zigzag sewing machines and then brought infringement suits against importers of Japanese machines, the Court found the three concerns to be conspiring in restraint of trade.

Patent pooling was an issue in another suit which the government brought against the General Electric Company. The basic patents on the electric lamp had expired, and GE had undertaken to perpetuate its control of the industry by employing later patents on such parts of the lamp as the filament and the frosting on the bulb. To this end, it had formed a patent pool with Westinghouse and granted licenses to four other producers, controlling the output and the prices of all six companies. These arrangements, while similar to those approved in 1926, though involving different patents and a larger number of licensees, were found by a district court in 1949 to violate both sections of the Sherman Act. General Electric, said the Court, had conspired with its licensees and had "unlawfully monopolized the incandescent electric lamp industry in the United States." [51]

Among the most important cases involving the operation of a patent pool is that of the Radio Corporation of America. Here, in a civil suit brought in 1954 and a criminal suit brought in 1958, the government charged that RCA had entered into agreements with A.T.&T., GE, and Westinghouse and with firms in other countries that gave it the exclusive right to grant licenses under more than 10,000 radio-purpose patents in the United States. As a result, other manufacturers of electronic equipment were made to depend upon RCA. In granting licenses, moreover, the company refused to license patents individually, but insisted on licensing all of the patents in a packaged group. RCA pleaded *nolo contendere* in the government's criminal case, paying a fine of $100,000, and accepted a consent decree in the civil suit. Under the terms of this decree, the company agreed to license its existing radio and TV patents royalty-free, to license its new patents at reasonable royalties, and to permit its licensees to obtain patents individually instead of requiring package deals. [52]

Remedies in Patent Cases

Employment of patents to eliminate competition has repeatedly been restrained by the courts. This has been true, of course, in the many cases in

49 / *Besser Mfg. Co.* v. *U.S.,* 343 U.S. 444.

50 / *U.S.* v. *Singer Mfg. Co.,* 374 U.S. 174.

51 / *U.S.* v. *General Electric Co.,* 82 F. Supp. 753.

52 / *U.S.* v. *Radio Corp. of America,* 1958 Trade Cases, Par. 69, 164.

which a court has found that a patent was not valid or was not infringed. In a number of cases, too, the Supreme Court has permitted defendants in infringement suits to show that patents had been used to violate the antitrust laws and then refused, on that ground, to enforce them.[53] The patents, though not invalidated, were rendered ineffective, and their use as an instrument of monopoly destroyed. The Court has also held that a defendant in an infringement suit, brought to enforce a patent that had been obtained through fraudulent representations, could sue the patentee for treble damages.[54] One such case led to the heaviest penalty ever incurred through abuse of the patent right. Here, Charles Pfizer & Co., a manufacturer of pharmaceuticals, had conspired with four other manufacturers to obtain a patent on tetracycline, an antibiotic, by misrepresenting its origin to the Patent Office. It had then licensed the other producers, forbidding them in its licenses to distribute the drug through packagers, who might compete in its sale. In this way, the group had been able to enforce a price of $30.60 for 100 capsules that had cost $3.87 to make. The companies were convicted of conspiracy in a criminal suit and fined $150,000 each. But, more important, they were sued for damages by governments, institutions, and individuals who had purchased tetracycline at the higher price, these suits being settled, in 1968, at a cost of $120 million.[55]

Judicial decisions and consent decrees in patent cases have been designed, not only to punish violators of the antitrust laws, but also to make markets more competitive by removing legal barriers to entry. The decree of the district court in the Hartford-Empire case[56] required the company to license all applicants under its patents, royalty-free. This decree was modified by the Supreme Court, in a 4 to 3 decision, to permit the collection of reasonable royalties, on the ground that their refusal would involve unconstitutional confiscation of the defendant's property. But the Court agreed, for the first time in history, to compulsory licensing.[57] In the National Lead case two years later, the government asked the Court to go beyond this precedent, reversing its position on the need for royalties. The Court, again by a 4 to 3 vote, refused to do so, but approved compulsory licensing, and intimated that it might agree to the elimination of royalties if this were the only way in which competition could be restored.[58]

Royalty-free licensing was first required, by a district court, in the case of the General Electric Company in 1953. Following the company's conviction in a criminal suit in 1949, the government asked that it be required to dispose of

53 / *Morton Salt Co.* v. *G.S. Suppiger Co.*, 314 U.S. 488 (1942); *B.B. Chemical Co.* v. *Ellis*, 314 U.S. 495 (1942); *Mercoid Corp.* v. *Mid-Continent Investment Co.*, 320 U.S. 661 (1944).

54 / *Walker Process Equipment Co.* v. *Food Machinery and Chemical Corp.*, 382 U.S. 172 (1965).

55 / See Peter M. Costello, "The Tetracycline Conspiracy," *Antitrust Law and Economics Review*, Vol. 1 (1968) pp. 13–44.

56 / *U.S.* v. *Hartford-Empire Co.*, 46 F. Supp. 541 (1942).

57 / *Hartford-Empire Co.* v. *U.S.*, 323 U.S. 386 (1945).

58 / *U.S.* v. *National Lead Co.*, 332 U.S. 319 (1947).

half of its productive facilities; to abandon the agency system under which it controlled the prices charged by its distributors; to dedicate to public use all of its existing patents covering the manufacture of electric light bulbs and parts; and to grant licenses under future patents in this field, on a reciprocal basis, at reasonable royalties. The court refused to dismember the company or to ban the agency system, but it did order the licensing of patents, with future patents to be made available at reasonable royalties and existing patents royalty-free. [59]

Similar provisions have been incorporated in consent decrees. Scores of such decrees have been accepted, providing for the licensing of all applicants, many of them for licensing without royalties. Under the typical decree, existing patents must be licensed royalty-free and future patents at reasonable royalties. Royalty charges are determined by agreement between the patent owner and the licensee or, failing this, are established by the courts. A consent decree accepted by General Motors in 1965, in a suit attacking its control of 85 percent of the output of buses, provided for royalty-free licensing of future as well as existing patents. This provision, the first of its kind, was part of a program designed to open the industry to competition.

Decrees in antitrust suits have called not only for the licensing of patents but also for the provision of necessary know-how. Owens-Corning Fiberglas was thus required to furnish its licensees, at nominal charge, with written manuals describing its machinery, materials, and processes. American Can was directed to provide any applicant, at cost, with "detailed working drawings, specifications of materials, prescribed production methods, and assembly blueprints," and if this should prove "inadequate to enable him satisfactorily to manufacture and assemble the machines and equipment covered thereby" to supply "further information, as the case requires, either (a) in writing, or (b) by making available a reasonable number of technical personnel for consultation . . . or (c) by permitting such applicant or his representative to visit defendant's machine shop where such machines and equipment are manufactured to observe the manufacture thereof." [60] Eastman Kodak agreed to provide other finishers of amateur color film with manuals describing its processing technology, to keep the manuals up to date by issuing annual supplements, and to provide technical representatives to assist competitors in using the methods described. [61] International Business Machines agreed to train outsiders in the techniques of making and using tabulating equipment and to provide the trade with its basic designs. [62] And General Electric was ordered to take similar steps to provide other manufacturers with the know-how required for the production of electric lamps.

[59] / U.S. v. General Electric, 115 F. Supp. 835.

[60] / U.S. v. American Can Co., Civil Action 26345-H, District Court of the U.S., Northern District of Cal., Final Judgment, June 22, 1950.

[61] / U.S. v. Eastman Kodak Co., 1954 Trade Cases, Par. 67, 920.

[62] / U.S. v. International Business Machines, Civil Action C-72-344, District Court of the U.S., Southern District of N.Y., Consent Decree, January 25, 1956.

PATENT REFORM

Many proposals have been advanced for the reform of the patent system, both through changes in the procedure whereby patents are granted and validated, and through changes in the substance of the patent law. Minor changes in procedure were made by Congress in 1939 and again in 1952. The period of use before application and the period during which an application might be amended were each cut from two years to one; the privilege of dropping and renewing applications was abolished; the time allowed for answering Patent Office queries was reduced; the interference procedure was simplified. Recommendations for a major revision of the law, prepared by a presidential study commission, were presented to Congress in 1967. Under the principal change proposed, a patent would be granted, in every case, to the first person to apply, thus eliminating interference proceedings and the usual three-year period of pendency between the time of an application and a patent grant. Thereafter, a patent could be challenged by another claimant. But only in this case would the Patent Office be compelled to search the prior art. This proposal was designed to make the process of granting patents more speedy and more thorough. The bill was opposed, however, by the patent bar and had not yet been enacted at the end of 1969.

The reforms so far adopted or considered by Congress are insignificant when compared with those effected by the courts. Judicial action has gone far toward protecting the public interest against abuses of the patent grant. There are many patents, however, that are never brought before the courts. And there may still be need for revision of the patent laws.

Checking the Multiplicity, Duration, and Concentration of Patents

The number of patent monopolies might be reduced by legislative changes in the standard of patentability. Patents might well be confined to inventions representing really significant advances in technology or granted only to persons who could show that substantial sums had been spent on research and development. Designs might better be left to protection through copyrights. And the patent privilege might be withdrawn from foods and medicines. The multiplicity of patents might also be reduced through changes in procedure. Patent applications might be published and hearings given to competitors, consumers, and antitrust officials in opposition to the patent grants. The Patent Office might be equipped with a larger staff at higher salaries and thus enabled to take more time and exercise more skill in passing on applications. Larger appropriations for this purpose might be financed by increasing patent fees. All of these measures, or any of them, should operate to check the excessive creation of legal monopolies.

The 17-year life of the patent is an anachronism, growing out of a handicraft economy and bearing no functional relation to the requirements of machine technology. There is no reason why the duration of protection should be the same in every case. The period permitted might well be related to the time required to recover the sums invested in research and development. Or basic inventions might be distinguished from mere improvements, major inventions from minor ones, and different terms allowed for each. The actual tenure of monopoly might at least be shortened by dating a patent from the day of application, or by checking delaying tactics and speeding up procedures in the Patent Office to lessen the period of pendency.

It has also been suggested that the monopolization of patent monopolies might be prevented by limiting the number of patents that may be assigned to a single holder, or by taxing accumulations of patents progressively. Such measures, however, would be crude in application, making no distinction among holdings that are used to monopolize a market, those that serve to strengthen one of many large competitors, and those that are made available to all the members of an industry. These measures could operate only to reduce investments made by larger corporations in industrial research and thus to hamper the advancement of technology. Where large accumulations of patents are used to monopolize an industry, the courts stand ready, under the antitrust laws, to provide a remedy by giving sanction to compulsory licensing.

Checking the Abuse of Patent Powers

Patent abuses, already checked by the decisions of the courts, might well be further checked by certain changes in the patent laws. The use of patent agreements to circumvent the antitrust laws might be discouraged by requiring that they be filed with the Department of Justice or the Federal Trade Commission, and made available to both enforcement agencies. The inclusion of restrictive provisions in patent licenses might conceivably be forbidden or the terms of such provisions limited by law. Price fixing in licenses might be made illegal per se, reversing the position taken by the Court in the General Electric case of 1926. Cross-licensing and pooling might be limited to cases where all applicants are licensed on the same terms and all pay the same rate of royalty. Legislation against restrictive provisions, however, might prevent a patent owner who wished to retain a monopoly in one field from licensing his patent for use in another and might close access to technology, in many other cases, by discouraging the issuance of licenses. If this were to be avoided, control of license contracts would have to be supplemented by compulsory licensing.

Compulsory licensing, as a general policy, would have serious disadvantages. It might impair the incentive to make substantial investments in research. It might make for secrecy, preventing the disclosure of advances in technology. Since the policy could be defeated by demanding exorbitant royalties, it would also be necessary to regulate these charges in accordance with some standard of reasonableness. This problem, of course, is not insoluble, as is shown by the experience of the courts in fixing royalties under antitrust decrees. Up to 1960, among 81 decrees requiring compulsory licensing with royalties, licenses had been requested and granted under only 50,[63] and there had been only six occasions in which a court had been asked to set a royalty rate.[64] But compulsory licensing, if it were general, would involve a heavy burden of administrative action and judicial review. Such a requirement, moreover, would work both ways, not only compelling the stronger competitor to license the weaker one, but also compelling the weak to license the strong. It may be doubted that protection of the public interest necessitates its general use.

There are cases, however, in which compulsory licensing may be desirable. It has proved to be a useful remedy where violators of the antitrust laws have been brought before the courts. It may be required, under the Atomic Energy Act, to prevent firms holding patents on nonmilitary uses of atomic energy from barring access to this new field of industrial activity. It might well be demanded where monopoly would imperil public health or safety or national security. It might be employed, after a proper interval, to prevent continued nonuse of patented technology. In this case, one argument against the requirement does not apply; the burden of fixing royalties would be slight. If it is true, as defenders of the patent system have always argued, that no inventions of commercial value are suppressed, there would be no requests for licenses. But if suppression does occur, the threat of compulsory licensing would induce the owner of an idle patent to put it to use. The public would derive the benefits that flow from new technology. And this is the purpose that the patent system was designed to serve.

TRADEMARKS

A product monopoly may be buttressed by a trademark as well as by a patent. Trademark rights, like patent rights, are enforced by bringing infringement suits. Such suits were entertained at common law. Statutory protection was subsequently given to trademarks by the legislatures of the states. The federal Constitution made no mention of trademarks. But Congress acted, in 1881, to protect marks used in foreign trade and, in 1905, to protect those used in interstate commerce. Infringement suits were still decided in accordance with the laws of the states. The first effective federal trademark law, the Lanham Act, was not passed until 1946.

The Act provides for the entry, on a Register at the Patent Office, of trademarks in the form of words or symbols used to distinguish the goods of a single seller, service marks in the form of devices used to identify a seller of services, certification marks that cover the goods or services of several sellers, and collective marks applied to sales made by the members of an association, such as a

---

63 / U.S. Senate, Committee on the Judiciary, Subcommittee on Patents, Trademarks, and Copyrights, *Compulsory Patent Licensing under Antitrust Judgments* (Washington, D.C.: Government Printing Office, 1960).

64 / Mark S. Massel, *Competition and Monopoly* (Washington, D.C.: Brookings Institution, 1962), p. 103.

cooperative. An application for registry must be accompanied by specimens of the mark, a description of the goods to which it is attached, a statement covering its past use, and a fee of $25. Where two persons claim similar marks, the Patent Office will hold hearings for the determination of priority. Once a mark is registered, an injured person may institute proceedings for its cancellation. Under the present law, however, marks cannot be contested after they have stood on the Register for five years. Initial registration is for 20 years and may be renewed, upon application, for further terms of like duration. Registry is not essential to the validity of a mark; it establishes no rights not previously recognized by law. What it does is to provide the registrant with prima facie evidence of ownership.

Trademarks and Competition

It is the purpose of a trademark, when widely advertised, to take a product out of competition by establishing strong consumer preference. In an industry that is highly competitive, this consequence may not be serious. But in one that is dominated by powerful firms, the investment that would be required to gain acceptance for competing brands may bar new entry to the field. When a mark is owned by a monopolist, moreover, it may serve to reinforce his power and to prolong his tenure of monopoly. A product may be protected by a patent and a trademark; the patent will expire, but the monopoly it has created may be perpetuated by the mark. During the life of the patent, the name given the product by its producer may have become the only one by which it can be bought. The customer who wants transparent glycerinated cellulose hydrate regenerated from viscose is likely to ask for cellophane. Where names have thus become generic, to be sure, the courts have held for the defendants in infringement suits. But litigation is a costly business: the patent on shredded wheat expired in 1912; the name was not found to be in the public domain until 1938; the case of *Kellogg* v. *National Biscuit* [65] had dragged through the courts for more than a quarter of a century. It is not every defendant who can afford to invest such sums to establish his right to compete.

Trademarks have been used successfully, where patents and copyrights failed, in the maintenance of resale prices, this practice having been approved by state and federal laws. They have been used to implement discriminatory pricing: methyl methacrylate was sold by Rohm & Haas to manufacturers as Lucite and Crystalite at 85 cents per pound, and to dentists as Vernonite and Crystalex at $45 per pound. They have been used to obtain exclusive markets: General Electric persuaded procurement agencies to establish specifications requiring Mazda bulbs, permitted Westinghouse to use the name, but denied its other licensees the right to do so. [66] Trademarks have also been used to effect a division of markets among the members of international cartels. Here, a mark is

65 / *Kellogg Co.* v. *National Biscuit Co.,* 305 U.S. 111.

66 / See S. Timberg, "Trade Marks, Monopoly, and the Restraint of Competition," *Law and Contemporary Problems,* Vol. XIV (1949), pp. 323-61.

advertised throughout the world, each participant is given the exclusive right to use it in his own territory, and anyone who oversteps the boundaries assigned to him is driven back by an infringement suit.

Trademarks and the Law

The Lanham Act was passed in 1946 after many years of agitation by trade associations and the trademark bar. The law contains a number of provisions that may be open to abuse. It permits concurrent registration of the same or similar marks by more than one concern, thus making possible their use as a device for sharing markets. It provides for the use of a mark by "related companies" when one "legitimately" controls the other and allows the owner of a mark to assign it when disposing of the good will or "part of the good will" of a business, thus opening the way to production and price control through restrictive licensing. The law approves certification marks, thus inviting attempts to exclude competitors from the market by refusing to certify their wares.

The bill that passed the House was criticized by the Department of Justice, and amendments were added in the Senate to meet the objections that were raised. As the law now stands, incontestible registry is denied to common descriptive names; a mark may be canceled if it has become the common name of a product on which a patent has expired; a person sued for infringement may defend himself by showing that a mark has been used to violate the antitrust laws; the Federal Trade Commission may bring proceedings for the cancellation of marks that are so employed.

Monopolistic practices involving trademarks have been enjoined in many cases by the courts. Contracts maintaining the resale price of trademarked goods were held to be unlawful in the Dr. Miles case [67] in 1911; their subsequent legalization will be discussed in Chapter 29. Decisions were rendered against the use of trademarks to promote discriminatory pricing in the Rohm & Haas case [68] in 1948 and against their use in excluding competitors from markets in the General Electric case [69] in 1949. In a number of cases involving the sharing of markets for trademarked goods by international cartels, decided from 1945 to 1950, the courts found such arrangements to be in violation of the Sherman Act, rejecting trademark licensing as a defense. [70]

COPYRIGHTS

Congress was authorized by the Constitution to give protection to authors as well as to inventors; it passed its first copyright law in 1790. This law, as subsequently amended and codified, applies not only to writers but also to

67 / *Dr. Miles Medical Co.* v. *John D. Park & Sons Co.*, 220 U.S. 373.

68 / *U.S.* v. *Rohm & Haas*, Civil Action No. 9068, District Court of the U.S., Eastern District of Pa.

69 / *U.S.* v. *General Electric Co.*, 82 F. Supp. 753.

70 / *U.S.* v. *Timken Roller Bearings Co.*, 83 F. Supp. 294 (1949).

composers, artists, photographers, dramatists, and producers of motion pictures. It covers not only the right to print, reprint, and copy, but also the right to translate, to dramatize, novelize, or put on film, to record music, broadcast it, or perform it in public for profit, to exhibit a movie or to produce a play. A copyright may be obtained by registering a covered work with the Copyright Office at the Library of Congress; no examination is undertaken and no legal assistance is required. It runs for 28 years and may be renewed for another 28. A copyright owner may enforce his rights by bringing suit against infringers. Willful infringement for profit is a criminal offense punishable by fine and imprisonment.

Copyrights and Competition

The consequences of legal monopoly may be serious in the case of patents; they are less so in the case of copyrights. A patent gives exclusive rights in an idea; a copyright covers only the particular form in which an idea is expressed. A patent may enable its owner to monopolize all the products of an industry; no such power is conferred upon the holder of a copyright. Basic patents have covered all aluminum, all telephones, all glass containers, and all electric lamps. Copyrights do not cover all books, all music, all pictures, or all plays. Each of them is confined to one among many items in a field that is actively competitive.

Copyrights have been used in a few cases, as patents have in many, to afford a legal basis for the extension of monopoly. Publishers have sought to maintain resale prices by bringing infringement suits against booksellers. Movie producers have employed block booking contracts to tie the sale of one copyrighted film to that of another. Competition among exhibitors of such films has been restricted by including identical terms in licenses. Competition between newspapers has been impaired by excluding publishers from membership in the Associated Press. The market for rights to commercial performances of music has been monopolized by the American Society of Composers, Authors, and Publishers.

The principal source of revenue from a piece of music is not the right to print or record it but to perform it for profit. With a piece of popular music, such performances may number in the tens of thousands. But popularity is ephemeral; demand may disappear as quickly as it came. In the absence of organization, composers and lyricists would find it difficult to collect the royalties to which they are entitled. As individuals they lack the means to detect and prosecute infringement and would be at a serious disadvantage in bargaining with such powerful interests as the radio and television networks and the motion picture companies. It was to provide them and their publishers with an instrument for collective action that ASCAP was established in 1914. The Society admitted to membership the authors and composers of five or more copyrighted works. It was managed by a self-perpetuating board of directors, half of them representing this group and half the publishers. The Society shortly came to enjoy a virtual monopoly of music rights. All copyrights were assigned to ASCAP; all license contracts were negotiated by ASCAP; all royalties were collected and pooled by ASCAP; the payments made to members depended on ASCAP's appraisal of the commercial value of their works.

ASCAP has been charged, from time to time, with various monopolistic practices. It discriminated among its licensees in charging royalties and among its members in distributing them. It refused to license the broadcasting of individual compositions, insisting on blanket licenses. It sought to collect royalties, not only from the networks for transcribing music, but also from individual stations for putting it on the air; not only from the producers of musical films, but also from their exhibitors. It entered into exclusive cross-licensing arrangements with similar societies in other countries, thus adding to the scope of its domestic rights. By monopolizing thousands of legal monopolies, it acquired and exploited market powers that go far beyond those accorded by a single copyright.

ASCAP has not had the field of copyrighted music to itself. Since the forties, it has had a rival in Broadcast Music, Inc., originally set up by the radio networks as an alternate source of supply. In 1964, there were 18,000 song writers entitled to share in royalties. Of these, half were affiliated with ASCAP and half with BMI. ASCAP has charged that BMI, too, has been guilty of unfair tactics, conspiring with the broadcasters to discriminate against ASCAP music in favor of that controlled by BMI.

Copyrights and the Courts

With copyrights, as with patents and trademarks, the courts have restrained abuses of monopoly power. They have held, for instance, that owners of copyrights on books could not require booksellers to adhere to listed prices;[71] that the copyright granted on Associated Press dispatches did not empower the AP to refuse access to its services;[72] and that copyrights on motion picture films did not justify the practice of tying one film to another by booking them in blocks.[73] With respect to ASCAP, however, enforcement of the antitrust laws has proved to be most difficult.

In 1941, ASCAP entered a plea of *nolo contendere* in a criminal suit and paid a fine of $35,000. At the same time, it accepted a consent decree in a civil suit.[74] This decree has been amended from time to time, following further litigation, always placing the society under further constraints. As it now stands, it governs relations between ASCAP and its customers, limiting the categories of users from whom the Society can demand royalties, requiring that compositions be licensed individually as well as in blocks, and providing for the determination of reasonable royalties. It also governs the relations between ASCAP and its

71 / *Bobbs-Merrill Co.* v. *Straus,* 210 U.S. 359.

72 / *Associated Press* v. *U.S.,* 326 U.S. 1.

73 / *U.S.* v. *Paramount Pictures,* 334 U.S. 141.

74 / *U.S.* v. *ASCAP,* Civil Action No. 13-95, District Court of the U.S., Southern District of N.Y., Civil Decree and Judgment.

members, prescribing eligibility for membership, giving members a voice in the Society's government, and controlling the distribution of royalty income. A consent decree with similarly detailed provisions, accepted in 1966, governs the activities of BMI.

Copyright Reform

The present copyright law was enacted in 1909. Since that time, electronic reproduction has developed means of communication that were then unknown: motion pictures with sound, radio and television, photocopying, tape recording, microform storage, new methods of projection, data banking and retrieval, and other applications of computer technology. These developments raise serious questions for copyright policy. How far are the new techniques to be covered by copyright law? How, given these techniques, is the author's property in his intellectual product to be protected?

One such question is presented, in particular, by cable or community antenna television. A CATV company building an aerial on some high place, takes broadcasts from the air and transmits them to subscribers by wire. The broadcasters pay royalties for the materials they use. The CATV stations do not. The broadcasters contend that CATV should be brought under the copyright law. This issue was presented to the Supreme Court by United Artists in a suit brought against a CATV station for infringing its copyright on motion picture films. The Court held for the defendant. A copyright, it said, covers the *performance* of a copyrighted work. The broadcasters of a movie put on a performance; CATV does not. It merely transmits the broadcaster's performance. It therefore cannot be convicted of infringement of a copyright.[75] This immunity, however, may be withdrawn by legislation or surrendered by agreement between broadcasters and CATV. The regulation of CATV is to be considered, at greater length, in Chapter 19.

A similar question is raised by the juke box. This machine plays copyrighted music for profit. The net income of the business, running to $500 million a year, is divided between the juke box operator and the owner of the location where the box is placed. But no royalties are paid to the owners of copyrights on the music that is played. Composers and record manufacturers contend that payments should be required.

A third such question is raised by systems of data storage and retrieval. This industry is still in its infancy. But it is possible that books, in time, will be reduced to microforms, stored in central depositories, located by computers, ordered by telephone, and delivered to any destination in the country, as printouts, by wire. Exemption of such systems from infringement liability would leave the author and the publisher with scant protection for their copyrighted work.

Another issue, different in character, is presented by photocopying. Photocopying machines, in wide use, make it possible for teachers to reproduce copy-

75 / *Fortnightly Corp.* v. *United Artists Television,* 392 U.S. 390 (1968).

righted materials for use in class-room instruction and over educational TV, for students to reproduce such materials for their own use, and for libraries to duplicate and store them. And this can be done without payment of royalties. Such reproduction is useful and should be permitted, within limits. But it could be carried so far as to deprive the author and the publisher of the income and the incentive that are essential to the production of copyrighted works. Somehow a line must be drawn between duplication that is permissible and duplication that is not. The courts have attempted to do this by enunciating a doctrine of fair use, approving reproduction of a reasonable portion of a copyrighted work for a legitimate purpose, while forbidding reproduction that competes in the market where the work is sold. But this rule is enforced only by infringement suits, and authors and publishers are not in a position to apprehend infringers and bring them into court. Such suits, in fact, are rare.

A bill recasting the copyright law, prepared by the Copyright Office over a period of 10 years, was presented to Congress in 1964. This measure would extend the duration of copyrighted protection to the owner's life plus 50 years, a term that is common abroad. It would require CATV stations to obtain permission for the transmission of copyrighted materials. It would require the operators of juke boxes to pay a royalty for every time a record is played. It would extend infringement liability to systems of data storage and retrieval. It would incorporate the fair use doctrine in cases of duplication of printed materials for educational purposes, permitting reasonable use for research, reporting, criticism, and teaching, but forbidding reproduction of a complete copy of a copyrighted work or the production of multiple copies of substantial excerpts, with similar provisions governing displays of visual materials, dramatic performances, and educational broadcasting. The bill embodying these provisions encountered strong opposition from CATV stations, juke box operators, and educators. It was passed by the House of Representatives in 1967. It was still in committee in the Senate at the end of 1969.

Chapter 9 EXCLUSION AND DISCRIMINATION

Two monopolistic practices, in particular, have been specifically attacked by the antitrust laws: the use of tying and exclusive contracts, and discrimination in price. These practices have a double significance. They affect the ability of one producer to compete with another in obtaining access to markets. They also affect the ability of one distributor to compete with another in obtaining and reselling supplies of goods. The way in which the applicable provisions of the law are enforced and interpreted will therefore determine the nature of competitive opportunities at the successive stages of production and distribution.

EXCLUSIVE CONTRACTS

Tying and exclusive contracts have been used, as was shown in Chapter 4, to obtain and extend a position of monopoly. Under the Sherman Act, such contracts were cancelled, in certain cases, by consent decrees and enjoined by decisions of the lower courts. But in a number of other cases monopolies obtained through tying contracts were allowed to stand. It was the position taken by the Supreme Court in these cases that led to the inclusion of Section 3, outlawing such contracts where their effect "may be to substantially lessen competition," in the Clayton Act. These contracts have since been attacked more often under this Section and less often under the Federal Trade Commission Act and the Sherman Act.

Tying Contracts

In the first order of the Federal Trade Commission to reach the Supreme Court, in the Gratz case[1] in 1920, a tying contract was involved. Gratz was the principal sales agent of Carnegie Steel, a subsidiary of U.S. Steel and the major producer of ties for binding cotton bales. He was also an agent for a company producing nearly half of the jute bagging used to wrap such bales. By refusing to fill orders for ties unless accompanied by orders for equivalent supplies of

1 / *FTC* v. *Gratz*, 235 U.S. 421.

bagging, he compelled dealers to turn to him for both commodities. The Commission, however, did not seek to prove that this arrangement substantially lessened competition or tended to create a monopoly in violation of the Clayton Act, but charged instead that it was an unfair method of competition, within the meaning of Section 5 of the Trade Commission Act. The Court rejected this contention, interpreting the latter Act so narrowly as to confine Commission orders to practices found "heretofore" to be unfair. Since tying contracts, as such, had not been held to be illegal, the order in the Gratz case was reversed. This interpretation of the Trade Commission Act has since been abandoned by the Court.

The Commission has issued orders against tying contracts in a number of cases, under Section 3 of the Clayton Act. But it is through suits instituted by the Department of Justice or by private litigants that the issue has been brought before the Court. In most of these cases one of the products tied by contract was protected by patent rights. Here it was obvious that the patented product was monopolized and that contractual arrangements tying another product to it tended to create a monopoly of the latter as well. In all such cases, the tying provisions have been condemned. A similar arrangement was outlawed by the Court in 1948, when it enjoined block booking in the motion picture industry. Contracts so tying one good to another as to extend the boundaries of monopoly have almost invariably been held to violate the law.

In the *Times-Picayune* case of 1953, discussed in Chapter 7, the Supreme Court laid down the rule that tying contracts were illegal per se in cases where the tying product was monopolized and an appreciable volume of trade in the tied product was restrained. But it permitted the defendant's contract to stand on the ground that the paper did not have a monopoly of the relevant market for the tying product. In 1958, however, the Court went on to extend the scope of the per se rule. The Northern Pacific Railway had included in leases for its land a provision requiring its tenants to ship the products of the land over its rails. Here, the company obviously did not possess a monopoly of the tying product—land. But the Court decided against it, holding that nothing more than "sufficient economic power to impose an appreciable restraint on free competition in the tied product" was needed to prove a violation of the law. There are certain practices, said the Court, "which because of their pernicious effect on competition and lack of any redeeming virtue are conclusively presumed to be unreasonable." Tying contracts, like price fixing, market sharing, and boycotts, were thus held to be illegal per se.[2]

Exclusive Dealing

Most of the orders issued by the Federal Trade Commission under Section 3 of the Clayton Act involve exclusive dealerships. And these have been reversed, in a number of cases, by the Court. In the most important of these, the Commission had issued 27 orders against refining companies who leased to retailers

2 / *Northern Pacific Railway Co.* v. *U.S.*, 356 U.S. 1.

of gasoline, at nominal rentals, tanks and pumps marked with their brand names, prohibiting their use in storing and selling gasoline produced by their competitors. This arrangement, however, did not prevent dealers from installing other tanks and pumps to handle other brands. And, though the cost of financing such installations handicapped independent refiners, the Court held that exclusion of their product from equipment financed by their competitors did not substantially lessen competition or tend toward monopoly.[3] An exclusive contract of a different type was found not to be illegal in a private suit involving General Motors in 1936. General Motors had forbidden dealers in Buicks and Chevrolets to use parts produced by other manufacturers in making repairs or even to offer them for sale. The Court found, however, that competition in the sale of parts had not been lessened and held that the company's contracts were needed to protect its warranty and preserve its goodwill.[4] In most other suits to come before the Court, exclusive dealerships have been enjoined. And here, since such arrangements are made illegal only where their effect "may be to substantially lessen competition or tend to create a monopoly," decisions have turned upon interpretations of this phrase.

Before 1947, in all of the cases where the rule against exclusive contracts was enforced, the seller employing such contracts dominated the markets in which he sold. In the Standard Fashion and Butterick cases[5] in 1922 and 1925, firms making two fifths of the dress patterns sold at retail excluded their competitors from the best stores in the cities and from the only outlets available in many smaller towns. In the Eastman Kodak case[6] in 1927, a firm producing more than nine tenths of the motion picture film made in the United States entered into an agreement with its customers, through an association of laboratories making motion picture prints, forbidding them to purchase film imported from abroad. In the Carter Carburetor case[7] in 1940, the principal manufacturer of carburetors gave discounts to dealers who bought exclusively from him and denied them to those who bought from his competitors. In the case of the Fashion Originators' Guild[8] in 1941, an association of dress manufacturers, whose 176 members made three fifths of the dresses sold at retail for $10.75 and up, sought to prevent "design piracy" by signing contracts with 12,000 retailers forbidding them to buy from imitators. In all of these cases, exclusive dealing was enjoined on the ground that its use by a dominant seller had substantially lessened competition and tended toward monopoly. In later cases, a less rigid criterion was employed.

The Test of Substantiality

In the International Salt case, mentioned in Chapter 8, where a contract

3 / *FTC* v. *Sinclair Refining Co.*, 261 U.S. 463.

4 / *Pick Mfg. Co.* v. *General Motors Corp.*, 299 U.S. 3.

5 / *Standard Fashion Co.* v. *Magrane-Houston Co.*, 258 U.S. 346; *Butterick Co.* v. *FTC*, 4 F. 2d 910, certiorari denied, 267 U.S. 602.

6 / *FTC* v. *Eastman Kodak Co.*, 247 U.S. 619.

7 / *FTC* v. *Carter Carburetor Corp.*, 112 F. 2d 722.

8 / *Fashion Originators' Guild* v. *FTC*, 312 U.S. 457.

tying the sale of salt to the lease of a patented salt dispenser was found to be illegal in 1947, the Supreme Court went on to say that

> . . . it is unreasonable, *per se,* to foreclose competitors from any substantial market. . . . The volume of business affected by these contracts cannot be said to be insignificant or insubstantial and the tendency of the agreements to the accomplishment of monopoly seems obvious. Under the law, agreements are forbidden which "tend to create a monopoly," and it is immaterial that the tendency is a creeping one rather than one that proceeds at full gallop; nor does the law wait for arrival at the goal before condemning the direction of the movement.[9]

This reasoning was applied to exclusive dealerships in the Standard Oil of California case in 1949.[10] Standard Oil, producing 23 percent of the gasoline sold in seven western states, contracted with some 6,000 independent dealers, handling less than 7 percent of the gasoline sold in the area, to fill all of their requirements for petroleum products and, in some cases, for tires, tubes, batteries, and other accessories. The lower court held Standard's contracts to be illegal on the ground that competition is substantially lessened when competitors are excluded from "a substantial number of outlets."[11] Standard appealed and the Supreme Court, in a 5 to 4 decision, affirmed the lower court's decree. The positions taken by the different judges illustrate the nature of the issue involved. Justice Douglas, in a separate dissent, argued that the requirements contracts should have been permitted, since they were "relatively innocuous as compared with the virulent growth of monopoly power" resulting from the probable alternatives: conversion of the exclusive dealerships into agencies or outright purchase of their businesses. The exclusive contract, he felt, "at least keeps the independents alive."[12] Justice Jackson took a different line. Exclusive contracts, he said, must be judged by their effect; they are illegal only when their effect "may be to substantially lessen competition," and here no evidence of this effect was introduced. The decree, therefore, was "but a guess in the dark," lacking "an adequate basis on which to upset long-standing and widely practiced business arrangements."[13] The majority thought otherwise. It is enough, said Justice Frankfurter, to prove "that competition has been foreclosed in a substantial share of the line of commerce affected." Standard's contracts created "a potential clog on competition," and it was the purpose of Section 3 of the Clayton Act to remove such an impediment "wherever, were it to become actual, it would impede a substantial amount of competitive activity."[14]

The precedent set by the Standard Stations decision was followed in the Richfield Oil case in 1951. Richfield's exclusive contracts with filling stations

9 / *International Salt Co.* v. *U.S.,* 332 U.S. 392, 396.

10 / *Standard Oil Co. of California* v. *U.S.,* 337 U.S. 293.

11 / *U.S.* v. *Standard Oil Co. of California,* 78 F. Supp. 850, 857.

12 / *Standard Oil Co. of California* v. *U.S.,* 337 U.S. 293, 319.

13 / *Ibid.,* p. 322.

14 / *Ibid.,* p. 314.

on the Pacific Coast accounted for but 3 percent of the gasoline sold in the area, but the rule of quantitative substantiality was applied and the contracts condemned. [15] In the light of these decisions it appeared that exclusive arrangements were to be outlawed per se. But later developments point the other way.

The severity of the rule of quantitative substantiality was mitigated, during the fifties, by the fact that the Federal Trade Commission declined to proceed against exclusive arrangements that appeared to be harmless, confining its orders to cases in which the probability of actual injury to competition could be shown. Then, in 1961, in the case of *Tampa Electric Co.* v. *Nashville Coal Co.,* [16] the Supreme Court modified its earlier position. Tampa had contracted to purchase from Nashville, for 20 years, all of the coal required for one of its generating stations. The Court assigned little importance to the fact that the contract involved a substantial sum of money, recognizing that it assured Tampa a steady source of supply and Nashville a steady market, while covering only 1 percent of the coal produced in the Nashville area, thus leaving to the Nashville company's competitors free access to the market as a whole. The decision made it clear that the Court was prepared, in exclusive dealing cases, to consider market factors other than the dollar volume of the trade concerned.

Dealer Franchises

Certain products, automobiles being the outstanding example, are distributed by their manufacturers through organizations of independently owned dealers. Each of the dealers receives from a manufacturer a franchise giving him the exclusive right to sell the manufacturer's product within a designated territory. Each of them promises, in turn, to devote his sales effort exclusively to the distribution of this product. The arrangement has marked advantages. It brings to the large-scale national enterprise the energies of small-scale local firms. It brings to the local businessmen the prestige, merchandising skill, managerial guidance, and financial strength of the national concern. There were 750 franchisers with 450,000 franchisees in the United States in 1967, including producers and distributors of tires, gasoline, shoes, and services such as those rendered by restaurants and motels. Together, they accounted for a quarter of the nation's retail sales.

Each of the parties to a franchise contract has his economic future at stake. The manufacturer depends upon the dealer to provide sales coverage, maintain stocks, handle trade-ins, perform servicing, make good on warranties, and preserve his reputation. The character of dealer performance in these respects determines the volume of the manufacturer's sales. To the dealer, on the other hand, retention of his franchise is a matter of life and death. Many controversies have arisen out of the manufacturer–dealer relationship, and some of them have come before the Congress and the courts.

15 / *U.S.* v. *Richfield Oil Corp.,* 99 F. Supp. 280 (1951), sustained *per curiam* 343 U.S. 922 (1952).

16 / 365 U.S. 320.

At hearings before a committee of the Senate in 1955, automobile dealers complained that manufacturers were coercing them, under threat of franchise termination, to increase their sales. Thereafter, the manufacturers changed the provisions of their franchises, extending them for terms of five years, making them cancelable only for cause, defining cause by spelling out objectively measurable criteria, and permitting dealers to appeal their decisions to an impartial umpire. Despite this reform, the dealers demanded legislation. The result was the Automobile Dealer Franchise Act of 1956. Under this law, dealers can collect damages if they can prove that manufacturers, when proposing to terminate a franchise, have not acted in good faith. Coercion, intimidation, or threats give evidence of bad faith; exposition, recommendation, or persuasion do not. Hearings were held in 1967 on a bill that would extend similar protection to franchisees in other industries. Experience under the automobile dealers' act, however, is not encouraging. Few damage suits have been brought, and the sums collected from cases won or settled have been small.

Most of the franchise suits brought before the courts have originated with the government and have been concerned with restrictions on territories and customers imposed on dealers in franchise contracts. In a leading case, decided by the Supreme Court in 1963, the White Motors Company, in selling trucks through franchised distributors, had assigned them territories, imposing penalties for sales outside, and had forbidden them to sell to certain customers. The government asked that these restrictions be adjudged illegal per se. The Court refused, allowing them to stand under a rule of reason. "Geographical restrictions," said Justice Douglas for the majority, "may be too dangerous to sanction, or they may be allowable protections against aggressive competitors, or the only practicable means a small company has for breaking into or staying in business." [17] The case was terminated, in 1964, by a consent decree under which the company agreed to discontinue its allocation of territories and customers.

A second case involving a franchise system came before the Court in 1966. Here, the General Motors franchise for Chevrolet dealers forbade them to establish branch locations. A number of dealers in Los Angeles had been selling cars through discount houses. By 1960, some 2,000 sales per year were being made in this way. Dealers' associations complained to General Motors, and GM thereupon warned its dealers that such sales must be discontinued since they violated the provision forbidding branch locations. This ruling was enforced by three dealers' associations who employed shoppers to purchase cars through the discount houses, and by GM, who then required the offending dealers to buy them back, sometimes at prices that involved a loss. This put an end to the discount sales of Chevrolets. The government then brought suit. The Supreme Court refused to pass on the legality of the franchise provision. But it found the action taken by GM and the dealers' associations for the purpose of eliminating sales through discounters to constitute a conspiracy in restraint of trade and thus to be in violation of the law. [18]

17 / *White Motors Co.* v. *U.S.*, 372 U.S. 253 (1963).
18 / *U.S.* v. *General Motors Corp.*, 384 U.S. 127.

The next defendant in a franchise suit was the Brown Shoe Co., the manufacturer whose acquisition of a chain of shoe stores had been found, as shown in Chapter 7, to violate the Celler-Kefauver Act. Brown had franchised 650 shoe stores, forbidding them to carry lines of shoes produced by other manufacturers in competition with its own. The Court held this limitation to be illegal, referring to its ruling in the earlier case that concentration in the industry must be checked in its incipiency.[19]

The Court spelled out its position on franchising in more detail in 1967 in the case of Arnold, Schwinn & Co., a manufacturer of bicycles. The company had undertaken to keep its bicycles out of the hands of discount houses by franchising its distributors. It entered into contracts with a score of wholesalers whom it treated as agents or consignees, limiting their sales to retailers in specified territories. It also franchised thousands of retailers, to whom its wholesalers made outright sales. It permitted them to buy only from these wholesalers and to sell only to consumers. The company's system thus imposed a vertical allocation of territories and customers. The Court held its confinement of sales to selected dealers to be legal as long as other brands were available to their competitors, thus accepting franchising as such. But it distinguished between the cases in which the company retained title to its goods, treating its wholesalers as agents or consignees, and the cases in which it surrendered title to retailers. In the former, it held the company's restrictions on territories and customers to be lawful unless unreasonable, following the rule laid down in the White Motors case. But in the latter, it held, as in the Brown Shoe case, that the vendor could not lawfully impose limitations on the vendee. Such limitations, it said, were illegal per se. The freedom of franchisers to allocate territories and customers was thus confined, under a rule of reason, to cases of agency and consignment sales. [20]

PRICE DISCRIMINATION

The sale of goods and services to different buyers at different prices is a common practice. Doctors, dentists, and undertakers customarily adjust their charges to the size of the customer's purse. Department stores sell merchandise at one price on the upper floors and at another in the basement. Railroads charge different rates to different shippers for hauling a ton a mile, and public utilities vary their charges for a cubic foot of gas or a kilowatt-hour of electricity. Farmers are paid one price for milk distributed to consumers and another for milk sold to producers of butter and cheese. Movie distributors collect more from one exhibitor than from another who shows the same film, their charges being based on box office receipts. Exporters sometimes charge lower prices abroad than they do in the United States. Manufacturers and wholesalers classify their customers and sell to each class at a different price. Discounts are commonly provided for promptness of payment and for purchases in quantity.

19 / *FTC* v. *Brown Shoe Co.*, 384 U.S. 316 (1966).
20 / *U.S.* v. *Arnold, Schwinn & Co.*, 388 U.S. 365.

Differentiation in prices frequently involves discrimination in the treatment accorded to different buyers; it does not invariably do so. The costs incurred in making different sales may differ; where prices are varied accordingly, the seller does not discriminate. Discrimination occurs most clearly when the same goods, of the same quality, are sold in the same quantity, at the same time, under the same conditions, and on the same terms, to different buyers at different prices. But it also occurs where costs differ and prices do not, and where differences in price are not proportionate to differences in cost. Discrimination may take the form of variation in the price itself, or the form of variation in the discounts accompanying a uniform price. It may also appear in differences in the quality of the goods and the character of the services provided by sellers and in the allowances made by sellers for services rendered them by buyers. Discrimination, in general, may be said to exist where all but one of the variables of different sales are identical, and also—if more than one variable differs—where the differences in one are not proportionate to those in another.

If markets were perfect, discrimination would be impossible, since every purchaser would buy at the lowest price and on the most favorable terms. If a seller is to discriminate, his market must therefore be divided into segments and each of them dealt with separately. This may be accomplished in a variety of ways. Buyers at different locations are separated by transport costs and, in the case of international trade, by artificial barriers. Customers are segregated according to the use they make of goods or services: those who drink milk are segregated from those who make it into butter, those who burn electricity at home from those who burn it in factories, those who ride in Pullman cars from those who ride in coaches, and those who ship lumber from those who ship television sets. Purchasers are separated by the time of day, the day of the week, or the season of the year: movies cost less in the daytime and long-distance calls at night; golf courses have lower rates on weekdays than on weekends; resort hotels are cheaper out of season, coal in the summer, and furs at the August sales. Buyers are separated by age, sex, and status: children are carried at half fare; ladies are admitted to ball games at reduced rates; students are given educational discounts when buying magazines. Consumers are segregated by ignorance and by variations in prestige, the same product being sold at different prices under different labels or in different shops. Distributors are classified according to the functions they perform and different discounts are given to those who sell at wholesale and at retail. In these and other ways, discrimination is made possible.

Forms of Discrimination

Discrimination may be open or secret, systematic or sporadic, permanent or temporary; it may be apparent in a structure of prices that is publicly announced and consistently adhered to over a long period of time; it may result occasionally from bargains struck in making individual sales. Discrimination may be purposive: it may be practiced by a monopolist who seeks to maximize his revenues by charging high prices where demand is inelastic and low prices where it is not, by a would-be monopolist who seeks to drive his rivals from local markets, or by a competitor who meets the different prices found in each part of his market or quotes the lower price required to make a sale; it may be designed to reduce costs by encouraging prompt payment, large orders, and off-peak use, to promote a new product, to invade a new market, or to expand sales by experimenting with elasticity of demand. Discrimination may be incidental; this is the case when a seller conforms to a delivered pricing system in his industry. It is the purpose of such a system to enable all sellers to charge identical prices at any destination. But the seller who conforms may charge some buyers more and others less for freight than the amounts he actually pays; his net return will be greater on the former sales than on the latter; in short, he will discriminate among his customers. Discrimination, in this case, is open, systematic, and permanent; but it is incidental to the purpose of monopoly.

The consequences of discrimination cannot be said to be always good or always bad. A number of cases may be distinguished for the purpose of analysis:

1. Discrimination by a single firm possessing a monopoly.
    a) In the absence of public regulation.
    b) Where rates and services are regulated by a public agency.
2. Discrimination by one of many sellers in an industry.
    a) Where incidental to collusion in fixing prices.
    b) Where undertaken independently.
        (1) Where it affects competition between the seller and his competitors.
        (2) Where it affects competition between the buyer and his competitors.

Discrimination by monopolists and its regulation by public authorities will be discussed in Chapter 14, the discrimination incidental to delivered pricing systems in Chapter 10. It is with purposive discrimination, undertaken independently by sellers facing competition, that we are here concerned.

The Uses and Abuses of Discrimination

The discount structures of sellers serve a variety of purposes. Discounts for cash cut costs by reducing the amount of credit that must be extended in making sales. Discounts based on the functions performed by buyers afford to wholesalers and retailers the margins that enable them to supply the seller with marketing services that he might otherwise be compelled to provide himself. Discounts based on the size of a single purchase encourage larger orders and thus reduce the cost involved in selling, accounting, collecting, packing, and delivery. Discounts related to the quantity purchased over several months may also cut costs by making possible the forward planning of production, maintaining output in off seasons, stabilizing operations, and reducing investment in inventories. Services rendered to buyers or allowances made to buyers for services rendered by them may pay for themselves by promoting sales. If concessions are justified by savings realized by sellers, they are not fairly to be called discriminatory. But large buyers may use superior bargaining power to exact concessions that are not so justified. And here discrimination will occur.

Discrimination may be judged by its influence on competition at either of two levels: that of the seller or that of the buyer. In either case, its consequences may be good or bad. At the seller's level, competition may be eliminated as prices are cut, in one market after another, and raised again when local rivals have been driven from the field. But competition may be strengthened where discrimination is employed to introduce new products, enter new markets, or feel out lower levels of demand, and where it is used to meet the lower prices of competitors. For reductions thus introduced and copied will eventually be generalized. "Sporadic, unsystematic discrimination," says Morris Adelman, "is one of the most powerful forces of competition in modern industrial markets. Like a high wind, it seizes on small openings and crevices in an 'orderly' price structure and tears it apart." [21]

The framers of the Clayton Act were concerned primarily with the effect of discrimination on competitors of the firm that gives a lower price, those of the Robinson-Patman Act with its effect on competitors of the firm receiving it. At this level, discrimination may strengthen or weaken competing channels of distribution by affecting the relative costs of different distributors. It may prevent equality of opportunity by giving an undeserved advantage to the larger buyer or to the smaller one. It may promote efficiency or subsidize inefficiency by favoring the buyer whose costs are low or the one whose costs are high. If opportunity is to be equalized and efficiency encouraged, the seller must recognize, in the prices charged each buyer, the savings to which the manner of his purchases entitles him. To do more would be to handicap the weak. To do less would be to handicap the strong. In the one case, monopoly would be promoted. In the other, the weak competitor would be protected, but competition itself would be impaired.

Discrimination under the Clayton Act

Section 2 of the Clayton Act made it unlawful "to discriminate in price between different purchasers of commodities . . . where the effect of such discrimination may be to substantially lessen competition or tend to create a monopoly *in any line of commerce.*" It provided, however, that this should not apply to discrimination "on account of differences in the grade, quality, or quantity of the commodity sold, *or* that makes only due allowance for differences in the cost of selling or transportation," or to discrimination "made in good faith to meet competition," and should not prevent sellers "from selecting their own customers in bona fide transactions and not in restraint of trade." The words here given in italics assumed particular importance in the subsequent interpretation of the law.

---

21 / M. A. Adelman, "Effective Competition and the Antitrust Laws," *Harvard Law Review,* Vol. LXI, pp. 1289-1350, esp. pp. 1331-32.

In the Mennen case in 1923 and in the Nabisco case in 1924, the phrase "in any line of commerce" was given a meaning so narrow that orders issued by the Federal Trade Commission were reversed. Mennen had refused to give its wholesale discount to a cooperative organization of retail druggists buying in equal quantities. National Biscuit had allowed the units of a chain to pool their purchases in claiming quantity discounts but refused to permit the members of an association of retailers to do so. The Commission found, in these cases, that discrimination had lessened competition with the favored distributors. The courts held, however, that the distributors were in a different line of commerce from Mennen or Nabisco, and found that competition with these concerns was not impaired.[22] This interpretation was reversed in the Van Camp case in 1929. American Can had refused Van Camp a discount granted another packing company, and Van Camp had sued for treble damages. The Supreme Court found for the plaintiff, holding that "any line of commerce" included the line where Van Camp competed with the other purchaser.[23] The Commission was encouraged by this decision to issue an order in a pending case against the Goodyear Tire and Rubber Company.

Goodyear had supplied Sears, Roebuck with tires like those sold elsewhere under a different trademark and with a different tread. Its price for filling all of Sears' requirements was cost plus 6 percent. To get the contract it had also paid a bonus in cash and Goodyear stock. After making allowance for differences in cost due to the quantities purchased and for savings in selling expenses, the Commission found that Goodyear's discrimination in favor of Sears ran between 12 and 22 percent of the price at which it sold to other distributors, enabling Sears to undersell them at retail by 20-25 percent. The Commission issued its order in 1933, contending that the difference in Goodyear's prices could not be justified by differences in cost. The final decision on Goodyear's appeal was not handed down until 1939, three years after the passage of the Robinson-Patman Act. It turned on a single word: "or." This word, said the court, made the phrase "on account of differences in . . . grade, quality, or quantity" completely independent of the phrase "makes only due allowance for differences in . . . cost," and thus permitted *any* difference in these factors to justify *any* difference in price.[24] The decision made it clear that discrimination could not have been prevented under the provisions of the Clayton Act.

This weakness of Section 2 was corrected when it was superseded in 1936 by the Robinson-Patman Act. Another one was not. The proviso preventing application of the law to sellers "selecting their own customers" is still available as a defense for powerful producers who may confine their sales to fabricators or distributors adhering to suggested policies or may coerce their weaker customers by threatening to withhold supplies. Railroads and public utilities are

22 / *Mennen Co.* v. *FTC,* 288 F. 774, certiorari denied, 262 U.S. 759; *National Biscuit Co.* v. *FTC,* 299 F. 733, certiorari denied, 266 U.S. 613.

23 / *Van Camp Co.* v. *American Can Co.,* 278 U.S. 245.

24 / *Goodyear Tire and Rubber Co.* v. *FTC,* 101 F. 2d 620, certiorari denied, 308 U.S. 557.

required to serve all comers. Manufacturers, even though controlling the bulk of an industry's output, are not.

Provisions of the Robinson-Patman Act

The Robinson–Patman Act contains a criminal and a civil section. The former (Section 3) makes three offenses punishable by fine and imprisonment. They are (1) charging different buyers different prices on sales that are otherwise identical, (2) selling more cheaply in one part of the country than in another, and (3) selling "at unreasonably low prices," whenever either of the latter things is done "for the purpose of destroying competition or eliminating a competitor." The first of these offenses is so narrowly defined as to be of little practical importance. The second is definite, but the third is vague: when are prices "unreasonably low"? The condition attached would make enforcement, if ever attempted, extremely difficult. It is only in the most flagrant of cases that a court would be likely to find in a cut in prices the purpose of "destroying competition or eliminating a competitor." It is in its civil section (Section 2) that the Act has been significant.

The law deals in part with specific forms of discrimination and in part with discrimination in general. Section 2-c forbids the seller to pay a broker's commission to the buyer himself or to an intermediary under his control. This prohibition is absolute: no exceptions are allowed. Section 2-d forbids the seller to make an allowance for services rendered him by the buyer unless it is made available to the latter's competitors "on proportionally equal terms." Section 2-e forbids the seller to furnish the buyer with facilities or services "not accorded to all purchasers on proportionally equal terms." Allowances, facilities, and services must thus be made proportionate to something, but what this may be the law does not attempt to say. These specific prohibitions serve to prevent evasion of the broader provisions of Section 2-a dealing with discrimination in general.

Section 2-a makes it illegal to discriminate in price, in selling goods of "like grade and quality," not only where the effect may be, as in the Clayton Act, "substantially to lessen competition or tend to create a monopoly," but also where it may be "to injure, destroy, or prevent competition with any person who either grants or knowingly receives the benefit of such discrimination, or with the customers of either of them." The new wording, it should be noted, does two things: it adds *injury to competitors* to the test of illegality, and it applies to competition not only with the one who gives the lower price but also with the one who gets it.

The law also changes the defenses that may be offered by a seller charged with discrimination. (1) Under the cost defense, provided in Section 2-a, he may show that the differentials in his price "make only due allowance for differences in the cost of manufacture, sale, or delivery resulting from the differing methods or quantities in which such commodities are . . . sold or delivered." (2) Under the good faith defense of Section 2-b, he may show that his lower price "was made in good faith to meet" not competition, as in the Clayton Act, but "an equally low price of a competitor." He may match a lower price, but may not undercut it.

A proviso in Section 2-a authorizes the Commission to fix limits beyond which discounts for larger quantities may not be given, even though justified by differences in cost, "where it finds that available purchasers in greater quantities are so few as to render differentials on account thereof unjustly discriminatory or promotive of monopoly."

And finally, the prohibitions of the Act are applied to buyers as well as to sellers. Section 2-f makes it unlawful for buyers "knowingly to induce or receive" a prohibited discrimination in price.

PRICE DISCRIMINATION BEFORE THE COURTS

Few cases have been brought under the criminal section of the Robinson-Patman Act, but many orders have been issued by the Federal Trade Commission under the civil sections of the law. During the first 20 years after the law was enacted, nearly half of these orders were issued under the brokerage section, another fifth under the section dealing with advertising allowances and services. Where these orders have been appealed, the Commission has almost invariably been upheld. But it is in connection with the remaining third of the Commission's orders, issued under the section dealing with discrimination in general, that the most important issues of interpretation have occurred. Here the courts have been called upon to define the concept of injury to competition, to decide upon the legitimacy of regional, functional, and quantity discounts, and to determine the availability of the cost defense and the good faith defense. The application of the law to discrimination in the distributive trades will be considered in the remainder of this chapter, its application to the discrimination inherent in delivered pricing systems in the next.

The Criminal Section

The enforcement agencies have rarely brought suit under Section 3, the criminal section of the Act. For years, enforcement of the section was left to private litigants who attacked the prices charged by their competitors in suits for triple damages. The door to such suits was closed, however, by a decision handed down by the Supreme Court in 1958. Section 3, unlike Section 2, said the Court, is not worded as an amendment to the Clayton Act. Since it is not a part of the antitrust laws, it affords no basis for private suits.[25] In the absence of public enforcement, Section 3 came to be regarded as a dead letter. In 1963, however, in a case brought by the government against the National Dairy Products Corporation, where the defendant argued that the vagueness of the section rendered it unconstitutional, the Supreme Court upheld its constitu-

25 / *Nashville Milk Co.* v. *Carnation Co.,* 355 U.S. 373.

tionality and remanded the case to a lower court for trial on the facts.[26] Bills have also been introduced in Congress to bring Section 3 within the antitrust laws, thus encouraging enforcement through private suits. But these have failed to pass.

Brokerage

Section 2-c of the Robinson-Patman Act, forbidding the payment of a broker's commission to anyone but an independent broker, has been so interpreted as to make such payments illegal per se. The prosecution is not required to prove that a payment has injured competition. The defendant is not permitted to justify the payment by showing savings in cost. And despite the phrase in the law that outlaws such payments "except for services rendered," he cannot escape conviction by showing that services have been performed. One of the first cases to come before the courts under this section involved the A&P. The company sought to justify its discounts, showing that its agents in the field not only served its purchasing department but also gave advice to sellers and aided them in disposing of their surpluses, and contending that sellers had been saved the cost of employing brokers' services. But the Court rejected this defense, finding the prohibition of such payments to be absolute.[27]

The law has been rigidly applied, not only where brokerage has been received by mass distributors, like the A&P, but also where it has been collected by independent intermediaries or cooperative buying groups and passed on to the benefit of many small concerns. In the Biddle case, an independent purchasing company sold market information and buying services to 2,400 clients, passing on to them in lower prices the commissions it obtained.[28] In the Quality Bakers case, brokerage was collected and transmitted by an agency set up by 70 bakers to make cooperative purchases of flour, equipment, and supplies.[29] In all such cases, payments that were helpful, not to mass distributors, but to small independent dealers, have been prohibited. In its enforcement, the law that was supposedly enacted to protect the independent dealer has boomeranged.

Allowances and Services

Sections 2-d and 2-e of the Robinson-Patman Act forbid the seller to allow discounts to the buyer for merchandising services rendered him by the buyer, or himself to render merchandising services to the buyer, unless such allowances or services are made available to all buyers "on proportionally equal terms." This does not mean that allowances must actually be made or services rendered to all buyers. It does mean, according to decisions made by the Commission, that

26 / U.S. v. National Dairy Products Corp., 372 U.S. 29.

27 / A&P v. FTC, 106 F. 2d 667 (1939), certiorari denied, 308 U.S. 625 (1940).

28 / Biddle Purchasing Co. v. FTC, 96 F. 2d 687 (1938), certiorari denied, 305 U.S. 634 (1938).

29 / Quality Bakers v. FTC, 114 F. 2d 393 (1940).

they cannot be given secretly; their availability must be publicly announced. Their terms cannot be such as to confine them to a few big buyers; they must be made available to all. If the form in which allowances or services are provided is such that some buyers cannot make use of them, sellers must offer genuine alternatives. Allowances, moreover, may be made only for services actually rendered, and they must not be substantially in excess of the cost of these services to the buyer or their value to the seller.

The courts in general have upheld the Commission when its orders under these subsections have been appealed. Here, again, proof of injury to competition is not required. Nor is discrimination to be justified by showing differences in cost or by proving the need—in good faith—to meet the offers of competitors. If allowances and services are not given "on proportionally equal terms," they are held to be illegal per se.

But proportional to what? There are various possibilities. One is proportionality to the dollar volume of purchases made by various customers. Another is proportionality to the cost to the buyer of the services rendered by him to the seller. Still another is proportionality to the value of such services to the seller. The Commission has employed proportionality to dollar volume as a rule of thumb.

The effect of enforcement of this section has apparently been to force some manufacturers to discontinue the use of demonstrators in larger sales outlets and to discourage them from experimenting, on a local basis, with new forms of sales promotion. In some cases, promotional allowances, instead of being made generally available, have been reduced or abandoned. Whether these changes have materially benefited the small retailer, it is impossible to say.

Injury to Competition

The prohibitions contained in the foregoing sections of the law are unqualified. But other forms of discounts, covered in Section 2-a, are illegal only when their effect "may" be "substantially" to injure competition. The application of the law thus turns on the meaning that is given to the words "may" and "substantially" and to injury to competition. The meaning given to the word "substantially" was discussed above when we considered the interpretation of Section 3. The word "may" has come to be interpreted as denoting reasonable probability. As for injury to competition, the law provides two tests, a broader and a narrower one. Under the broader test, discrimination is illegal "where the effect may be substantially to lessen competition or tend to create a monopoly." This test is thus concerned with the vitality of competition in general. Under the narrower test, discrimination is illegal where the effect may be "to injure, destroy, or prevent competition with any person who either grants or knowingly receives the benefit of such discrimination or with customers of either of them." This test is concerned with the impact of competition on particular classes of competitors. Discrimination is equally unlawful under either test. But it is more difficult to prove a substantial lessening of competition or tendency toward monopoly, easier to prove injury to classes of competitors. The Federal Trade Commission, in issuing price discrimination orders, has therefore emphasized the narrower test.

These tests are applied in judging the effect of discrimination on competition on either side of the market: between the seller and his competitors and between the buyer and his competitors. In orders dealing with the effect of discrimination on competition of the first type, the Commission has held that a discriminating seller's competitors were injured whenever trade was diverted from them to him and has inferred diversion from the mere existence of a difference in price. The result has been, in effect, to outlaw all price differences that are large enough to divert trade and thus to prohibit all price cuts save those extended to buyers as a whole.

In orders dealing with the effect of discrimination on competition between buyers and their competitors, the Commission has inferred, likewise, that competitors were injured whenever there has been a substantial difference in the prices they have paid. And it has held to this position in the face of evidence that the disfavored buyers have grown and prospered, and despite the buyers' testimony that they have not been hurt. In the view of the Commission, the only cases in which discrimination involves no injury to competition are those where a seller discriminates among noncompeting buyers or where his discrimination is minimal in amount. [30]

The Commission's use of the narrow test of injury was upheld by the Supreme Court in the Morton Salt case in 1948. Here, quantity discounts had been given to chain stores on a product that represented an insignificant share of the grocery business. But the Commission found that independent grocers had been injured, and the Court agreed. Morton's discounts, it said, had impaired "the competitive opportunities of certain merchants." Congress, in passing the Robinson-Patman Act, "was especially concerned with protecting small businesses." The law "was intended to justify a finding of injury to competition by a showing [in the words of a Senate report] of 'injury to the competitor victimized by the discrimination.'" [31]

Local Price Cutting

Where a firm that makes sales over a wide area competes with a firm whose sales are confined to a single locality, it may cut its price in this locality while maintaining it elsewhere. It may do so merely to meet a lower price in the local market, or it may undercut the local price in an effort to drive the local firm out of business. In either case, a lower profit margin or an actual loss in the local market may be offset by profits made elsewhere. In such cases, where local competitors have actually lost sales, the Federal Trade Commission has found injury to competition between sellers and has ordered the offending concerns to

30 / See Corwin D. Edwards, *The Price Discrimination Law* (Washington, D.C.: Brookings Institution, 1959), chap. xvi.

31 / *FTC* v. *Morton Salt Co.,* 334 U.S. 37, 46, 49.

cease and desist from discriminating in price. Its orders, in fact, have been so broad as to deny these concerns the right, at any time, for any purpose, to sell in different localities at different prices, and have thus placed on such competition stricter limits than the facts would seem to justify.

The legality of geographic price discrimination has been brought before the courts in a number of private damage suits. Where a company has sold at a lower price in one locality than in others for the apparent purpose of driving a local competitor out of business, violation of the Robinson-Patman Act has consistently been found.[32] But in a case where a company had set a lower price than it charged elsewhere in order to sell in a highly competitive local market, it was not held to violate the law.[33] In a later case, however, the Supreme Court took a less permissive line. The Utah Pie Company made and sold frozen fruit pies in Utah. Three larger companies shipped pies in from California. Utah undersold these concerns by 15 to 20 percent and obtained two thirds of the market. The Californians cut their prices in Utah to meet or undercut the prices charged by Utah Pie. As a result, Utah Pie's share of the market declined and its margin of profit was pinched. But it still outsold the other three concerns and was able to remain in business. The company nevertheless brought suit. A jury in a district court awarded it treble damages. The Court of Appeals reversed the verdict, holding that the evidence presented was insufficient to show the potentiality of injury to competition. The Supreme Court reversed this decision, inferring the potentiality of such injury from the mere persistence of geographic discrimination.[34] If this precedent is followed, it would appear to be virtually impossible for national or regional concerns to remain in local markets by persistently cutting prices there while maintaining them elsewhere.

Functional Discounts

Sellers have long followed the practice of classifying their customers, dividing them into noncompeting groups on the basis of the functions they perform—manufacturing, wholesaling, retailing—and giving a different discount to the members of each class. These discounts are usually graduated according to the buyer's position in the chain of distribution—larger discounts being given, for instance, to wholesalers and smaller discounts to retailers. They may thus be regarded as payment for different types of distributive services. The size of a buyer's discount does not depend upon the volume of his purchases or the costs incurred by the seller in serving him. It is governed solely by his status in the classification of the seller's customers.

Where buyers are not in competition with one another, discrimination between them is not in violation of the law. The Commission, accordingly, has never issued an order against a functional discount as such, but has explicitly

32 / *L. L. Moore* v. *Mead's Fine Bread Co.*, 347 U.S. 1012 (1954).

33 / *Balian Ice Cream Co.* v. *Arden Farms Co.*, 104 F. Supp. 796, 231 F. 2d 356, certiorari denied, 351 U.S. 672.

34 / *Utah Pie Co.* v. *Continental Baking Co.*, 386 U.S. 685 (1967).

held such discounts to be legitimate. The producers of spark plugs were thus permitted to charge lower prices to automobile manufacturers, who used them as original equipment, than to distributors of accessories, who sold them as replacement parts. Where different classes of buyers compete in reselling to the same customers, however, and where the members of one class compete with the customers of another, the law has been held to apply.

The degree of immunity afforded to functional discounts creates the possibility that sellers might evade the law relating to quantity discounts by establishing special customer classes for the purpose of granting discounts that could not be justified by differences in cost. The Commission has thus been forced to pass upon the methods by which customers are classified. In general, it has held that classifications may not be arbitrary, that they must conform strictly to the nature of the operations undertaken by different types of customers, and that buyers at the same level, such as independent retailers, mail order houses, and chain stores—must be put in the same class.

Where a customer performs more than one function, as in the case of one who sells at wholesale and at retail, it is necessary to determine which of the relevant discounts may be granted on his purchases. Here, the Commission has ruled that the larger discount allowed for any function may be applied only to the portion of an order for which that function alone is performed, and it has been upheld in this position by the courts. This principle, however, is difficult to enforce, since the seller, in applying different discounts to different portions of a sale, must take the buyer's word as to the quantities that will be handled in different ways, and the buyer has a strong incentive to overstate the quantity on which the higher discount will apply. The rule, moreover, is open to criticism, since it denies the split-function dealer the discount which he should receive for performing the wholesale function on that part of his purchases that he retails himself.

This question was involved in an order issued by the Commission against the Standard Oil Company of Indiana. Standard operated no service stations itself. It sold gasoline in tank wagon lots to retailers and in tank car lots to jobbers who resold it in tank wagons to retailers. It gave the jobbers a discount of 1½ cents a gallon. All of them made some sales at retail. One of them—Ned's in Detroit—operated exclusively as a cut-rate retailer. The Commission held that Standard was practicing illegal discrimination because its price to service stations was higher than its price to jobbers, or higher than the jobbers' price to service stations. It ordered Standard to deny the discount to jobbers on the part of the gasoline they sold at retail. It thus required the discount to be withheld from Ned's and required Standard to police the activities of the other distributors. The order operated to maintain a rigid stratification of functions in distribution, preventing Ned's and others from reducing the retail price of gasoline by combining the functions of wholesaler and retailer. It was reversed by the Supreme Court in 1958. [35]

35 / *FTC* v. *Standard Oil Co. (Indiana)*, 355 U.S. 396.

Volume and Quantity Discounts

Volume discounts are given on quantities purchased over periods of time, without regard to the size of individual orders or deliveries. They are designed to encourage customers to continue buying from a particular supplier. The Commission has forbidden such discounts, holding that cumulative purchases cannot be shown to cut the costs incurred in selling and delivering.

Quantity discounts are given on quantities purchased at a single time. These discounts, as such, were held by the Supreme Court, in the case of Bruce's Juices, not to be unlawful.[36] But quantity discounts have been prohibited, in many cases, by the FTC. The Commission, for instance, has forbidden larger discounts on orders placed by chains and cooperative buying agencies where deliveries are made to separate stores, finding no saving in costs. It is only discounts related to quantities delivered to one place at one time that have been found to be justified by differences in cost.

Even these discounts, in the circumstances of the Morton Salt case, were found to be in violation of the law. Morton's price per case of salt was $1.60 for less than carload lots and $1.50 for carloads of 1,035 cases each and was $1.50 for 5,000 cases and $1.35 for 50,000 cases when these were bought within a single year. Nominally the lower prices were equally available to all of the company's customers. But the only ones who bought enough salt in a year to get it for $1.35 were five large grocery chains. Independent retailers, competing with the chains, obtained supplies from wholesalers who had been required to pay $1.40 or $1.50. The Commission held these differences to be injurious to competition. It found the carload as well as the cumulative discounts to be unjustified by differences in cost. And it ordered the company to desist from selling to retailers at prices lower than those charged wholesalers whose customers compete with them. This order was sutained by the Supreme Court in a decision handed down in 1948.[37]

Quantity Limits

The Robinson-Patman Act authorizes the Federal Trade Commission to fix limits beyond which discounts for larger quantities may not be given, where "purchasers in greater quantities are so few as to render differentials on account thereof unjustly discriminatory or promotive of monopoly." For 15 years after the law was passed this authority was not exercised. But under pressure from independent dealers and members of Congress, hearings on a proposed order limiting discounts in the sale of tires and tubes were announced in October, 1949. Among 48,000 dealers making purchases from 27 manufacturers, the Commission found that 63, in the largest volume bracket, bought automobile

36 / *Bruce's Juices* v. *American Can Co.*, 330 U.S. 743 (1947).
37 / *FTC* v. *Morton Salt Co.*, 334 U.S. 37.

tires for 26-30 percent less than the prices paid by the smallest dealers, and truck tires for 32-40 percent less. Half of the business of distributing tires and tubes was in the hands of 2 percent of the distributors. The Commission held the industry's discount structure to be "unjustly discriminatory" and "promotive of monopoly" and issued an order in January, 1952, forbidding its members to grant larger discounts for quantities greater than a single carload of 20,000 pounds.

Goodrich appealed, contending that the lower prices offered larger dealers were voluntarily set to cover costs and yield a profit, that smaller dealers could enter the market and survive and grow, and that their share in the sale of tires and tubes had not declined for many years. It argued, too, that concentration is lower, the rate of entry higher, the life of enterprises longer, the share of them making profits larger, and the rate of failure lower in this field than in other businesses. In its final ruling on the case, the Court of Appeals nullified the Commission's order. Noting that 63 dealers obtained the larger discounts, it held that the Commission had failed to prove that this number was so small as to render the industry's price structure "unjustly discriminatory or promotive of monopoly." [38]

The Cost Defense

Differences in price are not unlawful if they make only due allowance for differences in the cost, per unit of output, of manufacture, sale, or delivery resulting from differences in methods of sale or delivery or in the quantities involved. The seller charged with discrimination may therefore defend himself by presenting a statement of costs. If he chooses to do so, he must bear the burden of proof. The burden is a heavy one. Where cost accounts are kept, they are not normally related to the costs involved in filling particular orders. Additional estimates must therefore be made for this purpose, and the expense involved in making them may be substantial. Nor is there any assurance that an accounting justification, however carefully prepared, will be accepted by the FTC. The Commission's accounting staff makes no field investigation of the seller's costs, but examines the figures he submits, sometimes calls for more, and recomputes his costs in its own way. It then offers its study, so prepared, in rebuttal of the seller's case.

The Commission has not hesitated to reject estimates of cost that have been offered in defense of differences in price. It has permitted discounts to be justified by savings in the costs of selling and delivering. But it has declined to recognize savings in the cost of manufacturing. It might be shown that particular orders have reduced the unit cost of output by making it possible to schedule production over longer periods, to buy materials when they are cheapest, to continue operations when demand is slack, and to avoid the risks involved in carrying inventories when manufacturing for stock. It might be argued, too, that the extra costs involved are all that need to be considered in fixing the

38 / *FTC* v. *B. F. Goodrich Co.*, 242 F. 2d 31 (1957).

price required to obtain an order, overhead having been recovered on earlier sales. The Commission, however, has adopted average total cost rather than marginal cost as its standard, requiring the cost of producing to fill an order to be computed by dividing total output into total expenditures, not by determining the added expenditure that it entails. Overhead, in other words, must be allocated uniformly to all the units sold.

In 1953, the FTC appointed a committee under Professor H. F. Taggart of the University of Michigan to study the cost accounting principles involved in "due allowance." In 1956, the committee brought in its report. It agreed that evidence of the marginal cost of serving a particular customer should not be accepted in justification of a lower price. But otherwise it urged the FTC to adopt a "broad approach" in evaluating studies of costs. The Committee advised against the requirement of exhaustive and expensive cost surveys, favored the approval of sampling techniques, and urged the acceptance of estimates prepared for customer classes rather than for individual customers. It recommended the admission of data from records other than books of account, of evidence regarding actual as well as recorded costs, and of estimates showing anticipated, as well as actual, costs. It held that lower prices should be justifiable by savings in the cost of manufacturing as well as in the cost of distribution. And it opposed the adoption of any standard method for allocating overhead. Great weight, said the Committee, should be accorded to cost studies made in good faith and in accordance with acceptable accounting doctrines. A mere showing that a different method would produce a narrower difference in cost should not suffice to overthrow the method that a seller has chosen to use.[39]

If all of the changes recommended in the Taggart report had been adopted and followed, the cost defense might well have come into greater use. But the report produced no great change in policy. The Commission has continued to be rigid in its interpretation of the cost proviso. It has accepted a cost justification, over the years, in only a handful of cases, rejected it in many more. Where the defense was rejected, moreover, the Commission's orders forbade all differences in price. A cost study that failed to justify a discount of 10 percent may have justified one of 5 percent; the order forbade the seller to give any discount at all. The cost defense is not only expensive; it has appeared to be futile. As a result, it has rarely been used.

The Good Faith Defense

The seller charged with illegal price discrimination has one more defense. He can argue that his lower price "was made in good faith to meet an equally low price of a competitor." Just as it sought to impair the cost defense, the FTC also undertook to whittle down the good faith defense. This was the issue on which the Commission was reversed by the Supreme Court in the case involving Standard Oil of Indiana, described above.

39 / Advisory Committee on Cost Justification, *Report to the Federal Trade Commission.*

Standard first had sought to justify its lower price to Ned's and other jobbers by presenting evidence as to its costs. This was rejected by the FTC. The company then advanced the defense that its price had been made "in good faith" to meet the offers made by its competitors. The Commission did not question this fact but contended that competition had nonetheless been injured. Standard replied that proof of meeting the price of a competitor afforded a complete defense. The Court of Appeals supported the Commission, holding this defense to be procedural rather than substantive, serving merely to shift to the Commission the burden of proof.[40] Under this ruling the Commission could charge discrimination, the respondent could advance the good faith defense, and the Commission would then be required to prove that competition had actually been harmed. The ruling was reversed, however, by the Supreme Court.[41] Good faith, said the Court, is a substantive defense. It can be refuted only by proving the absence of good faith. This might be done by showing that the competitor's lower price was itself known to be unlawful, or that his offer was not genuine, being made collusively for the purpose of excusing the defendant's price. But such matters are difficult to prove.

In 1953 the Commission issued its modified order against Standard of Indiana, again requiring that the discount be discontinued. Now, however, it attacked Standard's good faith defense on another ground. This defense, it said, could be used only to justify occasional price matching in particular instances. But Standard's discounts were a part of its established price structure and were regularly given to all of the buyers in a favored class. The Supreme Court agreed that the plea of good faith could not be accepted where discrimination was systematic. But it found that Standard had not adhered to a pricing system. Instead, it had given discounts to hold its customers when forced to do so by the lower prices offered them by its competitors. In this, it had acted in good faith.[42]

The good faith defense, however, has its limitations. It cannot be offered, as we have noted, in justification of an established discount structure. It cannot be used to justify a price that is lower than that charged by a competitor but only to meet his price. The discriminating seller must have knowledge of the price that he is meeting. And that price, in itself, must not be unlawfully discriminatory, a matter on which a competitor cannot be expected to be informed. The lower price can be used defensively to retain an old customer; it cannot be used aggressively to attract a new one. It can be used to meet a lower price charged by one's own competitors but not to enable one's customers to meet a lower price charged by their competitors. Thus, in 1963, when Sun Oil cut its price to the operator of one of its filling stations in Jacksonville to enable him to meet the price charged by an independent station across the street, the Supreme Court held this to be injurious to other Sun stations in the city and rejected

40 / *Standard Oil Co. (Indiana)* v. *FTC,* 173 F. 2d 210 (1949).
41 / *Standard Oil Co. (Indiana)* v. *FTC,* 340 U.S. 231.
42 / *FTC* v. *Standard Oil Co. (Indiana),* 355 U.S. 396 (1958).

Sun's good faith defense. [43] Given its limitations, this defense is rarely offered; it has even more rarely been accepted.

Buyers' Liability

The prohibition contained in Section 2 applies not only to sellers but also (under paragraph 2-f) to buyers who "knowingly" induce or receive an unlawful discrimination in price. This provision came before the Supreme Court in the Automatic Canteen case [44] in 1953. The Automatic Canteen Company leased candy dispensing machines to distributors and sold them candy for distribution, doing more than half of this business. It obtained discounts from 80 among 115 candy manufacturers, insisting on getting lower prices than those paid by its competitors. The FTC ordered the company to cease and desist from demanding these concessions. The company asserted that its lower prices were justified by the sellers' lower costs. The Commission asked for proof. The company replied that it could not reasonably be expected to prepare analyses of the costs of its suppliers. The Supreme Court agreed. The knowing receipt of a lower price, it held, did not in itself violate the Act. Knowledge that the lower price was unjustified would do so. But here, the burden of proof was on the Commission, not on the company.

Up to this time, buyers had been charged with illegal discrimination in few of the cases brought under Section 2. Now it appeared that buyers' liability could not be enforced. Buyers can still be prosecuted, however, where they knew that their discounts could not be justified. The Commission holds, moreover, that there are cases in which such knowledge can be assumed. This is true, for instance, where the price a buyer pays is one already found to be unlawful, where he makes his purchases in the same manner and in the same quantity as do his competitors, and where his experience in the trade should make it clear that a difference in price exceeds a difference in cost. And in this, the Commission has been upheld by the courts. [45]

ANTIDISCRIMINATION POLICY

In principle, the Robinson-Patman Act relates differences in price to differences in cost. But in many respects, the law departs from this principle. In some cases, it permits discrimination; in others, it even requires it. Sellers may legally discriminate among consumers and among business buyers who do not compete with one another. They may also charge identical prices where costs differ or give discounts that fail to reflect real differences in cost; it is illegal to discriminate in favor of the firm that buys in bulk, but legal to discriminate against it.

43 / *FTC* v. *Sun Oil Co.*, 371 U.S. 505.

44 / *Automatic Canteen Co.* v. *FTC*, 346 U.S. 61.

45 / *American Motors Specialties Co.* v. *FTC*, 298 F. 2d 225, certiorari denied, 364 U.S. 884 (1960).

Discrimination, moreover, is required when a broker's commission is denied a buyer who himself performs a broker's services, when allowances or services are withheld though they would pay for themselves by promoting sales, and when the Commission fixes limits beyond which discounts for quantity cannot be given though fully justified by differences in cost.

The Robinson-Patman Act was designed to reduce the buying advantages of the chain stores and other mass distributors. It was thus intended, not to prevent discrimination in general, but to prevent discrimination in favor of larger buyers and to permit or require discrimination in favor of smaller ones. It was concerned less with the maintenance of competition than with the survival of small competitors. It thus embodies a policy that has been characterized as "soft competition" in contrast to the "hard competition" demanded by the Sherman Act.

The Act attempts to limit the ability of the big buyer to use his bargaining power to obtain concessions in price. Its provisions, however, apply, in the main, not to the buyer who exacts a discount, but to the seller who grants it. Instead of moving directly to restrain the powerful buyer, it strikes at him over the shoulder of the seller.

Effects of the Robinson-Patman Act

From the point of view of the small retailer, the effects of the Robinson-Patman Act have been diverse. It has reduced the discriminatory advantages of mass distributors, virtually eliminating the payment of brokerage to any but independent brokers, making allowances and services more broadly available, and reducing the buyers' pressure for concessions of other types. But it has also worked against the interest of the small concern. It has encouraged the mass distributor to buy a plant's whole output or to manufacture a product for himself; here, his costs may be cut, but no discrimination is involved. The law, obviously, has not impeded the growth of the supermarket or the discount house. It has even been turned against the small retailer in many cases, being used to check the advantages of agencies buying collectively for independent firms. Whether it has operated, on balance, to help or to harm the small distributor, it is impossible to say.

The law has made for inefficiency, forcing the seller to use brokers when he does not need them, to buy services that he does not desire, and to provide services that have no use. It has moderated the vigor of competition. By requiring that discounts be justified by actual rather than potential differences in cost, it has discouraged price reductions that might profitably have been made. By outlawing the practice of setting lower prices, in some part of a market, to test the possibility of increasing sales, it may have prevented reductions that would soon have been generalized. Under conditions of oligopoly, it has barred the only form of competition that operates to lessen price rigidity. [46]

46 / See Edwards, *op. cit.*, Ch. 19.

Proposed Reforms

If the anti-price-discrimination statute is to be brought into harmony with the rest of the antitrust laws, there are many changes that should be made. Three sections of the act should be repealed: the criminal section because it is vague and useless; the brokerage section because it denies a broker's discount to others than independent brokers even though brokerage services are performed; the quantity limit section because it denies discounts that are justified by savings in cost. The section dealing with allowances and services should be made consistent with the other provisions of the law by relating such concessions to the cost of the services involved.

There is danger that a large firm may attempt to eliminate its smaller rivals by discriminatory sharpshooting. The prohibition of discrimination which injures competition at the seller's level should therefore be retained. But the narrow test of injury, which has to do with the effect of competition on particular groups of competitors, should be deleted and discrimination made unlawful only when it impairs the vigor of competition as a whole. The law should permit sporadic price discrimination but forbid persistent cuts in one substantial market when they are not extended to others or when deeper cuts are made in one market than in others. The cost defense should be liberalized. Freedom to make discriminatory price cuts should not be limited, as is now the case, to reductions made to meet the prices of competitors but should be extended to reductions that are designed to undercut them. The law should permit discrimination to be used, not only as a means of retaining old customers, but also as a means of attracting new ones.

There is danger, finally, that competition will be injured when large distributors use their bargaining power to exact from suppliers prices lower than those charged their competitors. Here, however, the law should be directed not against the seller but against the buyer. Here, again, the test of injury to competition should be the broader one. Buyers should be forbidden, in making purchases, to impose the condition that equally favorable terms are not to be granted to their competitors. Where buying in the same quantities as their competitors, and in the same way, they should be forbidden to accept, frequently or over a long period, prices that are substantially more favorable. Where quantities and selling methods differ, they should be forbidden to accept, persistently, larger discounts than can be justified by the savings involved. Here, the buyer's defense will depend upon the willingness of the seller to cooperate in presenting an analysis of costs. For this purpose, too, the cost defense should be liberalized. [47]

47 / *Ibid.*, chap. xx; see also Carl Kaysen and Donald F. Turner, *Antitrust Policy* (Cambridge, Mass.: Harvard University Press, 1959), pp. 183-88.

Chapter
10

DELIVERED PRICING

The forms of discrimination discussed in the preceding chapter arose, in the main, in cases where buyers fulfilled different functions or made their purchases in different quantities. Another form—geographic price discrimination—arises from the fact that sellers and buyers are often located at different points. In such a case the cost of goods at the buyer's destination includes not only the price of the goods themselves but also the charge that is made for their delivery. And it is this cost that is significant in making sales. As a consequence, a seller who seeks to extend the boundaries of his market or to compete for sales in markets that are nearer other sellers, may himself bear part or all of the charge for freight. In doing so he will realize less on sales made far away than on those made near at home. Accepting different net returns on sales to different destinations, he will discriminate between customers.

Such discrimination may be of small significance where goods are high in value and the cost of their delivery forms a small part of the price the buyer pays. Its importance may be great, however, where goods are so heavy or so bulky in relation to their value that the cost of transportation is a large part of the final price. Even here the consequences of discrimination will not be the same in every case. Where sellers act independently, making deliveries to different markets and accepting different net returns, competition in the markets where they sell may be increased. But where they act in concert, whether by explicit agreement or in accordance with a tacit understanding, discrimination may be incidental to arrangements whereby competition is inhibited. It is only in cases such as this that geographic price discrimination has come into conflict with antitrust.

GEOGRAPHIC PRICE STRUCTURES

Prices may be quoted either at the point where goods originate or at the point where they are delivered. Those quoted on the former basis are usually called "f.o.b. mill" or "f.o.b. shipping point" prices, since the seller, in this case, customarily agrees to deliver goods without charge to the conveyance provided— at his plant or at the nearest dock or railway station—by the buyer or a common carrier, i.e. to place them "free on board." Prices quoted at destinations are called "delivered prices" and include the cost of moving goods to the buyer's place of business or to the dock or station nearest him.

Prices quoted on a delivered basis usually involve discrimination; those quoted f.o.b. usually do not. But this is not invariably the case. Delivered pricing may sometimes be nondiscriminatory, and f.o.b. pricing may sometimes discriminate. The effects of various methods of pricing are revealed, as will be seen, not by the form of a seller's quotations, but by a comparison of the sums he realizes in making different sales.

Pricing Methods of Individual Sellers

An individual seller may independently adopt any one of a variety of geographic pricing practices. His choice will be influenced by the nature of his product, by the cost of transporting it to different markets, and by the character of competition in his trade. The resulting structure of prices will vary from case to case.

1. A seller may charge a uniform f.o.b. mill price. If he does so, buyers at different locations will incur different costs in purchasing his goods, and a buyer at any one location will find that his goods are more or less costly than those of his nearby or remote competitors. But the seller's return on every sale, regardless of the buyer's location, will be the same. He will not discriminate.

Alternatively, a seller may quote delivered prices but compute them by making a uniform charge for goods and adding, in every case, the precise amount he has paid for freight. The structure of his prices will, consequently, be the same as that described above. Though selling on a delivered basis, he will not discriminate. His policy will differ from that of the previous seller in only one respect; he retains title during transit and files with the carrier any claims for possible damages.

These methods of pricing are likely to be used both where goods are so low in value, in relation to their weight, that transportation costs confine their sale to local markets, and where goods are so high in value that transportation costs are not significant. They are also found where sellers are under no pressure to meet the figures at which buyers can obtain goods from nearby competitors. This will be the case where all of the sellers in a trade are located at the same center; where transportation rates are so adjusted that a buyer making purchases from sellers at different locations pays the same freight; where each of several sellers offers a highly differentiated product; and where a single seller possesses a monopoly. F.o.b. pricing has been employed in selling many goods, including textiles, leather, apparel, staple foodstuffs, standard drugs, household furniture, automobiles, and agricultural machinery.

2. A seller may quote the same delivered price at every destination in the United States. In this case the seller's price will include a charge to cover his average expenditure for freight. But this charge will be lower than the freight he pays on sales made far afield and higher than he pays on those made near at hand. His net return will vary, from sale to sale, with the distance of the buyer from his plant. In this sense he will discriminate.

Or a seller may quote a uniform f.o.b. price but make allowances for transportation, permitting his customers to deduct from their bills the full amount of freight that they have paid. Here, again, prices at different destinations will be the same, but the seller will collect less from those who are remote and more from those who are nearby. Though selling f.o.b., he will discriminate.

Such practices, known as "postage-stamp pricing," are used where goods are high in value and freight is relatively unimportant and particularly where the seller of a branded product that is nationally advertised desires to maintain a uniform resale price. They have been employed in selling such goods as hardware, tires and tubes, typewriters, electrical appliances, branded foodstuffs, drugs, cosmetics, soft drinks, candy bars, and cigarettes.

3. A seller may divide the country into zones, charging the same delivered price at every destination in a zone, but raising this price from zone to zone to cover the average cost of freight. He may pay the actual freight himself or direct the buyer to pay it and deduct it from his bill. In either case, the seller's average net return will be the same in every zone. But he will allow less freight than is paid at the farther boundary of a zone and more than is paid at the nearer one. At every boundary, moreover, he will allow less to buyers on the nearer side than he does to others just across the line. Within each zone and along each boundary, he will discriminate.

Zone pricing is likely to be used where the cost of transporting branded goods is so great as to prevent their sale throughout the country at a uniform delivered price. If freight is not too high, one price may be charged at all points east of the Mississippi or the Rockies and another at all points to the west. Where freight is more significant, however, zones may be greater in number and smaller in size. Zone pricing has been employed in selling such goods as refrigerators, washing machines, electric ranges, glass containers, paper products, paints, and business furniture.

4. A seller may meet the price at which a competitor closer to a market will make deliveries there. To do so, he may quote a delivered price that covers freight from his competitor's mill but pay the higher freight from his own mill. Or he may quote an f.o.b. price, or a delivered price that covers his own freight, and permit his customer to deduct from his bill the amount by which his freight exceeds that charged on shipments made by his competitor. In either case he is said to "absorb" freight. Where this is done, prices at different destinations will vary, but a buyer at any one of them may obtain goods at the same price from a distant seller as from a closer one. The seller's return, however, will differ from sale to sale, being lower where he absorbs freight and higher where he does not. Insofar as he follows this practice, he will discriminate.

A seller may absorb freight occasionally in order to make particular sales. He may do so temporarily in order to find employment for idle capacity. He may adopt freight absorption as a general policy. The practice is likely to be found in trades where products are standardized and sellers numerous, where investment is heavy and fixed costs high, and where the charge for transportation is a large part of the delivered price. It has been followed, among others, by sellers of lumber, bituminous coal, and gasoline.

Pricing Systems of Whole Industries

Delivered pricing systems may be said to exist where identical methods of delivered pricing are customarily followed in considerable detail by all of the members of an industry. They include single basing point systems, multiple basing point systems, systems involving what is known as the universal equalization of freight, and those establishing uniform price zones. Each of these systems may now be described.

1. Under a single basing point system, though production is carried on by different sellers at different points, the same location is used as the point of origin by every seller in computing the freight to be added to his base price in determining his delivered price. This system was once known to steel as Pittsburgh-plus, to corn syrup and malt as Chicago-plus, to cast iron soil pipe as Birmingham-plus, and to maple flooring as Cadillac-plus. Where it is used, delivered prices will vary from destination to destination. But if the base prices adopted by all sellers are identical, the delivered prices charged on any sale at any destination by all sellers, however distant, will also be identical. Given a common base price of $50 per ton, a single basing point at Pittsburgh, and the structure of freight rates assumed in Figure 10-1, the mills at Pittsburgh, Cleveland, and Chicago would all charge $50 in Pittsburgh, $54 in Cleveland, $56 in Detroit, and $58 in Chicago.

FIGURE 10-1
Single Basing Point System

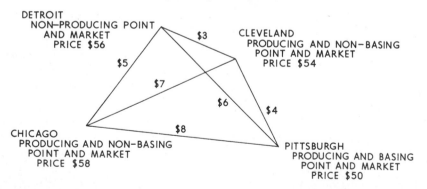

Under this system, a seller who ships by rail from the basing point will not discriminate. Since he will pay for freight to every destination the exact amount that he has charged, his net return on every sale will be the same. The nonbasing point seller, however, will discriminate. He will pay more than he charges for freight in selling to markets closer to the basing point, and less than he charges in selling to markets closer to himself. His net return will vary with the destination of his sales. Consider, in Table 10-1, the case of the seller located at

TABLE 10-1

Sales from Chicago to Pittsburgh, Cleveland, Detroit, and Chicago

	Pittsburgh	Cleveland	Detroit	Chicago
Base price	$50	$50	$50	$50
Plus freight from Pittsburgh . .	0	4	6	8
Delivered price	50	54	56	58
Minus freight from Chicago . .	8	7	5	0
Mill net realization at Chicago.	42	47	51	58
Freight absorption	8	3	..	..
Phantom freight.	..	..	1	8

Chicago. The seller realizes $16 more at Chicago than he charges at Pittsburgh. He does so because he pays $8 more freight than he charges at Pittsburgh and charges $8 more than he pays at Chicago. In the first case, he absorbs the difference in freight. In the second, he realizes what is known as "phantom freight." It is the freight absorption and the phantom freight involved, in varying amounts, in sales at different destinations that accounts for the discrimination in the structure of his net returns.

2. Under a multiple basing point system, two or more centers are used as points of origin in computing freight, but there are one or more centers of production that are not so employed. Here, the delivered price at any destination is the lowest one obtained by taking the base price of the product and adding the charge for freight from each of the surrounding basing points. On any sale, the place from which this charge is lowest is known as the governing basing point. As sales are made at different destinations, the governing basing point will shift from place to place. Here again prices differ from destination to destination, but if the base prices used by all sellers are identical, their delivered prices at any destination will be the same. If we modify our previous illustration by assuming that a second basing point is established at Chicago and a base price of $50 fixed there, the resulting structure of prices would be that shown in Figure 10-2. In this case, Pittsburgh is the governing point for Cleveland, and Chicago for Detroit.

Here, as under the previous system, the nonbasing point seller discriminates by collecting phantom freight when he sells in his own vicinity and absorbing freight when he sells in the vicinity of a basing point. But under this system there is no seller who does not discriminate. When he sells in the territory where his basing point governs, the basing point seller will pay the same amount he has charged for freight. But whenever he sells where another point governs, he will absorb freight. Under a multiple basing point system, there is no seller, such as the one at Pittsburgh under Pittsburgh-plus, whose net return on every sale will be the same. Variations are shown in Table 10-2. Here Cleveland discriminates by absorbing freight and collecting phantom freight, Pittsburgh and Chicago discriminate only by absorbing freight. Cleveland realizes $11 more when it sells at home than when it sells in Chicago, but the extremes of discrimination have been somewhat reduced by establishing Chicago as a second basing point.

FIGURE 10-2
Multiple Basing Point System

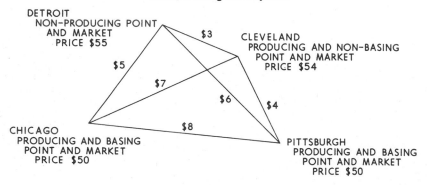

Multiple basing point systems have been used in selling steel, cement, lead, pulp, lumber, sugar, and other heavy goods. Under the system that is used in pricing sugar, seaboard cities where cane sugar is imported and refined are used as basing points, and prices at inland cities are computed by adding freight from these points. Though refineries producing sugar from beets are located at a score of centers in the midcontinent, none of them is used as a point of origin in the calculation of a price.

TABLE 10-2
Mill Net Realizations, Freight Absorption (–) and Phantom Freight (+) Experienced by Mills at Pittsburgh, Chicago, and Cleveland

	Pittsburgh	*Chicago*	*Cleveland*
In making sales at:			
Pittsburgh	$50	$42 (–8)	$46 (–4)
Chicago	42 (–8)	50	43 (–7)
Cleveland	50	47 (–3)	54 (+4)
Detroit.	49 (–1)	50	52 (+2)

3. The practice known as systematic freight equalization involves adherence to a plenary basing point system, in which every producing point is a basing point. Under such a system, every seller determines his delivered price at any destination by adding the base price and the freight rate on shipments from each of the nearby sellers and taking the lowest total as his own. Properly speaking, the practice is one of price equalization, since the charge for the goods themselves as well as that for their delivery is equalized. In this case, as in the

previous ones, prices at different destinations will differ, but those charged by all firms selling at any one destination will be the same. The character of this system may be shown by further modifying our illustration to establish Cleveland as a basing point, as well as Pittsburgh and Chicago. If a base price of $50 is adopted at each of these points, the structure of delivered prices will be that shown in Figure 10-3.

FIGURE 10-3

Plenary Basing Point System

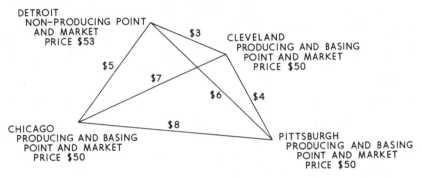

Plenary basing point systems have been used in the sale of salt, binder twine, milk cans, bottle caps, lime, gypsum plaster, window glass, and other building materials, and many heavy chemicals. Under such a system, the returns received by every seller will differ with the destinations of his sales. Since there are no nonbasing points, however, no seller will collect phantom freight by always charging for delivery from other locations than his own. A seller will discriminate only by absorbing freight, in varying amounts, as he sells in markets that are closer to his various competitors. This may be shown by recurring to our illustrative case (Table 10-3). One other fact should be noted: the difference between the highest and the lowest realization, which was $16 in the first case and $11 in the second, is now $8. By eliminating the nonbasing point, the extent of discrimination is further reduced.

TABLE 10-3

Mill Net Realizations and Freight Absorption Experienced by Mills at Pittsburgh, Chicago, and Cleveland

	Pittsburgh	Chicago	Cleveland
In making sales at:			
Pittsburgh	$50	$42 (−8)	$46 (−4)
Chicago	42 (−8)	50	43 (−7)
Cleveland	46 (−4)	43 (−7)	50
Detroit	47 (−3)	48 (−2)	50

4. A zone pricing system is a variant of the systems that are built on basing points. Under such a system, where common zones are recognized by all the sellers in a trade, delivered prices for each zone are computed by taking a base price and adding to it the average charge for freight from a basing point to each of the destinations within its boundaries. As a result, prices are uniform throughout each zone but differ from zone to zone, and the prices charged by every seller at any destination are the same. Here, again, the nonbasing point seller discriminates by realizing more when he sells at home and less when he sells near a basing point. But here, as in the case of zone pricing described above, every seller, including those at basing points, also discriminates among the destinations in each zone and between those lying along its boundaries. Zone pricing systems have been used in the sale of linseed oil, fertilizers, corn products, clay sewer pipe, power cable, and electrical machinery.

Implementing Delivered Pricing Systems

In those industries where delivered prices have regularly been matched by all sellers, the practice has usually been facilitated by some sort of an agreement or understanding with respect to many, if not all, of the factors that influence the prices that are charged. The possibility that variations in price may result from differences—whether deliberate or inadvertent—in the methods of selling and pricing employed by different members of the industry is thus removed.

The prices quoted to any buyer by different sellers would differ if any of them failed to sell on a delivered basis or to make an identical charge for delivery. This would be the case, for instance, if a seller at a nonbasing point were to give buyers the option of taking title at his plant and themselves providing for transportation, since nearby buyers would thus be enabled to obtain goods more cheaply from him than from his more distant competitors. It would be the case if a mill at one basing point were to permit a buyer to take title at some location where another point governed the delivered price and to divert a shipment to a destination at which its own price was governing, since the buyer might thus get goods for less money from the mill permitting such diversion than from those refusing to do so. It would also be the case if sellers were to employ different methods of computing freight, using different basing points, different price zones, different types of carriers, or rate books issued by different railroads. The seller who figured freight from a nearer basing point, or pushed zone boundaries outward, would quote a lower delivered price. The seller who charged for delivery by highway or waterway would quote a lower price than the one who charged for delivery by rail. And since the rate structures of different railways differ in detail, a seller who used the rate book issued by one road might charge less than one who used that issued by another.

Under delivered pricing systems, therefore, it has been the usual practice to quote prices only at destinations, refusing to give title at the points where goods are produced, or charging for freight even where buyers are permitted to haul them away in their own trucks. It has been usual for sellers to insist on delivery to final destinations, refusing to make allowances for diversion in transit. It has also been usual for sellers to recognize the same centers as basing points and to adopt the same zone boundaries, whether by formal agreement or by simple acquiescence in the leadership of larger firms. Sellers have customarily calculated their charges for delivery from common basing points on the assumption that goods will move exclusively by rail, collecting phantom freight where they are actually transported by highway or by waterway. In doing so, moreover, they have employed common freight books prepared by their trade associations in place of the schedules issued by the railroads themselves. And they have continued to use these books, after freight rates have been altered, until their associations have authorized a change. It is by methods such as these that the identity of the transportation charge included in each delivered price has been assured.

Prices could vary, of course, though charges made for delivering goods were identical, if those made for the goods themselves were not. Such variations would occur if different sellers were to use different base prices in calculating a delivered price. They would also occur if sellers were to make different adjustments for departures from the standard sizes and qualities for which base prices are announced, or if they were to offer different discounts, allowances, guarantees, or supplementary services. In basing point industries, however, the latter possibility has usually been removed by standardizing every element of a sale that might permit an indirect reduction of a price. In steel, for instance, there was open agreement on the "extras" that are added to the prices of standard products and the "deductions" that are subtracted from them in arriving at the prices of nonstandard goods. In cement, there was agreement on specifications, discount structures, and allowances for returned bags. It is only with respect to the base price itself that existence of agreement has always been denied. But this price, too, has usually been fixed through consultation or through leadership. Indeed, if this were not the case, there would be little point in seeking to control every other factor affecting the calculation of a delivered price. For it is in their contribution to the identity of prices charged at any destination that delivered pricing systems find their real significance.

THE NATURE AND ORIGIN OF BASING POINT SYSTEMS

For 30 to 40 years after World War I, the essential character of basing point pricing systems was a subject of continued controversy. The Federal Trade Commission attacked these systems, finding them to be in violation of the antitrust laws. Basing point industries, on the other hand, defended them, presenting arguments designed to show that they were vigorously competitive. At the same time, economists differed as to the causation of such systems, one school holding that they were highly artificial, resulting from deliberate collusion among sellers, another contending that they were quite natural, arising from the economic characteristics of the industries where they were found. We turn now to some of the pros and cons of these debates.

Competitive or Monopolistic?

The most complete statement of industry's case for basing point pricing is contained in a volume prepared by the United States Steel Corporation for presentation to the Temporary National Economic Committee in 1940.[1] The Corporation argued, first, that the system was perfectly competitive, as was shown by two facts: (a) The prices quoted by different sellers revealed the identity "which would result from 'perfect competition' in a single market at any one time."[2] (b) Each buyer was enabled to deal with many sellers; under f.o.b. pricing, he would be limited to one or a few, a situation which "certainly does not correspond to the assumptions of . . . 'perfect competition.' "[3]

It is true that the prices of steel and of cement were usually identical. During the thirties, when the purchasing agent for the Fort Peck Dam opened 10 sealed bids for reinforcing bars, each of them was for $253,633.80.[4] When the Navy Department opened 59 bids for steel pipe, each of them was for $6,001.83.[5] And when the Army Engineers opened 11 bids for cement at Tucumcari, New Mexico, each of them was for $3.286854 a barrel, identity being carried to the sixth decimal place.[6] Again in 1947, when the Illinois Department of Highways asked for bids on cement to be delivered in each of the 102 counties in the state, those submitted by eight companies were identical for each of the 102 deliveries.[7] Such identities cannot be attributed to mere chance. The mathematical probability of accidentally arriving at those reported in Illinois has been computed as 1 in 8 followed by 214 zeros, a possibility that is even more remote than the random selection of a single electron from the entire universe.[8] Identical prices may be a product of competition. They are more likely to reveal the presence of monopoly.

Under active competition, identity is a goal toward which prices are always moving but at which they seldom arrive and never stay. When one seller charges more than another, buyers shift their purchases. When a seller discriminates, charging one buyer more than another, the buyer so adjusts his operations as to obtain the lower price. Wherever prices differ, traders buy in the markets where goods are cheap and sell in those where they are dear. As a result of these forces, prices tend toward identity. But any seller can initiate a change. And constant change prevents identity from being attained or, if attained, from being pre-

---

1 / United States Steel Corp., *T.N.E.C. Papers*, Vol. III, *The Basing Point Method*, published by the Corporation, 1940.

2 / *Ibid.*, p. 36.

3 / *Ibid.*, p. 85.

4 / *New York Times*, February 20, 1939.

5 / *Annual Report of the Attorney General*, 1937, pp. 37-38.

6 / *Aetna Portland Cement Co.* v. *FTC*, 157 F. 2d 533 (1946), esp. p. 576.

7 / *Congressional Record*, May 31, 1950, p. 7961.

8 / *Ibid.*, computation by Professor C. O. Oakley of Haverford College as reported by Senator Paul H. Douglas.

served. Under a basing point system, on the other hand, identity of prices is an actuality. Buyers find no advantage in shifting their purchases. They cannot undermine discrimination by qualifying for a lower price. Traders cannot profit by buying in the cheaper markets and selling in the dearer ones. It is not through these forces that identity is achieved. Under such a system, moreover, most sellers take no initiative with respect to price. Changes, whether upward or downward, are usually announced by only one concern. As a result, identity of prices may persist for months and years at a time. Identical prices, when so attained and so preserved, give evidence not of competition but of agreement in restraint of trade.

So, too, with the argument that a basing point system brings many sellers within the reach of every buyer. This is indeed the case. But this does not prove that such a system fosters active competition. In fact, it proves the opposite. If firms selling heavy goods were really to compete, each one, enjoying lower transportation costs to points within its own vicinity, would undersell its distant rivals at these points. Those shipping by water would undersell those shipping by rail. Under basing point pricing, however, sellers forego the competitive advantage inherent in more favorable locations. Those who are not at basing points, though close to buyers in their own localities, make no attempt to underbid those who are far away. Those who are located on waterways include in their prices a charge for all-rail freight. Sellers at every center of production adhere to prices that enable outsiders to enter markets that would otherwise belong to them alone. This behavior, however, is said by the Corporation to be competitive: ". . . mills at a considerable distance from a basing point . . . behave competitively and naturally when they charge their customers a price which realizes that advantage. . . . They can scarcely be expected to offer lower prices. . . ."[9] "If the mill is the only one which can reach the destination by water, there is no competitive reason why it should give the benefit of the lower transportation cost to the customer. In fact, if it did so, it would be following some noncompetitive principle."[10] Competition, in this view, consists merely in meeting another's price, never in taking business away from him by undercutting it. But such forbearance would appear to most observers to betoken a reluctance to compete. If any buyer, under a basing point system, can obtain deliveries from every seller, it is because the absence of competition, under such a system, has resulted in a level of prices so high that everybody can afford to sell everywhere.

The argument just considered carries as its corollary the contention that f.o.b. pricing would result in the creation of a series of regional monopolies. According to the Corporation, ". . . freight rates would set up a wall between different producers and their markets, greatly limiting the area over which competition now takes place . . . buyers would be reduced to purchasing from the nearest mill . . . there would be very little or no choice . . . any single producer located at a distance from all other mills would have a virtual monopoly. . . . An isolated producer . . . would be able to charge high prices to consumers in his own

9 / U.S. Steel Corp., *op. cit.,* p. 59.
10 / *Ibid.,* p. 66.

area."[11] It is true, of course, that the consumer, under f.o.b. pricing, is likely to buy at the nearest mill. He does so to save freight. It is not true that he is prevented from buying from other mills. He may do so if he is willing to pay more freight. He certainly is not at the mercy of a monopolist. If a local mill makes all the sales made in its own vicinity, it is because its price, plus freight, is lower than the price, plus freight, of its nearest competitor. A monopolist exploits his position by charging more. The local mill retains its position only so long as it charges less. This is successful competition, not monopoly.

Natural or Artificial?

The United States Steel Corporation argued not only that the basing point system was competitive, but also that it had been "the natural result of basic economic conditions. . . ."[12] With respect to this matter, economists have divided into two opposing schools of thought. The first school, basing its analysis on the logic of competitive pricing, has held such systems to be an outgrowth of collusion. In a competitive market, according to this analysis, the rivalry of buyers and of sellers will tend to eliminate discrimination, since no buyer will continue to pay more than another and no seller will continue to accept less from one buyer than from another. Under basing point systems, however, discrimination persists, since buyers who are near at hand continue to pay more—in prices minus freight—than those who are far away, and sellers continue to accept less on distant sales than they could realize by making sales at home. It is clear, from this behavior, that such systems are not a product of competition. They must have originated, therefore, in conspiracy.[13]

The second school, applying the theory of oligopoly, has held that basing point pricing could evolve spontaneously, each seller who adopts it acting independently. According to this view, fewness of sellers always inhibits aggressive competition with respect to price, since any cut may instantly be matched, and the cutter's share in an industry's sales may not increase. An oligopolist, therefore, is unlikely to take initiative in reducing prices unless he feels certain that his industry's total sales will be enhanced. For if they are not, competition will be unprofitable and, if carried too far, may well prove to be ruinous. In the particular circumstances encountered in basing point industries, moreover, a seller who doubts his ability to make more sales by cutting prices will find that he can do so by absorbing freight. And this will offer him a happier alternative.

11 / Ibid., pp. 79, 84, 86.

12 / Ibid., pp. 22-31.

13 / See F. A. Fetter, The Masquerade of Monopoly (New York: Harcourt, Brace & Co., 1931), "The New Plea for Basing Point Monopoly," Journal of Political Economy, Vol. XLV (1937), p. 577, "Exit Basing Point Pricing," American Economic Review, Vol. XXXVIII (1948), p. 815; Vernon A. Mund, Open Markets (New York: Harper & Bros., 1948), "The Freight Allowed Method of Price Quotation," Quarterly Journal of Economics, Vol. LIV (1940), p. 232, "Monopolistic Competition and Public Price Policy," American Economic Review, Vol. XXXII (1942), p. 727; Fritz Machlup, The Basing Point System (Philadelphia: Blakiston Co., 1949).

A price cut would apply to every sale he made. As a result, if sales did not expand, his total revenues would fall. Freight absorption, on the other hand, reduces his return on but a fraction of his sales. And if his mill net realization on each such sale exceeds his marginal cost, it will enlarge his total revenues. Discrimination, therefore, comes about quite naturally. And adherence by sellers to a delivered pricing formula manifests nothing more than a rational adaptation to the facts of their environment.[14]

This analysis, it must be admitted, finds considerable support in the conditions found in industries where systems of basing point pricing have been employed. Take the case of steel, for instance: (1) The industry's technology requires production on a scale so great that capital costs obstruct new entry, giving the market to a few large firms. (2) Demand fluctuates with the cycle, leaving idle capacity when business activity declines. (3) Heavy investment carries high fixed costs, tempting each producer to put this capacity to work by reducing his price. (4) The industry's product is highly standardized and is bought in such quantities that a small difference in price may lead to a substantial shift in sales. In these circumstances, a lower price is almost certain to be met by one's competitors. Such a price, therefore, will not be advantageous unless it increases sales throughout the industry. (5) The demand for steel, however, is said to be inelastic. For one thing, the possibilities of substituting steel for other materials or other materials for steel are limited. For another, the demand for steel is derived, in the main, from the demand for goods in which steel is used. A reduction in its price may not be reflected in the prices of these goods. Or if it is, the cost of steel may be so small a part of their prices that a reduction will not affect the volume of their sales. In any case, the demand for these goods, too, is said to be low in elasticity. Machinery and equipment made of steel may find no market in depressions, however low their price. Many consumers' goods made of steel are luxuries and thus dispensable. Most of these goods are durable and the purchase of replacements may therefore be postponed. Sales may thus be unresponsive to a change in price. (6) But price cutting, though futile, might conceivably be carried to lengths that would prove to be disastrous. To make a particular sale, a seller would find it worth his while to quote any price that would more than cover his marginal costs. But such a price would fall far short of his average total costs. And if extended for any length of time to a major part of his output, it might well drive him into bankruptcy.

These conditions explain why firms producing steel are unlikely to engage in vigorous competition with respect to price. They do not explain why avoid-

---

14 / See J. M. Clark, "Basing Point Methods of Price Quoting," *Canadian Journal of Economics and Political Science,* Vol. IV (1938), p. 477, "Imperfect Competition Theory and Basing Point Problems," *American Economic Review,* Vol. XXXIII (1943), p. 283, "The Law and Economics of Basing Points," *American Economic Review,* Vol. XXXIX (1949), p. 430; C. R. Daugherty, M. G. de Chazeau, and S. S. Stratton, *The Economics of the Iron and Steel Industry* (New York: McGraw-Hill Book Co., 1937), Vol. I, chap. xii; Vol. II, chap. xxii; Arthur Smithies, "Aspects of the Basing Point Problem," *American Economic Review,* Vol. XXXII (1942), p. 705.

ance of competition took the form of quoting prices for delivery from a common basing point. This development may be attributed, in part, to the fact that changes in the geographic pattern of demand for steel may be rapid, while changes in the pattern of production must be slow. The location of construction projects, in particular, constantly shifts from place to place. Steel mills, on the contrary, are rooted to the ground. Production can move to growing markets only as new facilities are built. In the meantime, if all sales were made f.o.b. mill, one section of the country would be short of steel while another had a surplus of capacity. The basing point system solved this problem by establishing a structure of prices that enabled sellers tied to fixed locations to adjust their shipments to the movement of demand. The emergence of similar systems in other industries selling heavy building materials suggests that basing point systems usually originated in situations where such adjustments were required.[15]

It does not follow, however, that such systems are products of nature rather than works of art. In no case have they come alive full-blown, like Venus rising from the waves. There have been meetings held, agreements entered into, organizations formed, and rules laid down. The evidence of collusion is explicit and voluminous. The proceedings before the Federal Trade Commission in the case of the cement industry ran to 49,000 pages of testimony and 50,000 pages of exhibits.[16] The documentation with respect to steel is equally detailed, the system in this industry being identified, in its early years, with formal pooling arrangements and with a series of dinners, held between 1906 and 1911, at which Judge E. H. Gary, then president of U.S. Steel, presided over discussions of pricing policy. Nor has the subsequent quotation of identical prices been purely spontaneous, as the elaborate paraphernalia of standard prices and terms of sale, delivery to destination, all-rail freights, and common freight rate books, described above, will testify. Adherence to delivered pricing systems has been enforced, moreover, by the imposition of penalties. In the cement industry, any producer who cut his price might be punished by having his competitors quote a still lower price, using his plant as a basing point. Since he would make all of his sales from this point and each of them would make but few, they could thus inflict a serious loss on him at small cost to themselves. In the steel industry, too, according to the Federal Trade Commission, the potential punishment for any serious attempt to violate the basing point system was price raiding that soon brought the rebels to terms. If basing point pricing were a spontaneous outgrowth of natural causes, as some economists have argued, it would scarcely have been necessary to go to such lengths to insure that its requirements were observed. It is true, of course, that the conditions found in basing point industries do not make for active competition. But it does not follow that each member of such an industry will independently evolve the same sophisticated pricing formula. The theory of oligopoly shows that oligopolists are unlikely to compete. It does not prove that they are unlikely to conspire.

15 / See George J. Stigler, "A Theory of Delivered Price Systems," *American Economic Review,* Vol. XXXIX (1949), p. 1144.

16 / For a summary of this evidence, see George W. Stocking and Myron W. Watkins, *Monopoly and Free Enterprise* (New York: Twentieth Century Fund, 1951), pp. 193-216.

EFFECTS OF BASING POINT PRICING

Two of the consequences of basing point pricing have been described in defining the practice itself: (1) every seller quotes the same price at any destination, and (2) each seller (save those at a single basing point) discriminates by accepting different returns on sales to different destinations. Each of these consequences is the necessary complement of the other. Both of them are inherent in the very nature of the systems that have been employed. There are other effects of these systems, however, that remain to be explored. How have they influenced (1) the comparative industrial development of different sections of the country, (2) the number of firms and the extent of concentration in the basing point industries, and (3) the costs of production in these industries and the prices of their products? It is to these questions that we now turn.

The Location of Industry

The location of productive facilities is influenced by the comparative costs involved in reaching markets and in assembling raw materials. It may also be affected by the pricing system that an industry employs. In the case of cement, markets are most important, since limestone is widely scattered and abundant in supply. The pricing system, moreover, cannot affect the location of markets, since this is determined by the situation of construction projects where the product finds its major use. In the case of steel, materials have exercised a stronger pull, since iron ore and coking coal are concentrated geographically and the costs of transporting them are high. Location of the markets, on the other hand, depends in part on the location of the mills. Where steel is used in construction, to be sure, its market moves about from place to place. But steel is also used in making fabricated goods. And fabricators, in selecting their locations, compare the freight involved in making shipments with that included in the price of steel. Where the former is higher, they settle near their markets. Where the latter is higher, they settle near the mills. They may be attracted to any mill, whatever its location, if steel is sold f.o.b. But where fabricators have crowded around the mills in one city and avoided those in another, it is clear that a basing point system has been employed.

Under such a system, a fabricator who settled near a mill at a nonbasing point would have to pay for steel a price that covered phantom freight. His rivals at a basing point, however, would get their steel at the base price free of freight. He could not afford to absorb freight to compete near them. But they could afford to do so to compete near him. As a result, fabricators would settle only at a basing point. By doing so, they would enlarge the market at such a center, attracting new mills and leading mills already built there to expand. The location of mills and of fabricators, interacting, would both contribute to the same result.

Basing point pricing influences the location of the mills themselves in other ways. The system makes it unnecessary for them to settle near the market, since it eliminates competition in the delivered price. It attracts them to non-basing points, however, by holding out the prospect of collecting phantom freight. The major producers may find it profitable to build at these locations. But independent firms may be deterred from doing so by fear that the majors would shortly turn them into basing points. On balance, the system is likely to make for geographic concentration of capacity. Under a single basing point system, in particular, mills tend to settle at the basing point, since this is the one point in the country from which they can ship in every direction without absorbing freight. An artificial inducement to settlement at Pittsburgh was thus added to the natural advantages of that location by the institution of Pittsburgh-plus.

Basing point pricing serves to retard adjustment of industrial location to the steady migration of demand. It keeps mills at work in older centers by enabling them to reach the newer markets, and delays construction of capacity in regions where demand has grown. In this respect, of course, it is not without advantages, since it may be cheaper to produce and ship from existing plants that would otherwise be idle than to build new plants to do the job. But the system does more than this. By giving wider markets to firms located at a basing point, it induces further expansion there. And by keeping prices higher in areas around nonbasing points, it puts a brake on their industrial development. The growth of the South and the West was long retarded in this way by Pittsburgh-plus. The expansion of cities located on waterways has likewise been hampered by the practice of charging all-rail freight. The economic fortunes of whole regions may thus have been affected by industrial pricing policies.

The Structure of Industry

The influence of basing point systems on the number of firms and the extent of concentration in industries that have used them is a matter of dispute. On the one hand, it is said that such systems have operated to discourage the entry of new firms and the growth of smaller ones, particularly in outlying markets, by making it clear that any price they might announce, in developing these markets, would be met—automatically and immediately—by every other seller in the industry. On the other hand, it is noted that basing point pricing has usually been incidental to price leadership and that, typically, where a price leader has held an umbrella over a market, other firms have entered and expanded and the leader's share of the market has declined. This is what happened, under single and multiple basing point systems, in the case of steel. United States Steel accounted for two thirds of the ingots produced in 1901 and for only one third of those produced in 1938. It appears, therefore, that such systems, while prejudicial to entry and growth in outlying regions, are consistent with increasing numbers and declining concentration in an industry as a whole. It may be questioned, however, whether the community stands to gain from these developments so long as they are not reflected in competition with respect to price.

The Level of Costs and Prices

Basing point systems may influence the level of prices by affecting the costs of production or distribution or the margin of profit. Their influence on the costs of production, however, is not clear. By permitting mills to sell in wider markets, such systems may have enabled them to attain a larger scale of operations and thus a lower unit cost. But under a single basing point system this advantage is confined, in the main, to mills located at the basing point. And where multiple basing points are used, the advantage is offset by the fact that a seller not only gains business when he ships toward others, but also loses it when others ship toward him. The reduction of costs may be retarded, under either of these systems, by the absence of competitive pressures and penalties. It is even possible that inefficiency may be sheltered and improvements in efficiency impeded by maintaining basing points at locations where costs are high and refusing to establish them at locations where costs are low.

While the influence of basing point pricing on the costs of production is open to question, its influence on the costs of distribution is beyond dispute. By eliminating competition in price, it increases expenditures on salesmanship. By enabling sellers to ship to distant markets, and by making it possible for buyers— without incurring greater costs—to make their purchases from distant firms, it increases expenditures on freight. Transportation is used where it is not needed. Goods are hauled into cities where they could have been produced. Crosshauling is encouraged, the same goods moving in opposite directions over the same route at the same time. More costly methods of transport are used where cheaper methods are available. Goods that could move by water are moved instead by rail. All of this is wasteful, and all of it makes for higher costs.

These systems also make for higher margins of profit by preventing competition in price. Indirect price cutting is discouraged by standardization, direct price cutting by the practice of always meeting the lowest delivered price. Each seller is deterred from initiating a cut at his own base by the knowledge that such action would be futile, since his share of the market could not thereby be increased. No seller is deterred, however, from raising the price at his base, knowing that his share of the market will not suffer, since every other seller will do the same. The higher costs occasioned by these systems are thus accompanied by higher margins and the resulting level of prices is therefore higher than it otherwise would be.

ALTERNATIVES TO BASING POINT SYSTEMS

In passing judgment on single or multiple basing point systems, it would be well to consider them in the light of their alternatives. The major possibilities are three. The first is to abolish phantom freight by making every producing point a basing point and requiring freight to be computed by the mode of transport used, or by the cheapest of those available, while still permitting sellers systematically to equalize freight—and prices—at destinations, and thus to discriminate among their customers. The second is completely to outlaw geographic price discrimination, forbidding freight absorption as well as phantom freight by requiring that all sales be made f.o.b. mill. The third is to adopt an intermediate position, requiring that buyers be given the option of taking delivery at the mill, but permitting a seller to absorb freight, whenever he wishes, to make a distant sale. Each of these alternatives will be examined in its turn.

Systematic Freight Equalization

As compared with a single or multiple basing point system, one in which every producing point is made a basing point possesses certain possible advantages. If the base price at each of the former nonbasing points were to be raised to offset the reduction in freight, the structure of prices would be the same as it had been before. But if this is not done, the elimination of nonbasing points will remove an artificial handicap to the development of these areas and facilitate the gradual adjustment of industrial location to the migration of demand. And if the all-rail freight requirement is abolished, it will also do away with an impediment to the growth of cities located on waterways. Since freight must be absorbed in making sales near any distant mill, such sales will be less frequent and the wastes involved in needless transportation will thereby be reduced. The necessity of freight absorption will also limit the punitive invasion of markets and thus afford to independent firms a better opportunity to enter and survive.

The effect of such a system on the margin of profit and the level of prices, however, is less clear. The removal of traditional barriers to independent action may encourage producers to exercise initiative in pricing. And the abandonment of artificial aids to uniformity, such as common freight rate books, should also make for differences. But other sellers may still wait for a leader to announce any changes in base prices. And each of them may adopt as his own, at any destination, the lowest price that is quoted there. As a result, quotations will continue to be identical. And the level of prices may be as high and as rigid as before. Phantom freight will be eliminated. But systematic discrimination will still be practiced through variations in the amount of freight absorbed.

Compulsory F.O.B. Mill Pricing

The remedy for the evils of basing point pricing advocated by its severest critics is the requirement that each seller make all of his sales at a uniform price at the door of his mill, leaving to the buyer the arrangements for delivery. This requirement would do away with geographic price discrimination, giving the same return on every sale. It would confine each mill to a regional market, avoiding the wastes of crosshauling, and reducing the costs of competitive salesmanship. It would also cut costs by enabling the buyer to employ cheaper modes of transport where they were available. F.o.b. pricing would permit the economic location of new industrial facilities and promote the adjustment of capacity to shifts in the location of demand. It might do so, however, at some cost, hastening the construction of plants in newer markets while condemning those in older regions to partial idleness.

Those who advocate compulsory f.o.b. pricing argue that it would make for active competition. It is not certain, however, that this would be the case. The number of sellers in an industry might not be increased. Plants would be built at new locations, but they might not be built by new concerns. A smaller company, confined to a local market by the prohibition of freight absorption, might find it difficult to survive. A larger one, with greater resources and with its market geographically diversified, would be likely to have greater staying power. The smaller firm might be absorbed by the larger one, and concentration, instead of declining, would increase. The industrial pattern would still be that of oligopoly.

Under f.o.b. pricing, each center of production would have an exclusive market where its price plus freight was lowest, competing with others only where their markets overlapped. It could compete, not by absorbing freight, but only by reducing its base price. This action would extend the boundaries of its market and enlarge the areas in which it challenged its competitors. A seller at such a center might well assume that those at rival centers would retaliate. He would also realize that any reduction in his price, instead of being confined to a few transactions, would apply to all his sales. For both these reasons, he would hesitate to make a cut. Under the circumstances, competition is not to be avoided by precisely equalizing costs at destinations, since delivery methods and charges are beyond control. But markets may be roughly shared by fixing their boundaries through agreement on base price relationships. And, given oligopoly, it is not unlikely that agreement will be obtained.

It may be questioned, moreover, whether the prohibition of all freight absorption would be wise. When a producer has capacity standing idle, it is economical for him to absorb freight in competing for a sale as long as his mill net realization covers his marginal cost. And when new business is not to be had nearby but is obtainable far away, it seems unreasonable to forbid him to go after it. It should be remembered, too, that discrimination may serve as an entering wedge for competition. It may be used, not only to meet another's prices, but also to undercut them. To outlaw it completely would be to sacrifice one of the principal methods through which real rivalry in markets may occur.

F.O.B. Prices with Sporadic Freight Absorption

Under the third alternative, though sales would normally be made f.o.b. and buyers would always be given the option of taking title at the mill, a seller would be permitted to absorb freight, upon occasion, in competing for a distant sale. This alternative has more to commend it than either of the other two. It avoids the worst consequences of basing point pricing without incurring those of pricing f.o.b. It removes the artificial obstacles to economy in the selection of industrial locations and modes of transportation. It permits new plants to be constructed in areas of new demand. But it also permits old plants to follow the market by absorbing freight, leaving no useful capacity stranded in mandatory idleness. It allows for some crosshauling but wastes less transportation than do systems using basing points. It makes for diversity in costs, where markets overlap, by providing for different methods of delivery. And it works against market sharing through a frozen pattern of base price differentials by permitting one seller to invade another's market by absorbing freight. It thus preserves the function of discrimination as a means of undermining an established price. Of the possible methods of pricing, this affords the greatest opportunity for competition and the least assurance for monopoly.

BASING POINT SYSTEMS AND THE LAW

A basing point system might come into conflict with the antitrust laws in several different ways. First, it might be found to depend upon collusive agreement or conscious parallelism of action and thus to reveal a conspiracy in restraint of trade in violation of Section 1 of the Sherman Act. Or if imposed upon an industry by a dominant firm, it might be held to disclose an attempt to monopolize in violation of Section 2. In either case action would be brought by the Department of Justice under the provisions of the Sherman Act. Second, basing point pricing, involving the avoidance of competition through adherence to a common course of action, might be characterized as an unfair method of competition under Section 5 of the Federal Trade Commission Act. In this case action would be initiated by the FTC. Third, the geographic price discrimination resulting from such a system might be found to be injurious to competition and thus to be in violation of Section 2 of the Clayton Act as amended by the Robinson-Patman Act. And in this case action might be taken by either agency. However, though basing point systems had been in use since 1880, and the Sherman Act available since 1890, no decision was handed down by the Supreme Court in any case that clearly questioned the legality of such a system until 1945. To explain this delay it is necessary to review briefly the history of the government's relation to the principal basing point industries, steel and cement.

A Half Century of Indecision

Basing point pricing had its origin in 1880 when three independent producers began quoting delivered prices that were identical with those charged by the Carnegie company for steel beams. The practice was applied experimentally to a few products until 1890. By 1900 it had been extended to every concern and (with the exception of rails, which are picked up by the railways at the mills) to every product in the field. In 1901 the United States Steel Corporation was organized, and from then on the level of prices was effectively controlled, first through open agreements, then through the Gary dinners, and finally through price leadership. From 1901 to 1903 most steel was sold on a zone price basis. But thereafter all products but rails were priced at Pittsburgh-plus. In 1917, during World War I, the War Industries Board ordered the industry to establish a Chicago base. But the order was rescinded within a year at the suggestion of one of the members of the Board. His name was E. H. Gary.[17] In 1910 the Department of Justice had entered suit against the Corporation, charging it with illegal combination and monopolization of the industry. In 1915 this case was appealed to the Supreme Court, but the Court's decision was delayed until 1920 by the war. When it came, as we have seen, three judges held that the Corporation had violated the Sherman Act and four held that it had not. But the striking thing to note, in this connection, is the failure of the government to present any evidence concerning the basing point system or even to raise the issue of conspiracy. The nature and the significance of basing point pricing simply were not understood.

In 1919, immediately after the war, fabricators in the West and the South began to organize and to carry complaints to the Federal Trade Commission concerning the prices they were forced to pay for steel. In 1920, when the government returned the railways to their owners, a 40 percent increase in freight rates pushed these prices even higher by adding to the plus in Pittsburgh-plus. Protests mounted, resolutions condemning the basing point system were passed by the legislatures of 11 states, and 32 states joined in organizing the Associated States Opposing Pittsburgh-Plus.[18] In response to this pressure, the Commission issued an order, in 1924, directing U.S. Steel to cease and desist "from quoting for sale or selling . . . rolled steel products upon any other basing point than that where the products are manufactured or from which they are shipped." The Corporation then filed a statement promising to obey the order "insofar as it is practicable to do so"[19] and proceeded to set up a multiple basing point system in place of Pittsburgh-plus. The new system aided fabricators in the West and in the South by establishing bases at Chicago and Birmingham. But for many years, these gains were offset, in part, by making base prices higher at these centers than at Pittsburgh. Prices east of Pittsburgh were still Pittsburgh-plus; those west of Chicago were Chicago-plus. The Corporation plainly failed to obey the Commission's order. But the Commission made no attempt to have it enforced.

In 1933, under the provisions of the National Industrial Recovery Act (to be discussed at greater length in Chapter 28), the antitrust laws were suspended and a so-called code of fair competition was approved for steel as for other industries, by President Franklin D. Roosevelt. This code was administered by a Code Authority consisting of the Directors of the American Iron and Steel Institute. In this body, it should be noted, U.S. Steel and Bethlehem Steel had

17 / F. A. Fetter, *The Masquerade of Monopoly*, pp. 153-54.
18 / *Ibid.*, p. 157.
19 / *FTC, Practices of the Steel Industry*, 73d Cong., 2d Sess., Senate Doc. 159, p. 61.

more than half of the votes. The code required all producers to adhere to the multiple basing point system, charging all-rail freight, and empowered the Code Authority to pick the basing points, to publish an official freight rate book, and to issue a book prescribing uniform extras and deductions. The code further required producers to file their base prices and to wait ten days before making them effective, and it gave the Code Authority the power to investigate these prices, to find them unfair, and to direct producers to file new ones, or if they failed to do so, to tell them what their prices must be. The code, in effect, gave to U.S. Steel and Bethlehem the legal right to fix the price of steel. And it provided that other firms, if they departed from this price, should be fined $10 per ton on the steel they produced. As a result, the industry could not obey the Federal Trade Commission's order without violating the NRA code. And it could not adhere to the code without disobeying the FTC.

This situation persisted until the NRA was found to be unconstitutional in May of 1935, and the FTC order again came into force. The industry, however, continued to employ the multiple basing point system throughout the following decade. In 1938, when the Wheeler-Lea Amendment to the Trade Commission Act made all outstanding orders final unless appealed within 60 days, the Corporation filed an appeal. A decision in this case was again delayed, first by agreement, and secondly by the outbreak of another world war. And during the war, ironically enough, the mechanism afforded by the basing point system was used by the Office of Price Administration in establishing, not minimum prices, but maximum prices for steel.

In the case of cement the story is much the same. Here, in 1902, a multiple basing point system was established by the first of a series of trade associations, and in 1925, as we have seen, the activities of such an association were held by the Supreme Court to be within the law. [20] In this case the Department of Justice had shown that the prices charged at destinations were identical. But the Court had been impressed by the defendant's argument that identity of prices revealed the presence of active competition. And the Department had not charged that the basing point system had been employed as a means of carrying out a price-fixing conspiracy. From 1933 to 1935, as in the case of steel, the industry's system was legalized and enforced by a trade association acting as a code authority. Here, too, the system remained in force after the demise of NRA. In 1937, however, the Federal Trade Commission issued a complaint against the Cement Institute and 74 cement producers, following it in 1943 with an order to cease and desist from participating in an agreement to do any of the following things:

1. Quoting or selling cement at prices calculated or determined pursuant to or in accordance with the multiple basing-point delivered price system; or . . . any other plan or system which results in identical price quotations or prices for cement at points of quotation or sale. . . .

20 / See above, p. 123.

2. (a) Refusing or declining to quote or sell cement at the location of the producing mill. . . .

(b) Refusing . . . to allow purchasers to provide transportation by any means, at any cost, or to any place they may desire. . . .

(f) Quoting or selling cement at delivered prices which systematically include a common-carrier transportation factor greater or less than the actual cost of such common-carrier transportation from the point of shipment to destination.

(g) Quoting or selling cement at delivered prices which systematically include a freight factor representing transportation by a common carrier having higher rates than the means of transportation actually employed. . . .

(j) Collecting, compiling, circulating or exchanging information concerning common-carrier transportation charges . . . to be used as a factor in the price of cement. . . .

3. Discriminating in price . . . by systematically charging and accepting mill net prices which differ by the amounts necessary to produce [identical] delivered costs to purchasers. . . .[21]

The system thus outlawed by FTC was then being used by OPA in fixing ceiling prices for cement. The industry appealed the Commission's order, and in 1946 the Court of Appeals upheld it in part and reversed it in part. The government then appealed, and the final decision of the Supreme Court was handed down in 1948, after price control had been abandoned.

The cement order was a major move in a general campaign against basing point pricing which included orders against producers of corn products, malt, milk cans, crepe paper, rigid steel conduits, and bottle caps. A complaint was also issued, in 1947, against the American Iron and Steel Institute and 101 steel companies, the earlier action in that industry having been confined to U.S. Steel. The corn products cases were the first to reach the courts.

Basing Points before the Courts

The Corn Products Refining Co., with one plant making glucose at Chicago and another at Kansas City, sold this product to manufacturers of candy on the basis of Chicago-plus. The same practice was followed by other producers, including the A. E. Staley company of Decatur, Illinois. Each of these concerns was charged with price discrimination injurious to competition in violation of Section 2-a of the Clayton Act. Corn Products and Staley appealed the Trade Commission's orders, and in 1945 the two cases were finally decided by the Supreme Court on the same day.[22] The Court held that Corn Products at its Kansas City plant and Staley at Decatur had discriminated between customers,

---

21 / FTC Docket No. 3167.

22 / *Corn Products Refining Co.* v. *FTC,* 324 U.S. 726; *FTC* v. *A. E. Staley Manufacturing Co.,* 324 U.S. 746.

absorbing freight on some sales and collecting phantom freight on others, and that this discrimination had injured competition among candy manufacturers by helping those located near Chicago and harming those nearer Kansas City, Decatur, and other nonbasing points. The Court also rejected the defense, advanced under Section 2-b of the Clayton Act, that Staley's lower prices near Chicago were made "in good faith to meet the equally low prices of a competitor," finding that such prices had been quoted systematically. Individual adherence to a single basing point system was thus held to be in violation of the law.

In its next decision, handed down in the Cement Institute case in 1948, the Supreme Court sustained the Federal Trade Commission at every point.[23] The concerted maintenance of a basing point system, said the Court, "is an unfair method of competition prohibited by the Federal Trade Commission Act."[24] The Commission's finding of illegal agreement was supported by evidence "that the industry's Institute actively worked, in cooperation with various of its members, to maintain the multiple basing point delivered price system; that this pricing system is calculated to produce, and has produced, uniform prices and terms of sale throughout the country; and that all of the respondents have sold their cement substantially in accord with the pattern required by the multiple basing point system."[25] The system, being injurious to competition, was also held to be unlawful under the Clayton Act, since "a pricing system involving both phantom freight and freight absorption violates Section 2-a if . . . prices are computed for products actually shipped from one locality on the fiction that they were shipped from another."[26] The defense advanced under Section 2-b was again rejected on the ground that prices had been matched "as a practice rather than as a good faith effort to meet individually competitive situations."[27] Collective adherence to a multiple basing point system was held to be against the law.

Another case involving such a system came before a Court of Appeals in 1948. Here, the FTC had issued an order against fourteen manufacturers of rigid steel conduit, a form of pipe used as a shield for electrical wiring. Here, again, the order was brought under Section 5 of the Trade Commission Act. But in this case, the Commission had based its action on two separate counts. In the first count, as in previous cases, it charged the companies with conspiracy. But in the second, it contended that they had individually violated the Act "through their concurrent use of a formula method of making delivered price quotations with the knowledge that each did likewise. . . ." The second count was thus directed, not against agreement to use the basing point system, but against the use of the system as such. The court upheld the Commission on both points, finding strong evidence of agreement, but also going on to hold that concurrent

23 / *FTC* v. *Cement Institute*, 333 U.S. 683.
24 / *Ibid.*, p. 720.
25 / *Ibid.*, p. 716.
26 / *Ibid.*, p. 724.
27 / *Ibid.*, p. 725.

use of a basing point system might be regarded as an unfair method of competition in itself.[28] The decision was appealed but was allowed to stand when the Supreme Court divided 4 to 4 in 1949, presenting no opinions on the case.[29]

These decisions, in cement and other industries, led eventually to settlements in steel. In 1948 United States Steel signed a decree affirming and enforcing the order that had been issued by the Federal Trade Commission in 1924. And in 1951 the American Iron and Steel Institute and its members accepted an order, based on the complaint issued in 1947, forbidding them to participate in any planned common course of action to refuse to sell steel products f.o.b. mill, to exchange lists of base prices, extras and deductions, and freight factors for use in computing prices, or to fix prices in accordance with any formula which produces identical quotations. The order, however, specifically permitted freight absorption "when innocently and independently pursued, regularly or otherwise, with the result of promoting competition," and rejected identity of delivered prices at any destination as necessarily affording proof of violation of the law.[30] It was thus directed at collusion in the maintenance of a delivered pricing system, not at delivered pricing as such.

Basing Points before Congress

The decision of the Supreme Court in the cement case evoked a storm of protest. Leaders of the basing point industries were joined by the press and by members of Congress in viewing it with alarm. An investigation was launched by a subcommittee of the Senate. Witnesses for the industries insisted that the Commission's order required f.o.b. mill pricing, forbidding all freight absorption, though the Commission and the Court had plainly said that it did not. They contended that f.o.b. pricing would necessitate higher prices, and the cement and steel industries proceeded to prove the point by selling f.o.b. and setting their prices at the former base price level instead of setting them at average mill-net realization which would have been lower, since freight absorption had exceeded phantom freight; with demand strong, they shed crocodile tears as prices rose and profits grew. Witnesses asserted that the Court's decision would turn thriving industrial centers into ghost towns as industry was forced to migrate, moving out of many centers but, inexplicably, into none. They argued, too, that f.o.b. pricing would hurt little business and help big business, implying that the basing point system had been maintained as a species of philanthropy. And they insisted, finally, that the decision had created uncertainty and confusion as to the meaning of the law and that legislative "clarification" was required.

The industries' complaints were based, in part, at least, on the fact that the meaning of the law was all too clear. The independent, sporadic absorption of

28 / *Triangle Conduit & Cable Co.* v. *FTC*, 168 F. 2d 157.

29 / *Clayton Mark & Co.* v. *FTC*, 336 U.S. 956.

30 / FTC Order 5508, issued August 16, 1951.

freight to meet the lower prices of competitors was legal, even though involving discriminatory variations in a seller's net returns. The independent absorption of freight, even though persistent, was legal unless injury to competition could be shown. And where freight was an insignificant part of the delivered price, or where customers at different locations did not compete with one another, no such showing could be made. But the collusive and sustained observance of complex and rigid systems of delivered pricing had been found to be in violation of the law. And this was the major source of complaints of confusion and demands that the law be "clarified."

It must be admitted, however, that there remained, between the independent behavior that clearly was legal and the collective behavior that clearly was not, an area of some uncertainty. Suppose that an industry offered no evidence of meetings, correspondence, or conversation leading to agreement on a common pricing policy. Suppose that it had no nonbasing points, no all-rail freight requirement, no common freight-rate book. But suppose that the delivered prices quoted by one firm were matched first by another, then by a third, and then by a fourth, first occasionally, then frequently, and then invariably. At what stage in this process would the line be crossed between legality and illegality? This was a hypothetical question that could only be answered by decisions rendered by the courts from case to case.

Behind this question lay the possibility that basing point industries might come again to match delivered prices if the machinery of collusion could be rendered less conspicuous. Their ability to do so would depend upon the nature of the proof required to win a case. On this point, however, the decisions rendered by the courts by 1949 were quite discouraging. If prices were safely to be matched, therefore, some legislative "clarification" was required.

In 1950, after extended debate, a bill with this purpose was passed by Congress. The bill amended Section 5 of the Federal Trade Commission Act to say that "It shall not be an unfair method of competition . . . for a seller, acting independently, to quote or sell at delivered prices or to absorb freight. . . ." It also amended Section 2-a of the Clayton Act by adding "That it shall not be an unlawful discrimination in price for a seller, acting independently (a) to quote or sell at delivered prices if such prices are identical at different delivery points . . . or (b) to absorb freight to meet the equally low price of a competitor in good faith except where the effect . . . will be to substantially lessen competition." [31] At first glance, these amendments may appear to have been fairly innocent. But they would have handicapped the government in the prosecution of delivered pricing systems by placing on it a heavier burden of proof. The bill was vetoed by President Truman. [32] In 1951, a similar bill passed the Senate, the report that accompanied it stating explicitly that the

31 / 81st Cong., 1st Sess., S. 1008. The infinitive, split in 1914, united in 1936, was to be split again in 1950.

32 / The story of this legislation affords an excellent case study in practical politics. It has been well told by Earl Latham in *The Group Basis of Politics* (Ithaca, N.Y.: Cornell University Press, 1952).

identity of delivered prices achieved under a plenary basing point system was held to be lawful, and asserting that no adverse inference could be drawn from evidence as to its duration, frequency, regularity, or rigidity. This bill was never reported to the House. Other measures were introduced in the following years, but each of them died in committee. Congress thus failed to change the wording of the law.

Basing Points Today

Basing point systems are still subject to prosecution, but the ground for action against them has been modified. In the National Lead and Chain Institute cases,[33] decided in 1953, the Federal Trade Commission reversed its previous position regarding the discriminatory character of delivered pricing. The price that is relevant in determining the legality of discrimination, it now held, is not net realization at the mill but the price charged at the point of delivery. Under a basing point system, all buyers at the same destination are charged the same price. The seller, therefore, does not discriminate. Delivered pricing, accordingly, is no longer to be prosecuted under the Robinson-Patman Act. The new position was endorsed by the Attorney General's National Committee in its report on the antitrust laws in 1955. The real offense in basing point systems, said the Committee, is not the discrimination that may result from them, but the collusion that is involved in establishing and maintaining them. Such systems should therefore be attacked under Section 1 of the Sherman Act or Section 5 of the Federal Trade Commission Act.[34] Since it adopted this position, the FTC has issued fewer complaints against delivered pricing systems and has handed down no order against such a system unless it was shown to be conspiratorial. The new policy may make prosecution more difficult, but it has the virtue of distinguishing between those cases of geographic price discrimination which are legally actionable and those which are not.

The decision finally handed down by the Supreme Court in the National Lead case in 1957[35] operated, on the other hand, to strengthen the position of the government. The Federal Trade Commission had not only forbidden National Lead and others to conspire to use a zone pricing system but had also forbidden them to maintain such a system by adhering, as individuals, to the practice of matching delivered prices. The Court of Appeals had upheld the first part of the Commission's order but not the second. The Supreme Court, in a unanimous opinion, reversed this decision, upholding the order on both points. In doing so, it drew a line between sporadic matching of prices, which is legal, and systematic matching of prices, which is not.

What has been the practical effect of the government's campaign against systems of delivered pricing? The basing point system has not been reestablished.

33 / FTC Dockets 4874 and 5253.

34 / *Report of the Attorney General's National Committee to Study the Antitrust Laws,* pp. 209-19.

35 / *FTC* v. *National Lead Co.,* 352 U.S. 419.

The corn syrup industry quotes prices at each of its mills; prices at mills outside Chicago are relatively lower than before; the competitive position of outlying candymakers is accordingly improved. In cement, delivery can now be taken at the mill and at destinations other than construction sites; a third of the output moves by truck; delivered prices are not invariably equalized. In steel, too, sales are made f.o.b.; the all-rail freight charge and the common rate book have been abandoned; half of the steel moves by truck. [36] In periods of recession and to get particular orders, the basing point industries have again absorbed freight; they have done so on a smaller scale than before. This may be due, in some measure, to the decisions of the courts. It is also to be explained, however, by two other facts: increases in freight rates have made freight absorption less profitable; strong demand has made it less necessary.

Discrimination is still practiced in the heavy industries. It remains to be seen whether freight absorption will ever again become so general and so habitual as to effect a systematic matching of prices at each point of delivery. Certainly such a practice will be more difficult in the future than it was in the past. The common practices that assured identity in the charges made for delivery have been outlawed. It is no longer easy to match delivered prices instantly and invariably. It is clear, moreover, that phantom freight and nonbasing points are things of the past. Goods can now be shipped by the most efficient and economical mode of transport. Artificial handicaps to industrial location have been removed. Scores of cement plants have been built at new sites, and steel capacity has grown more rapidly in Cleveland and Detroit, in the South and the West, and along the eastern seaboard than at Pittsburgh and Chicago. And this is a substantial gain.

36 / Corwin D. Edwards, *The Price Discrimination Law* (Washington, D.C.: Brookings Institution, 1959), pp. 390-99; Simon H. Whitney, *Antitrust Policies* (New York: Twentieth Century Fund, 1958), Vol. I, pp. 276-81; Vol. II, pp. 276-77, 306-7.

Chapter 11 : ANTITRUST APPRAISED

The policy of maintaining competition has been criticized, from many points of view, by economists, lawyers, and businessmen. One group of critics holds that competition is undesirable; that the policy was mistaken from the start. A second group accepts the policy but complains that its application has been unfair, contending either that the antitrust laws are too vague, or that too many practices are held to be illegal per se. A third group accepts the provisions and the interpretation of the laws but finds their enforcement to be faulty, their penalties weak, and their remedies ineffective. According to a final group of critics, the effort to maintain competition has failed, as is shown by statistics revealing an increasing concentration of economic power. We now turn to a consideration of these respective views.

THE CASE AGAINST MAINTAINING COMPETITION

Those who hold the policy of maintaining competition to be unwise support their position with four arguments: (1) They take as the goal of policy the economist's abstraction known as perfect competition and complain that it is unattainable. (2) They assert that the economies of large-scale production are to be realized only by establishments so large that their owners will dominate the markets where they sell. (3) They contend that the research and development required for economic progress are to be expected only of firms possessing monopolistic powers. (4) They argue that action breaking large firms into smaller ones is futile, since the result is merely oligopoly, and oligopolists behave not like competitors but like monopolists. Each of these arguments will be examined in its turn.

Perfect Competition

It is the responsibility of antitrust to restore competition where it does not exist and to maintain it where it does. Is such an undertaking really feasible? The answer will depend upon the way in which competition is defined. If the economist's ideal of perfect competition is accepted as the goal, five conditions must be satisfied:

1. The commodity dealt in must consist of innumerable units, each identical with the others, so that buyers can shift quickly from one seller to another in order to obtain a lower price; the advantages offered by different buyers must also be uniform, so that sellers can shift quickly from one buyer to another in order to obtain a higher price.
2. The market in which the commodity is bought and sold must be well organized, trading must be continuous, and traders must be so well informed that every unit sold at the same time will sell at the same price.
3. Sellers and buyers must be numerous, each of them must be small, and the quantity supplied or demanded by any one of them must be so insignificant a part of the total supply or demand that no increase or decrease in his sales or purchases can appreciably affect the price.
4. There must be no restraint upon the independence of any seller or buyer, whether by custom, contract, collusion, the fear of reprisals by competitors, or otherwise; each one must be free to act in his own interest without regard for the interests of any of the others.
5. There must be no friction to impede the movement of resources from industry to industry, from product to product, or from firm to firm; investment must be speedily withdrawn from unsuccessful undertakings and transferred to those that promise a profit. There must be no barrier to entrance into the market; access must be granted to all sellers and all buyers at home and abroad.

Perfect competition, thus defined, never has existed and never can exist. An attempt to realize it in practice would require an atomization of industry that is not within the bounds of possiblity. The concept is useful merely as a standard by which to measure the varying degrees of imperfection that must always characterize the actual markets in which goods are bought and sold. It cannot be taken as a practical objective of public policy.

Effective Competition

Another concept, developed more recently by economists, defines competition in terms, not of perfection, but of workability, thus establishing a standard that is more nearly attainable. A market may be regarded as effectively competitive when it is characterized by conditions that afford to buyers and sellers real opportunities to protect themselves, each against the other. Effective competition may be produced by conditions that are less exacting than those demanded for perfection:

1. It need not involve the standardization of commodities; it does require the availability of products so closely related that they may be readily substituted, one for another. It does not require that the advantages offered by all buyers be identical; it does require that they differ so little that sellers will not hesitate to shift from one to another.

2. It does not require that markets be formally organized, that trading be continuous, or that all buyers and sellers be intelligent, educated, and equally well informed; it does require that information be available and that no action be taken to grant it to some traders and withhold it from others.
3. It does not require that traders be present in such numbers and limited to such a size that none of them has an appreciable influence on supply, demand, or price; it does require that traders be sufficiently numerous to offer to buyers and to sellers, respectively, a considerable number of genuine alternatives in sources of supply and demand, so that, by shifting their purchases or sales, they can substantially influence quality, service, and price.
4. It does not require emancipation from custom or isolation from contacts with competitors; it does require substantial independence of action: each trader must be free to adopt his own policy governing output, purchases, and price; traders must not take part in formal agreements or tacit understandings; power must not be so distributed that lack of resources or fear of retaliation prevent one trader from encroaching on the sales or the purchases of another.
5. It does not require that transference of resources be frictionless or instantaneous or that entry to the market be unimpeded by such natural obstacles as the cost of facilities and sales promotion or the experience and contacts of existing firms; it does require that transference and entry be unobstructed by artificial barriers and that no preferences be accorded or handicaps imposed.

Effective competition cannot be expected to insure complete flexibility or optimum economy in the use of resources. In a rough way, however, it can contribute toward these ends. By subjecting traders to its discipline, it can prevent deliberate curtailment of output and the survival of extremes of inefficiency. By affording access to genuine alternatives, it can protect the weaker trader against the worst of the bargains that might otherwise be imposed upon him by the stronger one. By holding open the door to opportunity, it can encourage experimentation in products, processes, and prices, and forestall the suppression of innovation by established firms. This concept, admittedly, is less precise than that of perfect competition. It is more useful, however, as a goal for public policy.

Economies of Scale in the Plant

Are the economies of large-scale production to be realized only through operation on a scale so great that competition cannot be maintained? In answering this question, it is necessary to distinguish between the advantages that pertain to size in an individual plant and those that pertain to size in a firm that may operate a number of plants. The economies of scale in a single plant will be considered first.

The large plant is generally assumed to possess certain marked advantages. It can effect a minute division of labor on the job. It can mechanize operations that would have been performed, on a smaller scale, by hand. It can install big, expensive, and highly specialized machines, provide them in great numbers, and arrange them in the proportions and in the sequences that are most conducive to continuous processes. It can utilize byproducts and reclaim waste materials. It can employ skilled technicians, specializing in research and development and in the various branches of management.

It cannot be doubted that such economies exist. But empirical studies of the subject are fragmentary and inconclusive. A few investigators have attempted to measure the unit costs of output, or the physical input required for output, in plants of various sizes in particular industries. But such inquiries encounter serious difficulties. The effect of size cannot be measured with precision unless all other things are equal, and they seldom are. The composition of the product or the technology of production may differ from plant to plant. A product is rarely the only one turned out by all of the plants concerned. Its share in the product-mix may be large for one plant and small for another. Its apparent cost will be strongly influenced by the methods employed in allocating overhead. Cases simple enough to permit the measurement of the effect of size alone are rare indeed. In a number of instances, investigators have found higher costs in the largest plants and lower costs in plants of medium size. But findings of this sort are scarcely to be generalized.

There are other indications that increasing size is not always advantageous. Big business typically expands, not by enlarging old plants but by building new ones, and the newer plants are not built on an ever larger scale. Indeed, there is a trend toward smaller size; in 67 among 115 industries from 1947 to 1958, the share of output coming from the eight largest plants actually declined.[1] In many fields, new developments in technology appear to make for operation on a smaller scale. Transport by truck and the ability to transmit electricity over long distances permit decentralization. New materials, such as the light metals, alloys, and plastics, and new processes, such as moulding, welding, stamping, and die-casting, require less heavy machinery than did older ones. Light, multipurpose machines—independently operated, readily transferred from product to product and moved from place to place, run at varying speeds and turned on and off at will—displace the massive, rigid installations of an earlier day.[2] The growth of technology, in the past, made for greater size. In many cases, now, it works the other way.

---

1 / U.S. Senate, Committee on the Judiciary, Subcommittee on Antitrust and Monopoly, *Hearings on Economic Concentration* (Washington, D.C.: Government Printing Office, 1966) Part 4, pp. 1536-56.

2 / David Hamburg, "Size of Enterprise and Technical Change," *Antitrust Law and Economic Review*, Vol. 1 (1967) pp. 43-52.

Even though lower costs can be obtained by a larger plant than by a smaller one, it does not follow that markets must be monopolized. Control over markets is usually achieved, not through the growth of a single plant, but by uniting several plants under common ownership. The size of plant required for efficiency and the scope of ownership required for monopoly are not to be confused. The advantages of size in the plant do not necessitate the attainment of greater size by the firm. They explain why Chevrolet can produce automobiles more cheaply than could the corner garage. They do not justify control by General Motors of Chevrolet, Pontiac, Oldsmobile, Buick, and Cadillac.

Joe S. Bain, in a significant study of this problem, took a representative sample of 20 industries and obtained engineering estimates on the plant size that had to be reached to obtain the lowest unit costs. Then he compared the output of such a plant with the total output of the industry. In 11 of the industries, he found that the low-cost plant would account for less than 2½ percent of the output, in 15 for less than 7½ percent, and in only one (typewriters) for more than 15 percent. Recognizing that the sales of some plants are limited to regional markets, he also compared the output of the low-cost plant with the total sales in its market. Here, he found that such a plant would supply less than 15 percent of the largest submarket in 18 industries; less than 15 percent of the smallest submarket in 12.[3] According to Richard B. Heflebower, the minimum optimal scale of plants embodying new technology may well be lower than the estimates made, for existing plants, by Bain's engineers. If this is true, the share of the market needed for efficient operation is even smaller than that computed by Bain.[4] In any case, Bain's study leaves little ground for the view that economies of size in the plant necessitate monopoly in the market.

Economies of Scale in the Firm

A firm with several plants may be a horizontal combination of plants performing similar functions, a vertical combination of plants performing successive functions, a conglomeration of plants performing unrelated functions, or some combination of the three. In each of these cases, there are said to be advantages in size. Horizontal combination may enable management to standardize products and procedures, give wider scope to know-how, and lift the poorer units in a chain up to the level of the best. It may permit specialization among plants and more intensive specialization in administration. Where plants are scattered, it may cut the costs of transport by eliminating cross freights. By making possible the use of a common selling organization, it may reduce the unit cost of sales. Vertical integration may improve control of quality and promise steadier operation by insuring regular delivery of materials and continued access to markets.

3 / Joe S. Bain, *Barriers to New Competition* (Cambridge, Mass.: Harvard University Press, 1956), chap. iii.

4 / R. B. Heflebower, "Barriers to New Competition," *American Economic Review*, Vol. XLVII (1957), pp. 363-72.

Even a conglomerate combination may cut costs by employing common facilities for research and marketing. In all of these cases, moreover, size may enable its possessor to obtain capital and credit more easily, to buy materials in larger quantities, and to spend more money on research.

But there are also disadvantages in size. Combination, in any form, requires more effort in coordination and necessitates larger expenditures on administrative overhead. A business may grow so cumbersome that no man can hope to manage it efficiently. It may be so vast, so scattered, and so diversified that no one can really know what is going on. Under these circumstances, the manager loses contact with actual operations and is forced, instead, to obtain his information from accounts and statistics, to issue orders from a distance, and to rely upon paper controls. He may be bogged down with memoranda, reports, and routine. He may hesitate to make decisions and waste time in interminable delays. His subordinates may dissipate their energies in duplicated effort. They may be entangled in red tape. They may shift responsibility to others, failing to act decisively because they fear to be reversed. A whole organization may be beset with nepotism, political maneuvering, factional warfare, and petty jealousies. So efficiency may be sacrificed to size, and management may grow lax or take refuge in inflexibility, resisting adjustment to changing conditions and refusing opportunity to new ideas.

A number of studies have been made of the relation between company size and profits, productivity, or unit costs, but the results have not been such that any firm conclusion would be justified. Some studies indicate that profits have fallen after mergers; others that multiplant companies have earned no more or even less than single-plant concerns. Others suggest that profits have increased with size; still others that the larger firms have done less well than somewhat smaller ones. Profits, however, are not a perfect index, being influenced by many factors other than size. But there are studies, too, which show that output per man-hour has not been increased by mergers, and that the largest firms, in a number of industries, do not have the lowest unit costs. When Bain sought to obtain estimates with respect to the economies of multiplant operation in his sample of 20 industries, he found that such economies were held to be perceptible but small in six, to be negligible or absent in six, and he was unable to get any estimates for the other eight. Such evidence does not support the view that the economies of size in the firm lead inevitably to monopoly.

A business may be too small to realize the economies that are implicit in modern technology; it may be too large to be administered with competence. Between these extremes there may be a size of optimum efficiency. But this size will differ from industry to industry. It may change, almost overnight, with the development of new methods of production and new techniques of management. And no one can locate the optimum in any industry at any time with any certainty. It may even be that any one of several sizes will display the same efficiency. There is no basis for supposing that the largest unit in an industry will necessarily have the lowest costs.

Even where a corporate giant is highly successful, its success may reveal the possession of acquisitive rather than productive advantages. It may have forced sellers to discriminate in its favor and buyers to pay a monopoly price. If integrated, it may have put the squeeze on independents. If diversified, it may have subsidized the losses of one activity with the earnings of another until it drove its rivals from the field. Its higher profits may reflect the banking connections that give it a preferred position as a borrower, and the financial resources that strengthen its hand in litigation, in advertising, and in relations with agencies of government. They may show that its size is advantageous to its stockholders but not to the rest of the community.

Size and Innovation

Many of the more important technical developments of recent years have come from industries where production is concentrated in the hands of a few large firms. Here, it is the corporate giant who has set the pace for change. New markets, new products, and new methods of production have been developed through industrial research. Here, as elsewhere, competition has been intensified through the development of substitutes. This "perennial gale of creative destruction" was hailed by Joseph Schumpeter as the source of economic progress.[5] It has led J. K. Galbraith to the happy conclusion that "a benign providence who, so far, has loved us for our worries, has made the modern industry of a few large firms an almost perfect instrument for inducing technical change."[6] Why should this be so? Is size essential to innovation? Is monopoly prerequisite to progress?

There is one way, certainly, in which size may contribute to innovation. The larger a firm, the greater is its capacity to finance research and development. Research is costly. The commercial exploitation of new inventions may require the prior investment of even larger sums. Du Pont is said to have spent 12 years and $27 million before it sold its first pound of nylon in 1940. A firm must be large to spend on such a scale.

The big concern has the ability to finance innovation; it does not necessarily do so. Scherer, in his study of 352 of the largest firms in the United States in 1955, found that the share of income devoted to research and development declined as size increased.[7] And Mansfield, in his study of the oil, drug, glass, and steel industries from 1945 to 1959, found a similar inverse relationship.[8]

5 / Joseph Schumpeter, *Capitalism, Socialism, and Democracy* (2d ed.; New York: Harper & Bros., 1947), chap. vii.

6 / J. K. Galbraith, *American Capitalism* (Boston: Houghton Mifflin Co., 1952), p. 91.

7 / See Werner Sichel, *Industrial Organization and Public Policy* (Boston, Mass.: Houghton Mifflin Co., 1967), pp. 246-60, Statement of F. M. Scherer before U.S. Senate Committee on the Judiciary, Subcommittee on Antitrust and Monopoly, 1965, Part 3, pp. 1188-1200.

8 / Edwin Mansfield, "Industrial Research and Development Expenditures," *Journal of Political Economy*, vol. 72 (1964), pp. 333-34.

Not only do larger firms spend a smaller share of income on research than smaller ones; they get a smaller return in patentable inventions per dollar spent. Schmookler, in his study of six industry groups in 1953, found that the larger firms in five of them spent more per patent obtained than did the smaller ones.[9] Scherer and Mansfield, in their studies, also found an inverse relationship between inventive output and firm size.[10] Innovation in the large firm appears to suffer from serious handicaps. The firm may be committed to earlier techniques. Its research may be less original than that of smaller companies. Its researchers may be less familiar with other aspects of the business. Managements may find it more difficult to coordinate their work and to evaluate their results. Research in the large firm, in short, encounters diseconomies of scale.

The big corporate laboratory is not the only—or necessarily the best—source of new ideas. When Jewkes, Sawers, and Stillerman studied the origin of the 60 most important inventions of recent years, they found that more than half of them came from independent inventors, less than half from corporate research, and even less from the research done by large concerns.[11] Such fundamental discoveries as nuclear fission, the transistor, and the laser were the work of small groups. And elsewhere, in recent years, there has been a proliferation of new enterprises that had their origin in small-scale research. Giant firm size, as Scherer observes, "is no prerequisite for the most vigorous inventive and innovative activity."[12]

As between industries, the rate of innovation is high in some cases where firms are large and low in others where firms are equally large. More than half of the money devoted to industrial research in the United States is invested in three industries: chemicals, electrical equipment, and aircraft. Other fields that are occupied by industrial giants—among them railway transport, telegraph service, anthracite coal, and the basic metals—have been notoriously backward. In the opinion of a firm of industrial engineers that analyzed the operations of U.S. Steel some years ago, the Corporation had been slow in introducing improvements in technology. Specifically, says George W. Stocking,

> . . . it was slow in introducing the continuous rolling mill; slow in getting into production of cold-rolled steel products; slow in recognizing the potentials of the wire business; slow to adopt the heat-treating process for the production of sheets; slow in getting into stainless steel products; slow in producing cold-rolled sheets; slow in tin-plate developments; slow in utilizing waste gases. . . .[13]

9 / See Sichel, *op. cit.*, pp. 261-69, Statement of Jacob Schmookler before U.S. Senate Committee on the Judiciary, Subcommittee on Antitrust and Monopoly, 1965, pp. 1257-64.

10 / Sichel, *op. cit.*, pp. 255-59; Edwin Mansfield, "Size of Firm, Market Structure, and Innovation," *Journal of Political Economy*, Vol. 71 (1963), pp. 565-68.

11 / John Jewkes, David Sawers, and Richard Stillerman, *The Sources of Invention* (London: Macmillan & Co., Ltd., 1958), chap. iv.

12 / Sichel, *op. cit.*, p. 260.

13 / *Hearings before the Subcommittee on Study of Monopoly Power, Committee on the Judiciary, House of Representatives* (81st Cong., 2d Sess.), Serial 14, Part 4 A, p. 967.

and so on. The most revolutionary development in the technology of steelmaking in recent years, the oxygen converter, was invented in 1950 by a foreign firm that was less than a third as large as a single plant of U.S. Steel. It was introduced into the United States by a firm that had only one percent of American steel capacity. It was not adopted by U.S. Steel until 1963, by Bethlehem until 1964.[14] The pygmies led; the giants lagged behind.

Monopoly and Innovation

Even if size in itself were invariably conducive to innovation, it would not follow that monopoly had a similar effect. Here, a distinction must be made between the monopolies—limited in scope and duration—that are granted under the patent system, and monopolization of a market as a whole. The patent monopoly may make for progress. Research is risky. The projects that do not pay off must be financed by those that do. Business might not take the chances involved if it were forced to bear the costs of failure but promptly deprived by competition of the offsetting profits of success. In this sense, innovation is fostered by monopoly. In a larger sense, it is not.

Investment in innovation depends not only upon the financial capacity of a business but also upon its motivation. There must be rewards to induce innovation; there must be penalties to compel it. Here, one finds a marked difference between the competitor and the monopolist. The competitor may be deterred from introducing new ideas by the fear that they will ultimately be copied by his rivals. But he is encouraged to innovate by the knowledge that he will make a temporary profit and by the hope that he will bring about a permanent expansion of the market. And he is compelled to innovate by the certainty that his rivals will supplant him if he does not. When they improve their products or cut their costs and prices, he must follow suit if he is to survive. It was under competition that such products as titanium, insulin, frozen foods, radios, television sets, and air conditioners were developed; that the technology of agriculture was revolutionized and the methods of retail distribution transformed.

So, too, with oligopoly. The management of the corporate giant is concerned with its prestige, with the full employment of its resources and the expansion of its markets, and with its reputation for progressiveness. It is also impelled to push research and development by the fear that other firms will beat it to the Patent Office and the market. There are rewards for those who get there first; there may be penalties for those who lag. It is under oligopoly that innovation has occurred in chemicals, automobiles, tires, business machines, and other manufactured goods.

With monopoly, it is otherwise. The monopolist may be encouraged to innovate by the fact that he can keep the profits to himself. But he is under no compulsion to do so. And with money already sunk in investments embodying an earlier technology, he may undertake to recover it before he makes a

---

14 / Walter Adams and Joel B. Dirlam, "Big Steel, Invention, and Innovation," *Quarterly Journal of Economics*, vol. 80 (1966), pp. 167-89.

change. There was progress, under monopoly, in the aluminum and shoe machinery industries, but its pace was less rapid than that attained in fields that were competitive. The monopolized telegraph industry was virtually stagnant for decades. Research has been conducted by the telephone monopoly, but it has been designed, in large measure, to enable A.T.&T. to enter fields other than telephony. The company postponed the introduction of improvements such as the hand set and the dial system for many years so that its old equipment might wear out before it was junked. Obsolescence must be recognized more promptly in a competitive industry. In short, size in a firm may be favorable to progress; monopoly in a market is not.

The Significance of Oligopoly

Efficiency and progress, as we have seen, depend to some extent on size. And size, though it seldom requires monopoly, does make for oligopoly. The policy of maintaining competition, say its critics, is thus unrealistic and futile. For oligopolists cannot be expected to compete.

In a field where sellers are few in number, each of them exerts a significant influence on supply and each of them must consider how the others may react to any initiative that he may take. Each seller, unless a recognized price leader, is likely to fear that an increase in his price will not be followed by his rivals. It may thus reduce his share of the market and his profits. Each seller fears, moreover, that a reduction in his price will promptly be matched. It will not increase his share of the market. It will increase his profits only if it adds to the total volume of sales. If he is convinced that demand is elastic, he may cut his price. Otherwise, he will not. An oligopolist therefore hesitates either to raise or to lower his price. An oligopoly price thus tends to be a rigid price.

So runs the theory. And, on the basis of this logic, it is argued that there is nothing to be gained from antitrust. Industries cannot be atomized without sacrificing efficiency and progress. But firms left big enough to be efficient and progressive will not compete. Agreements may be enjoined and combinations dissolved. Two or three large sellers may be broken into eight or ten. There may be no evidence of conspiracy, no monopoly, no apparent violation of the law—and still, no competition. So antitrust stands helpless in the face of oligopoly.

The theory, however, falls short of justifying this conclusion. It argues only that oligopoly price will be rigid. It does not explain how the price was first set at the level where it tends to stay. Originally, the price may well have been the outcome of competitive forces. The oligopolist, to be sure, is able to state the price at which he will sell. But when he does so, he simply expresses his judgment as to what the market will take. He must attempt to find a figure that will prove acceptable to buyers. He must assess the possible response of potential as well as actual competitors. His apparent independence is illusory. The market still has the final word.

Oligopoly price may be sluggish, but it does change. It rises under pressure from rising costs. It falls under pressure from excess capacity. The list price may be maintained, but discriminatory discounts may be given, in secret, to powerful buyers. And, as such concessions spread, they lead eventually to a downward revision of the list. Indeed, when Stigler studied price behavior under oligopoly, he found that oligopoly prices were not substantially more rigid than those established under other forms of market organization.[15]

In practice, an antitrust decree that increases the number of sellers in an industry may have marked advantages. Such a decree is unlikely to establish the conditions required for perfect competition. But it can lessen the prospect of uniformity in policy and afford to buyers a larger number of alternatives. The circumstances of individual sellers will seldom be the same. There will be differences in the range of products offered for sale, in location, in techniques of production, in efficiency and costs, in methods of computing costs, and in programs of research and development. The more sellers, the more likelihood of differences in judgment as to market prospects and elasticity of demand, with resulting differences in price and production policies. It requires only one seller to introduce an innovation in product, quality, or price. The larger the number of sellers, the more difficult it will be to negotiate and to enforce restrictive agreements; the better is the chance that one or more of them will take an independent line. Stigler, in his study of oligopoly pricing, found that price flexibility increased with the number of firms in an industry. And Kaysen and Turner report that "loose oligopoly structures such as oil refining and rayon appear to show more competitive behavior by large firms than do tight ones such as cigarettes and flat glass."[16] In short, oligopoly is generally to be preferred to monopoly and even as few as six or eight large sellers in a market to only three or four.

The rivalry of a few great firms, as was shown in the preceding section, is conducive to innovation—more so than monopoly, and more so, perhaps, than competition among many small concerns. A differential advantage achieved through innovation, unlike one resulting from a cut in prices, may be retained. Rivalry, under oligopoly, is therefore most likely to manifest itself in new technology. But the compulsion to exercise initiative will vary with the number in the field. By keeping the number as large as possible, antitrust can increase the likelihood that innovation will occur.

The power of oligopoly is not only tempered by rivalry on the sellers' side of the market but is also frequently offset by the existence, on the buyers' side of the market, of similar aggregations of power. In the case of producers' goods, for instance, a few salesmen representing oligopolists may deal, quite typically, with a few skilled purchasing agents representing oligopsonists. Iron ore is sold to steel mills; steel mill products to the manufacturers of locomotives, railway cars, automobiles, and machinery; locomotives and railway cars to the railroads; machinery to factories and public utilities; chemicals to industrial users; tire

15 / George J. Stigler, "The Kinky Oligopoly Demand Curve and Rigid Prices," *Journal of Political Economy,* Vol. LV (1947), pp. 432-49.

16 / Carl Kaysen and Donald F. Turner, *Antitrust Policy* (Cambridge, Mass.: Harvard University Press, 1959), p. 115.

fabrics to the rubber companies; and tires and plate glass to the automobile companies. So, too, with the wholesale markets for consumers' goods. Here, the mass distributors act as purchasing agents for the consumer, using their mass buying power, in his behalf, to force down the prices that highly concentrated producers might otherwise be disposed to charge. In all such cases, however, the power exerted by large buyers will vary directly with the numbers of the sellers with whom they deal. The more numerous the sellers, the better is the chance that one can be played off against another and a better price obtained. Here, again, there is a task for antitrust. By preventing sellers from combining, and by breaking up combinations where they have occurred, it can contribute to the successful exercise of countervailing power.

CRITICISMS OF ANTITRUST

The criticism of the antitrust laws most often voiced by businessmen is not that the policy they embody is wrong but that its application is unfair. There are two principal complaints. First, it is said that voluntary compliance with the laws is inhibited by the vagueness of their requirements and the ambiguity of their interpretation by the courts. It is argued further that managements, when considering a change in organization or method, have no way to determine whether it would be legal or not. The imposition of penalties for such offenses is therefore held to be unjust. Second, it is objected that the courts are holding too many forms of organization and too many business practices to be illegal per se when these should be judged, instead, by their effects. The two complaints are obviously inconsistent. If uncertainty is to be eliminated, offenses must be made explicit. If flexibility is to be preserved, precision must be sacrificed. The critics of antitrust should take one position or the other. They cannot logically occupy them both.

The complaint that antitrust is vague is partly disingenuous and partly justified. It is disingenuous when made regarding practices whose illegality is all too clear. But it has some force where the lawfulness of the issues presented by proposed arrangements has never been adjudicated, and where the meaning of the decisions rendered is ambiguous. This will be less true in cases involving restrictive agreements and coercive practices, more so in those involving combination, monopolization, and business size. The complaint that business organization and behavior should be judged, not by their form, but by their results is not without its merits. But it raises far more problems than it solves.

Three types of remedies are proposed. Under the first, the number of formal actions leading to the imposition of penalties would be sharply reduced and reliance placed, to a larger extent, upon informal processes. Under the second, the text of the laws would be reworded so explicitly that their meaning could not be misunderstood. Under the third, decisions as to the legality of business organization and practices would turn on evidence of their performance in the public interest. Each of these proposals appears to be reasonable. But each of them, on closer examination, will be found to be dangerous.

Informal Processes

A number of suggested reforms call for greater reliance upon informal processes. It has often been proposed that business be permitted to lay its plans before the Antitrust Division prior to their adoption and be granted immunity from prosecution where they are not disapproved. On the face of it, the case for prior administrative clearance is a persuasive one. The procedure could be inexpensive, expeditious, and flexible. It would look toward prevention rather than punishment. If the arrangements threatened to be harmful, they could be disapproved. If they were harmless, business would be permitted to go ahead without running the risk of prosecution. But the procedure would be open to abuse. In applications for clearance, something less than the whole truth might be told. A plan that looked innocent enough on paper might prove, in operation, to be less innocent than it had seemed. The scope of the immunity that was granted might be interpreted more broadly by business than by government. To guard against such abuses, the right to carry cases to the courts must be retained.

It has been urged, too, that cases initiated by the government, other than criminal actions, be settled in conference rather than submitted to litigation. Such a procedure would save time and money and might often prove effective in eliciting compliance. But it would conceal past violations of the law. And agreements as to future behavior might not be forthcoming when the threat of prosecution was not in view.

Making the Law Specific

If the statutes and decisions are vague and administrative discretion dangerous, why not rewrite prohibitions of antitrust in words made so precise that their intention would be plain? This solution, too, would be more difficult than it may seem. However numerous the restrictive practices described, precision of wording would limit the scope of the law, since any practices that differed in detail would then escape control. New forms of restraint could scarcely be foreseen; failure to anticipate and prohibit them would put a premium on their discovery. Many devices must be judged, moreover, not by their form but by their effects; the words defining their legality will therefore have to be indefinite. In such cases, revision of the statutes would be likely to alter the standards of legality. And where it did, every new phrase and word and punctuation mark would have to be interpreted. Such certainty as judicial construction has given to the law, over the years, would be discarded. Instead of being clarified, the meaning of antitrust would be shrouded, for decades, in new obscurity.

Proposals that the law be made more explicit have been advanced with respect to business organization as well as business practices. And it is here, as we have seen, that the greatest uncertainty remains. Some combinations have been found innocent and others guilty, some of the guilty broken up and others allowed to stand; the outcome of a dissolution suit, now as always, is beyond predictability. It is sometimes suggested, therefore, that a definite limit be placed on the permissible size of any firm in terms of its total assets, employment, output, or sales, or its share in those of an industry, or those related to a particular commodity.[17] It would then be perfectly clear that size in excess of the specified limit was illegal, and there would be no excuse for the government to fail to prosecute and no alternative for the courts but to dissolve. But here, again, the problem has been oversimplified.

Ceilings on Size

It would not be easy to establish a rigid limit for size. If such a limit were set in absolute terms—so many millions in assets or so many thousands of employees—its significance would vary from industry to industry. If set low enough to maintain competition in fields where the volume of sales and the scale of production were small, it would be lower than needed to maintain competition and might be too low to permit efficient operation in fields where they were large. If set high enough to preserve efficiency in the second case, it would afford no protection against monopoly in the first. If set at some intermediate point, it might check efficiency in the larger industry without checking monopoly in the smaller one. If a limit on size is not to be arbitrary, it must be relative rather than absolute in character.

If the limit set is to be relative, other difficulties will arise. What share of what—and where and when—shall be regarded as enough? What percentage shall be taken: 15, 20, 25, or 33? How shall the choice of any one of them be justified? Shall the figure be the same for every industry? If not, what principle of differentiation shall be used? What shall be used as a base: an industry or a product? If an industry, how shall it be defined? If the base is a product, where shall the line be drawn along the range of possible substitutes? What is the market within which the share to be measured is significant? How are its boundaries to be ascertained? The answers given to these questions will determine whether a particular firm appears to be large or small.

A limit on size, in relation to the market, would check concentration; it would be a crude weapon with which to attack monopoly. A concentration ratio reveals one fact about the situation in a market, but it does not tell everything that may be relevant. The manufacturer who makes the bulk of a product may be a hardened monopolist, or he may be a vigorous pioneer in a field that is shortly to become competitive. Entry for rivals may be obstructed or open; the threat of potential competition may be weak or strong. On the other side of the market, the oligopolistic seller may deal with actively competing buyers; he may also be faced by oligopsonists. A concentration ratio may wisely be employed to identify the fields that should be examined for further evidences of monopoly. It cannot be taken, in itself, as an index of monopoly power.

17 / See, for instance, Fred I. Raymond, *The Limitist* (New York: W. W. Norton & Co., 1947).

Even if these difficulties could be overcome, the wisdom of applying a rigid limit to size would be open to question. There may be advantages in size that such a limit would destroy. It may often be the case that lower costs and more rapid progress are to be attained by a larger firm than by a smaller one. Where the characteristics of an industry, in relation to the size of its market, are such that a firm could reach its optimum size without exceeding the statutory limit, these advantages could be retained. But where this is not the case, they would be sacrificed. As a firm approached the limit, moreover, its incentive to improve its product or reduce its costs and prices, thereby increasing its sales, would disappear. The law would thus induce stagnation and impose a rigid pattern of market sharing on the industry.

Standards of Legality

Legality, under the antitrust laws, might be judged by one of three standards: by a firm's behavior, by the structure of the market in which it deals, and by the character of its economic performance. Behavior is a matter of voluntary choice. Behavior that may be found to be illegal includes collusive price fixing, market sharing, the imposition of boycotts, and such practices as exclusive dealing and price discrimination. Market structure has to do with conditions external to the firm. Its use as a standard of legality would involve the definition of a product, determination of the boundaries of the market, of the number of sellers and buyers, their distribution according to size, their respective market shares, and discovery of possible barriers to entry and to growth. Performance has to do with the economic results of a firm's activities.

Adoption of performance as the standard of legality is advocated by a final group among the critics of antitrust. Legality, they say, should depend not upon the form of business organization or practices but upon their consequences. If the performance of business is in the public interest, this is all that needs to be required. For the attainment of such results fulfills the purpose of the law. [18]

Some who hold this view propose that the standard of performance be applied not only to combination and monopolization but also to collusive agreements and restrictive practices. Such a step would permit continuance of agreements to curtail output, assign quotas, and fix prices if it could be shown that their results had not been harmful. It would permit formation of new agreements of this sort if a court could be convinced that their terms were not unreasonable. This proposal would reverse the long-established interpretation of the law. For the American tradition of insisting on competition, it would substitute the European tolerance of the reasonable cartel.

Not all of the proponents of the standard of performance go this far. Most of them, probably, would confine its use to cases of combination and monopolization. Here, the proposal stands on firmer ground. As a practical matter, the employment of a rule of reason in such matters is inescapable; it would scarcely

18 / See Clare E. Griffin, *An Economic Approach to Antitrust Laws* (New York: American Enterprise Association, 1951).

be wise to break up "every" combination as the Sherman Act required. Such a rule has been continuously employed, in fact, since 1911. It is true that the courts, since 1945, have been less ready to condone monopoly. But the rule of reason persists. Under the present proposal, it would be recast in terms of performance in the public interest.

Market Performance

An effort to establish performance as the standard of legality would encounter serious difficulties. Agreement upon the tests by which to measure the performance of an enterprise would not be easy to obtain. Among the many questions to be raised, there might well be the following:

1. Is the enterprise using scarce resources economically? Is it wasting natural resources? Has it tied up more resources in productive facilities than its market is likely to require? Has it diverted resources, in excessive quantities, to the promotion of sales?
2. Is it producing efficiently? Are its plants of optimum size? Within the limits set by fixed equipment, is it employing the best available techniques? Are its costs, per unit of output, as low as they could be?
3. Does it operate steadily over time, at a high percentage of capacity, providing regular employment and a dependable flow of goods and services?
4. Is it contributing to economic progress? Is it investing substantial sums in research and development? Is it improving the quality of old products, introducing new products, and adopting new processes? Is it constantly reducing unit costs?
5. Are lower costs passed on in lower prices? Are profits sought through high margins on low volume or through low margins on high volume? Do prices and profits rise and fall as demand and output rise and fall, or are they rigidly maintained? Have profits for years been well above the average for industry in general, or have they yielded no more than a normal return?

To questions of this nature might be added many others, dealing with matters such as the treatment of labor, the promotion of friendly relations with other countries, and contributions to national defense.

It will be seen at once that most of these tests are qualitative in character, not lending themselves to measurement, but depending for their answers on individual judgment. How, for instance, is the propriety of expenditure on product variation or on sales promotion to be appraised? In many cases, too, the evidence obtainable would be ambiguous. Predatory price cutting is not readily to be distinguished from vigorous competition, monopolistic overcapacity from prudent anticipation of demand, deliberate suppression of technology from a wise decision to reject an inferior process, an unpromising product, or an improvement whose immediate adoption would be premature. The tests, moreover, differ in character and importance. In a given case, it is likely that some of the answers would be favorable and some adverse. It would be difficult to balance one against the other, or even to weigh them on a common scale. The summation, again, would require an exercise of judgment.

The proposal that large firms be judged by their performance is also open to criticism on other grounds. For one thing, it is designed to operate only as an escape. The suggestion is not that firms whose performance is poor be required to improve it but only that those whose performance is good be exempt from the penalties of antitrust. And there are doubtless many cases in which tests such as those of efficiency, progressiveness, and contribution to national defense could be used to condone monopoly. This approach, moreover, would impose upon the government a heavier burden of proof, requiring it to show not only that competition had been injured but also that performance had been poor. It would involve the enforcement agencies in the enterprise of offering advice and guidance to businessmen. It would necessitate repeated reappraisals of performance and would thus require continued supervision of business activity. If adopted, it would move away from the automatic safeguards of competition and toward administrative regulation as the method of control.

Market Structure

The proposal that legality be tested by performance is flatly rejected by many economists. Government, they say, should not be concerned with the results of business activity, but should confine itself to providing assurance of a fair field with no favors, leaving the results to take care of themselves. A firm should be judged not by the social consequences of its operations but by the power conferred by its position, not by market performance but by market structure. A combination should be held to be unreasonable whenever it has the power to exclude outsiders from the market, to coerce competitors, or to exploit suppliers or customers. And this should be true even though its power had never been abused or had been used affirmatively in the public interest. A company's contributions to the general welfare, however laudable, should not preserve it if they were not compelled by competition but were granted, instead, as a voluntary dispensation to the rest of the community. The power to do good implies the power to do evil. So the possession of power, in itself, should be the test of legality.

But market structure, too, has its shortcomings as a basis for judgment. The rigid application of any limit on occupancy of the market would encounter all of the difficulties considered above in discussing ceilings on size. It is by no means easy to obtain proper definitions and accurate measurements of the products and the markets to which such a limit would apply. Ratios can be computed showing the extent to which production is concentrated in the hands of a few large firms, but their significance is dubious. It cannot be assumed, in a particular case, that a low ratio reveals a situation that compels performance in the public interest while a high ratio reveals one that does not. A high degree of concentration may serve the public by conserving natural resources; it may harm the public by exacting excess profits; it bears little relation to realization of the economies of scale, to technical progress, or to market behavior. Nor can it be assumed that a low ratio invariably reveals a situation that is competitive while a high ratio reveals one that is not. Competition may be suppressed by collusion in a market where firms are many and small; it is sometimes vigorous in a market where they are few and large. The potential competition of firms that may enter the market must also be taken into account. The best that can be done is to make a shrewd guess, all things considered, as to whether there are enough sellers, enough substitutes, enough independence and rivalry in the market, and sufficient freedom of entry to afford the consumer real alternatives among which he may choose.

Market Behavior

The Sherman Act is a criminal statute. It brands certain forms of behavior—conspiring to restrain trade, monopolizing a market—as misdemeanors, punishable by fine and imprisonment. The guilt or innocence of a defendant must be judged, accordingly, by determining whether he has engaged in the forbidden behavior. In appraising behavior, the courts have looked into the question of intent. In some cases, evidence of intent may be needed; in others it is not. Conduct may be ambiguous, and evidence of intent may serve to illuminate the character of overt acts. What was the firm really doing? Was it merely engaging in vigorous competition, or was it inducing unfair discrimination in buying, and practicing discriminatory sharpshooting in selling, picking off its smaller competitors one by one? There are certain types of behavior, however—price fixing, market sharing, engaging in boycotts—so inherently anticompetitive that they can be held to be illegal in themselves. In such cases, behavior alone is the test. In cases of combination and monopolization, too, where structure and performance are also relevant, behavior must be taken into account.

The legality of combination and monopolization cannot be determined by a single standard. In arriving at final judgments, every sort of evidence that is available must be brought to bear. Evidence of market structure throws light on the extent of market power. Evidence of behavior shows how this power was obtained and how it has been employed. Evidence of performance, finally, reveals the results of structure and behavior and helps to interpret their significance.

Decisions as to legality must be made, inevitably, under a rule of reason, with each of these factors given such weight as seems to be wise. They will depend on human judgment, not always impartial, always fallible, varying from judge to judge and from case to case. Complete predictability, in the area of combination and monopolization, is not to be obtained. Uncertainty is inherent in the very nature of the problem with which the law must seek to deal.

WEAKNESSES OF ANTITRUST

A third group of critics endorses the policy of maintaining competition and accepts the form in which it has been embodied in the antitrust laws, but complains that these laws have not been properly enforced. It was commonly said, some years ago, that there was lack of vigor in the execution of the laws, lack of sympathy in their interpretation, and lack of courage in the imposition of penalties and the provision of remedies. There was some basis for these charges. From 1890 to 1935, enforcement was sporadic and halfhearted. The courts have always applied the laws to conspiracy, but from 1920 to 1945 they refused to apply them to monopolization. Imprisonment of offenders was rare; until 1959 no businessman had spent a day in jail for violation of the Sherman Act. Fines imposed on corporate offenders were insignificant, amounting typically to less than one tenth of one percent of a year's net profits. The courts did not hesitate to cancel collusive agreements among separate firms or to enjoin the restrictive practices of monopolists. But they were sparing in their use of the remedy of dissolution, rarely breaking up a business enterprise.

In later years, this picture has improved. Since 1935 the laws have been enforced with greater consistency and with greater vigor. Since 1945 the courts have applied them to monopolization as well as to conspiracy. Business offenders have been imprisoned; fines have been increased; settlements in treble damage suits have run into hundreds of millions.

All this represents real progress. But the execution of the antitrust laws still leaves much to be desired. There are shortcomings in the comprehensiveness, the consistency, and the competence of enforcement. And the courts are still reluctant to dissolve a going enterprise.

Shortcomings in Enforcement

Criticisms of the enforcement of antitrust are many. Responsibility is scattered among many agencies; their activities are not coordinated. Appropriations are inadequate; the staff is too small. Action by the Antitrust Division, instead of flowing from comprehensive and continued oversight of the economy, is based upon sporadic complaints. The number of cases brought can cover but a fraction of the violations of the law. Some violators are never called to account; others are prosecuted only after long delays. Litigation is unduly protracted. Prosecutors are more interested in winning legal victories than in achieving economic reforms. The judicial process is too much concerned with legal technicalities, too little with the provision of remedies. The skills of the economist are employed in preparation of the evidence required to win a case but not in the selection of cases for prosecution, the definition of economic issues, or the fashioning of final decrees. There has been no comprehensive study of the effects of these decrees; no continuing follow-up of their observance. Litigation, in short, has serious defects as a device for solving the problems of industrial organization and practices.[19]

The alternative would be to entrust enforcement of the antitrust laws to an administrative agency as has been done, in part, with the Federal Trade Commission. Such an agency, it is said, could be staffed with experts who would concentrate on the economic problems at hand. It could act on the basis of comprehensive oversight of the economy. It could develop and follow consistent policies. It could adopt procedures that would eliminate delays. All this may be possible, but no one can contend that it describes the performance of the Federal Trade Commission during more than half a century. On balance, the record of the Commission is even less impressive than is that of the Antitrust Division. It shares the shortcomings of the Division; it has further disabilities of its own. Litigation, whatever its limitations, is accorded greater respect by the business community than is administrative action. And it has been more effective in producing results.

Reluctance to Dissolve

The government and the courts have been forthright in their condemnation of monopoly, faltering in their use of dissolution as a remedy. It is this contrast between word and deed that is said to have turned notable legal victories, such as those in aluminum and cigarettes, into economic defeats.[20]

In the aluminum case, when it finally came back to the District Court for the preparation of a remedy, the government asked that Alcoa be broken into two separate, fully integrated firms. But the court refused. Between the day in 1945 when Judge Hand found Alcoa to possess an illegal monopoly and the day in 1950 when Judge Knox handed down his final decree, the government had sold to Reynolds and Kaiser war-built factories that enabled them to establish two new integrated companies, and Alcoa's share in the output of virgin aluminum had dropped to half. The court did not find competition so effective that relief was not required. It sought to strengthen Reynolds and Kaiser by striking from Alcoa's patent contracts a provision requiring them to license Alcoa under any patents that they might obtain. And it sought to introduce a fourth competitor into the American market by severing the ties of personal stock ownership that bound Alcoa and Aluminium, Ltd. of Canada. But Alcoa was not split in two. Aluminum, said the court, is vital to national defense. It must compete with other materials made by large concerns. Dismemberment of Alcoa's research staff and its managerial personnel would lessen its ability to do so.

In the Paramount Pictures and United Shoe Machinery cases, the courts first refused to accept the government's plea for dissolution, attempting to find

19 / See Mark S. Massel, *Competition and Monopoly* (Washington, D.C.: Brookings Institution, 1962).

20 / See Walter Adams, "The Aluminum Case: Legal Victory—Economic Defeat," *American Economic Review,* Vol. XLI (1951), pp. 915-23.

remedies in decrees enjoining various forms of monopolistic behavior. But when these proved to be inadequate, orders for dissolution were handed down. In the cigarette case, however, where the companies were convicted in a criminal suit, the government itself failed to follow through by entering a dissolution plea. And in the General Electric case, the court denied the government's request that the company be dissolved. The reluctance of the courts to order dissolution is to be explained by their uncertainty concerning the possible results. They have feared, first, that a reduction in size would impair efficiency and increase costs and, second, that it would restrain the progress of technology. In this, they may have been mistaken. But lacking definite assurance, they have hesitated to act. The courts have been influenced, too, by the fear that dissolution not only would punish those guilty of monopolization but also would injure innocent parties: workers whose wages were higher because of monopoly and investors who bought securities at prices that reflected the profits of monopoly. Doubting that consumers would gain, and fearing that workers and investors would lose, they have chosen not to take a chance.[21]

Difficulties with Dissolution

Where dissolution has been effected, its consequences have been open to dispute. In the case of Standard Oil, dissolved in 1911, the holding company distributed among its stockholders, on a pro rata basis, the shares of its subsidiaries. Though the successor companies were nominally independent, their owners were identical. These companies, moreover, were organized along state lines. A community of interest was thus maintained within a group of regional monopolies. The court's decree did serve, however, to discourage open collusion and to encourage the entry of new competitors. As time passed, the concentrated stockholdings were dispersed through inheritance and sale; new firms emerged, and the dominance of the Standard companies declined. The weakness of earlier dissolution decrees led the government to propose more drastic remedies. In later cases, the Antitrust Division requested not only that combinations be dissolved but also that the ownership, control, and management of each of the successor companies be completely and perpetually separated from the ownership, control, and management of any of the others.

The largest divestiture of ownership in history was that ordered by the Supreme Court in 1957 when it remanded the case of du Pont and General Motors to the District Court for the preparation of a decree. At that time, du Pont held 63 million shares of GM stock with a market value of $2.4 billion. Contrasting methods of disposing of these holdings were proposed by the government and by du Pont. Under the government's plan, different treatment would be accorded to Christiana and Delaware, du Pont family corporations that held two fifths of the du Pont shares, and to outsiders who held three fifths of these shares. Three fifths of du Pont's holdings of GM stock would be

---

21 / Donald Dewey, "Romance and Realism in Antitrust Policy," *Journal of Political Economy*, Vol. LXIII (1955), pp. 93-102.

distributed to the outsiders, over a period of ten years, in proportion to their holdings of du Pont stock. In the meantime, these persons would be authorized to vote the GM shares. The other two fifths of the GM stock, belonging to Christiana and Delaware, would be sold on the market—publicly or privately—during the ten years, with other du Pont stockholders being given an option to buy. In the interim, Christiana and Delaware would be denied the right to vote the GM stock. This plan was rejected by du Pont as being punitive in character. Under the du Pont proposal, the company would continue to hold its GM shares and receive dividends on them. The power to vote three fifths of these shares, however, would be transferred from du Pont to the outside owners of du Pont stock. The power to vote the other two fifths would be transferred, not to Christiana and Delaware, but to the holders of stock in these concerns, i.e., to members of the du Pont family. This plan was rejected by the government as being ineffective.

Two problems were raised by the government's proposal. The first was that of taxation. Forced sale of the du Pont's family's GM shares, as it occurred, would make their owners liable under the capital gains tax. Distribution of GM shares as dividends to owners of du Pont stock would be subject to taxation as personal income. The total tax bill was estimated in the hundreds of millions. The second problem was the possible effect of the divestiture on the market value of GM and du Pont stocks. Expert witnesses for the government testified that the market could absorb 2,000,000 additional shares of GM stock each year without a significant reduction in its price. Experts for the defense testified that the sale of GM stock in such quantities would drive its price down as much as 20 to 30 percent. They argued, further, that the prices of both GM and du Pont stocks would also be depressed by sales that their holders would be forced to make to get the money to pay their added income tax.

The District Court, in a decision handed down in 1959, refused to require divestiture. The government's proposal, said Judge La Buy, would be "unnecessarily harsh and punitive," since it would impose an "enormous" tax burden on "innocent" stockholders and would have a "serious impact" on the market value of du Pont and GM stocks. The remedy adopted by the court, however, went farther than that proposed by the defense. It required du Pont to pass on to its stockholders, on a pro rata basis, the right to vote the company's GM shares. It denied Christiana and Delaware the right to vote any GM stock held by or passed on to them.

The government appealed and, in 1961, the Supreme Court reversed the District Court, holding Judge La Buy's concern lest innocent investors be harmed to be irrelevant and divestment of voting rights alone to be inadequate. It ruled that the du Ponts must dispose of their GM stock within 10 years and returned the case to the District Court to work out the details.

In 1962, Congress passed a law providing tax relief. Under its terms, a du Pont stockholder receiving GM stock was to treat it not as income but as a return of capital, paying a tax only when he sold the GM shares (or if they had increased in value since he bought his du Pont shares) and being taxed only on his capital gain at the lower rate charged on such gains. This provision was said to cut the tax liability of du Pont stockholders from $1 billion to less than $500 million.

In the same year the court handed down its final order. The du Ponts had proposed that the GM shares held by du Pont, Christiana, and Delaware be distributed among the stockholders of these corporations, including members of the du Pont family group, and that 40 members of the group be required to dispose of their GM shares within 10 years, being denied the right to vote them in the meantime. The government had objected that the du Pont family included 75 GM shareholders who would still own 8 percent of GM stock. It asked that none of the GM stock held by the du Pont corporations be allowed to pass into their hands. The court took a middle ground. It required the corporations to distribute their GM shares within three years, permitting them to distribute such shares to members of the du Pont family. The 40 persons named by the du Ponts were required to sell their shares; the 35 other persons named by the government were not. The court held that its action would reduce the du Pont family interest in GM to less than 2 percent of GM voting stock and would thus end the likelihood of further du Pont domination of GM. The government finally acquiesced. The du Pont Corporation's distribution of GM shares to its stockholders had been completed by 1965. The effect of the operation on the market values of du Pont and GM securities was imperceptible.

THE ALLEGED FAILURE OF ANTITRUST

It is often asserted and widely believed that economic power, in the United States, is concentrated in the hands of a few corporate giants, that such concentration has been increasing over the years, and that, as a result, competition has virtually disappeared from the American economy. If this were indeed the case, it might well be said that antitrust had failed. But the situation, upon examination, is far less serious than has often been supposed. There is evidence, to be sure, that corporate wealth is concentrated in the hands of larger firms, but there is little to demonstrate that concentration has been increasing, and little to justify the assertion that competition has declined.

"The Concentration of Economic Power"

A number of statistical studies have revealed the existence of substantial concentration, in the hands of a few large firms, of employment, assets, output, or income (1) among all nonbanking corporations, (2) for manufacturing as a whole, and (3) within particular manufacturing industries. These studies afford some evidence regarding the extent to which control over financial resources is concentrated in the hands of large concerns. But they tell us little or nothing about the occurrence of monopoly and competition. The concentration figures for all nonbanking corporations apply to a heterogenous group that includes railroads and public utilities, whose monopoly powers are subject to public regulation, along with several companies, like Sears, Roebuck and the A&P, that operate in highly competitive fields. The figures for manufacturing as a whole apply likewise to an undifferentiated group, ranging all the way from industries that are virtually monopolized to those that are highly competitive. The concentration ratios for particular industries are based upon a classification, employed by the Census of Manufacturers, in which industries are defined, in part, according to the materials they use and the processes they employ. In some cases, firms manufacturing many different products are lumped together in a single category. In others, products that are closely competitive are listed as coming from different industries. Data on concentration within such categories afford little insight into the structure of markets for particular goods.

Other studies reveal concentration in the output, product by product, of manufactured goods. Such ratios are frequently misleading. In some cases, the degree of concentration is understated because the output figures are nationwide and markets are regional, or because dissimilar goods are lumped together in a common category. In others, the degree of concentration is overstated because the figures are confined to domestic output and the competition afforded by imports is ignored, because the figures are confined to new goods and the competition afforded by secondhand goods is ignored, and because products that may be readily substituted for one another, such as cane sugar and beet sugar or beer bottles and beer cans, are listed in unrelated categories. The significance of the ratios is obscured, too, by the fact that they pertain only to the largest four or eight firms and do not reveal whether the members of such groups are dominated by a single firm, or approach equality of power. It should be noted, finally, that the indexes of concentration are not indexes of monopoly. They may reveal the consequences of monopolistic restriction and exclusion or those of competitive innovation, market development, and reductions in cost and price. They may conceal the influence of potential competition, and the presence—on the other side of the market—of countervailing power. The studies of concentration fall far short of proving the monopoly that they are often said to prove.

"The Decline of Competition"

There is reason to believe that monopoly made rapid headway in the United States during the latter part of the 19th century. But there is nothing to support the view that it has continued to do so during the 20th. Indeed, all the evidence that is available appears to point the other way. G. Warren Nutter, in a pioneering study of the subject, comparing the extent of monopoly obtaining in 1899 and 1939, found that the relative importance of monopoly increased only in the case of financial enterprises, remained the same in agriculture, services, trade, contract construction, and public utilities, and declined in manufacturing, mining, transport, and communications. [22] M. A. Adelman, comparing the concentration of output in the economy in 1947 with that existing around 1901,

22 / G. Warren Nutter, *The Extent of Enterprise Monopoly in the United States* (Chicago: University of Chicago Press, 1951), pp. 35-43.

concluded that "The extent of concentration shows no tendency to grow, and it may possibly be declining. Any tendency either way, if it does exist, must be at the pace of glacial drift."[23] Joe S. Bain, writing in 1959, found that there was a marked increase in business concentration from the end of the Civil War to the early 1900's and a further increase, due to the growth of public utilities, from then until the middle 1930's, but that concentration had remained relatively stable since that time, both within the economy as a whole and within its principal sectors.[24] The staff of the Cabinet Committee on Price Stability, reporting in 1969 on an analysis of 213 industries, found that market concentration "has shown no marked tendency to increase or decrease between 1947 and 1966."[25] And G. Warren Nutter and Henry A. Einhorn, in the latest comprehensive study of the subject, finding that the share of output in the private sector of the economy that was attributable to monopolistic industries fell from 19 percent in 1889 to 18 percent in 1958 while the share attributable to competitive industries rose from 81 percent to 82 percent, conclude that "there is no evidence of a significant increase in the extent of monopoly" during the 20th century.[26]

These studies may not serve completely to demolish the decline-of-competition school of economics, but they have placed upon it a heavy burden of proof. Indeed, there are signs that our economy is becoming more rather than less competitive. The boundaries of products are constantly being pushed outward as industrial research provides us with an increasing variety of ready substitutes. Frozen foods compete with canned foods, and synthetic fibers with cotton, silk, and wool. In the case of durable goods, moreover, new products must meet the competition of products sold at second hand. New cars compete with used cars, and virgin metal competes with scrap. The boundaries of markets, too, are being steadily extended by the growth of transport and communication. Refrigeration brings the fruits of California into competition with those of Florida. Hard roads bring the downtown merchant into competition with the suburban shopping center, the local merchant into competition with those in other towns. The jurisdictional lines in distribution are repeatedly breaking down. The supermarket competes with the drugstore; the discount house with the specialty shop and the department store. These signs are present in abundance for all who have eyes to see.

The Extent of Monopoly and Competition

To what extent is the American economy monopolized; to what extent is it competitive? Two estimates were made for the year 1939. According to George

23 / M. A. Adelman, "The Measurement of Industrial Concentration," *Review of Economics and Statistics*, Vol. XXXIII (1951), p. 295.

24 / Joe S. Bain, *Industrial Organization* (New York: John Wiley & Sons, 1959), chap. vi.

25 / Cabinet Committee on Price Stability, Washington, D.C., 1969, Study Paper No. 2, p. 58.

26 / G. Warren Nutter and Henry A. Einhorn, *Enterprise Monopoly in the United States: 1899-1958* (New York: Columbia University Press, 1969), pp. 89-90.

Stigler, 27 percent of the income produced in that year came from industries controlled by individual monopolists or compulsory cartels and 73 percent from industries that were competitive or unclassifiable.[27] According to Nutter, 23 percent of nongovernmental production originated in monopolistic industries, including the public utilities, and 77 percent in competitive or nonprofit industries.[28] Both of these studies have been criticized in detail by Solomon Fabricant. "Yet whatever the outcome," he concludes, "the essential validity of their conclusion must stand. All the doubts that can be raised do not destroy, rather they support, the conclusion that there is no basis for believing that the economy of the United States is largely monopolistic. . . ."[29] The same conclusion would have held in 1958. In that year, according to Nutter and Einhorn, 21.5 percent of the nation's income was produced in the public sector, 15.9 percent in private industries that were monopolized, and 62.0 percent in competitive industries. In the private sector alone, 18 percent of the output came from industries that were monopolized; 82 percent from industries that were competitive.[30]

There are some industries, in the United States, in which a high degree of concentration is the general rule. Included here are communications and other public utility enterprises, but these are granted monopoly rights and subjected to public regulation. Included, also, are certain manufacturing industries, the four largest firms, in each case, accounting, for instance, in 1963, for nine tenths of the output of telephonic equipment, electric lamps, flat glass, and chewing gum; for three fourths of the output of motor vehicles, household refrigerators, sewing machines, washing machines, vacuum cleaners, linoleum, metal cans, typewriters, and cigarettes; for two thirds of the output of aluminum, explosives, detergents, tires, computers, phonograph records, and matches; and for half of the output of steel, aircraft, motorcycles and bicycles, storage batteries, glass containers, photographic equipment, and distilled liquors.[31] In all of these fields, a disproportionate share of the output is in the hands of a few firms. But oligopoly is by no means characteristic of industry as a whole. Even in manufacturing, there are many fields in which producers are numerous and the concentration of output is low: including, for example, textiles and apparel, foods and beverages, furniture and furnishings, household appliances, leather goods, pottery and porcelain wares, and printing and publishing. In mining, too, there are fields, such as copper, where concentration is high, but there are others, such as bituminous coal, where it is low. Aside from transport, utilities,

27 / George Stigler, *Five Lectures on Economic Problems* (London: Longmans, Green & Co., 1949), p. 50.

28 / Nutter, *op. cit.*, p. 20.

29 / Solomon Fabricant, "Is Monopoly Increasing?" *Journal of Economic History*, Vol. XIII (1953), pp. 89-96.

30 / Nutter and Einhorn, *loc. cit.*

31 / Bureau of the Census, *Concentration Ratios in Manufacturing Industry, 1963* (Washington, D.C.: Government Printing Office, 1966), Table 2.

and certain manufacturing and mining industries, a high degree of concentration is rare. All other fields—agriculture, forestry, fisheries, building construction, wholesale and retail distribution, and the service trades—are, in general, actively competitive.

THE VERDICT ON ANTITRUST

Observers differ in their appraisal of the effectiveness of antitrust. In one view, held by a minority, the program has been an utter failure. It has not maintained competition. It has not prevented increasing concentration of economic power. It has permitted markets, in general, to come under the control of cartels, monopolies, and oligopolies. This view finds scant support, as we have seen, in any evidence that is at hand. No one contends that antitrust has been a complete success. But most observers would agree that it is far from having been a complete failure.

Removing Barriers to Enterprise

Controversy over the remedy of dissolution has tended to obscure the most significant contribution that antitrust has made to the maintenance of a competitive economy. In case after case, where would-be competitors have found their entry to a market obstructed or their growth hampered by monopolistic practices, they have complained against such denials of opportunity. Under their pressure, the government has brought suit. And what the courts have done is to deprive the monopolist of the devices that he has used to obstruct their entry or hamper their growth. Patents have been opened to licensing, with and without royalties. Access to know-how has been assured. The sale, as well as the lease of machinery, has been required. Tying and exclusive contracts have been invalidated. The employment of integration to handicap nonintegrated competitors has been ended by divorcement. Artificial obstacles to enterprise have thus been cleared away, and the door thrown open to competition.

In the tin can industry, the dominant position occupied by American Can was based upon three practices. First, the company refused to sell its can-closing machines, leasing them to canners at a moderate rental. Second, it tied the lease of its machines to the purchase of its cans. Third, its contracts, running for many years, forbade the canners to purchase any cans from other firms. These practices were also followed by American's only important rival, Continental Can. In such a situation, it was virtually impossible for a newcomer to break into the business of making and selling cans. The consent decrees in the American and Continental cases knocked the props from under this duopoly. The companies agreed to sell their machines as well as lease them and, when leasing, to charge compensatory rentals; to sever the tie that bound the supply of machines to the sale of cans; and to limit exclusive contracts for cans to a single year. In addition, they agreed to grant royalty-free licenses under their patents, teach other manufacturers how to make canning machines, and teach canners how to service them. As a result, most canning machinery is now owned by canners, and anybody's cans can be closed on anybody's machines. The way has thus been opened for new firms to enter the can business and for canners, if they wish, to make their own cans. [32]

Similar decrees, outlawing the particular practices that have enabled a firm to exclude newcomers from a market, have been entered against a number of other defendants, notably United Shoe Machinery and International Business Machines. Such decrees have marked advantages. They raise none of the questions posed by dissolution. Instead of arousing the fear that innocent parties will be injured, they conform to the popular view that it is unjust for opportunity to be denied. Rather than attempting to compel the survivors of a former combination to compete with one another, they release competitive forces already in being. More feasible than dissolution, they may also be more effective.

An Ounce of Prevention

It is difficult to persuade the courts to break up combinations that have existed for many years. It is less difficult to persuade them to prevent combinations from coming into being. If Bethlehem had swallowed Youngstown before the passage of the Celler-Kefauver Act, it may be doubted that Judge Weinfeld would have ordered dissolution. But when confronted with a merger that was but a plan, he did not hesitate to forbid it. Here, the problem of possible harm to vested interests did not arise. The sole concern of the court was with the intent of the law. And the decisions that have followed, in case after case, have made it clear that the Supreme Court, too, is fully prepared to give effect to this intent. If the antimerger law is vigorously enforced, and if existing precedents are followed, it may well exert a powerful influence on the future structure of the American economy.

Antitrust as a Deterrent

In a careful study of 20 industries, published in 1958, Simon N. Whitney undertook to determine the consequences of antitrust decrees. Such a determination, he found, was rendered difficult by the simultaneous operation of many factors other than antitrust: for example,

> the tremendous rise in demand for gasoline and cigarettes which coincided with the period after the antitrust dissolutions and which contributed to reshaping these industries; the changes in meat packing and food merchandising after 1920 which made the antitrust issues of 1918–20 obsolete; the rise in freight rates and boom in demand following World War II which made the steel and cement mills quite willing to accept the orders against their basing point systems and go on an f.o.b. mill pricing basis; the decline

---

32 / James W. McKie, "The Decline of Monopoly in the Metal Container Industry," *American Economic Review*, Vol. XLV, No. 2 (1955), pp. 499-508.

in demand for anthracite which made the issue of railroad-mine disintegration seem unimportant; . . . the impact of television on the motion picture industry, far outweighing the impact of what seemed to be tremendously important antitrust decrees; the low level of railroad traffic and consequent decline in orders for Pullman cars which came just as the Pullman divorcement took place, and considerably reduced its importance; and the emergence of the king-size and filter-tip cigarettes, sharply modifying the dominance of three brands which had seemed impregnable to the Supreme Court in 1946. [33]

In some cases, the effects of antitrust suits were "unexpected and baffling," as when "steel and cement companies directed to drop the basing point method of pricing stopped absorbing freight and thereby increased their profits," and when "the railroads, under protection of court orders aimed in part to safeguard them against exorbitant terms in their contracts with the Pullman Company, found themselves saddled with all the headaches of the sleeping-car business." [34] On balance, however, Whitney concluded that the antitrust laws had made three important contributions to the maintenance of competition: they had prevented the cartelization of American industry along European lines; they had barred consolidations intended to enable firms to dominate their industries; they had helped to preserve freedom of entry and equality of opportunity. In all of this, moreover, their influence as a deterrent had been even more important than the visible consequences of their remedies. [35]

This is a judgment with which most economists would agree. Corwin D. Edwards concludes that the antitrust laws "made it necessary for monopolistic and collusive restraints of trade to be nominally secret. They prevented any general endorsement of such arrangements by public authorities or responsible business organizations and forestalled most efforts to make participation in private restrictions compulsory. . . . They thus prevented the appearance in the United States of a formally organized and state-supported cartel system." [36] Edward S. Mason finds that "the consideration of whether a particular course of business action may or may not be in violation of the antitrust acts is a persistent factor affecting business judgment." [37] And A. D. Neale, a British scholar, concludes from his study of the antitrust laws that "the operation of antitrust reflects pretty well the balance of opinion in the United States: first, that private unaccountable persons should not wield significant amounts of economic power; secondly, that should they seek to do so, they should be checked by a rule of law." [38]

33 / Simon N. Whitney, *Antitrust Policies* (New York: Twentieth Century Fund, 1958), Vol. II, p. 429.

34 / *Ibid.*, pp. 430-31.

35 / *Ibid.*, pp. 436-37.

36 / Corwin D. Edwards, *Maintaining Competition* (New York: McGraw-Hill Book Co., 1949), p. 294.

37 / *American Economic Review*, Vol. XXXIX (1949), 713.

38 / A. D. Neale, *The Antitrust Laws of the United States* (Cambridge, England: Cambridge University Press, 1962), p. 469.

Alternatives to Competition

It is unrealistic to pass judgment on the maintenance of competition, as its critics often do, without also considering the nature of the possible alternatives. What are they? In practice, laissez-faire is not among them. If monopoly cannot be prevented or eliminated, it will ultimately be subjected in one way or another to public control. In general, the choice lies between public enterprise and public regulation of private enterprise. There are particular cases, of course, in which these policies are unavoidable or even desirable. The question is not whether they should be used at all but whether they are to be preferred, as a general solution, to antitrust. Experience with public regulation and with public enterprise will be examined, respectively, in Parts III and IV of this book. It will be found there that these policies, too, have encountered difficulties and have achieved something less than complete success.

PART III

Controlling Monopoly by Regulation

Chapter 12   THE TASK OF REGULATION

It has been the general policy of government in the United States to maintain a competitive economy. Exceptions have been made, however, in the case of certain industries where monopoly has appeared to be inevitable and even desirable. Here, deprived of competition as an instrument of discipline, government has sought to protect the interests of consumers by itself undertaking to regulate rates and services.

The industries thus treated fall into two broad groups. In the first are those supplying water, electricity, gas, telephone, and transit services in local markets, together with those transmitting electricity and gas and providing communication by telephone and telegraph over long distances. Such industries are known as public utilities. They include many different companies. But each of these companies sells in a market where it possesses a monopoly. It can therefore be handled as a separate unit, its rates fixed with some precision at a level that will cover its costs and yield it a desired return. In the second group are industries providing interregional transport: railroads, motor carriers, water carriers, and airlines. The firms in these industries do not possess complete monopolies. Each type of carrier competes with many of the others, and most of them compete among themselves. Such firms cannot be treated separately; where they compete, their rates must correspond. Their costs, however, may not be the same. As a consequence, their earnings will differ, one receiving more, another less. In this case, regulation cannot yield precise results. But in both cases, the methods it uses are the same.

The problems that are common to all industries where rates and services are regulated will be considered in this chapter and the two that follow. Those that are peculiar to public utilities will be discussed in Chapter 15; those peculiar to transport, in Chapters 16 and 17; and those peculiar to communications in Chapter 18. One other industry—radio and television broadcasting—has been singled out for regulation, but for quite a different reason and in quite a different way. This story will be told in Chapter 19.

THE RATIONALE OF REGULATION

Regulation of rates and services was based, at the outset, on the assumption that the economic characteristics of the regulated industries were such as to set them apart from other businesses. These industries, it appeared, were naturally monopolistic. Their services were indispensable. They performed, as it were, a public function. The people, with no alternatives, depended upon them. Yet they operated as private enterprises, conducted for profit. Being free of competition, they could exploit their powers to the public detriment. Government was, therefore, compelled to intervene to safeguard the public interest. Regulation was thus a substitute for competition. Where competition was impossible, its purpose was to bring the benefits that competition would have brought.

Such was the logic of regulation. Even at the beginning, it was oversimplified. And with the passage of time, important amendments were required. But the logic still contains a core of truth.

Characteristics of Regulated Industries

In most of the industries subjected to regulation (railroads and public utilities, for instance, but not motor or water carriers) operations must be conducted on a large scale in order to attain low unit costs. Plants are huge and highly specialized, involving heavy investments and high fixed charges. They may be built in anticipation of demand. And until demand develops, their capacity will be but partly used. Plants must be big enough, in any case, to satisfy demand at its peak. The service they produce cannot be stored. In off-peak periods, therefore, capacity stands idle. But whatever the volume of output, fixed charges have to be met. In such a situation, cost per unit will diminish as volume is increased: the part of this cost that varies with output (materials, wages, etc.) may be unaffected, but the part that is constant (interest, administration, etc.) will decline. Volume may be increased by reducing rates. There is therefore a strong incentive to compete in price. But such competition may become destructive. For it will always be to the advantage of a company to keep on cutting prices—if it must do so to keep from losing business—as long as they continue to cover its variable costs and contribute something toward its overhead. Price warfare, if carried far enough, will drive an industry into bankruptcy, impairing its capacity to serve. More likely, this fate will be averted by combination or by agreement as to rates. These industries, thus, are said to be natural monopolies. And, as such, they are set apart for special treatment by the state.

As a justification for regulation, however, this argument has been over-emphasized. The railroads, after the Civil War, did engage in rate wars. But among the public utilities such warfare has been the exception rather than the rule. In both cases, combination and agreement have been usual. But, in this, the regulated industries are not unique. The steel industry, for instance, and the automobile industry involve large-scale production, heavy investment, and high fixed costs. They may have idle capacity and be tempted to put it to work by competing vigorously in price. Here, again, such competition could become destructive. And here, too, this outcome has been forestalled by combination and agreement, whether explicit or merely understood. This is the familiar pattern of oligopoly. The argument just recited could be used with equal force to justify the regulation of any industry where plants are costly and firms are few. The distinction between those that are regulated and those that are not must be made on other grounds.

In the case of public utilities there are other bases for monopoly. With most of them competition is confined by local market boundaries. It is limited, too, by the fact that their facilities must be located in city streets. There is a physical limit to the number of tracks that can be laid upon a street, the wires that can be strung above it, and the mains that can be buried below it. There is an even narrower limit to public tolerance of the nuisance that would be involved in duplicating such facilities. Some services, moreover, are of such a nature that competition would be undesirable. Urban transit is more convenient where cars are pooled and where connections can be made. Telephone service is more convenient where all subscribers are connected through the switchboards of a single company. Under such circumstances, monopoly is to be preferred.

But this alone does not explain control of rates and services. For competition has been lacking in other industries where regulation is unknown. The explanation lies, rather, in the buyer's disadvantage in bargaining. With steel, for instance, purchases are made, not by the ultimate consumer, but by oligopsonists who are able to protect themselves. With automobiles, they are made by the consumer, but they are nonessential, infrequent, and can be postponed. The availability of used cars, moreover, and variations in trade-in values afford him numerous alternatives. He does not demand protection by the state. With utility services, however, it is otherwise. They are essentials bought continuously by many small consumers. For them, the need is urgent and is not postponable. And there are no acceptable alternatives. The buyer must meet the seller's terms or go without. It is this that sets the public utilities apart, explaining why regulation is required.

Elsewhere, however, this explanation does not suffice. For transport, though increasingly competitive, is also increasingly controlled. Between those industries that are regulated and those that are not, no hard and fast line can be drawn by the economist. Nor has such a line been drawn by the courts.

Legal Status of Regulated Industries

For many years, as we saw in Chapter 2, the Supreme Court attempted to permit regulation where it seemed to be needed and to forbid it where it did not by placing in a separate category those industries that it found to be "affected with a public interest." For nearly half a century, from its decision in *Munn* v. *Illinois* in 1877 to that in the Wolff Packing Company case in 1923, the Court enlarged this category, being liberal in approving regulatory powers. But during the next decade it tightened up, repeatedly striking down the efforts of the states to regulate. There is, however, no clear principle by which to distinguish the cases in which the legislatures were upheld from those in which they were reversed. The tests of public interest most often mentioned by the Court were the essentiality of the service provided and the absence of competition in providing it. But neither of these criteria was followed with consistency. The rule of the law, in effect, was that an industry was affected with a public interest if the Court said so and was not if it said not.

Then in 1934 the Court handed down its decision in the Nebbia case, permitting the state of New York to fix a minimum price for milk even though the business of producing and distributing milk had none of the usual characteristics of a public utility. The doctrine of affectation with a public interest was thus discarded. As the law now stands, an industry can be regulated whenever the legislature decides to act. If some rates are controlled, it is because the people have demanded action. If others are uncontrolled, it is because they have not.

Purposes of Regulation

The crux of regulation is control of rates. The general level of rates is controlled to prevent monopolists from charging monopoly prices and obtaining monopoly profits, to promote wide use of the service, and to insure continued progress by requiring that gains in efficiency and advances in technology be passed on in lower rates. The structure of rates is controlled to prevent discrimination that would be unduly favorable to some consumers and unduly prejudicial to others. Service also must be controlled, to guarantee its availability and to make sure it is adequate in quantity and acceptable in quality. Otherwise, the ground gained in reducing rates might well be lost. If the quantity and quality of service are to be maintained, the financial stability of the regulated enterprise must be preserved. Rates cannot be set so low as to impair its credit. And its financial operations must be controlled. For all of these purposes, finally, it is necessary to regulate company accounts. For it is only through accurate accounting that control of rates and services and finances can be effectively administered.

THE REGULATORY COMMISSIONS

Industries have been regulated by the terms of decisions handed down by courts at common law, by the terms of franchises granted by cities and charters granted by states, and by the terms of ordinances enacted by city councils and statutes enacted by state legislatures. Each of these methods proved ineffective, as was seen in Chapter 2. Control by the courts was spasmodic and negative in character, coming only when suits were brought and injury was proved. Control by franchises and charters was clumsy and inflexible. Control by ordinances and statutes had the same defects. Governments eventually turned, therefore, to administrative regulation. In some cases, responsibility for such regulation is entrusted to a single official within an executive department. In the case of public utilities, it was entrusted to semi-independent commissions operating under general legislative powers. These bodies were to have the advantages of expertness, flexibility, and impartiality. They came to be the characteristic means by which rates and services are controlled.

The first commissions, with jurisdiction over railroads, were set up in the New England states before the Civil War. Their powers, however, were largely advisory. Railroad commissions with mandatory powers were first established in the Midwest in the early seventies. And in 1887 Congress established the Interstate Commerce Commission. Thereafter, the regulation of railroads passed largely into the hands of the federal government.

Commission regulation of public utilities was slower to develop. These services, in general, came later than the railroads. Abuses, until notorious, went unrecognized. Legislatures, in the absence of public clamor, were slow to act. The first utility commissions were set up in 1907 in Wisconsin and New York. Thereafter, in some states, the railroad commissions were given jurisdiction over public utilities. And in others, they were abolished and utility commissions set up in their place. By 1920 utilities had been brought under commission control in more than two thirds of the states. But the commissions were often limited in jurisdiction and in power. The need for regulation outran the ability to regulate. Then, after the market crash of 1929 and the financial scandals that followed, the state commissions were strengthened, their jurisdiction extended, and their powers increased.

Today there are commissions in all the states, most of them known as public utility or public service commissions, a few of them still as railroad commissions, and a few others as corporation commissions. There are also five federal commissions with authority over transportation and interstate utilities. The commission form of regulation is well entrenched.

The State Commissions

Among the state commissions in 1968, nearly all had jurisdiction over railroads, motor carriers, water, electricity, gas, and telephones, with half or more empowered to regulate street railways, taxicabs, and gas pipelines.[1] In general, the commissions had been given power to control rates, fixing them at reasonable levels and preventing undue discrimination, and to control the quantity and the quality of services. About four fifths of them were authorized to regulate utility finances, and all of them were empowered to control the methods of accounting and to require reports.

In size, the commissions range from one member in Oregon and Rhode Island to seven in Massachusetts and South Carolina; the usual number is three. Their members are appointed by the governor in 36 jurisdictions, most of them in the North, and elected by the people in 15, the latter being in the South and West. The qualifications required by law are few: membership usually must be bi-partisan, and members must be citizens and residents without financial interests in the regulated industries. But the members need not have training or experience in engineering, economics, accounting, or law. Few commissioners, in fact, have had technical competence. Elections are won through other qualities, and appointments are often made as a reward for political services. The salaries

1 / *Book of the States, 1968-69* (Chicago: Council of State Governments, 1969), p. 518.

paid commissioners are low. In 1967 there were three states that paid from $25,000 to $30,000, but there were eight that paid $10,000 or less and the median salary was around $15,000. These figures, obviously, do not compare to the payments made to officials of the regulated industries. The tenure of commissioners, finally, is short. The terms fixed by law run from 2 to 10 years; the term in three quarters of the states is 6 years. Some commissioners are reappointed, but most of them serve a single term or even less.

Some of the commissions are organized along functional lines, with divisions for rates, engineering, accounting, financial, and legal work; others are organized into separate divisions for different utilities; and still others into some combination of the two. The stronger commissions are staffed with technical experts, with fair salaries and some assurance of tenure. But, in general, the staffs are small and poorly trained. There were more than 500 staff members in two states in 1967, but there were fewer than 25 in fifteen states, the median numbering around 60. About half of the commissions had only two or three engineers, accountants, and attorneys on their staffs; some had none. Only five commissions had economists. Staff salaries varied, but most of the professional personnel were paid less than $11,000. Commission budgets are inadequate: in 1967 the total spent by all state commissions was $65 million, but a third of this was spent by three commissions with budgets of $5,000,000 to $10,000,000, while each of 20 commissions spent less than $400,000.[2] A utility corporation may spend far more than this to fight a single case. Litigation by the companies is financed by those who pay their rates. The commissions, too, are so financed: since 1930 their funds have come increasingly from levies imposed on the utilities.

The commissions have been given a measure of independence. Their membership is bipartisan, their terms are so staggered that no governor, in his own term, can appoint a majority, and their members cannot be removed without serious cause.

Commission Procedure

Much of the work done by the Commissions originates in complaints made by consumers. These deal, in the main, with the availability and quality of service, the accuracy of meters, and the application of different items in the schedule of rates. Such matters are handled informally, adjustments being obtained, in most cases, without undue delay. If bus service is irregular, if water pressure is low, and if complaints to the bus and water companies bring no improvement, an approach to the regulatory commission may well produce results. The commissions, however, make little effort to inform consumers concerning their availability to perform this service. Most consumers, in fact, are unaware that such commissions exist.

2 / Charles F. Phillips, Jr., *The Economics of Regulation,* Rev. Ed. (Homewood, Ill.: Richard D. Irwin, Inc., 1969), pp. 96-100.

More important cases have to do with the general level of rates. During periods when costs have been falling, such cases have been originated by complaints from city officials, large industrial users, or other consuming groups. Most commissions have the power to make investigations and institute proceedings on their own initiative. But many of them have lacked the will or the ability to do so, acting as if they were judicial bodies passively waiting for complaints. This attitude of impartiality has served the interest of the utilities, since consumers have usually lacked the knowledge and the resources that would enable them to bring a case. During periods of inflation, however, when costs are rising, requests for increases in rates are brought by the companies. And here, delay in action or refusal to act may work to their disadvantage, serving the consumer interest.

Rate-level cases may be handled informally or formally. Reductions have sometimes resulted from negotiations between commissioners and utility officials. In some instances, formal action has been avoided as long as there was any hope of obtaining an informal settlement. But concessions are more likely to be obtained if there is some prospect that formal measures will be used.

Formal cases take more time, require more work, and cost more money. They involve procedures that are specified by law, elaborated in administrative rulings, and subject to judicial review. Public notice must be given and formal hearings held. Witnesses may be subpoenaed and compelled to produce records and documents. Some commissions have left complainants to their own resources. Others have assisted them by conducting investigations and introducing evidence. Cases are prepared and argued by one division of a commission's staff; initial decisions may be made by an examiner; final decisions are made by the commission itself. These decisions must be accompanied by formal findings of facts. They may lead to orders requiring changes in rates and services. Such orders cannot be enforced by the commissions themselves. If not accepted, they must be taken to the courts.

Federal Regulatory Agencies

There are more than a dozen federal agencies that are charged with responsibility for regulating business activity. Some of them are independent commissions whose functions do not include the regulation of rates or services. Three of these agencies (the Federal Trade Commission, the National Labor Relations Board, and the Equal Employment Opportunity Commission) regulate particular aspects of business in general and three (the Federal Maritime Board, the Atomic Energy Commission, and the Securities and Exchange Commission) control the activities of particular businesses. There are also regulatory agencies within the departmental structure, not organized as commissions (the Food and Drug Administration, the Federal Aviation Administration, the Federal Water Pollution Control Administration, the Commodity Exchange Authority, and the Packers and Stockyards Administration), that have functions other than the regulation of rates and services. The functions of most of these agencies are considered, in their respective contexts, in various Parts of this book, discussion of the last two being omitted for want of space. There are four independent commissions, finally, (the Interstate Commerce Commission, the Federal Power Commission, the Federal Communications Commission, and the Civil Aeronautics Board) that regulate transport and utility rates and services. It is with the work of these four agencies that the present Part is primarily concerned.

The Interstate Commerce Commission is the oldest of the federal commissions. Set up in 1887, it now controls railroads, oil pipelines, interstate motor carriers and water carriers, and a number of other transport agencies such as freight forwarders and express companies. The Federal Power Commission, first created in 1920 with three cabinet officers as members, was reorganized in 1930 with full-time independent membership. It now has jurisdiction over power projects on navigable rivers, interstate transmission of electricity and natural gas, and determination of the field price of natural gas. The Federal Communications Commission, established in 1933, took over the regulation of interstate telephone and telegraph services from the ICC and that of radio and television from the Federal Radio Commission of 1927. The Civil Aeronautics Board, set up in 1938, controls entry into civil aviation, and routes, rates, and subsidies. The regulation of air traffic, safety, and other aspects of airline operations is in the hands of the Federal Aviation Administration.

The ICC has 11 members, the FCC has seven, and the FPC and the CAB each has five. Membership is bipartisan and members can have no financial interest in the industries they control. No other qualifications are established in the laws. Appointments are made by the President for overlapping terms running from five to seven years. Salaries are higher than those paid by the states, commissioners receiving $38,000 and commission chairmen $40,000 a year. The tenure of members of the ICC is fairly long; reappointment is common, commissioners serving, on the average, for more than 13 years. With the other agencies, however, this is not the case, members of the FPC typically serving for little more than a single term and members of the FCC and the CAB for only a fraction of a term. Appropriations for the work of the federal commissions are larger than those made for the commissions in the states, amounting to $27 million for the ICC, $14 million for the FPC, $18 million for the FCC, and $11 million for the CAB. Their staffs, too, are larger than those found in the states, numbering 1,900 for the ICC, 1,100 for the FPC, 1,400 for the FCC, and about 800 for the CAB. Observers have found commission personnel to be well qualified and conscientious. Their rate of turnover, however, is high. Work loads are growing and commission action is delayed.[3]

RATES AND EARNINGS

The regulation of rates has two aspects: control of the rate level and control of the rate structure. The former has to do with the size of a corporation's

3 / *Ibid.*, p. 104.

earnings. Here, the commissions are concerned that the return yielded by the rates be neither so high as to exploit consumers nor so low as to discourage investors. The rate structure has to do with the particular rates paid for different units of service by different classes of customers. Here, the problem is discrimination. The regulated industries are not forbidden to discriminate. But the commissions must take care lest the manner of discrimination be unfair or unreasonable, favoring some customers and harming others.

The Rate Level

The general level of rates should be high enough, first, to cover the current costs of operation and, second, to yield a proper return on the money invested in facilities. This return should be high enough to do two things. Looking backward, it should be fair to investors, avoiding impairment of the value of their property. Looking forward, it should preserve the credit standing of the regulated company so that it will be able to attract the capital it will need if its service is to be maintained, improved, and expanded in response to consumer demand. If earnings do more than this, the company will obtain monopoly profits at the expense of its customers. If they do less, its service will fall short in quantity and will decline in quality.

Control of the rate level involves three different processes. First, it is necessary to control operating expenses. These expenses are the largest sum that must be covered in the rates. If they are inflated, through dishonesty or inefficiency, the rates will be too high. To prevent this, methods of accounting must also be controlled. Second, it is necessary to determine the rate of return on investment that is to be taken as fair to consumers and investors and as adequate for the maintenance of credit. This rate is expressed as a percentage of the value of a company's property. Third, it is necessary to determine this value. This process involves the estimation of construction costs and the deduction of depreciation. Here, again, control of accounting is required, since inflation of the rate base would necessitate the allowance of larger earnings and higher rates. Methods of valuation differ, as do methods of allowing for depreciation. It is here that the major controversies over regulation centered for nearly half a century.

The commissions operate within the limits of the Constitution as it is interpreted by the courts. In its Fifth Amendment, the Constitution forbids the federal government to deprive any person of property without due process of law. In the Fourteenth Amendment, it imposes a similar prohibition on the states. The word "person," as we saw in Chapter 2, has been interpreted to mean corporation, the word "property" to mean corporate earnings and the value of corporate investment, and the words "due process" to comprehend not only the procedure followed in setting rates but also the adequacy of the rates themselves. The courts thus undertook to review the rates that the commissions set. Their concern, primarily, was to protect investors. Their attention was focused upon the adequacy of earnings. And in judging earnings, the issues brought before them usually related, not to the percentage adopted as a fair rate of return, but to the method used in measuring the rate base. The matter of valuation thus became the heart of the problem of controlling rates. It is only in recent years that the courts have left this matter to the discretion of the regulatory agencies.

Even now, control of rates is neither continuous nor tight. No effort is made to eliminate excessive earnings the moment they appear. Earnings are examined on complaint, or on commission initiative, perhaps no oftener than once in a decade. In the meantime, if demand has grown and costs have declined, returns that are excessive may be realized and retained. There is no assurance, however, that earnings will be adequate. As costs rise, commissions may be slow to grant corresponding increases in rates. And as demand falls, earnings may fall whatever the rates allowed. Surpluses are not seized and deficits are not made up as they appear.

These, in general, are the problems that must be faced in considering control of the level of rates. They are to be discussed in greater detail in Chapter 13.

The Rate Structure

The regulated company is a monopolist or a semimonopolist. It sells the same service to different classes of buyers. But it does not charge them all the same price. In part, the differences in price can be explained in terms of differences in cost. But, in large part, they cannot. And here, the company discriminates. Being a monopolist, it seeks to maximize its revenues by charging more where demand is strong and alternatives lacking, less where demand is weak and alternatives available. If such discrimination were forbidden, sales might well be smaller, costs higher, and prices therefore higher for consumers as a whole. Discrimination, thus, may be desirable, but it is also dangerous. The seller who discriminates may willfully favor one buyer over another, giving the former an unfair advantage and placing the latter under an unfair handicap. In regulated industries, therefore, the extent of discrimination that is practiced cannot be left to the companies but must be controlled by the commissions and the courts. The problems encountered in regulating the structure of rates will be considered in Chapter 14.

SERVICE, SAFETY, AND EFFICIENCY

"Service and efficiency," writes J. M. Clark, "are coordinate parts of any attempt to control prices; first, because it does the buyer no good to pay a lower price if the quality or quantity he gets for his money is lowered in the same proportion, giving him gas, for instance, of four fifths the former heating power for four fifths the former price. Second, it does the buyer no good to compel the producer to accept half the former net earnings if he gets in exchange a management half as efficient, for the poor management will add more to the costs of operation than the regulating commission can take away in reduced earnings."[4] In practice, the commissions have devoted some attention to quantity and quality of service and safety of operation but little to efficiency of management.

Quantity of Service

The quantitative controls over service are those relating to entry, extension, and abandonment. Where city streets are used, a company wishing to enter a utility industry must obtain a franchise from the city government. In all regulated industries, moreover, an entrant must apply to the relevant commission for a "certificate of public convenience and necessity." By denying certificates, it is thought, a commission can prevent speculative construction, overcapacity, and ruinous competition, thus assuring financial stability and continued service at regulated rates. But it may also impede progress by protecting old investments against the challenge of new technology.

A company with no competitors may be slow to expand its service even though demand has grown. Under regulation, however, expansion may be required. A commission cannot compel a concern to extend its operation into new territories. And it will take no initiative in ordering extensions within a region where operations are already under way. But it is likely to act, upon complaint, to force the concern, within this region, to extend to new customers the service it has been providing to older ones. It may not issue such an order where an extension would entail a substantial loss. But it may do so even though some loss would be incurred.

A commission cannot prevent a company from abandoning all its operations. But commissions can and do prohibit partial abandonments. This problem has been of small importance to the utility commissions, since they have been dealing, in the main, with expanding industries. It has been of great importance, however, to the ICC. Branch lines of railroads have become unprofitable as a result of exhaustion of resources, relocation of industry, and the increasing competition of motor carriers. The Commission has therefore been faced with many requests for abandonment. With a decline in the demand for passenger service, too, there have been requests for curtailment of the number of runs on main lines. The Commission has granted some of these requests but denied others, even though the services had to be rendered at a loss. Commissions may hesitate to require unprofitable extensions. But they are even more reluctant to deprive consumers of service they already have.

Quality of Service

The regulatory commissions are usually empowered to prescribe reasonable standards of service, requiring the regulated companies to conform. With most

4 / J. M. Clark, *Social Control of Business* (2d ed.; New York: McGraw-Hill Book Co., 1939), p. 337.

public utilities, these standards may include such matters as continuity of service, accuracy of meters, deposits and repayments, methods of billing, and the treatment of complaints. They may also define the quality of service in terms of technical dimensions and establish permissible limits of variation. For water, there may be standards of purity and pressure; for electricity, limits to variation in voltage; for gas, standards of heat content measured in British thermal units, limits to the percentage of impurities, and requirements as to the amount and steadiness of pressure. Telephone service, conceivably, could be controlled by limiting the number of subscribers on a line, specifying the amount and quality of equipment to be provided, reducing interference in transmission, and shortening the time required in completing calls. Urban transit, finally, might be governed by standards of cleanliness, ventilation, lighting and heating of cars, frequency of service, adherence to schedules, and adequacy of rush-hour service in terms of the ratio of seats to passengers and the number of square feet provided per standee.

The danger of prescribing service standards is that technology will be frozen, progress impeded, and managerial initiative impaired. This is a danger that the utility commissions have been able to avoid. In practice, little has been done in the way of developing and enforcing standards of quality. The utilities take the initiative, the commissions intervening only on complaint. The results, over the years, appear to have been good. Innovations in service have been numerous and the quality of service has been high. Since the mid-sixties, however, there have been massive power failures in the northeastern states and serious impairment of telephone service in metropolitan New York.

The railroads are a special case. Railroad freight service broke down completely during the First World War. Thereafter, the ICC was given extensive powers with respect to such matters as car supply, switching service, interconnection of carriers, interchange of traffic, the establishment of through routes and joint rates, and the joint use of terminals. As a result, and through the efforts of railroad managements, freight service was improved. But the quality of passenger service has steadily declined. Here, the powers granted to state and federal authorities have been inadequate and their exercise ineffective.

Safety

Along with service, regulation has to do with safety. This is true of all utilities. Prevention of explosion from gas leaks and of fire from unguarded wiring is a matter of public concern. Assurance of safety bulks large in the use of atomic energy as a fuel for the generation of electricity. But safety has been most important in the regulation of transport. Requirements are established, for all types of carriers, governing such matters as the character of equipment, the use of safety devices, the qualifications and hours of employees, the transportation of explosives, speed, and the investigation of accidents. Detailed regulations applying to railroads control the length of trains and the size of crews, provide for boiler inspection and the elimination or protection of grade crossings, and require the use of block signals, automatic couplers, and power brakes. It is in the case of aviation, however, that safety comes first of all. The safety work of the Federal Aviation Administration and the Civil Aeronautics Board will be described in Chapter 17.

Efficiency

Under private enterprise, efficiency and progress are normally evoked by the promise of profit and the penalty of loss. But where rates and earnings are regulated, the profit incentive is weakened or diverted to other ends. In the case of transport, a common rate is fixed for all of the carriers in a group. The carrier with lower costs earns more; the one with higher costs earns less. So some incentive is retained. But if the group as a whole reduces its costs, its rates will be cut. And if it increases them, its rates will be raised. In the case of public utilities, moreover, this procedure is applied to the individual firm. If regulation is tight, earnings cannot be enlarged by cutting costs. Let management be diligent in this cause, then rates will be reduced. Let it be indolent, then rates will be increased. There is no incentive to efficiency. Earnings, however, may be enlarged in other ways. The rate base can be expanded by unnecessary and extravagant investment. Operating expenses can be padded, property valuations inflated, and regulation obstructed by ceaseless litigation. But here, the profit incentive runs against the public interest.

If regulation were tight, efficiency would have to be sought through detailed supervision of operations. Orders would have to be issued and performance checked. The regulatory agencies would have to duplicate the central functions of management. In fact, however, regulation is not tight. With rate reductions lagging behind cost reductions, sometimes for many years, there is still an incentive to efficiency. But this incentive persists, not where regulation works well, but where it fails to work.

CORPORATE FINANCE AND INTERCORPORATE RELATIONS

Control of the finances of regulated companies is designed to protect consumers and investors by preventing overcapitalization, by maintaining a proper balance in capital structures, and by averting defeat of the purposes of regulation through various intercorporate relationships. It involves the power to disapprove security issues, to forbid combinations, and to supervise intercorporate transactions. In 1920 authority over the finances of railroads was given to the ICC. But until 1930 such authority with respect to public utilities was either lacking or was little exercised. Since that time, however, financial controls have been imposed by most of the states and by a number of federal agencies. Such controls are crucially important. Not only are they needed in themselves but they may also be employed in support of other regulatory activities. A request for approval of an issue of securities may afford an occasion for review of rates and services. Permission may be given on condition that rates be cut or services improved. Where these matters are settled through negotiation, a commission's power over security issues provides it with a stronger hand in bargaining.

Control of Capitalization

The base to which a percentage return is applied in computing a company's earnings is the value of the property it employs in rendering its service, not the value of its outstanding stocks and bonds. One might suppose, therefore, that overcapitalization would not matter, since the company's rates would not be affected if it were overcapitalized. But this, in fact, is not the case. Overcapitalization creates strong pressure for funds to use in paying interest and dividends. These funds may be obtained by charging high rates or giving poor service. The overcapitalized company is certain to seek high rates. If it is held to a fair return on its actual assets, it may have little or nothing left, after paying interest, to distribute in dividends. In this case, its stock will decline in value and it may be unable to raise further capital by selling new securities. With rates held down, the company may obtain the funds required for dividends by setting aside inadequate reserves for depreciation or by skimping maintenance. In either case, service eventually will suffer. Confronted with such a situation, a commission is likely to set rates at a level that will permit the payment of dividends on watered stock, preserving the company's credit and its ability to serve.

There is little that can be done about overcapitalization in the past. When companies go through bankruptcy and must be reorganized, however, water can be squeezed out, and the value of securities limited to the actual value of properties. In some cases, short of bankruptcy, voluntary revaluations may be obtained. But prevention of overcapitalization, in the main, has to do with new issues of securities, floated to finance new enterprises, combinations, and expanded operations by existing companies.

In controlling new issues, the commissions are concerned with their purposes, their size, and the cost of their distribution. Issues are not approved unless for necessary purposes and in amounts required to satisfy these purposes. Expenditure of the proceeds is supervised to make sure that they are used for the purposes approved. The costs of distribution are limited by fixing the minimum prices to be received by the issuers, by fixing the margins to be retained by the underwriters, and in some cases by requiring the placement of issues through competitive bidding.

Many railroad and utility companies have long had close relationships with particular banking houses, invariably employing these houses to market their securities. This practice has been defended on the ground that it assures the borrower sound advice and responsible service. It has been attacked on the ground that it gives the banker an excessive margin and the borrower a smaller share of the investor's dollar than he would otherwise receive. In 1926 competitive bidding for certain railway securities was required by the ICC. In 1939 and

1941 competitive bidding for issues under their jurisdiction was required by the FPC and the SEC. Similar requirements have been made by some of the state commissions. But this is not the general rule.

The Capital Structure

Regulation concerns itself not only with aggregate capitalization but also with the relative proportions of different types of securities and the terms on which they are issued. If too large a part of a company's capital is in the form of bonds, its fixed charges will be high and it will be less able to weather a depression. Its ability to meet future needs by borrowing will also be impaired. The commissions are therefore likely to limit the share of bonds, usually to half or thereabouts of total capital. To preserve a company's ability to raise new capital through sales of common stock, they may also maintain the value of outstanding common by limiting the fraction of preferred.

Protection of investors is an end in itself. But it is also undertaken to maintain a company's credit and thus its capacity to render service. The SEC and some of the state commissions now protect bondholders by regulating the provisions of bond indentures. They may attempt to insure the availability of funds to pay interest and principal by limiting the distribution of dividends and by requiring the accumulation of sinking funds. They may safeguard the value of mortgaged properties by specifying the provisions to be made for maintenance and depreciation. The commissions may also protect stockholders by preventing an inequitable distribution of voting power. To this end, they may forbid the issuance of nonvoting shares and of shares with multiple or contingent voting rights. In reorganizations, finally, the ICC and the SEC attempt to make sure that the relative rights of all classes of security holders are observed.

Combinations and Intercorporate Controls

One corporation may obtain the assets of another by leasing them or by getting a controlling interest in the latter's stock. Two or more corporations may be combined, in fact, through outright merger. Or a third corporation may combine them, in effect, by controlling their shares. All these forms of combination and acquisition of control are now subject to regulation, in one way or another, by public agencies. In the case of transport, the elimination of competition was forbidden, until 1920, under the Sherman Act. But it has been permitted, since that time, upon approval by the ICC and, in the case of airlines, by the CAB. In exercising supervision over these matters, the agencies concern themselves not only with the effect of their action on competition in service but also with its effect on the financial strength of the carriers and on the welfare of investors in their securities. When combination is permitted, total capitalization and the character of the capital structure can be controlled.

The most serious problems of intercorporate relationship are those created by the holding company. This device has been used, in many cases, as a means of defeating the purposes of regulation. The holding company votes the controlling shares in a subordinate operating company, elects its directors, and chooses its management. It then enters into business transactions with the operating company, borrowing from it, lending to it, and selling it properties, goods, and services. None of these transactions is the result of arm's-length bargaining. The holding company may borrow at a low rate of interest and lend at a high rate. It may charge exorbitant prices for properties, equipment, and supplies, and for construction, financing, management, and other services. By so doing, it pads the costs of the operating company and enlarges the base upon which earnings are allowed. As a result, so long as holding company charges are beyond the reach of the commissions, they must be covered by raising operating company rates. The holding company, moreover, may seek to enhance its revenues by forcing the operating company to make inadequate provisions for depreciation and maintenance and thus to pay larger dividends, impairing its ultimate strength. If regulation is to be effective, it is obvious that holding companies must be controlled. Before the thirties, such control was either lacking or seriously inadequate. In 1933 the ICC was given jurisdiction over railroad holding companies. In 1935 the SEC was given extensive powers with respect to public utility holding companies. The state commissions, too, were granted new authority. The holding company loophole was nearly if not entirely closed.

Interutility Competition

Regulation, in its origin, was justified by the absence of competition. Regulated industries, in general, are not supposed to be competitive. But many of them compete with industries offering alternative services: the railroads, pipelines, motor carriers, water carriers, and airlines with one another, gas with electricity, and the telephone with the telegraph. Such competition raises problems for the regulators. How far should they rely upon competition to protect the public interest; how far upon the imposition of administrative controls?

In the case of transport, as we shall see, government has assumed that the consumer would benefit if the service were in some sense competitive. Common ownership of competing media has been opposed. The ICC and the CAB, with power to permit the combination of unlike carriers, have rarely done so. Pooling of traffic by like carriers has been forbidden. Combination of such carriers has been kept under strict control. But government has resisted competition in rates, restricting entry into competing services and establishing minima below which their rates cannot be set.

With public utilities, this is not the case. Gas and electricity, telephone and telegraph, each stands on its own feet. As a result, when the earnings of one are high, its rates may be cut, thus making it difficult for the other to survive. Such a policy, however, would appear to be desirable. If competing services are on an equal footing, it gives the larger share of the market to the one with lower costs.

The states, in general, have permitted common ownership of gas and electric services. This arrangement is defended as reducing the costs of management, selling, billing, and collecting, and as permitting the use of each service for the most economical purposes. It is criticized as removing a possible incentive to improve service and cut rates, and as permitting the postponement of innovations so as to protect investments in existing plants. The SEC, in the process of reorganizing holding company systems, has generally put gas and electricity under separate managements. There has been combination within the telephone and telegraph industries, but not between the two. In the main, the federal commissions have sought to preserve competition between different media. An exception must be noted, however, in the case of the FCC. This agency has given radio licenses to newspapers, FM licenses to AM stations, TV licenses to radio stations, and also to motion picture companies. The problems presented here will be discussed in Chapter 19.

ACCOUNTS AND REPORTS

A commission must be equipped with accurate and informative accounts if it is to succeed in assuring reasonable rates, satisfactory service, and financial stability. To control the general level of rates, it needs to know operating expenses and the value of investments. To control the rate structure, it needs to know the costs of different types of service. To pass judgment on proposals for extension and abandonment, it needs information on the revenues and costs of particular operations. And to prevent overcapitalization, it requires information on all corporate assets and liabilities. If accounts were falsified or obscure, the commission would be seriously handicapped. Control of accounts, therefore, is essential to provide support in every other phase of its activities.

Abuses in Accounting

If operating expenses are padded without detection, the allowance made for them in fixing the level of rates will be too great, and rates and earnings will therefore be too high. This padding may be done in several ways. Accounts may not be properly segregated. Money spent in the interest of investors may be charged to consumers. Transactions with affiliated interests may not be properly identified. Expenditures for capital improvements may be included, in the guise of maintenance, in operating accounts. Excessive sums may be set aside each year in reserves for various purposes. Money spent in replacing worn-out equipment, though already covered in past contributions to depreciation reserves, may be charged again as current costs. In all of these ways, rates may be pushed up and elements of profit concealed in expense accounts.

If the rate base is padded, the amount of earnings that is added to expenses in fixing rates will be magnified. Here, again, a number of methods may be used. Properties may be entered at figures exceeding their actual cost. Intangible items may be included: good will, franchise value, and value as a going concern.

Properties may be sold back and forth among the members of a holding company system at ever increasing prices. Or their values may be written up without bothering to make a sale. Depreciation that has been charged to operating expenses may not be deducted from the valuation of assets. Property long since retired may be kept on the books. And rates will be boosted accordingly.

Through improper accounting, too, financial stability may be endangered by paying excessive dividends. Fictitious surplus accounts may be set up, and dividends apparently declared from surplus when really paid out of capital. Insufficient charges may be made for depreciation and dividends paid, though adequate provision for the replacement of worn-out property has not been made. Under retirement accounting, so called, no charges may be made for depreciation in bad years, keeping earnings and dividends high, and heavy charges made in good years, keeping earnings low and providing a justification for higher rates. Here, again, regulation will suffer a defeat.

Control of Accounting

For many years, companies subjected to regulation resisted supervision of their accounts as an invasion of privacy. But in this they were not upheld by the courts. Power to prescribe the form of accounts and the methods of accounting was eventually granted to all of the commissions, both federal and state. But there was no uniformity in the systems first prescribed. As a result, some companies had to keep several sets of books to conform to the differing requirements of different agencies. It was difficult to examine company accounts. And it was almost impossible to compare the operations of different concerns, private and public, large and small, and to appraise their relative efficiency. A movement toward the adoption of uniform systems finally got under way. Systems prescribed for gas and electric companies by the FPC and for telephone companies by the FCC in the middle thirties were approved by the National Association of Railroad and Utilities Commissioners.

The new systems went into complete detail, laying down clear accounting principles. They prescribed the categories to be used in classifying expenditures, distinguishing those chargeable to investors and to consumers, segregating those involving affiliated interests, and differentiating capital costs from operating costs. They required that property be entered in the books at its cost to the persons first devoting it to public service, thus eliminating subsequent write-ups in its value. They forbade retirement accounting, requiring instead that equal sums be set aside for depreciation in good years and in bad. In these and other ways, they sought to provide the regulators with a solid footing in facts.

All commissions require annual reports, prescribe their form, and specify the material they must contain. Some commissions examine the manner in which accounts are kept and check the accuracy of reports, making field audits from time to time. Others lack the resources with which to make such audits. And still others decline to make them, holding this to be an unwarranted invasion of the privacy of management. Accounting powers are universal, accounting systems adequate, but accounting requirements indifferently enforced.

| Chapter | THE RATE LEVEL |
| 13 | |

A number of different objectives might be sought by government in controlling the general level of rates in regulated industries. First, government might undertake to strike a balance between the interests of consumers and those of investors, fixing rates that would be low enough to prevent extortion of monopoly profits from the consumers but high enough to avoid injustice to the investors. Second, it might seek to promote the widest possible use of regulated services, setting rates at the lowest level consistent with the earnings required to attract the needed capital. These two objectives are not the same, since extortionate profits can be prevented not only where rates are low and volume large but also where rates are high and volume small; and also since earnings sufficient to attract new capital may differ from those required to compensate investors in the past. Third, government might attempt to increase consumption by encouraging the reduction of costs and rates through improvements in efficiency and progress in technology. And fourth, it might employ its control of rates as a means of stabilizing economic activity, raising them to retard a boom and reducing them to cushion a slump. In practice, however, only the first of these goals has been sought. Regulation has had to do, not with expansion of use, promotion of efficiency, advancement of technology, or stabilization of the economy, but solely with the question of earnings. At times, it has emphasized the interest of consumers; at other times, the interest of investors. But always, the balance of these interests has been the focus of its concern.

Thus motivated, control of the rate level requires the establishment of rates that, when multiplied by the expected volume of output, are calculated to yield enough revenue to cover all of the costs of operation and, in addition, to provide whatever earnings the regulators may find necessary and desirable. In measuring the adequacy of earnings, two factors are used: the value ascribed to the property of a regulated company, known as the rate base, and a percentage of this value, known as the rate of return. Establishment of the rates that will be required to yield the necessary revenues, at the volume assumed, thus involves three processes: (1) determination of the costs of operation, (2) determination of the rate base, and (3) determination of the rate of return. Each of these processes is discussed in one of the major parts of this chapter.

Rates, under this procedure, are fixed on a cost-plus basis. But costs, supposedly, are supervised. Efficient management is expected, and honest accounting is required. Return on investment, moreover, is not guaranteed. The regulators may overestimate future demand and underestimate future costs. Conditions may change and earnings, consequently, may fall short. But the shortage will not be made up by the government. Regulation, on the other hand, may underestimate demand and overestimate costs. And here, the surplus earnings that result will not be taken away. Control of earnings, finally, has to do with earnings as a whole; its limits do not apply to dividends. The interest paid on bonds and the dividends on preferred stock may be well below the rate of return allowed. From the sum remaining, therefore, dividends may be paid on common stock at a rate that is well above the one allowed. The declaration of dividends is sometimes supervised to safeguard the financial soundness of a company, but not to limit the profits of the owners of its shares.

COVERING THE COSTS OF OPERATION

Quantitatively, the costs of operation are more significant than the return allowed on investment. They add up to the largest sum that must be covered in fixing rates. In the case of public utilities, they may range from more than half to as much as three fourths of total revenues; in the case of railroads, from two thirds to more than four fifths. These costs include all types of operating expenses, plus annual charges for depreciation, plus taxes. Typically, operating expenses may run around 60 percent of revenues, depreciation around 5 percent, and taxes around 10 percent. Each of these categories will be considered in one of the sections that follow.

Operating Expenses

The need for controlling operating expenses might be questioned on the ground that regulated companies will find it in their own interest to keep expenses down. But this is not invariably the case. Expenditures made on behalf of investors may be charged to consumers. Managements may profit by voting themselves high salaries and substantial bonuses. Holding companies may gain by forcing their subsidiaries to purchase goods and services at excessive prices. In some cases, the groups controlling regulated companies may be incompetent. In others, they may be dishonest. To guard against such possibilities, expenses of operation must be supervised.

The legality of such supervision has long been recognized by the courts. In a railroad case[1] decided in 1892, the Supreme Court asserted that the legislative power was not "subservient to the discretion of any railroad corporation which may, by exorbitant and unreasonable salaries, or in some other improper way, transfer its earnings into what it is pleased to call 'operating expenses.' "[2] For a time during the twenties, the Court restricted the power of commissions to

1 / *Chicago & Grand Trunk Railway Co.* v. *Wellman*, 143 U.S. 339.

2 / *Ibid.*, p. 346.

regulate expenditures. In the Southwestern Bell case of 1923,[3] it forbade the Missouri Commission to question the payments made by Southwestern to its holding company, A.T.&T., saying, "The Commission is not the financial manager of the corporation, and it is not empowered to substitute its judgment for that of the directors of the corporation; nor can it ignore items charged by the utility as operating expenses unless there is an abuse of discretion in that regard by the corporate officers."[4] This rule would have made it virtually impossible to control the expenses resulting from intercompany transactions within a holding company system. It was revised, however, in the Illinois Bell decision[5] of 1930, the Court permitting the Illinois commission to reject the costs incurred through intrasystem purchases of goods and services. And in 1936, in a case involving the regulation of stockyard charges by the Secretary of Agriculture,[6] the Court gave broader scope to cost control, explicitly approving the Secretary's rejection of certain expenditures on the ground that they were unwise. Said Justice Roberts, "The contention is that the amount to be expended for these purposes is purely a question of managerial judgment. But . . . regulation cannot be frustrated by a requirement that the rate be made to compensate extravagant or unnecessary costs for these or any purposes."[7]

In practice, the commissions have not been vigorous in controlling costs. None of them has promulgated rules or established standards to govern expenditures. Only three or four of them have the power to require that budgets be submitted in advance. And even these lack budgetary control; they cannot prevent unwise expenditures from being made. Most commissions examine the reports that are periodically submitted on expenses incurred in the past. And if certain items seem improper, they may warn the companies concerned that they will not include them in computing future rates. But regulation may be so lax that the warnings will be ineffective. When rates are formally contested, expenses may be questioned. In such cases, however, the company will present its accounts as a record of established facts. And the representatives of the public will seldom be equipped to challenge the propriety of the items they contain. Upon occasion, certain items may be disallowed. But such control, at best, is indirect and weak.

Where it is exercised, the supervision of expenditures is selective. The prices and wages paid for goods and services bought in the open market are accepted as given. Inquiry is confined to matters where the interests of consumers and investors are obviously in conflict, and where the prices paid do not result from arm's-length bargaining. Questions may be raised, for instance, concerning the propriety of charging to consumers the costs of institutional advertising, political contributions, donations to charity, and other public relations activities, and

3 / *Southwestern Bell Telephone Co.* v. *Public Service Comsn. of Missouri,* 262 U.S. 276.

4 / *Ibid.,* p. 289.

5 / *Smith* v. *Illinois Bell Telephone Co.,* 282 U.S. 133.

6 / *Acker* v. *U.S.,* 298 U.S. 426.

7 / *Ibid.,* pp. 430-31.

the costs of litigation, particularly when it is designed to prevent reductions or to obtain increases in rates. Questions might also be raised concerning the legitimacy of salaries and bonuses, though this is seldom done. In recent years, however, commissions have inquired into transactions between affiliated corporations that might produce inflated costs. In some cases, intercorporate contracts must be submitted for approval. In others, the reasonableness of intercorporate payments must be proved. Certain expenses incurred by distributors of gas and electricity are regulated, moreover, by federal agencies: the wholesale prices charged for interstate transmission by the FPC, and holding company charges by the SEC. But no such control has been applied to the charges made by A.T.&T., the telephone holding company.

If the commissions were really to undertake to eliminate extravagant and unnecessary costs, they would have to go much further than they have gone in analyzing expenditures. In doing so, they might employ statistics of costs as a tool, comparing the expense ratios of different companies (expenses as a percentage of revenues), their expenses per unit of output, and their expenses per customer. Such comparisons would have to be used with some discretion, since conditions affecting the costs of different companies are not the same. But they would at least afford a point of departure for further analysis. A few commissions have used statistics as a tool but only to a limited extent. In general, these agencies have concerned themselves with the honesty but not with the wisdom of expenditures.

The commissions have usually taken the view that decisions respecting the wisdom of expenditures lie within the province of management. They have refused to substitute the judgment of regulators for that of managers. But the line they have sought to draw between regulation and management is unreal. The substantive problems with which the two must deal are the same. If regulation is to fulfill the function of competition as a disciplinarian, it must invade the sphere of management. Where it refuses to do so, there is no safeguard for the public interest. This is the inescapable dilemma of regulatory control.

Depreciation as a Cost

Depreciation has been defined by the National Association of Railroad and Utilities Commissioners as "the expiration or consumption, in whole or in part, of the service life, capacity, or utility of property resulting from the action of one or more of the forces operating to bring about the retirement of such property from service."[8] Physical depreciation is caused, through the passage of time, by forces such as wear and tear, rust, rot, and decay. Functional depreciation may come sooner: when facilities are rendered obsolete by innovations in technology, made inadequate by growth in demand, or condemned by changes in legal requirements. Depreciation may also result from contingencies

8 / National Association of Railroad and Utilities Commissioners, *Proceedings*, 1944, pp. 82-83.

such as disasters, accidents, and the disappearance of supplies: as, for instance, when exhaustion of natural resources deprives railroads of the traffic they were built to haul. Whatever its cause, depreciation involves destruction of the value of facilities used in the process of providing service. Unless the plants of regulated companies are to deteriorate, these facilities must be replaced. And provision for their replacement is properly to be charged to consumers as a cost of the service they receive.

Provision for maintenance, also, is a cost. But the two are not the same. Maintenance keeps facilities in good condition as long as they are kept in use. It supplies machines with necessary parts. It covers buildings with paint. But it does not provide the funds with which to replace the machines when they must be retired or the buildings when they must be torn down and rebuilt. This is the function of the depreciation charge.

Provision for replacement has been made in two quite different ways: through retirement accounting and through depreciation accounting. The former has been favored by the regulated companies, the latter by the regulatory agencies. Under retirement accounting, replacements are not charged to operating costs until they are actually made. Under depreciation accounting, reserves for replacement are built up by annual charges during the life of the facilities. Retirement accounting is said to be more flexible. And it is: it enables companies to make earnings look worse than they are in good years by making substantial replacements, thus forestalling possible demands for reductions in rates; it enables them to make earnings look better than they are in bad years, thus maintaining dividends at a higher figure than could be paid if the steady decline in the service value of facilities were recognized. This method of accounting permits managements to indulge in fair weather finance, enjoying profits today while jeopardizing financial strength tomorrow. It has therefore been rejected by all of the commissions. Depreciation accounting, with annual charges to meet declining values, is now generally required.

The size of the depreciation charge depends on three factors: (1) the difference between the cost of the facilities concerned and their probable salvage value, (2) the number of years during which this sum is written off, and (3) the method used in distributing the sum among these years. The facilities may be valued at their replacement cost or at their original cost. In the former case, the annual charge will fluctuate as prices change. In the latter, it can be stable. And this is what the commissions have preferred. At one time, the Supreme Court required that valuations be made at replacement cost,[9] but this decision has since been reversed.[10] Original-cost accounting is now the general rule. Salvage values are estimated and deducted. The length of depreciation periods is determined by engineering estimates of life expectancy. In practice, a separate charge is not computed for each item of property, but items are classified and an average charge applied to all those falling in each class. The provision for depreciation can be distributed over time, finally, in three different

9 / *United Railways and Electric Co.* v. *West,* 280 U.S. 234 (1930).

10 / *FPC* v. *Hope Natural Gas Co.,* 320 U.S. 591 (1944).

ways: (1) it can start high and decline from year to year, (2) it can start low and rise, and (3) it can remain the same. The first of these methods has theoretical advantages, but its use is prevented by practical difficulties. The choice has been between the other two.

Under the second method, a sinking fund is set up on a company's books and equal sums assigned to it each year. It is assumed that the fund is invested and interest earned. In practice, it is reinvested in the business, but interest is credited to it, compounding annually. As the fund grows, the interest payments rise. The total contributions for depreciation are therefore on a rising scale. These contributions are so computed that the basic payments plus the compound interest will be equal to the cost of assets at the time they are retired. Under the third method of distributing charges, equal amounts are assigned to a depreciation reserve each year. This reserve, too, is usually reinvested in the business. But it is not credited with interest. The annual contributions add up to the cost of the property retired. In either case, the capital costs of depreciating facilities are gradually transferred to operating costs. The sinking fund method is more complicated, the straight line method simpler. The latter is preferred by the commissions and is more widely used.

Depreciation has two related aspects: it is charged to operating costs; it must also be deducted from the rate base. Under the sinking fund method, the part of the fund attributable to interest has come from the owners of the company and has not been charged to operating costs. It is therefore not deducted from the base. But under the straight line method, all of the payments assigned to depreciation reserves are covered in costs; the full amount of accrued depreciation should therefore be deducted from the base. Otherwise, consumers would be paying for the same thing twice: once in costs and again in the return still allowed on an investment that has been charged to costs. Where accrued depreciation is deducted, the balance of interest between consumers and investors is not materially affected by differences in the size of the annual depreciation charge. If the charge is higher, consumers will pay more in costs and less in earnings. If it is lower, investors will get less in costs and more in earnings.

The Problem of Obsolescence

Changes in technology and shifts in demand may be as important as wear and tear in necessitating the retirement of facilities. But the rate of physical depreciation can be estimated, with some accuracy, by engineers, while the speed of obsolescence cannot be foreseen. As a consequence, no separate allowance is made for obsolescence in depreciation accounting. This factor is assumed to be covered in the general depreciation charge.

Failure to provide specifically for obsolescence may delay the introduction of improved equipment into regulated industries. Under competition, a firm is compelled to introduce improvements when its competitors do so. Under monopoly, too, it may choose to introduce them, being free to set its prices at levels that will recover the cost of the old equipment and cover depreciation charges on the new. But under regulation, such freedom is lacking. The regulated company cannot raise its rates without permission. It may not be permitted to charge enough to recover the cost of outmoded facilities if it retires them. It is therefore likely to keep them in use. The installation of new equipment may be postponed for many years until the old wears out. And, in the meantime, consumers will be denied the benefits that might have come from the advancement of technology.

This impediment would be removed, of course, if the depreciation of abandoned equipment were stopped, leaving it in the rate base. And this is done, in effect, when such equipment is defined as stand-by capacity and kept on the books. But this solution of the problem is unsatisfactory, since it compels consumers to pay a return, in perpetuity, on investments that have no use. A better procedure would be to permit obsolete equipment to be amortized while the equipment that replaced it was being depreciated at the normal rate. Amortization might be swift, full cost being recovered by the company before any benefits were passed on to consumers. Preferably, it would be slower, costs being recovered more gradually and some benefits accorded to consumers at an earlier date.

In practice, most commissions have done little or nothing about the recovery of investments in obsolete facilities. Regulation, as it is administered, thus operates to impede adoption of improvements in technology.

Taxes

In making rates, taxes—with but minor exceptions—are included in operating costs and deducted from revenues in determining earnings. This procedure has been required since 1922 by a decision of the Supreme Court.[11] It applies not only to taxes on property and on output, which normally are regarded as costs, but also to taxes on net income, which are not.

With respect to the first group of taxes, the question to be asked relates to their desirability as a source of public revenue. There can be no objection, to be sure, to imposing as heavy a burden on industries that are regulated as is borne by those that are not. But legislative bodies do not always stop at this point. They find in regulated services a convenient source of income and employ their producers, in effect, as tax collectors. In this way they unduly burden the consumers of such services and discourage the allocation of resources to the satisfaction of their wants. Here, policy in taxation is made without regard to its effect on regulation, and an artificial handicap is imposed on regulated industries.

With respect to taxes on net income, a different question is raised. Such taxes, generally, are supposed to be computed on the basis of earnings remaining after costs have been deducted from gross revenues. Their treatment, in this case

11 / *Galveston Electric Co.* v. *Galveston,* 258 U.S. 388.

as costs, favors investors in regulated companies, excusing them from taxes that investors in other industries are required to pay. It is true that unregulated companies may sometimes succeed in shifting their income taxes, in part at least, to consumers. But such shifting is not invariable or complete, and it is not endorsed by law.

Not only are rates raised when taxes on net income are treated as costs. They are kept high. The higher rates produce higher earnings. These produce higher taxes. And these must be covered again in cost. Excessive rates are thus perpetuated automatically. If this anomaly in regulation is to be corrected, such taxes must be excluded in computing operating costs.

FIXING THE RATE BASE

The process of determining the size of the rate base is known as valuation. Commissions and courts have often spoken of this process as one of finding the value of investments. As a matter of fact, these bodies do not find value; they make it. Companies that are regulated differ sharply in this respect from those that are not. In the latter case, value is not established by public authority. It is the result of market processes. The value of a company's property is determined by taking the revenue produced by the sales made at the price fixed in the market, deducting the costs incurred in the process, and capitalizing the remaining profits at the prevailing rate of interest. In the case of regulated companies this cannot be done. For the price on which the value is based is not fixed in the market; it is set by the regulators themselves. If they put it high, value will be high; if they put it low, value will be low. Value, in the commercial sense of the term, cannot be used as a basis for fixing rates. It is a consequence of prices, not a cause. Value for rate making is quite a different thing. It is established by regulation. It rests, not on the prices of products, but on estimates of the cost of productive properties. What we are concerned with, here, is not commercial value but the size of the rate base and the process by which it is fixed.

This process includes many steps. First, values must be assigned to forms of property that are tangible and reproducible, such as buildings and machines. A line must be drawn between items to be included as used and useful and those to be rejected as not. A decision must be made as to the costs to be employed in assigning values, whether those originally incurred, those required to reproduce the property, or something in between the two. Costs must be obtained from company books and records or an inventory taken and the items priced. A method must be adopted for computing depreciation, the computation made, and the resulting figure deducted from the cost of this part of the property. Second, a value must be assigned to land, an asset that is tangible but not reproducible. Here, a method of pricing must be determined and applied. And finally, decisions must be made as to the allowance of values for intangible assets. And where allowances are made, the values must be assigned.

In this process there are many opportunities to inflate the rate base and thus to increase permitted earnings by raising rates. Items may be improperly included: equipment not used or useful kept on the books, or various intangibles allowed. The items included may be overpriced: extravagant payments recognized, property transfers between affiliated corporations accepted at face value, facilities priced on the basis of imaginary costs of reproduction, and land priced not at what it cost but at what it would bring. These are the problems with which this part of the chapter is concerned.

The Judicial Rule of Fair Value

For half a century, in fixing the rate base, the commissions were dominated by the courts. In 1877, in its decision in the case of *Munn* v. *Illinois,* [12] the Supreme Court had taken the position that rate making was a legislative rather than a judicial function. But in 1886 it reversed this position, asserting that rates fixed under legislative authority were subject to judicial review and might be set aside if they were found, in violation of the Fifth or Fourteenth Amendments, to deprive investors of their property without due process of law. [13] And in 1894 for the first time it nullified the rates established by a state commission. [14] But the court set up no standard by which to judge the reasonableness of commission valuations until it handed down its decision in the famous case of *Smyth* v. *Ames* [15] in 1898.

The state of Nebraska had passed a law in 1893 setting up a Board of Transportation and giving it power to fix the rates charged for hauling freight. The railroads challenged the rates fixed by this body, claiming denial of due process. Some of these roads had been built during and after the Civil War when prices were much higher than in later years. The railroads contended, therefore, that they were entitled to a return on their original cost. William Jennings Bryan was the lawyer for the state. He sought to defend the contested rates by arguing that the railroads' property should be appraised at the lower level of reproduction cost. Thus, the issue was joined between two principles of valuation. And, since prices were falling, the companies embraced original cost and the government, reproduction cost.

The Supreme Court found the rates to be confiscatory on either basis. And then it went on, in a dictum not essential to its decision, to discuss the valuation of investments in regulated industries. This dictum later came to be of great importance, providing a basis for judicial review of rates for nearly 50 years. Said Justice Harlan:

> We hold . . . that the basis of all calculations as to the reasonableness of rates to be charged by a corporation . . . must be the fair value of the property being used by it for the convenience of the public. And, in order

12 / 94 U.S. 113.
13 / *Stone* v. *Farmers' Loan and Trust Co.,* 116 U.S. 307.
14 / *Reagan* v. *Farmers' Loan and Trust Co.,* 154 U.S. 362.
15 / 169 U.S. 466.

to ascertain that value, the original cost of construction, the amount expended in permanent improvements, the amount and market value of its bonds and stocks, the present as compared with the original cost of construction, the probable earning capacity of the property under particular rates prescribed by statute, and the sum required to meet operating expenses, are all matters for consideration, and are to be given such weight as may be just and right in each case. We do not say that there may not be other matters to be regarded in estimating the value of the property. What the company is entitled to ask is a fair return upon the value of that which it employs for the public convenience. On the other hand, what the public is entitled to demand is that no more be exacted from it . . . than the services rendered . . . are reasonably worth. [16]

This statement merits careful analysis. Rates, if they are to stand, must be high enough to afford a fair return on a fair value of invested capital. But fair return and fair value are not defined. Some of the items to be considered in determining fair value are enumerated. These include: (1) operating expenses, (2) earning capacity, (3) the market value of stocks and bonds, (4) original cost and money spent on improvements, and (5) "the present as compared with the original cost." And, lest something may have been forgotten, "We do not say that there may not be other matters to be regarded. . . ." Of the matters mentioned, however, (1) operating expenses are irrelevant, having nothing to do with the determination of the rate base; (2) earning capacity and (3) the market value of stocks and bonds are logical absurdities, since these depend upon the rates that are being fixed; (4) original cost and (5) present cost, while relevant and logical, are inconsistent, since the values to which they lead are far apart. What is fair value: original cost or present cost or some compromise between the two? The Court does not say. Both must be considered, and each must be given "such weight as may be just and right. . . ."

Some of the errors in the doctrine of *Smyth* v. *Ames* came to be corrected in the next few years. Operating costs were quietly dropped from the factors to be considered in appraising property. Earning capacity [17] and the value of stocks and bonds [18] were rejected as factors by the Court. Deduction for depreciation, overlooked by Justice Harlan, was added to the "matters to be regarded" in 1909. [19] Original cost and present cost remained as determinants of value.

It should be noted that the rule of *Smyth* v. *Ames*, in its time, was not calculated to justify excessive rates. Consideration of construction costs afforded a wholesome corrective to the tendency to set rates at levels that would validate inflated capitalizations. And consideration of "the present as compared with the original cost" provided a check for use in cases where original cost had been too high. The conversion of this rule into a device for raising rates was the work of later years.

16 / *Ibid.*, pp. 546-47.
17 / *Minnesota Rate Cases*, 230 U.S. 352, (1913).
18 / *Knoxville* v. *Knoxville Water Co.*, 212 U.S. 1 (1909).
19 / *Ibid.*

Judicial Emphasis on Reproduction Cost

Until World War I, regulated companies sought valuations based on original cost, while regulators favored reproduction cost. Then, with wartime inflation, prices soared and reproduction cost mounted. For many companies it came to be twice as high as original cost. As a result, the protagonists changed sides. The companies now contested commission orders in the courts, seeking to increase their profits by getting valuations based on reproduction cost. And the commissions defended their orders, basing their valuations on original cost. This controversy dominated regulation for the next 20 years, monopolizing the attention of the companies, the commissions, and the courts.

Until 1926 the Supreme Court took a middle ground. Its dicta seemed to favor reproduction cost. It insisted that this factor be considered. But it said that reproduction cost should not be given exclusive weight. And its decisions approved rates based on valuations that had given the factor minor weight. In one case, where prices had risen 110 percent, it accepted a valuation that had been raised 33 percent.[20] In another, where prices had risen 100 percent, it rejected a valuation that had been raised 25 percent.[21] The Court, however, was divided. The majority, under the leadership of Justice Butler, a railroad lawyer appointed to the Court by President Harding, came to give increasing emphasis to reproduction cost. The minority rejected this position. Its leading spokesman, Justice Brandeis, a well-known liberal appointed by President Wilson, wrote a series of dissenting opinions in which he argued that valuations should be based on prudent investment, i.e., on that part of the original cost that was prudently incurred. In this he was followed by other jurists, commission members, and academic authorities. The controversy thus came to be centered upon the respective merits of prudent investment and reproduction cost.

The high-water mark of reproduction cost valuation came with the Court's decision in the case of *McCardle* v. *Indianapolis Water Co.* in 1926. The original cost of the company's property was $10 million. Its reproduction cost was estimated at $22 million. The state commission allowed $15 million. The company claimed $19 million. The Court held that rates based on any valuation below $19 million would be confiscatory. At a return of 7 percent this permitted earnings of $1,330,000. Of this, some $525,000 was required to pay interest on bonds and dividends on preferred stock, leaving more than $805,000 to be paid on an original investment of $250,000 in common stock, an annual yield of more than 300 percent. Said Justice Butler: ". . . in determining present value, consideration must be given to prices and wages prevailing at the time of the investigation; and, . . . there must be an honest and intelligent forecast as to probable price and wage levels during a reasonable period in the immediate future." And again, "It is well established that values of utility properties

20 / *Galveston Electric Co.* v. *Galveston,* 258 U.S. 388 (1922).

21 / *Southwestern Bell Telephone Co.* v. *Public Service Commission of Missouri,* 262 U.S. 287 (1923).

fluctuate, and that owners must bear the decline and are entitled to the increase." [22]

In the O'Fallon case, [23] which followed in 1929, the Court repeated the fair value formula, setting aside the valuation of railroad properties that had been made over many years by the Interstate Commerce Commission, with meticulous care and at great expense, on the ground that insufficient consideration had been given to reproduction cost. But here, as elsewhere, the Court refused to say how much consideration of this factor was required.

The commissions, thus, were left in the dark. They had to allow a fair return on a fair value. But they had no way of telling what value the Court would accept as fair. Fair value, as Ben W. Lewis has remarked, was "the unpredictable product of incalculable considerations." [24] The Court found it by going into a trance, "embracing revelation as its technique of rate value determination." [25] In an effort to satisfy the undisclosed requirements of the law, the commissions undertook "to accord consideration to a modified reproduction cost figure as one among an assortment of irreconcilable elements to be transmuted into 'fair value' by the alchemy of mystic judgement," [26] arriving finally at a figure which bore "no derivative relation to any figures in evidence and no ascertainable relation to any functional purpose of rate making." [27]

The Economics of Reproduction Cost

The argument usually advanced in support of reproduction cost valuation was that it was needed to keep earnings in regulated industries in line with those in other industries and with changes in the cost of living. Other earnings rise during prosperity; if investors are to be treated fairly under regulation and the credit of regulated industries maintained, their earnings should be permitted to keep pace. And this can be accomplished by making changes in valuations to correspond with changes in construction costs.

So went the argument. There are questions that might be raised concerning the need for keeping earnings in line. But these will be considered later on. At the moment it is sufficient to point out three flaws. (1) The investor is said to be entitled to a constant return in goods and services. To provide it, his earnings in dollars should be adjusted in accordance with changes in the index of living costs. Reproduction cost valuation adjusts it in accordance with changes in the index of construction costs. The two are not the same. (2) It is not proposed that interest on bonds or dividends on preferred stock be changed as prices change. Dividends on common stock, under this method of valuation, will

22 / *McCardle* v. *Indianapolis Water Co.,* 272 U.S. 400, 408.

23 / *St. Louis and O'Fallon Railway Co.* v. *U.S.,* 279 U.S. 461.

24 / Leverett S. Lyon and Victor Abramson (eds.), *Government and Economic Life* (Washington, D.C.: Brookings Institution, 1940), p. 694.

25 / *Ibid.,* p. 699.

26 / *Ibid.,* p. 701.

27 / *Ibid.,* p. 692.

therefore change more than prices do. Assume a company with a valuation of $10 million and a return of 6 percent, producing earnings of $600,000. On $3 million of bonds at 4 percent, it pays $120,000. On $3 million of preferred stock at 5 percent, it pays $150,000. It has $330,000 left. On $4 million of common stock, it can pay 8¼ percent. Assume that the price level doubles. The company is revalued at $20 million. With its return still at 6 percent, it now earns $1,200,000. It still pays $270,000 on its bonds and its preferred stock. But it now has $930,000 left for its common. This gives it a yield of 23¼ percent. Prices have doubled, but dividends on common stock have tripled. (3) If the investor's earnings need to be kept in line with changing prices, this can be done, without touching the rate base, by varying the rate of return. In the case just given, earnings were raised from $600,000 to $1,200,000 by raising the valuation from $10 million to $20 million while leaving the rate of return at 6 percent. The same result could have been obtained by leaving the valuation at $10 million and raising the rate of return to 12 percent. Why not do it this way? The answer is not hard to find. Public opinion would be outraged if the rate of return to investors in regulated industries were doubled, advancing it to such a height. But it does not complain when the same effect is achieved through revaluation. For here, it does not realize what is going on. The companies center their attention on the rate base rather than the rate of return because valuation is a mystery and earnings can thus be boosted with greater ease.

Consider the uncertainties inherent in the concept of reproduction cost. (1) What is it that is being reproduced: a modern replacement for an old plant, the old plant in its original condition, or the old plant as it stands today? The assumption made in the McCardle case was that the company, starting fresh, would build its old plant in its depreciated condition,[28] a purely imaginary procedure in which sane managements are unlikely to engage. (2) Under what conditions is reproduction to occur: those originally existing or those existing at the present time? If the former, are allowances to be made to cover the possible cost, today, of cutting paths through forest long since razed, and hauling supplies by horse and wagon rather than train or truck? If the latter, are sums to be allowed for tearing down the buildings that might conceivably be standing where a railroad has its lines, or for ripping up and then relaying pavements that did not exist when a water company first laid its mains? Company lawyers have lively imaginations. And though the more absurd of their inventions have been rejected by the courts, a certain residue remains. (3) What methods of reproduction are to be assumed: simultaneous rebuilding of the whole plant involving large-scale operations and employing modern techniques, or piecemeal reconstruction on a small scale with techniques no longer in use? The latter assumption is the usual rule. And here, again, a procedure is imagined that no sane management would countenance. (4) What prices are to be taken as representing reproduction cost: the spot prices of a particular day, the average prices of a recent period, or figures based on forecasts of the future? If spot prices, they change from day to day; the chosen day may not be representative.

28 / *McCardle* v. *Indianapolis Water Co.*, 272 U.S. 400 at 417-18 (1926).

If average prices, they may be raised or lowered by changing the selected period. If either, the costs computed are those of the past and not the future. But if future prices are to be employed, valuation becomes a matter of guesswork, with the companies, presumably, guessing high and the commissions guessing low. Yet it was said by Justice Butler, speaking for the Court in the McCardle case, that forecasts of future prices should be made.

The case against reproduction cost valuation is conclusive. The principle facilitates manipulation of the rate base, capitalizing imaginary costs. The value it yields is uncertain, the estimates of companies and commissions being millions of dollars apart. The value is also unstable, being out of date before the valuation is completed and fluctuating widely over time. The valuation process is expensive, involving investigation and litigation respecting matters that could be taken, from existing records, as established facts. The process occasions protracted delays, cases dragging through the commissions and the courts for months and years. When costs are falling, adjustments in rates are thus postponed and excessive earnings retained, to the benefit of the investor. But when costs are rising, adjustments may be slow, too. And here, the investor will suffer; his enthusiasm for reproduction cost will wane. The principle works in only one direction: it is supported when prices rise but not when they decline.

Original cost valuation has none of these infirmities. The value it yields is definite and understandable, showing the actual sum invested in the business. This value is stable, affording a firm foundation on which the structure of regulation may be reared. If it is decided that earnings should be varied as prices change, this can be done, without disturbing the rate base, by altering the rate of return. Original cost valuation is simpler, quicker, and cheaper. It is not devoid of opportunities for controversy. Opinions may differ, for instance, as to actual investment versus prudent investment and as to investment cost versus first cost. Actual investment would accept at face value the figures shown on a company's books; prudent investment might reduce or eliminate certain items as dishonest or extravagant. Investment cost would accept as given the prices paid for productive facilities; first cost would ignore the prices set in transfers between affiliated companies, employing those paid when the facilities were first devoted to the public service. These differences are important, but in comparison with those arising under reproduction cost they are small. And finally, original cost is easily kept up to date. It is necessary only to add the cost of improvements and deduct the accrued depreciation shown on the books from year to year. Properties do not have to be revalued every time there is a change in rates. Action is speeded, and the expenses of regulation are reduced.

Judicial Abandonment of Reproduction Cost

During the thirties and the forties the Supreme Court moved away from reproduction cost. In the Los Angeles Gas and Electric case [29] in 1933, and in the Pacific Gas and Electric case [30] in 1938, the Court accepted valuations made

29 / *Los Angeles Gas and Electric Corp.* v. *Railroad Commission,* 289 U.S. 287.
30 / *Railroad Commission* v. *Pacific Gas and Electric Co.,* 302 U.S. 388.

by the California commission on the basis of original cost, holding the method employed to be within the discretion of that agency. And in the Natural Gas Pipeline case [31] in 1942, the Court upheld an order by the Federal Power Commission substantially reducing pipeline rates. The order was a temporary one, based on the company's own valuation, and did not raise the issue of original versus reproduction cost. But in the course of its opinion, the Court had this to say: "The Constitution does not bind rate-making bodies to the service of any formula or combination of formulas. Agencies to whom this legislative power has been delegated are free . . . to make the pragmatic adjustments which may be called for by particular circumstances." [32] And the significance of the decision was emphasized in a concurring opinion by Justices Black, Douglas, and Murphy:

> . . . we think this is an appropriate occasion to lay the ghost of *Smyth* v. *Ames*, . . . which has haunted utility regulation since 1898. . . .
>
> As we read the opinion of the Court, the Commission is now freed from the compulsion of admitting evidence on reproduction cost or of giving any weight to that element of "fair value." The Commission may now adopt, if it chooses, prudent investment as a rate base—the base long advocated by Mr. Justice Brandeis. [33]

In the next case, Justice Douglas spoke for the majority.

The FPC had ordered the Hope Natural Gas Company to reduce its rates by something more than 60 percent. Among other things, the company had contended that it should be allowed a return of 8 percent on a reproduction cost of $66 million. The Commission had allowed it a return of 6½ percent on an original cost of $33 million. Its action was upheld in 1944, in a five to three decision, by the Court. Said Justice Douglas: "Under the statutory standard of 'just and reasonable,' it is the result reached and not the method employed which is controlling. . . . It is not the theory but the impact of the rate order which counts. If the total effect of the rate order cannot be said to be unjust and unreasonable, judicial inquiry . . . is at an end." [34] In this case, the total effect of the order did not appear to be unjust. The company had accumulated substantial reserves. It could borrow new money by selling bonds at 3 percent. At the rates set, it would still be able to pay 8 percent on its stock. This satisfied the Court: "Rates which enable the company to operate successfully, to maintain its financial integrity, to attract capital, and to compensate its investors for risks assumed certainly cannot be condemned as invalid, even though they might produce only a meager return on the so-called 'fair value' rate base." [35] The rule of fair value was thus brought to an end. What was put in its place?

Clearly, the Court did not go back to the position of *Munn* v. *Illinois*. It gave more latitude to the commissions, but it retained the right of review. Commis-

31 / *Natural Gas Pipeline Co.* v. *FPC*, 315 U.S. 575.

32 / *Ibid.*, p. 586.

33 / *Ibid.*, pp. 602, 606.

34 / *FPC* v. *Hope Natural Gas Co.*, 320 U.S. 591, 602.

35 / *Ibid.*, p. 605.

sion orders, it said, will be upheld if their results are reasonable. But how are the commissions to know whether the Court will find them so? Certain results were mentioned; among them, the ability of a company to attract capital. But the Court did not say that these were the only results to be considered. And it gave no criteria by which they might be judged. Just where is the line to be drawn, for instance, between a return that enables a company to attract capital and one that does not? The Court left the development of standards to the commissions. But it would test the results of their work by standards of its own. And these standards were not divulged. The Court relaxed its grip on regulation. But it left the regulators in the dark.

The decision in the Hope case was nonetheless a landmark. It disposed of reproduction cost. It shifted attention from the rate base to the rate of return. It removed an impediment to effective regulation created by the federal courts. No rate-level case has reached the Supreme Court since Hope. Despite this decision, reproduction cost valuation was still required, in 1967, by the courts and employed by the commissions of 13 states. But original cost was the general rule. [36]

The Task of Valuation

Where the property in the rate base is valued at its original cost, the figures required may be obtained in one of two ways: they may be found in a company's books, or they may be computed by taking an inventory and then multiplying the items by the prices that were current at the time they were bought or built. The first of these methods obviously is less costly. But it cannot be used where records, for any reason, are unavailable or unreliable. This difficulty may be encountered where facilities were constructed before accounting was brought under commission control. It has less significance where construction has been more recent and accounts kept in accordance with commission rules. An original cost rate base, once obtained, can be kept up to date by reference to current accounts. An initial valuation based on reproduction cost can be made only by taking an inventory and multiplying the items in the list by present prices. It can be kept up to date, however, by employing an index of construction costs.

Inventories are taken by company engineers. Commissions may check them, by field inspections, if they have the funds to do so. More likely, they will accept them as they stand. Differences arise, however, concerning the inclusion of particular items. Rates are supposed to afford a return only on property that is used and useful in the regulated service. Facilities that have been dismantled or abandoned, together with those that are not related to the service, should therefore be excluded. But here, the judgments of the companies and the commissions may not be the same. The companies are likely to argue that obsolete equipment must be retained as stand-by capacity for use in case of

36 / U.S. Senate, Committee on Government Operations, *State Utility Commissions* (Washington, D.C.: Government Printing Office, 1967), p. 37.

need. The commissions may differ. Usually, however, the judgment of management is taken for granted. There has been little litigation on this point. Differences can arise, also, concerning the possible exclusion of certain expenditures
as imprudent. But here, again, few cases have been carried to the courts.

The cost of materials and equipment and that of the labor employed in
construction does not give the full measure of the investment in facilities. Money
has also been spent on other matters incidental to going into business: organization, legal services, engineering, supervision, and interest, insurance, and taxes
during construction. If these expenditures have not been charged to operating
costs, their inclusion in the rate base is usually allowed by law. In the past, lump
sums were allowed to cover such items, usually running around 15 percent of
the total value of a plant. In recent years, however, allowances have generally
been limited to figures supported by showings of actual cost.

The remaining steps in the process of appraising fixed assets are the deduction of depreciation and the addition of the value of land, which are discussed
below. An addition is also made for a current asset: working capital. Working
capital is required to bridge the gap between the time when a company pays
for what it buys and when it collects for what it sells. It may be measured by
subtracting current liabilities from current assets, or by adding up the operations
requiring outlays of cash. The question of working capital comes up in every
rate case, but the problem presented is a minor one.

Deduction of Depreciation

The fact that depreciation must be deducted to determine present value has
been recognized by the courts since 1909.[37] But the method of computing the
amount to be deducted has long been in dispute. The commissions have looked
on depreciation as an accounting matter, favoring deduction of the full amount
shown (under straight line accounting) in the depreciation reserve. The companies have argued that depreciation is an engineering matter, equipment retaining
its value as long as it can be operated efficiently, and that deductions should
therefore be based on engineering estimates, nothing being deducted unless
deterioration in efficiency is observed. In the history of regulation this dispute
has ranked second only to that between original cost and reproduction cost.

The procedure favored by the commissions is the sounder of the two. It
recognizes the steady exhaustion of capacity for service, due to all forms of
depreciation, and provides for the regular amortization of investment in facilities. It is simple and inexpensive. And it insures logical consistency in the
treatment of depreciation as an operating expense and as an item in the capital
accounts. The procedure supported by the companies, on the other hand, has
a number of defects. It takes no account of the fact of obsolescence or other
forms of functional depreciation involving a decline in value that is not reflected
in a loss of efficiency. It does not even recognize the full extent of physical
depreciation, since equipment, instead of deteriorating slowly, may break down

37 / *Knoxville v. Knoxville Water Co.,* 212 U.S. 1.

all at once. The procedure is complicated and costly, requiring appraisals by engineers. And it is illogical, requiring consumers to pay a return on an investment that they have already paid for in operating costs.

The companies have sought to have their cake and eat it too. When operating costs were under discussion, their experts have testified that their properties were depreciating at an alarming rate. And when the rate base was being fixed, the experts have testified again—and with a straight face—that scarcely any depreciation was to be observed. In both cases, it has been their purpose to raise the level of rates: first, by inflating operating costs; and second, by inflating the base on which a fair return must be allowed. And in the past, the Supreme Court has crowned their efforts with success.

In the New York Telephone case in 1926, Justice Butler, speaking for the majority, rejected the commission's effort to deduct accrued depreciation, saying: "The revenue paid by the customers for service belongs to the company. . . . Customers pay for service, not for the property used to render it. Their payments are not contributions to depreciation . . . or to capital of the company."[38] And in the McCardle case, he went on to approve the limitation of deductions to observed depreciation: "The testimony of competent valuation engineers who examined the property and made estimates in respect of its condition is to be preferred to mere calculations based on averages and assumed probabilities."[39] A few years later, however, the Court retreated from this position. In the Lindheimer case[40] in 1934, the Illinois Bell Telephone Company, with more than $48 million in its depreciation reserve, admitted less than $16 million as observed depreciation. Here, the Court recognized the relation between the annual charge for depreciation and the depreciation reserve, regarding both as excessive when measured by observed depreciation. And it proposed that the charge be reduced in fixing rates. But it did not accept the depreciation reserve as the proper measure of deductions for depreciation. Nor has it ever done so, explicitly. In the Hope case, however, the Court declared itself to be concerned only with the results, not with the methods of regulation. Since 1944, therefore, the commissions have been free to deduct the full reserve for depreciation in fixing the rate base.

Land

Land is of minor importance in the valuation of most transportation industries and municipal utilities. It is of major importance, however, in the cases of railroads and gas companies. Land differs from other items in the rate base, having no cost of production. But the dispute between original cost and present cost has been repeated in fixing a value for its cost of acquisition. And here, the decision went, at the outset, to the advocates of present cost.

38 / *Board of Pub. Util. Commissioners* v. *N.Y. Telephone Co.,* 271 U.S. 23, pp. 31-32.
39 / *McCardle* v. *Indianapolis Water Co.,* 272 U.S. 400, 416 (1926).
40 / *Lindheimer* v. *Illinois Bell Telephone Co.,* 292 U.S. 151.

In the Minnesota rate cases[41] in 1913 the Supreme Court permitted railroad land, acquired as a gift or at low prices, to be entered in the rate base at the market value of adjacent land, thus allowing investors an annual return upon the unearned increment. The railroads asked for even more. On the assumption that they would be forced to pay more than market value if acquiring their lands at present, they proposed that the value be computed by using a multiplier that would take this factor into account. But this was farther than the Court was willing to go.

Until 1954 the Federal Power Commission determined interstate pipeline rates by deducting from the figure at which the pipeline companies sold their gas another figure to cover the costs they incurred in producing it. In computing the latter figure, it valued the companies' gas lands on the basis of original cost. And in so doing, it was upheld, in 1934, by the Court.[42]

Intangibles

Not content to increase their earnings by overpricing tangible assets, regulated companies have also attempted further to inflate the rate base by adding intangibles: good will, franchise value, water rights, leaseholds, and value as a going concern. Inclusion of most of these items has long been rejected by the commissions and the courts. Good will is a capitalization of earnings that exceed a competitive return. To include it in the rate base would be to admit the failure of regulation to control the profits of publicly created and protected monopolies. So, too, with franchise value. Where a city has made a charge for a franchise, the sum invested belongs in the rate base. But this is rarely the case, franchises normally being granted as gifts. Inclusion of this item would require the public to pay a return, in perpetuity, on an appraisal of its generosity. The same is true of rights to the use of flowing water possessed by irrigation, power, and water companies.

The leases held by gas companies, permitting exploitation of deposits under private lands, are a special case. They have usually been bought and paid for. Their cost is properly recognized in valuing company properties. When gas is discovered, however, their value will rise. Should the increase be reflected in the valuation? Such a practice would afford an incentive to exploration—a stronger incentive, probably, than is required. It would also grant the companies an unearned increment on which to base an annual return. The Federal Power Commission, in connection with its determination of pipeline rates, has valued leaseholds, not at the price they would bring in the market, but at their original cost. And in this it was upheld in 1945 by the Supreme Court.[43]

Going-concern value, supposedly, represents an amount by which the value of a plant that is in operation exceeds that of an identical plant that is not.

41 / 230 U.S. 352.

42 / *Dayton Power and Light Co.* v. *Pub. Util. Commission,* 292 U.S. 290.

43 / *Colorado-Interstate Gas Co.* v. *FPC,* 324 U.S. 581; *Panhandle Eastern Pipe Line Co.* v. *FPC,* 324 U.S. 625.

But no reasonable measure of this value has ever been devised. A figure could be obtained, of course, by capitalizing excess earnings. But this, too, obviously, would be nothing but good will under a different name. So various rationalizations have been attempted. Going-concern value has been said to cover the costs of reproducing a business, apart from its physical facilities: creating an organization, recruiting and training personnel, developing administrative procedures, opening up a market, and educating customers. It has also been said to compensate a company for the losses it may have suffered in the early years of its development. But neither of these notions is really tenable. The costs said to be involved in reproducing a business have already been covered in operating expenses; to write them into the rate base would be to count them twice. The losses of previous years should scarcely be compensated if the excess profits of those years are not recoverable. And such losses, in any case, are not properly to be capitalized. There is something to be said for a policy of averaging earnings over time. But this cannot be retroactive. And it is better to be accomplished, not by manipulating the rate base, but by varying the rate of return. Going-concern value, in short, is purely hypothetical. It is the most intangible of all of the intangibles. Like the others, it capitalizes the amount by which earnings are permitted to exceed a reasonable return. But unlike the others, it has some plausibility.

Going-concern value has been recognized by the courts, accepted by the commissions, and generally included in valuations until recent years. In the Knoxville Water Company case [44] in 1909, the Supreme Court said that there was an "added value of the plant as a whole over the sum of the values of its component parts, which is attached to it because it is in active and successful operation and earning a return." [45] And in the Des Moines Gas Company case [46] in 1915, the Court found this "element of value in an assembled and established plant, doing business and earning money, over one not thus advanced" to be "self-evident." [47] In accordance with these and similar decisions, the commissions long followed the practice of making an arbitrary allowance for going value, usually adding 10 percent, more or less, to the value of physical facilities in arriving at the rate base. After 1933, however, the Supreme Court shifted its position. In the Los Angeles Gas and Electric case, [48] decided in that year, the Court upheld the California commission in rejecting an allowance of $9 million claimed by the company as going value. And in the Dayton Power and Light case [49] in 1934, it rejected a similar claim, saying that this intangible "is not something to be read into every balance sheet as a perfunctory addition." [50] As a result, the commissions no longer add a separate allowance for value as a

44 / Knoxville v. Knoxville Water Co., 212 U.S. 1.
45 / Ibid., p. 9.
46 / Des Moines Gas Co. v. Des Moines, 238 U.S. 153.
47 / Ibid., p. 165.
48 / Los Angeles Gas and Electric Co. v. R.R. Comn., 289 U.S. 287.
49 / Dayton Power and Light Co. v. Pub. Util. Comn. of Ohio, 292 U.S. 290.
50 / Ibid., p. 309.

going concern. But they may still be influenced by the concept when they fix the value of physical facilities.

FIXING THE RATE OF RETURN

In determining the earnings that are to be permitted, the rate of return is fully as important as the rate base. But it has received far less attention from the commissions and the courts. Under the decision in the Hope case, however, it is possible to hold the rate base steady. And when this is done, earnings will be influenced only by varying the rate of return. Attention has thus been shifted to the rate of return as an instrument for effecting the purposes of earnings control. Here, a number of problems arise. How should the rate of return required to attract new capital be determined? In fixing this rate, should each year be treated separately, or should returns be averaged over time? Should the level of rates and earnings be kept steady throughout the business cycle or raised and lowered as other prices and profits rise and fall? And, finally, should the rate of return be varied to afford an incentive to efficiency? These are the problems discussed below.

Fair Return in Practice

In its decision in the case of *Smyth* v. *Ames,* the Supreme Court listed the matters to be considered in determining fair value, but made no effort to define a fair return. In the Willcox case [51] in 1909, the Court remarked that a fair return is not the same in all cases but varies with circumstances, localities, and differences in risk. And in the Bluefield Waterworks case [52] in 1923, it went on to say that such a return

> . . . must be determined by the exercise of a fair and enlightened judgement, having regard to all relevant facts. A public utility is entitled to such rates as will permit it to earn a return . . . equal to that generally being made at the same time and in the same general part of the country on investments in other business undertakings which are attended by corresponding risks and uncertainties; but it has no constitutional rights to profits such as are realized or anticipated in highly profitable enterprises or speculative ventures. The return should be reasonably sufficient to assure confidence in the financial soundness of the utility and should be adequate, under efficient and economical management, to maintain and support its credit and enable it to raise the money necessary for the proper discharge of its public duties. A rate of return may be reasonable at one time, and become too high or too low by changes affecting opportunities for investment, the money market, and business conditions generally. [53]

51 / *Willcox* v. *Consolidated Gas Co.,* 212 U.S. 19.

52 / *Bluefield Waterworks and Improvement Co.* v. *Public Service Comn.,* 262 U.S. 679.

53 / *Ibid.,* pp. 692-93.

Here, as in *Smyth* v. *Ames,* the Court listed a number of factors for consideration. But it did not define them or indicate their relative weights. How, for instance, are other undertakings "attended by corresponding risks and uncertainties" to be identified? Under what circumstances is "confidence in the financial soundness" of an enterprise assured? When is the judgment employed in combining such factors to be regarded as "fair and enlightened"? The Court has provided no answers to these questions since 1923.

In principle, the rate of return allowed by the commissions and the courts has supposedly been set to equal that obtainable in other industries with comparable risks. In practice, this standard is not usable. Competitive industries have greater risks. There are unregulated industries with comparable risks, but they enjoy the profits of monopoly. In neither case can the rate of earnings be adopted here.

The return allowed to regulated companies may well be lower than that obtained in other fields. In general, the service sold by these concerns is an essential one, and their sales are steady, growing, and assured. The government grants them a monopoly, protecting them against the entry of competitors and against competition in rates. By regulating their finances, it gives assurance to investors that their savings will be safe. For all these reasons, the companies should be able to market their securities at a low rate of return. The rate, however, must be higher than that obtainable on riskless investments, such as government bonds. For these industries are not entirely free of risk. Through natural hazards (earthquakes, landslides, wind storms, floods, and fires) they may suffer losses not entirely covered by insurance. In business depressions, their revenues may decline. With shifts in industrial location, their markets may disappear. And with new developments in technology, they may encounter the competition of substitutes produced by other industries. The return allowed them is not guaranteed. This return, therefore, may be less than that obtainable in other ventures and must be more than that paid by the government. But this leaves considerable latitude for the determination of a rate.

The rate actually allowed by the commissions and the courts has been conventional or arbitrary, bearing no apparent relation to any statement of principles. It has usually been based on expert testimony, with little pretense of economic analysis. There has been no real study of the conditions governing investment decisions, the character of alternative investment opportunities, or the expectations that must be satisfied if new investments are to be made. Bankers and brokers appearing for the companies have given their opinion that future risks are likely to be great and that earnings, consequently, must be high if securities are to be sold. Witnesses for the public have pointed out that risks, in the past, have been small, and that the rate at which money can be borrowed is low. The commissions and the courts have then exercised their "enlightened judgement," coming up with a figure that they have rarely attempted to explain. Usually, this figure has fallen somewhere between 5½ and 8 percent. The allowed return has differed from state to state and from industry to industry and has varied over time. Among municipal utilities, it has been lowest for water companies, higher for electric companies, still higher for gas and telephone companies, and highest for street railways. The return has been reduced, though tardily, as the cost of money, in the market, has declined. During the twenties, for public utilities in general, it was cut from around 7½ percent to 7 percent; during the thirties, to 6 percent; and during the forties to 5½ percent.[54] In 1966, with market rates of interest rising, the return allowed electric utilities averaged 6.14 percent; that allowed gas utilities averaged 6.32 percent; that allowed other utilities ranged from 5.27 percent to 9.35 percent.[55]

The Attraction of Capital

In its decision in the Hope case, the Supreme Court suggested, as a test of the adequacy of earnings, the ability of a company to attract new capital. The importance of assuring this ability is not to be denied. If regulated undertakings are to keep pace with growing demand, modernize their equipment, and improve their facilities, they must be able to obtain more money from investors by selling bonds and stocks. In itself, this fact affords no standard by which the adequacy of earnings can be judged. Capital may be attracted at low rates or at high ones. But if the rate is lower or higher than is needed for the purpose, regulation has failed. To serve as a standard, it is necessary to take the lowest rate that will insure the needed investment. But how is this rate to be identified? The Court did not say. If the commissions are to use this standard, they must develop measures of their own.

When emphasis is placed on the attraction of new capital, the character of the capital structure must be taken into account. In the past this has rarely been done. A certain return has been fixed for the investment as a whole. The return on bonds and on preferred stock has been fixed by contract between the company and the investors. The return on common has been a residue, depending upon the relative magnitude of the three types of securities. Assume a company capitalized at $5 million and allowed a return of 6 percent, or $300,000, with bonds outstanding at 4 percent and preferred stock at 5 percent. If the company has $1 million in bonds, they get $40,000. If it has another $1 million in preferred stocks, they get $50,000. There is $210,000 left for $3 million of common, a return of 7 percent. But if the company has $2 million in bonds, they get $80,000. And if it has $2 million in preferred stocks, they get $100,000. This leaves $120,000 for $1 million of common, a return of 12 percent. Failure to consider the character of the capital structure thus has two undesirable effects. It encourages overissuance of bonds and preferred stocks, burdening companies with fixed charges and making them highly vulnerable to contractions in demand. And it forces consumers to pay the holders of common stocks a higher return than they would otherwise obtain.

In fixing a rate of return that will be sufficient to attract the necessary capital, a distinction should be made among types of securities, and each type given the return that it requires. In the case of bonds and preferred stocks

54 / Eli W. Clemens, *Economics and Public Utilities* (New York: Appleton-Century-Crofts, 1950), pp. 233-34.

55 / U.S. Senate, Committee on Government Operations, *op. cit.*, pp. 25-27.

already outstanding, this return is easily determined. It has been fixed by contract and is printed on the securities themselves. In the case of new issues, the return required will be fixed by the state of the market. And the terms of such issues, in general, are under commission control. It is only with respect to common stock that determination of an adequate return is difficult.

A standard of capital attraction looks toward the future, as the standard of fair value looked toward the past. The rate required to sell securities today may differ from that obtaining when earlier issues were sold. In the case of bonds and preferred stock, this fact is taken into account. Older issues may bear one rate and newer issues a different one. But in the case of common stock, this is not true. All holders of common get the same return. This return must be high enough to meet the expectations of investors in the future. May it ignore the expectations of investors in the past? Their money is already in hand. If the required return has fallen, it will yield them less than they had been permitted to expect. But there will be nothing for them to do but accept the smaller dividends or sell their shares and pocket the loss. Such a policy, however, would be less than fair. Considerations of equity are not to be forgotten. The rate of return, therefore, cannot be set with a view to the future alone. The treatment accorded past investments, moreover, may affect the decisions of those whose capital is sought today.

Fairness to former investors and attraction of new ones may not lead to the same return. A rate set for one of these purposes is likely to be too high or too low for the other. This dilemma could be avoided if common stocks were classified and given different rights to share in earnings, or if they could be issued at different prices and then paid the same dividends. But such arrangements have been subject to abuse and are now prohibited by law. John Bauer has proposed that common stocks, like other securities, be placed on a contractual basis, each issue bearing its appropriate return.[56] The proposal has obvious advantages. Old investors would be treated fairly, receiving what they had been permitted to expect. New shares would bear whatever rate was required to effect their sale. The amount of earnings needed would be definite. But there are also disadvantages. The risks that still remain in regulated industries prevent a fixed return on common stock. The return, of course, could be guaranteed. But in this case the function of taking risks would be assumed by government. A fixed return, moreover, would remove a possible incentive to efficiency. The holders of common would have no more reason to interest themselves in management than those of other securities. The normal functions of ownership would virtually disappear. A single rate of return for common stock, both old and new, would seem to be inevitable.

As a minimum, the return on common stock must be set at the level that is required to enable the regulated company to sell new shares. But how is this level to be ascertained? It is possible, of course, by examining the earnings-price ratio (showing the relation between annual earnings per share and the price at which a share is quoted on the market) or the dividends-price ratio (showing

56 / John Bauer, *Transforming Public Utility Regulation* (New York: Harper & Bros., 1950), chap. x.

the relation between the annual dividends per share and its market price) to determine the average return that sufficed to make such securities marketable in the past. But the problem is to discover the return that will be needed to attract new equity capital in the future. And this may differ.

The needed return will depend upon many factors, all of them uncertain. It will depend upon the character of anticipations as to future yields. It may be less affected by prospective dividends than by prospective earnings, since investors may be less interested in income than in a possible appreciation of capital values. It will be influenced by anticipations of earnings, not only in the utility industry, but also in other industries that compete with it for funds. Investors, moreover, may discount anticipated yields. They have, in fact, bid utility shares up to prices that result in earnings ratios as low as 5 percent and dividends as low as 2 percent. It does not follow, however, that capital can be attracted indefinitely at such rates, since these prices were evidently established in expectation of a continued upward trend in earnings. Market values reflect the market's psychology. And the market is volatile, its outlook changing from season to season, even from day to day.

In the circumstances, selection of a necessary rate of return is little more than guesswork. Neither the commissions nor the courts have any way of telling what the future earnings of industries competing for capital will be, what their dividend policies will be, or how far investors may go in discounting anticipated changes in yields. They have no basis, therefore, for determining the required level of earnings. The best that they can do is to fix a return that surely will be high enough to attract needed capital. But this, in fact, may be higher than is actually required. Control of the rate of return, in the nature of the case, cannot be tight.[57]

The Earnings Period

The period employed in controlling earnings is a single year. The volume sold in the previous year is multiplied by the prospective rates, the costs of that year are deducted, and the remaining income is taken as a percentage of the rate base. But the realization of this percentage is not assured. The commissions do not attempt to forecast the future. And if they did, they might not succeed. Demand may prove to be larger and costs smaller than they have assumed, or vice versa. Earnings may therefore be higher or lower than they have planned. But rates are not adjusted, in the next year, to compensate for these discrepancies. Earnings are not averaged, surpluses recaptured, or deficits made up. Each year is taken as sufficient in itself.

This procedure was required, until the thirties, by the decisions of the Supreme Court.[58] It is open to serious criticism. Where consumers, through

57 / See James C. Bonbright, *Principles of Public Utility Rates* (New York: Columbia University Press, 1961), pp. 246-56.

58 / *Knoxville* v. *Knoxville Water Co.,* 212 U.S. 1 (1909); *Galveston Electric Co.* v. *Galveston,* 258 U.S. 388 (1922); *Georgia Rwy. and Power Co.* v. *Comm.,* 263 U.S. 625 (1923); *Pub. Util. Comnrs.* v. *New York Telephone Co.,* 271 U.S. 23 (1926).

miscalculation by the commissions, have been forced to pay rates that have yielded more than a fair return, the surplus should not go to the companies. And where investors, conversely, have failed to realize a fair return, they should not be compelled to bear the loss. Where earnings fluctuate, securities are made more speculative and the cost of obtaining capital higher than need be. And where earnings are uncertain, managements are reluctant to experiment with price reductions that might prove advantageous to consumers and investors alike.

The alternative to discontinuous control of earnings is continuous control, taking a longer period and balancing the good years with the bad. Under such a policy, a reserve fund with maximum and minimum limits could be established. The excess earnings of one year would be paid into the fund. The deficient earnings of another would be supplemented by drawing on it. If the fund exceeded the maximum set, rates could be cut. If it fell below the minimum, they could be raised. Consumers and investors would both thus be protected against miscalculation by the commissions. Securities would be made less speculative and the cost of capital reduced. With recovery of possible losses assured, an obstacle to experimentation with lower rates would be removed.

Whatever the law, it is likely that commissions have always been influenced by past earnings in determining future rates. But there are only two or three places where plans have been adopted that provide for continuous control.

Policy in the Business Cycle

Adjustments to changes in the general level of prices, it was argued above, might better be made through the rate of return than through the rate base. It remains to consider whether such adjustments should be made at all. Should the prices fixed for regulated services and the earnings allowed investors in such services be held steady during prosperity and depression or kept in line with prices and earnings in other industries?

In the past, prices and earnings have not been completely rigid. Prices have been adjusted in response to changes in operating costs, and the rate of return has been modified in response to changes in interest rates. But the costs of regulated industries are relatively inflexible. Adjustments to changes have been tardy. And modifications in the rate of return have been slow and small. Prices and earnings, in these industries, have been less flexible than in other fields. Their prices have not kept pace with other prices. Their earnings have not been governed by changes in the cost of living or in the earnings obtainable elsewhere.

The relative rigidity of these prices may make for greater instability. When they are maintained in depression, investors get more and consumers are left with less than would otherwise be the case. But, of the two, investors have the lower propensity to spend. The effect of maintaining their incomes is therefore deflationary. On the other hand, when these prices are maintained in prosperity, investors get less and consumers are left with more than otherwise. And since consumers have a higher propensity to spend, the effect is inflationary. By altering these prices, during the successive phases of the business cycle, regulation could make some contribution toward reducing the fluctuations in business activity. By cutting prices in depression, shifting income from investors to consumers, it could help to cushion the slump. And by raising prices in prosperity, shifting income from consumers to investors, it could help to check a boom. If control were to be adapted to this purpose, investors would be given a low return in depression, a high return in prosperity, a fair return when averaged over the cycle as a whole. The importance of such a policy, however, is open to question. The possible variation in prices would not be large. The greatest cut possible in a depression would be the amount of dividends plus the annual depreciation charge. It is unlikely that all of this would be taken. And only a part of that taken would be shifted from money saved to money spent. The contribution to recovery would probably be small. So, too, with the effect of an increase in price during prosperity. Greater flexibility is probably desirable. But its significance as a stabilizer should not be overemphasized.

Two arguments are advanced in support of a policy of raising earnings during prosperity. The first is ethical: to be fair to investors, earnings should be kept in line with the prices of consumers' goods so that their real income will remain the same. The second is economic: earnings must be kept in line with those in other industries if capital is to be obtained. The ethical argument is untenable. The holders of bonds and preferred stocks are not paid in dollars of constant purchasing power. The holders of common stocks were never promised such a return. They have no real claim for preferential treatment. It should be noted, moreover, that investors advance this argument only when prices rise, never when they fall. The test of the economic argument is to be found in the market. The bonds and the preferred stocks of regulated companies, presumably, will be floated at prices that will sell them. The only question that arises is whether common can be sold. It is possible that investors will continue to buy shares that yield a smaller but a steadier return than that obtainable elsewhere. If so, earnings need not be increased. But it is also possible that the comparative yield of shares in regulated companies may be regarded so unfavorably that their market value will decline. In this case, if new shares are to find buyers, the rate of return should be increased.

Incentive to Efficiency

Under the present pattern of control, no effort is made to effect adjustments in the rate of returns so as to afford an incentive to efficiency. The same rate is allowed to companies that are well managed and to those that are not. If a company obtains a larger return than that allowed, it may keep the excess. And, with rate reductions lagging, this situation may persist for years. An incentive is thus afforded for cutting costs. But if rate reductions were prompt, this incentive would be substantially reduced. And if earnings control, instead of being discontinuous, were made continuous, averaging the good years with the bad, it would disappear.

An incentive could be provided if the commissions were to tie the rate of return to changes in costs, penalizing inefficiency by reducing the return as costs rise and rewarding efficiency by increasing the return as costs fall. In this way, the gains resulting from good management might be shared between consumers and investors. But such a program would not be easy to administer. Costs might rise, not through inefficiency but through causes, such as a decline in demand, that management was powerless to control. Costs might fall through causes, such as impairment of service, for which little credit was due. It would be necessary, therefore, to identify the gains resulting from efficiency. And for this purpose, standards of performance and methods of measurement would have to be devised. The application of such standards would be difficult. And it would take the commissions a long way into the domain of management.

Rewards for efficiency would not be questioned in the courts. But penalties for inefficiency would be appealed. And here, the standards and measurements employed would have to be submitted to review. The prospect is one that would not be welcomed by the companies, the commissions, or the courts themselves. An even more serious obstacle to the imposition of such penalties is to be found in their effect upon the ability of a company to attract new capital. A reduction in earnings would make it harder to sell securities. It would thus perpetuate antiquated methods and obstruct investments required in the public interest. The rate of return could be increased to reward efficiency, but it could not well be cut to penalize inefficiency.

THE RECORD OF EARNINGS CONTROL

Among the possible purposes of rate level control, regulation has shown little interest in the expansion of output and use, in the promotion of efficiency, or in the stabilization of economic activity. Its sole function has been that of striking a balance between the interests of consumers and investors, preventing the extortion of monopoly profits while preserving the ability of regulated companies to attract new capital. Of these two objectives, it is clear that the latter has been served. Where monopoly has persisted, as in the case of telephone, gas, and electric services, regulated companies have encountered no difficulty in selling their securities. But in preventing excessive earnings, regulation has had but limited success. In general, the rate of return obtained by regulated monopolies has been well above that required to pay interest on bonds and to maintain a market for preferred and common stocks.

The hand of regulation has been lax. Operating expenses have not been tightly controlled. Income taxes have been covered as a cost. Intangibles have been included in the rate base. Land has been overvalued. Facilities have been overpriced. Depreciation, already covered as an expense, has not always been deducted in the valuation of depreciated property. The rate of return allowed has been arbitrarily determined and set at a higher level than would have been required. And where earnings have exceeded this allowance, the surplus has been left with the regulated companies. Judged by the standards of the competitive market, regulation has fallen short. Competition, where it is present, affords a sterner discipline.

Chapter 14   THE RATE STRUCTURE

If a company were to sell its services at a uniform price per unit, without allowing for the differences in cost or in demand involved in making different sales, regulation could concern itself exclusively with problems of the rate level, ignoring those presented by the rate structure. But when a company classifies its services, charging different prices to different customers, and when it grants discounts to those who buy in greater quantities, the structure as well as the level of rates becomes a matter of concern. The rate level has to do only with total revenues, costs, and earnings: with assurance of equity in the relationship between investors as a group and consumers as a group. The rate structure has to do with particular charges: with equity in the relationships among consumers. Earnings that are fair both to investors and to consumers, as a whole, may be produced by rates that are differentiated in a variety of ways. One pattern of differentiation may be neutral in its effect upon competition among concerns that buy a common service, such as electric power or the movement of freight; another may give one competitor an unfair advantage and place a second under an unfair handicap. One pattern may require all customers to contribute, on an equitable basis, to the costs incurred in serving them; another may grant one group a subsidy and subject a second to a tax. The attention of regulators must therefore be directed, not only to the revenue produced by a company's rates, taken as an aggregate, but also to the rates themselves, taken individually; not only to the propriety of the earnings that they yield, but also to the consequences that flow from the ways in which they are related, one to another.

BASES OF PRICE DIFFERENTIATION

Differences in rates are based, in part, on differences in cost. It may cost less to serve one class of customers than another, to sell in larger quantities than in smaller ones. Differences in rates are also based, more largely, on differences in demand. Rates are set low where demand is elastic: where customers have less need for a service or less ability to pay for it, and where they can provide it for themselves or obtain it from a company's competitors. Rates are kept high where demand is inelastic: where the buyer's need and ability to pay are great, and where the seller possesses a monopoly.

321

If rates are proportioned to costs, some buyers will pay less than others, but the seller will not discriminate. Where his customers engage in competition, his position will be one of strict neutrality, affording none an artificial advantage, imposing on none an artificial handicap. As among consumers, he will play no favorites, subsidizing none and taxing none. But differences in rates may not be proportionate to differences in cost. At times they may be smaller; more often they will be larger. And here, discrimination will occur.

In part, discrimination is unavoidable. For it is usually impossible precisely to determine unit costs. Some costs are clearly identified with output and can readily be charged to particular kilowatt-hours or ton miles. This is true, for instance, of direct labor and of fuel. But other costs are jointly incurred in rendering different types of service. They do not vary directly with output, but decline in significance as output grows. These are the costs of capital—interest and depreciation—and administrative overhead. Where investments are heavy, as with railroads and electrical utilities, such costs are large. As a matter of accounting they must be allocated among the different units of service. But there is no correct way in which this may be done. The process of allocation necessarily involves an exercise of judgment. Whatever the result, it is open to dispute. Even if companies sought to make their rates proportionate to their costs, therefore, it would be impossible to tell for certain whether they had succeeded or failed.

Discrimination is not only inadvertent; it is also purposive. By discriminating among its customers, a company may expand its sales and enlarge its revenues. It may effect a fuller utilization of its facilities, spread its fixed costs over more units of output, and thus reduce its unit costs. Through larger revenues and lower costs, it may seek greater profits. Regulation, of course, is designed to keep profits within bounds. But for regulators, too, discrimination has its uses. It may be needed to enable a company to cover its costs and obtain a fair return on its investment. It may contribute to a lower general level of rates and to a wider use of regulated services. It may be employed to encourage uses that are thought to be socially desirable and to discourage those that are not.

Differences in Cost

In moving goods by rail, it can readily be shown that one ton is costlier than another. Goods that are bulky in relation to their weight take up more space than those whose density is high, goods that are irregular in size and shape take more space than those that can be stacked. Goods that must be loaded by hand cost more than those that can be loaded mechanically. Goods that require special equipment or services, such as refrigeration for fruit or watering for livestock, cost more than those that do not. Since railroads assume the risk of loss or damage, valuable goods cost more than cheap goods, small articles (being easily stolen) more than large ones, and fragile articles (being easily broken) more than sturdy ones. Since shippers themselves load goods moving in carloads, such shipments cost the railroads less than those in less-than-carload lots. And since regularity of movement permits economy in operation, goods moving in steady volume cost less than those that move sporadically.

It can be shown, too, that one mile is costlier than another. Terminal costs are as high for short hauls as for long hauls. Line costs may be higher, since short hauls involve fewer cars per train, poorer loading, and more frequent stops. Costs per mile, therefore, decline with distance, being lower for the longer hauls. Costs may even be unlike for equal distances. They are higher in the mountains than on the plains, in floodlands than on safer ground, and in the wintry North than in the sunny South. A mile costs more where traffic is sparse than where it is plentiful. It costs more where goods move in the direction of heavy traffic than where they move in the direction of empty cars.

In the sale of electricity, likewise, it can be shown that one kilowatt-hour costs more than another. The costs of this service, as they are presented by accountants, are divided into three categories: output costs, customer costs, and demand costs. Output costs are those incurred in the operation of a plant: the costs of labor, fuel, materials, and supplies. They vary with the volume of production. Customer costs are those incurred in reading meters, sending and collecting bills, keeping accounts, and the like. They vary with the number of customers. Demand costs are also known as readiness-to-serve costs. They are the overhead costs of capital and management involved in providing a plant that is large enough to meet the peak demand that may be made on it at any day and hour. They are thus a function of capacity. Differences in total cost per kilowatt-hour cannot be attributed to output costs, since they are roughly the same for each unit produced. They can be attributed, to some extent, to customer costs, since these costs decline, per kilowatt-hour, as a customer's consumption grows. Such differences, however, are not large enough to be of major significance. It is in demand costs, therefore, that the explanation for differences in cost per kilowatt-hour is mainly to be found. Investment in electric plants is heavy and overhead costs, accordingly, are high. The investment required depends upon the peak demand. A kilowatt-hour taken at the peak adds to the overhead; one taken at another time does not. The cost of the first, therefore, is higher than that of the second.

Utility accountants, in their analysis of costs, speak of the load factor of a utility system, the load factor of an individual customer, and the diversity factor of the system as a whole. The system's load factor is its average load expressed as a percentage of its peak load. Thus, if the average load over a period is 6,000 kilowatts and the peak at any moment is 9,000, the load factor is 66-2/3 percent. The customer's load factor is his average consumption expressed as a percentage of his maximum consumption. The system's diversity factor is determined by adding up the maximum demands of all of its customers, whenever they occur, and dividing this sum by the maximum demand made on the system as a whole at any one time. Thus, customer A may take one kilowatt at 8 a.m., customer B two kilowatts at noon, and customer C three kilowatts at 4 p.m., a total of six kilowatts; the maximum demand made on the system at any hour, however, may be three kilowatts; the diversity factor, therefore, is 2.

The average cost per kilowatt-hour will be reduced if the system's load factor can be raised. This may be accomplished in two ways: by improving the load factor of each customer or by raising the diversity factor. The customer's load factor may be improved by encouraging him to increase his consumption, using more power at off-peak hours. The diversity factor may be raised by attracting groups of customers whose maximum demands will be scattered, also coming at off-peak hours. Thus, there is in the nature of utility costs a basis for differentiating rates, setting them at different levels for different classes of customers, and reducing them as a customer buys in larger quantities.

Differences in Demand

The differentiation of rates is to be explained, in larger measure, by differences in demand. For some classes of customers and for some quantities of service, demand is relatively inelastic; for others, relatively elastic. In the first case, more money can be obtained if rates are kept high; in the second, if they are made low. Where a seller, by charging a single price, can make sufficient sales to keep his facilities fully employed and obtain sufficient revenue to cover his costs and earn a fair return, he will not be likely to discriminate among his customers. But a price set low enough to maintain full production may not yield sufficient revenue to cover costs. And one set high enough to cover costs may leave capacity in idleness. In such a case, the seller will find it to his advantage to discriminate.

Consider the monopolist whose situation is depicted in Table 14-1. The sales that he can make and the revenue he can obtain by selling all of his output at various prices are shown in the first three columns. His total costs are shown in the fourth. These include both the costs of capital and management that remain fixed whatever the volume of output and the costs of operation that vary with the quantity produced. And, for the sake of cimplicity, they are assumed to include a fair return on the investment in the plant. The final column shows the resulting profit, in excess of a fair return, or the resulting loss. The monopolist, if he sells at a single price, will choose the one that will yield him the greatest profit. In this situation he will charge $6 and produce 400 units. Let us assume, however, that his plant is big enough to turn out 2,000 units or more. He could sell this quantity at $2, but here he would not cover his costs. He could cover his costs at $5, but here he would be left with idle capacity. Suppose, however, that the seller discriminates. The result is shown in Table 14-2. Here, the prices, sales, and costs shown are the same as those in Table 14-1. But the seller divides his customers into separate groups and collects a different price from each. His total revenue is increased, as shown. And the resulting profit or loss (aside from a fair return) is sharply changed. Here, again, the monopolist will seek the greatest profit. But he will obtain it by creating a number of customer classes, charging those in the top group as much as $9 and selling to those in the bottom group for as little as $2. With such a scale of prices, he can operate close to full capacity. And he can raise his extra profit from $100 to $2,400.

Such discrimination cannot be practiced unless it is possible to divide the market, separating one sector from another, so that those charged the higher rate cannot buy in the low-rate sector, and so that those buying at the lower rate cannot resell in the high-rate sector. With transportation and public utilities, however, such a division is readily achieved. For these industries sell services, rather than transferable goods, and control their use by delivering them as they are consumed. If a railroad charges more for hauling textiles than for hauling

TABLE 14-1
An Unregulated Monopolist Selling at a Single Price

Price	Sales	Total Revenue	Total Cost	Profit or Loss
$9.00	100	$ 900	$1,400	−$ 500
8.00	200	1,600	1,750	− 150
7.00	300	2,100	2,050	50
6.00	400	2,400	2,300	100
5.00	500	2,500	2,500	0
4.00	700	2,800	3,000	− 200
3.00	1,000	3,000	3,400	− 400
2.50	1,400	3,500	4,100	− 600
2.00	2,000	4,000	5,000	− 1,000
1.50	2,800	4,200	6,400	− 2,200
1.00	3,600	3,600	8,000	− 4,400

coal, the textile manufacturer cannot get the lower rate by having his goods loaded onto coal cars. And if a gas or electric company charges a householder more than it charges a manufacturer, the householder cannot get the lower rate by connecting his dwelling with the factory's pipes or wires.

TABLE 14-2
An Unregulated Monopolist Discriminating in Price

Price	Sales	Sales in Each Class	Revenue from Each Class	Total Revenue	Total Cost	Profit or Loss
$9.00 . . .	100	100	$ 900	$ 900	$1,400	−$ 500
8.00 . . .	200	100	800	1,700	1,750	− 50
7.00 . . .	300	100	700	2,400	2,050	350
6.00 . . .	400	100	600	3,000	2,300	700
5.00 . . .	500	100	500	3,500	2,500	1,000
4.00 . . .	700	200	800	4,300	3,000	1,300
3.00 . . .	1,000	300	900	5,200	3,400	1,800
2.50 . . .	1,400	400	1,000	6,200	4,100	2,100
2.00 . . .	2,000	600	1,200	7,400	5,000	2,400
1.50 . . .	2,800	800	1,200	8,600	6,400	2,200
1.00 . . .	3,600	1,200	1,200	9,800	8,000	1,800

Discrimination is not without its limits. No group can be made to pay more than it believes the service to be worth. At higher prices, business would be diverted or destroyed. A ceiling is set, therefore, by what the traffic will bear. No sales will be made, on the other hand, for less than the added costs of labor, fuel, and supplies (the marginal variable costs) that they entail. Otherwise, the seller would make them at a loss. A floor is thus established by his out-of-pocket costs. Within these limits, however, the latitude for variation may be wide.

From his sales as a whole, the seller must recover not only the variable costs of operation but also the fixed costs of capital and administration. These costs are jointly incurred in serving all classes of customers. But they need not be charged equally against each unit sold. From some sales, it may be possible to recover a good bit more than average total costs; from others, a good bit less. As long as he gets something (above his variable costs) to contribute to his fixed costs and his profits, it will be worth the seller's while to cut his price, where he must do so, in order to obtain additional customers or to sell in larger quantities. He will therefore fix his charges, for different customers and for different quantities, in accordance with his judgment as to elasticity of demand. Where demand appears to be elastic, he will ask less toward overhead and profit; where it seems to be inelastic, he will take more.

The Case for Discrimination

Discrimination may have certain marked advantages. First, it may bring about a fuller employment of facilities and a wider consumption of services. Thus, in Table 14-2 we saw that output was raised from 400 units to 2,000 units. Second, discrimination may result in lower prices for all consumers. The price reductions in the lower groups need not be offset by price increases in the upper groups. At every level in the scale, including the highest, the price charged can be lower than would be the case if the seller did not discriminate. But this gain is unlikely to be realized unless rates and earnings are controlled.

Let us refer again to Table 14-2. Here, the monopolist obtained $2,400 beyond the fair return that we assumed to be included as a cost. He did so by taking from each class of customers all that the traffic would bear. He cut some prices from $6 to $5, $4, $3, and $2; he raised others from $6 to $7, $8, and $9. Now let us assume that rates are regulated. The regulatory agency limits earnings to a fair return. If the law were to prohibit discrimination, the price fixed would be $5, as is shown in Table 14-1, and 500 units would be produced and sold. But suppose the law permits discrimination. The results are shown in Table 14-3. Here, again, the prices, sales, and costs are the same as those previously shown. As in Table 14-2, consumers are classified and a different price charged in each class. But here, a fair return is obtained from a scale of prices that begins at $1.50. The volume of output is raised to 2,800 units. And every price in the scale, up to the top price of $3, is well below the $5 that would have to be charged if discrimination were not allowed. The customer who pays $3 is not harmed when the same service is sold to another for $1.50. On the contrary, he is helped, since this enables him to save $2 himself.

It is on this basis that discrimination has long been permitted in railroad and public utility rates. If the railroads, for instance, were to establish a uniform rate per ton at a figure that would cover average total costs, they would not improve the position of shippers whose commodities now bear the higher rates. In fact, they would worsen it. For producers of heavy and bulky low-value goods, that are now carried at low rates, could no longer afford to ship them. The volume of traffic would decline. All of the railroads' fixed charges would have to be met by the traffic that remained. The rates paid by high-value traffic would have to be raised. Shippers who now pay high rates should therefore be happy that other shippers are served at low rates.

TABLE 14-3

A Regulated Monopolist Discriminating in Price

Price	Sales	Sales in Each Class	Revenue from Each Class	Total Revenue	Total Cost	Profit or Loss
$3.00 ...	1,000	1,000	$3,000	$3,000	$3,400	−$400
2.50 ...	1,400	400	1,000	4,000	4,100	− 100
2.00 ...	2,000	600	1,200	5,200	5,000	200
1.50 ...	2,800	800	1,200	6,400	6,400	0
1.00 ...	3,600	1,200	1,200	7,600	8,000	− 400

For discrimination to be so justified, however, certain conditions must obtain. First, there must be a heavy investment entailing high fixed costs and a substantial amount of capacity standing in idleness, so that costs per unit can be reduced by spreading the fixed costs over a larger volume of output. Second, the lower rates must be needed to get business that would not otherwise exist. Third, they must be high enough to cover variable costs and contribute something to overhead. And fourth, the whole scale of rates must be regulated to keep earnings reasonable and to keep discrimination within bounds.

DISCRIMINATION IN PRACTICE

The rate structures of most industries rendering transportation and public utility services are highly differentiated. The differences found in them are based, in part, on differences in cost. But they are to be explained, in larger measure, by differences in demand. In the railroad and electric industries, in particular, discrimination is deliberate and detailed. The railroads discriminate among commodities and among hauls, charging more overhead to one ton or mile and less to another. The utility companies discriminate among customers, according to the uses made of their service and the quantities consumed, collecting more where they can get it and less where they cannot. Discrimination, in these industries, is a settled policy, practiced by the companies and accepted by the law.

Railroad Rates

Passenger fares show relatively little discrimination. Higher fares are charged in parlor and Pullman cars and lower fares on commutation trains. But the principle of classifying service, so common in Europe, is little used in the United States. Circuitous lines meet the fares of direct lines for service between competitive points, and lower fares are offered for special trips. But, in general, the railroads charge a uniform fare per mile. They practice discrimination, chiefly, in the structure of rates for freight.

More than 10,000 different commodities are hauled on the rails. These appear as some 25,000 commodity descriptions when differences in packing and manner of shipment are taken into account. There are freight stations at some 35,000 locations in the United States. Goods can move between these stations by scores or even hundreds of different routes. As a result, if rates were specified item by item and haul by haul, there could be tens of millions of separate rates. The structure of rates has been simplified, however, in two ways. First, the railroads have adopted systems of classifying commodities. Three standard systems were developed before 1890 by committees representing the carriers: one known as the "Official Classification" in the northeastern states, one in the South, and one in the West. There were seven regular classes in the Official Classification, twelve in the Southern, and ten in the Western, identical commodities being differently classified in the three regions. In 1952, regional classifications were superseded by a uniform classification, with 31 classes, in the area east of the Rocky Mountains. Under such systems, particular commodities packed in particular ways are assigned to particular classes and all commodities in the same class pay the same rate. Second, the computation of rates for different distances is also simplified. Rates based on cost would be less than proportionate to distance, as we have seen, since long hauls cost less per mile than short hauls. But distance rates are not made to conform precisely to differences in cost. Instead of being tapered mile by mile, they are reduced in mileage blocks. And rates for several points of origin or destination may be combined in common groups. In spite of these devices, the structure of rates remains a complicated one. There are some 75,000 freight tariffs in use in the United States. And a single tariff may run to more than a thousand pages.

The rate structure discriminates among commodities. The classes of freight are numbered from 400 to 13. Goods in classes above 100 move at multiples of the Class 100 rate. Those in classes below 100 move at percentages of that rate. But discrimination does not stop here. Most of the goods carried in less-than-carload lots pay the class rates. But some of them pay "exception ratings" which are much lower. These are ratings that were established for the purpose of meeting the competition of motor carriers in hauling light weight, valuable goods. Around 85 percent of all freight moves, in carload lots, at "commodity rates." These apply to the transportation, in large quantities, of specific commodities between specific points. Ton for ton, they are set far below other rates. This has long been done to make possible the movement of heavy, bulky, low-grade goods and, in particular, to meet the competition of water carriers. In the structure of rates as a whole, therefore, the differences between commodities are great. And these differences bear little relation to differences in cost. In a study made in 1960 the Interstate Commerce Commission compared the carload revenues from certain commodities with the full cost of hauling them, including overhead and return on investment, and found, for instance, that sugar beets were hauled at 42 percent of cost, pulpwood at 57 percent, fresh vegetables at 63 percent, gasoline at 77 percent, bituminous coal at 82 percent, baled cotton at 123 percent, pig iron at 138 percent, crude rubber at 160 percent, automobiles at 171 percent, cigarettes at 185 percent, liquors at 200 percent, and explosives at 324 percent.[1] The differences in the rates charged for transporting such commodities depend, not on differences in cost, but on differences in the elasticity of demand.

The rate structure discriminates, too, among hauls. Some discrimination is incidental to the practice of simplifying the structure by using distance blocks, relating rates to key points, and grouping points of origin and destination; more is a consequence of the policy of so fixing rates on particular hauls as to meet those charged by competing carriers and so fixing rates for particular locations as to equalize their competitive opportunities. Thus, a circuitous line will match the rate charged between two points by a direct line, and a railroad will match the rate charged between ports by a water carrier, maintaining higher rates at other points. And where two producing points are at unequal distances from a common source of raw material or a common market for their product, the more distant point will be given the same rate as the nearer one. These differences have nothing to do with costs: rates are lower where demand is made elastic by competition, higher where it is not.

The Rates of Other Carriers

Among other carriers, discrimination has been a serious problem only in the case of oil pipelines. These lines are owned and operated by the major refiners. But they also carry oil to independent refineries. In this situation there is danger that the majors may handicap the independents by charging high rates or imposing unreasonable restrictions on their services. The problem presented is a special one, having to do with competition in the oil industry.

With water carriers along the coasts and on the Great Lakes, the fixed costs of vessels and terminal services are substantial. The marginal cost of handling a particular shipment thus falls below its total unit cost. The shiplines are therefore under pressure to increase their cargoes by discriminating in their rates. They charge less where they meet the competition of rail and motor carriers;

1 / Cited in Charles F. Phillips, Jr., *The Economics of Regulation* (Homewood, Ill.: Richard D. Irwin, Inc., Rev. Ed., 1969), p. 322.

more where they do not. With inland water carriers, the fixed costs of barges and terminals are lower than with the others and there is less temptation to discriminate. Here, the freight classification established by the railroads is used and rates are based on railroad rates. Most traffic moves, however, on commodity rates. To compensate for slower service, these are set at a fixed differential—usually 20 percent—below rail rates. The discrimination found in the railway rate structure is thus reflected, at a lower level, in water rates.

In the case of motor carriers, where investment in rights of way is unnecessary and investment in rolling stock is smaller than with the railroads, fixed costs are low and marginal cost is close to total unit cost. It would thus be possible for these carriers to establish a nondiscriminatory rate structure—one that would closely conform to their unit costs. Instead of doing so, they have patterned their structure after that adopted by the railroads, with rates set at or near the discriminatory charges made for hauls by rail. The motor carriers discriminate, too, by using railway rather than highway distances in making rates, and by making greater reductions in rates for more-than-truckload shipments than are justified by savings in costs.

The airlines, like the truckers, need not invest in ways or terminals. But their investment in aircraft is substantial. They therefore have a strong incentive to establish a structure of rates that will keep their planes in the air rather than on the ground and flying well filled rather than poorly filled. Until 1948, all passengers were carried at a common rate, fares being determined by multiplying distances by a common charge per mile. Thereafter, different types of service were introduced and fares were differentiated to promote traffic. At present, lower fares are charged for coach services than for first class and even lower fares for youth, family, stand-by, and shuttle services. The structure of fares is discriminatory, favoring short hauls over long hauls, routes where the density of traffic is low over those where it is high, and first-class service over coach service. Air express rates are made proportionate to distance, in mileage blocks, but are subject to arbitrary minima for small shipments and for short hauls. Lower rates are charged for certain commodities, such as newspapers and securities. Air freight, offering slower service, is carried at lower rates than air express. Here, rates are higher for directions in which traffic is heavy and lower for directions in which it is light. The structure of rates is thus discriminatory both for express and for freight.

Electric Rates

In the early years of the service, electricity was sold at a uniform rate per kilowatt-hour. Then, as producers sought to extend their operations, they began to discriminate. In order to sell to groups who were unable or unwilling to buy at the established rate, they classified their customers, fixing a lower rate for the new customers, maintaining the higher rate for the older ones. And in order to encourage greater consumption by present customers, they fixed lower rates for larger quantities, maintaining the higher rate for smaller ones. As a result, the structure of electric rates came to be highly differentiated. Different classes were established for residential use, commercial light and power, industrial power, etc., and rates were differentiated from class to class. Within each class, moreover, consumption was divided into blocks, measured in kilowatt-hours, and rates were reduced in succeeding blocks. Thus, the average rate per kilowatt-hour charged for residential use might be 4 cents, for commercial use 3 cents, and for industrial use, 1½ cents. And among residential users, the charge for the first 50 kwh. per month might be 5 cents per kwh.; for the next 150 kwh., 3 cents; and for everything above 250 kwh., 2 cents. As a consequence of these distinctions, the spread between the upper and lower rates came to be substantial, industrial users being favored over residential users and large consumers over smaller ones.

The differences thus created have been modified with the passage of time, the ratio of domestic to commercial and industrial rates dropping from 1.93 to 1 in 1951 to 1.71 to 1 in 1964.[2] But discrimination persists, the differences corresponding, in general, to differences in the elasticity of demand. Big industrial users have the alternative of generating their own power; their demand, therefore, is highly elastic; their rates are low. Other users lack this alternative; their demand is less elastic; their rates are higher. Householders can use gas rather than electricity for cooking; for this purpose their demand is elastic; the additional kilowatt-hours used in cooking fall in the quantity blocks where rates are low. Householders, on the other hand, are unlikely to substitute gas, kerosene, or candles for electricity in lighting; their demand for this purpose is inelastic; the hours used in lighting fall in the first block where rates are high. Both customer classes and quantity blocks are set up by the utility companies on the basis of their judgment of what the traffic will bear.

The companies deny that they discriminate, defending their rates by presenting analyses of costs. Output costs (for labor, fuel, etc.) are distributed among customers in proportion to their consumption as measured by meters. Customer costs (for billing, collecting, etc.) are charged equally to each customer. And demand costs (for the investment necessitated by readiness to serve) are also calculated for individual customers. These costs may be measured by the number of switches a customer can turn on, the number of appliances he uses, or, more precisely, by a meter that has recorded his consumption at its half-hourly peak during the previous year.

The different costs may be shown on the consumer's bill. This is done, sometimes, under two-part or three-part rates, which are used most often in the sale of commercial and industrial power. Such systems, however, appear to be complicated and are employed less often in billing householders. Here, a one-part rate is generally used, but it is graduated downward in successive blocks. The recovery of customer costs may be assured by making a minimum charge (say $1 a month) though nothing is consumed, or by making a flat charge for the first block consumed (say $1 for the first 10 kwh.). Or it may be assumed

2 / William G. Shepherd and Thomas S. Gies, *Utility Regulation* (New York: Random House, 1966), p. 16.

that customer costs are recovered from the high rate charged in the first block. It is assumed, too, that demand costs are recovered in the earlier blocks. And it is therefore held that rates in these blocks must be high, while rates in later blocks—since they need cover only output costs—may properly be low.

Such a rate structure, however, is clearly discriminatory. The amount of money that must be invested in a utility business depends upon the size of the plant it must build, and the size of the plant is determined by the quantity of service it is called on to render during periods of peak demand. Those who use the service during such periods should therefore contribute more heavily than off-peak users toward meeting its capital costs. Under the usual block rate system, however, rates are not varied according to time of use. Some of those who pay the higher rates in the earlier blocks may consume this power off-peak, while some of those who pay the lower rates in the later blocks may consume this power on-peak. The system thus discriminates against the former in favor of the latter.

The crucial question, in judging the discriminatory character of a rate structure, is how the costs of capital (the demand costs of utility accounting) should be allocated. Some economists contend that discrimination is not to be avoided unless all such costs are charged to on-peak users and none of them to off-peak users. (This could be done by installing twin meters controlled by a time switch and charging a higher rate for the consumption shown by the on-peak meter than for that shown by the off-peak meter.) Other economists object that periods of peak demand are subject to constant change, and that allocation on this basis would therefore necessitate frequent and disturbing changes in the structure of rates. This difficulty could be overcome, however, by announcing changes in advance, at stated intervals, and making them gradually. More serious is the objection that the utility plant is required for the service of off-peak as well as on-peak users and that they should therefore contribute something toward its cost. But how much? The difficulty is that there is no correct method of distributing the costs of capital among the different classes and quantities of service. Any method employed will depend upon the judgment of the person who adopts it. And his judgment is likely to be influenced by his purposes.

The methods of allocating demand costs used by public utility companies have been designed to justify differences in rates by showing corresponding differences in costs, and thus to support the contention that the companies do not discriminate. The differences in the rates charged to different classes of customers were first defended on the ground that they corresponded to differences in their responsibility for peak demand. Householders, supposedly, paid high rates because they turned on their lights at the peak. And manufacturers got low rates because they operated their factories off the peak. In time, however, this argument ceased to serve. With the introduction of electrical appliances, householders came to use more power off-peak. And with the growth of industrial consumption, manufacturers created new peaks of their own. But the companies continued to charge high rates for residential use and low rates for industrial use, whether on the peak or off. A different rationalization was required.

The utilities now employ what is known as the noncoincident demand method of allocating overhead. For this purpose, they compute an aggregate maximum demand by adding together the separate maximum demands of all classes of buyers, although these demands may come at different times. Then they determine the percentage of this aggregate that is attributable to each class. And then, finally, they distribute their overhead costs in accordance with these percentages.

The method is based upon two fallacies. First, it involves circular reasoning. The differences in demand that are used as a guide in allocating costs are not independent of differences in rates, but are themselves determined by these differences. The companies first fix the rates they want to charge. These rates, in turn, affect the quantities demanded. These quantities are then used to govern the distribution of costs. And the costs are presented, finally, to justify the rates. Q.E.D. Second, the method does not make proper allowance for the factor of diversity. The concept of maximum coincident demand for a utility system as a whole is meaningful. The concept of aggregate noncoincident maximum demands of customer classes is not. A company does have to build a plant big enough to meet the peak of coincident demand. It does not have to build one big enough to meet the aggregate of noncoincident demands. For such demands, by definition, occur at different times. If a customer's maximum comes at the same time as the system's maximum, he may properly be charged with more responsibility for the size of the investment that is required. If it comes at any other time, he should be charged with less. But how much more and how much less is open to debate. The so-called demand costs assigned to individual customers under the noncoincident demand method of allocating overhead are arbitrary in character and are not to be accepted as justifying present differences in rates.[3]

The Rates of Other Utilities

The pattern of gas rates is similar to that of electric rates. Customers are classified and rates are varied in accordance with differences in the elasticity of demand. Lower rates are charged, for instance, for industrial than for domestic use, and for space heating and air conditioning than for cooking and water heating where competition is not so stiff. Overhead is allocated on the basis of noncoincident demands. Consumption is measured by meters and rates adjusted downward in successive blocks. But the pattern is simpler than with electricity, and the differentials involved are not as great. This may be attributed, in part, to an important difference in the character of the two services. Electricity must be produced as it is used; gas can be manufactured or imported and kept in storage. With gas, therefore, operations can be carried on with greater regularity. The load factor is less important, and there is less need to improve it by manipulating rates.

3 / Discrimination also results from an "objective rate plan" employed to encourage increased consumption. Here, customers who consume more than they did the year before pay a reduced rate; those who do not, pay the previous rate. Such discrimination may be temporary: if demand proves to be sufficiently elastic, the lower rate will be generalized.

Rates for water are even simpler than those for gas. Consumers are usually classified, consumption metered, and rates reduced in later blocks. But water companies are less interested than other utilities in promoting consumption. The load factor is not important. There are limits to available supplies. And most of the companies are owned and operated by city governments.

Rates for urban transport service are the simplest of all. A single fare, for any distance at any hour, is typical. But this does not avoid discrimination. Long hauls cost more than short hauls. Fares adjusted to costs would increase with distance, in successive zones. In other countries this is usually the case. In the United States, however, the single fare discriminates against the short-haul rider in favor of the long-haul one. In this industry, moreover, the load factor is highly important. The service has high peaks at rush hours and long periods between them when the plant is only partly used. Efforts have sometimes been made to improve this situation by selling passes at low fares, to be honored only during off-peak hours. But discounts are also given for weekly passes and for quantity purchases of tokens that are available for on-peak use. In general, transit fares discriminate against the off-peak user in favor of the on-peak one. The companies would gain if they could differentiate their fares by distance and by time of day. They retain the single-fare system because it is less expensive to administer.

In considering telephone rates, a distinction must be made between toll service and local exchange service. Differences in toll rates conform to differences in costs. Such rates vary with distance and duration. They are lower on station-to-station than on person-to-person calls. And they are lower off-peak, at night and Sundays, than on-peak during business hours. Local rates, however, bear little relation to costs. The level of these rates is based, not on the individual costs of local exchanges, but on the average cost of all the exchanges in a state. As a result, these rates discriminate against densely settled areas where unit costs are low in favor of sparsely settled areas where they are high. In the largest cities, local service is provided at a flat rate for an initial number of calls, with further charges made for added calls. But most local service is rendered at flat rates alone. Aside from coin box service, these rates are not proportioned to the number or duration of calls. Nor are they lowered during off-peak hours. Rates are differentiated, rather, in accordance with differences in the elasticity of demand. The monthly rentals charged for added equipment, for instance, ($1 to $1.25 for a "Princess" phone, 90 cents for an extension phone, and 35 cents for an extension cord) are based, not on costs, ($4.20 a year yields an astronomical return on the company's investment of a few pennies in a length of wire) but on the subscriber's docility. Business users are charged more than domestic users because they find the service indispensable. Domestic users are charged more for single party lines because they are willing to pay for added convenience. They are charged less for multiple-party lines because low rates are needed to bring about the widest possible use of the service. And the more widely the service is used, the more valuable it will be to those who can be made to pay the higher rates. The structure of telephone rates is deliberately discriminatory. And no effort has been made to conceal this fact beneath the cloak of an arbitrary allocation of costs.

REGULATION OF RAILWAY RATE STRUCTURES

When it is said that a regulatory agency "fixes" rates, this does not mean that the agency takes the initiative in setting each of the many particular rates that go to make up the rate structure. Such rates are initiated by the companies themselves. Railroad rates, for instance, are originated by the railroads, acting through their traffic associations. Proposed changes, usually involving reductions in particular rates designed to meet the competition of other carriers, are filed with the ICC. Unless the Commission suspends them, in response to protests or on its own motion, they take effect in 30 days. Individual shippers or organized groups of shippers may always complain concerning particular rates, and the Commission will review them. But the rates that come to it for action, though large in number, are probably less than 1 percent of all those in effect. When it acts in such cases, the Commission takes the other rates in the structure for granted, not questioning the propriety of the pattern as a whole. When a carrier applies for an increase in the general level of rates, however, the Commission may effect substantial modifications in the rate structure, permitting some rates to be raised more and others less.

The Interstate Commerce Act contains a number of provisions with respect to the structure of rates. Section 1 requires that the rates charged on particular goods and between particular points be "just and reasonable," and that the systems used in classifying goods be "just and reasonable." Section 2 prohibits discrimination between persons. Section 3 covers other forms of discrimination, making it illegal for a carrier to give any "undue or unreasonable preference or advantage" or to impose any "undue or unreasonable prejudice or disadvantage." Section 4 applies to a particular form of discrimination between places, forbidding a carrier, without express permission of the ICC, to charge more "for a shorter than for a longer distance over the same line, in the same direction, the shorter being included within the longer distance." Section 6 requires that rates be published and adhered to and forbids changes in rates without prior notice.

These requirements were first applied to the railroads. They have since been copied in regulating other carriers. But the ICC, in their enforcement, has concerned itself mainly with the structure of railroad rates. For it is here that the problem of discrimination has been most serious.

Particular Rates

A shipper may complain that the rate charged for a particular commodity or a particular haul is unjust or unreasonable, in violation of Section 1 of the Interstate Commerce Act. Such a complaint does not allege discrimination: it has to do, not with the relation between one rate and another, but with the propriety of a rate in and of itself. But the ICC has no absolute standard by which justice and reasonableness may be judged. It does not attempt, for instance, to determine the cost of carrying a particular commodity or making a particular haul. Instead, it compares the rate that has been questioned with some other rate in the structure, taking as its standard an analogous commodity or a haul of equal length.

The Commission will approve a difference in rates if it can be justified on either of two grounds. First, it may be shown that it corresponds to a difference in costs. Here, it should be noted, the determining factor is not the absolute cost of handling a particular shipment, but the difference in the cost of handling two. Second, a difference in rates may be justified by a difference in the value of the service to shippers. Thus, the Commission has long held that it is just and reasonable to charge more for handling finished goods than for handling raw materials and more for valuable goods than for cheaper goods. And since 1933 the agency has taken elasticity of demand into account under an amendment that requires it to consider the effect of rates upon the movement of traffic. In a few cases, finally, the Commission has based its decisions upon considerations of public welfare, approving lower rates, for instance, to encourage the shipment of such commodities as fertilizers and building materials. But this is the exception rather than the general rule.

When it finds a rate to be unreasonable, the ICC prescribes a maximum that may be charged. Before 1915 the Supreme Court permitted such maxima to be set low for particular goods, provided a railroad was able to obtain a fair return on its business as a whole. Thereafter, the Court held that maxima could not be set below the full cost of the service rendered, including overhead, since this would deprive the roads of property without due process of law.[4] In 1953, however, the Court appeared to return to its earlier position, not explicitly reversing its previous decisions, but holding that "the Due Process Clause should not be construed as a bar to the fixing of noncompensatory rates for carrying some commodities when the public interest is thereby served."[5] The railroads may not charge more than the maximum rates that are prescribed; they may charge less. But here, too, their freedom is limited. The ICC has power to fix minima as well as maxima. It may permit a road to set a rate at a figure that fails to cover its full costs. But it requires that all rates be reasonably compensatory. To this end, it forbids the setting of any rate at less than out-of-pocket costs. A just and reasonable rate, therefore, is not a specific figure but is one that comes within the limits that may be prescribed, not rising above a maximum that may cover or more than cover fully allocated costs, not falling below a minimum that covers only out-of-pocket costs.

Classification Systems

The three major systems of classifying commodities for the purpose of establishing class rates—the Official Classification in the Northeast, the Southern,

---

4 / *Northern Pacific Railway Co.* v. *North Dakota*, 236 U.S. 585 (1915).

5 / *Baltimore & Ohio Railroad Co.* v. *U.S.*, 345 U.S. 146, 150.

and the Western—were developed by the railroads in these regions before the turn of the century and were influenced by the economic conditions prevailing at the time. In each region the roads undertook to establish the structure of rates that would maximize their revenues. And this led to the adoption of different principles of classification and to the establishment of different rates for the same goods. The Northeast was a manufacturing region, and here the classification was so arranged as to encourage the exportation of manufactured goods. The South and the West were exporters of foodstuffs and raw materials, and here, with rates set low for such commodities, the roads augmented their revenues by setting them high for manufactured goods. As a result, class rates were higher in the South and much higher in the West than in the Northeast, though the cost of hauling goods was actually lower in the South and only moderately higher in the West. These discrepancies in the geographic structure of rates persisted for many years. They made it easier for manufacturers in the Northeast to ship to the border states and to the South and West, harder for those in the South and West to ship to the border states and to the Northeast and imposed an artificial handicap on industry in the South and West.

With the beginning of large-scale industrial development in the South and West during the thirties, the geographic discrimination in the classification systems came under vigorous attack. Complaints were made by the State of Georgia, by the Tennessee Valley Authority, and by the Antitrust Division. The fight was carried to the ICC, to the courts, and to the Congress. Action was opposed by the manufacturing interests and the railroads in the Northeast and by the railroads in the South and West. But in the Transportation Act of 1940 Congress provided explicitly that railroad rates should give no unreasonable preference to any region, district, or territory. In 1945 the ICC found the three existing classification systems to be unreasonable and issued a temporary order raising class rates in the Northeast and reducing them in the South and West, pending hearings on the establishment of a uniform classification for the country as a whole. Its action was challenged by the railroads but was upheld by the Supreme Court in 1947.[6] A uniform classification was then prepared and was finally put into effect, in the territory east of the Rocky Mountains, in 1952. It has operated to encourage the location of industry in accordance with factors other than discriminatory elements in railroad rates.

Control of Discrimination

Railroads have discriminated in three ways: between persons, between commodities, and between places. Discrimination between persons was once extensive. It is now forbidden by law. Rebates are no longer given to favored shippers at the expense of their competitors. There may still be some favoritism in the performance of service. But when it is disclosed, it is enjoined. Discrimination between commodities and between places is not forbidden as such but only when it is "undue" or "unreasonable." It is one of the principal functions of the

6 / *State of New York* v. *U.S.*, 331 U.S. 284.

ICC to determine the meaning that is to be assigned to these words, thus establishing the limits within which discrimination is to be permitted.

An action charging discrimination may be brought before the Commission by a shipper who complains that he is required to pay a higher rate than another shipper is permitted to pay. If he is to obtain a favorable decision, the complainant must show three things: (1) that there is a competitive relationship between his own commodity or location and the one that enjoys a lower rate, (2) that he has suffered (or is likely to suffer) serious injury as a result of the difference in rates, and (3) that the same railroad charges the two rates and would be able to correct the situation by changing one or both of them. The railroad, on the other hand, may argue that the difference in rates is nondiscriminatory, corresponding to a difference in costs. Or it may defend discrimination by presenting evidence that its service is more valuable to one shipper than to another, or that it encounters competition in serving the one and not the other. If the Commission fails to find undue discrimination, it will allow the rates to stand. But if it makes such a finding, it will order the railroad to remove the discrimination, permitting it to do so by reducing the higher rate, by raising the lower rate, or by doing both.

Cases involving discrimination between commodities arise where goods that may be substituted for one another compete in the same market and where competition between fabricators is affected by the relation of rates on raw materials to those on finished goods. With respect to substitutes, the Commission usually requires comparable rates. It has acted, for instance, to forbid higher rates for benzol than for gasoline, for linseed oil than for cottonseed oil, and for lard substitutes than for lard. With respect to raw materials and finished products, the relationship of rates may affect the location of industry, giving plants that are close to raw materials an advantage over those that are close to markets, or doing the reverse. The fortunes of different flour mills, for instance, will depend upon the rates fixed for livestock and meat. In such cases the Commission tends to eliminate any artificial advantage or disadvantage by relating differences in rates to differences in costs. In either type of case, however, exceptions may be made, the railroads being allowed to fix lower rates on commodities where they face competition than on those where they do not.

Discrimination between places had been built into the structure of freight rates long before the Interstate Commerce Act was passed. In the Northeast, rates were generally related to distance. But in the South, they were so established as to meet the competition of water carriers to various ports, and these ports served, in turn, as basing points in fixing rates to inland towns. As a result, rates throughout the South declined as traffic approached a waterway. On transcontinental traffic, moreover, rates were computed by taking the water rates from Atlantic to Pacific ports and adding to them rail rates for hauling goods back toward the East. Transcontinental rates therefore declined as traffic moved on toward the Pacific Coast. The Act forced a revision of this structure. Under its provisions, the ICC has adopted the principle of relating rates to distance. But it has permitted many exceptions to this general rule.

Cases of place discrimination fall into two categories. Those involving a higher charge "for a shorter than for a longer distance over the same line, in the same direction, the shorter being included within the longer distance" come under Section 4 of the Act, known as the long-and-short-haul clause. All other such cases come under Section 3, which deals with discrimination in general. Long-and-short-haul discrimination is forbidden unless expressly permitted by the ICC. In Section 4 cases, therefore, the burden of proof is on the railroad that seeks relief from this provision of the law. In Section 3 cases, however, the procedure is the same as that for discrimination among commodities. A shipper who complains of a higher rate than that charged at another place must show that the two places are in competition, that he is injured by the difference in rates, and that same railroad charges both rates and has the power to change them. And the railroad may defend

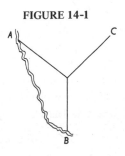

FIGURE 14-1

itself by showing differences in the cost of service, in the demand for service, and in the competition faced on the two hauls. The considerations that influence the Commission's decisions in cases brought under either Section are much the same.

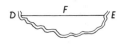

FIGURE 14-2

Discrimination may be permitted where there is competition between railroads and other carriers, between two railroads, or between two producing areas obtaining their raw material from a common source or selling in a common market. Thus, as shown in Figure 14-1, a railroad that runs from A to B may be permitted to meet the low rate of a water carrier operating on the river between these points without fixing an equally low rate on the equidistant haul from C to B. And, as shown in Figure 14-2, a railroad that runs from D to E may be permitted to meet the rate of a water carrier between these points, even though it would then be charging more for the shorter haul from D to F than for the longer haul from D to E. Similarly, as shown in Figure 14-3, railroad W that follows a circuitous route from G to H may be permitted to meet the rate of railroad X that follows a direct route, without fixing an equally low rate for the equidistant haul from I to H. And, as shown in Figure 14-4, railroad Y may be permitted to meet the rate of railroad Z from J to K, even though it would then be charging more for the shorter haul from J to L than for the longer haul from J to K. And finally, as shown in Figures 14-5 and

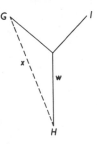

FIGURE 14-3

FIGURE 14-4

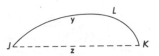

FIGURE 14-5

FIGURE 14-6

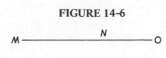

14-6, a railroad that serves the competing indus-trial centers M and N that draw their raw materials from the common source O or sell their product in the common market O may be permitted to reduce the rate at M to the figure charged at N.

Such discrimination has its limits. A railroad may fix a lower rate for one of two equidistant hauls or for a longer than for a shorter haul only when it is forced to do so to meet competition that arises from some natural advantage, such as that of a water carrier or a shorter rail line. Thus, as shown in Figure 14-7, railroad W will not be permitted to charge lower rates between P and Q where it competes with railroad X, a line of equal length, than between R and Q, where it has no competitor. And, as shown in Figure 14-8, railroads Y and Z

FIGURE 14-7   FIGURE 14-8

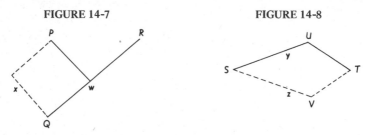

will not be permitted to charge less for the longer haul from S to T than for the shorter hauls from S to U and V, merely because they compete at T and not at U and V. A railroad may be permitted to equalize the competitive oppor-tunities of different places, as was done in Figures 14-5 and 14-6. But it cannot be required to do so. Thus, the producers at M have no legal right to demand that their rate be made the same as that at N. And opportunities can be equalized only by offsetting natural disadvantages, not by canceling natural advantages. In the cases shown in Figures 14-5 and 14-6, the railroad may reduce the rate at M to the level of that at N. It may not raise the rate at N to the level of that at M.

The decisions made by the ICC and reviewed by the courts, in cases such as these, determine when discrimination will be permitted and when it will not. But the line thus drawn between legality and illegality is not always clear. The limits of discrimination, at any time, will depend upon the composition and the judgment of the Commission and the courts.

Consequences of Discrimination

Discrimination among commodities, where it involves the establishment of lower rates for goods that otherwise would not move at all, may be of general benefit. It is of benefit to the carriers, since it enables them to enlarge their revenues, make fuller use of their facilities, reduce their unit costs, and improve their position with respect to earnings. It obviously benefits the producers of commodities that pay the lower rates. It even benefits the producers of those that pay the higher rates, for if the low-rate traffic did not move, they would have to pay all the overhead costs and provide all the earnings by themselves, and their rates would be higher still. It benefits the community as a whole, since goods are thus made generally available that otherwise would be confined to local areas.

Discrimination among commodities, however, is frequently designed, not to increase the volume of traffic, but merely to divert existing traffic from one carrier to another. Discrimination between places, also, usually has this effect. Such discrimination may benefit a particular carrier, enabling a railroad, for instance, to obtain traffic that would otherwise have moved by water or by highway or over another line. It obviously benefits the commodities and the places that enjoy the lower rates. It may even be said to benefit those that pay the higher rates. Thus, in Figures 14-1 through 14-4, the people of $C, F, I,$ and L are better off than they would be if the railroads serving them got none of the traffic between the competitive points, and were therefore forced to turn to them for more of the revenue required to cover costs and provide a fair return. But it cannot be said that such discrimination is of benefit to the community as a whole. What one carrier gains, another loses. The discriminating carrier gets more traffic and more revenue; the competing carrier gets less. With the former, costs and rates will be lowered. With the latter, they will be raised. The practice, moreover, has a social cost. It obstructs the allocation of traffic among different media in accordance with their relative economy. And it results in wasteful transport by roundabout routes.

Discrimination between places has another effect. It exerts a powerful influence on the location of industry. Where the disadvantage of distance from materials and markets is offset by lower rates, one community (such as M in Figures 14-5 and 14-6) may grow in importance while another (such as N) may be denied the growth it would otherwise have attained. Production may thus be diverted from more economic to less economic sites.

The less desirable consequences of discrimination are to be attributed to the competitive character of the transport industry. If transport were monopolized, goods would not be moved by rail where water was cheaper or by circuitous routes where direct routes were available. Nor would a transport monopoly, under public regulation, be so likely to promote the development of one community at the expense of another. But where transport is provided by many different carriers, each of them must be given an opportunity to go after competitive business and to develop new sources of revenue. And the forms of discrimination thus permitted will lead to waste. Competition, however, may have offsetting advantages. This question will be considered again in Chapter 17.

REGULATION OF PUBLIC UTILITY RATE STRUCTURES

With regard to the structure of rates, the laws that regulate public utilities usually follow the pattern of those that regulate railroads, requiring that particular rates be just and reasonable, that they be published, observed, and not changed without prior notice, and that discrimination be not unjust, unreasonable, or undue. But the state utility commissions have given much less attention to rate structures than has the ICC. Among the many possible structures that might serve equally well to cover costs and provide investors with a fair return, they have made no effort to discover and adopt the one that would best serve the public interest. Instead, they have left the initiative in fixing particular rates to the companies, accepted the pattern of rates established, subjected it to little scrutiny, and made little effort to have it modified.

Where the commissions act, it is usually in response to complaints. In such cases they must draw a line between the unreasonable discrimination that the law forbids and the reasonable discrimination that it allows. In doing so, however, they have developed no clear principles, but appear to have been guided, rather, by vague conceptions of equity. The commissions have frequently insisted that rate forms be simple and understandable. They have sometimes checked the multiplication of consumer classes and have even limited the differentials between them. In general, however, they have accepted classifications and differentials that have been based on differences in the elasticity of demand. Typically, they have compared the rate structure of one company with that of another and have held discrimination to be reasonable if it conformed to the customary pattern. The commissions have said that the establishment of particular rates is necessarily a matter of business judgment. But they have set up no standards in accordance with which such judgment must be exercised.

The commissions have generally held that differences in rates should be related to differences in costs. And they have sought to prevent the rate for any class from being set below its incremental or out-of-pocket cost. But they have laid down no rules to govern the allocation of overhead. Instead, most of them have accepted, without question, the theory of company accountants that allocates overhead in accordance with the proportionate responsibility of different customers for noncoincident demand. The commissions, moreover, have tended to favor discrimination where it has had the effect of expanding consumption and bringing about a fuller utilization of productive capacity. They have thus approved the creation of low-rate classes, the reduction of rates in successive quantity blocks, and the adoption of objective rate plans. As a result, the wide differentials established between classes, and between large and small users within these classes, have been allowed to stand. In the case of electricity, particularly, the low rates go to big business, where demand is elastic and where protection by government is not required. The high rates go to small business and to householders, where demand is inelastic and where such protection is really required. The law thus fails to give to those who need it most the aid it was intended to provide.

This failure is to be attributed to three main causes. First, the commissions have been compelled to devote most of their energy to the struggle over the level of rates and have had little of it left to spend in reforming the structure of rates. Second, they have been deceived by the methods of accounting that are employed to justify discrimination, not understanding the principles of demand on which discrimination is really based. And third, they have been deterred from overhauling the structure of rates by the fact that many of its parts have come to be deeply imbedded in business expectations. Reformation of the structure, according to different principles, would be helpful to those whose rates were lowered and to the community in general. But it would be harmful to those whose rates were raised and would therefore be politically unpopular.

The last of these difficulties could have been overcome by revising the structure gradually rather than suddenly. When costs fall, the general level of rates can be lowered. When they go up, it must be raised. On such occasions, the structure of rates can be so modified as to make it less discriminatory. When the general level is lowered, the higher rates in the structure can be reduced more, the lower rates less, and the differentials narrowed. When the general level is raised, the higher rates can be raised less, the lower rates more, and the differentials narrowed. But this has not been done. When the rate level has been changed, all the rates in the structure have moved together. The pattern of differentials has been preserved. The opportunity to lighten the impact of discrimination has been thrown away.

Chapter 15 REGULATION OF PUBLIC UTILITIES

In some states regulation of companies rendering one or another of the public utility services is left to local governments. In most cases, however, responsibility for such regulation is entrusted to state commissions. In the case of gas and electricity, local and state controls have been reinforced, since the middle thirties, by controls exercised by two federal agencies: the Federal Power Commission and the Securities and Exchange Commission. The present chapter is concerned, in the main, with regulation of electrical and gas utilities by the federal commissions.

CONTROL BY THE STATES

In a few states, notably New York, Wisconsin, Illinois, and California, at one time or another, the regulation of public utilities has been vigorous. But, by and large, regulation has not proved to be really adequate as a substitute for competition in fulfilling its functions of preventing monopoly prices and profits, checking discrimination, reducing costs, inducing technical progress, and promoting wider use of utility services. The limited effectiveness of state regulation and some of the reasons for its failures will be discussed below.

Effectiveness of State Regulation

It is virtually impossible to measure the results of utility regulation. Standards by which to measure service are difficult to develop and apply. Rates are quoted for standard units, but the meaning of comparisons between regulated and unregulated companies is obscured by differences in the structure of rates. In the case of electricity, for instance, the average charge per kilowatt-hour is affected by the methods used in classifying service and by the relative importance of different classes in total output. Comparisons can be made, of course, in terms of monthly bills for like quantities of like services. But their significance will still be open to dispute. Rates are affected by many factors other than the mechanism of control. There are differences in costs of generation between plants that are large and small, hydro and steam, close to coal and at a distance; differences in costs of transmission where plants are near to consumers and

344

where they are far away. In comparing private and public plants, moreover, it must be remembered that the bases for computing costs are not the same.

In general, rates have been lower in states where they were regulated than in states where they were not. George J. Stigler and Claire Friedland found this to be the case when they compared rates in adjacent states with and without regulation for the years 1912 to 1937. But they found that these differences had also obtained before regulation had been imposed. And they attributed the lower level of regulated rates to factors other than regulation: to differences in market size, in population density, and in the cost of fuel. They found no substantial differences in the structure of rates or in the ratio of domestic to industrial rates. In short, they were unable to discover that regulation had had any significant effects.[1]

There are generalizations that can be made, however, concerning electric rates. These rates have remained relatively stable over the years, declining moderately in response to decreasing costs and technological advances at a time when other consumer prices have been rising. The rates have varied widely from city to city, the highest figures being three times the lowest ones. In 1968, the average residential bill for 250 kilowatt-hours of electricity ranged from $3 in Eugene, Oregon to $10 in New York City. Finally, the rates charged for private power, under regulation, have generally been higher than those charged for public power. Private companies have cut their rates when faced with the example of public competition. And, at the lower level, consumption and earnings have increased. The force of example has thus been more effective as a regulator than the force of law.

Regulation, of course, is not designed to force rates down to the lowest level that will cover costs and yield a fair return, but merely to prevent the return from being too high. Even here, it has often failed. In the twenties, many electric and gas companies were realizing 20-30 percent per annum on their investment and a few as much as 50 or 100 percent or even more.[2] During the thirties, regulation was tightened and rates were cut. But in the forties and the fifties, the country's electrical utilities enjoyed a return averaging about 6 percent on their investment and a net income after dividends on preferred stock averaging about 10 percent on their common stock.[3] In 1965, the 192 principal electrical utilities averaged 7.39 percent on their investment. Eleven of these companies made over 12 percent, four over 14 percent, and one as much as 16 percent. In 1964, there were 35 companies that made more than 15 percent on their common stock and two others that made more than 20 percent.[4] The

1 / George J. Stigler and Claire Friedland, "What Can Regulators Regulate?" *Journal of Law and Economics,* Vol. 5 (1962), pp. 1-16.

2 / See Clair Wilcox, *Competition and Monopoly in American Industry* T.N.E.C. Monograph No. 21 (Washington, D.C.: Government Printing Office, 1940), pp. 94-95.

3 / James C. Bonbright, *Principles of Public Utility Rates* (New York: Columbia University Press, 1961), p. 282.

4 / U.S. Senate, Committee on Government Operations, *State Utility Commissions* (Washington, D.C.: Government Printing Office, 1967), p. 25; Lee Metcalf and Vic Reinemer, *Overcharge* (New York: David McKay Co., 1967), pp. 260-66, 287.

liberality of these returns was demonstrated by an upward trend in dividends and in the market value of utility shares. The prices commanded by these shares reveal that investors would provide capital for a yield much lower than the one they have obtained.

During most of the history of utility regulation, growth of demand and changes in technology have resulted in falling costs. Under these circumstances, excessive earnings have appeared. But reductions in rates have been resisted by the utilities. Regulation has lagged and the earnings have been preserved. But at times when revenues have declined, when costs have risen and earnings have dropped, applications for rate increases have been filed by the utilities and vigorously pressed. But commission action has not been speeded. Utility rates have eventually been permitted to rise, but not as fast or as far as other prices. For this happy outcome, however, the regulatory commissions can claim no credit. It has been a product, not of their wisdom and zeal, but of their lethargy. Regulation has been made more effective by its very ineffectiveness.

Shortcomings of State Regulation

The state commissions have done little to control the quality of utility services, in general leaving initiative to the companies and acting only on complaint. Most of them have manifested little interest in the structure of rates, accepting cost analyses advanced to rationalize discrimination, or entrusting the formulation of particular charges to the discretion of managements. All of them have been concerned with the level of rates. But few have sought to control operating expenses, the largest element in the rate level, by passing on them in advance. All have prescribed accounting systems, essential to rate control, but few have attempted to enforce them by audits in the field. Few have undertaken to develop criteria of equity or efficiency to govern earnings. And none has sought to maximize consumption by reducing rates to the lowest level that would yield a fair return. Instead, attention has been centered, in the past, on determining and preserving the value of utility properties. Some commissions, in making valuations, have accepted reproduction costs. Others, while giving such costs little weight, have made obeisance to the courts by going through the mumbo jumbo of the valuation ritual. Energy has been diverted from the purpose for which the laws were passed and the commissions formed.

Formal action is through a rate case. Some commissions initiate such cases. Others are passive, waiting for cases to be brought. In 1967, it was reported that four states had had no rate cases for eight years; that four others had had none for 13 years; that Delaware had had none since its commission was established in 1949; and that South Carolina had had none since 1933.[5] In rate case proceedings the contest between the company and the consumer is not an equal one. The company is represented by able lawyers, well paid, fortified with facts, and supported by a staff of expert witnesses. In some states the commission

5 / Metcalf and Reinemer, *op. cit.,* p. 31.

assists the consumer in preparing his case. In others, it does not. In both, his lawyers are poorly paid and inadequately reenforced. And if the consumer wins, the company can appeal—and appeal—and appeal. In the past, protracted litigation has been the rule. One telephone case dragged through the courts for 13 years. In such a situation, the commissions despaired of making progress through formal procedures and sought to salvage what they could by entering into negotiations with the companies.

Negotiation is faster and cheaper than litigation. And it may lead to cuts in rates. But there is no assurance that it will always protect the public interest. The negotiators meet behind closed doors; no record of their proceedings is released. The outcome will depend upon the zeal of the contending parties and on their skill in bargaining. The commission has certain advantages: it can threaten formal action, appeal to public opinion, or deny requests for extensions or abandonments or for the issuance of new securities. But the companies have the support of greater knowledge, financial resources, and staying power. They are therefore unlikely to concede as much as the law would have required. The rates agreed to may still be well in excess of costs; the profits they yield may be exorbitant. As the Power Committee of the Twentieth Century Fund remarked, "there is something fundamentally wrong with a system in which matters of such public moment are handled by public bodies in informal, and nearly always secret, conferences with interested executives."[6]

Causes of Failure

Responsibility for the failures of regulation cannot be charged to the commissions alone but must be shared by the courts, the legislatures, the executives, and the public at large. It was the courts that asserted their right to review the work of the commissions, stripped them of necessary powers, and reversed their decisions, always to the end of preventing or canceling reductions in rates. The explanation for their action is not far to seek. According to John Bauer, "the judges had been appointed extensively from prominent lawyers with successful corporation practice, who were heavily impregnated with private business perspectives. They had little consciousness of the public aspects of industry and little concern for the protection and advancement of public interest. Throughout the judicial domain, the dominant attitude was one of guardianship toward property and of vigilance against legislative and administrative encroachments."[7] It was thus by judicial action that the emphasis in regulation was shifted from the protection of consumers to the protection of property.

The legislatures have impeded regulation by denying the commissions adequate jurisdiction, powers, and funds. Even yet there are states where the control of particular services is left to local governments, where valuations must be

6 / *Electric Power and Government Policy* (New York: Twentieth Century Fund, 1948), p. 757.

7 / John Bauer, *Transforming Public Utility Regulation* (New York: Harper & Bros., 1950), p. 125.

based on cost of reproduction, and where power to control depreciation effectively is denied. In some states commissions cannot control security issues or other financial practices. And in most states they cannot require submission of budgets prior to action on expenditures. The courts, moreover, were given their opportunity to negate the work of the commissions by the failure of the legislatures to include clear standards in the laws. The commissions were simply instructed to establish rates at reasonable levels, but reasonableness was not defined. The door to judicial interpretation thus was opened wide.

The errors of courts and legislatures have been matched by those of the executives. Governors have made poor appointments, filling commissionerships with political hacks, unqualified by experience or interest for the work. In some cases they have even appointed men chosen by the utilities or have otherwise discouraged real enforcement of the law. By selling the consumer down the river, they have obtained political support.

And finally, the fault lies with the public: with consumers and with voters generally. No group has been organized to make sure that the commissions have adequate jurisdiction and powers, that they are well staffed and financed, that they act with vigor and dispatch. One reason is that the problem has not seemed to be serious. Utility rates are a small part of the consumer's budget; for many years, instead of being raised, they were reduced—the trouble was merely that reductions in rates did not keep pace with reductions in costs. This is not the sort of situation in which people are stirred to act. Another reason for public apathy, however, is to be found in the propaganda efforts of the utilities.

In hearings conducted by the Federal Trade Commission in the early thirties, trade associations of gas and electric companies were shown to have spent millions of dollars every year to influence public opinion. These bodies fed news and editorials to the press and used their control of advertising to prevent unfavorable publicity. They supplied friendly speakers for public meetings and kept unfriendly speakers from getting a hearing. They provided teaching materials to schools and colleges and sought to censor textbooks that they disapproved. They planted their propaganda in labor unions, granges, women's clubs, churches, and Sunday schools. According to one of their officials, they employed every means of communication but skywriting. And so they spread the word that tighter regulation was not required.[8] It took financial scandals of the greatest magnitude to overcome the confidence that they created and to arouse consumers from the lethargy this confidence induced.

After the disclosures of the thirties, the utilities were more discreet. But, according to Bauer, they continued their efforts to influence regulation.

First, they have maintained close and insistent political connections with both major parties. Second, they have watched constantly for their

---

8 / The evidence taken from utility records and presented by utility witnesses is summarized in Irston R. Barnes, *The Economics of Public Utility Regulation* (New York: F. S. Crofts & Co., 1942), chap. xxiii. The story is told more fully in Jack Levin, *Power Ethics* (New York: Alfred A. Knopf, 1931); and in Carl D. Thompson, *Confessions of the Power Trust* (New York: E. P. Dutton & Co., 1932).

own interest along the entire political front so as to get favorable actions and avoid unfavorable. Third, they have watched and promoted, or opposed, appointments, not only to the commissions but to the technical staffs. Fourth, they have sponsored favorable legislation and headed off unfavorable. Fifth, they have participated in quasi-public organizations and through them extended their influences into the communities and into political channels. Sixth, they have used extensive advertising and other means of publicity to stimulate favorable attitudes, and to prevent unfavorable news articles and editorial comments; seldom have newspapers printed squarely the public side in utility controversies. Seventh, the companies have kept close contact with the commissions, spreading graciousness and lures for their private advantage.

"While originally the companies were vigorously opposed to regulation," says Bauer, "they have come not only to accept it but largely to convert it into an instrument of protection for themselves."[9]

FEDERAL CONTROL OF HOLDING COMPANIES

Utility companies were first established on a small scale in local markets. In time these companies came to be combined in larger units. And eventually numbers of them were brought together, through ownership of stock, by holding companies. Some of these concerns performed no management function, serving merely to diversify investment risks. Others, however, provided their operating subsidiaries with a great variety of managerial services. Some of them controlled operating companies located in contiguous territories, where services could be coordinated through interconnections of facilities. But others exercised control over widely scattered properties, where unification of services was not a possibility. There were not only holding companies controlling operating companies but also superholding companies controlling holding companies. And, in some cases, the holding company structures were several stories high. This development had its most rapid growth in the years that followed World War I. By 1932, 16 top holding companies controlled more than three fourths of the electricity produced in the United States.

The combination of operating companies frequently has advantages. Where physical integration is possible, the combined markets may be served with a smaller investment in facilities; costs may be reduced by operating on a larger scale, and by improving capacity, load, and diversity factors; savings may be realized through economies in using fuel and labor, and by standardizing and exchanging equipment and supplies. Where properties are scattered, too, a larger enterprise may find it easier to sell securities and to borrow money from the banks. A holding company, moreover, may operate on a scale that enables it to employ experts in many fields of management that smaller operating companies could not afford. And it may provide its subsidiaries with skilled supervision,

9 / Bauer, *op. cit.,* p. 137.

technical advice, and a great variety of managerial services. But the growth of holding companies cannot be explained on these grounds alone. There were profits to be obtained in their promotion and operation. There were personal fortunes to be built. And this had little or nothing to do with the enhancement of efficiency.

Holding Company Abuses

An outstanding characteristic of the holding company structure was pyramiding: of control, of profits, and of losses. Let us see, first, how this structure facilitated the pyramiding of control.

1. Assume that there are 64 operating companies, each capitalized at $4 million, divided as follows: $2 million in 4 percent bonds, $1 million in 5 percent preferred stock, and $1 million in common. The total investment in these properties is $256 million. Each operating company can be controlled with half of its common, requiring an investment of $500,000. All 64 can be controlled with $32 million. This is 1/8 of the total investment.

2. Now divide the 64 operating companies into 16 groups of four each. Over each group set up a Father Holding Company. Each Father controls each of its operating companies with $500,000; all four with $2 million. It is capitalized at $2 million; of this, $1 million is in 5 percent preferred and $1 million in common. Each Father company can thus be controlled with $500,000. All 16 can be controlled with $8 million. The controlling share is 1/32 of the total investment.

3. Now divide the 16 Father companies into four groups of four each. Over each group set up a Grandfather Holding Company. Each Grandfather controls each of its Father companies with $500,000, all four with $2 million. Half of its capitalization of $2 million is in 5 percent preferred and half in common. Each Grandfather can thus be controlled with $500,000; all four of them with $2 million. This is 1/128 of the total investment.

4. Now set up a Great-Grandfather Holding Company to control the four Grandfather companies. It does so with an investment of $2 million. Its capitalization of $2 million is half in 5 percent preferred and half in common. It can be controlled with $500,000. This is 1/512 of the total investment.

5. Finally, set up a Great-Great-Grandfather Holding Company. Capitalize it at $500,000. Sell half of it in 5 percent preferred. The half that remains is 1/1,024 of the total investment. The investing public puts up $255,750,000. John Dough puts up $250,000 and runs the show.

If anything, this illustration understates the case. A larger part of the total capitalization could be in nonvoting securities. Control could be obtained with less than half the common. The money needed to buy the stock of one company could be borrowed, putting up the stock of another as security. The number of holding companies between the controlling interest and the operating properties could be multiplied indefinitely. In the Associated Gas and Electric structure there were 12 layers. In the Insull empire, one of the operating companies was controlled, at the top, by an investment of one two-hundredth of 1 percent.

It is easy to see how such a structure pyramided profits. To return to our illustration:

1. Assume that the 64 operating companies are allowed a return of 6 percent. On $256 million, this gives them $15,360,000. Of this amount, 4 percent must be paid on $128 million in bonds, or $5,120,000. Then 5 percent must be paid on $64 million of preferred, or $3,200,000. This leaves $7,040,000 to be distributed as dividends on $64 million of common, a return of 11 percent.
2. Half of this, or $3,520,000, goes to the 16 Father companies. They pay 5 percent on $16 million of preferred, or $800,000. This leaves them $2,720,000 to distribute on $16 million of common, a return of 17 percent.
3. Half of this, or $1,360,000, goes to the four Grandfather companies. They pay 5 percent on $4 million of preferred, or $200,000. This leaves them $1,160,000 for $4 million of common, a return of 29 percent.
4. Half of this, or $580,000, goes to the Great-Grandfather Company. This company pays 5 percent on $1 million of preferred, or $50,000. This leaves it $530,000 for $1 million of common, a return of 53 percent.
5. Half of this, or $265,000, goes to the Great-Great-Grandfather Company. It pays 5 percent on its $250,000 of preferred, or $12,500. It has $252,500 left for John Dough. On his investment of $250,000, he makes more than 100 percent.

This may explain why the control of a holding company structure was regarded as a prize. But pyramiding also had its risks. Let us assume that a mild recession brings a moderate reduction in the revenues of the operating companies. They still cover all of their expenses. But instead of earning 6 percent on their investment, they earn only 4 percent. What happens?

1. The 64 companies get $10,240,000. They pay $5,120,000 on their bonds, and $3,200,000 on their preferred. They have $1,920,000 left for their common, a return of 3 percent.
2. Half of this, or $960,000, goes to the Father companies. They pay $800,-000 on their preferred. They have $160,000 for $16 million of common, a return of 1 percent.
3. Half of this, or $80,000, goes to the Grandfather companies. They cannot meet the dividends on their preferred, let alone their common.
4. The income of the Great-Grandfather company and that of the Great-Great-Grandfather company is zero. They pay no dividends. They cannot even pay their bills. The companies go bankrupt. The house of cards comes tumbling down.

The holding company operators thus did something that would have seemed to be impossible: they took control of an industry that was guaranteed a legal monopoly of a necessary service and turned it into a highly speculative enterprise. From the soundest investment in the market, they converted utility shares, at the upper levels, into counters in a game of chance.

In this situation, there was an insistent drive for dividends. These could be obtained, in one way, through higher rates. Every dollar by which rates were changed was reflected in the dividends of the upper holding companies. These companies, therefore, were vigorous in resisting rate reductions and ingenious in finding ways by which rates could be increased. To this end, they padded the valuations of the operating companies, by making excessive charges for construction services, by causing properties to be sold back and forth at rising prices, by failing to make deductions for depreciation, and by writing up the value of the assets on the books. Dividends could be obtained, too, by reducing charges against income. And here, the holding companies indulged in fair-weather finance, neglecting to maintain their operating properties, failing to set aside reserves for depreciation, and building up fictitious surpluses. Dividends were thus paid out of capital, and the strength of the underlying enterprises was impaired.

The holding companies made money not only by collecting dividends but also through intercompany transactions. They borrowed money from the operating companies and loaned money to them. They handled the sale of their securities. They sold them equipment and supplies. They set up subsidiaries to provide them with engineering and managerial services. The prices paid in these transactions did not result from arm's length bargaining. The officers of the operating companies depended on the officers of the holding companies for their jobs. If they were asked to pay excessive prices, they did not complain. They did as they were told. In this way, holding company profits were hidden in operating company costs. And they were covered, of necessity, by the state commissions in setting the level of rates.

The Holding Company Act

Until 1930 the state commissions, in computing operating company expenses, were denied the right to disallow payments made to holding companies unless they could show them to be fraudulent. In that year the Supreme Court held, in the Smith Case,[10] that the commissions could look into the cost to the holding companies of the goods and services that they supplied, thus shifting to them the burden of proof. Thereafter, more than half of the states gave their commissions some power over holding company activities. Intrastate holding companies were brought under control. But the larger holding company systems were beyond the reach of the individual states.

In 1928 the Federal Trade Commission had been directed by Congress to investigate electric and gas utilities. In 1935 it published its final report,

---

10 / *Smith* v. *Illinois Bell Telephone Co.,* 282 U.S. 133.

summarizing more than seventy volumes of hearings and exhibits. Many holding company abuses were thus brought into glaring light. At the same time the largest holding company systems—Associated Gas and Electric, Insull, and Foshay in Minneapolis—had come down in ruins, scores of others were bankrupt, in receivership, or in default, and hundreds of thousands of investors had seen their savings disappear. The country was ripe for reform.

The Public Utility Act of 1935 had two parts. Title II was the law, discussed below, giving jurisdiction over interstate transmission of electricity to the FPC. Title I was the Public Utility Holding Company Act. This was the most stringent corrective measure ever applied to American business. It went beyond any other in requiring the reorganization of corporate structures and in forcing divestment of property. It made the Securities and Exchange Commission a potent regulator of electric and gas holding companies. Wherever abuses had been disclosed, it provided powers of control.

The Act defined a holding company as one holding 10 percent or more of the voting stock of another holding company or an operating company or having a "controlling influence over the management or policies" of such companies. It exempted those that were entirely intrastate or were predominantly operating companies with contiguous properties. The companies covered were required to register with the SEC and to file a statement showing all of the significant details of their structure and operations. The other provisions of the law fall into five categories: (1) The most severe provision was that of Section 11 (*b*) (2), generally known as the "death sentence," which provided for the elimination of the third and upper layers in the holding company structures, permitting Father and Grandfather companies, but forbidding Great-Grandfathers, Great-Great-Grandfathers, and remoter generations in the sequence of control. (2) Section 11 also empowered the SEC to effect the simplification of the remaining holding company structures through financial reorganization. The law then provided for the regulation of the reorganized concerns, authorizing the SEC to control (3) the operations of holding companies, (4) the dealings of their officers and directors, and (5) their relations with their subsidiaries.

To effect reorganizations, the companies were invited to prepare and submit their own plans. The Commission was then to hold hearings, approve or reject the proposals, or order them modified. In the absence of company initiative, it could prepare the plans itself. To force their adoption, it was required to obtain an order from a court. The Commission was instructed to confine each holding company organization to a single system of integrated operating companies and other businesses economically necessary or reasonably incidental thereto. It was authorized, however, to permit a holding company to control more than one system if (1) such control was needed to preserve substantial economies; (2) the systems were contiguous, being located on both sides of state or national borders; and (3) the resulting structure would not be so large as to impair local management, efficient operation, and effective regulation. In reorganizing corporations, the Commission was directed to do away with complications in their capital structure and to eliminate inequities in the distribution of voting power.

The regulatory powers conferred upon the SEC were extensive. Holding companies were required to follow methods of accounting prescribed by the Commission. They were required to obtain the Commission's approval before buying or selling assets or floating securities. They were forbidden to contribute to campaign funds or to engage in hidden lobbying activities. Their officers and directors were required to file their stockholdings and to make reports on changes. Profits realized on their dealings were made recoverable at law. Bankers were denied directorates unless such appointments were approved by the SEC. Holding companies were forbidden to borrow money from operating companies; their loans to these companies were subjected to control. Holding companies were forbidden, too, to perform various services for operating companies. For this purpose, mutual service companies, subordinate to the operating companies, were to be formed. All intercorporate contracts within a holding company system were brought under Commission control. And the Commission was further authorized to protect the operating companies against exploitation by controlling the declaration of dividends.

Holding Companies under the SEC

The constitutionality of the Holding Company Act was promptly challenged. The Electric Bond and Share Company refused to register, the SEC brought suit to compel it to do so, and the registration requirement was upheld by the Supreme Court. [11] The North American Company resisted reorganization, arguing that the disintegration provisions of the Act exceeded the powers conferred on Congress under the commerce clause and violated the Fifth Amendment by depriving the company of property without due process of law. This argument was rejected by the Court. [12] The American Power and Light Company then contested the simplification of its corporate structure, advancing the previous arguments and also contending that the law involved an unconstitutional delegation of legislative power. Again, the Court did not agree. [13] The SEC thus found itself on solid ground.

The Commission approached its task with caution. It was not until 1940 that voluntary disintegration plans were submitted and formal proceedings begun. By 1951 the Commission had undertaken the reformation of corporate structures including more than 200 holding companies and nearly 2,000 other companies. In 1952 it reported that 85 percent of the job was done. [14] In the upper levels some holding companies had reduced their holdings of operating company voting stocks to less than 10 percent, becoming investment companies. Others had merged with their subsidiaries. Still others had distributed their holdings to their stockholders or had sold them in the market and distributed

11 / *Electric Bond & Share Co.* v. *SEC,* 303 U.S. 419 (1938).

12 / *North American Co.* v. *SEC,* 327 U.S. 686 (1946).

13 / *American Power & Light Co.* v. *SEC,* 329 U.S. 90 (1946).

14 / *Report of the SEC to the Subcommittee on Monopoly of the Select Committee on Small Business, U.S. Senate* (83d Cong., 2d Sess.), Subcommittee Print No. 4, 1952.

cash, thus liquidating their affairs. Here, the duty of the SEC was plain: the upper levels had to go. Elsewhere, however, its task was more difficult.

Where were holding company systems to be dissolved and where allowed to stand? The Commission was strict in its enforcement of the principle of integration. It favored a compact system, confined to a single area, its facilities interconnected or capable of interconnection, its operations coordinated, and its management unified. It opposed the common control of electricity and gas, and the operation of companies providing other services, unless they could be shown to bear a functional relationship to the provision of electricity or gas. In permitting a holding company to control more than one utility system, it required that all three of the conditions laid down in the law be satisfied: (1) such control must be needed to preserve substantial economies, *and* (2) the systems must be contiguous, *and* (3) they must be small enough to permit local management, efficient operation, and effective regulation. In this way the many-tiered holding company systems with widely scattered properties were eliminated and the simpler, closely integrated systems were preserved. In the main, local utilities were restored to local managements. There are about 20 regional holding company systems remaining under Commission control.

The method by which divestment was to be effected had not been specified by law. Here initiative was left to the companies. Some holding companies sold their properties to other holding companies, to independent operators, or to local governments. Some sold their security holdings on the market. Some divided them among the owners of their shares. Whatever the method, it was supervised by the SEC, strict watch being kept on the expenses incurred, the fees collected, and the prices paid.

Along with the simplification of holding company systems went reorganization of the capital structures of individual companies. Here, the Commission scaled down overcapitalization, eliminated write-ups, required competitive bidding for new securities, and strengthened depreciation reserves. It retired excessive debt and insisted on substantial equity in common stock. It ordered inclusion in bond indentures of provisions to protect the holders of the bonds. And it sought to protect the rights of stockholders by insuring an equitable distribution of voting power. The reorganizations brought about by the SEC were not effected at the expense of the investor. Indeed, corporate finances were strengthened and the market value of utility shares was raised.

This sweeping reorganization of the electric and gas utility industries was a significant accomplishment. It did not in itself make the regulation of rates and services effective. But it removed a major obstacle to control. More than this, it showed that the problems encountered in dissolving corporate combinations are not insoluble, and thus provided a lesson for the critics of the Sherman Act.

Control of Intercorporate Transactions

Most state commissions now have authority over contracts between operating companies and other companies in holding company systems. In some states such contracts must have commission approval before they become effective. In others, they must be filed and may be disapproved. In general, the commissions pass judgment on the character of the services that are to be rendered and the charges that are to be made. They do not permit such charges to be fixed as a percentage of operating revenues but limit them to figures that do no more than cover the costs incurred and provide a reasonable return on the capital employed by companies rendering intercompany services. The expenditures and earnings of such companies, moreover, are subject to regulation by the SEC. Control of service charges, however, is less than rigorous. Intercompany contracts are presumed to be reasonable, and the commission that would hold them to be otherwise must bear the burden of proof. Control by the states, in most cases, is indirect, charges being influenced only by disallowing excessive amounts as expenses to be covered in fixing the level of operating company rates. Control by the SEC, in practice, does not go far beyond the requirement of periodic reports.

FEDERAL CONTROL OF ELECTRICITY

The Federal Power Commission was set up under the Water Power Act of 1920 to control the construction and operation of hydroelectric projects on navigable streams, jurisdiction over such waters under the commerce clause of the Constitution, as interpreted by the courts, belonging to the federal government. As originally constituted, the Commission was composed of the Secretaries of War, Interior, and Agriculture. This structure proved to be unwieldy, the cabinet members being occupied with other duties and the Commission's work being delegated almost entirely to its staff. In 1930 the law was amended to reorganize the body, providing for the appointment of five full-time commissioners, with bipartisan representation and five-year overlapping terms. Under Title II of the Public Utility Act of 1935, the Commission's jurisdiction was extended to cover the wholesale transmission of electricity in interstate commerce, and the body was authorized to draw up plans for regional power systems, to require interconnections, and to investigate and report on electric costs and rates. Under other legislation, the Commission was directed to pass upon the rates charged by certain federal hydro projects. And under the Natural Gas Act of 1938, it was empowered to regulate the interstate transmission and sale for resale of natural gas. In 1968 the agency had a staff of 1,100 and an appropriation of $15 million. Its activities relating to electricity will be discussed in this section. Its work in regulating natural gas, demanding the lion's share of its attention, will be considered in the next.

Control of Hydro Projects

Until 1920, licenses permitting the development of power on navigable rivers were granted by special acts of Congress. Such licenses were given in perpetuity, without charge, and with no provision for subsequent regulation of the licensees.

Valuable rights were thus squandered without regard for the national interest. This situation was vigorously denounced by Theodore Roosevelt. But it was not corrected until the passage in 1920 of the Water Power Act.

Under this law, responsibility for granting licenses is given to the FPC. In making such grants the Commission is to consider how the projects proposed would affect the use of water for other purposes, such as irrigation, navigation, and flood control. And it is to give priority to applications made by state and local governments. Licenses are to run up to 50 years, whereupon they may be renewed or granted to other applicants or the federal government can take over the properties involved, by mutual consent or by condemnation, paying a price that covers net investment exclusive of intangibles. Licensees must pay an annual rental to cover the cost of administration and the use of public lands. They must provide for other water uses and for the maintenance of their own facilities. After 20 years they must make annual payments into an amortization reserve. Licensees must conform to regulations imposed upon them by the states and by the FPC. The Commission is empowered to govern methods of accounting. And where no state agency exercises jurisdiction, it may regulate rates, services, and financial practices.

Since federal authority is limited to navigable waters, the Commission's power to control certain projects has been questioned on the ground that the streams involved were not navigable. But here, the courts have been liberal, defining navigability to cover streams that carry no commercial traffic and streams that might be navigated if they were improved, and even permitting the FPC to control the construction of dams on nonnavigable tributaries of navigable streams. [15] Under these interpretations, the Commission's jurisdiction has been broad.

In granting licenses, the Commission has examined projects in relation to the development of river basins as a whole and to all the purposes that such developments must serve. It has required that provision be made for recreational uses, for fish and wildlife conservation, for the maintenance of natural beauty and the preservation of historic sites. It has usually preferred projects making full use of the potential power to those allowing part of it to go to waste. During Democratic administrations, the Commission has favored public bodies over private applicants. Under the Republicans, licenses have been given, in important cases, to private firms. The Commission has consistently refused to grant licenses permitting the development of an entire watershed by a single company. But it has required applicants to present plans for interconnection with other lines.

The Commission has done little to regulate the rates and services of its licensees, leaving this task to the state commissions. It has prescribed a uniform system of accounting that not only must be used by companies under its jurisdiction but also has been approved by the association of state commissioners and adopted by many of the states. It has thus been influential in improving accounting practices, requiring properties to be valued at their original cost and

15 / See *Appalachian Power Co.* v. *U.S.*, 311 U.S. 377 (1940).

depreciation to be handled by making annual contributions to reserves. Its engineers have periodically inspected all projects under construction and in operation to insure compliance with license terms. And it has enforced the law's requirement regarding amortization.

Control of Interstate Transmission

In the thirties, nearly a fifth of the electricity consumed in the United States had moved across state lines. State commissions fixed the rates at which out-of-state companies sold to local consumers. But they were powerless to fix those at which out-of-state generators made sales in quantity to local distributors. When the Rhode Island commission attempted to fix the price that a Rhode Island generator charged a Massachusetts distributor, the Supreme Court held that neither state had jurisdiction over interstate commerce in electricity.[16] As a result, where current was generated in one state and distributed in another, the rates charged by the distributing company could not really be regulated, since the price that it paid for its power was beyond control.

This loophole was closed by Title II of the Public Utility Act of 1935. The FPC was given jurisdiction over electricity transported across state lines and sold for resale. It thus became a utility regulator as well as a conservation agency. Where the states lacked power, it was authorized to regulate rates and earnings, prescribe methods of accounting, and control financial operations, combinations, and the transfer of facilities. Upon complaint by a state, the Commission was empowered to order improvement of interstate service. It was also authorized to regulate discrimination in price between localities.

For three decades the FPC was not active in fixing interstate wholesale rates. Its electric rate staff consisted of four employees. It received few complaints; started no investigations on its own initiative. During the sixties, however, the Commission came to life. Investigations were undertaken. Hearings were held. Rate cuts were ordered, with consequent savings to consumers running into millions of dollars. This unaccustomed activity alarmed the industry. The Commission's jurisdiction was challenged, unsuccessfully, in the courts. A bill introduced in Congress would have exempted the utilities from control. It was not passed. At long last, regulation of interstate transmission was a reality.

Reliability of Service

Each electric company must command a large enough supply of power to enable it to satisfy its peak demand and to provide for possible emergencies. It may do so by maintaining a reserve of generating capacity. But it need not rely entirely on its own facilities. The peak and emergency demands on different companies may come at different times. They may therefore be met by interconnecting distribution systems or by pooling generating capacity. Such mea-

16 / *Rhode Island Public Utilities Commission* v. *Attleboro Steam and Electric Co.*, 273 U.S. 83 (1927).

sures not only increase the reliability of service but also reduce the investment that is required. All power systems are now connected with regional networks and there are a number of cases in which generating facilities are pooled. But these arrangements still fall short of realizing the full potentialities of co-ordination.

The FPC was required by its basic statute to draw up plans for interconnection of facilities on a regional basis and to promote their adoption. In fulfillment of this responsibility, it published a National Power Survey in 1964.[17] This was a thorough study resulting from a three-year investigation in which all segments of the industry had participated. Its proposals for coordinated development were designed to meet the country's need for electric power in 1980, when they were expected to be two and one half times as great as in 1964. Adoption of these proposals, said the Survey, would result in savings that could reduce the cost of electricity by nearly 27 percent, bringing the average price per unit down from 1.7 cents to 1.2 cents. The Commission's power to require interconnections, however, is limited. It may do so only upon application by a state commission or by a company transmitting electricity, and after due notice and hearing, but not on its own initiative. The force of the National Power Survey, therefore, was purely persuasive.

In the evening of November 9, 1965, the Northeastern part of the United States experienced the greatest power failure in history. All the lights went out in Rochester, then in Boston, then in New York until, within half an hour, 30 million people were plunged into darkness. The blackout lasted for 12 hours. In the morning of June 15, 1967, another massive failure cut off the power in an area of 5,000 square miles in the Middle-Atlantic states. It was 10 hours before service was restored. During the next two years there were 179 failures of lesser magnitude. The ability of the utilities to interconnect their systems with extra-high-voltage transmission lines had outrun their ability to handle larger loads. Overloading had not been detected. Failure had raced from point to point in a chain reaction. The switches that would have prevented the spread of disaster had not been thrown.

In the summer months of 1969, there were brownouts, with utility companies appealing to their customers to prevent total failures by turning off their air conditioners. Electric service was in short supply. The companies had not constructed adequate reserve capacity. They had underestimated the growth in demand occasioned by the spread of air conditioning. They had encountered regulatory obstacles and community opposition when they had sought to build plants that would be fired by nuclear energy. Their construction work had been held up by strikes and by delays in the delivery of heavy electrical equipment. Whatever the reasons, their service had ceased to be dependable.

In this situation, it was proposed that the Federal Power Commission be given authority to insure the reliability of service by taking steps that would avert blackouts and obviate the need for brownouts. An administration bill

17 / Federal Power Commission, *National Power Survey* (Washington, D.C.: Government Printing Office, 1964).

introduced into Congress would have empowered the Commission to require licenses for extra-high-voltage transmission lines, to establish minimum standards for such lines, and to inspect them in order to insure their consistency with these standards. It provided, also, for the establishment of regional industry councils to coordinate the utilities' plans for the provision of bulk power supply and would have authorized the Commission to insure such coordination by requiring interconnections between bulk power suppliers. The bill was the subject of hearings before committees in both houses in 1967, but was opposed by the utility companies and was not enacted into law.

FEDERAL CONTROL OF NATURAL GAS

Natural gas, obtained as a by-product in the search for oil, was wasted for many years, being blown off, burned, or devoted to inferior industrial uses in the vicinity of the oil fields. Little of it was shipped across state lines. Then, in the thirties, big new oil and gas fields were developed in regions remote from markets for gas. And, at the same time, the introduction of seamless pipe and other improvements in pipeline construction extended the distance over which gas could be economically transported from around 200 miles to 1,000 miles or more. High-pressure pipelines were built from the fields in the Southwest to every corner of the country. Now the major part of the gas produced moves in interstate commerce. Natural gas provides a third of the nation's energy. Of the gas that leaves the field, around two thirds goes into industrial uses; more than one third goes to 40 million commercial and residential consumers.

The gas industry falls into three divisions: production, transport, and distribution. Gas is distributed to consumers by local utility companies, whose operations are regulated by state or city governments. It is transported by pipeline companies, some of the lines being owned by producers and some of them by distributors. It is produced by oil and gas companies, a score of them, roughly, being corporate giants conducting integrated operations, some thousands of them being independents selling their output in the field. The pipeline companies produce a tenth of the gas they carry, obtain nine tenths of it from the independents. Of the industry's three stages, distribution involves the largest costs, transport far less, and production least of all. Of the price that the distributor pays the pipeline, two thirds to four fifths—depending on distance—is for transport; only a fifth to a third for the gas itself. But the cost of gas to the pipeline company and the company's charge for transport enter into the costs of local distributors and must be reflected in their rates.

Until 1938 state and local authorities were powerless to control the price that distributors paid for imported gas. Interstate pipelines, the Supreme Court held, were beyond their reach.[18] As a result, they were confined to regulating

---

18 / *West* v. *Kansas Natural Gas Co.*, 221 U.S. 229 (1911); *Haskell* v. *Kansas Natural Gas Co.*, 244 U.S. 217 (1912); *Public Utilities Comsn.* v. *Landon*, 249 U.S. 236 (1918); *Pennsylvania* v. *West Virginia*, 262 U.S. 553 (1923); *Barrett* v. *Kansas Natural Gas Co.*, 265 U.S. 298 (1924).

distribution charges. Controlled gas rates floated on top of the uncontrolled prices charged at the city gates. This escape, similar to the one found until 1935 in the interstate transmission of electricity, was closed by the Natural Gas Act of 1938.

The Natural Gas Act

The Act of 1938 brought the interstate transmission of natural gas and its sale for resale under the control of the FPC. The Act exempted the production and gathering of gas and its retail distribution. It established the usual pattern of rate control, requiring the pipeline companies to publish and adhere to their charges, giving prior notice of prospective changes, and empowering the Commission to suspend such changes, to fix "just and reasonable" rates, and to eliminate "undue" preferences. It also authorized the Commission to prescribe and enforce methods of accounting and to ascertain the "actual legitimate cost" of pipeline properties. As amended in 1942, the law requires the companies to obtain certificates from the FPC for interstate construction, acquisitions, extensions, and abandonments, and gives the Commission limited power to order extensions. The law carries no authority to regulate financial practices or combinations. And, unlike the Act of 1935 relating to electricity, it confers no power to order interconnections and makes no provision for studies directed toward the possible unification of facilities.

Regulation of Pipeline Rates

It is in the regulation of gas pipelines that the FPC has done its most important work. The Commission, over the years, has made substantial reductions in pipeline rates. In doing so, it has adhered to the principle of making valuations at original cost. It was the Commission's defense of this principle that led to the decisions of the Supreme Court in the Natural Gas Pipeline case in 1942 and the Hope Natural Gas case in 1944, repudiating the fair value doctrine of *Smyth* v. *Ames* and breaking its hold on the regulation of gas and other utilities.

Before money can be raised to build a pipeline or permission obtained from the PFC for its construction, the pipeline company must be assured a lasting supply of gas. To this end, it enters into contracts with producers for periods running as long as 20 years. Since market conditions for such a period cannot be foreseen, these contracts contain clauses providing for escalation of producer prices. Some of the escalation clauses are definite, requiring specific price increases on specific dates or reimbursement for larger taxes on production. Others are indefinite, requiring price increases whenever the contracting pipeline or another pipeline pays more to another producer or collects more from a distributor. Some provision for price adjustment is necessary in contracts running as long as 20 years. But indefinite escalation makes for spiraling inflation. In 1961, therefore, the FPC forbade all indefinite escalation clauses in future contracts save those providing for renegotiation of prices at five-year intervals.

Under the law, the pipeline companies can increase the price of gas to distributors before the FPC has acted on their requests for such increases. If the Commission subsequently disallows their requests, they must refund, with interest, the difference between the price collected and the price permitted. This situation has led to disputes between the pipeline companies and the distributors concerning the amount of refunds due.

Regulation of Gas Producers

The pipeline companies do not function as common carriers, transporting goods for others. They own the gas they carry, producing some of it themselves, buying most of it from independent producers. The FPC, in determining the charges made for transport, had to start, therefore, with the price of gas at the city gate, and then subtract from it the cost incurred or the price paid in obtaining gas in the field. It thus became involved not only in regulating the transport of gas but also in fixing the price of gas itself. And this stirred up a hornet's nest of politics.

At first the Commission confined itself to determining a value for gas produced by the integrated companies. For this purpose, it considered two alternatives: one was to use the price that was paid to independent producers; the other was to use the production costs of the integrated companies. It chose the second, computing the cost of producing gas by taking the companies' operating expenses and adding a return of 6 percent on the depreciated original cost of their producing properties. Its authority to take such action was challenged on the ground that the production and gathering of gas were exempted from control by the wording of the law. In 1945, however, the Supreme Court held that this exemption did not prevent the Commission from including the value of producing and gathering facilities in the rate base when fixing the transport charges of integrated companies. [19]

This decision protected consumers against increases in the price of gas where it was produced by integrated companies but not where it was produced by independents. The Commission's duty to take action in such cases was made an issue in a case involving the Phillips Petroleum Company. Phillips was the largest of the independent producers of gas. The company raised its price and was brought before the FPC upon complaint by the state of Wisconsin and the municipalities of Milwaukee, Kansas City, and Detroit. The Commission decided that it lacked the power to act. The plaintiffs appealed, and in 1954, the Supreme Court found Phillips to be a natural gas concern within the meaning of the Natural Gas Act, holding that exemption of the functions of production and gathering did not involve exemption of subsequent sales. It was therefore the Commission's duty to determine whether the prices charged by Phillips were just and reasonable. [20] Thus, for the first time in history, the Court directed a regulatory agency to increase the scope of its activities.

19 / *Colorado Interstate Gas Co.* v. *FPC*, 324 U.S. 581.

20 / *Phillips Petroleum Co.* v. *Wisconsin*, 347 U.S. 672.

The FPC was faced with the unwelcome task of fixing the prices charged by thousands of independent producers of gas. Within a month, the Commission issued an order freezing the wellhead price of natural gas sold for interstate transmission, requiring producers to apply for certificates and file their prices, and establishing control over future increases. By 1963, nearly 18,000 producers had applied for certificates. To lessen the burden of regulation, some 17,500 of the smaller producers were excused from keeping records and submitting reports in accordance with the system of accounting prescribed for other regulated concerns, and were allowed to file their applications for rate increases on simplified forms. As a usual matter, such increases were allowed to go into effect without objection by the FPC.

Regulation of the price of gas was vigorously resisted not only by gas producers but also by other members of the oil industry who saw in it an entering wedge to price control for oil. Efforts were made to negate the Court's decision by action in the state legislatures and the federal Congress. Laws were passed in Oklahoma and Kansas empowering state commissions to fix minimum prices that might be higher than the maximum prices fixed by the FPC, but these were held to violate the federal Constitution. [21] A bill was passed by Congress in 1953 exempting independent producers from control, but was vetoed by President Eisenhower when it was revealed that an oil company lawyer had attempted to influence a Senator's vote by offering a contribution to his campaign fund. A second bill, introduced in 1957, was never brought to a vote.

Fixing the Field Price of Gas

If the price charged for gas in the field is to be fixed by the FPC, how is this to be done? Originally, in determining the price of gas produced by the integrated companies, the Commission used the traditional method of fixing public utility rates: it calculated production costs and allowed, in addition, a fair return on the depreciated original value of the companies' producing properties. This process was complicated by the fact that the Commission's jurisdiction did not cover sales that were intrastate or sales to consumers, being confined to interstate sales made to distributors for resale to consumers. It was therefore necessary for the Commission to allocate costs between covered and uncovered sales. In doing so, it allocated all variable costs and half of the fixed costs (designated as commodity costs) in proportion to the annual volume of sales; the other half of fixed costs (designated as demand costs) in proportion to the peak period volume of sales. The resulting ceilings were thus based on an arbitrary exercise of judgment. But even if the Commission's jurisdiction had covered all sales of gas, it would have encountered difficulties in basing ceiling prices on computations of costs.

The traditional method of public utility rate control is not readily to be applied to an extractive industry. The production of electricity, for instance, is

21 / *Natural Gas Pipeline Co.* v. *Panoma Corp.*, 349 U.S. 44; *Cities Service Gas Co.* v. *Corporation Commission of Kansas,* 355 U.S. 391.

monopolistic; the production of gas is competitive. The cost of producing electricity can be determined precisely; the cost of producing gas cannot. Investment in a power plant involves little risk; investment in exploration for gas is highly speculative. With proper maintenance and replacement, the value of a power plant can be preserved; with depletion, the value of a gas field declines. In fixing the price of electricity, no thought need be given to possible exhaustion of supply; in fixing the price of gas, the need for conservation cannot well be ignored.

To determine cost for gas, the FPC must overcome a number of serious obstacles. The quality of gas is not uniform. The cost of producing it varies from field to field, from well to well, and from level to level in the same well. Part of the supply of gas comes from oil wells where it appears as a joint product along with oil. Part of it comes from gas wells, but much of this is a by-product of the search for oil. Determination of a cost for gas therefore involves an allocation of joint costs. Of the costs incurred in exploration, all are joint; of those incurred in development and production, as much as half are joint; of the total costs of such an operation, less than a third are clearly separable and more than two thirds are joint. The cost determined for gas is thus dependent upon the method chosen for use in allocating joint costs. Under one method, annual costs are allocated in proportion to the respective revenues received from sales of oil and gas, and fixed costs according to the respective values of reserves remaining in the ground. Under a second, joint costs are allocated in proportion to the British thermal unit content of these products. Under a third, they are divided in proportion to the respective costs of producing gas and oil from wells where they are produced alone. None of these methods is really defensible. Nor, in the very nature of the case, can costs so calculated ever be anything but arbitrary in character.

Further difficulties are encountered when an attempt is made to fix a value for a rate base and to find an appropriate rate of return. Evaluation of investment again involves the allocation of joint costs, and requires that proper allowance be made for depletion. Selection of a rate of return depends upon opinion as to risk and the inducement that is needed to overcome it. The price that is finally set will reflect a summation, not of objective facts but of subjective judgments. In this industry, moreover, the amount of money invested bears little relation to the amount of service rendered: a large investment may open dry holes; a small investment may produce a gusher. Whatever the usefulness of this procedure in fixing the rates of a producer of electricity, its application to an industry as competitive and as risky as the production of natural gas leaves much to be desired.

In 1954, the FPC attempted to abandon the traditional public utility procedure in fixing prices for the gas produced by integrated companies. In a case involving the Panhandle Eastern Pipeline Co.,[22] it valued the company's output of gas by determining a "fair field price." For this purpose, it took a weighted average of the prices paid by pipeline companies to independent producers in

22 / *In Re Panhandle Eastern Pipeline Co.*, FPC Opinion No. 269.

arm's-length bargaining in three gas fields. This method avoided the need for determining costs, evaluating investment, and deciding upon a reasonable return. By relating prices to one another rather than to costs, it also was designed to afford an incentive for the discovery of new reserves. The method was attacked, however, in a case brought by the City of Detroit and, in 1955, was held to be improper by a Court of Appeals. [23] Ceilings might be fixed by averaging field prices, said the Court, but evidence regarding investment and production costs and any added sums that might be needed to encourage exploration was still required. Determination of prices was again tied to computations of production costs.

Area Pricing

In the case of the integrated companies, it was difficult to fix a price for gas, company by company, on the basis of costs. In the case of independent producers, it was virtually impossible. Even if the theoretical objections to this procedure could be overcome, the administrative obstacles would still be insuperable. In 1960, the FPC had 3,200 requests for rate increases, filed by 570 producers, awaiting action. It estimated that, with a tripled staff, it would not be able to hear and decide these cases in less than 82 years. Finding the traditional method of fixing prices to be unworkable, the Commission announced that it had adopted an alternative approach. Under the new approach, known as area pricing, it delimited 23 producing areas and published tentative ceiling prices for each of them, based upon the prices that had prevailed from 1956 to 1958. It announced that requests for new prices and for escalated prices that were below these levels would be approved, but that producers asking for prices above them would have to bear the burden of proof. The effect was to lighten the Commission's burden by facilitating price adjustments below the ceilings while concentrating on those cases where the ceilings would be breached.

The FPC made its first area price determination for the Permian Basin of Texas and New Mexico in 1965. Here, it set two ceiling prices. One of them applied to gas from wells already in production and to gas produced in association with oil. The other applied to gas to be brought into production in the future, not in association with oil. Both ceilings were based on an average of costs plus a fair return on the investment in producing properties. The first ceiling was based on the average costs and the average investment reported in 1960 by all producers in the area for gas from wells already in production, no separate calculation being made for associated gas. The second ceiling was based on an industry-wide average of the costs incurred in producing new gas unmixed with oil. In calculating the investment base, the Commission assumed depletion over a period of 20 years. And it allowed a return, above costs, of 12 percent on investment. Using these methods, the Commission established a maximum of 14.5 cents per thousand cubic feet for old gas and for gas associated with oil; a maximum of 16.5 cents for new gas unmixed with oil. The first of these

23 / *City of Detroit* v. *FPC*, 230 F. 2d 810.

maxima was designed to prevent the realization of monopoly profits. The second was designed to afford an incentive for exploration and development. The Commission required producers to make refunds where prices had been above its maxima since 1965, and barred the operation of escalator clauses that would put future prices above its maxima. The price determination was promptly appealed to the courts and, in a decision handed down in 1968, the Supreme Court held that the Commission's method of establishing its ceilings did not exceed its authority, and that the resulting prices did not deny producers a reasonable return. [24]

In a second determination, for the Southern Louisiana Area, the FPC employed the same method, establishing a triple ceiling that set a maximum of 18.5 cents for old gas and for gas produced along with oil, a maximum of 19.5 cents for gas produced alone from wells opened before October 1, 1968, and a maximum of 20 cents for such gas from wells opened after that date. The Commission also announced that it would use the Permian Basin method in pricing new gas produced by the integrated companies and would reconsider its method of pricing their gas from wells already in production.

The Consumer's Interest in Field Price Control

The FPC finally developed a workable method of fixing maximum field prices for gas and its method was accepted by the courts. But serious questions remained. It may be asked, first, whether price control is needed to protect the consumer against monopoly. This would be the case if control over supply were concentrated in the hands of a few producers. But it is not. Producers number in the thousands, the degree of concentration is low, entry to the market is unobstructed, and there is no evidence of concerted action among producers to push prices up. Among the buyers of gas in any field, however, there are no more than two or three pipeline companies. When new fields are opened, more buyers bid for the supply. But the successful bidders are the only ones to lay in their lines. It may be possible for other buyers to enter, but such an occurrence is rare. The buyers' side of the market is thus characterized by oligopsony. But if oligopsony power is exercised, it should operate to push prices not up but down. Another factor, however, must be considered: gas is sold, as we have seen, under long-term contracts containing escalator clauses. The only prices being freely negotiated, therefore, are those between the buyers and sellers of new supplies. With demand growing and new supplies small, their prices tend constantly to rise. And these increases are communicated to the rest of the supply through escalation under the contracts. A price that is fixed in this way may be unfair to consumers in the sense that it affords producers a higher return than would be needed to induce new exploration and development. If the market is workably competitive, however, the price will not be much too high. Government ceilings would not appear to be required.

24 / *Permian Basin Area Rate Cases*, 390 U.S. 747.

It may be asked, too, whether the imposition of ceilings will operate to curtail the needed supply of gas. This will depend upon the level at which they are set. If increasing demand and increasing costs cause market prices to press against the ceilings, if action to raise them is delayed, and if they are actually enforced, they may have this effect. But if ceilings are kept above market prices, there will be no curtailment of supply. In this event, however, price control will have been unnecessary. The resources devoted to it will have gone to waste.

The Problem of Conservation

Gas is limited in quantity, exhaustible, and irreplaceable. It should therefore be used with economy. Today, however, consumption is increasing and much of the supply is directed into inferior uses where coal would suffice. Gas is employed, for example, as a raw material and as a fuel for industry when it might better be saved for commercial and residential purposes. This situation could be corrected by imposing direct control on the use of gas. It could also be improved by raising its price. A higher price would slow down the rate of exhaustion. And conservation, in this sense, may come to be required. Diversion from inferior to superior uses, moreover, is clearly to be desired. This, too, might be effected by a higher price. During the winter months, the demand for gas to be used in space heating keeps the pipelines operating at full capacity. In summer, demand declines, and the pipeline companies, to keep their facilities employed, sell gas at low prices for industrial use. If the price of gas were raised, industrial users would turn to substitutes. The companies, in order to operate their lines at capacity throughout the year, might then develop further facilities for summer storage in the North. The higher price would be borne by the consumer, and would give an unearned profit to the producer. The government, however, could tax this profit away. The cost of storage would necessitate a higher pipeline charge. This, too, would be borne by the consumer. But wasteful consumption would be curtailed and supplies thus made available for superior use. This fact, however, might not be persuasive. Some 40 million consumers have been induced to invest in gas-burning equipment. The political pressure exerted on their behalf is likely to be governed by their short-run interest in the maintenance of a low price.

Chapter 16

REGULATION OF TRANSPORT MONOPOLY

It is in the case of railroads that the federal government first undertook to regulate the operation of a private business. It is here that government has had its longest experience as a regulator and its greatest powers, that its regulatory activities have been most extensive, most intensive, and most detailed. It is here that regulation has been most effective and attended by the greatest measure of prestige. The story of this experience therefore has particular significance. An account of the changing relationship between the government and the railroads is given in this chapter. An account of public regulation of other transport media and of national policy respecting transport as a whole will be presented in the next.

PUBLIC AID TO RAILWAYS 1850-70

In its first stage, the policy of government toward railroads was to promote construction. Its motivation was solely that of opening up the country and speeding its settlement. To this end, assistance was provided by local, state, and federal governments. Local and state aid took the form of purchases of stock at figures above its market value, loans at low rates of interest, guarantees of railroad bonds, donations of cash, land, equipment, materials, and labor, and exemption from taxes. Federal aid took the form of grants of right of way through the public domain and freedom to use materials on the domain, such as timber and stone; of low-interest loans; and, more important, of extensive gifts of public lands. From 1850 on, 72 such transfers were effected, more than 130 million acres being involved. Most of this went to a few transcontinental lines, two thirds of it to the predecessors of five of the present roads. In some cases, receipts from land grants covered a major part of the construction costs. As a consequence of public aid, roads were built before there was traffic to support them. Fortunes were made through financial manipulation by their promoters, and heavy losses were sustained by those who bought their shares. But the country was opened and its settlement assured.

Estimates of the total of public aid vary, according to the basis of computation, from $600 million to $1,500 million. Against these sums, however, an offset must be made. Railroads receiving land grants were required, thereafter,

368

to carry freight for the government at reduced rates. And this obligation was not suspended until 1946. It is possible that the government by that time had saved as much on transport costs as it had spent on public aid.

STATE REGULATION OF RAIL MONOPOLY 1871-87

During the years of railroad building, little thought had been given to the possible need for regulation. Several roads were built in every section of the country, and it was assumed that competition between them would protect the public interest. But competition proved, instead, to be ruinous. And it led, shortly, to collusive agreements among the railroad companies. The level of rates was raised, and discrimination was practiced between persons, between products, and between communities. The public attitude toward the railroads changed from benevolence to hostility. Shippers demanded protection. And for this, they turned first to the legislatures of the states.

The Emergence of Monopoly

The economic characteristics of the railroad business were such as to lead the roads into destructive competition. Their investment in plant and equipment was large. The annual cost of this investment was high. This cost, in the short run, was fixed, not varying with the volume of traffic. Operating expenses, too, were largely fixed: plant and equipment had to be maintained and administrative charges met whether volume was large or small. Fixed costs, as a fraction of total costs, in the railway industry, may be as low as a fourth or a fifth when capacity is fully used. But they may be as high as half or two thirds when utilization is incomplete. With overexpansion, in the early years, much capacity stood idle and fixed costs were high. There was pressure, therefore, to increase volume by reducing rates. Greater volume, though at lower rates, might lead to greater earnings, since fixed costs could thus be spread over more units, and total unit costs, thereby, would fall. Rate cuts, however, might not stop at total unit costs. To obtain a particular shipment, rather than lose it to a competitor, it would be advantageous to keep on cutting the rate as long as it yielded enough to cover the variable costs involved—for extra fuel and labor—and contributed something toward meeting overhead. If a minor part of a railroad's traffic were carried on this basis, its revenues might thus be maximized. But if a major part were so handled, it would be headed for bankruptcy. And this is what happened during the sixties and the seventies. Rate wars, breaking out among the roads between the Atlantic and Chicago, between Chicago and the Pacific, and in the South, carried rates to a fraction of their former levels and threatened the industry with disaster. Monopolistic agreements were the result.

Agreements among the railroads first took the form of understandings with regard to rates. When these proved ineffective, they were superseded by market-sharing arrangements known as pools. These were of two major types: traffic pools and money pools. Where traffic was pooled, competitive shipments were divided among the participating carriers in accordance with agreed percentages, the distribution being effected by employing certain large shippers (such as Swift, Armour, and Standard Oil) as "eveners," granting them rebates on their rates, and so directing their shipments that quotas would be filled. Where money was pooled, shipments were not controlled, but earnings from competitive traffic were divided into shares on which the railroads had agreed. In either case, competition was ended and rates were raised. And with monopolistic pricing thus established, discrimination was widely practiced as a means of maximizing total revenues. All shippers were affected by the higher rates, and some shippers were unfairly handicapped by favors granted their competitors.

Resentment against the railroads, arising during the seventies, was strongest among the farmers of the Midwest, and was given expression through the granges. Farm prices had been falling as a result of overexpansion, and high freight rates were blamed. It was felt that the farmer would get more of the sums paid in the market if the railroads hauling his crops there were required to take less. Dissatisfaction was created, too, by discrimination, by losses resulting from financial manipulation, by political scandals, and by the arrogance of railroad managements. The granges therefore demanded action, first by the states and then by the federal government.

The Granger Laws

Common carriers had long been given a special status at common law in judgments handed down on cases brought before the courts, being required to serve all comers at reasonable rates, avoiding discrimination among those whose circumstances were the same. The railroads had also been subjected to control through the provisions of their charters and through the activities of state commissions which had been set up, in some cases, as early as the thirties and the forties. But these methods were ineffective: the courts did not act unless a plaintiff carried through a suit; the charters were limited and inflexible; the commissions were confined to such matters as appraising property taken under eminent domain, reporting on charter violations, and enforcing safety laws. Until the granger laws were passed in the early seventies, there was no real control over rates.

Such laws were enacted in Illinois, Iowa, Wisconsin, and Minnesota between 1871 and 1874. In general, they either fixed maximum rates at low and rigid levels, or set up a commission and empowered it to fix these rates at levels which were reasonable. The laws were upheld by the courts. But they were bitterly attacked by the railroads, being held responsible for bringing on the business depression of 1873. Within a few years they had been repealed or replaced. But the setback for regulation was only temporary. New laws were enacted during the eighties, establishing state commissions with substantial powers. By 1887 commissions were in operation in 25 states.

During these years, the farmers had been pressing, too, for action by the federal government. Such action was finally precipitated by a decision handed down by the Supreme Court in the Wabash case[1] in 1886. The Wabash railroad had been found guilty of violating the law of Illinois by charging more for a shorter haul from one town in Illinois to New York than it charged for a longer haul from another. The Court reversed this verdict on the ground that the shipments in question could not be regulated by the state, since the Constitution gave exclusive jurisdiction over interstate commerce to the federal government. Where traffic was confined within its borders, a state could act. But where it crossed state lines, the Congress alone had power.

FEDERAL REGULATION OF RAIL MONOPOLY 1887-1917

In 1872 a committee known as the Windom committee was appointed by the Senate to investigate the possibility of reducing the cost of transport from the Midwest to the East. In 1874 this committee made its report, charging that rail rates were extortionate and recommending that the government own and operate some railroads as a means of controlling the charges made by their competitors. No action was taken. In 1885 the Senate appointed a second committee—the Cullom committee—to consider proposals for federal regulation. In 1886 the report of this committee condemned discrimination in railroad rates, urged legislation to control it, and recommended that a commission be established to enforce its terms. In 1887, following the Wabash decision, this proposal was enacted into law.

The Act to Regulate Commerce, 1887

The Interstate Commerce Act, as it came to be known, initially applied to common carriers transporting passengers or property in interstate or foreign commerce wholly by rail or, in cases of continuous movements under common control, partly by rail and partly by water. The law forbade the pooling of traffic or earnings. It required that the rates established by carriers be "reasonable" and "just," leaving the definition of these terms ultimately to the courts. It also required that rates be published and adhered to and that prior notice be given before they were increased. The Act contained a number of provisions designed to limit discrimination. It prohibited rebates to favored shippers and (with minor exceptions) all other forms of discrimination among persons. It curbed discrimination among commodities and among places by forbidding carriers to give "any undue or unreasonable preference or advantage" or to impose "any undue or unreasonable prejudice or disadvantage," leaving it to the courts again to determine when discrimination was undue or unreasonable. The law specifically attacked one form of discrimination between places, forbidding the railroads—unless granted special permission to do so—to charge more for a shorter haul than for a longer haul, when the one was contained within the other, over the same line in the same direction. This prohibition was qualified,

1 / *Wabash, St. Louis & Pacific Railway Co.* v. *Illinois,* 188 U.S. 557 (1886).

however, by the proviso that the two hauls be "under substantially similar circumstances and conditions."

The Act created an Interstate Commerce Commission and set forth its powers. The Commission was authorized to undertake investigations upon complaint by shippers or upon its own initiative. It was empowered to compel witnesses to testify, to demand the production of books and documents, to prescribe uniform systems of accounting, and to require annual reports. Where it found that the law had been violated, the Commission was authorized to issue an order directing the carrier in question to cease and desist from the illegal activity. If its order was not obeyed, it could apply for an enforcing order to a federal court. In such proceedings the Commission's findings of fact were to be taken as prima facie evidence. Carriers were made liable for damages sustained as a result of violations of the Act, and the Commission was empowered to determine the amount of such damages. Certain violations, such as the granting of rebates, were made punishable by fine and imprisonment, and here the Commission was to assist in prosecuting cases brought before the courts.

Emasculation of the Act of 1887

The new commission made a good beginning toward enforcement of the law. But its efforts were soon obstructed by the courts. When it found a rate to be too high, the Commission specified the rate that should be charged. But the Supreme Court held, in 1897, that it had no power to do so.[2] As a result, a rate that was found unreasonable could be cut a fraction of a cent and maintained at this level until another case was brought, the process being repeated again and again. The Commission was thus deprived of any real power over the level of rates. So, too, with discrimination. The law provided that the testimony of a witness could not be held against him in a later suit. But when action was taken against the granting of rebates, a shipper refused to testify, claiming protection against self-incrimination under the Fifth Amendment to the Constitution. And in this he was upheld.[3] The evidence required for preventing personal discrimination was thus made difficult to obtain. Enforcement of the prohibition of higher rates for shorter than for longer hauls was also blocked. This prohibition applied only "under substantially similar circumstances and conditions." And the Supreme Court, in another case[4] decided in 1897, held that competition between railroads and between trading centers was a factor in making conditions dissimilar. Since this competition was the source of most long-and-short-haul discrimination, its prevention was thus brought to a halt. The Commission's orders, finally, were not binding in themselves but had to be taken to the courts for enforcement. Here, decisions were delayed for months and years. In the meantime, rates found to be unreasonable continued in effect. The Commis-

2 / ICC v. Cincinnati, New Orleans, and Texas Pacific Railway Co., 167 U.S. 479.

3 / Counselman v. Hitchcock, 142 U.S. 547 (1892).

4 / ICC v. Alabama Midland Railway Co., 168 U.S. 144.

sion's rulings were thus ignored, and shippers were discouraged from bringing new complaints.

The ICC, throughout its second decade, found itself confined, in the main, to conducting research and making advisory reports. The law was amended in 1893 to compel witnesses to testify without risk of self-incrimination, and in 1903 to give suits brought under its provisions priority in the courts. It was amended, too, by the Elkins Act of 1903 to make recipients of rebates as well as railroads and their officers and agents liable in cases of personal discrimination. But the Commission was not granted real powers until the passage of the Hepburn Act in 1906 and the Mann-Elkins Act in 1910.

Strengthening the ICC 1906-10

The Hepburn Act undid some of the damage that had been done by the courts. (1) It authorized the Commission, when rates were found to be unreasonable, to specify the legal maxima. (2) It contained many provisions designed to prevent personal discrimination. It gave the Commission jurisdiction over industrial railroads and private car lines and empowered it to control divisions of rates and charges made for switching and for special services rendered by shippers and by carriers. It forbade free passes, except to railway employees. It increased the liability of recipients of rebates and the criminal penalties that could be imposed. (3) The law forbade railroads to haul (except for their own use) goods they had themselves produced. This provision, known as the commodities clause, was designed to remove the advantage in car service and rates enjoyed by railroad-owned anthracite mines over their independent competitors. (4) The law sought to prevent railroads from refusing to interchange traffic with water carriers by empowering the Commission to require the establishment of joint routes, to fix joint rates, and to determine how they should be divided. (5) The law strengthened the ICC in other ways. It required that all accounts be kept in such forms as the Commission might prescribe. It provided heavy penalties for delay and falsification in the submission of reports. And it made the Commission's orders effective after 30 days, with noncompliance punishable thereafter by a fine of $5,000 per day, thus putting on the railroads the burden of appealing to the courts.

The Mann-Elkins Act made other significant changes in the law. (1) Under the Act of 1887, the ICC had been unable to pass upon a rate until after it had been put into effect. When rates were rising and complaints were numerous, this meant that unreasonable charges could be collected for many months before the Commission was able to act. When action was finally taken, moreover, these charges would have been passed on in product prices and restitution was therefore difficult if not impossible to effect. The new Act corrected this situation by giving the Commission power to suspend proposed increases, for a stated period, while it considered their legality. The burden of justifying higher rates was thus put on the carriers. (2) When one rate was cut, under the original Act, the railroads could compensate for the reduction by raising another. Now the

Commission was empowered, on its own motion, to consider the schedule of rates as a whole. (3) The Commission was also authorized to control the system used in classifying freight. And finally (4) the loophole found by the court in the long-and-short-haul prohibition was closed. The phrase "under substantially similar circumstances and conditions" was dropped from the law. The effectiveness of the prohibition was thus restored, and the formulation of policy to govern exceptions was left, in the main, to the ICC.

The new laws rehabilitated the Commission. Its orders, in general, came to be accepted by the courts. Other legislation followed. In 1912 the railroads were forbidden to own or operate vessels passing through the Panama Canal. In 1913 the ICC was directed to determine the value of railway properties. In 1917 it was authorized to require the roads to establish reasonable rules to govern the provision of freight cars and, if need be, to prescribe such rules itself. Concerning the valuation act, a further word should be said.

The Railway Valuation

The Act of 1887 had provided that rates should be reasonable and just. The Supreme Court had held in the case of *Smyth* v. *Ames* in 1898, that reason and justice required the allowance of a fair return on a fair value. But the value of the railroads was unknown. Until the Hepburn and Mann-Elkins Acts were passed, this did not matter, since the ICC had been left with little power over rates. But with regulation strengthened, the need for determining value was recognized.

The Valuation Act of 1913 directed the Commission to ascertain the value of every railroad in the United States. For each piece of property, other than land, used by each road it was to determine the original cost to date, the cost of reproduction, and the cost of reproduction less depreciation. In the case of land, it was to determine value both at the time of its dedication and at the time of its valuation. And to these sums, it was to add a proper value for intangibles. A tentative value, as of 1913, was to be announced. If there were protests, public hearings were to be held. A final value was then to be adopted and thereafter kept up to date.

The initial valuation was expected to take three years. In the end it took almost 20 and cost more than $50 million. In 1933 the work of bringing the 1913 valuation up to date was still to be done. And by this time, as we shall see, the requirement that rates be fixed to yield a fair return on a fair value had been dropped.

State and Federal Jurisdiction

As the power of the ICC increased, that of the state commissions declined. In the Wabash case the Court had drawn a line between interstate and intrastate traffic, assigning the one to the federal government and the other to the states. But points of conflict remained: the two types of traffic were intermingled, the rates charged for one affecting those that could be charged for the other. When intrastate rates were set at levels that disturbed the pattern of interstate rates, the ICC ordered them changed, and the issue of jurisdiction was carried to the courts. In the Shreveport Rate Case,[5] decided in 1914, the Texas commission had fixed rates for traffic from Dallas and Houston to northeast Texas that were lower than those fixed by the ICC for traffic from Shreveport, Louisiana, and the ICC had issued an order rescinding the intrastate rates on the ground that they were unduly preferential to Dallas and Houston and unduly prejudicial to to Shreveport. Its power to do so was upheld by the Supreme Court. The Commission was thus given jurisdiction over intrastate as well as interstate rates whenever an influence on interstate commerce could be shown. And in nearly all important cases such a showing could be made. In fixing rates, the state commissions were, therefore, relegated to a minor role.

The state commissions, however, have not abandoned the field of transport. They regulate intrastate carriage by highway, waterway, and air. They exercise some control over safety and service on the railroads. And they still fix rates where lines are wholly intrastate. But in every phase of railway regulation, for 50 years, the dominance of the ICC has been assured.

MANAGERIAL SUPERVISION OF RAIL MONOPOLY 1918-33

Up to World War I, regulation took the form of judicial action designed to protect shippers against extortion and discrimination. The ICC exercised no affirmative authority over railway management. It was charged with no positive responsibility to maintain earnings. With the coming of war, service broke down, and the government was forced to operate the railroads, paying them a fixed return. When the war ended, new legislation was required. Arrangements had to be made to effect the reversion to private operation. Gaps in the regulatory structure had to be closed. There was need, for instance, for more effective control of service and for authority to regulate the issuance of securities. Attention had to be given, too, to the financial needs of the railroads. New capital was sought, but earnings were declining and credit was impaired. There followed a complete revision of the law, increasing the powers of the Commission and charging it with new responsibilities. A different phase in the history of regulation was begun.

Government Operation 1918-20

When America entered the war in 1917 the demand for railway service was substantially increased. Men, materials, and equipment had to be moved, in quantity and without delay, to army camps, to war industries, and to Atlantic ports. The railroads, under their separate managements, proved to be incapable of doing the job. Each of them sought profit for itself. It therefore hoarded cars

5 / *Houston, East and West Texas Railway Co.* v. *U.S.,* 234 U.S. 342.

when they were needed on other lines. It routed shipments over its own tracks and through terminals when other lines made it possible for terminals to be bypassed. As a result, the movement of supplies was impeded by car shortage and terminal congestion; the breakdown of transport threatened to prevent the successful prosecution of the war. The government took over the railroads on December 28, 1917.

The United States Railroad Administration operated the railway system as a single unit. It eliminated needless duplication of facilities and services. It pooled rolling stock and used it where there was the greatest need. It economized equipment, establishing priorities for freight and insuring that cars were fully loaded by fixing sailing days. It speeded service, making shipments by the shortest routes and bypassing crowded terminals. It succeeded in moving the men and the materials that were required to win the war. And this was its purpose.

The government paid each railroad company a rental for its properties. It undertook to maintain these properties, returning them in as good condition as it found them, and to make necessary improvements for which the roads would pay. The management of operations, subject to government orders, was left to the officials of the roads. Whether the railroads were better off or worse off after this experience is a matter of dispute. The government, certainly, lost money. But this was because it failed to raise its rates, as wages and other costs increased. The record affords little or no evidence concerning the desirability of public ownership. It does show, however, that unification can make for greater efficiency.

Transportation Act of 1920

The provisions of the Transportation Act of 1920 fall into three categories: those that were designed to facilitate a return to private operation, those that involved a further extension of the powers and duties of the ICC, and those that represented a major departure in regulatory policy. It is only with the second and the third that we are here concerned.

The Commission was given new authority over service, securities, and rates. It was empowered to order unification in the event of an emergency, to require joint use of terminals, and to establish rules respecting the use of locomotives and cars. Its permission was required before a railroad could build a new line or extend an old one, abandon service on all its lines or any part of them, or obtain new capital by selling its securities. As a means of preventing destructive competition and discrimination, the Commission was authorized to establish minimum as well as maximum rates. And in finding a rate unreasonable, it was empowered to fix, not merely a maximum, but the exact rate that should be charged. The Act also reinforced the long-and-short-haul clause, giving statutory effect to policies that the Commission had followed in granting exceptions to its general rule.

In other provisions the Act departed from previous policy. It recognized that the task of fixing rates for railroads differs from that of fixing rates for public utilities. Every gas or electric company has a monopoly in the community it serves. Separate rates can be set for each of them at a level that will guarantee it a fair return. Most railroads, however, compete with other roads at various points along their lines. Different rates cannot be fixed for different roads. If this were done, the road with the higher rates would get no business. Rail rates, therefore, must be set at a common level. But common rates, applied to different roads, will not yield similar returns. The roads may differ as to volume of traffic, conditions of cost, and structure of capital. One may be strong, another weak. When rates are set for both, the one may prosper, but no profit for the other can be guaranteed. It was to the solution of the problem presented by this situation that the attention of those who framed the Transportation Act of 1920 was turned.

The Act set up a new rule to govern the making of rates, directing the ICC to fix them "so that carriers as a whole (or as a whole in each of such rate groups or territories as the Commission may from time to time designate) will, under honest, efficient, and economical management . . . earn an aggregate annual net railway operating income equal, as nearly as may be, to a fair return upon the aggregate value of the railway property of such carriers. . . ." Congress set 5½ percent as the figure to be taken as a fair return for the first two years, authorizing the Commission in its discretion to raise it to as much as 6 percent. Several things should be noted about this rule. It required the ICC to look into the honesty, efficiency, and economy with which the railroads were managed. It imposed on the Commission an affirmative obligation with respect to railway earnings. But it did not guarantee that the roads as a whole would actually realize the profit that the rates were intended to provide. And it did not guarantee that any road, taken by itself, would make ends meet. The problem of the strong and weak roads still remained.

Three solutions were attempted. (1) Under a provision known as the recapture clause, a road that earned more than 6 percent on the value of its property in any year was permitted to keep half of the excess, putting it in a reserve fund from which it could pay interest and dividends. But it was required to turn the other half over to the ICC to be placed in a revolving fund from which loans (at 6 percent interest) could be made to weaker roads. (2) The Commission was directed, in determining how rates on joint hauls should be divided, to give special consideration to the need of weaker roads for revenues. (3) Combination, once forbidden, was now encouraged. The ICC was empowered to permit pools, if they would improve service and reduce costs, and to permit one railroad to control another, if it appeared that the public interest would be served. It was instructed to prepare a plan for consolidation of the railroads into a limited number of competitive systems of approximately equal strength. Thereafter, it was to approve combinations that conformed to its plan and disapprove those that did not. In all of these ways, the railway system as a whole was to be strengthened, the weak roads being aided or absorbed at the expense of the strong.

Results of the Act of 1920

The transitional provisions of the Act of 1920 and those that strengthened the Commission were successful. The new rule of rate making and the efforts to solve the strong-and-weak road problem were not. Despite the obligation imposed on the ICC to fix rates that would yield the roads from 5½ to 6 percent on their investment, their average earnings did not reach this figure, and the rule was supplanted in 1933. The recapture clause, the division of joint rates, and the combination program did not succeed in strengthening the railway system by bringing the stronger roads to the support of the weak.

The power of the government to capture excess earnings, when challenged, was upheld by the Supreme Court.[6] But the plan worked badly. The weaker roads got little aid from money for which they had to pay as much as 6 percent. The stronger roads curtailed the profits subject to recapture by increasing their expenditures. With earnings computed as a percentage of property values, they contested the Commission's valuations in the courts. The major consequence of the plan was litigation. Acknowledged to be a failure, it was repealed in 1933.

The provision directing the ICC to favor the weaker roads in dividing joint rates was also upheld by the Court.[7] This plan, too, proved to have its limitations. Divisions were possible only where carriers made connections and were significant only where traffic was interchanged in substantial quantities. The share of a joint rate left to a stronger road could not be cut so far as to be confiscatory. Such a road, moreover, might reduce joint hauls by inducing shippers to route their goods in other ways. And a weak road might hesitate to offend a strong one by insisting on a larger share. The plan was doubtless of some assistance. But it lacked the strength to solve the problem in itself.

In 1921 the ICC published a tentative plan for consolidation of the railroads, held hearings on it, and issued its final plan in 1929. This called for the creation of two systems in New England, a line along the Atlantic coast, a system in the South, five trunk lines from the Atlantic to Chicago, five regional systems in the central and northwestern states, and five transcontinental lines from Chicago to the Pacific, a total of 19. These systems were to realize some of the advantages of unification. They were to compete with one another in rendering service. And each of them was to be strong enough to earn a fair return at a common level of rates. Combinations in accordance with this plan were not to be required. But where voluntarily proposed, they were to be approved. Such combinations, however, did not occur. The shareholders of the stronger roads displayed an understandable reluctance to risk curtailment of their earnings by taking on the burdens of the weaker ones. The major systems, on the other hand, were eager to absorb the strongest of the shorter lines. The combinations

6 / *Dayton-Goose Creek Railway Co.* v. *U.S.*, 263 U.S. 456 (1924).
7 / *New England Divisions Case*, 261 U.S. 184 (1923).

they sought, in general, were not according to the plan. But these were the combinations that actually occurred. The ICC had been given no jurisdiction over holding companies, and consolidation was effected by setting up such companies to purchase railroad shares. This loophole was closed in 1933 when the law was amended to give the Commission authority over all combinations, however achieved, including those effected through holding companies. But there were still no proposals for mergers conforming to the pattern the Commission had proposed. And finally in 1940 the requirement that combinations conform to a plan drawn up in advance was dropped from the law. Thereafter, with consolidations as with other acquisitions of control, the Commission could grant approval when it appeared to be in the public interest. The project of creating a score of competing railway systems, comparable in strength, was thus abandoned.

The Depression and the Railroads

The railroads were hard hit by the depression of the thirties. Car loadings fell off; from 1929 to 1932 gross revenues were cut in half. If their capitalization had been in stocks, the roads would have been in a better position to sustain this loss. But 56 percent of their capitalization, in 1932, was in bonds, bearing an average interest charge of 4.58 percent. In many cases, though operating costs were covered, interest could not be paid. By 1938 as many as 111 railroads, with more than 30 percent of the country's mileage, had become insolvent and were in receivership. Railway bonds had been a major outlet for conservative investment. Nine tenths of them were held by institutional investors: savings banks, insurance companies, university endowments, and the like. The railway problem thus became, not that of protecting the shippers against the railroads, but that of protecting the holders of railroad securities against financial loss.

Several things were done to meet this situation. In 1932 the Hoover administration set up the Reconstruction Finance Corporation and empowered it to make loans to the railroads, among others. In the next ten years such loans reached a total of $850 million, enabling many roads to stave off bankruptcy. In 1933 Congress sought to facilitate the reorganization of railway companies by adding a new section (Section 77) to the Bankruptcy Act of 1898. In 1933, also, Congress embodied emergency provisions in a statute making major changes in railroad law.

The Emergency Transportation Act of 1933 included sections, mentioned above, repealing the recapture clause and bringing holding companies within the jurisdiction of the ICC. It replaced the 1920 rule of rate making with a new rule that will be discussed below. It also sought to improve the financial condition of the railroads by reducing their costs. To this end, the Act provided for the appointment of a Federal Coordinator of Transportation, to be chosen from the members of the ICC, and for the creation of regional committees representing railway managements. These agencies were to cut costs by eliminating wastes and by reducing duplication of facilities and services. A serious limitation was imposed, however, upon their powers. No action could be taken that would reduce the volume of railway employment or the wages of any railway employee. The results of the program were meager. The committees could not agree upon economies to be effected. The Coordinator made some valuable reports. But he did little coordination. The make-work limitation in the law, adopted to satisfy labor, tied his hands behind his back.

ADJUSTMENT TO TRANSPORT COMPETITION 1938-58

For 60 years the regulation of railroads was based on the assumption that they possessed monopolistic powers and that shippers therefore required protection against exorbitant and discriminatory rates. In regulating rates it was further assumed that substitutes for railway service were not available and that rates could therefore be set at whatever level might be required to enable the roads to cover their costs and obtain a fair return. With the emergence of increasing competition from other carriers—by pipeline, highway, waterway, and air— these assumptions lost validity. Many shippers, by substituting other modes of transport, were now able to protect themselves. And increases in rates, instead of yielding an assured return, might lead to a decline in revenues. This was a fundamental change, and one to which policy had to be adjusted. The process of adjustment began in 1933.

Emergence of Competition

From 1916 to 1939 the railroads' share of intercity freight ton-miles dropped from more than 77 percent to less than 63 percent; their share of intercity common-carrier passenger miles dropped from 98 percent to less than 66 percent. In the case of freight, they lost business to the pipelines and the trucks; in the case of passengers, primarily to the buses, though they began also to experience competition from the airlines. The situation was worse than these figures would indicate, since the railroads tended to lose the part of their business that paid them best and to keep the part that paid them least. They lost to the highways valuable merchandise on which the rates were high, retaining commodities moved in bulk on which the rates were low. They lost to the airlines long-distance, first-class passenger traffic which was profitable, retaining commutation traffic which was not. They suffered, too, from the development of Diesel and hydroelectric power, since oil moved by pipe and electricity moved by wire competed with coal, the bulk of which moved by rail.

The competitors of the railways have certain marked advantages. The pipelines have lower costs. So do the water carriers, though their service is slow and subject to interruption. The airlines have greater speed, but at a somewhat greater risk. The motor carriers have lower costs on short hauls, higher costs on long hauls. But they have greater flexibility, giving faster service and superior convenience, avoiding the costs of packing and rehandling by operating from door to door.

Faced with such competition, the railroads might have retained a larger share of traffic by introducing improvements of their own. Buses and trucks might have been used to a greater extent as feeders, supplementing instead of substituting for movement by rail. Door-to-door service might have been developed at an earlier date, and packing and handling reduced by loading standard containers or trailers on flat cars for longer hauls. Freight might have been speeded and passenger service made more attractive and more convenient. In all of these respects, improvements came 20 years too late. The railroads sought, rather, to increase their revenues by obtaining permission to raise their rates. Instead of improving their competitive position, they worsened it. They suffered the effects of managerial inertia, ingrained through years of monopoly and regulation.

The 1933 Rule of Rate Making

The new rule of rate making, contained in the Emergency Transportation Act of 1933, recognized that competition had created greater elasticity in the demand for railway services, and that earnings, therefore, could no longer be assured by raising the level of railway rates. It directed the ICC, in fixing rates, to "give due consideration, among other factors, to the effect of rates on the movement of traffic; to the need, in the public interest, of adequate and efficient transportation service at the lowest cost consistent with the furnishing of such service; and to the need of revenues sufficient to enable the carriers, under honest, economical, and efficient management, to provide such service." The rule still required the Commission to look into the honesty, economy, and efficiency with which the railroads were managed. But it no longer contained an affirmative obligation to provide the railroads with a fixed return. After 35 years of regulation based upon the doctrine of fair value, and after 20 years of costly valuation work, it abandoned value as a factor to be taken into account. The new rule was functional in character, providing for rates that would attract business, assure adequate service and cover its necessary cost, and establish earnings at a level required to insure railway credit, so that new capital could be obtained. In introducing these factors into its consideration, the rule accorded a broad new area of discretion to the ICC.

The rule required the Commission to consider the effect of rates on the movement of traffic not only when passing on requests for changes in the general level of rates but also when acting on rates charged for particular shipments. The Commission might thus reject the railroads' application for a general increase on the ground that higher rates would divert traffic from the railroads to other carriers. It might also disapprove reduction of the rate for a particular shipment on the ground that the lower rate would divert traffic from other carriers to the railroads.

Extension of Control to Other Carriers

Up to 1935, pipelines and some ships operated by railroad companies were the only carriers other than railroads controlled by the ICC. Carriers by water and by air were subject to some safety regulation by the federal government. And these, together with motor carriers, were subject to safety regulation and to some economic regulation by the states. Common carriers by water on the Great Lakes and in the coastwise and intercoastal trades were subject to the jurisdiction of the United States Shipping Board. But other carriers on these waters and all carriers on other inland waters were uncontrolled. Air service was supervised, to some extent, by the Postmaster-General, and the rates paid for carrying mail were fixed by the ICC. But aviation, otherwise, was free of economic regulation. And the federal government had no power of any sort over the railroads' most serious competitor: the motor carrier.

The next few years were marked by a significant expansion of federal control. In 1935 interstate motor carriers were brought within the jurisdiction of the ICC. In 1938 carriers by air were subjected to economic regulation under a Civil Aeronautics Board. In 1940 all of the interstate transport by water was brought within the jurisdiction of the ICC. In all of these cases, the familiar pattern of control, developed over the years through experience with the railroads, was applied, with minor changes in detail, to the other carriers. In the case of motor and water carriers, the 1933 rule of rate making was adopted without change. In the case of aviation, it was modified in one respect, directing the CAB, in fixing rates, to consider the need of each company, taken separately, rather than that of the industry as a whole, for revenue sufficient to enable it to provide adequate and efficient service.

The extension of control to these carriers was caused by factors differing radically from those that explained its application, a half century earlier, to the railroads. At that time shippers had complained of poor service, high rates, and unjust discrimination. But now shippers were well satisfied with the treatment they were receiving at the hands of carriers by highway, by water, and by air. The pressure for regulation came, not from consumers, but from producers. It had its origin, not in the abuses of monopoly, but in the fact that competition was hard to take.

Transportation Act of 1940

The railroad problem had now become a transport problem, and regulation had moved on from railroads alone to transport as a whole. This change was recognized by the statement that was put at the head of the Interstate Commerce Act by an amendment contained in the Transportation Act of 1940. It was then declared to be the policy of Congress

. . . to provide for fair and impartial regulation of all modes of transportation subject to the provisions of the Act, so administered as to recognize and preserve the inherent advantages of each; to promote safe, adequate, economical, and efficient service and foster sound economic conditions in transportation and among the several carriers . . . to the end of developing, co-ordinating, and preserving a national transportation system by water, highway, and rail, as well as other means, adequate to meet the needs of the commerce of the United States. . . .

All forms of transport were to be developed. Regulation was to be impartial. The emphasis was on the system as a whole. And this still stands as the expression of national transport policy.

The Act of 1940 made certain changes, already mentioned, in the law. It eliminated the requirement that combinations conform to a prior plan. It brought water carriers under the jurisdiction of the ICC. In addition, the Act made a number of other changes in substance and in procedure. It amended the long-and-short-haul clause in further detail. It made clear the power of the ICC to prevent discrimination among regions and directed the Commission to examine the interterritorial structure of rates. And it put the burden of proof on the carriers in proposing reductions as well as increases in rates.

Railway Rate Bureaus

Changes in the general level of railway rates cannot be made without the approval of the ICC. And changes in the structure of rates may be ordered by the Commission in response to complaints. But individual rates are initiated by the roads themselves. In taking such action, each road might act independently. In practice, it does not. For many years, particular changes have been effected through the medium of trade associations known as rate bureaus. A road proposing a new rate takes its proposal to one of these bureaus. The proposal is examined by bureau employees, who forward it to large shippers and to competing roads. If any object, the rate is considered by a committee of traffic officers. Their decision is subject to a series of appeals. The final action of the bureau takes the form of a recommendation to the carriers concerned. Legally, each of them retains the right to make a change, even though the bureau disapproves. In practice, none of them is likely to do so. Rates will not be changed unless competing roads agree. This machinery operates as a cartel, removing the making of rates from the hands of individual managements. Its effect is to make rates higher and more rigid than they otherwise would be. Rate bureaus, long used by the railroads, have also been set up by other types of carriers.

In 1944 the Department of Justice brought a suit against the Western Association of Railway Executives, the American Association of Railroads, and a number of western roads, charging that the establishment of rates through bureaus was in violation of the Sherman Act; and the state of Georgia brought another suit in which the legality of such activities was attacked. In the light of existing precedents, there was little doubt that the bureaus would be held to violate the law. The railroads therefore turned to Congress for exemption. The Reed-Bulwinkle Act, granting their request, was passed over the veto of President Truman in 1948.

The new law made rate agreements subject to approval by the ICC. It left shippers free to carry complaints to the Commission, and authorized the Attorney General to take cases before that agency. The law was defended as maintaining order in the making of rates and bringing all aspects of the process within the jurisdiction of a single body. It was attacked as assigning further responsibilities to a body that lacked the ability and the inclination to discharge them in the public interest. The Commission could scarcely begin to review the thousands of individual rates on which the bureaus might act. And it was less likely than competition to force reductions in such rates.

SALVAGING THE RAILROADS, 1958–

The railroads prospered during World War II; they were in trouble again in the fifties. They were losing traffic; their earnings were low. Their efforts to improve their situation were handicapped by competition, by regulation, and by other forces beyond their control. The railroad problem came to be one of finding methods whereby the financial health of the carriers could be restored and their services preserved. To this end, steps were taken to afford the railroad companies somewhat greater freedom to take action that was calculated to increase their revenues and to reduce their costs.

The Railroads' Plight

The railroads enjoyed good earnings during World War II. Traffic was heavy and, with the war being fought on two fronts, it moved to the West as well as to the East. Expansion of motor carriage was limited by shortages of trucks, parts, and tires. Coastwise water haulage was curtailed as ships were sunk and, until more pipelines could be built, the railroads had to carry oil from the producing regions to the refineries. The great bulk of wartime freight was moved by rail.

Earnings were down again in the fifties; the railroads' return on their investment averaged 3.6 percent during the decade. It stood at 2.8 percent in 1958, the railroads ranking at the bottom of the list of major industries. With earnings low or nonexistent, the roads could not attract the capital required for the improvement of their plants. In the South and West, where business was good and hauls were long, the problem was not quite so serious. In the Northeast, however, where hauls were shorter and highway competition heavy, it was acute.

The railroads made money hauling freight, but they sustained heavy losses in hauling passengers. According to the method of accounting used by the ICC, which charges part of the annual cost of tracks, signals, property taxes, etc., to the passenger service, these losses amounted to $724 million in 1957. If no charges were made for the use of the railway plant, they would still have amounted to $370 million. In other words, the railroads would have been $370 million better off if they had quit carrying passengers. Most serious of all was the drain imposed by commutation services, requiring multitrack stations on costly downtown sites, hundreds of cars, and hundreds of employees, all of them being fully employed for only 20 hours a week and mostly standing idle for the other 148. For some roads, there was danger that the losses on passenger traffic would come to exceed the earnings on freight. And when this happened, the roads would go bankrupt.

The major cause of declining earnings was the continued loss of traffic to competing carriers. The railroads' share of freight traffic dropped from 75 percent in 1929 to 45 percent in 1959. Intercity movements of passengers were only one tenth by common carrier, nine tenths of them being effected by private automobile. Of the common-carrier business, the railroads' share dropped from 77 percent in 1929 to 29 percent in 1959.

The railroads were caught in a vise. They were not entirely free either to increase their earnings or to reduce their costs. They might obtain permission to raise the level of their rates, but competition would prevent them from doing so. They could not get more business by reducing particular rates because the ICC would limit their cuts. Some of their competitors were subject to similar regulation, but large numbers of carriers were exempt. The railroads could not escape the losses incurred in carrying passengers because they were forbidden to discontinue unprofitable services without obtaining the permission of the ICC or— in the case of intrastate services—that of the state utility commissions. They were compelled, under union work rules, to employ workmen they did not need—keeping firemen on diesel engines that had no fires to be stoked—and to pay a full day's pay for less than a full day's work. The cost of such featherbedding was said to run to more than $500 million per year, and this cost could not be cut without running the risk of a paralyzing strike. The railroads could not cut costs by merging their operations without first obtaining the approval of the ICC. They could not avoid the federal excise tax of 3 percent on their freight rates, the tax of 10 percent on their passenger fares, or the heavier burden of real estate taxes imposed on them by state and local governments.

The Rate-Making Rule of 1958

In exercising its power to fix minimum rates for particular shipments, the ICC forbade the railroads to undercut the rates charged by the trucks or the barge lines, even though lower rates would have more than covered the railroads' out-of-pocket costs. Its purpose was to limit the use of rate discrimination as a means of diverting traffic from the highways and waterways to the rails. But in serving this purpose, it denied the railroads their principal opportunity to increase their revenues. This limitation was modified by Congress when it passed the Transportation Act of 1958. The new law amended the 1933 rule of rate making by adding this provision: "Rates of a carrier shall not be held up to a particular level to protect the traffic of any other mode of transportation, giving due consideration to the objectives of national transportation policy. . . ."

The new rule was intended to help the railroads by enabling them to compete for a larger share of traffic. But the ICC and the courts have blunted its effect. The Commission has approved rate cuts on competitive shipments, but its orders have sanctioned few cuts that went below the railroads' average total costs, including a full allocation of overhead. In 1963 the Supreme Court set aside the Commission's rejection of a cut made by the New Haven Railroad, saying, "If a carrier is prohibited from establishing a reduced rate that is not detrimental to its own revenue requirements merely because the rate will divert traffic from others, then the carrier is thwarted from asserting its own inherent advantages of cost and service.[8] But the Court did not say how inherent advantages were to be measured, whether by average total costs or by out-of-pocket costs, including no charge for overhead. The next case to come before the Court involved the rates established by the Southern Railroad for carrying grain. Most of this traffic had been handled by trucks and by barges that were exempt from rate control. In an effort to compete for the business, the railroad designed a new hopper car, known as the Big John. Made of aluminum, it had twice the capacity and half the weight of the old box car and could be loaded and unloaded more easily and at lower cost. In 1961 the Southern proposed to cut its rates on movements of grain in trains of such cars by as much as 66 percent. Its proposal was fought by southern elevators and millers who saw grain moving more cheaply to the east, by the truckers and the barge lines, and, on behalf of the barge lines, by the TVA. The issue was disputed before the ICC and the courts for the next four years. In 1963 the Commission disapproved Southern's rates, holding them to be insufficiently compensatory. In 1965 a district court rejected this decision, finding the evidence on which the Commission based its action to be inadequate. The Supreme Court agreed, returning the case to the ICC for further consideration.[9] And finally, the Commission reversed itself, deciding that the rates were legal after all. They were thus allowed to take effect. This was a victory for the railroads. But the Court's next decision was a defeat. Ingot molds had been moved from Pittsburgh to Steelton, Kentucky by barge and truck for a charge of $5.11 per ton. In 1963 the Pennsylvania and the Louisville and Nashville Railroads cut their joint rate on this shipment from $11.86 to $5.11. The barge and truck lines complained, contending that the railroads' move violated national transportation policy by depriving them of their inherent advantage. The ICC found that the railroads' out-of-pocket costs on the shipment were $4.49; their fully-allocated costs $7.59. It rejected their argument that rates were legal if they covered out-of-pocket costs, holding that they must cover fully-allocated costs. The Commission was reversed by a district court that found its choice of fully-allocated costs to have inadequate support.

8 / ICC v. New York, New Haven & Hartford R.R. Co., 372 U.S. 744, 759.

9 / Arrow Transportation Co. v. Cincinnati, New Orleans, and Texas Pacific Ry Co., 379 U.S. 642 (1965).

But it was finally upheld, in 1968, by the Supreme Court, which ruled that the selection of a method of costing whereby to determine inherent advantage was within the authority of the ICC.[10] Given the policy of the Commission and the Court's reluctance to call it into question, it would appear that the railroads' freedom to compete for traffic by cutting rates is to be strictly limited.

Reduction in Costs

The railroads have also been aided through measures that have enabled them to reduce their costs. In the Act of 1958, Congress empowered the ICC to permit curtailment of intrastate services where state commissions had acted adversely or failed to act. Abandonment of a number of unprofitable services was thus approved. Interstate passenger service, also, has been sharply curtailed. From 1958 to 1968 the number of scheduled intercity passenger trains was cut by three fifths. On more than a third of the routes served in 1958 the service was completely eliminated. Two states were left with no passenger service by rail.

The 3 percent excise tax on freight rates was discontinued in 1958, the 10 percent tax on passenger fares in 1962. At the same time, a number of states and cities moved to reduce the burden of commutation services.

In 1963, following a four-year dispute between railroad managements and labor unions on the modification of work rules, Congress enacted a law requiring arbitration. After public hearings, the arbitration board gave the roads the right gradually to eliminate firemen on freight and yard diesel engines and to reduce the number of brakemen on train crews. The men displaced were to be offered severance pay, retraining, or employment in other jobs. The new rules went into effect in 1964.

The most ambitious step taken to save the railroads was the approval of mergers. The ICC, long opposed to railway combinations, reversed its policy, granting 33 and denying only five of 38 applications on which it acted from 1955 to 1968. Of these, the most important were the combinations of the Chesapeake and Ohio and the Baltimore and Ohio in 1962, of the Norfolk and Western and the Nickel Plate in 1964, and of the Pennsylvania and the New York Central in 1966. The last of these mergers, before the Commission and the courts for six years, was finally approved by the Supreme Court in 1968. A merger of the Great Northern, the Northern Pacific, and the Chicago, Burlington & Quincy, first proposed in 1955, was still before the Court in 1969. Other applications were pending. Rail combinations were said to open the way to large savings. Terminals could be consolidated and junctions eliminated. Duplicate repair and maintenance services could be dropped. Shipments could be forwarded over routes that had lower gradients, fewer curves, and shorter mileages. It should be possible to operate fewer and heavier trains with greater economy in the use of locomotives and with car loadings substantially improved. There should be savings, too, in labor costs and in sales and administration. Such

10 / *American Commercial Lines* v. *Louisville & Nashville Ry Co.*, 392 U.S. 571.

economies are doubtless possible, but they are not yet in evidence. In 1970, the Penn Central went into bankruptcy.

The railroads' share of intercity traffic continued to decline in the sixties, their share of ton miles dropping from 45.5 percent in 1959 to 41.5 percent in 1967; their share of common carrier passenger miles from 28.8 percent to 11.7 percent. They made money hauling freight but continued to lose money hauling passengers. In 1929, there were about 20,000 passenger trains in the United States; in 1970, there were only 420 and the railroads had petitioned the ICC for permission to discontinue more than 100 of these. In that year, Congress enacted legislation to create a quasi-public corporation, supported by federal grants, loans, and loan guarantees, to contract with the railroads to take over their passenger business and to operate such of their services as were deemed essential. Roads not choosing to participate would be required to maintain existing services for another five years.

Railway Modernization

A number of measures would improve the railroads' condition by modernizing their operations. Terminals and freight yards can be automated. Specialized freight cars, such as the Big John and the automobile rack car, can be designed for particular shipments. Unit trains can be introduced for large shippers. Trains can be shuttled, on tight schedules, between single points of origin and destination. Such innovations are already under way. Among them, the most promising is piggybacking. This is a coordinated truck-rail operation in which tractor-trailers are used for pick-up and delivery and the trailers are loaded onto rail flatcars for the line haul. It combines the greater flexibility of trucking at terminals with the lower cost of rail hauls over long distances. When this service was introduced, the truckers complained, and it was not until 1954 that the ICC permitted the railroads to take this business. Piggybacking still accounts for a very small share of car loadings. But it grew, during the sixties, at a rate of 18 percent per year. If this expansion continues, much of the long-haul traffic that has been lost to the highways may be recovered by the rails.

It should be possible, too, to lure passengers back. Rail terminals are more accessible than airports. Rail schedules are more dependable than those of airlines. Railway coaches can be more comfortable and less confining than are buses and planes. Travel by rail is faster than by bus. Door to door, on shorter distances, it can be nearly as fast as by plane. Per passenger mile, its costs are less than those of any other medium. In other countries—in Japan, for instance, in Western Europe, and in Canada—passenger service is far superior to that in the United States. Trains are run on jolt-free roadbeds at speeds above 100 miles per hour, and services offered travellers compare with those provided by the airlines. In this country, by contrast, it would appear that the railroads have deliberately sought to scuttle their passenger services. Their stations and their coaches are antiquated, uncomfortable, and dirty. Their sleeping car and diner services have been dropped. Their fares have been raised. By making their service less attractive and more expensive, they have driven their customers away. And then they have used their loss of traffic to justify applications for abandonment.[11] One attempt at modernization is under way. High-speed service with improved equipment has been introduced by the Penn Central in the Northeast corridor between Boston and Washington, with federal support being provided under a law enacted in 1965. But the railroad's management of this project has been halfhearted and its potentialities are far from being realized. If the rails are to play their proper role in the intercity movement of passengers, a billion or two must be spent in rebuilding their plant from the roadbed up. This is by no means impossible. A nation that can put men on the moon should be able to solve the lesser problems and to meet the lesser costs involved in moving them from place to place on the surface of the earth.

THE PERSISTENCE OF REGULATION

The railroads are still under tight control. They cannot sell a bond or a share of stock without permission, extend or abandon a line, curtail a service, raise their rates, or, in particular cases, reduce a rate. The ICC is authorized to inquire into the honesty, efficiency, and economy with which they are managed, a function which—if really fulfilled—would involve a virtual duplication of managements. This is not done. But, as things are, decisions that in other industries are left exclusively to management must here be shared with the Commission. On crucial issues of business policy—the desirability of expanding or contracting operations, of raising or lowering rates—the Commission may reject the judgments of management and substitute its own. Or it may delay action while deciding what position it shall take. In either case, the consequences may be serious.

Under the 1933 rule of rate making, the ICC must consider the effect of rates on the movement of traffic. In doing so, it has made its own guesses as to elasticity of demand. In this connection, it has given weight to the competitive position of the railroads, their public relations, and the state of the nation's economy. During depression, it has undertaken to estimate how changes in rates would affect the confidence of business. During prosperity, it has sought to judge how they would influence inflationary trends. All these are matters respecting which judgments may differ. If the Commission rejects the views of management, the consequences may be good or bad: where its judgment is superior, the railroads will gain; where its judgment is inferior, they will lose. But when losses occur, nobody can be held responsible: the stockholders of the railroads may complain, but their directors have a perfect alibi, and the members of the ICC are out of reach.

In most cases, the Commission has finally accepted the views of management. But many months have elapsed before it has done so. And in the meantime, costs have risen while revenues have lagged. Losses have been incurred, and

11 / See Peter Lyon, *To Hell in a Daycoach* (Philadelphia: J. B. Lippincott Co., 1968).

railway credit has been impaired. The funds required for improvement have not been obtained. But here, again, the railway managements cannot be held accountable; neither can the members of the ICC. It may therefore be concluded that this—to paraphrase the familiar saying—is an undesirable way to run a railroad.

Chapter 17

REGULATION OF
TRANSPORT COMPETITION

Government does two things with respect to transport: it promotes and it regulates. It promotes the development of various modes of transport by extending public aid. It regulates all modes of transport, controlling entry, combination, services, and rates. Transport policy, as distinct from railroad policy, must comprehend all types of carriers. And it must include promotion as well as regulation. In regulation, the nation's policy, as enunciated by the Congress, is one of impartiality. In promotion, however, each type of carrier is considered separately; no effort is made to adopt a program that will be comprehensive in itself or consistent with impartial regulation.

Four modes of commercial transport compete with the railroads: oil pipelines, motor carriers, water carriers, and air carriers. The pipelines differ from the other carriers in important respects. Their costs are so much lower than those of the railroads that the latter cannot hope to compete in the movement of oil. There is no complaint, however, that pipeline competition is unfair. The pipelines, unlike the railroads' other competitors, have never been subsidized. The real problem raised by the pipelines is how they affect competition in the oil industry, not in the transport industries. For this reason, regulation of the pipelines by the ICC will not be considered here. It is the purpose of this chapter, first, to outline the methods employed in promoting and regulating motor carriers, water carriers, and air carriers and, second, to consider the problems involved in developing a comprehensive and consistent policy for transport as a whole.

MOTOR CARRIERS

The most serious competitors of the railroads are the motor carriers. Their competition, according to the railroads, is unfair. The railroads must provide their own ways, buying the land, building the roadbed, tunnels, and bridges, laying the track, meeting the costs of maintenance, paying interest on their investment, and contributing through property taxes to the support of every county and city they pass through. The motor carriers, on the other hand, operate on ways acquired, constructed, and maintained at public expense, having no investment to make and no property taxes to pay. As users of the highways, to be sure, they are subject to other taxes that are levied to meet the costs of construction and maintenance. But the railroads contend that the motor carriers do not pay their share of these costs. And the motor carriers argue, just as vigorously, that they do.

Meeting Highway Costs

It may be doubted that intercity transport should be required to meet all highway costs. Roads have other uses: they give access to land, facilitate community services, and promote performance of many of the functions of government. They raise property values and thus increase taxpaying ability. Local roads, particularly, are properly to be financed from general revenues. But intercity highways are used primarily for long-distance transport, and their users might well be expected to defray their costs. Before World War I, all highway costs were met, in the main, by taxes on property. But since that time, they have been met increasingly by levies on users: motor license fees, gasoline taxes, and the like. Most of the money spent by states on highways comes from these sources, the rest being obtained mostly in the form of grants from the federal government. When allowance is made for the other purposes served by highways, it is generally agreed that operators of motor vehicles, as a whole, now bear a fair share of their costs. But this burden must be divided again between private vehicles and commercial carriers. Do trucks pay their proper share of user costs?

In the earlier years, commercial traffic was subsidized by other users of the roads. Today, lighter trucks pay their way. But diesels and tractor-trailer combinations do not. The heavier vehicles pay higher taxes, but they also necessitate larger expenditures. They require longer radius curves, wider traffic lanes, and special passing lanes on steeper grades. They carry heavier axle loads and chalk up more ton-miles. So the highways must be made wider and stronger, repaired more often, and replaced sooner on their account. The trucks, however, do not fall far short of meeting their full share of highway costs. According to Merton J. Peck and John R. Meyer, they would have paid their way in the late fifties if user taxes had been increased by one cent per mile. And this would have raised trucking costs by no more than 3 percent.[1]

The Motor Carrier Industry

The railroads (aside from those operated as industrial facilities) are all common carriers. With motor vehicles, this is not the case. Such vehicles must be divided, first, into private carriers and carriers for hire. Of all the trucks on the road, more than nine tenths are in the first category and less than a tenth in the second. The latter group must be divided, again, into contract carriers and common carriers. The contract carrier hauls goods in quantity, under special contract, for a single large shipper or, at most, for a very few. It is only the

1 / John R. Meyer, *The Economics of Competition in the Transportation Industries* (Cambridge, Mass.: Harvard University Press, 1960), p. 85.

common carrier who holds himself out to serve the public generally. Contract carriers account for a minor part and common carriers for a major part of intercity tonnage hauled for hire.

The trucking industry is characterized by large numbers of small concerns. There are more than 15,000 companies. Some of them are big, operating huge fleets, a score of them taking in more than $20 million a year. But most of the companies are small, many of them operating less than a dozen trucks, two thirds of them taking in less than $200,000. In the absence of public intervention, the industry would be highly competitive. Unlike the railroads, where a few oligopolists provide service on any route, the number of motor carriers can be expanded indefinitely. Equipment can be shifted readily from route to route. In the absence of regulation, new entry would be easy; the cost of capital required is low. With railroads, investment in plant is three times as great as annual revenue. In trucking, it is but a ninth as great. Fixed costs, accordingly, are low. Of annual expenses, less than a tenth are constant; more than nine tenths vary with the amount of business done. Economies of scale are small. There is little temptation to increase volume by discriminating or by cutting rates. There is little likelihood of destructive competition leading to monopoly.

Regulation by the States

For many years the states have regulated motor carriers in order to control the use of their roads and to insure safety. To this end they have established standards governing the width, length, height, and weight of vehicles, their lights, brakes, and other equipment, the speed at which they may be driven, the age of their drivers, and the number of hours that a driver may work. Beginning in the twenties, the states also undertook to regulate the business of common carriers, requiring certificates of convenience and necessity for entry and applying controls, in varying degrees, to services, rates, accounts, and securities. They soon found, however, that the carriers could evade their regulations by operating under contracts. They sought, therefore, to bring contract carriers under control. At first, the courts resisted their attempts. But the state of Texas hit upon the device of requiring permits rather than certificates of public convenience and necessity for contract operations. And the Supreme Court, in a case decided in 1932,[2] allowed its law to stand. All but three of the states now require certificates of common carriers and permits of contract carriers and regulate their services and rates.

In the case of highways, unlike that of railways, intrastate business is still within the exclusive jurisdiction of the states. And interstate carriers must obey the laws controlling traffic on state highways and pay the taxes levied for their use. But in 1925, when Michigan attempted to exclude an interstate carrier by refusing it the right to operate, the Supreme Court held that regulation of interstate commerce was beyond the power of the state.[3] There was pressure, there-

2 / *Stephenson* v. *Binford*, 287 U.S. 251 (1932).

3 / *Michigan Public Utilities Commission* v. *Duke*, 266 U.S. 570.

after, for federal legislation, from the railroads, the bus lines, some truckers, and the state commissions. But it was 10 years before a federal law was passed.

Motor Carrier Act of 1935

The Motor Carrier Act of 1935 applies unequally to different carriers. All interstate carriers are subject to such regulations governing safety of operation as the Interstate Commerce Commission may prescribe. But private carriers are under no further control. And many carriers for hire are specifically exempt. Among them are vehicles used in local transit operations, those used incidentally by railways, shipping companies, and airlines, and those owned and operated by farmers and agricultural cooperatives. More important is the exemption, under political pressure, of carriers transporting agricultural commodities, horticultural products, livestock, and fish, but not products that are made from them.

The remaining provisions of the law apply to those contract and common carriers that are not exempt. Both must carry liability insurance. And for both, the ICC is given power to prescribe methods of accounting, require reports, control the issuance of securities where capitalization exceeds $1 million, and approve or disapprove combinations and acquisitions of control. But beyond this, the two are treated differently, the law being looser for contract carriers and tighter for common carriers.

Entry is regulated. A grandfather clause protects the rights of firms in operation before the law was passed. Contract carriers must obtain permits. Common carriers must obtain certificates, for which more stringent conditions are laid down. A company cannot be given the right to carry on both types of operation unless good cause is shown. Dual operation might be abused, affording the carrier an opportunity to discriminate by hauling goods for favored shippers under contract at lower rates. The ability to offer both types of service, moreover, would give the operator an advantage over his competitors in soliciting business.

Rates are controlled. Contract carriers must file their minimum charges and may not charge less. The Commission may fix a legal minimum, but not a maximum. Common carriers, on the other hand, are subject to much the same pattern of control as are the railroads. Their rates must be reasonable and not unduly discriminatory. They must be published and observed, and notice must be given before a change. The Commission can suspend proposed changes and fix minima, maxima, and specific rates.

The control of common carriers by motor differs in certain respects, however, from the control of carriers by rail. The ICC is specifically denied the power to fix the rates charged on intrastate hauls. It cannot require through routes or joint rates. It cannot prevent the discontinuance of service. And the law contains no long-and-short-haul clause. In one respect, a heavier obligation is imposed: truckers must obtain insurance on the goods they carry; the responsibility of railroads for loss or damage is assumed.

Motor Carriers under the ICC

In 1963 there were some 15,000 trucking companies with 900,000 vehicles subject to economic control by the ICC. At the same time there were nearly 125,000 operators with close to a million trucks placed beyond control by the exemptions granted to private carriers and to those transporting agricultural commodities. These exemptions have afforded ample opportunity for evasion of the law. Truckers have qualified as private carriers by pretending to buy their loads at point of origin and to sell them at destination. They have claimed the agricultural exemption not only when hauling crops from farm to market but also when hauling processed foods from factory to distributor. As a result, carriers controlled by the ICC account for only a third of highway freight and those beyond control for two thirds.

To administer the law, the Commission set up a Bureau of Motor Carriers, with a sizable staff in Washington and in the field. For many months, the Bureau was engaged in defining its jurisdiction and determining which companies were subject to which controls. It had to pass on thousands of applications for permits and certificates, determining in each case whether the applicant fell within the provisions of the grandfather clause. In later years the Commission has been concerned, in the main, with controlling new entry, combinations, and rates.

Control of Supply

In controlling entry, the Commission's policy is restrictive. Applicants for new operating authority, for alternate routes, and for extensions of existing routes are required to prove that the proposed service is really needed, that the services already available are inadequate, and that adequate service cannot be provided by carriers already in the field. They are asked to justify their applications in detail: to defend the financing they propose, the equipment they intend to use, and the schedule they plan to follow. For small concerns, the obstacles created by this procedure are almost insurmountable. Decisions, moreover, may be delayed for months or years. Certificates may then be refused on the ground that adequate service can be rendered by established truckers, or even that rail service is available. Where operating rights are granted, they may be strictly limited. Operators may be confined to hauling particular goods between particular points. They may be required to follow circuitous routes, forbidden to serve intermediate points, and denied the right to carry cargo on the return haul. They are thus prevented from reducing costs by filling empty space. By cutting operating rights into bits and pieces, the ICC condemns the carriers to inefficiency. In considering whether to issue a certificate of public convenience and necessity, the Commission directs its attention only to necessity, ignoring convenience. Its purpose is not to serve the interests of shippers but to protect the position of established trucking companies.[4]

With regard to mergers, the Commission's policy is described by Walter Adams as "vague and vascillating." According to Professor Adams,

> What is embraced in one opinion as a natural and inevitable result of the economic facts of life is rejected in a second as not to be in the public interest. Where the fears of competitors are airily waved aside in one instance, the probable plight of competitors is of great importance in another. The Commission approves some acquisitions (usually by large carriers) because nothing has been adduced to show that they are contrary to the public interest. It rejects other acquisitions (usually by small carriers) because they are not shown to be consistent with the public interest.[5]

Though the Commission's rationalization of its decisions may be faulty, the effect of these decisions is clear. The number of certified motor carriers has steadily declined, and the business has come increasingly to be concentrated in the hands of larger firms.

Control of Rates

With regard to rates, too, the effect of Commission action has been to make the industry less competitive. In passing on requests for changes in the general level of rates, the Commission concerns itself, as in the case of the railroads, not with individual companies, but with the carriers as a whole. But here, its standard is a different one. It does not judge the rate level by measuring the return upon the carriers' investment, since investment in the industry is so small in relation to revenue that rates calculated to yield a fixed return might not suffice to cover costs. Instead, it seeks to insure an operating ratio that will afford a safe margin of revenues over costs, generally holding a ratio of 95 (costs being 95 percent of revenue) to be reasonable. In acting on particular rates, the Commission employs the same principles, in the main, that it does with the railroads. But here it is more concerned with fixing minima than maxima. To prevent destructive competition within the trucking industry, it has put a floor under rates. In doing so, it has placed less emphasis on marginal costs and more on covering fully allocated costs. But it has acted tardily, permitting rates to drop a long way before it has called a halt. Changes in motor carrier rates, as with the railroads, are agreed upon in rate bureaus before being proposed to the ICC. Here, the burden of proof is on the carrier who proposes to cut a rate. And

4 / See *Competition, Regulation, and the Public Interest in the Motor Carrier Industry*, Report of the Select Committee on Small Business, U.S. Senate (84th Cong., 2d Sess., Senate Report No. 1693, 1956).

5 / Walter Adams, "The Role of Competition in the Regulated Industries," *American Economic Review*, Vol. XLVIII, No. 2 (1958), pp. 527-43 at p. 531.

if a rate is cut without the approval of the bureau, the Commission may suspend it. The structure of rates conforms, not to costs, but to that established, on a value-of-service basis, by the railroads. In considering individual rates, therefore, the Commission has been influenced less by motor carrier costs than by competing railway rates. As a result, traffic is allocated uneconomically, much intercity freight moving by truck that could be carried more cheaply by rail, and much freight being hauled by private truck that could be handled more cheaply by common carrier. The Commission has generally followed the rule of maintaining parity of rates between competing media. With rates held equal, competition is confined to service, and this gives an advantage to the trucks. But the Commission's purpose in fixing rates, as in controlling entry, has been to protect established interests in both the trucking and the railroad industries.[6]

WATER CARRIERS

Transport by water falls into a number of different categories, each of them involving a different type of cargo and carrier. Transoceanic shipping does not compete in the domestic market and will not be considered here. Included in domestic transport are coastwise oceanic shipping, intercoastal shipping through the Panama Canal, and shipping on the Great Lakes, the Mississippi River system, and other inland waterways. Coastwise shipping carries an eighth as much tonnage as the railways, four fifths of this being in tankers carrying oil. Intercoastal shipping is much smaller in volume; its relative importance has declined. Carriers on the Great Lakes handle less than a fifth as much as the railroads, most of it being in iron ore, coal, and grain. Carriers on other inland waterways handle less than a tenth as much tonnage as moves by rail.

Public Aid to Waterways

For carriers on the oceans and on the Great Lakes, ways are provided by nature. For those on other inland waters, they are provided by government. For both, harbors are improved and port facilities maintained at public expense. Appropriations for waterways were made, at an early date, by state and local governments. Appropriations have been voted by Congress every year or so for the past century. Improvements have not been made in accordance with any comprehensive plan, the contents of the Congressional pork barrel being determined, from time to time, by trading votes. Investment in these improvements is far in excess of anything that could be justified by economic need. Save for the Panama Canal and the St. Lawrence Seaway, waterways are free of tolls. User charges, comparable to those imposed on motor carriers, are unknown. The rates charged by water carriers, therefore, need cover only the costs of their equipment and its operation. The costs involved in providing their ways, if any,

6 / See Ernest W. Williams, Jr., *The Regulation of Rail-Motor Rate Competition* (New York: Harper & Bros., 1958).

are met by the taxpayer. But even if they were met by the shipping companies, the costs of water transport would be below those incurred in hauling goods by rail.

The Shipping Industry

The shipping business, like the trucking business, is divided among private, contract, and common carriers. The private carriers transport their own goods, such as petroleum and iron ore, in vessels designed for the purpose. The contract carriers also transport bulk cargoes in specialized craft, often serving under charter or operating as tramps. The common carriers handle specialized or general cargoes, operating on schedule over fixed routes. All three types of carriers use the same waterways and compete for the same business. As in the case of motor carriers, entry is easy, the cost of capital being low. Fixed charges, too, are low. There is little tendency toward ruinous competition, ending in combination and monopoly. In the absence of regulation, the industry would continue to be competitive.

Regulation of Water Carriers

Under the Shipping Act of 1916, the United States Shipping Board and its successor, the Maritime Commission, were given authority over common carriers on the Great Lakes and in the coastwise trade and both common and contract carriers in the intercoastal trade. But until 1940 contract carriers, aside from the intercoastal trade, and all carriers on rivers and canals were uncontrolled.

Control was imposed by the Transportation Act of 1940. Jurisdiction over transoceanic shipping alone was assigned to the Maritime Commission (later to the Maritime Board). Jurisdiction over water carriers in interstate commerce was given to the ICC. But the great bulk of such traffic was exempted from the requirements of the law. The carriers granted exemption include small craft, ferries, and ships operated incidentally by railroads and trucking companies, all private carriers, contract carriers whose cargoes and vessels are so specialized that they do not compete with common carriers, and common carriers whose cargoes consist of three or fewer commodities in bulk. Altogether, nine tenths of the tonnage is exempt.

Where the law applies, its provisions are similar to those established for motor carriers. Entry is controlled, contract carriers being required to obtain permits and common carriers to obtain certificates. Unless specially approved by the ICC, no company may have both. The rights of those existing when the law was passed are protected by a grandfather clause. Methods of accounting may be prescribed, and reports required. Pools and combinations may be approved or disapproved. Jurisdiction over rates charged in intrastate traffic is left to the states. Interstate rates are controlled, the methods differing for contract and common carriers. Both must publish their rates and observe them, giving prior notice of a change. The Commission can suspend proposed rates pending an investigation. For contract carriers, it can fix minimum rates, but not maxima. For common carriers, the familiar pattern applies. Rates must be just and reasonable, without unjust discrimination or undue preference or prejudice. The Commission can fix maxima as well as minima. Here, as with railroads but not with motor carriers, the long-and-short-haul clause is made effective, and through routes with joint rates may be required. As with motor carriers, the Commission cannot prevent abandonment. And here, it is given no power over the issuance of securities.

In its administration of the Act of 1940 the Commission has had to define the groups that are exempt, distinguish between contract and common carriers, and determine the applicability of the grandfather clause. In the few cases where new firms have applied for entry, it has granted permits and certificates over the objection of existing interests, but refused them where it appeared that traffic was not sufficient to support the applicants and those already in the field. The Commission has had little occasion to prescribe rates. The water carriers set their rates at a fixed differential—as much as 20 percent—below those charged on competing hauls by rail. This saving keeps shippers from asking that rates be lowered; rail competition prevents the carriers from asking that they be raised. The Commission, on the other hand, has sometimes forbidden cuts in rail rates in order to keep competing water carriers in business.

CIVIL AVIATION

Of all the competitors of the railroads, the airlines have shown the most rapid growth. In 1918 the government began to operate airmail routes. In 1926 it began letting airmail contracts to private lines. The development of commercial aviation dates from this time. The growth of the industry was further stimulated by the great volume of traffic created by World War II. From 1940 to 1950 the quantity of mail carried increased five times, passenger miles six times, and express and freight tonnage 50 times. By 1968, commercial airlines were serving 500 cities with 2,500 planes. In that year, they did six times as much passenger business as the railroads, accounting for 87 billion passenger miles to the rail-roads' 15 billion.

Public Aid to Aviation

Airways, like highways and waterways, are provided by government. An airway is a route, ten miles or more in width, equipped with aids to navigation: beacon lights, radio ranges, communications facilities, weather reports, and emergency landing fields. The airway system is maintained and operated by the federal government. It is used not only by common carriers but also by military aircraft and private planes. The airlines contribute to its support by paying a federal tax on gasoline. This payment has been found to fall short of their share of airway costs, but only by $6 million a year.[7] To this extent, their use of the airways has been subsidized.

Airports, too, are publicly financed. Half of their construction cost is provided by local governments, half by the federal government. The airlines make no contribution toward interest or amortization. Operating costs at the largest airports are nearly met by revenues from landing fees, rentals, and the sale of fuel. But elsewhere, these revenues fall far short of costs; deficits are met by local governments. In 1970, Congress enacted and President Nixon signed a bill authorizing the appropriation of $5 billion in federal funds to be used, over the next five years, to automate air traffic control and to match local expenditures for the construction and modernization of airports.

The airlines are not only subsidized indirectly through government maintenance of the airways and government contributions to the capital and operating costs of airports; they are subsidized directly through payments designed to cover the amount by which a line's revenues fail to cover its costs and yield a fair return on its investment. From 1938 to 1957, such subsidies were paid to all the airlines in the United States. Since then, they have been confined to local-service, territorial, and helicopter operations. In 1965, this subsidy stood at $84 million, in 1968 at $59 million.

The Aviation Industry

On the airways, as on the highways and waterways, there are private, contract, and common carriers. The common carriers are of three types: scheduled carriers and supplemental carriers, handling both passengers and cargo, and carriers handling cargo alone. The scheduled carriers operate on established schedules over regular routes between fixed termini. They include two groups: the trunk lines, eleven of them in 1969, handling 90 percent of the passenger business, the four largest (American, Eastern, Trans-World, and United) having two thirds of this; and the feeder lines, nine in number, rendering local services. The supplemental lines, known formerly as the nonskeds, are not confined to fixed routes and are not supposed to operate with any regularity. There were twelve such lines in 1969, accounting for 7 percent of passenger mileage. There were five all-cargo lines. Airline revenues are obtained primarily by carrying passengers. In 1968 the trunk lines got nine tenths of their revenues from this source, the other tenth from carrying freight, express, and mail.

In their economic characteristics the air carriers lie somewhere between the railroads and the trucking companies. They need make no investment in airways or airports. But planes are costly and depreciate rapidly. The annual cost of capital, therefore, is lower than for railways and higher than for motor carriers. Investment, however, is flexible: planes can be shifted from route to route or transferred to other lines by lease or sale. Operating costs vary with volume, but not directly: flying expenses, half of the total, decline with size of plane and

7 / Meyer, *op. cit.,* p. 144.

length of flight; ground expenses, the other half, are more nearly constant. Given the level of fixed costs, there may be some tendency toward destructive competition and the emergence of monopoly. But the industry is not one in which economies of scale are such as to demand great size. Entry, unless restricted by law, is quite possible. Without regulation, it is likely that the industry would be effectively competitive.

The Pattern of Regulation

Aviation, when intrastate, is subject to regulation by the states. But commercial flights, in general, cross state lines, bringing the industry as a whole within the jurisdiction of the federal government. Federal safety regulation began in 1926, and certain forms of economic regulation, by the Post Office and the ICC, in 1934. But unified and comprehensive regulation dates from the Civil Aeronautics Act of 1938. Under this Act, aviation was made subject to control by two federal agencies. A Civil Aeronautics Administration, in the Department of Commerce, was given two functions. It was to promote aviation, establishing and maintaining the airway system, and planning and administering the airport program. It was to enforce safety rules, testing aircraft, examining airmen, controlling air traffic, and investigating accidents. A Civil Aeronautics Board, a semi-independent agency composed of five members appointed by the President and also located in the Department of Commerce, was charged primarily with responsibility for economic regulation. It was empowered to control entry, to establish routes, to regulate rates, and to determine airmail payments and subsidies. The Board was also authorized to prescribe safety rules and to investigate accidents.

This setup was changed in 1958 when Congress created an independent Federal Aviation Agency, outside the Department of Commerce, and transferred to it all of the functions previously assigned to the CAA, together with the responsibility for prescribing safety rules, previously assigned to the CAB. The Board was left, however, with its economic powers. Its responsibility for the investigation of accidents was transferred, in 1967, to a National Transportation Safety Board in the Department of Transportation.

With respect to safety, all flying is brought within the scope of the law. With respect to economic matters, however, control is limited to common carriers. The CAB, moreover, is empowered to grant exemptions from control. The law follows the usual pattern of regulation, with certain differences. Entry requires a certificate of public convenience and necessity, the rights of carriers in business when the Act was passed being preserved by a grandfather clause. Abandonment also requires permission; and pooling, combination, and intercorporate relationships are subjected to control. Rates must be just and reasonable, without undue preference or prejudice. They must be published and observed and notice given before a change. Changes can be suspended, and the CAB can fix maximum rates or minima or both. The long-and-short-haul clause does not apply. As in the case of water carriers, no power is given to control the issuance of securities.

Air Safety

Responsibility for safety is now concentrated in the Federal Aviation Administration, successor to the Federal Aviation Agency. To carry on its work, the FAA has a budget 40 times as large as that of the ICC and a staff numbering 45,000 employees. The CAB, by comparison, is small in size.

The FAA makes and enforces safety rules. It establishes its control by requiring that licenses, known as certificates, be obtained for planes and their equipment, and for mechanics, pilots, and members of air crews. It tests and rates aircraft. Where the safety of a particular make of plane is questioned, it can suspend its certificate, keeping all planes of this make on the ground. The agency inspects maintenance operations, examines and rates mechanics. It tests pilots and members of their crews, maintains surveillance over their performance. It can reprimand them, suspend them, or require their dismissal by revoking their certificates.

The FAA directs traffic in the air. For this purpose, it maintains a staff of 15,000 traffic controllers at more than 300 airports and at a score of control centers in between. It governs flying by two sets of regulations: visual flight rules and instrument flight rules. Under VFR, the pilot is responsible for preventing collisions by seeing other planes and avoiding them. Flying under these rules is forbidden at major airports and in weather when visibility is poor. The IFR apply to every flight originating or terminating at an FAA-controlled port or flying at an altitude of more than 18,000 feet. A pilot operating under IFR submits his flight plan to an FAA control center, giving his proposed route and altitude. Before it clears the flight, the center makes sure that no other plane is flying this route at this altitude at this time. The pilot must also get a take-off clearance from the FAA traffic tower. After taking off, he reports his course, speed, and altitude every thousand feet as he climbs. A controller guides him by radio until he clears the vicinity of the airport when he is turned over to the route control centers along the path of his flight. Orders given him by radio then determine his direction, altitude, and speed. He is separated by three miles horizontally and 1,000 feet vertically from other planes. He follows an FAA radio range beam which confines him to a narrow path or, under a system called area navigation, now coming into use, he may shift his signal so as to take a broader path. He receives FAA weather information and keeps reporting his position along the way. On arriving at his destination, he again gets clearance from an FAA controller for his approach and landing.

The record of safety in flying has steadily improved, the rate of fatalities during the sixties being less than one in every 100 million passenger miles, making travel by air liners safer than by automobiles. But there are still serious accidents. There are one or more collisions each year and large numbers of near misses. And danger is growing. There is increasing congestion at major airports, with 14,000 takeoffs and landings at Kennedy airport in New York each day.

Planes are getting larger and faster. When they are on a collision course, time is too short to avert a crash.

Greater safety can be assured in several ways. The number of common carrier flights at the busiest airports can be limited. Use of these ports by personal aircraft can be restricted. More ports and more runways can be built. Instruments sending fuller information from planes to controllers can be generally required. Landing approach spacing can be computerized, so that planes of different speeds can come in safely at 30-second intervals. Ultimately, all flight plans can be fed into computers and instantly coordinated, increasing the speed and the accuracy of traffic control. But these measures will be costly and they will take time.

Development and promotion of new safety systems is a function of the FAA, as are search and rescue operations where accidents have occurred. Investigation of the causes of accidents is assigned to the National Transportation Safety Board. This arrangement is based upon the theory that the FAA, in its promulgation and administration of air safety rules, might itself be guilty of negligence and might therefore seek to shift the blame. The Board, accordingly, is authorized to make an independent investigation, in case of serious accident, and to determine responsibility.

Control of Entry

Until 1938 there was no legal barrier to entry to civil aviation. Airmail contracts were let by competitive bidding. But anyone who wished to operate without a contract was free to do so. Under the Civil Aeronautics Act, entry is controlled by the CAB. Certification of the lines in existence in 1938 was required by a grandfather clause in the law. But action on applications covering new operations is within the discretion of the Board. Such applications have included proposals for new trunk lines, new feeder lines, and all-cargo carriers.

In the years since it was founded, the Board has received more than 150 applications for the creation of new trunk lines, but has not approved a single one. The business remains in the hands of the grandfather companies. Through bankruptcies and mergers, their number has been reduced from 16 to 11.

The Board has been generous, on the other hand, in granting certificates to small carriers providing local and feeder services. Here, its policy has been costly. With such services, traffic has been sparse, revenues have been inadequate to cover costs, and subsidies accordingly have been high. But the local lines provide the only service obtainable in some 300 cities. Their traffic is increasing, and they are coming to depend on subsidies for a declining share of their revenues.

The most violent controversy with regard to the Board's policies governing entry raged around the nonskeds. A blanket exemption, granted to these carriers in 1938, was intended to apply to operations that were irregular in character and limited in extent. After World War II, however, the number of nonskeds rose to 150, and they provided service with fair regularity on an increasing scale.

Many of these carriers were operated by former Army pilots, flying secondhand planes. They were attacked as affording inferior safety and skimming the cream off the market to the detriment of the scheduled lines. They were defended as exemplifying the virtues of small competitive enterprise. It was clear, however, that exemption of their operations was inconsistent with enforcement of regulation for the industry as a whole. In successive steps, beginning in 1947, the Board tightened its control. In 1955, it created the category of "supplemental air carrier" and, under this designation, made temporary grants of limited rights, permitting the nonskeds to make charter flights without limit, but no more than ten flights per month between any two points. In 1962, Congress revoked these temporary rights and authorized the CAB to grant permanent certificates. Under this authority, the Board certified 15 lines, (12 of them still in operation in 1969) largely for the purpose of providing charter flights.

The Board has certified five all-cargo carriers. These concerns have difficulty in meeting the competition of the passenger lines which transport cargo in the bellies of their planes. They account for a sixth of air cargo ton miles, the supplemental carriers for around a fourth, and the passenger lines for three fifths.

Control of Routes

The CAB controls entry not only into the airline business but also into the provision of service on particular routes. The Board has not undertaken to design an ideal network of routes. Instead, it has confined itself to acting on applications from the airlines for permission to fly between particular points. It has promulgated no standards to govern the allocation of routes. It has not said how much traffic there must be before a second carrier will be admitted, or what it considers to be the optimum number of carriers on a route. In general, its policy has been to have two or more lines compete in rendering service between each pair of cities on trunk routes. Where it judges service to be inadequate, it admits another line. Where it fears that competition would seriously impair the earnings of existing carriers, it refuses to do so. In periods when earnings are large, it grants route requests. When earnings are small, it denies them. The Board has granted monopoly rights on local service routes. It has sought to employ its control over routes as a means of insuring the strength of the several lines. To this end, it has permitted the weaker lines to lengthen their routes and to participate in service between points where traffic is heavy.

The Board devotes a major part of its time and energy to consideration of route applications. But it is unlikely that the numbers of carriers it admits to particular routes differs materially from the numbers there would have been in the absence of regulation. The Board's control over routes has operated, in the main, to delay adjustment to shifting demand. And it has done so at a considerable cost in manpower and in money.[8]

8 / Richard E. Caves, *Air Transport and Its Regulators* (Cambridge, Mass.: Harvard University Press, 1962), chap. ix.

Control of Service

The CAB has both discouraged and encouraged competition in service. When coach service was introduced, it feared that lower fares would impair the carriers' financial strength. It therefore sought to limit the quality of the service, requiring high-density seating and confining flights to night hours. The Board, in controlling routes, has permitted fewer types and classes of service than might otherwise have been available: shuttle services, for instance, and cheaper flights in older and slower planes. Its policies, on the other hand, have speeded the introduction of new equipment. The Board has allowed rapid write-offs for the depreciation of new planes, permitted their owners to charge higher fares, and forbidden them to cut their fares on older planes. It has also used its control over routes as leverage in promoting modernization. As a result, the industry's rate of innovation may well have been more rapid than it would have been in the absence of regulation. But the competition thus fostered has been competition in comfort, convenience, and speed, not in economy.[9]

Control of Subsidies

From 1938 to 1953 the subsidies given to the airlines were paid by the Post Office in the form of excessive rates for carrying the mail. The rates were fixed by the CAB; the resulting subsidy was hidden in the postal deficit. In 1951, the CAB began reporting the airmail pay and the airline subsidy separately. In 1953, President Eisenhower transferred responsibility for paying the subsidy from the Post Office to the CAB.

For many years, the Board devoted more attention to determining the amounts to be paid for carrying the mail or distributed as subsidies than to fixing fares. It established two methods of payment for airmail: a service rate and a need rate. The service rate is paid to lines that are self-supporting. It is based on estimates of cost per pound-mile, involving an allocation of joint costs between mail and other services. This rate may or may not be held to contain an element of subsidy, depending on one's judgment regarding the method of allocation that is used.

The need rate goes to carriers that are frankly subsidized. This rate takes several forms. An "open rate" is computed separately for each line. This is done by adding together all costs, subtracting all revenues, and adding a return on past and future investment to cover the cost of capital. This method of subsidization offers no incentive to efficiency but encourages the carrier to spend excessive sums on expansion, innovation, and sales promotion, since these outlays will be underwritten by the government. The Board attempts to limit such extravagance, refusing to recognize excessive expenditures in computing subsidy rates. But it cannot really prevent waste and inefficiency in management.

9 / *Ibid.,* chap. x.

Two other methods of calculating the need rate are designed to offer the carriers an incentive to efficiency. A "closed rate," which is most common, is negotiated with each carrier, assuring it a definite sum. If the carrier cuts its costs, it can keep the money it saves. A group rate, computed for the lines in each of four groups, sets the level of subsidy according to the economic characteristics of the group as a whole. The lines that make a profit larger than the average are allowed to keep it. Under these procedures, the airlines gain, not by increasing costs, but by reducing them.

Direct subsidies are declining in importance. Subsidies to domestic carriers rose from $10 million in 1938 to a high of $84 million in 1965. But the subsidies paid before World War II provided the trunk lines with a quarter of their gross revenues; those paid today account for less than 3 percent of the industry's revenues. The trunk lines have been off subsidy since 1957. Subsidies to the local lines, over the past 20 years, have amounted to three quarters of a billion. But these payments are declining. The locals, too, may become self-sufficient in the course of time.

Control of Fares

Originally, air fares were based on first-class rail fares, so that the airlines might compete for passengers. They have borne little relation to costs, since deficits, if they occurred, would be covered by subsidies. When earnings have been low, an increase in the general level of fares has been requested by the carriers. When earnings have been high, a reduction in the general level of fares may have been made by the CAB. Initiative in proposing changes in particular fares is taken by the carriers. In aviation, the procedure differs from that followed by the railroads and the trucking companies. Collusion in fare making is frowned upon by the CAB. Requests for changes in fares are not discussed and agreed upon before they are presented to the Board.

The CAB paid little attention to the level of fares before 1957. Airline earnings could be controlled by allocating routes and by fixing subsidies. But when the trunk lines went off subsidy in 1957, it became necessary to adopt a policy regarding fares. The Board therefore made a General Passenger Fare Investigation, announcing its results in 1960. The investigation dealt only with the general level of fares. Here, procedures were prescribed and standards established to govern the computation of allowable earnings. The airlines had proposed that earnings be computed, as they are for motor carriers, as a percentage of revenues. The Board rejected this approach, calculating earnings, as is generally done, as a return on investment. To determine the needed rate of return, the Board ascertained the respective shares of debt and equity in the capital structures of the airlines and estimated the rate that was needed to attract each type of capital. As the rate to be allowed, it took a weighted average of the two. The resulting return for the Big Four was 4.5 percent on debt, 16 percent on equity, and 10.25 percent overall; for the other trunk lines, 5.5 percent on debt, 18 percent on equity, and 11.125 percent overall; for the local carriers, 5.5 percent on debt, 21.35 percent on equity, and an average, for the different carriers, running from 9 to 12.75 percent overall. The Board thus established a measure of reasonableness for earnings. In the mid sixties, when the average earnings of the trunk lines had climbed above 10 percent, they requested an increase in the level of fares. The CAB refused to grant it. In the late sixties, however, when heavy investments had been made in jumbo jets, when labor and material costs were inflated, and when planes were flying partly full, airline earnings fell. The CAB approved two fare increases, totalling more than 10 percent, in 1969.

For many years, the Board's control of the structure of fares was sporadic, casual, and uninformed. It had no demand or cost data on which to base its decisions; no standards by which to judge the propriety of particular rates. The fare structure was modified from time to time, on an ad hoc basis, at the initiative of the carriers. Lower charges were fixed for coaches than for first-class flights. Promotional fares were introduced for family groups, for military personnel, for youths, for excursions, and for stand-by services. But there was no consistent pattern. As a part of its passenger fare investigation, made before 1960, the Board announced its intention to examine the structure as well as the level of fares. But its report on this part of its study did not appear until 1968. The Board then proposed that fares be based on costs, beginning with a common terminal charge for each trip, to cover the costs of takeoff and landing, and adding a charge per mile, tapering with distance, with first-class fares set at 125 percent of coach fares and promotional fares continued at their current discounts. A foundation for a rational structure of fares has thus been laid.

REGULATING COMPETITIVE MEDIA

In the beginning, the task of regulating the railroads, like that of regulating public utilities, was one of controlling a business possessing monopoly power. As other types of carriers came to offer serious competition, the familiar pattern of regulation was applied to each of them in turn. But the nature of the problem facing the regulators underwent a fundamental change. Entry could no longer be controlled, combinations judged, and rates fixed, solely with a view to the effect of action on a single type of carrier. Regulation, unless strictly impartial, would influence the allocation of traffic, thus affecting the comparative development of competing services. But impartiality, in the face of conflicting policies regarding promotion, was not to be achieved.

Control of Supply

Control of entry was first undertaken to protect the solvency of a regulated monopoly. It is now practiced to govern the adjustment of supply to demand in a competitive industry. In the cases of pipelines, water carriers, and airlines, this control has not been so employed as to inhibit competition. In the case of motor carriers, it has. Trucking companies have been denied certificates. And where certificates have been granted, they have frequently limited operating rights.

Limitations on the supply of trucking service have their defenders. They are said to prevent destructive competition, impairment of service, and instability of rates. They are said, too, to permit attainment of the most economical scale of operation. But each of these arguments is open to question. The character of the industry's costs is such that destructive competition is unlikely to occur. Alternatives are so readily available that service is unlikely to be impaired. Uncertainty as to rates may be harmful to shippers, but this can be avoided by requiring prior notice of changes rather than eliminating competition from the field. There may not be significant economies in large-scale operation. But if there are, it should be possible for firms to grow in size without the aid of artificial barriers to small competitors. Control of the supply of trucking operates to freeze technology, preserving outmoded forms of transport and delaying the development of superior services. One fact, however, should be noted: the damage that regulation can do, in this regard, is limited by its inability to control the private carrier.

Control of supply operates in another way to obstruct adjustment to change. Carriers other than railroads are permitted to confine themselves to traffic they find to be profitable. The motor carriers do not haul goods that are low in value; the water carriers do not take goods in small lots; the airlines discourage unprofitable business by charging high rates. Each of them has the freedom to pick and choose. The railroads, however, are required to keep on handling business that yields no profit or even involves a loss. They must haul low-value goods that will move only at low rates. They must maintain service on branch lines that have ceased to pay their way. They must continue to carry commuters even though they would be better off if the commutation service were dropped. The railroads are thus victims, as well as beneficiaries, of quantitative controls.

Control of Combination

Where rail, motor, and water carriers are concerned, the control of combination is within the jurisdiction of the ICC. Where airlines are involved, it is within the jurisdiction of the CAB. The combination of like carriers and the combination of unlike carriers raise quite different problems. In the first case, the issue is whether to permit the elimination of possible competition in service as well as rates between firms who employ the same technology. In the second, it is whether to permit the elimination of competition, not only in service, but also in rates and in technology.

With respect to the railroads, until 1920 the government pursued two different policies. It recognized the existence of monopoly and regulated rates. But, at the same time, it forbade pooling under the Interstate Commerce Act and combination under the Sherman Act. The two policies were inconsistent. If regulation were effective, there would be little point in maintaining competition. If competition were maintained, there would be little need to regulate. Under the Transportation Act of 1920, this anomaly was brought to an end. Pooling and combination were made permissive, subject to approval by the ICC. And this precedent was followed, in later years, with other carriers.

The combination of unlike carriers may also be approved. But here, in general, approval has been withheld. The ICC has permitted railroads to acquire supplementary motor services but not competing ones. And the CAB has refused to permit control of airlines by surface carriers. In the interest of progress, they have required the different transport media to compete. But such competition makes for optimum economy only when the competitors are put on an equal footing. And this has never been done.

Control of Rates

As monopolists, the railroads tended to differentiate their rates in accordance with the value of the services they rendered, charging in each case what the traffic would bear. As a regulator, the ICC sought to prevent the rate level from going too high and the rate structure from becoming too discriminatory by fixing legal maxima. With the growth of competition, the pattern of railroad rates began to change. As motor carriers took over goods with higher values that had moved at higher rates, the railroads cut these rates to check the loss. They reduced their less-than-carload rates, graduating these rates by size of shipment, and introducing all-commodity rates for mixed carloads. As water carriers cut into the business of hauling goods with lower values, the railroads cut rates on their competing hauls. For moving such goods in trainloads, they established rates below their carload rates. Where goods could be handled more cheaply by other carriers, they fought to keep them on the rails. Where their competitors were subsidized, they met the rates resulting from the subsidy. The structure of railroad rates was still discriminatory. But the nature of the discrimination had changed. Lower rates were charged on the goods that now could be moved by other carriers, higher rates on the goods that could be moved by rail alone. Insofar as more profitable traffic was lost, rates had to be raised on the traffic that remained. And as rates were raised, the competition of other carriers grew more keen. In this situation, the task of regulation came to be less one of fixing maximum rates than of fixing minima.

As long as the government confined itself to fixing maximum rates, traffic was allocated among the different types of carriers in accordance with the choices of shippers, made in response to the rates that were charged. But as soon as the government began to fix minima, the allocation of traffic came under the influence of public policy. It is the purpose of this policy, as enunciated by Congress, "to provide for fair and impartial regulation of all modes of transportation . . . so administered as to recognize and preserve the inherent advantages of each. . . ." In fixing minimum rates, how is this to be done?

The ICC sought to satisfy the requirement by a policy that assured each medium of transport its accustomed share of traffic. Starting with an established structure of rates, it permitted one type of carrier to meet the rates set by another where these rates covered fully allocated costs, provided that, in doing so, the first carrier did not go below its own out-of-pocket costs. But it did not permit one type of carrier to undercut the rates set by another, even though a lower rate would have covered its out-of-pocket costs. This policy permitted the railroads, for instance, to discriminate by fixing lower rates for competitive traffic. But it put a limit to discrimination: the railroads' rates could be as low as those charged by water or motor carriers; they could not be lower. The Commission thus undertook, not to promote competition, but to protect competitors.

For economy in transport, freight should be hauled by the carrier with the lowest costs. The railroads' marginal or out-of-pocket costs will often fall below the fully allocated costs of their rivals. If they are permitted to compete by fixing rates that more than cover their marginal costs, they will make money by doing so. If they are not allowed to compete on this basis, unused capacity will be condemned to idleness. The gainer from such a policy will not be the shipper but the carriers with higher costs. In adopting this policy, the Commission may have succeeded in satisfying the legislative requirement of fairness and impartiality; it did not succeed in preserving the inherent advantages of each type of carrier. Given idle capacity, the railroads' ability to profit by carrying extra traffic at rates that cover little more than costs is an inherent advantage of the industry. Refusal to permit them to do so deprived them of this advantage. When the railroads were forbidden to undercut the rates charged by truckers, for instance, they were denied the one competitive weapon with which they might have countered the superior service offered by the trucks. As a result of this policy, traffic has been allocated uneconomically. The railroads have a cost advantage on hauls of more than 20 tons for distances over 200 miles. But under the Commission's rules, most shipments under 40 tons, whatever the distance, are carried by truck. Services are duplicated and costs are kept higher than they need to be.

A reversal of this policy was made possible by Congress when it provided, in the Transportation Act of 1958, that the rates of one type of carrier are not to be held up to prevent the diversion of traffic from another. But the ICC, as we saw in Chapter 16, has dragged its feet in applying the new rule. If the rule were finally made effective, the Commission could no longer deny the railroads the right to undercut the rates that are charged by truckers and water carriers as long as the railroads' rates were high enough to cover their marginal costs. What would be the result? The other carriers have feared that the railroads would overhaul their rate structures, drastically cutting their rates on competitive traffic and compensating for these cuts by raising their rates on noncompetitive traffic. These fears would seem to be exaggerated. There would doubtless be a substantial shift of traffic from the highways to the rails, with the truckers gaining low-volume, short-haul business but losing high-volume, long-haul business. The water carriers, with their low costs, would not be so hard hit. The railroads, moreover, are still subject to maximum rate controls. They might not be permitted substantially to increase the rates they charge on noncompetitive traffic. And though some increases were granted, they might not be able to meet all their overhead with the revenue derived from such goods. Some of this burden would therefore have to be carried by competitive traffic. Wherever the railroads put their rates, the truckers would still have the advantage of superior service. With lower costs of packing, loading, and unloading, with greater flexibility and higher speed, they are not likely to be driven from the field. Minimum rate regulation based on out-of-pocket costs can be fair and impartial. It can also preserve the inherent advantages of different types of carriers.

Promotion versus Regulation

If minimum rate making is to be impartial, permitting traffic to be allocated in accordance with inherent advantages, the real costs of each type of carrier must be reflected in its money costs. But insofar as carriers are subsidized, their money costs will not reflect their real costs. Rates will be based on artificial rather than inherent advantages. Traffic will be allocated, not in accordance with comparative economy of operation, but in proportion to the sizes of the subsidies. The effort to achieve impartiality in regulation will be set at naught.

This, in fact, is the case. The railroads have to cover all their costs. Their competitors are not always required to do so. Diesel trucks and tractor-trailer combinations, as we have seen, fall short of meeting their full share of highway costs. Water carriers are not required to pay for the use of the waterways. Air carriers do not cover the costs of the airports or the airways. And local lines, in addition, are paid an outright subsidy. As a result, facilities are expanded where costs are high and traffic is diverted from carriers whose costs are low.

The promotion of different forms of transport has been subject to no comprehensive plan. Money has been voted separately for highways, waterways, and airways without regard to its effect on transport as a whole. Until the Department of Transportation was set up in 1967, administration, too, was uncoordinated. Nowhere in government was there an agency possessing overall responsibility for transport promotion. Nowhere was any effort made to achieve consistency between regulation and promotion in accordance with the stated purposes of national transport policy.

TOWARD ECONOMY IN TRANSPORT

Each of the modes of transport has its particular advantages. Motor carriers are best adapted to moving light goods in small quantities, making short hauls, providing feeder services, and meeting the need for flexibility. Water carriers have the lowest costs where freight is hauled in bulk for long distances and speed is not required. The airlines enjoy superiority in carrying passengers and valuable goods for long distances at high speeds. The railroads are needed to carry passengers where distances are too short for travel by air and traffic too congested for travel by road. They are at their best in hauling freight for long distances in carload lots at intermediate speeds. Here, their scope, speed, and dependability are greater than those of the water carriers and their costs lower than those of the motor carriers. The railroads get three times as many ton-miles per worker and more than three times as many ton-miles per gallon of fuel than do the trucks. Greater economy would be realized in transport if each of these media could be given the work that it is best equipped to do. This might be accomplished in one of two ways: administratively, by bringing the several transport media under common control, or through the market, by equalizing competitive opportunities.

Coordination of Services

Administrative coordination could be effected by transport companies operating railroads, trucks and buses, ships and planes. Unnecessary duplication of facilities could thus be eliminated, useless capacity abandoned, and capital requirements reduced. For each shipment, the managers of such an enterprise would presumably employ the method that would move it with the greatest convenience and economy. Provision would be made for interconnection of different services at common termini. Trucks and buses would be used for pick-up and delivery, supplementing longer hauls by railways, waterways, and airlines. Interchangeable containers could be used, carried on flatcars, and loaded onto ships. A complete service could be offered, at the lowest possible cost, adapted to the needs of the customer.

This might be accomplished by a company possessing a national or regional monopoly. With such an organization, savings could be realized, too, through unification of facilities, joint use of equipment, elimination of duplicate services, and the like. But the stimulus of competition would be lacking. Stagnation, rather than progress, might be the result.

The different modes of transport might also be combined and operated together, in any area, by each of a number of different companies. This form of organization has been favored by the railroads. It would preserve competition in service, if not in rates. It would simplify regulation by eliminating the competitive inequality of different carriers. But the plan has one great danger. It might impede the development of carriage by highway, by water, and by air. The transport companies would be dominated by railroad interests, since their major investment would be in rail facilities. They might well hesitate to employ the other media if these facilities were partly idle. The railroads, moreover, have been notoriously unprogressive. It is mainly through the competition of other media that their service has been improved. If this competition were to be ended, they might sink back into their rut. But with entry easy for the other carriers, this should not occur. The potentiality of competition would persist.

The creation of multimodal transport companies is obstructed by statutory provisions and administrative rulings that limit intermodal combinations to those where the operations of one type of carrier are "auxiliary and supplemental" to those of another. This solution to the transport problem would require a reversal in public policy. The organization of transport oligopolies, moreover, would appear to be barred by the action taken by the ICC in approving mergers of railroad companies. These combinations have created regional rail monopolies that would have to be dissolved if intercompany rather than intermodal competition were to be made the rule. And no such reversal is likely to occur.

Equalizing Competitive Opportunities

If transport is to be competitive, it is important that the independence of the different types of carriers be preserved. But if traffic is to be allocated among these carriers in accordance with their inherent advantages, they must be put on an equal footing with regard to costs. This might be done in one of two ways. The motor, water, and air carriers could be charged for the use of public facilities. Or the railroads could be given aid that would be comparable to that now given their competitors.

User charges have the advantage of collecting the cost of transport facilities from the people who use them instead of imposing it on the general taxpayer. Their effect on competition among the different media depends upon the way in which they are computed. Here, there are three possibilities: (1) The other carriers might be asked to pay charges equivalent to the burden borne by the railroads. In this case, they would be expected not only to meet their share of the costs incurred by the government in providing them with facilities but also to cover costs the government had not incurred: interest on land though no land had been bought, interest on investment though it had been financed in whole or in part by taxation rather than by borrowing, interest at commercial rates though money had been borrowed at government rates, and taxes on property though no such taxes had been paid. This method of computation would protect the railroads, but it would subject the other carriers to an artificial handicap. (2) The users of public facilities might merely be required to pay their own share of the costs actually incurred by the government. Such costs would not include the imputed interest or taxes mentioned above. Their allocation among different purposes (such as flood control, irrigation, power production, and navigation) and among different classes of users (such as automobiles and light and heavy trucks and buses) would be difficult. But once this problem was solved, the subsidization of competing carriers through government outlays would be brought to an end. This, however, would not require the users of public facilities to meet their full economic costs. For these include the cost of capital, not only when borrowed, but also when provided by the taxpayer. (3) User charges could be set to cover economic costs, including interest actually paid by the government and interest imputed, at the same rate, on capital provided by the taxpayer. But even here, the competitors of the railroads would enjoy an advantage. They would have to meet only a part of the cost of jointly used facilities. This cost would include interest but at the low rate paid by the government. It would include no taxes.

If the users of public facilities were required to pay tolls that would cover their full share of the costs of construction and maintenance, the allocation of traffic among the different transport media would change. The motor carriers and the water carriers could pay such charges and continue to compete. The airlines could continue to serve the major cities. But air service to hundreds of smaller cities would be dropped. If this service is desired, it must be subsidized.

Competition might be equalized, alternatively, by aiding the railroads. Local governments might exempt them from taxes on their roadways, or the federal government might give them money to offset the taxes that they pay. Or the government could purchase their facilities, assuring them continued use. It could then provide ways to all types of carriers without charge, or impose charges that would result in comparable costs. Even if the railroads were required to finance the government's outlay, their fixed costs would be reduced: the interest rate would be lower, and there would be no property taxes to pay. This suggestion raises many problems that cannot now be explored. It is opposed by the railroads, who see in it an entering wedge for public ownership.

Less Regulation or More?

The regulation of transport was undertaken when the railroads were monopolists. Now that the industry is competitive, it may well be asked whether regulation, instead of being extended, should not be dropped. The answer is, in part, that competition is not complete. There are still hauls that can be made only by rail. And though competition has changed the pattern of discrimination, protection against undue discrimination is still required. The railroads, moreover, possess much greater resources than their competitors. In the absence of regulation, they might engage in unfair competition, driving their weaker rivals from the field. They might refuse, for instance, to interchange shipments with other carriers. They might slash rates on competing traffic or establish competing services, conducting them at a loss. With their competitors eliminated, they might then proceed to regain and to exploit their position of monopoly.

Complete deregulation would have pronounced effects. It would benefit most railroads, water carriers, and producers in population centers. By improving the allocation of traffic, eliminating excess capacity, and accelerating technical progress, it would benefit society as a whole. But it would be harmful to other interests: the trucking companies, producers in poor locations, and shippers of agricultural and bulk commodities whose rates might now be raised as others were lowered. These interests are politically vocal. A change that they oppose is unlikely to be made.

Few would propose that regulation be abandoned; the issue is whether it should be tightened or relaxed. Those who favor tighter regulation point out that the railroads are completely covered by the law while other carriers are partially exempt: trucks transporting agricultural commodities, livestock, and fish, and water carriers transporting a few commodities in bulk. It is noted, too, that the control of contract carriers is weak and that of common carriers often incomplete: there is no federal control, for instance, over intrastate traffic by media other than railroads, over the issuance of securities by water carriers and airlines, or over the abandonment of motor or water services. To achieve effective and impartial regulation, it is said, these gaps in the law should be closed. If this were done, the Interstate Commerce Commission's minimum rate regulations could be made more effective and its control over the allocation of traffic secured.

A view more frequently expressed is that regulation should be relaxed. Several proposals are made: (1) Restriction of entry into the motor transport industry should be abandoned; the industry's economic characteristics are not such that destructive competition would occur if entry were free. (2) Limitations on trucking rights should be removed; truckers should be permitted to haul any cargo in either direction over any route, cutting their costs by filling empty space. (3) Control over air routes should be discontinued; supply should be free to adjust to changes in demand; the energy that is wasted on route proceedings should be devoted to more vital tasks. (4) The railroads should be given greater freedom to abandon unprofitable services; if a service that is socially necessary cannot pay its way, as is the case with commutation, it should be subsidized by the communities that require it, not by other people who ship or travel by rail. (5) Railroads should not be permitted to suppress the competition of air or water carriers by bringing them under control, but combinations of rail and water and motor carriers should be approved to the end that coordinated motor-rail-motor and motor-water-motor services can be supplied. (6) Rules that obstruct innovations in technology should be abandoned. In particular, the way should be opened to a wider use of piggy-backing services. (7) Collusion should be forbidden in fixing rates; rate bureaus should be made subject to the antitrust laws. (8) Where agricultural commodities and goods moving in bulk are exempt from rate control, the same exemption should be extended to the railways as to motor and water carriers; the scope of regulation for each mode of transport should be the same. (9) The power to fix minimum rates for truckers should be withdrawn; the structure of costs in this industry is such that there is little temptation to discriminate. Maximum and minimum rate controls for the railroads, however, should be retained, otherwise rates on noncompetitive traffic may be set too high and rates on competitive traffic too low; control is needed if discrimination is to be kept within bounds. (10) The clause in the 1933 rule of rate making that required the ICC to consider "the effect of rates on the movement of traffic" should be repealed; decisions concerning the probable effect of rates on revenues should be returned to transport managements, eliminating duplication of the managerial function with its consequent delays. All of these proposals point toward less reliance on regulation and more on competition. And this is the direction in which official recommendations for changes in policy have moved in recent years.

The Department of Transportation

The Department of Transportation, set up in 1967, brought under common direction 35 federal agencies having to do, in one way or another, with transport. Some of its functions are purely administrative: management of the Coast Guard, the St. Lawrence Seaway, the Alaska Railroad, the car service operations of the ICC, and safety regulation for surface and air carriers. Other functions involve the administration of certain promotional programs and planning for the promotion of transport as a whole. The Department includes, for instance, the Highway Administration, the Federal Aviation Administration, and the Office of High-Speed Ground Transportation. But its ability to develop a comprehensive plan for transport is limited by its lack of jurisdiction over the Maritime Administration, that grants subsidies for ship construction and operation, and over the Army Corps of Engineers, that promotes the development of inland waterways. Nor is the Department in a position to bring about consistency of promotional and regulatory policies. Its authority does not extend to regulation. Control of entry, combinations, routes, and rates is left with the ICC and the CAB. But the scope of the Department's operations and its location in the structure of government may, nonetheless, enable it eventually to exert a strong influence on the development of policy. And since it is concerned with several modes of transport rather than a single one, it may come to speak for the coordinated promotion and regulation of transport as a whole.

Chapter 18 REGULATION OF COMMUNICATIONS

The field of communications is broad and varied. In some cases, as with telephone and telegraph, communications are carried principally by wire. In others, as with radio, they are carried by air waves. In some cases, as with telephone and telegraph, firms providing communications services function as common carriers. In others, as with broadcasting, they have no such obligation. The duties of the Federal Communications Commission, as the principal regulatory agency, are therefore numerous and diverse.

Whatever the medium of communication, the regulatory agency controls entry to the field. In the case of common carriers by wire, this control is designed to maintain essential services by preventing destructive competition—resulting from heavy investment and high fixed charges—that would endanger solvency and impair credit. In broadcasting, on the other hand, investments are generally smaller, fixed costs lower, and destructive competition less likely to occur. Here, control of entry is necessitated by the fact that the number of channels in the radio spectrum is limited and demand for their use exceeds the supply. With wireless common-carrier communication, too, air space must be allocated. In both cases, the agency must make and enforce traffic rules.

In communications, as elsewhere, the rates charged by common carriers for the use of their services might be excessive or discriminatory and the services unsatisfactory in quantity and quality. Such rates and services, as with other public utilities, are subjected to control. In broadcasting, however, rates are not controlled. The broadcaster serves the consumer without charge; there is no rate to be fixed. The broadcaster's services are scrutinized in granting or denying him the right to use the air, but they are not regulated in detail.

BACKGROUND OF COMMUNICATIONS REGULATION

The types of common carrier communications services are numerous and varied. The earliest was one-way, person-to-person service, providing a printed record: telegraphy. Then came two-way communication by voice: telephony, soon and still the dominant medium. These services were gradually extended from short to long distances, from domestic to transoceanic communications, first through the use of cables and then by radio. In later years, the communications companies have also come to provide a variety of services to other businesses. Teletypewriter service enables the subscriber to type out messages that are transmitted as electronic impulses and translated, at the receiving end, into printed form. Facsimile transmission enables him to send material that is received simultaneously in picture form. Programs are forwarded by air for television networks from point-of-origin to broadcasting stations. And, with the advance of technology, the list of services continues to grow.

The Communications Industries

The dominant form of communications is telephony and the giant of the telephone industry, serving 93 million of the nation's 110 million telephones, is the American Telephone & Telegraph Co., controlling the Bell system, popularly known as "Ma Bell." A.T.&T. is a holding company, owning the voting stock in 23 regional operating companies that provide 84 percent of the nation's local telephone service, deriving two thirds of its revenue from this business. Through its long-lines department, the corporation provides 98 percent of the long-distance service. It also supplies teletype and telephoto services and private-line services and has a virtual monopoly of the transmission of television programs. Through its manufacturing subsidiary, Western Electric, the company accounts for 80 percent of the nation's output of telephonic equipment. Jointly, the two concerns own the Bell Telephone Laboratories, the nation's largest organization for electronic research. The Bell system is completely integrated, the president of A.T.&T. being empowered to vote its stock in the subsidiaries and to select their directors and officers. The parent company is thus in direct and complete control.

A.T.&T. is the biggest corporation in the country. Its business operations are greater in magnitude than those of many states. In 1969, the company had 3,000,000 stockholders and 900,000 employees. Its assets amounted to $44 billion; its operating revenues to more than $15 billion, and its net income to some $2.2 billion.

There are 2,000 other telephone companies, servicing 17 million phones, mostly in smaller towns and rural areas. There are also other holding companies, the General Telephone and Electronics Corporation, with 40 subsidiaries serving 9 million phones in 34 states being the largest. This concern also provides other wire services, as does A.T.&T., and has a subsidiary which manufactures electronic equipment.

In the one-way transmission of personal messages providing a printed record by wire, Western Union has a monopoly. This business accounts for half of its revenues. The company also competes with the Bell system in the provision of wire services other than telephony, deriving the other half of its income from this business. By comparison, however, Western Union is a pygmy, its revenues amounting to less than 3 percent of those of A.T.&T.

Development of Communications Industries

Signals were first transmitted electronically by wire by Samuel F. B. Morse in 1835. The first telegraph line was strung between Washington and Baltimore in 1843. Thereafter, telegraphy soon came to be used in the dispatching of trains and the transmission of news, 50 companies being engaged in this enterprise by 1851. Many of these concerns were subsidized, being permitted, without charge, to string their lines along the rights-of-way of land-grant railways. A number of these enterprises were combined to form the Western Union Telegraph Company in 1856.

Invention of the telephone was claimed by Daniel Drawbaugh, Elisha Gray, and Alexander Graham Bell. Drawbaugh's telephone was invented in 1869 and put to work in 1871. Bell first transmitted voice by wire in 1875. Patent litigation ensued. The Bell interests acquired the Gray as well as the Bell rights and sued Drawbaugh for infringement. Bell won its suit in the Supreme Court in 1887. It then proceeded with the construction of telephone lines.

A war for survival followed. Western Union, then the stronger company, barred Bell's lines from the railway rights-of-way and sued Bell for infringement of its patent. But Bell successfully resisted the attack. The patent suit was settled out of court in 1879. The communications business was divided between the two concerns, Western Union taking record communications for itself and leaving voice communications to Bell.

Bell then went on to establish its dominance over the telephone industry. Up to 1898, it brought infringement suits against 600 small local companies, converting the losers into licensees. It refused to sell telephonic equipment manufactured by Western Electric to independent companies, refused to connect them to its long distance lines, and drove them out of business by undercutting their rates. Bell bought the shares of its licensees and those of independent companies. Where no such companies existed, it encouraged local promoters to establish them, assisted their development, and then acquired control. Proceeding ruthlessly over the years, it virtually monopolized the business of telephony.

In telegraphy, a second company, Postal Telegraph, was established in 1881 to compete with Western Union. Postal was at a disadvantage because Western Union's contracts with the railroads gave that company an exclusive right to use their rights-of-way for its lines and their stations for its offices. Western Union kept four fifths of the business; Postal Telegraph acquired one fifth. Both companies prospered until the thirties; both lost money during the depression; Postal Telegraph went into bankruptcy. It was clear that the business would not support two concerns. Legislation was therefore enacted by Congress permitting them to merge. The merger was effected in 1943, Western Union thus obtaining its monopoly of telegraphy. But the personal-message telegraph business, faced by the competition of air mail and two-way communication by phone, steadily declined. As the Bell system prospered, Western Union fell on bad days. It was only its competition with A.T.&T. in providing other types of services that enabled it to survive.

The Beginnings of Regulation

From around the turn of the century the telephone business, being largely intrastate in character, was regulated by state utility commissions, the pattern of control being the same as that described above in the case of electricity. In 1910, under the Mann-Elkins Act, companies providing interstate telephone and telegraph services were subjected to regulation by the Interstate Commerce Commission. This body was concerned primarily with railroads and took little interest in the communications industries, acting only in response to complaints. During more than 20 years of jurisdiction over interstate telephony, it never instituted a proceeding to reduce rates. In 1927, the regulation of radio broadcasting was entrusted to a Federal Radio Commission and in 1934 the functions nominally exercised by the ICC in regulating interstate telephone and telegraph companies and those performed by the FRC in regulating broadcasting were brought together under the Federal Communications Commission, a new agency set up under the Federal Communications Act. It is only with the Commission's regulation of common carriers that we are here concerned.

In this field, the usual pattern of control applies. Commission approval must be obtained for entry and for curtailment or discontinuance of service. Carriers must furnish service on request. Rates must be just and reasonable, must be published and observed, and notice given prior to a change. The FCC can suspend proposed changes upon complaint or at its own initiative, and can prescribe maxima and minima. There may be no unjust discrimination in rates or services. The Commission may require interconnections and through rates and determine the division of such rates between participating companies. Accounts are subject to control, appropriate methods of valuation may be employed, and means of providing for depreciation may be prescribed. The Commission has jurisdiction over combinations. It has no authority, however, over security sales or corporate reorganizations, and no control over intercompany contracts or the declaration of dividends.

REGULATION OF TELEPHONE INDUSTRY

Regulatory jurisdiction over the telephone industry is shared by the state utility commissions and the Federal Communications Commission. Jurisdiction over purely intrastate services, and thus over most local services, lies with the state commissions. Jurisdiction over local services that cross state lines, a minor part of such business, and over long-distance service, lies with the FCC. Bell's associated companies are thus regulated, in the main, by the state agencies, its long-lines department by the FCC. This duplication creates a number of problems for regulation. The costs of integrated services must be allocated between intrastate and interstate operations and rates must be set at levels required to cover the costs of each. Investments, too, must be allocated and a fair return allowed on a fair value in each case. The federal agency assists the states in seeking to solve these problems. But it appears that the state commissions have been weaker than the FCC and that intrastate rates have been set at levels higher than those permitted for interstate services.

Quality of Service

Until recently, the commissions, state and federal, did not concern themselves with the quality of telephone service. This service, in the United States, was said to be the best on earth. Certainly, great strides had been made in its convenience and reliability. Four fifths of Bell subscribers were on private lines. Subscribers were directly dialing all of their local calls and nine tenths of their long-distance calls. Long distance connections were effected, on the average, in less than a minute. Further improvements were on the way: abbreviated dialing for numbers frequently called, the automatic transfer of calls from one phone to another, the simultaneous transmission of picture and voice. The record was impressive. But telephone service was still subject to annoyance and even to abuse. The telephone companies permitted its use for merchandising, for solicitation of funds, and for the dissemination of recorded propaganda. They gave no assurance of privacy; wires might be tapped or bugged not only by law-enforcement agencies but also by private detectives and even by telephone employees, checking on the character of the service supplied. Then, in 1969, the quality of the service, particularly in New York City, sharply declined. There were widespread complaints of delays in the installation of new phones, of delayed dial tones, unintelligible beeps, protracted busy signals, wrong numbers, lines crossed, connections cut off, and phones going dead. One exchange was blacked out; none of its subscribers could be reached. New York Bell had not foreseen the growth in demand for its services and had failed to provide the facilities that were required. Hearings on the quality of intrastate service were now held by the New York commission and an inquiry into the quality of interstate service was initiated by the FCC. The Bell system belatedly undertook to make the increased investments required to meet the growing demand.

Rate Regulation by State Commissions

Regulation of telephone rates by state commissions, said John Bauer in 1950, "has in fact been far less effective than that of the other local utilities."[1] These agencies, said Joseph C. Goulden in 1968, "give . . . short shrift to telephone matters. One lawyer, a secretary, an economist who works part-time for another agency—such is the typical state staff."[2] The commissions have been ill-equipped to cope with the complexities of technology, corporate organization, and inter-

1 / John Bauer, *Transforming Public Utility Regulation* (New York: Harper & Bros., 1950), p. 337.

2 / Joseph C. Goulden, *Monopoly* (New York: G. P. Putnam's Sons, 1968), p. 302.

governmental relations found in this industry. They "lack the zest for vigorous, independent inquiry."[3] C. Emery Troxel, having reviewed company requests for rate increases brought before the Michigan commission from 1949 to 1961, found that the commission had held rates down, granting the companies less than they had asked.[4] But state commissions, on the other hand, have taken little or no initiative in reducing the level of rates.

The level of intrastate rates is comparatively high, the charges made for calls running 20 to 30 percent above those made for comparable interstate calls. This discrepancy is to be explained, in large part, by the ability of the telephone holding company to require the associated operating companies to purchase goods and services that it supplies at whatever prices it may fix, thus enhancing its revenues by increasing their costs. These costs must be covered in fixing their rates. But the commissions are powerless to control them. No agency is authorized to regulate Western Electric, or A.T.&T., to fix their charges, to control their costs, or even to prescribe the form of their accounts. Since the Supreme Court handed down its decision in the Smith case in 1930,[5] the commissions have been permitted to inquire into the nature of the services rendered by these companies, to judge the reasonableness of their charges, and to disallow unreasonable charges as expenses to be covered in fixing rates. In practice, however, none of these agencies is able to obtain the information or to make the findings that would be required. Dealings between the operating companies, on the one hand, and the holding company and its research and manufacturing subsidiaries, on the other, are not controlled.

The commissions have taken little interest in the formulation of rate structures, leaving the associated companies a free hand to adopt whatever patterns they may choose. In practice, the rates charged for different local services differ widely. But they bear little relation to differences in cost, being related, rather, to differences in the elasticity of demand. Business users are charged more than residential users because they find the service indispensable. Residential users are charged 35 cents a month for having their phones on extra-long cords, 90 cents a month for extension phones, $1 to $1.25 a month for colored instruments, and so on, these charges being justified, not by differences in cost, but only by the failure of subscribers to object. The structure of local telephone rates is deliberately discriminatory, but the commissions lay down no rules to govern discrimination, make no effort to bring it under control.

Holding Company Policies

In 1935, the Federal Communications Commission was directed by Congress to investigate the telephone industry. Its inquiry, according to Charles F. Phillips, Jr., "was, without doubt, the most intensive, extensive, and compre-

3 / *Ibid.,* p. 306.

4 / C. Emery Troxel, "Telephone Regulation in Michigan," in William G. Shepherd and Thomas S. Gies, *Utility Regulation* (New York: Random House, 1966), pp. 141-86.

5 / *Smith* v. *Illinois Bell Telephone Co.,* 282 U.S. 133.

hensive probe by a regulatory agency of an industry under its jurisdiction."[6] Some 300 lawyers, accountants, and engineers were engaged in the work over a period of four years. The basic record included 8,500 pages of testimony, 2,000 exhibits, and 77 staff studies. The Commission's final report was published in 1939.[7] It disclosed no such financial scandals as those found by the Federal Trade Commission in the electrical industry. But it did give evidence that A.T.&T. had taken advantage of its opportunity to increase profits, at the expense of the consumer, by padding the operating expenses and the property valuations of the associated companies.

A.T.&T. rendered various services to its associated companies, giving advice on the construction and operation of their properties, carrying on research through the Bell Laboratories and obtaining patents, raising and holding funds to meet their financial needs, and managing the assets of the parent company. For these services, it charged the associated companies a license fee amounting to 1.5 percent of their gross revenues. Some of the activities financed by this fee (those relating to research and patenting, for instance) may have contributed more to the revenues of A.T.&T. than to those of its subsidiaries. But the company's books were not kept in such a way as to permit their segregation. Subscribers to telephone service may thus have been required, through their rates, to finance activities whereby A.T.&T. made profits in fields other than telephony.[8]

The Commission found that the parent company, in prescribing methods of accounting, had required its subsidiaries to include in operating expenses depreciation charges known to be in excess of actual requirements but had forbidden them to deduct more than a part of depreciation reserves in arriving at the valuation of their properties. Annual charges for depreciation had not been reduced by an amount sufficient to compensate for the increasing length of life of the telephone plant. These charges were close to a fifth of the expenses involved in operating the system and thus significantly affected the consumer's bill. Reserves, built up out of such charges, represented nearly 30 percent of the investment in the telephone plant. But only "observable" depreciation was deducted in determining the rate base, and the depreciation "observed" amounted to only 7 to 12 percent, instead of 30 percent, of property values. To the extent to which reserves, accumulated from rates paid by subscribers, were not deducted from the base upon which further rate payments were computed, the subscribers were compelled to pay the company a return on money which they themselves had contributed.[9]

A.T.&T. handled the financing of the whole system. It made advances to the associated companies, supplied them with the capital which they required, and

6 / Charles F. Phillips, Jr., *The Economics of Regulation* (rev. ed.; Homewood, Ill.: Richard D. Irwin, Inc., 1969), pp. 658-59.

7 / Federal Communications Commission, *Investigation of the Telephone Industry* (Washington, D.C.: Government Printing Office, 1939).

8 / *Ibid.*, chap. vi.

9 / *Ibid.*, chap. xi.

charged them for the costs incurred in the process. Year after year, the company collected interest at a fixed rate, neither altering its charge with fluctuations in the rates charged by other lenders nor permitting its subsidiaries to enter the money market on their own. Insofar as its policy increased the price they had to pay for capital, it was reflected in the telephone subscriber's rates.[10]

A.T.&T. was found to have issued instructions which compelled the associated companies to purchase practically all of their apparatus, equipment, and plant materials from Western Electric. Six small independent producers of such supplies, subsisting largely on the business which Western gave them, were in no position really to compete with it. Since Western obtained its orders without competitive bidding, it was not forced to sell at a competitive price. The company's cost accounts did not afford an authentic basis for testing the reasonableness of the prices which it set upon specific products. Its prices, moreover, bore no apparent relation to its own statement of costs. Both costs and prices for many items were above those reported by independent firms. Western Electric profits had never been subject to any sort of public control. From 1882 to 1936 the company realized a net income on cash paid-in capital that exceeded 20 percent in 41 years, 50 percent in 25 years, and 100 percent in 6 years. To the extent that Western's charges were excessive, the excess entered into the property valuations and operating expenses of the associated companies and thus compelled the state commissions to fix rates that yielded something more than a fair return.[11]

Finally, the facilities employed by A.T.&T. and its subsidiaries in rendering long-distance service so overlapped that it was virtually impossible to determine how much of their cost should be charged to the Long Lines Department of the holding company and how much to the associated local companies. And it was therefore practically impossible to judge either the reasonableness of the tolls charged or the fairness with which the resulting revenues were divided. The tolls may well have been too high. And they may have been so divided as to divert revenues from the associated companies to the Long Lines Department, thus necessitating higher local rates.[12]

Regulation by the FCC

In the years that followed, the FCC succeeded, through negotiations with A.T.&T., in obtaining some rectification of most of the abuses revealed by its study in 1939. The values of operating properties were restated in terms of original cost, reducing the base on which a fair return had to be allowed. Depreciation accounting was brought into conformity with Commission standards, thus cutting operating costs. The prices charged by Western Electric were reduced. The method of apportioning long-distance earnings between the associ-

10 / *Ibid.*, chap. xv.

11 / *Ibid.*, chap. x.

12 / *Ibid.*, chap. xii.

ated companies and the Long Lines Department was so altered as to give the former a larger share.

The Commission has attained a considerable measure of success in regulating the interstate operations of A.T.&T. Until 1966, it held no formal hearings on the propriety of the company's rates. It made no determination as to the value of the company's investment or the return to be allowed thereon; no effort to fix the level or the structure of its rates. Instead, it adopted a procedure known as "constant surveillance," meeting periodically with company officials to discuss matters of substance, and arriving at compromises through negotiation. In this way, from 1940 to 1965, 50 major cuts were made in long-distance rates, amounting altogether to $1.5 billion per year and lowering their general level by 22 percent. Included in these actions was one that established a countrywide charge of $1 for long-distance calls made at night.

But the problem of telephone regulation had not been finally solved. Roger C. Cramton, Professor of Law at the University of Michigan, after examining the regulation of interstate rates from 1953 to 1962, concluded that "a detailed look at the methods and mechanics of regulation suggests strong doubts concerning its effectiveness: disputed issues have been compromised by the Commission after negotiation with the Bell System; standards for determining allowable expense, items includible in investment, and cost of capital have never been determined. . ."[13] Booz, Allen & Hamilton, a firm of management consultants, in a report prepared for the Bureau of the Budget in 1962, asserted that the FCC was not organized, staffed, or equipped to do a thorough regulatory job; that its investigations of costs were superficial; that it had developed no criteria to govern rates of return; and that it was therefore unable to determine the reasonableness of telephone rates.[14] And Nicholas Johnson, a member of the Commission, said in 1967, "There is substantial question in my mind whether the David-FCC is capable of 'regulating' the Goliath-Bell in anything other than the most superficial terms."[15]

CURRENT ISSUES IN REGULATION

The Federal Communications Commission, on its own initiative, instituted an investigation of the telegraph industry in 1962. The focus of the Commission's concern was with the condition and the prospects of Western Union. The personal message business, where the company had a monopoly, had been steadily declining. In its other services, the company faced the powerful competition of A.T.&T. The recommendations contained in the report of the Commission's Common Carrier Bureau, released in 1965, were designed so to strengthen the company as to assure its survival and to promote its further growth.

13 / Roger C. Cramton, "The Effectiveness of Economic Regulation: A Legal View," *American Economic Review,* Vol. LIV, No. 3 (1964), pp. 182-91, at p. 187.

14 / *New York Times,* April 25, 1962.

15 / Goulden, *op. cit.,* p. 294.

One among the issues considered in the investigation was Western Union's charge that A.T.&T. discriminated unfairly in fixing the structure of its rates, exacting a high return for those services where it enjoyed a monopoly and accepting a low return for those where other companies sought to compete. If the validity of this complaint were to be judged, it would be necessary to investigate Bell's rates. The FCC ordered such an investigation in 1965.

This inquiry was designed to be comprehensive in scope and thorough in detail. It sought, first, to determine the revenue requirements of A.T.&T. and to ascertain whether its overall charges were just and reasonable. To this end, it examined the general level of Bell's rates, looking into the propriety of the company's costs and deciding upon the rate of return needed to attract new capital. Second, the inquiry sought to ascertain whether the company's charges for different categories of service were just and reasonable; whether they subjected any of its customers to undue discrimination. To this end, it undertook to analyze the structure of Bell's rates. And finally, the inquiry was intended to provide the information that would enable the FCC to determine whether it should prescribe the charges to be made for Bell's interstate services.

This investigation was without precedent in the telephone industry. Its announcement evoked predictions of disaster and cries of outrage from A.T.&T. and from other members of the business community. The Commission, said A.T.&T., should continue to adhere to the tried-and-true method of constant surveillance under which rates were negotiated rather than ordered. The company formally requested the FCC to abandon the investigation. The Commission refused; the inquiry was begun in 1966.

The Rate Level

The FCC directed its attention, first, to the determination of Bell's rate base and its rate of return. The company argued that its rate base should include (1) investment in plant under construction, (2) the value of supplies and materials on hand, and (3) its balance of working capital. In its first report on the investigation, in 1967, the Commission accepted the first of these items, rejected the other two. Two other matters affecting the rate base were held for further study: the propriety of Western Electric's prices and the legitimacy of Bell's division of costs between intrastate and interstate services.

The return on Bell's investment, in recent years, had been running between 7.5 and 8 percent. The company now contended that it required a return of 8 to 8.5 percent to permit it to earn 10 to 11 percent on its common stock. This was necessary, it argued, to enable it to compete with other industries in raising capital. The company's contention was not accepted. For one thing, A.T.&T., with a nationwide monopoly of an essential service, should be able to attract capital at a lower rate than that required by other concerns. For another, it would be able to obtain money more cheaply if it were to alter its capital structure, raising more than the existing third of its funds by selling bonds, less than the existing two thirds by selling stocks. The Commission therefore decided that a fair return on Bell's overall investment would be 7.5 percent.

On the basis of these decisions, the FCC ordered A.T.&T. to cut its long-distance rates by an average of 3 percent, the cut amounting to $120 million per year. This was done in October, 1967. A further cut in these rates, averaging 4 percent and amounting to a total of $150 million a year was agreed upon by the Commission and the company in 1969 and took effect in 1970.

The Problem of Western Electric

The Western Electric Company, with $2.7 billion in assets, 177,000 employees, and $4 billion in annual sales, is one of the largest manufacturing enterprises in the United States. A wholly-owned subsidiary of A.T.&T., it supplies nearly all of the telephonic equipment required by the companies in the Bell System. If Western's charges were excessive, they would inflate the rate bases and operating expenses of these companies, thus necessitating a higher level of rates. This problem, as we have seen, was one with which the FCC was concerned when it made its report on the telephone industry in 1939. This report revealed serious abuses and led to substantial reforms. But the problem remained.

To solve this problem, two different approaches have been proposed. The first would disintegrate the holding company system, introducing an element of competition into the determination of operating company costs. This is the approach that was taken by the Antitrust Division of the Department of Justice in 1949 when it filed a complaint under the Sherman Act, asking that Western Electric be divorced from A.T.&T. and split into three separate companies, that A.T.&T. be compelled to grant licenses to other manufacturers under its patents, and that all manufacturers be required to make their sales by competitive bidding.[16] The consent decree accepted in this case in 1956 did not go so far. It aided General Telephone and other manufacturers of telephonic equipment by requiring A.T.&T. to license them under its patents, licenses under old patents being royalty-free and those under new patents at reasonable royalties. It required Western to maintain an adequate system of cost accounts. But it did not require disintegration. Nor did it open the Bell market to competitive bidding. Instead, it permitted A.T.&T. to retain control, keeping Western as its manufacturing subsidiary. This decree was denounced by an antitrust subcommittee of the House of Representatives in 1959 as a "blot on the enforcement history of the antitrust laws."[17] But the government's pressure did have some effect: the prices charged by Western Electric were reduced by 5 percent between 1950 and 1968.

Under a second approach to the problem, intercompany transactions in the

16 / *U.S.* v. *Western Electric Co.,* District Court of U.S., District of N.J., Civil Action No. 17-49, *Complaint,* January 14, 1949.

17 / *New York Times,* May 26, 1959.

holding company system would be supervised in the telephone industry as they are in the electric and gas industries. Federal regulation would be extended to all sales by Western Electric, fixing its charges to cover its costs and providing a fair return on the investment in its properties.

Present arrangements stop far short of this. Western Electric, under the terms of the consent decree, must follow the accounting procedures that are prescribed by FCC and must report on its financial operations and its manufacturing costs. The FCC and the state commissions review its prices and its profits and take them into account in determining the level of rates, disallowing any charges which they find to be excessive. But none of the commissions has the power to prescribe what charges may be made. Further inquiry into this problem is promised at a later stage of the investigation of the telephone industry that was initiated by the FCC in 1965.

The Rate Structure

Until the sixties there was no sharp differentiation in the rates charged by A.T.&T. for various types of interstate services, those for each service bearing a similar relation to its costs. During the forties, Western Union and A.T.&T. had each constructed a microwave (radio-relay) system to carry a portion of its messages. Then, in 1959, the FCC ruled that airspace in the band above 890 megacylces might be used for communication by private operators. This opened the door to competition with the private carriers. And it led A.T.&T. to overhaul the structure of its rates. Rates for telephonic communication were not changed. But rates for teletypewriter service (TWX) and private line service were cut and a new class of private line service (TELPAK) was introduced, providing volume discounts for the full use of packages of channels between specific points for a month or more at a time. As a result, rates for these services were set at 51 to 85 percent of their previous levels.

This differentiation in the pattern of Bell's rates led Western Union to complain that A.T.&T. was engaging in unfair competition, using its monopoly of telephonic service to subsidize its TWX and private line telegraphic services. Consequently, as a part of its investigation of the telegraph industry, the FCC requested A.T.&T. to report to it on its investment, expenses, revenues, and earnings in each of seven categories of interstate service, showing its net earnings, in each case, as a return on the portion of its investment allocated to that service.

Bell's report on its seven-way cost study was submitted in 1965. It revealed a wide discrepancy in earnings from the different services. The average rate of return for all of the services stood at 7.5 percent. The rate for the telephone service was 10 percent; that for TWX was 2.9 percent; that for TELPAK was 0.3 percent. These figures lent support to Western Union's charge that Bell was engaging in undue discrimination in its competition for the private line business.

The Commission's staff shared this view. Bell, they argued, should be required to set its rate for each service at a level that would cover its fully-allocated costs and yield it a fair return on its investment. To this end, the Commission should proceed to establish minimum rates.

This policy would be rejected by most economists. Prices, they hold, should be permitted to respond to differences in the elasticity of demand. Where demand is inelastic, they may be high. Where it is elastic, they may be low. Here, prices should be set, not to cover fully-allocated costs but to cover marginal costs. Where prices are set high enough to cover fully-allocated costs, they discourage full use of the available service. Where they are set low enough to do little more than cover marginal cost, they encourage wider use. In the former case, pricing is used to preserve the weak competitor. In the latter, it is used to serve the interest of the consumer.

The Problem of Western Union

From 1945 to 1970, the number of Western Union's telegraph offices fell from 3,500 to 1,400. By 1966, the volume of the personal message business had declined by 70 percent. The company's financial condition was impaired; its future existence jeopardized.

The decline in the message business was attributable, in part, to the rise of competitive services: air mail and speedier and cheaper telephonic communication. It was also attributable, in considerable part, to the declining quality and the increasing price of the telegraph service. Formerly, telegrams were promptly delivered to the recipient by personal messenger. Now they were telephoned to anyone who might answer at his number and forwarded to him by ordinary mail. The rates charged for this worsened service were raised 11 times between 1945 and 1964, being more than doubled over the period. The charge for a 15-word telegram in 1951 was 40 percent below that for a three-minute telephone call; in 1964, it was 30 percent above that for such a call. Instead of experimenting with the possibilities of promotional pricing, the company deliberately priced itself out of the market. Proceeding on the assumption that its public message business would continue to decline and would shortly disappear, an assumption that—given its policies—was doubtless correct, it turned its attention to other services.

Western Union now offered leased-wire services to business and government, provided teleprinter services, and sought to expand its participation in the new computer-based information storage, retrieval, and transmission services. Content to jettison its public message business, it looked for its future toward these fields.

It had long been FCC policy to keep Western Union alive and healthy. How was this to be done? One possibility, as we have seen, was to establish minimum rates that would preserve the company by handicapping its rivals in seeking competitive business. A second was to transfer Bell's TWX service to Western Union, leaving Bell with its monopoly of voice communication and giving Western Union a monopoly of message record services. This proposal was made by the staff of the FCC and by a committee of Congress. It led to protracted negotiations between the two companies which ended with Bell's agreement to the transfer. This move should strengthen Western Union financially. It will deprive the consumer of the advantage of possible competition in services and in rates.

A third possibility was to improve Western Union's personal message service. Most or all of the company's remaining offices could be closed. Windows for the receipt of telegrams could be opened in post offices. Telegrams could be delivered by the postal special delivery service. A mailgram service could be introduced, with messages forwarded overnight for delivery with the morning's mail. Service could be speeded and rates cut. All of this is conceivable, but whether it would happen within the context of post office operations, as described in Chapter 23, is open to debate.

CHANGING TECHNOLOGY AND EMERGING COMPETITION

In the past decade, a revolution in technology has shaken the communications industries. Changes have been rapid and sweeping. Broad new channels of communication have been opened by massive research and development. The coaxial cable, once carrying 5,000 messages at a time, now carries 30,000. Microwave circuits, too, are multiplying by many fold the number of channels available. Communications satellites are being equipped with capacities in the range of 5,000 to 10,000 voice circuits. Where formerly voice and record communications were separate, it is now possible to put them both on the same circuit, switching at will from one to the other. Computers are now able to store information, retrieve it, and transmit it over high capacity circuits for business and general use. Electronic developments are creating new solid-state circuits. The laser device, producing an intense highly directional beam of light, has been proved capable of carrying vast amounts of information. In the millimeter waveguide pipe, as many as 250,000 circuits are feasible. These and other innovations still to come promise to change the traditional structure of the communications industries and to alter the pattern of government regulation of these industries in ways that are as yet unforeseen.

Communications Satellites

The radio signals that carry television programs from networks to broadcasters travel for limited distances before they lose power. To reach distant broadcasters, they must be intercepted, amplified, and passed on. For overland transmission, this function has been performed, through a system of relay stations, by A.T.&T. Until the sixties, however, overseas transmission was impossible. Then it was accomplished through the development of the communications satellite. Placed in orbit by rocket, the satellite serves as a relay station to receive, amplify, and forward not only TV programs but also telephonic, telegraphic, and other forms of instantaneous communications, their signals being put into the air from ground stations on one side of the ocean and picked up by stations on the other. The first of these satellites, developed by A.T.&T., was launched from Cape Kennedy in 1962. By 1969, there were seven in orbit, three over the Atlantic, three over the Pacific, and one over the Indian Ocean, tied in with 40 ground stations in 25 countries. Monstrous new satellites, planned for 1971, will multiply the capacity of the system by five.

With transmission of communications by satellite an accomplished fact, the question arose as to who should own and operate them. Three possibilities were considered. (1) The system might be owned by the existing common carriers. This was rejected because it could lead to domination by A.T.&T. and discrimination against other carriers. (2) The system might be owned by a government corporation. This was rejected because it threatened to put the camel's nose of socialism under the tent of communications. (3) The system might be owned jointly by the communications companies and by other private investors and made subject to public regulation. This was the alternative—an awkward compromise—that was adopted by the Congress.

The Communications Satellite Act of 1962 provides for the creation of a new type of legal entity: a private joint venture, half of its stock owned by American and foreign communications carriers, half by private investors; 6 of its 15 directors elected by the carriers, 6 by the private investors, and 3 appointed by the President of the United States. The corporation is a common carrier, selling its services to other common carriers, American and foreign. It is granted a monopoly of this business; is expected to earn a profit and pay dividends. The corporation is regulated by the American government. The National Aeronautics and Space Agency launches its satellites. The FCC regulates its rates and prevents it from discriminating among the users of its service. The Antitrust Division forestalls monopolistic agreements among the carriers and the imposition of barriers to entry.

At the outset, the Communications Satellite Corporation (Comsat) was a highly speculative investment. But it soon became a great success. It proved to be completely reliable—more so than conventional radio or marine cables. It came to handle not only television transmission but a large part of transoceanic telephone messages and growing traffic in other fields. By 1968 it was earning a profit and its shares had tripled in value.

Proposals for the creation of a system of satellites to handle domestic communications originated in the interests of various groups in its possible use in relaying television programs. In 1966, the Ford Foundation proposed that a nonprofit corporation be created to operate a system of satellites to forward commercial TV programs for a fee and educational programs without charge. Comsat objected to this proposal, contending that its monopoly of this field covered domestic as well as transoceanic communications. It countered with the proposal that it be authorized to establish a multipurpose domestic system, handling other forms of communication along with TV programs. It offered to provide one channel without charge for demonstrations of educational TV broadcasts. Comsat threatened to supersede A.T.&T. as the principal carrier of TV shows, a development that was not acceptable to A.T.&T. The television networks, on the other hand, finding that the cost of operating a satellite system would be lower than the charge made by A.T.&T. for the use of its ground relay system, proposed that the door be opened to the creation of a number of independent systems to forward TV programs, handling noncommercial programs without charge.

These proposals raised a number of questions of policy. Should the domestic satellites be confined to a special service or should they serve a variety of purposes? Who should own and operate them? Should a single system be granted a monopoly or should several systems be created to compete? Should the operators be strictly controlled by the government? In 1969, after having considered these issues, the FCC was about to give Comsat a green light when the White House intervened, rejecting Comsat's claim to a monopoly and ruling that domestic satellite systems should be owned and operated on a competitive basis by independent companies with a minimum of government regulation. It instructed the Commission to proceed along this line. At mid-1970 the first domestic satellite system was still to be set up.

Telephone Attachments

Until 1969, the Bell system forbade its subscribers to attach to their phones, by electrical, inductive, or acoustical means, any equipment not provided by Bell, contending that such attachments might impair the quality of its service. The company thus attempted to prevent the use of one-piece Swedish handsets, of antique handsets, of Hush-a-phones that enabled users to converse without being heard by other persons in the room, and of other non-Bell devices. Such restrictions curbed the growth of independent phone systems and helped A.T.&T. to maintain its monopolies of the long-distance telephone and television transmission markets.

Bell's rule was challenged by the Carterphone Company, the manufacturer of a coupling device that plugged two-way mobile radio communications systems into subscribers' telephone lines, so that any phone could be used to communicate with radio-dispatched vehicles. A.T.&T. had put Carter out of business by harassing its customers. Carter brought suit under the antitrust laws and the court referred the question to the FCC. In 1968, the Commission outlawed Bell's attachment rule, holding it to be unreasonable and discriminatory. The telephone subscriber, said the Commission, has the right to attach any device that serves his convenience without detriment to others.

This decision made possible the use of a variety of devices, not only those that tied radio communications systems into telephone lines but also devices such as tape recorders, push-button phones, small-business switchboards, and closed-circuit TV, and devices that permit abbreviated dialing, talking by phone through speakers located anywhere in a room, switching office calls to home phones, and the like. The decision put an end to Bell's monopoly in all such fields and opened the way to competitive development.

Microwave Communications

The Federal Communications Commission's "Above 890" ruling in 1959 not only removed the barriers to the installation and operation of microwave systems for private use, but also permitted the establishment of common-carrier systems, offering their services to many users. In 1969, the Commission approved the application of Microwave Communications, Inc. to set up such a service between Chicago and St. Louis. The company proposed to provide interoffice and interplant voice and record communications in bulk, to transmit computer data, and to relay television programs. In all of this, it proposed to compete with A.T.&T. and Western Union, and to offer its services at prices well below those they had charged.

The Commission's approval of this application led to further developments in the field. MCI applied for a number of extensions, looking toward the construction of a network connecting the nation's largest cities. And these were but a few of more than 500 applications presented to the FCC. In July 1970, the Commission solicited public comments on a staff proposal that it open the business of private bulk communications to general competition. In this field, the Bell and Western Union monopolies may soon be at an end.

Computers and Communications

The uses foreseen for computers, in the years ahead, stretch the imagination. Computers, it is predicted, will soak up information from distant sources, sift it, and pump it out in the form of statistical summaries, econometric analyses, legal precedents, and medical diagnoses. They will cull libraries for bibliographical materials, assemble research data, and transmit them in microform printouts, displacing books. They will supply a steady flow of information on current events, displacing newspapers. They will keep the family's accounts, pay its bills, and do its banking, creating a cashless, checkless economy. They will serve the myriad interests of business, science, education, and government, and those of the average man. These predictions, to be sure, appear to be extravagant, but some part of them may well be realized.

Many computers will function in place; tie-ins with communications facilities will not be required. But it is believed that half of the computers in use in 1975 will have such tie-ins. Data will be assembled by the computer over wires or microwaves and transmitted to their users in the same way. A terminal on a subscriber's telephone line will connect him with distant information banks. Computer services of every kind will be delivered to their users by communications common carriers.

There is a growing industry supplying computer services; communications carriers, along with others, are entering the field. A.T.&T. is forbidden, by its consent decree, to participate in industries outside communications. It cannot compete in selling computer services, but it can, and does, provide computer operators with transmission facilities. Nearly all of the remaining carriers have gone into the data processing and banking business. And data processors, on the other hand, are entering the communications field. Western Union is drawing over a third of its revenue from data transmission. General Telephone and Electronics is building a data services network. Microwave Communications, Inc. is planning to enter the field. These and other companies look forward to becoming mass movers of information for business and government.

The ultimate structure of the computer-communications industries is unknown. Computer and communications companies may be kept separate; computer services may be rendered by communications carriers; or integrated and nonintegrated operations may both occupy the field. Whatever the pattern, there will be problems for regulation. Should government control the prices charged for computer services? The computer industry, of itself, may be effectively competitive so that regulation of its rates is not required. Should government control the prices charged for the transmission of computer data? Communications carriers tend to be monopolistic; their rates for this service, as for others, will be controlled. But what of the integrated computer-communications company that competes with the nonintegrated computer company? Will it not have an unfair competitive advantage? Might it not employ its control of communications facilities as a means of undercutting its rivals in the computer business? And, if so, how is this to be prevented? Should government forbid the entry of communications carriers into data processing? Or should it permit such combinations but regulate combined computer-communications rates? Or should it attempt to separate the two services, determining the costs and fixing the rates of each? Should government assume responsibility for the quality of computer service as well as that of communications service? Should it undertake, for instance, to insure the privacy and the security of the information that is stored?

So far, the position taken by the Antitrust Division and the FCC on these issues has been that data processing services, of themselves, should not be regulated as common carriers; that communications companies should not themselves offer such services, but should be permitted to set up arm's length subsidiaries to do so; and that combined services whose primary purpose is communications should be subject to control. But the industry is still in its infancy, and this cannot be taken as the final word.

FUTURE COMMUNICATIONS POLICY

The rates and services of communications common carriers were first subjected to regulation because they enjoyed monopolies of essential services. This is still the case with personal two-way voice communication, both local and long distance. Here, monopoly is to be preferred because of its greater convenience and lower cost. The level and the structure of its rates must therefore be subjected to control. But it does not follow that monopoly should be extended to other communications services. In the provision, for instance, of record communications and data transmission, the relaying of television programs, and so on, innovations in technology have opened the way to competition. Here, public policy has alternatives. It can undertake to protect existing enterprises by barring entry and establishing minimum rates, as it has done in the case of transport. Or it can rely upon competitive forces as its means of control. If the unhappy lesson of transport regulation has been learned, it will adopt the latter course.

Chapter 19 | REGULATION OF BROADCASTING

It was the need for allocation of scarce airspace among competing claimants that forced the government to regulate broadcasting. And it was the need to grant or to refuse licenses for this purpose that compelled the regulators to make a series of decisions establishing policies to govern broadcasting. Were licenses to be granted for a few powerful stations in urban centers or for many weaker stations in smaller communities? Were they to be granted for broadcasts embodying new technologies: for frequency modulation as well as amplitude modulation, for television as well as radio, for color as well as black and white? Were licenses to broadcast to be granted to owners of other communications media? Were they to be concentrated in the hands of a few concerns or scattered among many? What were to be the contractual relations between the networks and their affiliated stations? How was airspace to be divided between educational broadcasting and commercial broadcasting? How were the interests of regional, ethnic, and cultural minorities to be served? How was freedom of the air to be assured and its abuse controlled? How was the broadcasting of obscenity, of lotteries, and of violence to be prevented without resort to censorship? How, if at all, were excesses of advertising to be kept within bounds? Under what circumstances were license renewals to be denied or licenses revoked? These questions, and others, were not anticipated, were not thought through in advance. Instead, they were thrust upon the regulators by the pressure of events. And they have been answered reluctantly and tardily. It is with such questions and their answers that the present chapter is concerned.

BACKGROUND OF REGULATION

Communication by radio dates from the discoveries of Guglielmo Marconi in Italy around the turn of the century and from subsequent developments by Ambrose Fleming in England and by Lee De Forest and E. H. Armstrong, among others, in the United States. The first public broadcast in this country, using the method of amplitude modulation, occurred in 1920 when Westinghouse station KDKA in Pittsburgh announced the election of Warren G. Harding. Other stations were soon established by Westinghouse, General Electric, and A.T.&T. It was assumed, at this time, that broadcasting was to be financed by manufacturers of receiving sets and, perhaps, by educational institutions and city governments. Then, in 1922, commercial broadcasting was inaugurated by the A.T.&T. station, WEAF in New York, and radio shortly became an advertising medium. The first network was set up by A.T.&T. in 1923. Then, following an agreement with GE, Westinghouse, and their patent-holding company, RCA, in 1926, A.T.&T. withdrew from the field, its network being taken over by an RCA subsidiary, the National Broadcasting Company. The Columbia Broadcasting System was set up in the following year. Network domination of the broadcasting business dates from this time. Frequency modulation broadcasting, on a commercial basis, was authorized in 1940, television in 1941, and color television in 1951. The business has grown phenomenally. There were 7,500 broadcasting stations in the United States in 1969 and receiving sets in more than 60 million homes. Radio and television programs were reaching almost all of the country's population.

Beginnings of Control

Regulation was first applied to broadcasting under the authority of an act passed in 1912 which was designed to control the use of air waves in telegraphy and telephony. Under this law, persons transmitting radio messages were required to obtain licenses from the Secretary of Commerce, and operation without a license was made a misdemeanor. As the law was worded, it was not clear whether the Secretary had the power to refuse licenses or was obliged to grant them to all who might apply. But Herbert Hoover, when Secretary, sought to employ this authority to control the number of licensees. He called a conference of broadcasters and negotiated an allocation of frequencies. Under this allocation, the Zenith Radio Corporation of Chicago was put on the same frequency as General Electric and limited to two hours of broadcasting per week. Zenith jumped to another channel, and Hoover brought suit to enjoin it from broadcasting. The court decided for the company in 1926, and Hoover appealed to the Attorney General for a ruling as to his powers. The Attorney General replied that the Secretary had no authority, under the Act of 1912, to withhold licenses or to designate frequencies, prescribe hours of operation, or limit station power. Hoover therefore abandoned his attempt to regulate the industry. The result was pandemonium. Within the next few months, some 200 new stations went on the air, each of them using any frequency it chose. Interference was general, and the usefulness of radio as a medium of communication was virtually destroyed. In desperation, the industry turned to the government, demanding public action to bring order out of chaos in the air.

The Radio Act of 1927 forbade broadcasting without a license, set up a Federal Radio Commission to pass on applications for licenses, and authorized it to assign wave lengths, fix hours of operation, and control station power. Licenses were to be granted only where the Commission found that this would serve the "public interest, convenience, or necessity." They were limited to three years and were subject to revocation. The Commission thus held the power of life and death over every station in the industry. But this power was not exercised with a firm hand. By 1927 the commercial interests were thoroughly entrenched. The broadcasting business had become an advertising medium, and the organization of programs had been taken over by the network companies. The Commission did not attempt to alter the established pattern of control. It gave the best channels, the best hours, and the highest power to the commercial interests, assigning poor channels, off hours, and lower power for educational broadcasting. It did little or nothing to improve or maintain the quality of broadcast services or to protect the broadcasting privilege against abuse. The Commission's timidity is to be explained, in part, by the fact that its appropriations were small and its tenure uncertain. Its authority was granted by Congress, in 1927, 1928, and 1929, for a year at a time, and was not made permanent until 1930. The agency was abolished when its functions were taken over by the Federal Communications Commission under the Communications Act of 1934.

Broadcasting under the Communications Act

The sections of the Communications Act dealing with radio and television follow the pattern established by the Radio Act of 1927. The law requires broadcasters to obtain licenses from the FCC and authorizes the Commission to classify stations, prescribe their services, assign their frequencies, determine their locations, and fix their power. It instructs the Commission to bring about an efficient and equitable distribution of radio services among states and communities. Licenses cannot be granted to aliens, to foreign corporations, to domestic corporations controlled by foreigners, to representatives of foreign governments, or to persons found guilty of violating the antitrust laws. The Commission is empowered to inquire into the technical, financial, and moral responsibility of other applicants, the quality of their broadcasting apparatus, the qualifications of their technical personnel, and the value of their services to listeners. The standard governing the issuance of licenses is still that of "public interest, convenience, or necessity." It is the stated purpose of the Act to provide for the use of radio channels by private enterprises "but not the ownership thereof." Licenses cannot be transferred or assigned without Commission approval. They are limited, as before, to three years and may be renewed, modified, or revoked. The broadcasting of lotteries and of obscene, indecent, or profane language is prohibited, and a station that provides time to one candidate for public office is required to afford equal opportunities to rival candidates. But the Commission is forbidden to censor programs or to interfere with the right of free speech.

The Commission has occupied itself, in the main, with the problem of allocating air space and with the difficult issues of policy which this involves. It has granted and renewed licenses and approved transfers of broadcasting properties. It has policed the air to apprehend illegal operators and enjoin their activities. But it has shown great reluctance to interfere with broadcasting operations, rarely employing its power to deny renewal of licenses. Despite its moderation, however, the FCC has been a center of violent controversy. The commercial interests in radio and TV are not harmonious. Whatever the issue before the Commission and whatever its decision, someone is certain to be dissatisfied. As a result, the agency has constantly been subject to attack.

Interests in Broadcasting

The groups with a stake in broadcasting are many and diverse. They may be identified as follows:

1. The broadcasting stations. Among some 7,500 broadcasting stations in the United States, there are more than 6,600 radio stations (4,200 of them AM and 2,400 FM) and 800 television stations, around 7,000 of the total commercial and 500 noncommercial. A few of these stations are owned by the networks, but 99 percent are independent. The typical radio station is a small-scale business. It may have a gross income of less than $200,000 a year. A television station is a larger enterprise, requiring an initial investment of $2 million or more. It obtains its revenue, in part, by selling time to advertisers, in larger part, by selling it to networks. The business is highly profitable. In 1960, the four stations in the San Francisco Bay area made 220 percent on the depreciated value of their investment.[1] The broadcaster's most valuable asset is his license, giving him an exclusive right to a portion of the air, which he gets as a present from the government. Stations are bought and sold at figures far in excess of their physical worth, the difference being a capitalization of their monopoly rights. In 1958 the Columbia Broadcasting System bought station WCAU from the Philadelphia *Evening Bulletin* for $20,000,000. Of this, it paid $4,400,000 for the station's physical assets, $3,000,000 for its AM and FM licenses, and $12,600,000 for its TV license.[2] Substantial gains are realized in such transactions, and vested interests are established, making it almost certain that licenses, once granted, will always be renewed.

2. The networks. There are a number of national and regional networks in radio, three national networks in television. These concerns operate 19 radio and 15 TV stations and have contractual relations with more than half of the independent radio stations and nearly all of the TV stations. They buy time from these stations in retail lots and sell it to advertisers at wholesale. They provide commercial and sustaining programs to their affiliates. At one time, they originated half of the material broadcast by radio. With the coming of TV, local radio stations came increasingly to fill their programs with recorded music. But now the networks are responsible for half of the material broadcast over TV and nine tenths of that broadcast during the prime evening hours. These enterprises, too, are highly profitable. In 1967, the three TV networks and their own stations made a profit of $160 million. Their net income, after federal taxes, was 56.5 percent of the value of their investment in tangible property.[3]

1 / Newton N. Minow, *Equal Time* (New York: Atheneum, 1964), p. 125.

2 / *New York Times*, July 24, 1958.

3 / Federal Communications Commission, *Annual Report, 1968*, pp. 121, 126.

3. The advertisers. These are the merchants and the manufacturers who buy time on local stations and on national networks to sell their wares. In some cases, they merely pay for spot announcements. In others, they finance elaborate shows. In 1968, advertisers spent over $3 billion on television. Paying the piper, they were able to call the tune.

4. The advertising agencies. These are the concerns that plan the national advertising campaigns, dream up the slogans, and compose the commercials. In the heyday of radio, they produced nearly all of the network shows, arranged to put them on the air, and sold them to the advertisers. With television, time became so costly that few advertisers could afford to purchase an entire show. Now the agencies buy minutes of time on the networks for their clients as they buy inches of space for them in magazines, selecting among the programs that the networks make available.

5. The program producers. The networks themselves produce all of the public affairs and sports programs and a fifth of the prime-time entertainment programs. They buy four fifths of the latter programs from independent producers: from motion picture companies and TV program packagers. The typical television series is a joint product, its formula being threshed out by the producer, the advertising agency, the network, and the sponsor.

6. The rating services. These enterprises undertake to determine, through sampling techniques, how many sets are tuned in to what programs at particular times. Their ratings are taken as revealing the size of the audience that the networks have for sale. They thus determine the rates that can be charged for time. The program that gets a high rating stays on the air; the program that gets a lower one is dropped.

A number of other groups have a financial interest in commercial broadcasting: (7) the amusement industry, including the performers, the agents who represent them, the associations that collect royalties for the owners of music copyrights, and the unions of musicians, actors, and technical personnel; (8) the concerns that relay TV programs: A.T.&T., Comsat, and domestic satellites still to come; (9) cable television companies that offer increasing competition to conventional TV; (10) the manufacturers and (11) the distributors of receiving sets, with money tied up in inventories embodying an earlier technology; (12) the repair men, small-scale operators for whose services the consumer pays many millions of dollars a year, some of them making repairs when none are needed and charging more for their work than it is worth. There are also noncommercial interests in broadcasting: (13) educational and public service broadcasters and (14) the philanthropic foundations that contribute to their support.

15. And finally, the listener and the looker. There are radio sets in 99.7 percent of American homes, television sets in 98.5 percent, color television sets in 35.7 percent, and other receivers in tens of millions of automobiles and in millions of public places. The average television receiver is in use six hours a day. Watching it is the forgotten man, woman, and child of commercial TV. The station, the network, the sponsor, the advertising agency, and the program producer try to give him what they think he wants. But the government gives

him little thought. Supposedly, he gets his entertainment free. Actually, he does not. His investment in television receivers amounts to more than $20 billion. His expenditure on electricity runs to $3 billion a year. His total bill for services and repairs is unknown. His financial stake in broadcasting is many times as large as that of all the other groups combined. And he pays for his programs when he buys the goods they advertise. But the other groups are organized to exert political pressure and the listener-looker is not. As a result, the government serves their interests more than his.

ALLOCATION OF AIRSPACE

Some air channels are reserved by the government for its own use, mostly for national defense. All of the channels remaining are allocated by the FCC. In assigning frequencies to different applicants, the Commission must consider the relative importance of various purposes: safety at sea and in the air, police and disaster operations, dispatching of trucks and taxis, telephonic connection with trains and ships and with subscribers in remote areas, communication by ranchers and foresters, and chatter by amateurs, as well as educational and commercial broadcasting. All of these require consideration, and their respective claims must be weighed, one against the other, in granting exclusive rights to the use of channels in the air. In practice, less than a tenth of the channels are assigned for purposes other than broadcasting, the great bulk of them being allocated to radio and TV.

The AM Allocation

Radio and television broadcasts are carried by electromagnetic waves emitted from an electric circuit in which the magnitude of the current is constantly being changed. The frequency of the waves depends upon the frequency of the oscillations employed, slow oscillations producing long waves with low frequencies, rapid oscillations producing short waves with high frequencies. The frequencies are measured in waves per second, the units of measurement used being kilocycles (thousands of cycles) and megacycles (millions of cycles). The spectrum available for practical use extends from the low frequencies where broadcasts are disturbed by static to the high frequencies where physical limitations make broadcasting increasingly difficult. The standard AM broadcast band has been assigned to the middle frequencies between 550 and 1,600 kilocycles per second. To avoid interference in such broadcasting, it is necessary to give each channel a width of ten kilocycles. There is thus room for 106 channels in the standard band. The number of stations that may occupy these channels depends upon the hours during which they may broadcast and the amount of power they may use. With the hours and the power originally permitted, there was room for some 3,000 AM stations in the United States. The number of applicants for AM licenses was many times this figure. The FCC, therefore, had to pick and choose. And since licenses were costless and profitable, its task was that of giving valuable prizes to a few and denying opportunity to many more. The Commission's problem was the same, as we shall see, when it undertook to allocate space in the higher frequencies for FM and TV.

One question that had to be answered in making the AM allocation was that of station power. At stake here were the issues of monopoly versus competition in broadcasting, availability of service to listeners in different regions, availability of the medium for local uses, and cultural standardization versus cultural diversity. It was the intention of Congress that the industry should be competitive and that every region in the country should be served. But these objectives were in conflict. If the power permitted were low, the number of stations could be large, but listeners in remote and sparsely settled regions would not be reached by broadcasts. If the power were high, every region could be reached, but the number of stations would be small. Broadcasting, moreover, would tend to be concentrated in a few large cities. Matters of state and local interest would not get on the air. Broadcasts would be devoted primarily to making sales in mass markets. Programs would not be designed to meet the needs of rural listeners. Everything would be cast in the standard mold of Broadway and Hollywood.

The Commission might have escaped this dilemma by giving high power in some channels and low power in others. From 1934 to 1939, in fact, it did permit WLW in Cincinnati to broadcast experimentally at 500 kilowatts. But it was felt that high-power stations would be given an unfair advantage over their low-power competitors. So, in 1939, the permission was withdrawn. Under the regulations adopted, stations were divided into three classes, local, regional, and clear channel, the local stations being assigned as much as 250 watts, the regional stations from 1 to 5 kilowatts, and the clear channel stations from 10 to 50 kilowatts, some 60 of them operating at the higher power. On this basis, too, the opportunities for earnings were unequal. And regional diversity was not really protected, since the development of network broadcasting insured the uniformity that low power was intended to prevent.

Similar issues were encountered in fixing broadcast hours. A radio transmitter emits waves that behave in two different ways: ground waves that travel near the surface of the earth and sky waves that go off into the air. At night, the sky waves are reflected back to earth by the ionosphere. As a result, an AM channel can be used by several stations without interference during the day but not at night. If all stations were permitted to operate around the clock, rural areas would not get clear reception after dark. But if this privilege were given to some stations and not to others, the former would be favored and the latter handicapped. Here, there was a compromise. By international agreement, certain channels were reserved for the exclusive use of single stations at night and other stations assigned to these channels were confined to daytime hours. Reception in rural areas was thus given some protection. But the clear-channel stations were limited in power. They were located, moreover, in major cities, and their programs were designed to appeal to an urban audience. As a result, there were still some parts of the country in which reception was lacking or inadequate and many others in which local interests were not served.

The FM Allocation

In AM broadcasting, sound is transmitted by varying the amplitude of the carrier wave. With frequency modulation, the amplitude of the wave is kept the same and its frequency varied. The band allotted to FM broadcasting is in the higher frequencies between 88 and 108 megacycles per second. Since each FM channel requires a width of 400 kilocycles, there is room in this band for 50 channels, as compared with the 106 available for AM. But high-frequency waves, instead of traveling along the ground, pass off into space. With such waves, also, the elimination of static requires less power. As a result, stations can be located closer together without interference, and more stations can share the same channel. Thus, with 50 channels, it should be possible to have 2,000 stations broadcasting on FM. The introduction of FM, therefore, was expected substantially to increase the number of stations, providing more opportunities for local interests, and making the industry more competitive. Reception of FM, moreover, is superior to that of AM, since it does not fade, is beyond the reach of most static, and is relatively free from interference.

Commission approval of FM broadcasting was opposed by the owners of existing AM stations. Approval was given, however, in 1940. But despite the superiority of FM reception, the expected growth of this method of broadcasting did not occur. Listeners who had already invested in AM receivers were reluctant to convert. And new buyers found that AM sets were cheaper than FM sets. As a result, the AM stations held the mass audience and the national advertising business, while the independent FM stations reached fewer listeners and obtained less revenue by selling time. The number of FM stations broadcasting commercially reached 737 in 1949 but fell to 530 in 1956. From this low point, FM recovered, reaching more than 2,400 stations by 1970. Some FM stations (a minority of the total) devote themselves to the broadcasting of good music, some of it live, most of it recorded. Since 1961, moreover, they have improved the quality of their reproduction by broadcasting stereophonically. But the great majority of FM stations is operated by AM broadcasters and has been employed for simultaneous transmission of their AM programs, consisting largely of music that appeals to the jukebox trade. The FCC took the position that this practice wasted scarce airspace. It therefore ruled that, beginning in 1967, the owners of AM stations in cities of more than 100,000 population would not be permitted to duplicate more than half of their programs on their FM affiliates.

The TV Allocation

The space originally allotted for television by the FCC fell in the very high frequency band between 54 and 216 megacycles per second. This space overlapped that assigned to FM broadcasts, leaving 12 channels of the width required for TV. There were 37 stations operating in these channels in 1948 and 71 others under construction, a total of 108. Stations were already encountering interference, and the demand for further space was far in excess of the supply. It appeared to be possible, however, to increase the number of channels available by making use of the ultra high frequencies (UHF). But before this could be done, it was necessary to determine the feasibility of UHF broadcasting and to fix the width of channels, the distance between stations, and the amount of power to be used. At the same time, it was desirable to reconsider the allocation of very high frequency (VHF) space to TV. The Commission therefore imposed a freeze on TV, granting no more construction permits and no new licenses. A new allocation was worked out during the next three years, and the freeze was lifted in the spring of 1952.

The TV allocation retained the 12 channels in the VHF band and created 70 new channels, each 6,000 kilocycles wide, located between 470 and 890 megacycles in the UHF band, making 82 channels in all. The distance required between stations differed for different geographic zones, running from 170 to 220 miles for VHF and from 155 to 205 miles for UHF. The power permitted on different VHF channels ran from 100 to 316 kilowatts; that permitted UHF stations was 1,000 kilowatts. On this basis, there was room for 2,051 television stations in 1,275 different communities, 619 of them on VHF and 1,432 on UHF. When the freeze was lifted, there was a land rush of applicants for licenses. The Commission established a system of priorities to govern its consideration of applications, giving first priority to cities more than 40 miles from an existing station and considering these in order of population. In the next 18 months, it authorized 453 new stations, 178 in the VHF band and 275 in the UHF band.

The new allocation, however, did not work out as was expected. The UHF stations ran into the same difficulty as was first encountered by FM. Nearly all of the television receivers in use were built for VHF. Of the new sets produced, moreover, most were equipped for VHF alone and few for both VHF and UHF. If the owners of VHF sets were to receive UHF broadcasts, they had to invest in converters, additional antennas, etc., and this was an investment that few were willing to make. The UHF stations were thus caught in a vicious circle: lacking an audience, they could not obtain large advertising revenues; lacking revenues, they could not finance popular programs; lacking such programs, they could not attract an audience. As a result, the stations were forced to fight an uphill battle for survival. Some of them surrendered their licenses. There were many applicants for the few spots still available in VHF, few for the many available in UHF.

This development could have been avoided in a number of different ways: (1) All television stations could have been moved into the UHF band. But this would have rendered most TV sets obsolete and would therefore have been highly unpopular. (2) Some cities could have been assigned exclusively to VHF and others to UHF, instead of putting most of them on both. But this would have favored the owners of sets in the former cities and penalized those in the latter. (3) The power of VHF stations could have been reduced and that of UHF stations increased. But this, too, would have involved discrimination, favoring those closer to VHF stations and penalizing those farther away. The FCC chose the method that would arouse the least objection at the time.

In the years after the television allocation, the pressure to obtain TV licenses increased. This pressure resulted from the scarcity of possible assignments. But the scarcity was artificial: beside the 12 VHF channels for which the applicants were contending, the 70 UHF channels lay virtually unused. It became increasingly apparent that something had to be done. In 1962, upon the recommendation of the FCC, Congress amended the Federal Communications Act to require that all television sets manufactured after April, 1964, be equipped to pick up Channels 2 to 83. The short-run effect of this requirement was small. As long as people continued using sets that could be tuned only to Channels 2 to 13, applications for licenses in the 70 UHF channels were few. At present, however, half of the sets in use are equipped to receive UHF. In time, as new sets are purchased and obsolete sets replaced, the audience on UHF will grow and the number of TV stations will be steadily increased.

CONTROL OF TECHNOLOGY

The FCC has one responsibility that makes its position unique among regulatory agencies: it controls the rate of technical change. The introduction of each new development in broadcasting depends upon the willingness of the Commission to approve the facilities to be employed, to provide a channel for experimental use, and eventually to assign channels for general broadcasting. This responsibility is inescapable: control of access to the air involves control of the purposes for which it is used. But the responsibility is a difficult one to discharge. Approval of innovations may render existing equipment obsolete. It may commit the industry prematurely to inferior techniques. Refusal to approve, on the other hand, is bound to give rise to charges of bureaucratic obstructiveness. Here, as elsewhere, the Commission is sure to be damned if it does and damned if it doesn't.

Introduction of FM and TV

The Commission first had to face the problem of innovation when it approved FM broadcasting. Its AM licensees opposed its action on the ground that large sums had been invested in AM transmitters and receivers whose usefulness would be destroyed. But FM was found to have great technical advantages, and channels were provided for its use.

The problem was raised again by the introduction of TV. Here, the Commission had to decide whether to establish standards for equipment, requiring all broadcasters to conform, or to permit different companies to develop and use facilities of different types. The Commission refused to standardize, fearing to freeze a changing art. It encouraged experimentation, but delayed commercial broadcasting. This, though unpopular, was wise. The relation of receiver and transmitter is that of lock and key. If receivers embodying a particular method of telecasting had been widely sold, the development of other methods might have been foreclosed. The Commission, in seeking to promote improvement of the art, might have found itself presented with a *fait accompli.* So the allocation of channels for commercial broadcasts was postponed. At the same time, the materials that would have been required for television were made unavailable by World War II. By the time the war had ended and commercial telecasting was approved, the research that was basic to its development had been done. The Commission thus gained the advantage of delay without being forced to bear the blame. The Commission's control of technology did not involve it in serious conflict until it was forced to choose between rival systems of introducing color into TV.

Introduction of Color

In 1950 CBS had developed a method of broadcasting in color, known as a field sequential system, involving the use of a spinning, synchronized disc attached to the television receiver and alternately flashing green, red, and blue, which the viewer's brain translated into colored pictures. At the same time, RCA was working on a dot sequential system in which the pictures were formed, as they are in color printing, by a multitude of colored dots. The CBS system was incompatible, i.e., broadcasts in color by this method could not be received on existing sets in black and white. The RCA system would be compatible; broadcasts could be received in black and white. CBS applied for permission to use its system in initiating color telecasts. Its application was opposed by RCA, by NBC, and by most of the other interests in the industry.

Against approval of the application, it was argued that receiving sets in the hands of consumers and those in the stocks of merchants and manufacturers would be made obsolete, and that the industry would be committed, by hasty action, to an inferior method of color broadcasting. In support of the application, it was urged that pictures, being available in color, should be enjoyed without delay. In October, 1950, after 62 days of hearings, 10,000 pages of testimony, and 265 exhibits, the Commission gave its approval for broadcasts in color by CBS. Thereupon, a suit for an injunction was brought by RCA. In May, 1951, the Commission was upheld by the Supreme Court, Mr. Justice Black asserting that its action was not capricious and that the Court would not reverse it on the ground that it might have been unwise.[4] The right of CBS to go ahead was clear. In October, 1951, however, the Office of Defense Mobilization requested the company to postpone development of color on the ground that the materials involved were needed in the Korean War. The company complied.

The television industry took advantage of the respite thus provided to set up a national committee that represented all the interests involved. This body undertook to perfect a method of color casting that would be fully compatible. Its final product, based on the dot sequential system originated by RCA, was

4 / *RCA* v. *U.S.,* 341 U.S. 412.

presented to the Commission for approval. In December, 1953, the Commission reversed itself, accepting the system for general use. It offered to hold hearings on this decision if there were any objection, but CBS did not object. A superior technique was finally adopted. But it was not the one that the Commission first approved.

COMPETITION AND MONOPOLY

It was the policy of Congress, when it passed the Communications Act, to favor competition in radio. This policy was designed to afford opportunities for small business, to deny monopoly profits to licensees, to provide service for all states and communities, and to prevent concentrated control of an important medium of communication. The issue of competition versus monopoly has repeatedly been presented to the FCC. It was raised when the Commission decided whether to permit stations to be controlled by owners of competing media—radio stations by newspapers and television stations by motion picture producers or exhibitors—when it determined the number, power, and control of AM stations, when it considered applications for joint control of AM and FM stations and of radio and TV, and when it examined the relationship of the stations and the networks. It is to these decisions that we now turn.

Competition between Media

In communication, as also in transport, the question arises as to whether different media should be required to compete with one another or be permitted to combine. This issue first presented itself to the FCC in connection with applications for broadcasting licenses and purchases of stations by owners of newspapers. Radio and newspapers compete, of course, both in the dissemination of news and in the sale of advertising services. It was, therefore, feared that newspaper ownership of broadcasting facilities might result in the suppression of competition and the creation of local monopolies. The Commission made a study of this problem between 1941 and 1944 and finally decided to issue no general rule. In practice, it has tended to favor other applicants where there is only one newspaper in a town. But it has not refused a license to a newspaper where it faces competition, or even where it possesses a monopoly, if it is the only applicant. Nor has the Commission sought to prevent newspapers from purchasing broadcasting properties. As a consequence, each of 256 newspapers owns a broadcasting station in the same city, a newspaper owns the only radio station in each of 68 cities, and the only television station in 11.[5]

A similar problem is created by the competition of television with motion picture producers and exhibitors in the entertainment business. The movie interests have substantial investments in production and exhibition facilities. If permitted to control TV, they might seek to protect themselves by retarding the development of their competitor. In 1952 the Commission was asked to

5 / *Business Week*, April 4, 1970.

approve a merger of the American Broadcasting Company with Paramount Theaters. Both companies had resulted from dissolutions in antitrust cases: ABC had separated from NBC and Paramount Theaters from Paramount Pictures. But the Commission gave its approval, in the hope that the combination would create a stronger competitor for NBC and CBS. In 1967, however, acquisition of ABC by International Telephone and Telegraph, designed to diversify I.T.&T. securities holdings and to strengthen ABC's competitive position in broadcasting, after first having been approved by FCC, was subsequently forbidden when the Antitrust Division threatened suit. There was danger, said the Division, that I.T.&T. would use its financial leverage to force ABC to carry advertising for its other subsidiaries, and that its foreign interests would affect the way that ABC would treat the news.

Competition among Stations

The Commission has generally sought to maximize the number of broadcasting stations. Wherever possible, it has granted two or more licenses in each community. In doing so, it has been upheld by the Supreme Court. In the Sanders case,[6] where a station had contested the granting of a second license in a city, the Court held, in 1940, that radio was not a public utility, that control of entry was not designed to protect licensees against competition, and that the Commission, in granting a license, was not required to consider the effect of its action upon competitors.

The Commission has also sought to prevent concentration in station ownership. It has limited the number of stations, wherever located, that it would license to a single broadcaster. It has refused to grant more than one license to a single licensee in the same service (AM, FM, or TV) in the same community. And in 1970 it adopted a rule forbidding broadcasters, in the future, to acquire more than one outlet, whatever the service, in one community, and proposed a rule requiring owners of more than one medium in a market to reduce their holdings to one of them within a year. The FCC, however, has not followed the policy of enforcing competition between different types of broadcasting. It was assumed, at one time, that FM licenses would go to large numbers of independent operators. But the Commission eventually yielded to pressure from AM stations, granting more than 90 percent of the FM licenses to such concerns. So, too, with television: the capital and the enterprise for TV broadcasts came from the radio industry, and the TV licenses were granted, in the main, to radio licensees. Despite the Commission's nominal allegiance to competition, broadcast facilities have come to be concentrated increasingly in the hands of multiple owners and cross-channel empires.

The Networks in Radio

Before the advent of TV, half of the radio stations in the United States were

6 / *FCC* v. *Sanders Bros. Radio Stations,* 309 U.S. 470 (1940).

owned by or affiliated with one of the national networks, which provided them with programs that took up half of their time. The FCC had no jurisdiction over the networks as such, but it could influence them indirectly through its power to control the stations they owned and those they served. Following complaints from broadcasters, the Commission launched an investigation of network practices in 1938 and issued a report revealing various abuses in 1941.

The contracts which controlled the relationship between the major networks and their outlets contained provisions which worked to the detriment of competing networks and station operators. They ran for 5 or 10 years and might be renewed by the networks—but not by the stations—on 30 days' notice. The network typically took an option on the station's time, obtaining the right to make use of preferred hours for broadcasting. On 28 days' notice it might require the station to sell it any one of the contracted hours, even though this forced the operator to cancel an arrangement with a local customer, thus running the risk of losing his patronage. The usual contract forbade a station to accept a program from another network, thus denying it the right to obtain profitable business and preventing new networks from getting a foothold in the industry. It also forbade the station to accept programs from national advertisers for local broadcasting at rates below those which the network charged for the station's time, thus preventing it from competing for national advertising. These provisions were found by the Commission to stifle competition and to make the station a servant of the network rather than an instrument for serving the public interest.[7]

The Commission acted to correct these abuses, issuing rules to govern the relationship of networks and stations under its power to grant or withhold station licenses. The new rules limited network contracts to two years. They modified the option clauses, increasing the length of notice required and giving stations greater freedom to reject network programs. They outlawed the exclusive affiliation clause, enabling other stations to obtain network programs. They forbade the networks to control the rates charged by their affiliates in competing for advertising business.

The new rules were welcomed by independent broadcasters; they were vigorously resisted by NBC and CBS. In hearings before a committee of the Senate, the companies argued that the rules would cripple if not paralyze broadcasting, threaten the very existence of networks, create anarchy in the air, and encourage the government to socialize the industry. In a suit brought to enjoin enforcement of the rules, they contended that the Commission had exceeded its authority, acted arbitrarily and capriciously, and taken their property without due process of law. This position was rejected by the Congress and the Courts, the Commission's contract regulations being upheld by the Supreme Court in 1943.[8] As a result of these developments, the position of the affiliated stations was substantially improved. But NBC and CBS retained their dominance. Their prophecies of doom were not fulfilled.

7 / See FCC, *Report on Chain Broadcasting*, 1941.
8 / *National Broadcasting Co.* v. *U.S.*, 319 U.S. 190.

The Networks in TV

The networks dominate television as they once dominated radio. They have their own TV stations in the major cities. They have affiliation contracts with most of the other stations in the country. They provide most of the program material. They make three fourths of the sales of advertising time. The networks' power to grant or withhold affiliation gives them an upper hand in bargaining with station owners, and a marked advantage over independent producers of programs and sellers of time. The networks still are not subject to direct control by the FCC.

Network broadcasting was the subject, during the fifties, of a thoroughgoing report by a study staff set up by the FCC. Attention was centered on two practices: option time and "must buy." The option time provisions in the networks' contracts with their affiliates, in conformity with the rules adopted in 1941, enabled them, by giving 56 days' notice, to displace other programs and advertisers during any three of the five hours in the morning, the afternoon, and the evening, and the nine hours at night. The very risk of such displacement, the investigators found, discouraged advertisers from buying time through station representatives rather than networks, and deprived independent producers of a potential market for their services. The "must buy" requirement was imposed on advertisers by two of the networks: NBC and CBS. Under this arrangement, the networks refused to permit an advertiser to select the stations that would carry his program, but insisted on selling the time of 50 or more stations as a group. This compelled the advertiser to buy time in markets where he might not be selling, and to use a network affiliate in cities where he might have preferred to use another network or an independent competitor. By preventing stations, advertisers, and producers from dealing directly with one another, these practices concentrated control in the networks and obstructed independent entry to the field.

To these criticisms, the networks replied that their business practices were needed to maintain the high quality of their programming. Option time was needed, they said, to enable them to deliver an assured audience to the advertiser. "Must buy" was needed to enable them to collect sufficient revenue to cover their costs. Outlawry of these practices would deprive the public of the programs it preferred. If the networks were indeed giving the public what it preferred, however, one might well ask why restrictive arrangements were required. In this case, it might be assumed, stations would carry the network programs without being compelled to do so by the enforcement of options, and advertisers would purchase network time without being compelled to do so by "must buy."

The Network Study Staff, in its report to the FCC, recommended that "must buy" be prohibited and that option time be abolished. Under this pressure, NBC and CBS dropped their "must buy" requirements but made no change in option time. In 1960, the FCC, holding option time to be essential to successful network operation, issued an order reducing the number of hours that could be optioned, in any segment of the day, from three to two and a half, thus giving local stations a bit more freedom in the selection of programs. In 1963, after the Commission's membership had been changed, it voted 6 to 1 to abolish option time.

In 1970, the FCC took another step that was designed to lessen network dominance. It adopted a rule, to take effect in the fall of 1971, requiring TV stations in the country's 50 top markets to fill at least one of their four nightly prime-time hours with nonnetwork material, leaving the nets with only three fourths of their former market. It was not likely that such a change would improve program quality, but it would open the way to independent program production and time sales, thus making the industry more competitive.

Investigators of the network problem have frequently recommended that the FCC be empowered to regulate network practices by applying its rules, not indirectly through the stations, but directly to the nets. A number of bills conferring this power have been introduced in Congress, but none of them has passed.

POLICY AND PRACTICE IN LICENSING

The Federal Communications Commission has it within its power to confer upon selected persons, as a gift, monopoly rights in the use of the air. These rights are worth hundreds of thousands—in some cases millions—of dollars. As matters stand, the demand for them exceeds the supply. In distributing its prizes, the Commission must find some way to pick and choose. Here, Congress has given it little help. The Communications Act merely requires that applications "set forth such facts as the Commission . . . may prescribe as to the citizenship, character, and financial, technical, and other qualifications of the applicant . . ." and states that grants must serve the "public convenience, interest, or necessity. . . ." It is left to the Commission to develop its own standards of financial dependability and engineering practice and its own criteria for judging the public interest. This the Commission has done, after a fashion. But its policy and its practice have left much to be desired.

Criteria for Licensing

In cases where there is only one applicant for a license, the FCC need only assure itself that he is an American citizen, of good character, that he meets its minimum financial and technical standards, that he does not already own a station in the same area, and does not own the maximum number of stations permitted by the Commission's multiple ownership rule, and that he does not propose to broadcast lotteries or obscenity. The applicant's character may be questioned if he makes deliberate misstatements or if he has been connected with left-wing groups. But otherwise, a license will be issued as a matter of course. In cases where there are several applicants, however, the Commission's problem is one of choosing among claimants, all of whom are qualified. In doing so, it must have criteria to guide and to justify its choice.

The matters that the Commission takes into consideration, in addition to diversification of ownership, already discussed, are: (1) the residence of applicants, (2) the character of ownership and management, (3) broadcasting experience, (4) the nature of proposed programs, and (5) past performance. Nominally, it has preferred local ownership to outside ownership, integrated owner operation to dispersed ownership and delegated operation, experienced operators to inexperienced ones, those promising better programs to those promising poorer ones, and those whose performance has been good to those whose performance has been bad.

These criteria are open to criticism in themselves. The criterion of proposed programming is virtually useless. All of the applicants will promise programs of educational value, local programs of civic interest, and entertainment of high quality. In the case of radio, all of them will play records. In the case of television, all of them will broadcast the same network programs. The choice is one between tweedledum and tweedledee. The criterion of past performance is imprecise. Here, judgment is wholly subjective; no objective tests are specified. The several criteria, moreover, are inconsistent. The criteria of local ownership and owner management favor the local applicant. The criterion of broadcasting experience may favor an outsider. No weight is assigned to the criteria. There is no way to tell, when they are in conflict, which is to prevail. By their very nature, the criteria are subject to manipulation. And they have been manipulated by the FCC.

Practice in Licensing

The decisions of an administrative agency should be prompt. They should be based upon the record in the case. They should be explicitly justified in the light of principle and precedent. It was shown, in a Congressional investigation in 1958, that the Commission's decisions on license applications met none of these tests. A decision might be delayed for as long as five years. A case was first heard and an opinion prepared by an expert trial examiner. But the Commission's final decision might ignore the record of the hearings and the opinion of the examiner, being taken on other grounds. Decisions were not written by the Commissioners themselves but were drafted by a special staff whose task it was to rationalize the Commission's choice. The nominal criteria were not consistently applied. In some cases, the emphasis was on local ownership; in others, on broadcasting experience. In some, programming plans were emphasized; in others, their significance was minimized. The Commission's criteria, said Professor Louis L. Jaffe of the Harvard Law School, had become "spurious criteria, used to justify results otherwise arrived at."[9] They were "announced only to be

9 / Louis L. Jaffe, "The Scandal in TV Licensing," *Harper's Magazine,* September, 1957, pp. 77-84, at p. 79.

ignored, ingeniously explained away, or so occasionally applied that their very application seems a mockery of justice."[10]

The pretense that grants were made in accordance with established principles was called into further question by the fact that a winning applicant might be permitted to sell his license, at a substantial profit, to an unsuccessful contestant who did not satisfy the conditions on which the original grant was nominally made. Thus, a license granted to an applicant in Denver on the ground of local ownership was sold to an outsider within four months at a profit of 2,400 percent, and the acquisition was approved by the FCC on the ground of the buyer's broadcasting experience.[11] In some cases, it appeared that applications were made for the sole purpose of being bought off by competing applicants; in others, for the purpose of selling out once a license was conferred.

It was also shown in the Congressional hearings that members of the Commission, in the performance of their duties, had not adhered to the highest standards of morality. They had discussed the merits of pending cases in private with certain of the applicants, as if a judge were to discuss a pending decision in private with one of the litigants. They had accepted favors—in the form of color television sets, fees for speeches, and entertainment for themselves and their wives—from the industry they were supposed to regulate. It was charged that one Commissioner had demanded $50,000 as the price of his vote for a television license. It was shown that another had accepted substantial sums from a lawyer representing an applicant on whom a license was then conferred. As a result of this disclosure, the Commissioner was discharged and a number of television awards were set aside by the courts.

Reform of Licensing

An alternative to the present method of licensing is readily available. Channels needed for noncommercial use—for public safety and education—could be reserved; those remaining available for commercial exploitation could be auctioned off. Applicants for these channels would be required, as they are now, to satisfy the requirements for eligibility. Where there was only one applicant for a license, it could be issued to him without charge. But where there were two or more applicants, the license would go to the highest bidder. Rights for the use of airspace could be leased for limited periods, their rental being determined by the levels of the successful bids.

Such a system would have many advantages. It would speed action. It would save the cost of lengthy Commission proceedings. It would put an end to the hypocrisy inherent in presenting and considering promises of performance. It would obviate the need for rationalizing license grants in terms of dubious and conflicting criteria. It would relieve applicants of the temptation to resort to bribery or to the use of political pressure, Congressmen of demands that they

10 / *Ibid.*, p. 84.
11 / *New York Times,* March 9, 1958.

exert such pressure, and Commissioners of the need to resist the temptation of bribery and the pressure of politics. The value of the licenses, instead of enriching individuals, would go to the government. [12]

PROGRAM CONTENT

Under the terms of the Communications Act, the FCC is specifically denied the power of censorship. But it is also authorized, in granting or renewing station licenses to determine whether the "public interest, convenience, or necessity would be served. . . ." In passing on applications for new licenses, it may therefore consider the character of program service that is promised. And in passing on applications for renewals, it may consider the character of programs provided in the past. The Commission, thus, may not require a script to be submitted for approval in advance of a performance. But it may refuse renewal of a license on the ground that past performances have failed to serve the public interest. This power, if it were really used, would enable the Commission—for better or for worse—to influence freedom of speech and the quality of programs on the air.

Freedom of the Air

The FCC is forbidden to interfere with the right of free speech. But it does not follow that the air is free. Broadcasting stations are not regarded as common carriers. Access to the microphone or the TV camera cannot be demanded, in general, as a legal right. But there are rules regarding such access that broadcasters must observe.

A special rule applies to the provision of broadcasting time to candidates for public office. If a station gives time, without charge, to one candidate, the law requires that it give equal time to all other candidates, many of whom may appeal to tiny minorities. The cost to broadcasters might well be prohibitive. The rule was suspended by Congress in 1960 to make possible the Kennedy-Nixon debates, but was then restored. It stands, therefore, as an obstacle to such exchanges. Instead of giving time, broadcasters may sell it. But if they sell it to one candidate, they must make it available, on equal terms, to others. As a result, candidates who have ample funds get on the air, while those who lack them do not. Minority views are thus denied a hearing. For this dilemma, no solution has been found.

Another question was raised when a licensee broadcast his own opinions on issues and candidates to the exclusion of opposing views. The right of a newspaper publisher to do so is unquestioned. Is a similar right conferred on the broadcast licensee? This question was brought before the FCC in 1941 in a case involving a station in Boston. The Commission ruled that the air space allotted

12 / See Harvey J. Levin, "The Radio Spectrum Resource," *Journal of Law and Economics,* vol. XI (1968), pp. 433-501, and "Spectrum Allocation Without Markets," *American Economic Review,* vol. LX No. 2 (1970), pp. 209-18.

to a licensee was part of the public domain and could not be used as if it were his private property. To employ it in the public interest, balanced discussion was required. The station itself was not to be an advocate. This ruling was denounced by the broadcasting industry, and in 1949 it was superseded by a policy statement known as the fairness doctrine.

The fairness doctrine requires that broadcasting stations devote a reasonable amount of time to controversial public issues and that, in doing so, they afford opposing sides an equal opportunity to be heard. It permits a station to endorse a candidate for office but requires it to afford other candidates an opportunity to reply. In cases where an attack is made on the honor or integrity of any person or group, the doctrine also requires that those attacked be given an opportunity to reply.

These rules have been applied in a number of cases. In 1967, the FCC required stations broadcasting cigarette advertisements to allot time to cancer and heart societies to warn of the dangers of smoking cigarettes. In 1968, the Commission required a station attacking the leftist W. E. B. Du Bois clubs and another station attacking the rightist John Birch Society to allow time for replies. And in 1969, in a case where the Commission had ordered a station in York, Pennsylvania to provide time to Fred J. Cook to respond to a personal attack by Rev. Billy James Hargis, the Supreme Court enforced its order and upheld the constitutionality of the fairness doctrine.[13] In 1970, after President Nixon had made five appearances over all the national networks in prime evening time to defend his conduct of the war in Indo-China, the FCC made a further application of the fairness doctrine, ordering the networks to afford congressional critics of the war a similar opportunity to be heard.

One danger is that discussion of disputed issues will not be balanced. Another is that they will not be discussed at all. Broadcasters, advertising agencies, and advertisers are all engaged in salesmanship. And salesmen do not lightly run the risk of giving offense to customers. Censorship is forbidden to the FCC, but it may legally be practiced by commercial interests. The wonder is, in such a situation, that American broadcasting is fairly free. Controversial issues are aired. Opposing points of view are heard. Persons attacked are given a chance to reply. Some subjects may be taboo; criticism of advertising and advertisers is certain to be rare. But criticism of politics and politicians is common. The air, indeed, may well be freer than would be the case if the Commission held a tighter rein.

Quality of Programs

The only provisions of the Communications Act governing the character of radio and television programs are those that forbid the broadcasting of "any obscene, indecent, or profane language" and "any advertisement of or information concerning any lottery, gift enterprise, or similar scheme, offering prizes dependent in whole or in part upon lot or chance. . . ." No standards respecting

13 / *Red Lion Broadcasting Co. v. FCC*, 395 U.S. 367.

the balance of material to be broadcast or the quality of individual programs have been established by the FCC. Determination of the nation's radio and television fare is left to commercial interests.

People engaged in selling merchandise are certain to seek the largest possible audience. And in order to obtain it, they are likely to appeal to the lowest common denominator of intelligence, education, and taste. A few good programs are available. But the general character of the fare provided on TV is that described by FCC Chairman Minow when he addressed the National Association of Broadcasters in 1961:

> I invite you to sit down in front of your television set when your station goes on the air . . . and keep your eyes glued to that set until the station signs off. I can assure you that you will observe a vast wasteland. You will see a procession of game shows, violence, audience participation shows, formula comedies about totally unbelievable families, blood and thunder, mayhem, violence, sadism, murder, Western badmen, Western goodmen, private eyes, gangsters, more violence, and cartoons.[14]

Similarly, the National Commission on the Causes and Prevention of Violence, having analyzed the dramatic programs shown in prime time on the three networks during sample weeks in 1967 and 1968, found that acts of violence averaged 15 per hour of viewing. The Commission concluded that

> a constant diet of violent behavior on television has an adverse effect on human character and attitudes. Violence on television encourages violent forms of behavior and fosters moral and social values about violence in daily life which are unacceptable in a civilized society.[15]

Such material, certainly, should not occupy the air to the virtual exclusion of public affairs, science, philosophy, literature, dramas, ballets, symphonies, and the graphic arts. With other media—books, magazines, newspapers, theater, and movies—some part of the output is addressed to the cultivated minority. With radio, this audience is partly served by FM. But with commercial television, minority interests and tastes are generally ignored. The advertising agencies review all scripts in advance, scrutinizing plot and dialogue, and check on all rehearsals to prevent the showing of anything that might be harmful to the sponsor. The integrity of TV as a medium of artistic expression is sacrificed to its utility as a medium for selling goods.

"It is inconceivable that we should allow so great a possibility for service, for news, for entertainment, for education, and for vital commercial purposes to be drowned in advertising chatter."[16] So said Herbert Hoover, then Secretary of Commerce with responsibility for the regulation of radio, in 1922. Today,

14 / *New York Times,* May 9, 1961.

15 / National Commission on the Causes and Prevention of Violence, *To Establish Justice, to Insure Domestic Tranquility* (Washington, D.C.: Government Printing Office, 1969), chap. viii, p. 199.

16 / Quoted in Minow, *op. cit.,* p. 11.

advertising chatter fills a large part of every broadcast hour. Commercials are too numerous, following one another without interruption. They are too long, running to several minutes of straight sales talk. They are too frequent, coming not only at station breaks, but being inserted in the middle of a program and woven into the program itself. They are too loud, power being stepped up so that the sound will follow the viewer if he attempts to escape. Many of them are deceptive; many are disgusting. The excesses of advertising abuse the privilege that is given to broadcasters by the government.

Control of Programs

Little has been done by the FCC to raise the quality of programs. In 1946 the Commission issued a report on the *Public Service Responsibility of Broadcast Licensees,* known as the Blue Book, pointing out that the performance of radio stations, by and large, was falling short of the promises they had made when they applied for licenses. Broadcasters were not providing listeners with a balanced offering. They were not serving the interests of their own communities. Advertising abuses were common and serious. The Commission's indictment was sweeping and well documented. But the agency did not attempt to employ its powers to correct the evils it disclosed. The Blue Book was first denounced and then ignored by the broadcasters. It was never followed up by the FCC.

In 1949 the Commission issued rules prohibiting giveaway shows, under the provision of the law forbidding lotteries. Enforcement was resisted by the networks, the case being appealed eventually to the Supreme Court. The Court decided unanimously for the networks, holding that giveaway shows were not lotteries.[17] The Commission's first attempt to prevent the prostitution of the airwaves thus came to naught.

In 1958, it was disclosed that radio disk jockeys had collected money, known as "payola," from producers of popular records for putting them on the air. At the same time, it was revealed that a TV show in which contestants vied for prizes running into hundreds of thousands of dollars was a fake, the participants being rehearsed in the parts they were to play. These would not appear to be matters of great moment. But the scandal rocked the country. The upshot was a law, enacted in 1960, which prohibited payola and the rigging of quiz shows, making it a crime, punishable by fine or imprisonment, to broadcast material for which payment had been received without announcing that fact or to prearrange the outcome of a contest. By the time this law was passed, the big-money quiz shows had been off the air for many months.

For nearly 30 years, the FCC did nothing to curb the abuses of advertising. Then, in 1963, it voted 4 to 3 to hold hearings on the adoption of a rule that would confine the time devoted to commercials within the limits set by the National Association of Broadcasters in its own code. The Commission's proposal was denounced, at the hearings, by the broadcasters and by other business

17 / *FCC* v. *American Broadcasting Co., Columbia Broadcasting System, National Broadcasting Co.,* 347 U.S. 284.

groups. The House of Representatives, by a vote of 317 to 43, passed a bill forbidding the FCC ever to impose any limitation on the time devoted to commercials. Thereupon, the Commission terminated its proceedings. In 1965, the Commission issued a policy statement directing broadcasters to eliminate objectionable loudness in commercials, implying that this would be one of the bases on which their performance in the public interest would be judged. But, as yet, no licensee has been denied a renewal on the ground that his commercials were too loud or too long.

Revocation of Licenses

The FCC, until recently, was reluctant to punish licensees for minor infractions of its rules. The only penalty it could impose was revocation of their licenses, and this was too severe to fit the crimes. This situation was corrected by Congress in 1960 when it authorized the Commission, instead of revoking a license, to renew it for a probationary period shorter than the normal three years, and to levy fines of $1,000 or less for each day of an offense, up to a total of $10,000. The Commission can now use fines and probationary renewals for lesser offenses, license revocations for more serious ones.

The FCC has clear authority to refuse renewal of a license. But the penalty of revocation has rarely been used. The Federal Radio Commission did revoke the licenses of two quacks who were broadcasting prescriptions and selling patent medicines over the air. And it took similar action in the case of a Protestant clergyman who used his station to make violent attacks on the Catholic Church and on various citizens of Los Angeles. Upon appeal, this action was upheld.[18] In general, however, licenses have been permanent. Whatever the behavior of the licensee, his rights have been automatically renewed. It was not until 1969 that the FCC refused to renew the license of a major TV station. In that year, it revoked the license of WHDH in Boston, awarding it to another applicant who gave assurance of superior programming. And it cancelled its renewal of the license of WPIX in New York, following charges that the station had falsified its broadcasts of the news. In 1969, too, a Court of Appeals upheld the right of groups of citizens to protest renewals of licenses. Four years earlier, Negro, church, and other groups in Jackson, Mississippi complained that Station WLBT had engaged in blatant racial discrimination in its programming and asked that its license be revoked. Instead of taking such action, the FCC renewed the license for a probationary period of a single year, advising the station to mend its ways. The case was appealed and, in 1969, Judge (now Chief Justice) Warren E. Burger directed the Commission to cancel the license and to invite other applications for the award. The judge denounced the Commission for its favoritism toward established broadcasters and its hostility toward those protesting a renewal of their rights.

These developments alarmed the broadcast licensees. As usual, Congress

18 / *Trinity Methodist Church, South* v. *Federal Radio Commission*, 62 F. 2d 850 (1932).

rushed to their rescue. A bill introduced by Senator John O. Pastore of Rhode Island would have forbidden new applications for a license held by an established broadcaster unless the FCC had first taken the initiative to revoke it. The measure would have operated to give existing licensees assurances of permanent monopoly. In 1970, however, the FCC announced that it would not entertain challenges to broadcasting licenses whose holders "substantially" met the programming needs of their communities. In effect, this statement superseded the Pastore bill. It left the door open to protests against license renewals. But it assured licensees whose performance was no more than adequate that their continued tenure would not be disturbed.

DIVERSITY IN BROADCASTING

The fare afforded by radio and television could be improved by offering the listener and the viewer a greater number of alternatives. This has been the purpose of rules adopted by the FCC, such as those reserving channels for educational broadcasting, limiting the duplication of programs on AM and FM, and requiring TV stations to devote one of the four prime night hours to non-network programs. It was the purpose of the law requiring manufacturers to equip TV sets to receive UHF as well as VHF. A greater variety of programs could also be provided by introducing Subscription TV, Cable TV, and noncommercial broadcasting. The FCC was slow to make channels available for Subscription TV; the future of such a service is not promising. The Commission was also reluctant to acquiesce in the growth of Cable TV. And it played little part in the initiation of noncommercial broadcasting. But it is in the last two fields that the most promising developments in broadcasting are likely to come.

Subscription TV

An alternative to television programs financed by advertisers could be provided in the form of programs paid for by viewers, variously known as Subscription TV, Toll TV, or Pay TV. Here, the producer broadcasts a scrambled image which the subscriber unscrambles by purchasing a gadget which he applies to his receiving set. Promoters of such systems applied to the FCC in the early fifties for channels on which to give them a trial. Their applications were vigorously opposed by established broadcasters, by movie exhibitors, and by members of Congress. In the face of this opposition, no allocation was made for 10 years. Then a channel was assigned for an experiment in Hartford, Connecticut by Zenith Radio and RKO. The experiment lasted from 1962 to 1969. During this period, it offered four hours of entertainment each night, including theatrical productions, night club acts, first-run movies, live sports, and no commercials. But it enrolled only 5,000 to 7,000 subscribers in a city of 275,000 homes. Financially, it was a failure, as other experiments had been where programs had been delivered to subscribers over telephone wires.

In 1969, the FCC finally announced that it was prepared to allocate channels in major cities for Subscription TV. But it protected established broadcasters by hedging its offer with numerous restrictions. The Commission's rules were upheld by the Supreme Court in 1970. At last, there was a settled policy on Pay TV. But there was no Pay TV. Nor was it likely that there ever would be.

Cable TV

A cable TV system is built around a master antenna, erected on some high place, which picks up near and distant signals from the air, amplifies them, and transmits them to subscribers' receiving sets over a network of coaxial cables. There were 2,300 such systems in 1969, serving 3.5 million of the nation's homes. The first of them were located in remote towns or mountainous areas where reception was poor. Here, subscribers paid $10 or so for installation of the wires and $5 or so a month for the service. Later systems have been set up to overcome the interference created by high buildings in cities. Here, the costs of installation are greater and the charges are higher.

Cable TV has marked advantages. It increases the choices available to the viewer, carrying 20 or more signals from stations both near and far. It improves the quality of his reception. It can supply programs to meet the particular needs of local communities and minority groups. Potentially, it can provide a number of other services: continuous weather, news, and market reporting, meter reading, supermarket shopping, alarm systems, video telephony, computer connection, etc.

But Cable TV encounters serious obstacles. By importing signals from distant broadcasters, it competes with local stations. And by duplicating local broadcasts, it cuts the size of their audiences and reduces their revenues. It thus evokes their opposition. By relaying programs covered by copyrights, it also incurs the opposition of the copyright owners. In cities, moreover, it must obtain franchises and rent duct space to lay its cables under the streets and must pay landlords and building operators in order to install and maintain its wiring.

The jurisdiction originally given to the FCC by Congress covered broadcasting over the air. But Cable TV transmits its programs by wire. It was thus questionable whether such systems were subject to Commission control. For some years, the Commission left this issue to be decided by the Congress. But eventually, in the absence of Congressional action, it asserted its authority, holding that the impact of Cable TV on other broadcasters was too serious to be ignored. On this basis, it issued orders limiting the services that could be offered by cable companies. The Southwestern Cable Company appealed and the Commission's assumption of power was upheld, in 1968, by the Supreme Court. The provisions of the law, said the Court, are broad enough to cover all forms of electronic communication.[19]

For some time, the FCC undertook to protect established broadcasters by imposing restrictions on Cable TV. In 1966, it ruled (1) that no Cable TV station could bring distant signals into the top 100 TV markets without first

19 / *U.S. v. Southwestern Cable Co.,* 392 U.S. 157.

convincing it that this would not impede the growth of new UHF stations and would not develop into Pay TV; (2) that Cable TV stations would have to carry the programs of local broadcasters at their request; and (3) that they could not rebroadcast network programs carried by local stations on the same day. In 1968, the Commission proposed further restrictions: (1) forbidding operation in the top 100 markets without the consent of existing broadcasters, (2) limiting the right to duplicate programs in urban areas, (3) limiting the number of channels a station could carry in rural areas, and (4) forbidding retransmission of signals from distant stations unless their permission was first obtained.

But later developments have been more favorable to Cable TV. In 1970, the Commission voted tentatively to adopt a new statement of policy. It would lift its earlier restrictions, permitting virtually unlimited importation of out-of-town programs. It would require a Cable TV station, before importing distant beams, to carry all the local signals and to provide four additional channels, one for the use of the city government, one for community groups, one to lease to the general public, and one for its own programs. The Commission had ruled that Cable TV stations with 3,500 or more subscribers must originate some programs on a local basis beginning in 1971. And it had directed such stations to fill the breaks on imported programs by selling time to local advertisers. It now proposed to use the funds obtained by selling time to indemnify UHF stations for their anticipated loss of markets and to compensate copyright owners for the use of their materials. The FCC has approved a system that transmits its signals in suburban areas not by wire but by microwave and is expected to do so as a matter of general policy.

The Commission has also undertaken to preserve competition in the cable business. It has forbidden TV licensees to acquire control of cable systems in their own broadcast areas and has considered limiting the ownership of such systems by other mass media. It has also considered limiting the number of systems that may be owned by a single firm. Such rules are consistent, in principle, with those that have governed radio and TV.

Educational Broadcasting

In the Communications Act of 1934, Congress directed the FCC to consider the desirability of reserving a number of radio channels for educational broadcasting. The Commission decided not to do so. It acted, in part, on the assurance of commercial licensees that educational programs would be broadcast by their stations. A committee of educators and broadcasters was established for the purpose of promoting such programs. But education was relegated to the poorest hours of the day and was dropped entirely when programs yielding advertising revenue became available. Education fared better in the FM allocation, where profits were not so promising and commercial pressures not so intense. In 1968, there were 363 licenses outstanding for noncommercial FM stations, many of them confining their broadcasts to a college campus or a small college town. But the real struggle over educational broadcasting centered in the allocation of space for TV. The educators asked that a fourth of the TV channels be reserved for their use, supporting their request with detailed evidence of the dearth of educational material being broadcast by commercial licensees. The commercial broadcasters opposed this reservation, arguing that educators were incompetent to produce TV programs and that space assigned them would go to waste. In its final allocation, the Commission set aside a tenth of the TV channels for education, eventually providing for 356 educational licenses, most of them in the UHF band.

Television has great potentialities for education: for classroom instruction, for extension courses, and for adult education. There are more than 400 closed-circuit systems in operation in educational institutions. But educators have been slow to apply for broadcasting licenses. In 1968, there were 164 stations on the air, with nearly 200 allocations still going begging. The principal obstacle has been the lack of financial resources. Nonprofit stations are forbidden to meet any part of their costs by selling time to advertisers. Educational TV has received grants, running to $150 million, from the Ford Foundation, mostly for the support of NET, an organization which serves as a producer of educational programs and as a distribution system for local stations. But these stations have had to finance themselves, in the main, by obtaining appropriations from school boards, city councils, and state legislatures. And these bodies have been laggard and niggardly. If the potentialities of education TV are to be realized, it must have a massive infusion of funds.

Public TV

In 1967, a commission composed of eminent citizens appointed by the Carnegie Corporation, a philanthropic foundation, presented a report on noncommercial television. The commission did not concern itself with the use of TV as an instrument for formal instruction, but directed its attention, rather, to its use as a medium for general enlightenment. It proposed that a nonprofit corporation be chartered by the federal government to create and operate a nationwide system of Public TV, to be based on the existing educational stations. The corporation would have 12 directors, 6 of them appointed by the President and 6 chosen by the presidential appointees. It would add to the number and improve the facilities of local stations, produce public-interest programs, and make them available for broadcasting. It would maintain local autonomy over programming and encourage program diversity. The corporation would be financed by the revenue from a 5 percent tax on new TV sets, yielding around $100 million a year.

This proposal, in general, was enacted into law when Congress passed the Public Broadcasting Act of 1967. The measure created a Public Broadcasting Act of 1967. The measure created a Public Broadcasting Corporation, as had been recommended, and directed it to facilitate the development of noncommercial broadcasting. But Congress did not impose the recommended tax. Instead, it appropriated a paltry $9 million from general revenues for the fiscal year 1969 and $15 million for 1970. The PCB still has no assurance of continued life, being required to apply for a new authorization and an appropriation each year.

The Corporation, in its short life, has made grants to strengthen local noncommercial stations. It has invested in the study of public TV audiences and the training of TV personnel. It has supported program production by NET and by individual stations. It has set up a subsidiary, the Public Broadcasting Service, to make interconnections and to handle the national distribution of its programs. The signals of nearly 200 public TV stations can already be received by three fourths of the nation's households. They actually reach a third of these, giving the system an audience of 45 million people.

The future of Public TV will depend upon the character of its programming. Rather than mere entertainment, it will devote itself, without commercial interruption, to the arts, the sciences, and the interpretation of events. If its programs are dull, timorous, and didactic, its audience will be small and it will pose no competitive threat to commercial TV. If they are exciting, disturbing, and inspiring, it will attract some part of the commercial audience, incur the enmity of the commercial broadcasters, and evoke hostile action by their friends in Congress. If public TV, as a medium of the highest quality, is to prosper, it must build a loyal constituency of its own.

Chapter
20

REGULATION APPRAISED

Critics of the policy of maintaining competition, while stressing the shortcomings of antitrust, are likely to ignore the many problems raised by its alternatives: public regulation and public enterprise. These problems are fully as serious as those raised by antitrust. If a wise choice is to be made among the possible methods of control, it is important that they be faced. The problems of public enterprise will be considered in the next part of this book. American experience with public regulation has been reviewed, in considerable detail, in the earlier chapters of this part. The means of regulation, its weaknesses in operation, its inherent limitations, and the character of its results are now to be examined in more general terms.

THE REGULATORY COMMISSION

The task of regulating an industry, when undertaken in this country, may sometimes be assigned to one of the departments of the state or federal government under the direction of a single executive. It is usually assigned, however, to a commission of three to seven members set up for the special purpose outside the departmental structure. The law customarily provides that the members of such a body shall represent both major parties, that they shall serve for long and overlapping terms, that they cannot be discharged unless for malfeasance or neglect of duty, and that their decisions shall be subject, not to executive veto, but only to judicial review. The status accorded to the regulatory commission is thus designed to assure it an independence similar to that enjoyed by the judiciary.

This arrangement was once assumed to have a number of advantages. The specialization of the agency and its independent status were supposed to assure the appointment of persons who are experts in the field. This was supposed, in turn, to enable the agency to adopt procedures that would be less formal and more flexible than those employed by the courts and to carry on its business with greater dispatch. The multiple membership of the agency, including men with varying experience and points of view, was supposed to make for greater soundness of judgment. Its overlapping terms were thought to give it continuity of policy. Its independence, freeing its members from political pressures, was supposed to assure their devotion to the public interest and their impartiality in the settlement of private disputes.

All of these assumptions have now been called into question by political scientists. Leading scholars in the field have come to ask whether expertness is really desirable, whether several heads are indeed better than one, whether independence is in fact attainable, and, if so, whether it is to be desired.

Is Expertness Desirable?

The expert is a specialist, highly skilled by training and experience within a narrow field. He is best used in a post where policy is prescribed and the scope of his discretion limited. His proper function is that of analyzing complex data and making individual determinations in accordance with settled principles. The members of a regulatory commission, on the other hand, are given broad discretion to define the public interest in the light of ambiguous statutory goals. Their task is largely that of formulating policy. And this calls for social judgment rather than expertise. As a policymaker, the expert is miscast. His special competence does not relate to definition of the public interest. His professionalism afflicts him with myopia. He views the problems of regulation through the blinders of his specialized techniques. Put him in command, and regulation will tend to be inflexible. It is important that experts be on a commission's staff. These specialists, of course, will not agree. The lawyers, the economists, and the engineers, within the limits of their disciplines, will offer varying advice. The commissioners themselves should be equipped to take a broader view. The expert, it has been said, should be on tap but not on top.

Are Several Heads Better Than One?

The members of a regulatory commission fulfill three quite different functions. One is judicial in character: they must adjudicate private disputes. A second is legislative: they must formulate public policy. The third is executive: in some cases, a commission is required to perform purely administrative tasks; in every case, the commissioners must manage the operations of their own agency. As a means of settling disputes, the multimembered commission has the advantage of protecting participants against the possibility of arbitrary decisions. As a means of formulating policy, also, it may have the advantage of assuring that consideration is given to conflicting points of view. But compromise takes time, and the process is likely to prevent incisive decision and vigorous action. As a device for administration, moreover, the multiheaded agency has nothing to recommend it. It is bound to be badly managed. Lines of authority and responsibility are blurred. Conflicting orders are given. Some work is duplicated; other work remains undone. Commissioners are bogged down in the minutiae of operations when they should be giving their attention to adjudication and the formulation of policy. These difficulties could be overcome, as has been done in certain cases, by designating one member of the commission as its chairman and assigning administrative authority to him, or by delegating administration to a general manager, subject to the authority of the commission as a whole. But the shortcomings of the multimembered agency as a device for formulating policy would still remain.

Is Independence Attainable?

A commission is certain to be subjected to pressure on behalf of the industries it is supposed to regulate. The privileges that it can grant or withhold may be worth millions to them. Its decisions affect their earnings and the value of their properties. They will seek its favors. They will attempt to prevent unfavorable action, to delay it, modify it, or reverse it. To this end, they will undertake, in every way that is open, to influence the commission's policies. They may approach commissioners directly. They may put pressure on them indirectly, through the governor or the President or through members of the legislature or the Congress. They may enlist public support for their demands by conducting propaganda campaigns.

The notion that a regulatory commission can be insulated against such pressures is politically naïve. The independence of such an agency is more nominal than real. The executive appoints—and may or may not reappoint—its members. The law may require bipartisanship, but a governor or a president can select from either party members who are sympathetic to his views. He thus can strongly influence a commission's policy. President Kennedy strengthened the federal commissions by appointing tough regulators to their chairmanships; President Johnson followed suit. But the appointments made by his successor, according to *Business Week,* put "a clear Nixon stamp on the regulatory agencies—frankly political with a strong conservative tinge."[1] An executive will not often intervene to affect commission action on particular cases. But he will determine its general tone.

A commission gets its legal authority and its financial support from the legislature or the Congress. One of these bodies, at the behest of a regulated industry, can investigate the agency, intimidating its personnel and paralyzing its operations. It can refuse to confirm nominees for appointment or reappointment, cut the agency's appropriations, restrict the character of its expenditures, and curtail its jurisdiction and powers. When a commission is given to understand that an influential legislator is opposed to its policies, they are likely to be reconsidered. When it is told that such a person is interested in a pending case, action is certain to be quickened and a sympathetic hearing assured.

A regulatory agency cannot rely for strength on expertness alone. If it is to survive and prosper, it must have political support. It may have the backing of a strong executive. But this is not usually the case. A governor or a president may give whole-hearted support to an agency when it is first established. But his attention will shift to other matters when its operations become routine. A

1 / *Business Week,* September 20, 1969, p. 47.

president will come to be preoccupied with questions of national security, foreign relations, economic stability, and social welfare. He will not see the chairman of a commission from one year to the next. He will not concern himself with its operations unless some scandal is disclosed.[2]

Failing executive support, a commission may develop its own contacts in the legislative branch. Going to the source of power, it may seek support among offsetting pressure groups, or undertake to sell its program to the country as a whole. An aggressive effort to enlist popular support, however, is likely to be forbidden by law or the funds required to finance it denied. Without such support, there is only one more place for the agency to turn. To insure its own survival, it must seek the backing of those it is supposed to regulate. With their aid, it can get its members reappointed, its budget enlarged, and its powers maintained. For this support, the regulatory agency must pay a price. To some extent, it must resolve disputed issues in favor of the regulated industry. In some measure, it must yield to the industry's views on policy.

Even though the regulator does not consciously surrender to the regulatees, he may come, through subtler influences, to share their views. He is continuously concerned with their problems. He constantly associates with their managements. It is not surprising if he comes to see their problems sympathetically and to accept their outlook as his own. The regulatory agency is likely to become industry-minded, losing the perspective of the public interest. Impartiality in regulation cannot be assured.

Is Independence Desirable?

Regulation is an intensely political process. It is not confined to the elimination of abuses and the settlement of disputes. It also deals with matters that are of central importance in the economy. It interferes with freedom of management, limits the rights of property, and affects the level of profits. It serves as a vehicle of economic change. The regulatory agency fashions public policy. It cannot and should not be taken out of politics. Public bodies must be held accountable. With independence, power might be abused. To prevent abuse, the agency should be subject to political control. This, in contrast to the case once made for the independent commission, is the view of students of public administration today.

WEAKNESSES OF REGULATION

Our judgment of commission regulation need not be based on a priori reasoning alone. Experience with this device in the United States is an extensive one. In the case of public utilities, it stretches over more than 60 years; in the case of transport, almost 90. In the first case, the problem has been the relatively simple one of regulating firms possessing complete monopolies of essential

2 / See William L. Cary, *Politics and the Regulatory Agencies* (New York: McGraw-Hill Book Co., 1967), chap. 1.

services in local markets. In the second, it has been the more difficult one of regulating a competitive industry. In neither case has the undertaking been attended by conspicuous success.

The Results of Regulation

The utility commissions, in the states, have taken little or no initiative in developing standards to govern the quality of service. In acting on the general level of rates, they have exercised no real control over operating costs. They have prescribed methods of accounting but have not regularly audited company accounts. In determining the rate base, they were handicapped for a quarter of a century by litigation. In fixing the rate of return, they have developed no clear principles. In general, they have set price levels on a cost-plus basis, establishing no connection between earnings and efficiency. They have centered their attention on the task of allowing a return that is fair to past investors and setting rates at a level that does not exploit consumers. But they have permitted earnings well in excess of those required to market new securities. And they have made no effort to promote consumption by reducing rates to the lowest level at which a fair return could be obtained. Expansion of use has been prompted, in recent years, less by the processes of regulation than by the demonstration, through the policies adopted by public power projects, that wider sales and higher profits are to be realized at lower rates. The commissions, finally, have left to the utilities all initiative with respect to the structure of rates. Large users have been favored, small users burdened, and discrimination justified through the sophistry of cost accounts. State regulation, in general, has afforded scant protection to the consumer of utility services.

In the case of transport, in addition to difficulties such as those discussed above, there are others arising from competition between the different media and between individual carriers. It is national policy, enunciated by the Congress, that regulation is to be impartial and traffic allocated among the different media in accordance with their inherent advantages. But there is no coordination of promotion and regulation, of the several promotional programs, or of the regulation of surface carriers and air carriers. The allocation of traffic is distorted by differential subsidization. And this is then offset, in part, by discrimination in the structure of rates. To aid the railroads, the ICC bars entry into trucking, limits the goods that truckers may carry, prescribes the points they may follow, raises their costs and puts a floor under their rates. To aid the truckers and the water carriers, it has retarded innovations in rail technology and forbidden profitable reductions in rail rates. The ICC is said to be railroad-minded. But it may have harmed as much as it has helped. The railroads have been regulated for decades, intensively and sympathetically. Their state, in comparison with that of other industries, is not a happy one. Regulation has been less damaging to the airlines. But the CAB has devoted its energies, at considerable cost, to route determinations that have delayed adjustment to shifting demand, resulting finally in a pattern little different than would have obtained if the carriers had been given freedom of choice.

In the case of radio and television, monopoly rights worth millions have been given away. The recipients of these favors have openly violated their pledges regarding the character and quality of their broadcasting services. Yet little has been done, in more than 40 years, to require them to keep their word.

In a few states, from time to time, utility commissions have earned a reputation for vigor and effectiveness. But, by and large, the verdict of scholars on the performance of such bodies has damned them with faint praise. In the words of John Bauer: "The wonder is that regulation has worked as well as it has. Although far from satisfactory, it has not been a complete and unmitigated failure. While the commissions have not measured up to high standards, perhaps they have done, in the main, the best they could under all the circumstances. They have carried on their work in an easygoing, nonalert way, but they have seldom deliberately flouted the public interest. . . ."[3] In his study of the federal regulatory commissions, Marver H. Bernstein concludes that "the commissions have not been satisfactory instruments of governmental regulation of business." These bodies, he finds,

> have proved to be more susceptible to private pressures, to manipulation for private purposes, and to administrative and public apathy than other types of governmental organizations. They have lacked an affirmative concept of the public interest. The effectiveness of regulation of business by commission hangs by a thin thread. As a method for ordering economic relationships in society short of governmental ownership and operation, it has not proved itself.[4]

And the editors of *Business Week,* reviewing the "dismal record of indecision, confusion, and delay [that] has made existing regulation a failure," conclude that "the whole, elaborate regulatory machine is on the point of collapse. Almost no one, either in government or business, thinks the agencies are doing even a passable job."[5]

External Limitations

The weaknesses of the commissions are to be attributed in large part to matters that are beyond their control—to the limitations that are placed upon them by the legislative, executive, and judicial branches of the government, and to the lack of popular support.

From the legislature, a commission needs a mandate that clearly defines its

3 / John Bauer, *Transforming Public Utility Regulation* (New York: Harper & Bros., 1950), pp. 137-38.

4 / Marver H. Bernstein, *Regulating Business by Independent Commission* (Princeton, N.J.: Princeton University Press, 1955), pp. 294, 296.

5 / *Business Week,* February 28, 1970, p. 132. See also pp. 60-73.

objectives, a grant of ample jurisdiction and sufficient powers, authority to pay the salaries that are required to attract and hold able men, and appropriations adequate to enable it fully to meet its responsibilities. Too often the legislative bodies are unable or unwilling to make their mandate clear. Beset by conflicting pressures that cannot be readily resolved, they pass the buck, adopting a statement of purpose that is couched in vague and general terms and leaving to the commission the task of making its goals precise. The effect is to lay the commission open to attack on the ground that it seeks to exceed its legal authority. The legislature may also deny the agency full jurisdiction and requisite powers, restrict its salaries, and limit the size of its staff, holding its budget far below the sums it really needs. Grandly ordering the agency to do a job, it may meanly withhold the tools with which to do it.

From the executive, a commission needs well-qualified appointees, political leadership, and continuous support. Commissioners should be not only competent and honest but they should be imaginative, forceful, and devoted to the public welfare. With salaries low, the executive is handicapped in attracting able men. In a few cases, men of outstanding ability have served on state and federal commissions. But this has not been the general rule. Governors and presidents have used these appointments as a means of discharging political obligations: rewarding campaign workers and providing employment to unsuccessful candidates. It is rarely that appointees have been qualified for their posts by training or experience. Temperamentally, they have been characterized by a lack of imagination, an excess of caution, a distaste for forceful action, an inclination to temporize, to play it safe, to let well enough alone. The typical state commissioner, says Emery Troxel, "appears more satisfied with things as they are than with good regulatory effects, more interested in his politics than in his knowledge and expertness. In general, the states are sending nice political-minded boys to do a job that calls for wise and determined men.[6] Appointments to the ICC, according to the Task Force of the Hoover Commission on governmental organization, "have been of mixed quality. Not a few have been political. . . . The Commission has always had a nucleus of very able members, but appointees have only rarely been the best men available."[7] Governors and presidents, moreover, have largely confined themselves to making these appointments. Save in the earliest years of a commission's life, they have offered little political leadership and provided little political support.

From the courts, a commission needs decisions that uphold its authority. But judicial review, in years past, has frequently been hostile. The safeguard of due process has been applied not only to procedure but also to substance, and procedural requirements have sometimes been unduly hampering.

6 / Emery Troxel, *Economics of Public Utilities* (New York: Rinehart & Co., Inc., 1947), p. 88.

7 / Commission on Organization of the Executive Branch of the Government, *Task Force Report on Regulatory Commissions* (Washington, D.C.: Government Printing Office, 1949), pp. 84-85.

From the public, finally, a commission needs continuing support. Without this, it will find itself in trouble with the legislature, the executive, and even with the courts. But people, in general, have little enthusiasm for regulation. When flagrant abuses are disclosed, they will demand enactment of a law. But once the law is passed, and a commission created to enforce it, their attention will turn to other things. The only group that will maintain its interest in the commission's work will be the industry it was set up to regulate.

Internal Shortcomings

The causes of commission weakness are internal as well as external. Properly to perform its function, a commission should have integrity in handling its cases, competence in managing its operations, imagination in planning its program, initiative in carrying out its plans, and vigor in enforcing its orders. To some degree, commissions have been found wanting in each of these respects.

There have been instances in which commissioners have taken bribes. But these are no more common than among public officials in other fields. Dishonesty is more prevalent, however, when it appears in subtler forms. Commissioners have yielded to pressure from the governor or the White House; from members of the legislature or the Congress. They have permitted industry representatives to confer with them privately in furtherance of their interests regarding matters that should have been discussed only in public where all those concerned were given an equal opportunity to hear and be heard. They have accepted lavish entertainment and costly gifts. Serving for low salaries for limited terms, they see well-paid lifetime jobs awaiting them in the regulated industries. And they may let these factors influence the decisions that they make. The commissions, in general, have not attained the standards of integrity expected of the courts.

A supposed advantage of the regulatory commission is its ability to dispose of matters informally and, in formal cases, to adopt procedures that are simpler than those employed in the courts. But commission proceedings, in fact, are criticized as being legalistic, inflexible, and ponderous. Witnesses are examined and cross-examined at length. Exhibits are piled high. The resulting records are voluminous. And each commissioner must study the record before a decision can be made. With a large and growing work load, action is inordinately delayed. In the CAB, in 1960, the average age of dockets closed by formal proceedings was 32 months. In the ICC, contested proceedings ran from 18 to 36 months. In the FCC, proceedings had been pending for more than three years. In the FPC, the backlog of pending cases in 1959 was four times as great as in 1957.[8]

A commission typically takes little or no initiative in searching out and promoting the public interest. Its attitude is passive; its approach to its task is

8 / James M. Landis, *Report on Regulatory Agencies to the President-Elect* (Reprinted by U.S. Senate, Committee on the Judiciary [Washington, D.C.: Government Printing Office, 1960]), pp. 5-6.

judicialized. It acts in response to complaints that may be brought before it and to requests made by the regulated industry, assuming that the public interest will somehow emerge from the adjudication of private disputes.

A commission is likely to be timid. Encountering strong opposition, it may postpone action. Finding action unpopular, it may reverse its course. Thus, the FCC stalled for years before it finally permitted subscription-TV. It proposed that the time devoted to commercials be limited to that allowed by the broadcasters' own rules, but backed down when Congressmen complained. Its handling of applications for license renewal has been cautious in the extreme.

Absorbed with routine matters, the typical commission lacks the time or the will to anticipate foreseeable problems and prepare for their solution. It undertakes no research, plans no program in advance. The ICC did not prepare itself to cope with the situation that was created by increasing competition in transport. The CAB did not prepare to solve the problems created by the termination of trunk-line subsidies. A commission may even fail to develop general standards to guide its action in individual cases. The ICC failed to define the standards of cost that it employed in fixing minimum rates. The CAB enunciated no criteria to control its certification of air routes. The FCC revealed the criteria that were said to govern its allocation of frequencies, but these, as we have seen, are spurious.

Most of the state commissions confine themselves to keeping up with the daily load of work, as John Bauer has put it, "in an easygoing nonalert way." These bodies, says Troxel, "seem to be apathetic and do not press for funds, statutory powers, and other means of improvement."[9] In his study of the federal commissions, Bernstein also notes the "static quality of regulation and the inertia and apathy that gradually overtake the regulatory process," and he continues: "Although tradition, precedent, and custom harden into blind routine in all types of social organization, the commission seems to be peculiarly susceptible to the disease of 'administrative arteriosclerosis.' "[10]

If the provisions of a regulatory statute are to be observed, voluntary compliance must be invited through educational effort and involuntary compliance enforced through investigation and the application of appropriate penalties. Among the regulatory commissions, the enforcement program of the SEC has been outstanding. The Commission has put its emphasis on education. At the same time, it has maintained a continuous check on stock market transactions and the operations of securities dealers, ferreting out violations and moving to impose penalties. The enforcement programs of other commissions, by contrast, are lacking in imagination and vigor. Voluntary compliance is neglected; policing is understaffed and poorly financed. A law having been passed, it is left to enforce itself.

The Life Cycle of Regulation

Political scientists have come to describe the evolution of the regulatory

9 / Troxel, *op. cit.,* p. 88.

10 / Bernstein, *op. cit.,* pp. 100-101.

commission in terms of a biological metaphor. The life cycle of such an agency, they say, has its periods of gestation, of vigorous youth, of settled maturity, and decrepit old age. But here the analogy breaks down: commissions do not die; they ossify.

When a commission is first established, it may well act with vigor. It then has popular support. It is likely to be staffed with men of vision, courage, and skill. Born in an environment of conflict, it has the strength and the will to do battle with the regulated industry. If it moves with speed, it may effect significant reforms. The SEC, given extraordinary powers and striking while the iron still glowed with the heat of public indignation, imposed the requirement of truthful disclosure on the securities markets, established its supervision of trading on the securities exchanges, and effected a thorough reorganization of the electrical utility industry. The FPC and the FCC, in their early years, provided leadership in the improvement of accounting practices. The FPC fought through the cases that finally disposed of the reproduction cost method of evaluating utility properties. The FCC conducted thorough investigations of the telephone and radio broadcasting industries and brought about important reforms in the relationship between the telephone holding company and the associated operating companies and in that between the radio networks and the broadcasting stations.

Such things may happen during a commission's youth. In time, however, the agency matures. The force that gave it impetus is spent. The quality of its personnel declines. It loses its taste for conflict. Divorced from other sources of support, it turns for strength to the industry it regulates. Through constant contact, it comes to accept the industry's standards as its own. Among the federal commissions, only the SEC appears usually to have received high marks from external examiners. The FPC sought to escape its legal obligation to fix the field price of gas. The FCC took little action to check the flagrant abuses of the broadcasting privilege. Caves, in his study of the CAB, found "no clear trend toward more and more willingness to accept the industry's outlook," but he did find "an unwillingness to 'rock the boat.'" The Board, he says, "has not sought out bold and imaginative policies with chances of great success but also with chances of great failure and strong repercussions in the industry. It has not tried to stir public discussion of the 'public interest' in air transport policy as an alternative to taking a plausible public interest view that has never diverged too far from the interests of the carrier managements themselves."[11] It should be noted that, with imaginative and vigorous new leadership, a dormant commission may take a new lease on life, as did the FPC and the FCC in the early sixties. But such improvement is no more likely to be lasting than was the vigor of the agency's early years.

In its old age, the commission loses all contact with the public interest. It envisages its function as that of protecting the health and welfare of the regulated industry and maintaining its own status as the industry's protector. It ceases to adapt its thinking to external change. Its policies are encrusted with tradition; its procedures hardened into routine. It comes to be institutionalized,

11 / Richard E. Caves, *Air Transport and its Regulators* (Cambridge, Mass.: Harvard University Press, 1962), pp. 289, 298.

embodying vested interests and seeming to have values in itself. Its members come to be more concerned with preserving its existence than with forwarding its purposes.

This description would seem to fit the ICC. The oldest of the federal commissions, it won a reputation in its early years for expertness and impartiality. Over the decades, it has steadily grown in size, in power, and in the scope of its responsibilities. But the Commission's policies are obsolete. Instead of adapting them to the changing needs of a growing economy, it has devoted its efforts to the preservation of the status quo, obstructing the evolution of a coordinated system of transport, enforcing inefficiency, delaying innovation, and increasing costs. The Commission's procedures are ponderous, its deliberations protracted. Its critics describe it as apathetic, lethargic, torpid, moribund, suffering a marasmus[12]—defined by Webster as a "progressive emaciation and general wasting due to enfeebled constitution rather than any specific or ascertainable cause." And there are few outside the Commission's halls who come to its defense.

Reform of Regulation

Proposals for the reform of regulation have come from several quarters. Executives and legislators, impelled by disclosures of corruption, have proposed the creation of safeguards whereby honesty may be assured. Students of public administration, impressed by evidence of administrative inefficiency, have proposed that the regulatory function be reorganized. Members of the bar, suspicious of procedures that differ from those of the courts, have proposed that the regulatory process be further judicialized.

The need for additional measures to insure the integrity of regulation was made clear by disclosures of corruption in 1958. The retention of conflicting interests was already forbidden to commissioners and their staffs by the regulatory statutes. Acceptance of bribes was against the law. Now, the SEC promulgated a code of ethics forbidding its members to discuss pending cases with outsiders, instructing them to refuse lavish gifts or lavish hospitality, and directing them to "reject any efforts by the executive or legislative branches of the government to affect their independent determination of any matter being considered by this commission." In 1961, President Kennedy issued an executive order forbidding commissioners and the heads of other agencies to take private employment incompatible with their public duties, to receive any payment except from the government for official services, or to accept gifts under defined circumstances, and requiring each agency to issue similar orders to its employees. And in 1962, on his recommendation, Congress passed a law forbidding officials to accept outside compensation in connection with cases before their agencies and disqualifying former officials from appearing as agents or attorneys on matters connected with their former duties.

12 / See Samuel P. Huntington, "The Marasmus of the ICC," *Yale Law Journal,* Vol. LXI (1952), pp. 467-509.

To improve commission management, speed action, and reduce delay, a number of measures have been proposed by experts in public administration. First, they recommend that the membership of the larger commissions be reduced—from 11 in the ICC and 7 in the FCC to 3 or 5. Second, they recommend that all administrative authority be assigned to a chairman appointed by the chief executive. Among the federal commissions, this had been done by 1969 in all except the ICC where the chairmanship still revolved, year by year, among the 11 members. Third, they recommend that responsibility for making decisions in individual cases be delegated to hearing examiners, with the commissioners themselves acting only by choice or on appeal, as is now the practice of the FCC and the CAB. And finally, they urge that the regulatory agencies establish research sections and set up policy-planning staffs.

Critics of the regulatory agencies have complained that the several functions assigned to the commissions—the administration of detailed regulations, the planning of policy, and the adjudication of disputes—are incompatible. Administrative duties may dissipate the energy that should be devoted to adjudication. The bias implicit in policymaking may warp the judgment needed in settling disputes. This reasoning has led to proposals that each of the federal commissions be split, the administrative and policymaking functions being transferred to an executive department and the judicial function remaining independent.[13] This proposal is open to question. Transfers of routine administrative functions has much to recommend it. But in the regulatory agencies, as in the executive departments, policy grows case by case out of decisions that are taken through adjudication. The two would appear to be so intimately related that their divorcement is neither feasible nor desirable.

A second familiar complaint has been that the regulatory commissions serve both as prosecutor and as judge, the first of these functions destroying the impartiality required for the proper performance of the second. Segregation of these functions, too, has been proposed, their performance to be placed in separate agencies: prosecution within an executive department and adjudication in an independent commission. When Congress acted on the problem, it did not go this far, seeking only to insure the independence of the judicial function within the commissions themselves. Under the Administrative Procedure Act of 1946, the appointment, promotions, salaries, and tenure of hearing examiners are determined by the Civil Service Commission; the regulatory commissions are forbidden to transfer the examiners to other duties and are required to assign cases to them in rotation. There is no evidence that these requirements have had significant effects. The regulatory agencies were already leaning over backward to judicialize their procedures. Private interests, were not, in fact, abused.[14]

13 / This proposal was endorsed by Louis J. Hector on his retirement from the CAB in 1960 and by Newton Minow on his retirement from the FCC in 1963. It has been rejected by William L. Cary, former Chairman of the SEC. See Louis J. Hector, "Problems of the CAB and the Independent Regulatory Commissions," *Yale Law Journal,* Vol. LXLX (1960), pp. 931-64; Newton N. Minow, *Equal Time* (New York: Atheneum, 1964), pp. 279-89; Cary, *op. cit.,* chap. 5.

14 / On the reform of regulatory agencies, see Emmette S. Redford, *American Government and the Economy* (New York: Macmillan Co., 1965), chap. xxv.

INHERENT DEFECTS OF REGULATION

The failures of regulation as a method of compelling performance in the public interest are not to be attributed solely to the commission form of organization, to vague objectives and limited powers, to mediocre personnel and inadequate appropriations, to apathetic administration, judicial hostility, and the lack of popular support. If these defects could be remedied, to be sure, regulation would be more effective. But it would still fall short of the standard set by competition. For the difficulties of regulation are largely inherent in the nature of the undertaking itself.

Regulation as a Substitute for Competition

Taking the place of competition as the method of control, regulation should be expected to yield comparable results. It should not only prevent the regulated industry from charging a monopoly price, impairing the quality of its service, and enjoying a monopoly profit. It should provide an incentive to adopt new methods, to improve quality, to increase efficiency and cut costs, to develop mass markets and expand output by selling at a lower price. It does none of these things.

Regulation, at best, is a pallid substitute for competition. It cannot prescribe quality, force efficiency, or require innovation, because such action would invade the sphere of management. But when it leaves these matters to the discretion of industry, it denies consumers the protection that competition would afford. Regulation cannot set prices below an industry's costs however excessive they may be. Competition does so, and the high-cost company is compelled to discover means whereby its costs can be reduced. Regulation does not enlarge consumption by setting prices at the lowest level consistent with a fair return. Competition has this effect. Regulation fails to encourage performance in the public interest by offering rewards and penalties. Competition offers both.

Regulation is static, backward-looking, preoccupied with the problems of the past. It does nothing to stimulate change, seeking to maintain order on the basis of the old technology. It is slow to adapt to change; new problems appear, but regulatory thinking lags. Competition, by contrast, is dynamic. It was not the state commissions that cut the price and multiplied the consumption of electricity in the region bordering on the Tennessee Valley, but the yardstick competition of the TVA. It was not the ICC that overhauled the structure of railroad rates, but the competition of the trucks. It was not the CAB that sparked the low-fare air-coach service, but the competition of the nonskeds. If left to regulation, none of these innovations would have occurred.

Regulation is slower than competition. It must satisfy the requirements of due process: investigate, give notice, hold hearings, study the record, make findings, issue orders, permit appeals. All this takes time and delays action. In some cases, delay may be harmful, as when it permits earnings to rise well above or to fall far below the return required to attract new capital. In other cases, it may be helpful, as when it brakes an inflationary spiral of wages and prices. But here, the merit of regulation lies, not in its efficiency, but in its inefficiency.

Regulation-Mindedness

Industry-mindedness is said to afflict the regulatory commission when cut off from political support. Regulation-mindedness is endemic to regulation as such. The regulator's business is to make regulation successful and keep it so. If the effectiveness of his controls is weakened by the freedom of firms beyond his jurisdiction, he seeks wider jurisdiction. If the applicability of his controls is lessened by changing circumstances, he seeks tighter controls. It does not occur to him that the ultimate purpose of regulation might be better served if jurisdiction were narrowed or controls relaxed. His presumption favors expansion of coverage and elaboration of detail. The regulator's concern is less with the purpose of regulation than with the instrument of regulation itself.

Two or more regulated industries may offer services that can be substituted for one another, such as electricity and gas, telephone and telegraph, AM and FM radio and TV, and transport by railway, waterway, and highway, and by air. Here, it should be possible to afford the public some protection by maintaining competition between them. But increasingly, those imposing regulation in one field have sought to preserve its effectiveness by obstructing competition from another. When the highways came to protect shippers against the railways, the reaction was not to relax the regulation of the rails, but to suppress the competition of the trucks.

So, too, with competition within a regulated industry. For many years, though all railroads were regulated, it was the policy of government to provide the public with further protection by maintaining competition between them. Such a policy could readily have been applied to transport by highway and by air. But now, rate bureaus are legalized for rail and motor carriers, entry into the highway and air transport industries is restricted, and mergers of carriers in each of these industries are approved. The safeguards of competition, though available, have been discarded, and reliance placed upon the creation and the control of monopoly.

As the method of regulation has changed, its purpose, too, has changed. From seeking to protect the consumer against high rates and poor service, it has come to protect the regulated industry against low rates and impaired earnings. From the correction and prevention of abuses, it has come to insure the industry's prosperity. From supervision in the public interest, its orientation has come to be that of management.

Power without Responsibility

In the case described, the regulated industry comes, in the end, to have two masters: its own management and the regulatory agency. Essential functions of management are duplicated. Managerial decisions are reviewed. Where the regulatory agency finds them to be wise, it allows them to stand. Where it finds them to be unwise, it exercises a veto power. It thus acts to protect management against the consequences of its own mistakes.

If there were assurance that the business judgment of commissioners would be superior to that of managers in more than half of the cases (weighted by their importance), we might conclude that duality of management would produce a net gain. But commissioners, in fact, are unlikely to be the better businessmen. And even if they were, there would be offsetting costs.

Duplication costs money; two managements impose a heavier administrative burden than does one. Negotiation between the managements takes time; decisions are inevitably delayed. Division of authority saps the vitality of an enterprise; diverts energy from the solution of external problems to the prosecution of internal disputes. Managements come to direct their attention more to outsmarting the regulators than to introducing innovations, improving service, and reducing costs.

Regulation dissipates responsibility. The ICC is required, in setting rates, to consider their probable effect upon the volume of traffic. In doing so, it may substitute its own judgment for that of railway managements. And here, if earnings fall, there is no one whom the owners of the roads can hold responsible. The managements are deprived of power; the Commission has power but lacks responsibility. And even if managements are not reversed, decisions are often so delayed that substantial losses are sustained. In cases such as this, management escapes accountability by blaming the regulators. And the regulators are not made accountable by law.

PART IV

Controlling Monopoly by
Public Enterprise

Chapter 21   FIELDS OF PUBLIC ENTERPRISE ·

The methods employed by government to insure that the activities of business are so conducted as to serve the general interest have included the maintenance of competition, the regulation of private enterprise, and public ownership and operation of industry. Where competition has proved to be unworkable and where regulation has failed, private enterprise has given way to public enterprise. The problems presented by the maintenance of competition and by the regulation of business have been examined in the preceding chapters; those presented by government ownership and operation will be considered in Part IV. In the present chapter we shall review the enterprises owned and operated by governments in other countries and by the federal, state, and local governments in the United States. In the next two chapters we shall examine, in greater detail, the most important cases of federal government enterprise: public power projects, the atomic energy industry, and the post office. In the final chapter we shall analyze some of the problems that have emerged from experience with public enterprise at home and abroad.

THE MEANING OF PUBLIC ENTERPRISE

Public enterprise is difficult to define. Some of the activities of government are regarded as examples of such enterprise, and others are not. But the line between the two is not an easy one to draw. According to one definition, public enterprise is said to involve provision by government of goods or services that might also be provided privately. But this distinction excludes the postal service, which has always enjoyed a monopoly but is generally thought to be a public enterprise. And it includes the school system, which competes with private education but is not usually designated as a public enterprise. According to the definition that is commonly given, a governmental activity may or may not be called a public enterprise, depending upon how it is financed. Some goods and services produced by government are distributed to users in return for individual payments in the same way as sales are made by private firms. Others are distributed without charge, and their costs recovered through taxation. In the first case, government is said to be engaging in enterprise; in the second, it is not. But when the line is drawn here, activities that are otherwise identical may fall

481

on opposite sides. Thus, a road financed by charging tolls will be defined as a public enterprise and one financed by collecting taxes will not. And this is true even though the taxes imposed, such as motor vehicle license fees and taxes on motor fuels, are designed to make collections from users in proportion to the character and quantity of their use. There are services, moreover, where the prices charged are not set high enough to cover total costs, their deficits being met through taxation. This has been the case, for instance, with the Post Office and with certain urban transit systems. But self-support cannot be made the test of public enterprise. For, if it were, the same activity would be included in one year and excluded in another, depending upon whether it had operated in the black or in the red. Nor can collection of some part of the cost of a service from its users be made the test. For in this case, a small matriculation or diploma fee would suffice to classify a city college or a state university as a public enterprise, even though its costs were defrayed almost entirely from general revenues.

In the nature of the case, any definition of public enterprise must be arbitrary. No such definition will be attempted here. But in the discussion that follows, little or no consideration will be given to the traditional activities of government such as the provision of roads and streets, police and fire protection, and public education, attention being directed, in the main, to those activities that are businesslike in character, involving services that might be provided commercially. It is with the use of public enterprise as an alternative to competition or to regulation that we are here concerned.

PUBLIC ENTERPRISE IN OTHER COUNTRIES

Public enterprise, varying in scope, is found in every country in the world. In certain fields—transport, communications, and municipal services—it has long been usual. The movement toward nationalization was speeded, in the 20th century, by war, depression, and war. World War I brought communism to Russia. World War II brought it to the countries of Central Europe and to China. The wars and the depression contributed to the spread of public enterprise outside the communist region—in Western Europe and in the underdeveloped areas. Such enterprise, in its present scope, extends from its traditional fields to new industries such as aviation, radio, and television, and to mining, manufacturing, and trade. The tide of nationalization reached its high point during the years of postwar reconstruction in the forties. With disillusionment in the fifties, it started to recede.

Traditional Fields of Public Enterprise

For more than a century governments have monopolized certain industries, operating them as sources of public revenue. From 10 to 20 countries, in each case, have thus monopolized tobacco, matches, alcoholic beverages, and salt. In the Latin countries of Europe and America, in Australia, and elsewhere, governments finance themselves, in part, by conducting public lotteries, having nationalized the gambling industry.

Another long-established field of public enterprise is transport and communication. Highways and port facilities have been publicly provided everywhere. The railroads of Belgium, Italy, Germany, and Switzerland were taken over by governments in the latter years of the 19th century. All those of France were taken over by 1937. The railroads of more than 50 countries, including all the major powers but Britain and the United States, were nationalized before World War II. Urban transit systems have been predominantly governmental. Post offices have always been national undertakings; the telegraph systems, in most countries, have been developed by the postal authorities. In Germany the telephone service was developed by the state telegraph system. Elsewhere in Europe the telephones were taken over around the turn of the century.

Public utilities, throughout the world, have long been owned by governments. Water supply, in nearly all large cities, is a public responsibility. Gas and electricity were publicly provided in more than three fourths of the cities of Germany and in more than half of those in Great Britain before 1930. Regional systems for the generation and transmission of electricity were operated by governments in Canada, New Zealand, and South Africa. The Central Electricity Board, in Great Britain, was given a monopoly of transmission lines by a Conservative government in 1926.

Housing has been supplied by governments for longer periods and in greater quantities in Europe than in the United States. In England public housing was first permitted by law in 1851. In Germany and the Netherlands, it dates from 1901. Elsewhere it had its origin in the shortages that followed World War I. In most countries, the governments undertook to stimulate construction by co-operatives, limited-dividend societies, and other private builders by providing subsidies in the form of cheap land, tax exemption, and low-interest loans. But in some cases—notably in the city of Vienna—housing was built and operated by the governments themselves. In Great Britain, between the two world wars, a fourth of the new housing, including virtually all of the rental housing, was constructed by local authorities.

The Nationalization Movement

The movement toward public ownership was quickened during the thirties and particularly during the forties. It made its appearance not only in the advanced economies of Western Europe but also in underdeveloped areas throughout the world. Its causes were various. In Britain it found its origin in the tradition of a socialist party, finally come to power, and in proposals for industrial reorganization designed to enhance efficiency. In France it sprang from the syndicalist philosophy that calls for the seizure of power by organized labor and from a desire to punish capitalists who had collaborated with the enemy during World War II. In Italy it began with an effort to protect private enterprises from the consequences of the Great Depression by providing governmental aid. In the underdeveloped areas it gave expression to a worldwide revolt against colonialism and imperialism and to nationalistic demands for economic independence. But however diverse its causes, it led, in every case, to a marked expansion in the scope of public enterprise.

The nationalization program of the Labor Party in Great Britain, effected through measures adopted in 1946, 1947, and 1948, included finance (the Bank of England), Commonwealth communications (civil aviation, cables, and radio), public utilities (gas and electricity), transport (carriers by rail, by water, and by road), a depressed industry (coal), and another industry that fell into none of these categories (iron and steel). Some of these measures were not controversial. But others, such as those relating to road haulage and to iron and steel, were highly so. The program was carried out by a socialist government. But it was not envisaged as a part of a revolution that would bring about a completely socialized economy. Each case was argued on its merits. And the argument for nationalization ran in terms of its possible contribution to productive efficiency and public responsibility. Coal mining, for instance, was to be made more efficient through reorganization and modernization. The iron and steel industry, already monopolized, was to be made more responsible by transferring its controlling shares from private owners to the government. But Britain was still to have a mixed economy, a fifth of it—more or less—being operated by the state, four fifths of it by private enterprise.

In France the postwar nationalizations included the Bank of France and the four largest commercial banks, the 34 largest insurance companies, as much of the coal, gas, and electrical industries as still remained in private hands, the Renault works, and a company manufacturing engines for airplanes. In addition, the government extended its participation in mixed companies in a number of different fields: aviation, shipping, motion pictures, broadcasting, news service, chemicals, and petroleum. The French program was inspired by leftists—trade unionists, socialists, and communists—who had played a large part in the resistance movement in France and among the Free French abroad. Nationalization was seen by these groups as affording the means to three ends. It was to promote economic reconstruction. It was to transfer economic power from the capitalists to the workers. And in some cases, such as the Renault works and the airplane engine company, it was to punish collaborators. In these cases, the properties were confiscated. But in France, as in Great Britain, compensation was the rule.

In Italy industries were made public less by design than by default. An Institute for Industrial Reconstruction was set up during the depression of the thirties to extend financial aid to ailing industries. This agency, with its subsidiaries, came to hold the shares of many Italian companies. These holdings, moreover, were continued and increased during and after the war. As a result, the Institute controls a substantial part of Italian industry, owning nearly all of the stock in shipbuilding, most of that in iron and steel, and a large part of that in the manufacture of transport equipment, electrical equipment, tractors, and machine tools. In addition, the government owns the country's five largest banks, the railroads and the airlines, the telephone, telegraph, radio, and television systems, the motion picture studios, the coal mines, and the petroleum industry. Public enterprise, though adopted without reference to any logical pattern, is thus as extensive in Italy as it is in Britain or in France.

In the underdeveloped countries, nationalization has been a means of freeing domestic industry from foreign control. The railway, urban transit, power, and communications systems of these countries have usually been provided by foreign capital. Exploitation of their natural resources has also been undertaken by foreigners. In some cases, the governments of such countries have expelled the foreign owners by buying their shares. In other cases, foreign properties have been taken by force. Here, nationalism has been the motive and socialism has merely been the means.

Among all underdeveloped countries, further industrial development is a major goal of policy. But industrialization requires large amounts of capital. And apart from the production of oil, the prospects for investment are so uncertain that funds are no longer provided by foreign enterprise. Development from internal sources, moreover, is handicapped by a shortage of voluntary savings, an absence of capital markets, and a lack of domestic entrepreneurs. In this situation, the governments of backward countries raise funds for development by taxation or inflation and by borrowing from the governments of advanced countries or from international agencies. In some cases, they set up banks to finance private ventures. In others, they assume the responsibilities of entrepreneurship. Here, they may go into partnership with private enterprise, or provide management themselves. In some cases, the governments plan to retain control. In others, they set up new undertakings and operate them for a time, with a view to selling them to private firms. Here, again, nationalism is the motive and socialism but a means.

The Scope of Public Enterprise

The fields in which public enterprise is most common, in the noncommunist world, are banking, transport, communications, and public utilities. In nearly all countries, the central banks are owned by governments; in some countries, other banks and insurance companies have been nationalized. Almost all of the railroads outside of the United States are public undertakings. Commercial airlines, with few exceptions, are government-owned. Telephone and telegraph services, too, are usually governmental. Radio and television broadcasting is a public enterprise in most countries, being wholly private only in Latin America. Urban transit and electricity are characteristically provided by governments. Rental housing, in cities, is widely accepted as a public responsibility.

Several governments are engaged in mining, in manufacturing, and in foreign trade. Great Britain, France, and Italy operate coal mines. Turkey is in the business of mining coal, copper, chrome, and manganese. Tin is produced by Bolivia, and oil by Mexico. The oil resources of South America and the Middle

East are owned and their exploitation controlled by governments. Fifteen of the 200 largest industrial enterprises in noncommunist countries outside the United States are government-owned, being engaged in the production of chemicals, petroleum products, and iron and steel.[1] Public enterprise in manufacturing is found most often in the less developed countries. In India, for instance, the government produces iron and steel, machine tools, locomotives and railway cars, communications equipment, fertilizers, antibiotics, and insecticides. State trading has long been employed by countries that export foodstuffs and raw materials as a means of increasing the prices and incomes of their producers.

Denationalization

In the underdeveloped countries, the process of nationalization is continuing. In Great Britain and in Western Europe, it appears to have run its course. The high hopes held out at the end of the war have failed of fulfillment. Consumers, workers, and politicans alike have been disillusioned. There has been a widespread loss of faith in the benefits of public enterprise. As a result, the proponents of nationalization have come to regard the process as completed and have ceased to urge its extension to other fields. In Britain, the process was reversed when a Conservative government returned the trucking industry and the iron and steel mills to private ownership. But denationalization, too, appears to be finished. The Labor Party, again in power, renationalized steel in 1967. And now, as with the other industries taken over by Labor, the Conservatives permitted public enterprise to stand. In France, though the national industries are criticized, there has been no move to return them to private hands.

PUBLIC ENTERPRISE IN THE UNITED STATES

In the United States, as in other countries, the activities of government have steadily grown in variety and in extent. Services that were once provided by private enterprise have come increasingly to be supplied by public agencies free of charge. Cities, today, provide not only for streets and police and fire protection but also for harbor facilities, sewage disposal, and the removal of garbage and trash; not only for elementary instruction but also for school lunches, playgrounds, medical examinations, public clinics, and hospital beds; for colleges, libraries, museums, zoos, parks, bathing beaches, swimming pools, golf courses, and free concerts by bands and orchestras. State governments, too, provide not only for highways and prisons but also for parks, forests, hospitals, universities, and various programs of social security. The federal government, apart from such activities as the maintenance of national parks, libraries, and museums, does not itself provide free services. But it contributes, through grants in aid, to the provision of such services by the cities and the states.

Services rendered commercially, as well as those provided without charge, have passed from private into public hands. The operation of city water systems

1 / *Fortune*, September 15, 1967, pp. 140 ff.

and the provision of water for irrigation are now predominantly governmental responsibilities. And government has entered increasingly into the provision of such services as credit, insurance, housing, and electricity. These developments reflect a striking change, over time, in public attitudes. The trend has clearly been toward giving wider scope to production by agencies of government.

Character and Extent of Public Enterprise

The character of public enterprise differs from industry to industry. It differs, first, as to scope. In some cases, as with the postal service, government has monopolized an entire field. In others, as with the generation and distribution of electricity, it has monopolized particular markets but left most markets in private hands. In still others, notably in the field of insurance, it has entered into competition with private firms. Public enterprise also differs as to form. In some fields, such as the postal service and electric light and power, government has both owned and operated productive facilities. In others, such as atomic energy, it has provided facilities that have been operated under contract by private concerns.

Public enterprise, in all its forms, still plays a minor role in the American economy. In 1968, enterprises owned and operated by state and local governments accounted for 0.45 percent of the nation's income, federal enterprises for 0.92 percent, all public enterprises for only 1.37 percent. State and local enterprises accounted for 0.63 percent of the persons employed in production, federal enterprises for 1.14 percent, all public enterprises for only 1.77 percent.[2] "Creeping socialism," denounced with such vigor by businessmen and politicians, still had a long way to creep.

Causes of Public Enterprise

The establishment of public enterprises, in the United States, is not to be attributed to socialist ideology. For, in this country, the doctrines of socialism have never been embraced by more than a tiny minority. Nor have such enterprises been created to afford a source of public revenue. In other countries, governments have been financed, in part, by profits derived from state monopolies of products such as tobacco, matches, and salt. But here, state and municipal liquor stores are almost the only example of public enterprises operated for a profit. And even they are justified as means of controlling the use of alcohol.

The real causes of public enterprise in America are many and varied: (1) Productive activities of the greatest magnitude have been undertaken because they were deemed essential to the prosecution of warfare and to national defense. This was the origin of the first dam thrown across the Tennessee River, at Muscle Shoals, Alabama, during World War I. It was the origin of the atomic energy and synthetic rubber plants built during World War II. It explains the great shipbuilding programs undertaken during both world wars. (2) Other

2 | *Survey of Current Business,* July, 1969, pp. 21, 39.

activities were inaugurated for the purpose of pulling the country out of the Great Depression. This was the beginning of the Reconstruction Finance Corporation and other lending agencies, of public housing, and of large-scale river valley developments. (3) Some public enterprises have been created because private business saw little prospect of profit in a field. This was the case with the Alaska Railroad, with crop insurance, and with the provision of electricity in small towns and rural areas. (4) In other instances, the cost of an undertaking has been so high and its risks so great that it could not be privately financed. This was true of the Panama Canal and the river valley developments. It would have been true of atomic energy in time of peace. (5) The acquisition of many enterprises has been incidental to undertakings established for other purposes. Dams built to provide water for irrigation have also provided water power for the generation of electricity. Operation of the Panama Canal has also involved operation of the Panama Railroad. The maintenance of prisons has necessitated the creation of prison industries. (6) At times, governments have been forced to take over an industry by the breakdown of operations under private management. This has been the case with streetcar and subway systems in certain cities. It was the case with the railroads during World War I.

Under all these circumstances, the inauguration of public enterprises has been less a matter of choice than of necessity. But there are cases where deliberate choices have been made. (7) Some enterprises are designed to conserve the nation's resources: state and national forests, irrigation works, and public administration of grazing lands. (8) Others are related to programs of social welfare: public education, housing, health, and social insurance. (9) In some cases, public ownership and operation have been stimulated by the revelation of abuses under private enterprise and by the failure of regulation to keep rates and earnings from going too high. This was true of electricity in the thirties. Here, the use of public plants as yardsticks by which to measure private operations was one of the arguments advanced for their establishment. (10) There are a few cases where it appears that public enterprise is to be attributed solely to the view that the nature of a service is such as to require its socialization. This doubtless explains monopolization of the postal service by the federal government and of water distribution by many municipalities. But the logic of this policy has not been carried very far. The arguments advanced for public enterprise, in these cases, would seem to apply with equal force to the telephone service and the distribution of milk. It can merely be recorded as a historic fact that socialism has been adopted for communication by mail and not by telephone, for supplying water and not for delivering milk.

Obstacles to Public Enterprise

Expansion of public enterprise has not been hampered by the courts. Where governments obtain property by exercising the right of eminent domain, state and federal constitutions require that the taking be for public use and that just compensation be paid. And where new facilities are built or existing facilities purchased in a voluntary sale, the expenditures must be made for a public purpose or to promote the general welfare. But the courts have seldom obstructed public enterprise by requiring excessive compensation. And they have accepted the judgment of legislative bodies as to public purposes. The Supreme Court of the United States upheld the establishment of a municipal fuel yard by the city of Portland, Maine, in 1917,[3] socialization of banking, grain storing, milling, and other enterprises by the state of North Dakota in 1920,[4] initiation of a wholesale and retail gasoline business by the city of Lincoln, Nebraska, in 1927,[5] and the right of the federal government to engage in the business of generating, transmitting, and distributing hydroelectric power in 1936.[6]

Public enterprise has been limited more often by the legislatures than by the courts. In the past, cities were frequently prevented from obtaining the funds required to purchase or construct a utility plant by legal restrictions on their borrowing power. During the thirties, however, many of these restrictions were removed. Cities were authorized to issue bonds outside their debt limits for the purpose of acquiring utility properties, the issues to be serviced from utility revenues. They were permitted to sell utility services beyond their boundaries. Provision was made, too, for the creation of special authorities with broad jurisdiction and added borrowing power. Today, as a result, there are fewer legal barriers to local government enterprise.

The most serious obstacle to a further extension of public ownership and operation lies in the state of public opinion. The American people, in years of prosperity, look upon public enterprise with suspicion and upon private enterprise with admiration or, at least, with tolerance. This may be due, in part, to the persistence and the skill with which propaganda unfavorable to public enterprise has been disseminated by private interests. It is also due, in large measure, to the demonstrated ability of private enterprise to render satisfactory service at an acceptable price.

Public Competition with Private Enterprise

Business organizations, such as the United States Chamber of Commerce and the National Association of Manufacturers, have complained, from time to time, concerning government competition with private firms. Such competition, they contend, is unfair, since public enterprises may enjoy lower costs and may even be conducted at a loss. Toward the end of the Hoover administration, a special committee was set up by the House of Representatives to investigate the problem. The committee held extensive hearings and built up a long record of cases, coming to the conclusion that "The entrance of the government into commercial and industrial undertakings, backed by public credit and resources and its military and civilian personnel, for the purpose of competing with the

3 / *Jones* v. *City of Portland,* 245 U.S. 217.

4 / *Green* v. *Frazier,* 253 U.S. 233.

5 / *Standard Oil Co.* v. *City of Lincoln,* 275 U.S. 504.

6 / *Ashwander* v. *TVA,* 297 U.S. 288.

business establishments and the opportunities of livelihood of its citizens is . . . repugnant to our fundamental democratic institutions and aspirations."[7] It therefore recommended that such activities be abandoned and that a standing committee of Congress be established to guard against "unwise and unprofitable encroachments" upon private enterprise. This report was followed by a great expansion of governmental undertakings during the depression and the war. Then, in 1953, another committee of the House held hearings on the same subject, taking four volumes of testimony from witnesses who complained that the federal government was producing some 275 different types of goods and services. The list included such items as anchor chains, brushes and brooms, cleaning and pressing, Diesel engines, furniture, greenhouses, harness shops, ice cream, laundries, mattresses, paint, rope, seeds, tailoring, and woodworking. It appeared to be quite shocking until subjected to analysis.

In some cases, as with the Post Office and atomic energy, government has always had a monopoly. In others, as with crop insurance, private enterprise has no desire to compete. In a few, as with electricity, government has taken over monopolies from private owners. This may be resented, but it is not a case of public competition with private enterprise. There are other goods and services, however, that are produced both by government and by private firms. But some of them are sold in separate markets: low-rent housing to tenants who cannot afford to pay commercial rentals, public loans to borrowers who cannot obtain credit from private lenders. The public and private agencies do not compete. Other things are produced by government for its own use: paint and rope by the Navy, mail bags by the Post Office, munitions by the arsenals, and local services in the Canal Zone and on army posts. Such items are numerous. They make up most of the list compiled by the committee of the House. Perhaps the government should buy these things instead of making them. But the practice complained of here is the common business practice of vertical integration, not competition with private enterprise. Such competition has occurred in a few cases: the former postal savings system with private savings banks, city colleges and state universities with private institutions, public recreational facilities with the commercial amusement industry. But these cases are comparatively rare. The real grievance is not that government has competed unfairly, but that it has excluded private enterprise from certain profit-making opportunities.

LOCAL GOVERNMENT ENTERPRISES

Local governments, in the United States, engage in a great variety of activities that might be carried on by private enterprise. All of them maintain elementary and secondary schools. Many of them support colleges, libraries, museums, parks, playgrounds, zoos, golf courses, bathing beaches, and swimming pools. Some of them operate public markets, wharves, docks, coalyards, ice plants, slaughterhouses, laundries, and cemeteries. A few run liquor stores, telephone

7 / *Report of the Special Committee Appointed to Investigate Government Competition with Private Enterprise* (72d Cong., 2d Sess., House Report 1985, 1933), p. 18.

systems, and gas plants. Among cities of more than 5,000 population, more than two thirds own their water systems. Water is supplied by a private company in Indianapolis, by the government in every other city of any size. In this field, public enterprise is generally accepted. In three others, it has given rise to controversy. These are urban transit, electrical distribution, and low-rent housing, where cities have entered on a substantial scale.

Urban Transit

In nearly a hundred cities in the United States, and in all but one or two of the larger cities, the transit systems are publicly owned. In some cities transit has been a public enterprise for many years. In others, public ownership has been necessitated by the inability of private companies to make ends meet. The industry, in recent times, has suffered from a steady decline in demand. This has been a consequence, clearly, of the widespread ownership and use of private automobiles. As riders have shifted from mass to individual transport, traffic congestion has increased and the quality of transit service has declined. With fewer riders, the quantity of service also has been curtailed. Costs per passenger have risen, and fares have had to be increased. The combination of poorer service and higher fares has contributed to a further contraction of demand. Private operators, in some cases, have been saved from bankruptcy by public subsidies. Or cities, to maintain an essential service, have bought them out.

The financial record of the municipal systems is not a happy one. Costs have risen, but politicians have curried favor with the voters by opposing higher fares and the taxpayers have financed the deficit. Until World War II the 5-cent fare was traditional in the United States. During the forties, fares were doubled; by 1955 the systems in 50 cities were charging 20 cents. And even at this level, nearly all of the larger systems were operating at a loss.[8] In New York, the fare was held at 5 cents until 1948, at 10 cents until 1953. The system ran a deficit of $46 million in 1953. A Transit Authority was then established and directed to make ends meet. It raised the fare to 15 cents, then to 20 cents, earning a surplus in the early sixties. But at the end of the decade, it was again in the red, running a deficit of $120 million in 1969. It raised its fare to 30 cents in 1970.

The problem of urban transit is complicated by the fact that municipal boundaries are not coterminous with the areas to be served. If transit is to be planned and provided for a metropolitan area as a whole, an instrument whose jurisdiction reaches beyond the city limits must be found. This has been done in Boston where the Commonwealth of Massachusetts has operated the transit system of the metropolitan region since 1918. A number of such authorities have been set up to deal with the urban transit crisis of recent years: one to provide rapid transit in three counties around the San Francisco Bay, another to supply transportation in Southeast Pennsylvania, a third to control transit

8 / Wilfred Owen, *The Metropolitan Transportation Problem* (Washington, D.C.: Brookings Institution, 1956), pp. 127-33.

facilities in New York City and surrounding counties in the state. A fourth body, the Washington Metropolitan Transit Authority, crossing state lines to include the District of Columbia and counties in Maryland and Virginia, has been set up under an interstate compact, with Congressional approval, to provide a system of rapid transit lines for the national capital area.

Municipal Electric Systems

Among cities of more than 5,000 in 1967, electricity was distributed by 506, accounting for 5 percent of such sales. The largest city in the group was Los Angeles. The greatest concentration of such cities was in the Tennessee Valley. Included also were Seattle and Tacoma in Washington; Austin and San Antonio in Texas; Lansing and Kalamazoo in Michigan; Cleveland and Columbus in Ohio; and Kansas City, Missouri; Springfield, Illinois; Ft. Wayne, Indiana; Jacksonville, Florida; and Holyoke, Massachusetts.

Public ownership, in this field, grew steadily until the twenties, largely in small towns where private enterprise had not come in. It declined during the twenties, as many municipal systems were bought up by private concerns or holding companies. This movement was checked during the thirties when the federal government began aggressively to promote municipal ownership. From 1933 to 1938 the Public Works Administration financed the acquisition and construction of power facilities, making grants to cover 45 percent of their cost and loans to cover part or all of the other 55 percent. And municipalities, along with rural cooperatives, were accorded a preference in the sale of federal power. Many of the city systems date from this time.

The relative efficiency of public and private power systems, in American cities, has been a matter of protracted controversy. It is possible, by a judicious selection of cases for comparison, to construct an argument for either side. And this has frequently been done. But where impartial appraisals are available, the evidence is mixed. When public and private systems, in general, are compared, the former make a poor showing because their average size is smaller, and smaller plants have higher unit costs. A more significant comparison can be made between public and private systems of greater size.

It is difficult to compare the quality of service because there are no measures that can readily be applied. But it is possible to compare rates, and here it is found that public rates are usually lower than private rates. In 1967, the average charge made by private companies was 2.31 cents per kwh; the average charge by public companies was 1.49 cents.[9] The lower rates, moreover, appear to be a consequence of lower costs. When 16 large public systems and 19 large private systems were compared for the Twentieth Century Fund, it was shown that the former had slightly higher costs for generation and transmission but substantially lower costs for sales promotion, customer accounting, bill collecting, and general administration, with lower total costs as a result. And the

9 / Federal Power Commission, *Statistics of Publicly Owned Electric Utilities in the United States, 1967.*

public systems had made adequate provisions for depreciation and, unlike the private systems, had devoted large sums to the retirement of their debts.[10] On the other hand, as is often pointed out, private systems pay taxes and public systems are tax exempt. The latter frequently render free services, such as water pumping and street lighting, to city governments. But the cost of such services may not equal the taxes that private companies are required to pay. The public systems enjoy an even greater advantage in their ability to borrow at a lower interest rate. And this, indeed, may go far toward explaining their lower costs and rates. When all these matters are taken into account, however, the municipal systems appear to have been run with marked success.

Public Housing

The beginning of large-scale public housing in the United States dates from the Great Depression. The federal government began, in 1933, to finance the construction of houses as a means of increasing employment. At first, it confined itself to making loans to private, limited-dividend housing corporations. But progress, through these agencies, was slow. Then the government itself bought large tracts of land in cities, often involving the clearance of slums, and built large-scale housing developments, renting apartments to families in the lower-income groups. This was emergency action, designed to promote recovery. The 50 projects constructed in some 30 cities during this period were later transferred to municipal governments. Construction of public housing as a permanent policy dates from the Housing Act of 1937. Here, the purpose was to provide low-rent housing for the poor.

As amended in later years, the Act of 1937 authorizes the federal government to extend financial aid to local governments in providing housing to low-income families. The law calls for the creation of municipal housing authorities whose function it is to assemble the land required for new housing developments, design the structures, let contracts for their construction, and own and operate the finished dwellings. Such authorities have been created in more than 1,500 communities. The federal government approves the sites selected, sets and enforces standards governing the quality and cost of construction, and makes loans and grants to the local authorities.

Local governments are required by the law to contribute 10 percent of the capital invested in each project. They raise this money by selling bonds whose interest is exempt from the federal income tax. Their contribution thus includes a federal subsidy. The federal government is authorized to put up 90 percent of the capital required. Its contribution may take the form of an outright grant or an annual payment. In practice, it has been the latter. The federal payments are made each year for 40 years. They cover the cost of interest and amortization on the local bonds. The local authorities collect the rents from the projects and meet their operating costs. They exempt the projects from property taxes

10 / *Electric Power and Government Policy* (New York: Twentieth Century Fund, 1948), pp. 405-9.

but their losses here are offset by payments in lieu of taxes made in practice at federal expense. In effect, the federal government contributes virtually all of the capital required for a project. The local government is supposed to break even on the operating costs.

In absolute numbers, public housing is impressive. There were around 750,000 dwellings under public management in 1969. The annual number of public housing starts, depending on congressional appropriations, has run between 30,000 and 90,000, standing at 35,000 in recent years. Relatively, public housing is of small significance, accounting for only 1.5 percent of the stock of urban dwellings and sheltering little more than 1 percent of the families in the country as a whole.

The supply of public housing falls far short of the demand. It could be rationed by raising the rents, but this would defeat the purpose of providing low-rent housing for the poor. The rationing is therefore done administratively. Entry is limited to families whose incomes are less than five times the rents, preference being given to applicants of good character in accordance with the urgency of their needs. Continued occupancy is limited to families whose incomes, following entry, do not increase by more than 25 percent. The median income of public housing tenants is less than $2,500 a year. Many are broken families. A quarter are over 65 years of age. A quarter are on relief. The average cost of operating a unit of public housing in the mid-sixties was $70 per month. The average rent was $44. The housing obviously was provided, not on a commercial basis, but as a form of public charity.

Public housing is widely held to be a failure. The initial cost of public housing units has been inordinately high. Some of them, having been poorly maintained, are now in a state of physical decay. Many of the housing authorities are facing deficits, their operating costs having come to exceed their income from rents. So these costs, as well as the capital costs, are now to be subsidized by the federal government under legislation enacted in 1969. Public housing has been costly. And, more seriously, it has failed to effect the social rehabilitation of the low-income families for whom it was designed. If the problem of housing these people is really to be solved, other approaches must be found.

STATE GOVERNMENT ENTERPRISES

Most states maintain public parks and forests. All states run factories in their prisons, making products such as bags and binder twine for sale to farmers, automobile license plates, and a variety of other goods for public use. But the major business enterprises in which the states are now engaged are the maintenance of insurance services, the operation of liquor stores, the provision of transport facilities, and—in two cases—the generation of electricity.

State Insurance Programs

All of the states administer compulsory unemployment compensation systems, collecting payroll taxes from employers and paying benefits to the unemployed. These are large-scale operations. But, being a form of social insurance, they differ in character from those conducted by private companies. Another form of insurance written by state, as well as private, companies provides compensation for workmen suffering industrial injuries. Under laws passed since 1911, all states now require employers to make payments to workers in cases of disabling accidents or occupational disease. And they further require employers to give proof of their ability to make such payments or to carry insurance to cover the risk. In 32 states, such insurance is written only by private companies. But in 18 states there are state funds. In 12 of these, the state funds compete with private insurers. In 6, they have a monopoly. Where the two compete, the private insurers solicit the better risks, leaving the poorer ones to the states. Where the state funds have a monopoly, their costs and their rates are lower than those of the private companies in other states.

State Liquor Stores

With the repeal of the 18th Amendment in 1933, control of the liquor traffic was returned to the states. Two different methods of control were then adopted: the licensing of private distributors and distribution by the state itself. The latter method was advocated as a means of eliminating private profit from the sale of liquor and thus preventing expansion of consumption by removing the incentive to stimulate demand. Seventeen states went into the business of selling liquor at wholesale, 16 of them also selling at retail. Three of these states monopolized distribution. The rest permitted some private traffic, usually monopolizing package sales of hard liquor but licensing drinking places and distributors of beer.

State liquor store systems occupy an ambiguous position. They are supposed to serve both as regulators of the use of liquor and as merchandisers of the stuff. The former function has had little of their attention; the latter a great deal. The state stores do not advertise their products, leaving that to the manufacturers. Their prices are not raised to discourage intemperance. Per capita consumption of liquor is as high in states that have state stores as in those that do not. The stores have been highly profitable, their earnings running to more than 20 percent on sales. The states that operate such stores have made more money from the liquor traffic than those that sell licenses to private distributors. The stores are important, not as a means of encouraging temperance, but as a source of public revenue.[11]

Transport and Terminal Facilities

The state of New York has long maintained a system of barge canals, 525 miles in length, which it operates at public expense, charging no tolls. All state governments have built and maintained highways, financing this activity by

---

11 / Julian L. Simon, "The Economic Effects of State Monopoly of Packaged Liquor Retailing," *Journal of Political Economy* LXXIV (1966), pp. 188-94.

charging license fees and taxing motor fuels. With the growing demand for multilane superhighways in later years, these revenues proved inadequate and many states went back to the practice, abandoned a century before, of collecting tolls. The first—and the longest—of modern toll roads, the Pennsylvania Turnpike, was opened to traffic in 1940. There are now 29 states with toll roads and 25 with toll bridges and tunnels. The roads, in most cases, are planned, built, and operated by semiautonomous agencies that function as business entities, selling bonds, collecting tolls, and using their revenues to cover their costs and retire their debts. The roads, in general, have been money-makers, the New Jersey Turnpike, the most heavily travelled, taking in more than $100,000,000 a year. It is unlikely, however, that more such roads will be built. The major routes are now served, most of them by free roads that are comparable in character. As the toll roads pay off their bonds, they will be incorporated into the larger system of free highways.

Terminal facilities for rail, motor, air, and water carriers are integral parts of the transport system. Some of these facilities are provided by private enterprise, some by municipalities, some by state governments, and some by regional authorities. Harbor facilities at ocean ports—wharves, docks, warehouses, and the like—are usually owned by state governments. At New Orleans a State Board of Port Commissioners, formed in 1896, operates grain elevators, coffee terminals, banana conveyors, cranes, derricks, a belt-line railway, a canal, and a free-trade zone where goods can be imported, processed, and exported duty-free. In some cases, an agency has been set up by two or more states to provide the facilities required along a common waterway. Of these, the most important is the Port of New York Authority.

The Port of New York Authority was established, under an interstate compact between the states of New York and New Jersey, in 1921. Its activities are directed by a board of 12 commissioners, 6 appointed by the governor of each state, to serve for terms of 6 years, without pay. They are administered by a general manager appointed by the board. The Authority is empowered to plan, lease, buy, or build all types of terminal and transport facilities. It can finance construction by selling bonds, fix and collect tolls, and use its revenues to defray operating expenses and to pay interest and amortize its debts. In 1930 the Authority acquired the Holland Tunnel, which had been built in 1927, and in the next 10 years it built the Lincoln Tunnel and the George Washington Bridge. It now owns six bridges and tunnels, six marine terminals, two truck terminals, two bus terminals, an airport, and the Trans-Hudson Railway System, a commuter line which it acquired in 1962. It operates the Newark, La Guardia, and Kennedy International airports under lease. It is building a world trade center in Lower Manhattan, consisting of two 110-story skyscrapers, to be completed in 1972 at a cost of $270 million. In 1970 its assets were valued at more than $2 billion. Its gross operating revenues were more than $200 million; its net revenues more than $100 million.

The Authority has lost money on its truck and bus terminals, its airports, and its railway. But it has made substantial profits by charging high tolls on its tunnels and bridges. These structures have long since been paid for. Their present revenues are used to finance other projects. The authority is frequently criticized for its policy of investing in lucrative ventures such as the world trade center while refusing to support mass transit in the metropolitan area. It replies that it must maintain its credit standing by confining its investments to projects that will pay their own way. The Authority is also cited as a model of public enterprise. But its success must be attributed, in part, at least, to its monopoly power and to its freedom from regulation in fixing rates.

State Power Systems

Multipurpose projects, including the generation and sale of hydroelectric power, have been constructed by state governments in Nebraska and New York. The people of Nebraska are served exclusively by publicly owned electrical utilities. Three large irrigation and power projects were built during the thirties, their lines being connected to form a common pool. A number of towns were operating their own power plants, and lines were being built in rural areas by REA cooperatives. Then, in 1939, a Consumers' Public Power District was formed to acquire the properties of several private companies. And in 1946 the Omaha Public Power District was set up to take over the facilities of the Nebraska Power Co. in Omaha and in many other towns. With this, electricity in Nebraska was completely socialized.

In New York, a State Power Authority was created by the legislature when Franklin D. Roosevelt was governor in 1931, and the water power within its boundaries was declared to be a resource of the state. The Authority was directed to build dams, generate power, and sell it in wholesale quantities. The Authority has generated power at the International Rapids of the St. Lawrence River since 1958 and at Niagara Falls since 1961. Its development of these resources is described in Chapter 22.

FEDERAL GOVERNMENT ENTERPRISES

Outstanding among the businesslike enterprises operated by the federal government are the generation and distribution of electricity, the production of nuclear fuels and promotion of their use in producing electric power, and the operation of the postal system. These are to be considered in some detail in Chapters 22 and 23. Other federal enterprises include (1) carrying on the administration of public lands, (2) lending and guaranteeing loans, (3) providing insurance against a number of different risks, (4) buying and selling commodities, (5) supplying transport facilities and operating transport services, and (6) engaging in manufacturing. These activities are briefly reviewed below.

Administration of Public Lands

The federal government owns 750 million acres of land, half of this in Alaska and most of the rest in 11 western states. Aside from the communist countries, it is the biggest landlord on earth. As a landlord, however, it is unique, taking more interest in the use to which land is put than in the revenue it yields. Its concern is with the conservation of resources. It permits extractive industries to operate on public lands, but controls the methods that they use.

The national forests, covering 186 million acres in 44 states, are managed by the Forest Service in the Department of Agriculture. The Service sells standing timber to private loggers, supervises logging operations, issues grazing permits, collects fees, and controls methods of grazing. The other public lands are administered by bureaus in the Department of the Interior. The Fish and Wildlife Service is responsible for the management of more than 27 million acres contained in some 200 refuges for waterfowl and 40 refuges for other types of wildlife, and for the propagation of fish in some 100 hatcheries. The National Park Service manages more than 25 million acres, including 31 national parks and around 170 monuments and other sites of natural or historical interest. The Service grants concessions to private enterprises for the operation of tourist facilities. The Office of Indian Affairs acts as a trustee for the 56 million acres of Indian lands. The Bureau of Reclamation controls land held for irrigation, running from 10 million to 15 million acres in different years. It builds and operates dams and ditches, sells land, supplies water, and collects water rents. The Bureau of Land Management administers the rest of the public domain, including 170 million acres of range lands. Here, it issues grazing permits and collects grazing fees. The Secretary of the Interior also grants leases to mining companies for the exploitation of oil and gas and other minerals on public lands and collects mining royalties.

This activity is not carried on for profit, but it does afford a test of the capacity of government for large-scale management. Here, the quality of its performance appears to have been high.

Federal Lending Agencies

In 1955 the Hoover Commission found 104 agencies with 40,000 employees and $17 billion in federal funds engaged in the business of making loans or providing insurance against various types of risk. Much of the government's activity in this field has been directed toward broadening the availability and increasing the stability of credit by promoting the formation of mutual institutions controlling central credit reservoirs where risks are pooled. The first of these institutions was the Federal Reserve System, set up in 1913. In this case, the capital of the central banks was subscribed by the existing national banks whose membership in the system was required by law. In other cases, the initial capital was provided by the government. This was the pattern followed in setting up the Federal Land Bank System in 1916, the Federal Intermediate Credit Bank System in 1923, the Federal Home Loan Bank System in 1932, and the system of Production Credit Corporations in 1933. The stock of the Land Banks, the Home Loan Banks, and the Production Credit Corporations is now owned by member associations; the government no longer contributes to their support. The Intermediate Credit Banks, too, are moving toward member ownership.

Each of these organizations serves financial institutions; none of them lends directly to individual borrowers. Direct loans are made, however, by a number of federal agencies. Three of them lend to farmers. The Banks for Cooperatives make loans to finance the activities of agricultural marketing associations. The Rural Electrification Administration makes loans to finance the construction and operation of electric lines and telephone lines by rural electrification cooperatives. The Farmers' Home Administration makes loans to small farmers to help them buy their farms, improve their farming operations, and achieve self-support. Each of these operations is subsidized.

Direct loans are also made to businessmen. For 20 years the Reconstruction Finance Corporation was the largest lender in the United States. The RFC was established, on a temporary basis, in 1932, to check financial disaster by extending emergency aid to such enterprises as railroads, banks, and insurance companies. But its life was repeatedly extended and its powers enlarged. During the thirties, it was employed to finance relief and recovery programs; during the war, to finance the procurement of strategic materials and the construction of industrial facilities. In 1948, its powers were again enlarged, enabling it to lend to any state or local government, to any public agency, to any financial institution, and to any business enterprise in the United States. According to the investigators who reported to the Hoover Commission in 1949, the Corporation's record during the depression was highly satisfactory and the functions assigned to it during the war were well performed.[12] Soon thereafter, the RFC came into bad odor; it appeared that the quality of its management had declined and that dubious loans had been made on the basis of political influence. As a consequence, a bill was passed in 1953 putting the agency into liquidation. In 20 years, the RFC had made 640,000 loans and lent or spent $48,740 million. It had suffered defaults on only 1 percent of its loans, and had paid more than a billion dollars into the Treasury; its remaining assets were valued at $700 million.

Two agencies still make business loans. The Export-Import Bank lends to to American traders and their foreign customers. The Small Business Administration lends to meet the capital needs of small concerns. Here, as with the loans to farmers, there is an element of subsidy.

In some cases, financial agencies have been established by the government to serve as instruments in carrying out programs that have not been expected to pay their own way. Subsidiaries set up by the RFC distributed money for relief during the depression and provided facilities for production and procured marginal supplies of essential materials at high costs during the war, the losses incurred in the process being canceled by acts of Congress. The Commodity Credit Corporation is required to make loans to support the prices of agricul-

12 / Commission on Organization of the Executive Branch of the Government, *Task Force Report on Lending Agencies* (Washington, D.C.: Government Printing Office, 1949), pp. 21-22.

tural commodities at levels fixed by law, even though substantial losses may result. The Public Housing Administration is authorized to make both loans and grants to finance the construction and operation of low-rent housing by city governments.

Federal Insuring Agencies

Insurance programs have been inaugurated to serve a number of different purposes. The Federal Deposit Insurance Corporation was set up, in 1933, to restore and maintain confidence in the banks. The Corporation insures deposits up to $20,000 in all banks belonging to the Federal Reserve System and in other banks that wish to be insured. Four programs have been adopted to increase the availability of credit for private housing. The Federal Savings and Loan Corporation insures accounts in savings and loan associations. The Federal Housing Administration insures home mortgages that are held by financial institutions. The Veterans Administration guarantees loans that are made to finance the purchase of homes by veterans. The Federal National Mortgage Association, once publicly owned but now private, buys mortgages underwritten by these agencies and sells them to investors. The government also offers property insurance to farmers, to shipping companies, and to Americans investing abroad. The Federal Crop Insurance Corporation insures crop yields against drought and other natural risks. The Maritime Administration insures loans made by private lenders to finance the construction and reconditioning of merchant ships. The Export-Import Bank insures foreign investors against the risks of inconvertibility and expropriation.

Through the Veterans Administration and the Social Security Administration, the government carries on the largest life and annuity insurance operations to be found on earth. In 1968 the VA had 6 million life insurance policies in force and paid out $4.6 billion in benefits to aged veterans and survivors of veterans. The SSA system of old-age, survivorship, and disability insurance enrolled around 70 million workers and paid out $24.6 billion to more than 18 million beneficiaries. In paying benefits, the operations of these agencies resemble those of private companies, but they are differently financed. With veterans' insurance, as with private insurance, the benefits are covered by the premiums, but the administrative costs are borne by the taxpayer. Under the social security system, benefits are related to the wages on which taxes have been paid, but they are computed less generously for younger than for older workers, for well-paid than for poorly paid workers, and for bachelors than for workers with dependents. Social insurance, resting on the taxing power, thus differs from insurance sold by private companies.

Federal Trading Agencies

During World War II the government was deeply involved in foreign trade. It purchased equipment and supplies at home and shipped them to its allies abroad.

It purchased and imported strategic materials. After the war, the government took the position that trade should be returned to private hands. But it continues to buy and sell commodities on a substantial scale.

The government's principal trading agencies are the Commodity Credit Corporation and the General Services Administration. Agricultural commodities are acquired by the CCC and given away or sold at a loss. The GSA contracts for expanded production of minerals in the United States. It imports minerals and other strategic materials. It manages the nation's stockpile of these materials, making sales and purchases to rotate supplies of perishable goods. In 1970, the value of its stockpile was estimated at $7 billion, of which $2.6 billion was in excess of the nation's needs. Its sales had run to $250 million a year.

Federal Transport Enterprises

The federal government owns and operates two railroads, one in the Panama Canal Zone and one in Alaska. The Panama Railroad Company was acquired in 1904, the purchase being incidental to the construction of the canal. In addition to running a railroad across the isthmus, the company operated a ship line between New York and the Canal Zone and soon came to operate most of the business enterprises in the zone, including fueling plants, terminal services, public utility systems, hotels, restaurants, commissaries, and recreational facilities. Up to June 30, 1947, the company had met its costs from its own revenues and had paid $25 million in dividends to the Treasury. In 1948 the railroad company lost its identity, being absorbed by the Panama Canal Company which now operates the canal itself and all other public enterprises in the zone.

Provision for the construction of a railroad to promote the development of the territory of Alaska was made in 1914. Until the forties, the roadbed, structures, and equipment were primitive in character and operations were conducted at a loss. Between 1945 and 1953 the road was rebuilt and reequipped, bringing the government's investment to a total of $500 million. Since 1957, the road has earned a profit, though paying no interest on the investment.

During World War I the government built merchant ships and operated them commercially. After the war, it sold as many as it could, but much of the fleet remained in public hands. In 1936, Congress set up a Maritime Commission, authorizing it to build ships and charter them to private lines for operation on essential trade routes. The building program called for the construction of 50 ships a year. During World War II this program was expanded. From 1939 to 1946, the Commission built 5,600 ships. In 1946, Congress authorized the sale of these ships at a fraction of their cost. On this basis, hundreds of them were sold. But other hundreds are still held by the government in an emergency reserve. Ships have been withdrawn from this reserve and operated by agents under contract with the government to meet the needs for transport created by the war in Korea, by the closing of the Suez Canal, by the shipment of wheat to forestall starvation in India and Pakistan, and by the war in Vietnam.

From 1918 to 1953, the government operated a barge line on the Mississippi,

Missouri, and Illinois rivers. This undertaking was started during World War I and continued thereafter as a means of interesting private capital in the development of inland water transport. Whether through this example or not, more than a hundred private barge lines were brought into operation. But the government line was not financially successful, its loss on an investment of $20 million running to $7 million by 1953. This record is to be explained, in part, at least, by the facts that its equipment was antiquated and that Congress required it to continue certain services that were clearly unprofitable. For many years, it was the policy of Congress to sell the line, but there were no takers. Finally, in 1953, a sale was effected, the properties, including some new equipment, going for $9 million to a private concern.

Transport and communications services have been operated since World War II by the Army, Navy, and Air Force, passengers and cargo being carried by the Military Sea Transport Service and passengers by the Military Airlift Command. The services also operate worldwide networks of communications, comparable in character and scale to those provided by private companies.

Federal Manufacturing Enterprises

The government is also involved in manufacturing activities. The Navy builds ships and produces paint, rope, ships' stores, and the like. The Army and the Navy manufacture weapons, ammunition, uniforms, and other military goods. The Post Office makes its own mail bags. Federal prisons operate industries to provide their inmates with employment and to train them for later life. In all of these cases, government produces for its own use. Elsewhere, however, goods made in publicly owned factories are offered for general sale.

The Government Printing Office is the biggest printing plant on earth, with acres of floor space and thousands of employees. The Office does $200 million or more of business each year, always operating in the black. The Superintendent of Documents handles sales, buying documents at cost from the Printing Office and selling them at a markup of 50 percent. He distributes some 60 million publications a year, returning a substantial profit to the Treasury.

The government has engaged, from time to time, in a variety of other manufacturing activities. Since 1933, the Tennessee Valley Authority has produced fertilizers. Since 1921, the Bureau of Mines has produced helium, a gas that is used in military, atomic, and space projects. Until 1938, it monopolized this business. Then, in 1960, it changed its policy, setting its price high enough to encourage production by private firms. As a result, these firms took over the market and the government's output went into a growing stockpile. The Bureau has now shut down three of its five helium purification plants. The cost of the program to the Treasury has run to $50 million a year. From 1944 to 1954 the Bureau also operated pilot plants for the production of titanium and zirconium and the extraction of petroleum from oil shales, leaving the field to private enterprise when the development phase was past. Through the Virgin Islands Company, created in 1934 to provide employment and promote recovery in the islands, the government went into the business of producing sugar, molasses, and rum. It lost money on sugar, made money on rum. In 1949, however, Congress forbade it to manufacture alcoholic beverages; its distillery was leased to another concern and was subsequently sold.

Other industries were established by the government in World War II to produce essential materials; rubber, tin, and nickel. The government invested some $70 million in the construction of 29 synthetic rubber plants, raising the capacity of this industry from around 8,000 tons to more than a million tons a year. The plants were operated, under contract, by oil and rubber companies at cost plus a fixed fee. They were sold to private firms in 1955. A smelter was built in Texas City, Texas, to produce pig tin from Bolivian concentrates. It was operated for some years by the government, being sold to a private firm in 1957. The nickel plant at Nicaro, Cuba, was built, at a cost of $90 million, to process Cuban ores. It was being operated for the American government by a private contractor when diplomatic relations with Cuba were broken in 1960.

Chapter 22 PUBLIC POWER PROJECTS

For more than 60 years the federal government has been in the business of generating and selling electric power. Since the thirties its operations have come to be conducted on a major scale. Over all, it now accounts for 14 percent of the electricity generated in the United States. The government entered this business, as it were, by the back door. Its involvement, on the present scale, was not deliberately planned. Rivers were dammed for other purposes: to store water for urban and industrial consumption, to maintain channels for navigation, to provide water for irrigation, to prevent floods. The first big dam on the Tennessee was built to insure a supply of nitrates for the manufacture of munitions during World War I, the dams on the Lower Colorado to supply water to the cities of southern California and the farms of the arid Southwest, the first dams on the Columbia to create employment and to stimulate recovery from the Great Depression, the later dams on the Tennessee to promote the region's economic and social development. Whatever the reasons for their construction, the dams afforded a source of power. So government went into the business of producing and selling electricity. And in the Tennessee Valley, when the supply of power from hydroelectric installations fell short of the demand, it went on to produce power from steam. But here, as elsewhere, government's entry into the power business was a by-product of its effort to control the flow of water in river valleys.

RIVER VALLEY DEVELOPMENT

In earlier years, each step that government took in developing the resources of a river basin had a single purpose: water supply, navigation, irrigation, flood control. But it came to be seen, in time, that these purposes were interrelated. The waters of a river could be held back to conserve supplies and to check floods; they could be released to meet the needs of urban and industrial consumers, to maintain navigation, and to irrigate farms; and, incidentally, they could be run through turbines to produce power. If dams were to be built for any of these purposes, it was evident that all of them should be kept in mind. So government came to plan for multipurpose development, viewing the needs and the resources of a river valley as a whole.

Single-Purpose Development

Congress first undertook to promote navigation when other modes of transport were unknown. It has continued to do so, with little regard for the economy of transport as a whole, asking water carriers to make no payment for the ways that it provides. Responding to local pressures, it has made an annual appropriation for river and harbor improvements in legislation that has long been known as the pork barrel bill. Since the beginning of the 19th century, Congress has assigned this function to the Army Corps of Engineers. In addition to its military duties, the Corps has dredged river beds to deepen channels, built dams to even the flow of water between seasons, dug canals, and installed locks, and has continued to operate and to maintain these facilities. The Corps has built a number of major structures, among them Bonneville Dam on the Columbia, Fort Peck Dam on the Missouri, and the Barnhart Island Dam on the St. Lawrence.

For a century, the government concerned itself only with navigation. Then, in the Reclamation Act of 1902, Congress established the Bureau of Reclamation in the Department of the Interior and authorized it to construct irrigation works in the 17 states west of the 100th meridian. The cost of these projects was supposed to be recovered from farmers whose land was supplied with water. But payments were so arranged that the farmers were heavily subsidized. In its early years, the Bureau's undertakings were few in number and moderate in size, attracting little public attention. Then, beginning in 1929 with the construction of Hoover Dam on the Lower Colorado, it built a number of gigantic structures, among them Shasta Dam on the Sacramento and Grand Coulee Dam on the Columbia, involving irrigation, water supply, flood control, navigation, and incidental power production throughout whole river valleys.

Flood Control

Flood control work was undertaken by the Army Corps of Engineers as early as 1917 and was greatly expanded after the Mississippi flood of 1927. The government's responsibility for the prevention of flood damage was given formal recognition by Congress in the Flood Control Act of 1936. Under this law, the Corps of Engineers was directed to make studies of the nation's waterways and to draw up plans for their improvement and was authorized to build flood control works of all kinds.

Floods are not completely to be prevented: rains may fall on frozen or saturated ground and snows may melt more rapidly than they can be absorbed. But damage from floods can be substantially reduced. The use of flood plains can be zoned and heavy investment forbidden in regions where the risk of loss is high. Warnings can be issued, and people evacuated before the waters rise. But these measures are unpopular and have not been attempted; hazardous occupancy has been preserved. Levees and flood walls can be built, and river channels deepened, widened, and straightened. These are the works that have been emphasized by the Corps of Engineers. But such measures are of limited effect. A levee or a flood wall—if it holds—may save a sheltered area. But it will do so by diverting flood waters to unprotected lands across and down the stream. Channel improvements may carry the waters past a city only to spread them on the lands below. If floods are really to be controlled, waters must be held upstream to be released more gradually. This can be done by building storage dams and by improving the management of land along the watersheds.

Under natural conditions, water was held where it fell. The forest cover delayed the melting of the snow, checked evaporation, cut the velocity of the wind, held the soil in place, and held the water in the soil. The grass cover, too, held soil and water. The runoff was retarded, underground reservoirs were replenished, and floods were checked. With the coming of civilization, these defenses were destroyed. Clear cutting of timber disclosed the forest floor to sun, wind, and rain. Careless logging left skid trails and invited fires. Overgrazing killed the seedlings and packed the earth, destroying its absorptive power. On the grasslands, too, overgrazing and careless cultivation removed the spongelike cover and exposed the soil. The hillsides and the lowlands were eroded, soil washed and blown away. Now the water, instead of sinking into the ground, evaporated and ran off. The water table was lowered; the valleys were inundated with recurring floods. To hold back the floods, it now is necessary to improve the management of forests and of soils.

Responsibility for watershed management was assigned to the Department of Agriculture by the Flood Control Act of 1936, the first funds for the purpose being appropriated in 1946. The Department's authority was reaffirmed by the Watershed Protection and Flood Prevention Act of 1954. Under this law, the Soil Conservation Service has undertaken to retard the runoff of water by promoting the adoption of such methods of land treatment as terracing, contour plowing, strip cropping, and providing grassed floodways, and by building dams on small streams.

The champions of big dams and those of little dams have been engaged for years in vigorous debate, the big dam faction supporting the Corps of Engineers, the little dam faction backing the Soil Conservation Service. Of the two programs, that of the Engineers is by far the larger. During one year in the sixties, it built half again as many structures as did the SCS, at a cost 13 times as great.

Multipurpose Development

A single dam may serve a number of purposes. A system of dams in a river basin can do even better. It can keep a channel at the depth required for navigation, supply water for irrigation, and hold floods in check. It can provide water for domestic and industrial use. It can produce hydroelectric power. More than this, the lakes created behind the dams afford new opportunities for fish and wildlife and sites for recreational activities. By raising and lowering water levels by inches, the larvae of mosquitoes can be stranded and the spread of disease controlled. In this way, and by checking stream pollution, public health can be improved. These purposes are interdependent. Action to serve any one of them affects the ability of the system to serve others. The need to compromise among them necessitates unified planning and control.

The multipurpose character of river valley development was recognized by Congress in 1920 when it set up the Federal Power Commission and directed it to make provision for other needs when granting licenses for the construction of dams to generate power. It was further recognized in 1927 when Congress, in the River and Harbor Act, directed the Corps of Engineers to report on the possible development of river basins for navigation, flood control, irrigation, and power. Multipurpose projects have been built on many rivers by the Engineers and by the Bureau of Reclamation. But the concept of basinwide planning for the development of water resources finds its fullest expression in the work of the Tennessee Valley Authority.

The water control system of the TVA includes 32 dams, 12 of them single-purpose structures and 20 of them serving multiple purposes. The volume of water in reservoirs and streams throughout the river basin is centrally controlled, being subject to adjustment from day to day and even from hour to hour. Floods are held back from the Tennessee, the Ohio, and the Mississippi; waters are impounded in the winter and the spring and released in the summer and the fall. During the dry season, in earlier years, the Tennessee dropped to a depth of two feet at Chattanooga and a foot and a half at Knoxville. Now an 11-foot channel is maintained throughout the year, supporting navigation for 630 miles from Knoxville to the river's mouth. From its hydroelectric plants the system produces more than 20 billion kilowatt-hours of power. The hillsides of the valley have been reforested, and the erosion of its soil brought under control. Malaria, once common in the region, has virtually disappeared. Progress has been made in sanitation through the Authority's studies of stream pollution and through the installation, under state laws, of sewage treatment plants. Fish have been propagated, and preserves established for wildfowl. Lakes and parks have been opened to recreational use. The possibilities of multipurpose development have thus been fully demonstrated by the TVA.

Criteria for Investment in Valley Development

Valley projects, in all parts of the country, are constantly being proposed by regional pressure groups. The total cost of these projects would be far in excess of the funds available for their construction. A way must therefore be found to determine which are to be undertaken and, among these, which are to be given priority. Under the Reclamation Act of 1902, Congress established the test of financial feasibility. Irrigation works were not to be built unless it could be shown that their users could repay their cost. But repayment of interest was never required, and, with successive amendments, annual repayments of principal were so reduced that the test was rendered meaningless. Then, in the Flood Control Act of 1936, Congress set up another test. The benefits to be derived from proposed projects were to be measured and the projects undertaken only "if the benefits to whomsoever they may accrue are in excess of the estimated costs." Under the law, this test must be used by the Corps of Engineers and the Soil Conservation Service. It has also been adopted by the Bureau of Reclamation.

In estimating benefits, these agencies have established three categories: tangible benefits—primary and secondary—and intangible benefits. Tangible benefits are those that can be measured in money: primary benefits being those that would flow directly from the project under consideration; secondary benefits those that flow indirectly from a project. In the case of irrigation, for instance, they include the gains of the millers and the bakers who would turn an added supply of wheat into flour and bread, the gains of the carriers and the distributors who would handle these products, and those of the other businessmen who would sell to them. The law, as we noted, provides for the inclusion of benefits "to whomsoever they may accrue." Intangible benefits, finally, are those to which a monetary value cannot be assigned. Included in this category are such matters as the saving of life that would result from the prevention of floods.

Direct benefits are valued at the prices that the beneficiaries would presumably be willing to pay to obtain them, these prices being determined, where possible, by finding those of the cheapest alternatives. Power is valued at the price that would have to be paid if it were purchased from a steam plant. The benefit of navigation is determined by estimating the prospective traffic and multiplying it by the rate that would be charged if the goods were to move by rail; the benefit of irrigation by estimating the resulting increase in agricultural output and multiplying it by the prevailing price. The benefit of flood control is computed by predicting the magnitude of the floods to be averted, appraising the damage they would have done, and adding the gains that would be realized if property in the flood plain could be put to better use.

The estimation of costs follows the same pattern. Primary costs are those that would be incurred in constructing, operating, and maintaining a project, taken at the prevailing market rates, plus the value of properties that would have to be abandoned if land were flooded and the amount of taxes that would have to be foregone. Secondary costs are those associated with secondary benefits. In the case of irrigation, cited above, they would be the added costs of the millers, bakers, carriers, distributors, and other businessmen.

In appraising a project, the agencies compute a ratio of tangible benefits and costs, with benefits as the numerator and costs as the denominator. If the ratio is greater than 1, the project is said to be justified. Intangible benefits are described in writing, but their role in the guidance of investment is a minor one.

Use of the ratio of benefit to cost as a criterion for investment is open to question. A favorable ratio shows that some return will be realized, but it does not show what the rate of the return will be. It does not distinguish, for instance, between an investment that will yield 6 percent and one that will yield 3 percent. It therefore discriminates against projects where capital requirements are low and operating costs high in favor of those where operating costs are low and capital requirements high. But this point need not detain us here. Our present concern is with the way in which the criterion is employed.

Practice in Determining Investment

Local groups desiring river improvements take their proposals to their Congressmen. Provisions for the study of these proposals are included in appropriation bills. Surveys are then made and hearings held by the agencies concerned. Reports are prepared analyzing benefits and costs. Where the ratios are favorable, the projects are approved. Such ratios are likely to be found: the agencies are under pressure to find them; the size of their budgets depends upon their success in doing so. The number of projects approved therefore exceeds the number that can be built. But the ratio of benefit to cost is not employed in choosing among them; projects with higher ratios are not preferred to those with lower ones. The ratio is merely used to establish eligibility. Thereafter, the choice is political. The projects built are the ones for which Congress votes the funds.

Favorable ratios can be manufactured by overstating benefits and by understating costs. Benefits may be overstated by including secondary benefits. In the case of irrigation, for instance, the gains of the millers, bakers, etc., can properly be counted if these producers would not otherwise have been employed. They can be regarded, under any circumstances, as a benefit to the region in question. But in times of full employment they should not be counted as a benefit to the economy as a whole. Primary benefits, too, can be overstated. Generous estimates can be made of the increase in crops that will result from irrigation, the increase in traffic that will follow improvements in navigation, and the amount of damage that will be prevented by controlling floods. In the case of irrigation, moreover, the prices used in computing the value of increased output are those maintained by government supports. Here, too, some benefits are counted twice: the increase in the value of land resulting from larger crops is counted as well as the increase in the value of the crops themselves.

Costs, on the other hand, may be understated. Here, the most important item is the cost of capital. In figuring this cost, the development agencies use the rate of interest that must be paid by the government. The Corps of Engineers, in years past, has used 3 percent; the Bureau of Reclamation, 2.5 percent. Such rates did not cover the real cost of the capital employed. The real cost is measured by the interest that would have been earned if the capital, instead of being taken by the government, could have been invested in the private sector of the economy. Measured in this way, the cost would have been 5 or 6 percent.

If benefits and costs could be measured with greater accuracy, the benefit-cost ratio would be a better guide. This might be done if the task were transferred to an agency that would have no selfish interest in the findings it would make. As it is, the process operates to justify such projects as groups with political influence may desire. Some of those undertaken could doubtless be justified if stricter standards were employed; others probably could not.

Organization for Valley Development

The purposes served by the development of a river valley are indivisible. If development is undertaken for any one of them—flood control, water supply, irrigation, navigation, power production, sanitation, recreation—it affects them all. The purposes, moreover, are competitive. Water diverted for upstream irrigation does not produce downstream power. A reservoir kept full affords the greatest head for power; a reservoir that is emptied provides the greatest space for storing floods. The works installed in a river basin are functionally interdependent. Dams built upstream for storage maintain a steadier flow, increasing the output of power at dams downstream. Construction of Hungry Horse Dam on the Flathead River increased the output of power at dams below it on the Flathead and the Columbia by four times the amount produced at Hungry Horse itself. A river basin is an hydraulic unit. Its dams should be planned as parts of a common system; the detention and release of its waters directed by a common management.

Among the purposes for which a river valley is developed, few can be served by private enterprise. Hydroelectric power can be produced and sold on the market. Water, though usually supplied by public agencies, could also be supplied by private firms. But the other services—the prevention of floods, the provision of channels for navigation, the promotion of public health, the propagation of fish, the protection of wildlife, the provision of parks—cannot be sold commercially: supplied to those who would be willing to pay for them and withheld from those who would not. These services must be rendered, if at all, to the people of a valley as a whole. They must be rendered, therefore, by an agency of government.

Power, as was said, can be privately produced and sold. But if this is done, it is unlikely that the other purposes of valley development will be adequately served, since they may require the release of water that would make for greater output, sales, and profits if retained. It is unlikely, moreover, that the potential power of a river will be fully developed. A private concern will build a dam or two at advantageous sites. It will not build a system of dams throughout a drainage basin. Nor will it invest in upstream storage that increases the output of power at downstream plants. If these things are to be done, a river's power must be developed by public enterprise.

A drainage basin may lie within the borders of a single state. In such a case, development may well be undertaken by state government. A great river system, however, will flow through many states. Its development cannot be undertaken by any one of them. States in a drainage basin have attempted to solve their common problems in a variety of ways. They have adopted common policies in the control of small streams. They have passed reciprocal laws. They have also entered into compacts, approved by Congress under Article I, Section 10 of the Constitution, to develop interstate rivers and govern the distribution of their waters. New York, New Jersey, Pennsylvania, Delaware, and the federal government set up a Delaware River Basin Commission in 1961 to coordinate their activities in developing the water resources of the Delaware and to control their use. On the Rio Grande since 1939, and on the Upper Colorado since 1949, water has been apportioned by an interstate commission with a chairman appointed by the President. In no case, however, have states set up a common agency and given it the power to plan and direct the development of a river valley. If such an agency is to exist, it must be created by the federal government.

In summary, river valley development, to be fully effective, should be administered by a single federal agency. There is but one example of this form of organization: the Tennessee Valley Authority. Other valleys have been developed by the federal government, but in no other case is there unified control. The Army Corps of Engineers, the Bureau of Reclamation, and the Soil Conservation Service all operate in the same valleys, each with its own purpose, its own legislation, and its own political backing, none with authority to carry out the development of a valley as a whole.

Politics in Valley Development

The interests of groups who use the water of a river system are frequently in conflict. Nobody opposes the dredging of channels or the building of levees and flood walls. And so, though inferior to other methods of dealing with floods, they continue to be built. But dams give rise to contention. Upstream and downstream users compete in claiming water for agricultural, industrial, and domestic use. Farmers want small dams that will cut the risk of farming by preventing small and frequent floods; cities want big dams that will avert disaster by preventing large occasional floods. Farmers want water diverted for irrigation; barge operators want it released for navigation. Dams wanted for these purposes are said to threaten the destruction of fisheries. Wherever dams are proposed, owners whose lands would be submerged are certain to object.

In this atmosphere of conflict, the federal agencies are partisans. The Army Corps of Engineers represents the interest of downstream cities. It has the backing of the National Rivers and Harbors Congress. Building public works in local communities, it is the darling of Congressional committees. Responsible to the Secretary of the Army, it is subject to no civilian control. The Bureau of Reclamation represents the interest of farmers in the arid West. It has the backing of the National Reclamation Association and the support of the 34 Senators from its 17 Western States. The Soil Conservation Service represents the interest of upstream farmers who want small dams. Compared with the other agencies, it does not have strong political support. The Corps and the Bureau, each with its national pressure group and its Congressional contacts, have great political strength.

Although these agencies operate in the same river basins, there is no effective coordination of their work. Interagency committees have been established, in Washington and in the basins, but they do not function as common planning authorities. Committee members represent their respective agencies; any decision they make can be reversed by their superiors. Action depends upon unanimous agreement; each agency has the veto power. In the circumstances, little can be expected. Some compromises may be negotiated; no common planning will be done. Policymaking will be attuned to the separate demands of local interests, not to the welfare of the country as a whole.

To integrate valley development, two proposals have been made: that all the federal agencies dealing with water resources be brought together in a single department; and that semiautonomous authorities be set up in other river valleys on the model of the TVA. Each of these proposals has encountered determined opposition. There are local interests that stand to gain from interagency competition. There are vested interests in established agencies. Except for the Tennessee, the prospects for integrated valley development are far from bright.

ISSUES IN POWER DEVELOPMENT

The promotion of navigation on inland waterways has its critics. But there are few who question the desirability of irrigation and none who question the need for flood control. When dams are built for any of these purposes, moreover, there is general agreement that the force of the falling water should be used to generate electricity. But here the agreement ends. A number of issues are in dispute. Should hydroelectric power be generated, transmitted, or distributed by public agencies? At what price should public power be sold? Do the prices charged for such power cover its cost? Should these prices be used as a yardstick by which to judge the prices charged by private companies? Should public agencies be permitted to produce power from steam, to increase their output as demand grows, to extend their operations beyond the valleys they have served?

Disposition of Power

The federal government, having built a dam over which water flows in steady and substantial volume, can dispose of the water's power in a number of different ways: (1) It can sell the falling water to a private company, permitting it to build and operate the generating facilities. (2) It can sell the water to an agency of state or local government. (3) It can build the generating facilities itself and lease them to a private company. (4) It can lease them to a state or local agency. (5) It can operate the generating facilities, selling power at the plant to a private concern. (6) It can sell the power to a state or local agency. (7) It can build and operate transmission lines, selling its power to private distributors. (8) It can sell the power, at this stage, to municipal or cooperative distributors. (9) It can distribute power itself. The business community, obviously, will prefer the alternatives that would permit the generation, transmission, and distribution of power by private concerns, and will oppose those that would permit these functions to be performed by public or cooperative enterprise.

Practice in disposing of power has differed from project to project. In all cases, the government has built the generating facilities. On the Colorado, it has leased the facilities at Hoover Dam to two different operators, a private concern and a municipality, who generate, transmit, and distribute the power. Elsewhere, it has built its own transmission lines. In most cases, it sells power directly to industrial users. On the Columbia, it sells most of the remaining power to private distributors, a minor part to municipalities and cooperatives. On the Tennessee, it sells nearly all of the remaining power to municipalities and cooperatives, a negligible amount to private distributors.

It has long been the policy of Congress to require that preference be given to governmental and cooperative distributors in the sale of power produced by federal agencies. A preference clause was written into the Reclamation Act in 1906, and one has been included in every relevant law enacted in the following years. In conformity with this requirement, contracts for the sale of power to private companies have been made for limited periods so that, upon their expiration, sales can be made instead to such public and cooperative distributors as may apply. For many years, the preferential clause had little significance, being applied only to surplus power not needed for pumping water at irrigation dams of moderate size. Its purpose was to enable struggling municipal and rural systems to attain the size and strength already possessed by private firms. Since 1933, however, the government has come to produce large quantities of power, and has used preference in the sale of this power as a means of promoting municipal and cooperative ownership of distribution systems. As a result, these systems have grown in number and in size. The private power industry has therefore fought the preference clause. Its retention and the manner of its administration have become an issue of partisan politics.

Price Policy

In setting the level of rates to be charged for power produced at a multi-purpose project, a public agency can adopt one of three policies. First, it can set its rates at the level of those charged by private companies. If its plant is located in a sparsely settled region, its sales at these rates are likely to be small and much of its capacity unused. But if its plant is located where demand is large, it may recover its costs and earn a profit. In this case, the profit may be used to pay off the government's investment in the multipurpose structures, not only meeting the cost of producing power but also subsidizing navigation, irrigation, and flood control. This is the policy that was adopted in pricing the first power sold at Hoover Dam.

Second, the agency can set rates at a level designed to cover the separate cost of producing power and part of the cost of the common facilities. This, in fact, is what Congress has usually directed such agencies to do. But the policy has its drawbacks. It requires an allocation of the common costs of multipurpose projects, an undertaking whose difficulties are to be considered later on. This policy, too, might require a plant in a sparsely settled region to charge rates so high that its capacity would not be fully used. In practice, moreover, an agency must decide upon its initial rates before its costs can be known. It must therefore fix them on some other basis and determine later whether it has met its costs.

Third, the agency can set its rates at a level designed to promote the widest possible use of power, thus assuring full use of its facilities. This, too, is a rule that Congress has laid down. Since the elasticity of demand is unknown, an agency that follows this rule must make a guess. If it assumes that demand is inelastic, the level at which it sets its rates will be high. If it assumes that demand is elastic, the level will be low. In this case, it will take a chance. This is something that a private company would hesitate to do, since an error in judgment would result in a loss. Here, the public agency has an advantage: if it errs, the taxpayer will foot the bill. The agency is therefore free to create a market by setting low rates. If it succeeds, its income may suffice not only to cover the separate cost of producing power but also to pay off some part of the cost of the common facilities. This policy may enable a plant in a sparsely settled region to attract new industry. It is the policy that was adopted by the TVA in the Tennessee Valley and by the Bonneville Power Administration on the Columbia.

If low rates are to promote consumption, they must be made effective not only when power is sold to distributors but also when it is sold to consumers. The agency producing power must therefore follow through to regulate its distributors, controlling their rates, services, earnings, finances, and accounts. This is done, for instance, through the contracts entered into between the TVA and the municipalities and cooperatives that distribute its power.

The structure of a public agency's rates is likely to be discriminatory, though differing from the pattern adopted by private companies. Lower rates will be charged for larger quantities of power as a means of promoting greater use, but reductions may stop when a moderate quantity is reached. Different rates will be charged to different classes of users, but domestic consumers may get lower rates than commercial establishments; industrial rates may be kept low to attract new factories. Power will be sold at a uniform price to buyers at different locations, no charge being made for the difference in transmission costs. All of the towns in a region will be given an equal opportunity to share in its development.

Allocation of Joint Costs

When a public agency seeks to promote the widest possible use of power, it will set its rates below those charged by private companies. The companies will complain that the agency's rates fail to cover its costs. The agency will demonstrate that its rates do cover the separable costs of producing power: the cost of operating and maintaining the generating plants and transmission lines, together with interest on the money invested in these facilities and payments to amortize the principal. But the companies will reply that the rates do not cover a proper share of the cost of jointly used facilities: of the dams that were built not only to produce power but also to provide for navigation and irrigation and to prevent floods. The debate thus turns on the question of how these costs should be met.

At one extreme, there is the view, sometimes expressed by the private companies, that all of the cost of these dams should be charged to power and none of it to other purposes. This would transfer from the taxpayer to the power consumer the cost of subsidizing navigation, irrigation, and flood control. At the other extreme, there is the view, once espoused by proponents of public power, that all of the cost should be charged to the purposes for which the dams were supposedly built and none of it to power. This would compel the taxpayer to subsidize the power consumer. Between the two extremes, a number of methods have been proposed for allocating to power its proper share of the joint costs.

Each of these methods is open to criticism. (1) It is suggested that an equal charge be made for each of the purposes for which a dam is used. This would be workable but purely arbitrary. (2) It is suggested that contributions to joint costs be made proportionate to the separable costs of the various uses of common facilities. This, too, would be workable but arbitrary. (3) It is proposed that the contributions be made proportionate to the benefits received by the users of different services. This is justifiable but unworkable. The benefits of some services are difficult to measure. The benefits of others can be measured by the prices which they bring. But since these prices are in question, this method would involve circular reasoning. (4) It is proposed that the alternative cost of building a single-purpose dam for each of the purposes served by a project (where this would be economically justifiable) be computed, and contributions to joint costs made proportionate to their respective shares in the total of single-purpose costs. The use of alternative possibilities as a basis for allocation has a certain logic. But this procedure necessitates an estimation of the cost of imaginary projects, an exercise in which personal judgment has free play and differences of opinion are certain to result. (5) It is proposed that the share of joint cost charged to each purpose be made proportionate to its use of reservoir capacity. This, too, makes sense. But the cost of different layers in a reservoir is difficult to estimate. The use of reservoir capacity for different purposes is even more so, since it differs from season to season and from day to day. The usefulness of a reservoir in producing power depends, moreover, not only on the volume of water that passes through the turbines but also on the head of water behind the dam. If this procedure were to be used, costs would have to be allocated, in the end, in accordance with an arbitrary rule. Choice among the methods of allocation is a matter of judgment. The final decision, whatever its nature, will be open to dispute.

The allocation of joint costs is unnecessary. It has no function in setting the rates to be charged for power. These rates will be set at the level required to attain full utilization of capacity. They must cover the separable cost of producing power. They may well make a further contribution to the Treasury, but this does not require the allocation of costs. Cost allocation, here, has only one significance. It is raised as an issue when comparisons are made between the rates that are charged for public and for private power.

Yardstick Regulation

In the early years of the New Deal, public rates were frequently put forth as a yardstick by which to measure the propriety of private rates. State regulation of private rates was said to be ineffective, and comparison with public rates was offered as a means of tightening control. But such comparisons are open to question. Costs differ from steam plants to hydro plants, from private operation to public operation, from single-purpose projects to those with many purposes. And here the insoluble problem of allocating joint costs becomes a crucial one. As a result, truly comparable figures are not to be obtained. If public rates are low, therefore, it does not follow that private rates should be set at similar amounts. In objecting to the yardstick propaganda of the period, the private companies had a legitimate complaint. It should be noted, however, that the example set by public projects was a salutary one. Low public rates disclosed the existence of a vast potential market. They were copied by private companies. And they led to larger sales and greater profits. The public rates were not fair yardsticks. But public projects, like the TVA, did serve as pacesetters for private industry.

Expansion of Power Operations

The sale of hydroelectric power by government has been defended on the ground that such power is a by-product of projects undertaken for other purposes. But government does not confine itself to hydro power. Its multipurpose projects operate under a handicap. Since the flow of water is regulated to meet such needs as flood control and navigation, the quantity released varies from time to time. At one time, there may be too much to put through the turbines, the rest of it washing over the dams; at others, there may be so little that turbines are shut down. As a result, output is irregular. To give its customers dependable service, the government may build steam plants to "firm up" the supply. The electricity produced by these plants will not be a by-product.

The scale on which power is produced by a public agency is likely to increase. If the agency were to share the market of a region with private companies, it would not have to enlarge its own output to keep pace with growing demand. But where it monopolizes the market, it must do so. In time, the power produced at its hydro plants will be fully utilized. To meet the demand, it will have to produce more power by steam. Instead of merely selling surplus power, it will be running a big utility company. It is possible, too, that its attractive rates will make it easy for such an agency to expand, extending its operations from the region where it was first established into surrounding territory.

In all of this, the private utility industry sees a threat to its survival. It therefore seeks to limit the growth of public power. To this end, it asks that public agencies be denied the right to finance new power plants by reinvesting their earnings or by selling securities on the market, being compelled instead to request the Congress to appropriate the funds for each new plant they need. It asks, too, that the growth of such agencies be kept within fixed boundaries. These limitations are resisted by the regions that benefit from public power. Like the preference clause, they give rise to continued political debate.

THE TENNESSEE VALLEY AUTHORITY

In the volume of water that it carries, the Tennessee is fourth among the rivers of the United States. Rising in the Blue Ridge Mountains, it flows 800 miles to the Ohio, draining parts of Virginia, North Carolina, Kentucky, Georgia, Alabama, and Mississippi, as well as Tennessee. The first federal installations on the river, consisting of two nitrate plants, a steam power plant, and Wilson Dam at Muscle Shoals, were constructed during World War I. After the war private companies offered to buy the properties, but their bids were rejected as inadequate. At the same time, Senator George W. Norris, Republican, of Nebraska was urging public operation of the facilities at Muscle Shoals and further development of the resources of the Tennessee. Bills embodying this program were passed by Congress but were vetoed by President Coolidge in 1928 and by President Hoover in 1931. For years, the power and nitrate plants stood idle and the power contained in water falling over Wilson Dam was allowed to go to waste. Then, with the New Deal in 1933, a bill was enacted by Congress and signed by President Roosevelt to carry out the program that Senator Norris had proposed. The first of the new dams to be planned and built under the program was named Norris Dam.

The primary purposes of the new law, as set forth by Congress, were flood control and navigation. The third purpose stated was that of providing for "the maximum generation of electric power" insofar as this was "consistent with flood control and navigation." It was declared to be public policy to use the plants at Muscle Shoals to "improve, increase, and cheapen the production of fertilizer and fertilizer ingredients." And, more broadly, it was said to be the intention of Congress to conserve and develop the resources of the valley and to promote the economic and social well-being of its people.

To carry out this program, the law created a semiautonomous agency in the form of a corporation, designed to combine the prerogatives of government with the flexibility of private enterprise: the Tennessee Valley Authority. The policies of the Authority, within the law, are determined by a Board of Directors consisting of three members appointed by the President, subject to approval by the Senate, for overlapping terms of nine years. Detailed administration is delegated to a General Manager who is appointed and held responsible by the Board. The Authority is freed from Civil Service regulations in selecting and managing its personnel. Unlike most other federal enterprises, it does not depend on annual appropriations to cover its operating costs in producing power but meets them from its own commercial revenues. The Authority must obtain approval from the Bureau of the Budget for its administrative expenses and on its plans for new construction and from the Treasury for the terms on which it borrows. Its books are audited by the General Accounting Office. But its operations are not regulated by state or federal utility commissions. Compared with most federal enterprises, it is generally free of external controls.

The TVA Power Program

The TVA operates an integrated multipurpose water system. It maintains its reservoirs at levels that leave room to store floods. It releases water in the quantities needed to maintain navigation. Within these limits, it uses water to produce power. Under its enabling act, the agency was instructed to put its power activities on a self-supporting basis. It was required to give preference to public and cooperative nonprofit bodies in selling its power. It was authorized to lease, buy, or build transmission lines to reach the market. It was permitted to control prices charged by its distributors.

In building up its transmission and distribution systems, the TVA encountered determined resistance from the Commonwealth and Southern system whose subsidiaries were already operating in the valley. These companies wanted TVA to sell its power to them, but this would have violated the clear intent of the law. TVA did not undertake to duplicate their facilities; in cooperation with the cities in the region, it sought to buy them out. But its offer to purchase the properties at original cost less depreciation, as determined by an independent audit, was rejected as inadequate, their owners demanding prices that would cover the capital value of their earning power. TVA then proposed that public and private power be pooled and sold at a common rate. The companies refused, demanding a division of the field. Negotiations ended in disagreement. TVA then embarked on an aggressive sales campaign, making contracts with large industrial users and promoting the formation of competing municipal systems and rural electrification cooperatives. The companies brought a number of suits, seeking to prevent the TVA and the cities from going into the business of distributing power. To check the growth of cooperatives, they built spite lines designed to skim the cream from the rural market. The TVA was finally victorious, winning its lawsuits, building up its rural market, and purchasing private facilities at prices between those it had offered and those their owners had asked. It thus acquired a territory of 80,000 square miles, twice as large as the drainage basin of the Tennessee, with a population of 5,000,000 of whom 1,500,000 were then consumers of electricity.

The TVA inherited the dam and steam plant at Muscle Shoals and bought six dams from private companies. Its first new dams—Norris and Wheeler—were designed by the Bureau of Reclamation. The Authority then organized its own engineering staff and built 20 more dams itself. In addition to the dams it owns, TVA exercises control, by agreement, over the storage and release of water at six dams owned by the Aluminum Company of America. The Authority has built a number of steam plants to meet the growth in demand. Its installed capacity in 1968 was 18.2 million kilowatts. Less than a fourth of the power it sells is hydroelectric; more than three fourths is produced by steam. New thermal plants now under construction, all larger than any in operation, two of them using atomic fuel, will carry the system's capacity to 28 million kilowatts by 1974. The TVA sells 22 percent of its output to other federal agencies, the most important being the Atomic Energy Commission, 23 percent of it to private industries, and 55 percent to distributors, 157 in number, 102 of them municipalities, 53 rural cooperatives, and two small private companies.

In answer to a question at a press conference in the summer of 1953, President Eisenhower cited the TVA as an example of what he meant by "creeping socialism." In a sense, the characterization was justified. The project is certainly socialistic. And it has moved from place to place. The TVA started with a series of multipurpose dams. To transport incidental power, it built transmission lines. To obtain an assured market, it promoted public ownership of distribution facilities. To avoid duplication, it bought out private companies, thus obtaining a regional monopoly. To "firm up" its power supply, it built steam plants. To keep pace with growing demands, as any private enterprise would have done, it built more steam plants. Far from creeping, it proceeded at a walk or even at a run.

In fixing its initial rates, the TVA deliberately sought to promote expansion in the use of power, assuming demand to be elastic and setting its charges at a level designed to create a market that would enable it to produce at full capacity. In regulating the rates of its distributors, too, it required that they be set at levels designed, not to yield a profit that would finance the other activities of local governments and reduce their taxes, but to increase the use of power and contribute to the valley's economic development.

The low-rate policy, thus established, has been continued. In 1967 residential consumers in the Tennessee Valley bought electricity for less than half of the nation's average rate: .87 cents per kilowatt-hour compared with 2.02 cents. The policy has been successful. From 1933 to 1965, in the region, the number of farms electrified rose from 3 percent to more than 99 percent. The use of domestic power, per customer per annum, rose from an average of 600 kilowatt-hours to 12,400, a figure more than twice as high as that for the nation as a whole. The total consumption of power rose from 1.5 billion kilowatt-hours to 85 billion, increasing 56 times.

Are TVA Consumers Subsidized?

It is often charged that the customers of TVA are subsidized. In support of this charge, it is said (1) that the Authority does not pay taxes, (2) that it does not pay a proper share of the joint cost of the multipurpose facilities or charge to power a proper share of joint administrative costs, and (3) that it does not pay the market rate of interest on capital provided by the government. Each of these points requires examination.

The TVA itself pays to state and local governments, in lieu of taxes, 5 percent of the revenue it collects from customers other than the federal government. Its distributors make such payments as the laws of their states require. In 1967, these payments, taken together, amounted to more than $30,000,000. This was 7.2 percent of total revenue. The taxes paid by neighboring private utilities ranged from 4 to 10 percent of revenue. The TVA does not pay the federal tax on corporate net income, which is a tax on private profit rather than a cost. But it is repaying the government's investment in its plant, a charge the private companies are not required to meet. If the Authority enjoys an advantage on this score, it is not very great.

There is no question that TVA rates have covered the costs of building and operating the facilities that are used exclusively in producing power. This includes the steam plants that turn out three fourths of the power, the hydroelectric plants, and the transmission lines. The only question that can be raised is whether the Authority is paying its proper share of the cost of the multipurpose dams and charging enough of the cost of general administration to power. Using the alternate justifiable expenditure method of allocation described above, and recomputing the allocation each time a new dam is built, it has arrived at a distribution that allots 27 percent of the cost of the dams to navigation, 31 percent to flood control, and 42 percent to power. Correspondingly, it charges 30 percent of the cost of general administration to navigation, 30 percent to flood control, and 40 percent to power. Whether this is the proper allocation is a matter of opinion. Since this issue is now relevant only to a minor part of the cost of a minor part of the supply of TVA power, it has lost whatever importance it may once have seemed to have.

On the bonds that it issued to finance the purchase of private properties and on those that it may issue to finance the construction of new facilities, the TVA must pay the rate of interest that the market requires. On the capital provided by the Treasury, it need only pay the rate at which funds are borrowed by the government. Since this is lower than the rate that private companies must pay, they may argue that the difference amounts to a subsidy. The use of the term in this connection can be questioned, but the advantage given the Authority cannot. The private companies, on the other hand, when granted the privilege of accelerated amortization receive what amounts to an interest-free loan from the government. The pot, in this case, is calling the kettle black.

The subsidy given consumers of TVA power, if any, is small indeed. In the 25 years from 1933 to 1958, the Authority earned an average return of 4 percent on the government's investment in its power establishment. It invested $470 million of its earnings in new facilities and paid more than $250 million into the Treasury. Under legislation enacted by Congress in 1959, the Authority must pay off the remaining $1 billion of its debt in the next 45 years. Its annual payments since that date have run well ahead of those required.

Nonpower Activities

There has been no serious flood on the Tennessee since the system of TVA dams was completed; the level of flood waters on the Ohio and the Mississippi has been reduced accordingly. The ton-miles of shipping carried by the river is many times as large as in 1933. Aside from its water control activities, the TVA has worked a transformation in the valley that has made it a model which is admired, studied, and copied in the development of backward areas throughout the world. Before 1933 the standard of living in the region was low; per capita income was 40 percent of the national average. There was little industry, production being predominantly agricultural. The soil was eroded and lacking in fertility. Public facilities for health, education, and recreation were poor. For 20 years, the Authority functioned as a regional planning agency, studying the resources of the valley and providing technical assistance for their development. By 1968, per capita income had been raised to 70 percent of the national average. The availability of power had attracted new industries. Employment had increased more rapidly than in other parts of the Southeast. The creation of a series of lakes had provided opportunities for fish and wildlife and for recreation. Erosion had been checked through reforestation and the introduction of soil-conserving practices. Dairy herds had been improved by providing better pasturage. Crop yields had been increased through fertilization. The TVA was engaged in an extensive program of chemical research and in the production and promotion of concentrated fertilizers, its results being made available to farmers everywhere and to other fertilizer manufacturers. In cooperation with state and local agencies, it had contributed to marked improvements in public health, education, and other activities of government. Its success in these undertakings is attested by the virtually unanimous support accorded it by the people of the valley.

The TVA since 1953

The TVA was a favorite child of the New Deal. No love was wasted on it by the party that came into power in 1953. Instead, a determined effort was made to halt its growth. Its appropriation was cut; its request for funds to build a new steam plant at Memphis was refused. In 1954, when the expansion of atomic energy operations had created an added demand for TVA power, President Eisenhower directed the Atomic Energy Commission to enter into a contract with two utility holding companies (through E. H. Dixon and E. A. Yates, their presidents) to build a private steam plant at West Memphis, Arkansas, to feed into the TVA transmission lines some 600,000 kilowatts of power to replace like quantities that the TVA would supply to the AEC. An investigation was launched in 1955 after Congress was retaken by the Democrats. It was then disclosed that a man employed by the Dixon-Yates combination had also served as an adviser to the government and participated in the drafting of the contract. At the same time, the citizens of Memphis voted to approve a bond issue of $100 million to enable the city to build a steam plant of its own. With the questionable origin of the deal disclosed and the plant in West Memphis made unnecessary, the government canceled the contract.

Since 1953, Congress has made no appropriations to finance new power facilities. But in 1956 it authorized TVA to invest its earnings in such facilities, and in 1959 it gave the Authority permission to raise new capital by selling up to $750 million in revenue bonds. At the same time, it forbade the agency to extend its operations more than five miles beyond its existing boundaries. TVA is thus allowed to grow but not to spread.

Long-time friends of TVA complain that its character has changed. It is now more interested in the production of electricity, they say, than in the other purposes for which it was originally created. There is some basis for this criticism. But it should be noted that many of the social activities initiated by the Authority have been taken over by the region's state and local governments. The environment in which the agency now operates differs markedly from the one into which it was born in 1933.

OTHER VALLEY DEVELOPMENTS

Water control structures have been built on many of the rivers of the United States by the Bureau of Reclamation and the Corps of Engineers. Multipurpose systems comparable to those in the Tennessee Valley have been built in the basins of the Colorado, the Columbia, the Missouri, and on the St. Lawrence. But in no other valley is there an integrated water control and public power system comparable to that of the Tennessee. On the lower Colorado, where dams for water supply and irrigation were built by the Bureau of Reclamation, the power is sold at the damsite. On the Columbia and the Missouri, irrigation works have been built and operated by the Bureau and flood control and navigation works by the Corps of Engineers. On the Columbia, the power produced at all the dams is transmitted and sold by a single authority, the Bonneville Power Administration. On the Missouri, there is no common authority. On the St. Lawrence, an international river, the navigation works are operated, for the United States, by the federal government, the power plants by the State Power Authority of New York.

The Colorado River

The demand for development of the Colorado River came primarily from the people of southern California who sought water supply, irrigation, and power. Development of the river waited upon agreement, among the states in the valley, regarding the division of its waters. A dispute between the upper-basin states (Wyoming, Utah, Colorado, and New Mexico) and the lower-basin states (Arizona, Nevada, and California) was settled in 1922 by a compact that provided for an equal division of the flow. But Arizona and California could not agree upon a division of the lower basin's share. The way to the river's development was finally opened when Congress, in the Boulder Canyon Act of 1928, assigned three fifths of the lower basin's water to California and authorized construction of the dams and the canals despite Arizona's refusal to join the other states in ratifying the compact. In 1949, the upper basin states reached an agreement that gave Colorado about half of their share, and in 1956 Congress approved a development program that provides for a series of storage dams to regularize the flow of the Colorado and to supply water to the upper-basin states for irrigation and for industrial and municipal purposes, its cost to be met, in part, by the sale of power.

The largest of the structures on the Lower Colorado is a dam in Boulder Canyon, 726 feet high, which backs up the water of the river for 115 miles and has an installed power capacity of more than a million kilowatts. Authorized by Congress in 1928 and completed by the Bureau of Reclamation in 1936, it was christened Hoover Dam by the Republicans, rechristened Boulder Dam by the Democrats, and re-rechristened Hoover Dam by the Republicans. Downstream there are a number of smaller dams and a canal that diverts water from the Colorado into irrigation works in southern California. Parker Dam, 155 miles below Hoover Dam, was built by the Metropolitan Water District, an agency established in 1928 by 13 cities in southern California. From here, the MWD pumps water through an aqueduct 230 miles long to a reservoir from which it supplies the local water systems.

Proposals for additional structures on the Colorado have evoked the opposition of conservationists. A dam planned for Echo Park in the upper basin would have submerged the Dinosaur National Monument. And dams proposed for Marble Gorge and Bridge Canyon, designed to provide more water for Arizona, would have obliterated stretches of the magnificent scenery of the Grand Canyon. Each of these projects was modified to satisfy the conservationists.

When it provided for the construction of Hoover Dam, Congress required the Secretary of the Interior, before installing power facilities, to make contracts for the sale of power that would insure recovery of their cost, with interest. It authorized the Secretary to dispose of power in any one of three ways: (1) by building and operating the power plants; (2) by selling rights to falling water, permitting the purchasers to build and operate the plants; and (3) by building the plants and contracting for their operation by lessees. Of these alternatives, the Secretary chose the third. The government built two power plants. The one on the Arizona side of the river was leased to the City of Los Angeles, and the one on the Nevada side to Southern California Edison. The lessees had to build and operate their own transmission lines.

The Act of 1928 required the Secretary to charge the highest price obtainable for power, fixing it on the basis of competitive alternatives. The price initially set in the 50-year contracts with the two lessees was thus based on the alternative cost of generating steam power at Los Angeles. This price was designed to yield a profit. Of $165 million spent on the dam, $25 million was charged to flood control. Revenue from power was to amortize the other $140 million at at 4 percent in 50 years. Investment in generating equipment was to be amortized in 10 years. None of the cost of the dam was to be charged to irrigation or water supply. Power consumers were to subsidize these purposes. Under these arrangements, there was no thought of using public competition as a means of reducing private utility rates or increasing the consumption of electricity.

In 1940 the original contracts were modified. Improvements in technology had reduced the alternative cost of generating steam power. Comparison with the lower rates charged for power generated on the Tennessee and the Columbia had given rise to public complaints. The new provisions extended the period for amortizing generating facilities from 10 years to 50 and—more important—cut the interest rate from 4 percent to 3. The price of power from Hoover Dam was thus reduced. But the arrangements otherwise remained the same.

Development of the lower Colorado has done much for the states of the Southwest. It has brought desert land into agricultural production. At Lake Mead, behind Boulder Dam, it has created a major recreational area. By supplying water to Arizona and to Southern California, it has permitted an expansion of population in the area. And by supplying power, it has contributed to industrial growth.

The Columbia River

The Columbia River with its tributaries—the most important being the Snake—drains an area of 260,000 square miles, part of it in Canada, most of it in the states of Montana, Idaho, Washington, and Oregon. Plans for the development of this basin have called for a series of 33 dams surpassing those of the TVA, with an ultimate hydroelectric capacity of 17.6 million kilowatts. Construction here was started in the thirties. Bonneville Dam, on the lower Columbia, was built and has been operated by the Army Engineers, its primary function being that of promoting navigation. The dam is equipped with ship locks and with fish ladders that enable salmon and other fish to swim upstream to their spawning grounds. The Grand Coulee Dam, on the upper Columbia, is one of the biggest structures on earth, standing 450 feet high, measuring 4,300 feet at its crest, and creating a lake that stretches for 150 miles on the Canadian border. The dam was built and has been operated by the Bureau of Reclamation; it serves the purposes of stream control and irrigation. Power generated at the dam is used to pump water from the Columbia up into the Grand Coulee, a dry river bed 2 to 6 miles wide and 27 miles long between cliffs 600 feet high, which affords a natural reservoir whence water is released to irrigate a million acres of desert land in central Washington. The John Day Dam, even larger than the Grand Coulee, comes into production in 1971.

A key structure in the government's plan for the development of the basin was a high dam at Hell's Canyon on the Snake. A request for a license to build three small dams on this stretch of the river was presented to the Federal Power Commission by the Idaho Power Company. The high dam required a larger investment but promised to be more efficient in producing power, promoting navigation, and controlling floods. The three small dams would produce a million kilowatts of power and would increase downstream production by 181,000 kilowatts; the high dam would produce 900,000 kilowatts and increase downstream production by 774,000 kilowatts, a difference of 459,000 kilowatts. The high dam would provide 3 million acre-feet more water storage for navigation and flood control. The Truman administration therefore objected to the grant of a license to Idaho Power. But when Eisenhower took office, private power was favored and the objection was removed. In 1955 the Power Commission granted the license and the three small dams were built. Some of the water control and power potential of the Columbia was lost. Under the terms of a treaty with Canada, four storage dams are being built, three of them north of the border. These installations will regularize the river's flow. They will also increase the generation of power downstream by 2.8 million kilowatts. The extra power is to be divided between the two countries.

Water control operations in the Valley are handled by the Corps of Engineers and the Bureau of Reclamation. The power produced is sold by the Bonneville Power Administration which owns and operates the transmission lines. An effort is made to coordinate the work of these bodies through an interagency committee. Proposals have been made at times for the creation of a Columbia Valley Authority, but opposition by vested interests is strong; the cumbersome setup is retained.

The BPA was directed by Congress to give preference to public distributors and was authorized to regulate their rates. Seattle and Tacoma, two of the largest cities in the region, already had municipal plants, and there has been some growth of distribution by other cities and cooperatives. In 1968, 46.5 percent of BPA power was sold to such customers and to the federal government, 33.5 percent to private industries, and 10.6 percent to private utility companies. Bonneville rates are less than half the national average; home and farm consumption in the region is two and a half times the national average. These rates, like those charged by the TVA, are not designed to yield a profit but are expected to cover the separable cost and part of the joint costs involved in producing power. In this case, the task of allocating joint costs has been assigned by Congress to the Federal Power Commission. For the facilities in use in 1953, these costs were allocated 7 percent to flood control, 7 percent to navigation, 25 percent to irrigation, and 61 percent to power. The low rates charged by BPA were thus covering all of the costs of the power business and three fifths of the cost of the multipurpose dams.

In the Pacific Northwest, as in the Tennessee Valley, the hydroelectric resources will soon be fully exploited. It will therefore be necessary to augment them by building thermal plants, fired by coal or by nuclear energy. And this raises a familiar problem: are these plants to be owned and operated by the government or by private enterprise? Under a plan proposed in the early sixties, the Atomic Energy Commission would have installed a power reactor at its plutonium plant in Hanford, Washington, operated it with by-product steam from the plant, and sold electricity to the BPA. The plan was rejected by Congress. Instead, the power plant was built by 16 private utility companies and operated with steam purchased from the AEC. In 1968, it was announced that the private companies, the municipal and county systems, and the BPA had agreed upon a 20-year $15 billion program to construct another 40 million kilowatt hours of generating capacity in the Northwest. The new thermal plants will be built and operated by the private companies and the public systems.

Most of the hydro power will be produced and the transmission lines will be operated by the BPA. Bonneville power will be tied in with Southwestern power by four lines, two of them already in operation, exchanging energy to meet peak demands.

The Missouri River

The Missouri basin comprises a sixth of the land in the United States, including part or all of 10 states. Two comprehensive plans were proposed for the development of the valley, one by General Lewis A. Pick of the Army Corps of Engineers, the other by W. Glenn Sloan of the Bureau of Reclamation. The Pick plan was designed to meet the needs of the people of the lower valley, it emphasized navigation and flood control. The Sloan plan appealed to the people of the upper valley; it put its emphasis on irrigation. A compromise was finally effected between the two. The Pick-Sloan plan included 138 projects for flood control, navigation, irrigation, and hydroelectric power, with 1,500 miles of levees, a navigation channel, six big dams and many smaller ones on the main stream and its tributaries. It was a plan of water control, with no regard to soil conservation, fish and wildlife preservation, recreation, or public health. Initiation of the projected works was authorized by Congress in the Flood Control Act of 1944. The first of the structures completed, the Fort Peck Dam in Montana, was designed for water storage. The largest earth-filled dam in the world, it was built by the Corps of Engineers. There are now a score of hydroelectric plants in operation in the valley. Under the present setup, each of these installations is handled separately, the Bureau of Reclamation marketing the surplus power.

Development of the valley has given rise to continued controversy. The upstream states complain that the Corps of Engineers controls the flow of water from its reservoirs in such a way as to favor downstream navigation over upstream irrigation and power. They favor the construction of more dams on the upper river, creating a step series of lakes united by locks, to permit slack-water navigation and provide more water for irrigation and power, with downstream navigation supported by the free flow of water released upstream. The lower basin states oppose this project, holding that it would delay navigation and increase its cost. The controversy is yet to be resolved.

Operating in the valley, along with the Corps of Engineers and the Bureau of Reclamation, are the Soil Conservation Service, the Fish and Wildlife Service, the Public Health Service, the Federal Power Commission, and a number of state agencies, their jurisdictions overlapping and their interests frequently in conflict. Here, as on the Columbia, there is an interagency committee. Holding meetings of 50 to 100 people about 10 times a year, each time in a different city, the committee cannot serve as a coordinating body. To fulfill this function, bills have been presented to Congress establishing a Missouri Valley Authority, with power to plan and direct the valley's development. Here, again, the bills have been successfully opposed: by the existing federal agencies, the contractors who work for them, the Congressional committees who handle their appropriations, the governments of the valley states, and the private power companies, all of them with an interest in keeping things as they are. An alternative proposal, advanced by the valley states, called for the creation of a joint commission under an interstate compact, with 10 votes for the states and 10 for the federal government, to review and approve or disapprove the programs of the federal agencies. This proposal, giving the states coordinate power in the supervision of federal projects, was passed by the Senate but defeated in the House. A final plan was recommended by the Missouri Basin Survey Commission in its monumental report on Missouri: *Land and Water,* issued in 1953. Under this plan, an administrative body would be established by the federal government and empowered to control the work done in the valley by all of the federal agencies participating in its development. The Commission's recommendation was ignored.

The St. Lawrence River

Agitation for a channel to carry ocean-going ships between the Great Lakes and the Atlantic began as early as 1895. Construction of such a seaway, with some canals on the American side and some on the Canadian side of the St. Lawrence, was recommended by an International Joint Commission and by the Corps of Engineers in 1926. Efforts to secure Congressional approval for the project were defeated in 1933, in 1941, and in 1948, having evoked the opposition of the railroads, the coal miners, and the port cities on the Gulf and Atlantic coasts. The government of Canada, despairing of American cooperation, finally announced its intention of building the seaway on its own side of the border. Thus prodded, Congress authorized American participation in the project in 1954.

The Seaway Act of that year set up a federal corporation to cooperate with a Canadian body in building, operating, and maintaining the necessary dams, canals, and locks along the International Rapids. This project, together with the existing canals at Niagara Falls and Sault Ste. Marie and other channel and harbor improvements along the Great Lakes, would eventually provide a 27-foot channel from the lake ports to the open sea. The Seaway itself was completed and opened to traffic in 1959. Its users were to pay tolls which are designed to cover the costs of operation, maintenance, and interest and to amortize the investment in navigation facilities in 50 years. The traffic generated by the project has been smaller and its costs larger than expected. After 10 years of operation, it had accumulated a deficit of $40 million. It seemed unlikely that the undertaking would pay its own way until the channels connecting the lakes were deepened and the lake ports equipped to handle ocean-going ships.

One feature of the project is the Barnhart Island Dam which made it possible to produce 1,880,000 kilowatts of hydroelectric power. On the Canadian side of the border, the power development was handled by the Hydroelectric Power Commission of Ontario, a public agency established in 1906. On the American side, a license to develop the power was granted by the Federal Power Commission to the State Power Authority of New York. Construction was completed in 1958. The SPA is selling most of its power to industries in the vicinity and to private distributors in New York and Vermont. It was prepared to sell to municipal and cooperative distributors, but few of them applied.

At Niagara Falls, a three-way fight for the privilege of further developing the power resources on the American side was carried on, in the fifties, among the private power interests, the State Power Authority, and the advocates of federal development. The private interests withdrew from the contest after one of their plants was destroyed by a rockslide. The issue of state versus federal development was decided in 1957 when Congress authorized the FPC to give a license to the state. The SPA has built a plant with a capacity of 1.8 million kilowatts. Production here began in 1961. The Authority sells this power, in the main, to industrial users and to private distributors, to whom it has agreed to deliver a substantial block of power for years to come. All savings in the cost of power are passed on to consumers in lower rates.

PUBLIC POWER POLICY

On many of the issues discussed in this book, it is difficult to distinguish between the position of the Republicans and that of the Democrats. This is the case, for instance, with the maintenance of competition, the prevention of fraud, the subsidization of business and agriculture, the acceptance of unionization and collective bargaining, and the regulation of transport and communications. It is not the case with public enterprise in power. The Democrats have promoted public power. The Republicans have opposed it.

The New Deal was no friend to the private power industry. In the Public Utility Holding Company Act of 1935, as we saw in Chapter 15, it subjected the industry's corporate structure to drastic reorganization and its intercorporate relations to continuing control. At the same time, it built dams and began itself to generate and sell electric power. Under Hoover, the power produced at Boulder Canyon was sold at the dam. Under Roosevelt and Truman, the government built its own transmission lines. It encouraged municipalities to buy or build distribution systems and, during the depression, helped them to do so by making loans and grants. It pushed the extension of service into rural areas by making long-term low-interest loans to rural electrification cooperatives. It gave to municipal and cooperative distributors assurance of priority in the sale of its power. Instead of leaving the field to private enterprise, it actively promoted public ownership. Under Hoover, the power produced at Hoover Dam was sold at a price designed to yield a profit that would subsidize irrigation and flood control. Under Roosevelt and Truman, rates were set at levels that were calculated to maximize consumption. They were designed, not to yield a profit, but to forward economic and social development. This policy, while unpopular with private utility companies, was nonetheless defensible. In certain regions, it displaced or forestalled private enterprise. In setting rates, it took risks that private enterprise could not afford to take. But it did succeed in promoting regional development in a way that private enterprise would not have done.

The Republicans steadily opposed the growth of public power. In 1940, they gave their presidential nomination to Wendell Willkie who, as president of Commonwealth and Southern, had come to national prominence by leading the private utility industry in its fight against the TVA. When the party returned to power, in 1953, the new Congress reduced the budgets of the TVA, the Rural Electrification Administration, the Bureau of Reclamation, and the Army Corps of Engineers. It canceled all new projects and put a stop to some that were already under way. Ex-President Hoover asserted that the objective of public power policy "should be to get the federal government out of the business of generating and distributing power as soon as possible." President Eisenhower was not prepared to go that far. The TVA, he told his press conference, had to be accepted as an historic fact. The sale of the system, he thought, would be a pretty drastic step. Through the Dixon-Yates deal, however, the new administration sought to divert growing demand of the Tennessee Valley from the TVA to a private company. At Hell's Canyon, it prevented a greater output of power by dropping the plan for a high public dam and approving three small private dams. The philosophy behind these moves was set forth in a formal statement announcing the adoption of a "partnership power policy."

Under this policy, the primary responsibility for meeting the power needs of any region was said to rest with the people of that region. The federal government would finish the projects already under construction. But in the case of new projects, it would give priority to local public or private enterprise. Where flood control, navigation, or irrigation were involved, it would enter into partnership with local interests, paying for the part of the projects that could not be met by the sale of power. Only where such projects were clearly beyond the means of local groups would the federal government carry the cost alone.

In 1955 the second Hoover Commission made a number of recommendations on public power. It proposed (1) that the power plants at multipurpose dams be built by private companies or, failing this, that they be built by the government and leased to private companies or, failing this, that power be generated by the government and sold at the damsite; (2) that insofar as possible no more transmission lines be built; (3) that preference for public distributors be discontinued and power sold on equal terms to private companies; (4) that no more steam plants be built, the steam power needed being purchased instead from private companies; and (5) that public power be sold at rates that would cover taxes as high as those paid by private companies. The Commission's Task Force went even further, recommending that the government invite proposals for the sale or lease of all of its power facilities.

This report embodied the most extreme position taken by the foes of public power. Instead of adopting its recommendations, the administration moved the other way. In approving development of the Upper Colorado, it committed the government to a long-term project of the greatest magnitude. In permitting the TVA to raise capital by selling securities on the market, it abandoned its fight to prevent the agency from meeting the growing demand, within that region, for public power.

In 1964, the Republican candidate for the presidency, Senator Goldwater, again proposed that the TVA be sold to private utility interests or, at least, that the steam plants be put up for sale. The issue did not prove to be a popular one.

In the Kennedy and Johnson administrations, the partnership power policy gave way to the policy of "competitive cooperation." This policy envisages the peaceful coexistence of private and public power systems, each seeking to outdo the other, both being interconnected by regional systems—or a nationwide system—of long-distance transmission lines. Public power was no longer an issue when the Republicans returned to office in 1969. The hatchet had finally been buried.

Chapter 23

GOVERNMENT MONOPOLIES: THE POST OFFICE; ATOMIC ENERGY

Two important public enterprises remain to be considered: the Post Office and the atomic energy industry. In some respects the two are similar. Both are owned by the federal government. Each has a monopoly. Neither is operated like a private business. Both involve substantial investments of public funds. Both entail losses that are charged against the Treasury. Both have been embroiled in politics. In neither is the present organization of the enterprise felt to be satisfactory. In other respects the two undertakings differ. The postal service dates from the foundation of the republic; the atomic energy industry from the Second World War. The Post Office is a department of the government; the Atomic Energy Commission is an independent agency. The work of the Post Office is done by civil servants; the work of the atomic energy industry is done, in the main, by employees of private contractors under the supervision of the AEC. The Post Office makes no effort to stimulate private enterprise in communications; the AEC promotes the use of nuclear energy as a fuel by private electrical utilities. The Post Office regulates no other enterprise; the AEC has extensive regulatory responsibilities. Few people would contend that the Post Office has been well managed; most observers would agree that the task of managing the atomic energy program has been well done.

THE POSTAL SERVICE

The Post Office is traditionally a public enterprise. The postal service, wrote Adam Smith in 1776, "is perhaps the only mercantile project which has been successfully managed by, I believe, every sort of government. The capital to be advanced is not very considerable. There is no mystery in the business. The returns are not only certain, but immediate."[1] Congress was given the power by Article I, Section 8 of the Constitution "To establish Post Offices and post Roads," and a postal system, including 74 post offices, was established by the first Congress in 1789. The system was originally set up as a separate agency under the President. In 1829, the Postmaster General was admitted to the Cabinet. And in 1872, the Post Office was made a department of the government.

1 / *The Wealth of Nations*, Book V, chap. ii, Part I.

531

In the early days of the republic, the postal service had a vital function to fulfill. In the absence of modern means of communication, it afforded the only tie that bound the country together, uniting the wilderness with the capital, scattered settlements with centers of trade and finance. It contributed to a sense of national identity, to economic and political unity. It was a basic instrument of public policy.

Today the Post Office is one of many media of communication. It is a big business—one of the biggest on earth, with 44,000 offices, over 700,000 employees, and a budget of $7 billion a year. It delivers mail each weekday to nearly every business and household in the land, handling 80 billion pieces each year. Only 14 percent of this is personal correspondence. A tenth is newspapers or magazines. More than a fourth is advertising matter. Almost half involves business transactions: orders, invoices, bills, checks, and the like. The volume of such materials is twice as great today as it was 20 years ago. And it promises to keep on growing at an increasing rate.

Organization and Administration

The Post Office Department was organized much as a private business would be organized, with responsibility nominally centered in the Postmaster General and a hierarchy of subordinates responsible to him. But the Department was not run as a private business would be run. It could not select its own personnel. The upper positions were filled through political patronage; the remaining jobs were controlled by the Civil Service Commission. The Department did not set the rates it charged. All rates but those for parcel post were fixed by Congress. Parcel post rates were fixed by the Interstate Commerce Commission. The Department did not determine the amounts it spent. Salaries were fixed by Congress. Funds for post office buildings were included in the annual appropriations for public works. The Post Office made contracts with private carriers for transport of the mail. The amounts it paid the railroads were fixed by the Interstate Commerce Commission. The sums it paid the airlines were fixed by the Civil Aeronautics Board. Postal revenues could not be used to defray the costs of the service; they had to be paid into the Treasury. To finance its activities, the Department had to present its budget requests to the Bureau of the Budget and to appropriations committees of the House and Senate and have funds voted it by Congress in appropriation bills. Funds for the Post Office were broken down, by purposes, into some 60 different appropriations, and each expenditure had to be charged against the appropriation under which it had been authorized. The Department's books were checked by the General Accounting Office to make sure that no unauthorized expenditures were made.

The individual postmaster could not operate his office as if it were a business. He was bound hand and foot by the rules contained in *Postal Laws & Regulations,* a book that weighed nearly three pounds and ran close to a thousand pages. Until recently the Department's administration was highly centralized. Every postmaster got his instructions directly from Washington and made his reports directly to Washington. However urgent the repairs required in an emergency, the postmaster could not pay for them by transferring money from one account to another without first obtaining permission from Washington. Whatever his need for equipment, he could not buy it without authority from Washington.

The post office at Seattle one time badly needed a tow truck for its own breakdowns. Washington, however, wouldn't approve the purchase. Then the Seattle postmaster learned he could buy an Army-surplus tow truck, new, for $1.00. So he went ahead and bought it? Oh, no. He had to write Washington for approval. But Washington answered: "No." Thought the postmaster then: "I'll buy it myself; give it to the Department." But he couldn't—not without first writing to Washington. And the answer on that too was "No." The number of breakdowns in Seattle didn't require a tow truck, Washington believed; and it was contrary to procedure to allow any local postmaster on the scene to act on his own judgment and initiative.[2]

This situation stood in marked contrast to the pattern of organization that characterized large-scale private industry. If it were operated as a private enterprise, administration of the postal service would long since have been delegated to regional headquarters, and the individual postmaster would have been accorded a larger measure of responsibility.

When the Post Office was investigated by former President Hoover's Commission on Organization of the Executive Branch of the Government in 1949, it was employing none of the techniques of modern management. It had no management engineering. It was doing no research on the service needs and desires of its patrons, and little or no research on methods of handling and transporting mail. It was giving little formal training to its personnel. Its accounting system was antiquated; its cost controls rudimentary. It had no standards by which to measure performance on the job. To its question, "What is wrong with the Post Office?" the commission answered, "(a) The administrative structure is obsolete and overcentralized. (b) A maze of outmoded laws, regulations and traditions freezes progress and stifles proper administration. (c) . . . it lacks the freedom and flexibility essential to good business operation."[3] And when President Johnson's Commission on Postal Organization reported in 1968, it found the management structure of the Post Office to be "archaic" and "inappropriate," said that "In appearance, many people are responsible for running the Post Office; in fact, no one is" and that "the nominal managers of the postal service do not have the authority to run the postal service," and concluded that "the present organization of the Post Office prevents it from being managed properly."[4]

2 / C. Lester Walker, "So They're Re-doing the Post Office," *Harper's Magazine,* June, 1951, pp. 37-45, esp. p. 39.

3 / Commission on Organization of the Executive Branch of the Government, *The Post Office* (Washington, D.C.: Government Printing Office, 1949), p. 3.

4 / The President's Commission on Postal Organization, *Towards Postal Excellence* (Washington, D.C.: Government Printing Office, 1968), pp. 31, 33, 34, 46.

Post Office Personnel

The personnel practices of the postal system were open to serious criticism. The best men seldom got the postal jobs. The Postmaster General, with few exceptions, was appointed, not because of his experience in postal administration, but as a reward for his service as a politician. He functioned, traditionally, as the chief patronage dispenser of the national administration. Candidates for individual postmasterships could establish their eligibility by passing a Civil Service examination. But the candidates appointed by the President were selected, with the advice of Congressmen and local politicians, from among the top three found eligible. A third of the postmasters appointed in the sixties came from the career service; two thirds were political hacks. Workers employed at lower levels were, in general, poorly educated and inexperienced. Nor were their deficiencies overcome by training on the job. The time devoted to such training averaged only eight hours per man per year, and half of this was on the man's own time.

So, too, with other aspects of labor policy. The wages paid to postal workers compared favorably with those paid men for similar work in private industry. The workers were organized, but they were not allowed to strike. They did not bargain with the Post Office concerning their pay. They put pressure, instead, on members of Congress. And here, given their numbers, it had its effect. Opportunity for advancement within the service was small. A postal worker, whatever his performance, could not be transferred to a larger office outside the district where he lived. Four fifths of the workers retired at the grade at which they were hired. Working conditions, in urban offices, were described as appalling. Buildings were antiquated, dismal, and dirty, with inadequate lighting, heating, and ventilation. They were overcrowded, with too few lockers and washrooms and paltry health services. Modern methods of personnel relations were unknown. Supervision was authoritarian. There was intense antagonism, in some places, between supervisors and subordinates, with the former suffering physical attacks. In this context, the morale of the work force was low and its rate of turnover high—as high as 23 percent per year. In private industry, labor productivity has steadily advanced; in the Post Office it had stood still.[5]

Quality of Service

The Post Office, over the years, has steadily expanded the scope of its services. Starting with the general delivery window, it went on to urban free delivery in 1863 and to rural free delivery in 1896. Starting with letters and papers, it took on parcel post in 1913. And, from time to time, it added such services as registry, special delivery, money orders, parcel insurance, c.o.d. collection, and airmail. Measured against the service provided a century or more

5 / *Ibid.*, pp. 98-120.

ago, the Post Office had progressed. But measured against the possibilities, its progress had been slow. In recent years it had even lost some ground.

Four or five deliveries a day are common in Europe; six are the rule in Japan. But here, in 1950, deliveries in residential areas were cut from two to one. Only 64 percent of first-class mail was delivered the next day. A letter mailed in Washington, D.C. on Monday evening was delivered in New York City on Wednesday morning, 40 hours later, having travelled at five miles an hour, a speed about half that attained by the Pony Express more than a century ago. Delivery of first-class mail was not hastened by affixing airmail stamps; nine tenths of such mail was forwarded by air regardless of the postage it bore. On shorter distances, on the other hand, airmail might slow delivery down. Mail crossing a city might move more slowly than mail crossing the country; more slowly, indeed, than a man could walk. The nation built more highways, more airports, faster cars and faster planes, but the mails still moved at a snail's pace.

In Chicago, in October, 1966, the largest post office in the world was virtually paralyzed for a period of three weeks. Ten million pieces of mail were set aside, unprocessed and undeliverable. There was concern that the accumulation would have to be burned or dumped in the lake. What went wrong? First, there was an unanticipated explosion of bulk mailings. Second, there were failures of equipment. One loading dock was under repair. Elevators and conveyor belts were broken down. Half of the tractor fleet was out of service. Third, there were failures of personnel. Some employees had been laid off in disciplinary actions resulting from labor disputes. Others, in large numbers, had reported sick, absenting themselves from work. A number of supervisors had retired. The office was forbidden to fill its vacancies by paying overtime. There was no postmaster on the job. This conjuncture of circumstances was without precedent. But, given the persistence of its basic causes, the paralysis could recur—and spread.

Technical Progress

The experts who studied the Post Office for the Hoover Commission in 1949 found that it had done little to improve its methods of handling materials. Instead of being racked in modern containers and hoisted and hauled with jacks and trucks of modern design, mail was still transported in bags. Instead of being sorted by machine, it was sorted by hand. Though the burden of door-to-door delivery could have been lessened and delivery speeded by the development of light motorized vehicles, the postman still carried the mail in a sack on his back. "While it can be shown that over the years postal methods have been improved and costs reduced," said the experts, "it has been an uninspired and low-geared effort which progressive businessmen would regard as mediocre."[6]

6 / Commission on Organization of the Executive Branch of the Government, *Task Force Report on the Post Office* (Washington, D.C.: Government Printing Office, 1949), p. 33.

Progress toward modernization was made during the fifties and the sixties. Introduction of the ZIP-Code system, identifying by number every post office and metropolitan delivery station in the United States, accelerated the sorting process (partly by enabling large mailers to use their electronic equipment to presort their mail), and facilitated shipment directly to destination, eliminating handling en route. Movement of mail was also speeded by persuading large mailers to deliver letters to the post office early in the day, reducing the early evening peak, by concentrating sorting operations at regional centers, and by installing conveyor systems to deliver mail to the upper floors of high-rise buildings. Machines have been developed to face and cancel letters and to enable clerks to sort them, at the rate of 3,600 an hour, by punching keys that route them by mechanical carriers to their proper sacks. Another machine, an optical character reader with a cathode ray scanner, locates and reads the zip code numbers on printed or typed addresses and directs the coded letters, at the rate of 36,000 an hour, to one or another of 277 bins, leaving the 30 percent that bear no number to be sorted manually. But mail in most offices was still handled as it was a century ago, with letters sorted into pigeon holes by hand. In 1969, there were key punch sorters in only 40 offices and optical character readers in only 10.

New equipment is costly. It could not be bought without Congressional approval. And Congress, however open-handed elsewhere, had been stingy where the Post Office was concerned. The system was woefully undercapitalized. The net fixed assets of the telephone system amounted to $35,620 per employee; those of the postal system to $1,145. The share of the telephone budget that was allocated to capital investment was 34 percent, the share of the postal budget assigned to this purpose was 2.2 percent. If it were properly to fulfill its function, the Post Office should have had an infusion of $5 billion in new capital. But if it were to get these funds, Congressional policy had to be reversed.

The Post Office had devoted some attention, in recent years, to the design of physical facilities. It had done little in the way of market research. It had projected future demand for its services as a whole. But it did not know what new services might be wanted; what people would be willing to pay, for instance, to get next-day delivery for urgent mail. It thus might be leaving the public with unmet needs.

Postal Rates and Deficits

For a quarter of a century after the Post Office was established, it was operated as a business and returned an annual profit. But since that time, Congress emphasized expansion of the service and made little effort to insure that rates should cover costs. In all but a few years the Department has operated at a deficit. During the sixties the deficit exceeded $8 billion; in 1967, it stood at $1.2 billion. And these figures understated the loss, since the Department's accounts included no allowance for the government's contribution to the pension fund, no interest charge on the sums invested in postal facilities, and no provision for depreciation. The deficits could have been wiped out by cutting costs. The President's Commission on Postal Organization asserted in 1968 that "at least 20 percent of postal costs—well over a billion dollars a year at present volumes—would be saved if the Post Office management were freed to plan and finance postal operations and capital investment strictly in accord with postal needs."[7] But this would have required a transformation of existing organization and procedure. The deficits could have been eliminated, too, if somebody had raised postal rates, but the Postmaster General could not and the Congress usually would not. And when Congress did raise rates, belatedly, the gain in revenue was offset, in major part, by increases in wages.

The structure of postal rates did not conform to the costs incurred in carrying different classes of mail. Changes in rates were proposed by the President. They were considered by committees of the Senate and the House. Increases in second and third class rates were opposed by lobbies of publishers and advertisers. Increases in first-class rates encountered no such opposition. The resulting structure of rates was not entirely without justification. It did reflect differences in the number and weight of pieces mailed. It made some allowance for distance. Flat rates to all domestic destinations were fixed for letters, postcards, newspapers and magazines, books, and other materials weighing eight ounces or less. But rates graduated by zones were fixed for parcel post. There were charges for special services and allowances for presorting and low priority in handling. Some mail was carried free: that sent by members of Congress and by agencies of the federal government and books and records for the blind.

Every class of mail handled by the Department, except letters, was carried at a loss. Airmail letters, according to the Department's estimates, had been carried at 121 percent of cost, other letters at 103 percent, advertising matter at 67 percent, and periodicals at 25 percent. In the fiscal year 1963, the Post Office is said to have made a profit of $162 million in carrying first-class mail and airmail; incurred a loss of $922 million in carrying other classes of mail and in maintaining rural services.[8] The inadequacy of the rate level and the character of the rate structure forced the taxpayer and the letter writer to subsidize other users of the service.

It would certainly have been reasonable to require the postal service as a whole to support itself, and to require commercial users of the service, in particular, to pay their own way. It would scarcely be desirable, however, to require every service rendered by the Post Office to cover its cost. Delivery routes in remote and sparsely settled regions, for example, must be maintained at a loss as a matter of public policy. But specific appropriations should be made for such purposes. In principle, no class of mail should be carried for less than the long-run variable cost of the service rendered, and some charges should be

7 / President's Commission on Postal Organization, *op. cit.*, p. 24.

8 / Joint Economic Committee, *Subsidy and Subsidy-Effect Programs of the U.S. Government* (Washington, D.C.: Government Printing Office, 1965), p. 66. See also Morton S. Baratz, *The Economics of the Postal Service* (Washington, D.C.: Public Affairs Press, 1962).

set, in accordance with the value of the service to the user, at a level that would enable the system to recover both its variable cost and the fixed costs of the service as a whole. But the Post Office did not really know enough about its costs and the demand for its services to establish a pattern of rates that would conform to these rules.

Postal Reform

In 1967, the Postmaster General, Lawrence F. O'Brien, proposed that the Post Office be removed from the cabinet and set up as a government corporation like the TVA, to be governed by an independent board of directors, insulated from politics and administered, on a business basis, by a professional executive. The next year, the President's Commission on Postal Organization, headed by Frederick R. Kappel, formerly chairman of the board of A.T.&T., made detailed recommendations designed to carry this proposal into effect. (1) A postal corporation, owned entirely by the federal government, was to be chartered by Congress to operate the postal system on a self-supporting basis. It was to be governed by a board of nine directors, six of them appointed by the President and three selected by the other six, one of them to serve as chief executive officer. (2) Postmasters were to be appointed without regard to politics. Postal employees were to be transferred from the civil service to a new career service within the corporation. Wages, fringe benefits, and working conditions were to be determined by collective bargaining. (3) A modern cost accounting system was to be installed, so that rates could be related to the costs of different classes of service. Rates were to be initiated, following studies of costs and demands and after public hearings, by a staff of rate experts appointed by the board of directors. They were to be promulgated by the board, to take effect unless vetoed by Congress within 60 days. (4) The corporation was to meet its needs for capital by going to the market to sell its bonds.[9]

In 1969, President Nixon submitted to Congress a draft of a Postal Services Act that differed in detail but not in essential principle from these recommendations. And in 1970, prodded by a strike of postal employees, Congress voted substantial increases in wages and enacted a program of postal reform. The new law set up a U.S. Postal Service as an independent establishment within the government, to be operated by a board of 11 members, 9 of them to be appointed by the President and 2—a Postmaster General and a Deputy P.M.G.— to be chosen by the other 9. Wages are determined by collective bargaining, subject, in the absence of agreement, to binding arbitration. Rates are fixed by a separate commission of five members, subject to veto by a unanimous vote of the governing board. Subsidies are to be phased out so that the Postal Service will be self-supporting by the end of 15 years. The Service is authorized to meet its needs for capital improvements by borrowing, up to $2 billion a year, in the market. The conditions essential to a businesslike administration of the

9 / President's Commission on Postal Organization, *op. cit.,* pp. 53-64.

postal system, free from politics, are thus provided. How they will work out in practice remains to be seen.

THE ATOMIC ENERGY INDUSTRY

On August 6, 1945, President Truman announced that an atomic bomb had been exploded over Hiroshima. More than 70,000 people had been killed; as many more had been wounded; a sizable city had virtually been destroyed. On August 9, a second bomb was exploded over Nagasaki. On August 10, Japan surrendered. These dramatic events marked the culmination of an enterprise in which the government of the United States had been engaged for the previous five years. In 1939 Albert Einstein had written to President Roosevelt, informing him that scientists had succeeded in splitting the atom, thus releasing a force of potential military use. In 1940 the government initiated a program of atomic research. In 1942 the first self-sustaining nuclear chain reaction was achieved in a laboratory at the University of Chicago. In the next year work was started on a wartime program that eventually cost nearly $2 billion. Great plants were built to manufacture bomb materials at secret cities in Tennessee and in the State of Washington. A secret laboratory was built atop a mesa in New Mexico where physicists devised the bomb. On July 16, 1945, the first bomb was exploded experimentally on the desert in New Mexico. Within a month World War II had come to an end. The American people were faced with a new problem. How, now, was the power they had unleashed to be controlled?

All of the atomic facilities had been built and were owned and operated by the government. There was general agreement that this should continue to be the case. The processes employed were dangerous in themselves; the products were weapons; secrecy was demanded; tight control was required. But what agency should be given authority to exercise control? During the war, the program had been administered by the Manhattan Engineer District, a unit established for the purpose by the Army Corps of Engineers. Now, the question was whether control should be left with the military or turned over to civilians. Atomic energy could be used in weapons. It might also come to be employed for peaceful purposes. Military control might hamper these developments. A bill prepared in the Pentagon would have perpetuated such control. It evoked determined opposition. The measure finally enacted by Congress provided for control by a commission of civilians, with decisions affecting military uses to be made in consultation with a liaison committee representing the armed services.

Atomic Energy Act of 1946

The Atomic Energy Commission, set up by the new law, consists of five members appointed by the President, with the consent of the Senate, for terms of five years each, their terms being so arranged that one appointment is to be made each year. The Commission is a policy board, with administrative authority being delegated to a general manager. The Commission is advised by the Military

Liaison Committee and by a General Advisory Committee of civilian scientists. Its work is subject to oversight by a Joint Committee composed of nine members of the Senate and nine of the House of Representatives, its chairmanship rotating between the two.

The law permitted private enterprise in mining and concentrating the ores—uranium and thorium—from which fissionable materials are produced. But from this point on, every step was kept under strict control. Until the law was amended in 1954, private ownership of fissionable materials, of facilities for their production, and of patents covering the productive processes was forbidden. The production, exportation, and importation of such materials were made government monopolies. The Commission was empowered to issue licenses to govern the sale and delivery of the original ores, the manufacture of facilities for the production of fissionables, and the manufacture of equipment for their use. It was authorized to lend or lease fissionables, in safe quantities, with or without charge, for research, medical therapy, or industrial use. The Commission retained title to such materials and controlled their transfer. It might also distribute radioactive by-products for use in research, medicine, and industry. Persons engaging in regulated activities without its permission were subject to heavy penalties.

The Manhattan Engineer District did not itself conduct the researches, construct the facilities, or carry on the operations through which the materials for the atomic weapon were produced. Instead, it accomplished its purpose by entering into agreements with private contractors. Continuance of this procedure was authorized by the Act of 1946. The Atomic Energy Commission may itself engage in research, construction, and production, or it may employ private contractors. Its contractors must submit reports, permit inspection, and obey its regulations respecting safety and security. But the terms of its contracts, in the main, are within its own discretion. Competitive bidding is not required.

Under the law, all information concerning the manufacture or utilization of atomic weapons, the production of fissionable materials, and the use of such materials in the production of power was classified as restricted. The Commission was authorized to declassify such data as it determined might be published without endangering national security. Disclosure of restricted information was punishable by fines up to $20,000 and by imprisonment up to 20 years. Disclosure with intent to injure the United States was punishable by death or by imprisonment for life.

The Act of 1946 was without precedent. It sought to provide in advance for the development and control of a new source of power. It established a public monopoly in a new and growing industry. It made a sweeping delegation of authority to a governmental agency. And it required this body to carry on its operations in strictest secrecy. This policy was hazardous, but it was felt to be essential to national security.

Atomic Energy Act of 1954

Between 1946 and 1954 there were significant changes affecting atomic policy. The Communist powers came to present a serious threat to the security of the United States and other nations of the West. The Soviet Union succeeded in developing atomic weapons of its own. The western powers joined in organizations dedicated to their mutual defense. Canada, Great Britain, and others among these nations embarked upon atomic programs. The people of many countries looked upon the armament race between the great powers with growing fear. Those of the underdeveloped countries, in particular, complained that the new source of energy was being put to destructive rather than constructive use. The powers of the East and those of the West came to compete for the friendship of neutral states. In the meantime the United States had accumulated a huge store of weapons. It had demonstrated the feasibility of employing atomic energy to produce industrial power. And it had the capacity to devote a part of its resources to this activity. Given this situation, President Eisenhower proposed, in February, 1954, that Congress amend the atomic energy law.

The changes recommended by the President were three: (1) The secrecy required under the Act of 1946 was to be relaxed to permit the government to share with its military allies a limited amount of information concerning atomic weapons that were to be used for mutual defense. (2) It was to be relaxed, too, to allow the exchange of knowledge with friendly nations concerning the peaceful uses of atomic energy, thus opening the way to the constructive use of such energy in other parts of the world. (3) The limitations on private possession of fissionable materials, atomic facilities, and patents relating to atomic technology were to be relaxed to permit and encourage private enterprise to undertake the generation of industrial power from nuclear fuel.

The first two of these recommendations gave rise to little controversy, and the powers requested by the President were written into the law. The proposals relating to employment of the atom by private enterprise, however, evoked a long debate. Private ownership of patents was opposed on the ground that it would give the first companies permitted to enter the field an unfair advantage over those that might seek to enter later on. The issue of public versus private power was thrown into the debate. The proponents of public power sought to confer on the Atomic Energy Commission itself the right to generate and sell electricity, to give other public agencies, such as the TVA, the same opportunity that was given private enterprise to employ atomic energy for this purpose, and to maintain the principle that municipal and cooperative distributors be given preference in buying publicly generated power.

As the law was finally passed, in August, 1954, it permits the private construction, ownership, and operation of atomic power plants, the private possession and use of nuclear fuel, and the private sale of by-product material, all under license by the AEC. It permits the private ownership of patents, but provides, in certain cases, for compulsory licensing. The law forbids the Commission to go into the commercial power business, but allows it to sell the power that it may generate at experimental installations. It grants public agencies an equal right with private utilities to apply to the AEC for licenses. And it maintains the principle of preference for municipal and cooperative distributors.

The Atomic Energy Commission

The first members of the Atomic Energy Commission were appointed by President Truman, with David E. Lilienthal of the Tennessee Valley Authority as chairman. They were confirmed by the Senate in November, 1946, after protracted hearings. The Commission took over the assets of the Manhattan District on January 1, 1947. It acquired establishments with a capital investment of $1,400,000,000, including a weapons research laboratory and a town of 9,000 at Los Alamos, New Mexico, production plants, a research laboratory, and a town of 36,000 at Oak Ridge, Tennessee, and another plant and town of 17,000 at Hanford, Washington. It inherited a contract system with 5,000 government employees and 50,000 contractor employees. It was entrusted with the knowledge required to produce fissionable materials and atomic bombs. It was given custody of the nation's stock of bombs.

The Commission's responsibilities are many and heavy: (1) It must provide for the production and storage of such kinds and quantities of weapons as the President decides may be required. (2) It must promote the discovery, mining, and initial processing of uranium and thorium, license their production and shipment, purchase and import them, and provide for their handling and storage. (3) If larger supplies of fissionable materials are required, it must decide what processes to use in producing them, what plants to build, and where to locate them. It must build the plants itself or select private builders, make contracts with them, and supervise their work. It must license the manufacturers of the equipment it installs. (4) It must operate the plants producing fissionables or select private operators, enter into contracts, and check on performance to insure compliance with their terms. (5) It must store fissionables, allocate supplies not required for military purposes among claimants for research, medicine, and industry, and regulate such uses by issuing licenses. It must also handle the distribution of radioactive by-products, by gift or sale. (6) It must pass on applications from private firms or from other public agencies to build and operate atomic power plants. (7) It must provide such operators with nuclear fuel. (8) It must control their sale of by-product material. (9) It must so regulate the production and use of all atomic materials as to protect the health and safety of workers and surrounding communities. (10) It must stimulate and support research in nuclear physics and in the possible applications of atomic energy, conducting such research itself or entering into contracts with private laboratories. And here, again, its contractors must be supervised. (11) It must examine the information in its possession to determine what is to be kept secret and what may be disclosed. (12) It must take elaborate precautions to insure security, subjecting its employees and those of its contractors to extensive investigation by the Civil Service Commission and the FBI. For a time, the AEC also had to manage the towns it inherited from the Manhattan District, a responsibility which it has escaped by selling properties to local owners and by promoting the formation of local governments.

The facilities controlled by the AEC represent an investment of close to $10 billion. Its annual budget exceeds $2 billion. It has installations in more than half of the states. To supplement the plants at Oak Ridge and Hanford, it had built large plants for the processing of nuclear materials at Portsmouth and Fernald in Ohio, at Paducah, Kentucky, and on the Savannah River in South Carolina, and smaller plants at eight other points. The Commission has a plant to manufacture weapons at Sandia in New Mexico, a number of testing ranges, and a score of centers for research and development. By any measure, the industry is one of the first magnitude.

The Contract System

Of the total amount spent on the atomic energy program in a year, less than 5 percent goes to support the AEC and more than 95 percent goes to its contractors. In 1970 the Commission itself had 7,000 employees, its contractors 125,000. Research was carried on, plants were constructed, ores were processed, fissionable materials were produced, components of weapons were manufactured—all by contractors. The Commission's research work has been done, largely, by universities, by independent agencies, and by industrial laboratories. The plants have been operated by such concerns as Union Carbide, General Electric, Goodrich, du Pont, Bendix, and A.T.&T. The government has provided the facilities, the raw materials, the working capital, and the overall direction; the contractors have supplied the labor and the management.

A minor part of the Commission's contracts have been let by publishing specifications and inviting competitive bids. This method, resulting in awards at prices fixed in advance, has been used in constructing such facilities as roads, office buildings, and warehouses, and in buying standard equipment and supplies. For most expenditures, competitive bidding was ruled out at the beginning by the urgency of the projects, by their novelty and complexity, by the need for flexibility, and by the overriding requirement of secrecy. Contractors were selected by a few men on the basis of their personal judgment as to speed, reliability, and secrecy. In later years, selection came to be based on more formal criteria: ability to handle operations on a large scale, willingness to assign the work to well-qualified managerial and technical personnel, past experience and reputation, and enthusiasm for the job. The terms of contracts, specifying the standards that are to be maintained, the personnel that is to be used, the costs that are to be reimbursed, and the fees that are to be paid, are settled by negotiation. In the case of research, the contracts have usually called for reimbursement of costs. In the case of construction and operation of productive facilities, they have called for cost plus a fixed fee. (Cost plus a percentage of cost was forbidden by the Act of 1946, since this method of payment provides a positive incentive to inflate costs.) The nature of the fixed fee has varied from contract to contract. In some, it has been set at one dollar; in others, at an agreed share of home office expenses; in still others, at an amount running between 3 and 7 percent of the estimated value of the contract. This payment has been regarded, in every case, as compensation for management, not as a reward for taking risks, since all the risks are shouldered by the government.

The Commission's relation to its contractors is somewhat similar to that of a parent company to its subsidiaries. The contractors provide the services of scientists, engineers, administrators, managers, and laborers. The Commission gives general guidance, sets goals for output and costs, and requires reports. It seeks to insure prudence in the use of public funds. It advances money to its contractors and audits their accounts. It supervises their operations to enforce compliance with the terms of their contracts and with the provisions of the law. It must protect workers and the public against hazards to health and safety. And it must preserve national security by checking on contractor personnel and keeping strict account of all atomic materials. The Commission has decentralized its supervisory activities, maintaining a staff at every site where work is done. Local officials are authorized to make decisions on the spot, subject to Commission review on major issues of policy.

The contract system is similar to that employed in other cases of government procurement, particularly in purchasing defense material. Here, it was unavoidable at the outset. Adopted by the Manhattan District, it enabled the government to call on the organization, personnel, and know-how of private industry, and thus to get into production more quickly than it otherwise could have done. Continued by the AEC, it kept a going enterprise in operation, avoiding the disruption that would have been occasioned by substituting public managements. The system still has its advantages. The Commission is relieved of the burden of administrative detail. The contractors are not handicapped by bureaucratic rules. Operating outside the governmental salary scale, they are able to attract and hold managerial and technical personnel of superior ability. Moreover, by enabling private enterprise to obtain experience in handling atomic materials, the contract system facilitates the eventual termination of the government's monopoly of the industry.

But the system also has its disadvantages. The cost-plus contract affords no incentive for efficiency, promising no penalty when costs are high and no reward when costs are low. Costs may be padded; a fixed-price contract that is frankly calculated to provide a profit may well be cheaper in the end. The need for supervision creates a serious dilemma. If control is lax, the public interest in safety and economy may suffer. If it is strict, the advantage of managerial flexibility may be lost. In the heroic days of the Manhattan District, the emphasis was not on costs or on controls but on getting the job done. Decisions were prompt and agreements verbal, with details to be filled in later on. Such procedure, while necessary in fighting a war, is not acceptable in time of peace. Commission control of contractor performance has come to be increasingly pervasive and detailed. It places more emphasis on assuring legal protection for the AEC than on increasing productivity. When it was shown, at one time, that General Electric had 8,000 employees at Hanford and the Commission only 340, a Senator asked how it could control so many with so few. He might have asked, with equal justice, how the GE management could function with so many people at its elbow, checking on its every move. Between the dangers of too little supervision and too much, the AEC must follow an uncertain course. And finally, the system makes for oligopoly rather than competition in the future of the industry. The contracts go, of necessity, to a few large firms. For years the major contracts were let to only seven concerns. And this is understandable. It is easier for the Commission to negotiate with those already possessing technical ability and large productive capacity than to educate and finance their smaller rivals. It is easier to supervise a handful of market leaders than to police an entire industry. But this means that the favored few are given a head start over their competitors in obtaining knowledge and experience in a whole new field of industrial technology. The AEC has made some effort to correct this situation. In 1964, for instance, it segmented the General Electric contract at Hanford and distributed parts among a number of smaller firms. But its influence, in general, has been to concentrate the industry.[10]

Technical Progress

There can be no question that, in the case of atomic energy, a monopoly (and, what is more, a government monopoly) has made rapid strides in the advancement of technology. There has been striking progress, first of all, in the development of atomic weapons. The bomb that devastated Hiroshima had an explosive force equivalent to 15,000-20,000 tons of TNT. This, however, was an early model and is now regarded as inefficient. The destructive power of a hydrogen bomb is a thousand times as great. This power is measured in megatons, each equivalent to 1 million tons of TNT. One bomb may pack a force of 20 megatons, more than six times as much as all the explosives used in World War II. One such bomb, exploded over a city, could destroy everything within an area of 50 square miles, cause destruction by blast or fire within 2,000 square miles, and produce a lethal radioactive fallout over 7,000 square miles. Atomic explosives have also been adapted to other types of weapons, for use on a smaller scale. The stockpile of strategic nuclear warheads is said to run to more than 4,000, with accompanying supplies of tactical weapons running into the tens of thousands.

Ways have been found, too, to use the atom as a source of power. Experimental reactors employing a number of different techniques have been built and operated with success. Atomic power has been applied to marine propulsion: the first of a fleet of submarines, able to cruise indefinitely without refueling, was launched in 1955, the first merchant ship in 1959, vessels of other types in the sixties. Atomic engines were designed for the propulsion of rockets. Packaged power plants were built to be flown to disaster areas. Nuclear-fueled unmanned weather stations were established in the Arctic and the Antarctic. A full-scale plant producing electricity for commercial use went into operation in

10 / Richard A. Tybout, *Government Contracting in Atomic Energy* (Ann Arbor, Mich.: University of Michigan Press, 1956); Harold Orlans, *Contracting for Atoms* (Washington, D.C.: Brookings Institution, 1967.)

1957. Twenty-eight more plants, embodying different reactor designs, were in operation or scheduled for operation in 1970.

There has been progress in other peaceful uses of atomic energy. A notable contribution has been made to agriculture, industry, and medicine by radioactive isotopes, a by-product of nuclear fission distributed at cost by the AEC. When small amounts of these isotopes are introduced into large quantities of an element, the progress of the element through biological or industrial processes can be traced by using Geiger counters or similar devices. Such methods have been employed in studying the way in which plants use fertilizers and other materials contained in soils. They have been employed in industry to study the wear of cutting tools, gears, and pistons, the composition of mixtures, and the combustion of fuels. They have been used, too, in measuring the thickness of materials, detecting flaws in castings, tracing flows of liquids, spotting leaks in pipelines, and revealing poisonous fumes. They have been employed extensively in medical research and in the diagnosis and treatment of disease. Research is exploring still other possibilities: the use of radiation to induce genetic changes in plants, to preserve foodstuffs, and to initiate chemical processes; the use of reactors to provide heat for buildings and for industrial operations; the use of atomic explosions to excavate harbors, canals, and reservoirs, to shatter sub-terranean rock formations, releasing deposits of oil and gas, and to liquefy oil shales so that they can be pumped from underground. Eventually, these and other uses of atomic energy may come to be more important than its use as a source of power.

Secrecy

In its early years, the AEC carried on its operations, in the main, in secrecy. Disclosure of restricted information was forbidden, under extreme penalties, by the Act of 1946, in the mistaken belief that the nation's security was to be assured by keeping to itself "the secret" of the bomb. The Commission, in exercising its power to declassify information, tended to lean over backward to avoid political attack. Information was withheld from the American people even though it was known to their potential enemies.

When the myth of American monopoly of atomic knowledge was destroyed by explosions in the Soviet Union, the pressure for supersecrecy was relaxed. In the Act of 1954, Congress permitted information regarding military applications to be shared with allied governments and information regarding peaceful uses to be generally disclosed. Since that time, the AEC has made steady progress with the work of declassification. Volumes have been published, conferences held, and courses of instruction offered on various aspects of atomic technology. Much that once was hidden may now be seen. But a large part of the Commission's work is still secret.

Far from serving the national interest, secrecy may be harmful. The conditions imposed in its name may prevent the program from attracting and holding able scientists. The erection of barriers to the interchange of knowledge may well retard the progress of technology. Secrecy also prevents free entry to the industry. The Commission's contractors and the groups that plan to produce atomic power are given access to classified material once they have been investigated and cleared. But access is denied to others who could make an equal contribution to the field. A privilege to some, it is a handicap to their competitors. Secrecy, finally, prevents an adequate check on extravagance, inefficiency, and even corruption. It facilitates concealment of mistakes. It confuses the need for security with mere distaste for criticism of administrative policy.

Congress and the AEC

The AEC is subject to supervision by the Joint Committee on Atomic Energy, composed of members of the Senate and the House. The Committee, when established, was expected to protect the public interest by developing expertise in a field where the technology was unfamiliar and the problems new, and by serving as a watchdog in a field where public funds were being spent in secrecy. Relationships between the Committee and the Commission have gone through several phases, sometimes being hostile and sometimes harmonious, as the personalities involved and the issues raised have changed. Starting out as an ineffectual body, dealing with matters of minor importance, the Committee became a powerful one, taking the lead in forming major policies.

In its early years, when secrecy was emphasized, the Committee was informed of major policy decisions and received reports on subsequent performance. But it had no adequate basis for appraising policy or performance and no effective means of exercising control. It did not know the size of the atomic stockpile, the current rate of output, or the unit cost of production. It did not pass on the Commission's budget, this function being left to appropriations committees that acted almost entirely in the dark. The tenuous character of Congressional control, in this period, was revealed by the Joint Committee's investigation of the Commission in 1949 in response to a political charge of "incredible mismanagement." In six weeks of hearings, the testimony given related to peripheral matters—the wisdom of providing a pipeline to obtain gas, the cost of constructing certain buildings, the administration of government towns, the exportation of isotopes, and one or two alleged breaches of security—and not to the essential core of the Commission's work.

Beginning with the fifties, the Joint Committee began to assert itself. During the Truman administration, in opposition to the AEC, it demanded a crash program to speed production of the hydrogen bomb; it was upheld, in this, by the President. During the Eisenhower administration, with secrecy relaxed, the Committee informed itself more fully on details of the program and participated more openly in the discussion of policy. With interest shifting from military to civilian applications of atomic power, it operated under fewer constraints. Then, when the President directed the AEC to enter into the Dixon-Yates contract, described in Chapter 22, the Commission and the Joint Committee were thrown into the thick of the fight between public and private power.

This was a fight that could not have been avoided. The physical feasibility of producing electricity with atomic heat had been shown; its economic feasibility remained in doubt. The AEC was confronted with two issues, how rapidly should the development of commercial power be pushed; should it be undertaken by private or by public enterprise? The Commission decided to go slow. It built a number of small experimental reactors but declined, with a single exception, to build big ones. It held that the initiative in developing commercial power should be left to the private utilities, with the government standing by to help. The Joint Committee, on the other hand, wanted development pushed. It demanded that the Commission try out several types of reactors and that it build and operate big plants itself.

The Eisenhower administration sought to employ the peaceful uses of atomic energy as an instrument of foreign policy. At the same time, it sought to leave to private industry the development of power production from atomic fuel. The two purposes were inconsistent. Foreign policy called for speedy development. Private development resulted in delay. It was concern for foreign policy, in the main, that motivated the Joint Committee in demanding a more aggressive developmental program with larger participation by the government. The forced development of atomic power was not necessitated by an imminent shortage of other fuels in the United States. It was desired as a mark of national prestige. It was demanded as a means of extending aid to friendly nations and thus contributing to national security. This struggle went on for years, with Congress forcing on the Commission a more ambitious program and larger appropriations than it asked. With the peaceful uses of atomic energy increasing in importance, the Joint Committee took the lead in formulating policy.

Among Congressional committees, the JCAE is unique. It deals with a program that is specialized and technical. It has acquired a considerable competence in the field. Its expertise has come to be recognized by the Congress and the country. It is thus in a position to promote the programs of the AEC by standing as their champion; to defeat them by standing in opposition. The Joint Committee participates in the deliberations of the AEC, relating not only to general policies but to details of particular projects. It influences the character of programs before they are adopted or announced. It has come to operate, in effect, as a board of directors for the atomic enterprise, with the AEC functioning in an administrative capacity.

ATOM-FIRED ELECTRIC POWER

The atomic power plants now being built embody the familiar methods of turning heat into steam and steam into electricity. They therefore employ equipment of conventional design: boilers, turbines, generators, transformers, and transmission lines. The only change is the substitution of the nuclear reactor for the coal-burning furnace as a source of heat and of fissionable material for coal as a fuel. Within the reactors presently in operation, the fuel, in rods of enriched uranium, is sprayed with neutrons and its atoms are split, releasing part of their energy in the form of heat and part in the form of more neutrons to sustain a chain reaction. This reaction is moderated by water surrounding the rods, relaying heat to make steam. A second generation of reactors, known as breeders, to be built in the eighties, will use a plutonium alloy as a fuel. This material will fission when bombarded with fast neutrons, producing heat that will be picked up by a coolant at 800° Fahrenheit and used to make steam. The excess neutrons obtained in the process will be used to breed new fuel in a blanket of U 238 surrounding the reactor's core. The breeder reactor will thus produce plutonium as well as power, creating more fuel than it uses up. Both types of reactors have the disadvantage of necessitating elaborate precautions against radiation and requiring costly provisions for the disposition of radioactive waste.

A third development, if it comes, will be farther in the future. In the explosion of the atomic bomb, energy was released by the fission of heavy atoms. In the explosion of the hydrogen bomb, far greater energy was released by the fusion of light atoms. Fusion would have advantages over fission as a source of power. Producing no fission fragments, it involves no risk of radiation and no problem of disposition of radioactive waste. The material used in its production, deuterium, is present in limitless quantities in the waters of the sea. But there are formidable obstacles to be surmounted if fusion is to be controlled. It takes intense heat, amounting to tens of millions of degrees, to set the process going; the hydrogen bomb was triggered by exploding an atomic bomb. And once the process starts, it is difficult if not impossible to control it. This may be done by preparing a plasma containing deuterium atoms and compressing it within a powerful magnetic field. If the plasma can be held long enough in a stable state, its deuterium atoms will fuse, releasing a searing heat that can be used in turning water into steam. Scientists have made some progress toward the development of this technology, but it will be another 20 years or more before fusion can be harnessed to produce commercial power. In the meantime, reactors embodying various techniques for inducing fission will be used. There is no question that power can be produced by such methods. The question is whether it can be produced at a cost that will make it pay.

Economic Feasibility of Atomic Power

In an atomic power plant, the cost of the related facilities for generating and transmitting electricity is the same as that incurred in a conventional plant. The cost of the reactor itself is greater than that of a coal-burning furnace. A spacious site is required for safety. Shields of lead and concrete have to be installed. Provision has to be made for the disposal of waste materials. All of this makes for a large investment and thus for a high annual charge for capital. This disadvantage may be offset, however, by savings in the cost of fuel. Atomic fuel, potentially, is cheap. A single pound of U-235 can produce as much heat as 1,500 tons of coal. Money can be saved in the costs of transport, handling, and storage as well as in the price of the fuel itself. If atomic power is to compete with power produced in other ways, the cost of the reactor, or the cost of the fuel, or both, must be reduced.

Power produced at atomic plants has not yet been fully competitive with that produced by other means. The cost of power at nuclear plants with capacities up to 800,000 kilowatts has run from 7 to 10 mills per kilowatt hour; the cost at conventional plants has run between 4 and 9 mills. At these figures, nuclear power has been competitive only in areas, such as New England, Florida, and California, where the price of conventional fuel is high. But the cost of power at plants now coming into operation is expected to be between 5 and 7 mills, its cost at plants planned for the seventies less than 5 mills.[11] The TVA, adjacent to low-cost coal mines, is building the largest nuclear plant on earth, with a capacity of more than 3 million kilowatts. It expects to save $8 million a year by using nuclear fission instead of burning coal to generate heat. Given this outlook, power produced by existing types of nuclear reactors should be competitive in most of the country by 1980.

The development that will make power from atomic plants even cheaper than power from other sources is the perfection of the breeder reactor. The plutonium produced along with power by this reactor can be removed and sold for use as fuel elsewhere. The cost of fuel can therefore be sharply reduced. It is expected that breeder reactors will be in wide use by 1985. When this happens, power from the atom should undersell power from any other fuel.

Promotion of Atomic Power

The development of an atomic power industry could be undertaken by the government itself. It could be left to private enterprise. It could be promoted by various forms of public aid. The first of these alternatives was rejected. It was believed, at the time, that private enterprise, if given access to restricted information, would promptly take the initiative in building atomic power plants and, through its productive genius, would shortly put the cost of atomic power at a level where it could compete. This did not prove to be the case. The power companies were assured an ample supply of other fuels; they had no need for atomic heat. The investment required to produce it was heavy, the venture risky, and its success uncertain; it threatened to cut profits or to raise rates. There was only one reason to undertake it: if private industry did not build atomic power plants, it was likely that the government would build them; public power would continue to grow. But even so, the companies were not prepared to bear the risk alone. Private development required substantial public aid.

In 1951 and 1952, private enterprise was invited to investigate the possibility of producing atomic power. A number of teams, each consisting of a power producer and an equipment manufacturer, studied the problem and submitted

11 / Charles F. Phillips, Jr., *The Economics of Regulation* (Homewood, Ill.: Richard D. Irwin, Inc., 1969), pp. 591-92.

proposals. Most of these plans involved the construction of dual-purpose plants, with a company operating the reactor, using the heat and selling plutonium to the government for military use, or with the government operating the reactor, producing plutonium, and selling the company the heat. The government, however, announced that it was already producing all the plutonium it needed and that it could not commit itself to purchase or produce any more. With this announcement, the dual-purpose reactor approach was abandoned.

In 1953, Congress authorized construction of the first large-scale nuclear power plant at Shippingport, Pennsylvania. This plant, with a capacity of 60,000 kilowatts, supplies electricity to the Duquesne Light Company at Pittsburgh. In 1955, acting under authority of the Atomic Energy Act of 1954, permitting private ownership of atomic reactors and private use, under lease, of atomic fuels, the AEC invited utility companies to submit proposals for the construction of several central station plants and a number of smaller plants, offering to assist their builders in a variety of ways. This invitation led to the construction of three central station plants and four smaller ones. Again in 1957, the Commission invited proposals for a number of reactor prototypes, offering added financial inducements to encourage their construction. Four more projects were undertaken in response to this request. It should be noted that a few plants were also being built by utility companies on their own initiative. But, on the whole, the response of private industry was disappointing.

The Joint Committee, seeking to speed the development of civilian power, proposed that the government build and operate prototype plants. The Eisenhower administration, opposed to public power, resisted these proposals. It preferred to wait for private development and sought to induce it by offering added public aid. This policy left to private interests the initiative in deciding what projects were to be undertaken. It required protracted negotiations and resulted in delays. Meantime, the JCAE kept pressing for governmental action.

The upshot of this dispute was an announcement by the AEC, in 1960, of a 10-year program directed toward making atomic power competitive in some parts of the country by 1970 and in other countries, where fuel costs are higher, at an even earlier date. The program was to go through successive stages of experimental, prototype, and full-scale plants. It was to emphasize the reactor types that appeared to be most nearly competitive. Where a type was promising and proposals for its construction were not forthcoming from private companies, the AEC was to build the prototypes itself, but it was not to build and operate full-scale plants. The program thus represented a victory for the JCAE.

There were 29 plants in the United States producing electricity from nuclear fuel or scheduled to do so in 1970, their total capacity standing at nearly 10 million kilowatts or about 3 percent of the nation's total. These plants embodied nearly all of the promising reactor prototypes. They ranged in scale from 22,000 to 1 million kilowatts. A few of them were owned and operated by public power systems or by rural cooperatives; most of them by private power companies. Another 55 plants were scheduled for operation by 1975, bringing the atom's share of power generation to 10 percent. The AEC estimated that nuclear power would provide a third of the nation's generating capacity by 1980. The Commission's promotional efforts must be accounted a success.

Subsidization

The use of atomic fuel by the private power industry has been heavily subsidized. The plant at Shippingport cost $120 million. The Duquesne Light Company provided the site, invested $15 million in the generating equipment, and contributed $5 million toward the cost of the reactor. The government put up the other $100 million. In return for its investment, it obtained experience in operating a large reactor. For the power produced at Shippingport to be sold at the price of other Duquesne power, five sixths or more of its cost was subsidized.

The AEC was forbidden, by the Act of 1954, to contribute to the capital cost of any other privately owned reactors. But it was permitted to provide assistance in many other ways. It did research and development work and gave its findings to industry free of charge. It paid reactor operators for the technical and economic data they provided. In some cases, the AEC built and operated a reactor, providing steam to a privately owned generator. In others, it provided nuclear fuel for a privately owned reactor without charge.

Some utility companies paid for their plants themselves and paid the AEC for the use of its fuel. But these companies, too, were subsidized. State regulatory commissions permitted them to include their expenditures on research and development as costs to be covered by their rates. They took advantage of the provision for accelerated amortization in the federal income tax. These costs were met by their customers and by the Treasury. In addition, Congress acted, in 1957, to provide, at a nominal charge, $500 million in insurance against catastrophic accidents, thus assuming most of this risk. Finally, there has been a hidden subsidy in the prices charged by the AEC for fuel.

Up to 1965, the Commission charged two prices and paid one. It charged, first, for the U-235 that was consumed in the course of generating power and, second, for the use of the fissionable material in which it was contained, and it paid for the plutonium that was produced as a by-product of the process. Its charge for the U-235 was supposed to cover its cost. It included the price paid by the AEC for uranium concentrates and the cost of enriching them, comprising a share of the Commission's overhead, of the cost of its capital, of depreciation, and a return on its investment. It was computed on the basis of fully allocated rather than marginal cost. The propriety of this price cannot be appraised because the Commission's costs are kept secret. It is believed, however, to have been set too high. The price was reduced from its earlier level in 1961 and in 1962. The rental charged for the use of fissionable material was supposedly set on the basis of its value to the user. This charge was first fixed at 4 percent of the cost of the material. It was raised in 1961 to 4.75 percent. Since utility companies normally allow 6 to 12 percent or more for the cost of their inventory of fuel, this charge involved a substantial subsidy. The price paid for plutonium, finally, was based upon its estimated value as a fuel. Since the cost of producing plutonium is secret, this price, too, cannot be appraised, but it may well have contained an element of subsidy.[12]

When all of these subsidies are taken together, it is clear that the private atomic power industry has not stood on its own feet. In 1964, however, Congress amended the Atomic Energy Act to permit power companies to own fissionable materials as well as lease them. Under this amendment, the companies can either buy enriched materials from the AEC or buy uranium concentrates from private producers and take them to an AEC plant to be enriched for payment of a fee. And, beginning in 1970, reactor operators were required to purchase rather than rent the fuels they use. Private plants can also be established for the chemical processing of spent fuel. Whether or not these arrangements will eliminate the subsidy formerly provided by the low rental charge for fuel will depend on how the AEC fixes the price of the fuel it sells and the fee it collects for enriching other fuel. If the subsidy is eliminated, there will be an increase in the cost of electricity generated from atomic fuel amounting to a fraction of a cent per kilowatt hour.

Regulation of Atomic Power

The AEC is related to the atomic energy industry in three quite different ways. As a manufacturer of atomic weapons, isotopes, and reactor fuels, it functions as an entrepreneur. Here, it provides the capital, directs the undertaking, and assumes the risks. But it does not operate like other public enterprises: most of its work is done, under contract, by private firms. In its relation to the power industry, the Commission functions as a promoter, stimulating action, providing knowledge, and extending financial aid. As atomic power increases in importance, it will come increasingly to take on the character of a regulatory agency.

Unless opinion changes, atomic power plants will be owned and operated, in the main, by private enterprise. If the industry is to be completely private, however, it will have to be given the right to produce its own fuel or to purchase it from commercial sources of supply. To this end, the government will have to relinquish its monopoly of the manufacture of fissionable materials. Until recently, no such change appeared to be within the bounds of possibility. It had long been held that the production of fissionables so intimately affected the nation's security that it could not safely be placed in private hands. The atomic power industry, therefore, would have to depend upon the government for its fuels. But this is no longer felt to be the case. The government's stockpile of atomic weapons is oversized and its demand for fissionable materials has declined. The power industry's demand, on the other hand, is growing and will continue to grow. The atomic industry's function, in the future, is evidently to

12 / See Philip Mullenbach, *Civilian Nuclear Power* (New York: Twentieth Century Fund, 1963), pp. 71-73, 166-75.

be that of supplying fuel to the producers of electric power. And the AEC can be depended upon to prevent the diversion of fissionable materials to dangerous uses by supervising their production and sale. The government is therefore preparing to sell some of its atomic plants to private firms. In 1969, President Nixon directed the AEC to operate the plants at Oak Ridge, Paducah, and Portsmouth as separate entities and to prepare them for eventual sale. When these and similar facilities are sold, the peaceful uses of the atom will have been transferred, almost entirely, to the private sector.

The industry that uses the atom to produce electricity will necessarily operate under tight controls. To protect workers and the public against extraordinary hazards, it will have to conform to detailed health and safety regulations prescribed and enforced by state and local authorities and by the AEC. A company that wishes to build a nuclear reactor will have to get approval from the AEC for its location and design. The Commission will inspect construction while it is under way. It will test the functioning of the reactor before it is cleared. The company will then have to get AEC permission to operate the plant, and to possess, transport, and process nuclear fuels and to dispose of their by-products. The Commission will license those who run the reactor, maintain continuous surveillance over its operation and, in case of emergency, can order it to be shut down. And, finally, under state and federal laws, as is the case with power produced in any other way, the company will be subject to regulation, by state utility commissions and by the Federal Power Commission, of the services it renders and the rates at which it sells.

So, too, with private plants that produce or reprocess fissionable materials. Here, again, there are threats to health and safety. And there is danger, too, that such materials may be smuggled out to other governments to build up nuclear arsenals around the world. To protect against these dangers, strict inspection will be required. The private suppliers of fissionable materials, moreover, will not be numerous enough to make the industry effectively competitive. So, in order to protect the power industry and its customers from excessive charges, the prices fixed for these materials will have to be controlled. The industry will be one in which business enterprise is kept within the strictest bounds.

FUTURE ADMINISTRATION OF THE ATOMIC PROGRAM

The several functions of the AEC—military and civilian, research manufacturing, promotion, and regulation—are inconsistent. It has therefore been proposed that the Commission be dismembered; its functions distributed among other agencies. For some of these functions, moreover, the commission form of organization does not appear to be appropriate. Here, it has frequently been proposed that the Commission be superseded by a single administrator. None of these proposals has yet commended itself to the Congress. But, eventually, some change in the administration of the program is likely to be enacted into law.

Chapter 24

PUBLIC ENTERPRISE APPRAISED

The method employed in the development of atomic energy, described in the previous chapter, has been that of government ownership and private operation under government contracts. This experience is not unique. Production by private contractors, using their own facilities, has been the method commonly employed in handling the construction of public works and in procuring equipment and supplies in time of war. Productive facilities have also been provided by government, in certain fields, for use by private firms. This was the case, in World War II, with synthetic rubber and with a number of other goods whose output was required. But public enterprise, more frequently, has involved operation as well as ownership by government.

It is with the problems raised by public operation that the present chapter is concerned. How—without the reward of profit or the penalty of bankruptcy—are efficiency and progress to be obtained? How—when there is a monopoly, even though it be a government monopoly—are the interests of the consumer to be protected? And how—given the inconsistency of productive efficiency and public accountability—is the inevitable conflict between efficiency and accountability to be resolved?

EFFICIENCY AND PROGRESS

In the writings of socialists, in the past, much was said concerning the shortcomings of private enterprise, but little or nothing concerning those of public enterprise. In the writings of socialism's critics, on the other hand, the inevitable failures of public enterprise were asserted, but little was offered in the way of proof. Discussion of the merits and demerits of public enterprise thus had an air of unreality. But with the spread of nationalization, in recent years, the difficulties inherent in government operation of industry have come increasingly to be recognized. Evidence is accumulating on problems of organization and management, on factors affecting efficiency and costs, and on the influence that public operation exerts on the morale of labor and on the advancement of technology. In England, particularly, and also in the United States, the issues raised by public enterprise are being brought into a clearer light.

555

Comparisons of Efficiency

Comparisons have sometimes been made of similar industries administered by private and by public managements. It is possible, for instance, to compare the railroad, airline, telephone and telegraph, and radio and television services provided privately in the United States with those provided publicly abroad. It is possible, too, to compare private transit, water, gas, and electric utility services in some American cities with similar public undertakings in others. But so many variables are involved, in every case, that sweeping generalizations concerning relative efficiency cannot be justified.

When quality of service is compared, the judgments made are largely subjective. It would be possible, of course, to measure the speed and frequency of trains, planes, and transit vehicles, their adherence to schedules, and their records of accidents, the time required to make a telephone connection or to deliver a telegram, the pressure and purity of water, the heating value of gas, the constancy of electric current, the number of stations providing broadcasts, the number of hours they are on the air, and the frequency and duration of interruptions to all these services. But such comparisons are seldom made. And with respect to other matters, such as comfort and cleanliness of transport equipment, the convenience of all types of public services, and the courtesy of service personnel, methods of measurement are not available. In the case of broadcasting, in particular, objective standards are lacking. One viewer may prefer the vaudeville and violence of commercial programs, another the intellectual fare of educational TV. The difference cannot be measured; it is a matter of taste.

Rates can be compared, but such comparisons may be misleading. Where the quality of service differs, there is no comparable unit to which the rates can be applied. Rate structures are complicated; charges vary with customer classes, with types of service, and with quantities consumed. It is therefore difficult to find, in different schedules, particular rates that are properly to be compared. And even though services and rates were standardized, comparisons might not be meaningful. A high rate might cover costs and yield a profit; a low rate might be subsidized. Subsidization may have been necessitated by failures of management; it may have been adopted as a deliberate policy. In either case, with one enterprise expected to pay its own way and another supported, in part, by taxes, their rates cannot be taken as an index of their relative efficiency.

So, too, with comparisons of cost. The conditions under which private and public enterprises provide their services may differ in many respects, and these differences will be reflected in differences in costs. Transport costs, for instance, will be influenced by the density of traffic and the character of the terrain, telephone costs by the size of the exchanges, and water costs by the accessibility of adequate supplies. Electric costs will vary with differences in the method of generation, the scale of operation, and the degree of physical integration. In the case of multipurpose projects, as was seen in Chapter 22, they will depend upon the principle that may be used in allocating some part of the joint costs to the business of producing power. Costs will be affected, too, by differences in the burden of taxes, in the charges for capital, and in the policies adopted in depreciating assets and retiring debts. As a consequence, where the costs of private and public enterprises differ, it is difficult to determine how much of the difference is properly to be attributed to factors such as these and how much to differences in the efficiency of managements.

There is no basis, in the evidence available, for asserting that greater efficiency is always to be attained by private or by public enterprise. Examples can be adduced to support a case for either side of the argument. Observers of the performance of the nationalized industries in Britain, for instance, are inclined to agree that gas, electricity, and road haulage have been well run and that railways and coal mines have not. But this judgment would doubtless be passed on the performance of the same industries, under private enterprise, in the United States. No conclusion is justified. It is possible, however, to recognize some of the factors that influence efficiency and costs.

Factors Affecting Costs

Public enterprise has certain advantages that may make for lower costs. For one thing, it can effect economies by unifying and coordinating competitive services. When the government operated the railroads, during World War I, it eliminated competing trains and circuitous routes, pooled locomotives and cars, and required the common use of terminals and shops. If the government were to operate all types of carriers, it could doubtless establish common terminals, dovetail transport by water, air, road, and rail, and employ shorter hauls by buses and trucks to supplement longer hauls by trains. In the same way, if a city were to undertake the distribution of milk, it could realize substantial savings by eliminating parallel delivery routes. In all such cases, moreover, costs could be cut by eliminating competition in advertising and in other methods of promoting sales. All this, however, is less an argument for public enterprise than for monopoly. The savings promised could also be realized by private enterprise under public control. But, in either case, there might be offsetting losses. For the regulatory force of competition would be gone.

A second advantage of public enterprise is its ability to obtain capital at a lower price. The risks are underwritten by the taxpayer. Hence, bonds issued by agencies of government can be sold at a low interest rate. The annual charge for borrowed money, accordingly, is lower for public than for private enterprise. This advantage is offset, of course, to the extent that government pays excessive sums in acquiring private properties or adopts extravagant standards in constructing new facilities. Also, since public enterprises, unlike private companies, are usually required to pay back the funds invested in them, their charges for capital will be higher during the years when this is being done. But once the investment is paid off, these charges—compared with those of private firms—will be low indeed. Another fact, however, must be noted. The capitalization of a private enterprise is likely to be partly in bonds that bear a fixed return and partly in preferred and common stocks whose owners need not be given dividends in years when profits are not earned. The capitalization of a public enterprise will be exclusively in bonds. As a result, its payments to its creditors must be as large in bad years as in good. Its capital cost, though low, will be inflexible. Its legal obligation, during a depression, may be heavier than that of a private firm.

Another advantage sometimes claimed for public enterprise is the abandonment of regulation and the saving of its costs. With complete authority in public hands, it is said, there will no longer be need for detailed supervision with the virtual duplication of managements that it has sometimes involved. But monopoly, though public, will still have to be supervised to insure efficiency and progress, to prevent dishonesty and undue discrimination, and to protect consumers against poor service and excessive rates. And such supervision will entail substantial costs.

Along with the factors that may tend to make the costs of public undertakings low, there are a number of others that operate to make them high. There is danger, first, that public agencies will pay too much for their supplies. These agencies may call for competitive bids. They may buy on cost-plus contracts. But they will usually pay top prices. Sellers may discriminate in favor of large private buyers. They will seldom discriminate in favor of the government. Public bodies, moreover, have frequently been forced by state or federal law to purchase certain goods or to make their purchases from certain sellers despite the fact that they are high in price. Under the "Buy American" Act of 1933, as it has been administered, federal agencies are required to buy domestic goods unless their prices exceed those of imported goods by more than a specified percentage after the tariffs on imports have been paid. No private buyer suffers such a handicap.

Second, it is likely that public enterprises will spend too much for labor. They may be compelled to take on workers as a means of relieving unemployment. They may be required to retain more workers than they need. They may be forced, by the demands of political patronage, to discharge people who are competent and well trained in order to make room for those who are incompetent and untrained. They must meet the costs involved in civil service processes and security investigations. From all of this, private concerns are free. Top salaries are lower in public than in private employment. But the number of salaried workers is likely to be larger. And the wages of other workers, if not higher, are as high. Labor is organized to exert political, as well as economic, pressure. And such pressure may add to costs by raising wages, cutting hours, and providing a variety of special benefits.

Third, and finally, public enterprise may be prevented from taking action that would reduce its costs. Removal from uneconomic locations or abandonment of unprofitable services are likely to be forestalled by pressure politics. Unification of facilities, reorganization of operations, and modification of the methods of production may well be forbidden if they would threaten propertied interests or reduce the volume of employment in a trade. Public enterprise, being public, may often be governed by policies that do not make for economy.

When these disadvantages have been noted, it must be said that the difference between private and public enterprise is often not as great as the discussion would suggest. Private industries, too, are subject to political pressures that inflate their costs. With the railroads, for instance, labor has been accorded special benefits by law. And economies that would have lessened employment were forbidden by the Transportation Act of 1933. In these respects, the nationalization of railways would involve but little change.

Forms of Organization

Three major forms of organization have been used for the administration of public enterprise: the government department, the public corporation, and the mixed corporation. Of these, the first has had the longest history and the widest use. Departmental administration has typically been employed in the management of state and local enterprise in the United States. It has been used by the federal government in management of the Post Office, the social insurance system, and public lands. Under this form of organization, departments are divided into bureaus, bureaus into branches, branches into sections, and so on. But the layers and lines of authority are well defined. There is a single administrator: the department head. He may be advised by a staff of specialists. But he alone is held responsible for the execution of legislative policies. Departmental management thus makes for strict accountability. But it is subject to political pressures and handicapped by bureaucratic controls. Its advantages and disadvantages will be considered, at some length, later on.

The public corporation is established as a separate legal entity. It functions like a private business, entering into contracts, acquiring and holding property, bringing suits and being sued. Its creditors can enforce their rights without obtaining the government's permission to sue or proceeding through the Court of Claims. The corporation's stock is usually held by the Treasury. The members of its board are appointed by the government, usually for long and overlapping terms, to afford assurance of continuity. Its management is appointed by the board and is made responsible to the board. The corporation is granted a considerable measure of autonomy with respect to its financial operations, its purchases, its personnel, and the general conduct of its business. It thus has the advantage of being insulated, to some extent, from political pressures and being freed, in part, from bureaucratic controls. But it may also escape accountability. This problem, too, will be considered later on.

The public corporation has been extensively employed in Europe for many years. It is the device adopted for the administration of all of the industries nationalized by Great Britain and many of those nationalized by France since World War II. Its history in this country, beginning with the Bank of North America in 1781 and the United States Bank in 1791, includes the creation of several emergency corporations during World War I, and the establishment of the Port of New York Authority in 1921. Such corporations multiplied during the Great Depression and World War II, conspicuous among them being the Reconstruction Finance Corporation and the TVA. The Hoover Commission, in 1949, recommended the incorporation of a number of other federal activities. The corporate form has thus come to be widely regarded as most desirable for the administration of public enterprise.

In the mixed corporation, stock is owned both by private investors and by the government, and the board of directors includes representatives of both private and public interests. Where a majority of the stock is publicly owned, this form of organization may differ little, in operation, from the preceding one. Where a minority of the ownership is public, the government's power is limited, but its participation will enable it to exert some influence on policy. Mixed ownership has seldom been adopted, on its merits, as a permanent form of organization. It has usually resulted from the acquisition of partial shareholdings or the extension of public aid to depressed industries. In certain cases, as with the federal home loan banks and the intermediate credit banks, it has been used, during a period of transition, to promote the development of new forms of private enterprise. The device has been widely employed in Europe, characterizing much of the nationalization effected in France and most of that in Italy. It has been little used in Great Britain or the United States.

Administrative Boards

In some cases a public corporation is located within a government department and its directorate is composed, in whole or in part, of officials of the department. This is true, for instance, of the Panama Canal Company and the Commodity Credit Corporation. In such cases, there is departmental control of policy and the corporate device is employed simply as a means of delegating the management of operations. Elsewhere, however, corporations are independent of the departmental structure.

The boards of public corporations may be small or large; their members serving full-time or part-time, with or without compensation. In France board membership is part-time and unpaid. In Great Britain and the United States it is usually full-time and salaried. In Great Britain the boards are small, when compared with those of private companies. In the United States they are even smaller, numbering typically from three to five. The number of directors of the TVA, for instance, is three.

The large, part-time, unpaid board can deal only with matters of policy. But when a board is small, full-time, and salaried, its members may become deeply involved in administrative details. Such a development is undesirable, since administration is handled better by a single official than by a board. And there is another function which the board itself must perform: that of planning developments and programs and making determinations of policy. The typical board, like that of the TVA, has avoided this pitfall, delegating administration to a general manager and confining itself to planning and policy.

In France the boards of the nationalized industries have been designed to be representative of different interest groups, members being appointed by the various ministries to speak for workers, consumers, and the government. This arrangement, based on the traditional syndicalist philosophy of the French trade unions, is not conducive to good administration. The members of an administrative board should have a common purpose, owing allegiance only to the enterprise they serve. The members of tripartite boards are loyal, not to their corporations, but to their outside interests. The boards are thus divided, devoting themselves to bargaining and negotiation instead of directing their efforts toward the adoption of common policies.

In practice, the French boards have not played the part they were expected to play. Their part-time, unpaid members have lacked the knowledge and time required for administration, and the motivation and opportunity to learn. As a result, responsibility has devolved upon the government. Decisions as to policy are made by ministers. The public members on the boards are civil servants who take no action unless it is approved by ministers. The other members serve, in effect, in an advisory capacity. On paper, the boards run the nationalized industries; actually, they do not. The independence of the public corporations, in France, is therefore more nominal than real.

In Great Britain, too, there have been complaints concerning the corporate boards. Among the first appointees, many were the same businessmen who ran the industries before they were nationalized. Others were drawn from the ranks of labor and from the civil service. As these men have retired, their places have been filled by promotion from within the national industries. The salaries paid have not been adequate to attract executives from other fields. The industries, it is said, are coming to be run by an inbred technocracy. The question raised by objective observers is not whether board members, in general, are competent, but whether they possess sufficient breadth of view. The boards, it is felt, should not be composed of technical specialists, but of persons of diverse abilities whose interests are in broad issues of public policy.

It has been the experience in the United States that public agencies, when first established, attract administrators of high ability. As time goes by, however, public attention shifts to other activities, and men of superior talents are attracted by newer agencies. The older undertakings offer less of a challenge; they are handicapped in hiring and holding men of ability by the limits placed on government salaries. As a result, they fail to maintain the quality of their administrative personnel. And even though honesty be preserved, imagination and vigor are lost. This process of deterioration has been observed, over the years, in many public agencies. It offers a persisting threat to the efficiency of public enterprise.

Overcentralization

A common characteristic of undertakings of great size is a tendency toward excessive centralization in management. This tendency is widely regarded, in

American business, as one of the disadvantages of operating on a large scale. Decentralization of administration is therefore a usual objective of business policy. But in government, overcentralization persists. In the United States, as we have seen, the Post Office is a case in point. In Great Britain, instead of nationalizing different companies separately, Parliament organized each industry as a whole. But it left the internal structure of the industries to be determined by their boards. Administration, thus, could legally have been decentralized. But the boards believed in bigness as a means of insuring efficiency. Regional and local units were established for the performance of certain administrative functions. But there was little delegation of real authority. So, in Britain, it is said that "everything is run from Whitehall" just as it is said, in this country, that "everything is run from Washington."

Centralized administration undoubtedly has its advantages during a period when the principal tasks to be accomplished are those of reorganizing an industry, modernizing its methods, and effecting overall changes in policy. But, once established, it is likely to endure. And it is certain, in many ways, to be prejudicial to efficiency. Overcentralization makes for inflexibility, preventing adjustments which a local situation may require. It forestalls the exercise of individual initiative, subjecting subordinates to remote, impersonal controls. It involves protracted delays, provoking a feeling of frustration and impairing morale. There are some functions, to be sure, that must be centralized. But there are many more than can and should be delegated to officials down the line. The usual failure of large-scale public enterprise to make such delegations is one of its principal shortcomings.

Labor Relations

A major argument advanced in support of proposals for the nationalization of industry has been the contribution it is supposed to make to productive efficiency by improving labor morale. A nationalized industry, it is said, does not belong to the employer but to the people as a whole. Its employees are engaged, not in producing profits for investors, but in promoting the welfare of the entire community. Workers, no longer governed autocratically, are invited to participate in management. Suspicion and hostility give way to willing cooperation. And, as a result, there is a rise in productivity. So runs the argument. It has not been borne out by the experience of nationalized industries in Great Britain or in France.

In both countries, the wages paid by public corporations are determined by collective bargaining. In Great Britain, nationwide agreements are effected by bargaining between the unions and the boards. In France, the unions do not negotiate with the boards, since they are represented on the boards and would therefore be dealing with themselves. They bargain, instead, with the officials of the corporations, under the supervision of their respective ministries. In both cases, the agreements are concluded, in effect, between organized labor and the state. As a purchaser of labor, the state may be less inclined to resist the demands of the unions than private employers would have been. But the nego-tiators appear as adversaries, just as they do in bargaining with private industries.

In France the interest of workers in matters such as health, safety, education, and welfare is presumably protected by their representation on the boards. In Great Britain the public corporations are required to establish machinery for joint consultation in these fields. Such consultation could lead, through close cooperation, to determinations which would limit the independence of unions and of managements. In practice, it has been approached with the psychology of bargaining. In some cases, it has been resisted by administrators as a threat to their authority. In others, delays resulting from centralization of the power to make decisions have given consultation an appearance of futility. The program, in the eyes of most observers, has failed to give the workers any feeling of participation in the government of industry.

Nationalization, in operation, has made little difference in the relations between employers and employees. It has not affected the position of the worker at the mine or in the factory. It has not changed the attitude of labor. It has not removed suspicion or hostility. It has not improved morale. It has not reduced soldiering, lessened absenteeism, or done away with strikes. It has not significantly raised productivity.

Advancement of Technology

When government takes over an established private industry, it inherits the industry's achievements in the development of technology. When it creates a new industry, it is inspired to develop methods of its own. But when an enter-prise has long been operated by government, there is no assurance that contin-ued improvements will be made. There is no profit incentive to encourage innovation. There may not even be investment in research.

Atomic energy, as a government monopoly, has made great strides in the advancement of technology. The TVA, too, has made progress through research. But progress, in both cases, has been stimulated by competition—in the case of atomic energy, by the threat of more rapid development by a potential enemy; in the case of the TVA, by the hostility of the private power industry. Where government is secure in a monopoly, on the other hand, progress is less likely to occur. With the Post Office, little has been invested in research, innovation has been tardy, and newer methods have not been brought into general use. Such backwardness has also been found in private industries: in coal, for instance, and in the railway, Pullman, and telegraph services. But, by and large, it would be generally agreed that public is less progressive than private enterprise.

PUBLIC ENTERPRISE AND THE CONSUMER

It is not to be assumed that the interests of consumers in the performance of an enterprise will be adequately safeguarded by virtue of the fact that it is owned and operated by the government. If there is competition, consumers will be afforded protection by the availability of alternatives. But if there is not, they may suffer the consequences of monopoly. The quality of service may be low. The level of prices may be high. The structure of prices may be unduly discriminatory. Nor are consumers fully protected by their right to vote. The ballot lacks precision as a method of control. And votes are also cast by members of producer and consumer groups whose interests differ from those of consumers as a whole. If consumers are really to have protection, some other method will be required.

The Price Level

As a matter of policy, a public enterprise may be operated at a loss, its rates being set to cover but a portion of its costs, and its deficit being met from other sources of public revenue. Or it may be operated at a profit; its rates being kept high, and its earnings used to defray the costs of other public activities. Or it may be required merely to pay its own way, its rates being designed to cover all its costs, but to yield no surplus for other purposes.

Operation at a loss may be adopted as a method of providing consumers with goods or services for which they cannot pay; low-rent housing is thus provided for families in the lower income groups. It may be used as a means of subsidizing an industry; newspapers and magazines are thus delivered at less than cost. Such a policy may be justified on the ground that the community derives benefits from an undertaking that cannot be fully financed by the price that can be charged. Public housing, for instance, may improve health and reduce delinquency. But the policy has its disadvantages. A low price on water supply may lead to greater cleanliness, but it may also lead to wasteful use. The subsidy afforded the users of the service must be financed by other taxes; the consequence of the transfer will depend upon the incidence of the taxes that are used. Where an enterprise need not meet its costs, moreover, there is no basis for judging the efficiency with which it is administered. An alternative is available: in the case of housing, for instance, tenants can be charged a rental that will cover costs, and provided aid in the form of an income supplement. If this were done, the transfer from the taxpayer to the recipient of public charity would be made clear, and the housing enterprise could be required to stand on its own feet.

Operation at a profit may be designed to check consumption; state liquor stores have kept their prices high. It may be employed as a means of providing revenue: some cities with municipal electric plants have cut their taxes, financing their normal functions by charging high electric rates. This policy may be defended, in some cases, on the ground that revenue is needed to defray the social costs resulting from an enterprise. It may be argued, for instance, that the consumption of liquor necessitates higher expenditures on police protection and that these expenditures are properly to be met by charging a high liquor price. But it can scarcely be contended that municipal activities are best to be financed from profits made on electricity or on water. High prices curtail use; in the case of liquor this may be desirable; in the case of electricity and water it is not. And finally, prices kept well above cost afford no compulsion to efficiency, no penalty for inefficiency.

If there is to be an adequate basis for judging the economy and efficiency with which a public enterprise is conducted, it should be required to pay its own way. Its prices should be set at a level that is calculated to yield sufficient revenue to enable it to meet its operating costs, replace outworn and obsolete equipment, maintain a reserve against contingencies, and provide for necessary expansion. Its goal, over the years, should be that of showing neither a profit nor a loss. Such a policy will lead it to supply the volume of service that is socially desired; to economize in its use of scarce resources. The best means of promoting the efficiency of an enterprise is to be found in its annual statement of profit and loss.

Costs may be covered by selling a smaller quantity at a higher price or a larger quantity at a lower one. A private enterprise may content itself with the smaller volume, hesitating to cut prices because it fears to take a chance on the elasticity of demand. A public enterprise will be more likely to run the risk. If demand proves to be inelastic, it will not go bankrupt. Its loss will be made up by appropriations from other public revenues. If demand proves to be elastic, however, it will expand its service and continue to cover its costs.

But there is no assurance, under public enterprise, that rates will be lowered by reducing costs. Indeed, there is danger that they will steadily be raised to cover steadily increasing costs. Labor is organized, economically and politically, to demand higher wages and other benefits. A private enterprise, if faced by competition, would be constrained to resist such demands by the threat of bankruptcy. A public monopoly encounters no such threat. And there may be little or no resistance to passing repeated wage increases on to the consumer in higher rates.

A public enterprise, moreover, may not be permitted to cover its costs. Politicians may seek to curry favor by keeping rates so low that a service must be provided at a loss. This has been the case, in the United States, with the postal service and with transit systems operated by municipalities. In Britain, too, though the prices of nationalized industries are supposed to cover their costs, the government, on the eve of an election, has refused to make the necessary increases in coal prices and transport rates. Where workers and consumers are both exerting pressure, wages may be pushed up and prices held down. The consequence will be a deficit that has to be met by the taxpayer.

The Price Structure

A public enterprise is no more likely than a private enterprise to charge the same amount for every unit sold. A public power plant will not make a flat charge per kilowatt-hour. A public railroad will not make a flat charge per ton-mile. For one thing, the costs involved in selling different units will differ, and prices will be adjusted to cover differences in cost. They will be higher where purchases are made in small quantities; lower where service is consumed off-peak. For another thing, the demands of different consumers will differ in elasticity and—where there is idle capacity—prices will make allowance for such differences. Nothing will be sold for less than marginal cost, but some customers will be charged more than average total cost and others charged less. Overhead will not be spread evenly, but will be allocated in accordance with elasticity of demand. Where customers lack alternatives, rates will be high; where they possess them, rates will be low. The use of the service will thus be maximized, and costs and profits, in general, kept lower than they otherwise would be. Even though the enterprise be public, the structure of its prices will resemble that of a regulated private monopoly.

Both public and private enterprises will discriminate for economic reasons. But a public enterprise may also discriminate to serve political purposes. Such purposes may be commendable. School children are transported without charge by city transit systems. Books and records for the blind are delivered for nothing by the Post Office. The principle could be extended. Electricity could be supplied at a high price to gambling dens, at a low price to churches and hospitals. The railroads could charge high rates for hauling slot machines and low rates for hauling hymnals and medicines. The government could thus discourage activities that were considered bad, encourage those that were considered good. But here, too, its purpose might better be accomplished in another way. Taxes and subsidies should be made visible, not hidden in the structure of rates. Worthy causes should be supported by the taxpayer, not by the users of public services. In the interest of economy and efficiency, public enterprises should be permitted to base their rates on business principles alone.

Such enterprises may discriminate in favor of worthy causes. There is greater danger that they will be required to discriminate in favor of powerful pressure groups. The prices charged by public enterprises need not be fixed by legislation. But postal rates have always been so fixed, and others, such as railroad rates, might also be. The structure of freight rates, if thrown to Congress for determination, would afford even greater opportunities for political manipulation than did the tariff in the past. The railroads might well be required to favor particular communities and commodities, the lowest rates going to those with the greatest political power. The farmers, it may be presumed, would get such rates on everything they bought and sold. And other users of the service would be taxed, in higher rates, to finance the subsidy.

Consumer Protection

Under private enterprise, the consumer is protected against poor service, high prices, and undue discrimination in two different ways: by competition and by regulation. Under public enterprise, such protection is also possible. A nationalized industry could be organized as a number of competing units. Or separate organizations could be established for competing services, such as gas and electricity; communication by mail, telephone, telegraph, and radio; and transport by rail, road, water, and air. Or, failing this, such industries could be organized as monopolies and independent tribunals authorized to regulate their services and rates. In most cases of nationalization, however, the consumer has been given protection in neither way.

In Great Britain, for instance, the emphasis has been on unification and coordination. The purpose has been efficiency; a consequence has been monopoly. Within each of the national industries, the organization is highly centralized. Gas and electricity are separate. But the Transport Commission, at the outset, controlled haulage by railway, highway, and waterway. Shippers were permitted to select their mode of transport. But their freedom of choice was more nominal than real. For the government decided what services were to be provided and what rates were to be charged. And its interest was in physical integration, not in the allocation of traffic in accordance with comparative costs.

So, too, with regulation. In Great Britain the rates charged by the Transport Commission are reviewed by the Transport Tribunal as were those charged, before nationalization, by the railroad companies. With other public industries, however, the prices fixed by managements are final, no formal provision being made for their control. In this country the rates of municipal utilities are subject to commission regulation in some states but not in others. Those of the Bonneville Power Administration and certain other projects must be approved by the Federal Power Commission. But this requirement is designed to assure the taxpayer—and the private power industry—that rates will not be set too low, not to assure the consumer that they will not be set too high. In general, the prices fixed by public enterprises are not reviewed by other agencies. The consumer is afforded less of an opportunity to protect himself against public monopoly than against private monopoly.

In Britain the government has sought to give consumers a voice by setting up a consumers' council or a system of national and regional or local councils in each of the nationalized industries. The councils are part-time bodies, holding meetings monthly or quarterly. Their membership, appointed by the respective ministries, is designed to be broadly representative. It is their function to receive, investigate, and settle consumer complaints. They may merely call the complaints to the attention of managements or they may make recommendations to managements or attempt to work out settlements themselves. They may also give advice on questions submitted to them by managements, raise questions of their own, and make recommendations to the ministries. In practice, the councils have been ineffective. They have been little known or used, receiving few complaints. They have been wanting in vigor, meeting infrequently and being poorly staffed. They have not been independent, relying on the public enterprises for their quarters, information, and facilities. They have had no means of enforcing their recommendations, lacking the support of an organized pressure group. Having sought, in many cases, to explain the policies of national industries to the public, they have come to be regarded as mouthpieces of managements.

EFFICIENCY VERSUS ACCOUNTABILITY

A public enterprise should be administered efficiently. It should be held, in the fulfillment of its function, to strict accountability. But these two purposes are not consistent. For the rules established in the name of accountability are often prejudicial to efficiency. And the independence required for efficiency may carry with it freedom from accountability. This is the dilemma on which attention has been centered in the debate on the administration of public enterprises both in Great Britain and in the United States.

The Government Department

There is danger that the managers of public enterprises will be irresponsible, taking actions not authorized by law, or that they will be dishonest, enriching themselves through favoritism and fraud. There is danger, too, that political parties will seek to gain and hold office by firing government workers, however efficient, and giving their jobs to party followers. To guard against these dangers, certain controls have been imposed upon the budgets, accounts, and personnel practices of government agencies. Such controls apply to the departmental administration of public enterprise in the United States.

A department of the federal government must prepare its annual budget well in advance, itemizing its proposed expenditures. This budget is presented to the Budget Bureau to be analyzed, modified, and approved. It goes next to the appropriations committees of the House of Representatives and the Senate where it is further modified. From there it goes to the House, subsequently to the Senate, then to a conference committee, and finally back to the House and the Senate to be enacted in amended form. The department is thus given authority to spend particular funds for particular purposes within a fiscal year. It cannot borrow on its own responsibility to obtain new equipment or to expand its working capital. It cannot transfer unexpended sums from one appropriation item to another. It must draw all its funds from the Treasury and return all its earnings to the Treasury. While it is carrying on its operations in one year, it must be going through this process to obtain appropriations for the year ahead.

All expenditures made by a department are audited, at a later date, by the General Accounting Office. This agency, under a Controller General, is responsible to the Congress. It appraises the manner in which federal agencies discharge their responsibilities, attempting to insure that expenditures are made only for purposes authorized by law. The Office interprets the laws and issues rulings to which departments must conform.

In hiring, promoting, transferring, and firing personnel, the departments are subject to control by the Civil Service Commission. Not all jobs are under Civil Service, but for those that are, job descriptions must be prepared and job classifications obtained. And they must then be filled by persons whose qualifications the Commission has approved. Unless an agency is being abolished or reduced in size, employees cannot be discharged without observing prescribed procedures. And even when there is a reduction in force, discharges must be made in accordance with the priorities established on the Commission's retention register.

The Civil Service regulations may make a public enterprise less vulnerable to political pressure. The budgetary controls may make it more so. For these controls can be applied by Congress for purposes other than that of insuring honesty, economy, and efficiency in administration. They can be used—and have been used—to force an enterprise to favor powerful pressure groups. The administrator who resists such pressures, in the public interest, may have his appropriation cut. He may be denied the right to make expenditures for certain purposes. Nor are the personnel of a public agency immune from political attack. Persons appointed or reappointed to positions requiring Senatorial approval may be denied confirmation. And all public employees, including civil servants, may find themselves accused of incompetence, dishonesty, immorality, and disloyalty, subjected to inquisitions by ambitious politicians, their reputations blackened, under cover of Congressional immunity, in an effort to profit from personal publicity. These handicaps are not experienced by private enterprise.

The Costs of Bureaucracy

In operation, the controls established to insure accountability are clumsy and sluggish. In controlling budgets, the committees on appropriations and the houses of Congress lack the knowledge and the time required for adequate review. In the committee hearings and in the Congressional debates, the questions asked and the issues raised are likely to be irrelevant, petty, or partisan. If a budget is reduced, a flat percentage cut may be applied across the board, because the legislators are unable to distinguish between activities that are important and those that are not. Where distinctions are made, an integral part of a program may be denied support because an administrator has offended politicians who are thus enabled to obtain revenge. The process of making appropriations, far from being informed and precise, is usually arbitrary and even capricious. And it is always slow.

The rules governing public expenditures, issued by the General Accounting Office, are voluminous and meticulous. At one time, the audit of such expenditures, made by the Office, was designed to give assurance that every penny had been spent with strict legality. Sums spent in good faith might subsequently be disallowed. An official who had paid for a taxi on a business trip, for instance, might be denied a refund, months later, on the ground that he could have ridden on a bus. In later years, the Office has placed its emphasis on broader appraisals of agency performance, leaving such audits to the agencies themselves. But the public administrator still may feel that it is more interested in observance of legal restrictions than in economy or efficiency.

To the administrator, too, the regulations of the Civil Service Commission appear to be designed to make it impossible for him to obtain or to retain competent personnel. He cannot employ a man, however able, until the Commission gives its consent. And the processes of investigation, examination, clearance, and approval may go on for months. Instead of the man he wants, the administrator may be forced to take another, whose talents are inferior, but whose paper qualifications come closer to satisfying the Commission's rules. When budgets are cut, the man last hired, though the best man in the office, will be the first to go. Some chairwarmer dating from an earlier administration will have superior retention rights. If a man is attacked politically, he can be dropped. But if he is merely incompetent, the Commission will come to his defense. Discharge is made so difficult that the administrator may abandon the attempt, finding it simpler to move the undesirable employee to an empty room without a function, a title, a secretary, or a phone. The Commission, by withholding jobs from political patronage, may protect the public enterprise from a fate that would be worse. But to the administrator, attempting to carry out a program, the fate it leaves him with is bad enough.

In general, these controls obstruct good management. First, they carry the constant threat of reversal of policy. It is difficult or impossible to go on with projects, already initiated, when appropriations are curtailed or funds denied. It is difficult, too, to plan for the future when there is no assurance of continuity. Second, the controls involve delays. Where responsibility is centralized, decisions are taken to the top, and months may elapse before they come back down. In the meantime, the enterprise is unable to adjust to change. Action is suspended while papers move, deliberately, from desk to desk until the final signature has been obtained. Third, the controls provide no means for judging efficiency. The system of accounting used does not require that revenues shall cover costs. Nor does it analyze the costs themselves. An enterprise, thus controlled, may go on indefinitely operating at a loss, its costs far higher than they need to be. Fourth, and finally, the controls circumscribe the discretion and curb the initiative of managements. And so they discourage imagination, repress enthusiasm, and smother innovation. Strict accountability is assured by binding an enterprise with red tape. But another thing assured is immobility.

The Public Corporation

The public corporation was once envisaged as an entity that would be independent of the established departments of government and would be freed from hampering controls. Its autonomy was to be assured by entrusting its administration to a separate board, with members appointed for long and overlapping terms. Its freedom was to involve exemption from the procedures usually governing budgets and appropriations, from supervision by the General Accounting Office, and from Civil Service regulations as to personnel. The corporation was to obtain its initial capital from the Treasury and was to seek Congressional approval for expansion of its facilities. But otherwise it was to be self-supporting, paying its bills with the proceeds of its sales. It was not to be required to obtain its current revenues through Congressional appropriations or to turn its income over to the Treasury. In command of its own resources, it was to determine its own expenditures. Freed from the General Accounting Office, the corporation was to make its purchases and sales in accordance with its judgment of market opportunities. Freed from Civil Service, it was to make its own decisions in handling its employees.

This independence was expected to carry with it a number of advantages. It would protect an enterprise from partisan interference and enable it better to resist the demands of pressure groups. It would make for continuity of policy. It would permit quicker action and greater flexibility. It would promote the adoption of businesslike methods of accounting, making it possible to apply commercial standards in judging economy and efficiency. It would encourage initiative and open the way to innovation. In short, it would enable the administrators of a public enterprise to run it as a private business would be run.

This is still the way the public corporation is regarded in Great Britain. But the freedom of such bodies has been steadily whittled down in the United States. Many of them have lost their independent status, being subordinated to government departments. All of them have been required by law, first, to submit their administrative expenses—a small but crucial part of their total expenditures—to the Bureau of the Budget for approval and, subsequently, to have them appropriated by Congress. All but the TVA, the Federal Reserve Board, and the Federal Deposit Insurance Corporation have been brought under Civil Service. And under the Government Corporation Control Act of 1945, all federal corporations must submit business-type budgets each year in order to obtain approval of their programs as a whole from the President and from Congress. Their accounts, moreover, are subjected to a business-type audit by the General Accounting Office. These requirements have clearly limited the freedom of the public corporation. Whether they have impaired its advantages as an agency of administration is still a matter of dispute.

The Problem of Accountability

In Great Britain the public corporation retains more freedom than it does in the United States. But there, too, it is recognized that the independence that makes for efficiency may also make for irresponsibility. And the major issue debated, under nationalization, is how a balance can be struck between the two objectives of businesslike management and political accountability.

Each of the public corporations in Britain was located within a ministry. The minister was empowered to appoint the members of its board. He was to prescribe the form of its records, accounts, and reports. He was to inspect its establishments and make sure that certain regulations, such as those relating to health and safety, were observed. The corporation was required to submit reports to the minister; some of its actions, including plans for reorganization, expansion, and borrowing, had to be submitted for his approval. The minister was authorized to issue formal directives to the board. In this way, policy was supposed to be made public and responsibility for policy made clear. But the minister was expected to refrain from day-to-day interference in the management of the business.

In practice, things have not worked out this way. Ministerial directives are seldom issued. But ministerial control over corporate management is direct, continuous, and detailed. Ministers meet informally with the chairmen of their boards. They explain the government's policies, make clear that managerial decisions must conform. Where business judgment and political judgment differ, the minister tells the chairman what to do. And the chairman, being beholden to the minister for his appointment, acts accordingly. [1]

The boards are responsible to the ministers, and the ministers to Parliament. But control by Parliament is lax. Departments of government have long been held accountable, under the Parliamentary system, by the device of raising questions about their operations to be answered by ministers during the question period in the House of Commons. This procedure, indeed, is taken so seriously that a member's threat to raise a question may induce an official to modify his policies. But with the public corporations, Labor and Conservative ministers alike have refused to answer questions concerning day-to-day operations. They are required to answer questions on policy, but they have the power to decide what is policy and what is a matter of detail. Responsible in fact for managerial decisions, they can avoid meeting that responsibility. The annual reports of the corporations can be debated in Parliament, but the reports are tardy and the information they provide is insufficient to afford a basis for judgment. Instead of dealing with basic policies, the debates are likely to be confined to petty details.

It is charged, in Britain, that this situation, in effect, hands the corporate boards and the ministers a blank check to be filled out, for better or worse, at their pleasure. "Britain's industrial structure," says *The Economist,* "is now composed of a large number of private industries over which the state has considerable powers of control and a small number of public industries over which it has no control whatsoever."[2] To deal with this problem, a select committee was established by the House of Commons in 1957 to investigate and report, from time to time, on any of the national industries. The committee's jurisdiction is broad, and its authority limited. By 1964, it had held hearings on each of the nationalized industries, questioned their ministers and their boards, studied their records, and issued comprehensive reports, together with recommendations for reform. The Committee's work was competent, its recommendations well considered. Following this procedure, however, a national industry can be investigated only once in seven years. And the Committee's recommendations have been ignored by the boards, the ministers, and the Parliament. The problem of accountability has not been solved.

A fundamental difficulty remains. Even though mechanisms for controlling

1 / See Michael Shanks (ed.), *The Lessons of Public Enterprise* (London: Jonathan Cape, 1963), chaps. v., xiv.

2 / *The Economist,* May 19, 1956, p. 668.

the performance of public enterprises may be provided, standards of appraisal may not. With nationalization, the yardstick of competition is abandoned and the market rendered ineffective as an arbiter of cost and price. There are no agreed criteria by which to judge success or failure, no way to tell how well an enterprise has done or how much better it might have done. Accountability may be enforced, but accountability for what? Parliament may exercise its right to act, but it will still be acting in the dark.

CHANGE OF OWNERSHIP

Some enterprises have been public from the beginning: the Post Office in all countries, the telegraph and telephone systems in Western Europe, and atomic energy in the United States. Others, once private, have been socialized. Still others, once public, have been privatized. The processes of nationalization and denationalization give rise to problems of their own.

Nationalization

In some cases, governments have come to participate in business by extending aid to private companies that were heading into bankruptcy. In others, they have seized the properties of foreigners or traitors. In still others, they have seized all private properties. But aside from confiscation and revolution, nationalization has usually involved the payment of compensation for enterprises purchased by governments at forced or voluntary sales. The issues raised by the process have had to do with the amount to be paid and the form in which the payment was to be made.

In Great Britain the sale of the industries was forced, the procedure being to vest ownership in the government as of a certain day. In some cases—coal, transport, gas, and electricity—the government acquired an industry's assets, the former companies being left to enter another business, to continue as investment agencies, or to liquidate their holdings, as they chose. In others, such as iron and steel, it acquired the shares of corporations, superseding the former owners in control. Usually, the amount of compensation paid was fixed by Parliament. Matters of detail could be submitted to arbitration, but the level of payments could not be challenged in the courts. In general, the payments were designed to leave the former owners with securities of the same value or with earnings of the same size as they had before. The new securities, however, were bonds bearing a fixed rate of interest rather than stocks yielding a variable return, the risks of the enterprises being transferred to the taxpayer. The methods employed in effecting nationalization gave rise to little or no litigation and to little public criticism or debate.

In the United States, if the owners of a private enterprise were forced to sell it to a government, they would have the right, under state and federal constitutions, to appeal the amount of their compensation to the courts. In practice, most public enterprises have been initiated by governments. And where private assets have been acquired, it has been through voluntary sale. Here, the price has been arrived at through negotiation. And the government, instead of paying too little, is as likely to have paid too much.

Denationalization

In the event of denationalization, a frequent procedure has been to set up a liquidation agency and charge it with responsibility for selling the government properties. This has been done, for instance, in the case of the iron and steel mills and the trucking industry in Great Britain and in that of the synthetic rubber plants in the United States. In such cases, the seller may be under pressure to make a sale, while the buyer is under no compulsion to buy. As a result, the price may be low. The government loses money on the deal, and the companies that buy its properties are subsidized. In Britain, after 1953, when the government attempted to dispose of road haulage, it found itself unable to sell its long-distance lines, with their garages and terminals. It therefore kept a fleet of 9,000 trucks and remained in this part of the business. It succeeded, however, in selling the rest of its trucks. But in doing so, it incurred a loss of £12 million. When the government sought to dispose of its 90 steel mills, it was more successful. Here, it merely held the voting stock. The former corporations, with their properties and managements, were still intact. Of the smaller mills, some were sold back to their former owners, others to fabricators. With the big mills, stock was sold to investors through banking syndicates at prices that were generally satisfactory. It did not appear that the government would sustain a loss. In the United States, there have been no disposals of entire industries. The only important sales have been those of war-built facilities. Here, the government has usually suffered a heavy loss. On the ships built during World War II, the loss was $2.8 billion; on the steel plants, $490 million. Disposal of the synthetic rubber plants was an exception to the general rule. The government had built 27 plants at a cost of $260 million; a Rubber Producing Facilities Disposal Commission, set up in 1953, succeeded in selling 25 of them by 1955 for $270 million.

The way in which public assets are sold will affect the future structure of an industry. If all the sales are made to a single company, the government may get a better price, but the industry may be monopolized. If sales can be made to many buyers, even though at a comparative loss, the industry may become competitive. This is a consideration which influenced the government of the United States in disposing of war assets, such as its aluminum plants. For nearly 50 years before 1940, the Aluminum Company of America produced 100 percent of the nation's output of primary aluminum. In 1950, Alcoa produced only 50 percent, Reynolds about 30 percent, and Kaiser about 20 percent. The change in the structure of the industry was a result of the policy adopted by the government in selling the facilities it had built during the war.

The success of denationalization may be imperiled by the threat of an opposition party, if returned to power, to renationalize. This makes it more difficult for the government to find buyers. And if an industry, once sold, is renationalized, it may be doubted that it can ever be denationalized again. The British steel industry was nationalized by a Labor government in 1951, denationalized by a Conservative government in 1953, and renationalized by Labor in 1967. The first nationalization gave rise to violent political controversy. The renationalization evoked little enthusiasm among the Laborites themselves and aroused little excitement in the country as a whole. The government appointed Conservatives and executives of the former private companies to run the industry, and the new management embarked upon an ambitious program of expansion and modernization. Socialism, in the British steel industry, was here to stay.

PART V

Setting the Plane of Competition

Chapter 25 : PROTECTING CONSUMERS AGAINST FRAUD

To make sure that private enterprise serves the public interest, government has insisted, wherever possible, that competition be maintained. But the maintenance of competition, in itself, is not enough. The public interest is also affected by the methods used when firms compete. (1) Goods may be adulterated and their value misrepresented. Information may be withheld and markets manipulated. Underhanded tactics may be employed in diverting patronage. Such methods are unfair to competitors. They are harmful to consumers. (2) Sellers seeking present profits and buyers seeking present satisfactions may waste scarce natural resources, thus impairing the well-being of future generations and endangering their security. (3) Competing sellers may also seek advantage by inflicting damage on human resources, exploiting the labor of children, maintaining conditions of work that imperil the health and safety of employees, requiring long hours and paying wages that fall below the minimum needed for healthful and decent living, providing no security against accident, illness, unemployment, or dependent old age.

Each of these practices operates to drag the better firms down to the level of the worst. Government, therefore, seeks not only to maintain competition but also to protect the scrupulous businessman against his unscrupulous rival, thus insuring the integrity of markets and raising the plane upon which firms compete. The next three chapters, constituting Part V of this book, are concerned with governmental programs that establish the plane of competition. The present chapter deals with measures that protect consumers of goods and services against fraud and deception on the part of sellers. The next chapter has to do with measures that extend similar protection to investors. Chapter 27 is devoted to the conservation of natural resources. The establishment of minimum standards for the protection of labor will be discussed, along with other labor problems, in Chapter 30.

THE CONSUMER AND THE LAW

The large enterprise, as a buyer, whether it be a business organization, a public institution, or an agency of government, is unlikely to be defrauded or deceived by other enterprises, as sellers, since it customarily places little or no reliance on any representation that they may make. Instead, it employs skilled purchasing agents who specialize in the goods it buys, lays down specifications to govern quality and performance, and conducts tests in its own laboratories to make sure that the specifications are met. The ultimate consumer, however, does not do his buying in this way. His purchasing agent—the housewife—is usually selected for her competence in other fields. The goods that he must buy are so many, so varied, and so complex that he can scarcely expect her to become an expert on all—if on any—of them. He cannot hope to establish his own specifications or to make his own tests. He is rarely in a position to judge quality or performance or even, perhaps, to protect himself against short measure and short weight. He must rely, therefore, upon the representations that are made by the manufacturers who produce the goods he buys and the merchants who distribute them. As a result, he may be persuaded to purchase articles that are harmful or dangerous or simply worthless, to accept one quantity or quality in the guise of another, and to pay far more for what he gets than it is really worth. Placing his confidence in the word of the seller, he may often be protected by the latter's interest in preserving a reputation. But he may sometimes be defrauded and deceived. And it is against fraud and deception that action has been taken, over the years, at common law and through legislation by local, state, and federal governments.

The Consumer at Common Law

Centuries ago, the position of the consumer, at common law, was encompassed within the meaning of the phrase *caveat emptor:* "Let the buyer beware." Under this rule, the buyer was held to be able to protect himself and was therefore denied damages if he brought suit. The doctrine was developed, however, in cases involving the purchase of familiar articles, displayed in plain sight, so that an appraisal of their value could be made. As time passed, it ceased to fit the facts. Goods became less simple and markets more impersonal; spot transactions gave way to the conclusion of contracts for future performance; the buyer was forced to rely increasingly upon the seller's honesty. This change was given recognition by the courts, and *caveat emptor* came to be modified by the legal rules of fraud, warranty, and negligence.

Under the rule of fraud, contracts were invalidated, at an early date, where it was shown that one of the parties had been tricked into signing different terms than he had thought, and damages came to be awarded where it could be proved that sellers had willfully made statements that they knew to be false. Proof of fraud was by no means easy to establish. But actions under the other rules were more readily sustained. Warranty was held to be expressed in written or oral statements made by a seller or his agent at the time of sale, or implied where goods were sold for future delivery; and if goods were not as represented, the buyer was upheld in refusing to accept or pay for them, or in keeping them and suing under his contract, asking damages for its breach or demanding performance in accordance with its terms. Under the rule of negligence, it was held that a seller was bound to reveal to buyers any defects hidden in his product of which he knew or should have known, and a buyer injured by his failure to do so might recover damages.

The consumer was thus afforded some protection at common law. But the law applied only to injury in the past; it contributed little to the prevention of injury in the future. And it was called into play only when buyers were sufficiently harmed and angered, and sufficiently well to do, to take the initiative and bear the cost involved in bringing suits. If the consumer is really to be protected, prohibitions against fraud and deception must be written into statutes, accompanied by penalties, and enforced by public officials at public expense.

Establishment of Legal Standards

Legislators have undertaken to protect the buyer, first of all, by establishing legal standards. They have set up standards of weight and measure and container size and fill. In some cases, they have provided standards of identity for commodities and minimum standards of composition, quality, and performance. In others, they have provided for the creation of standard grades.

Congress was given power, by the Constitution, to enact laws establishing standards of weight and measure. In general, it has failed to do so, leaving this responsibility to the states. It has acted, however, in a few cases, defining the ampere, volt, watt, and other electrical measures, the barrel as a unit of dry measure, and other containers for fruits and vegetables.

The states, too, have acted to prescribe standard containers for certain products, such as fruits, vegetables, milk, and cream, and standard weights for others, such as a loaf of bread and a ton of coal. State and local governments have long assumed responsibility for the supervision of weights and measures in general. In the usual case, a state official issues regulations establishing specifications and tolerances for all weights, measures, and weighing and measuring devices, such as gasoline pumps and merchants' scales. Local officials inspect all new devices and test all old ones once or twice a year. Devices found to be inaccurate are seized and destroyed. Persons convicted of giving short weight or measure may be fined or jailed. Compliance with legal standards, however, is less than universal. The funds provided for administration are usually meager. The fines imposed are small, and jail sentences are rare. Honesty in weights and measures is to be attributed more to voluntary observance of the laws than to the vigor with which they are enforced.[1]

Standards have been created not only for the units by which goods are weighed or measured but also for the goods themselves. Standards of quality, usually for goods bought or sold by farmers, have been established by certain of the states. Congress has empowered the Food and Drug Administration to devise

---

1 / For a survey of the enforcement of weights and measures laws, see Leland J. Gordon, *Weights and Measures and the Consumer* (Mount Vernon, N.Y.: Consumers Union of the United States, 1966), Part IV.

standards of identity for foods and drugs. Observance of these standards is not obligatory, but departure from them must be disclosed.

In the case of certain goods, principally agricultural commodities, Congress has gone on to require standard grades, empowering the Secretary of Agriculture to establish grades for cotton, tobacco, grains, and other agricultural products. The use of such grades is required in organized commodities markets, where goods are bought unseen and contracts made for future delivery. Elsewhere, in general, they need not be used; but if they are, misrepresentation of the grade of goods is forbidden by law.

Requirement of Truthful Disclosure

Both state and federal governments have enacted laws forbidding sellers to misrepresent their goods and requiring them to disclose facts whose concealment might be harmful to their customers. Many have required that packages be so labeled as to show the weight of their contents and that certain goods, such as animal feeds, be so labeled as to reveal their composition. Congress has prohibited the misbranding of foods, drugs, and cosmetics. Misrepresentation was among the unfair methods of competition outlawed by the Federal Trade Commission Act and among the deceptive practices outlawed by the Wheeler-Lea Act. Disclosure of identity, composition, quality, or the presence of harmful ingredients is required in the cases of foods and drugs, insecticides and fungicides, viruses, serums, and toxins, caustic poisons, alcoholic beverages, fur products, wool and other textile fiber products, and hazardous household substances.

The requirements with respect to labeling vary from case to case. It is usually provided that true weight and measure must be shown. For alcoholic beverages, and for animal feeds, disclosure of composition is required. For drugs, composition need be shown only if they depart from standards established by law. But here, as with cosmetics, caustic poisons, insecticides, and fungicides, the presence of dangerous ingredients must be revealed, and warnings must be given and instructions provided for their proper use. For foods, failure to satisfy minimum standards must be disclosed. For most products, however, the law contents itself with the negative provision that misrepresentation is not to be allowed. But there are cases in which affirmative disclosures are required.

Under the Federal Alcohol Administration Act, the producer of alcoholic beverages must obtain from the Internal Revenue Service certificates approving the labels that he puts on his bottles. Not only must the labels avoid deceptive statements; they must provide adequate information concerning origin and quality. Similar rules apply to statements made in advertisements.

Under the Wool Products Labeling Act of 1939, labels must be affixed to products containing wool (with certain exceptions, such as carpets, rugs, and upholstery) showing the percentages of new wool, reused or reprocessed wool, and other fibers or fillers that are used. Refusal to provide this information is made punishable by fine or imprisonment, and falsification is made a violation of Section 5 of the Federal Trade Commission Act. It has been the purpose of the law not so much to protect consumers against misrepresentation as to protect wool growers against the competition of other fibers and weavers of woolens against the competition of other goods.

Under the Fur Products Labeling Act, passed in February, 1951, the Federal Trade Commission was directed to hold public hearings to determine the true English names of furs and to issue a Fur Products Name Guide by February, 1952. Sellers were required to use these names on labels attached to fur products after August, 1952, and also to state whether the furs contained in such products were new or used, if they had come from bellies, tails, or paws, and if they had been dyed or bleached.

The Textile Products Identification Act of 1958 applies to yarns, fabrics, and household articles such as apparel, floor coverings, draperies, and beddings made from natural or synthetic fibers other than wool. The law requires sellers of such products to affix labels revealing the percentage by weight of each fiber they contain. Synthetic fibers must be identified by one of 16 generic names worked out by the FTC in cooperation with members of the trade. Misbranding is forbidden under penalty of fine or imprisonment.

The Hazardous Substances Labeling Act was passed in 1960 and became effective in 1962. The Act empowers the Food and Drug Administration to find such household products as cleaning agents, paint removers, and polishes to be hazardous and to require that warnings be printed on their labels if they contain substances which are toxic, corrosive, irritating, flammable, or likely to generate pressure through heat or decomposition, and if they may cause personal injury as a result of normal handling or use, including ingestion by children. Producers failing to give such warnings can be fined $500 and imprisoned for 90 days. Goods lacking the labels can be seized and withdrawn from sale.

Another law requiring truthful disclosure, enacted in 1958, has to do not with the quality of a product but with its price. Under the Automobile Information Disclosure Act, manufacturers are required to put tags on new passenger cars and station wagons showing the suggested retail price of the car, the price of each piece of extra equipment, and the cost of transport to the dealer. The law was designed to put a stop to the dealer's practice of inflating the nominal price of a new car and thus misrepresenting the trade-in allowance actually given on an old car. As a consequence, the net price paid by the buyer is not affected, but the deal doesn't look as good to him as it did before.

Truth in Packaging

With the spread of self-service markets, competition at retail came increasingly to take the form of competition in packaging. And competition in packaging came, all too often, to involve deception. Packages were made to look bigger than they really were: glass jars with thick walls, indented bottoms, and irregular or magnifying shapes; boxes enlarged and slack-filled. The quantity in a package was reduced, while its size and price were kept the same. Nonstandard weights and measures were used to prevent comparisons; the "king-size" 15-ounce bottle held less than the ordinary pint. Packages were printed with "cents off" labels, though the retailer was not obliged to make the cut; the economy package might well carry a higher price.

Existing federal law required truthful labeling only for liquor and for foods and drugs. It did not cover the many other packaged products that crowded the supermarket shelves. To afford the housewife protection in this area as well, Congress passed the Fair Packaging and Labeling Act of 1966. Under this law, the Food and Drug Administration and the Federal Trade Commission, in their respective jurisdictions, can require disclosure of the net quantity in every package, specifying type size, contrasting background, and conspicuous position. The FTC can also regulate "cents off" and other bargain claims. The Act outlaws the "jumbo pound" and the "giant quart." Where the number of "servings" in a package is stated, it requires that the size of a serving be defined. Except for cosmetics, the law requires that the ingredients of packaged products be listed by their common names in the order of the quantities contained. An effort to empower the FDA and FTC to standardize the sizes and weights of packages was passed by the Senate but defeated in the House. Enforcement of the law has been slow in getting under way. Appropriations for the purpose have been miniscule.

Truth in Lending

The consumer who borrowed money or bought an article on the installment plan was faced, until recently, with an incomprehensible variety of credit charges. If he borrowed $100 to be repaid in monthly installments, the alternatives offered him might have been described as follows:

1. No interest rate is quoted. The borrower is told that the charge will be $10 down and $10 per month. The cost of the credit is not disclosed.
2. An interest charge is added. The borrower is told that the cost of credit will be 6 percent of the $100 loan. The actual rate is close to 12 percent, because the interest quoted applies to the original amount of the loan and not to the balance that declines each month as the installments are paid.
3. A discount rate is deducted. Instead of paying $6 for $100, a rate of 6 percent, the borrower pays $6 for $94, a rate of 6.38 percent. And here, again, as he repays his debt, the charge for the credit he actually receives goes up to nearly 12 percent.
4. Interest is represented as a simple monthly rate, being quoted at 1, 2, 3, or 4 percent per month. The actual charge, of course, is 12 times this, or 12, 24, 36, or 48 percent per year.
5. Lenders start with an interest charge but add on fees for services, such as investigation of credit risks and processing of loans, which add to the cost of credit, thus making the interest rate that has been quoted quite meaningless.

To protect the borrower by making the cost of credit intelligible and cost comparisons possible, Congress enacted the Consumer Credit Protection Act of 1968. Under this measure, all businessmen regularly making loans to consumers are required to disclose the actual cost of credit, in writing, at the time of each transaction, expressing it in two ways: as an absolute sum in dollars and cents and as a percentage of the amount financed, computed as a simple annual rate on the unpaid balance. Sellers must provide similar data when credit is advertised. Exceptions are made for petty transactions and special provision is made for reporting the cost of credit provided through revolving accounts by department stores. The law contains special provisions designed to curb extreme cases of deception and extortion by unscrupulous lenders. It protects homeowners who unknowingly sign second mortgages to finance repairs by giving them three days in which to change their minds. It limits the share of a worker's pay that a creditor can attach through legal action. It makes extortion by loan sharks a federal crime, subject to $10,000 fine and 20 years imprisonment. Willful violation of other provisions of the law is punishable by a $5,000 fine and one year in prison and may subject an offender to civil suits for damages. Enforcement, in their respective fields, is left to nine different federal agencies.

Protection of Public Health and Safety

There are some goods and services whose sale may be so harmful to the health and safety of consumers that protective measures going far beyond mere grading and labeling are required. Measures of this sort adopted by the states are so numerous that it is possible to do no more than indicate their general character. The production, possession, and sale of narcotics is usually regulated; the sale of drugs without a doctor's prescription is forbidden; and the sale of poisons is controlled. Adulteration of foods and drugs is generally prohibited, as is the use of arsenic in spraying fruits and vegetables. Inspection of meat and fish and the pasteurization of milk are made compulsory. The sale of second-hand bedding is restricted, and the sterilization of hair and feathers used in new bedding is customarily required. Standards of cleanliness, enforced by inspection, are established for food-dispensing establishments—such as dairies, canneries, bakeries, meat markets, and restaurants—and for clinics, dispensaries, barber shops, and swimming pools. Standards of professional competence are employed in granting and refusing licenses to physicians, dentists, midwives, nurses, pharmacists, optometrists, and chiropodists. And the list is not by any means complete.

The sale of certain goods has been subjected to stringent controls by the federal government. In one case the law has required, since 1907, that goods be inspected and approved before they can be offered for sale. Under the provisions of the Meat Inspection Act of that year, slaughtering, packing, and canning plants that ship meat across state lines are inspected by veterinarians from the Department of Agriculture. Animals are inspected before, and carcasses after, slaughter; diseased meat is destroyed and pure meat stamped "U.S. Government Inspected" and released for sale. Federal inspection covers 85 percent of the national supply of meat. The other 15 percent is intrastate. In some states, inspection has been voluntary; in others, nonexistent. Conditions in packing plants have threatened public health. In 1967, however, Congress extended federal standards to intrastate establishments. It authorized federal grants to enable the states to initiate or to improve inspection. And it empowered the Department of Agriculture to impose federal inspection where the states failed to act. Under the Poultry Products Inspection Act of 1957, the Department also inspects poultry sold in interstate commerce, examining each lot before slaughter and each bird afterward, and supervising sanitation and processing. Here, as with meat, the federal government acted, in 1968, to strengthen inspection in markets that are intrastate. Establishments processing sea foods may, at their request, be inspected by the Bureau of Commercial Fisheries of the Department of the Interior, and may then display a shield indicating that their products have been prepared under its rules. But such requests are rarely made.

The Flammable Fabrics Act was passed in 1953 after a number of persons had been seriously burned as a result of the ignition of garments made of synthetic materials. Under the provisions of this law, the production or distribution of any article of apparel which is "so highly flammable as to be dangerous when worn" is made illegal under the Federal Trade Commission Act. The Commission may institute proceedings to enjoin the manufacture or sale of such articles and to confiscate existing stocks. The provisions of the law were extended, in 1968, to cover bedding, draperies, and other interior furnishings. And under legislation enacted in 1966 and 1969, the government may ban the sale of children's toys that are highly dangerous.

In 1966, following publication by Ralph Nader of a best seller called *Unsafe at Any Speed* and subsequent public hearings, Congress enacted a National Traffic and Motor Vehicle Safety Act. The law directed the National Highway Safety Bureau to prescribe safety features to be included and safety standards to be met in all new motor vehicles and tires. These features may include such items as impact-absorbing steering columns, front-seat head rests, comprehensive interior padding, recessed knobs and handles, rupture resistant fuel tanks, glare reduction and rear-window defogging. The standards are designed to reduce the likelihood of crashes, to reduce the frequency and severity of injuries during crashes, and to insure safety from fire following a crash. The law also required manufacturers whose vehicles and tires proved, in operation, to be defective, to recall them from their owners to rectify the defects. The penalty for failing to do so is set at $1,000 per car up to a total of $140,000. The first standards were issued in January, 1968. Automobile manufacturers have recalled millions of cars for repair since the law took effect.

Further action to insure public safety has been proposed. A National Commission on Public Safety, set up by Congress, reported in 1970 that consumer products such as fireworks, glass bottles, household chemicals, power tools, rotary lawnmowers, and color television sets carried unacceptable risks and recommended that an independent federal agency be created to promulgate and enforce safety standards for such products and to enjoin the distribution of products that failed to meet them. In the same year, the Federal Trade Commission proposed the creation of still another agency to set standards for the quality of new automobiles and parts and to enforce these standards by checking on performance and imposing penalties where they were not met.

Protection against Swindlers

Action has been taken, too, to protect the consumer against financial loss. Since 1872, federal law has prohibited the use of the mails to defraud. Each year, inspectors for the Post Office investigate cases where glasses have been fitted by mail; fake cures sold to sufferers from cancer, tuberculosis, and other serious ailments; and money collected for worthless insurance policies, stocks in nonexistent mining ventures, and the clearance of title to mythical estates. The Post Office grants a hearing to any person accused of such practices and, if it finds him guilty, may issue a fraud order, instructing postmasters not to cash money orders made out to him or to deliver letters addressed to him, but to return them instead to their senders, stamped "Fraudulent!" Serious cases may be turned over to the Department of Justice for criminal prosecutions, leading to fines up to $1,000 or imprisonment up to five years or both. Fraud orders are issued and convictions obtained by the hundreds every year. But action against false statements is handicapped by the need to prove that they were made with fraudulent intent. At best, the Post Office can exclude no more than a minor fraction of illegal letters from the mails. Lacking the right of censorship, it acts upon complaint. In many cases the victims of fraud do not complain. Where they do, the swindler named in an order need only change his name and address to resume his business. The Post Office can keep him from collecting money through the mail. It cannot prevent him from advertising in newspapers or magazines or from mailing third-class matter to promote over-the-counter sales.

The states, also, have undertaken to protect buyers against fraud. Most of them have made it a criminal offense to obtain money under false pretenses. Most of them have adopted a uniform sales act, prescribing a standard form for sales contracts and defining the obligations of warranty. The states have acted, too, to protect small borrowers against extortion, bringing institutions making small loans, such as personal finance companies, industrial banks, credit unions, and remedial loan societies, under the jurisdiction of state banking departments. In earlier years, necessitous and uninformed borrowers were cruelly exploited by loan sharks. They were charged exorbitant rates of interest and kept continually in debt with threats of attachments of wages and personal property. The small loans business is now controlled, however, by a Uniform Small Loan Law which has been adopted by most of the states. Under this law, lenders are licensed, the rates that they may charge are limited, and their ability to obtain repayment by attaching wages and property is curbed. Small loans are still costly, but the ethics of the lenders have been greatly improved.

FOODS, DRUGS, AND COSMETICS

For nearly half a century, the federal government has undertaken to protect consumers against impurities in foods and drugs. Today, the food and drug laws are taken for granted. But for decades, their enactment was bitterly opposed by the industries concerned. The need for such legislation first became apparent about 1880 with the growth of large-scale food processing industries, concealing foods in cans where their quality could not be judged, and employing harmful substances to improve their appearance and to preserve them for sale in mass markets, and with the development of a patent medicine industry, dispensing dangerous and habit-forming drugs. The first bill calling for regulation was introduced in Congress in 1890, and during the next 25 years, nearly 150 other bills were introduced. But the public was apathetic, the opposition determined, and the bills were shelved. Then public attention was captured as the problem was dramatized. Dr. Harvey W. Wiley, the chief chemist of the Department of Agriculture, organized within his staff a "poison squad," whose members volunteered to eat foods currently being offered for sale, and reported to the press, from day to day, on the state of their health. Upton Sinclair wrote a novel, *The Jungle,* picturing the filth found by his characters in the Chicago packing plants and describing the sale of diseased cattle as clean meat. Samuel Hopkins Adams published a series of articles in *Collier's* exposing the patent medicine business. At last, the country was aroused. The General Federation of Women's Clubs organized and directed a widespread and effective drive for the enactment of a law. The Pure Food and Drugs Act, drafted by Dr. Wiley, was finally passed in 1906. Enforcement of the law was assigned to the Department of Agriculture, and Dr. Wiley was put in charge.

The Food and Drugs Act of 1906

The Act forbade adulteration and misbranding of foods and drugs sold in interstate commerce. Food was defined as adulterated if it contained decomposed or putrid animal or vegetable substances or parts of diseased animals, if it had been so mixed or colored as to conceal its inferiority, if ingredients had been added that made it injurious to health, or if valuable constituents had been removed and others substituted or mixed with it so as to impair its quality or strength. Candy was said to be adulterated if it contained various mineral substances, poisonous colors or flavors, liquors, drugs, or other harmful materials. Drugs were adulterated if they fell below the standards laid down in the United States Pharmacopoeia or the National Formulary or any other standards under which they were sold. Foods and drugs were declared to be misbranded if their packages or labels bore statements which were "false or misleading in any particular," if one was sold under the name of another, if the contents of packages had been removed and others substituted, or if the presence of certain narcotics or stimulants was not revealed. Food was also misbranded if its weight or measure was not plainly shown; drugs, if their packages or labels bore false claims of curative effects. The law authorized the seizure and forfeiture of adulterated or misbranded foods and drugs and made adulteration or misbranding a misdemeanor punishable by a fine of not more than $200 for the first offense, and a fine of not more than $300 or imprisonment for not more than one year, or both, for each subsequent offense.

As passed, the law was a substantial achievement; in operation, it proved to have a number of serious weaknesses. It failed to cover the growing trade in cosmetics or the sale of therapeutic devices such as sun lamps, orthopedic shoes, bust developers, and electric belts. It exempted foods sold under proprietary names and those labeled as compounds, imitations, or blends. Since it gave the Food and Drug Administration no authority to establish standards of identity for foods, it handicapped the Administration in proving that they were misbranded. Since it failed to authorize inspection of food processing plants, it prevented action to improve the conditions under which foodstuffs were prepared. The law did not control false advertising claims; it applied only to the statements made on the package containing the food or drug or the label affixed to it. In 1911, moreover, the Supreme Court held that the prohibition of statements that were "false or misleading in any particular" was limited to statements of fact concerning the identity or quality of a product and did not extend to claims concerning its beneficial effects.[2] This decision led to the adoption of a corrective amendment in 1912. But the amendment, through the efforts of the patent medicine lobby, forbade statements that were both "false and fraudulent," thus imposing on the Administration the burden of proving fraudulent intent. The law was administered by a small staff with an inadequate budget, operating under continuous pressure from the manufacturers whom it was supposed to regulate. Convictions were difficult to obtain, prison sentences were rare, and the fines imposed were so small as to amount to little more than a modest license fee.

A drive for stronger legislation got under way in the twenties and the thirties with the publication of a large number of books on the abuses of advertising. In its office in Washington, the Food and Drug Administration set up a museum that came to be known as the Chamber of Horrors. Here, in a series of exhibits, could be seen samples seized from foods on public sale—filthy candy, decayed fruit, worm-eaten nuts, butter full of maggots, and raisins infested with insects; samples of patent medicines to cure every known disease, with testimonials from their users, accompanied by copies of their death certificates; and samples of cosmetics—eye-lash beautifiers containing poisonous aniline dyes, hair removers containing thallium acetate, and hair tonics, freckle removers, ointments, and salves containing mercury or other dangerous ingredients—together with photographs of women who had been blinded, paralyzed, or permanently disfigured by their use.

In 1933, Rexford G. Tugwell was appointed Assistant Secretary of Agricul-

2 / *U.S.* v. *Johnson*, 221 U.S. 488.

ture and shortly thereafter sponsored the enactment of a new law. Associations of food, drug, patent medicine, and cosmetic manufacturers raised a slush fund of $500,000, lined up the press, attacked the Tugwell bill as un-American, and denounced Tugwell himself as a subversive character. By such tactics, the lobbyists succeeded in delaying action for five years. In the autumn of 1937, however, a drug manufacturer who wished to distribute sulfanilamide in liquid form added a deadly poison—diethylene glycol—as a solvent and put it on the market as Elixir Sulfanilamide, making no effort to test the mixture for toxicity. Of the 240 gallons made, the first 6 sold were found to be the certain cause of 73 deaths in 15 states and the probable cause of 20 others. At the same rate, distribution of the entire batch would have killed 3,720 people. The Food and Drug Administration seized the remaining stock and prosecuted the manufacturer. But it would have been powerless to act before the tragedy occurred. The shock of this experience contributed heavily to the enactment of a new law in 1938.

The Food, Drug, and Cosmetic Act of 1938

The Act of 1938 strengthened the earlier definitions of adulteration and misbranding. Food was now defined as adulterated if it contained any poisonous or deleterious substance, if it was colored with coal tars not approved by the Food and Drug Administration, if it was prepared under conditions that might result in contamination with filth or injury to health, or if it was packed in containers composed of substances that might make it injurious. Candy could no longer contain metallic trinkets or other inedible materials. The wording that defined misbranding to cover statements that were "false or misleading in any particular" was restored. Under an amendment adopted in 1930, the Administration had been authorized to establish standards of "quality, condition and/or fill of container" for canned goods, and such goods were said to be misbranded if failures to meet these standards were not disclosed. Now the Administration was empowered to set up minimum standards of identity and fill for all foodstuffs, and disclosure of failure to meet them was required. The exemption formerly granted to foods sold under brand names was withdrawn, and for foods, as for drugs, it was provided that the ingredients of those departing from established standards must be shown. Foods and drugs were both defined as misbranded if their containers were so made or filled as to mislead the purchaser. For drugs, moreover, the law required inclusion on the label of directions for use and warning against misuse.

The scope of the law was extended to cover cosmetics and therapeutic devices. A cosmetic was declared to be adulterated if it "is or may be injurious" under customary or prescribed conditions of use, and to be misbranded—as with foods and drugs—if its label bore statements that were "false or misleading in any particular." Here, again, deceptive containers were forbidden. But the rules for cosmetics were less stringent than those for foods and drugs. Soaps were exempted. In the case of hair dyes, the use of coal-tar colors was permitted if their labels stated that they might irritate the skin, gave directions for making skin tests, and warned that use on eyebrows and eyelashes could lead to blindness. In general, no provision was made for the establishment of standards, and the disclosure of ingredients was not required.

The law was strengthened, however, in other ways. The government was authorized to inspect factories producing foods, drugs, devices, and cosmetics. Where the processing of foodstuffs might involve a risk of contamination so serious as to menace public health, it was empowered to license manufacturers and to establish standards of sanitation as a condition for granting licenses. Drug concerns developing new drugs were required to obtain approval from the Food and Drug Administration before putting them on sale, and the Administration was authorized to deny approval to drugs that had not been tested and to those that were found to be unsafe. Penalties for violation of the law were increased to $1,000 or a year's imprisonment or both for an unwitting or negligent first offense, and to $10,000 or three years or both for offenses involving intent to defraud or mislead. At the same time, the advertising of foods, drugs, and cosmetics was brought under the supervision of the Federal Trade Commission by the Wheeler-Lea Act, discussed below.

Chemical Additives Amendments

With the continued growth of food processing industries, producing on a large scale for distribution to mass markets, there has been increasing use of chemicals in bakery products, salad dressings, peanut butter, ice cream, soft drinks, and many other foods. Chemicals are added for a variety of purposes: to facilitate processing, to compensate for the loss of nutrients—vitamins, proteins, and minerals—in processing, to prevent deterioration or preserve an appearance of freshness, and to improve color or taste. Until 1958, if the FDA had established a standard that excluded a chemical from a product, the use of the chemical might be discontinued by the producer or, if continued, had to be acknowledged on the label. And where it could be proved that a chemical had injured the consumers of a product, its use could be stopped. But chemicals could still be introduced into the nation's food supply without making prior tests to determine whether they were safe. Among 704 chemicals so used in 1950, the FDA and the Public Health Service found that 428 were known to be safe; the safety of the other 276 was unknown.[3]

For many years, flour was bleached with nitrogen trichloride to make it white, and the use of this chemical was continued for several years after it was discovered, in 1946, that dogs fed bread baked from flour so treated developed canine hysteria. Nutritive elements are still removed in the process of preserving flour for commercial distribution and then restored, in part, in the process of "enriching" bread with chemicals. Bread has also been given a more enduring appearance of softness by the use of emulsifying agents such as the poly-

3 / Select Committee to Investigate the Use of Chemicals in Foods and Cosmetics, *Report on Food* (82d Cong., 2d Sess., House Report 2356), p. 4.

oxyethylene stearates. There are many other cases in which materials added to foods have been found to have been harmful. An agent used to prevent frozen peaches from turning brown was found to be highly toxic. Sodium nitrate, used to keep the color of meat from fading, was found to damage the blood of experimental animals. The synthetic hormone stilbestrol, used to fatten chickens, was found to induce cancer in rats.

The Administration's power over the use of chemical additives in foods was strengthened when Congress passed the Food Additives Amendment of 1958. A processor who wishes to add a chemical to a food now bears the burden of proving that it is safe. To do so, he must pretest it by feeding it to animals and submit the results of his tests to the FDA. If an additive is found to cause cancer, its use in any quantity is forbidden. In other cases, the Administration will establish tolerances, specifying the quantities in which a chemical may be used. As a general rule, such a tolerance is set at 1 percent of the smallest quantity found to have had harmful effects. Under the terms of the law, the safety of additives in use before 1958 had to be established by 1960; the safety of new additives had to be proven before they were used. Food processors predicted that the law would ruin the industry. In initiating its enforcement, however, the FDA exempted some 600 chemicals as safe, permitted continued use of some 200 others during the period required for testing, and banned the use of only half a dozen until their safety could be proved. Critics of the measure question whether tests applied to animals afford an adequate indication of the safety with which chemicals can be consumed by humans. But the law, whatever its limitations, marks a great advance over what had gone before.

The 1958 amendment did not apply to color additives. In 1959, the FDA, having found that coal-tar colors used in lipsticks had damaged the kidneys, liver and spleen of laboratory rats, ordered all lipsticks containing any of 17 such colors taken off the market. Cosmetic manufacturers protested that the colors were harmless in the quantities in which they were used. But under the Act of 1938, which then applied, the FDA had no alternative but completely to forbid their use. This situation led to the enactment of the Color Additives Amendment of 1960. Under this measure, color additives cannot be applied to foods, drugs, or cosmetics if their use, in any quantity, is found to have caused cancer. Otherwise, unless exempted by the FDA, they can be used only within tolerances which the Administration fixes as safe and only from batches which it has cleared as safe.

The Pesticides Amendments

Pesticides and herbicides are poisons that are used extensively by farmers to kill insects, rodents, and other pests that destroy crops and to kill weeds that retard their growth, and by public authorities to destroy such insect pests as mosquitos, moths, beetles, and fire ants, and to keep down weeds along highways. Residues of these poisons are left on foods to be eaten by man. Other quantities are inhaled or absorbed through the skin. Accumulated over the years, they may cause chronic poisoning or induce cancer.

Under the Pesticide Amendment of 1954, a manufacturer of such poisons is required to apply to the Department of Agriculture and the FDA for registration and for the establishment of tolerances. In his application, he must show how the poison is to be used and what amounts are apt to remain on a food crop. He must report on its toxicity and cancerous effects as revealed by laboratory tests. The Department of Agriculture evaluates the usefulness of the poison and estimates the residue that is likely to remain from its use. The FDA then evaluates the data on its toxicity and its cancer-producing effects, and establishes tolerances, indicating the residue that may safely remain on foods. If there is danger of cancer, it fixes a tolerance of zero. In 1959, the law was further amended to require that warnings be printed on the labels of potentially hazardous pesticides and herbicides and instructions given for their safe use. But under these amendments, as they stood until 1964, the government was required to register the poisons and clear them for use unless it could prove that they had done actual harm.

In 1962, the late Rachel Carson published a series of articles in the *New Yorker,* later appearing as a Book of the Month, under the title "Silent Spring." Her book was a vigorous protest against the massive spraying of crops and weeds with dangerous chemicals and a warning concerning the danger of such spraying to bees, birds, wild and domestic animals, and human beings. Chemical manufacturers ridiculed her thesis and were supported in their position by the Department of Agriculture.

President Kennedy ordered an independent study to be made by a panel of eminent scientists. The panel, reporting in 1963, endorsed the continued use of pesticides and herbicides but agreed with Miss Carson that the gaps in our knowledge concerning their long-term effects, particularly on reproduction and heredity, are so large that great conservatism is desirable in permitting mass spraying and in setting tolerances for residues on foods. The panel recommended cutting down on the use of the most toxic pesticides until more knowledge could be obtained concerning their effects.

There was mounting evidence against pesticides in the following years: there was a series of fish kills on the lower Mississippi; residues were found in foodstuffs, in cow's milk, and in mothers' milk. The Department of Agriculture lost its enthusiasm for massive spraying and shifted its interest to biological methods of controlling pests. The Act was amended, in 1964, to empower the Secretary of Agriculture to suspend or cancel the registration of a pesticide or herbicide whenever the article or its label do not conform to the requirements of the law. Agriculture's enforcement of the law was less than vigorous. In 1968, the General Accounting Office charged that the Department had failed to prosecute violators and had not recalled unregistered, adulterated, and misbranded goods.[4]

4 / *New York Times,* September 17, 1968.

Decisions as to the permissible use of pesticides were subsequently shifted to a committee composed of the Secretaries of Agriculture, Interior, and Health, Education, and Welfare. At the end of 1969, the Secretary of HEW announced that the government was phasing out all but the most essential use of DDT over the next two years, cutting it to less than a tenth of the former volume. The government now has the power to keep off the market substances that have not been proven to be effective and safe. It still cannot control the way in which pesticides and herbicides are employed once they are cleared for use. The law merely gives assurance that the chemicals will be safe if they are used as directed.

The Drug Amendment of 1962

During the years 1959 through 1961, the Senate Subcommittee on Antitrust and Monopoly, under the chairmanship of Estes Kefauver, investigated the drug manufacturing industry. The committee found that drugs put on the market were sometimes ineffective and unsafe, that they were misrepresented, and that they were overpriced.

The procedure employed in clearing a drug for sale under the Act of 1938 was as follows: The drug manufacturer was required to present evidence to the FDA, not that the drug was effective, but that it was safe. To obtain such evidence, he first tested the drug on animals. If these tests revealed no harmful effects, he sent the drug to a number of physicians, of his own choosing, asking them to test it on their patients. The FDA did not control the planning of these tests or supervise their execution. The physicians making the tests might or might not be properly qualified. They might or might not tell their patients that they were being used as guinea pigs. Only a small minority of the physicians invited to make such tests may have done so. Those who did so may not have kept systematic records of the results. Their reports may have been inadequate. Some of them may even have reported favorable results, for a fee, without actually making the tests. On the basis of the evidence thus obtained, the manufacturer presented his application for approval to the FDA. If the officer who examined the application gave his approval, the drug was cleared for use. If he disapproved, he had to obtain the support of his superiors in the Administration before the application could be denied. Unless the FDA acted within 60 days, or at most within 180 days, the drug automatically became eligible for sale.

All drugs have some side effects. Caution must therefore be exercised in their use. But the committee found that nine tenths of drug advertising made no mention of side effects or undertook to minimize them. Public health was thereby endangered.

New drugs may be patented in the United States. Other drug manufacturers can be prevented from competing with the patent holder by bringing infringement suits. The monopoly position thus obtained is reinforced by identifying drugs by trade names rather than by their generic names. These devices have been employed as a means of obtaining high prices and profits. Drugs have been sold at higher prices to individual consumers than to the government, at home than abroad, and under trade names than under generic names. The committee found one pill that was produced at $1.57 a bottle and sold at $17.90, a markup of 1,118 percent; another with a markup of 7,079 percent. It found that drug manufacturers, as a whole, averaged a return, after income taxes, of 18.9 percent on their investment, a figure twice that realized by manufacturers in general, and that three of the major drug companies had made profits of 33 to 38 percent after taxes.[5]

Senator Kefauver introduced legislation designed to correct these abuses. His bill was opposed by the Pharmaceutical Manufacturers Association and by the American Medical Association. Substitute measures that would so seriously have weakened the provisions of the Kefauver bill as to destroy its value were introduced in the Senate and in the House. Drug reform was to be put on the shelf.

At this juncture, it became known that the use of a sleeping pill called thalidomide by pregnant women in West Germany had resulted in the birth of more than 7,000 babies lacking arms or legs. An American drug manufacturer had applied for permission to sell the drug in the United States. In the absence of experimental evidence from American tests showing the drug to be unsafe, the FDA lacked authority to forbid its sale. Each time the application came up for action, however, Dr. Frances O. Kelsey, an FDA examiner, ruled that it was incomplete and sent it back for more information. Dr. Kelsey was put under heavy pressure by the drug industry and its Congressional allies to give her approval, but she stood firm. Then it came to be known that the manufacturer had sent 2,500,000 of the pills to 1,267 physicians in the United States for experimental use. Nobody knew how many pregnant American women may have taken them. But one such woman went to Sweden to obtain an abortion, and it was learned that her child, if born, would have been deformed. Thalidomide thus provided the shock that demolished the opposition to the Kefauver bill and made possible the enactment of the Drug Amendments of 1962.

Under the resulting law: (1) All drug factories are to be inspected at least biennially. (2) Drug manufacturers must maintain quality by following good manufacturing practices, as defined by the FDA. (3) The Administration can forbid the testing of drugs on humans if it finds that clinical testing on animals has not been adequate. (4) A physician must get the consent of his patients before giving them experimental drugs, unless he decides that this is not feasible or not in a patient's interest. (5) All antibiotics must be tested, batch by batch, for strength and purity. (6) A manufacturer applying for approval of a drug must prove not only that it is safe but also that it is effective. (7) No drug can be put on the market until it has been specifically approved by the FDA. (8) Drug manufacturers must keep records on clinical experience with the use of drugs and report on this experience upon request. (9) Drug labels and advertisements must contain information on injurious side effects. (10) They must pre-

5 / See *Administered Prices: Drugs* (87th Cong., 1st Sess., Senate Report 448, 1961); Richard Harris, "Annals of Legislation," *New Yorker,* March 14, 21, 28, 1964; Estes Kefauver, *In a Few Hands* (New York: Pantheon Books, 1965), chap. i.

sent the generic names of drugs in type at least half as large as that used for their trade names. (11) The FDA is authorized to review all generic names and establish simpler ones where they are needed. (12) The FDA may summarily remove a drug from the market if it has evidence that it carries an imminent threat to health.

Senator Kefauver had proposed that a manufacturer be required to grant licenses to other manufacturers under any drug patent after an initial period of three years, or in any case, where he was selling a drug at more than 500 percent of its cost of production. This provision was killed in the Senate. The law still provides no protection against exorbitant prices or profits.

In its enforcement of the new law, the FDA has laid down detailed rules to govern the testing of drugs on animals and on humans. It has directed manufacturers to maintain records of clinical experience with respect to the safety of new drugs. It has asked them to report not only on the effectiveness of new drugs but also on that of all drugs introduced since passage of the Act of 1938, showing that the claims made on labels and in promotional literature are justified. It has undertaken surveillance of the advertising of prescription drugs, making sure that their effectiveness is not misrepresented and that information on their side effects is not withheld. In 1970, the FDA issued a leaflet to be given to women purchasing birth-control pills, specifying the cases in which such pills should not be used and indicating the risks involved in their use.

The Food and Drug Administration

The work load of the FDA is large and varied. Within a year, it examines hundreds of applications to certify new drugs and new food additives and tests thousands of batches of antibiotics and color additives, rejecting a minor fraction and clearing the rest for sale. In the same period, it inspects half of the 14,000 drug establishments in the United States and more than a third of the 88,000 food establishments. It examines thousands of lots of raw agricultural products, checking on residues of pesticides. It prepares standards by which to judge adulteration of foods, holds hearings on them, modifies them where necessary, and adopts them for use. It investigates tens of thousands of reports of poisonings attributed to drugs, chemical additives, cosmetics, pesticides, and hazardous household substances. It maintains surveillance over drugs after they have been cleared for use, recalling hundreds of them from the market and sending warning letters to physicians where it finds them to be unsafe. It undertakes to prevent illegal sales of prescription drugs by pharmacists and by dope peddlers.

The FDA has been an object of constant criticism. Drug manufacturers complain of unduly stringent standards and undue delay in the approval of new drugs. Consumers charge that there is laxity in testing and that unfavorable test results have been suppressed. It was disclosed in 1969 that a fourth to a half of the tests conducted by drug manufacturers for FDA were made in Southern prisons by a single testing company whose tests were cursory and almost uniformly favorable.[6] The FDA was aware of this situation but had not acted to rectify it.

Goods produced in violation of the law can be seized and persons guilty of violation fined and imprisoned. Each year FDA inspectors make hundreds of seizures of filthy and decomposed foods, of hazardous substances lacking adequate warnings, of harmful drugs and fraudulent cancer cures, scores of seizures of foods containing excessive pesticide residues, of foods containing illegal additives, of poisonous cosmetics, and fraudulent devices for the treatment of disease. Violators are turned over to the Department of Justice for prosecution. The record indicates that many offenders are found to be in violation again and again, that criminal penalties are sought only in the most flagrant cases, and that the sentences imposed by the courts are so light as to have little effect as a deterrent.[7]

The FDA is understaffed and underfinanced, its personnel for 1969 standing at 4,250, its appropriation at $73 million. Its leadership, since 1966, has been strong but constantly changing, with three different commissioners in four years. It has been repeatedly reorganized but has never had the active interest and support of the head of its Department. In 1969 a study panel appointed by the Commissioner reported that the agency was unable to develop the kind of concerted and coordinated efforts needed to deal adequately and simultaneously with its myriad problems. "We are currently not equipped," it said, "to cope with the challenge."[8]

UNFAIR METHODS OF COMPETITION

When the courts developed rules condemning unfair methods of competition as violations of the common law, and when the Congress forbade employment of such methods, in Section 5 of the Federal Trade Commission Act, it was not so much their purpose to protect the consumer as to serve the interest of business by protecting the scrupulous businessman against his unscrupulous competitor. Protection of the consumer was not explicitly made a function of the Commission until the Wheeler-Lea Amendment was passed in 1938. But protection of business has been its duty both before and since.

A number of orders issued by the Commission have directed businessmen to cease and desist from molesting their competitors in a variety of ways: by spying on them and stealing their trade secrets, by threatening them with litigation, by spreading false rumors about their credit, by disparaging their products, by inducing their customers to break contracts, and by bribing purchasing agents and salesmen to obstruct the distribution of their competitors' goods. The number of such orders has not been large, and some of them have been reversed upon appeal. In a larger number of orders, businessmen have been

6 / *New York Times,* August 13, 1969.

7 / On the abuses of the drug industry and the performance of FDA, see Morton Mintz, *The Therapeutic Nightmare* (Boston, Mass.: Houghton-Mifflin Co., 1965).

8 / *Business Week,* August 6, 1969, pp. 104-6.

directed to abandon misrepresentation, and here the Commission has almost invariably been upheld. Orders against misrepresentation serve to protect consumers. But until 1938 this was not their legal purpose. Under the law, as it then stood, they were issued to safeguard competitors against deceitful diversion of patronage. Any protection that they might afford to consumers was purely incidental.

Preventing Misrepresentation

The number of cases in which the FTC has taken action against misrepresentation runs into the thousands. Orders have been issued repeatedly, over the years, involving practices such as these:

1. Misrepresenting the character, composition, or quality of goods: passing off one good as another—cotton as linen, rayon as silk, woodchuck as mink, rabbit as seal, gumwood as mahogany, and veneers as solid wood—selling imitations as originals, seconds as prime quality, adulterated goods as pure, and secondhand goods as new.
2. Misrepresenting the geographic origin of goods: giving the impression that quality is high by claiming a familiar source, such as Havana for cigars not made in Cuba and Panama for hats not made in Panama.
3. Falsely claiming endorsement of goods: suggesting that impartial and responsible persons have investigated and approved their quality—describing goods, for instance, as "Government Issue" or "U.S. Regulation" when they are not, or intimating that they have been endorsed by the Boy Scouts or the Red Cross.
4. Misrepresenting the usefulness of goods: making false statements concerning the curative powers of patent medicines, the corrective properties of various devices, or the beautifying effects of cosmetics, or failing to disclose the potential harmfulness of drugs.
5. Misrepresenting the real price of goods: advertising an article sold only in combination with others as "Free," indicating that goods are being sold below cost when they are not, or suggesting that bargains are being offered by first marking prices up and then marking them down.
6. Misrepresenting the nature of the seller's business: claiming a status that implies a higher quality or a lower price, as is the case, for instance, when blenders of whiskey claim to be distillers, when manufacturers of clothing describe themselves as weavers, and when dealers in furniture parade as manufacturers.

The Commission has also proceeded against another method of sales promotion that would appear to be socially undesirable, ordering manufacturers of penny candies to cease and desist from providing retailers with selling schemes, accompanied by advertising displays, whereby the quantity or price of candy obtained by school children was determined by chance. Here, though no misrepresentation was involved, it was held that inculcation of the gambling spirit was harmful, that children were unable to protect themselves, and that scrupulous manufacturers might be forced to adopt the practice in order to avoid the loss of sales to their less scrupulous competitors.

Unfair Methods and the Courts

In general, the Commission's authority to issue orders against misrepresentation has been upheld when these orders have been appealed to the courts. In the Winsted Hosiery case[9] in 1922, the Supreme Court upheld an order against a manufacturer who sold socks containing little or no wool under such names as cashmere, merino, worsted, and wool. In the Royal Milling case[10] in 1933, it upheld an order directing a concern that merely mixed and blended flour to desist from representing itself as a milling company. In the Algoma Lumber case[11] in 1934, it supported the Commission in ordering a number of West Coast lumbermen to discontinue the practice of describing yellow pine as "California White Pine." And in the Keppel case,[12] in the same year, it sanctioned an order against the sale, in interstate commerce, of candy to be resold through lotteries. In the Standard Education Society case[13] in 1937, the Court upheld an order requiring the publisher of an encyclopaedia to stop representing that sets were being given free to selected buyers for advertising purposes and that payments asked of them covered nothing but the cost of periodic loose-leaf supplements. And in 1941, the Supreme Court refused to review decisions of a lower court upholding the Commission in ordering Ford and General Motors to desist from claiming that their interest rate on installment sales was 6 percent when, in fact, the 6 percent was figured on their original loans, ignoring monthly payments, and the actual rate of interest on balances remaining unpaid was 11.5 percent.[14]

But the Commission has not always been so fortunate when it has appeared before the courts. The law itself is clear enough. In plain words, "unfair methods of competition in commerce are hereby declared unlawful" and action is authorized "if it shall appear to the Commission that a proceeding by it . . . would be to the interest of the public. . . ." But the Supreme Court has curbed the Commission, from time to time, by holding that a method it has proscribed was not "unfair," that it was not harmful to "competition," that it was not "in" commerce, or that action against it was not in the public interest.

In the Gratz case[15] in 1920, where an order had been issued against a con-

9 / *FTC v. Winsted Hosiery Co.,* 258 U.S. 483.

10 / *FTC v. Royal Milling Co.,* 288 U.S. 212.

11 / *FTC v. Algoma Lumber Co.,* 291 U.S. 67.

12 / *FTC v. R. F. Keppel & Bro.,* 291 U.S. 304.

13 / *FTC v. Standard Education Society,* 302 U.S. 112.

14 / *General Motors Corp. v. FTC,* 114 F. 2d 33 (1940); certiorari denied, 312 U.S. 682 (1941); *Ford Motor Co. v. FTC,* 120 F. 2d 175 (1941); certiorari denied, 314 U.S. 668 (1941).

15 / *FTC v. Gratz,* 253 U.S. 421.

tract that tied the sale of bagging to the sale of baling ties, the Court held that the use of a tying contract (though it might be illegal under the Clayton Act) was not an unfair method of competition, within the meaning of the Trade Commission Act, since the words *unfair methods* "are clearly inapplicable to practices never heretofore regarded as opposed to good morals because characterized by deception, bad faith, fraud, or oppression, or as against public policy. . . ." The law was thus amended by the insertion of the word "heretofore" and the principle established that the Commission could not issue orders against new forms of unfairness, but could act only where it could find a precedent in common or statute law. This interpretation stood until the Court handed down its decision in the Keppel case[16] in 1934: "We cannot say that the Commission's jurisdiction extends only to those types of practices which happen to have been litigated before this Court. Neither the language nor the history of the Act suggests that Congress intended to confine the forbidden methods to fixed and unyielding categories." The restrictive rule of the Gratz case was thus reversed after nearly 15 years.

In the Raladam case[17] in 1931, the Commission had ordered the makers of Marmola to cease and desist from claiming that the product could be safely administered or that it would reduce obesity. The Court agreed that the advertising was unfair and the Commission's action in the public interest but held the order invalid on the ground that "competition" had not been damaged, since there was no evidence of the existence of truthful manufacturers of slenderizing preparations who might be harmed by Raladam's mendacity. The Commission was thus denied the right to protect consumers against misrepresentation where it was the general practice in a trade. This position was reversed in a second case involving the Raladam Company[18] in 1942. But the loophole had already been plugged by Congress when it passed the Wheeler-Lea Act in 1938.

Two other decisions, imposing limits on the Commission's powers, still stand. In the Klesner case[19] in 1929, where each of two small merchants in Washington, D.C., called his store "The Shade Shop" and the Commission had ordered one of them to desist, the Court reversed the order on the ground that the controversy was a private one, to be settled by a private suit, and that no "specific and substantial" public interest was involved. In the Bunte case[20] in 1941, the Court reversed an order against a manufacturer who was making candy in Illinois for sale by lottery in Illinois, on the ground that his activity, while it affected commerce, was not "in" commerce, as the law required. These decisions have been regretted as limiting the Commission's jurisdiction. But they may also have the advantage of directing its attention from a multitude of petty cases to a smaller number of more important ones.

16 / *FTC* v. *R. F. Keppel & Bro.*, 291 U.S. 304.

17 / *FTC* v. *Raladam Co.*, 283 U.S. 643.

18 / *FTC* v. *Raladam Co.*, 316 U.S. 149.

19 / *FTC* v. *Klesner*, 280 U.S. 19.

20 / *FTC* v. *Bunte Bros., Inc.*, 312 U.S. 349.

DECEPTIVE ADVERTISING

Since the adoption of the Wheeler-Lea Amendment in 1938, Section 5 of the Trade Commission Act has forbidden, not only unfair methods of competition, but also deceptive acts or practices in the sale of goods in general, and four new sections—12 to 15 inclusive—have empowered the Commission to move against false advertisements of foods, drugs, corrective or curative devices, and cosmetics, in particular. Protection of the consumer, for its own sake, has thus become a major part of the Commission's work.

The Commission's Powers

The law provides more methods of dealing with falsehood in the advertising of foods, drugs, devices, and cosmetics than in the advertising of other goods. For goods in general, the FTC may employ its usual procedures, accepting assurances of discontinuance, issuing complaints and orders, and suing to obtain the imposition of a civil penalty where an order has been disobeyed. For foods, drugs, devices, and cosmetics, the Wheeler-Lea Act empowered the Commission to ask a district court to issue an injunction to stop dissemination of a false advertisement, pending the completion of its own action in the case. And it made dissemination of such advertisements a crime, punishable by a fine up to $5,000 or imprisonment up to six months or both for the first offense, and by fine up to $10,000, or imprisonment up to a year, or both, for a subsequent offense, if it could be shown either (1) that the use of misrepresented products had been injurious to health, or (2) that misrepresentation was undertaken with intent to defraud or mislead. It is difficult, however, to prove that misrepresentation caused injury or that it was intentional. Criminal suits are therefore likely to be few.

A different standard is established for judging falsehood in advertising under the Wheeler-Lea Act than for judging misbranding under the Food, Drug, and Cosmetic Act. A good is misbranded if its label is "false or misleading in any particular." An advertisement is false if it is "misleading in a material respect." The latter standard is obviously weaker than the former one. But the law also provides that advertisements shall be judged not only by statements made but also by those "suggested," and by the extent to which they fail to reveal "material" facts. The force of the law thus turns on what statements or suggestions, and what omissions, are to be regarded as "material." Depending on the judgment of the courts, the amount of misrepresentation permitted under this standard may be large or small.

The Control of Advertising

In the course of a year, the FTC receives thousands of complaints concerning deceptive advertising and, among these, investigates a few hundred. It examines hundreds of thousands of printed advertisements and radio and TV commercials, and questions one in 15 or 20. From all this, less than 500 items may lead to action. When action is taken, an inquiry is first made by correspondence. If the matter cannot be settled in this way, it is referred to one of the Commission's field offices for an investigation and report. Samples of the advertiser's products may then be obtained and turned over to technical agencies of the government— such as the Food and Drug Administration, the Public Health Service, or the Bureau of Standards—for analysis. Where evidence of misrepresentation is thus developed, the Commission may go forward with a case.

In a great majority of instances, actions against false or misleading advertising are dropped when the Commission receives written assurance that statements to which it has objected will no longer be made. A smaller number of cases (a hundred or more during a year) go through the mill of complaint, hearing, and formal order. Various manufacturers have agreed, for example, or the Commission has ordered them, to desist from representing:

that Regelex, a calendar device, provides an unfailing method of birth control;

that Beau-T-form Maternity Garments enable a woman to maintain the youthfulness of her figure during pregnancy, eliminate the discomforts of pregnancy, or promote easy or safe delivery;

that Nurserytyme crib mattresses will keep a baby's spine straight, materially help a child develop properly, or have an appreciable effect on a child's future health;

that Dry-Tabs, a drug preparation, will correct the bed-wetting habit;

that Fashion-Glo Bust Cream will beneficially affect the structure and firmness of the breast;

that Herbold Pomade will color the roots of the hair and prevent the hair from becoming gray;

that Nu Maid Margarine provides the user with increased pep, energy, vitality, vigor, strength, or endurance;

that Carter's Little Liver Pills will have any therapeutic action on any condition, disease, or disorder of the liver; that it will increase or beneficially influence the formation, secretion, or flow of bile; that it is a cure, remedy, or competent or effective treatment of those conditions in which an individual feels "down and out," "blue," "down in the dumps," "worn out," "sunk," "all in," "mean," "low," "cross," "tired," "miserable," "grouchy," "cranky," "peevish," "fagged out," "grumpy," or "rundown";

that J-O Paste will rid the premises of rats and that rats consuming the product will leave the premises to die;

that Ever-Seal caskets afford the body permanent protection against the elements.

Every such assurance or order applies only to the company that it names. Where similar misrepresentations are made by many firms, action leading to orders must be taken case by case. The FTC has sought to meet this problem by issuing statements of policy that apply to whole industries or to certain practices that are followed by firms in different fields. It has issued a guide distinguishing statements that should not be made from those that could be made in advertising automobile tires, for instance, and another attacking the widespread practice of stating fictitiously high prices, then pretending to offer substantial bargains. Such guides may persuade advertisers to modify their claims; they also indicate the grounds on which the Commission may issue a complaint.

Weaknesses of Control

The effectiveness of the Commission's efforts to check falsehood in advertising is open to question. The usual case is closed by an assurance of discontinuance, which is nothing more than a slap on the wrist. An order carries no penalty for past deceptions and does nothing to prevent future ones. In one notorious case, the FTC, beginning in 1959, investigated claims by the manufacturer of Geritol that his product cured tiredness, loss of strength, run-down feeling, nervousness, and irritability by providing iron to "tired blood." In 1962, the Commission issued a formal complaint. In 1965, it issued an order to cease and desist. In 1967, this order was upheld by a circuit court, making it final and binding. In 1968, the Commission ruled that the manufacturer had violated the order. In 1969, it asked the Department of Justice to bring suit to compel compliance. In 1970, the Department sued, asking that the manufacturer be fined $500,000 and his advertising agency another $500,000 for violations of the Commission's order. In all this time the company continued to advertise the iron in Geritol as a remedy for bad blood.

The FTC may sue for an injunction to prevent false advertising of foods and drugs under Section 12 of its Act but it cannot do so in the case of other products under Section 5. It has often been recommended that this power be extended to Section 5. But it must be noted that the Commission has scarcely ever sought an injunction under Section 12. It should be noted, too, that a civil penalty for violating a Commission order against false advertising is seldom sought and that a criminal prosecution is virtually unknown.

The FTC has suffered a number of reverses upon appeal. The courts have tended to accept a good bit of misrepresentation as a matter of course. In the Ostermoor case[21] in 1927, a lower court reversed the Commission's order against an advertisement that pictured the filling of a mattress, when liberated, as fanning out to many times the thickness of the mattress itself. Said the court, ". . . the slightest pictorial exaggeration of the qualities of an article cannot be deemed to be . . . a misrepresentation. . . . The time-honored custom of at least merely slight puffing . . . has not come under a legal ban." And this precedent was followed in later cases, the courts permitting one concern to

21 / *Ostermoor & Co.* v. *FTC,* 16 F. 2d 962.

advertise a "perfect" lubricant that will operate a car for an "amazing" distance,[22] and another to represent a cure for obesity as "easy," "simple," and "safe."[23] In 1953, however, a court upheld a Commission order directing the Book-of-the-Month Club to desist from advertising as "Free" a book sent to a subscriber who could obtain it only by signing a contract to purchase four other books during the year.[24] In 1957, in a case where the FTC had found that a manufacturer's claims that his shoe insert aided "balance," "stance," and "posture," eliminated foot fatigue, and improved health were, in fact, deceptive, and a lower court had held that they were mere puffing, the Supreme Court held that the Commission's findings of fact should be final and directed that its order be enforced.[25] In 1959, after 16 years of litigation, a Court of Appeals finally sustained the Commission's order that the word "Liver" be dropped from the name of Carter's Little Liver Pills.[26] And in 1965, the Supreme Court upheld a Commission order in one of a number of cases involving the use of deceptive demonstrations in television commercials. In this case, the Colgate-Palmolive Company had pretended to show that an application of its Rapid-Shave cream made it possible to shave sandpaper clean with a single razor stroke, but instead of sandpaper it had used a prop made of plexiglas sprinkled with sand. The court held that the use of such a prop involved material deception.[27]

The FTC, although aided by these decisions, still has an uphill fight. The Commission, rather than the advertiser, bears the burden of proof. It must draw a difficult line between harmless exaggeration and harmful deception. It must base its orders on evidence that the advertiser's claims are false and on testimony that they are, in fact, deceptive. When orders are issued, cases won, and sanctions imposed, moreover, they apply only to the company that makes the advertised product, not to the advertising agency that prepares the misleading copy, to the publisher who prints it, or to the station that broadcasts it. And then the advertiser need only drop the old campaign and embark upon a new one as deceptive as the last. The Commission cannot require the publication of retractions. It cannot censor copy in advance. And it can scarcely be expected to keep pace with the inventive copywriters in the advertising agencies. The control that it exerts may moderate some of the more serious abuses of advertising. But it is not to be described as rigorous.

Cigarette Labels and Advertisements

In January, 1964, a panel of 10 outstanding scientists and physicians, selected from a list of 150 by a process designed to insure their impartiality and asked by the Surgeon General of the United States to survey the voluminous evidence

22 / *Kidder Oil Co.* v. *FTC,* 117 F. 2d 894 (1941).

23 / *Carlay Co.* v. *FTC,* 153 F. 2d 493 (1946).

24 / *Book-of-the-Month Club* v. *FTC,* 202 F. 2d 486.

25 / *FTC* v. *Sewell,* 353 U.S. 969.

26 / *Carter Products, Inc.* v. *FTC,* 288 F. 2d 461.

27 / *FTC* v. *Colgate-Palmolive Co.,* 377 U.S. 942.

regarding the relation between cigarette smoking and health, made a unanimous report, running to 387 pages.[28] The panel found that the average male cigarette smoker ran a 9- to 10-fold greater risk, and a heavy smoker ran a 20-fold greater risk of developing lung cancer than did a nonsmoker, that the cigarette smoker also ran a greater risk of dying from pulmonary and coronary diseases, and that smoking thus operated to shorten human life.

Within a week, the FTC announced hearings on proposals to regulate cigarette labeling and advertising. In June, following these hearings, the commission announced that, beginning on January 1, 1965, it would deem it a deceptive practice to sell cigarettes in packs or cartons that failed to carry a label reading, "Caution: Cigarette smoking is dangerous to health. It may cause death from cancer and other diseases" or alternative wording to the same effect. Beginning July 1, 1965, moreover, it would deem it a deceptive practice to omit this warning from cigarette advertisements.

This announcement led to the formation, in Congress, of a powerful bloc of tobacco-state Senators and Representatives, determined to defend cigarettes down to the last butt. In response to their pressure, the FTC postponed the effective date of its labeling order so that Congress might consider legislation to supersede it. This legislation, as enacted by Congress and signed by President Johnson in July, 1965, required that each pack of cigarettes bear this warning: "Caution: cigarette smoking *may* (Italics supplied) be hazardous to your health," with no mention of its contribution to the death rate. And it went on to forbid the Federal Trade Commission and the government of any state or city to impose any regulation on the advertising of cigarettes for the next four years.

Statistical, clinical, and pathological evidence on the significance of cigarette smoking as a cause of death from lung cancer, coronary heart disease, and other ailments accumulated over the following years. Government and business both responded. In 1967, the Federal Communications Commission ordered all radio and TV stations carrying cigarette commercials to broadcast offsetting announcements regarding the perils of smoking. In 1968, the Federal Trade Commission recommended that all cigarette advertising on radio and TV be discontinued. In 1969, the broadcasting networks proposed to phase out all cigarette advertising over a period of four years. The cigarette industry agreed to terminate all advertising on radio and TV by September, 1970. In that year, Congress took final action. It strengthened the wording of the warning on cigarette packages. It outlawed the advertising of cigarettes on radio and television broadcasts after January 1, 1971. It forbade the FTC (unless expressly permitted to do so) to require health warnings in other cigarette advertising before January 1, 1972.

28 / *Smoking and Health, Report of the Advisory Committee to the Surgeon-General of the Public Health Service,* Department of Health, Education, and Welfare.

Chapter 26

PROTECTING INVESTORS AGAINST FRAUD

When a person puts his money in a bank, buys a life insurance policy, or purchases stocks or bonds, he must depend upon the competence and integrity of those with whom he deals. His bank might be mismanaged, and its assets stolen; he cannot himself examine its books or inspect its vaults. His insurance contract might carry, in small type, provisions that would limit his potential benefits; lacking the knowledge to analyze it, he is likely to take the agent's word. His insurance company might gamble with his savings; he cannot check on its investment policies. The new issues of stocks and bonds offered him by security salesmen might represent no actual undertaking, might not be backed by genuine assets, or might be overpriced. The market on which he buys and sells old issues might be so rigged that he would pay more and take less for them than they were worth. If his corporation prospers, the earnings that should come to him might be diverted to insiders. If it goes bankrupt, the assets that should be his on reorganization might be so shuffled as to go to someone else. If he were to attempt to diversify his risks by buying shares in an investment company, he might find it run by bankers as a dumping ground for issues that the market had refused. Stocks and bonds, like foods and drugs, may be adulterated and misbranded. The buyer of securities, like those who purchase other goods, may be ill equipped to protect himself against the seller who misrepresents his wares. It is for these reasons that government has moved, first at common law and then through state and federal legislation, to safeguard the interests of investors by regulating banks, savings institutions, and life insurance companies, by preventing misrepresentation in the sale of securities, by regulating securities dealers, investment companies, and the securities exchanges, by defining the responsibilities of corporate directors, officers, and trustees, and by controlling the processes of bankruptcy.

BANKS AND SAVINGS INSTITUTIONS

With banks and savings institutions, as in other fields, regulation has been tightened following widespread losses and revelations of abuse. In commercial banking, the American system, with thousands of independent banks operating under state as well as national charters, long made for insecurity. In 1920, there were 30,000 banks in the United States; during the twenties more than 5,000 of these banks failed, most of them in small towns suffering from the effects of agricultural depression. At the same time, city banks, taking advantage of rising prices, made loans to finance speculation in real estate and in securities. When the market crashed in 1929, the value of their collateral declined. Their reserves were depleted; they were unable to meet the demands of their depositors. There were runs on the banks; 8,000 banks failed from 1920 to 1933. Bank holidays were declared by state after state and finally by the federal government. No depositor could get a penny from his account until the banks were reopened during the early days of the New Deal. Deposits in the stronger banks were unimpaired; depositors in the weaker banks suffered heavy losses. A Senate Report[1] revealed serious breaches of trust by bank officials. Certain large commercial banks had set up investment affiliates and sponsored dubious securities; instead of giving impartial investment advice to their customers, they had pressed them to buy securities in which they themselves had an interest. They had paid excessive compensation to their officers; had extended large loans, with inadequate collateral or no collateral, to directors and officers to enable them to finance their private speculations. In some cases, officials, acting on the basis of inside information, had sold short the stock of their own banks, reaping a profit as other stockholders lost. It was this experience that led to the creation of the Federal Deposit Insurance Corporation and to the passage of the Banking Act of 1933.

In the case of life insurance, a thorough investigation of the principal companies was made in 1905 by the Armstrong Committee of the New York State legislature with Charles Evans Hughes, later Chief Justice of the United States Supreme Court, serving as its counsel. The committee's report,[2] published in 10 volumes, disclosed serious abuses. The companies were controlled, not by their stockholders or policyholders, but by self-perpetuating directorates. They had overpaid their officers and made lavish expenditures on unnecessary buildings. They had made extravagant investments, reported fictitious assets, and manipulated insurance funds. They had bought into banks, where they had maintained large inactive balances, reducing company earnings at the expense of shareholders and policy owners. They had refused to pay legitimate claims. They had maintained well-financed lobbies in state capitals to fend off corrective legislation. The Committee's recommendations for reform were embodied in the New York State insurance law of 1906, and this served as a model that was copied by many other states.

Bank Deposits and Savings Accounts

Commercial banks have been regulated for a longer time and in greater detail

1 / U.S. Senate, Committee on Banking and Currency, *Stock Exchange Practices* (Washington, D.C.: Government Printing Office, 1934), pp. 163-221.

2 / *Report of the Joint Committee of the Senate and Assembly of The State of New York, Appointed to Investigate the Affairs of Life Insurance Companies*, 1906.

than any other business. Freedom to set up national banks is controlled by the federal government; freedom to set up state banks, under varying standards, by the several states. The operations of banks are subject to continuous scrutiny. Those of national banks are supervised by the Comptroller of the Currency, the Federal Reserve System, and the Federal Deposit Insurance Corporation. The Comptroller of the Currency grants charters to national banks, controls changes in their status, requires periodic reports, conducts examinations, and may enforce his regulations by taking action to remove bank officers, force receiverships, and revoke charters. The Federal Reserve System performs a central banking function for all national banks and for those state banks, some 1,500 in number, that have chosen to join it. It conducts examinations of all member banks. The Federal Deposit Insurance Corporation insures the first $20,000 in each deposit in all national banks, in state banks belonging to the Federal Reserve System, and in other state banks that have joined the FDIC. It insures deposits in 96 percent of the banks in the country, providing protection for three fifths of the money in deposit accounts. It has thus put an end to the danger of crises produced by runs on banks. The Corporation examines insured state banks that do not belong to the Federal Reserve System. The banking departments of state governments supervise the banks that they have chartered in their respective states; they conduct the only examination of state banks that do not belong to the FDIC. Regulatory power is thus distributed among many agencies, operating under different laws and applying different standards. Each bank, of course, must satisfy the standards that the strictest agency controlling it may apply. Experts in public administration believe, however, that the three federal agencies should be brought under common direction and federal authority over state banks increased.

Controls over banks extend to every aspect of their operations. Their capitalization is controlled to insure their soundness and the equitable distribution of voting power. The quantity of their lending and the size of their reserves are controlled to stabilize the supply of deposit currency and the volume of business activity. Payment of interest on demand deposits and at more than a specified rate on time deposits is forbidden, to prevent the dissipation of banking resources through competition for business. The quality of bank loans is controlled to assure their safety. Commercial banks are given greater latitude than savings banks in choosing their investments. But the Banking Act of 1933 limited the loans that a national bank can make to any of its officers, forbade such a bank to lend more than a tenth of its capital and surplus to any one borrower, and required national banks to divorce their securities affiliates. The structure of the banking system is also controlled. National banks are permitted to set up statewide branches only in those states where banks are permitted to do so. Bank holding companies are required to divest themselves of nonbanking interests; transactions between such holding companies and their subsidiaries are supervised; their acquisition of new subsidiaries must be approved. Banks are forbidden to merge without first obtaining the permission, in their respective jurisdictions, of the Comptroller of the Currency, the Federal Reserve System, or the FDIC.

Bank examinations are conducted without giving prior notice. Such an examination is not a substitute for an independent audit of a bank's accounts. Nor is it undertaken primarily to detect embezzlement, though examiners may, and sometimes do, apprehend embezzlers in the course of their work. It is the purpose of examination, rather, to determine whether a bank is conforming to the requirements of law and is following sound banking policies and practices. The examiners study the bank's loans and investments and appraise its assets. If departures from legal requirements or from sound banking principles are found, they demand immediate correction. Given the controls imposed by law, enforced by examinations, and reinforced by insurance, the safety of bank deposits is now assured.

Protection is extended, also, to accounts in savings banks and in building and loan associations. Savings banks with state charters are supervised by the state banking departments; those with federal charters by the federal banking authorities. Savings banks are usually required to confine their investments to assets that are presumed to carry little risk. State savings banks are permitted, and federal savings banks are required, to insure their deposits with the FDIC. Building and loan associations with state charters are supervised by the state banking departments, those with federal charters by the Home Loan Bank Board. Accounts in the state associations may be, and those in the federal associations must be, insured by the Federal Savings and Loan Insurance Corporation, created for this purpose in 1934. Regulation of these associations was strengthened in 1968 when Congress empowered the FSLIC to supervise the practices of holding companies controlling their shares.

Life Insurance

A life insurance policy may take the form of term insurance, with premiums rising or benefits declining as the expectancy of life grows shorter with the passage of time. The usual policy, however, calls for the payment of the same premium each year. During the earlier years of the policy, this premium not only covers the cost of the promised benefit but also pays money into a savings account. During the later years, the premium falls short of the cost of the benefit, the difference being made up by income from the savings account. It is with the safety of the savings accumulated under the ordinary life insurance contract, as well as with the value and the cost of the insurance, that we are here concerned.

For many years, it was held that the business of writing insurance policies was intrastate in character and, therefore, was not covered by the Sherman Act. In 1944, however, the Supreme Court found that the operations of fire insurance companies involved the transmission of communications, documents, and money in interstate commerce and concluded that the Sherman Act applied.[3] The insurance interests then sought complete exemption from the law. In this they were not wholly successful. The McCarran Act, passed in 1945, suspended

3 / *U.S. v. South-Eastern Underwriters Assn.*, 322 U.S. 533.

enforcement of the antitrust laws against rate agreements among insurance companies for a period of three years, making them applicable thereafter but only "to the extent that such business is not regulated by state law." There are certain collusive practices, such as agreements among insurance companies not to file lower rates and boycotts denying reinsurance privileges to those who do so, which can still be prosecuted under the Sherman Act. And mergers of insurance companies located in different states, being beyond state control, can probably be prevented under the Celler-Kefauver Act.

Insurance is unique in the extent to which the task of regulation has been delegated to the states. The McCarran Act stimulated the passage of new regulatory laws, many of them patterned on a model statute prepared by the insurance companies. How well does the resulting pattern of regulation protect the policyholder's interests?

State regulation is concerned, primarily, with the financial soundness of the insurance companies. State insurance commissioners determine the capital a company must have, require the maintenance of adequate reserves, prescribe accounting methods, check on the value of assets, and control investment policies. They enforce these controls by requiring companies to make deposits of securities, by calling for annual reports, and by conducting examinations of company accounts.

State regulation is concerned, secondarily, with the fairness of trade practices. To assure integrity and responsibility, brokers and agents are required to obtain licenses, and those who cannot satisfy administrative standards are excluded from the field. To prevent discrimination, tying clauses, requiring one party to a transaction to purchase insurance from the other, and the rebating of premiums to favored purchasers of insurance are banned. To check misrepresentation, policy forms are simplified and standardized or limited to those that the commissioner may approve. An effort is made to assure fairness in the settlement of disputed claims, some states seeking to avoid the time and cost of litigation by providing machinery to arbitrate disputes.

Regulation has to do, finally, with the determination of rates. Here, the choice lies between competition, on the one hand, and cooperation under public supervision, on the other. Cooperation has been chosen on the ground that competition might drive rates down to a level that would impair the ability of the companies to pay their claims. The laws provide only that rates shall not be excessive (whatever that may mean) and shall not discriminate among the purchasers of policies. The rates of fire and casualty insurance companies are prepared by private rating bureaus, filed with the state insurance commissioner, and made effective when approved by him. Commissioners have sometimes succeeded in preventing increases and bringing about reductions in rates. Membership in rating bureaus is required in a few states but not in most. Some states forbid agreements to adhere to bureau rates. Independent filing is generally permitted, and deviations from bureau rates have increased. In the case of life insurance, rate bureaus are not needed. All of the companies use the same mortality table as the basis for their rates. The relative cost of mutual and participating policies issued by different companies depends upon the comparative size of their year-end dividends.

The administration of the regulatory laws is strong in some states, weak in others. But the policyholder is protected by the fact that his company must meet the standards established in every state—and thus in the strictest state—in which it operates. On the whole, state regulation has operated to assure financial soundness and to discourage unfair practices. As far as rates are concerned, there is little danger of monopoly; entry to the insurance business is unobstructed, the number of competitors is large, and the degree of concentration is low.[4]

SECURITIES DISTRIBUTORS

When new securities are offered for public sale, their distribution is commonly managed by an investment banker. If the issue is large, the banker will organize a syndicate of investment houses to join with him in selling it, some of it to their own customers, some of it to dealers, who will retail it to other investors. An investor, in purchasing a security, will be influenced by representations made to him by the bankers, by the dealers and their salesmen, or by investment advisers. Any of these people may have an interest that conflicts with his own. They may seek to persuade him to buy a security whose value is dubious or to pay too high a price. They may misrepresent the worth of a security or neglect to disclose information that is essential to its evaluation. It is the investor's helplessness in such a situation that has led both state and federal governments to act to afford him some protection. This movement started, more than a half century ago, with the enactment of laws by the states. It gained momentum, after the financial debacle of 1929, with the passage of the federal securities legislation of the thirties and the creation of the Securities and Exchange Commission. It continued, following a comprehensive study of the securities markets made for the SEC in the early sixties, with the enactment by Congress of amendments to the securities laws and the adoption by the SEC and the National Association of Securities Dealers of new rules to govern securities distributors.

The Blue-Sky Laws

The distribution of securities has been regulated by the states since 1911, when Kansas passed the first of the so-called "blue-sky" laws, to prevent promoters, in the words of one legislator, from selling shares "in the bright blue sky itself." Such laws had been enacted by all the states except Nevada by 1933. In a few states, these laws merely provide that the fraudulent sale of securities

4 / There is widespread public dissatisfaction with one type of insurance: insurance against automobile accidents. Too much attention is devoted to determination of legal responsibility. The payment of indemnities is too long delayed. The insurance costs too much. Settlements could be speeded and costs cut if indemnification were related to injury without regard to legal fault. On this basis, a law providing for the payment of medical bills and loss of income, up to $2,000, was enacted in Massachusetts in 1970.

shall be a criminal offense, empower the Attorney General to prosecute offenders, and authorize the courts to grant injunctions and to impose penalties. In most cases, however, the laws require dealers in securities to obtain licenses, excluding nonlicensed dealers from the trade. They also require that securities themselves be registered before they can be sold within a state. Registrants must file extensive information, and registry may be denied where issues are fraudulent or registration statements falsified.

These laws have afforded scant protection to investors. The funds provided for their enforcement have rarely been adequate to finance a real analysis of the statements that are filed. Little effort has been made to censor security prospectuses, the only documents that buyers see. The laws do not prevent mismanagement of corporations, once their securities have been sold. Nor do they regulate the subsequent transfer of these securities. Many transactions escape control, moreover, since the jurisdiction of state authorities does not extend to sales across state lines. It remained for Congress to make the first effective provision for the protection of investors when it enacted the securities laws in the early years of the New Deal.

Abuses in the Securities Markets

The speculative boom that followed World War I came to an abrupt end with the stock market crash in October, 1929. In the course of the next few years, the value of stocks listed on the New York Exchange fell from $89 billion to $15 billion and the value of bonds listed from $49 billion to $30 billion, representing a total loss to investors—on paper, at least—of $93 billion. At the same time, purchasers of stocks in public utility holding companies, investment trusts, and other ventures, and buyers of bonds issued by real estate promoters, foreign corporations, and foreign governments, took further losses as the issuers went bankrupt or defaulted on the payments that were due. Holders of stocks in the Insull companies, one of the great utility empires, lost nearly $740 million. Holders of shares in 22 investment trusts saw their value drop from $560 million to $50 million. Americans who bought debentures issued by Ivar Kreuger, the Swedish match monopolist, recovered $10 million on the $250 million they had paid. At the depth of the depression, three fifths of the real estate mortgage bonds outstanding, two fifths of the bonds of foreign corporations, and a third of those of foreign governments were in default.

This financial debacle led to a series of investigations: to hearings before the Senate Committee on Banking and Currency, running to 12,000 pages of testimony and exhibits, on the practices of commercial banks, investment bankers, and the stock exchanges; to an inquiry by the Federal Trade Commission, filling more than 70 volumes, on the practices of public utility holding companies; and, subsequently, to studies by the Securities and Exchange Commission dealing with the practices of trustees who held the securities backing corporate bonds, and with those of investment advisers and investment trusts. Out of these investigations there came startling disclosures of misrepresentation, manipulation, incompetence, and irresponsibility on the part of many who had been conspicuous as leaders in finance. These revelations, reported in the press in circumstantial detail, gave rise to insistent demands for financial reforms. And Congress, in the next few years, enacted a series of laws that were tailor-made to prevent abuses of the types that had been found.

Requirement of Truthful Disclosure

It was revealed, in the hearings of the thirties, that investment bankers had misrepresented the securities they sold, had concealed significant facts, and had dressed the market, buying some of these securities to make them appear more valuable than they really were; that they had discriminated among investors, offering lower prices to preferred lists of favored purchasers; and that they had obtained excessive margins for themselves. To prevent such practices, Congress enacted the Securities Act of 1933, bringing public offerings of new securities under control. Administration of the law has been entrusted, since 1934, to the Securities and Exchange Commission set up under the Securities Exchange Act of that year.

Where securities worth more than $300,000 are publicly offered for sale in interstate commerce or through the mails, the issuer must file a registration statement with the SEC, disclosing the information the investor needs to enable him objectively to appraise their value. In the case of corporate securities, he must disclose the provisions of the corporation's charter, outline its capital structure, explain the relation of the new security to others then outstanding, describe the scope and character of the company's business, tell how the funds raised by the new issue are to be employed, reveal any material contracts to which the corporation is a party, list its directors and officers together with the sums that they are paid, describe any cases in which such persons have had an interest in things the company has bought, list the principal holders of the company's stock, list those who have options to purchase its securities, tell what stock has been given for services or properties other than cash, name the underwriters of the issue, reveal the size of their commissions, and show the yield of the security to the issuer as well as its cost to the purchaser. In the case of foreign bonds, similar information is required, including data on the purpose for which the funds are to be used, the legal status of the issue, the financial condition of the borrower, and his past record in making payments on his debts.

The SEC makes a thorough examination of registration statements and security prospectuses. And where it finds that false or misleading statements have been made or material facts withheld, it may issue an order suspending a security's sale. But this is the extent of its responsibility. The Commission does not undertake to advise investors as to the merits of securities. It has no power to prevent the sale of any stock or bond, however dubious, as long as full disclosure has been made. Its function is merely to insure that sellers tell the truth, the whole truth, and nothing but the truth.

Where securities are covered by the law, sale without registration is made a criminal offense. In addition, purchasers of securities who suffer losses are permitted to bring civil suits against those who signed the registration statements and, if they can prove that their losses resulted from falsification or conceal- ment, are entitled to return the securities and recover the money paid, plus interest, minus any earnings received, or to collect damages equal to the sums lost on securities they have sold. Individuals signing a registration statement— directors, underwriters, appraisers, accountants, and engineers—can avoid per- sonal liability by showing that they exercised reasonable care in judging and confirming its validity. But liability cannot be avoided by the issuing corporation itself. Suits for recovery must be brought within three years of the original sale of the securities concerned and within one year of the discovery that misrepre- sentation had occurred.

Related Reforms

The authority of the Securities and Exchange Commission was extended to cover public utility holding companies in 1935, associations of securities dealers in 1938, trustees of security issues in 1939, and investment companies and investment advisers in 1940. The Public Utility Holding Company Act finds its greatest significance in strengthening state regulation of public utility rates and was discussed, in that connection, in Chapter 15. This measure, and the three discussed below, were outgrowths of the investigations of the thirties and were designed to check the abuses they disclosed.

Securities are sold in over-the-counter markets by thousands of dealers. It did not appear to be practicable to require the SEC to control the detailed op- erations of all of these concerns. Instead, the dealers were asked to take responsibility for self-regulation, acting through a representative organization under the Commission's general supervision. Under the Maloney Act of 1938, a dealers' association must register with the SEC, admit all qualified applicants to membership, provide for democratic self-government, and obtain Commission approval for its rules. These rules must forbid manipulation and deception and require fair trading practices. The association must discipline its members for infractions of the rules, with the SEC acting as a court of appeals. The National Association of Securities Dealers, organized under the provisions of the Maloney Act, includes in its membership 95 percent of all securities dealers and takes responsibility for detailed regulation of the trade.

It was disclosed, in the investigations of the thirties, that trustees of securities held as backing for corporate bonds had failed in some cases, to protect the bondholders' interests. They had permitted the debtor in the Kreuger case, for instance, to withdraw superior securities and substitute inferior or even worth- less ones. They had inserted provisions in trust indentures designed to relieve themselves of legal responsibility. The Trust Indenture Act of 1939 was designed to exclude from trusteeship of a corporate mortgage anyone who has an interest adverse to that of holders of the corporation's bonds, and to prevent trustees of such securities from avoiding responsibility. The law sets up standards of eligibility for trustees and requires them to make full disclosure of the terms of trust indentures. It defines the obligations that trustees must assume. And it empowers the SEC to regulate the operations in which they are permitted to engage.

Organizations known as investment companies, investment trusts, or mutual funds sell their own shares to investors and use the money thus obtained to purchase a variety of securities in a large number of other enterprises, thus giving the investor the greater safety afforded by diversity. A study of these concerns, undertaken by the SEC in 1935, revealed that investment companies organized and run by investment bankers had been forced to absorb securities for which the bankers could find no other market, to make needless purchases and sales in order to yield the bankers a commission, and to pay the bankers excessive fees for managing their affairs. Investment advisers, like sellers of securities, had sometimes had interests adverse to those of their clients, which they had failed to disclose. The Investment Companies and Investment Advisers Act of 1940 requires investment trusts and investment advisers to register with the SEC. It provides that two fifths of the directors of an investment trust must be independent of security underwriters, brokers, or advisers, and forbids such trusts to use their funds to finance affiliated bankers or security distributors. It authorizes the Commission to supervise transactions between the trusts and affiliated interests, to regulate the charges made for managing their affairs, and periodically to inspect their books. The law also forbids investment advisers to defraud their clients, to make profit sharing arrangements with them, or to assign their contracts to other persons without their consent, and requires any adviser who acts as a principal in a transaction to inform his client of the fact. Violations of the law are made a criminal offense, punishable by fine and imprisonment.

The Special Study of the Securities Markets

In the years that followed World War II, there was a surge of speculative fever in the United States, with investors demanding shares in unseasoned companies in glamour industries in hope of realizing a quick rise in price. There was a spectacular growth in the volume of business done on over-the-counter markets. Much of this business was in new issues by small companies not yet appropriate for popular participation. The securities involved were not listed on organized exchanges; their issuers were exempt from the reporting requirements imposed by the Securities Exchange Act of 1934. There was no evidence of the pervasive sort of fraudulent activity that was disclosed in the thirties. But there was evidence of grave abuses requiring additional controls.

In 1961, stimulated by disclosures of manipulative activity leading to expulsion of members of the American Stock Exchange and serious shortcomings in the government of the Exchange itself, Congress directed the SEC to undertake a comprehensive investigation of the securities markets. To make this study, the Commission employed a group of lawyers, economists, and statisticians from outside its own staff. The result of their two-year investigation, published in 1963, was a report that ran to 5,400 pages, covering the distribution of new securities and its regulation by the NASD, the practices of mutual funds, trading on over-the-counter markets, trading on organized exchanges and its regulation by the exchange authorities, and the effect of exemptions granted under the securities law.[5] The *Report of Special Study* contained 175 recommendations for further reforms. Some of them could be effected by tightening the policing of the securities markets by associations such as the NASD and the New York Stock Exchange and some of this has since been done. Other recommendations could be effected by promulgating new rules under existing Commission authority; a number of these rules have now been issued. A final group of recommendations called for new legislation; many of them were embodied in the Securities Acts Amendments of 1964.

Qualifications of Dealers and Salesmen

Entry into the securities business has been unrestricted. Many new firms, acting as brokers for others and as dealers on their own account, have been attracted to the business in recent years. The capital invested in some of these firms has been only nominal or unduly small. Their owners have seemingly been unaware of their obligations to investors. Their salesmen, though inexperienced, have undertaken to serve as investment advisers, even engaging in financial and estate planning. Their supervisors have failed to keep the salesman under control. In some cases, unscrupulous operators known in the trade as boiler-room floaters have engaged in high-pressure salesmanship. Some of the broker-dealer firms have remained outside the self-regulatory association of securities dealers.

The *Report of Special Study* recommended control of entry to the securities business. It would establish minimum capital requirements for broker-dealers and minimum experience requirements for principals and supervisors. It would require licensing of supervisors and salesmen, on the basis of standards encompassing competence, character, integrity, and financial responsibility, administered by local committees similar to those that govern admission to the bar. It would deny licenses to persons who had violated SEC regulations and to those who had been convicted, during the 10 previous years, of theft or embezzlement. It would make membership in a self-regulatory group prerequisite for registration as a broker-dealer or an investment adviser.

The Securities Acts Amendments of 1964 authorized the SEC to establish minimum capital requirements for members of broker-dealer firms and standards of competence, training, and experience for members and their employees. The Commission, acting on this authority, established capital requirements and adopted a rule requiring examinations of securities salesmen, analysts, supervisors, investment advisers, and advertising and public relations personnel, covering altogether some 23,000 employees of 450 firms. The amendments did not

5 / *Report of Special Study of Securities Markets of the Securities and Exchange Commission* (Washington, D.C.: Government Printing Office, 1963), Parts 1-5.

compel broker-dealers or investment advisers to become members of the NASD, but they gave the Commission power directly to regulate the activities of those who did not choose to do so.

Selling Practices

The *Report of Special Study* disclosed that the compensation of securities salesmen had depended on the volume of their sales, putting them under pressure to sell, and that some salesmen had, accordingly, been guilty of practices that were harmful to their customers, overtrading their accounts, recommending unsuitable issues, misrepresenting their value, and concealing material facts. It indicated that broker-dealers and the NASD had failed to uncover these abuses and prevent their repetition. It recommended that the compensation of salesmen be tied less closely to the volume of their sales; that more emphasis be placed on the suitability of securities to the needs of the customer; and that salesmen's performance be supervised more strictly by their employers and by the NASD. It also proposed that the SEC be given direct disciplinary controls over individuals in the securities business. Under the law as it then existed, the only penalty available to the Commission was complete withdrawal of the right to do business, a punishment so severe that it could not often be invoked. The *Report of Special Study* proposed that the SEC be authorized to impose lighter penalties for minor infringements of its rules. The Securities Acts Amendments of 1964 authorized the NASD and the SEC to proceed directly against employees of broker-dealers and empowered the SEC to employ sanctions, such as temporary suspension, short of complete revocation of the right to do business.

The investigators found that broker-dealers and investment advisers had sought to promote securities sales by disseminating published advice, giving little information on the research on which it had been based or pretending to research that had not been made. In some cases, they found that the public relations departments or consultants of issuing corporations had sought to stimulate the sale of new issues by publishing glowing descriptions of possible products and optimistic projections of sales and earnings; that they had traded in the securities they were touting. The *Report of Special Study* recommended that the SEC adopt rules requiring disclosure of the compensation received and the securities or options held by public relations firms and that legislation be enacted providing penalties for the reckless or intentional dissemination of false or misleading statements or unwarranted forecasts. No such legislation has been forthcoming, but behavior in this area is said to have been improved through ethical guidelines issued within the trade and through decisions handed down by the courts.

Distributor Self-Regulation

The pattern of regulation in the securities markets is unique in its reliance on trade associations to establish many of the rules, do much of the policing, and take most of the disciplinary action, leaving to the SEC responsibility for general supervision of these activities. The reasons for the adoption of this pattern are clear. Securities dealers are not exempt from the antitrust laws. They are not public utilities; they have no franchises. Their prices are not controlled. The volume of their business is such that the SEC could not hope to regulate it directly. Delegation of regulatory power may involve some impairment of competition. But it is believed that Commission oversight will prevent excesses. And there is no barrier to entry to the field. The Commission's investigators found that the NASD, through its rules of fair practice, enforced by travelling examiners, had succeeded in raising the standards of responsibility in the trade. They did find, however, that the Association had fallen short of providing investors with the measure of protection that they need, and that the SEC, preoccupied with day-to-day problems, had not adequately performed its task of continuing oversight. The NASD functions through member committees and, as a result, there have been delays in handling disciplinary cases and disparities in the penalties imposed. The Association, moreover, makes no public reports on the action it takes. The investigators recommended that the NASD enlarge its staff, delegate much of its disciplinary function to the staff, and report on actions taken. The Securities Acts Amendments of 1964 gave the SEC new power to alter NASD rules regarding organization, eligibility for membership, and discipline. The Association has since been reorganized and its operations strengthened.

Mutual Funds

Mutual funds are said to offer two advantages: diversification of holdings, reducing risks, and expert investment guidance resulting in higher returns. The advantage of diversification is real; the funds have a larger and more varied holding of securities than the usual investor would be able to acquire. The advantage of expert guidance is open to question; the earnings of representative funds, over the years, have been no higher than those that could have been obtained from a random selection of securities. The funds have grown rapidly in recent years. From 1940 to 1969, the number of their stockholders grew from 296,000 to 4 million, the value of their holdings from $2.5 billion to $40 billion. Two reports on the operation of these concerns (one made for the SEC by the Wharton School of Finance of the University of Pennsylvania and one by the Commission's investigatory panel) have revealed a number of abuses.

Sales of fund shares are sometimes made under contracts which commit the purchaser to continue buying such shares over a period of years. Some of these sales have been made under a practice known as "front-end loading," which means that half of the amount paid by the purchaser in the first year goes to pay the salesman's commission and only half goes to purchase shares. This practice affords a strong incentive to high-pressure salesmanship. It also involves serious losses for those investors who have to withdraw from their contracts in the early years of the contracts. And this is a possibility concerning which the investors have not been informed. Salesmen have also augmented their commission incomes by persuading investors to switch, at some cost, from one fund to another. The SEC Study recommended that the Investment Companies Act of 1940 be amended to forbid front-end loading, and that the Commission adopt a rule forbidding deception in connection with recommendations to switch funds.

Instead of buying and selling securities directly, where they could do so, the funds make their purchases and sales through broker-dealers. The commissions thus paid the dealers give them an added incentive to push the sale of the fund's own shares. But they involve a diversion of money that could have been retained for the benefit of the funds' shareholders. The Study recommended that the NASD amend its rules to prevent the interposition of unneeded brokers in buying and selling securities.

A mutual fund is typically managed, under contract, by an investment advisory concern that collects a fee of 0.5 percent of the fund's average total net assets over the year as its charge for this service. The investigators found that these fees bore no relation to the costs involved in managing the funds or to their performance and that they were higher than those paid for handling other accounts of comparable size. They urged that determination of these charges be brought under control.

The investigators found, finally, that fund officials and advisers had traded in the same issues as those bought and sold for the funds, thus raising the question of possible conflicts of interest. They recommended that the funds keep track of trading by insiders and that such trading be policed by the NASD.

The SEC report on mutual funds was published at the end of 1966. For the next three years, the Commission negotiated with the industry, seeking agreement on legislative reforms. In this, it failed and the issue went to the Congress. Action was finally taken in 1970. The law now limits front-end loading and imposes on fund managements a standard of fiduciary responsibility in setting management fees.[6]

THE SECURITIES EXCHANGES

Old security issues are traded on organized exchanges and on over-the-counter markets. The organized exchanges include the New York Stock Exchange, the American Exchange, and a number of regional exchanges. Trading on the New York Stock Exchange, the most important of these markets, is limited to shares in some 1,500 well-established widely owned corporations who satisfy its listing requirements. The exchange originated as a private club. Membership is still obtained by purchasing one of some 1,300 seats at a price that runs around $200,000. Trading is confined to members: brokers who execute purchase and sale orders for others, specialists in certain stocks who not only execute orders for others but also buy and sell for their own accounts, floor traders who deal primarily for their own accounts, and odd-lot dealers

6 / See also Irwin Friend, Marshall Blume, and Jean Crockett, *Mutual Funds and Other Institutional Investors* (New York: Twentieth Century Fund, 1970).

who buy from and sell to their customers in lots of less than 100 shares. The exchange is governed by a board elected by its members. Unlisted stocks, the shares of banks, insurance companies, and mutual funds, and corporate and government bonds are traded on over-the-counter markets. These markets lack formal organization; they consist of 4,000 dealers, getting in touch with one another by telephone, handling some 50,000 issues, quoting prices on some 8,000 of them each day.

The Securities Exchange Act

There were revelations, in the thirties, of malpractice on the securities exchanges. Traders had manipulated the markets, acquiring securities and forming pools which drove their prices up, by circulating favorable publicity through tipsters and financial columnists, by making wash sales (nominal transactions in which no securities changed hands), and by matching orders (buying through one broker and selling through another) both at steadily rising quotations, thus creating the appearance of an active market, then unloading their holdings at the peak of prices, withdrawing their support, and possibly buying again when prices had declined. To put an end to such abuses, trading on the exchanges was subjected to supervision by the SEC.

Under the Securities Exchange Act of 1934, stock exchanges, dealers, and brokers, and listed securities are required to be registered. A number of manipulative devices—market pools, wash sales, and the dissemination of false and misleading information—are flatly prohibited. Other trading practices, such as price pegging (buying securities so that quoted prices will not fall), short selling (contracting to deliver securities the seller does not possess), dealing in options ("puts" and "calls" that give one party the privilege of requiring another, respectively, to buy or sell securities at a stated price), and trading by stock exchange members for their own accounts are made subject to regulation by the SEC. An exchange that violates the law or rules laid down by the Commission may be fined up to $500,000, or closed temporarily or permanently by having its registration suspended or withdrawn. Members or officers of an exchange, when found to be in violation, may be suspended or expelled. Corporations that fail to obey the law and regulations may have their securities denied the trading privilege by suspension or cancellation of registry. Persons found guilty of willful violation may be fined up to $10,000 or imprisoned up to two years or both. Persons responsible for misrepresentation, in statements filed with the Commission, may be sued by investors who have suffered losses and, unless they can prove they acted in good faith, may be forced to pay them actual damages.

Trading on Organized Exchanges

The *Report of Special Study of the Securities Markets,* published in 1963, covered the regulation of trading on organized exchanges and found it to be defective in providing protection for investors. Half of the transactions on these exchanges involve purchases or sales by specialists and other members trading for their own accounts. Such transactions operate to maintain a continuous market, but they involve potential conflicts of interest.

The specialists are assigned by the exchanges to deal in certain securities. It is their function to stabilize the prices of these securities by buying when the prices are falling and selling when they are rising. The specialist makes about half of his profit from the commissions he collects as a broker, half by trading for his own account. His position as a broker gives him an advantage in acting as a trader. He has exclusive access to his book of orders to sell and buy. These orders give him inside information on how the market is going to move. He may take a position as a trader in anticipation of market movements. He may even influence such movements. The specialist opens trading at the beginning of the day. When orders to buy exceed orders to sell and the markets should open higher than it closed the day before, he may start with a lower price and lead the market down. When orders to sell exceed orders to buy, he may do the opposite.

The specialist may well be tempted to put his personal interest above his obligation to the exchange. Specialists, in fact, have tended to neglect inactive stocks, concentrating on a minority of issues. In some cases, instead of stabilizing the market they have destabilized it, buying for their own account on the rise and selling on the fall. In two market breaks, the first in the spring of 1962 and the second following President Kennedy's assassination in November, 1963, some specialists walked away from the market or accelerated its decline by dumping their shares. In some cases, too, specialists have lacked the capital that would enable them adequately to perform their stabilizing function.

Following recommendations made in its *Report of Special Study,* the SEC announced new rules to govern specialists in 1964. The rules require that specialists observe their obligation to buy and sell for their own account whenever it is necessary to maintain a fair and orderly market; that they refrain from selling their own shares on a declining market; and, when sales have been made, that they reenter declining markets with price-supporting purchases. The rules forbid the specialist to make the first transaction of the day at a price which is inconsistent with the supply and demand situation revealed by his book. The rules, finally, require specialists to carry three times the previous amount of capital to support their market-stabilizing operations.

Floor traders have no market function or responsibility. Having ready access to information, they use it for their own gain. They tend to concentrate on the more active issues, increasing market swings by buying on the rise and selling on the fall. They are an anachronism, a vestige of the day when the exchange was less a public market than a private club. The *Report of Special Study* recommended that they be banned by 1965. Negotiations between the SEC and the New York Stock Exchange led to a compromise. Under the new rules, floor traders are not to be eliminated, but three fourths of their transactions must serve to stabilize the market and they must have a capital, for this purpose, of at least $250,000.

Transactions by odd-lot dealers make up a tenth of the volume on the New York Stock Exchange. This trading is handled by two firms. The prices they pay and charge their customers are determined by the last round-lot sale minus or plus a differential which they fix themselves. These prices are thus set by a duopoly which is regulated neither by the stock exchange nor by the SEC. The odd-lot dealers profit particularly through offsetting transactions. They have opposed the automation of trading, which would open the way to competition and reduce their margins. The *Report of Special Study* recommended that the exchange regulate odd-lot markups, adopt rules controlling offsetting transactions, and require surveillance of such transactions. The Exchange has since adopted rules bringing these matters under control.

Exchange Self-Regulation

The Securities Exchange Act of 1934 brought about a fundamental alteration in the status of the New York Stock Exchange, transforming it from a private club into a body charged with public responsibilities. The Exchange was now expected to require its members to comply with the provisions of the Act, with its own rules, and with rules adopted by the SEC, and to discipline those who failed to do so. The Commission was empowered to initiate new rules dealing with a long list of substantive matters. Instead of employing its coercive powers, however, it chose to proceed by suggesting that desired reforms be effected by the Exchange itself. At the beginning, the SEC urged the Exchange to reform its organization, appointing public members to its governing board and employing a salaried president, and proposed a number of changes in its rules. The Exchange dragged its feet on these reforms until the Commission threatened to put them into effect under its own powers. The Exchange then set up a committee to recommend reorganization and new procedures; changes were subsequently made.

The authors of the *Report of Special Study* found that the Exchange had provided constructive and vigorous leadership in creating an honest market. They commended, in particular, its initiation of standards to govern the compensation of underwriters, its establishment of qualifications for securities dealers, its administration of rules fixing capital requirements for traders, and its enforcement of regulations regarding proxy solicitation, truthful disclosure, and financial reporting, which are prerequisite to the listing of securities. In all of these matters, they found that the Exchange had made a significant contribution to investor protection. They recommended that the pattern of self-regulation be retained.

In certain respects, however, the investigators found that the self-regulatory activity of the Exchange left much to be desired. It had failed to focus on the conflict of interest inherent in the operations of specialists, to recognize the problem of public responsibility raised by the privileged position of floor traders, or to impose needed controls on odd-lot trading. It had dealt severely with infractions of its rules where interests of other members were concerned, but had been unduly tender where the interests of investors were at stake, relying on admonition rather than punishment, and failing to publish its findings as to violations or to report on the disciplinary action it had taken. It had been more concerned to shield the members of the club from public criticism than to make sure that standards of public responsibility were enforced. The *Report of Special Study* recommended that customer complaints be seriously investigated, that punishments be appropriate to the infraction involved, and that violations resulting in the imposition of penalties be publicly reported. The Exchange has since moved in this direction.

The investigators proposed another reform. Finding the Exchange to be so organized as to give floor professionals a disproportionate influence in its government, they recommended that voting power be so distributed and the composition of the governing board and the principal committees of the Exchange so altered as to assure more representation to traders dealing directly with the public. Here one significant change occurred in 1969 when the Exchange agreed to permit its member firms to "go public," i.e., to incorporate and offer their shares for general ownership.

Stock Exchanges and Antitrust Laws

Restrictive activity by the New York Stock Exchange was successfully attacked in 1963 under the antitrust laws. The Exchange had ordered its members to sever private wire connections with nonmembers. A broker in Dallas, thus deprived of wire service, sued the Exchange for triple damages. The Supreme Court found for the plaintiff, holding the action of the Exchange to be in violation of the Sherman Act.[7]

In other suits, antitrust was less successful. Plaintiffs had charged that the establishment of minimum commission rates by the Exchange and its refusal to permit members to share commissions with nonmembers constituted conspiracies in restraint of trade. The courts disagreed, holding that the Congressional delegation of power to supervise the exchanges to the SEC implicitly exempted the exchanges from the antitrust laws. They distinguished these cases from the Silver case by arguing that exclusion from wire service was harmful while enforced observance of minimum commission rates was not. This left the power to regulate commission rates to the SEC.

The SEC held hearings in 1968 on whether the Exchange should be permitted to fix minimum commissions. The Antitrust Division argued that these rates should be determined by free competition. The Exchange argued that considerations of financial soundness required that they be fixed. Another problem presented itself, having to do with the structure rather than the level of rates. A large share of securities purchases and sales had come to be made by institutional investors: mutual funds, insurance companies, pension trusts, and the like. And these concerns bypassed the NYSE, trading in what was called a "third

---

7 / *Silver* v. *New York Stock Exchange*, 373 U.S. 341.

market." They bought and sold in large quantities but, under Exchange rules, they could not be charged lower commissions. The institutional traders therefore took their business to regional exchanges where lower fees were permitted. The NYSE favored changing its rules to permit quantity discounts. Brokers opposed substantial cuts. In another development, mutual funds directed that part of the commissions paid by them be diverted to designated brokers. This "give-up" was permitted under NYSE rules. It served to reward those brokers who pushed the sale of mutual fund shares. But it appeared to the Antitrust Division to be a form of reciprocal dealing and thus be in violation of the antitrust laws. It was also opposed by SEC. The probable outcome of these controversies is as follows: The exchanges will be permitted to fix brokers' commissions. The commissions it fixes will be regulated by the SEC. The structure of commissions will include quantity discounts, with commissions on large quantities below the present level and commissions on small quantities above it. Give-ups will be forbidden.

Over-the-Counter Markets

The volume of business in over-the-counter markets where unlisted issues are traded has increased manifold since World War II. More issues are being traded and more broker-dealers are participating. Quotations on wholesale transactions in these markets have been provided to members of the trade by a National Quotations Bureau, a private monopoly subject to no public regulation. The SEC investigators found that broker-dealers had sometimes reported fictitious quotations to the Bureau in order to give securities an illusory value.

The over-the-counter bid-and-asked quotations published in the daily press did not represent actual transactions. They were sponsored by an NASD committee that took the wholesale quotations and added a markup. The resulting quotations were confusing and deceptive. The Securities Acts Amendments of 1964 required registered securities associations to adopt rules designed to produce fair and informative retail quotations for unlisted securities. The NASD subsequently worked out a plan under which the bid-and-asked quotations were replaced by a single accurate price for issues traded nationally. Quotations on regional issues were to conform to this pattern later on.

THE CORPORATE INSIDER

The modern corporation is characterized by wide diffusion of nominal ownership and narrow concentration of actual control. If the capitalization of a corporation is all in voting common stock, control can be exercised by one share more than half of those outstanding. If it is half in voting common and half in nonvoting preferred, control can be exercised by one share more than a fourth. If the capitalization is one third common, one third preferred, and one third bonds, control lies with those who hold a bit more than a sixth of it. This would be true if more than half of the common were required for control. But such is rarely the case. Many shares are held by persons who make no effort to exercise control—by speculators who are constantly shifting their holdings, by investment institutions seeking only to diversify their risks, by scattered owners whose activities are limited to cashing their dividend checks and signing their proxy certificates. Control may thus be held by those who own a 4th of the common, representing but a 12th of the total investment, or an 8th representing a 24th, or even less. In practice, control over the largest corporations is exercised, through operation of the proxy machinery, by minority stockholdings or by self-perpetuating managements with as little as 5 percent or even 1 percent of the outstanding shares. In some cases, moreover, concentration has been facilitated by the issuance of common stock with no vote and other classes of stock with multiple votes, and carried even further by pyramiding through successive layers of holding companies.

The danger in this situation is that the few who are in control will so employ their power as to divert the earnings of a corporation from its many owners to themselves. This has been done, in the past, in a variety of ways. Managements have voted themselves huge salaries and secret bonuses. Directors and officers have borrowed from their corporations at low rates of interest, bought from them at low prices, and sold to them at high prices. Insiders, possessing information that was not supplied to others, have profited by selling their stock before a dividend was to be passed and by purchasing stock before a dividend was to be declared. Dividends have been withheld and surpluses accumulated, in one year; payments that should have gone to holders of noncumulative preferred stock have been distributed, instead, to holders of common, in the next. Earnings have been diverted, too, by enabling insiders to acquire more shares, at favorable prices, when prospects improved, and by denying to other owners the right to buy such issues and thus to maintain their proportionate claim to dividends. And these manipulations have been shielded by impublicity; by the issuance of no reports, of delayed reports, of inadequate reports, and of reports that have misrepresented the finances of the companies concerned.

When corporations have gone through bankruptcy, there have been further opportunities for gain. Reorganization was effected, until 1933, through receiverships established by courts of equity. It was not the duty of a receiver to reorganize a bankrupt company but only to keep it in operation and to conserve its assets while reorganization plans were prepared by its creditors. For this purpose, protective committees were set up to represent the interests of investors holding different classes of securities, such holders were invited to deposit their securities together with proxy powers, and reorganization committees were then appointed to formulate and propose specific plans. When such a plan was approved by a court, the process was completed by transferring the bankrupt's property to a new corporation through a foreclosure sale.

In these procedures, inside interests were often dominant. They would select a person sympathetic to the company's management to act as its receiver and persuade a friendly judge to appoint him to the post. They would take the initiative in setting up committees that nominally represented the interests of investors, in soliciting proxies, and in obtaining the deposit of securities. They would lead reorganization committees to propose new plans designed to keep them in control. Investors would be advised to accept securities of smaller value than those they previously held. New securities, with superior rights, would be floated to raise additional capital. And the very bankers who had distributed the earlier issues would handle the new flotations and pocket generous commissions on the deal. Profits would also be made by persons using inside information for trading in the company's securities. Excessive fees would be collected, with the approval of the court, by the receiver, by committee members, by bankers serving as depositaries, and by lawyers representing the many groups concerned. And when the receivership had ended, investors would again find themselves in possession of a crippled enterprise, saddled with debt, and left in the control of those who had ruined it before.

It was to protect financial lambs, thus shorn and reshorn, that further controls were adopted in the early years of the New Deal. And these controls, it should be noted, have gone some distance toward preventing the repetition of abuses that were all too common in the past.

Checking the Diversion of Earnings

The courts have shown a disposition, since the thirties, to hold corporate directors to a stricter standard of accountability. The position of a director has come increasingly to be likened to that of a trustee. And the fiduciary relationship has been held to require, not only fidelity to the interests of stockholders, avoiding personal gain at their expense, but also the exercise of considerable care and diligence in protecting them against loss. Instead of escaping responsibility merely by pleading that they had acted in good faith, directors have been held to liability for negligent mismanagement.

Concentration of control and diversion of earnings have also been checked by legislation. The issuance of nonvoting common stock has been forbidden by several states and, in cases of corporate reorganization, by Congress in the Chandler Bankruptcy Act of 1938. Pyramiding of control through the holding company device, in the case of public utilities, has been limited by the Public Utility Holding Company Act of 1935 and subjected to regulation by the SEC. This law and others already mentioned contain provisions that make it easier for investors to protect themselves against insiders whose interests may differ from their own. Publication of informative reports was required, by the Securities Act of 1933, of corporations making public offerings of new securities. It was also required, by the Securities Exchange Act of 1934, of all firms whose securities are listed on a registered exchange. Solicitation of proxies by such companies, under the latter act, must conform to rules laid down by the SEC. Proxy statements must be truthful; proposals advanced by stockholders who oppose the management must be included and submitted to a vote. Speculation by insiders in the shares of their own concerns is handicapped by provisions, contained in the Securities Exchange Act, the Public Utility Holding Company Act, and the Investment Company Act, that apply to directors, officers, and owners of a tenth or more of the stock in any corporation covered by these laws. Such persons are forbidden to sell the stock of their companies short. They are required to make frequent reports on changes in their ownership. And if any of them makes a profit by buying his company's stock and selling it within six months (or by selling the stock and rebuying it), his gain can be recovered for the company through a suit brought by the company itself or by any of its stockholders. Diversion of earnings by transactions between concerns within a holding company structure is also prevented, in the case of public utilities, by provisions of the Act of 1935 that make all such transactions subject to approval by the SEC.

The Commission has brought suit against corporate officials who have taken advantage of inside information to profit at the expense of other shareholders. In one of the most important of these cases, in 1965, it sued the Texas Gulf Sulphur Company and 13 of its directors, officers, and employees, charging that the company had discovered a rich deposit of copper and zinc on November 12, 1963; that the insiders had then purchased or taken options on 127,000 shares of its stock and that friends whom they tipped off had acquired 28,000 more; that the company had put out misleading information on the strike on April 13, 1964; that it had finally disclosed the true character of its discovery on April 16; and that the price of Texas Gulf Stock had thereupon risen from $17 to $34 a share. The SEC asked the court to require the insiders to make restitution to persons who, in ignorance, had incurred losses during this period by selling the stock to them or to their friends. In the final decision in the case, in 1970, the court ordered 10 of the defendants to make restitution to the company in amounts ranging from $2,300 to $96,000 plus interest at 6 percent from the date of the offense. The decision also provided a basis for other suits against Texas Gulf by persons who had sold its stock to other buyers between April 13, when it had issued misleading publicity, and April 16, when it had told the truth.

In another important action, in 1968, the SEC charged Merrill Lynch, Pierce, Fenner & Smith, the nation's largest brokerage house, 14 of its officers and 15 of its customers with violation of the law. Merrill Lynch, acting as an underwriter for Douglas Aircraft, learned that Douglas earnings would decline in the last half of 1966. It passed this information on to the 15 customers (large investment companies), enabling them to avoid losses by selling Douglas stock or to make profits, estimated at $4.5 million, by selling it short. It withheld this information from its other customers who presumably sustained losses. Following administrative hearings, Merrill Lynch accepted a consent order under which the firm's New York sales office was closed for 21 days and its West Coast underwriting office for 15, at a cost of around $1 million, nine of its officers were censured and six were suspended for three weeks without pay. The SEC could have imposed a stiffer penalty. But the case did serve to establish the principle that inside information is not to be used by a broker to enable certain customers to profit in the market at the expense of others. If he reveals such information to any of his customers, he must reveal it to all of them.

Extending the Scope of the Law

Corporations whose shares were not listed on an organized exchange were exempt from the proxy solicitation and financial reporting requirements of the Securities Exchange Act of 1934, and from its limitations on stock trading by corporate insiders. The investigators found, in 1963, that one fourth of the corporations issuing stock sold over the counter sent no financial reports to shareholders and that proxy solicitations gave no information on nominees for directorships. The Securities Acts Amendments of 1964 extended controls on financial reporting, proxy solicitation, and insider trading to companies selling securities over the counter if they had more than $1 million in assets and more than 750 stockholders, a figure which fell to 500 at the end of two years.

The *Report of Special Study* stated that one fifth of all banks sent no financial data to their shareholders; that 97 percent of their proxy solicitations gave no information on nominees for directorships, and that 92 percent of the solicitations did not even give the names of such nominees. It recommended that proxy solicitation and financial reporting requirements be extended to banks and to insurance companies. The Amendments of 1964 did extend the requirements to banks but assigned their administration to the federal banking authorities rather than to the SEC. They did not extend the requirements to insurance companies, leaving this matter to be regulated by the states.

Purely intrastate distributions of securities are exempt from the registration provisions of the Securities Act of 1933 but not from its prohibitions against fraud. The SEC cannot police these prohibitions, however, since it has no way to learn that an intrastate offering exists. The Study recommended that persons offering securities for intrastate sale be required to notify the SEC. The Commission would then be able to check on possible fraud in their distribution. Congress declined to enact this requirement into law.

Bankruptcy and Reorganization

Where debtors are able to pay their debts, government stands ready to enforce the contracts they have made. But where, through incompetence or misfortune, they have lost their ability to pay, such contracts cannot be enforced. Here, government serves as an umpire, safeguarding the interests of debtors and creditors alike. It refuses creditors the right to seize all of a debtor's assets, depriving him of the means of self-support and denying him an opportunity to make another start. It forbids the debtor to hide his assets, to change their location, or to transfer their ownership in an effort to defraud his creditors. It prevents one creditor from taking possession of assets to which another has an equal claim. In some cases, it liquidates the debtor's assets and seeks to distribute the proceeds, with an even hand, among his creditors. In others, it attempts to effect a compromise that will lighten the debtor's burden by persuading his creditors to extend the maturity and reduce the size of their claims. Where the debtor is a corporate enterprise, it may undertake to keep the business in operation and to improve its prospects by reorganizing its financial structure, easing its debts but giving the holders of each of its securities an opportunity to participate fairly in its future returns. These things are done, through the courts, under the provisions of the bankruptcy laws.

Congress was given power, by the Constitution, "to establish uniform laws on the subject of Bankruptcies." During most of the 19th century, however, it left this matter to the several states. A permanent federal bankruptcy law was not enacted until 1898. This law endured, without significant amendments, for nearly 40 years. It provided not only for liquidation and distribution of a debtor's assets but also for an agreement scaling down his debts, and the latter procedure was frequently employed in settling cases involving small concerns. But the law made no provision for the reorganization of larger corporations, and such reorganizations came increasingly to be effected through equity receiverships. It was the exposure of abuses that had grown up under this system that led to the amendment of the Bankruptcy Act during the thirties, most notably by the Chandler Act of 1938.

The Chandler Act applies to industrial and utility corporations and prescribes the procedure that must be followed if the debts of such a corporation exceed $250,000 and it is to be reorganized. The law limits the activities of insiders and provides extensive safeguards for other holders of securities. It requires the court to appoint a disinterested person as trustee, excluding from this post all creditors, stockholders, directors, officers, and employees of the company, its lawyers, and its bankers. It requires all those who seek to represent the interests of investors to file sworn statements and empowers the court to supervise their operations and to pass upon the compensation they receive. It charges the trustees with sole responsibility for formulating the plan of reorganization and presenting it to the court, after notifying the interested parties and considering whatever proposals they may make. It directs the court to hold a hearing on the trustee's plan and where a corporation's debts exceed $3 million to obtain an opinion from the SEC. When the plan is approved by the court, the law provides that it shall be submitted to the company's creditors and stockholders, together with the court's opinion and the Commission's report. If creditors with two thirds of the company's debt and owners with half of its stock agree, the plan then goes into effect.[8]

THE SECURITIES AND EXCHANGE COMMISSION

The SEC is a small agency with a big job. With a staff numbering a few hundred professionals, it is expected to supervise all of the aspects of the securities business in the United States: the securities distributors, the invest-

---

8 / Reorganization procedure for railroads is governed by amendments adopted in 1933 and 1935 and differs in detail from that described above. Here, the law manifests somewhat less concern for the safety of the investor, and the preparation of opinions on reorganization plans is assigned to the Interstate Commerce Commission rather than the SEC.

ment companies, the exchanges, the behavior of corporate officials themselves. Its task is constantly growing in volume and changing in character. Congress has delegated to the Commission broad discretionary authority to regulate by making rules. But the Commission has chosen, of necessity, to fulfill its function in so far as possible through self-regulation. It has placed its emphasis on prevention rather than punishment.

Each year the SEC receives and analyzes thousands of registration statements (4,700 in 1969) and processes the median statement within 44 calendar days. Each year, too, it passes on thousands of proxy statements submitted by managements and by groups opposing managements. And it acts on thousands of complaints from investors concerning the conduct of broker-dealers, investment advisers, and investment funds. In this way, it has protected investors against misrepresentation and forced the disclosure of facts that were withheld. The Commission's very existence has doubtless prevented fraudulent representations that otherwise would have been made.

The SEC has kept trading on the exchanges under surveillance and has investigated irregularities that have occurred. It constantly feeds information on stock transactions into computers that are programmed to give warning whenever the price of a stock departs from an established norm, i.e., when it suddenly moves by more than 10 percent, either up or down. In such a case, the Commission seeks to find reasons for the change. These may be obvious: a favorable earnings report, a pending merger. But where such changes are unexplained, the Commission takes the case to the Exchange to determine whether manipulative activity may be under way. If investigation reveals an infraction by a member firm, the Exchange will take corrective action. In a churning market, it may not always be possible to detect trading patterns that would reveal manipulation. But with oversight so constant and pervasive, it is unlikely that manipulation of the sort experienced in the twenties could be carried on overtly or on a major scale.

The Commission's supervision of exchange self-regulation, however, has been open to criticism. According to the authors of the *Report of Special Study:*

> The Commission has not established an effective system of regular surveillance of the exchanges' enforcement and disciplinary activities. In general it has equipped itself, its personnel and procedures, only for the more passive role of surveying whatever is brought to its attention through reporting systems.[9]
>
> An insufficient portion of the attention and energies of the Commission and its staff . . . has been devoted to . . . continuous examination of changing market circumstances and regulatory needs, appraisal and reappraisal of the adequacy of existing regulatory measures, and evaluation and oversight of the operations of self-regulatory organizations. Although the Commission's Division of Trading and Exchanges . . . has been manned by persons of great competence and dedication, it does not appear to have

9 / *Report of Special Study of Securities Markets of the SEC,* Part V, p. 199.

been adequately staffed or organized to fulfill its potential and necessary role. . . .[10]

The Commission's most serious failure occurred in the case of the American Exchange. Here, control had been assumed by a self-perpetuating group of specialists. Attention was centered on increasing the volume of listings without regard to their quality. American Exchange officials and members had profited from inside information given them by listed companies and by purchasing the shares of these companies at prices lower than those charged on the Exchange. The rules of the American Exchange were neither observed nor enforced. The whole machinery of self-regulation broke down. None of this was detected by the SEC in time to be prevented. When the scandal was finally aired, the Commission required that the American Exchange be reorganized and its rules revised. The Exchange, accordingly, adopted a new constitution, installed a new management, adopted stricter listing standards, imposed tighter controls on traders, and took disciplinary action against violators of its rules.

In general, the prestige of the SEC has been high. The Commission has succeeded to a degree unusual in a regulatory agency in enlisting the cooperation and winning the respect of the enterprises that it regulates. It has enjoyed greater freedom than most such agencies from political attack. It has been ranked by scholars as the most successful of the federal agencies. In 1949, a task force of the Hoover Commission on governmental organization reported that the SEC "has combined knowledge of the field, judgment and reasonable consistency of policy with freedom from partisan political pressures." In sum, the task force found the SEC to be "an outstanding example of the independent commission at its best."[11] And this is a verdict that would hold today.

What is the explanation? First, the Commission's purpose is clear and is generally approved. It is to make securities markets honest. The Commission has no monopoly rights to give away; no competitor to protect against his rivals. Its only service is to the truth. Second, the Commission has operated in a field where it has been possible, as it would not be possible, for instance, in the regulation of broadcasting, to delegate a major part of the regulatory detail to the industry itself, and this has spared its energies for other work. Third, the SEC, during most of its life, has had strong leadership, and it has succeeded in retaining a nucleus of highly qualified, experienced, professional staff. None of the other regulatory agencies has been so fortunate.

In a letter mailed to leaders of the securities business during his campaign for the presidency in 1968, Richard M. Nixon denounced proposals sponsored by the SEC for the regulation of brokers' commissions and the control of mutual funds and promised to put an end to "heavy-handed bureaucratic regulatory schemes." This statement created some apprehension at the time. But there is no evidence, as yet, that the Commission's teeth are to be pulled.

10 / *Ibid.,* p. 201.

11 / Commission on Organization of the Executive Branch of the Government, *Task Force Report on Regulatory Commissions* (Washington, D.C.: Government Printing Office, 1949), p. 144.

Chapter 27 CONSERVING NATURAL RESOURCES

In the exploitation of natural resources, competition cannot be relied upon to protect the public interest. Here, competing producers may cut the trees off hillsides, permitting the rains to wash the topsoil from farm lands, to shoal streams and clog reservoirs, and to flood the cities in the valleys below. They may scramble for petroleum, blowing natural gas into the air, flooding the pools with water, and leaving much of the oil underground. They may draw heavily upon supplies of water for use in agriculture or industry, lowering the water table for a whole community. They may pour wastes into the streams and lakes, destroying fisheries; release them into the air, endangering human life. In cases such as these the general welfare is endangered, and action to conserve resources must be taken by government.

THE NEED FOR CONSERVATION

When the first white men came to this continent, resources were so abundant in relation to needs that no thought had to be given to economy in their use. What man desired was his for the taking, and whatever was taken, there was more to take. And so, for more than two centuries, natural wealth was wasted recklessly. It was converted into private fortunes. It was destroyed for the pleasure of destroying it. In time, as population expanded and as levels of living rose, requirements increased and resources grew scarce. It came to be realized that profligacy was no longer possible. And out of this realization came the popular demand that waste be prevented and natural wealth conserved. The conservation movement had its origin in the abuses of the past.

The Rape of a Continent

Three centuries ago half of the land that now comprises the United States was in timber—unbroken tracts of virgin forest stretching for hundreds of miles, dense stands of white pine to the north, yellow pine to the south, and softwoods in the far west, with giant trees centuries old, measuring from 5 to 10 feet through and towering 200 and even 300 feet into the air. Between the forests lay the grasslands of the Great Plains with deep layers of fertile soil built up over the ages as grasses rotted where they died. Everywhere, save in the deserts, water was plentiful, its surface flow controlled, its underground sources replenished by moisture-holding roots and leaves. The streams ran clear; rivers, lakes, and oceans teemed with fish. Plains and forests abounded with wildlife; great herds of buffalo, elk, and antelope roamed the prairies; countless flocks of wild fowl crossed the skies. Beneath the surface lay rich deposits of minerals: metals readily accessible, coal in quantity, oil and gas held in vast reservoirs waiting only to be tapped.

Upon this natural paradise the white man fell with weapons of destruction, chopping, plowing, and shooting his way from east to west. The forests he regarded as a nuisance, felling giant trees to clear the land for planting, stripping them to get bark for tanning, burning them to get lye for soap. For generations he cut the forests clean, leaving dry slash to burn and scorch the soil, sparing no trees to scatter seeds and start new growth. By 1850 the center of logging had moved from Maine to New York, by 1860 to Pennsylvania, by 1870 to the region of the Great Lakes, by 1900 to the pineries of the South, by 1930 to the Pacific Coast. What axe and fire did to the forests, the plow, cattle, and sheep did to the hillsides and the plains. Plowing and overgrazing destroyed the grasses, removing the soil's protective cover, exposing it to wind and water, and leaving it to blow and wash away. The rain, instead of renewing stores of water underground, increasingly ran off the surface. Rivers were yellowed with silt, poisoned with industrial wastes, turned into open sewers. Fish were destroyed by pollution of the inland streams, by overfishing of the lakes and seas. The giant sturgeon of the Chesapeake Bay were slaughtered for their roe, their bodies thrown to rot along the shore. The numbers of birds and animals were reduced by the destruction of their natural habitat—the cutting of forests, the plowing of grasslands, and the drainage of swamps. Wildlife was eliminated, too, by trap and gun, to provide food and clothing, to protect crops and livestock, and merely for the pleasure of the sport. The egret was killed for its plumes, thousands of buffalo for their tongues, and elk to get two teeth to dangle from a chain. Methods of mining were equally destructive: the more accessible deposits were taken, the richer veins exploited, the poorer ones allowed to go to waste; gas was blown away and oil left underground.

Our resources, as a consequence, have been depleted. Nine tenths of our virgin timber has been cut. Great stands have been turned into inferior second growth, or into worthless brush, unsightly stumps, and bare rock. Nearly a third of our topsoil has washed or blown away. Erosion is said to have destroyed or seriously impoverished some 280 million acres of crop and range land, an area equal to that of six midwestern states. The water table has been lowered; in the arid West and the industrial East, particularly, populations have approached the limits of supply. Important fisheries have been exhausted; catches have declined; species once plentiful have all but disappeared. Many forms of wildlife have been extinguished, among them the passenger pigeon, the great auk, the heath hen, and the Labrador duck; others would be extinct if not protected by the law. Minerals, too, have been moving toward exhaustion at a rapidly quickening pace. For most of them consumption in the United States since World War I has been greater than that in all the world in all the years before. From 1900 to 1950 the annual use of all materials increased 5 times, the use of crude oil 30 times. In that half century more copper, lead, and zinc was taken than was left in known reserves. Once self-sufficient in the basic metals, we must now import to satisfy our needs. The cream has been skimmed from our resources; the day when they could be taken for granted has long been past.

Not only has man reduced the quantity of natural resources; he has impaired the quality of what remains. He has polluted the waters with industrial wastes; with pesticides, detergents, and sewage. He has polluted the air with noxious fumes; with soot, dust, and chemicals. He has disfigured the landscape; raised the level of noise, in urban areas, close to the limits of human tolerance.

Alarmed by what he has done to his natural environment, man has sought to conserve it. His efforts have been tardy and intermittent. Their emphasis has shifted from time to time.

The Conservation Movement

The demand for conservation of natural resources came first from geographers and foresters, from nature lovers and sportsmen, and from citizens aroused by evidence of wanton waste. It concerned itself, primarily, with preservation of the forests and with protection of wildlife and fisheries. The first measure adopted by Congress in this field, in 1871, created a Commissioner of Fish and Fisheries. The second, in 1872, established the Yellowstone National Park, to provide "for the preservation, from injury or spoilation, of all timber, mineral deposits, natural curiosities or wonders within said park, and their retention in their natural condition" to serve "as a public park or pleasuring ground for the benefit and enjoyment of the people." This was followed, in 1888, by a law facilitating the irrigation of arid lands; in 1890, by one creating Yosemite National Park; and in 1891, by one that authorized the President to issue proclamations withdrawing public lands from entry, to be held as forest reserves. Such withdrawals were subsequently made by Harrison, Cleveland, and McKinley; a forestry bureau was set up in the Department of Agriculture in 1897, and Gifford Pinchot was appointed as its chief in 1898.

It was through the crusading zeal of Pinchot, in the administration of Theodore Roosevelt, that conservation was made a national issue. "The forest and water problems," said Roosevelt in his first message to Congress, "are perhaps the most vital internal questions of the United States." A number of important measures followed. More national parks were created. The forest reserves were greatly enlarged. In 1902 Congress provided for the construction of irrigation projects by the federal government; in 1903, for the creation of national wildlife refuges; in 1905, for the establishment of the Forest Service; in 1906, for the protection of Alaskan fisheries. In 1908 the movement was given further impetus by the endorsement of conservation measures in the platforms of both major parties.

Carried forward under Taft and Wilson, the movement received a setback when public attention was diverted by World War I, and when Albert B. Fall, Secretary of the Interior in the Harding administration, was convicted of accepting bribes to turn the navy's oil reserves at Elk Hills, California, and Teapot Dome, Wyoming, over to private companies. Interest was again aroused, however, during the thirties, when drought and wind filled the air with clouds of dust, and when the "Okies," driven from the Dust Bowl of the Great Plains, set forth upon the trek to California described by John Steinbeck in *The Grapes of Wrath.* Now a second crusader appeared, under a second Roosevelt, this time preaching the gospel of conservation of the soil. Through speeches, magazine articles, and motion pictures like *The Plow That Broke the Plains* and *The River,* Hugh H. Bennett took his message to the people. Through the Soil Conservation Service of the Department of Agriculture, established under his leadership, he left his mark upon the land. The New Deal will be remembered, too, for the Taylor Grazing Act—marking the first attempt to prevent overgrazing on the public range—for extension of the system of national parks and monuments, for the work of the young men enrolled during the Great Depression in the Civilian Conservation Corps, for reforestation, and for the inauguration of great projects—beginning with the TVA—for reclamation, rehabilitation, and flood control.

The public interest in conservation again lagged during and after World War II. There were still a score and more of national organizations representing the interests of their members in the parks and forests, in wildlife, birds, and fisheries, and in other forms of natural wealth. Significant reports were issued by the President's Water Policy Resources Commission in 1950 and by the President's Materials Policy Commission in 1952. But the people were apathetic. The war had made heavy inroads on their natural resources, but they still enjoyed prosperity. Materials might be exhausted, but they were confident that science would produce synthetic substitutes. Public regulation came to be viewed with suspicion. A drive to sabotage the Taylor Grazing Act succeeded. A protracted struggle between state and federal governments for the control of off-shore oil did not appear to raise a ripple of concern.

It was not until the Johnson Administration that conservation again moved to the center of the stage. Now it was directed toward the needs of an urban society, the quality of the environment, the aesthetics of land use. It sought to prevent pollution of water and air; to restore the beauty of the countryside by landscaping highways, eliminating billboards, and removing or screening automobile graveyards and roadside junkyards. It undertook to increase the facilities available for recreation: wilderness areas; seashores and lakeshores; national, city, and roadside parks.

With the coming of the seventies, the conservation movement had widespread support. There was popular opposition to the construction of dams that would submerge scenic and historic areas; of highways and jetports that would destroy parklands and refuges for wildlife; of atomic power plants that would discharge heated water into rivers, raising their temperature and destroying aquatic life.

There was general concern with the extent and consequences of pollution of water and air. There was alarm concerning overpopulation and the declining resource base. Conservation became a popular issue and politicians vied for recognition as conservationists. Hundreds of bills were introduced in Congress; dozens of hearings were held; appropriations for conservation programs exceeded the administration's requests. A Council on Environmental Quality was set up by Congress in 1969. With the bandwagon rolling, President Nixon climbed aboard.[1]

Future Requirements and Resources

The United States will be confronted, in the years that lie ahead, with the problem of maintaining a growing population, at a rising level of living, on a fixed base of natural resources. By the year 2000 the country's population will be around 300 million. Its gross national product, increasing at less than 4 percent per year, will be four times that of 1960. To support production at this rate, its annual consumption of farm products and its withdrawals of fresh water will have to be doubled, its consumption of timber nearly tripled, its consumption of metals and of energy tripled.[2] And both materials and power must come from resources that have finite limits, some of them largely exhausted, others approaching exhaustion at a rapid rate.

Natural resources may be divided, according to the nature of the problems presented by increasing requirements, into three major groups: (1) those that are inexhaustible, such as solar energy and water power; (2) those that are exhaustible but replaceable, such as forests, grasslands, wildlife (if not exterminated), and the fertility of the soil; and (3) those that are exhaustible and irreplaceable, such as minerals (including metals and fuels) and the soil itself. The minerals may be further divided into (a) those that are relatively plentiful in the United States, such as coal, and (b) those that are relatively scarce, such as oil and gas. With respect to the first group of resources no need for conservation will arise. With respect to the second, the need is for avoidance of waste in exploitation and attention to renewal of supply. It is principally in the third category, and particularly in its second subdivision, that there is danger of serious shortages.

But sober judgment, even here, supports no prophecy of doom. If materials grow scarce they may be imported—at least in peacetime—from abroad. With intensified effort and with new techniques of exploration, further deposits may be disclosed at home. With improved methods of recovery, more may be obtained from known reserves. Deposits of lower grade may be exploited, synthetic substitutes developed, and more plentiful materials employed in place of scarcer ones. By reclaiming scrap the same materials may be used again and again. Supplies may be stretched, moreover, through greater economy in use. The problem to be faced in the future will not be that of unsatisfied wants but that

1 / See Frank E. Smith, *The Politics of Conservation* (New York: Pantheon, 1967).

2 / Hans H. Landsberg, *Natural Resources for U.S. Growth* (Baltimore: Johns Hopkins University Press, 1964).

of rising costs. This problem should be soluble, though difficult. But for its solution continued attention to conservation will be required.

The Meaning of Conservation

Conservation has two different meanings. According to the first, it is enforced nonuse, requiring the present generation to abstain from exploiting natural resources so that they may be preserved for exploitation by other generations later on. According to the second, it is avoidance of waste. But waste also has two meanings. The one is expressed in physical terms: in this sense, waste occurs whenever resources are lost that might have been recovered by the most efficient methods available, even though their value may fail to cover the necessary cost. The second meaning is economic: here, waste is said to occur when resources are lost whose value would have covered the cost of saving them.

Conservation, conceived of as nonuse or as avoidance of physical waste, may be appropriate in certain cases: the preservation of the redwoods, of wilderness areas, of wildlife, of natural curiosities and national monuments, and of resources required, at any cost, for national defense. But it is not appropriate for forests, soils, and waters, or for minerals, in general, as was shown by the President's Materials Policy Commission in 1952:

> One popular fallacy is to regard our resource base as a fixed inventory which, when used up, will leave society with no means of survival. A related fallacy is that physical waste equals economic waste: the feeling that it is wasteful to use materials in ways that make them disappear. This attitude can lead to devoting a dollar's worth of work to "saving" a few cents worth of waste paper and old string. These fallacies together lead to a hairshirt concept of conservation which makes it synonymous with hoarding. . . .
> Conservation is something very different from simply leaving oil in the ground or trees in the forests on the theory that by sacrificing lower value uses today we will leave something for the higher value uses of tomorrow when supplies will be scarcer. Using resources today is an essential part of making our economy grow; materials which become embodied in today's capital goods, for example, are put to work and help make tomorrow's production higher. Hoarding resources in the expectation of more important uses later involves a sacrifice that may never be recouped; technological changes and new resource discoveries may alter a situation completely. It may not be wise to refrain from using zinc today if our grandchildren will not know what to do with it tomorrow.[3]

True conservation, then, may be defined as the management of publicly owned resources and the supervision of privately owned resources in the general interest. In various cases it may involve the preservation of unique resources for

3 / President's Materials Policy Commission, *Resources for Freedom* (Washington, D.C.: Government Printing Office, 1952), Vol I, p. 21.

continued enjoyment or insurance against emergencies, the development of new resources through drainage, irrigation, and similar activities, the restoration of damaged resources and the prevention of future damage through reforestation, improvements in cultivation, control of pollution, and the like, and the maintenance of renewable resources by making renewal coincident with use. In every case, including that of nonrenewable resources, it requires avoidance of economic waste.

THE PUBLIC DOMAIN

The areas comprising the public domain of the United States were acquired, first, by cession to the federal government of lands extending to the Mississippi claimed by the 13 original states, and then, in 1802, by purchase of claims to lands beyond the Mississippi from France. They were subsequently extended by the purchase of Florida from Spain in 1819, the occupation of the Northwest Territory in 1846, and the cession of vast southwestern regions by Mexico in 1848, supplemented by purchase from Mexico in 1853. Title to many of these lands was confirmed through conquest and through treaties with the Indian tribes. In this way, a century ago, the federal government came to own 1,442 million acres, or three fourths of the area then within the boundaries of the United States. These holdings were further augmented by the purchase of Alaska, involving another 378 million acres, from Russia in 1867.

Having come into possession of such vast areas, the government was faced with the following problems. Should its lands be held or disposed of? If held, how should they be administered? If disposed of, what should be the terms? Of the 1.8 billion acres that once constituted the public domain, a billion acres have been transferred from federal ownership, while 750 million acres, a third of the nation's area, remain in federal hands. Policy in the disposal and in the reservation of public lands will be discussed in this section. Policy in the administration of such lands will be considered, in connection with the discussion of particular resources, later on.

Disposal of Public Lands

Some sales of public land were made to settlers, for as little as 75 cents an acre, before the federal government was formed. But disposition on a major scale did not occur until the public domain had been established and surveyed, laid out in townships, and divided into sections of 640 acres each. Thereafter, the dominant policy was that of transferring ownership to state governments and to private interests. Large tracts of land were given to the states to encourage education, reclamation, and other public activities, and to railroad companies to promote the nation's economic development. Until 1862, aside from such grants, disposal of public lands was regarded mainly as a source of revenue. Sales were made at first in tracts of a section each, then in half sections, in quarter sections, and finally in eighths. The price stood at $2 an acre until

1820 and at $1.25 from 1820 on. Under the Homestead Act of 1862, emphasis shifted from the provision of revenue to the promotion of settlement. In accordance with laws enacted in 1830 and in 1841, squatters had long been granted prior purchase rights. But now, title to a quarter section might be obtained, without payment, by five years occupancy and improvement of the land. The people were thus invited to help themselves, and land was divided among them on the basis of first come, first served.

This policy, already generous, was later made even more so. Under the Timber Culture Act of 1873, an individual was authorized to obtain 160 acres of land by planting trees on 40; under the Timber and Stone Act of 1878, by planting trees on 10. Under the latter law, moreover, he was entitled to purchase a quarter section of valuable timber land on the Pacific Coast for $2.50 per acre. Under the Desert Land Act of 1877, one who promised to irrigate arid land was permitted to buy 640 acres, and later 320 acres, at $1.25 an acre. In 1909, a homesteader was enabled to acquire a half section of such land, and in 1916, a full section, without charge. In 1912, too, the period of occupancy required under the Homestead Act was reduced from five years to three.

The provisions of these laws, though lenient, were frequently ignored. The public domain was not adequately policed. The conditions governing its exploitation were not effectively enforced. Land was occupied without registry. Timber was cut, for decades, over wide areas, by trespassers. Title to tracts many times the size of a quarter section, or a section, was obtained through dummy entries by railroad, lumber, and mining companies. Great stands of timber and rich deposits of minerals were thus turned over to private interests for as little as $1.25 an acre or, under the Homestead Act, for nothing at all.

Reservation and Extension of Public Lands

With the growth of the conservation movement, from the end of the 19th century, there came to be increasing support for the view that the public lands remaining, instead of being turned over to homesteaders or left open to unregulated grazing, should be reserved for public uses and administered by agencies of government. Earlier, reservations had been made for occupancy by the Indian tribes and for the establishment of Yellowstone and Yosemite parks. But the policy of reservation really dates from 1891, when Congress authorized the President to issue proclamations reserving forest lands. Under this authority, 46 million acres were reserved by Harrison, Cleveland, and McKinley, 148 million by Theodore Roosevelt. Reservations came to be made, too, by Congress itself or by the Executive under enabling acts, for other national parks and monuments, for wildlife refuges, for irrigation projects, and for power sites. And finally, after 1934, more than 142 million acres of range lands were withdrawn from alienation under the Taylor Grazing Act.

Not only has the public domain increasingly been closed to private ownership but its size has been augmented by purchases from private owners and by private gifts, amounting to 50 million acres or more. The homestead laws are still on the books. But, outside Alaska, there is little land now open to entry. And, save for unsuspected mineral wealth, this land is virtually valueless.

The policy of reservation has always met with vigorous local opposition. Ninety-six percent of the land remaining in the public domain lies within the borders of 11 western states. And here it comprises more than half of the total area. The states concerned complain that federal ownership of their resources deprives them of needed revenues. The government has met this argument, in part, by sharing with the states the monies it collects from licensees who operate on public lands. But the real basis for opposition is a fundamental one. The lumbering, grazing, and mining interests desire to have the public domain offered for sale, or at least turned over to the states, so that they may exploit it with fewer restraints than would be imposed by the federal government. For this reason, the reservation of public lands has constantly been under attack. Threats to national parks and monuments have also appeared in the form of plans to submerge them by constructing dams to control the flow of rivers, provide water for irrigation and domestic use, and generate electricity; threats to wildlife refuges in the form of plans to convert them into weapons-testing sites for the armed services. These threats, too, have usually been defeated when they have aroused the resistance of recreational interests, sportsmen, and conservationists.

The Submerged Coastal Lands

Along the nation's coasts and stretching out to sea from the low tide mark there lies a strip of land that is under relatively shallow water, known as the continental shelf. In width it averages some 30 miles, varying from narrow ledges to sections in the Gulf of Mexico that reach as far as 250 miles before they drop into the deeps. For three miles out this area has been held by international law to fall within our national boundaries. But, until recently, it has not mattered whether it belonged to the federal government or to the states. In practice, the states have regulated the taking of clams, oysters, shrimps, crabs, sponges, and other forms of marine life from these waters, and the federal government has acquiesced. But no real issue of ownership was raised until the thirties, when rich deposits of oil were discovered in the Pacific off the coast of California and in the Gulf of Mexico off the shores of Texas and Louisiana. It was this discovery that gave rise to protracted controversy over title to the tidelands, so called despite the fact that the right of the states to areas between the high and low tide marks had never been a matter of dispute.

The states concerned enacted laws asserting their ownership of offshore oil. By this authority they licensed drilling and collected royalties. Bills claiming federal ownership were introduced in Congress from time to time but failed to pass. Then, in 1945, President Truman issued a proclamation asserting the supremacy of federal rights, and the Attorney General brought suit against the state of California asking for invalidation of its law. In 1946, while this case was pending, Congress passed a quitclaim bill relinquishing the lands in question to the states. The bill was vetoed, and the veto was sustained. Then, in 1947, the Supreme Court handed down its decision, denying title to California without giving it clearly to the federal government, but asserting that the latter "has paramount rights in and power over that belt, an incident to which is full dominion over the resources of the soil under that water area . . ."[4] The government then sued the states of Texas and Louisiana and, in 1950, was again upheld. In 1952, Congress passed a second quitclaim bill, characterized by the President as "robbery in broad daylight—and on a colossal scale." Again the bill was vetoed and the veto sustained. Then in 1953, after weeks of hearings and a month of Senate debate, a third bill was passed by Congress and signed by President Eisenhower.

The constitutionality of the new law was challenged by the states of Rhode Island and Alabama and was upheld by the Supreme Court on the ground that the right to dispose of property belonging to the United States "is vested in Congress without limitation."[5] But this left another issue to be settled. The law transferred to the coastal states title to those offshore lands that lay within their "historic boundaries." But the location of these boundaries was in dispute. Was it set at three miles or at three leagues (or 10½ miles)? Was it to be measured from the low-water mark existing today or from that existing when a state joined the Union? Was it to be measured from the mainland or from outlying islands? Was it to run in a straight line or was it to follow the indentations of the shore? The answers to these questions were left to the Supreme Court. In the meantime, the Gulf states proceeded to grant leases and to collect royalties on the lands they claimed. In 1957, the federal government brought suit against them, rejecting their claims to lands beyond the three-mile limit and asking that royalties collected on such lands be turned over to the federal treasury. In 1960, the Court held that the historic boundaries of Florida and Texas extended three leagues into the Gulf but that those of the other states extended only three miles.[6] Louisiana was thus required to relinquish millions in accumulated royalties that had been held in escrow. In subsequent decisions the Court rejected California's claim that its historic boundaries extended into the Pacific for three miles beyond its most distant islands, some 50 miles beyond its coast, and the claim of Texas that its boundaries reached for three leagues beyond artificial jetties built offshore. It appears, however, that a major part of the proven reserves of off-shore oil has been given to the coastal states.

Recreational Lands

In 1962, a Congressional commission on outdoor recreational resources, under the chairmanship of Laurance S. Rockefeller, presented a long-range program designed to meet the growing need for such facilities. The commission

---

4 / *U.S.* v. *California*, 332 U.S. 19, 38-39.

5 / *Alabama* v. *Texas, Louisiana, Florida, California*, 347 U.S. 272 (1954).

6 / *U.S.* v. *Louisiana, Texas, Mississippi, Alabama, Florida*, 363 U.S. 1.

recommended not only that existing recreational areas be preserved but also that additional ocean and lake shores and other recreational lands near major population centers be acquired by federal, state, and local governments. This proposal was embodied in the Land and Water Conservation Fund Act of 1965. Under this law, money received by the federal government from several sources (receipts from the sale of surplus lands, entrance fees at national recreational areas, charges for the use of camp sites, and a tax on fuel used by motor boats) is kept in a separate fund. Two fifths of this fund is to be used by the government to purchase outdoor recreational facilities near urban areas. Three fifths of it is to be granted to the states, on a matching basis, for the same purpose. It was expected that this provision would make possible the expenditure of as much as $2 billion on such facilities in the next 10 years.

FORESTS

The forests of the United States were long treated as if they were mines to be exhausted rather than lands to be kept producing annual crops. Careless logging destroyed the smaller trees and left the ground covered with slash and brush, inviting fires that killed the seed trees and burned the soil itself. Clear cutting, too, killed the seed trees and the seedlings, and comparatively little replanting was done. Methods of lumbering have been improved, in recent years, and some of the more flagrant wastes reduced. But it was estimated in the fifties that disease still destroyed a billion cubic feet of wood a year and fire destroyed a half billion more. Half of the timber cut and sawed was wasted in the process: one fourth of the material contained in a tree was left in the woods; another fourth was left at the mill.[7] The annual growth still runs little ahead of the annual cut, being only half of that needed to satisfy future demands. Forest conservation, therefore, requires increased disease and fire protection, improved techniques and greater care in logging, fuller utilization of the wood that is taken, and replanting at twice the rate that presently obtains.

If timber is to be regarded not as a mineral but as a crop, the forests must be so managed that their yield will be sustained. A tree suitable for pulpwood can be grown in from 15 to 40 years; one suitable for lumber will take from 50 to 80 years. To obtain the greatest possible output, in the long run, those trees—and only those trees—should be taken that are ripe for use. And for every tree that is cut, another should be planted to take its place. If 50 years were the period required for growth, one fiftieth of a stand would be cut and one fiftieth replanted every year. The harvest would thus be reaped, but the forest would remain. This is the meaning of sustained yield management.

The possibilities of conserving the forests depend upon the character of their ownership. A third of the forest land in the United States is publicly owned, more than 180 million acres being owned by the federal government. Two thirds is private property. Of this land, a fifth is in large tracts held by pulp and

7 / President's Materials Policy Commission, *op. cit.,* chap. 8.

lumber companies. The rest is in scattered patches, nearly half of it in woodlots on several million farms. For the public forests, adoption of conservation measures is merely a matter of good management. For private holdings, it may require the imposition of controls. Where holdings are large, controls are clearly feasible. Where holdings are small and scattered, they are difficult to enforce.

Administration of Public Forests

The timber in the national forests is not withheld from use but is exploited in accordance with the sustained yield principle. Standing timber is sold to private loggers on the basis of competitive bids. Contracts may specify the types and sizes of trees that are to be taken, or government foresters may mark the trees that are to be cut. Contractors are forbidden to injure the remaining trees and are required to dispose of all inflammable slash. Operations are policed by the foresters, and observance of regulations is enforced.

Two criticisms have been made of federal forest policy. The first had to do with the size of the permitted cut. The government's fifth of the commercial forest land contains more than half of the standing timber. But it has accounted for less than a third of the annual cut. The private forests are being seriously depleted. But the public forests have not been drawn upon as extensively as sustained yield management would allow. Trees that were overripe were allowed to stand, impeding the surrounding growth. The difficulty here, in part at least, was that of inaccessibility.

A second issue arose, in the Pacific Northwest, in connection with the building of access roads. For many years, the government confined itself to selling timber rights, and the major lumber companies built the railroads, and later the dirt roads, over which the logs were hauled. Then the government itself began to build better all-purpose forest roads. As a result, many smaller loggers were enabled to reach the timber and haul it away by truck. The number of bidders increased, and prices tended to rise. The larger companies, therefore, denounced the construction of public roads as socialistic and demanded that it be stopped. The smaller ones, on the other hand, demanded that more such roads be built. The question here was not whether or how the trees were to be cut but at what price and by whom.

In recent years, this conflict has subsided. The prices of timber products have risen. More access roads have been constructed. The cut of timber in the national forests has been sharply increased. Sales of this timber now exceed $200 million a year.

State Regulation of Private Forests

The standards of private forestry in the United States, though greatly improved in recent years, still leave much to be desired. On many of the larger properties, owned by pulp and lumber companies, the practices are good. Trained foresters are employed, and timber is treated as an annual crop. But on the smaller patches, where most of the trees are found, the practices are generally poor. Timber, when sold, is cut clean and little replanting is done.

Most of the timber states, particularly those in the North and the West, now have well-supported forestry departments. All of the states have laws designed to protect their forests against fire and disease. Some of them also seek to regulate private forest practices. In 1970, there were nine states with laws promoting improvement in methods of lumbering. In some cases, these laws provided for the issuance of rules by state officials. In others, they left establishment of standards to local committees of lumbermen. In most cases, the laws were regarded as "educational" in character; penalties for noncompliance were not imposed. In only a few states, notably Oregon, Washington, and California, were mandatory regulations established and enforced. Here, cutting was forbidden below a certain diameter, retention of seed trees was ordered, and replanting was required.

Federal Regulation of Private Forests

The federal government has no authority directly to regulate private forest management. But it has sought indirectly to promote the adoption of conservation practices. It has aided the states in forest research and education, in fire protection and pest control, and in the provision of planting stock. Under the provisions of the Norris-Doxey Act of 1937, it has encouraged the improvement of forestry in rural areas, particularly on farm wood lots. This program now covers 4 million owners of 300 million wooded acres, participating in several hundred cooperative projects, comprising three to five counties. Each of these projects is provided with a resident forester who renders technical assistance to woodlot owners, advising them on cutting, planting, management, and marketing. Under the provisions of the Sustained Yield Act of 1944, the government has also sought to influence the practices employed on larger private forest lands. This law permits the Forest Service to grant long-term exclusive contracts for cutting trees in public forests to operators who will agree to the establishment, under federal supervision, of sustained yield units that will include adjacent private properties. Such agreements, running from 50 to 100 years, are designed to purchase conformity with conservation practices by giving private operators the assurance of continued timber supplies. This plan, however, has not fulfilled its purpose. Only six agreements had been concluded by 1970. The smaller operators have opposed the program on the ground that it will grant the larger ones perpetual monopolies within the public forests. The larger operators, on the other hand, have hesitated to accept extension of federal supervision to the methods used on private lands.

Conservationists have often contended that forest resources are to be conserved only by taking more forest lands into public ownership, and agencies such as the Forest Service and the National Resources Board recommended, during the thirties, that some 200 million acres be added to existing public forest areas. In later years, attention has shifted to means of increasing public control over private cutting practices. Bills introduced in Congress have provided for the establishment of national standards, for federal grants to enable the states to enforce them, and for federal enforcement where the states might fail to act. Whether state cooperation should thus be coerced, and whether enforcement, on this basis, would be effective, is still a matter of dispute.

SOILS AND WATERS

Conservation of the soil aims to prevent exhaustion of fertility and the loss of the soil itself by controlling methods of grazing and cultivation. Conservation of water seeks to maintain an adequate and steady supply by retarding the runoff and controlling floods. Conservation also enlarges the area available for cultivation by irrigating arid land. Since grazing is largely done on the public domain, it is subject to regulation by the federal government. Cultivation, being done on private lands, is influenced indirectly by the law. Control of water usually involves a drainage basin that extends beyond the boundaries of a single state. State programs to control the supply of water thus require federal support. And large-scale projects designed to hold water in storage, to provide for irrigation, and to prevent floods have been constructed by federal agencies and financed by federal funds.

Administration of Public Grazing Lands

During the 19th century, ranchers turned their livestock loose to graze on public lands. They obtained no permits, observed no rules, and paid no fees. Legally they were in trespass, but no attempt was made to keep them off. As the public domain was sold and given to settlers, the better half of the range lands, producing two thirds of the feed, was taken into private ownership. The poorer half, producing a third of the feed, remained in public hands. This half was still grazed, without permission, regulation, or payment. In some cases, ranchers even sought to fence it, holding that years of uncontested trespass conferred proprietary rights. Control of grazing in national forests was finally inaugurated in 1900; control of grazing on the public range in 1934. Ranchers still drive their herds into the forests and onto the range lands for part of every year. But now permits must be obtained, regulations observed, and payments made.

Priority in obtaining permits for grazing in the forests is given to those whose stock has grazed there in the past. But permits are granted as a privilege, not a right. They are limited to 10 years, are not transferable, and may be revoked. Holders of permits must obey the regulations of the Forest Service. The length of the grazing season and the numbers of livestock admitted are rigidly controlled. The season is shortened and the numbers curtailed, if need be, to protect the forest floor. A fee is charged per animal unit per month in accordance with a formula based on the prices of cattle and sheep in relation to the prices of other goods. The resulting figure is lower, however, than the charges made for grazing on private lands. And the Forest Service cares for and improves the range.

Under the Taylor Grazing Act of 1934, the remaining public range lands, amounting eventually to 158 million acres, were withheld from alienation, and provision was made for their administration by a Grazing Service in the Department of the Interior. Grazing districts were created and advisory boards of local stockmen established to cooperate in making grazing rules. Permits were granted to cover specified numbers of livestock during certain months of the year. Priority was given to past users, and the permits were confined to those who could feed and water stock in the months when it was off the range. These rights, unlike those granted by the Forest Service, were transferable and could thus be capitalized and sold. The fees charged were nominal: 8 cents per head for cattle and horses, one fifth as much for sheep and goats. The Grazing Service was to undertake reseeding and improvement of the forage on the range.

Under pressure from stockmen, control of grazing has repeatedly been subject to political attack. During the forties, Senator McCarran of Nevada launched an investigation of Grazing Service "bureaucracy" that ran for seven years. As a result, the agency's appropriation was cut from more than $1 million in 1945–46 to around $500,000 in 1947–48 and its staff from 250 to 86, leaving but 50 men to supervise 158 million acres of grazing lands. In effect, the senator's campaign repealed the Taylor Grazing Act, delivering the grazing districts into the hands of the local boards of stockmen and leaving the Washington office too weak to exercise control. This served the special interest of the users of the range but sacrificed the general interest in the conservation of the soil. In 1946, Representative (later Senator) Barrett of Wyoming started a similar investigation of the Forest Service, directed toward transferring control of grazing in the forests to local livestock boards. And again in 1953 and 1954, a bill supported by President Eisenhower would have made forest grazing permits permanent and transferable and permitted their holders to construct improvements, excluding newcomers and establishing private property rights on forest lands. A storm of opposition was aroused; the conservationists fought to save the forests as they had not fought to save the soil.[8]

The Grazing Service has now been absorbed by the Bureau of Land Management in the Department of the Interior. In recent years, the Bureau has persuaded Congress to permit it to raise its fees, relating them to the prices of livestock. By 1968 the fees had been increased to 33 cents per animal per month. The Bureau then proposed that they be raised, over a 10-year period to $1.23. As usual, it encountered strong opposition from organized stockmen. The Bureau's appropriation has been increased. Its income now enables it to carry out a more effective program of range improvement and grazing control.

8 / See E. Louise Peffer, *The Closing of the Public Domain* (Stanford, Calif.: Stanford University Press, 1951), chap. xv; and articles by Bernard De Voto in *Harper's Magazine* for January and June, 1947, January and July, 1948, and August, 1954.

Soil Conservation

On land that is under cultivation, the techniques of conservation include the preservation of fertility through fertilization and crop rotation, and the preservation of the soil itself—against wind erosion by planting trees to serve as windbreaks, and against water erosion by terracing sloping fields, by planting crops on the contour, by planting strips of sod-forming grasses and legumes between intertilled crops, by planting wide grassed runways to retard the runoff, by building check dams and diversion channels, and by rotating crops to leave absorbent organic matter in the soil. Farmers cannot be ordered to adopt these practices, but they may be persuaded to do so by undertaking educational programs and by purchasing cooperation with public funds. And this is what the federal government has done. For many years, it has carried on research and education through the Department of Agriculture, the state experiment stations and agricultural colleges, and the agricultural extension service. Beginning with the thirties, it has initiated three more programs in the name of conservation: under the Soil Conservation Act of 1935, the Soil Conservation and Domestic Allotment Act of 1936, and the Soil Bank Act of 1956.

The Act of 1935 established the Soil Conservation Service, and this agency, under H. H. Bennett, embarked upon a program of setting up demonstration projects and providing technical assistance, on a voluntary basis, to combat erosion of the soil. To this end, it sought and obtained the cooperation of the states. Thus, laws were passed by all the states permitting farmers to organize soil conservation districts and administer them as units of local government. At the request of such a district, the technicians of the Soil Conservation Service will make a survey and draw up a work plan for the district and for each of its farms, classifying the land according to its suitability for cultivation and showing the proper use for every field. Working together, a technician and a farmer will determine how to fertilize his soil, how to rotate his crops, where to terrace, where to plant on the contour, where to plant in strips, and where to drain. On the basis of his plan, the farmer will conclude an agreement with the conservation district, which then may help him to obtain equipment, fertilizers, planting stock, and seeds. The character of the program has varied from region to region with differences in the character of the land. It has also changed over the years, its emphasis shifting from soil conservation alone to a broader concern with land use management. By 1968, nearly 3,000 districts had been created, including 97 percent of the nation's farms and 93 percent of its farmland; nearly 2 million farmers were cooperating in the program. Its cost to the federal government was running around $100 million a year.[9]

The Soil Conservation and Domestic Allotment Act of 1936 was employed by the New Deal as a means of maintaining agricultural incomes after the

9 / R. Burnell Held and Marion Clawson, *Soil Conservation in Perspective* (Baltimore, Md.: Johns Hopkins Press, 1965).

Agricultural Adjustment Act of 1933 was found to be unconstitutional. Under the Act of 1933, "benefits" had been paid to farmers who cooperated in raising prices by curtailing the acreage of certain basic crops. Under the new law, "conservation payments" were made to farmers who cooperated in conserving the soil by restricting their planting of "soil-depleting" crops. Under both laws, the crops in question were the same. The Agricultural Conservation Program was thus set up alongside the Soil Conservation Service, and local committees of farmers were created to participate in its administration. During World War II, foods and fibres grew scarce, and emphasis was shifted from curtailment of output to soil-conserving practices. Attention has been directed, however, less toward the prevention of erosion than toward the preservation of fertility. Farmers have been paid for doing things they would have done in any case, i.e., for adopting such profitable practices as liming their fields and planting winter crops. The payments, made with the approval of the local committees, have gone to some 3 million farmers at the rate of $200 million to $250 million a year.

The principal purpose of the Soil Bank program, set up in 1956 for a period of three years, was to curtail the production of basic crops. Farmers were paid to take their land out of wheat, corn, cotton, rice, tobacco, and peanuts and put it in an "acreage reserve" on which they were permitted to graze livestock or produce other crops. They were also paid to put land in a "conservation reserve" on which grazing and cultivation were forbidden. Here, grass and trees were to be grown and water stored. The program cost $725 million in 1957 and $825 million in 1958. The major part of this money was spent on the acreage reserve, a program which ended with the 1958 crop year. The conservation reserve cost $300 million in 1963 and $200 million in 1964.

Of these three programs, that of the Soil Conservation Service has been functionally directed toward the conservation of the soil. The purposes of the other two have been mixed and their value as conservation measures less clear. But it is to them, rather than to the SCS, that the big money has gone.

Water Conservation

Water has many uses. Without withdrawal from streams or natural reservoirs, it provides a habitat for fish, places for recreation, channels for navigation, and means for the disposal of human and industrial wastes. Withdrawn, it quenches thirst, promotes sanitation, irrigates crop lands, supports livestock, generates electricity, and contributes heavily to industrial operations, cooling, washing, and grading materials and products, and entering into a growing number of chemical processes. In the West, water is used more largely for irrigation; in the East, for industry.

To be available for withdrawal uses, water must be captured and controlled. Of an average annual precipitation of 30 inches in the United States, however, 21½ inches disappear through evaporation, arc caught by foliage, or run off into the oceans; of the remaining 8½ inches, most goes underground; only an inch or so is intercepted and consumed. In the country as a whole, five sixths of the water used is taken from the surface and one sixth from under ground. The arid West, however, depends more heavily upon the latter source. Here, the shortage of water is acute. Population has outrun supply, and the water table has fallen as competitive pumping has drawn off water more rapidly than it has been replaced. Many of the populous industrial areas of the country, too, are approaching the limits of pure water supplies. Streams are polluted, their flow diminished, water tables lowered, and ground waters ruined (along the coasts) by the incursion of salt from the seas. As a result, water for urban and industrial uses must be drawn from greater distances and freed of impurities at constantly increasing costs. In 1964, the United States consumed over 350 billion gallons of water per day; in 1980, it will require 600 billion; that year's dependable supply is forecast at 515 billion.

Means must be found whereby the supply of water can be increased. Rainfall may be precipitated by seeding clouds from airplanes. Potable water is now being produced successfully—though at high cost—under a governmental program in which a number of plants have experimented with methods of removing salt from brackish water and from sea water. It should be possible to reduce evaporation by draining swamps and to divert water to man's use by destroying water-loving plants. It may become necessary to practice economy in use, recycling water for repeated uses, rationing users in accordance with a system of priorities, asking industry to adopt techniques that call for smaller quantities, reserving purer water for more important purposes, and leaving contaminated water for use where purity is not required. The water conservation measures so far adopted by government have been confined, however, to improvement of soil and forest practices on watersheds, construction of storage reservoirs, and abatement of stream pollution.

MINERALS

Mineral resources include the metals (iron, the ferrous alloys, copper, lead, zinc, bauxite, and other nonferrous ores), the mineral fuels (coal, oil, and gas), and many other valuable materials: stone, clay, gypsum, salt, sulfur, graphite, fluorspar, phosphates, potash, and the like. Deposits of these materials are exhaustible and irreplaceable. For some of them (such as iron, nickel, molybdenum, coal, limestone, clay, gypsum, salt, phosphates, and potash), the supply in North America is large enough to satisfy foreseeable demands. In the case of coal, the United States has 40 percent of the world's known reserves and has mined less than 3 percent of its supply. But for some minerals (such as manganese, chromite, tungsten, tin, antimony, mica, quartz crystals, and industrial diamonds), deposits are lacking or deficient. For others (iron, copper, lead, zinc, etc.), depletion of domestic supplies has necessitated increasing reliance on imports. And now the United States, though it produces half of the world's output of petroleum, is also importing oil from overseas.

Declining supplies lead to high prices, and these, in turn, make for greater economy in production and in use. Where minerals essential to national defense are not available in ample quantities, however, action by government may be required. Materials may be bought abroad and held in strategic stockpiles. They might well be withheld from less important uses and allocated to more important ones. Recovery from scrap, resort to lower grade deposits, and development of substitutes might be encouraged by paying subsidies. Government might undertake, moreover, to reduce the wastes involved in extraction and processing. So far, however, aside from oil and gas, it has not attempted to influence mineral technology.

Public regulation of the mining industries, in general, has been confined to operations occurring on public lands. Regulation outside these areas has been limited to two industries. Minimum prices were fixed for bituminous coal during the depression of the thirties. The production of petroleum has been controlled for 50 years.

Control of Mining on Public Lands

For purposes of control, minerals found on public lands fall into three groups. Uranium, under the Atomic Energy Act, is reserved to the federal government. Oil, gas, coal, and certain other minerals may be exploited by private operators in accordance with the terms of leases granted under the Mineral Leasing Act. Access to other minerals found on the public domain is governed by the Mining Law of 1872. Under this law, as it then stood, one who located such minerals could claim possession of a tract of 20 acres by setting up markers on its boundaries, and might obtain a patent recording his title by paying $5 an acre and spending $500 on development. The patentee was then permitted to mine his deposit until it was exhausted. In doing so, he might make ugly gashes in the landscape, destroy the topsoil, and pollute the streams. But he was not required to restore the land to its previous condition or to compensate for the damage he had done. The law was originally intended to afford a stimulus to exploration. But it ceased to bear a significant relationship to the production of minerals. Most claims were unpatented, and in such cases no more than 2 percent of the properties were being mined. Even where claims were patented, there were mines on only 15 percent. The law was used, in fact, to obtain possession of lands for lumbering, grazing, and recreational purposes. This abuse was finally corrected by Congress in 1955. As the law now stands, a mining claim gives no right to use of the land for other purposes until a mine has been proved and title transferred.

Under the Mineral Leasing Act, first passed in 1920, the Secretary of the Interior is empowered to grant leases for the exploitation of oil and gas and certain other minerals on public lands. Where there is no known geologic structure containing such minerals, he may grant exclusive rights to conduct explorations in designated regions for limited periods at a moderate charge. Where oil and gas are known to exist, however, leases are granted on the basis of competitive bids. Such leases give access to land only insofar as it is needed for mineral operations; they require lessees to avoid damage to timber and inter-ference with forage and to prevent soil erosion and water pollution. They also provide for regulation of the spacing and drilling of wells. Where a pool lies under private as well as public lands, the Secretary may enter into an agreement with private owners for its development as a unit. Where a pool lies entirely within the public domain, or where a prospective lessee of public land holds title to adjacent private land, he may require unitization as a condition of grant-ing a lease. Drilling operations are inspected and the provisions of leases en-forced by the Geological Survey.

The most important of the current issues of minerals policy has to do with the conditions that are to govern the exploitation of oil shales in Wyoming, Colorado, and Utah. The technology of exploitation is still to be developed. But the oil in these shales may be five times the size of the world's known reserves, its value exceeding $300 billion. Four fifths of the deposits lie under federal lands. The oil industry seeks leases to exploit them, observing government rules and paying royalties. Conservationists contend that their exploitation should be managed by a public agency (or possibly by a semipublic agency such as Comsat) with the oil companies doing the work under contract and the profits going to the government. The issue is still in dispute.

Regulation of Mining Industries

There are wastes in mining. Recovery of ore from open pits, as with iron and copper, is virtually complete. Recovery of coal by stripping runs from 75 to 95 percent. But recovery from underground operations is only partial. Poorer veins are not worked; material is left in walls or pillars or abandoned as the roof caves in. In the case of coal, one half is taken and the other half is lost. But the physical waste is not all economic waste. For most of the material lost would have been recovered if the price were high enough. To improve the extraction of such materials, government has relied upon the forces of the market place.

Aside from safety requirements, the public regulation of methods of mining has been confined, almost exclusively, to oil and gas. Upon these minerals the United States now depends for most of its supply of energy, for its lubricants, and for raw materials for its industries. Essential in time of peace, they are vital to the nation's defense in time of war. And it is in the extraction of oil and gas that the most serious wastes of mining have occurred. Government has therefore acted to conserve supplies by regulating methods of mining on private land, where 95 percent of the oil and gas is produced.

Wastes in Mining Oil and Gas

Deposits of crude petroleum are found, at depths varying from a few hundred to several thousand feet, in reservoirs of irregular shape lying between successive folds of rock. In these deposits, oil occurs with gas and water, the three being separated in accordance with their specific gravities: the gas above, the water below, and the oil between. When the rock that seals a reservoir is punctured by drilling, the oil is forced to the surface by the pressure of expanding gas. If wells are so placed, in relation to the conformation of the underlying strata, as to make full use of this pressure, a maximum of oil and gas will be recovered at a minimum of cost. But if they are not, the gas may be permitted to escape, its pressure will be wasted, and the oil will have to be brought up, at higher cost, by pumps. A pool of oil, moreover, is a geologic unit. If wells are properly spaced, and rates of flow adjusted, gas pressure can be so distributed as to economize its use. But if wells are close together and operated independently, gas and its pressure may both be thrown away. For economy in exploitation, a pool should be under common management.

Between the boundaries of a pool of oil, created some millions of years ago and lying a mile or more beneath the surface of the earth, and the property lines drawn on the surface sometime within the last century or two, there is no necessary relationship. Under Roman law and under the Napoleonic Code, the title to land pertained only to the surface; subsurface rights were retained by the state. Under English law, however, since the time of Queen Elizabeth I, ownership of the surface has been held to carry with it ownership of everything that lies beneath. And this doctrine was carried over into the law of the American colonies and the United States. When metals or coal were found beneath a man's land, therefore, it was clear that they belonged to him. But oil and gas do not stay put; they move from place to place. And so, when they were found, it was necessary for the courts to decide whether they belonged to the man who owned the land around a well or to his neighbors. Conflicting precedents were available. One was the doctrine of riparian right which gave those owning lands that touched on running streams an equal interest in the preservation of their flow. A second was an English rule, dating from 1843, giving the owner of a water well the right to withdraw percolating waters from beneath the ground. A third was the law of capture, giving ownership of wildlife to those who should reduce it to possession. Of these, the courts rejected the first and chose the other two. Fugacious minerals, they reasoned, are similar to percolating waters, to prowling beasts and migratory birds. Let a man seize them as they cross his land, and they belong to him.

It followed from this rule that a landowner could drill for oil wherever he pleased, as often as he pleased, and as speedily and as carelessly as he pleased, without regard to the geology of the underlying reservoir, in order to take its wealth before it could be taken by the owners of adjacent lands. Or, in leasing rights to another, he could provide for termination of the lease if the latter failed to drill and operate his wells in such a manner as to withdraw the greatest possible amount of oil. The consequences of the law of capture may be illustrated by the sketch on page 653. If the section of a pool shown were to be exploited as a unit, with a view to assuring maximum recovery at minimum cost, drilling would proceed slowly, wells being placed in accordance with the conformation of the reservoir, spaced to take full advantage of gas pressure, and carefully cased to prevent water from flooding the pool. There would be no well on the land of C. The gas trapped at this point would be used to drive the oil up through the wells of B and D. Assume, however, that property lines are drawn as indicated by the markers on the surface and the dotted lines below. Now C, sinking a well, strikes gas. He finds no market for it in his vicinity. He cannot store it. And if he leaves it underground, it will go to work producing oil, not for him, but for B and D. So he blows it off, in order to reach the oil. All of the owners move so swiftly that they cannot drill with care. Most of them case their wells effectively to seal off water. But D does not. So water from above now

FIGURE 27-1

Cross-Section Sketch Showing the Occurrence and Mining of Oil and Gas

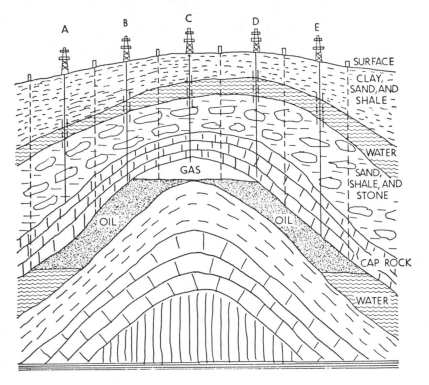

floods the pool. Water also advances from below. It could be held back, and more oil pumped out, if A and E would pump in air. But they have no incentive to do so, since the costs would be charged to them and the profits collected by B, C, and D. So gas is thrown away, and oil mixed with water and left underground. The situation has been even worse than that depicted here. For wells have been drilled, not at the center of each man's property, but to offset one another at its outer limits, the feet of derricks all but touching along the boundaries.

The wastes resulting from competitive exploitation are numerous. First, there are those involving an actual loss of gas and oil: the venting and flaring of gas that could have been captured and used as a fuel, the waste of natural gasoline mixed with the gas, the destruction of oil through carelessness by flooding and by fire, the abandonment of recoverable oil, and the loss through runoff, seepage, and evaporation of oil stored above ground. Second, there are wastes in costs that are higher than they need to be; such costs are involved in the use of capital and labor to construct offsetting wells, to make and install pumps to do the work that could have been done by gas, and to build tanks for storing oil that could have been left in storage underground. And third, there are the wastes involved when scarce, exhaustible materials are produced in such quantities that they are put to inferior uses instead of being held for more important ones: when oil, for instance, replaces coal in heating buildings and driving locomotives instead of being held as a fuel for motor vehicles and airplanes, and when gas is used in making carbon black. Great progress has been made, in recent years, in reducing many of these wastes. Less gas is blown off; more oil recovered. And natural gas is now being piped from the Southwest to northern and eastern markets in quantities exceeding those consumed at home. But wastes persist, and steps directed toward prevention have been taken by the oil-producing states.

Conservation of Oil and Gas

Laws were enacted at an early date to prevent some of the more obvious forms of waste. Pennsylvania, in 1878, required that wells be plugged upon abandonment, and Indiana, in 1891, prohibited the flaring of natural gas. Similar laws were passed, during the nineties, by other states, but none was vigorously enforced. Real regulation dates from the enactment of a statute by Texas, in 1919, giving the Railroad Commission of that state authority to issue orders preventing physical waste. By 1940, conservation laws had been passed by all of the major oil-producing states. Under these laws, typically, waste is condemned and regulatory powers conferred upon administrative agencies.

The rules issued by these bodies cover such matters as the spacing of wells, the methods of drilling, casing, shooting, and plugging wells, the flaring of gas at the wellhead, the open storage of oil, and the establishment of oil-gas and oil-water ratios. They may also require repressuring of pools with air, gas, or water to achieve secondary recovery. The rules governing spacing may establish, as drilling units, areas that can be drained most economically by single wells, may permit a well to be drilled in the center of such a unit and forbid drilling along its boundaries, and, where different owners hold title to land within a drilling unit, may require them to pool their interests in a single well. Such regulations are policed by the requirement of permits for drilling, by supervision of drilling operations, by field inspections, and by gas-oil ratio and pressure tests. There is no question that these measures have produced results. The grossest wastes have been stopped; the flaring of gas has been sharply reduced, and the recovery of oil substantially increased. But it cannot be said that waste has been ended and the final goal of conservation reached.

Conservation requires unitization: the careful determination of the boundaries of a reservoir, the location of wells in accordance with its geological peculiarities, and regulation of the flow from each well to maintain pressure throughout the field. To this end, the law of capture must be abandoned, a pool placed under common management, and property owners assigned proportionate shares in total royalties. But unitization, in general, is not compulsory. In some states, as has been noted, pooling of interests in a drilling unit may be required. But this principle is not usually extended to an entire field. In some states, too, voluntary unitization agreements have been exempted from the antitrust laws. But agreement here must be unanimous: if one landowner holds out, the project fails. In Oklahoma, a unitization order can be proposed if owners of more than half of a pool request it, but will not become effective if owners of more than 37 percent object. In Louisiana, an order cannot be issued if owners of more than 25 percent object. In Texas, where production is greatest, unitization cannot be required.[10]

ENVIRONMENTAL QUALITY

Man's impairment of his environment, with industrialization, urbanization, and continued population growth, has come to be a matter of major public concern. Attention centered, first, on pollution of water, went on, soon, to pollution of air, now encompasses all aspects of environmental quality.

The nation's streams are polluted with wastes discharged by steel and paper mills, oil refineries, packing plants, canneries, and the like, with pesticides and herbicides washed off the farmer's fields, with detergents discharged by households, and with sewage dumped by local governments. There were 1,582 communities in 1969 that provided no treatment for human wastes; 2,117 that provided only primary treatment. Cities have treated and used the waters that have been polluted by those that lie along the streams above them and, in turn, discharged their sewers into the waters used by those below. Normally, the streams would have cleansed themselves of such pollutants. But now their quantity is so great that this cannot occur. The consequences are serious. The organic pollutants provide food for the growth of algae which rob the waters of their oxygen. Inert materials—dirt, oil films, and other industrial wastes—cut off the light of the sun, inhibiting other growth. The fish, deprived of oxygen and food, die out. The fisheries of Lake Erie, it is said, are gone beyond recovery. Ponds and lakeshores are coated in green slime. The beds of rivers lie deep in oily muck.

Even more serious is pollution of the air. Dense clouds of smoke and soot,

10 / Erich W. Zimmerman, *Conservation in the Production of Petroleum* (New Haven, Conn.: Yale University Press, 1957); Wallace F. Lovejoy and Paul T. Homan, *Economic Aspects of Oil Conservation Regulation* (Baltimore, Md.: Johns Hopkins Press, 1967), chap. 4.

noxious fumes and deadly chemicals are discharged into the air by factories and power plants, by incinerators and burning dumps, by commercial and residential buildings, by automobiles, trucks, and airplanes. Under favorable conditions, these pollutants are dispersed, in part, by the winds. But when there is a temperature inversion, with a warmer layer of upper air preventing cooler air on the ground from rising, the concentration of pollutants becomes dangerously high. At worst, it may be lethal, as at Donora, Pennsylvania where it left 20 dead one day in 1948, or at New York City where it killed 80 one day in 1966. Short of this, contaminants in the air attack property, darkening paint, corroding metal, embrittling rubber, and disintegrating stone. They damage crops and injure livestock. And what is worse, they do harm to human lungs, increasing the incidence of respiratory diseases and shortening the span of life.

Nor is this all. There is the destruction of natural beauty: loggers denuding the hillsides, mines building up slag heaps, stripmines cutting great gashes through the landscape. There is the assault on the wilderness: superhighways driven through the forests, jet ports built in wildlife refuges. There is the creation of ugliness: the mountains of industrial and household wastes, the junk yards, billboards, and hideous commercial enterprises that line our roadsides. And there is noise—unceasing and increasing noise.

Water Pollution

Progress toward the abatement of water pollution has been slow. Under the Water Pollution Control Act of 1948, Congress provided for federal loans to afford local governments an incentive to construct sewage treatment works. But each loan was subject to a ceiling of $250,000. And during the whole period from 1948 to 1956, Congress appropriated only $11 million for the purpose. Thereafter, the ceiling was raised, with the federal government making matching grants, meeting 30 to 55 percent of the cost of local projects. Appropriations, too, were increased, reaching $100 million in 1964, $200 million in 1968, and $800 million in 1970. Federal aid had been extended for 9,000 projects by 1970. The results of these expenditures were disappointing. The General Accounting Office, appraising the program in 1969, found little improvement in the quality of water in eight rivers where abatement work had been carried on for a decade. On one river, where $7.7 million had been spent on sewage disposal plants, pollution had been reduced by 3 percent. At the same time, the factories along the stream had increased their discharge of wastes by 350 percent.[11]

Action has been taken with regard to industrial as well as governmental pollution. Under the Act of 1948 the Public Health Service might find any pollution of waters that endangered the health of persons in another state to be a public nuisance and might move to bring it under control. A time-consuming procedure was required. First, the Surgeon General conferred with officials of the offending government or industry and suggested remedial measures. Second,

11 / *New York Times,* November 8, 1969.

if his suggestions were not heeded, he named a board which held a public hearing and prepared a report with recommendations for reform. Third, on the basis of this report, the Secretary of Health, Education, and Welfare issued an order embodying the recommendations, with a schedule of dates on which compliance would be required. Fourth, if compliance with his order did not follow, he might ask the Attorney General to bring suit in a federal court to have it enforced.

For many years, this law was not carried out. It was not until 1959 that the Secretary issued an order against pollution. By 1964, however, the Public Health Service had initiated action in 30 cases, involving more than 600 towns and 700 industrial establishments. The Secretary had taken the final step of bringing suit in only one case (St. Joseph, Missouri), and this had been settled out of court. Ability of the federal government to enforce the law against state and local authorities had not been put to a test.

In 1965, Congress passed the Federal Water Quality Act, setting up a new Water Pollution Control Administration in the Department of the Interior. Under this law, the states were given two years in which to establish standards of quality for all interstate waters, and to adopt enforcement procedures. Where the states failed to act, or where their action was found to be inadequate, the WPCA was authorized to issue orders and to take violators of its orders into court. All of the states submitted the required quality standards. Half were found to be acceptable; half were rejected as inadequate. The WPCA proceeded with public hearings and arrived at agreements with a number of local governments and industries, giving them time to prepare and initiate abatement action. It also issued orders in 50 abatement cases, involving some 2,000 communities and 2,000 industries, between 1966 and 1970. Its orders are enforceable by the courts.[12]

In a message to Congress in 1970, President Nixon recommended a tougher attack on pollution. In the next four years he would have the federal government put up $4 billion and state and local governments $6 billion to finance construction of municipal waste treatment works. And he would impose precise effluent limits on all municipal and industrial sources of pollution with violations punishable by fines of up to $10,000 per day.

Air Pollution

Pollution of the air was first attacked by city and state governments. By 1968 there were abatement ordinances in 130 cities and abatement statutes in 46 states. In some communities, notably Pittsburgh and Los Angeles, substantial progress was made. But many cities had no programs and, in others, enforcement was far from adequate. Local action was handicapped, too, by the fact that air pollutants move across state lines. This difficulty might be overcome by adopting an interstate compact and setting up a common agency to deal with pollution in a region as a whole. This was done by the states of New York, Connecti-

12 / See Marshall I. Goldman, Ed., *Controlling Pollution* (Englewood Cliffs, N.J.: Prentice-Hall, Inc., 1967).

cut, New Jersey, Pennsylvania, and Delaware in 1967. Another approach is through action by the federal government.

In the Clean Air Act of 1965, Congress provided for federal grants to local agencies to meet up to two thirds of the cost of pollution control programs, authorizing only $74 million for the purpose over a period of 10 years. It also empowered the Secretary of Health, Education, and Welfare, when local officials should complain that their communities were endangered by pollution from across their borders, or when he had reason to believe this to be the case, to call a conference of the bodies concerned, and to make a report on the situation, together with recommendations for its rectification. If no action followed, the Secretary was authorized to call a public hearing, to make formal findings, and to transmit them to the industries and agencies concerned. If there was still no action, he might request the Attorney General to bring suit to enforce abatement.

This was obviously a cautious approach to the problem. But in the following years, Congress went farther. In 1965, it directed the Secretary to establish standards to control emissions from motor vehicles, the source of 60 percent of the pollutants in the country as a whole and 85 percent in urban areas. The first standards issued applied to the 1968 models and stiffer standards were imposed in 1969. Manufacturers failing to meet these standards were made subject to a fine of $1,000 per vehicle. Within a decade the law will substantially reduce the quantity of pollutants in the air. But in the meantime emissions from vehicles manufactured before 1968 will be uncontrolled.

The Air Quality Act of 1967 ordered the Secretary to map the country's atmospheric regions, setting up pollution control regions where the atmospheric regions cross state lines. It created a National Center for Air Pollution Control and directed it to establish air quality criteria to serve as a basis for standards to be put into effect by the states. If state action proves to be inadequate, the Secretary of HEW can go to the courts to obtain injunctions. In cases of emergencies involving serious threats to health, he is empowered to shut down factories, to halt motor traffic, and to cut off air pollution from any other source.

The National Air Quality Act of 1970 goes even farther. It requires the manufacturers of automobiles so to design new cars as to reduce the emission of pollutants by 90 percent and sets a deadline for the attainment of this goal. It requires the builders of new industrial establishments to incorporate pollution control devices of the highest standard known. It directs the Secretary of HEW to promulgate national air quality standards for ten major pollutants, gives the states nine months in which to adopt plans for meeting these standards, and requires that they be implemented within another five and a half years. It empowers the Secretary to prohibit all emissions of hazardous substances not covered by the standards. And it makes willful violators of the law subject to punishment by fines and imprisonment.

In sum, this legislation marks significant progress toward pollution control.

Its effectiveness will depend upon the size of the appropriations made for its enforcement and the vigor with which the work of enforcement is carried on.[13]

Wilderness and Wildlife

In 1964, after the opposition of mining, logging, and grazing interests had kept it in committee for a decade, Congress finally passed "An Act to establish a National Wilderness Preservation System for the permanent good of the whole people," defining a wilderness as

> an area where the earth and its community of life are untrammeled by man, where man himself is a visitor who does not remain. An area . . . retaining its primeval character and influence, without permanent improvements or human habitation, which . . . has outstanding opportunities for solitude or a primitive and unconfined type of recreation . . .

Under this measure, 9 million acres then in national forests were designated by the Forest Service to be set aside as wilderness; provision was also made whereby other lands, not exceeding 5 million acres, then in the forests or in national parks or monuments, wildlife refuges, or game ranges could be added to the wilderness during the next 10 years. The law bore the marks of compromises that were exacted as the price of its enactment. Existing grazing rights are to be observed and lumbering permitted, under control of the Forest Service. Prospecting and mining are to be continued, under lease, until 1985. Reservoirs may be created and power plants and transmission lines built by the federal government. Apart from these exceptions, the lands are to be preserved as wilderness, crossed by no permanent roads, entered by no motorized transport, containing no structures of any kind. Commercial enterprises are to be limited to those that are needed to facilitate recreational use. In 1968, Congress followed up this action by establishing a system of wild rivers, sections of which are to be maintained in their natural state, and provided for the creation of a nationwide system of wilderness trails.

All of the states have departments or commissions for the conservation of fish and game whose activities are financed in part by the sale of hunting and fishing licenses and in part by grants of funds derived from federal taxes on fishing tackle, guns, and ammunition. Such agencies maintain wildlife refuges and hunting preserves, operate fish hatcheries, and stock the lakes and streams, each spring, with fish. They regulate hunting and fishing by sportsmen and the taking of seafoods such as lobsters, oysters, clams, and shrimp by commercial fishermen. State laws forbid the hunting of certain species (quail, wood duck, canvasback, and redhead) and control the time when others may be taken, the methods that may be used, the sex and size that may be killed or kept, and the quantities that hunters or fishermen may take. Hunting and fishing are permitted

13 / See Harold Wolozin, Ed., *The Economics of Air Pollution* (New York: W. W. Norton & Co., 1966).

at certain seasons but not allowed at others, particularly during breeding times. The caliber and load of guns is regulated; the use of live decoys, bait, ferrets, fires, snares, nets, and dynamite, and the shooting of wildfowl at night are prohibited. Limits are established for the sportsman's kill or catch, both for the day and for the hunting or fishing season as a whole. These regulations are enforced by game wardens, and violators may be punished by fine and imprisonment.

The federal government has also contributed to the conservation of wildlife and fisheries. In 1903, it established the first national wildlife refuge. In 1913, it concluded a treaty with Canada for the protection of migratory birds. The Fish and Wildlife service now operates some 400 refuges, some of them for big game and smaller animals, most of them providing food and cover for waterfowl and other birds. The government has controlled the taking of sponges in waters off the coast of Florida since 1906. It has also entered into treaties controlling fishing in international waters, protecting the seals of the Pribilof Islands since 1911, restricting the killing of whales since 1935, and governing fisheries in the Great Lakes and in the Pacific Northwest.

Highway Beauty

Governmental concern for environmental quality has extended, finally, to the aesthetics of the nation's highways. In 1965, at the urging of President Johnson, Congress enacted a highway beauty law. Under this measure, billboards within 660 feet of an interstate highway were to be eliminated and junkyards within 1,000 feet of such a highway were to be screened by 1970. The federal government was to pay three fourths, the states one fourth of the costs involved. States that failed to cooperate were to forfeit 10 percent of their federal highway aid. Some progress was made, under the program, toward screening junkyards, improving roadside rest areas, and landscaping scenic strips. But the opposition of the billboard interests was too strong to overcome. An exception was made in the law for customary usage in commercial areas and the definition of such usage and areas was left to local and state governments. The penalty for noncompliance was never imposed. The funds provided for enforcement of the law were insignificant. Of 839,000 illegal billboards, only 750 had been removed by 1970.

PART VI

Moderating Competition

Chapter 28

DEPARTURES FROM ANTITRUST

Although the maintenance of competition has long been the policy of the United States, expressed in the common law since colonial times and embodied in statutory law for four fifths of a century, it has not been followed with consistency. There have been other policies, some of them pursued for many years, others adopted during the Great Depression of the thirties, that restrained competition and made for monopoly. There have been periods of national emergency, of depression and war, when the policy of maintaining competition has been abandoned and the antitrust laws temporarily suspended in whole or in part. From time to time, moreover, particular groups have been exempted from the provisions of antitrust. In some cases these groups have been subjected to alternative forms of control. In others, they have been given a virtual license of monopoly. Several of these departures from the policy of preserving competition will be outlined in the present chapter; others will be examined, at greater length, in the chapters which follow.

POLICIES INCONSISTENT WITH ANTITRUST

Policies inconsistent with antitrust have been pursued by federal, state, and local governments. The conflict between the patent system and the antitrust laws was discussed, in some detail, in Chapter 8. The tariff has excluded foreign competitors from American markets for more than a century. Federal policies with respect to taxation, procurement, agriculture, and labor have restrained competition during the past four decades. State corporation laws have facilitated corporate combination. State laws and local ordinances have excluded outsiders from state and local markets and from entry into sheltered trades. In some cases restraint of competition has been an incidental consequence of measures adopted for other purposes. In others, as with the laws restricting access to markets, it has been deliberate.

Barriers to International Trade

The United States has imposed duties on imports throughout its history. But its emphasis until the Civil War was on a tariff for revenue. Thereafter, rates were raised by Republican administrations, to protect the rising manufacturing interests in the North, reduced by Democratic administrations to help the agricultural exporters of the South, and raised again by the Republicans. Duties reached their highest point under the Hawley-Smoot Act of 1930 which carried them to an average of 52 percent of the value of imported goods. Then, in 1934, Congress passed the Reciprocal Trade Agreements Act, giving the President power to reduce tariffs by as much as half of the 1930 rates in return for comparable reductions in the rates that other countries imposed on American goods. From then until 1945, the average duty on American imports was cut, in 29 bilateral negotiations, to 28 percent. In 1945, Congress empowered the President to cut duties, in further negotiations, by as much as half of the 1945 rates. In 1947 the United States and 22 other nations, meeting in Geneva, established the General Agreement on Tariffs and Trade, generally known as the GATT. In successive meetings, other nations joined in this agreement until it came to cover four fifths of the world's trade. As a result of these negotiations (and also as a result of a rise in the prices of goods paying duties set, not at a fixed percentage of value, but at a fixed amount per gallon, dollar, or pound), the average weight of the American tariff was cut to 12 percent.

At this point, in 1951, the movement toward freer trade was checked. There was a realignment of political forces, with exporters of manufactured goods in the Republican North favoring lower tariffs and representatives of new industries established in the Democratic South demanding higher ones. During the fifties, these forces stood at stalemate. Those favoring lower tariffs could not get the votes to proceed with the trade agreements program. Those demanding higher tariffs could not get the votes to destroy it. They did succeed, however, in robbing it of strength. The President's power to cut duties was reduced to 5 percent per year. A so-called "peril point" provision was written into the law that made it politically difficult for him to go even this far. Numerous escape clauses were inserted, under which particular duties reduced in negotiations could again be raised. One of these empowers the President to raise a duty if the Secretary of Agriculture finds that imports imperil domestic price supports. Another empowers him to do so if the defense authorities find that imports imperil national security, and this escape was amended in 1958 to say that the welfare of every industry in the nation, however frivolous its product, affects its security. A third escape empowers the President to raise a duty if the Tariff Commission finds that imports threaten to injure domestic producers. Under this escape, a prosperous company could demand a higher tariff if it could show that sales of one among many of its products might not increase as rapidly in the future as sales of competing imports. Under these escapes, the President acted to check the importation into the United States, among other things, of watches, bicycles, fuel oil, carpets, and glass. An international agreement was negotiated imposing quotas on imports of textiles. It appeared to be easier to raise barriers to trade than to lower them.

This trend was checked with the passage of the Trade Expansion Act of 1962.

Under this measure, the President was empowered to cut duties, in reciprocal negotiations, by as much as half of their existing level and, in certain cases, to remove them entirely. The "peril point" provision was repealed. The escapes for agriculture and defense were retained, but the escape for producers threatened with injury was tightened, injury being defined as idling of plant, unemployment of labor, and inability to operate at a profit. The President was given the alternative of assisting firms and workers to adjust to increased imports instead of restoring duties to their former level. Armed with this power, the administration entered into protracted negotiations, running from 1963 to 1967, with the other members of the GATT. As a result, the remaining duties on most American imports were cut, the average reduction amounting to another 38 percent, with one fifth of this reduction to be made each year over a period of five years.

American trade policy is still protective. The duties on some products are virtually prohibitive. There are still rates that stand at 50 percent or more, those on coal tar dyes running to 300 and 400 percent of actual value. Nor are duties themselves the only barrier. Imports are obstructed by the methods of customs administration. Tariffs are raised by putting goods in classes that bear higher rates and by overstating the values to which the rates apply. Marks of origin are required to be affixed in ways that add unreasonably to costs. Importers are discouraged by excessive red tape and interminable delays. Sanitary regulations are sometimes used to exclude products that are not so much contaminated as competitive. In some cases, internal taxes and regulations have been so devised as to discriminate against imported goods. Procurement agencies, under rules adopted pursuant to the Buy American Act of 1933, are forbidden to buy abroad unless the domestic price exceeds the foreign price by more than a specified percentage. Countries receiving aid from the United States cannot use this money to buy in the cheapest market but must spend it for American goods. Quotas are imposed on imports of fuel oil and sugar as well as textiles, and there is persistent pressure to apply them to other goods.

The trade policy of the United States is less restrictive than that of many other countries, where quota systems and exchange controls, governing the use of foreign monies, are frequently employed. But it is still inconsistent with America's position as the world's greatest creditor, with her interest in retaining export markets, and with her commitment to assist the poorer nations of the world in their economic development. And it is inconsistent with the maintenance of competition.

Barriers to imports exclude foreign competitors from the domestic market. They make it easier for domestic producers to obtain and perpetuate monopolies and to enforce restrictive agreements. Where rivalry does arise, they protect high costs at home against the competition of lower costs abroad. They exact from the consumer, in a higher price, a profit for monopoly and a subsidy for inefficiency. They are foreign to basic principles of market freedom and private enterprise.

Tax Policy

Competition has also been restricted by taxation. In some cases, the effect was intended. This was true, for example, of the federal tax formerly imposed on oleomargarine, of the tax imposed on bituminous coal producers who did not adhere to the minimum prices fixed by the government under laws enacted in 1935 and 1937, and of state taxes on chain stores. In other cases the effect, though inadvertent, has been the same.

There are several ways in which the present structure of federal taxes may operate to discourage the establishment of new firms, to hamper the growth of small firms, and to promote the combination of existing firms. The personal income tax, with its progressive rates, discourages investment in new, uncertain undertakings, favors investment in bonds and in the shares of old, established firms. The fact that capital gains are taxed at a lower rate than the larger incomes may stimulate investment in enterprises whose future growth appears to be assured. But it may also induce the owner of a family business to sell it, during his lifetime, to a large competitor who can offer an exchange of shares or ready cash. The tax on corporate income, at a high flat rate, obstructs the growth of smaller firms more seriously than that of larger ones. It discourages the reinvestment of earnings, the principal means by which the growth of smaller firms can be financed. It does this, first, by reducing the profits to be expected from reinvestment, and second, by reducing the earnings from which such reinvestment can be made. At the same time, it prevents the smaller company from financing expansion by selling securities, since it impairs the attractiveness of its shares. The tax does permit a corporation to carry the losses of some years forward or backward to offset the profits of others, and this reduces the weight with which it falls on risky undertakings, but it affords no aid to new concerns. It permits the diversified company to offset high returns on one product with low returns or losses on another, an alternative that is not open to the single-product firm. The tax, finally, encourages mergers, since the losses of an unprofitable partner to a merger can be subtracted, in computing taxable income, from the gains of a profitable one. The estate tax, finally, may force the aging owner of a family enterprise to offer it for sale. And, if he does, a large competitor is likely to be the purchaser. None of these effects was intended by the framers of the tax laws. But all of them may discourage competition and promote monopoly.[1]

Procurement Policy

When government is suddenly compelled to embark upon a large new program of expenditure, as is the case, for instance, when it must mobilize for war, it is

---

1 / See J. Keith Butters and John V. Lintner, *Effect of Federal Taxes on Growing Enterprises* (Boston: Graduate School of Business Administration, Harvard University, 1945).

likely to make its purchases, in disproportionate amounts, from larger firms. During World War II, in the United States, 33 companies obtained more than half, by value, of the prime war supply contracts, and 10 of them obtained 30 percent. The government made an effort, through the Smaller War Plants Corporation, to encourage the placement of subcontracts with smaller firms, but concentration of its business was the general rule. Again in 1968, during the war in Vietnam, the hundred largest defense contractors got two thirds of the contracts. These concerns got more than $50 million each; five of them got more than a billion each. A tenth of the defense procurement dollars were spent on a competitive basis; nine tenths were spent under contracts that were negotiated individually.[2]

All this is understandable. Orders for military items are novel and complex. Big companies have established reputations for competence and reliability. They have their representatives in Washington. They keep themselves informed concerning government requirements. They make their offers at the proper time and place and in the proper form. They approach public officials on the basis of personal acquaintanceship. Procurement agencies, by dealing with them, can cover more ground and do it in a shorter time. Small suppliers, by contrast, are numerous, scattered, and unknown. They must be recruited, instructed, and supervised. To put them to work requires a larger organization, consumes more effort, and involves delay. It is not surprising that the market leaders get the lion's share of the business.[3]

The consequences of this development are described by Walter Adams and Horace M. Gray in the following words:

> In a period of mobilization, a company which receives prime contracts secures thereby the instruments of economic power. It has the opportunity of earning profits on the production of goods with an assured market. It gets priorities and allocations on materials, parts, and components which are naturally scarce in a defense economy. It has the power of determining how much subcontracting is to be done and who the subcontractors are to be. It is placed in a favorable position to apply for special tax amortization privileges for the expansion of productive facilities. It acquires the technical skill and knowhow which become strong selling points in the negotiations for future contracts with the government. In short, the companies receiving the bulk of government orders in an emergency can strengthen their relative position vis-a-vis their smaller competitors and potential competitors in a peacetime economy.[4]

Procurement policy, directed necessarily toward other objectives, thus makes for concentration and monopoly.

2 / Joint Economic Committee, *The Economics of Military Procurement* (Washington, D.C.: Government Printing Office, 1969).

3 / See Corwin D. Edwards, "Antimonopoly Policy during Rearmament," *American Economic Review,* May, 1952, pp. 404-17.

4 / Walter Adams and Horace M. Gray, *Monopoly in America* (New York: Macmillan Co., 1955).

Agricultural Policy

American agricultural policy since 1929 has sought to maintain the prices of agricultural products at levels higher than those that would result from the interplay of the forces of demand and supply in free markets. To this end the government has made loans and purchases, taken supplies off the market, diverted them to noncommercial uses, and dumped them abroad, paid farmers to restrict the quantities produced and marketed, approved agreements fixing prices and controlling sales, and compelled producers and distributors to adhere to their terms. These are the techniques of monopoly. If adopted by businessmen, they could be prosecuted as restraints of trade. Here, they are approved as methods of approaching "parity." The methods employed to raise the farmer's prices and increase his income will be examined in Chapter 31. At this point, it suffices to point out that the policies now applied to business and to agriculture are not only inconsistent; they are antithetical.

Labor Policy

A similar inconsistency exists in labor policy. When businessmen combine and agree to control the supply of goods and services in order to raise their prices, their action is condemned as a conspiracy in restraint of trade. When workers combine and agree to control the supply of labor in order to raise their wages, a different rule applies. The organization of labor has been permitted by the courts for more than a hundred years. It has been encouraged and protected by Congress for more than 30 years. Employers have been required by law to grant recognition to labor unions and to engage in collective bargaining.

Freedom to organize is avowedly designed to afford labor equality of bargaining power. But this policy, it must be admitted, departs from the concept of a free market for labor. Instead of creating a situation in which many sellers deal with many buyers, it accepts monopoly as a counterweight for monopsony. The policy, moreover, frequently threatens the maintenance of competition in the market for the goods and services that labor produces. And here it comes into conflict with the policy of antitrust. The problems presented by this conflict will be considered in Chapter 30.

State Corporation Laws

Until the middle of the last century, most corporations obtained their charters through specific enactments by state legislatures. By 1850, however, many states had adopted general incorporation laws, and by 1875 such laws provided the usual method of incorporation. Until 1889 these laws did not permit one corporation to control another by owning its shares. In that year New Jersey amended its laws to authorize such holdings. Other states, competing for the business of selling corporate charters, shortly followed suit. No limits were placed upon the purpose of intercorporate stock ownership or on its scope.

The new laws facilitated corporate combination and concentration of control. To effect a combination it was no longer necessary to persuade the owners of a corporation's assets to vote in favor of their sale. Control could be obtained more simply and more cheaply by acquiring a majority or a working minority of its voting stock. In this way competing companies could be brought under common ownership, they could be linked through common subsidiaries, and a single company could spawn subsidiaries of its own. Holding companies could be pyramided, layer upon layer, with control concentrated at the apex and extended over a widening base. Control could be exercised, moreover, to withhold dividends and reinvest earnings, thus contributing to further growth. All of these developments have made for size and for monopoly. A policy that came to be embodied in state incorporation laws, contemporaneously with the passage of the Sherman Act, has thus run counter to the purposes of antitrust.

Barriers to Nonlocal Trade

The federal constitution forbids the imposition of duties on trade between the states. In the case of alcoholic beverages, however, the 21st Amendment (abolishing national prohibition) permits state governments to restrict imports as a means of regulating the liquor business. Many states have used this power not so much to check the consumption of intoxicants as to prevent producers outside their borders from competing with local maltsters, brewers, vintners, distillers, and growers of hops, grapes, and grains. In the case of other goods, as well, though no such exception has been made, legislators have discovered various means of protecting producers located in one state or city from the competition of those located in another.

Many states have protected local dairy interests by forbidding the sale of yellow margarine and by imposing heavy taxes on the production and sale of uncolored margarine. They have protected local nurseries by employing their horticultural laws to curtail the importation of nursery stock. At one time, the federal government was imposing quarantines against 11 plant diseases and insect pests, the states against 239. Some states, through grading and labeling requirements, have restricted imports of chickens and eggs. Florida has defined "fresh dressed poultry" as poultry slaughtered in Florida; and Florida, Georgia, and Arizona have each defined "fresh eggs" as eggs laid within the state. A number of states maintain rigorous standards in grading fruits and vegetables and exclude those falling in the lower grades. Georgia has empowered its agricultural authorities to embargo out-of-state fruits and vegetables when they believe the domestic supply to be sufficient for the markets of the state. State laws have handicapped out-of-state truckers. Some states have discriminated against trucks that come in loaded, prepared to sell, in favor of those that come in empty, prepared to buy. The Buy American Act has its counterpart in state law. Nearly every state requires that some sort of preference be shown to residents in making public purchases. State agencies and institutions have thus been forced to hire local labor, award contracts to local bidders, and purchase supplies from local firms. City councils have taken similar action. Urban markets for fluid milk have been closed to all producers but those whose dairies have been inspected and approved by local health authorities, a measure that limits competition when applications for inspection are refused. Building ordinances, likewise, though ostensibly designed to eliminate hazards to health and safety, have contained provisions which operate to exclude from local markets materials produced by outsiders and to compel builders to use materials produced by local firms.

These measures have the same defects as do the barriers to international trade. In fact, they may be more harmful, since the area they leave open to freedom of competition is a smaller one. As we move from "Buy American" through "Buy Indianan" and "Buy Middletown" to "Buy Main Street," the consequences differ, not in kind, but in degree.

Barriers to Certain Occupations

Entry into professions affecting public health and safety—medicine, nursing, pharmacy, and the like—has long been regulated by the states. Qualifications have been established, examinations given, and licenses required. Over the years, this form of control has gradually been extended until, today, there are as many as 75 trades where entry is restricted by law. All of the states require licenses of accountants, architects, attorneys, chiropodists, dentists, embalmers, engineers, nurses, optometrists, osteopaths, pharmacists, physicians, teachers, and veterinarians, and most of them license barbers, beauticians, chiropractors, funeral directors, surveyors, and salesmen of insurance and real estate. A number of states also license such tradesmen as plumbers, dry cleaners, horseshoers, tree surgeons, automobile salesmen, and photographers. Altogether, there are more than 1,200 occupational license laws, averaging 25 per state.

Most of these laws have been enacted, not in response to popular demand, but at the behest of organized producer groups. "The shoe fitter's responsibility is the very foundation of a child's health," read an advertisement published in the daily papers of New York in 1953. ". . . the Juvenile Shoe Guild is actively campaigning for state licensing of children's shoe fitters." The boards that administer the laws are usually composed predominantly of members of the trades concerned. In some cases, the governor must appoint licensed practitioners; in others, a trade association picks the board. The powers of these bodies differ. Some are advisory: qualifications are established, examinations given, and licenses issued and revoked, in name, at least, by public officials. Others have complete authority. In general, the states exercise little or no control.[5]

Some of these laws are doubtless needed to protect public safety, health, and

5 / "Occupational Licensing Legislation in the States," *State Government,* December, 1952, pp. 275-80.

morals. But many of them are obviously designed to limit competition. And all of them can be diverted to this end. The standards established for admission to a trade may be unnecessarily severe. Extensive educational requirements have been set up for barbers, and 10 years of experience or a college degree asked for plumbers. Licensing may be employed as a means of defining the jurisdiction of competing trades. Some states have refused to license drug stores to freeze ice cream or to serve meals. Others have confined the sale of such products as bicarbonate of soda, witch hazel, iodine, and Epsom salts to licensed pharmacists. These statutes, finally, may be used to enforce agreements with respect to price. In Nebraska, under a law enacted in 1937, automobile dealers were licensed, and "willfully or habitually making excessive trade-in allowances" was declared to be a sufficient ground for denying or revoking licenses. In Oklahoma, minimum prices are set for dry cleaners and those who charge less are subject to license revocation, a fine of $500, and imprisonment for 30 days.

Many of these laws are inconsistent with the policy of maintaining competition. If this policy is to prevail, such laws should be repealed. Where consumers need to be informed concerning the qualifications of tradesmen, the issuance of certificates should usually suffice. Uncertified practitioners should not be excluded from a trade. Where licensing is really needed, the states should assume responsibility for preventing its abuse.

SUSPENSION OF ANTITRUST IN DEPRESSION

Between 1929 and 1932 the national income of the United States fell from $90 billion to $40 billion. The Federal Reserve Board's index of industrial output fell from 110 to 58. By 1933 nearly 15 million workers were unemployed. By March 4, 1933, every bank in the country had been closed. On that day Franklin D. Roosevelt was inaugurated President. The new administration immediately embarked upon an ambitious program designed to effect reform, provide relief, and promote recovery. To the last of these ends, the banks were reopened and bank deposits guaranteed. The dollar was devalued to encourage export trade. Public expenditures were increased: money was distributed to persons on relief and paid out in wages to those employed on public works. Farm incomes were enlarged, by paying subsidies and by curtailing output to raise prices, on the assumption that the prices farmers received had fallen too far in relation to the prices farmers paid. It was in this context that the National Industrial Recovery Act was signed into law on June 16, 1933.

It was the avowed purpose of the new law to stimulate recovery by increasing consumer demand. Demand was to be increased by increasing purchasing power. Purchasing power was to be increased by increasing employment and raising wages. Employment was to be increased by establishing maximum hours. Wages were to be raised by establishing legal minima and by requiring union recognition and collective bargaining. To enable businessmen to pay higher wages to more workers, they were to be protected against "chiselers" (i.e., competitors) who might undercut their prices. And to afford them this protection, the antitrust laws were to be suspended. Codes of "fair competition" were to be drawn up, industry by industry, setting forth the maximum hours and the minimum wages, guaranteeing collective bargaining, and establishing the rules whereby the chiselers were to be controlled. But prices were not to be raised. Said Mr. Roosevelt:

> I am fully aware that wage increases will eventually raise costs, but I ask that managements first give consideration to the improvement of operating figures by greatly increased sales to be expected from the rising purchasing power of the public. . . . If we now inflate prices as fast and as far as we increase wages, the whole project will be set at naught. We cannot hope for the full effect of this plan unless, in these first critical months, and even at the expense of full initial profits, we defer price increases as long as possible.[6]

Such was the logic of the law, described by the President as "the most important and far-reaching legislation ever enacted by the American Congress."

The new program was not conceived by the President's academic advisers, the so-called "brain trust." It had its origin in a deal between organized labor and organized business. Labor had long sought maximum hour and minimum wage limits, union recognition, and collective bargaining. Business was seeking the right of "self-government," meaning freedom to make and enforce rules restricting competition, to be obtained by suspending the prohibitions of anti-trust. Gerard Swope, President of the General Electric Company, had published a widely discussed plan for a nationwide "coordination of production and consumption" through legalized cooperation in controlling prices and methods of competition. The United States Chamber of Commerce had issued a report proposing revision of the antitrust laws to permit similar programs of economic planning. According to the Chamber's president, Henry I. Harriman, "The time has come when we should ease up on these laws and, under proper governmental supervision, allow manufacturers and people in trade to agree among themselves on these basic conditions of a fair price for the commodity, a fair wage, and a fair dividend."[7] When it passed the National Industrial Recovery Act, the Congress heeded this advice.

NIRA and NRA

The law specified that all the codes must provide for maximum hours, minimum wages, and collective bargaining. Beyond that, it left initiative in formulating their provisions to trade associations, requiring only that such groups truly represent their trades, do not restrict admission, and do not eliminate or oppress small competitors. When codes were approved by the

6 / As quoted in L. S. Lyon and Others, *The National Recovery Administration* (Washington, D.C.: Brookings Institution, 1935), p. 758.

7 / 73d Cong., 1st Sess., House of Representatives, Ways and Means Committee, *Hearings on National Industrial Recovery*, p. 134.

President, violation of their terms became an unfair method of competition, punishable as a misdemeanor by a fine of $500 for each offense. All practices permitted were exempted from antitrust.

The National Industrial Recovery Act was administered by the National Recovery Administration. At its head, during the first year, was General Hugh S. Johnson, a former cavalry officer. Beneath him were 55 deputy administrators, most of them businessmen, each of them responsible for a different segment of industry. Advising these officials were a research division, a legal division, and three advisory boards, representing the interests of industry, labor, and the consumer. This organization, set up almost over night, proceeded at high speed to codify labor standards and trade practices throughout American industry.

The program was launched with a great fanfare. Pending the completion of the codes, a President's Reemployment Agreement, containing minimum labor standards, was signed by more than two million employers. These firms were permitted to display the emblem of the Blue Eagle at their places of business and to affix it to their goods. The public was invited, in effect, to boycott those who failed to do so. In the meantime, the work of drafting the codes got under way.

Trade Associations and Code Authorities

At the beginning, the NRA had no policies to govern the character of the provisions offered and accepted for inclusion in the codes. The first drafts were drawn up by the trade associations. They were a product of negotiation between these associations and organized labor, each conceding terms to the other in return for agreement to the terms that it sought for itself. These drafts were discussed informally with the deputy administrators, who acted not as guardians of the public interest but merely as arbitrators of disputes. Later drafts went to public hearings where the proposed provisions could be criticized. Then, when needed modifications had been made, the final drafts were handed to the deputies. If the Industry and Labor Advisory Boards had found them acceptable, they were approved. If the Consumers' Advisory Board had objected, its protest was ignored. The industry and labor boards had organized backing; the consumers' board did not. When the codes were approved by the deputies, they were rubber stamped by the administrator and the President and given the effect of law.

The codes were administered by bodies known as code authorities. These bodies were largely composed of or selected by trade associations. The personnel and the policy of the authorities were controlled by trade associations. In three cases out of four, the code authority secretary and the trade association secretary bore the same name and did business at the same address. Code administration was usually financed by mandatory assessments against each of the firms in an industry. In the garment trades, collection of the levy was assured by the requirement that a label purchased from the code authority must be sewn in every garment sold. The program thus involved a virtual delegation to trade associations of the powers of government, including in some cases, the power to tax.

The NRA undertook, in its own words, "to build up and strengthen trade associations throughout all commerce and industry."[8] It conferred new powers and immunities on strong associations, invigorated weak associations, aroused moribund associations, consolidated small associations, and called some 800 new associations into life. It sought to employ these agencies as instruments in the promotion of industrial recovery. But many of the provisions which it permitted them to write into their codes were ill designed to achieve this end.

Codes of Fair Competition

The NRA approved 557 basic codes, 189 supplementary codes, 109 divisional codes, and 19 codes entered into jointly with the Agricultural Adjustment Administration—a grand total of 874. The codes spelled out more than a thousand different kinds of provisions for the regulation of 150 different types of competitive practices. In addition to the mandatory labor provisions, they set forth rules condemning a number of trade practices that had long been held to be unfair. Here, the authors drew upon the texts of trade association codes of ethics, trade practice conference agreements with the Federal Trade Commission, and orders issued by the FTC. Thus, the codes denounced various forms of misrepresentation, forbade defamation of competitors, inducing breach of contract, and commercial bribery, and prohibited design piracy, espionage, vexatious litigation, and the enticement of employees. These provisions added little to existing law. They were in the tradition of established policy.

But the codes did not stop here. They went on to control terms of sale, prices, markets, production, capacity, and the channels of distribution. In the name of fair competition, they required adherence to practices that the Federal Trade Commission and the courts had held to be unfair. They perverted the concept of unfairness in competition by extending it to competition itself. Industry by industry, they were designed by a majority to curb the competitive propensities of an obstreperous minority. Item by item, they copied the pattern of the European cartel.

Control of Terms of Sale

All of the codes contained provisions which governed the terms and conditions of sale, subjecting to detailed regulation in various combinations such matters as quotation, bid, order, contract, and invoice forms, bidding and awarding procedures, customers classifications, trade, quantity, and cash discounts, bill datings, credit practices, installment sales, deferred payments, interest charges, guaranties of quality, guaranties against price declines, long-term contracts, options, time and form of payments, returns of merchandise, sales on consignment, sales on trial or approval, cancellation of contracts, trade-in

8 / NRA Bulletin No. 7, January 22, 1934.

allowances, advertising allowances, supplementary services, combination sales, rebates, premiums, free deals, containers, coupons, samples, prizes, absorption of freight, delivery of better qualities or larger quantities than those specified, sale of seconds and of used, damaged, rebuilt, overhauled, obsolete, and discontinued goods, the payment of fees and commissions, and the maintenance of resale prices. In general, these provisions were designed to affect the allocation of business between trades and among the firms within a trade and to prevent the granting of any indirect concession which would operate to reduce a price.

Control of Prices

More than 85 percent of the codes contained some provision for the direct or indirect control of price. A dozen of them permitted the code authorities to establish minimum prices without regard to costs of production and without approval by the NRA. The code for the bituminous coal industry, for instance, stated that "the selling of coal under a fair market price . . . is hereby declared to be . . . in violation of this code. . . . The fair market price of coal . . . shall be the minimum prices . . . which may be established . . . by the respective code authorities." Another two dozen codes empowered the authorities to fix prices equal to the "lowest reasonable" costs of a "representative" firm, to become effective when approved by NRA. In iron and steel, and in a few other industries, the codes legalized basing point systems of delivered pricing, specifying each of the elements of the pricing formulas and prescribing their use. In iron and steel, moreover, the code provided that

> The board of directors shall have the power . . . to investigate any base price for any product . . . filed by members of the code. . . . If the board of directors, after such investigation, shall determine that such base price is an unfair base price . . . the board of directors may require the member of the code . . . to file a new list showing a fair base price. . . . If such member of the code shall not . . . file a new list . . . the board of directors shall have the power to fix a fair base price. . . .

In the paper tag industry, too, a price reporting provision was employed as a method of fixing a common price. The code for this industry forbade producers who did not file prices to sell below the lowest price filed by any of their competitors. In practice, prices were filed by a single large concern.

The fixing of prices was usually less overt. Some 200 codes permitted code authorities to establish minimum prices only to prevent "destructive price cutting" and to do so only in the event of an "emergency." These limitations, however, had little significance. The concepts were never clearly defined. "An emergency," it was said, "is something that is declared by a code authority." As the coal dealers put it, "We have always had an emergency in retail solid fuel." The code for this trade became effective on February 26, 1934; the authority declared an emergency on March 1, 1934, and proceeded to fix prices based on the "lowest reasonable costs" of selling coal. Emergencies were also declared in several other trades, affording their members an opportunity to arrive at "cost determinations" which could be used to justify high minimum prices. The history of NRA gives evidence that they made the most of this opportunity.

In the codes for the wholesale and retail trades, price fixing took the form of provisions for "loss limitation." In some cases, these provisions forbade the distributor to sell goods for less than they cost him. In others, they required him to add a markup based upon some estimate of distribution costs. In still others, they compelled him to charge a price set by the producer or by the wholesaler from whom he bought. It is likely that provisions of the second type and it is certain that those of the third type involved something more than the mere limitation of loss.

The type of price-fixing provision which was most widely adopted, under NRA, was that which provided for "cost protection." Three fifths of the codes prohibited sales below "cost." The effect of such a provision would depend, of course, upon the standard of cost that was employed. If a firm were forbidden to sell below its own cost, it might be undercut by a lower-cost competitor. If it were forbidden to sell below the cost of its lowest-cost competitor, the provision would not serve to raise the prices of the trade. If it were forbidden to sell below an average cost computed for the trade, the result would depend on the method of computation. Did all firms report or was a sample used? If the latter, was the sample representative? Were the reports honest, or were they padded? Was the average a simple one or was it weighted? If the latter, were the proper weights applied? Was the figure taken as representative a mean, a median, or a mode? Were the reports and the computations taken at face value, or were they subjected to an independent audit? Depending on the answers to these questions, the prices set by this provision would be high or low.

More than half of the codes provided for the establishment of a standard costing system. More than 50 of them forbade sales below some average of cost, the rest forbade sales below the seller's individual cost. In many cases the procedure followed in the determination of an average cost led to the establishment of an arbitrary minimum price. In the printing industry, the code authority collected data from 200-odd printers among some 17,000 and issued "cost determination schedules" in the form of catalogues which set forth minimum prices rather than costs. In the paint industry, the authority sent questionnaires to 160 among some 2,000 firms, rejected 34 of the 74 replies, and employed the 40 remaining (which included no data on certain of the industry's products and no returns from some of its more important members) in arriving at figures which were said to represent "the lowest reasonable cost of manufacturers, large and small, throughout the industry." So, too, with the adoption of a common formula for use in the determination of individual costs. In the limestone industry, the code authority prescribed itemized costs for successive operations that added up, in every case, to a uniform total. In the trucking industry, the authority drew up a schedule of costs in dollars and cents, and truckers whose rates fell below the resulting figures were charged with violation of the code. This procedure was known to the industry as "cost education." In some cases, finally, the code provided not only for uniform costs but also for a uniform markup. Thus, the code of the waterproofing industry forbade its members to sell below "allowable cost" plus a "reasonable" percentage to be determined by the code authority, and the code of the brick industry forbade selling below "direct factory cost" plus an item called "weighted average indirect allowable cost," this item being stated by the code authority in terms of dollars at a figure which was uniform throughout the industry.

Two thirds of the codes provided for the establishment of open price-reporting systems. Most of these systems were of a character that would probably have been outlawed under the earlier decisions of the courts. Nearly half of them gave no information to buyers. Most of them required the filing of identified price lists. Most of them also required sellers to adhere to the prices they had filed until new filings became effective, and three fourths of them required a waiting period before a new filing was permitted to take effect. In many cases the price-reporting systems afforded a convenient medium through which the price-fixing provisions could be policed.

Allocation of Markets

A number of codes contained provisions which were designed to effect an allocation of markets among the members of a trade. Some of them prohibited freight allowances, thus preventing sellers from entering distant markets by absorbing freight. Others prohibited "dumping," forbidding firms to sell outside their "normal market areas" at prices lower than those "customarily" charged within such areas and granting code authorities the power to determine which areas were "normal" and which prices "customary." Still others divided the country into zones and forbade producers located in one zone to sell in another below the prices charged by producers located there. Thus, the code for the salt-producing industry provided that "the minimum prices established in any marketing field by any producer in that field shall be the lowest prices at which any producer shall sell in that field. . . ." Such provisions, in effect, set up a tariff wall around each of the designated areas.

Control of Production

Ninety-one codes provided for the restriction of output and the distribution of available business among the firms in a trade. A few codes limited the size of inventories, compelling manufacturers to confine their operations to the volume permitted by current sales. Sixty codes, most of them in the textile industry, imposed limitations on the number of hours or shifts per day, or the number of hours or days per week, during which machines or plants might be operated, thus curtailing production and allocating the resulting volume of business on the basis of capacity. A half dozen codes, including those for the petroleum, lumber, copper, and glass container industries, provided for the limitation of production in accordance with estimates of total demand, and for the assignment of production quotas on the basis of present capacity or past production or sales.

Control of Capacity

Some 50 codes imposed limitations upon the construction, conversion, or relocation of productive capacity, or made some provision for the imposition of such limitations. In some cases, the provision of new facilities and the inauguration of new services were forbidden. The code for the iron and steel industry provided that "it is the consensus of opinion in the industry that, until such time as the demand for its products cannot adequately be met by the fullest possible use of existing capacities for producing pig iron and steel ingots, such capacities should not be increased. Accordingly . . . none of the members of the code shall initiate the construction of any new blast furnace or open hearth or Bessemer steel capacity." A number of transit codes forbade the opening of new routes or the extension of existing ones. In other cases, additions to capacity required the permission of the code authority or the approval of the NRA, thus giving these bodies control over entry to the industry and the relative growth of different companies.

Control of the Channels of Distribution

The codes for the wholesale and retail trades were designed, in general, to check the development of competing channels of distribution. They established mandatory markups and so defined the trades as to include the mass distributors. They limited the discounts that could be given to distributors buying in quantity. They established customer classes and specified the discounts that should be given to each class. They required, for instance, that a discount of only 25 percent be given to retailers and a discount of 50 percent to wholesalers. They forbade manufacturers to assume distributive functions or to sell their goods to certain classes of distributors. They specified the customers that might be served by wholesalers and those that were reserved to retailers. These provisions were enforced against manufacturers and wholesalers by rules forbidding distributors to buy from those who disobeyed their terms.

Penalties

Adherence to code requirements was enforced not only by penalties provided in the law but also by sanctions established in the codes. The requirements imposed on manufacturers by distributors and on wholesalers by retailers were enforced by organized boycotts. Twenty-six industries bound their members to pay "liquidated damages" into the treasury of the code authority in the event of a violation. The iron and steel code contained the following provision:

Recognizing that the violation by any member of the code of any provision (dealing with base prices, delivered prices, or terms of sale) will disrupt the normal course of fair competition in the industry and cause serious damage to other members of the code and that it will be impossible fairly to assess the amount of such damage to any member of the code, it is hereby agreed by and among all members of the code that each member of the code which shall violate any such provision shall pay to the Treasurer . . . as and for liquidated damages the sum of $10 per ton of any products sold in violation of any such provision.

In this case, as in others, it appears that the "liquidated damages" were really fines imposed on violators of the code rather than payments made to injured parties to reimburse them for losses actually sustained.

The End of NRA

It soon became clear that the power conferred upon the trade associations by the law had been abused. Despite the President's plea that price increases be postponed, business had made the most of its monopolistic opportunities. Complaints began to be heard. They came not only from customers, when prices had been raised, but also from competitors when their opportunities had been curtailed by the restraints imposed upon them by their industries. In the spring of 1934, the President appointed a committee, under the eminent lawyer, Clarence Darrow, to investigate. The committee's report condemned the whole undertaking, denouncing it as "monopoly sustained by government" and as "a regimented organization for exploitation." In the fall of 1934, General Johnson was replaced by an administrative board of seven members, including representatives of business, labor, and the consumer. Thereafter, NRA policy was radically revised. Provisions of the sort that had been written into the earlier codes were no longer granted. Applications for the approval of activities requiring specific sanction were denied. But the new policy was not applied to the existing codes. They were allowed to stand.

As written, the law was due to expire in the summer of 1935. The President asked Congress to extend its life for two more years. Hearings were held by the Senate, and it appeared that the powers conferred by the law, if extended at all, would be sharply modified. While Congressional action was still pending, the Supreme Court handed down its decision on the Schechter case.[9] The Court was unanimous. The law involved an unconstitutional invasion of intrastate commerce and an unconstitutional delegation of legislative power. The NRA was put to death on May 27, 1935.

An Appraisal of NRA

NRA must be given credit for the improvement of labor standards in the United States. The codes initiated the maximum hours, minimum wages, and prohibition of child labor that were continued, in 1935, by the Fair Labor

9 / *Schechter* v. *U.S.*, 295 U.S. 495 (1935).

Standards Act, and the union recognition and collective bargaining that were continued by the National Labor Relations Act. The code authorities manifested little interest in enforcing the labor provisions of the codes, confining their attention to the suppression of competitive practices. But the NRA itself undertook enforcement of these provisions, and here it attained a modicum of success.

The trade practice provisions of the codes were administered most effectively in industries that had not been vigorously competitive: those that were disciplined by powerful trade associations or dominated by a few large firms. Here, the legal sanction was not needed; suspension of the antitrust laws was all that was required. In more competitive industries, however, where firms were small and numerous and trade associations weak, enforcement of the codes was difficult if not impossible. And here they tended to break down.

The National Industrial Recovery Act contributed little, if anything, to recovery. The substitution of action—even if ill-advised—for inaction may have made for a restoration of confidence. The building of floors under wages and prices may have convinced businessmen that the bottom had been reached. But prices rose more rapidly than wages, checking the expansion of purchasing power. Industrial prices rose with agricultural prices, thus preventing the restoration of the balance that the Agricultural Adjustment Act was designed to achieve. The price increases, adding to costs, may well have discouraged ventures that business would otherwise have regarded as feasible. It is certain that they did so in the vital construction industries. Other measures adopted by the New Deal undoubtedly stimulated business activity: the agricultural program, devaluation, and deficit spending. But it was the conclusion of the economists of the Brookings Institution that the "Recovery" Act itself "on the whole retarded recovery."[10]

The NRA did serve one useful purpose. It provided the country with a demonstration of the character and the consequences of cartelization. It showed that industry, when given the power of "self-government," could not be trusted to exercise it in the public interest; that enterprise would be handicapped and vested interest protected, progress obstructed, and stagnation assured. It showed that businessmen, if given a blank check to be filled out, would proceed to commit economic suicide, pricing themselves out of the market and encouraging consumers to turn to substitutes: to oil when the price of coal was boosted and to mechanical refrigerators when the price of ice was raised. It showed, moreover, that enforcement of limitations on competition required a greater degree of regimentation than business was prepared to take, and that supervision adequate to protect the public interest would require an enormous organization, to be supported at a heavy cost.

It is probable that the NRA was like a vaccination, giving the United States a mild case of the cartel disease and immunizing it against the disease itself. It is certain that—as long as this experience remains in memory—there are few who would welcome its return. If American industry, in general, is again to be cartelized, the movement will have to take a different form.

10 / Lyon and Others, *op. cit.,* p. 873.

The Philosophy of Cost Protection

One idea persists. Admittedly such practices as price fixing, market sharing, production control, and curtailment of capacity are reprehensible. But is not cost protection to be justified? Surely, sale below cost must be maliciously destructive and its prohibition, therefore, must be reasonable.

This view is based upon a false assumption as to the essential character of "costs." It assumes that costs are objective figures, scientifically ascertained by impersonal accountants, and set forth in precise terms on which all accountants would agree. But this is not the case. Costs are purposive: they are instruments of business policy. Cost accountants are employed by managements and will show whatever it may be that managements want shown. Costs are based on judgments, and judgments may differ. There may be different opinions, first, as to what should be included in costs: how much overcapitalization, how much obsolete capacity, how large an expenditure on sales promotion and public relations, what level of executive salaries. Opinions may differ, second, on how to measure the items that are included in costs. Are raw materials to be charged at the prices paid for those used in a product, at the prices paid for the last ones purchased, or at current replacement cost? Is a particular expenditure to be charged to the costs of operation or to the cost of capital? Is capital to be entered at its original cost or at its reproduction cost? Is it to be depreciated by writing off an equal sum during each year of its estimated life, larger sums in the beginning that taper off in later years, or larger sums in years when business is good? And, by the way, how estimate an asset's estimated life? Opinions may differ, finally, as to the distribution of overhead costs among joint products. Should they be made proportionate to material costs or labor costs or both, related to power consumed, machine-hours used, or floor space occupied, or allocated in accordance with any one of several other principles? As men's judgments differ, so will their estimates of costs. To forbid sales below cost, therefore, is to set as a minimum price a figure that is not objective but is one that accountants can manipulate.

The cost protection philosophy, moreover, ignores the economic function of cost and price. It assumes that cost is immutable and price adjustable; that cost, therefore, must always be taken as cause and price as effect. And this assumption, too, is false. For cause and effect may operate the other way around. If price falls below cost, it is possible that cost may be reduced. New materials may be employed, new methods discovered, wastes eliminated, and efficiency increased. The cost of capital may be reduced, by writing down excessive valuations, or by putting overvalued assets through the wringer of bankruptcy. This, after all, is the disciplinary function of the cost-price relationship. If price were never permitted to fall below cost, there would be no business failures, no compulsion to adjust production to changing demands, no penalty for waste and inefficiency. Business, under a system of private enterprise, is driven by the carrot of profit and by the stick of loss. Cost protection would leave the carrot, but it would take away the stick.

EXCEPTIONS TO ANTITRUST

A number of industries and business practices have been exempted, over the years, from the provisions of the antitrust laws. In some cases monopoly has been accepted as inevitable or desirable and government has undertaken the regulation of rates and services. This is true of transport and public utilities, whose control was discussed in Part III. In other cases it has appeared that the members of a trade, far from possessing the powers of monopolists, are at a disadvantage in bargaining. And here, instead of attempting to restore competition to both sides of the market, Congress has approved the principle of bilateral monopoly. This solution has been adopted in the case of labor unions and agricultural cooperatives. In still other cases, industries have appeared to be chronically distressed. The demand for their products has declined, substitutes have displaced them, changing technology has made established methods obsolete, and competition has induced recurring bankruptcies. Here, Congress has sought to afford relief by permitting such industries to curtail output, share markets, and fix prices. Bituminous coal will illustrate the point. And finally, there are cases where exemptions are to be explained by the ability of well-organized trades to exert political power. There are businessmen who take the view that competition, though desirable for others, is not appropriate for themselves. And there are politicians who give lip service to the maintenance of competition but are open to persuasion that exceptions should be made. Those made on behalf of retailers of branded goods and producers of petroleum will be discussed, respectively, in Chapters 29 and 32.

Labor and Agriculture in the Clayton Act

In a number of cases brought under the Sherman Act, the courts have condemned certain restrictive activities of labor unions and agricultural cooperatives. It was argued, before 1914, that some of these decisions raised doubts concerning the right of such bodies to exist. There was also hope, among unions and cooperatives, that legislative approval of their existence might be interpreted as endorsing their activities. So, in response to the demands of labor and agriculture, the following provision was written into Section 6 of the Clayton Act: "Nothing contained in the antitrust laws shall be construed to forbid the existence and operation of labor, agricultural, or horticultural organizations, instituted for the purposes of mutual help and not . . . conducted for profits, or to forbid or restrain individual members of such organizations from carrying out the legitimate objects thereof; nor shall such organizations, or the members thereof, be held or construed to be illegal combinations or conspiracies in restraint of trade under the antitrust laws." This provision clearly exempted unions and cooperatives per se. But it was not interpreted to grant complete immunity. The exemption was expressly limited to the "legitimate objects" of such groups. And these objects were not held to include restraint of trade.

Agricultural and Fisheries Cooperatives

During the twenties, many of the states enacted a uniform statute permitting the formation of agricultural cooperatives and prescribing their legal structure. This measure limited the return that could be paid on an association's capital and required that each owner of its shares be given a single vote. In 1922, Congress broadened the antitrust exemption it had given to cooperatives by passing the Capper-Volstead Act. Under this law, "farmers" are permitted to employ such associations as common agencies in sorting, grading, and packing their crops, in producing such foodstuffs as butter, cheese, and canned goods, in marketing their output, and in fixing prices and terms of sale. This privilege is confined to associations operated for mutual benefit, each of whose members has a single vote or whose dividends are limited to 8 percent per year, and whose supplies are drawn predominantly from within their membership. One other safeguard is provided: "If the Secretary of Agriculture shall have reason to believe that any such association monopolizes or restrains trade . . . to such an extent that the price of any agricultural product is unduly enhanced," he may issue a complaint, hold a hearing, and issue an order to cease and desist which, upon noncompliance, he may request the Attorney General to enforce.

This exemption has not been held to permit cooperatives to conspire with other distributors, to fix resale prices, or to discriminate unlawfully among their customers. But it is nonetheless a sweeping one, enabling cooperatives to make exclusive contracts with hundreds of farmers and to combine in the establishment of common marketing agencies. It encompasses not only farming operations but also manufacturing establishments engaged in processing agricultural commodities. The safeguard embodied in the law affords but scant protection against abuse. No criterion is established by which to judge whether prices have been "unduly" enhanced. The Secretary of Agriculture, moreover, may be expected to view the activities of agricultural cooperatives with a not unsympathetic eye. It should be noted, too, that such associations were authorized by the Cooperative Marketing Act of 1926 to collect, disseminate, and interpret trade statistics, an activity that has brought many a trade association into conflict with antitrust.

The significance of these arrangements varies from product to product. Where producers are widely scattered, as is the case with the great staple products, cooperatives are unlikely to control enough of the supply to dictate the price. But where producers are geographically concentrated, as they are in the cases of fruits, vegetables, nuts, and milk, a cooperative may possess monopolistic powers. In the one case, the laws exempting cooperatives from antitrust may serve merely to equalize the bargaining power of sellers and buyers of agricultural commodities. In the other, they may grant a license to monopoly. In either case, they extend to agriculture a privilege that is denied to industry. Except for Appalachian Coals, joint selling agencies in the domestic market have been held, under the Sherman Act, to be illegal per se.

Under the Fisheries Cooperative Marketing Act of 1934, an exemption similar to that of the Capper-Volstead Act was extended to fishermen. Here, the authority to serve complaints and issue orders if prices were "unduly" enhanced was conferred upon the Secretary of Commerce, to be transferred in 1939 to the Secretary of the Interior. But here, a different situation exists. Fishermen, typically, are independent proprietors, holding title to their boats and selling their catch to fish dealers and canners. Some of them have financed their boats by mortgaging them to the canners and some of them may work part-time as laborers in the canneries. In general, fishermen have not availed themselves of the privilege of forming cooperatives. More often, they have come together in labor unions, sometimes combining with cannery workers, to bargain with the fish dealers and canners. But the substance of their bargains relates, not to wages for their labor, but to the price of the product which they sell. In 1949 it was held that fishermen could not claim exemption from antitrust as members of labor unions, since their relation to the purchasers of fish was not that of employees.[11] The way remains open, however, to obtain exemption by establishing fisheries cooperatives. And here, as in agriculture, there is danger of abuse.

Under the provisions of the agricultural marketing agreements legislation of the 1930's, cooperatives were further authorized to enter into agreements with the processors and distributors of agricultural commodities to control their sale and price, and the Secretary of Agriculture was empowered to order them to do so. This legislation, providing for the establishment of both voluntary and compulsory cartels, will be considered in Chapter 32.

Agreements and Combinations in Transport and Communications

Transoceanic shipping rates have customarily been fixed by agreement among the ship lines of different countries meeting in shipping conferences. Under the Shipping Act of 1916, American lines participating in these agreements were granted exemption from the antitrust laws. The Act required that the agreements be filed with the U.S. Shipping Board (now the Federal Maritime Commission) and authorized the Board to modify or cancel rates, in services touching American ports, that it found to be discriminatory or unfair. In 1964, the Commission found that conference agreements were operating to the disadvantage of the United States. Rates were lower on cargoes coming from Europe than on those going to Europe. They were lower on cargoes going to South America from Europe than on those going there from the United States. Under a dual rate system, permitted by the FMC, shippers were offered service at 10 to 15 percent below the normal rate if they would sign exclusive contracts with conference members, thus preventing nonconference lines from competing for their business. In an attempt to meet this situation, the Commission ordered the shipping companies to submit for its inspection their rate schedules and their contract terms. The foreign companies refused to do so. The Commission

11 / *U.S.* v. *Local 36, I.F.A.W.A.,* 177 F. 2d 320.

countered by threatening to close American ports to their ships. This move led, predictably, to protests by other governments. The Commission was unable to enforce its rules. The law thus gives a free hand to international shipping cartels.

The passenger fares charged by international airlines have similarly been set, since 1945, region by region, in annual conferences by members of the International Air Transport Association. Every airline in a region belongs to its conference and has a vote. Agreements must be unanimous and must be approved by each carrier's government, in the United States by the Civil Aeronautics Board. Generally, the foreign lines and governments have favored higher fares; the American lines and the C.A.B., lower fares. Any line can make a unilateral cut, but such action is discouraged by the fact that its landing rights in other countries may be revoked. The IATA thus functions as a loosely controlled price cartel.[12]

Exemption from antitrust is also afforded to domestic transport, immunity being granted to railway traffic associations by the Reed-Bulwinkle Act of 1948. Railroad rates had been regulated by the Interstate Commerce Commission since 1887. But the Commission acted only on the cases that were brought before it and, in practice, reviewed less than 1 percent of the specific rates. Presumably each carrier was to take the initiative in fixing its charges. But, for many years, all changes in rates had been submitted to traffic associations set up by the carriers for this purpose and were not made effective unless approved. The Supreme Court had held, repeatedly, that the antitrust laws applied to the railroads. So, in 1944, the Department of Justice brought suit against a railroad traffic association under the Sherman Act. The railroads thereupon demanded exemption. Congress complied; the Bulwinkle Bill was passed. Its significance was discussed in Chapter 16. The rates charged by motor carriers are fixed through traffic associations in the same way. The fares charged by domestic air carriers are not.

The combination of competing railroads, motor carriers, and water carriers is permitted by law when approved by the Interstate Commerce Commission; the combination of competing airlines when approved by the Civil Aeronautics Board. The combination of communications companies is permitted when approved by the Federal Communications Commission. In each of these cases, the combined company is subject to the jurisdiction of a regulatory agency.

Export Trade Associations

In 1918, Congress passed the Webb-Pomerene Act, exempting from the antitrust laws any "association entered into for the sole purpose of engaging in export trade," thus legalizing combinations for making sales abroad. The Act expressly forbade the members of such associations to interfere with the exports of nonmembers or to take joint action in making sales in the domestic market, warning them not to "enter into any agreement, understanding, or conspiracy

12 / Mahlon R. Straszheim, *The International Airline Industry* (Washington, D.C.: Brookings Institution, 1969).

or do any act which artificially or intentionally enhances or depresses prices within the United States . . . or which substantially lessens competition within the United States or otherwise restrains trade therein." Associations were directed to file their charters, bylaws, agreements, and other data with the Federal Trade Commission and to make periodic reports to that body. The Commission was not authorized to issue orders to cease and desist from violations of the law, but it was permitted to investigate association activities and to recommend readjustments that would bring them within the scope of the exemption.

For more than 20 years, supervision of these associations by the FTC was only nominal. The documents required were kept on file; the names of the associations and the value of their exports were reported annually. This work was the responsibility of a single employee. It was not until the forties that the Commission undertook to investigate association activities and to effect readjustments that would bring them into conformity with the law.

Webb-Pomerene associations, over the years, have numbered around 30. Normally they have handled less than 5 percent of the goods exported from the United States. Most of the earlier associations were operating agencies, making sales abroad, allocating orders at home, assembling and shipping goods, making collections, and remitting payments to their members. It was generally assumed that mere price and quota agreements were not permitted by the law. In 1924, however, in response to a letter from a group of silver producers, the FTC declared that an association need not "perform all the operations of selling its members' product to a foreign buyer" but might be engaged solely "in allotting export orders . . . and in fixing prices at which the individual members shall sell. . . ." From that time, most associations have left to their members the work of making sales, shipping goods, and collecting payments, confining themselves to the task of fixing prices or assigning quotas or both.

The Webb-Pomerene Act did not say whether export trade associations might participate in international cartels. But in its silver letter, the FTC asserted that it saw no reason why such an association "might not adopt a trade arrangement with non-nationals reaching the same market, providing this market was not the domestic market of the United States. . . ." A number of associations joined in cartel agreements on the strength of this interpretation of the law. In 1939, however, the Department of Justice initiated a campaign against division of world markets by international cartels. And in 1945, in its decision in the case of the Alkali Export Association, the Supreme Court held that the association's participation in such arrangements was illegal, since the Webb-Pomerene Act was intended to promote competition rather than collusion in the markets of the world.[13] Ten years later, in a letter to another trade association, the FTC formally reversed the position taken in the silver letter, announcing that agreements restricting American exports and excluding foreign competitors from American markets were not among the activities exempted by the Act.

13 / U.S. v. Alkali Export Assn., 325 U.S. 196.

A number of arguments have been advanced in support of this exemption: (1) By combining, exporters can reduce the cost of making foreign sales; they can save money on advertising, selling, and handling, on freight, insurance, storage, and the like. (2) Combination will enable small American exporters to compete more effectively with larger ones. (3) Foreign sellers are united in cartels. Americans would find it difficult to compete with them if they, too, were not permitted to combine. (4) Foreign buyers are also cartelized. In the absence of combination, American sellers would be at a disadvantage in bargaining.

If associations actually engaged in physical operations, the first of these arguments would have some validity. But most of them do not. If associations were usually composed of smaller firms, the second argument also would have some point. In practice they have been formed more frequently by larger companies. The third argument is dubious. The cartelization of foreign sellers should not make it difficult for Americans to sell abroad. Quite the contrary: cartels raise prices and this should make it easier to compete. The last argument, too, is open to question. Foreign buyers may be cartelized, but the American firms that have combined to deal with them have seldom been weaklings needing help.

The antitrust exemption granted to export trade associations has done little to remove obstacles to American exports or to enable small businesses to participate more fully in export trade. It has been applied to so narrow a range of products as to question its necessity. The exemption might well be repealed or, if retained, should be confined to associations of small concerns that actually function as joint sales agencies.[14]

Insurance

In 1920, Congress exempted from the antitrust laws combinations of marine insurance companies. The share of marine insurance carried with American companies was a minor one, and the action was designed to encourage their development. The exemption was complete; no administrative approval was required. Presumably, however, such combinations would face the competition of foreign insurance companies.

For many years, it was held that the business of writing domestic insurance policies was intrastate in character and, therefore, was not covered by the Sherman Act. In 1944, however, the Supreme Court found that the operations of fire insurance companies involved the transmission of communications, documents, and money in interstate commerce and concluded that the Sherman Act applied.[15] The insurance interests then sought complete exemption from the law. In this they were not wholly successful. The McCarran Act, passed in 1945, suspended enforcement of the antitrust laws against rate agreements among insurance companies for a period of three years, making them applicable there-

14 / See Federal Trade Commission, Staff Report, *Webb-Pomerene Association: A 50-Year Review* (Washington, D.C.: Government Printing Office, 1967).

15 / *U.S.* v. *South-Eastern Underwriters Assn.*, 322 U.S. 533.

after but only "to the extent that such business is not regulated by state law." This exemption was given broad scope by the Supreme Court in 1958, when it put an end to a Federal Trade Commission campaign against deceptive advertising of accident and health insurance policies, holding that the Commission had jurisdiction over such advertising only in states whose laws did not forbid it.[16] There are certain collusive practices, however, such as agreements among insurance companies not to file lower rates and boycotts denying reinsurance privileges to those who do so, which can still be prosecuted under the Sherman Act. And mergers of insurance companies located in different states, being beyond state control, can probably be prevented under the Celler-Kefauver Act. The character of state regulation of the insurance business was discussed in Chapter 26.

Bank Mergers

When the Celler-Kefauver Act, amending Section 7 of the Clayton Act, was passed in 1950, it was assumed that the new law did not apply to mergers of banks. In 1960, however, Congress undertook to make the exemption explicit by passing a Bank Merger Act. Under this measure, banks were permitted to merge if they obtained approval from the competent banking authorities: national banks from the Controller of the Currency, state banks belonging to the Federal Reserve System from the Board of Governors, and other insured banks from the Federal Deposit Insurance Corporation. Around 1960, there was a wave of bank mergers and, despite the new law, the Department of Justice brought a number of suits. In the leading case, the Supreme Court found that a merger of the Philadelphia Bank and the Girard Trust Company, though approved by the Controller of the Currency, was in violation of Section 7.[17] Thereupon, Congress sought to restore to the banking authorities the power to approve mergers. In the Bank Merger Act of 1966, it established common criteria to govern the legality of mergers, whether in action taken by the banking authorities or in decisions made, under the antitrust laws, by the courts. Under these criteria, the authorities were permitted to approve a merger whose effects "may be substantially to lessen competition or tend to create a monopoly" where they found that these effects "are clearly outweighed in the public interest by the probable effect of the transaction in meeting the convenience and needs of the community." The merger movement continued and the Department of Justice brought more suits, losing a number of them in the lower courts. Then, in 1967, the Supreme Court handed down a unanimous decision, outlawing mergers of banks in Houston and in Philadelphia.[18] The Court rejected the contention of the Controller of the Currency that the Department of Justice was powerless to proceed against a merger bearing his approval. It held

16 / *FTC* v. *National Casualty Co.,* 357 U.S. 560.

17 / *U.S.* v. *Philadelphia National Bank,* 374 U.S. 321 (1963).

18 / *U.S.* v. *First City National Bank* and *U.S.* v. *Provident National Bank,* 386 U.S. 361 (1967).

that proponents of mergers under the Bank Merger Act were required to prove that the anticompetitive effects of the mergers are clearly outweighed by their benefits to the community. And it found that, in this case, they had failed to do so. The Bank Merger Act of 1966 has failed, as did the Act of 1960, to open as wide an escape from the antitrust laws as was sought.

Newspapers

The mortality rate among newspapers in American cities has been high, due largely to the competition of radio and television. In many cities, only one or two remain. In a score or more of cities, two papers, while maintaining nominal independence, have entered into agreements involving joint operations, price fixing, and profit sharing. The Department of Justice brought suit against one such agreement in Tucson, Arizona. The Supreme Court, in a decision handed down in 1969, held the agreement to be in violation of the Sherman Act. [19] Newspaper publishers then descended on Congress, demanding exemption from the law. It was important, they said, to remove the threat of bankruptcy so that independent editorial policies could be maintained. But they did not explain how such independence could be assured if operations were to be merged and profits shared. Congress responded, in 1970, by exempting existing agreements between pairs of papers covering joint mechanical and business (but not editorial) operations and future agreements of this sort where one of the papers involved may be found by the Department of Justice to be facing bankruptcy.

Professional Sports

When the Supreme Court held, in 1957, that professional football, like boxing, wrestling, and basketball, was subject to the Sherman Act, although it had held, in 1953, that professional baseball was not, it admitted that its ruling might appear to be "unrealistic, inconsistent, or illogical" but left the problem to Congress to be solved. Two solutions were proposed. The first would have brought baseball within the scope of the Sherman Act. The second would have exempted football, basketball, and hockey, along with baseball, from the law. Bills embodying each of these approaches have been introduced at successive sessions of Congress. None of them has been enacted. The anomaly remains.

Baseball presents a peculiar problem for antitrust. In the market for players' services, the clubs do not compete. Under the "reserve rule," in force since the 1880's, no club bids against another. A club may sell a player's contract, but he cannot offer his services for sale. He has to take what his club offers him or quit. A club may exclude a good player from major league competition by holding him on a minor team, but he has no recourse. If he jumps his contract, he is blacklisted and nobody will hire him. If these practices were brought under the Sherman Act, they would undoubtedly be held to violate the law. But free

19 / *Citizen Publishing Co.* v. *U.S.,* Supreme Court of the U.S., October Term 1968, No. 243 (1969).

competition in the market for players might well destroy the sport. If the richest club were free, each year, to hire the best players, and were thus to win all its games, the sport would cease to be competitive and public interest would decline. This situation was recognized by Congressman Celler, whose bill would have permitted the practices described above to continue if the clubs could prove, in each court case, that they were "reasonably necessary" to the equalization of competitive playing strength. This principle, however, has not been enacted into law. The exemption of baseball is complete.

Exceptions to State Antitrust Laws

The legislatures of the several states have granted numerous exceptions under their respective antitrust laws, usually acting on behalf of farmers, retailers, and the local service trades. Most states permit agricultural marketing agreements and many permit the establishment of minimum prices for milk. In all but four states, the maintenance of resale prices has been legalized, at one time or another, and in many states, merchants have been forbidden to sell at prices that fall below their costs. A number of states have authorized the establishment of minimum prices for alcoholic beverages, for gasoline, and for barbering, shoe repairing, laundering, cleaning and dyeing, and other service trades. These exemptions apply, in the main, to fields that would normally be highly competitive. Their effect is to be felt in local markets for consumers' goods and services.

The Scope of Exceptions

According to Kaysen and Turner, 18.4 percent of the nation's income originated, in 1954, in sectors of the economy that are exempt from antitrust. These sectors, therefore, "cannot be dismissed as involving only a few special situations."[20] It should be noted, however, that 12 percent of income was produced in that year by public enterprise or in industries that were subject to regulatory controls, leaving only 6.4 percent coming from industries where exemption was not accompanied by such controls. In national policy, the maintenance of competition or the substitution of regulation or public enterprise are still the general rule. Unregulated monopoly is the exception. Taken together, the trades exempted are less important than those still subject to the law.

20 / Carl Kaysen and Donald F. Turner, *Antitrust Policy* (Cambridge, Mass.: Harvard University Press, 1959), p. 42.

Chapter

29

CURBING COMPETITION IN DISTRIBUTION

One of the principal fields in which both state and federal governments have departed from the policy of maintaining competition is that of wholesale and retail distribution. The members of these trades are numerous and, when organized, politically powerful. Every legislator has scores, hundreds, or even thousands of grocers, druggists, and other tradesmen in his district. When any of these groups speaks with a single voice, he listens. And when the voice demands suppression of competition, he is likely to agree that competition should be suppressed. The result is seen in the body of legislation with which this chapter is concerned.

THE COMPETITIVE STRUGGLE

In the absence of public intervention the distributive trades are highly competitive. There is no obstacle to entry to the field. Capital requirements, particularly in retailing, are low. The necessary equipment is inexpensive and may be bought at second hand. Stocks of goods are abundant; sources of supply are numerous and widely scattered; credit is readily available. Labor may be provided by unskilled workers hired at low wages, by the retailer himself, and by members of his family. The processes of distribution are simple. Technical training and managerial experience are not required. New types of distributive agencies are continually springing into life. The field is in a constant state of flux.

In the United States in 1963 there were more than 2 million establishments engaged in distribution, some 300,000 of them in wholesaling and 1,700,000 in retailing. Among the retail outlets, 200,000 belonged to chains; 1,500,000 were operated by one-store firms. One fourth of all retail sales were made by the chains; three fourths by the independents. There are large firms in retailing, but they do not monopolize the field. Among variety stores in 1963, the four largest firms made 56 percent of the sales; among food stores, 22 percent; among general merchandise stores, 18 percent.[1] Most retail outlets are small, their sales running around $100,000 per year. The business is highly competitive. There is competition between stores of the same type and between stores of different

1 / *U.S. Census of Business, 1963, Retail Trade,* Summary Statistics, Part 1.

types: drug stores compete with hardware stores, hardware stores with auto supply stores, auto supply stores with variety stores, variety stores with candy stores, candy stores with food stores, food stores with tobacco stores, and tobacco stores with drug stores. Wholesale markets, in general, are national or regional; retail markets are local. But even in the latter case the number of competitors usually is large. Hard roads and automobiles, moreover, have brought the local merchant into competition with the door-to-door salesman, the roadside stand, the supermarket, the department store, and the specialty shop. And even in isolated communities he must compete with Sears, Roebuck and Montgomery Ward.

Changing Patterns of Distribution

In the 19th century, the trading post and the peddler gave way to the general store, the general store to the specialized store. The channel of distribution then established ran from the manufacturer through the wholesaler to the retailer and on to the consumer. In the 20th century, this channel was bypassed with increasing frequency as the manufacturer began to sell directly to the retailer and even to the consumer, until a large part of his goods came to be distributed in this way.[2] The principal factor in this development was the growth of the large-scale retailer: the mail order house, the department store, and the chain. Of these, the most important was the chain. This form of organization grew rapidly in the twenties, reaching its peak in the thirties with 80,000 chain grocery stores. Thereafter, the number of these stores declined. A&P, with 15,400 stores in 1929 was down to 4,500 in 1964. But this development reflected the displacement of smaller stores by larger ones. Supermarkets, introduced during the thirties and expanded during the forties, came to handle more than two thirds of the grocery business. They were joined, in the fifties and the sixties, by the shopping center and the discount house.

The mass distributor has made life more difficult for the manufacturer, the wholesaler, and the independent retailer. He has bought directly, eliminating the wholesaler. He has demanded substantial discounts on his purchases, threatening otherwise to enter production in competition with the manufacturer. When making goods for himself and when buying them from others, he has sold them under his private brand. He has reduced prices at retail by introducing the methods of self-service and cash and carry, and by seeking his profit in a small margin on a large turnover, thus undercutting the independent retailer. Sometimes, to attract customers, he has sold well-known goods at a loss, annoying both their manufacturers and their other distributors.

His suppliers and his rivals have shaped their tactics accordingly. The manufacturer has sought to secure the loyalty of the consumer by spending large sums to advertise his brand. The wholesaler, too, has branded and advertised the goods he handles. And he has attempted to bind his customers to him by organizing

2 / *U.S. Census of Business, Wholesale Trade, 1963,* Summary Statistics, Part 1.

voluntary chains. The independent retailer, finally, has formed cooperative buying groups in an effort to claim the discounts obtainable by purchasing in quantity. He has copied the methods of self-service and cash and carry. And he has aligned his fortunes with those of the manufacturer and the wholesaler by pushing the sale of national brands. But neither the wholesaler nor the retailer has been content to rely on methods such as these. Instead, they have turned to the states and to the federal government for help.

The Attack on the Mass Distributor

One of the first steps taken on behalf of the independent merchant was to impose an artificial handicap on the mass distributor by subjecting him to a discriminatory tax. Beginning in the 1920's, laws taxing chain stores were enacted in 29 states. This tax was typically imposed on every store in a chain at a rate which rose with the number of stores maintained within a state. In Louisiana, however, the rate rose with the number of stores in a chain, wherever located. This was upheld as a valid method of classification by the Supreme Court of the United States[3] and was copied by a number of other states. Bills were introduced in Congress calling for the imposition of federal taxes at higher rates but failed to pass. One of them would have taxed each store in a chain of more than 500 stores at the rate of $1,000 multiplied by the number of states in which the chain was operating. At the time, this would have imposed on the A&P a levy of $470,000,000, turning its net profit of $80,000,000 into a loss of $390,000,000. The chain store taxes failed to accomplish their purpose. Instead of destroying the chains they made them more efficient, resulting in the elimination of less profitable units and stimulating the development of supermarkets. The taxes were dropped by 15 states, being found unconstitutional by some and repealed by others. In 1965 only 14 such laws remained.

A second approach was to reduce the buying advantages of the mass distributor. This was attempted in the provisions of the NRA codes that denied the wholesaler's discount to retailers and limited quantity discounts and advertising allowances. It was continued in the Robinson-Patman Act in 1936. This law was drafted by the counsel for an association of wholesale grocers. Its effect, as we have seen in Chapter 9, has been to handicap the competitors of the old-line wholesaler, not only the chain store, but also the wholesale cooperatives and other buying agencies that serve the independent retailer. Suppliers are forbidden to pass on to distributors savings that result from the elimination of brokerage services in making a sale. They may not render services to distributors or pay distributors for services rendered them, unless such services or payments are available "on proportionally equal terms" to all. Different prices may be charged for different quantities insofar as they make only due allowance for differences in cost. But the discounts thus obtainable are limited by the methods permitted in the computation of cost. And the Federal Trade Commission may establish

3 / *A.&P.* v. *Grosjean,* 301 U.S. 412 (1927).

limits beyond which differences in price are forbidden even though justified by differences in cost. One of the first orders issued under the Robinson-Patman Act involved the A&P. In this case the Supreme Court upheld the brokerage section of the law and enjoined the A&P from accepting a broker's discount. But the attack on the buying advantages of the chain did not stop here. In 1949 the Department of Justice initiated a civil suit asking that the company be dissolved as an illegal combination under the provisions of the Sherman Act. The issues presented by this suit are considered, in some detail, below.

A third method of protecting the independent merchant has been that of restricting the freedom of the mass distributor to reduce the prices at which he sells. There were provisions in the NRA codes permitting resale price maintenance, forbidding sales below cost, and requiring the addition of a minimum markup. Then, resale price maintenance was legalized by most states and the federal government, and minimum markup laws enacted by many of the states. The significance of this legislation is to be considered in the present chapter.

THE A&P CASE

The Great Atlantic and Pacific Tea Company was founded in 1859. Ninety years later it was a gigantic holding company with retail subsidiaries operating close to 5,000 stores in more than 3,000 cities in 40 states, with manufacturing subsidiaries producing a minor but substantial share of the goods it sold, and with wholesale subsidiaries making its purchases. Of the latter the most important was the Atlantic Commission Company, a broker dealing in fruits and vegetables not only for A&P but also for other distributors. The company was handling less than 7 percent of the groceries sold in the United States, but more than half of those sold in a few cities, and more than a third of those sold in a good many others. It had served as a pioneer in introducing new techniques of distribution, improving sanitation in the sale of foodstuffs, making seasonal foods available throughout the year, local foods available throughout the country, and foods once consumed only by the rich available to all. It had kept its margin low, receiving this commendation in 1946 from Judge Walter Lindley in a federal district court: "To buy, sell, and distribute to a substantial portion of 130 million people one and three-quarters billion dollars worth of food annually at a profit of 1¼ cents on each dollar is an achievement one may well be proud of."[4]

In 1944 the government initiated a criminal suit against the A&P under the Sherman Act. In 1946 the company was found guilty by Judge Lindley and fined $175,000. On appeal the conviction was sustained,[5] and A&P paid its fine, not carrying the case to the Supreme Court. Thereupon, in 1949, the govern-

4 / U.S. v. N.Y. Great A.&P. Tea Co., 67 F. Supp. 626.
5 / 173 F. 2d 79 (1949).

ment brought a civil suit, asking that the company be enjoined from illegal practices in buying and selling and that it be dissolved, cutting off its manufacturing activities, abolishing its central purchasing agencies—including ACCO—and splitting its retail operations into seven parts.

Practices in Selling

The government's complaint centered on the sales policies, the buying advantages, and the vertical integration of the A&P. With respect to selling, it charged that the company engaged in temporary, local price cutting, deliberately taking losses to drive out competition in some areas and recouping them by charging higher prices in others. It was said, too, that the company undertook to expand its volume by selling below cost, instead of computing prices by first determining its costs and then adding a margin of profit.

It is true that the prices charged by A&P had varied from store to store. The company admitted that, from market to market, it met the prices charged by its competitors. It may even have made deeper cuts in markets where cuts were being made by other stores. As a result, its prices would be lower where its competition was tougher. The scope of its operations and the magnitude of its financial resources, moreover, were such as to enable it to carry particular outlets for long periods at a loss. But there was no evidence that the company had increased its share of the market by employing geographic price discrimination to drive out local competitors. And if losses were deliberately incurred in some areas, it would have been difficult to find others where they could be recouped. In every market where the A&P operated it had to face competitors.

It is true, too, that the company had reduced its margins and its prices in an effort to increase its sales. And in this it succeeded. With larger volume, costs were reduced and aggregate profits were increased. But such behavior was scarcely to be criticized. Competitive sellers are normally to be expected to expand their sales by taking advantage of elasticity of demand. To insist on cost-plus pricing, as the government appeared to do, was not to promote competition but to stifle it.

"Defendants," said the government in its complaint, "have regularly undersold . . . competing retailers. . . ." And A&P published its reply in full-page advertisements in more than 2,000 daily and weekly newspapers throughout the United States: "To this charge we plead *guilty*. We confess that for the past 90 years we have constantly stepped up the efficiency of our operations in order to give our customers more and more good food for their money." But this exchange was not entirely fair to the government. "Defendants," said the complaint, "by coercing and receiving unlawful buying preferences, have become enabled to and have regularly undersold . . . competing retailers. . . ."[6] The emphasis was on the company's advantages in buying.

6 / Civil Action 52-139, S.D. N.Y., September 15, 1949.

Advantages in Buying

The A&P has always sought, in one way or another, to buy at prices lower than those that were paid by its competitors. Before the Robinson-Patman Act was passed, it demanded a broker's discount. When this was outlawed, it asked that the prices it paid be cut by a similar amount. When this was forbidden by the FTC, it announced that it would buy only from suppliers who would sell direct and not through brokers. The company insisted on substantial allowances for advertising the products it handled and on discounts for other services it rendered their producers. Operating its own warehouses, it induced suppliers to add to their charges when making store-door deliveries to its competitors. But whatever the form of these concessions, the important thing is that they enabled A&P to obtain its goods at a lower price.

This gave the company an advantage. But was it an unfair advantage? Or did the government seek to subject the company to an unfair handicap? A&P performed a broker's services; it was denied a broker's commission. It provided suppliers with advertising and other services; the allowances it could receive on this account were limited. It bought in quantity; whether its discounts involved discrimination required analyses of its suppliers' costs. But all these matters were fully covered by the Robinson-Patman Act. Why go beyond this to seek the company's dissolution under the Sherman Act?

The government charged that A&P obtained its preferential prices by coercing its suppliers. It was said to do so by threatening to manufacture for itself. There is no question that the company's buyers were tough traders. And it is certain that their position was strengthened by the availability of an alternative. But opinions differ as to whether their operations were properly to be described as coercion or merely as successful bargaining. It is interesting, too, to note the identity of those who were said to be coerced. In some cases, they were large and powerful processors. Here, the mass distributor exacted concessions from oligopolists to pass them on, at retail, in a lower price. If this be coercion, consumers would welcome more of it. In other cases, to be sure, the suppliers were small concerns. But, in general, A&P bought no more than a tenth of the foodstuffs sold in national markets and no more than a fifth of those sold in regional markets. If suppliers disliked its offers, they could sell to someone else.[7]

Vertical Integration

The government's final complaint had to do with the vertical integration of A&P. In selling the products of its factories, the company was said to charge higher prices to its competitors than to its own outlets, employing the higher profits made on the former sales to offset the lower profits or losses realized on

---

7 / On this point see Richard B. Heflebower, "Mass Distribution: A Phase of Bilateral Oligopoly or of Competition?" *American Economic Review*, Vol. XLVII, No. 2 (1957), pp. 274-85.

the latter. Its retail operations were thus held to be subsidized by its gains from manufacturing. It would seem, however, that the company was justified in charging less when distributing goods through its own outlets, since this process entailed none of the costs of soliciting business and transferring ownership. There is doubt, moreover, that its factories really subsidized its stores.

Strictly speaking, the A&P did not "sell" and its stores did not "buy" the goods A&P made itself. The figure that it entered in its books, when making such a transfer, was an accounting fiction, not a market reality. By reducing this figure it could have eliminated the apparent profits of its factories and augmented the profits of its stores. And, as a result, the charge that the former operation was being used to subsidize the latter could no longer have been made. This charge could have been brought, with equal logic, against any integrated firm. For it was the government's contention that the use of profits realized by one subsidiary to offset the losses incurred by another is an abuse inherent in integration. Certainly, such a practice is inherent. But it may be questioned whether it is an abuse.

A similar issue was presented by the activities of the Atlantic Commission Company. But here there were further charges. ACCO served both as a purchasing agent for A&P and as a broker handling shipments made by suppliers to the competitors of A&P. The two functions were said to be inconsistent, and the company's dual position was said to have been abused. As a broker, ACCO should have devoted itself solely to the interests of its clients. But, as a purchasing agent, it sought to get fruit and vegetables of better quality at lower prices for A&P. The company sought also to induce suppliers of produce to sell through it exclusively and to induce jobbers to buy through it exclusively. And insofar as it succeeded, it cut its rivals off from other sources of supply. It was this division of interest and abuse of power that was emphasized by the district court in its decision in the criminal case. But ACCO never came close to obtaining a monopoly. So one might ask, if its customers were really victimized, why they failed to take their business elsewhere. It would appear, if ACCO had not served them, that they would have been no better off.

The Central Issue

The growth of A&P and similar chains made the grocery business more competitive. It improved the methods and cut the costs of distribution. It gave the consumer a better product at a lower price. And this is precisely what competition is supposed to do. The chains, moreover, carry no threat of monopoly. Their share of the business is a minor one, and it has not increased for many years. New competitors have entered the market, with new methods, and the door stands open to the entry of many more. The purpose of the government's suit, therefore, was not to enforce competition or to prevent monopoly. It was to protect the independent grocer against the competition of the chains. The attack was on the advantages of size. The legal issue was whether these advantages so seriously restricted the competitive opportunities of small merchants as to constitute restraint of trade. The issue of public policy was whether the small competitor should be protected at the risk of impairing the vigor of competition, or competition preserved at the risk of harming the small competitor.

The Consent Decree

The civil suit was settled by a consent decree in January, 1954.[8] The government accepted less than it had asked. The retail chain was not broken up. The manufacturing operations were not cut off. But A&P was enjoined on several points: (1) In selling, the company was forbidden to fix a low markup for particular stores with the purpose of eliminating local competition by having them operate at a loss. Such intent, however, was not to be inferred from the mere fact of operation at a loss. It must be proved if the company is ever to be convicted of violating the decree. And this will not be easy to do. (2) In buying, A&P was forbidden to require its suppliers to stop selling food to its competitors through brokers, to stop offering discounts to these competitors, and to raise the prices charged them. And it was further forbidden to obtain discounts by combining the quantities purchased by two or more of the 37 units in which it grouped its stores, except in certain cases where savings in costs might be shown. (3) With respect to integration, A&P agreed to dissolve the Atlantic Commission Company. And it was forbidden, thereafter, to buy any food for competitors or to sell any food to competitors, except that processed in its own plants.

The decree, in its detail, subjected A&P to many limitations that did not apply to its competitors. It does not appear, however, to have imposed a serious handicap. Many observers take the view that the dissolution of ACCO did the company more good than harm. During the sixties, with a profit margin of 1 percent, A&P sales ran over $5 billion a year; its profits between $50 million and $60 million.[9]

RESALE PRICE MAINTENANCE

Resale price maintenance is an arrangement under which the seller of a product identified by a brand name or trademark sets a minimum price below which the buyer may not go in making a subsequent sale. The person who sets the price may be the producer or a distributor of the product in question. The persons whose prices are thus to be controlled are those who sell the product at retail. It is the purpose of the practice to prevent retailers from competing in the prices charged for branded goods.

Freedom to maintain resale prices was first sought by manufacturers. Certain retailers had sold well-known branded goods at low prices as a means of attracting customers. Other dealers, when meeting these prices, obtained small margins

8 / Civil Action 52-139, S.D. N.Y., Consent Decree, January 19, 1954.

9 / *Business Week,* June 5, 1965, p. 90.

on such goods. This threatened to make their distribution unprofitable, and manufacturers feared that dealers might fail to push them or even drop them from their stocks. They therefore sought to insure the loyalty of their distributors by preventing reductions in price.

Before the 1930's, resale price maintenance had repeatedly been condemned by the courts, being held both to violate the Sherman Act and to be an unfair method of competition under the Federal Trade Commission Act. Producers had attempted to obtain legal sanction for the practice by bringing infringement suits against those who undercut the prices printed on their products, charging violation of patents and copyrights, and by entering into contracts with their distributors, but to no avail.[10] There were but two methods of maintaining resale prices that the courts allowed: (1) Manufacturers could refuse to sell to price cutters.[11] Indeed, their freedom to do so was guaranteed by Section 2 of the Clayton Act, which gives to "persons engaged in selling goods, wares, or merchandise in commerce the right to select their own customers in *bona fide* transactions and not in restraint of trade." But refusal to sell could not be used to enforce an illegal agreement to maintain a resale price.[12] And it could not be carried to the extent of spying on distributors and threatening to withhold supplies.[13] (2) Producers were permitted to fix the prices at which their products could be sold by agents.[14] But agency could not be used as a mere subterfuge; the permission was limited to cases where an agent did not take title but acted solely on behalf of his principal. The maintenance of resale prices was thus severely circumscribed by law. And the Federal Trade Commission had undertaken to prevent the practice by issuing scores of complaints and orders to cease and desist.

As time went on, manufacturers lost interest in fixing the prices at which their goods could be sold. A substantial portion of their output came to be marketed, at cut prices, by mass distributors. And these concerns possessed the alternative—if prices were set too high—of entering into competition by producing under private brands. It was therefore desirable for the manufacturer to retain the favor of the price cutter as well as that of the dealer who wanted prices maintained. So he retreated into neutrality, abandoning his efforts to change the law.

The initiative was now taken by trade associations representing the interests of independent retailers, with the National Association of Retail Druggists in the lead. Until 1931 repeated attempts to get bills permitting resale price maintenance through Congress had ended in failure, and the practice had been approved by New Jersey but by no other state. Then the retailers' associations

10 / See *Bobbs-Merrill Co.* v. *Straus,* 210 U.S. 339 (1908); *Dr. Miles Medical Co.* v. *John D. Park & Sons Co.,* 220 U.S. 373 (1911); *Bauer* v. *O'Donnell,* 229 U.S. 1 (1913); *Straus* v. *Victor Co.,* 243 U.S. 490 (1917).

11 / *U.S.* v. *Colgate & Co.,* 250 U.S. 300 (1919).

12 / *U.S.* v. *A. Schroeder's Sons, Inc.,* 252 U.S. 85 (1920).

13 / *Beechnut Packing Co.* v. *F.T.C.,* 247 U.S. 441 (1922).

14 / *U.S.* v. *General Electric Co.,* 272 U.S. 476 (1926).

started moving on the legislatures. And within a few years price maintenance had been legalized by nearly all of them, under the euphemism of "fair trade."

State Fair Trade Laws

The first of the new laws was enacted in California in 1931. It exempted from the state's antitrust act any contract wherein the seller of a branded product bound the buyer, when reselling it, to charge the price the former specified. The law proved ineffective because retailers who did not sign contracts undercut the prices charged by those who did. An amendment was therefore adopted in 1933, incorporating a provision known as the nonsigner's clause: "Wilfully and knowingly advertising, offering for sale, or selling any commodity at less than the price stipulated in any contract entered into pursuant to . . . the Act, whether the person so advertising, offering for sale or selling is or is not a party to such a contract, is unfair competition and is actionable at the suit of any person damaged thereby."[15] Contracts maintaining resale prices were thus made binding, not only on retailers who had signed them, but also on those who had refused to do so. The terms of a contract accepted by a single dealer might thereby be made to govern the prices charged by every dealer in the state.

The California law, including the nonsigner's clause, was shortly copied by other states. The validity of such enactments was upheld by the Supreme Court of the United States, in 1936, in the case of *Old Dearborn Distributing Co.* v. *Seagram Distillers Corp.*[16] The manufacturer, said Justice Sutherland, had made a substantial investment in advertising his brand. The good will thus acquired was a species of property that belonged to him. When he made a sale, he parted with his product, but not with his good will. When distributors cut his prices, they impaired his good will and thus inflicted damage on his property. Prevention of such damage was a proper subject for legislation. And then came this clincher: "There is nothing in the Act to preclude the purchaser from removing the mark or brand from the commodity—thus separating the physical property, which he owns, from the good will, which is the property of another—and then selling the commodity at his own price, provided he can do so without utilizing the good will of the latter as an aid to that end."[17] The laws that had been enacted at the behest of retailers were thus justified in terms of the rights of manufacturers. The decision stimulated the spread of retail price fixing. By 1941 all the states but Missouri, Texas, and Vermont—a fourth exception being the District of Columbia—had fair trade laws.

More than half of these laws followed the California act, most of the others being based on a model statute drafted by the National Association of Retail Druggists. Under both drafts, a first seller not only might bind a second one but might also require him to bind a third. According to the California pattern,

15 / *California Statutes,* 1933, chap. 250.
16 / 299 U.S. 183.
17 / 299 U.S. 183, 195.

prices might be fixed by the producers of branded products or, failing this, by their wholesale distributors. The N.A.R.D. model confined this power to the owner of a trademark and to distributors to whom he delegated authority. This draft permitted producers to bind themselves to refuse to sell, both to price cutters and to those who bought from them. It also copied Justice Sutherland, explicitly permitting distributors to undercut established prices if identifying brands had been removed.

The laws placed no limit on the level at which a seller might set a resale price. They made no reference to the costs of distribution or to the reasonableness of the margins that might be allowed. The contracts they authorized, however, were confined to those involving vertical agreements among manufacturers, wholesalers, and retailers. Horizontal agreements among producers or among distributors were usually forbidden. A product, to be covered, had to be "in free and open competition" with similar goods produced by other firms.

Exceptions to price fixing requirements were typically made to permit reductions when selling damaged goods, closing out a line, liquidating a business, or making a sale under the order of a court. Enforcement was not by public officials. The laws were not criminal statutes. In general, they carried no penalties. What they did was merely to exempt resale price maintenance contracts from state antitrust laws, giving persons injured by violations of such contracts the right to bring suit for injunctions and damages. Adherence to fixed prices, therefore, was privately policed.

Fair Trade in Operation

The statutes legalizing resale price maintenance were whipped through the legislatures at breakneck speed. There is no record of hearings having been held in 40 states. There is no transcript of hearings available in any state. The California law was supposed to contain a provision authorizing a producer to require "any dealer" to maintain a stipulated price. The text enacted, however, was garbled. Instead of "any dealer," it read "in delivery," so that the authorization made no sense. The care with which the laws were considered is indicated by the fact that this version was passed by the House and the Senate and signed by the governor, not only in California, but also in Arizona, Iowa, Louisiana, New Jersey, New York, Pennsylvania, and Tennessee. The N.A.R.D. held the hoop and cracked the whip. The legislators and the executives obediently jumped.

High-pressure tactics were used, too, in persuading reluctant manufacturers to enter into contracts, at prices providing margins that distributors desired. Committees of distributors visited the manufacturers, reviewed the contracts they proposed to issue, and discussed the adequacy of the margins they allowed. In the drug trade the goal was a margin of 33 1/3 percent, i.e., a markup of 50 percent. Manufacturers, in turn, received assurance that the prices being set by their competitors were equal to their own. Nominally they did not join in horizontal agreements. The effect, however, was the same. There were rewards for those who cooperated and penalties for those who did not. Retailers' associations circulated white lists of manufacturers who signed contracts, advising dealers to push their goods, giving them window and counter displays, special advertising, and extra sales effort. They issued black lists of those who failed to sign, the black lists carrying with them the threat of boycotts. When the makers of Pepsodent refused to enter contracts, "Pepsodent went under the counter in practically every California drug store . . . and . . . clear across the country. . . . Rapidly, other brands . . . forged ahead. . . . Result: a few months later, Pepsodent returned to the fold. . . ."[18]

There was similar cooperation in enforcement. Fair trade committees, set up by the druggists, distributed lists of contract prices, sought to persuade individual druggists to abide by them, policed the trade to discover price cutters, and turned them over to manufacturers for prosecution. In Connecticut, the committee agreed "to police all contracts . . . through the service of a well-organized group of 65 investigation and enforcement captains, located in strategic points throughout the state, under a full-time director of enforcement. . . ." Under this arrangement, when price cutting was reported to a captain, "he first contacts the dealer complained of in an effort to have him increase his price. If this procedure fails . . . the director of enforcement . . . authorizes the captain to make several purchases from the dealer . . . in the presence of a witness. Affidavits as to the purchases are then made and sent to the manufacturer involved, whose problem it then becomes to have the dealer increase his price." This system worked so well, according to the secretary of the committee, that "it has not been necessary to warn any dealer a second time."[19]

The Miller-Tydings Act

The fair trade laws permitted resale price maintenance when both of the parties to a contract were in the same state. But such contracts were held to violate the federal antitrust laws when the parties were in different states. And the great bulk of branded goods sold at retail had moved across state lines. If resale prices were to be maintained it was necessary to amend the federal laws. This was accomplished in 1937 by attaching a rider to the District of Columbia Appropriations Act, which was passed just before the Congress adjourned. President Roosevelt was thus forced either to accept the rider or to deprive the District government of the revenues required to finance its activities. He therefore recorded his objection to the substance of the measure and to the manner of its enactment but signed it into law.

Such was the origin of the Miller-Tydings Amendment to the Sherman Act. The amendment exempted from the federal antitrust laws interstate contracts fixing resale prices within those states where intrastate contracts had been legalized. As a result, the Federal Trade Commission and the Department of

18 / *Business Week,* August 28, 1937, pp. 37, 44.

19 / Federal Trade Commission, *Resale Price Maintenance* (Washington, D.C.: Government Printing Office, 1945), p. 244.

Justice could still prosecute persons attempting to maintain resale prices in three states and the District of Columbia, but not in the other 45 states. The law applied only to products "in free and open competition" with others of the same type, and forbade agreements between manufacturers, between wholesalers, or between retailers.

The validity of this amendment was not successfully called into question until 1951. In that year, the Supreme Court handed down its decision in the cases of *Schwegmann Bros.* v. *Calvert Corp.* and *Schwegmann Bros.* v. *Seagram Distillers Corp.*[20] Schwegmann operated a supermarket in New Orleans. The state of Louisiana had a fair trade law, including a nonsigner's clause. Calvert and Seagram made contracts with other retailers of whisky in the state, fixing the price of fifths at $4.24. Schwegmann refused to sign and sold them at $3.35. Calvert and Seagram sued, and Schwegmann appealed. The Court held that the Miller-Tydings Act applied only to those distributors who had accepted interstate contracts. The Act contained no reference to the nonsigner's clauses in the state laws, and therefore did not permit control of the prices at which nonsigners resold goods brought in from other states. In the words of Justice Douglas, "Contracts or agreements convey the idea of a cooperative arrangement, not a program whereby recalcitrants are dragged in by the heels and compelled to submit to price fixing." Such a program, he said, "is not price fixing by contract or agreement; that is price fixing by compulsion; that is not following the path of consensual agreement; that is resort to coercion."

The Schwegmann decision knocked the prop from under the structure of fair trade. Within a week, R. H. Macy & Co. of New York announced reductions in the prices of some 6,000 branded goods. Gimbel Brothers met the cuts. Macy's went lower, and other stores joined in. A major price war was under way. In one day prices were cut as much as 30 percent. Palm Beach suits went from $29.95 to $16.87, Underwood typewriters from $92.50 to $65.99, Waterman fountain pens from $3.95 to $1.59, and Bayer aspirin from 59 cents to 4 cents. Such prices produced a buying wave that rivaled the Christmas rush. Battalions of police were assigned to keep the crowds of shoppers in control. The contagion spread to Detroit, Denver, New Orleans, and 40 other cities.[21] The warfare came to an end, within six weeks, when stocks had been exhausted and manufacturers refused to replenish them. Some cynics took the view that merchants had employed price cuts as a method of advertising and had welcomed them as a means of disposing of swollen inventories. In any case they had proved to be costly. Prices soon moved back toward their earlier levels. And Macy's announced a change in its traditional policy of undercutting other stores by 6 percent: "We endeavor, with reasonable exceptions which include goods price-controlled by the manufacturer, to save our customers at least six percent for cash."

The price war afforded the proponents of fair trade a dramatic illustration of

20 / 341 U.S. 384.

21 / Survey by Dun & Bradstreet, reported in *Congressional Record,* July 1, 1952, pp. 8937-39.

the need for Congressional action to undo the damage that the court had done. Bills were introduced with the potent backing of the American Fair Trade Council, representing the manufacturers of branded goods, and the Bureau of Education on Fair Trade, organized by the druggists to represent their interests and those of other associations of distributors. The enactment of these bills was opposed at public hearings by Schwegmann and Macy, by the Department of Justice and the American Bar Association, by organizations of labor and agriculture, and by many other groups. But the druggists had not forgotten how to get results. Congress was overwhelmed with letters, telegrams, phone calls, and delegations of visitors. The McGuire-Keogh Fair Trade Enabling Act passed the House by a vote of 196 to 10 and the Senate by a vote of 64 to 16.

The McGuire-Keogh Act

The new law was an amendment to Section 5 of the Federal Trade Commission Act. Like the Miller-Tydings Act, it exempted from all the antitrust laws interstate contracts fixing resale prices within the states where intrastate contracts are allowed, confined this exemption to products "in free and open competition," and forbade agreements between competitors. But it went beyond this to permit the enforcement of interstate contracts against all of the dealers in a state when such contracts have been signed by any one of them. In short, it reversed the Schwegmann decision by extending the federal exemption to cover the nonsigner's clause.

After this law was enacted, Eli Lilly & Co. fixed a resale price of $2.83 on a bottle of insulin. Schwegmann sold it for $2.08. Lilly sued, under the Louisiana law, and was granted an injunction by the state court. Schwegmann appealed to the federal courts, contending that the nonsigners provisions in the state and federal laws were unconstitutional. He lost his case in the Court of Appeals[22] and, in 1953, the Supreme Court refused him a hearing.[23] A year later, the Court refused to review the decisions of lower courts upholding the New York, New Jersey, and federal laws in cases appealed by Sam Goody, a dealer in phonograph records, and S. Klein, a department store operator in New York and Newark. Refusal to review did not affirm the validity of these decisions, but it did permit them to stand. In 1963, Hudson Distributors, having refused to abide by contracts issued by Eli Lilly and by the Upjohn Company and signed by 1,400 drug retailers, asked the Supreme Court to find the nonsigner's clause in the fair trade law of Ohio to be invalid. The Court refused, finding the clause to be in conformity with the McGuire-Keogh Act. "Whether it is good policy to permit such laws," said the Court, "is for Congress to decide."[24]

22 / *Schwegmann* v. *Eli Lilly & Co.*, 205 F. 2d 788 (1953).

23 / 346 U.S. 856.

24 / *Hudson Distributors* v. *Upjohn Co.*; *Hudson Distributors* v. *Eli Lilly & Co.*, 377 U.S. 386 (1964).

Erosion of Fair Trade

Opponents of resale price fixing continued to fight the fair trade laws in the state courts. In many states, the laws were upheld. But in 26 states, by 1967, they were rendered inoperative by decisions that either threw them out entirely or nullified the nonsigner's clause. And in five states, the whole law or the non-signer's clause was repealed by the legislature. As a result, price maintenance contracts remained enforceable in only 16 of the 46 states (now including Hawaii) that had legalized them.

An even more serious blow was dealt fair trade in 1957 by the Supreme Court of the United States. Masters, a discount house located in the District of Columbia, had shipped General Electric appliances to buyers in New York, charging them less than the maintained price. General Electric brought suit, and Masters carried the case to the Court of Appeals. This body held that Masters' sales were made not in New York but in the District of Columbia and therefore were not governed by the New York law. Upon appeal, the Supreme Court refused review.[25] Price cutters were thus enabled to avoid state fair trade laws by shipping goods in from areas where such laws were not in force. As a consequence, price maintenance was publicly abandoned, in 1958, by the leading manufacturers of electrical appliances and other costly consumers goods.

The druggists were little affected by the price cutting that followed these developments. But the N.A.R.D., sensing a threat, was quick to act. Having met reverses in the states, it again turned to Washington. Here, it tried a new approach, seeking enactment of a federal statute that would empower manufacturers to fix retail prices throughout the United States simply by giving written notice. This scheme was embodied in a Quality Stabilization Bill, so-called although it had nothing whatsoever to do with quality. Under its provisions, the owner of a brand name would notify retailers of the branded good regarding the price at which they would be permitted to sell. If a retailer then sold at a lower price, the brand owner could revoke his right to handle the good, offering to buy back his remaining inventory. If the retailer persisted in selling below the established price, the brand owner could sue for an injunction forbidding him to do so and for the recovery of damages. If the legislature of any state so decided, however, the federal statute would not apply within its boundaries. This bill was introduced at every session of Congress during the early sixties. It never came to a vote in either house.

The Case Pro

The case for resale price maintenance is based upon a criticism of the loss leader. A leader is a well-known product with a well-known price that is sold

25 / *General Electric Co.* v. *Masters Mail Order Co.*, 244 F 2d. 681 (1957); 355 U.S. 824 (1959).

below this price for the purpose of attracting customers. A loss leader, properly speaking, would be a leader that was sold at a loss. But it is seldom clear, when the term is used, whether it is taken to mean that a product is being sold at less than the markup customary in the trade, at less than the seller's markup on other goods, at less than invoice cost plus distribution cost, or simply at less than invoice cost. In the first two cases, there would seem to be no ground for criticism, since there is no reason why all dealers should use the same markup or why any dealer should apply the same markup to all his goods. If loss means sale at less than invoice cost plus distribution cost, the term is robbed of precision by the uncertain judgments involved in computing distribution cost. If loss means sale below invoice cost, however, the meaning is precise. But is such a practice to be condemned? Loss-leader selling is simply an alternative method of sales promotion. A dealer, seeking to increase his sales, might spend his promotional money either on advertising or on selling something for less than it cost. In the first case the consumer would get a picture on a billboard; in the second, a product at a lower price. Why should the one be permitted and the other prohibited?

First, say the advocates of fair trade, because the loss leader harms the consumer. When an article is sold by other dealers for $3.50 and by Macy, say, for $1.79, the consumer gets the false impression that comparable savings are to be obtained on everything in Macy's store. So, along with the leader, he is induced to buy a lot of other goods on which he does not save a cent. Price cutting, moreover, is inconvenient, since it forces the customer to higgle over his purchases. The maintained price, on the other hand, protects the consumer by preventing deception. And it saves his time by obviating the necessity of higgling. It may be doubted, however, that the consumer is deceived as often by actual bargains as he is by advertising. And this is an activity that the fair traders, for all their zeal in fighting misrepresentation, do not propose to touch. Loss-leader prices, moreover, are stated and adhered to by the seller, leaving no room for bargaining. And the convenience of maintained prices, in general, may well be offset by their height.

Second, it is said, loss-leader selling is harmful to the manufacturer. The case usually cited is that of the Ingersoll watch, "the watch that made the dollar famous."

> Some retailers throughout the country decided to use the Ingersoll watch as a loss leader. They began to sell it for less than a dollar. The price went down and down as competition increased, until it was finally selling for 57 cents, far below the wholesale price. The retailers who were selling it at that price were making up their losses on sales of other merchandise in their large stores. . . . Small business retailers were forced to drop the Ingersoll dollar watch. They could not sell it if they charged more than 57 cents, and they could not afford to sell the watch at that price and take the loss involved in each sale. The

result was that the manufacturer lost his market and was forced out of business.[26]

The watch, presumably, had lost its usefulness as a leader for the larger stores. And, since consumers had been led to value it at 57 cents, it could never again be sold for a dollar. The end of Ingersoll occurred some time before World War I. But the case, according to fair traders, is not unique. Indeed, they say, "the annals of American manufacturing are replete with examples of products which have been price-slashed out of existence."[27] The Federal Trade Commission, however, has professed its inability to identify such products. And further doubt is cast upon the statement by the curious apathy of the manufacturer. For the manufacturer, with his very survival at stake, is content to leave it to the retailer to bear the brunt of the battle for fair trade.

The loss leader, finally, is said to be harmful to the retailer. Price cutters feature different articles, each of them shifting from one to another. Small dealers are forced to meet their prices on line after line. And, in doing so, they are driven inexorably toward bankruptcy. Price maintenance, runs the argument, is needed to keep the little merchant alive. And, in fact, there may be instances where this is true. If the book department at Macy's, for instance, were to cut its prices on best sellers, the small book dealer might find it difficult to survive. But there is no evidence that substantial numbers of merchants have been put out of business by loss-leader competition alone. And it is significant that small stores are to be found in the District of Columbia and in Missouri, Texas, and Vermont.

It should be noted, finally, that resale price maintenance goes far beyond the prevention of selling at a loss. This purpose could be accomplished by forbidding sales below invoice cost or by requiring a minimum markup to cover distribution cost. But the fair trade laws permit the establishment of a uniform markup bearing no relation to cost. They seek to eliminate all possibility of competition at the retail level by enforcing a minimum price.

The Case Con

Resale price maintenance is to be criticized, first, because it facilitates price fixing agreements among manufacturers. The legal provisions requiring that products be "in free and open competition" and forbidding horizontal understandings are really without effect. Each maker of competitive products may sign a different contract with a different distributor. But none of them will do so until the distributors assure him that the price he sets is the same as that

26 / Senate Small Business Committee, quoted in *Congressional Record,* July 1, 1952, pp. 8935-36.

27 / Committee on Small Business, House of Representatives, *Fair Trade: the Problem and the Issues* (82d Cong., 2d Sess., House Report No. 1292, 1952), p. 38.

established by his rivals. Manufacturers need not conspire with one another. But the result is as it would be if they did.

Second, fair trade suppresses competition in retailing. It denies the consumer the lower prices made possible by greater efficiency, by larger volume, by simpler service, by cheaper equipment and lower rents. It compels the low-cost seller to charge as much as the high-cost one, the high-turnover seller as much as the one whose turnover is low, the cash-and-carry store as much as one providing credit and delivery, the store in a slum as much as the shop on Park Avenue. And this is accomplished, under the aegis of the law, without giving the appearance of conspiracy.

Third, the system tends to freeze the channels of distribution, retarding the advancement of technology. To preserve the independent merchant, it deprives the mass distributor of his principal appeal. By preventing tough competition in price, it makes for soft competition in the form of advertising and salesmanship, costly facilities, and nonessential services. "The crux of the problem of resale price maintenance," concluded a committee set up to study the problem in Canada, "is whether the consumer should reap the benefits of the most efficient forms of retailing or . . . should be forced to pay more in order to make retailing . . . a more comfortable occupation. . . ."[28]

Consequences of Fair Trade

When the fair trade laws were enacted, the average level of retail drug prices rose. But manufacturers, in general, did not adopt their nominal resale prices as those to be legally maintained. Instead, they sought to fix on figures high enough to satisfy the independent retailers and low enough to hold the business of the mass distributors, tending to set them between the highest and the lowest previously charged. The legal minima then became the actual prices in both types of outlets. And, as a result, prices rose in downtown department stores, cut-rate stores, and chains, but fell in smaller independent outlets in outlying neighborhoods and in small towns. The increases, however, outweighed the declines, and the general level rose.

Characteristically, for drugs and liquors, prices in markets where they are fixed are higher than those in markets where they are free. Among 117 drug items checked in 1948, in Maryland and the District of Columbia, 29 cost a seventh less, 38 cost a quarter less, and 35 cost a third less in the District. The average cost of 54 drug items was 16.2 percent less in St. Louis, Missouri, than in East St. Louis, Illinois.[29] And the average price of 77 items covered in a survey made by the Department of Justice in 1956 was 27 percent below the fair trade price in eight cities where resale prices were not maintained.[30]

28 / *Resale Price Maintenance, An Interim Report of the Committee to Study Combines Legislation* (Ottawa, 1951), p. 16.

29 / *Fortune,* January, 1949, p. 70.

30 / Statement by Assistant Attorney General Robert A. Bicks before Senate Committee on Interstate and Foreign Commerce, June 16, 1959.

It may be questioned whether price maintenance has really aided the independent retailer. Margins may be raised. But higher prices, by cutting the volume of sales and by increasing the costs of selling, may limit total profits. Price competition, suppressed on certain goods, may merely shift to others whose prices cannot be controlled. Private brands, at low prices, may be offered by mass distributors, and the independent, bound by his contracts, may find himself unable to compete. High margins, moreover, may attract newcomers to a trade. Gross profit margins on food items run around 19 percent, those on drug and toilet items around 30 percent. As a result, the number of food stores carrying drugs and toiletries rose from 37 percent to 85 percent of all such stores in the 10 years ending in 1952.[31] Drug and toilet items were added, too, by other types of retailers. So the druggists' volume had to be shared with growing numbers of competitors. Resale price maintenance alone, it seems, will not suffice. In England, after this system was adopted, the numbers of merchants selling proprietary medicines increased so rapidly that the chemists requested their makers to restrict their distribution to members of the chemist's trade. In the United States, the N.A.R.D. may well come to demand, in time, that the sale of all drugs and toiletries be confined by law to registered pharmacists.

For the manufacturer the gains from fair trade are even more dubious. If he resists the pressure of the retailers' association and refuses to maintain resale prices, he may be excluded from independent outlets. If he yields and enters into contracts, he will be under further pressure to increase the independent's margin by setting his prices high. If he sets them too high, he may cut his volume. And he may provoke increasing competition from private brands. While insuring the loyalty of the independent, he may lose his outlet through the mass distributor.

Scope and Enforceability

Resale price maintenance can do neither as much good nor as much harm as the arguments for and against it would suggest. There are limits to its applicability. And, even where it is applicable, there are difficulties in its enforcement.

Resale prices can be maintained only in the case of goods that are standardized, branded, and easily identifiable, that are widely used and frequently purchased, and whose cost to the consumer is neither insignificant nor very large. They cannot readily be maintained where the cost of raw materials is a major part of total costs and where this cost is subject to substantial and repeated fluctuations. Price maintenance thus appears to be inapplicable to clothing, furniture, hardware, jewelry, and notions, and to such foodstuffs as meat, flour, sugar, and canned fruits and vegetables. It has been used, mainly, in the cases of drugs, cosmetics, liquor, tobacco, and books, together with such other products as electrical appliances, auto accessories, photographic equipment,

31 / *Business Week,* February 16, 1952, pp. 158 ff.

phonograph records, and sporting goods. And these do not add up to more than 10 percent, by value, of the products sold at retail in the United States.

Maintained prices can be evaded in many different ways. Goods may be offered, under the permitted exceptions, as having been damaged, or as belonging to lines that are being dropped. Price cutters may offer premiums, coupons, gifts, bonuses, bargain combinations, and special deals. Prices on costly appliances such as refrigerators and television sets are particularly difficult to enforce. Prices may be cut, in effect, by making liberal trade-in allowances: the purchaser of a vacuum cleaner may be allowed $20 for his old broom. Retailers regularly give discounts on expensive items to employees, friends, and steady customers. Manufacturers and jobbers make sales at retail, charging less than the retail price. Discount houses, their volume growing steadily, operate openly in cities within fair trade jurisdictions, offering electrical appliances, household equipment, and other price-maintained goods at figures far below the standard price. In such a situation, it may be questioned how much of an effort the manufacturer is likely to make to enforce the prices he may fix. In 1948, the General Electric Company hired detectives to purchase its products from discount houses, brought suits, and obtained injunctions. But the houses continued to operate. Such concerns must be on guard against making sales to spotters, must expect to be taken to court, and must be prepared to pay an occasional fine. But with substantial profits obtainable when sales are made at a markup of 25 percent instead of 45 percent, this may be treated as a minor cost. Most manufacturers continue to supply them; they buy in quantity and pay cash.

PROMOTIONAL DEVICES

The chain supermarket, in its earlier years, operated on a markup of 15 percent. It carried a small inventory; made its profit from a rapid turnover. Today, its markup is still lower than that obtained in other retail fields. Its prices are 3 percent below those charged by independent stores. But its margin has risen, standing at 19 percent. This increase is to be attributed, in the main, to a rise in costs. The proliferation of brands has compelled the supermarket to carry a larger inventory and has enlarged its overhead. And competition has led it to adopt promotional devices that have increased its expenses and raised the prices it must charge.[32]

Trading Stamps

Trading stamps are sold to retailers by companies that undertake to redeem them in merchandise. They are distributed to consumers with half of the groceries sold in the United States. For every dollar she spends, the shopper gets

---

32 / John P. Doll, V. James Rhodes, and Jerry G. West, *Economics of Agricultural Production, Markets, and Policy* (Homewood, Ill.: Richard D. Irwin, Inc., 1968), chap. 14.

2½ cents worth of stamps. Four families out of five accumulate and redeem the stamps, the goods acquired in this way being valued at some $90,000,000 a year.

The cost of stamps to the retailer runs around 2 percent of his gross sales. This cost would be covered if the stamps diverted enough patronage from his competitors to increase his sales by 12 to 15 percent. The first stores to use stamps as bait may have realized such a gain. They were thus enabled to distribute stamps without raising their prices. But when all stores came to use stamps, none of them could gain a larger share of sales. All of them therefore found it necessary to recoup their higher costs by charging higher prices.

The consumer is now forced to pay an extra 2 percent for her groceries, taking stamps in return, whether she wants them or not. She may protest, asking that the practice be discontinued. The retailer might be willing to comply. But he is unable to do so. If he acts alone, he will lose business to his competitors. If he enters an agreement to stop giving stamps, he may be convicted of participating in a conspiracy in restraint of trade. So he finds himself trapped.

The legislatures of 20 states have acted to regulate the trading stamp business. In Kansas, use of the stamps is prohibited. In Washington, Wisconsin, and Wyoming, the stamps can be redeemed only in cash. In 16 other states, the consumer must be given the option of redeeming them in cash rather than in merchandise. Measures with similar provisions have been introduced in other legislatures and in Congress. The movement promises to afford the consumer and the retailer an avenue of escape.

Lotteries

Games of chance, with big prizes, have come to be widely used as customer bait, along with trading stamps, by supermarkets and filling stations. These games resemble trading stamps in their effects on the merchant's costs and prices. They also raise the additional problem of misrepresentation. The chance of winning a prize is small: the chance of winning $1,000 in a visit to a retail outlet is only 1.2 in a million. But this fact is not disclosed. In some cases, according to the Federal Trade Commission, fewer prizes have been given than were advertised. The prizes have not been equally distributed among the stores in a chain. The winnings have been concentrated in the early weeks of the game. And retailers have continued to advertise the game after all the prizes have been paid.

The FTC issued rules, effective late in 1969, to regulate the operation of these games. Retailers who use the games must inform consumers that their chances of winning are small. They must identify the area in which a game is being played and list the prizes to be paid there. They must make sure that prize-winning tickets are distributed at random. The Commission holds misrepresentation and manipulation of the games to be deceptive practices and is prepared to move against them under Section 5 of the Federal Trade Commission Act.

These rules may insure that the games will be honest. They do not protect consumers against the need to pay higher prices to cover the retailer's higher costs. In some states, however, the games are open to attack under long-standing laws forbidding lotteries. Maryland, in response to the spread of supermarket and filling station games, passed a law forbidding them in 1969. Other states may follow.

REGULATION OF LIQUOR DEALERS

In 16 states, liquor is sold at retail by state monopolies. In 34 states it is sold by private distributors. Here, no one may enter the business without obtaining a license from a state authority. And prices are kept high by permitting or requiring resale price maintenance or establishing legal minima. The nominal purpose of these measures is to promote temperance by limiting consumption. But there is no evidence that they have this effect.

Curtailment of entry and maintenance of prices make for large profits. And these profits are capitalized in determining the prices at which licensed properties are sold. As a result, licenses are highly valuable. And, since they are given without charge, the demand for them exceeds the supply. The standards that supposedly govern the grant of licenses are vague and inconsistent. Officials who make the grants depend, therefore, on complicated legal requirements. Their decisions may be long delayed. In some cases, they have been influenced by the payment of bribes.

There are a number of possible alternatives. Liquor might be distributed, as in other states, by a state monopoly. If the number of stores is to be limited, licenses might be sold at auction, with the profit going, not to merchants, but to the state. Or requirements might be laid down to assure against abuses in the operation of the stores, and licenses granted to all applicants who met them, with prices uncontrolled and the number of stores determined by competition. Any one of these alternatives would be preferable to the methods of allocation that now obtain.

| Chapter | GOVERNMENT AND LABOR |
| 30 | |

In the case of labor, government has departed from the rule of competition. Where workers have not been able to organize to protect themselves against bad working conditions, long hours, and low wages, it has established minimum standards to govern the terms of their employment. Where they have been able to organize, it has encouraged them to do so. Granting monopolistic powers to labor unions, it has been forced increasingly to regulate them, imposing controls upon their dealings with employers, with workers, and with the community at large.

MINIMUM LABOR STANDARDS

Legislation on behalf of labor had its origin, more than a century ago, in humanitarian efforts to check the obvious abuses of industrialism. Children had been employed in mines and factories, which stunted their growth and deprived them of educational opportunity. Women had been put to work, for long hours and at night, under conditions that were harmful to morals and at tasks that impaired their strength. Men, too, had been exposed to industrial accident and occupational disease, working in surroundings that imperiled their safety and their health. Correction of these abuses was the purpose of the early labor laws. From this beginning, government went on in later years to establish maximum hours and minimum wages for labor in general, to protect members of minority groups against discrimination in opportunities for employment, and to provide insurance against the risks of industrial accident, unemployment, dependency and illness in old age, total disability, and survivorship.

Protection for Women and Children

Child labor laws in the United States date from a statute adopted in Massachusetts in 1842 establishing a 10-hour day for children under 12 years old employed in factories. From this beginning, the states went on gradually to extend and tighten their regulations, excluding children from certain employments, requiring attendance at school, raising age limits, reducing hour limits, and establishing minimum wages. Today such laws are found in all the states, a typical statute requiring school attendance until 16 and forbidding employment in factories or stores (during school hours or at night) before 16 and in mines before 18. Where employment is permitted, the laws fix maximum hours and many of them provide for a minimum wage. In general, agriculture, domestic service, and street trades are exempt, and provision for enforcement is inadequate. Since 1938, the employment of children under 16, or under 18 in hazardous occupations, has been forbidden by the federal government in industries covered by the Fair Labor Standards Act.

The first statute to regulate the employment of women, in this country, was enacted by New Hampshire in 1847. Such legislation, too, was gradually extended, beginning with laws establishing maximum hours, going on to forbid the use of women in occupations that would endanger their morals, their safety, or their health, and providing finally for the determination of a minimum wage. By 1965, there were statutes fixing maximum hours for women in 43 states and statutes fixing minimum wages in 38 states. In a few states, the minimum wage is fixed by statute; in most, by an administrative agency. Here, different minima are fixed for different occupations. The laws have their greatest significance in retail distribution and in the service trades.

Protection against Industrial Hazards

The states have long sought to protect men, as well as women and children, against the risks of industrial accident and occupational disease. Beginning with Massachusetts in 1877, they have enacted laws calling for the installation of safety appliances, the inauguration of safety inspections, and the adoption of other precautions against accidents; laws regulating dangerous processes and forbidding the use of harmful materials; and laws requiring certain standards of sanitation, ventilation, and illumination. Such laws now typically provide for the establishment of rules and regulations by an administrative agency and for their enforcement by periodic inspection of industrial facilities. In few states, however, is adequate provision made for the financing of inspection services.

Protection is also afforded by laws prohibiting the employment in certain occupations—such as tunneling under air pressure—of men who lack the strength to do the work; by laws requiring the observance in other occupations—such as truck driving—of periods of rest; and by laws establishing maximum hours in many hazardous industries. Despite these preventive measures, industrial accidents continue to occur, depriving the worker of his income and imposing on him the added cost of medical care. These hazards are met, in part, by workmen's compensation laws, found since 1948 in all the states. Under these laws, employers are required to pay benefits to workmen suffering from industrial accidents or occupational diseases. In half of the states, they must carry insurance against this risk. In the other half, they are given the option of proving their ability to pay.

Maximum Hours and Minimum Wages

Maximum hours and minimum wages have been fixed by law not only to protect women and children and men employed in hazardous trades, but also to raise the level of wages for workers in general. Such requirements are defended as a means of establishing fair standards of employment, protecting workers who lack the power to protect themselves. Work beyond the hours fixed, instead of being forbidden, in the interest of safety and health, is merely penalized by requiring that time-and-a-half be paid for overtime. Maximum hour requirements have thus come to serve as a means of increasing take-home pay.

General wage and hour laws were enacted by a few of the states before they were adopted by the federal government. The federal laws were first applied to particular groups: employers under government contracts, employers covered by NRA codes, bituminous coal operators, companies operating subsidized ships, and subsidized producers of sugar beets. The first comprehensive wage and hour law was the Fair Labor Standards Act of 1938.

The Fair Labor Standards Act applies to workers employed in occupations in or affecting interstate commerce, save those specifically exempted, such as administrative and professional personnel, outside salesmen, workers rendering personal services, and those processing agricultural commodities. The scope of the law has been repeatedly extended. It now covers 50 million of 62 million nonsupervisory employees. The minimum wage has been repeatedly increased. As originally written, the law cut maximum hours from 44 in 1938 to 40 in 1940 and raised minimum wages from 25 cents an hour in 1938 to 40 cents in 1945. The minimum set for wages was raised to 75 cents in 1949, to $1 in 1955, to $1.25 in 1961, and to $1.30 for farm labor and $1.60 for all other labor to take effect in 1971. The law is enforced by the Department of Labor. If an employer pays less than the minimum wage, the Department is empowered to collect the difference and turn it over to his employees. Willful violators are subject to a fine of up to $10,000 for the first offense and to a fine plus six months imprisonment for the second. The Department, however, can barely begin to enforce the law, its staff being too small to inspect more than a 20th of the establishments under its jurisdiction in any year. Where it has made inspections, it has found half of the concerns examined to be in violation. And from these concerns it has collected less than half of the back wages that were due.

The minima set under state and federal wage laws are so far below the wages actually paid that they have little significance for most American industries. They have operated, however, to raise the level of wages in such local enterprises as laundries, cleaning establishments, and retail stores, and in sawmills, canneries, hosiery mills, cigar factories and other industries, particularly in the southern states, where wages have been notoriously low. If set too far above prevailing levels, minimum wages will result in unemployment. In practice, the wage requirements have been moderate and the employment effect, while perceptible, has not been great.

Fair Employment Practices

Since 1945, laws forbidding discrimination in employment have been enacted by 34 states and 50 cities. The laws cover discrimination by employers in hiring, firing, promoting, and determining compensation, by labor unions in admitting members, and by employment agencies in classifying and referring employees. They forbid discrimination on the basis of race, creed, color, or national origin. Under a typical statute, a worker who suffers from discrimination may file a complaint with an administrative agency. An effort will then be made to obtain an adjustment through conciliation. If this fails, the agency is empowered to hold a public hearing and issue an order directing an offender to cease and desist from discriminatory practices. Such orders can be enforced by the courts. The agencies concerned have proceeded with caution. Few cases have resulted in an order, and fewer have been carried to the courts. Reliance has been placed, in the main, on conciliation and the enlistment of voluntary support. But substantial progress is said to have been made in opening to members of minority groups opportunities that had previously been closed.

In 1964, under the Civil Rights Act, Congress made it an "unlawful employment practice" for any employer, employment agency, or labor organization in industries in interstate commerce to discriminate in matters affecting employment because of race, color, religion, sex, or national origin. The method provided for enforcement of the law is cumbersome. An Equal Employment Opportunity Commission, set up under the statute, can act only where there is no state law or where a state has failed to act for 60 days. The Commission then seeks to obtain a settlement through conciliation. If this fails, it informs the complaining workman, who may then bring suit or request the Attorney General to sue on his behalf. And where he perceives a general pattern of discrimination, the Attorney General may bring suit on his own initiative. But the Commission, unlike those of the states, lacks the power to issue an order to cease and desist. Despite this limitation, the agency has made some progress, persuading a number of large firms to modify their employment practices. At the same time, the Attorney General has filed suits against employers and labor unions, charging a general pattern of discrimination in each case. Late in 1970, bills giving the EEOC power to issue cease-and-desist orders had been passed in both the Senate and the House. It appeared that this power was soon to be conferred.

Social Insurance

Alongside the legislation outlined above there has developed a comprehensive program of social insurance. In addition to laws requiring compensation in the case of industrial accidents, all the states now have laws providing for payments in the event of unemployment. These measures now cover two thirds of all workers. Benefits are paid after the first week of unemployment and may last, in most states, as long as 26 weeks. They are supposed to amount to half of the previous weekly wage, but dollar limits prevent workers from obtaining this much in all but a few states. Benefits are financed by a tax on payrolls.

The federal government's system of social insurance, inaugurated in 1935, has been steadily expanded: its coverage enlarged from two thirds to nine tenths of those who are gainfully employed, its protection extended from retirement to survivorship to disability and to sickness in old age, and the size of its benefits increased. The system now pays benefits to workers on retirement, to those who are totally disabled, and to the surviving dependents of those who have died. The size of these benefits is related to the worker's previous earnings and the number of his dependents. Hospital care for the aged is provided under the Medicare program enacted in 1965. All of the foregoing benefits are financed by taxes on the workers' wages and on the employers' payrolls. Through the payroll tax, insurance against the risks of labor have been made a cost to be covered in the prices of goods. Medical benefits for the aged, other than those for hospital care, are provided by Medicare under a voluntary system, with the pensioner and the government sharing the cost. Taken together, these measures afford the great majority of workers with protection against all forms of insecurity except the risk that medical costs will be incurred and income lost before retirement through an accident or illness that does not originate on the job.

POLICY TOWARD UNIONIZATION

In establishing minimum standards for labor, through laws controlling the employment of women and children, requiring provision for health, safety, and security, and setting moderate limits on hours and wages, government sets a plane for competition, as it does in checking unfair methods of competition, through the work of the Federal Trade Commission. It may curtail the supply of goods and services that would have been produced under substandard conditions of employment. But it leaves wide latitude for the operation of competition as a regulatory force. When it goes on, however, to promote the organization of labor, and when it seeks to equalize the bargaining power of workers and employers, government abandons competition as a regulator and is driven, eventually, to adopt administrative controls.

The policy of government toward the organization of labor, in the United States, falls into four periods. In the first, government discouraged unionization, putting its weight on the side of the employer. In the second, it permitted unionization, but sought to achieve a position of neutrality between the employer and the worker. In the third, it promoted unionization, shifting its weight to the side of the worker. In the fourth and final period, it has attempted to equalize the bargaining power of the employer and the worker by regulating the relations of management and labor in growing detail. Here, it has appeared to be groping toward a middle ground.

Discouragement of Unionization

Unionization has been controlled by statute for less than 35 years. But unions had been brought before the courts, in criminal and civil suits, during the previous century, and their activities regulated under the common law. Until 1842, the courts held the mere existence of a labor organization to constitute an illegal conspiracy. In that year, the Supreme Court of Massachusetts set a new precedent, holding that questions of legality were raised, not by unions as such, but by the character of their activities.[1] Thereafter, the courts sought to distinguish between legal and illegal strikes, according to their purposes, and between lawful and unlawful uses of the boycott and forms of picketing.

For 90 years, unions were tolerated. But the law gave no protection to the right of workers to organize. Employers were not required to recognize the unions or to engage in collective bargaining. On the contrary, they were permitted to obstruct unionization and to interfere with union activities. And they did so by requiring workers, as a condition of employment, to sign "yellow-dog" contracts which forbade union membership, by spying on their workers, by discharging union members, and by circulating blacklists to prevent them from obtaining other jobs.

Not only did government give a free hand to employers but it gave them positive support. Union meetings were forbidden by local authorities, and union organizers driven out of town. Company police were clothed with legal authority. Local and state police and federal troops were used against strikers. Sweeping injunctions were issued by the courts, prohibiting anyone from interfering in any way with an employer's business. Originally designed to ward off damage that was threatened to property, these orders came to be employed as weapons for breaking strikes. The leadership of strikes was enjoined, the payment of strike benefits forbidden, and picketing prohibited. Such an injunction was temporary, and the court eventually held a public hearing to determine whether it should be made permanent. But by this time, the strike had been lost. The purpose of the order had been served.

Neutrality toward Unionization

In 1914, Congress sought to curb the use of the injunction against labor by including a list of strike activities in the Clayton Act and forbidding the federal courts to enjoin them when carried on "peaceably" and "lawfully." The courts, however, continued to issue injunctions, holding that the activities they enjoined were neither peaceable nor lawful. The provision, in effect, was nullified.

In 1932, Congress accomplished its purpose. The Norris-LaGuardia Act, passed in that year, established beyond question the legality of unionization and collective bargaining, asserted the right of unions to freedom from inter-

1 / *Commonwealth* v. *Hunt*, 4 Metcalf 111.

ference by employers, and made "yellow-dog" contracts unenforceable. It forbade the federal courts to enjoin union membership, strikes, peaceful picketing, or the payment of strike benefits, when these activities are undertaken by persons "participating or interested in" a labor dispute. At the same time, it changed the procedure to be followed in issuing injunctions, making them more difficult to obtain.

The Norris-LaGuardia Act marked the beginning of a statute law of labor relations. It was later modified, as we shall see, by certain provisions of the Taft-Hartley Act. It was followed, in the thirties, by the passage of anti-injunction laws in the major industrial states. The purpose of this body of legislation was not to give an advantage to labor but rather to remove the handicaps it had suffered in the past. It was not long, however, until government shifted its weight to labor's side of the scales.

Promotion of Unionization

In 1933, it became the policy of the United States to promote the organization of labor. This policy was first embodied in the National Industrial Recovery Act. Employers were required, by this law, to recognize the right of employees "to organize and bargain collectively through representatives of their own choosing," and were forbidden to interfere with this process, or to require that workers join a company union or refrain from joining an independent union in order to get a job. In 1935, when the NIRA was found to be unconstitutional, this policy was reaffirmed and elaborated by Congress in the National Labor Relations Act, better known as the Wagner Act.

Under the Wagner Act, again, employers were required to grant recognition to labor unions and to engage in collective bargaining. The law also forbade, as "unfair labor practices," a number of methods by which employers had attempted, in the past, to prevent labor from organizing. These practices included interference with unionization, domination or support of a union, discrimination against the members of a union, and refusal to bargain with their legal representatives. Where more than one union claimed to represent the workers, the issue was to be decided by a secret ballot. The law set up a National Labor Relations Board and empowered it to conduct representation elections and to enforce the rules against unfair labor practices by investigating complaints, holding public hearings, and issuing cease-and-desist orders that were enforceable, upon appeal, by the courts. The constitutionality of the measure was upheld by the Supreme Court in 1937.[2]

The Wagner Act was one-sided. It outlawed none of the practices of unions, only those of employers. It gave to unions, but not to employers, the right to appeal to the NLRB. It was deliberately designed to clear the way for unionization by removing the obstacles remaining in its path. In this, it was successful. The NLRB held 50,000 representation elections and handled 45,000 unfair

2 / *NLRB* v. *Jones & Laughlin Steel Corp.*, 301 U.S. 1.

practice cases in the next 12 years. Union membership increased from less than 3 million in 1933 to more than 15 million in 1947.

The Wagner Act was not amended for a dozen years. It came, in this time, to be generally accepted. During much of the period, however, the demand for labor was increased and its supply restricted by World War II. At the war's end, controls on inflation were removed. Prices shot up; their rise was followed by a wave of strikes. Public opinion came to be increasingly concerned with the practices of labor. There was criticism, in particular, of the unequal provisions of the Wagner Act. Restrictive legislation dealing with the tactics used in strikes was passed by nearly all the states. The movement culminated, in 1947, with the passage by Congress of the Labor Management Relations Act, known as the Taft-Hartley Act.

Regulation of Union-Management Relations

An attempt was made, in the Taft-Hartley Act, to approach a balance between the rights and duties of employers and those of employees. The law retained the rights that had been given to labor by the Wagner Act. But to the former list of unfair practices of employers it added a parallel list of unfair practices of unions. The law forbade the closed shop, where workers not members of the union cannot be employed. But it permitted the union shop, where such workers can be employed but must join the union after they are hired. The Act made it an unfair practice for a union to interfere with a worker's right to abstain from membership, or to force employers to discriminate against non-unionists, except as required by a valid agreement establishing a union shop. It gave employers, as well as unions, the right to present their views concerning the desirability of unionization to their employees, and the right to petition the NLRB for an election. It made it an unfair practice for unions, as well as for employers, to refuse to bargain. In addition, the Act contained provisions designed to protect union members against misconduct by their leaders and to protect innocent bystanders in labor disputes. These are to be considered later on.

The Taft-Hartley Act was denounced by the unions as a "slave labor law." It was made an issue in the presidential campaigns of 1948 and 1952. A determined effort to repeal it was defeated in 1949. Repeated attempts drastically to amend it were made, without success, between 1951 and 1954. The Act eventually came to be accepted as an established fact. In practice, it does not appear seriously to have checked the growth of unions or to have put them at a disadvantage in bargaining. Relations between management and labor, since its enactment, have generally been good. Wages have been raised in successive contracts. Millions of workers have been assured benefits, in addition to those they will get from the government, under private unemployment and retirement plans. The sobriquet "slave labor" has been dropped.

The National Labor Relations Board

Case-by-case application of the labor relations laws is the work of the National Labor Relations Board, an independent agency consisting of five members appointed by the President. The Board's General Counsel, also appointed by the President, has final authority to determine whether complaints are to be dismissed or prosecutions initiated. The Board itself, aided by a staff of trial examiners, functions as an administrative tribunal, passing judgment on the cases that are brought. The agency has a heavy work load: it may determine the representative bargaining unit in as many as 13,000 cases in a year and handle as many as 17,000 complaints regarding unfair labor practices. To carry this load, it has more than a thousand employees, three fourths of them in Washington and one fourth in 30 regional offices. But its staff is not large enough to enable it to keep up with the volume of its work. Representation cases, delegated to the field offices, are handled promptly, usually being concluded in less than three months. But unfair practice cases are not finally determined, on the average, in less than a year and a half. Even at this rate, action is swifter than with other regulatory agencies. But the nature of the problems presented is such that the damage sought to be averted may already have been done before a decision is reached.

In handling cases where the representative character of a union is in question, the Board conducts elections. If a union gets a majority of the votes in such an election, the Board certifies it as the exclusive bargaining agent for all of the employees. Here, it must define the bargaining unit, deciding whether to hold a single election for all of a company's employees or separate elections in each of its plants, a single election within a plant or separate elections in each of its departments, a single election for all of the workers in such a unit or separate elections for the members of skilled crafts. The Board's decisions in these cases may determine whether one union or another or no union wins the vote.

The unfair labor practice cases involve complaints that employers have interfered with the formation or the independence of unions or the freedom of workers to belong to them; that unions have employed coercion in inducing workers to join; that employers or unions have sought to influence the outcome of labor disputes by resorting to unfair tactics; that they have failed to bargain, in good faith, concerning matters that should be subject to collective determination. These complaints require the Board to answer such questions as the following: Did particular forms of behavior by employers or union leaders illegally restrain or coerce workers in deciding whether to join a union? Did an employer overstep the proper limits of free speech? Did he fire or refuse to hire a worker because he was incompetent or lazy or because he was engaging in union activity? Is a particular strike to be held illegal; a case of picketing or a boycott condemned? Is it unfair for an employer to lock his workers out, to replace them with others, to subcontract his work to other firms, to close his plant, to move to another town? Under what circumstances is an employer to be compelled to rehire a striker or permitted to refuse to do so? What must an employer do to bargain in good faith? Need he merely meet with union representatives, refusing to accept their demands, or must he present information in support of his refusal and make counterproposals of his own? May he make an offer on a take-it-or-leave-it basis or must he consider alternatives? Is it fair for him to take unilateral action, raising wages before negotiations are to start or after they are under way? Is it fair for him to deal separately with union locals, bypassing their national organization; to appeal to union members over the heads of their officers? On what matters is the employer compelled to bargain: wages, hours, and working conditions alone or these plus house rents, paid vacations, Christmas bonuses, group insurance, pensions, and stock-purchase plans?

Of the complaints of unfair practices that are brought to the General Counsel, two thirds are likely to be withdrawn or dismissed. Of the remaining third, one in seven may be settled in the regional offices, the other six referred to Washington. Here they will first be heard by a trial examiner, who will make a report with findings of fact, the relevant provisions of law, and recommendations for a decision. The General Counsel and the respondent in a case may accept this report or may file exceptions, as is usually done, with the Board. The Board must then decide the case; it makes between 1,000 and 1,500 such decisions in the course of a year. Its only power is to issue an order to cease and desist. A party so ordered may appeal to the courts. If he refuses to comply with an order, the Board may ask the court to compel him to do so. Some 200 unfair practice cases are thus carried to the courts each year. In most of these cases, the Board has been upheld. The orders that it issues, together with the decisions of the courts, determine the content of the law.

It will be seen that enforcement of the labor relations laws has injected the government into the heart of union-management relations, imposing detailed controls on the behavior of employers and unions, on bargaining procedures, and on the content of collective agreements. The law also threatens to involve the government in the administration of such agreements. Formerly, a labor contract partook of the nature of a treaty between sovereign powers. Disputes arising under it were handled informally through private machinery for the settlement of grievances or were referred to arbitration. The great majority of such disputes is still handled in this way. But under the Taft-Hartley Act, either party to a labor contract can bring suit for violation of its terms. The way has thus been opened to transplant the substance of such contracts from the field of private agreement to that of public law.

UNIONS AND THE WORKER

Unions serve the interests of the worker in many ways. They represent him more effectively than he could represent himself. They may get him shorter hours, better working conditions, higher wages, and other benefits. They handle individual grievances, freeing the worker from dictation by the foreman and protecting him against arbitrary discharge. They give the worker status in the community, a voice in the determination of policies that affect him, a sense of participation in economic and political affairs. For all of this, they take less than 1 percent of his wages in dues.

But the story also has another side. Where a worker must be a member of a union to hold a job, refusal of membership may exclude him from a trade. Or, alternatively, membership may be forced upon him against his will. Union leaders, moreover, are not subject to democratic control. As a result, there is danger that they will discriminate among their members, suppressing freedom of speech and denying due process of law; that they will fail effectively to represent the worker's interest; that they will even defraud the worker, enriching themselves at his expense. To deal with these problems, provisions have been written into state and federal law.

Exclusion from Membership

It is only in the skilled crafts that restrictions on admission to union membership are to be found. They take the form of high initiation fees and strict apprenticeship requirements. In 1959, seven unions in the building trades had initiation fees that averaged $75. The fees charged by plumbers' locals ranged from $20 to $300. Such charges serve, of course, to keep out workers who cannot lay the money on the line. Fourteen unions had apprenticeship requirements calling for long periods of training. These are maintained not so much to insure the quality of service as to restrict the competition for jobs. Where there is a closed or union shop, denial of union membership means denial of employment. Where membership is denied, moreover, the unions make no provision for appeal.[3] Excessive initiation fees are forbidden by the Taft-Hartley Act. Excessive apprenticeship requirements are not against the law.

Until 1964, workers were also excluded from union membership on the ground of race. In four of the railroad brotherhoods, constitutional provisions excluded Negroes. In nine other unions, applicants for admission to a local had to be approved by a vote of its members. In the Railroad Trainmen, for instance, applicants could be blackballed by three of the members of a lodge. This provision made it easy to exclude the members of minority groups. Such discrimination has been forbidden for many years under state fair employment practices laws. It is now forbidden by the Civil Rights Act of 1964. It was also held, in 1964, to be an unfair labor practice under the Taft-Hartley Act. The NLRB was thus empowered to prohibit it by issuing orders enforceable in the courts.

Compulsion of Membership

The worker's participation in union activities is not always voluntary. Instead

3 / See Leo Bromwich, *Union Constitutions* (New York: Fund for the Republic, 1959).

of permitting nonunionists freely to decide whether they wish to join, unionists may put pressure on them by refusing to work with them or to transport or work on materials produced by them; unions may even compel workers to join by obtaining a closed or union shop. Instead of permitting their members to decide whether they are getting enough from membership to justify continued payment of their dues, unions may force them to pay by persuading their employers to adopt a checkoff system under which the worker's dues are deducted before he gets his wages and sent directly to the union treasury.

These measures have been adopted in the name of union security. In their support, it is argued, first, that freedom of choice would enable some workers to take a free ride, enjoying the benefits of unionization without contributing to its costs. It is not true, however, that all workers share such benefits. As between regions and between firms, workers who are in a stronger position may gain from an increase in wages; those who are in a weaker position may lose their jobs. Within a firm, too, workers who have seniority may gain; those who lack it may be dropped. The closed or union shop and the checkoff exact a contribution not only from those who may profit from the activities of a union but also from those who may lose. A second argument has more force: if union security were not assured, unions would be forced to attract new members and to induce the payment of dues by pressing every grievance and making extravagant demands; responsible union leadership would be more difficult to obtain.

Solutions for the problem of involuntary participation in unions have been sought by Congress and by the legislatures of the states. In the Taft-Hartley Act, Congress forbade employers to withhold the worker's union dues from his wages unless he gave his written consent. It provided that union contracts should not require a closed shop or require a union shop unless it was approved by a majority vote. In practice, the closed shop has continued to exist, particularly for construction workers, seamen, and longshoremen whose employment is intermittent and thus affords no other means of recognition for seniority. The union shop was favored by the provision requiring elections, since it won such large majorities that employers could not refuse to accept it. The provision was repealed in 1951. The Act also permitted workers to request elections whereby unions could be decertified as bargaining agents, but such requests have rarely been made. The fundamental conflict of interest between unions and their members that had been assumed by Congress was not found to exist.

Section 14b of the Taft-Hartley Act outlawed contracts compelling union membership in states whose laws forbade them, thus opening the way to the enactment of right-to-work laws by the states. These measures outlaw the closed and union shops by forbidding requirement of union membership as a condition of hiring or continued employment. They have been supported by employers and opposed by labor in the belief that they would reduce the union's power. By 1965, such laws had been enacted by 21 states and were still in effect in 19 states, all of them in the South and West. In that year, repeal of Section 14b was recommended by President Johnson. This would have nullified the right-to-work laws and permitted, within the states affected, the reestablishment of the union shop. The repealer passed the House but was rejected by the Senate.

In practice, the laws had but little effect. In some industries, in these states, the unions were too weak to negotiate a union shop, even if its legality were clear. In others, though not required to do so, the workers continued to maintain their union membership. In some cases, where unions would have been strong enough to obtain a union shop, a small minority of workers remained outside. Here, the unions had to resort to persuasion to get them to join and to keep them in the fold. The laws did not prevent unionization or interfere with collective bargaining. They neither fulfilled the hopes of employers nor justified the fears of labor.[4]

Relations within Unions

The government of unions, while democratic in form, is autocratic in reality. The rank and file of union members are apathetic, few of them attending meetings unless a strike or a new contract is to be put to a vote. Union managements perpetuate themselves through their control of the electoral machinery. Union presidents typically remain in office all their lives, too firmly entrenched to be dislodged. In this respect, the union resembles the corporation. And here, as in the corporation, there is danger that insiders will abuse their power.

Union leaders have taken money from employers for signing what are known as "sweetheart" contracts because they give the workers less than could have been obtained. They have borrowed union money to finance their business deals. They have profited from deals in which the union's interest differed from their own. They have embezzled union funds. These, to be sure, are the offenses of a small minority. But here, as with corporations, there is need for protection against conflicts of interest.

Within the union, power may be abused in other ways. Elections may be rigged. Dues may be raised without the consent of a majority. Freedom of speech may be denied. Workers may be charged with violating union rules and arbitrarily fined or expelled from membership. Here, again, there is need for assurance of democratic processes.

Congress attempted to deal with some of these problems in the Taft-Hartley Act. It required unions to render financial reports and to file information concerning the compensation of their officers. The data, however, were merely deposited; no check was made upon their accuracy. The law did not enforce accountability for union funds; it had little effect upon financial practices. The Act also required that reports be made regarding the procedures used in holding elections, conducting meetings, and imposing union discipline. This, too, had little effect; the procedures were not changed.

The law was strengthened by the Landrum-Griffin Act of 1959. This measure

4 / Frederic Myers, *"Right to Work" in Practice* (New York: Fund for the Republic, 1959).

was designed to protect members of unions against improper conduct by their officers. First, it provides safeguards against diversion of union funds, requiring more detailed reports on financial matters, making union officers responsible as fiduciaries, requiring that those who handle funds be bonded, and forbidding unions to make loans to their officers resulting in an indebtedness of more than $2,000. Second, it provides safeguards against possible conflicts of interest, forbidding union officers to request or receive various types of payment from employers and requiring such officers and employers to report on any payments that are made. Third, it regulates the internal government of unions, requiring periodic elections by secret ballot and insuring the member's right to vote, making it necessary to obtain majority approval before increasing dues, assuring due process in disciplinary actions, and guaranteeing freedom of speech in union meetings. If these rights are denied, members may sue for an injunction to enforce them. If violence is employed in their denial, the guilty officers are subject to criminal penalties.

UNIONS AND THE INNOCENT BYSTANDER

Persons who are not themselves involved in differences between unions and employers may nonetheless be harmed by these disputes. If the disputants fail to come to agreement, neutrals may be hurt by strikes. If they succeed in agreeing, neutrals may be asked to finance a higher wage by paying a higher price. In either case, government may be forced to intervene.

A strike is not to be regarded as an unfortunate failure in the process of collective bargaining; it is essential to that process. The threat of a strike must always be present if labor is to enforce its demands, and strikes must be called upon occasion to prove that the threat is not a bluff. When this occurs, innocent bystanders are bound to be hurt.

It is not only the intransigent employer who is hit by a strike; an employer who participates fully in collective bargaining may be struck by a rival union, picketed by a minority group, or hurt by a strike or a boycott directed against another firm. A strike may also be harmful to workers who are not involved: to other workers in a plant where a single craft has struck; to workers supplying it with materials or handling its products. In most cases, a strike does little harm to the consumer: the products involved may be dispensable; substitutes may be available; adequate stocks may be on hand. In some cases, however, a service is essential, lacks a substitute, and must be rendered continuously. The interruption of such a service may do great harm. A strike may also involve disorder and violence, damaging a whole community. To deal with these problems, government has undertaken to confine the strike, outlawing its use for certain purposes, and to promote the settlement of industrial disputes.

Where unions and employers come promptly to agreement, nobody is hurt by a strike. But agreement may be reached at the cost of an inflated price. Here, too, government has intervened. In time of war, particularly, it has sought both to maintain essential production and to check inflation by arbitrating wage disputes.

Limitation of Strikes and Boycotts

Strikes and picketing, as such, are not held to be unlawful. But when undertaken in pursuit of an unlawful purpose, they may be banned. Strikes called in violation of union contracts, jurisdictional strikes, and sympathetic strikes, together with secondary boycotts, were banned by the Taft-Hartley Act.

The employer was authorized, in case of a strike in violation of a union contract, to bring suit to enforce observance of the contract or to obtain damages for its breach. Such suits, in fact, are rarely brought. Employers are reluctant to sue the unions with which they deal.

An employer who has recognized one union may be struck by a rival union that claims to have jurisdiction over his employees. Under the Wagner Act, the employer was helpless in such a case. Under the Taft-Hartley Act, he can petition the NLRB for an election to determine which of the unions represents a majority. The jurisdictional strike, once a serious problem, has all but disappeared.

An employer who has no dispute with his employees may be struck when they walk out to show their sympathy with strikers in another plant. He may also be hurt when they refuse to work on materials coming from or going to a plant involved in a dispute. Both of these practices—the sympathetic strike and the secondary boycott—were outlawed by the Taft-Hartley Act. Here, again, the employer was authorized to sue for damages, a right that has been little used.

One form of the secondary boycott is the refusal of truckers to haul "hot cargo"—goods moving to or from a struck plant. In contracts between the Teamsters' union and the trucking companies, the Teamsters obtained the companies' agreement not to question this practice under the secondary boycott provision of the Taft-Hartley Act. As a result, the provision was virtually nullified.

The hot cargo clause was outlawed by the Landrum–Griffin Act in 1959. It is now illegal for a union and an employer to enter into an agreement under which the employer must refrain from using or transporting the products of another employer. Exceptions are made in the cases of the garment and construction industries, where the letting out of work to subcontractors is the general rule. Elsewhere, the practice of coercing one employer by exerting pressure on another is against the law.

An employer may be picketed not only by a union that represents a majority of his employees but also by one that represents a minority or none of them. Picketing may be used as a means of promoting organization or forcing union recognition. It may even be used as a means of exacting tribute. Whatever its purpose, the refusal of truckers, in particular, to cross a picket line makes it a weapon of great effectiveness.

The right to picket, like the secondary boycott, was circumscribed by the Landrum-Griffin Act. It is now unlawful for a union to picket an employer for whom the NLRB has held an election within the 12 preceding months, or to picket an employer who has a contract with another union that is lawfully recognized as representing a majority of his employees. The abuses of organizational and recognition picketing have thus been curbed.

Mediation, Investigation, and Publicity

To promote the settlement of industrial disputes, government has relied, in the main, upon the provision of facilities for mediation and the requirement of a waiting period during which it makes an investigation and publishes a report. In neither case does it deny the right to strike or dictate the terms of a settlement.

Mediation services are maintained by the federal government and by the major industrial states. These services are authorized to intervene in disputes at the request of either party or upon their own initiative. It is the function of the mediator to ascertain, in confidence, the concessions that each of the disputants is prepared to make and, upon this basis, to propose a settlement to which both of the parties will agree. In most cases, the mediator succeeds in this attempt. Where he fails, the strike goes on.

For industries where a strike would create a national emergency by imperiling health or safety, the Taft-Hartley Act provides additional procedures. Here, if mediation fails, the Attorney General may obtain an injunction postponing a strike for 80 days. During this time, an impartial board appointed by the President will investigate the dispute and publish a report, making no recommendation for a settlement. Thereafter, the NLRB will poll the employees to determine whether they are willing to accept the last offer made by the employer. When this has been done, the injunction will be dissolved and the workers will be free to go on strike. These procedures have not been effective in settling disputes. In every case where workers have been polled on the employer's last offer, they have voted overwhelmingly to reject it. In half the cases where the law has been used, the disputes have not been settled during the cooling-off period. The Act provides no machinery through which to effect a settlement. Presidents, under political pressure to avoid public inconvenience and disorder, have therefore resorted to *ad hoc* measures for restoring peace. The price that they have paid has usually been acceptance, in some measure, of labor's demands.

Compulsory Arbitration and Seizure

Government has sometimes denied workers the right to strike, particularly in essential industries and in time of war. Where this is done, unions and employers are required to submit disputes to arbitration, and a board is established to determine the content of the wage bargain. This pattern was originated in Australia in 1904. It was copied by Kansas in 1920 but found unconstitutional in 1923, and has reappeared in a few states since 1947. It was adopted by the federal government in World War II.

Under the Railway Labor Act of 1926, special arrangements are made for dealing with strikes on the railways and the airlines. The President may request the unions not to strike during a cooling-off period of 60 days. He then appoints a board to investigate and report. The board's recommendations are not binding, the unions remaining free to go on strike. If they do so, the President's only recourse is to ask Congress for special legislation to keep the trains running or the planes flying. Such legislation was enacted in 1963 and again in 1967. In both cases, arbitration was required.

Compulsory arbitration is likely to put an end to collective bargaining. Unions and employers, instead of conceding points in negotiations, will submit their disputes to the government. Here, they may get better terms. If not, they can blame the arbitrators. So the terms of employment contracts come to be written in Washington and in the capitals of the states. When this occurs, the market is abandoned and regulation accepted in its place. Voluntary observance of terms adopted by mutual consent gives way to enforced compliance with terms conforming to legal precedent. With wages fixed by government, unions and employers compete for control of the wage machinery. The terms of employment respond to the exercise of political power.

In compulsory arbitration, unions are likely to have the upper hand, particularly where production is essential and labor scarce, as is the case in time of war. Men cannot well be forced to work. Policemen and soldiers cannot dig the coal, make the steel, and run the trains. In the circumstances, wages will be raised. The government's decision may still be unacceptable to the workers; it may be resisted by the employer. In some way, it must be enforced. The method used has been the seizure of the industries concerned.

Companies were seized to enforce decisions in labor disputes, under war powers granted the President by Congress, on three occasions in World War I and on 60 during and after World War II. When the steel industry was seized by President Truman in 1952, however, these powers had expired and the seizure was held to be unconstitutional. If seizure were genuine, it would raise many questions of administrative organization and procedure and property rights. In fact, it has been a mere formality. Private managements have continued to run their own concerns, and private owners have continued to receive their dividends. When the properties have been returned, however, their owners have had to accept an increase in wages as an accomplished fact. Seizure has been a means of giving the unions, in large part at least, the terms their economic and political power has enabled them to demand, and forcing employers to acquiesce. The fact is that the best brains in labor relations have come up with no adequate solution to the problem of industrial disputes.

UNIONS AND THE CONSUMER

Businessmen are forbidden, under the antitrust laws, to combine to fix the prices they get for their goods. At the same time, workmen are permitted, under the labor laws, to organize and to bargain collectively to fix the wages they get for their services. In the one case, monopoly is forbidden—to protect the consumer. In the other, it is permitted—to protect the worker. However inconsistent, these are established national policies. The consumer, as we have seen, is helped by business competition. Is he hurt by labor monopoly?

Whatever the effect of unions, it is confined to particular fields. Nine tenths of the workers in transport and public utilities, four fifths of those in building construction, and two thirds of those in mining are organized. But three fifths of those in manufacturing and nine tenths of those in distribution and the service trades are not. In some industries and in some regions, labor is powerful; in others, it is weak.

Where unions are strong, they may harm the consumer in three principal ways: First, they may raise prices directly by restricting competition in the markets for the products they make. Second, they may raise prices indirectly by reducing the productivity of labor and increasing its cost. Third, they may do so by restricting competition in the market for labor, thus raising wages and again increasing labor cost. These possibilities are examined in the section which follows.

Monopolization of Product Markets

Unions have sometimes restricted competition in product markets by acting on their own. Unions in the building trades have obstructed entry by outsiders and by new concerns. Unions of barbers and beauticians have specified the prices their employers were to charge. Union fishermen have refused to supply fish to canners except at the prices they have fixed. The United Mine Workers curtailed the supply of coal, in the forties, by calling the miners out on "holidays."

Unions have also conspired with employers to restrict competition in the markets for their products. Union locals in the building trades, in return for a monopoly of the labor market, have protected contractors from outside competition by refusing to install equipment produced in other cities. They have limited the number of competitors in a market by refusing to supply labor to new concerns. They have enforced collusive bidding arrangements by withholding labor from employers who did not cooperate. The sanction that enforces such arrangements is the strike. These practices are not characteristic of unions in general, being found principally in fields where employers are themselves too numerous and too small to restrict competition but where labor is so well organized that it has the power to do so.

The object of an agreement between a union and an individual employer is to put an end to competition among the workers in his plant. Such an agreement, however, need not impair the competition existing between the employer and his rivals in the sale of goods. But a union may bargain with all of the firms that sell in a market, making each of its contracts in identical terms. Here, the labor element in costs becomes uniform and rigid, and competition based on differences in wages disappears. When employers agree on common wages, they are also likely to agree on prices whereby the wages can be paid. Wage rates, moreover, may be established at levels that some concerns cannot afford. These producers will go out of business, and production will be concentrated in the hands of those that may remain. Wage levels, finally, may be set so high as to discourage the entry of new competitors, and exclusive occupancy of a market by the parties to a wage agreement may thus be assured. In these ways, unionization may restrain competition, not only in the market for labor, but also in the market for goods.

Unions under the Antitrust Laws

It is principally in the case of labor that interpretation now limits the boundaries of antitrust. The Sherman Act was originally directed toward restraints by industry. But unions were not exempted, and in the Danbury Hatters' case in 1908, the Court awarded damages to an employer who had been injured by a secondary boycott.[5] This led to the inclusion in the Clayton Act of a section providing that unions, as such, shall not "be held or construed to be illegal combinations or conspiracies in restraint of trade." In subsequent decisions, however, the Court continued to apply the law to union activities, permitting labor organization, strikes, and picketing, but forbidding secondary boycotts,[6] intentional interference with the movement of nonunion goods,[7] and agreement with other groups to control the supplies and the prices of goods and services.[8] But activities not including other groups, following decisions handed down in the Apex case of 1940 and the Hutcheson case in 1941, would now appear to be outside the law. In the Apex case, the Court held that a sit-down strike, involving the seizure of a hosiery plant, destruction of property, and interference with shipments, did not violate the Sherman Act because it did not monopolize the supply or control the price of hosiery.[9] And in the Hutcheson case, where a carpenters' union had gone on strike and conducted a boycott against Anheuser-Busch because the brewing company had employed the members of a machinists' union to install machinery, the Court found that the law did not apply "so long as a union acts in its self interest and does not combine with non-labor groups."[10] This position was reaffirmed in the Allen Bradley case in 1945.[11] Here, though the Court upheld the government in condemning a conspiracy involving an electrical workers' union, equipment manufacturers, and contractors, it went on to say that "the same labor union

5 / *Loewe* v. *Lawlor,* 208 U.S. 274.

6 / *Duplex Printing Press Co.* v. *Deering,* 254 U.S. 443 (1921).

7 / *United Mine Workers* v. *Coronado Coal Co.,* 259 U.S. 344 (1922).

8 / *U.S.* v. *Brims,* 272 U.S. 549 (1926); *Local 167* v. *U.S.,* 291 U.S. 293 (1934); *U.S.* v. *Borden Co.,* 308 U.S. 188 (1939).

9 / *Apex Hosiery Co.* v. *Leader,* 310 U.S. 469.

10 / *U.S.* v. *Hutcheson,* 312 U.S. 219.

11 / *Allen Bradley Co.* v. *Local Union No. 3,* 325 U.S. 797.

activities may or may not be in violation of the Sherman Act, dependent upon whether the union acts alone or in combination with business groups." The immunity now granted to labor by the law extends beyond the market for labor to the markets for other goods and services. Interference with competition in such markets, though forbidden to employers acting alone and to employers and organized workers acting together, is permitted to organized workers acting alone. Unions are thus granted the privilege of monopolizing product markets. This privilege, denied to business, is not essential to unionization or to collective bargaining. Congress could take it away by amending the law. But, so far, attempts to do this have failed.

Where identical terms governing labor costs are written into the contracts that a union signs with competing employers the line between legality and illegality is the same as that in the cases discussed above. If a union, acting independently, undertakes to obtain identical terms in its contracts with each of the firms in an industry, its behavior is legal, whatever the consequences may be. But if it conspires with some firms to impose on others conditions that will make it difficult for them to compete, it will be found to violate the Sherman Act. A case involving such a conspiracy came before the Supreme Court in 1965. The United Mine Workers had entered into a contract with the Bituminous Coal Operators Association under which it had accepted mechanization of the mines in return for higher wages and contributions to its welfare fund. It had then insisted, in bargaining with weaker operators, on acceptance of contracts containing identical terms, thus threatening to drive them out of business. One of these operators brought suit for triple damages under the Sherman Act and was awarded $270,000 by a lower court. The Supreme Court, finding that the union and the operators' association had conspired to restrain trade, affirmed the decision. [12]

The Productivity of Labor

Unions in various industries have attempted to make work for their members by adopting practices that have operated to reduce the productivity of labor and thus to increase its cost. First, they have resisted technological innovation, obstructing the adoption of new methods and refusing to work with new tools. Unions have sometimes made it unprofitable to introduce new machines by limiting their speed and by demanding that their operators be paid a higher wage. Unions in the building trades have refused to install precut lumber and preglazed windows. Painters have refused to use spray guns. Second, unions have limited the amount of work that a man is permitted to do. The crew of a freight train travels 100 miles and the crew of a passenger train 150 miles to do a full day's work; at the end of three or four hours, the men draw eight hours' pay. Third, unions have required the employment of unneeded labor. The air pilots and the engineers once insisted that four men (three pilots and an

12 / *United Mine Workers* v. *Pennington*, 381 U.S. 657.

engineer) be carried in the cockpit of a jet plane where there was work for only three. Members of the musician's union have been paid to sit in the wings while a phonograph was played offstage. Fourth, unions have required the performance of unnecessary work. Plumbers have required that the thread be cut off pipes and the pipes rethreaded. When material comes to a publisher already set up, printers have insisted on making a duplicate known as a bogus which is then thrown away. Here, again, the practices described are not characteristic of unions in general. They are confined, in the main, to fields where traditional skills are vulnerable to technical change. They are particularly notorious in railway transport, in building construction, and in printing.

Labor practices impairing productivity have been approved, in a number of cases, by the courts. Some of these practices, known as featherbedding, were outlawed by a provision of the Taft-Hartley Act that made it an unfair labor practice to exact payment for services that are not performed. But in a case involving the requirement of a printers' bogus, the Supreme Court held, in 1943, that this provision does not apply to rules requiring work, however unnecessary, as long as the work is actually done.[13] And in cases where union contracts in the construction trades contained clauses prohibiting the use of prefabricated materials, the court held, in 1967, that is was not a violation of the law for the union to go on strike to prevent employers from using such materials or from subcontracting their manufacture to other firms.[14]

In contrast to these practices, there are ways in which unions make for greater productivity. In some cases, too few in number, unions have invested in research and cooperated with management in the improvement of technology. More generally, by giving assurance of security, unions may reduce the need for restrictive practices. By providing machinery for the settlement of grievances, they may improve the worker's morale. By exerting pressure for higher wages, they may stimulate the employer to find new means of increasing efficiency and cutting costs. The net effect of these influences cannot be ascertained. It may be noted, however, that the growth of labor organization has coincided with a marked expansion in the output of industry.

Monopolization of Labor Markets

Unions may raise the prices the consumer pays for certain goods and services by restricting competition in product markets and by reducing labor's productivity. They may exert a wider influence by monopolizing labor markets, raising wages, and increasing production costs. What is the probable effect of labor monopoly? In answering this question, a distinction must be made between the cases in which a union bargains with a single firm and those in which it bargains with all of the firms that sell in a common market.

It is generally conceded, today, that the workers employed by a single firm

13 / *American Newspaper Publishers Assn.* v. *NLRB,* 345 U.S. 100.

14 / *National Woodwork Manufacturers Assn.* v. *NLRB,* 386 U.S. 612; *Houston Contractors Assn.* v. *NLRB,* 386 U.S. 664.

should be permitted to organize and to bargain collectively. If forced to sell their labor as competitors, they would be at a disadvantage in dealing with a buyer who is a monopsonist. To the worker, the job is vital; to the employer, though labor is needed, the individual laborer is not. Without reserves to support him during prolonged negotiations, the worker must shortly come to terms; the employer can better afford to wait. The worker lacks market information and negotiating skill; the employer possesses both. In such a situation, a fair bargain is not to be obtained. It has thus appeared that bargaining power must be equalized. It is obvious, however, that employers cannot be so completely atomized that their power will not exceed that of employees. It follows, therefore, that labor must be permitted to combine.

But a union need not confine itself to bargaining with a single employer; it may bargain with all of the companies in an industry. And here, as we have seen, the inclusion in contracts with these concerns of terms creating common labor costs may operate to lessen competition in the product markets where they sell. This possibility has led to the proposal that the labor laws be so amended as to confine the right of collective bargaining to unions representing the employees of a single firm. Politically, such a proposal is unreal. Economically, it is impractical. Such action would require the dismemberment of national unions. It would compel the reconstruction of established bargaining machinery. It would be difficult if not impossible to enforce.

Aside from industries that are geographically concentrated or those that are serving purely local markets, multifirm bargaining is not widespread. On a national scale, it is confined to a few such industries as steel and automobiles. Even here, its prohibition would have little effect. The wages set in one union's bargain with Bethlehem would still be the same as those set in another's bargain with U.S. Steel. The wages fixed for General Motors would correspond to those agreed upon by Ford. The nationwide pattern of wage rates, in such industries, results less from the form that is taken by bargaining than from the economic forces that underlie it. Given this pattern, firms may compete on other bases, but not on that of wage costs.

The Level of Wages

Unions, by definition, are monopolies. They suppress competition in the sale of labor as does a cartel in the sale of goods. By making membership a requisite for employment, unions bar nonmembers from the market for labor. By setting up exclusive bargaining units, they deny employers access to alternative labor supplies. By fixing a standard rate of wages, they deny employment to workers who are worth less and would be willing to work for less. By striking, they withdraw the supply of labor completely. By picketing, they dissuade nonmembers from competing for their jobs. By controlling the supply of labor, they seek to fix its price.

One would expect the monopoly power of unions to be reflected in the level of wages, but empirical studies of the influence of unions on wages have yielded inconclusive results. When wages in union industries are compared with those in nonunion industries, union wages are found to be higher, but the significance of this comparison is obscured by the fact that unions are found in dynamic industries in the North; unorganized workers in traditional industries in the South. When union wages are compared with nonunion wages for workers in the same occupation, industry, and region, it is found that union wages generally are higher, but they are not invariably so, and the difference, in any case, is slight. When the size of wage increases in union and nonunion industries is compared, it appears that increases received by union members are not much larger than those received by nonunionists. Some unions, in particular fields, have made extraordinary gains. This is true in building construction and in trucking, where the unions are large and powerful and the employers, by comparison, small and weak. It is true in such large-scale manufacturing industries as steel and automobiles, where the unions are strong enough to exact a share in the profits of oligopoly. But for unions in general, the measurable gains are small.[15]

The process of collective bargaining may well create the impression that union gains are greater than is actually the case. In the very nature of the process, the extent of disagreement between the union and the employer is exaggerated. The union demands more than it expects to get. The employer refuses, and offers less than he expects to give. The final bargain may set a wage no higher than would be obtained if the market were competitive. But it exceeds the employer's offer and enables the union to claim a victory.

There are limits, in the market, to union power. If union wages are raised too far above nonunion wages, nonunion firms may appear and grow. If wages in general are pushed too high, employers may substitute machinery. If wages and prices are raised too far, sales may fall off. If profits are cut too much, investment may decline. The consequence of higher wages may be lower employment. This outcome may be accepted by labor as a matter of deliberate choice. The possibility, in any case, is not safely to be ignored.

Cost-Push Inflation

Critics of unions have come, in recent years, to charge them with a major part of the blame for continued inflation. Wages, they point out, have risen more rapidly than the productivity of labor. Labor costs per unit of output have thus been increased, and the prices of products have had to be raised to cover their higher costs. In a business recession, it is said, employers resist the efforts of unions to increase wages. But during prosperity, they do not. To maintain profits, they must maintain production. To maintain production, they must accede to labor's demands. Higher wages are the cause; higher prices are the effect.

15 / See H. Gregg Lewis, *Unionism and Relative Wages in the United States* (Chicago: University of Chicago Press, 1963), chaps. III and IV, and Frank C. Pierson, *Unions in Postwar America* (New York: Random House, 1967), chaps. III, IV, and V.

But labor does not always get higher wages simply because it wants them. It also gets them because demand is strong. In some fields, where unions are powerful, wages have risen even though demand is weak. But in others, where demand is strong, wages have risen even though labor is unorganized. In the first case, the cause of inflation is the push of cost. In the second, it is the pull of demand. For business in general, both factors are likely to be present, exerting their pressure in the same direction at the same time.

Unions, by demanding higher wages, do make some contribution to inflation. But this is not its only or its major cause. Of greater importance are the factors that sustain demand. Foremost among them are the nation's commitment to maintain full employment and the direction of monetary and fiscal policies toward that end. In the political struggles that led to the adoption of this commitment, labor played a leading role. And here its responsibility for inflation is not to be denied.

Chapter 31

CONTROLLING AGRICULTURE

During the past 40 years, the federal government has largely removed one basic industry—agriculture—from the market economy and subjected it to the processes of central planning and authoritarian control. It has supported the prices of certain crops by making loans or purchases, thus accumulating surpluses which it has given away or sold at a loss, and by controlling the quantities that might be produced and sold. It has made direct payments to farmers for taking land out of production, and to supplement the incomes they obtain by selling their crops at the prices fixed by the market. It has helped producers of some commodities to establish and maintain production and price cartels. The price support and direct payment programs are considered in the present chapter. The cartel programs are described in the chapter that follows.

THE FARM PROBLEM

The case for controls in agriculture is usually based on three arguments. First, it is said that farmers, as a group, get incomes that are lower than those received by other groups in the community. Second, it is contended that farmers, unable themselves to monopolize their markets, are exploited by business and labor monopolists from whom they buy and to whom they sell, and should, therefore, be aided by government in obtaining monopoly power. Third, it is asserted that agriculture is basic to the whole economy, providing the foundation upon which the prosperity of other industries depends, and that its claim to public favor is thus unique.

Each of these arguments is open to question. As for the first, it is true that average income is lower in agriculture than in other pursuits. But the average conceals many incomes that are high as well as many that are low. As for the second argument, most of the markets in which the farmer buys and sells are, in fact, competitive. And where they are not, it would be better to make them so than to give the farmer a monopoly. Agriculture, finally, is no more fundamental than many other industries. It could be argued, with equal logic, that the prosperity of the economy depends upon that of mining or manufacturing. True, agriculture feeds us. But we are in no danger of running short of food. And even in the case of food, supply requires not only the services of farming but also those of transporting, processing, and merchandising. Politically, the claim of agriculture may be persuasive. As a matter of economics, it is not unique.

Agriculture, however, is not without its problems. Though the incomes of many farmers may be ample, there are still pockets of rural poverty. For all farmers, the prices of agricultural products are unreliable as guides to production. Prices and incomes are unstable. In its secular trend, the growth of agricultural output, stimulated by improvements in technology, has outstripped the growth of demand, and surpluses have mounted. It is to these problems that we now turn.

The Structure of Agriculture

In the absence of public intervention, the producers of most agricultural commodities would be powerless to fix the prices at which they sell. In agriculture as a whole and in each of its branches, producing units are numerous, the typical unit is small, and the degree of concentration in production is low. Each of the major crops is grown on hundreds of thousands, a few of them on millions, of farms, and these numbers may readily be increased. For any of the major crops, the eight or ten largest producers account for but a minor fraction of 1 percent of total output. None of them controls a part of the supply large enough to enable him, by curtailing output, appreciably to affect the price. No group of farmers, acting in concert, is likely to control enough of a supply to enable it to fix a price, since curtailment of output, by holding out the promise of higher returns, would encourage nonparticipation among its members and stimulate expansion among outsiders. The agricultural economy, if left to itself, is a competitive economy.

The picture brought to mind by the word "farm" is that of an enterprise of moderate size producing several familiar commodities such as corn, wheat, cotton, tobacco, hogs, cattle, poultry, milk, and eggs. But among the 3 million units called farms, there is great diversity in the nature of the product, in the character of the processes of production, in the degree of specialization, and in the scale of operations. The term comprehends the production of feed grains and livestock in the Corn Belt, of wheat on the Great Plains, of cotton and tobacco in the South, and of range livestock in the Southwest. It covers the dairy farms of New England, the Middle Atlantic, and the Lake States; the citrus groves of Florida and California; and the apple orchards of Virginia and Washington. It includes the producers of ducks on Long Island, sugar cane in Louisiana, and tree nuts on the Pacific Coast. With 200 different products, grown under widely differing conditions, there is no such thing, in actuality, as a typical farmer or an average farm.

Two thirds of all farms, or about 2 million, are operated by their owners, three fifths of them debt-free, two fifths encumbered with mortgages. One fifth, or more than 500,000, is operated by tenants, rents being paid by some of them in cash, by others in shares of agricultural products. This group is divided, in turn, into those who have their own equipment and plan their own operations and others, called sharecroppers, numbering 250,000, who contribute nothing but their labor and are paid not in wages but in shares of the crop.

A few thousand farms are operated by salaried managers. The great majority are family farms. A family farm is usually defined as an enterprise of such size that it can be financed, managed, and operated, with little or no hired help, by a farmer and the members of his family. Here, the farmer is owner, manager, and worker, his residence is both a home and an office, his wife and children are partners and fellow laborers. His income from farming and other sources may go into a common pool; his operating costs and his living expenses may be met from the same account. The family farm thus differs in character from other businesses. It combines a productive enterprise with a mode of life.

As farms are defined by the Census, they include suburban homes whose occupants have industrial employment and do a little farming on the side and farms occupied by aged owners who are in semiretirement. More than a third of the 3 million farms in the country fall into this category, their operations being part-time or nominal. When these are subtracted, there remain 2 million full-time farms. In this group, however, there are more than 500,000 farms that afford little more than subsistence to the farmer and his family. This leaves around 1,500,000 commercial farms. And of these, three fifths account for nine tenths of agricultural output. This is commercial agriculture. And it is to serve the interests of commercial agriculture that price and production legislation has been devised.

The Level of Farm Income

For agriculture as a whole, the problem presented to public policy is not that of relative poverty. Proponents of agricultural legislation have made much of statistics that purport to show that people on farms have incomes that are much lower than those received by nonfarm groups. But this quotient of low income has been obtained by overstating the number of farm folk in the divisor and understating the aggregate farm income in the dividend. The divisor has been inflated by including people who work in town and live on suburban tracts that the Census classifies as farms. It has been enlarged, too, by the fact that the farm population includes a larger fraction than does the nonfarm population of persons under 20 and over 65. The dividend, on the other hand, has been deflated by underestimating the rental value of farm homes, by computing the value of food produced and consumed on the farm not at the price the urban consumer pays but at the price the farmer gets, which is only two fifths as high, and by ignoring the fact that a larger part of farm than nonfarm income is tax-exempt. When the necessary corrections are made, the contrast in income per capita becomes less striking.

Studies of the average money incomes of all farm families show them to be lower than those of nonfarm families. This is particularly true of families on part-time and subsistence farms and on the 500,000 commercial farms whose sales are less than $5,000 a year. But the 1 million farmers whose sales exceed this amount have average money incomes as high as those of nonfarmers. Their real incomes are higher than those of nonfarm people, since the real incomes of farmers and nonfarmers are equal when the money incomes of farmers stand, according to various estimates, between 70 and 90 percent of those of nonfarmers. Another factor, too, must be taken into account. Farmers own real estate which increases in value. This increment is regarded by the farmer as a part of his income. But it is not included in statistical comparisons of incomes on and off the farms.

The Unreliability of Farm Prices

It is the function of prices to guide producers in allocating resources to the production of various goods. Where more is demanded, rising prices are supposed to call forth more production; where less is demanded, falling prices are supposed to warn producers to contract. In agriculture, however, this function is performed imperfectly. When the farmer is deciding what quantities of what commodities to plant, the prices he has to guide him are those obtained for crops produced the year before. These prices are not likely to be repeated; they were the consequence of conditions that are subject to change. A high price for one commodity may have resulted from a drought; the season ahead may be a rainy one. A low price for another may have been caused by a bumper crop; in the coming harvest, yields may fall. Where a price is high, other farmers may increase their plantings and drive it down; it might be wiser not to go along. Where a price is low, others may contract their acreage and drive it up; the farmer who plants as much as ever may do very well. Production, therefore, responds but slowly to changes in price relationships. And the individual farmer may miss the market every time, never producing more or less until everyone else decides to do the same.

The Instability of Farm Income

In general, the trouble with the farmer's income is not its level but its undependability. Supply is uncertain: the same acreage, cultivated in the same way, may yield more one year and less the next; a crop as a whole may be good, but on particular farms that crop may be destroyed by drought, flood, hail, disease, or pests. Demand is unreliable: foreign markets may be closed; business depression may cut the quantities of foods and fibers that will be consumed at home. These are forces that the farmer is powerless to control. But they may drive his income down to levels that impair his standard of living, prevent him from paying his taxes, the installments on his machinery, and the interest on his mortgage, and finally deprive him of his farm. It was the fear of such a disaster, more than anything else, that brought the farmer to a point where he was unwilling to entrust his fortunes to the market. And this fear had its basis in the bitter experience of the past.

The prices of agricultural commodities fluctuate more violently than prices of manufactured goods. This fact is to be attributed, in the main, to the relative inelasticity of their demand and supply. Where demand and supply are elastic, changes in price are limited. When price goes up, demand contracts, supply expands, and the rise is checked. When price goes down, demand expands, supply contracts, and the decline is stopped. With agriculture it is otherwise. For some commodities, such as meats and fruits, demand is fairly elastic. But for most, a change in price does not result in a proportionate change—or anything approaching a proportionate change—in the amount consumed.[1] Foods, in general, are necessaries. If prices are high, consumers may eat less, but they will still eat. If prices are low, consumers may eat more, but most of the money they save will be spent for other things. So, too, with supply. When prices, in general, go up, agricultural output is increased. Workers leave the farms, attracted by the higher returns obtainable in industry. But farmers increase their investment in land, fertilizer, and machinery. When prices fall, however, output is maintained. With unemployment, workers drift back to the farms. And farmers continue to produce. Interest, rent, and taxes must be paid. Land, equipment, and family labor can be put to work without expense. They might better be employed than left in partial idleness. Replacement and repair of buildings and machinery can be postponed. Fertilization can be skimped. As long as the cost of seed and feed remains below the price at which an individual farmer sells his output, he can maximize his income by producing at full capacity. And, unless the law forbids it, this is what farmers in general will do. It follows that supply is relatively elastic but demand inelastic as prices rise and that both are inelastic as prices fall. As a result, increases in price are only partially arrested, and declines are allowed to go unchecked. So swings from low to high and high to low are both repeated and extreme.

The Agricultural Revolution

There have been striking gains, in recent years, in the productivity of American agriculture. Farming is said to have changed more in the last 25 years than in the previous two centuries. New seeds, new fertilizers, and new pesticides have been developed; the breeds and feeds of livestock and poultry have been improved. More capital has been invested in farming, and more machinery introduced. As a result, yields per acre of crop land doubled between 1930 and 1960, the yield of wheat per acre rising from 14 bushels to 24, that of corn from 26 bushels to 54, and that of cotton from 171 pounds to 440. There were similar increases in eggs per hen and pounds of milk per cow. Output per man-hour more than quadrupled, rising at a rate of 5 percent per year. A generation ago, in the corn belt, a man could till 80 acres of land; with modern machinery, he can easily handle 240. Before World War I, it took 15 hours of labor to grow and harvest an acre of wheat; now it takes four. In

---

1 / Elasticity of demand runs between 0.1 and 0.3 for wheat, cotton, tobacco, milk, sugar, and potatoes, around 0.5 for feed grains, and from 0.6 to 3.0 for meats and fruits.

1940, a farmer fed 10 people; today he feeds 33. From 1940 to 1966, aggregate inputs in agriculture rose by 8 percent; outputs increased by 61 percent.

The growth of demand for agricultural products, in general, has not kept pace with the growth of supply. Population has not expanded as rapidly as output. Income has grown, but with each 10 percent that is added to his income, the consumer increases his expenditure for food by only 2 percent, and much of this does not reach the farmer but goes for processing and packaging. There is a limit to the stretch of the stomach. The consumption of food, in pounds per capita, has even fallen off, taste having shifted from starches, fats, and other staples to fresh vegetables, fruits, and better cuts of meat. At the same time, the demand for feed crops has been cut by the disappearance of the horse, and the demand for natural fibers restrained by the invention of synthetic substitutes.

Despite the limitations of demand, farmers have kept on producing many crops in quantities larger than they could sell at prices they found to be acceptable. In consequence, agriculture's major problem has been one of technological unemployment. Given the new technology, the nation has had too many of its resources in farming. To put it bluntly, there have been too many farmers on too many farms.

EVOLUTION OF PARITY AND PRICE SUPPORTS

The two decades before World War I were a golden era for American agriculture. Markets grew as industry expanded. On the farms, prices and incomes rose. Prosperity was sustained, uninterrupted, for the longest period the farmer had ever known. With the outbreak of war, production of foodstuffs in Western Europe suffered, and supplies from the Argentine and Australia were cut off by a shortage of shipping. The United States was called upon to feed her allies. Farm prices rose sharply, farm output was expanded, and farm debt grew, as new acres were bought on credit and the prices of crops were capitalized in the price of land. When the war ended, the farms of Europe came back into production and shipments from Argentina and Australia were resumed. Markets disappeared and prices dropped.

American agriculture did not participate in the prosperity that followed the war. And when the Great Depression struck, agriculture went from bad to worse. Demand at home collapsed, and prices continued to fall. The cash income of farmers dropped from $11 billion in 1929 to $5 billion in 1933. Farm families suffered hardships, and farms were lost through sales for delinquent taxes and foreclosures of mortgages. It was in this experience of prolonged and deepening depression that government support of agricultural prices had its birth.

Forerunners of Parity

The first method of increasing prices to be adopted after World War I was that of raising tariffs on imports of agricultural commodities. This was done under President Harding in 1921 and 1922. The method was effective for some products, such as sugar and wool, where consumption exceeded domestic production and foreign producers competed in the American market. For the great export crops, such as cotton, tobacco, wheat, and pork, it was completely ineffective. Here, production exceeded consumption. And where duties were imposed, they served only to keep out supplies that had never come in. If the prices of these commodities were to be boosted, another method had to be found.

Attention now turned to the invention of devices that would make it possible to sell an export crop at a higher price at home than that obtainable abroad. The most important of these proposals, the McNary-Haugen Plan, would have established a government export corporation with a large revolving fund to be used in purchasing agricultural products in the American market in quantities sufficient to raise domestic prices to the levels desired. The stocks thus accumulated would then be sold abroad at the world price. The money lost in the process would be recovered by imposing a tax on the sales made at home. This plan was enacted by Congress and vetoed by President Coolidge in 1927 and again in 1929.

The Agricultural Marketing Act of 1929, adopted during the Hoover administration, rejected this approach, seeking instead to promote the orderly marketing of agricultural commodities by stabilizing their prices. The Act created a Federal Farm Board, with a revolving fund of $500 million, and empowered it to support the stabilization activities of farmers' cooperative marketing associations. The Board entered the market in the fall of 1929, buying cotton at 16 cents a pound and wheat at $1.15 to $1.25 a bushel. By the summer of 1931, cotton had fallen to 6 cents and wheat to 39 cents, and the Board was holding 3,500,000 bales of cotton and 257 million bushels of wheat. Its revolving fund no longer revolving, the Board stopped buying. The harvest of 1931 produced a bumper crop, and prices fell to the lowest levels of the century. In this market, the Board unloaded. Its losses ran between $300 million and $400 million. The Farm Board's failure is readily explained. Stabilization through storage is feasible where funds are ample and surpluses are soon to be followed by shortages. The Board's funds were limited, and it dealt in commodities that were always in surplus and never in short supply. Even this might work, however, if production were controlled. The Board did appeal to farmers to kill off part of their livestock, plow under part of their cotton, and curtail their acreage of other crops. Its exhortations were ignored. Production was maintained, and prices continued to fall.

The First AAA, 1933

The Roosevelt administration took over from the earlier farm plans the notion, known as "equality for agriculture," that the prices of agricultural commodities should be raised to levels that would bear the same relation to the prices of other goods as that existing in the years before World War I. Rechristened as "parity," this idea was embraced as the goal of New Deal farm policy. In the Agricultural Adjustment Act of 1933, the first of the New Deal farm measures, parity was defined as the establishment of "prices to farmers at a level that will give agricultural commodities a purchasing power with respect to articles farmers buy equivalent to the purchasing power of agricultural commodities in the base period . . . August, 1909–July, 1914," with later base dates adopted for tobacco and, subsequently, for a few other commodities.

Parity, under the new program, was to be sought, in part, through loan, purchase, and storage operations like those of the Farm Board. A Commodity Credit Corporation was established and authorized to make loans on agricultural commodities. The CCC immediately went into operation, lending 10 cents a pound on cotton and 45 cents a bushel on corn. It made "nonrecourse" loans. If the prices went above 10 cents or 45 cents, the farmer could pay off his debt, repossess his crop, sell it, and pocket the difference. If prices fell below these figures, he could default on his payment, keep the money loaned him, and let the government take the loss. From his point of view, the proposition was "heads, I win; tails, you lose." What was involved in the lending operation, in reality, was the establishment of a minimum price.

But the Farm Board debacle was not forgotten. Production was to be controlled. The Agricultural Adjustment Act denominated as "basic" seven commodities: wheat, cotton, corn, hogs, rice, tobacco, and dairy products. For these commodities, the Secretary of Agriculture was empowered to curtail production by entering into voluntary contracts with farmers under which each of them would agree to restrict his acreage of a particular crop or his breeding and feeding of a specific type of livestock to a fixed percentage of the quantities obtaining in a base period. And the Secretary was further authorized to make payments, in the form of rentals for acres taken out of production or other benefits in cash, to those farmers who were willing to cooperate. Farm income was thus to be enhanced in two ways: (1) by higher prices resulting from curtailment of output, and (2) by checks drawn on the Treasury of the United States. The law provided for funds to make these payments by imposing a tax on the processors of the basic commodities, such as ginners of cotton, millers of wheat, and packers of meat.

In 1933, the government's first contracts with planters of cotton and tobacco required them to plow under a portion of their growing crops. At the same time, the government bought 6,200,000 little pigs and 222,000 pregnant sows, distributing part of this stock through relief agencies, turning part of it into grease and fertilizer, some of which was dumped in the Mississippi when tankage facilities were overtaxed. For other commodities and in later years, however, the contracts controlled the number of acres to be planted by individual farmers and the heads of livestock to be produced. Persuaded by official propaganda and tempted by cash benefits, farmers signed contracts to cover half of the acreage of corn; three fourths of that of wheat, cotton, and tobacco; and three fourths of the output of pork. The program was thought to be successful. There was a moderate decline in the output of cotton, tobacco, and other crops, and a sharp decline in the output of wheat and corn. Prices rose, and the CCC escaped disaster. Its stocks of cotton mounted, but its loans on corn paid off.

For this good fortune, some credit may be given to control of acreage, a great deal more to lack of rain.

The Soil Conservation Stopgap

In January, 1936, in the Hoosac Mills Case, the Supreme Court held the production control provisions of the Agricultural Adjustment Act of 1933 to be unconstitutional on the ground that the processing tax was employed, not to serve the general welfare, but in the interest of a particular group, and that the benefit payments it financed were used to purchase conformity with a program which the powers, delegated to Congress by the Constitution, gave it no authority to enact.[2] The administration then cast about for a method by which its program could be continued without running afoul of the Court. The result was the Soil Conservation and Domestic Allotment Act of 1936.

Payments were made, under this law, for such soil-building practices as applying fertilizer and turning green manure. They were also made for taking specified portions of acreage out of soil-depleting crops and putting them into soil-conserving crops. The soil-depleting crops, by some coincidence, were the very ones whose output the government had previously been seeking to curtail. The soil-conserving crops were unmarketable grasses and legumes.

The law was a hurried stopgap. It was concerned less with conserving the soil than with conserving the program of benefit payments for production control. For this purpose, however, it was a clumsy instrument. It was followed by a second Agricultural Adjustment Act in 1938.

The Second AAA, 1938

The new law directed the Commodity Credit Corporation to make non-recourse loans on corn, wheat, and cotton at 52 percent to 75 percent of parity whenever supplies should rise above certain levels or prices fall below certain levels. Price pegging, for these crops, was thus made mandatory. Supports for other commodities remained permissive.

The Act of 1938 directed the Secretary of Agriculture, whenever he should find that the output of corn, wheat, tobacco, or rice exceeded the quantity normally produced by a specified percentage, to fix the amount that could be marketed. If two thirds of the growers approved the plan in a referendum, the total would then be broken down into quotas for every state, county, and farm. Acreage allotments would be prepared, a farmer's marketing quota being defined as the amount produced on the acres permitted him. Commodities produced in excess of the quotas could not be sold, bartered, given away, or fed to stock, but had to be destroyed or stored. Farmers who kept within their quotas were eligible for commodity loans, for soil conservation payments, and for parity payments based on their allotted acreage. Those who exceeded their quotas were penalized by a heavy tax.

2 / *U.S.* v. *Butler,* 297 U.S. 1.

This pattern of control was upheld by the Supreme Court, first on the ground that the marketing quotas controlled commerce rather than production,[3] and later on the ground that production on individual farms affected prices in nationwide markets, and that the regulation of such prices was within the power of Congress.[4] The Act of 1938 was still in operation when World War II brought back prosperity.

Wartime Goals and Controls

From 1939 to 1945, while wholesale prices on nonfarm commodities rose 28 percent, the prices paid to farmers rose 112 percent. In 1943, the parity ratio with 100 as its goal, stood at 113. In 1945, the ratio of farm to nonfarm income per capita, on the 1909-14 base, stood at 151; compared with city folk, farmers were half again as well off as they had been in the golden era before World War I. The farmer had obtained everything he had asked for, and a great deal more. But parity and price supports had taken root.

With the coming of war, surpluses gave way to shortages, falling prices to rising prices, deflation to inflation. The CCC was happily enabled to unload its holdings at a profit. But there was need for a reversal in policy. The problem now was to increase supply, restrain demand, and put ceilings over prices. But the farmers' friends in Congress saw to it that the prices of agricultural commodities were controlled with less severity than those of other goods.

There were not only ceilings over prices but there were floors under them. But price supports were now used, not to increase farm incomes, but to encourage farmers to divert production from crops that were needed less to those that were needed more. In 1941, the Secretary of Agriculture announced the levels at which the government intended to support the prices of hogs, dairy products, chickens, and eggs. Thereafter, such action came to be taken as a matter of course, being extended to scores of other commodities. The prices announced were supported by loans and purchase guarantees.

In 1941, Congress raised the mandatory loan rate to 85 percent of parity for all commodities whose output the Secretary of Agriculture had requested farmers to increase. In 1942, it raised the mandatory supports to 90 percent of parity (later boosting that for cotton to 92½ percent) and required that they be kept there for two years after the President should declare the war to be at an end. President Truman made this declaration on December 31, 1946. By then, come depression or prosperity, government control of agriculture was here to stay.

PRICE SUPPORTS IN OPERATION

During the past decades, the pattern of price supports has undergone repeated

---

3 / *Mulford* v. *Smith*, 307 U.S. 38 (1939).
4 / *Wickard* v. *Filburn*, 317 U.S. 111 (1942).

changes in detail. But in broad outline it has remained the same. It has included: (1) the computation of price goals for farm products in terms of 1909-14 purchasing-power parity, (2) a program of mandatory and permissive loans and purchases designed to maintain farm prices at fixed percentages of parity, (3) provision for the disposition of resulting surpluses, and (4) control of the quantities of commodities produced and sold. Each of these elements of the program will now be subjected to further analysis.

Parity Price

The concept of parity was put in a nutshell by a cattle raiser interviewed on a television program: "If a man could take a bushel of corn to town in 1912 and sell it and buy him a shirt, he should be able to take a bushel of corn to town today and buy a shirt." This, indeed, was the general idea. But in operation it is not as simple as it seems.

From the thirties until the fifties, parity was determined by multiplying the average price that farmers received for a commodity in 1909-14 by an index of prices that farmers paid for goods they bought, expressed as a percentage of the average prices prevailing in 1909-14. This formula came to have an unfortunate effect: it operated to obstruct adjustment of production to changes in demand. The demand for wheat and other field crops had declined; the demand for meats, dairy products, fruits, and vegetables had risen. The parity formula kept the prices of the former products high and those of the latter low, thus discouraging the transfer of resources from the one field to the other. In 1948, Congress provided for the adoption of a modernized formula. This formula retained the 1909-14 ratio between farm and nonfarm prices as the goal for agricultural products as a whole. But it changed the relative parity prices of particular products so as to reflect changes in demand, reducing the price of wheat, for instance, and raising that of meat.

The change did not take effect at once. To ease the shift from the old parity to the new, a figure known as transitional parity was computed by reducing old parity at the rate of 5 percent per year. As long as the transitional parity price of a commodity exceeded its modern parity price, the transitional price remained in effect. When it fell below, the modern parity price took effect. The shift occurred at different dates for different commodities. Now, however, the old formula has been generally superseded by the new.

The process involved in computing a parity price may be illustrated by showing how such a price was determined for hogs, per 100 pounds, in January, 1958:

 a) Determine the average price received by farmers for the commodity during the preceding 10 years. For hogs, this was $18.90

 b) Compute an index of the average prices received by farmers for all agricultural commodities during the same 10 years,

using the prices received in 1909-14 as 100. In January,
1958, this index stood at   262

c) Divide (a) by (b). This gives an "adjusted base price" for
hogs of. . . . . $ 7.21

d) Compute an index of prices paid by farmers, taking those
paid in 1909-14 as 100. In January, 1958, this index
stood at   301

e) Multiply (c) by (d) and divide by 100. The parity price for
hogs is $21.70

Parity, or $21.70, was the price to which the farmer was held to be justly entitled. Support prices, however, were set at less than parity. If fixed, in this case, at 80 percent, the price would be $17.36.

Parity price is said to be a just price. But, at best, the figure rests on fallible human judgment. And, at worst, it is subject to deliberate manipulation. Parity can be raised by shifting the base date from 1909-14 to some other period when price relationships were more favorable, and this has been done in the case of certain commodities. It can be raised by boosting the index of prices paid, and this was done when Congress required, at one time or another, that interest, taxes, freight rates, and wages be added. Before 1950, this index included 170 commodities used in farm production and in farm family living. Since then, it has included some 340. Each of these commodities is given a weight in making the computation. The index of prices received has included 52 agricultural commodities, each of which is given its own weight. The height of a parity price is influenced by the items chosen for inclusion in these indexes and by the weights assigned them. These decisions are made by the statisticians of the Department of Agriculture.

In addition to computing the parity index and parity prices, the Department also computes a general parity ratio. This is the ratio of the index of prices received by farmers to the index of prices paid. It is designed to reveal, in a single figure, how farmers are faring in relation to other groups in the community. The base upon which all of these figures are prepared is now 60 years in the past. It has been proposed, therefore, that it be changed to a number of more recent years. This would be an improvement. But it should be noted that the old base would be built into the new, for the prices of recent years have been influenced by supports related to the parities of the past.

Issues in Price Supports

The program of price supports has given rise to issues that have been fought over, during three decades, at successive sessions of Congress. Which commodities shall have their prices supported? Shall the provision of supports be left to the discretion of the Secretary of Agriculture or shall supports be made mandatory by Congress? Shall supports be flexible, with lower and upper limits specified within which the Secretary may fix them, or shall rigid levels of support be written into law? And finally, how high shall the supports be?

Some 200 different commodities are produced on American farms. Of these, only six—wheat, corn, cotton, tobacco, rice, and peanuts—are designated as "basic" and these, together with certain nonbasic products, receive supports. The supported commodities accounted for 42 percent of farm market sales in 1967; the nonsupported commodities for 58 percent. What determines whether a price is supported or not? The answer is simple: the price of a commodity will be supported if its producers can corral a majority of votes in each of the houses of Congress. The price-supported commodities are referred to, with reason, as "the political commodities."

If the provision of supports were left to the discretion of the Secretary of Agriculture, he might conceivably decide not to support the price of some commodity in some year when it was in excess supply. If supports are mandatory, the Secretary must provide them, however large the supply may be. Supports were discretionary under the Act of 1933. They were made mandatory in 1938 for wheat, corn, and cotton, but not for other crops; mandatory in 1941 for all crops whose production had been increased during the war. They have been mandatory for basics and for designated nonbasics, including milk and butterfat, and discretionary for other commodities since the mid-fifties.

When supports, even though mandatory, are flexible, the Secretary can set them at the upper limit specified when supplies are small, at the lower limit when supplies are large, using price, within these limits, as a guide to future production. Before World War II, supports were flexible; under the Act of 1938, they could be set anywhere between 52 and 75 percent of parity. In 1941 and 1942, Congress made the supports of war-expanded crops completely rigid, setting them first at 85 and then at 90 percent of parity. Between 1948 and 1958, Congress repeatedly fought over the issue of flexibility. In 1948, it set the limits of supports at 60 to 90 percent of parity; in 1949, at 75 to 90 percent; for 1955, at 82½ to 90 percent; and from 1956, again at 75 to 90 percent. The latitude permitted for discretion has been limited.

In the depression, parity price was regarded as a distant goal, to be approached in the fullness of time; supports stood at 66 percent of parity. During the war, parity price became a figure that had to be exceeded by a considerable margin before inflation could be restrained; prices rose to 113 percent of parity. Since the war, parity has been used to justify the levels at which prices have been pegged; supports at 75 to 90 percent of parity have been the general rule.

Loans, Purchases, and Storage

Storage operations have often been advocated as a means of stabilizing prices, i.e., reducing the amplitude of price fluctuations over time. If this were its purpose, the government would attempt to estimate the prices that would achieve a long-run equilibrium between supply and demand, establish a price range below and above this level, buy when prices fell under the lower limit, and sell when they rose over the upper one. Supplies would thus be withdrawn from the market and put into storage in seasons when output was large, released from storage and returned to the market in seasons when output was small. The farmer would enjoy a stabler price, the consumer a steadier supply. The government would aim to break even, its profits covering its costs.

Under the price support program, the purpose has been a different one. Lending, buying, and storing have been employed, not to stabilize prices, but to raise them. With prices set above the equilibrium level, production has been encouraged, stocks have been accumulated, and these accumulations have had to be unloaded at a loss.

The CCC has had its own storage bins. It has rented commercial warehouse space. It permits the farmer to store commodities on the farm, sending its inspectors to seal his bins and cribs. With other facilities exhausted, it has stored millions of bushels of wheat in unused airplane hangars, in abandoned movie theaters, and in the holds of hundreds of merchant ships riding at anchor on Puget Sound and on the Columbia River, the Hudson, and the James. Its storage costs alone have run to a million dollars a day.

The losses incurred in storage vary with the character of the commodities involved. They are lower for durable products and higher for perishable ones. Cotton can be kept for years if stored in a dry place. Grain can be kept for two or three years before it begins to deteriorate. But meat, eggs, dairy products, fruit, and vegetables spoil rapidly, require refrigeration, and cannot be kept in growing quantities without excessive costs. It is with such commodities that the government has had its unhappiest experience. From 1943 to 1950, it was required to support the price of potatoes. A tenth of the potatoes acquired were transferred to schools and relief agencies. Nine tenths went into livestock feed, alcohol, flour, starch, and spoilage. Millions of bushels were dumped to rot or covered with kerosene and burned. Other millions were dyed blue, to keep them out of commercial channels, and sold back to farmers at a pittance for use as feed and fertilizer. The loss on potatoes was $600 million.

From its establishment in 1933 up to June 30, 1964, the cost to the Commodity Credit Corporation of acquiring, transporting, storing, and selling agricultural commodities, including interest on its investment and losses on its sales, was $35 billion. During the years from 1933 to 1943, its gains exceeded its losses. But this was due to good luck rather than good management. On two occasions, the Corporation was enabled to rid itself of excessive holdings at good prices by fortuitous events: in 1934, by a drought; in the early forties, by World War II. Since that time, the agency has operated at a loss, averaging $300 million a year during the late forties, rising to $1 billion a year during the fifties, and to $3 billion a year during the sixties. Its inventories have run as high as $9 billion. It has had $2 billion to $3 billion tied up in wheat alone, holding more than a billion bushels, equivalent to a year's crop, with another harvest on the way.

Surplus Disposal

When the government sets a price above the level that would balance demand and supply, it creates a surplus. If the surplus is not to be destroyed, it must be disposed of in some other way. The method of disposition most popular with Congressmen is dumping abroad. This gives the foreign consumer American foods and fibers at low prices at the expense of the American taxpayer. But subsidized competition is resented by the foreign producer. This, in itself, would not bother the Congressmen. But economic aggression evokes retaliation, closes foreign markets to American exporters, and endangers international diplomacy.

Great ingenuity has been exercised to overcome this difficulty. Agricultural surpluses, instead of being dumped on commercial markets, are turned over to other governments, being donated to relieve victims of disasters or "sold" not for dollars but for foreign currencies. As much as a third of American agricultural exports have been handled in this way. The procedure does not enlarge the market for agricultural commodities but merely replaces commercial sales. Much of the foreign currency acquired remains unused. Part of it is given to the governments of underdeveloped countries in the form of loans or grants to finance their development. It is doubtless desirable for the United States to aid the underdeveloped countries. But such a policy should be adopted on its merits. It should not be merely incidental to the disposition of surpluses created by the nation's agricultural policy.

Surpluses are also dumped at home. First, they are turned over to state educational authorities who distribute them through school lunches. Nearly 20 million school children, from poor families, get this food without charge or at prices that cover but a fraction of its cost. School authorities have resisted, with some success, the efforts of the Department of Agriculture to force upon them whatever foods have happened, at the time, to be in greatest oversupply, accepting only those for which there was nutritional need. The program has, therefore, operated to improve nutrition, making, in particular, for a substantial increase in the consumption of milk. Second, surpluses are given to state and local welfare authorities for distribution to some 3 million needy people: inmates of charitable institutions and other recipients of public aid. Here, the foods distributed are those that happen to be in surplus, bearing little relation to dietary need. Third, surplus food is distributed to another 3 million needy people through a stamp plan, first employed between 1939 and 1943 and revived in 1961. Under this plan, a recipient of public aid can buy, for $64, stamps that he can use at retail stores to purchase food worth $100. The retailer recovers their value from the government. The plan has two advantages: it employs commercial channels in distributing relief; it preserves the recipient's freedom of choice. But it may be doubted that the consumption of foodstuffs is increased by either of these programs; the money saved is likely to be spent on products other than food. Each of these schemes provides an outlet for agricultural surpluses that is socially acceptable. Certainly, it is better to use supplies in this way than to destroy them or to subsidize their competition with commodities produced abroad. But, taken together, these devices make but a small addition to demand. Their contribution to the reduction of agricultural surpluses is minimal.

Control of Production

With support prices set high, the losses incurred through surplus disposal can be kept within limits only if production is controlled. Attempts have, therefore, been made to accomplish this purpose by curtailing the acreage that may be planted to particular crops and by establishing quotas to control the quantities that may be marketed. Under the Act of 1933, benefit payments were made to farmers who voluntarily contracted to reduce their acreage by stipulated percentages. Under the Act of 1938, the price of a commodity was not supported unless two thirds of its producers voted to accept marketing quotas that would limit the quantities they could sell. Thereafter, those who kept within their quotas received full price supports; those who exceeded them were penalized. But the quotas were not set in physical units such as bushels or pounds. Instead, the quantity a farmer was to be permitted to sell was divided by his average yield per acre in earlier years to determine the number of acres he would be permitted to plant, and his marketing quota became the amount, however large, that he could produce on his allotted acres. Restriction of acreage thus remained the method of reducing output. Congress, moreover, imposed limits on acreage curtailment. In the case of wheat, total allotments could not be cut below 55 million acres no matter how large the surplus might be, and farmers producing wheat on 15 acres or less could maintain or increase their output without incurring a penalty. Similar limits on acreage control were enacted for cotton, rice, and peanuts.

Reduction of acreage has not brought about a proportionate reduction of output. From 1953 to 1963, a cut of 33 percent in acres planted caused a drop of only 3 percent in the output of wheat; a cut of 45 percent in acres caused a drop of only 6 percent in the output of cotton; a cut of 40 percent in acres failed to change the output of tobacco; a cut of 14 percent in acres was followed by an increase of 42 percent in the output of corn. The explanation for this failure is not far to seek. Land is but one of the inputs contributing to agricultural output; more labor and more capital can be combined with less land to obtain the same output or an even larger one. The farmer retires his poorest acres and retains his best. Under the stimulus of higher prices, he cultivates his land more intensively, using better seeds, planting the rows closer together, pouring on more fertilizer, and applying more pesticides. Yields per acre are increased and output is maintained.

For production to be effectively controlled, quotas must be set in physical units. These quotas may be enforced by giving certificates to farmers to cover the quantities they are permitted to sell. Sale or purchase of commodities unaccompanied by certificates can be forbidden by law. Quantities sold within quotas will bring the support price. Quantities in excess of quotas can be made subject to a punitive tax. With tight controls, production can be cut. Such controls were provided by Congress for cotton and tobacco in 1934 and for potatoes in 1935. They were repealed in 1936 when the Supreme Court found the Agricultural Adjustment Act to be unconstitutional. Tight controls have been applied to sugar since 1934.

Tight controls, effectively enforced, would reduce the costs involved in acquiring, transporting, storing, and selling surplus commodities. They would lessen the international problems that are created by dumping surpluses abroad. They would reduce the burden that price supports impose upon the taxpayer. They would not lessen the consumer's load. They would make for rigidity in the allocation of resources, obstructing adjustment to changes in demand and cost. If the output of one crop were successfully curtailed, the farmer would use his land and labor to produce another. New surpluses would appear, and these, in turn, would have to be controlled. The process could logically end, in the phrase of Henry A. Wallace, only when every plowed field had its permit sticking to its post.

Land Retirement

Government has repeatedly attempted, with scant success, to curtail the output of particular crops by reducing the acreage devoted to their production. As an alternative, it has undertaken to remove land from production entirely. It has done so by renting land or by buying it, by acquiring portions of farms or by retiring whole farms.

During the thirties, the government purchased and retired 12 million acres of marginal farm lands. The effect of this operation on agricultural output was imperceptible. A second land retirement effort was made under the Soil Bank Act of 1956. Under this law, the government offered to make rental payments to farmers who would enter into contracts to take land out of production. These payments covered the farmer's normal profit on the acres under contract, an incentive bonus, and the cost of conservation practices. The law set up two programs: an acreage reserve and a conservation reserve.

The acreage reserve was an emergency program designed to reduce surpluses of basic crops by making one-year contracts to retire the land on which they were produced. More than 21 million acres were placed in this reserve in 1957. But reduction in acres was offset, in large measure, by increases in yields. Save for corn, however, the program succeeded in effecting a moderate reduction in the output of basic crops. It did so at great expense. Payments amounted to more than $600 million in 1957 and nearly $700 million in 1958. In a few cases, the rents paid to farmers were very large. There were 67 who collected more than $50,000 each, two of them more than $270,000 each. In 1957, Congress put a limit of $3,000 on individual payments. As a result, in 1958, many of the larger farmers failed to renew their contracts. The acreage reserve was discontinued.

The conservation reserve was a long-run program designed to retire land from crop production under 3- to 15-year contracts, putting it into grass, trees, and water storage. Here, the contracts covered retirement of whole farms as well as parts of farms. By 1960, nearly 29 million acres, about 6 percent of the country's plowland, had been placed in this reserve. Retirement of whole farms under the program evoked the opposition of merchants and townspeople in rural communities, who saw in it a threat to the basis of their livelihood. Their fears were shared by their Congressmen. The government's authority to write new land retirement contracts was terminated. The effect of the conservation reserve on agricultural output is not known.

Land retirement is popular with farmers; it is easier to administer than production controls; it costs less than price supports. But the undertaking has serious disadvantages. Retirement of parts of farms, as we have seen, has little effect on output, since the poorer acres are retired and yields on the better acres are increased. Retirement of whole farms presents a dilemma. If the more productive farms are retired and marginal farms left in operation, output will be curtailed, but agricultural efficiency will be impaired. If marginal farms are retired, the effect on output will be small. But these are the farms that the government is more likely to get. Land that is poor and land that is owned by elderly farmers and by part-time farmers will be offered for rent; land that is highly productive will not. The cost of retirement, moreover, will be high. If the government continues to support the prices of agricultural commodities, it will be bidding against itself. Its rentals will have to be high enough to compete with the profits that can be made by remaining in production and selling at supported prices. Rents will have to be raised as the government seeks to acquire increasing quantities of land. Rental, over the years, will cost as much as purchase, and will leave the farmer with title to his farm. The principal beneficiary of land retirement will be the landowner.

PARITY AND PRICE SUPPORTS APPRAISED

The program of price supports, with its goal of parity, may be appraised, first, in terms of its basic philosophy, its economic logic, and its possible results. Is parity ethically justifiable? Is the support of product prices an appropriate means to the end of farm welfare? Is it more likely to help or to harm the farmer in the long run? The program may be appraised, second, in terms of actual experience. What has it cost the taxpayer and the consumer? How has it affected agricultural productivity? How has it influenced the allocation of resources within agriculture and between agriculture and the rest of the economy? By the first test, the program must be condemned. By the second, it does not come off so badly.

The Ethics of Parity

Parity is presented as a precise statistical expression of ultimate justice in the distribution of income among producing groups. Some doubt is thrown on the purity of the concept by the brazen way in which its statistics have been manipulated by the Congress. But it is still maintained that farmers as a group should get the same share of the nation's income, and that farmers as individuals should stand in the same relationship to nonfarmers, as they did in some period in the past.

It is nonsense to argue that the share of income going to any group should always remain the same. And this holds for farmers as it does for lamplighters, glass blowers, and livery stable keepers. As technology advances and income grows, the share of a single industry should decline. A steady shrinkage in the fraction spent for foods and fibers, in particular, is the mark of a progressive community. There are few who would argue that the farmer's share in income should have been frozen at the fraction he received before the Revolution or the Civil War. There is no greater logic in the contention that it should be frozen at the fraction he received before World War I or, indeed, at that he gets today. If the farmer's relative worth to society is declining, there is no ethical principle to support the proposition that his relative income should be maintained. And the farmer has no better claim to such protection than any other group in the community.

The parity to which the price supports are tied, moreover, is not one of income per farmer but rather one of price per hundredweight, per bushel, and per pound. Parity, said the cattleman, means that a bushel of corn should always buy a shirt. Here, the concept of justice attaches itself to a relationship among inanimate objects. Morality is said to require that the values at which such objects exchange should always be the same. This is to say that a television set should always bring three suits of clothes. Such a proposition is recognized at once as fallacious. But if not a TV set, why a bushel of corn? If the demand for a product or the cost of producing it goes down, it should command less of other products in return. It has no moral claim to more. To grant such a claim is to pervert the pricing mechanism, helping the producers of one product, hurting the producers of another, and harming the consumers of both.

Parity cannot be justified as establishing justice between farmers and non-farmers or between agricultural products and other goods. In operation, it creates inequities among the farmers themselves. The prices of a few crops are supported; the prices of most crops are not. The parity formula, moreover, is more favorable to some crops than to others. If all were supported at the same percentage of parity, there would be inequities. But the percentages of support, also, are varied. And these variations find their sole explanation in differences in political power.

The benefits of the program are not distributed on the basis of need. The larger incomes resulting from higher prices and governmental payments are proportioned to the farmer's scale of operations. Farmers in the middle- and upper-income brackets, 1 million of them, get four fifths of the subsidy. Farmers with smaller incomes, 2 million of them, get one fifth. It is possible to explain this distribution in terms of economics or politics. It would be difficult to justify it in terms of ethics.

Consequences for the Farmer

There is no assurance that the program, in the long run, will succeed in accomplishing its purposes. The price supports, as we have seen, defeat the purpose of acreage controls by providing a powerful incentive to increase yields.

The higher prices that help producers of grains also harm producers of livestock and poultry who must pay more for their feeds. There is danger, too, that the farmer will price himself out of the market. And where he does not, there is danger that what is gained in the higher prices charged for crops will be lost in other ways.

By insisting that the price of cotton be maintained at an artificial level, the American planter has acted to deprive himself of his former share of the market, both abroad and at home. He has encouraged the expansion of competitive acreage in Latin America, Africa, and Asia. Foreign production rose from 11 million bales in 1932 to 40 million in 1967. The prices obtained, by law, for cotton have also tended to stimulate the substitution of competitive materials. The quality of rayon has been improved; its price set lower than that of cotton. As the market for fabrics has grown, it is the production of synthetic rather than natural fibers that has increased. Cotton's place has been taken by rayon not only in apparel but also in fabric for tires. Cotton has also been superseded by paper in products such as towels, napkins, tissues, packages, and bags. Long faced with growing competition, the cotton grower has seemingly been bent on self-destruction. Confronted with the development of synthetic fibers, the wool grower has exhibited a similarly suicidal bent. So, too, with the dairy farmer. In 1940, butter had nine tenths of the market for spreads and margarine only a tenth. By 1963, margarine had three fifths of the market and butter only two fifths.

In cases such as these, an artificial level of prices cannot permanently be maintained. In others, this may be possible. But the advantage obtained by the farmer may be dissipated by attracting new entrants or by inflating the value of land. With tobacco, for instance, where an acre yields a gross income 20 times that yielded by an acre of wheat or corn, farmers have crowded in to share in the profits; allotments are now given to nearly 600,000 farms. As a consequence the size of the individual allotment has declined, the average for Burley tobacco dropping from 1.58 acres in 1948 to 1.16 in 1963. Where an advantage remains, it is capitalized in determining the prices charged for land. Without a quota, tobacco land may sell for $50 an acre; with a quota it will bring $2,500 or more. Here, the capital value of the added income resulting from the quota is appropriated by the man who owned the land at the time when the quota was imposed. The farmer who subsequently buys the land pays for the value of the quota as he would for any other form of property. Thereafter, though price is inflated by monopolistic restriction of output, he receives but a competitive return.

Cost to Taxpayers and Consumers

In the fiscal years from 1932 through 1969, the cost of all agricultural programs to the taxpayer was over $88 billion. The cost has mounted steadily over the years. During the thirties the average annual expenditure was $471 million; during the forties it was $841 million; during the fifties, $2.2 billion;

and during the sixties, $5.4 billion.[5] The cost of the farm programs is equal to nearly half of the net income that farmers receive from all their operations.

It is difficult to estimate the cost of the programs to the consumer. The prices of some products in some years have been raised. And the increases have been pyramided as the products have passed through the hands of wholesalers and retailers. But this effect has been offset, in some measure, by another development. There has been a marked advance, as we have seen, in agricultural productivity. Instead of declining, agricultural output has risen. This development is a consequence of heavy investments in improved technology. And these investments may be attributed, in large part, to the confidence inspired by price supports.

Malallocation of Resources

Prices should not be regarded as ends in themselves but as means to an end. Their proper function is that of effecting economy in the allocation of resources. As demand falls and as costs fall, prices should fall. And this decline should warn producers to divert resources to the production of other goods. When prices are supported at levels unjustified by demand and costs, this does not happen. Producers keep on turning out commodities that are wanted less instead of shifting to the production of those that are wanted more.

This is what tends to happen under the program of price supports. Resources are allocated, not in accordance with the dictates of the market, but in response to the pushes and pulls of politics. The logical consequence is malallocation, in agriculture itself, and in the community as a whole. The accidental price relationships of the historic past are congealed within a rigid mold. The alteration of taste and the improvement of technology are willfully ignored, as if agriculture should be impervious to change. As a result, instead of moving into industry, where their labor would be more productive, farmers are invited to remain in agriculture where it is less so. And instead of providing the consumer with the foods he wants, they are encouraged to keep on producing foods that have to be sold at a loss or given away.

In practice, however, the program has not prevented a shift of labor from agriculture to industry. From 1940 to 1970, the number of farms was cut by half. The number of people on farms was cut by two thirds, from 30 million to 10 million; from 23 percent of the population to 5 percent. This movement was stimulated, of course, by industrial prosperity. Under less favorable circumstances, it would not have occurred.

The program has had a more serious effect upon the allocation of resources within the agricultural economy. Marketing quotas and acreage allotments have

5 / Joint Economic Committee, *Subsidy and Subsidy-like Programs of the U.S. Government* (Washington, D.C.: Government Printing Office, 1960), p. 29, and *Subsidy and Subsidy-Effect Programs of the U.S. Government* (Washington, D.C.: Government Printing Office, 1965), p. 35. Data for later years from Legislative Reference Service, Library of Congress.

retarded shifts in production that would normally have occurred, with changes in opportunities and in ownership, on the individual farm. They have perpetuated cultivation on a scale too small for maximum efficiency. They have frozen the location of production among regions and among farms. The use of an historic base in fixing quotas and allotments has permitted continued cultivation of land where yields are low and prevented expansion on lands where yields are high. So, larger quantities of fertilizer have been needed, and the community has obtained a smaller product at a higher cost.

DIRECT PAYMENTS

Government has augmented the incomes of farmers not only by supporting the prices at which they sell but also by giving them checks drawn on the Treasury. Direct payments have been made in various forms and for various purposes. Under the simplest form of such a system, the farmer sells his products on the market for whatever they will bring. At the end of the year, he calculates the income he would have received if he had sold them at the promised percentage of parity. He subtracts from this the income he actually received. He then sends the government a bill for the difference. And the government, after auditing his accounts, sends him a check.

Direct payments were made under the original Agricultural Adjustment Act, benefit payments to farmers who contracted to reduce their acreage being relied upon to close a large part of the gap between market price and parity price. Such payments have been made since 1934 to producers of sugar beets and cane under a production quota system described in Chapter 32. They have been made since 1936 under the Soil Conservation Act to farmers who agree to adopt soil-building practices. They have been made since 1954 to producers of wool. Direct payments were made under the soil bank program adopted in 1956 to farmers who contracted to take land out of production. They have come to assume increasing importance, during the sixties, in programs designed to enhance the incomes of growers of feed grains, wheat, and cotton.

The Wool Program

The wool program is designed to encourage domestic production of wool at a yearly level of 300 pounds. Under this program, the Secretary of Agriculture fixes an incentive price for wool at a figure that may be as high as 110 percent of parity. The domestic producer sells his clip on the market at the going price, a figure that exceeds the world price by the amount of the tariff. He receives the difference in a check from the Treasury. The tariff on wool has cost the consumer some $25 million a year. The visible subsidy has cost the taxpayer another $35 million. By thus spending $60 million, the American people have made it possible for a small number of sheepmen to remain in an occupation where their efficiency is low and their costs high.

Farm Programs in the Sixties

In 1962, in its programs for feed grains and for wheat, the government began moving away from high price supports toward lower supports, exposing the farmer, in some measure, to the operation of the market. The lower supports were supplemented by direct payments, cushioning the impact of the shift. The payments were made to farmers who diverted acreage from these crops to non-agricultural purposes and to farmers who confined their production to the acres allotted them, being based on the resulting yield. The payments were thus designed to separate income supports from the price mechanism and to provide an incentive to keep production within bounds.

Under the feed grains program, as it operated in 1964, the government supported the price of corn by making loans at the rate of $1.10 per bushel and paid another 15 cents per bushel directly. The program for wheat was more complicated. Here, a multiple price system obtained. The government supported the price of wheat at $1.30 per bushel. This was the price that the farmer got for the part of his crop that was used for feed. For the part that was exported, the farmer got the support price and was also given a certificate to cover the difference between this price and the price in the world market. The exporter was required to purchase these certificates to cover his shipments. The certificates were priced at 25 cents in 1964, giving the farmer $1.55 for the part of his crop that was sold abroad. On the part that went into human consumption at home, the farmer got the support price and was given a certificate to cover the difference between this price and the price paid by the domestic consumer. The miller was required to purchase these certificates to cover the quantity of wheat that he turned into flour. The miller's certificate was priced at 70 cents, giving the farmer $2 for the part of his crop that was consumed domestically. In sum, the farmer got the support price of $1.30 for all of his crop, plus a direct payment of 25 cents for the part that was exported and a direct payment of 70 cents for the part that was consumed at home.

The Food and Agriculture Act of 1965 governed farm programs from the beginning of 1966 to the end of 1970. The law afforded different treatment to the producers of different commodities. It provided no price supports or direct payments to producers of livestock, fruit, and vegetables. It continued price supports for producers of certain basic commodities: rice, tobacco, and peanuts. It continued the subsidies paid to the producers of sugar and wool. It incorporated, in modified form, the dual systems of price supports and direct payments established in 1962 for feed grains and for wheat. It introduced a similar system for cotton.

Under the cotton program, price supports were cut, in 1966, from 30 cents per pound to 21 cents, making it possible for American cotton to compete in world markets. Direct payments were made to growers who retired an eighth of their acres, at the rate of 9½ cents a pound on the part of the crop that was sold at home, with further payments to those who made still further cuts in acreage.

Supports for such major crops as feed grains, wheat, and cotton thus moved closer to the prices fixed by forces operating in the market. The farmer's income was supplemented by direct payments. And these payments were conditioned on the diversion of farmland, in accordance with government acreage allotments, from the production of crops to other purposes.

A new agricultural law, enacted in 1970, continues for another three years the existing program of price supports plus direct payments for basic crops. Under a new provision, known as a "set-aside," it requires farmers to keep some acreage idle in order to qualify for these benefits. But it permits them to use their remaining acres for any crops they may choose to grow and sell without a subsidy. It thus takes another step toward free markets.

Direct Payments: Pro and Con

There is much to be said for direct payments as an alternative to price supports. The cost to the community may be lower. The expenses incurred in storing commodities are avoided; the whole supply moves into consumption; none of it spoils in storage; none of it is destroyed. The method can be used with commodities that are perishable as well as with those that are durable. Prices on the domestic market are lower; the consumer's burden is reduced. Commodities are sold on world markets on the same price basis as at home; the appearance of export dumping is avoided. The subsidy is made visible; it must be debated and voted each year.

But there are also disadvantages. A system that makes it easy to subsidize perishables may make for larger costs. A subsidy paid directly will be fully as powerful as one paid indirectly in stimulating increased output. The consumer's burden may go down; the taxpayer's burden will go up. There will still be surpluses to export; they will still cause international friction; they will still be attributable to artificial stimulation of production by the government. The visibility of the subsidy does not commend it to the farmer. Farmers have taken many payments from the government. But they still feel that prices obtained in the market are earned, even though the market has been rigged. It offends their pride to be offered a subsidy—in any form that can be recognized. Moreover, when subsidies are brought into the open, there is danger that they will be cut off.

In 1969, direct payments to three million farmers amounted to $3.5 billion. There were 353 farmers each of whom received $100,000 or more. There was one cotton grower who received checks from the Treasury amounting to $3.3 million; another who received $4.4 million. Such a largess, bestowed at his expense, strikes the taxpayer as being scandalous and he demands that it be curtailed. There were moves in Congress in 1968 and 1969 to limit direct payments to $20,000 per farmer per crop, but they failed to pass. In 1970, Congress finally established a limit of $55,000. Such a ceiling may invite evasion or avoidance. Farmers may split their farms or diversify their crops in order to qualify for multiple payments. They may drop out of the program and expand their output. Direct payments thus present the government with a dilemma. If they are large enough to be effective in controlling output, they invite political attack. If they are small enough to be tolerated, they are likely to be ineffective.

The cost of direct payments to the government, in any case, will be greater than that of price supports. And as production grows, the cost will increase. Direct payments will therefore be more likely than price supports to lead to the imposition of mandatory production controls.

Chapter 32

COMPULSORY CARTELS

In industries where producers are numerous and well organized, pressures are frequently brought to bear on government to adopt measures designed to lessen competition. In most cases, as we saw in Chapters 28 and 29, the measures adopted have merely freed the industries concerned from laws that had forbidden them to impose their own restraints. There are cases, however, in which restraints on competition, developed by an industry, are given legal status and enforced for it by government. Some of these take the form of cartels with whose restrictions all the members of an industry are compelled by law to comply. It is with such arrangements that the present chapter is concerned.

THE BACKGROUND OF CARTELIZATION

A cartel is an association of independent enterprises in the same or similar branches of industry, formed for the purpose of increasing the profits of its members by subjecting their competitive activities to some form of common control. The members of such an association remain under separate ownership, retaining their freedom of action with respect to matters which are not included, and surrendering it only in respect to matters which are included, within the scope of their agreement. The distinguishing characteristic of the cartel is the fact that this agreement invariably requires the substitution of common policies for independent policies affecting the determination of production and price.

Types of Cartels

The principal types of cartels, differentiated according to the methods which they employ, may be outlined as follows:

1. Associations that attempt to control the conditions surrounding a sale:
    a) Standardization cartels, engaged in the simplification and standardization of products.
    b) Term-fixing cartels, devoted to the regulation of such matters as conditions of delivery, time of payment, discounts, options, free

deals, return privileges, and quality guaranties and guaranties against price declines.

2. Associations that undertake to fix prices:

   a) Trademark cartels that unite the producers of branded goods in boycotts directed against distributors who undercut the stated resale price.

   b) Calculation cartels that promote the adoption of common methods of cost accounting, common estimates of cost, and common margins of profit.

   c) Minimum-price and uniform-price cartels that circulate lists of prices, hold meetings for the discussion of prices, set up committees to issue detailed schedules of prices, and police their members to enforce adherence to such prices.

3. Associations that undertake to allocate among their members particular productive activities, sales territories, and customers:

   a) Specialization cartels that assign to certain members the exclusive right to produce certain varieties of an industry's products.

   b) Zone cartels that assign to certain members the exclusive right to sell in certain markets.

   c) Customer-preservation cartels that reserve for each member the exclusive right to sell to his former customers.

   d) Order-allocation cartels that decide in the case of each submission of bids which member's bid shall be lowest.

4. Associations that undertake to award each member a fixed share of the business:

   a) Plant-restriction cartels that limit the number of hours during which plants may be operated, limit the number of machines that may be employed, and prohibit the installation of new machines.

   b) Fixed-production-share cartels and fixed-marketing-share cartels that assign quotas to each of their members and impose, upon those who produce or sell more than their quotas permit, fines whose payment is guaranteed by previous deposits.

   c) Production-equalization cartels and marketing-equalization cartels that assign production or marketing quotas and either operate equalization pools, making collections from those who exceed their quotas and payments to those who fail to attain them, or readjust quotas in succeeding periods, reducing the shares of those who exceed them and increasing the shares of those who keep within them.

   d) Profit-sharing cartels that operate profit pools, collecting part or all of their members' profits and redistributing them upon some predetermined basis.

   e) Syndicates that employ common agencies either to negotiate sales for their members and allocate orders among them or to distribute part or all of their output, fixing terms and prices, assigning quotas, and dividing profits.

The methods employed by a cartel may place it within more than one of these categories. Cartels of all types attempt, for instance, to regulate the terms of sale. But few cartels stop here; the tendency has been to move on from those forms of control that are simple and mild to those that are complex and stringent.

Enforcement of Restraints

If a cartel succeeds in restricting output and raising prices, some of its members may be tempted to increase their earnings by exceeding their quotas or by undercutting the prices that are set. They may secretly violate the terms of the agreement or they may openly withdraw from membership. If this happens, on any scale, the established prices can no longer be maintained. If a cartel succeeds in enlarging the profits of its members, new firms will enter the field. If they are excluded from membership in the cartel, they can undercut its price. If they are admitted, the output allowed will have to be divided among more producers, each of them receiving a smaller share. Prices may be kept high, but profits will decline. To prevent these things from happening, some means of enforcement must be found.

Cartel restrictions are usually enforced by persuasion backed by various forms of economic pressure. A cartel may be in a position to discipline its members by revoking licenses granted under patents which it holds in a common pool, by imposing fines against money which it holds on deposit, or by withholding payments from equalization pools, profit pools, sales receipts, or other funds which it controls. It may be able to compel outsiders to become members or even drive them out of business by offering loyalty discounts to customers who do not deal with them, by boycotting suppliers who sell to them and customers who buy from them, or by making exclusive contracts with suppliers and with customers which cut them off from access to materials and supplies. If private enforcement, employing such methods, does not suffice, a cartel will seek to have its system of restrictions enforced by the state.

Cartels Abroad

In most industrial countries, outside of the United States, cartels have never been illegal. As a result, by the outbreak of World War II, this form of organization had come to dominate their industry and trade. Cartelization enjoyed its longest history and reached its highest development in prewar Germany. Dating from the 1870's, the movement advanced through successive stages with the approval of successive governments until practically every form of business activity that lent itself to cartelization, from the extractive industries, through heavy and light manufactures, transportation, and construction, to the wholesale and retail trades, was organized into one or more cartels. In France, after the eighties, business was brought together in *comptoirs,* which functioned variously as joint purchasing offices, common export agencies, zone cartels, quota cartels, and selling syndicates. In Belgium, likewise, cartelization dated from the end of the 19th century. Elsewhere in Europe, the movement did not assume extensive proportions until after World War I. In Italy, as in Germany, during the thirties the cartel structure served as an instrument in carrying out the economic policies of the totalitarian state. In Japan, where industrialism had been imposed upon a feudal society, the control of industry was in the hands of a few great families. In Great Britain, the policy of freedom of trade long impeded the progress of cartelization by compelling British businessmen to meet the competition of foreigners. The abandonment of that policy, in the Great Depression of the thirties, provoked a rapid transition to a predominantly cartelized economy. By the end of the decade, complete cartels fixing prices, limiting output, assigning quotas, operating equalization pools, and imposing fines against penalty deposits, controlled the cement, coal, and iron and steel industries, and agreements governing prices, capacity, and output were found in many other fields.

After World War II, there was a marked shift in policy. At the end of the war, the victorious Allies undertook, with indifferent success, to decartelize the economies of Germany and Japan. The countries of Western Europe experienced a rapid recovery, ushering in a long period of prosperity. Some of their leaders came to see in the cartel restrictions that had characterized the prewar depression a barrier to the expansion of international trade, a handicap to increasing productivity, and thus a threat to their continued growth. As a result, laws were enacted that brought cartel activities under a measure of public control. Such laws had been adopted by 20 countries in Western Europe by the end of 1964, and provisions for the regulation of cartels had been written into the treaties establishing the European Coal and Steel Community and the European Economic Community. The laws differ in method and in effectiveness. Few of them forbid cartel restrictions. All of them seek to insure that such restrictions will not be unduly harmful to the public interest. They aim, not to keep prices free, but to keep them fair. Under various laws, cartel agreements are made public by requiring that they be registered, restrictions contrary to public policy are made unenforceable through private suit, or a public agency is empowered to order that they be deleted or modified. Under each of these laws, the government's approach to the problem of cartel restraints is tentative. Under none of them has it taken on the character of a crusade. There are still cartels in Western Europe, and they still agree on terms of sale, fix prices, rig bids, limit productive capacity, allocate markets and customers, assign quotas, and enforce these restraints by giving loyalty discounts, entering into exclusive contracts, and imposing collective boycotts. But it is more important to recognize that cartel agreements today are fewer in number and less restrictive in character than was the case before World War II.[1]

Cartels in the United States

Associations of independent business enterprises in the United States are never called cartels. They are known, instead, as trade associations. But the

1 / Corwin D. Edwards, *Control of Cartels and Monopolies* (Dobbs Ferry, N.Y.: Oceana Publications, Inc., 1967).

activities of some of these associations have closely paralleled those of European cartels. When they have confined themselves to mutually beneficial activities that have not restrained competition, trade associations have remained within the law. But where they have gone on to fix prices, restrict output, or share markets, they have run afoul of antitrust. It was only from 1933 to 1935, under the National Recovery Administration, that such restrictions were generally approved. Then, under the so-called codes of fair competition, American industry was effectively cartelized. (The activities of trade associations were discussed in Chapter 4, their status under the antitrust laws in Chapter 6, their exemption from antitrust under NRA in Chapter 28.) For industry in general, this experience was terminated by a unanimous decision of the Supreme Court. But for particular industries, cartels were reestablished under new laws.

One such case was that of bituminous coal. Here, a sick industry was to be made well by fixing minimum prices and forcing producers to cooperate in observing them by imposing a punitive tax on those who failed to do so. An attempt to establish such prices under a law enacted in 1935 was aborted when the law was held to be unconstitutional. A second attempt, under a law passed in 1937, involved the establishment of prices by a government commission on the basis of proposals made by district boards elected by the coal operators. This was done with scientific precision and with meticulous regard for the requirements of due process. The commission determined the weighted average cost of producing coal in each of 23 producing districts and in each of 10 minimum price areas, and considered producer price proposals based upon these costs. It prepared an elaborate classification of kinds, grades, and sizes of coal and made a painstaking study of the sources of every type of coal that was sold in each of the country's market areas. It then coordinated the proposed prices where coal produced in different districts competed for sale in common market areas. At each step in the process, it gave due notice, held preliminary hearings, issued findings of fact and formal determinations, and then held final hearings. In this way, it established a consistent schedule of minimum prices for every type of coal produced in every region in the United States and sold in every market in every season for every type of use—about 400,000 separate prices in all. This work took three years; it was completed in 1940. By then, the world was at war. The demand for coal was growing and its price was rising. The schedule of prices, prepared at such great pains, was no longer needed to keep prices from going down. But it was very useful in keeping prices from going up. It was used for this purpose by the Office of Price Administration throughout the war. And this, in fact, was the only use it ever had. The price-fixing law was allowed to expire in 1943.

Three other cases of postwar cartelization survive. They are found in the production of petroleum, in the production of sugar, and in the marketing of agricultural commodities produced within limited geographic areas, such as fruits, nuts, and vegetables, or sold within limited markets, such as milk. Here, competition in production or in price has been, or may be, forbidden and the restrictions imposed are enforced by government itself. And here, though it calls them by different names, the United States embraces compulsory cartels.

PETROLEUM PRORATIONING

In the operation of pipelines and refineries, the oil industry has often revealed the characteristics of monopoly. But in the production of crude petroleum, it has been competitive. The major companies normally account for half of the supply, but the number of independent producers runs into the thousands, known reserves are substantial, improvements in mining are enlarging recovery, and exploration is constantly going on. When a new field has been opened, competitive exploitation has had two effects. First, it has resulted in serious waste. Second, it has operated to expand the output of crude oil and to depress its price. Public control has thus been sought not only by conservationists interested in preventing waste but also by producers interested in maintaining price.

When oil producers first experienced a decline of prices resulting from the opening of large new fields, they sought to protect their incomes by entering into voluntary agreements for the control of output. But such agreements tended to break down as outsiders kept on producing and insiders either withdrew or failed to keep their word. Not only were the agreements unenforceable but they might be held to violate the Sherman Act. The industry, therefore, undertook to legalize the restrictions and to enforce them by enlisting the coercive power of government. The result has been a body of state and federal legislation setting up an elaborate system of prorationing. This is producer legislation, designed to serve a producer interest. In the oil states and in the nation, its enactment is a tribute less to the political power of the major oil companies than to that of organizations representing the thousands of independent producers of petroleum.

Development of State Prorationing

The first law designed to maintain the price of oil by curtailing production was enacted in Oklahoma in 1915. The law forbade "economic waste" as well as physical waste, and defined it as production in excess of "reasonable market demands." It authorized the state's Corporation Commission to determine allowable output and to prorate it among well owners in proportion to the potential capacity of their wells. The law was enacted to reduce an oversupply of oil. But the growth of demand in World War I did away with the surplus, and the plan was not put into effect. The law is significant, however, as the one that set the pattern for prorationing.

With the coming of depression in the thirties, the demand for oil declined. This experience, in itself, was unfamiliar to the industry. At the same time, moreover, lush new fields were brought into production. Output in east Texas jumped from nothing in 1930 to more than a million barrels a day in 1931, an amount exceeding the total output of Oklahoma or California. Prices plummeted: the average price of Mid-Continent crude (36° gravity) fell from $1.229 a barrel at the beginning of 1930 to $0.239 in the summer of 1931, sales being made, in some cases, for less than a dime. Under a law passed in 1919, the Texas Railroad Commission had the authority to reduce physical waste but not to control economic waste. But something had to be done. Acting without waiting for Congressional approval, the governors of Oklahoma, Kansas, and Texas made a compact to restrict production, and set up an advisory committee to determine the output that each of their states was to be allowed. In Oklahoma, the proration law was resurrected and the Corporation Commission put to work dividing the state's allotment among its wells. In Texas, also, though legal authority was wanting, the Railroad Commission began prorationing. The orders issued by these bodies were resisted. In both states, they were enforced by declaring martial law. In 1932, the Supreme Court declared this measure to be invalid.[2] But it upheld the Oklahoma statute on the assumption that prorationing was a method of conservation, thus coming within the power of the state.[3] Texas amended its earlier law to authorize prorationing. And within a few years, most of the other oil-producing states had fallen into line.

The typical proration law prohibits waste, defines it to include not only physical but also economic waste, defines the latter as production in excess of "reasonable market demand," and empowers a state commission to restrict output and apportion that allowed among fields and among producers in a pool. The only important oil state to lack such a statute has been California. And here, a similar program has been administered by a voluntary committee of oil producers.

State action, taken by itself, has two serious weaknesses. It provides no method for determining the size of the total market or the shares to be allotted to individual states. And it affords no means of compelling the states to keep within their shares. A single state, if its output were substantial, could destroy the program by refusing to cooperate. To complete the structure of control, and to insure its effectiveness, the oil producers therefore turned for help to the federal government.

Development of Federal Regulation

Federal action to control the output of petroleum was first proposed by an Oil Conservation Board set up, in 1924, by President Coolidge. In 1933, this lead was followed under the NIRA. The program adopted for the oil industry imposed controls at every stage of its operations: production, refining, and marketing. To regulate supplies, limitations were placed on imports, on withdrawals from storage, and on the output of crude. The industry's code provided

2 / *Sterling* v. *Constantin*, 287 U.S. 378.

3 / *Champlin Refining Co.* v. *Corporation Commission of Oklahoma*, 286 U.S. 210 (1932).

for periodic determination by a federal agency (the Bureau of Mines) of the amounts required to balance consumer demand, for allocation of these amounts among the producing states, and for prorationing among pools and wells by state authorities. And where the states should fail to limit output, it authorized the federal government to act.

Unlike the other codes, this one was not turned over for administration to the industry. Nor was it entrusted to the NRA. Instead, the code was placed under Harold L. Ickes, then Secretary of the Interior, who served as Petroleum Administrator, and was managed by officials of his department, with a committee of oil producers serving in an advisory capacity. In this case, the abuses experienced in many other industries did not appear. But the code did provide the oil producers with the mechanism they required to establish a nationwide system of production control.

The Recovery Act itself did more than this. In Section 9c, it empowered the President to prohibit interstate shipments of petroleum that had been produced in violation of state laws. "Hot oil," turned out in excess of state quotas, was to be excluded from interstate commerce, and restriction of output was thus to be enforced. In 1933, the President required that oil offered for shipment be covered by affidavits in which the sellers swore that it had been produced within their quotas. In 1934, when this system had broken down, he set up a Federal Tender Board to issue certificates of clearance that had to be shown before petroleum or its products were permitted to move across state lines. This system worked. But in January, 1935, the Supreme Court found Section 9c to be unconstitutional, on the ground that it involved an invalid delegation of power, since the authority conferred on the President was not accompanied by standards adequate to govern its use.[4] In the next month, Congress restored the executive's power to prohibit interstate shipments in excess of state quotas by passing the Connally Hot Oil Act. The new law contained procedural safeguards and was upheld by a Circuit Court of Appeals in 1936.[5] Unquestioned before the Supreme Court, its constitutionality has since been assumed.

In May, 1935, the Schechter decision destroyed the petroleum code along with the codes administered by NRA. But the nationwide system of controlling production survived. The Bureau of Mines continued to make its estimates of demand. And the power to regulate interstate shipments was continued under the Connally Act.

The Present Pattern of Control

Responsibility for control of the production of crude petroleum is taken by the governments of the oil-producing states. The procedure followed by the regulatory agency in such a state is this: (1) It determines total output for the state by forecasting total demand at the prevailing price, using the estimates

---

4 / *Panama Refining Co.* v. *Ryan*, 293 U.S. 388.

5 / *Griswold* v. *President of the United States*, 82 F. 2d 922.

made by the Bureau of Mines and such other data as it may choose. (2) It subtracts from this total the probable output of wells that are exempted from control: wells producing small quantities, those producing on artificial lift, those in secondary recovery, etc. (3) It divides the remainder of the state's allowable output, in accordance with the provisions of an allocation formula, among the remaining wells, determining the output allowed each pool by multiplying that allowed per well by the number of wells in the pool. (4) At the middle of each month, it issues an order, fixing the allowable output for the coming month. Formerly, Texas set its quotas in terms of the number of days per month in which wells were permitted to produce. This proved, however, to be a clumsy method of control and, in 1963, Texas joined the other states in fixing its quotas as a percentage of the total output allowed. Following this procedure, in June, 1966, prorated wells were producing at 34 percent of capacity in Texas, at 35 percent in Louisiana, and at 38 percent in Oklahoma.

In this operation, the Texas Railroad Commission occupies a position of peculiar importance. Texas is the largest domestic producer of crude petroleum. The large buyers regard Texas as their residual source of supply. The figure at which this marginal output changes hands becomes the prevailing price. The Railroad Commission permits the state's producers to turn out just enough to keep this price at the highest level that consumers—and the federal government— will tolerate. In doing so, it requires these producers to assume the cost of sales foregone and confers a benefit on producers in other states. By thus serving as a balance wheel, Texas insures the stability of the prorationing system as a whole.[6]

Control by the states is aided by the federal government. The Bureau of Mines makes its monthly forecasts of consumer demands for gasoline, fuel oil, and other petroleum products, translates these forecasts into an estimate of the demand for crude, and divides this total into separate estimates for the producing states. It then transmits its estimates to the regulatory agencies of the states. The Bureau's forecast of total demand is an estimate of the quantity that will be bought at the prevailing price. It does not show how much less would be bought if the price were raised or how much more would be bought if it were reduced. It assumes the legitimacy of price fixing, accepting without question the proposition that price should be taken as given and supply adjusted to demand. The estimates for the several states, though presented as estimates of demand, are really nothing of the sort, since there is no such thing as a demand for oil produced in a particular state. They are suggested quotas, based on past output or present capacity.

The prorationing program would break down, of course, if the states did not compel producers to keep within their quotas. Here, the federal government stands ready to aid in enforcing state restraints by preventing interstate shipments in excess of state quotas. In practice, however, the states have succeeded in bringing production under control and the exercise of federal authority is not required.

6 / James E. Jensen, "Texas: Balance Wheel in Control of Crude Oil Supply," *Land Economics* XLI (1965), pp. 271-75.

Methods of Quota Allocation

The economic effects of prorationing depend upon the principles of quota allocation that are employed. A possible standard to govern allocation is provided by the concept of the Maximum Efficient Rate (MER) of production. This is a rate that involves no economic waste, permitting no loss of output whose value would be greater than the cost of avoiding the loss. It treats a pool as a unit, spacing and operating wells so as to make the greatest possible use of natural drives to bring oil to the surface. The power of these drives falls as output rises. If production is held below the MER, output will be postponed, but there will be no economic loss. But if it is allowed to exceed the MER, there will be avoidable underground waste through loss of ultimate recovery.

In practice, the allocation of quotas bears no relation to any scientific determination of the MER. It is motivated by considerations not of efficiency but of equity. Owners of property rights on the surface are numerous and politically powerful. The allocating authorities seek to assure to each of them his fair share of the wealth in the pool below.

The individual well rather than the whole pool is taken as the unit for prorationing. A quota is allowed for every well. Determination of these quotas on a basis that is fair to every property owner is difficult. First, quotas may be fixed on a flat basis per well. But this is unfair unless the wells in a field are evenly spaced and pressure throughout the reservoir is uniform. It rewards the owner who has drilled a large number of wells and penalizes the one who has not. And it requires that pressure be kept under one tract to drive up oil under another. Second, quotas may be based on the potential output of each well, and the potential measured by running at full capacity. This gives larger quotas on tracts where pressure is greater. But the process of measurement is wasteful. And this method, like the other, puts a premium on the duplication of wells. The only safeguard against such duplication is found in spacing regulations. In Oklahoma, since 1959, no more than one well is permitted on 40 acres and surface owners within such an area may be compelled to pool their interests in its yield. In Texas, however, three fourths of the wells are spaced on a 20-acre basis and, under exceptions to the 20-acre rule, wells are drilled on areas as small as city lots. The cost of such excessive drilling in the country as a whole is said to run as high as $1 billion a year. Third, the quota for each well can be made proportionate to the area it drains. Thus, in Louisiana, a larger quota is allowed where a well drains 40 acres rather than 20, or 80 rather than 40. This lessens the incentive to drill additional wells. But it discriminates among owners unless reservoir conditions under tracts of equal size are uniform.

In practice, the basic tool employed in allocation is a depth factor adjusted by an acreage factor. The top allowable for a well varies with its depth modified by its proximity to other wells. The permitted output is a percentage of this figure. The depth factor is without clear justification. It is true that it costs more to drill a deeper well; the factor thus may afford an incentive for such drilling. But deeper pools may not contain more oil, be under stronger pressure, or have larger yields. The depth brackets are arbitrary in character, bearing no relation to MER. The method is administratively convenient. It persists because nobody objects.[7]

Quota allocation, far from being based on technical principles, is complicated by another factor. Due to political pressure, smaller wells may be exempt from control. In Texas, for instance, wells producing less than 20 barrels a day are exempt from orders curtailing output, half of the wells in the state being uncontrolled. This has two important consequences. It again affords producers an incentive to increase their output by drilling unneeded wells. And it favors production from poor high-cost pools over that from rich low-cost pools; production by numerous small concerns over that by the major oil companies. In Texas, in 1960, 43 percent of the output came from wells that were exempt, only 57 percent from wells that were controlled. The exempt wells are permitted to run freely. The controlled wells were allowed to produce, until 1963, on only eight or ten days in any month. Production from flush fields has thus been held down to a third or a fourth of their MER.[8]

Stabilization and Conservation

The objective of prorationing is stabilization, not conservation. The two are not identical. Conservation, it will be remembered, has various meanings: (1) postponement of consumption, (2) complete recovery, and (3) recovery wherever price will cover cost. Stabilization also has different meanings. Nominally, it seeks only to moderate the fluctuations in price. In practice, it seeks a higher level.

Does stabilization contribute to conservation? In some respects, it does. By restricting the supply of oil and raising its price, it may check inferior uses at present and hold larger reserves for superior uses in the future. By keeping stripper wells in operation, it may insure a larger ultimate recovery. By curtailing flush flows, it saves the cost involved in storage above ground. But these advantages could be obtained in other ways. And here, they are offset by the fact that stabilization causes waste. When total output is made to depend upon the quantity that can be sold at a fixed price, it bears no necessary relation to the quantities required for economical recovery. When every well receives a quota and spacing is not subjected to rigorous control, excessive drilling is encouraged, there is needless duplication of investment, and the efficiency of production is impaired. Real conservation requires the unitary operation of a pool. But prorationing differs from unitization. It is concerned with equity among property owners, not with maximum recovery at minimum cost. Insofar as stabilization makes for conservation, it does so incidentally and accidentally. Its real objective is a higher price.

7 / Wallace F. Lovejoy and Paul T. Homan, *Economic Aspects of Oil Conservation Regulation* (Baltimore, Md.: Johns Hopkins Press, 1967), chap. 6.

8 / See James W. McKie and S. L. McDonald, "Petroleum Conservation in Theory and Practice," *Quarterly Journal of Economics*, Vol. LXXVI (1962), pp. 98-121.

THE SUGAR QUOTA SYSTEM

The continental United States has always consumed more sugar than it has produced, importing a major part of its supply, some of it from Hawaii, Puerto Rico, the Virgin Islands, and the Philippines; more of it, until 1960, from Cuba. Sugar is produced at low cost from cane grown in tropical and semitropical regions; at high cost from beets grown in the western states. In the absence of artificial arrangements, the beet sugar industry would disappear. Sugar beets and cane are grown by less than 3 percent of the farmers on the mainland and account for less than 1 percent of farm income. But these farmers are located in 19 states and influence the votes of 38 Senators. For many years, they have been sheltered from foreign competition by barriers to imports.

Until the turn of the century, sugar was admitted duty-free from offshore possessions and at a preferential rate 20 percent below the general tariff from Cuba. Then protective duties were imposed, bringing the rate on sugar up to 1 2/3 cents a pound. After World War I, the United States increased its duties, the rate rising to 2½ cents; that on Cuban sugar to 2 cents. In a series of trade agreements concluded between 1934 and 1948, this rate was cut to .5 cents. And with Philippine independence, duties were gradually reimposed on sugar coming from that country. But the tariff is no longer of major significance. The right to sell sugar in the American market has come to be controlled in another way.

The Pattern of Control

The sugar quota system, as it has evolved in laws enacted since 1934, includes six major elements: (1) The Secretary of Agriculture makes an annual estimate of the total quantity of sugar demanded for consumption in the United States. (2) The law divides this quantity between domestic and foreign sources. (3) The domestic share is divided into market quotas on the basis of past sales, being distributed among producing areas, the area quotas between cane and beet producers, the beet quotas among factory districts, and cane and beet quotas, converted into acreage allotments, among individual growers. (4) Cash subsidies are paid to farmers who keep within their allotments. These payments have run around $50 million a year. To be eligible for a subsidy, a farmer must employ no child labor—once common in the beet fields—and observe such minimum wages as the Secretary may require. (5) An excise tax is levied on imports and domestic output to finance the payment of subsidies. (6) Quotas are imposed on refined, as well as raw, sugar, and on that coming not only from foreign countries but also from islands under the American flag. The only purpose of this provision is to obtain support for the scheme from mainland refiners.

The marketing quotas, under this system, depend upon the Secretary's annual estimates of total demand. The law directs him, in making these estimates, to take into account (1) the amount of sugar consumed during the previous year, (2) deficits or surpluses in sugar inventories, (3) changes in population, (4) the level and trend of consumer purchasing power, and (5) the relation between changes, since 1947, in the price of refined sugar and in the general cost of living, with a view to maintaining "prices which will not be excessive to consumers and which will fairly and equitably maintain and protect the domestic sugar industry." These standards are vague enough to leave the Secretary considerable latitude. Hearings are held, at which consumers propose that the figure adopted be large so that the price of sugar may be low and domestic producers propose that the figure be small so that the price may be high. The Secretary presumably then selects a figure that will bring political forces into balance and proclaims it to be the consumption requirement for the coming year. It is assumed, of course, that price and demand are fixed and that supply alone is adjustable.

Determination of National Quotas

Under the law as it was first enacted in 1934, the Secretary of Agriculture was directed to divide the market between foreign and domestic producers by selecting as a base the three years within the period 1925-34 that he deemed to be "most representative." The increased duties in the Hawley-Smoot Tariff Act of 1930 had operated to cut the share of foreign producers in the American market from 54 percent to 30 percent and to increase the share of other off-shore producers and that of domestic producers from 46 percent to 70 percent. The Secretary came to the conclusion that the three years that followed the enactment of the Hawley-Smoot Act were "most representative."

In 1937, the division of the market between foreign and domestic producers was written into the statute. The former were given 29 percent of the market, the Philippines 15 percent, and other insular and domestic producers 56 percent. The law provided further that the latter share should never fall below 3,715,000 tons.

During World War II, the quota system was suspended. Sugar from the Philippines was cut off; its share in the American market fell to virtually nothing. That of Cuba rose to 45 percent. When quotas were reimposed after the war, the shares of domestic producers were again increased, that of the Philippines restored, but to a smaller figure than before, and that of Cuba cut back from its wartime level.

The Act of 1948 again divided the market, now giving domestic areas and the Philippines absolute quotas totaling 5,418,000 tons and providing that requirements in excess of this amount should be divided between Cuba and other countries in the ratio of 96 percent to 4 percent. The foreign producers' share of the market fluctuated with the Secretary's estimates of total requirements. At 7,500,000 tons, Cuba got 28 percent; at 8 million tons she got 31 percent.

Under an amendment adopted in 1956, the basis of allocation was changed again. The basic need for sugar was set at 8,350,000 tons; the fixed quota of domestic producers at 5,424,000 tons. Cuba was given 96 percent of the difference, a fixed quota of 2,806,960 tons. Above the figure of 8,350,000 tons, the domestic areas were allotted 55 percent, Cuba 29.6 percent, and other foreign countries 15.4 percent. Under this formula, Cuba's share of the American market in 1960 was set at 3,119,665 tons, one third of the total national requirement of 9,400,000 tons.

The system worked in many ways to Cuba's advantage. In supplying a third of the American market, she received prices that ran from 2 to 2½ cents a pound above those prevailing elsewhere. This gave her an added income of about $125 million a year. In addition, she retained her tariff advantage of 20 percent, which was worth another $8 million. In sum, she collected $133 million more than she would have received for her sugar on the world market.

In 1960, following the Cuban revolution and the deterioration of Cuban-American relations, imports of sugar from Cuba were barred by President Eisenhower and the Cuban quota divided among other suppliers. In 1962, Congress again revised the method of dividing the market, this time giving absolute quotas to domestic producers and to the Philippines, permitting the distribution of half of Cuba's previous share among other countries, and retaining the other half, amounting to 1,500,000 tons, in a global quota, to be restored to Cuba in the event that diplomatic relations were resumed, and to be available, in the meantime, for additional imports from other suppliers. The law subjected imports from other countries to a fee equal to the difference between the world price of sugar and its price in the United States, thus denying them the bonus that Cuba had formerly enjoyed. The new formula governing allocation, as it was applied in 1964, gave 58 percent of the market to areas producing under the American flag and 42 percent to foreigners.

In 1964, Congress failed to extend the law. The import fee expired. The Secretary of Agriculture, acting under his administrative powers, imposed the quotas. In 1965, however, Congress enacted a new law, allotting shares in the American market for the years through 1971. This measure gave two thirds of the market, then set at a total of 9.7 million tons, to American producers (nearly a third of it to producers of sugar beets) and a third to producers abroad. The law discontinued the reservation made for Cuba and fixed absolute quotas for more than 30 countries. Different allocations were proposed by the Administration and by the Agriculture Committees of the Senate and the House, under pressure from lobbyists representing the consuming countries. Under the allocation finally adopted, two thirds of the foreign quota went to countries of Latin America, nearly a third to the Philippines, and an eighth to countries in Africa and Asia. An effort to capture part of the difference between the foreign and domestic price by reimposing an import fee was defeated, giving the foreign producers a subsidy of more than $200 million a year.

Effects of the Quota System

In its influence on America's relations with other countries, the consequences of the sugar quota system are serious. Division of the import quota among the countries that are allowed to sell in the United States makes inevitably for ill will. Withdrawal of a quota as a means of exerting diplomatic pressure, as was done in Cuba (and for a time in the Dominican Republic) is an act of economic warfare. The enlarged quotas granted to domestic producers and to foreign suppliers since 1960 cannot well be taken away. Cuba, America's most economic and most convenient source of supply, has permanently lost her former place in the American market. Even under the friendliest of governments, the position which she once enjoyed can never be regained.

The economic effects of the system are equally serious. It establishes a rigid cartel. It imposes market quotas and acreage allotments on the farmers without asking their consent. It penalizes production in greater quantities than the allotments may allow. It subsidizes a tiny minority of American farmers, rewarding them for wasting the nation's resources by expanding an uneconomic industry. Since 1934, it has increased the acreage devoted to sugar beets by more than 40 percent and the output of beet sugar by more than 130 percent. The program's benefit to American growers of sugar cane and beets amounts to $200 million a year. Its cost to American taxpayers and consumers runs around $800 million, more than $80 million of this to pay for its administration and to finance the subsidies; more than $700 million in higher prices.

MARKETING AGREEMENTS AND ORDERS

For most agricultural commodities, producers are numerous and scattered. They cannot combine to control the prices of their crops. Government has therefore controlled the prices for them, through the various devices described in Chapter 31. For a few commodities, however, producing areas or markets are limited in size. Here, producers are few enough in number and close enough together to exercise control themselves. In these cases, government has permitted them to do so. Such permission has been given by the laws of many states. It was given by the federal government under the Agricultural Marketing Agreements Act of 1937.

The Act of 1937 empowers the Secretary of Agriculture to enter into marketing agreements and to issue marketing orders. The persons whose activities are regulated by such agreements and orders are the handlers (processors and distributors) of agricultural commodities. The controls imposed thus apply not only to producers' cooperatives that handle their members' products but also to individual proprietors, partnerships, and corporations engaged in manufacturing and marketing. Agreements take the form of contracts between the Secretary and individual handlers; they do not apply to those who do not accept them. But orders are binding on all handlers of a commodity, whether they agree to them or not. Agreements function as voluntary cartels; orders as compulsory cartels. Both are exempt from the provisions of the antitrust laws.

Agreement and Order Procedures

The issuance of agreements and orders proceeds through the following steps: (1) Producers, acting through their cooperatives, agree upon a program and present it to the Secretary of Agriculture. (2) The Secretary holds public hearings, considers the evidence presented pro and con, and prepares an agreement. (3) If the agreement is to be accepted voluntarily, he submits it to the handlers for signature. If compulsion is required, he puts it to a vote. (4) If two thirds of the producers and half of the handlers involved accept it (or three fourths and four fifths, respectively, for California citrus fruits), he issues an order. And with producer approval, he may also issue an order even though the handlers disapprove.

Agreements and orders are used to control the supply and price of special commodities. They have frequently been applied to vegetables, fruits, and nuts and sometimes to products such as hops and honey bees. A proposal to impose an order on the sale of turkeys was voted down by their producers in 1962. The most important commodity covered—always by orders—is milk. At any time, there may be 75 orders in effect for milk and around 40 agreements for all of the other commodities.

In the case of milk, orders are administered by a public official appointed by the Secretary of Agriculture. For the other commodities, agreements are administered by committees elected by growers and handlers of the products concerned. In neither case is any representation accorded to consumers. Enforcement is effected through civil suits for injunctions or triple damages and through criminal prosecutions leading to fines.

Control for Special Crops

Agreements and orders for products other than milk may not fix prices directly. But they may contain trade practice provisions similar to those found in the NRA codes. And they sometimes require that prices be filed and forbid sales below filed prices until after the expiration of a waiting period. The method usually adopted, however, is that of influencing price by controlling supply.

Supply has been controlled in three principal ways: (1) Daily or weekly shipments have been regulated so as to even out the rate at which commodities move to market. This has been done in the case of perishables, such as citrus fruits. Here the whole supply is sold, but sales are regularized to avoid gluts and scarcities. The fluctuation of prices is reduced; their general level is not substantially increased. Producer incomes are stabilized; dealers are assured steadier supplies; consumers are deprived of an opportunity to buy at bargain prices during periods of surplus. (2) The supplies of several commodities have been controlled by regulating their quality so as to prevent the shipment of substandard grades, sizes, and maturities. In this case, rejects are withheld from the market and diverted to inferior uses or destroyed. Producer prices and incomes are likely to be increased, and consumers are clearly denied an opportunity to buy the less expensive grades. (3) For certain more durable commodities, the quantity that can be sold during a season has been fixed and each producer given a quota related to a historic base. Here, surpluses have been diverted to other uses or pooled in storage for future sale. Such arrangements may be successful, in the short run, where a commodity has no unregulated substitutes and where enlargement of its supply takes many years and requires a substantial investment, as is the case with tree crops. These controls raise prices to consumers and, where demand is inelastic, increase the incomes of producers. But in the long run, if they induce an increase in supply, as they have done with nuts, they make for even greater surpluses and lead to demands for even more drastic action, such as the imposition of an embargo on competing imports. Whatever the method used, it is the purpose of the controls to improve the position of the producer at the expense of the consumer. A producer-oriented department runs the program; the consumer has no voice.

MILK MARKET CONTROLS

Dairying is the most important single source of agricultural income. Milk is produced commercially on more than a million farms, most of them in states near urban centers in the East and Middle West. Its supply remains about the same from year to year, depending upon the number of cows and the output per cow. A higher price does not quickly increase the number of cows: three years elapse from the time a cow is bred until her heifer begins to give milk. A lower price does not reduce the number; cows could be slaughtered, but the price of meat is also likely to be low. Changes in price, moreover, have little effect on bovine physiology. The supply of milk fluctuates with the seasons, rising as much as a third above the yearly average in the spring when calves are born and cows are put out on green pasture, and falling as much as a fourth below it in the fall.

The demand for milk has a high degree of income elasticity, rising and falling with prosperity and depression. But it is said to have a low degree of price elasticity, sales falling less than proportionately when prices are increased and rising less than proportionately when prices are reduced. Consumption is fairly steady throughout the year, falling but 5 percent below and rising but 5 percent above the annual average.

Half of all milk is consumed in fluid form. Half is sold to manufacturers who turn it into butter, cheese, and concentrated and powdered products. These two markets differ in their susceptibility to control. Because milk is heavy and bulky in relation to its value, the cost of transport is high. Because it is easily contaminated and affords a medium favorable to the growth of bacteria, city governments require that dairies be inspected and that milk sold in its original form be pasteurized. The region from which a city draws its milk, known as its milkshed, is, therefore, limited in size both by the economic factor of transport cost and by the political factor of inspection requirements. Entry into the business of distributing milk is also limited by the cost of pasteurization facilities. In recent years, with changes in technology, milk has come to move in bulk tank trucks to large bottling and distributing plants, serving wider market areas. But the urban market for fluid milk is still a sheltered one, lending itself to the application of private and public controls. In its manufactured forms, however, milk can be shipped more cheaply, lasts longer, and carries less of a threat to public health. This market for milk is, therefore, a wide one and is less readily subjected to control.

Urban Milk Markets

Most of the milk sold in a typical city is distributed by two or three large concerns. As sellers, the distributors behave as oligopolists. They compete in the duplication of delivery services, in brand names, advertising, and salesmanship. They seldom compete in price. Despite the fact that supply varies widely from season to season, the price of milk remains the same throughout the year. And every company delivering milk to the doorstep charges the same amount.

Where price competition has entered the market, it has come from delivery through stores. Here, a saving of several cents a quart is possible. But since the large distributors have invested heavily in delivery facilities, they have generally sought to check store sales. To this end, they have urged adoption of regulations fixing retail prices, forbidding the sale of milk over the counter at a price lower than that charged for delivery, and discriminating against paper containers, the use of which facilitates its sale through stores.

In buying milk the large distributors appear as oligopsonists. Its sellers are thousands of dairy farms. Unorganized, the farmer would be at a disadvantage in making his sale; organized, he can bargain collectively for better terms. Milk producers have, therefore, established cooperative associations and, through these associations, have entered into negotiations with distributors for the purpose of determining the farmer's price. Such associations now control two thirds of the milk that is offered for sale in all the major markets in the United States.

These associations have served the milk producer in another way. The payments he receives are based upon an f.o.b. price at the city plant, which is subject to deductions for haulage, terminal, and other charges. They depend, also, upon the quality of his milk and the uses to which it is put. Distributors might defraud the farmer by deducting from his payments transportation and other charges in excess of those actually incurred, by understating the quality of his milk, and by misrepresenting the shares going into different types of use. It is the function of the cooperatives to prevent such abuses by inspecting company records and accounts.

Milk Price Structures

For the purpose of fixing the prices to be paid producers, milk is classified according to use. Class I, which brings the highest price, contains milk that is sold fresh for consumption in fluid form. The other classes, which bring less, contain milk that goes through various manufacturing processes before it is consumed. Class I milk would normally bring more than other milk because the transport charges restrict its supply and sanitary precautions add to its cost. But these factors alone do not explain its higher price. Distributors are willing to pay more for Class I milk because they can charge more for it. And they can charge more because demand in the urban market is inelastic, because supply is under their control, and because inspection and pasteurization requirements protect them from the entry of competitors. Distributors cannot pay as much for milk in other classes because the markets where they sell it are highly competitive and they cannot control its price. The structure of milk prices is thus deliberately discriminatory, with markets separated and prices adjusted to variations in the conditions of demand and supply. In theory the farmer receives different prices for different gallons of identical milk, depending upon where they are ultimately sold. In practice he gets a single price, known as a blended price, which is an average of the prices for the different classes weighted by the quantities sold in each class.

The classified price plan is usually supplemented by a pooling arrangement. If a distributor were to sell more of one farmer's milk and less of another's in Class I and were to pay them accordingly, the former would receive a higher and the latter a lower blended price. This is prevented by the establishment of individual handler pools. Under such an arrangement, the blended price is computed by weighting the class prices in proportion to all of the distributor's sales, and the price he pays to every farmer is the same. But another difficulty remains. Different distributors may sell different fractions of their milk in various classes. A farmer may, therefore, get a different blended price from one distributor than his neighbor gets from another one. This is prevented by the establishment of market-wide pools. Here, the blended price is computed by weighting the class prices in proportion to all of the sales in the market, and the price paid by every distributor to every farmer is the same. Standing alone, this arrangement might be unfair as among distributors, since the fractions sold by different distributors in different classes might not be the same. All of them would pay the market average in buying milk, but some of them might get more and some of them less than the market average in selling it. To meet this situation, a market-wide pool is usually accompanied by an equalization pool, with distributors who sell more than the market average in Class I paying in, and those who sell less drawing out. As a result, each distributor not only pays the market average on his purchases but also gets the market average on his sales.

This pattern is further complicated by the fact that farmers are often paid in accordance with the provisions of a "base-rating" or "base-and-surplus" plan. Under such a plan, each farmer is assigned a quota corresponding to his low production during the fall and winter months and is paid throughout the year at the Class I price for "base" milk, produced within his quota, and at a lower price for "surplus" milk, produced in excess of his quota. As a result, the prices paid to different farmers will differ. And this is the purpose of the plan. But the returns realized by different distributors may also differ, since one will pay a higher average price for milk than another if his producers' bases are larger in relation to his Class I sales. Here, again, the problem is solved by setting up an equalization fund, with distributors whose Class I sales exceed their producers' bases paying in and those whose producers' bases exceed their Class I sales drawing out.

The base-and-surplus plan was designed, originally, to reduce seasonal fluctuations in supply by giving farmers an incentive to even out the freshening of their cows. But it has also come to be employed, at times, as a means of restricting and allocating output and excluding new producers from the field. By refusing to revise quotas from year to year, thus compelling farmers who have expanded output to accept a lower price for their additional supply, producers' associations have sometimes checked production and imposed pecuniary penalties on those who sought to obtain a larger share of the market. By refusing to assign quotas to newcomers, thus depressing the prices that can be obtained for months or years, they have sought to monopolize markets, discouraging the entry of competitors.

Public Intervention in Milk Markets

Producers of milk fared better than other farmers in the decade that followed World War I. The break in prices, with depression, was less severe for dairy products than for other agricultural commodities. But producers were dissatisfied. They were also well organized. In state capitals and in Washington their pleas for aid fell on sympathetic ears.

More than half of the states enacted temporary or permanent milk control laws, beginning in 1933. These laws typically established a milk control board, composed of representatives of producers and distributors, and gave it regulatory powers. It was the purpose of these measures, in general, to increase the incomes of producers by underwriting the prices negotiated between producer associations and distributors, by regulating output, and by obstructing entry, and to maintain the margins of distributors, by fixing resale prices and by preventing the development of competing methods of sale. The power of a state government to fix prices for milk was upheld by the Supreme Court of the United States in the Nebbia case in 1934.[9]

Action was also taken by the federal government. Marketing agreements were established, under the first AAA, for 15 markets in 1933. In general, these agreements gave legal effect to collective bargains establishing producer prices, checked output and obstructed entry by adopting the base-and-surplus plan, and enlisted the cooperation of distributors by fixing retail prices and by imposing handicaps on their unorthodox competitors. The base-and-surplus plan was eliminated from the agreements in 1934 and the effort to control retail prices was abandoned. In 1937, rules governing the federal regulation of milk markets were spelled out in the Agricultural Marketing Agreements Act.

Under this law, the federal government can regulate markets when interstate commerce is involved. It can act only by order, and only when two thirds of the producers consent. It cannot limit the size of a milkshed (although local health

9 / *Nebbia* v. *New York,* 291 U.S. 502.

authorities still may do so). Its orders must classify milk according to use and prescribe the method of fixing the price of each class. They may provide either for an individual-handler pool or for a market-wide pool, but in the latter case, they must also provide for the equalization of returns. The prices set in an order must equal parity or, at the discretion of the Secretary of Agriculture, an amount which he deems adequate to insure "a sufficient quantity of pure and wholesome milk." They must also reflect the price of feeds and other economic conditions which affect supply and demand. And they must be in the public interest. These standards are so vague as to leave the Secretary free to adopt any price upon which producers and distributors agree. Enforcement of such prices through federal orders was upheld by the Supreme Court in the Rock Royal case in 1939.[10]

Federal Milk Market Orders

Milk markets are usually under federal orders where cities are located near state borders and where milk is drawn from more than one state. Nearly all of the great urban markets for milk were under federal orders in 1968. Each of the 74 orders then in effect delineated the market area it covered, defined the classes of milk, set forth the price of each class or the formula to be used in computing it, described the manner of pooling, required the presentation of reports on the quantities of milk that were sold for different uses, prescribed the method of payment, and provided for the auditing of distributor records and accounts. Each of the orders provided, further, for the appointment of a market administrator and for the imposition of assessments to cover the costs of administration.

Prices, under such orders, have been fixed in two principal ways: by administrative determinations following public hearings, and by adjustment in accordance with the provisions of a formula. Under the first of these methods, there have been delays in adapting prices to changing conditions, since alterations cannot be made without new hearings, and the hearing procedure is costly, cumbersome, and time consuming. Under the second, adaptation is continuous and automatic, and hearings need be held only to consider the provisions of the formula. But this method also has its difficulties. Factors that are relevant to the price of milk must be agreed upon, and the data they call for must be obtained. The formula may have to be set aside to meet conditions that arise in an emergency, such as a sudden drought. Producers are likely to accept a formula when it puts their prices up; they are less likely to do so when it puts their prices down. In fact, the prices in effect under a third of the market orders in recent years have not been those set by the market administrators but those negotiated, at higher levels, by producers and distributors.

The price of Class I milk in all the major markets is now fixed by formula. In two thirds of the market orders, under the formula that has had the longest and

10 / *U.S.* v. *Rock Royal Cooperative, Inc.,* 307 U.S. 553.

widest use, this price is determined by taking as a base the average price currently paid for milk by manufacturers of dairy products in Minnesota and Wisconsin and adding a differential to cover something more than the extra costs of sanitation, transport, and handling involved in supplying milk for Class I use. In Chicago, in 1966, the price paid for manufacturing milk was $3.20 per cwt; the price paid under this formula for identical milk for fluid consumption was $4.24. The advantage of the formula is that it adjusts the price in the sheltered Class I market to changes in demand and supply by relating it to the price of manufacturing milk. As a result, the Class I price is not maintained at a level that diverts a growing share of milk to other classes, depressing their prices and thus causing the blended price of milk to fall.

After World War II, the competition of margarine drove down the price of butter and hence the price that butter manufacturers would pay for milk. As a result, the formulas that tied the price of Class I milk to that of manufacturing milk lost their popularity. Since that time, a third of the major milk markets have adopted new formulas in which the Class I price has been cut loose from that of manufacturing milk and related to other factors such as the cost of feed, the prices of other agricultural products, the general level of commodity prices, and disposable income per capita. Under such formulas, the Class I price was raised when the share of milk going to other markets contracted and lowered when it expanded, thus keeping it from getting too far out of line. But under none of these formulas was it possible to keep the blended price from falling as the price of manufacturing milk went down.

All of the formulas were modified by adjustments designed to lessen seasonal fluctuations in supply and by premiums for higher quality and for convenience of location. Where milksheds overlapped, moreover, farmers found that differences in the formulas made it advantageous for them to ship first to one market and then to another.

The price of manufacturing milk, to which the Class I price is related in most milk market formulas, does not itself reflect the play of free market forces. For the government supports the price by purchasing, in the form of butter, cheese, and dry milk powder, 3 to 9 percent of the milk produced in the United States, at prices that yield the farmer 75 to 90 percent of parity. It supports the price, too, by imposing quotas on imports of dairy products. The whole structure of fluid milk prices is thus erected on a foundation that is held up by artificial props.

State Milk Controls

The prices paid to milk producers are fixed by public agencies under the laws of 20 states. Such laws are used where the milkshed for a market lies entirely within the boundaries of a single state. They may be used in preference to federal orders where producers or distributors desire to impose restrictions that federal orders do not permit, such as production control and retail price fixing. And they may also be used as a supplement to federal orders. In general, the procedures employed in preparing state milk orders are similar to those adopted under federal controls. In areas not covered by federal orders, the state administrator may not employ a pricing formula. But he is likely to adopt a price that corresponds to those established in nearby federal markets. Prices set by the states have tended to be higher than those set by the federal government. But where a market has operated under both federal and state orders, their provisions have been made consistent and the same person has been appointed as administrator by both governments.

Resale prices are fixed for milk under the laws of 15 states. Sales below cost are forbidden by the laws of 10 other states. Such laws have been demanded by distributors as a condition for their acceptance of the producer prices that federal and state orders may require. In some cases, resale prices have been fixed on the basis of statements made by the distributors or informal inquiries by state authorities. In others, they have been based on studies of the costs of distribution, sometimes being set at levels designed to cover the costs of the least efficient distributors.[11]

Distributors' margins are also protected by regulations that restrain competition. Such regulations have made prices as high for sales across the counter as for home delivery or limited the difference between the two. They have also prohibited sales in large containers, required dealers to charge as much or more per quart when they sold milk in paper containers as when they sold it in bottles, and forbidden or limited discounts for sale in quantity. In Minnesota, a law enacted in 1957 requires wholesale distributors to file their prices and to adhere to the prices they file. It prohibits 17 specific methods by which the distributors might engage in nonprice competition when selling to retailers. And state officials, acting under its provisions, bring distributors and retailers together to obtain agreements eliminating competition from the field. The law, over a period of 10 years, has operated to check the trend toward lower costs in distribution. It has kept high-cost operators in business. It has harmed consumers without observable benefit to producers.[12]

Effects of Milk Controls

The programs of milk control adopted by the federal government and by the states have been designed to maintain the incomes of producers and distributors at the expense of consumers. In accordance with the usual procedure, consumers have been privileged to present statements at public hearings. But these statements, in most cases, have been confined to expressions of the opinion that prices should be low, while those prepared on behalf of producers' associations by accountants and statisticians have been replete with tables, charts, and graphs

11 / U.S. Department of Agriculture, Economic Research Service, Agricultural Economic Report No. 152, *Government's Role in Pricing Fluid Milk in the United States* (Washington, D.C.: Government Printing Office, 1968).

12 / Ronald D. Knutson, "The Economic Consequences of the Minnesota Dairy Industry Unfair Trade Practices Act," *Journal of Law and Economics,* XII (2) (1969), pp. 377-89.

which demonstrate convincingly why prices should be high. The decisions that follow these hearings, moreover, are made by officials who owe the very existence of their agencies and their jobs to the producer pressure groups. Under the circumstance, the hearing accorded to consumers can be little more than a matter of form.

The milk control laws are discriminatory in character. They create two classes of producers: a favored class, selling in urban fluid markets for the Class I price and dumping its surpluses in the market for manufacturing milk, and a disfavored class, selling only for the manufacturing price. Those in the first class get more income for their effort than those in the second.

Federal and state controls doubtless assure the farmer producing under a market order a higher price than he would otherwise obtain for Class I milk. But they may not give him a higher blended price. The high Class I price may encourage production and discourage consumption. Less of the farmer's milk may be sold for fluid use; more of it for manufacturing. The blended price, accordingly, will fall. State controls maintain the margins of distributors and thus make sure that a higher Class I price is reflected in a higher retail price. By checking the introduction of less expensive methods of distribution, they keep the price of milk at a figure higher than that consumers otherwise would pay. The controls, however, have not caused this price to rise more rapidly than those of other foods. As income has grown, the consumption of fluid milk has also grown. The use of canned and powdered milk has increased even more, since the controls force those who use fresh milk to subsidize those who use milk in other forms.

Milk markets cannot be freed of all controls. The farmer sells his milk to oligopsonists. He must, therefore, be permitted to organize and to bargain collectively. In the public interest, moreover, the bargaining process must be supervised by government. In markets under federal orders, the procedure employed in fixing the producer's price is a proper one. The requirement of public hearings is designed to prevent abuses. The use of formulas permits flexibility in administration. The formulas, of course, should not attempt to divorce the price of Class I milk from the underlying forces of supply and demand but should be so devised as to respond to changes as they occur. One thing more is needed: the consumer interest should be represented more effectively. The further measures, adopted under state laws, to protect distributors from competition, preserve their methods of doing business, and maintain their margins, are useless to producers and harmful to consumers. They should be repealed.[13]

13 / Reuben A. Kessell, "Economic Effects of Federal Regulation of Milk Markets," *Journal of Law and Economics,* X (1967), pp. 51-78.

PROMOTION AND
SUBSIDIZATION

Government has subsidized private enterprise, in transport, in industry, and in agriculture, throughout the nation's history. In some cases, it has done so for the purpose of promoting activities deemed socially desirable that otherwise might not have been undertaken. In others, it has done so in response to pressures from groups that were politically powerful. Once granted, subsidies tend to persist. Today, they result in the transfer of many billions of dollars, each year, from the rest of the community to their beneficiaries. In some cases, subsidization is readily justified. In others, its justification is dubious. In all cases, however, it is defended in terms of the contributions, real or imagined, that it makes to the well-being of society as a whole.

FORMS OF SUBSIDIZATION

Some subsidies are direct and visible; others are indirect and hidden. In the former cases, government has made outright gifts: grants of public lands or payments from the treasury. More often, it has given aid in less open ways: by rendering services for which it makes no charge, by selling goods and services for less than they are worth, by buying goods and services for more than they are worth, and by exempting some enterprises from taxes that others must pay. In all of these cases, the cost of the subsidy has been borne, in the end, by the taxpayer. Acting indirectly, government has subsidized enterprise by sheltering it from the full force of competition and by granting it the privilege of uncontrolled monopoly. And here, the cost of the subsidy has been borne by the consumer in a higher price.

Free Services

One of the more important of the many services rendered by government to business is that of providing it with useful information. State and federal governments—particularly the latter—are the principal source of the statistical reports that are used by businessmen in their daily operations. The *Statistical Abstract of the United States,* its annual issue running to more than a thousand pages of fine type, serves as little more than an index to the vast quantities of statistics that are collected, analyzed, and published periodically by the Bureau of the Census and other offices of the Department of Commerce, by the Bureau of Mines, the Bureau of Agricultural Economics, the Bureau of Labor Statistics, the Bureau of Internal Revenue, the Interstate Commerce Commission, the Securities and Exchange Commission, the Federal Reserve System, and many other public agencies. Economic trends are reported regularly by such publications as the *Survey of Current Business,* the *Federal Reserve Bulletin,* and the *Monthly Labor Review.* Special studies, covering many phases of business activity, are listed in each number of the *Monthly Catalogue of Government Documents.* Maps, charts, and other aids to navigation are published by the Coast and Geodetic Survey. Estimates of prospective crops are released by the Crop Reporting Service. And weather forecasts—of great importance not only to agriculture but also to shipping, aviation, and other businesses—are issued daily by the Weather Bureau.

Government also carries on research and releases its findings for commercial use. The Geological Survey and the Bureau of Mines, the Forest Service, and the Fish and Wildlife Service, together with similar agencies in many states, function in effect as laboratories for the mining, lumbering, and fishing industries. The Tennessee Valley Authority has developed new chemical fertilizers and given its formulas to the fertilizer industry. The National Bureau of Standards engages in physical research, conducts tests, and establishes industrial standards when requested to do so by two thirds of the members of a trade.

The federal government has long assisted business in making sales in foreign markets through the efforts of the Department of Commerce at home and those of the consular service abroad. It also promotes foreign investment. American firms with funds invested in other countries may be injured by discriminatory legislation or administrative action that add to their costs, by exchange controls that prevent the transmission of their earnings, or by failure to provide adequate, prompt, and effective compensation in the event of nationalization. To protect them, investment treaties are negotiated with other governments and representations are made through diplomatic channels by the Department of State.

All of these services are promotional in character. They do not seriously affect the allocation of resources or interfere with the regulatory power of competition.

Sales at Low Prices

Goods have frequently been sold by government to business enterprises for less than they were worth. During the 19th century, valuable mining and timberlands were sold for a song. Merchant ships built by the government during the two world wars were subsequently sold to private operators at a fraction of their cost. After World War II, other property that had cost the government $15 billion was sold by the War Assets Administration for $4 billion.[1] In the case of

1 / Joint Economic Committee, *Subsidy and Subsidy-Effect Programs of the U.S. Government* (Washington, D.C.: Government Printing Office, 1965), p. 79.

iron and steel, 116 units costing $750 million went for $260 million, or about 35 cents on the dollar.[2] In disposing of surplus materials, the emphasis was on speed, not price. Airplanes were sold for less than the value of the gasoline left in their tanks, and brand-new machinery, never uncrated, was sold for scrap. Insofar as the prices paid for such goods fell short of actual market values, their purchasers were subsidized.

So, too, with the sale of public services. When government engages in lending, guaranteeing, and insuring operations, the fees it charges frequently fail to cover its total costs, the administration of such programs being financed by the taxpayers. Government has subsidized private forestry, not only by supporting research and education, but also by providing it with fire protection, with planting stock, and with technical assistance for less than cost. Government has subsidized the livestock industries by permitting sheep and cattle to graze in national forests and on other public lands for fees below those charged on private ranges. It has subsidized advertisers and the publishers of newspapers and magazines by delivering their products at a loss. In 1970, for instance, the subsidy involved was more than $545 million. In the postman's bag are pounds of periodicals that denounce the government for paying subsidies, but not (it may be assumed) for subsidizing publishers.

Purchases at High Prices

Government also subsidizes business by buying goods and paying more for them than they are worth. Under the Buy American Act of 1933, procurement officers must purchase goods produced in the United States unless their price exceeds the price of goods produced abroad by more than a specified percentage. Contracts for war production have usually been let, under the pressure of emergency requirements, not through competitive bidding, but on the basis of cost-plus-a-fixed-fee or cost-plus-a-percentage-of-cost. In both cases, profits may have been increased by padding costs, and in the latter, in particular, the incentive to do so was obviously strong. Under many contracts, high prices have been reduced through renegotiation. Wartime profits, in general, have been subject to the excess profits tax. But it is still likely that the government, on a major part of its procurement, has paid substantially more than a competitive price. At the end of World War II, moreover, the emphasis in settling terminated contracts was not on economy but on speed. As a result, the settlements were generous, a few of them involving fraud, but more providing a substantial subsidy.

To insure national security, the government has undertaken to build up stockpiles of strategic materials produced abroad to which this country might be denied access in time of war. In 1965, these stockpiles consisted of 76 commodities, ranging from asbestos to zirconium and including goose feathers

2 / *Iron and Steel Plants, Disposal Status as of December 31, 1950* (Washington, D.C.: General Services Administration, 1951).

and castor oil, many of them bought in quantities well in excess of probable needs. Holdings acquired at a cost of $8.5 billion were then valued at $7.8 billion, representing a paper loss of $700 million.[3]

During the fifties, under pressure from mining interests, purchases of lead and zinc were shifted from foreign to domestic producers, diverting the stockpiling program from its original purpose to that of subsidizing domestic mining companies. From 1954 to 1958, the government spent $200 million for unneeded lead and zinc, bringing the stockpile of lead to 455 percent and that of zinc to 887 percent of estimated requirements. In 1961, Congress provided for an outright subsidy under which lead producers were paid 75 percent of the difference between the market price of 11 cents a pound and a target price of 14½ cents, and zinc producers were paid 55 percent of the difference between the market price of 11½ cents and a target price of 14½ cents, payments to a single producer being limited to an output set at 1,500 tons in 1961 and declining to 600 tons in 1965.

In the case of one product, the government not only paid an excessive price but was compelled, for many years, to buy supplies for which it had no need. From 1878 to 1903, under the Bland-Allison Act and the Sherman Silver Purchase Act, the Treasury was required to buy specific quantities of silver each month, and the metal thus acquired was added to the stock of money. In 1933, under the Thomas Amendment to the Agricultural Adjustment Act, purchases again were authorized; and in 1934, Congress directed that they be continued until silver should provide a third of the metal backing for the currency. In 1932, the market price of silver had stood at 24.5 cents per ounce. In 1934, the Treasury's buying price was set at 50 cents; in 1939 at 71.11 cents; and in 1946 at 90.5 cents. As a result, production of the metal was tripled. For many years, the whole domestic output was diverted to the government, the silver used by industry being imported at lower prices from abroad. The metal was dug from the ground in the mountain states only to be buried again at West Point, New York. There, it was utterly useless, contributing nothing to the value of the currency. The sums paid for it, running into the billions, represented nothing but a subsidy to the mining industry.

After the mid-fifties, the demand for silver for industrial uses increased. The metal came to be in short supply; its price rose. In 1956 and again in 1961, the government checked this increase by making sales from its accumulated stock. In 1963, Congress formally brought the silver purchase program to an end. It authorized the government to retire the part of its currency that consisted of Silver Certificates (largely in the form of one-dollar bills, exchangeable for silver on demand) and to replace them with Federal Reserve Notes. In 1965, it authorized the substitution of other metals for silver in minting dimes and quarters and reduction of the silver content of half dollars. Now, after 30 years of governmental price support, the producers of silver were on their own.

3 / *New York Times*, January 10, 1965.

Reduction of Taxes

Reduction of taxes below the figures other enterprises are required to pay has been employed by governments as a means of subsidizing favored companies or industries. Exemption from property and business taxes for 5, 10, or 15 years has been used by state and local governments to attract new industries. Several states have authorized their subdivisions to issue tax-exempt securities to build and equip factories for rental to new concerns, which can then deduct their rents from income in computing the federal corporate income tax. Reduction of liability under the corporate income tax has also been used by the federal government to stimulate construction of new industrial capacity and to encourage mining operations.

Corporations constructing facilities deemed essential to production for national defense have been granted permission, during both world wars and again under the Revenue Act of 1950, to deduct a fifth of the cost of such facilities from taxable income each year for five years, instead of making smaller deductions throughout their lifetime, as would otherwise have been required. Until 1954, an equal share of the depreciation had to be written off each year. Thereafter, more rapid write-offs were permitted in earlier years. In 1962, in order to promote business recovery, the privilege was extended to industries in general. If tax rates continued high, a corporation that adopted this practice could postpone tax payments but not escape them, since it would be unable to write off the cost of new facilities in their sixth and later years. In effect, however, it would have been granted an interest-free loan by the government. If tax rates fell, the corporation's gain would be greater, since it would minimize its tax in years when rates were high, postponing it to years when rates were low. In either case, accelerated amortization operated to provide a subsidy.

The favorite of the tax law is the mining industry. Not only may mining companies deduct the costs of exploration and development—successful and unsuccessful, tangible and intangible—as current expenses in computing taxable income. They are also given the option of making arbitrary deductions, up to half of net income, for depletion of wasting assets (at rates that have run from 5 percent of gross income for coal, sand, gravel, stone, and oyster shells through 15 percent for the metals and 23 percent for sulfur and bauxite to 27½ percent— now 22 percent—for oil and gas) instead of deducting the depletion that actually occurs. The depletion allowance, moreover, may be deducted year after year, even though every dollar invested in the property has long since been written off. The arrangement has deprived the Treasury of revenue running to $1.5 billion a year.

Exclusion of Competitors

Longest in duration and broadest in scope among the means of subsidizing industries in the United States is the tariff. When foreign competitors are excluded from the domestic market, higher prices can be charged and income thus transferred from the consumer to the domestic producer. Where such restrictions are really needed to enable an industry to survive, the subsidy does not enrich the protected companies but serves only to divert resources from more productive to less productive employments. Where they are not needed, they contribute unnecessarily to the profits of the favored firms. Tariffs do appear to be needed by such minor industries as china, pottery, glassware, cutlery, lace, and leather goods. They do not appear to be needed by such major industries as iron and steel, automobiles, machinery, electrical equipment, chemicals, and rubber goods.

Government has also aided favored enterprises by forbidding domestic rivals to enter the field. It has denied entry, as we have seen, to trucking companies and to airlines, and has delayed the entry of Pay TV and Cable TV. It has thus maintained the charges and protected the earnings of established carriers. Out-of-state competitors are sometimes excluded from regional markets, and out-of-town competitors from local markets by restrictive statutes or ordinances. In magnitude, these measures have less serious consequences than does the tariff. In principle, however, they are the same.

SUBSIDIES TO TRANSPORT

Government has made its greatest promotional effort in the field of transport. It contributed heavily to the construction of railways and has provided highways, waterways, and airways at public expense. It has paid cash subsidies to merchant shipping and to the airlines. In fact, the only form of transport it has not aided, in one way or another, is that provided by the pipelines.

Subsidies to Railroads

American railroads, during the 19th century, were the recipients of grants amounting to 183 million acres of public lands, some of them valuable mining and timber properties. They were also aided by cash contributions, by tax exemptions, and by governmental subscriptions to their securities. Altogether, the aid extended to railroads by federal, state, and local governments is said to have amounted to $1,282 million. As a result, the railroad network was extended and the West opened to development more rapidly than it would have been by private enterprise alone. Until 1946, the land-grant railroads were required to carry government traffic at preferential rates. By that time, the rate reductions made by these roads and by their competitors had amounted to more than $1,000 million, about four fifths of the sums they had derived from the original grants.

In recent years, while making money by hauling freight, the railroads have lost money on their passenger business. The quality of this service has steadily declined; much of it has been discontinued. In 1956, Congress passed a High Speed Ground Transportation Act under which the government was to finance experimentation with modern passenger transport in the corridor between Boston and Washington. There was some improvement in service, but the possibilities were far from being realized. The railroads then proposed that nearly all intercity passenger services be abandoned. In 1970, Congress responded by enacting a law that would set up a quasi-public corporation to take over the passenger business and to operate the essential passenger services. The enterprise would be supported, in part, by federal loans and grants. With this program under way, the railroads would again be subsidized.

Subsidies to Highway Transport

The ways of carriers other than railroads and pipelines are provided by government. From 1940 to 1964, the federal government spent more than $50 billion on highways, waterways, and airways, more than half of it on highways. For 1971, the federal expenditure on highways, matched in part by the states, reached $4.5 billion. In the beginning, all motor traffic was subsidized. But for many years the taxes imposed on highway users have sufficed to cover highway costs. The burden, however, has been distributed unequally. Passenger cars were long required to pay more and trucks less than their proper share of these costs. As a result, the trucking industry was subsidized.

In 1956, the federal government adopted the policy of requiring each group of highway users to make payments to cover its share of highway costs. To this end, it has imposed a variety of taxes on commercial vehicles, tires and tubes, and motor fuels. But these taxes still fall less heavily on heavy tractor-trailer combinations than on light trucks and on diesel-powered than on gasoline-powered trucks. When this situation is rectified, subsidization of the trucking business will be brought to an end.

Subsidies to Shipping

Coastwise and intercoastal shipping has been reserved, since the early days of the republic, to vessels flying the American flag. Such protection has also been afforded, since the turn of the century, to trade with noncontiguous possessions of the United States. Exclusion of competitors thus operates, indirectly, to subsidize American concerns.

Transoceanic shipping has been subsidized in many different ways. First, it has been granted cargo preferences. In 1904, Congress required that goods purchased for the Army or Navy be carried in American vessels. In 1934, it expressed its desire that exports financed by government loans be carried in such vessels. And in 1954, it required that at least half of the tonnage of all goods procured by the government or supplied by it, through loans or grants, to other governments be transported under the American flag. American shipping companies, protected from foreign competition, have thus obtained a subsidy in the form of higher freights, paid from funds that were nominally appropriated for other purposes, such as the provision of foreign aid. This subsidy has amounted to $100 million a year.

Second, the transoceanic lines have been enabled to acquire ships on terms that have cut their capital costs. Ships that were built for the government have been sold to private operators at a few cents on the dollar. After World War II, 843 ships that had cost $4,400 million were sold for $1,776 million, representing two fifths of their original cost and a fourth to a fifth of their replacement cost.[4] Not only have ships been provided at bargain prices; the government gives generous trade-in allowances on old vessels and offers easy-payment plans. Three fourths of the price a company must pay may be loaned to it by the government, these loans being made on terms that themselves involve a subsidy.

Third, the shipping companies are given a tax subsidy, being permitted to put part or all of their earnings and capital gains into reserve funds on which they can draw to purchase new ships. The income thus sequestered is exempted from the corporate income tax.

Fourth, the operating costs of passenger and cargo liners providing scheduled service on established routes are also subsidized. For many years, a subsidy was hidden in excessive payments made for carrying the mails. Under the Merchant Marine Act of 1936, it was brought into the open. An "operating differential subsidy" has since been paid to cover the difference in cost in operating under the American rather than a foreign flag. In 1969, this subsidy was being paid to 15 companies operating 13 passenger liners and some 300 cargo ships. It met a fourth of their operating costs. From 1954 to 1969, the subsidy paid to keep these ships afloat rose from $100 million a year to $200 million. Under legislation enacted in 1970, the operating differential subsidy is expected to amount to $6 billion during the next decade.

Subsidies to Aviation

Commercial aviation is subsidized by the provision of airways and airports at public expense. The airlines do not fall far short of meeting their share of the cost of maintaining the airways and operating the larger airports. But they do not meet the operating costs of smaller airports or contribute toward the capital costs of any airports. Some airlines are supported, too, by the payment of operating subsidies, designed to make up the difference between their expenditures and their revenues and to provide a fair return on their investment. Until 1958, the subsidies went to all the scheduled airlines; since then they have gone only to lines rendering local and feeder services. These payments amounted to $59 million in 1968.

A new subsidy for civil aviation has been introduced in the form of government support for the development of a supersonic passenger plane. This plane, longer than a football field, is designed to carry 300 passengers at 1,800 miles

4 / Joint Economic Committee, *op. cit.,* p. 53.

per hour, saving four hours on a transatlantic flight. The government put up 90 percent of the cost of its development. By 1971, its contribution would amount to more than $1 billion. If the private capital needed to finance the construction of such planes were not forthcoming, the government might foot the bill, raising its contribution to as much as $4 billion. And if the planes should fail to pay their way, operating subsidies were likely to follow. The transoceanic airlines, off subsidies for a dozen years, would go back on.

SUBSIDIES TO BUSINESS

Business has always depended, of course, upon functions fulfilled for it by government: upon the provision of legal status for the business unit, the main-tenance of a monetary system, the establishment of standards and grades of quantity and quality, the enforcement of contracts, the protection of creditors in bankruptcy, the preservation of order, the guardianship of public health and safety, and the assurance of national security. But the contribution of govern-ment to the prosperity of business has gone far beyond this: to the grant—over the years—of billions upon billions of dollars in subsidies.

Government has undertaken, in several ways, to promote the establishment and growth of small businesses. Through various agencies, it has offered informa-tion and advice on problems of business management. In wartime, it has helped small plants to obtain government contracts. To increase the availability of capital, it has underwritten loans made by financial institutions and has itself made loans to small concerns. To enable small firms to grow by reinvesting earnings, it has lightened the impact of the corporate income tax. During the sixties, in an effort to encourage the redevelopment of depressed areas, govern-ment provided small plants entering these areas with industrial sites, with exemption from local taxes, and with long-term, low-interest loans. But the sum total of such aid is paltry when compared with that extended, over the years, to big business.

Large concerns are the principal beneficiaries of the various forms of sub-sidization outlined above: sales at low prices, purchases at high prices, tax reduction, and the exclusion of competitors. There are major industries, some of them including gigantic firms, that lean heavily on the government for support.

Subsidies to Shipbuilders

Under the Merchant Marine Act of 1936, shipping companies receiving operating subsidies were required to have their ships built in American yards. This put them at a competitive disadvantage, since the cost of building ships in the United States was twice as great as that of building them abroad. The law therefore authorized the government to contribute, as a "construction differ-ential subsidy," the difference between American and foreign costs. Until 1960, the government's contribution normally could not exceed half of the cost. In

1960, its share was raised to 55 percent; in 1962 to 60 percent. The largest ship to be subsidized under this law was the liner "United States," built at a cost of $76.8 million. Of this, $32.9 million was put up by the United States Lines, $43.9 million by the taxpayers. From 1937, when the program began, to 1968, the government paid out nearly $1 billion in construction subsidies; in 1968, more than $100 million. At that time, the Johnson Administration proposed that the American construction requirement be dropped, permitting shipping companies to purchase ships built in foreign yards. The Nixon Administration rejected this proposal. Under a new law, enacted in 1970, cargo liners are to be built in American yards at the rate of 30 ships a year for the next 10 years, with the government's contribution to their cost dropping from 55 percent at the beginning to 35 percent in the mid-seventies. The law was expected to cost the taxpayer $2.7 billion for construction subsidies during the next decade.[5]

Promotion of Housing

Since the thirties, the federal government has sought to promote the construction of housing by increasing the availability of credit. It does not lend money directly to builders or to buyers. But through a number of agencies, performing a variety of functions, it has made itself a major factor in the field of housing finance. By granting federal charters to savings and loan associations and insuring their deposits, it has increased the volume of savings flowing through these agencies. By insuring payments on housing loans, it has enlarged the supply of mortgage money. By creating a secondary market for mortgages, it has insured the liquidity of lending institutions and freed their funds to make more loans. Not only has government enhanced the supply of housing credit; it has eased its terms. It has made loan ratios higher, down payments smaller, maturities longer, and interest rates lower. All this has operated to produce more houses.

In one way or another, the government has come to underwrite a large part of the home mortgage debt. In the main, its activities have been self-supporting, making no charge against the federal budget. But so many mortgages have been guaranteed at so high a percentage of property values that a decline in realty prices could cause a serious loss. By assuming a large share of the risk of housing credit, the government has aided large numbers of homeowners. At the same time, it has contributed substantially to the prosperity of house builders, real estate brokers, and mortgage lenders.

Promotion of Atomic Power

As we saw in Chapter 23, the creation of an industry to use atomic reactors as a source of heat in generating electricity required the subsidization of private power companies. The government bore the cost of research, running to $2.5

5 / On subsidies to shipping and shipbuilding, see Samuel A. Lawrence, *United States Merchant Shipping: Policies and Politics* (Washington, D.C.: Brookings Institution, 1966).

billion, and made its findings freely available to the industry. In a few cases, it contributed to the cost of building the reactors. In every case, it supplied atomic fuel at a rental charge so low as to involve a subsidy. A further subsidy may have been hidden in the price it paid for byproduct plutonium. The cost of insurance against catastrophic accidents, finally, was largely borne by the government.

Subsidies to the Oil Industry

The largest beneficiary of subsidies, aside from agriculture, is the oil industry. Its favors from government include reductions in its liability for taxes, quantitative restrictions on competitive imports, and permission to curtail domestic output. Under the corporate income tax law, the industry may write off most of the intangible costs of drilling oil wells in a single year instead of spreading them—as other industries must do—over the life of the assets, this privilege resulting in a tax saving of some $300 million per year. And from 1925 until 1969, the industry could deduct from income, under the percentage depletion provision described above, 27.5 percent of the value of its properties, up to half of its income, each year. Other industries pay the government half of their profits; the oil industry has paid only 6 or 7 percent. This favor has provided a subsidy of $1.5 billion per year. An attack was made on the depletion allowance when Congress debated the so-called tax reform bill of 1969, but its opponents succeeded only in reducing it from 27½ percent to 22 percent.

Quotas were imposed on the importation of crude oil and oil products in 1959. They now limit such importation to 12.2 percent of domestic output. As a result, the particular firms who have been given permission to do so have been able to import oil at $2 a barrel and sell it at $3.30, making a handsome profit on the deal. Altogether, the quota system has raised the price of oil to American consumers by $6 billion a year and has increased the income of American producers by $4 billion. A task force of the Nixon cabinet, set up to examine this program, reported at the end of 1969, recommending that the quota system be discontinued, thus eliminating the need to allocate the quotas among numerous applicants, and that tariffs on imports be imposed in their place. At mid-1970, with legislation pending to forbid such action, the Administration announced that the quota system would be retained.

The total of the subsidies received by the oil industry in the form of tax favors and import restrictions runs to $6 billion a year. In addition, as we saw in Chapter 32, the industry is exempted from the antitrust laws and permitted to curtail its output under state prorationing laws. These arrangements are obviously inconsistent. The tax allowances and the import controls increase the industry's profits and thus afford an incentive for greater investment. The prorationing programs cut back the larger output that would otherwise result. The net effect is to saddle the industry with excess capacity and to inflate its costs.

SUBSIDIES TO AGRICULTURE

Government, in the United States, has aided agriculture for a century and more. Since the thirties, its assistance has taken the form, in part, of cash payments from the Treasury: payments to producers of particular crops such as sugar and wool, and payments to farmers in general for retiring acreage, restricting output, and using soil-conserving practices. It has also taken the form, in larger part, of measures designed to raise the prices of the things the farmer sells. This has been done, as we have seen, by making loans and purchases, by restricting imports and by subsidizing exports, by curtailing the quantities produced, and by imposing controls on marketing. Public expenditures on such programs have run to more than $5 billion a year. But this is not all: government has also extended aid in other ways. It has supplied free land and services, financed educational research and education, provided water for irrigation, increased the supply of credit, promoted rural electrification, insured crops, and ameliorated rural poverty. Expenditures on these activities have approached another $1 billion a year. The programs that have aided agriculture by making direct payments and by raising prices were discussed, in some detail, in Chapter 31. Those that extend aid in other ways are considered, more briefly, below.

Free Land and Services

Government stimulated agricultural settlement, for more than a century, by selling land to farmers at low prices and by giving it away. Until 1819, land was sold at $2 an acre, first in tracts of 640 acres, then 320, and finally 160. In 1819, the price was cut to $1.25 and the acreage to 80. Under laws enacted in 1830 and 1841, squatters were given preemptive rights. And under the Homestead Act of 1862, farm families were given title to 160 acres each if they settled on the land and cultivated it for a period of five years. In 1902, the size of homesteads was increased to 320 acres where settlers undertook to irrigate arid land; in 1916, it was raised to 640 acres in the case of grazing lands. In 1902, also, government began to make more land available by building irrigation works. In the next 50 years, more than 4 million acres were reclaimed and opened to settlement. At the same time, land was made more accessible by the construction of farm to market roads.

Government also provides the farmer with a number of free services. It delivers the mail to his home, however remote, with no extra charge. It supplies him with current market information through its crop and livestock reporting service. It facilitates the distribution of his products by establishing standards and grades of quantity and quality. It protects him against loss from insect pests and plant and animal diseases. It finances agricultural research and education.

In 1862, when it passed the Homestead Act, Congress also set up the Department of Agriculture and passed the Morrill Land-Grant College Act, donating land to the states for the endowment of agricultural colleges. It subsequently extended federal aid to the states, under the Hatch Act of 1887, for agricultural experiment stations and, under the Smith-Lever Act of 1914, for agricultural extension work. The Department of Agriculture, with over 100,000 employees, now functions as a gigantic agricultural service agency. Research in soil chemistry and plant and animal biology, in the improvement of fertilizers and feeds, in the control of pests and diseases, and in other aspects of agricultural technology is conducted by the Department and by the state experiment stations. Education in agricultural methods is provided to students by the land-grant colleges and is carried to the farmer through farmers' institutes, through demonstration projects, and through instruction on the farm, by thousands of country agents employed jointly by the Department and the colleges.

The desirability of these subsidies is never questioned. Free land hastened the settlement of the country. Farm-to-market roads and rural mail delivery have bound it together. Other services, it is thought, must be provided by government because farmers are too small and too scattered to provide them for themselves. Industrial research is financed by private enterprise, even where firms are small. But agricultural research is financed by the taxpayer. And education is supported more generously for agriculture than for any other calling.

Irrigation

The earliest irrigation projects were built and operated through private enterprise, and the first irrigation laws were designed to encourage this type of activity. With the passage of the Newlands Act in 1902, however, a Bureau of Reclamation was established in the Department of the Interior and authorized to construct irrigation systems in 17 western states and the territory of Alaska. The first of these systems were small, being confined to the single purpose of irrigating agricultural land. In later years, however, the Bureau came to undertake gigantic projects, such as those at Hoover Dam on the Colorado and at the Grand Coulee on the Columbia, involving not only irrigation but also power production, navigation, and flood control. At the present time, half of the crop land in the West is irrigated and, of this, a fourth is irrigated by water from federal projects.

Under the Newlands Act, public land was temporarily reserved for irrigation and then reopened to entry, with homesteads limited to the size required to support a family, no more than 160 acres being given to any settler. In the region of the Grand Coulee, land was purchased by the government and resold, with similar limits on size. Recipients were chosen by lot, preference being given to veterans. After an initial period of development, settlers are expected to repay, in annual installments, the cost of constructing the irrigation works, thus obtaining title to water rights. The government has sought to prevent speculators from profiting by selling land at prices which reflect the value of irrigation. Since 1926, no sale has carried water rights until half of the annual installments have been paid, unless the Bureau has first approved its price as containing no increment of value based on irrigability.

The owners of irrigated land are heavily subsidized. They have never been asked to pay interest on the government's investment in irrigation works. The time allowed them to pay the principal, moreover, has repeatedly been extended. It was set at 10 years in 1902, at 20 years in 1914, at 40 years in 1926, and at 50 years in 1939. With each extension, the significance of the interest subsidy has been increased. The settler now pays nothing for the first 10 years and 2½ percent of the principal annually for the next 40 years. If we assume that the money it invested cost the government as little as 2½ percent a year, the interest on the unamortized balance, during 50 years, would exceed the principal. The settler would thus be paying barely half of the amount the project cost the government. At a higher rate of interest, his share would be even less. Nor need he pay all of the principal. In the case of multiple-purpose projects, until 1952 the interest collected from power companies was applied to the cost of constructing a project as a whole and the payments required of owners of irrigated land were reduced accordingly. In 1952, this arrangement was modified. The settler's annual charge depends on his ability to pay. His period of payment may thus be extended beyond 50 years. The interest collected from power companies and other users of water is now employed initially to pay their share of the construction cost. Thereafter, it can still be used to pay off the remaining irrigation debt. The beneficiaries of federal irrigation projects are thus required to meet but a minor part of their cost. The major part is met by the taxpayers and by other water users. The size of the subsidy is hidden, however, by the intricacies of public accounting.[6]

The irrigation subsidy operates, of course, to increase the acreage devoted to the production of foods and fibers. Ironically, it has been paid at a time when the government has sought to solve the problem of mounting agricultural surpluses by paying farmers other millions to retire land from cultivation and to curtail their plantings of the major crops.

Agricultural Credit

Ever since World War I, the government has payed a major role in the provision of agricultural credit. In part, it has sought to meet the needs arising in periods of emergency. When farmers have been hit by drought, it has made loans to enable them to support their families and keep their farms in production. During the Great Depression, it set up an agency to refinance farm mortgages, bringing quick relief to farmers and to their creditors. In larger part, the government has undertaken to promote the formation of permanent institutions, under cooperative ownership, to meet the normal credit needs of agriculture. These needs are, first, for long-term credit to finance the purchase and enlargement of farms and the construction of farm buildings and, second, for intermediate-term credit to finance purchases of feed, seed, fertilizer, livestock, and farm machinery, and the processing and marketing of agricultural commodities. To meet these needs, the government set up an elaborate structure

6 / See Otto Eckstein, *Water Resource Development* (Cambridge, Mass.: Harvard University Press, 1958), chap. viii.

of credit institutions: a system of federal land banks to provide long-term credit in 1916, a system of intermediate credit banks in 1923, a parallel system of production credit corporations and a system of banks for cooperatives in 1933, all of these institutions being brought under the supervision of a Farm Credit Administration. The initial capital for each of the systems was provided by the government. But their stock has gradually passed, or is passing, into the hands of their member banks or corporations. The agricultural credit structure is unnecessarily complicated and might well be simplified. But it serves the purposes for which it was set up and now comes close to paying its own way. The government's contributions to its creation would appear to have been justified.

Rural Electrification

In 1934, only a tenth of the farms in the United States had electricity. Thirty years later, 98 percent of them had been electrified. Half were served by private companies and half through public agencies. But the initiative that brought about the change was taken by the government. The private companies had long been reluctant to extend their lines into sparsely populated rural areas. They were encouraged to do so by the example set them by the Rural Electrification Administration.

The REA, first created by executive order in 1935, was given statutory authority in 1936. Its primary function has been that of making loans to cooperative associations set up to build and operate electrical facilities. But it has also provided these associations with legal, construction, engineering, and other advisory services. Its loans have usually financed the erection of transmission and distribution lines to carry purchased power. In some cases, however, they have also covered generating plants. The cooperatives are given legal preference in purchasing power from projects operated by the federal government. Title to the facilities financed by REA is held by these associations. The loans are being paid off, at 2 percent interest, over periods of 35 years. And when payments are completed, the properties will pass into debt-free private ownership.

The program has been a highly successful one. Loans have been extended to more than a thousand cooperatives and REA systems are serving some 6 million customers in 46 states. Electricity has been carried to the farms, costs and rates have been cut, and consumption has been increased. Payments have run ahead of schedule.

A similar program was initiated in 1949 to extend telephone service into rural areas. Following the same pattern, it is administered by the REA. This program, too, has been successful, increasing the fraction of farm homes with telephones from a third to three fourths.

These gains, however, have been subsidized. The money that is loaned to the cooperatives at 2 percent has cost the government as much as 7 percent. The difference has amounted to hundreds of millions of dollars every year. In view of the present strength of the cooperatives, it may well be asked whether this subvention is still required.

Crop Insurance

A farmer's crop may fall off seriously in any year through no fault of his own. He may plant the same seed with the same fertilizer on the same land and cultivate it in the same way. But his yield may be diminished by forces that he is powerless to control: by drought, flood, freezing temperature, wind, hail, plant disease, and insect pest. His risks of loss are like those met in other fields by purchasing insurance policies. But insurance companies have not attempted to provide indemnities against declines in yields resulting from hazards other than wind and hail. They have lacked both the data required to determine risks and the assurance of breadth and diversity of coverage. All-risk crop insurance was, therefore, unavailable until it was provided by the federal government.

The Federal Crop Insurance Corporation was established in 1938 and was authorized to sell insurance anywhere in the nation. It wrote its first insurance on wheat in 1939 and on cotton in 1941. Its losses, in its early years, were heavy. By 1944, its indemnities had exceeded its premiums by $37 million. The program was then discontinued by Congress, but was soon reestablished on a smaller scale, being limited to a few crops. Again, there were losses, amounting to $23 million by the end of 1947. Again, the program was revised by Congress, this time being limited to 375 counties. The Corporation was directed to charge premiums that would cover its indemnities, building up reserves in good years to meet the losses incurred in bad. Thereafter, as it gained experience, it was permitted gradually to expand its coverage. In 1955, the Corporation was authorized to reinsure the risks of private crop insurers. But private participation in the program did not materialize.

In 1967, the FCIC had nearly $800 million of insurance outstanding on 24 crops in 1,363 counties. It insured against most of the farmer's risks: bad weather, plant diseases, and insect infestation. It wrote policies both on individual crops and on all of a farmer's crops, insuring single crops at 75 percent of their yield in earlier years and multiple crops at a specified dollar value. It varied its premiums in accordance with the risk, adjusting them as its experience changed. For the period from 1948 through 1967, the Corporation's premiums exceeded its indemnities. But in 1968, it sustained a loss of $14 million on its insurance of wheat, cotton, and citrus fruits. The program is subsidized. Its administrative costs, up to $12 million a year, are met by the government.

Crop insurance still has its weaknesses. Operations are on a limited scale, with a small fraction of the farmers covered and a small fraction of the acreage in any crop insured. There is an adverse selection of risks, farmers on poor land coming in and farmers on good land staying out. Coverage should be expanded, and participation increased.

Aid to Low-Income Farmers

Commercial farmers, in comfortable circumstances, have been the chief beneficiaries of the programs described above. There are other farmers, in comparative poverty, who present a problem of their own. Working small plots of poor land, with obsolete methods and limited equipment, they earn a meager living. Farmers in this group require a different sort of aid. Some of them should be helped to find employment off the farm. Those who remain should be helped to raise their productivity. Another governmental program now serves these purposes.

The Farmers Home Administration, established in 1946 to succeed the Farm Security Administration, set up in 1937, makes loans to rural communities, to farm cooperatives, and to individual farmers, and insures repayment of loans that are made by private lenders. Its loans to local governments finance the construction of water and sewer systems, housing, and recreational facilities. Its loans to cooperatives finance irrigation and drainage projects, the erection of grain elevators, and the acquisition of heavy equipment. Its loans to the farmers themselves serve a number of purposes. There are long-term loans to enable the farmers to buy land and to enlarge their holdings, to construct farm buildings, and to develop soil and water resources. There are loans, for shorter terms, to enable them to buy farm equipment, livestock, feeds, seeds, fertilizers, and insecticides. These loans are made on easy terms, with long maturities, and low interest rates. But most important is the fact that their use is supervised in order to make sure that their intended purposes are served. Members of the FHA staff visit the borrowers, help them to prepare farm plans, advise them on their choice of crops and methods of cultivation, make recommendations on farm management, and work out a schedule for repayment of the debt. In this way, the agency has put hundreds of thousands of small farm families on their feet.

Given the nature of this program, the record of repayment has been remarkably good. Nine tenths of the borrowers have made their payments on schedule. Loans written off as losses have been less than 1 percent of those made. The agency's annual loss on loans outstanding may run between $5 million and $10 million. The government's expenditure on the program is greater than this, since borrowers are not required to meet the cost of administration. This cost is particularly high in the case of supervised loans, where the agency provides the borrowers with educational assistance. The cost of administration has amounted to $60 million a year. The program thus involves an annual subsidy of $65 million to $70 million to farm families in the low-income group. These expenditures are small indeed when compared with those made on behalf of farmers who are well-to-do.

APPRAISAL OF SUBSIDIES

To say that an enterprise is subsidized is not necessarily to condemn it. Some subsidies, to be sure, serve only to confer favors on politically powerful groups at the expense of the community as a whole. But other subsidies are promotional in character, being designed to encourage the development of productive activities that are inadequately supplied and are generally held to be desirable.

The line between the two, however, is not an easy one to draw. Promotional subsidies, once granted, tend to persist long after the need for them is past. And all subsidies are presented to the public in terms of their contribution, real or imagined, to the general good. The value of some subsidies is unquestioned; the merits of many others are open to debate. A number of questions must be asked in every case: (1) Is the purpose for which the subsidy is paid a worthy one? (2) Granted the worth of the purpose, is the subsidy really needed? (3) Granted the need for the subsidy, is it charged to the consumer or to the taxpayer? (4) However financed, is the subsidy hidden or provided openly? (5) However provided, what are its probable effects? The first of these questions is political, the remaining ones economic in character.

The Politics of Subsidies

Worthiness of purpose, of course, is a matter of judgment and is not to be determined by a scientific rule. It would generally be agreed, however, that many of the purposes for which subsidies have been provided are worthy ones: the construction of railways to speed the opening and settlement of the West; the development of commercial aviation; the protection during infancy of industries that could later stand alone; the promotion of peaceful applications of atomic energy; the creation of institutions to meet the credit needs of agriculture, housing, and small business; agricultural research and education; rural electrification; the initiation of crop insurance; the alleviation of rural poverty. It would be agreed, too, by almost everyone except the interests involved, that no useful purpose was served, in the past, by paying fancy prices for silver to be dug up in the West and reburied in the East; that no useful purpose is served today by barring imports that would compete with the output of powerful domestic industries, by requiring procurement officers to buy from domestic suppliers at prices higher than those charged abroad, by inducing expansion of the oil industry when output from existing properties is strictly curtailed, by subsidizing the production of lead and zinc. But the desirability of many other subsidies is open to debate:

Should the Post Office be required to carry periodicals and advertising matter at a loss? Pro: the circulation of periodicals enlightens the electorate and binds the country together; advertising stimulates demand and thus increases production and employment. Con: the principal beneficiaries of low rates on periodicals are scarcely to be described as journals of enlightenment; reduction in the volume of direct-mail advertising matter would be a boon not only to the Post Office but also to its recipients.

Should irrigation be provided at a price that does not cover its cost? Pro: irrigation increases the area of land under cultivation; opens new opportunities to farm families. Con: irrigation runs counter to agricultural policy in general which seeks to retire existing acreage and to curtail the output coming from the acres that remain.

Should American cargoes be carried under the American flag? Pro: a national flag fleet is needed to promote sales abroad, to deliver exported goods, to protect shippers against exorbitant freights and discriminatory practices. Con: shipping companies are common carriers, not merchandisers; their ships are not to be compared to the delivery trucks of retail firms; as members of shipping conferences, they combine with foreign companies to keep rates high and to maintain rate structures that discriminate against the trade of the United States. Pro: an American merchant marine is needed to serve the Navy in time of war. Con: at the outbreak of war, enemy ships seized in America's ports or those of her allies or captured at sea would be available for her defense; American ships seized in enemy ports or captured at sea would be lost; previous registry would be without significance.

Should merchant ships be built in the United States? Pro: American shipyards should be kept in operation in peacetime so that they will be ready to build the merchant ships that will be needed in time of war. Con: this argument assumes another war of attrition; it has been rendered obsolete by the changing technology of warfare.

Should air service be supplied to regions where it cannot pay its way? Pro: the local airlines feed traffic to the trunk lines; people in smaller places are as much entitled to rapid transport as those in larger ones. Con: subsidization of local airlines deprives branch rail lines and bus lines of needed business; if passengers are unwilling to meet the cost of air service, they should go by rail or bus.

Should the government subsidize the development of a supersonic transport plane? Pro: the SST is needed to maintain American leadership in the manufacture of civilian aircraft. Con: the noise produced by such a plane would be unbearable. The racket from its engines, when taking off, would be four times that produced by present jets. The plane would be followed in flight by a sonic boom, deafening people and destroying property within a radius of 50 miles. The vapor it discharged into the stratosphere might adversely affect the climate of the earth. And this would be done to enable a handful of wealthy people to cross the Atlantic in four hours less time.

Subsidization results from political pressure. If pressure is not applied in support of a cause, however worthy, it will not be subsidized. But if an effective lobby is maintained on Capitol Hill, a dubious purpose will not prevent a subsidy from being paid.

The Economics of Subsidies

If an undertaking is deemed desirable, we may still ask whether a subsidy is required for its support. In some cases, a subsidy is clearly needed if an undertaking is to be maintained. The subsidy paid to shipbuilders is a case in point. American shipyards, it would seem, cannot compete on an equal basis with other countries. Ships are usually made to order, in small numbers. Standardization and mass production, in which Americans excel, are rarely feasible. Costs in the United States have been twice as high as those abroad. If a shipbuilding industry is to exist in the United States, it must be subsidized. Subsidies are also needed, for the time being, to support crop insurance and local airlines.

In some cases it may be questioned whether a subsidy has ever been needed to accomplish the purpose for which it has been given. Shipping, under more progressive management, might have been able to pay its own way. Ship design, port facilities, and cargo-handling devices all could be improved. More freight could be prepacked for loading in containers. Ships could be loaded to a higher fraction of capacity, sailing full and down. Time in port, standing idle, could be reduced and time at sea, earning money, increased. Subsidization has not sufficed to keep American merchant ships afloat. The number of ships flying the American flag has steadily declined. Since World War II, the share of American trade carried by such vessels has fallen from 60 percent to less than 10 percent. What has been needed is less an infusion of funds from the Treasury than a revolution in management.

This is not the only case where a subsidy is paid though it is not needed, or where a subsidy, once needed, is continued after need for it has ceased. Heavy trucks would continue to roll if they were required to meet their full share of highway costs. Oil would be discovered and developed even though its producers were taxed at the same rate other corporations have to pay. Rural electric systems would continue to function even though their interest cost was not subsidized. The great American industries would continue to make substantial profits even though the tariffs that protect them were removed. All these subsidies could be discontinued without risk of loss to the community as a whole. But where political pressure is applied by subsidy seekers, Congress may not insist upon convincing proof of need.

If a subsidy is to be paid, for whatever reason, it is desirable that it be financed, not by the consumer, but by the taxpayer. When subsidies are paid by the consumer in higher prices—as is the case with those provided by the tariff and by the program of agricultural price supports discussed in Chapter 31—the incidence of the burden is regressive, the higher prices resting lightly on those whose incomes are large and heavily on those whose incomes are small. When subsidies are provided directly by the government, on the other hand, their cost can be distributed among the taxpayers in accordance with their ability to pay.

However it is financed, a subsidy should not be hidden but provided frankly and openly. Recipients prefer the hidden subsidy. Its existence can be obscured; its costs concealed. Being collected indirectly, it may require no formal justification, no annual round of hearings, reports, debates, and votes. And thus it stands a better chance of a protracted life. By the same token, the public interest demands an open subsidy, one that is plainly labeled and understood, that must be defended and appropriated year by year. Such a subsidy cannot survive in the absence of knowledge and consent. In this respect, the payments to shipping and aviation are almost the only ones that cannot be criticized.

Finally, even though subsidies are provided openly, on proof of need, for desirable purposes, they may have unfortunate effects. Since they come, not from the market, but from the public purse, they may divert the attention of managements from the cultivation of customers to the cultivation of Congressmen. Being paid, in general, when losses are incurred and not when profits are shown, they reward incompetence and penalize efficiency. Instead of encouraging the producer to stand on his own feet, they invite him to lean upon the state. Rather than progress, they make for lethargy.

PART VII

Which Controls?

Chapter 34

HOW CONTROL MONOPOLY?

When it seeks to control monopoly, government chooses among three policies: the maintenance of competition, the regulation of monopolistic enterprise, and the administration of monopolistic undertakings by public enterprise. Its choice may relate to the economy in general: shall resources be allocated through the market or by agencies of government? In time of war, there is little opportunity for choice; allocation must be directed by the state. In peacetime, however, choice is possible. Allocation can be left to the market, and policy can deal with the facilitation of market processes and with the prevention of harmful results. Choices are more often made in particular cases: is a certain industry, characterized by monopoly, to be broken into competing parts, to be regulated by a public agency, or to be taken over by the government?

No policy can be applied across the board. Competition cannot be enforced where the service rendered must be under unified control. Rates and services cannot easily be regulated or public operation undertaken in fields where firms are small and numerous, and competition normally intense. Private enterprise cannot always be preserved in areas where health and safety are in danger or where national security is at stake. Each of the controls available is likely to have some use. The choice as to policy is one of relative emphasis: which of the controls are to be regarded as exceptions and which as the general rule? In the United States, as we have seen, regulation and public enterprise are the exceptions; the maintenance of competition is the general rule.

COMPREHENSIVE NONCOMPETITIVE CONTROLS

A number of large-scale oligopolistic industries have economic characteristics similar to those that led to regulation of the railroads: heavy investment, high fixed costs, and excess capacity, resulting in pressure to obtain added business by cutting prices below total costs, and leading to destructive competition unless prevented by overt or tacit collusion. This is true, to some extent, of steel, copper, aluminum, cement, automobiles, farm machinery, electrical equipment, chemicals, oil refining, meat packing, tin cans, cigarettes, soap, and a score of other manufacturing industries. The difficulties encountered in applying the

809

antitrust laws in such cases have sometimes led economists to conclude that these industries must ultimately be subjected to regulation, with an Interstate Steel Commission, presumably, controlling the steel industry, a Federal Automobile Commission regulating the automobile industry, and so on. The prospect is forbidding. Regulation has been rewarded with scant success in the industries where it has already been applied. It would encounter even greater difficulties in those to which it would be extended. And its extension on so large a scale would necessitate abandonment of the market as a coordinator in favor of central planning and authoritarian control.

The Greater Difficulty of the Task

In public utilities, transport, and communications, the task of regulation has been difficult enough. In manufacturing, it would be even more so. Here, it would be necessary to deal with numerous enterprises differing in size, in corporate structure, in degree of integration, in number and location of establishments, in number and proportionate output of different products, and in technology, efficiency, and costs. If control were to be effective, it would have to be extended to every aspect of business policy: to the size and character of investment, to the adequacy of expenditures on research, to the propriety of expenditures on sales promotion, to the desirability of changes in style, to the level and structure of prices, and to the size and distribution of earnings. Regulation might begin more modestly, but its final stage, if the history of the railroads is a guide, would be the virtual duplication of managements.

The regulatory agency would be called upon to control efficiency and to govern the rate of change. In doing so, it would have to strike a balance between the interests of consumers and those of investors, finding answers to questions such as these:

1. Should prices be set at levels that would only cover the costs of low-cost firms, promoting efficiency but inflicting losses on investors in high-cost firms, or should they be set at levels that would cover the higher costs, protecting investors but denying consumers the benefits of efficiency?
2. When demand declines, should adjustment be speeded by cutting prices at the expense of investors or postponed by restricting output or maintaining prices at the expense of consumers? When demand rises, should prices be raised, giving a windfall profit to investors, or should prices be maintained and output rationed to protect consumers?
3. When the price of materials is falling, should the price of the product be based on actual cost, protecting investors, or on replacement cost, benefiting consumers? When the price of materials is rising, should the price of the product be based on actual cost, protecting consumers, or on replacement cost, giving a windfall to investors?
4. Should new products and new technology be introduced promptly, serving consumers but harming investors in outmoded products and obsolete

technology, or should innovation be retarded, protecting investors but denying consumers the benefits of progress?

5. If old capacity is standing idle, should investment in new capacity be delayed to protect investors or should it be permitted in the interest of consumers?

Nor are these the only decisions that the regulatory agency would be called upon to make. It would have to fix the prices of natural resources, weighing the claims of the present against those of the future in determining how rapidly such resources were to be consumed. It would have to establish criteria of efficiency, selecting the more efficient among the applicants for entry to the industry, refusing entry on the ground of inefficiency. All of these are decisions that must be accepted when made by the market, but that would lead to endless controversy, prolonged delay, and dubious results if subjected to the requirements of due process and submitted to the pressures of politics.

Market Economy or Planned Economy?

Where the share of publicly owned or regulated industry in the economy is small, the overall direction of economic activity can be left to the market. But if the share of production brought under regulation or ownership were large, the many interrelationships of the industries concerned would necessitate co-ordination of the controls. Resources would have to be allocated among rival claimants, the output of one industry dovetailed with the requirements of another, and the prices established for different industries and different markets brought into some sort of harmony. The policy of socialization or regulation, if consistently pursued, could end only in comprehensive economic planning and the authoritative direction of economic activity. The question that is ultimately posed by any proposal to abandon the maintenance of competition as a general policy is that of making a choice between the market economy and the planned economy.

The issues involved in such a choice are numerous and difficult. The more important ones are listed here:

1. Would resources, in a planned economy, be allocated in accordance with the wishes of consumers, with those of a majority of voters, with those of the bureaucracy, or with those of pressure groups?

2. Could a high level of output be maintained, or would the performance of the economy be impaired by overcentralization of decisions, by the complexity of central planning, by the isolation and ignorance of the planners, by conflict, compromise, confusion, and delay, by the clumsiness and the rigidity of the controls, by the costs of bureaucratic overhead, and by the lack of tests by which success or failure could be judged?

3. Could progress be assured, or would it be restrained by the absence of incentives, by the need for agreements, by the opposition of vested interests, and by reluctance to assume responsibility for taking risks?

4. Could stability be maintained, or would changes in administration (with policy uncertain for months before elections) and changes in plan by existing administration (with new plans hatched in secrecy and sprung without warning) make for greater instability?

5. Could trade with other nations be expanded and economic differences adjusted peaceably, or would the desire to protect the domestic plan from the disrupting effect of change abroad lead to isolation, and would the conversion of differences arising between private traders into differences between governments lead to irritation and ill will?

6. Could public morality be maintained, or would the larger number of permissions required and regulations imposed result in more bribery, black marketeering, bootlegging, and disrespect for law?

7. Could group conflict be prevented, or would the fact that each group's share in income was determined by the state intensify such conflict and reduce the nation's strength by threatening its unity?

8. Finally, and most important, could individual freedom be preserved, or would the centralization of power facilitate coercion of conformity?

These questions are too complex to be debated here. But their character should serve to show that any proposal generally to abandon competition as a regulator must go to the fundamentals of our society.

Experience with Wartime Controls

Judgment as to the nature of comprehensive controls is not entirely a matter of conjecture. Such controls were applied in the United States during World War II. For more than three years, prices and wages were fixed, consumers' goods rationed, and materials allocated by agencies of government. There are lessons to be drawn from this experience.

Three principal methods were used in controlling prices. Where products were standardized, markets well organized, and information readily available, maximum prices were set in dollars and cents. Where products could not be standardized, as in the case of building construction, custom-made goods, and repair work, formulas embodying various cost and profit factors were prescribed for sellers to use in computing the prices they might charge. For most goods and services, prices were frozen at existing levels, being set at the highest figures charged in March, 1943. Where new goods were introduced and where new sellers entered the market, their ceilings were related, in various ways to those of goods and firms already there.

Price ceilings, once set, had to be adjusted. The general freeze reduced the margins of distributors who were selling in March on the basis of prices they had paid for goods in earlier months. It perpetuated differences due to chance, catching some sellers with prices that were abnormally low. It created shortages in some localities. As costs rose, moreover, the ceilings left high-price firms in business, threatened to eliminate their low-price competitors. They cut off needed segments of supply. Ceilings were, therefore, adjusted by administrative action, and higher prices were charged when permission was obtained.

Price controls were effective in some fields, ineffective in others. It was possible to enforce dollars-and-cents ceilings, difficult to enforce freezes, and virtually impossible to enforce ceilings that were to be computed by sellers through the use of formulas. Controls were effective where production was concentrated in the hands of a few large firms and where prices had been fixed through open or tacit agreement before the war. They were ineffective where producers were small and numerous and where industries had been actively competitive. Ceilings were evaded by reducing the quality of goods sold at the ceiling price, by moving goods, such as dresses, from a lower into a higher price class, by reducing discounts, and by worsening other terms of sale. In some trades and in some regions, ceilings were simply ignored.

With labor scarce and wages free, the cost of labor rose. With prices frozen, profits declined. If ceilings on prices were to be preserved, wages had to be controlled. This, too, was done by imposing a base-date freeze. And here, again, adjustments had to be made, raising substandard wages, permitting increases for merit and for length of service, and removing differentials between plants, industries, and communities. Adjustments were always upward. The principal contribution of wage control to the stabilization of prices was bureaucratic delay.

With prices frozen, the market could no longer perform its accustomed function of rationing consumers' goods and allocating raw materials. This function had to be fulfilled by setting up administrative agencies, devising administrative mechanisms, and adopting administrative procedures. The rationing authorities determined the needs of various classes of consumers for various kinds of goods and supplied them with certificates and coupons to use, along with money, in making purchases. The allocation authorities determined what goods were to be produced and allotted to their producers orders that enabled them to obtain the materials required for their production. These controls were cumbersome. They were evaded in various ways. They brought the allocators and the price controllers into frequent conflict. But they worked, after a fashion, for a time.

The wartime controls were supported by patriotism. They were tolerated as temporary. But, even so, they encountered serious obstacles. Price control, in particular, was subjected to continuous political attack. Congress, in response to such pressures, acted repeatedly to handicap the Office of Price Administration by denying it necessary powers. It forbade the imposition of ceilings on agricultural commodities until their prices exceeded 110 percent of parity. It forbade the standardization of products to which the ceilings applied. It prohibited the establishment of official grades and the requirement of informative labels. It required the OPA to set prices at levels that would cover costs and yield a profit, not on industry's operations as a whole, but on each of its products, taken separately. It required the OPA to remove professional economists from administrative posts, replacing them with businessmen.

If the application of controls was difficult in time of war, it would be even more so in time of peace. Freezes would become increasingly inoperable as the base dates to which they were tied receded farther into the past; they would have to be superseded by controls that were more complex and more difficult to apply. The services of unpaid volunteers in the administration of rationing and the enforcement of retail price ceilings, provided as a contribution to the war effort, would not be forthcoming, on a permanent basis, in time of peace; this work would have to be done by an army of salaried employees. Arbitrary decisions, justifiable in an emergency, would not be tolerated; the requirements of due process would have to be scrupulously observed.

Under the pressure of war, controls were accepted as a necessary evil. But few of those who lived through this experience would welcome its repetition as a matter of deliberate choice. The more one sees of administrative controls, the greater becomes his admiration of the market as an allocator.

SELECTIVE NONCOMPETITIVE CONTROLS

Though noncompetitive controls may be rejected for the economy as a whole, they may be needed in solving the problems presented by monopoly in particular industries. There are certain fields in which the nature of the service rendered is such as to necessitate unified administration. This is true of utility services: water, gas, electricity, urban transit, and telephone. Here, the consumer cannot be protected by competition. But he cannot be left without protection, since the services are essential and he would be at the mercy of monopolists. The quality of the services might suffer. The general level of the rates charged might be too high. The structure of rates might be unfairly discriminatory. In transport, the shipper would be protected by competition on some hauls but not on others. The quality of transport service might be kept high and the general level of rates low by competition. But here, too, in the absence of controls, the consumer would be the victim of undue discrimination. In cases such as these, the choice lies, not between competition and noncompetitive controls, but between private enterprise under regulation and public enterprise. In such cases, which of the controls is to be preferred? And how can its performance be improved?

Shortcomings of Noncompetitive Controls

The results of rate and service regulation, over the years, as they were summarized in Chapter 20, were found to range from fair to poor. The utility commissions in the states have done little to insure the quality of service. Their performance with respect to the general level of rates has been weak. They have exercised no real control over operating costs. They have enunciated no clear principles to govern the allowable rate of return. They have permitted earnings much higher than those required to market new securities. They have set rates on a cost-plus basis, developing no incentive for efficiency. They have made no effort to increase consumption by reducing rates to the lowest level that would yield a fair return. With respect to the structure of rates, they have left the initiative to the utilities. The small user has suffered from discrimination. State regulation, in short, has afforded scant protection to the consumer of utility services.

The performance of the federal utility commissions, in fields other than surface transport, has been somewhat more impressive. The Federal Power Commission and the Federal Communications Commission established tighter controls over utility accounting. The Securities and Exchange Commission effected a thorough reorganization of the corporate structure of the electric utility industry. The FPC, though tardily and reluctantly, tightened its control over interstate transmission of electricity and developed a workable price-fixing program for natural gas. The FCC brought about successive reductions in long-distance telephone rates. It protected broadcasters in their dealings with the networks in radio and TV. But the record is not unblemished. The Civil Aeronautics Board has established no criteria to govern the allocation of routes. It has speeded investment in costlier equipment but retarded the introduction of new services. It has been slow to develop principles to control the level and the structure of rates. The FCC has given away monopoly rights worth millions of dollars, nominally in accordance with criteria that really are spurious, its action, in some cases, being tainted by corruption. The public interest in the character of broadcasting has been poorly served.

In the case of surface transport, the Interstate Commerce Commission faces the problem of competition among different media. The Commission is directed by Congress to be impartial in its regulation, so that traffic will be allocated among these media in accordance with their inherent advantages. But such an allocation is prevented by differential subsidization. And the effects of this subsidization are then offset, in part, by discrimination in the structure of rates. Once set up to protect shippers against rail monopolies, the ICC now undertakes to protect railroads, truckers, and barge lines against one another. Its concern today is less with the consumer's welfare than with the carrier's prosperity.

This record would be better if the regulatory agencies had been stronger and if they had adopted wiser policies. But some of the defects of regulation are inherent in its very nature, as we saw in Chapter 20. Regulation does not prescribe the quality of service or require innovation. It sets prices to cover costs, wherever they may be. It does not induce efficiency; it offers no incentive to good administration, imposes no penalty on incompetence. It comes to serve the interests of the regulated industries. It is backward-looking, slow to adapt to change. It expands controls when it could contract them. It exercises power without accepting responsibility. Its operations are cumbersome and costly, its decisions made only after long delays.

No such generalizations concerning public enterprise would be justified. Sometimes it has been efficient and progressive; sometimes it has not. At best, it raises serious problems. Public enterprise has all of the disadvantages of size: overcentralization, delay, impersonality, rigidity. It has the disadvantages of monopoly. How is the consumer to be protected against poor quality, high prices, and discrimination? How is progress in technology to be assured? Public enterprise, moreover, has the added disadvantages of politics. Group pressures may inflate costs, keeping the payments made for facilities, supplies, and labor high. They may depress revenues, keeping the general level of charges for services low. They may lead to unfair discrimination. They may obstruct the adoption of improvements in those cases where improvements are proposed. Public enterprise, finally, is faced with the dilemma of efficiency versus accountability. For efficiency, it must be free to exercise initiative. For accountability, it must be bound with red tape.

Experience leads to the conclusion that the noncompetitive controls should be confined to those cases where their use is unavoidable or their desirability so clear as to sustain a heavy burden of proof. Sound judgment supports tradition in its reliance on the maintenance of competition as the general rule.

Where Regulation? Where Public Enterprise?

There are circumstances under which a service, if it is to be provided at all, must be rendered by public enterprise. (1) The scale of a project may be so large, the capital demanded so great, and the period required for its recovery so long that private enterprise cannot attempt it. The construction of a canal across the Isthmus of Panama is a case in point. (2) An undertaking, though socially desirable, may never be expected to yield a profit. This is true of the maintenance of public forests, range lands, national parks, wilderness areas, and wildlife refuges. (3) It may be impossible to collect the costs of a project from its beneficiaries. Examples are flood control and increases in the power generated at dams downstream when a river's flow is stabilized by building dams upstream. (4) The successful performance of a service may require compulsory participation; its contributions and its benefits may involve redistribution. This is the case with social insurance. (5) A project may be deliberately designed to incur losses in order to promote new fields of business activity. This was done, for instance, in developing the complex of credit institutions in agriculture and in housing. (6) An essential service provided by private enterprise may have broken down. This has happened to urban transit in a number of cities. Under none of these circumstances is the alternative of regulated private enterprise desirable or possible.

There are certain fields, such as those listed above, in which public enterprise is inevitable. There are other fields in which the desirability of public enterprise has never been questioned: among them, the provision of roads, waterways, airways, and postal services. There are still other fields in which the desirability of public enterprise, once disputed, is now taken for granted: education and recreation, for instance; insurance against unemployment, dependent old age, and survivorship; the promotion of private enterprises by rediscounting or insuring loans; the ownership of national parks and forests; and the construction of works for irrigation, navigation, and flood control. There are but few fields in which the propriety of public enterprise is at issue, in the United States, at the present time: production—such as the Navy's manufacture of paint—that is incidental to the operation of governmental agencies and is said to deprive private business of profit-making opportunities, low-rent urban housing, health insurance, and the generation of electricity at hydro plants, conventional steam plants, and atomic power plants, its transmission, and its distribution.

Where public enterprise and regulation are both possible, there is no clear rule to govern the choice between them. A stronger case can be made for public enterprise where an industry is mature, its product standardized, and its operations reduced to routine, so that little imagination or initiative are required; where its capital input is large and its labor input small and technically specialized, so that it can realize the advantage of a low interest rate and avoid the disadvantage of political patronage; and where its operations are so concentrated that they can readily be subjected to central control. A stronger case can be made for regulation where an industry is new and growing; where its capital input is relatively small and its labor input relatively large; and where its operations are dispersed.

These and other considerations can be weighed. But no certain answer is to be obtained. Public enterprise and regulation each has its advantages and disadvantages. It cannot be said that one would always work better than the other. It is not even possible to predict with confidence which would be better in a particular case. If one of the controls is working badly, the other can be tried. If one is working at all well, those who propose to substitute the other should bear the burden of proof.

Strengthening Noncompetitive Controls

The reforms that have been adopted to improve regulation and the proposals most often made for further reform relate to regulatory structure and procedure. The members of an agency's staff that prosecute cases have been separated from the members that decide them, so that impartiality may be assured. The initial steps in decision making have been delegated to trial examiners, so that commissioners can speed decisions by concentrating on the cases that require review. It has been proposed, in addition, that the regulatory commission be replaced by two bodies: a tribunal that would concern itself exclusively with adjudication and a single administrator who would formulate policies and direct programs. Desirable as such reforms may be, they do not go to the heart of regulation.

More fundamental changes are needed. In some cases, existing policy should be reversed. Broadcasting licenses, for instance, instead of being given away should be auctioned to the highest bidder. Control of entry and rates in surface transport should not be used to preserve for each of the transport media its accustomed share of traffic. Determination of airline routes, instead of requiring protracted legal proceedings, should be left to the carriers. In general, there should be clearer definitions of purpose, by legislative bodies and by the commissions themselves. Criteria should be adopted and published to govern the determination of a fair return and the discrimination that is to be permitted, in other fields as well as transport, in the structure of rates. Greater efforts should be made to develop and apply substitutes for the incentives to efficiency and innovation that are present in competitive industries. There is need for continuing research, to appraise the results of regulation and to afford knowledge of current and coming developments in the regulated industries. There is need, too, for planning directed toward the adaptation of policy to impending change. The commissions, obviously, should devote their energies, not to promoting the welfare of the industries they regulate, but to protecting the interests of consumers. They should take more initiative, display more vigor and courage. To this end, it goes without saying, they should be given stronger support by legislative bodies and by chief executives: adequate jurisdiction and power, larger appropriations, better appointments, higher salaries, and longer tenure. Little of this will be accorded them if consumers are uninformed and indifferent; much of it if there is active popular support.

Where regulated industries have been exempted from the antitrust laws, it is important that regulation assume the full burden of control. The jurisdiction of the regulatory agency should cover all of the area that is exempt, so that none of it escapes entirely from control. The agency should discharge its full responsibility. This has not always been done. In 1921, for instance, the Packers and Stockyards Act transferred enforcement of the law against unfair methods of competition and deceptive practices, for this area, from the Federal Trade Commission to the Department of Agriculture. From 1950 to 1957, the FTC referred to the Department some 30 complaints against concerns defined by the law as packers. The Department took no significant action on any of them. In 1958, when the Commission could not, and the Department did not, proceed against a packer for advertising his margarine as "freshly churned," the dairy industry persuaded Congress to amend the law, returning to the FTC jurisdiction over packinghouse products other than meats and leaving with Agriculture jurisdiction over meats. In 1960, 40 years after it had been charged with this responsibility, the Department initiated enforcement activities. Where such negligence is tolerated, the industry that is nominally regulated escapes from all control.

Public enterprise, as well as regulation, can be improved. Administrative efficiency can be enhanced by avoiding the traditional departmental organization with its hampering political controls and by employing in its place the semiautonomous public corporation, with accountability assured by public oversight. The conflict between efficiency and accountability can somehow be compromised. Efficiency can be tested by pricing to cover costs, over the years, earning no profit and incurring no loss. Here, again, it is obvious that able administrators should be appointed, adequate salaries paid, and long tenure assured.

Neither regulation nor public enterprise necessitates complete abandonment of competition as a method of control. Competition may be eliminated within a regulated or a public industry, but two or more such industries, producing substitutes, can still compete with one another, as is the case, for instance, with electricity and gas, and with transport by rail, highway, water, and air. Indeed, as interindustry competition grows, the reins of regulation can be and should be relaxed. There can be competition, finally, among the methods of control. The results of regulation and of public enterprise, in the same field, can each be used, where conditions are comparable, as a yardstick with which to measure the performance of the other. Competition can thus supplement the noncompetitive controls.

REINFORCING THE MAINTENANCE OF COMPETITION

If the maintenance of competition is to continue as the general policy in the United States, there is much that could be done to enhance its effectiveness. Some of the exceptions to the antitrust laws could be repealed. Antitrust measures that are in conflict with the central purpose of the laws could be modified. The Sherman Act could be reformulated to attack unreasonable market power. Steps could be taken to strengthen the organization and improve the procedures of antitrust. Competition could be promoted not only by taking negative action to prevent restraints but also by acting positively to promote the creation and growth of new enterprises. Competition could be reinforced by changing tariff, tax, patent, and corporation laws. Inconsistent policies in other areas could be brought into harmony with competitive policy. This policy, finally, could be given a more authoritative voice within the counsels of the government.

Attacking Anticompetitive Behavior

There are exceptions to the antitrust laws whose repeal would be favored by most economists. These include the compulsory cartelization of oil, of sugar, and of milk; the voluntary cartelization of transport services through rate bureaus and of various agricultural commodities under the Agricultural Marketing Agreements Act. There would be strong support, too, for an amendment that would put action by labor unions to restrict competition in product markets within the scope of antitrust. On one matter, economic opinion would be virtually unanimous: the state and federal laws permitting resale price maintenance should be repealed.

Agreements to fix prices, restrict output, and share markets are already held to be illegal per se. Here, the antitrust laws need no strengthening. But the list of per se offenses might well be extended to include such practices as industry-wide conformity to listed prices and common refusal to sell to distributors who do not resell at a suggested price.

Two other laws should be modified to bring them into harmony with the central purpose of antitrust. Export associations set up under the Webb-Pomerene Act should be permitted where they are used by small firms for the actual handling of foreign sales, but forbidden where they are used by large firms as a cover for participation in international cartels. The Robinson-Patman Act should be so revised that it will apply not only to the seller who gives unjustifiable discounts but also to the buyer who exacts them. The test of injury should be broadened, making discrimination unlawful not when it injures competitors but when it impairs the vigor of competition as a whole. The cost defense should be liberalized. Freedom to make discriminatory price cuts should not be limited to those made to meet the prices of competitors but extended to those designed to undercut such prices. The criminal section, the brokerage section, and the quantity limit section of the law should be repealed.

Much has been done, in recent years, but more could still be done to raise the plane of competition. The FTC should be given more ample powers to cope with abuses in advertising. Consumers of many kinds of packaged goods should be given the protection of standard grades and informative labels.

None of these suggestions is really radical. Each of them is consistent with what has gone before. But in another area of antitrust law, a fundamental change in policy has been proposed.

Attacking Unreasonable Market Power

Carl Kaysen and Donald F. Turner propose that the focus of the law, where it deals with the problems created by a firm's great size be shifted from market conduct to market structure. Instead of forbidding the act of monopolization, they would forbid the possession of unreasonable market power. They would define market power as the persistent ability of a firm to restrict output or to fix prices without losing a substantial share of the market, or without losing substantial profits or incurring heavier losses because competitors had increased their output or reduced their prices. They would find evidence of market power in the persistence of behavior that differed from the behavior that competition would compel: in the persistent failure of prices to fall when demand declined, when costs fell, and when capacity stood idle; in the persistence of abnormally high profits and in the failure of such profits to induce rivals to enter the market. They would establish a legal presumption that market power existed where a firm had made 50 percent or more of the sales in a market for five years or more, or where four firms had made 80 percent or more of the sales, permitting defendants to rebut this presumption by presenting evidence to the contrary. They would hold market power to be unreasonable unless it could be attributed, entirely or almost entirely, to economies of scale that could not be realized if firms were larger in number and smaller in size, to the legal exercise of basic patent rights, to the introduction of new products, processes, or marketing techniques, to superior quality, to lower prices, or to extraordinary efficiency. Where market power was found to exist and to be unreasonable, they would have the law instruct the courts to employ the remedy of dissolution as a matter of course, breaking larger companies into smaller ones that would still be large enough to be efficient and progressive.[1]

A similar approach would be employed in dealing with prospective mergers. A merger would be banned if it were likely to create or to increase unreasonable market power. A presumption would be established that any merger resulting in control of 20 percent or more of a market would confer such power. This presumption could be rebutted by showing that the merger would make for greater efficiency and progressiveness.

A similar approach was taken by a White House Task Force on Antitrust Policy whose report was released in 1969. This body proposed enactment of a law that would require the government to identify as oligopolistic any industry in which four or fewer firms (*a*) had 70 percent of the market in seven of the last 10 years and in four of the last five years and in which (*b*) the industry's sales and the leaders' share in the last five years had not fallen 20 percent below the figures for the previous five years. In such industries the oligopolists would be given a year in which to formulate their own deconcentration plans. Thereafter, the Department of Justice would sue to compel deconcentration within five years (through divestiture, removal of barriers to entry, patent licensing, and the like) so that no firm would be left with a market share of more than 12 percent. But such deconcentration would not be ordered by the courts in cases where the defendants could establish that it would result in a substantial loss of the economies of scale.[2]

In practical application, the proposed approach raises many questions. How, for instance, are a product and its market to be defined and measured? How are the courts to assess economies of scale? How are they to weigh the factors that determine market power? But the approach also has marked advantages. It could clarify the purpose of the law and make its application more predictable. It would turn attention away from the past misconduct of individuals and toward the future performance of the economy. It would strike directly at oligopoly, now so largely outside the law. It would not sacrifice efficiency and progress to obtain competition but would assure the benefits of competition where efficiency and progress would not be impaired.

Strengthening Antitrust

A number of changes in organization and procedure would strengthen the enforcement of antitrust. Instead of continuing the present duplication of responsibility, the Federal Trade Commission could be given jurisdiction over cases involving unfair methods of competition, deceptive practices, price discrimination, and exclusive dealing, with the Antitrust Division assuming full

---

1 / Carl Kaysen and Donald F. Turner, *Antitrust Policy* (Cambridge, Mass.: Harvard University Press, 1959), pp. 75-82, 91-93, 111-18, 265-70.

2 / *Report of the White House Task Force on Antitrust Policy,* 1968 (unpublished manuscript).

responsibility for cases involving restrictive agreements, monopolization, and mergers. The Division could make more comprehensive economic investigations, relying on them rather than on voluntary complaints as its normal source of information on violations of the law. Firms planning to merge could be required to notify the Division before the merger was to take effect. The Division could make more use of economic analysis in choosing cases for prosecution, devoting less effort to those that promised easy legal victories and more to those that would significantly affect the competitiveness of the economy. It could make more use of economists, too, in defining the economic issues in cases brought to trial and in translating economic data into terms intelligible to the courts. The courts, in turn, could employ economists to review materials submitted by litigants, to make independent studies of matters in dispute, and to present their conclusions in open court, subject to examination by both sides. Criminal prosecutions and triple damage suits could be limited to per se offenses where intent to violate the law was shown; in other cases, the government should ask for nothing more than civil remedies. Such remedies could be improved by bringing expert knowledge of business organization and practices to bear, more widely, in the formulation of new decrees, and by conducting systematic and continued studies of the effects of past decrees. The effectiveness of decrees could be enhanced, moreover, by regularly policing observance of their terms.

Consistency of Policy

The burden of maintaining competition cannot be borne by antitrust alone. The competitiveness of the economy is affected by many other measures adopted by the government: by tariffs that exclude foreign goods, by patents that confer monopolies that are broader in scope and longer in duration than would be needed to promote research and development, by quirks in the tax laws that make for industrial concentration, by subsidies that favor one competitor over another, by policies that favor large firms in awarding government contracts, procuring materials, and disposing of surpluses, by policies that restrain competition among farmers and among laborers, and by programs that seek to attain stability, not through monetary and fiscal action, but by restricting production and fixing prices. The competitiveness of the economy is also affected by the policies of state and local governments: by laws that relate to incorporation, and by those that exclude outsiders from local markets and from sheltered trades. Competition is affected, too, when industries are granted exemption from the antitrust laws. In some cases, the exemptions have not been accompanied by alternative controls. In others, the controls provided have been designed to serve the interests of particular groups rather than those of the community as a whole. In still others, controls have been designed to serve the public interest, but the regulatory agencies reflect the attitudes of the industries they are supposed to regulate, or the methods of regulation do not afford an adequate substitute for the safeguards of competition. The policy of maintaining competition is but one among many. Where policies are in conflict, there is no assurance that it will prevail.

Action affecting the competitiveness of the economy is taken not only by the Antitrust Division but also by a score of other agencies. The provisions of agricultural marketing agreements and the competitive behavior of packers and stockyards and of agricultural marketing cooperatives are controlled by the Department of Agriculture. Fisheries cooperatives and actions affecting the oil industry come under the Department of the Interior. The importation and wholesale distribution of alcoholic beverages are policed by the Treasury. Mergers and rate agreements in transport are controlled by the Interstate Commerce Commission, the Civil Aeronautics Board, and the Federal Maritime Commission; mergers in the interstate gas and electric industries by the Federal Power Commission; and mergers in the communications industries by the Federal Communications Commission. Mergers in banking fall within the respective jurisdictions of the Comptroller of the Currency, the Federal Reserve Board, and the Federal Deposit Insurance Corporation. Decisions affecting the maintenance of competition are made by still other agencies: decisions on the letting of contracts by the Defense Department, the Atomic Energy Commission, and the National Aeronautics and Space Agency; decisions on stockpile purchases and on the disposition of public property by the General Services Administration. But nowhere in the government is there an officer or even an interagency committee charged with responsibility or given authority to maintain general oversight of competitive conditions in the economy, to look at national policy as a whole, to draw up a comprehensive program, to coordinate the programs of separate agencies, to resolve conflicts, or to eliminate inconsistencies.

The voices that speak for competition, in the federal government, are a long way down the line. The special interests of business, labor, and agriculture are represented in the President's cabinet; the general interest in maintaining a free economy is not. There is an adviser on consumer interests in the Executive Office of the President, but she functions as a public relations officer, having no administrative authority and only a modest influence on policy. It is frequently proposed that a Department of the Consumer be established in the government, presumably incorporating those agencies whose programs are designed to assure the consumer's safety and to protect him against fraud. Such a move should help to raise the plane of competition, but it would do little to strengthen the maintenance of competition itself. If this is to be done, policy should be unified and given expression in the upper councils of the government. To this end, all matters affecting the competitiveness of the economy should be coordinated through an interagency committee whose members should represent all of the bodies operating in the field. Issues of executive policy should be discussed by this committee, and positions prepared for approval and promulgation by the President. Proposals for legislation should be made by the committee, and prospective legislation submitted to it for advice. The committee's chairman should have a voice at the highest level of the administration.

Promoting Competition

Government can promote the maintenance of competition through methods other than those afforded by antitrust. It can encourage the creation and growth of new and small enterprise. It can change the relevant provisions of tariff, patent, tax, and corporation laws.

Government has moved, as noted in Chapter 33, to aid new and small business. It has sought, by creating lending institutions, to increase the availability of equity capital. It has modified the tax laws to permit the reinvestment of earnings. It has aided small firms in obtaining government contracts. It has given them advice on management. All of this has been on a modest scale. But the area is one in which more might well be done. Government could encourage the provision, on a commercial or cooperative basis, of research services and management and marketing advice, or it might provide such services itself. It has long performed this function for the farmer. There seems to be no reason, in principle, why it should not perform it for the small businessman. Small enterprises now number around 5 million, being particularly active in construction, millwork, and metalwork, and in transport, finance, specialty retailing, and the service trades. But the contribution that small business can make to the competitiveness of concentrated industries is marginal. There are other measures, however, whose impact would be great.

Domestic monopolies could be exposed to foreign competition by removing protective tariffs. The number of patents a firm is permitted to hold could be limited, the duration of patents reduced, and licensing made compulsory. The provisions of the income tax laws that encourage industrial concentration could be changed. The barriers that are raised, in many fields, to the entry and growth of new firms by heavy expenditures on advertising could be lowered by imposing limits on such expenditures or by taxing them at a progressive rate. Concentration of control through intercorporate stockholdings could be checked by taxing such holdings, by revising state corporation laws, by requiring federal charters, and by reorganizing holding company structures in other industries as was done in the case of gas and electric utilities. The monopolistic powers of private enterprises could be curbed by promoting competition by cooperative associations and by providing yardstick competition by public enterprise. Most of these proposals have their disadvantages. Few of them would now command political support. But they serve to illustrate the point that the policy of maintaining competition, if taken seriously, need not be impotent.

Chapter 35   HOW MUCH COMPETITION?

The maintenance of competition is the general policy in the United States. But, as we have seen, it is not applied consistently throughout the economy. Wherever competition really hurts, steps are taken to moderate its force. Indeed, it would seem that restriction of competition, condemned as restraint of trade when practiced by business in general, is approved as collective bargaining for labor, as parity for agriculture, and as fair trade for the independent retailer. It is with the significance of these departures from competition that the present chapter is concerned.

GOALS OF POLICY

Competition is not an end in itself, but a means to an end. The end which it serves is consumer welfare. But this is not the only goal of public policy. There are other goals—economic, political, and social—which man strives to attain. These goals and the goal of consumer welfare are sometimes consistent, sometimes inconsistent. When they diverge, man must make a choice. His choice will depend upon his judgment of values. It may permit the maintenance of competition. It may require that competition be modified.

Consumer Welfare

It is the purpose of the policy of maintaining competition to serve the interest of men as consumers rather than their interest as producers. As consumers, men want to get more for their money. And so they desire a larger output of goods high in quality and low in price. As producers, men want to get more money. And they may do so, at times, by curtailing output, impairing quality, and raising price. As consumers, all men are interested in having a bigger pie. As producers, each of them is interested in getting a bigger slice, even if it means a smaller pie. The producer interest is a special interest that sets one group against another. The consumer interest is a general interest that all men have in common.

If consumer welfare is taken as the goal, production is to be guided by free consumer choice. There is to be a high rate of economic growth. Poverty is to be eliminated. Levels of living are to rise. Health is to be improved. Men are to have more leisure in which to enjoy more goods and services. Opportunities for education and recreation are to be enlarged. The goal is materialistic, but it is not entirely so. For material well-being provides the means for scientific inquiry and artistic expression and creates a wider audience for literature and the arts.

The consumer interest is served by efficiency in production and by progress in technology. Waste is to be reduced, and costs cut. Invention is to be encouraged, new methods developed, and new products introduced. Efficiency requires freedom of entry to markets and freedom of exit by the route of bankruptcy. Progress demands acceptance of innovation and adaptation to change. Efficiency and progress are induced by the lure of profit. They are compelled by competition.

Other Goals of Policy

The consumer interest and the public interest are not always to be identified. Man, in his capacity as a consumer, is not concerned with national security. As a citizen, he must yield it precedence over other goals. The preservation of the social order must—and always does—come first. This does not mean that every plea for privilege advanced in the name of national defense need be accepted as legitimate. Patriotism, to paraphrase Dr. Johnson, is the last refuge of the monopolist.

The consumer interest is satisfied if the national product is large. Society may also be concerned with the way in which this product is distributed. Moral philosophers have long debated the meaning of justice in distribution and have not agreed. But most laymen would hold that it requires, not equality of wealth and income, but avoidance of the extremes of inequality—of the misery of the very poor beside the luxury of the very rich. They would ask that goods be distributed widely, not to equalize material well-being, but to afford each man an equal opportunity to develop his capacities for the enjoyment of life and his talents for the service of society.

The consumer interest is an interest of the present. The consumer may acquiesce in wasteful methods of exploiting natural resources if they provide him, at the moment, with a large supply at a low price. The public interest takes a longer view. It is concerned not only with the present generation but with the next and with those to follow. It measures today's convenience against tomorrow's need.

The consumer, as a consumer, is indifferent to the health and welfare of the worker. He may be content with low prices made possible by child labor, dangerous working conditions, long hours, and low wages. It may, therefore, be deemed desirable to protect those workers who cannot protect themselves and to strengthen labor in its dealings with employers by insuring its right to organize and to bargain collectively.

The consumer, as such, is also unconcerned with instability and insecurity. But ever since the grim depression of the thirties, assurance of stability and security have been among the major goals of public policy. Business activity is to be maintained at a steadily rising level, avoiding both inflation and deflation, boom and bust. Those in the labor force who are able and willing to work are to be given opportunities for employment. Those whose income may be cut off through misfortune are to have a measure of support.

Economic change, though beneficial to consumers, may be harsh in its impact on producers. Innovation may deprive small businessmen and farmers of their sources of livelihood. Its incidence in human hardship and social unrest may make its moderation seem desirable. Considerations other than those of efficiency and progress may be involved. People may wish to preserve the independent merchant and the family farm as bulwarks of individualism and democracy. They may wish, at least, to retard the speed of economic adjustment and to socialize its cost.

Choice and Compromise

The goals of public policy are often in conflict. Production that makes for higher levels of living may be stimulated by incentives that make for inequality in distribution; approaches toward equality may dampen the incentives for production. Innovation that improves the well-being of consumers may create insecurity for producers; measures that assure security may hamper innovation. Where this happens, a choice must be made between the goals that are in conflict, or a way must be found to effect a compromise. Man must decide how much of equality and stability he is willing to sacrifice to obtain efficiency and progress; how much of efficiency and progress he is willing to sacrifice to insure equality and stability.

In some cases, choice or compromise may be explicit. But often, the conflict is not admitted or even recognized. Different goals are sought in different fields: in the field of big business, on the one hand, and in those of small business, agriculture, and labor on the other. Or different goals may be sought in the same field: conservation of petroleum, for instance, and stabilization of the income of oil producers. Here, choice or compromise must be effected in the process of day-to-day administration. Public policy does not always conform to the requirements of logical consistency. But despite its lack of logic, it still may work.

POLITICAL PRESSURE GROUPS

Government responds to organized political pressure. Such pressure may be applied, at times, by socially minded groups. It was through the activity of such groups that government came to concern itself, for instance, with the welfare of unorganized labor and the conservation of natural resources. Pressure may also come from consumers on behalf of measures designed to raise the level of living. But consumers are poorly organized and usually ineffective. The strongest pressures that beat upon the government are those that come from powerful producer groups. Consumers are interested in goods in general; their interest in the products of particular industries is likely to be weak. The interest of producers, on the contrary, is concentrated on the revenue to be obtained from a particular product. The members of producer groups are bound together by the fact that all of them derive their income from a common source. Their interest, accordingly, is compelling, and producers organize to make it felt.

Producer pressure groups have two purposes: to stimulate action that will help their members and to prevent action that would harm them. For these purposes, they maintain lobbies in the state and national capitals. Through such organizations, they keep constant watch on the processes of legislation, preparing bills for introduction and checking on bills that are introduced by others, following bills through committee hearings and action to the floor of each house, estimating prospective votes, and rallying their forces to insure enactment or defeat. At the same time, they keep in contact with administrators, attempting to influence appointments, decisions as to policy, and the use of the veto power. To attain their ends, they employ the arts of persuasion, in public and in private. If need be, they resort to coercion, threatening withdrawal of political support. Here, their strength depends upon their ability to influence elections by contributing to campaign funds, by getting out the votes of their members, and by enlisting wider support through all of the devices of publicity. Their work is highly specialized, employing the skills of experts. It is carried on, as we have seen, with great effect.

Organized Business

Each group of enterprises in the United States—manufacturers, distributors, and servicemen; miners, lumbermen, and fishermen; builders, realtors, and mortgagors; bankers, brokers, and insurers; transport companies and public utilities; publishers, broadcasters, exhibitors, and the like—has its trade association, dedicated to the promotion of its interests. These bodies number in the thousands. Some of them are powerful; some are comparatively weak. All of them are on the job 12 months a year. The achievements of such bodies are evidenced by the success of the National Association of Retail Druggists in whipping resale price maintenance through the legislatures of 45 states and the Congress in Washington, by the success of the Committee of American Steamship Lines in obtaining shipping subsidies, and by the success of the associations of petroleum producers in getting percentage depletion, prorationing, import curbs, and the transfer of the offshore oil lands to the states.

There are organizations, too, that specialize in particular aspects of public policy, such as taxation and international trade. Thus, the Trade Relations Council (formerly the American Tariff League) and the Nationwide Committee on Import-Export Policy bring together manufacturers of china, pottery, glassware, watches, textiles, and other products who are interested in restricting imports. These groups have been highly effective, in past years, in curtailing the

President's power to negotiate trade agreements and in opening escapes from agreements already made.

There are organizations, finally, that undertake to speak for business as a whole. Of these, the Chamber of Commerce is more comprehensive in its scope, the National Association of Manufacturers more limited. But both have a diverse membership with varying interests. They tend, therefore, to focus on broad issues where their members are agreed: on labor policy, for instance, and on public regulation and public enterprise. Here, their opinion carries weight.

In numbers, businessmen form a small fraction of the electorate. But they are keenly conscious of their common interests. They command substantial financial resources. They enjoy considerable prestige. They have ready access to officials in the legislative and executive branches of government. Their political influence, therefore, is disproportionately large.

Organized Labor

Of the laborers outside of agriculture in the United States, more than 70 percent are unorganized. Less than 30 percent, some 17 million in number, are organized. There are around 200 national unions, varying in size and strength. Ten of them have half of the members, three of them—the Teamsters, the Automobile Workers, and the Steel Workers—having more than a million each. The hundred smallest unions, on the other hand, each with fewer than 25,000 members, account for only 5 percent of union membership.

Individual unions have used political, as well as economic, means to serve the interests of their members. Unions in the building trades have sought enactment of restrictive building codes. The railway brotherhoods have lobbied for train-limit and full-crew laws, worked for the taxation and regulation of truckers, and opposed construction of the St. Lawrence Seaway. The mine workers twice succeeded in getting price-fixing laws. They have fought the development of hydroelectric power and urged curtailment of imports of fuel oil. Unions in many industries have lined up with their employers in opposing tariff cuts. The seamen's unions have joined with the shipping companies in seeking subsidies.

There is now one comprehensive organization of labor: the American Federation of Labor and Congress of Industrial Organizations. This body has as its affiliates a large minority of unions with a large majority of union members. Some important unions, however, do not belong, notably the Mine Workers, the Automobile Workers, and the Teamsters. The AFL–CIO is a loose federation without the power to dictate policy to the constituent unions, whose individual interests may diverge. It does undertake, however, to speak for labor as a whole. In its earlier years, the AFL fought for free public education, for hour and wage legislation, and for the elimination of child labor. In 1933, it joined with the Chamber of Commerce to sponsor the NRA, and in 1935, it pushed the passage of the Wagner Act, recognizing the right of collective bargaining and setting up the National Labor Relations Board. Before they combined, the AFL and CIO both supported the development of the social security system and the adoption, in the Employment Act of 1946, of full employment as a goal of national policy. The AFL long sought to exert political influence by endorsing candidates for office. But the organization is unable to deliver the labor vote.

Union members and their families constitute more than a fourth of the electorate. But labor is less effective politically than is business. Its power has fluctuated, rising in the thirties and falling in the forties and the fifties. Labor was unable to prevent the passage of the Taft-Hartley Act over President Truman's veto in 1947 or the enactment of right-to-work laws by the legislatures of 21 states. It failed in its all-out effort to unseat Senator Taft in 1950 and failed repeatedly to force repeal of the "slave labor" law. It failed to block the passage of the Landrum-Griffin Act in 1959. One explanation for the limited political effectiveness of labor lies in the fact that its organization is concentrated in the Northeast, the Midwest, and on the Pacific Coast. Its lack of power in the South and in the West deprives it of ability to control a number of crucial Congressional votes. Union membership, moreover, has declined, not only relatively but absolutely, having fallen from 18.5 million, or 36 percent of the nonfarm labor force, at its peak to 17 million or only 28 percent today.

Organized Agriculture

There are four comprehensive organizations in agriculture—the National Grange, the American Farm Bureau Federation, the Farmers' Union, and the National Farmers' Organization. A fraternal and social organization with a conservative tradition, the Grange is the oldest of these bodies. Its members, numbering more than 800,000, are mostly fruit and vegetable growers, dairymen and poultrymen, concentrated in New England and the Middle Atlantic States. The Farm Bureau had its origin in the county farm bureaus set up to support the county agents of the agricultural extension service. Today, with 1,600,000 members in 49 states, centered in the corn belt of the Midwest and the cotton South, it is the largest of the agricultural pressure groups. The Farm Bureau represents the interests of large commercial farmers, rejecting high price supports and production controls and opposing programs to aid small farmers and farm laborers. The Farmers' Union, with 250,000 members, has its main strength among the Wheat growers of the Great Plains. It has taken the lead in the battle for high price supports. With an interest in small farmers, too, it has fought for various forms of federal aid. The National Farmers' Organization, the youngest of the four, seeks to have farm prices fixed through collective bargaining. These bodies exert their influence in determining the character of agricultural policy as a whole. More powerful in determining the details of agricultural legislation are the associations that promote the interests of producers of particular commodities, such as the National Milk Producers' Federation, the National Association of Wheat Growers, and the National Cotton Council. Measures affecting the producers of these commodities are not adopted without their consent.

The farm organizations pressed for enactment of agricultural legislation during the twenties. They helped draft the Agricultural Adjustment Act of 1933. Ever since that time, they have played a major role in the formulation of agricultural policy. The organizations are closely allied with the agricultural committees of Congress and with the various branches of the Department of Agriculture. They provide the Department with personnel and keep in constant touch with its affairs. The farmers participate, too, in the administration of agricultural programs through committees elected in 3,000 rural counties. The attitude of farmers toward the Department of Agriculture differs from that of businessmen toward the Department of Commerce or workers toward the Department of Labor. The farmers look upon the Department as an agency belonging to them, dedicated to their welfare, and serving their interests.

Farmers and their families are only 5 percent of the country's population. But their political power is greater than their numbers would suggest. This is due in part to the fact that they have the support of business interests in the rural areas—merchants, bankers, implement dealers, operators of grain elevators and cotton gins, and the like. It is due, also, to the character of our governmental structure. Agriculture has been overrepresented in the state legislatures and in the halls of Congress. This situation is being corrected, partially and tardily, as the states move to comply with the decision of the Supreme Court that requires them to revise electoral districts so that legislative representation will be proportionate to population, and as Congressional districts are reformed following the decennial censuses. But in the Senate, New York and California each has two votes, while 20 rural states, with a total population smaller than either of them, have 40 votes. This structure cannot be changed without a constitutional amendment, and the amending process is such that it cannot be changed without the farmer's consent. The overrepresentation of agriculture is certain to persist.

RESPONSE TO GROUP PRESSURES

Businessmen, laborers, and farmers are numerous, and they have the right to vote. It would be unrealistic to suppose that they would not employ this right to serve what they conceive to be their interests. The question is not whether action to moderate competition will be taken in their behalf, but how. The efforts of other citizens should be directed, not toward preventing all such action, but toward assuring that it takes a form that is consistent with the general interest. Where a producer group attempts to enrich its members at their expense, other citizens may well resist. But where such a group seeks only to insure the security of its members, the community may find it wise to co-operate in programs designed to reduce uncertainty, to protect small producers, and to ease adjustment to change. Two other tasks are imposed on government by the organization of producer groups: it must seek to equalize bargaining power; it must undertake to settle disputes. These are the matters to be considered in the sections which follow.

Conferring Special Favors

Special favors, as we have seen, are conferred on organized producers at the expense of the taxpayer. Subsidies are provided for shipping companies, stockpile purchases for mining companies, percentage depletion for oil companies, and price supports for farmers. Favors are conferred, too, at the expense of the consumer. Competitors are excluded from the market by the tariff; they are handicapped by those provisions of the Robinson-Patman Act that require discrimination against large buyers. Compulsory cartels are established for producers of sugar and milk; voluntary cartels may be set up by producers of other agricultural commodities. The price of oil is maintained by controlling its supply. The resale prices of branded goods may be fixed by the owners of brand names. Other examples of such action come readily to mind. In all of this, the rule of competition is abrogated. In none of it is the public interest readily to be discerned. But these are not the only ways in which government may respond to the demands of pressure groups.

Reducing Uncertainty

Government may seek to afford producers a greater measure of security. The farmer, in particular, is plagued by uncertainty. He cannot depend on last year's prices as guides for this year's plantings. His prices and his income are subject to violent fluctuations. They may be seriously depressed by a cyclical decline in demand, by a bumper crop that increases total supply, or by natural hazards that reduce his own supply. All of these matters are beyond the farmer's control. All of them point to needs for social action. To make price dependable as a guide to future production, supports might be announced from season to season on the basis, not of past parity, but of prospective demand and supply. To make income more stable, fluctuations in demand might be offset by collecting taxes in prosperity and distributing benefits in depression; fluctuations in supply might be offset by buying for storage in years of surplus and selling from stores in years of shortage, not raising the long-run level of prices but only narrowing their spread; losses due to natural hazards might be offset by crop insurance.

Such measures would require extensive intervention in the market. But they would reduce uncertainty. They would make for further gains in productivity. They would be more consistent than is the present program with the principles of a competitive economy.

Preserving Small Producers

In manufacturing, it has never been the policy of government to preserve the family factory. In agriculture, where policy has professedly been directed toward the preservation of the family farm, the measures adopted have favored the big farmer rather than the little one. In distribution, however, steps have actually been taken to preserve the independent retailer.

In distribution, the threat of monopoly comes, not from big business, but from little business. It is at the behest of small merchants, combined in groups to exert political pressure, that competition has been harnessed lest it be too tough. Despite the general profession of faith in freedom of enterprise, the legislative bodies of local, state, and national governments have acted repeatedly to limit entry into sheltered occupations and local markets, to increase the costs of strong competitors by imposing discriminatory taxes, to prevent them from obtaining concessions in the prices paid for their supplies, to put a floor under the prices at which retailers can resell, and to permit complete elimination of competition in the resale prices of branded goods. Laws such as these are designed not so much to maintain competition as to preserve individual competitors. They have properly been described as making for "soft competition," in contrast to the "hard competition" demanded by the Sherman Act.

In defense of such measures, it is argued that equality of competitive opportunity cannot be assured unless the advantages enjoyed by the stronger competitors are taken away. The large, diversified distributor and the small, specialized distributor do not compete on equal terms. The large concern has greater bargaining power than the small one and thus can purchase at a lower price. The diversified concern, by drawing on other resources, can sustain losses where its specialized competitor would be destroyed. All this may be true. We must remember, however, that the gains of size and diversity in distribution are shared with the consumer, bringing him more goods for less money, as competition is supposed to do.

But if the small and specialized distributor cannot survive the struggle, there may be other values that are lost. It is possible that smallness and independence, though inefficient and costly, should be preserved for their own sake. When the independent merchant is displaced by an agency or an outlet controlled or owned by the manufacturer, as Justice Douglas remarked in the Standard Stations case, ". . . entrepreneurs become employees of absentee owners. Then there is a serious loss in citizenship. Local leadership is diluted. He who was a leader in the village becomes dependent on outsiders for his action and policy. Clerks responsible to a superior in a distant place take the place of resident proprietors beholden to no one."[1] In the same way, it might be argued that the little merchant should be protected from the chain store, the supermarket, and the discount house so that he may fulfill the responsibilities of civic leadership.

Perhaps this view should be dismissed as mere nostalgia for a vanished past. But if it is accepted, there should be no confusion as to the goal of policy. The preservation of competitors may have some value in itself. But it is not the preservation of competition and should not be permitted to masquerade as such. If this is to be the policy, it should be adopted in full awareness of the price that the consumer will be forced to pay.

1 / *Standard Oil Co. of California* v. *U.S.,* 337 U.S. 293, 319.

Easing Adjustment to Change

In some cases, large numbers of small producers may suffer hardship as a consequence of change. There may be a long-run decline in demand or increasing competition from substitutes, from new locations and new technology. A whole industry may be sick, with an unhappy history of destructive competition: excess capacity, pressure to cut prices, sales below costs, persistent losses, bankruptcy followed by reorganization followed by repeated bankruptcy. The industry may be concentrated geographically, its prosperity determining the welfare of whole communities. Its productive facilities may not be readily convertible to other uses; its labor force not easily relocated or trained for other jobs. Ultimately, in such a case, adjustment to change will be inevitable and desirable. Immediately, it can be effected only at the cost of serious inconvenience or actual distress. The groups affected are, therefore, likely to demand that barriers be placed in the way of change.

The remedy usually proposed and often adopted, in such a situation, is that of fixing minimum prices or restricting output and assigning market shares. For a time, such action may lend support to incomes. But in the long run, it can only serve to intensify the crisis, cutting the industry's sales and increasing those of its competitors. Even if it were effective, resistance to change would be undesirable. People should not be kept indefinitely in the wrong places, using the wrong methods to produce the wrong things. Better remedies might be found in the encouragement of migration, in the creation of new industries, or through investment in research to develop new uses for an old product, improve its acceptability, and reduce its cost.

Where a local industry is obviously dying, there is much to be said for public action to ease the process of adjustment and share the cost of change. The duration of unemployment benefits might be extended and workers aided in moving to new locations and acquiring new skills. Companies might be assisted in finding new opportunities and granted loans to cover the cost of converting their facilities. Such a policy was embodied in the Trade Adjustment Act of 1962 as a means of easing adjustment to reductions in tariff rates. It might well be applied wherever change results in widespread hardship, cushioning the impact of change on the individual while preserving its benefits for society as a whole.

Equalizing Bargaining Power

Where buyers are large and strong and sellers numerous and weak, the sellers are at a disadvantage in bargaining. In such a situation, there are two ways in which bargaining power might be equalized: the power of the buyers might be reduced by forcing them to compete; the power of the sellers might be increased by permitting them to combine. The first of these solutions is not always available; the power of the milk distributor is not to be reduced to that of the individual milk producer; the power of the employer is not to be reduced to that of the individual worker. Government has, therefore, encouraged the organization of milk producers into cooperatives and the organization of workers into unions. In these cases, indeed, such a policy was inescapable. So the community has abandoned competition as a regulator and has acquiesced, instead, in the development of countervailing power, ranging monopoly against monopsony.

The policy presents its problems. The equalization of power may not be possible. There is no way to tell when power is equal. There can be no certainty that equality—and nothing more—will be attained. In the case of labor, for instance, monopoly may undercompensate or overcompensate for monopsony. Unions may stay weak where employers are strong, grow strong where employers are weak. Though the balance is shifted, imbalance in bargaining may persist.

The effort to equalize power will involve the government increasingly in the bargaining process. And when it is clear that workers or employers are to be strengthened by public action, each will attempt to influence the state. It is scarcely probable that government, under such pressures, will adhere to its purpose of equalizing power. More likely, it will shift its weight from one side to the other as the contending forces push and pull. There are inequalities of power, not only in markets, but also in politics.

If power can indeed be equalized, buyers and sellers will be unable to exploit one another, but they may combine to exploit someone else. Cooperative associations may protect the milk producer against the milk distributor, but the two may join hands to make the housewife pay a higher price for milk. The United Mine Workers may protect the miners against the operators, but the two may agree to restrict the supply and raise the price of coal. This is likely to occur, particularly, in periods when inflation makes it easy for the buyer to pass on his higher cost in a higher price. If the consumer is to be protected against this outcome, competition must be maintained or prices regulated in the market where the buyer subsequently sells.

Settling Disputes

Where bargaining between unions and employers is disorderly and where strikes result in the interruption of essential services, government may be forced to seek a settlement of their disputes. Here, again, it may experience difficulty in maintaining a position of impartiality. Where it serves as a mediator, government must act impartially, since it lacks the authority to impose its will. Where it investigates disputes and makes reports, government may well maintain a scrupulous neutrality. But here, it may also slant its findings in an effort to enlist support for the outcome it desires. And where arbitration is compulsory, government may favor the employer, or the worker, and compel the other one to acquiesce.

The impartiality of an arbitrator is not to be assumed. If the political power of employers and employees is evenly divided, he can preserve his position by dividing his decisions, throwing half of them to one side and half to the other. But if power is unequal, he is likely to favor the side that controls his appointment, his budget, and his legal authority. Employers and workers will, therefore, strive to capture the arbitral machinery. And decisions will go to those who win the votes.

SIGNIFICANCE OF CURBS TO COMPETITION

The policy of government toward the different segments of the economy has differed. The maintenance of competition has been the general rule. But the force of competition has been moderated in important fields, notably in the cases of distribution, agriculture, and labor. This inconsistency, however, is not without its logic. In general, enforcement of competition has been the policy where producers are few in number and large in size, and where their power to do harm to others, accordingly, is great. Competition has been moderated, on the other hand, where producers are many in number and small in size, and where their power, as individuals, is insignificant. This action has been taken, in general, to alleviate hardship, to maintain equality of opportunity, and to provide assurance of security.

It cannot be said, as yet, that the measures moderating competition have imposed a heavy burden on consumers. But the moderation of competition—in the cases of agriculture and labor, in particular—still carries serious social risks. It is taking determination of the distribution of income out of the marketplace and subjecting it to the pressures of politics. It is confronting the community with the threat of continuous inflation.

The Cost to the Consumer

The measures adopted by government in the fields of distribution, agriculture, and labor are clearly inconsistent with the policy of maintaining competition, but it would be easy to exaggerate their harmful effects. Their purposes may be open to criticism, but the underlying competitive forces are often so strong that these purposes are but partly realized. Certainly, it cannot be said that the consequences of these measures have been so serious that competition has ceased to be the general rule.

In the field of distribution, clearly, the competitive forces have proved too powerful for legislation to control. The chain store taxes were a failure. The effects of limits on discounts have been avoided, in many cases, by vertical integration, by the purchase of a factory's entire output, and by the development of private brands. Minimum markup laws, in operation, have not perceptibly affected the level of prices. Resale price maintenance, though fairly effective for drugs and toiletries, has proved to be unenforceable in the case of household appliances. The years since these measures were adopted have seen the rise of the supermarket and the discount house. There is small likelihood, in such a situation, that competition can be driven from the field.

In the case of agriculture, though policy is faulty in principle and costly to the taxpayer, it has probably not been harmful, in practice, to the consumer. By reducing uncertainty, it has operated to increase investment, to improve technology, to raise productivity, and to maintain output at prices that the consumer has been able and willing to pay. At the same time, it has permitted the transfer of resources, on a substantial scale, from agriculture into other fields. If it has slowed this movement, it has served but to soften the impact of change.

Labor policy, too, though favorable to monopolistic combination, has not done perceptible harm to the consumer. It is still to be demonstrated statistically, at least, that organization has caused wages to rise more rapidly in union than in nonunion industries. Higher wages, moreover, need not be passed on to the consumer in higher prices if confined to gains in productivity. They cannot be passed on, in any case, unless demand is strong. If prices rise, the explanation is not to be found in labor policy alone.

From Market to Legislature

The organization of business, agriculture, and labor into effective pressure groups may not as yet have done much harm. But it still gives ground for apprehension. Increasingly, determination of the shares of income is being taken from the market and turned over to the state. And this is a trend that promises, eventually, to change the essential character of our society.

In the market economy, the income of the individual is determined by the forces of demand and supply, prices and costs. Where the consumer's demand for a good increases, the producer's income will rise. Where it declines, his income will fall. Where a producer is efficient, his income will be high. Where he is inefficient, it will be low. These differences in income will leave some men worse off than others. But they will appear to these men to be the consequences of impersonal forces, not of political choice. They will, therefore, be accepted as a given fact, and individuals will adjust to them. Men will move out of the production of goods that are wanted less and into the production of goods that are wanted more. They will undertake to improve their efficiency. Differences in income will thus serve to direct the allocation of resources in accordance with consumer preferences.

In a polity of pressure groups, on the other hand, the income of the individual will be fixed by the state. The mechanism that determines it will no longer appear to him to be impersonal in character. If a man's income declines, or if it is smaller than he desires, he will feel that the government is to blame. Instead of recognizing that he is producing the wrong thing, or is inefficient, he will attribute the unsatisfactory size of his income to the policies adopted by the party in power. And, in a democratic society, such policies are subject to change. Those who are able to exert political pressure will, therefore, demand and get higher incomes. Those who are not will get smaller ones. Differences in income will cease to perform their proper function in guiding the allocation of resources, checking waste, and rewarding economy. Instead of shifting to the production of wanted goods, or improving their efficiency, producers will seek to increase their incomes by putting pressure on the state. The allocation of resources will be effected through the processes of central planning and authoritarian control.

In such a society, if democratic institutions survive, order will be maintained only by achieving a balance of power among political pressure groups. If business, labor, and agriculture can each be satisfied, there will be peace. But it does not follow that the general interest will be served. For the pressure groups may merely be conspiring to exploit those in society who still remain unorganized. No one of these groups can gain unless there are others who will lose.

The Threat of Inflation

A society that is dominated by producer pressure groups is confronted by the threat of continuous inflation. There are mechanisms already built into our economy that have this effect. Organized labor strikes for higher wages. Employers, to meet the larger wage bill, raise their prices. If sales fall off and employment declines, government eases credit and runs a budgetary deficit, injecting enough purchasing power into the system to put the idle back to work. Resources, once again, are fully employed, with prices up. Higher prices for things the farmers buy raise the index of parity. Government, with agricultural prices tied to parity, raises the level of price supports. Higher prices for food raise the index of the cost of living. Escalator clauses in union contracts then come into play. Wages move up again. The stage is set for a repeat performance.

Inflation could be prevented. It could be checked by tightening credit, raising taxes, and reducing public expenditures. But these steps would reduce employment, sales, and profits. The medicine may well seem worse than the disease. Given the political power of labor, business, and agriculture, it is not likely to be taken. Inflation could also be checked by imposing direct controls on wages and prices. This has been done, after a fashion, in time of war. But to adopt such controls as permanent measures, in peacetime, would be to change the character of the economy. This remedy, too, is politically unacceptable. The conclusion is fairly clear: it is likely that the level of prices will continue to rise.

POLICIES IN PERSPECTIVE

In their total effect, in the perspective of history, the policies of government toward business in the United States appear to have been sound. Comprehensive planning and control of economic activity have been confined to time of war. The essential characteristics of a market economy have been preserved. Public enterprise has been limited, in general, to fields where it was really needed, and in some of them it has done well. Public regulation has been restricted in the main, to fields where it was unavoidable. The plane of competition has been raised by a growing body of laws protecting consumers, investors, and workers, and conserving natural resources. The force of competition has been moderated in the cases of labor, agriculture, and the distribution trades. But this has been done without great social cost and without destroying the fundamentally competitive character of the economy. The antitrust laws have been influential in preserving market freedom. The courts have been consistent in their condemnation of restrictive agreements and monopolistic practices. They have been effective in striking down barriers to competitive enterprise. They have displayed discretion and common sense in dealing with combination and monopoly.

The American economy—whether because of these policies or despite them—is vigorous, productive, and progressive. "Judged by performance," wrote John Maurice Clark, "this defective system has somehow achieved an advancing productiveness that has placed it in the forefront of the world's economies, and has diffused the benefits of increasing real income among the population to an extent undreamed of, even as recently as the beginning of the present century" and at a speed "more rapid than that achieved on a sustained basis by any other economic system."[2] The United States has achieved the longest span of life, the best standard of health, the greatest amount of leisure, the widest spread of education, and the highest level of living ever found, in combination, on earth. It has been moving, at the same time, toward greater stability in production, greater security for the individual, and greater equality in the distribution of income and opportunity. The policies that have promoted—or permitted—these developments cannot have been far wrong.

2 / J. M. Clark, *Competition as a Dynamic Process* (Washington, D.C.: Brookings Institution, 1961), pp. 5, 77.

INDEXES

INDEX OF CASES

INDEX OF NAMES

INDEX OF SUBJECTS

This book has been set in 10 point Press Roman, leaded 2 points. Part numbers and titles and chapter numbers are in 16 point Helvetica italic. Chapter titles are in 16 point Helvetica caps. The size of the type page is 27 by 46½ picas.